THE HISTORY OF BETHLEM

— ·◆· —

'Stunning. At last Bethlem has the comprehensive history it deserves, firmly grounded in a wider social and political context. With a deft touch the authors have unpicked the tapestry of myth and misconception surrounding Bethlem, to reveal the intricate twists and turns of its various existences. Psychiatric historiography has been considerably enriched.'

Nick Hervey, co-author of Masters of Bedlam,
The Transformation of the Mad-Doctoring Trade

Bethlem Hospital is a unique institution. Now seven hundred and fifty years old, it has been continuously involved in the care of the mentally ill since at least 1400 – as such it has a strong claim to be the oldest foundation in Europe with an unbroken history of sheltering and treating the mentally disturbed. *The History of Bethlem* is a scholarly history of this key establishment, looking at Bethlem's role within the caring institutions of London and Britain and its place in the history of psychiatry.

Bethlem is not simply Europe's oldest psychiatric establishment; it is the most famous and the most notorious, assuming many guises over its 750-year history. It began as a religious foundation in the context of the Crusades. It became a hospital for the insane by chance, survived complex battles between Crown and Papacy, Parliament and the Corporation of the City of London, and gained great prominence for many years as Britain's only lunatic hospital.

The name of Bethlem turned into everyday speech and became part of a national culture. From Shakespeare's time, 'Bedlam' was becoming detached from the institution and assuming a life and a persona of its own, with connotations of turmoil, confusion and cacophony.

Bethlem transcended locality and became a national and international institution. Based upon a full use of the Bethlem archives, *The History of Bethlem* is a long overdue re-evaluation of its history. This comprehensive volume explores Bethlem in the context of the history of Britain, London, hospitals and psychiatry.

The authors are **Jonathan Andrews**, Lecturer in the History of Medicine at Oxford Brookes University; **Asa Briggs**, Emeritus Professor of History and Vice-Chancellor of the University of Sussex; **Roy Porter**, Professor in the Social History of Medicine, The Wellcome Institute, London; **Penelope Tucker**, Research Fellow, the Wellcome Institute, London and **Keir Waddington**, Research Fellow, Queen Mary & Westfield College.

THE HISTORY OF
BETHLEM

*Jonathan Andrews, Asa Briggs, Roy Porter,
Penny Tucker and Keir Waddington*

London and New York

First published in 1997
by Routledge
11 New Fetter Lane, London EC4P 4EE

Simultaneously published in the USA and Canada
by Routledge
29 West 35th Street, New York, NY 10001

Typeset in Garamond by
RefineCatch Limited, Bungay, Suffolk

Printed and bound in Great Britain by
TJ International Ltd, Padstow, Cornwall

British Library Cataloguing in Publication Data
A catalogue record for this book is available from the British Library

Library of Congress Cataloguing in Publication Data
The history of Bethlem / Jonathan Andrews . . . [et al.].
Includes bibliographical references and index.
1. Bethlem Royal Hospital (London, England)—History.
2. Psychiatric hospitals—England—London—History.   1. Andrews,
Jonathan, 1961–   .
[DNLM: 1. Bethlem Royal Hospital (London, England)   2. Hospitals,
Psychiatric—history—England.   WM 28 FE5 1997]
RC450.G72L728   1997
362.2′1′09421—DC21   96–52471
DNLM/DLC   CIP

ISBN 0–415–01773–4

CONTENTS

———•◦•———

— Contents —

PART III: 1783–1900

PART IV: 1900 to the present

PART V: Appendices

PLATES

— ⬩ ◆ ⬩ —

— *Plates* —

FIGURES

—◆—

TABLES

———— •◆• ————

ACKNOWLEDGEMENTS

———— •◦• ————

Rather like the story of Bethlem itself, the history of this history of Bethlem is lengthy and complex, and this is not the place to tell its tale; suffice to say that the team of authors are collectively deeply grateful to all we have dealt with at Bethlem and the Maudsley for their eager cooperation, patience, tolerance and understanding. Special thanks must go to Eric Byers, the Chief Executive, for his help in making facilities and materials available; and to Miss Patricia Allderidge, the Archivist, for her unrivalled expertise and her unflagging enthusiasm for Bethlem, its history and its archives.

The staffs of many libraries and other institutions have been exceedingly helpful. We would like to make special mention of all those who have helped us at the Guildhall, the Public Record Office (both Chancery Lane and Kew), the Corporation of London Record Office, the Greater London Record Office and the British Library. While the authors have made every effort to contact copyright holders of material used in this volume, they would be grateful to hear from any they were unable to contact.

Penny Tucker would particularly like to thank the following for comment, advice, or for allowing advance sight of articles: Drs Caroline Barron, Sandra Cavallo, John Clark, Natsu Hattori, Peregrine Horden, Derek Keene, Marie-Anne Kinselbach, Carole Rawcliffe, David Roffe, Christina Vanja, Nicholas Vincent; for making drawings, Caroline Overy; and Ms Ellie Phillips.

Jonathan Andrews extends his special thanks to Dr F. J. G. Jefferiss, Matthew Craske, Rosemary Weinstein, Len Smith, Akihito Suzuki and Helen Bradley and many others whose comments and suggestions proved very helpful.

Keir Waddington is grateful to many. In researching the twentieth-century history of Bethlem, invaluable help on the 1930 buildings has been provided by Kaye Bagshaw of the RIBA. Jennifer Haynes offered careful guidance through the Foulkes and Sargant papers at CMAC, Wellcome Institute, and the staff of the Wellcome Institute Library, British Library and the Greater London Record Office have proved helpful and supportive.

Asa Briggs would like to thank L. H. W. Paine for his earlier commitment to and interest in the writing of Bethlem's history. In addition, thanks are due to Peter Bartlett, Abigail Beach, W. F. Bynum, Ann Dally, Martin Daunton, Anne Digby, Anne

Hardy, Juliet Hurn, Cheryce Kramer, Caroline Overy, Frank Prochaska, Andrew Scull, Trevor Turner and David Wright for their useful comments and reading of the text. A debt is also owed to all those who agreed to be interviewed for this book, a list too long to mention.

The Wellcome Trust generously provided the funds which have allowed Penny Tucker and Keir Waddington to conduct their researches.

At Routledge, Heather McCallum and Ruth Jeavons have been great sources of encouragement, while the superb index is due to Zeb Korycinska.

It remains to say that the interpretations offered in the ensuing book are those of the authors alone; the Bethlem and Maudsley NHS Trust is in no way responsible for the opinions that follow.

ABBREVIATIONS

———— •◆• ————

AR	*Annual Register*
BAR	*Bethlem Admission Registers*
BCGM	Bethlem Court of Governors Minutes
BGCM	Bethlem Grand Committee Minutes
BIAR	Bethlem Incurables' Admission Registers
BL	British Library
BMA	British Medical Association
BMJ	*British Medical Journal*
BRH	Bethlem Royal Hospital, Monks Orchard Road, Eden Park, Beckenham, Kent
BRHA	Bethlem Royal Hospital Archives (at BRH address)
BSA	*Bethlem Steward's Accounts*
BSB	Bethlem Salary Books
BSCM	Bethlem Sub Committee Minutes
BwellGCM	Bridewell General Committee Minutes
CA Rep.	Court of Aldermen Repertories
CGJ	*The Covent Garden Journal*
Citizen	*The Citizen Of The World*
CLRO	Corporation of London Records Office, Guildhall
CSPD	*Calendar of State Papers Domestic*
CUP	Cambridge University Press
DHSS	Department of Health and Social Security
DNB	*Dictionary of National Biography*
DPM	Diploma in Psychological Medicine
EMS	Emergency Medical Service
GCCM	*Guy's Hospital Court of Committee Minutes*
Ghall	Guildhall Library, London
GLRO	Greater London Record Office
GM	*The Gentleman's Magazine*
GNC	General Nursing Council
GPI	General Paralysis of the Insane
JMS	*Journal of Mental Science*

LCC	London County Council
LEP	*The London Evening Post*
MEC	Medical Executive Committee
MIETS	Mental Impairment Evaluation and Treatment Service
MRC	Medical Research Council
MPA	Medico-Psychological Association
MTO	Management Team of Officers
NHS	National Health Service
OUP	Oxford University Press
PCC	Prerogative Court of Canterbury
PCR	Privy Council Registers
PP	*Parliamentary Papers*
PRO	Public Record Office, Chancery Lane, London
PRO Kew	Public Record Office, Kew Gardens
q.n.	Quire number
RAWP	Resources Allocation Working Party
RC	Royal Commission
RHB	Regional Health/Hospital Board
SEMRHB	South East Metropolitan Regional Hospital Board
SETRHA	South East Thames Regional Health Authority
SHA	Special Health Authority
SLGCM	St Luke's Hospital General Committee Minutes
SLHCM	St Luke's House Committee Minutes
SM	London Sessions Minutes
SP	*State Papers Domestic*

CHAPTER ONE

INTRODUCTION

———— ·•· ————

Bethlem is a unique institution. Now seven hundred and fifty years old, it has been continuously involved in the care of the mentally ill since at least the 1400s – in other words for nearly six hundred years. As such it has a strong claim to be the oldest foundation in Europe with an unbroken history of sheltering and treating the mentally disturbed. Facilities for the mad were set up in Spain from the early fifteenth century, beginning in Valencia in 1409, but such establishments were not to enjoy a continuous thread. In most of Western Europe it was the sixteenth century which brought comparable developments, and some regions did not develop independent psychiatric facilities until the nineteenth century. Many medieval institutions housed mad people from time to time, but few specialized in their care and won a reputation for it.[1]

Bethlem is not simply Europe's oldest psychiatric establishment; it is the most famous – or, what for long amounted to the same thing, the most notorious. Certain psychiatric hospitals were to achieve prominence within the profession – the York Retreat, or Illenau in the German state of Baden, both in their distinctive ways regarded as model environments at particular moments in the evolution of psychiatry. Some have provided the stage for dramatic episodes in the history of psychiatry – for instance Bicêtre in Paris, where Philippe Pinel supposedly struck the chains off the lunatics in a magnificent emancipatory gesture during the French Revolution.[2] Others, so to speak, had greatness thrust upon them because of the illustrious patients who happened to have been detained there – the name of Charenton is now indelibly printed upon the public mind thanks to its association with the Marquis de Sade. Nevertheless, it is arguably only the name of Bethlem that has actually turned into everyday speech and become part of a national culture. In English parlance 'Bedlam' – as in 'Bedlam mad' or later expressions like 'utter bedlam' – was becoming, from around Shakespeare's time, detached from the institution and assuming a life and a persona of its own, with connotations of turmoil, confusion and cacophony. It was perfectly natural in the early years of the Industrial Revolution for a blast-furnace in the West Midlands – well over a hundred miles away from Bethlem Hospital itself – to be christened 'Bedlam', just as it is still utterly natural to speak, for example, of the rush-hour or the January sales as being 'like Bedlam'.[3] While English-speakers give these usages no thought, it is interesting that equivalent sayings barely exist as commonplaces in any other language or culture. A resident of Berlin, Bordeaux or Boston can of course speak colloquially of someone being about to be packed off to this or that local asylum, but that is the point: it seems that only Bethlem transcended locality and became a 'national institution' – in both senses of that term.

Indeed, more than national – *international*. For over a century Bethlem was one of the sights of London on any serious tourist's itinerary, along with the Tower and Westminster Abbey; and it is easy to find examples of eighteenth- and nineteenth-century continental psychiatrists invoking the example of the Hospital, mainly in a positive light and often as part of a propaganda campaign to encourage their own prince or burgermasters to endow a comparably imposing establishment.

Given that Bethlem became a national institution – indeed became *Bedlam* – it is very odd that its history has been so little studied and that beyond a limited repertoire of lurid incidents, so little is known about its real history. Its archivist, Patricia Allderidge, has offered a plausible explanation for this: 'historians of psychiatry', she has observed, 'actually do not want to know about Bethlem as a historical fact because Bethlem as a reach-me-down cliché is far more useful. It has, after all, fulfilled this role in the popular imagination throughout much of its existence'. There is, in other words, an assumption that the truth about Bethlem is, somehow, almost instinctively too familiar to need any real investigation – and that goes with the supposition that all the hand-me-down tales *must* somehow be true otherwise they wouldn't be so widely in circulation.[4]

Dangers lurk here. In the Middle Ages everyone knew that the Jews poisoned the wells, thus causing the Black Death. In the early modern period everyone knew that witches went off on their orgiastic sabbaths with Satan;[5] under the *ancien régime* everyone knew the Bastille was crammed with political prisoners, oppressed by torture and torments. And in much the same way every schoolperson proverbially knows that Bethlem was a scandalous hellhole that systematically neglected its patients and, when it was not neglecting them, inflicted upon them cruel and unnatural therapies. Ten years back, as Allderidge also noted, a reviewer wrote of Bethlem's staff that 'they did not even pretend to offer either refuge, good care, or cure': a statement at first blush so bizarre – a hospital that didn't even *pretend* to look after its patients? – that it could only have been written in the unspoken belief that nothing could be too bad to say about the Hospital.

All sorts of pseudo-facts reinforce the 'bad Bethlem' myth. Take sightseeing; that was indeed openly permitted back in the seventeenth and eighteenth centuries, as is documented below in Chapter 13 – in 1610 Lord Percy recorded going to see the lions in the Tower, the show of Bethlem, and the fireworks at the Artillery Gardens. In those days there was nothing odd about permitting or encouraging such a spectacle: all the world was a stage and visiting Bethlem was regarded as edifying for the same reasons as attending hangings. But distinguished scholars have taken this one stage further and computed that in the seventeenth century the hospital entertained as many as 96,000 visitors a year. Here, as Allderidge has pointed out, we must pause. How do we know? There were no turnstiles or visitors' books. It's a figure arrived at by some foolish deductions from the finances – inflated to absurd proportions, one suspects, so as to highlight the sense of freakshow. The result is that such facts become articles of faith, repeated like mantras, from one book to another. Very recently the following appeared:

> As late as 1815, the Bethlehem madhouse exhibited lunatics every Sunday, admission one penny. The annual revenue from these visits amounted to £400, which amounts to an astonishing 96,000 admissions a year.[6]

Not one single 'fact' in that statement happens to be factual.

It is particularly intriguing that little serious historical investigation has been conducted into Bethlem, given that histories of Bethlem actually started very early – over two hundred years ago, which is, of course, long before most asylums were founded let alone acquired a history that could be written up. In 1783 there appeared *An Historical Account of the Origin, Progress and Present State of Bethlem Hospital*, penned by the Revd Thomas Bowen, who was the chaplain to Bridewell (see Chapter 20). This was, however, less a real history than the Georgian version of a glossy promotional coffee-table work, a public-relations exercise setting Bethlem in a shining light for fund-raising purposes.[7]

The first full-length history was the work of a Bethlem chaplain, the Revd Edward O'Donoghue, whose *The Story of Bethlehem Hospital from its Foundation in 1247* came out in 1914, was never reprinted, and so is rather rare.[8] O'Donoghue was a quirky and superstitious man. A one-time member of the Charity Organization Society, he was a sympathetic listener and friend of the patients and a keen journalist who played a major role in keeping the Hospital's journal going.

His *Story of Bethlehem* is a curiosity, written in a style by turns affected, archaic, chatty and condescending; the historian takes sides, turns history into a pageant of saints and sinners, parades his whimsical prejudices and comes up with some bizarre speculations. Yet, while largely neglecting the institution's later records, his work had the very real merit of delving into the early archival sources, casting light on much that had been quite obscure. The Governors, rather than have the murkier episodes of its history raked over yet again, wanted generally to let sleeping dogs lie. Although they judged the book unsuitable to be given to the patients, they did order some 2,000 copies for distribution.

Perhaps because of the existence of O'Donoghue's leisurely look at the byways of Bethlem, its history then attracted virtually no attention for half a century, though a pot-boiling and often inaccurate book came out in 1972,[9] and growing attention was paid to Bethlem's image by literary scholars, for instance by R. R. Reed in his *Bedlam on the Jacobean Stage*.[10] During the last twenty years Patricia Allderidge has herself published a number of original and challenging articles, both debunking old Bethlem myths and exploring aspects of its history, and Jonathan Andrews has produced a doctoral dissertation covering the years 1634 to 1770, strongly arguing that the time is long overdue for a serious re-evaluation. David Russell's *Scenes from Bedlam* has developed these ideas, focusing on patients and their carers from the mid-sixteenth century. While he does not attempt to write a history of Bethlem he does give a broad overview, although less is said about Bethlem in the twentieth century where the focus is on the Maudsley, training and research.[11] Yet, despite the fact that British psychiatry without Bethlem is like Hamlet without the mad prince, Bethlem has remained essentially ignored.

Psychiatry's history has enjoyed a remarkable surge of interest in the last couple of decades – in part due to the intense public debates over the state of psychiatry itself and particularly the future and fate of psychiatric institutions.[12] Professional historians have argued that psychiatric history as traditionally written by (practising or retired) psychiatrists has tended to be 'Whiggish', that is to say anachronistic and triumphalist, interpreting and judging the past in terms of the present, and complacently taking for granted a tale of progress; psychiatrists have countered that such revisionist or radical historians are no less anachronistically judgmental in their often highly critical stance. Such debates continue to rage, and doubtless the information provided by this book might be used to lend support to either side.[13]

But it is important to stress at the outset that current historical controversies respecting psychiatric hospitals since around 1800 – questions of institutionalization and subsequent deinstitutionalization – are not, and should not be central to this history of Bethlem. That is to some degree because Bethlem was not, of course, founded as a lunatic asylum. During its first century it had no deranged people at all; and at least till the Reformation it served a variety of other purposes as well as giving shelter to the mad. It is also because, even with respect to the insane, Bethlem does not fit into the patterns standardly visible elsewhere. True, since around 1850 Bethlem has in most ways integrated itself within the British psychiatric world, yet major differences remained; while many public institutions were growing huge, housing thousands of patients, Bethlem stayed very small indeed.

The history of a typical British lunatic asylum or psychiatric history might run like this. Mumerset County Asylum was founded in the first half of the nineteenth century in response to the stresses and strains of an urbanizing society with a rapidly rising population; the medical profession gradually imposed its authority on the institution – even their vision of what asylums 'ought to be', to borrow part of the title of Dr W. A. F. Browne's early-Victorian book.[14] The asylum rose in prominence, it grew in numbers of inmates, and daunting problems emerged, including the counter-productive effects of institutionalization and expansion themselves. Stagnation followed in the latter part of the nineteenth century, punctuated after the First World War by intermittent attempts at reform, with attempts to integrate it better within the community, leading perhaps, as a result of internal and external pressures, to closure in the late 1980s.[15]

If this thumbnail sketch might serve as a recognizable asylum profile, the crucial point is that Bethlem corresponds to it in almost no respect at all. It would be pointless to recite at this juncture all the ways in which Bethlem breaks the mould – that is one of the aims of the body of the book. The point is not simply one of its exceptional longevity – of the fact that Bethlem has a past that long antedates the average private asylum or county asylum, and hence established traditions of its own and carved out a unique niche for itself within the 'trade in lunacy'.[16] It is also that even during the nineteenth and twentieth centuries Bethlem was often conspicuous in its attempts to be distinctive from and independent of other institutions. This is a path it has followed with considerable success; in an age in which many institutions have closed down, Bethlem is very much alive and well – and growing. There are clichés about Bethlem which may be confirmed by the research set out in this book; but few stereotypes about asylums in general apply to Bethlem.

This may be put another way: this history of Bethlem is intended not solely or even primarily as a contribution to the history of psychiatry, for much of Bethlem's history impinges only marginally on the rise of psychiatry as such (a term in this country only a century old). The nuts and bolts of Bethlem's functioning – its administration, finances, officials, entrance policies, charity regulations and so forth – have been almost totally neglected. Historians have hitherto concentrated on the image of Bethlem – on *Bedlam*. This book focuses on the institution itself and how it operated, as well as on the dialogue between institution and image. It thus inaugurates the proper historical analysis of the institution; and not least, unlike many accounts of psychiatic institutions, it takes the story right up to the present day.

That most English of Marxist historians, E. P. Thompson, once wrote of the 'peculiarities of the English';[17] while avoiding a nostalgic evocation of eccentricity he thereby pointed to certain extremely distinctive features of English history. It is in that spirit that we offer this study of an institution which, like so many other English institutions (one thinks of the monarchy or of Parliament), has gradually evolved under a multitude of pressures and tensions, has changed and changed again almost out of recognition, yet still has maintained a certain strand of continuity, captured not least in ambiguous attitudes towards its own past. Our aim is neither to apply a coat of whitewash nor to paint it black; it is to show what has made one particular institution live and assume a series of personalities.

NOTES

1 Of course assorted hospitals and monasteries took in the occasional lunatic before Bethlem. What is here being discussed is the emergence of an institution that came to be recognized as specializing in the insane. For the mad in early medieval Europe see Penelope E. R. Doob, *Nebuchadnezzar's Children: Conventions of Madness in Middle English Literature* (New Haven and London: Yale University Press, 1974); Christopher Paul Philo, 'The Space Reserved for Insanity: Studies in the Historical Geography of the Mad-Business in England and Wales' (University of Cambridge, Ph.D. thesis, 1990). Islam developed hospitals for the insane before Christendom: see Michael W. Dols, 'Insanity and Its Treatment in Islamic Society', *Medical History*, xxxi (1987), 1–14; *idem, Manjūn: The Madman in Medieval Islamic Society* (Oxford: Clarendon Press, 1992); the early Spanish asylums developed under Islamic stimulus.

   For the chronology of the founding of institutions for the insane, see J. G. Howells (ed.), *World History of Psychiatry* (New York: Brunner/Mazel, 1968); Roy Porter, 'Madness and its Institutions', in Andrew Wear (ed.), *Medicine in Society* (Cambridge: CUP, 1992), 277–301. The village of Geel in the Netherlands was boarding mad people as an adjunct to its religious shrine from perhaps the twelfth century: William Llewellyn Parry-Jones, 'The Model of Geel Lunatic Colony and its Influence on the Nineteenth Century Asylum System in Britain', in Andrew Scull (ed.), *Madhouses, Mad-Doctors and Madmen* (London: Athlone Press; Philadelphia: University of Pennsylvania Press, 1981), 201–17.

2 That this is an essentially fictitious event is demonstrated by Dora B. Weiner, '"*Le Geste de Pinel*": The History of a Psychiatric Myth', in Mark S. Micale and Roy Porter (eds), *Discovering the History of Psychiatry* (New York and Oxford: OUP, 1994), 343–7.

3 The great water-colourist John Sell Cotman painted the Bedlam Furnace near Madeley in the Severn Gorge; his painting is reproduced in Ann Bermingham, *Landscape and Ideology: The English Rustic Tradition 1740–1860* (Berkeley: University of California Press, 1986), 82. The Methodist preacher John Fletcher of Madeley was famous for his millennial prophesies, saying 'our earth's the bedlam of the universe, where reason (undiseas'd in heaven) runs

mad' (quoted in Stephen Daniels, *Fields of Vision: Landscape Imagery and National Identity in England and the United States* (Cambridge: Polity Press, 1993), 70). For further examples of metaphoric, proverbial and jesting uses of the term see Roy Porter, *Mind Forg'd Manacles: Madness and Psychiatry in England from Restoration to Regency* (London, Athlone Press, 1987; paperback edition, Penguin, 1990); Natsu Hattori, '"The Pleasure of your Bedlam"; The Theatre of Madness in the Renaissance', *History of Psychiatry*, vi (1995), 283–308.

4 Patricia H. Allderidge, 'Bedlam: Fact or Fantasy?', in W. F. Bynum, Roy Porter and Michael Shepherd (eds), *The Anatomy of Madness*, vol. 2 (London: Tavistock, 1985), 17–33, esp. pp. 18–21.

5 And, it should be added, many radical American feminists today know that around nine million witches were burnt to death in Europe in the early modern period as part of the witch-craze. For an account of how this ludicrous figure – the real figure is probably under 100,000 (which is of course 100,000 too many) – achieved prominence amongst modern feminists, see James Sharpe, *Instruments of Darkness: Witchcraft in England 1550–1750* (London: Hamish Hamilton, 1996), 169f.; and Jonathan Barry, Marianne Hester and Gareth Roberts (eds), *Witchcraft in Early Modern Europe: Studies in Culture and Belief* (Cambridge: CUP, 1996), 288f.

6 Robert Youngson and Ian Scott, *Medical Blunders* (London: Robinson, 1995), 286. The book might better have been named *Historical Blunders*.

7 Thomas Bowen, *An Historical Account of the Origin, Progress and Present State of Bethlem Hospital* (London: For the Governors, 1783).

8 E. G. O'Donoghue, *The Story of Bethlehem Hospital from its Foundation in 1247* (London: T. Fisher Unwin, 1914). Edward O'Donoghue (or Gerald, as he preferred to be known) went on to write the history of Bethlem's sister institution: *Bridewell Hospital, Palace, Prison Schools from the Earliest Times to the End of the Reign of Elizabeth* (London: Bodley Head, 1923).

9 A. Masters, *Bedlam* (London: Michael Joseph, 1972). It is remarkable that Bethlem isn't even mentioned in certain standard histories, for instance Franz G. Alexander and Sheldon T. Selesnick's *The History of Psychiatry: An Evaluation of Psychiatric Thought and Practice from Pre-historic Times to the Present* (London: George Allen & Unwin, 1967). The oddest omission of all is the entire neglect of Bethlem in Michel Foucault's *La Folie et la Déraison: Histoire de la Folie à l'Age Classique* (Paris: Librairie Plon, 1961); trans. and abridged as *Madness and Civilization: A History of Insanity in the Age of Reason*, trans. by Richard Howard (New York: Random House, 1965; London: Tavistock Publications, 1967).

10 R. R. Reed, *Bedlam on the Jacobean Stage* (Cambridge, Mass.: Harvard University Press, 1952); this was followed by works like Max Byrd's *Visits to Bedlam: Madness and Literature in the Eighteenth Century* (Columbia: University of South Carolina Press, 1974); more recently see Natsu Hattori, *op. cit.*, and her 'Performing Cures: Practice and Interplay in Theatre and Medicine of the English Renaissance' (D.Phil., University of Oxford, 1995).

11 Patricia Allderidge, 'Richard Dadd 1817–1886: Painter and Patient', *Medical History*, xiv (1970), 308–13; *eadem*, 'Criminal Insanity: Bethlem to Broadmoor', *Proceedings of the Royal Society of Medicine*, lxvii (1974), 897–904; *eadem*, 'Management and Mismanagement at Bedlam, 1547–1633', in Charles Webster (ed.), *Health, Medicine and Mortality in the Sixteenth Century* (Cambridge: CUP, 1979), 141–64; *eadem*, 'Hospitals, Madhouses and Asylums: Cycles in the Care of the Insane', *British Journal for Psychiatry*, cxxxiv (1979), 321–34, reprinted in R. M. Murray and T. H. Turner (eds), *Lectures on the History of Psychiatry* (London: Gaskell, 1990), 28–46; *eadem*, 'The Foundation of the Maudsley Hospital', in German E. Berrios and Hugh Freeman (eds), *150 Years of British Psychiatry, 1841–1991* (London: Gaskell, 1991), 79–88; *eadem*, 'Sketches in Bedlam', in Leonie de Goei and Joost Vijselaar (eds), *Proceedings of the 1st European Congress on the History of Psychiatry and Mental Health Care* (Rotterdam: Erasmus, 1993), 76–82; Jonathan Andrews, 'Bedlam Revisited: A History of Bethlem Hospital *c.* 1634–*c.* 1770' (Ph.D. diss., London University, 1991). D. Russell, *Scenes from Bedlam* (London: Baillière Tindall, 1996) provides a further account.

12 The most thorough attempt to explore new directions in the history of psychiatry is Mark Micale and Roy Porter (eds), *Discovering the History of Psychiatry* (New York: OUP, 1994).

13 See for instance H. Mersky, 'Somatic Treatments, Ignorance and the Historiography of

Psychiatry', *History of Psychiatry*, v (1994), 387–92; J. L. Crammer, 'English Asylums and English Doctors: Where Scull is Wrong', *History of Psychiatry*, v (1994), 103–16; Andrew Scull, 'Psychiatrists and Historical "Facts": Part One: The Historiography of Somatic Treatments', *History of Psychiatry*, v (1995), 225–41; *idem*, 'Psychiatrists and Historical "Facts": Part Two: Re-writing the History of Asylumdom', *History of Psychiatry*, v (1995), 387–94.

14 W. A. F. Browne, *What Asylums Were, Are and Ought to Be: Being the Substance of Five Lectures Delivered Before the Managers of the Montrose Royal Lunatic Asylum* (Edinburgh: Black, 1837; reprinted Routledge, 1991, with an introduction by Andrew Scull).

15 For evidence from particular asylum histories that confirm this general vignette see, for example, Andrew Scull, *The Most Solitary of Afflictions: Madness and Society in Britain, 1700–1900* (New Haven, Conn. and London: Yale University Press, 1993) and his *Decarceration: Community Treatment and the Deviant – A Radical View*, 2nd edn (Oxford: Polity Press; New Brunswick, N.J.: Rutgers University Press, 1984).

16 William Llewellyn Parry-Jones, *The Trade in Lunacy: A Study of Private Madhouses in England in the Eighteenth and Nineteenth Centuries* (London: Routledge & Kegan Paul, 1971).

17 See E. P. Thompson, 'The Peculiarities of the English', in *The Poverty of Theory and Other Essays* (London: Merlin Press, 1978), 35–91. For some reflections on such myth-making see Raphael Samuel and Paul Thompson (eds), *The Myths We Live By* (London and New York: Routledge, 1990); Roy Porter (ed.), *Myths of the English* (Cambridge: Polity Press, 1992).

PART I

1247–1633

CHAPTER TWO

BACKGROUND

—— •◦• ——

INTRODUCTION

Why should anyone, other than historians or perhaps just medical historians, trouble to read about the very early history of Bethlem Hospital?

The simple answer is that institutions, just as much as individuals and nations, are shaped by their history. This shaping process generates an organizational mentality which has to be understood by anyone seeking to work in or with, or to change, the organization. And in order to understand the organization and what makes it tick, one must understand how it has become what it is today: its history.

But does one really need to look back hundreds of years, to a time when Bethlem was a completely different institution – in fact, not really an 'institution' at all? The alternative might be to choose some other starting-point, and an argument could be made for the 1630s. It was from 1633, when the Hospital was first managed by an employee of the City of London instead of being granted to an individual who made what profits he could from it, and when the Physicianship (medical management) and Keepership (administration) became distinct and separate offices, that Bethlem began to take a more modern form. But 1633 certainly did not represent a complete break with the past. Much of what happened afterwards was a consequence of previous attitudes of mind and ways of doing things. In 1633, Bethlem already had a 'corporate culture', and it is impossible to grasp why its Governors acted as they did in the seventeenth century and beyond without appreciating what that culture was.

Second, one of the things which makes Bethlem so fascinating is that this ancient institution is like an old lady with a very strong and distinctly perverse character. Throughout Bethlem's history, patterns weave. One such pattern is that Bethlem has its *alter ego*, Bedlam. Down the years, at least since the early seventeenth century, 'Bethlem' and 'Bedlam' have danced together, if not always in harmony. It is possible that it was partly as a result of a decision taken by the Governors in the 1590s to encourage visiting that Bedlam, the metaphor for a world gone mad (as opposed to a familiar name for the place, or a word for madhouses generally), developed at all. In our own century, we find those Governors' successors doing their utmost to obliterate the unwelcome associations which the Hospital's *alter ego* conjured up in the popular mind.

And of course in a looking-glass world, things do not happen as expected.

Bethlem's history is full of the unexpected. It owes its existence to the unlikely combination of a London alderman, Simon fitzMary, whose political career was, even by the standards of the mid-thirteenth century, turbulent, and the Italian holder of a near-eastern episcopate. It owes its present specialization, as far as one can tell, to an accident. The process by which the modern Royal Hospital became the great psychiatric institution it is today is obscure, was unpredictable at the outset, and was directed by chance rather than intent.

Aspects of Bethlem's development can be understood only if one appreciates the accidental, and sometimes rather eccentric, nature of that development. Because Bethlem was not designed for the role it eventually assumed, administrative development tended to lag behind functional changes, creating mismatches. It is moreover important to understand, and to keep in mind, just how small Bethlem was at the outset, and how poor, compared to other London religious institutions which later became the great City hospitals. Its development was inevitably constricted by its early poverty, just as its small size resulted in its government being delegated to the Governors, first, of Christ's Hospital, and then of Bridewell, the City's first great reformatory. Another of the constant themes of Bethlem's history is the way that it has for so much of its existence been the little sister of some larger or in other ways dominant institution.

Finally, the very particular circumstances and concerns of the mid-thirteenth century, and the way that society had developed in the two or three centuries beforehand, are critical both to the fact that Bethlem was founded at all, and to the form that foundation took. Some of the background circumstances and concerns arose as a result of large matters: international warfare, dissent within the Catholic Church, the emergence of societies which needed warriors to defend and project their power, and suffered from internal violence. Others were personal, and can now only be guessed at. Factors of this type continued to play a major part in Bethlem's history for several more centuries. Again, it is the large matters which have left the most obvious traces and can most easily be identified today. These included the wars between England and France; the tensions which arose because the claims of popes to universal authority and to financial support from churches throughout Christendom came increasingly to conflict with nationalistic ideas and the desire of English kings, churchmen and peoples alike to escape papal interference and demands; and disputes between English kings and the City of London over control of the Hospital, its revenues and its offices. Individual motives, largely invisible though they are to us, probably had even more impact on the way Bethlem developed. Bethlem cannot be understood in isolation from its history; and its history cannot be understood in isolation from that of the world around it.

HISTORICAL CONTEXT

Europe, 900–1247

The world into which Bethlem Hospital was born is a difficult one for us to imagine today. Its birthyear, 1247, sits about halfway through the Middle Ages (say, 900 to

1500). This of itself lends it no especial importance. If one had to choose one moment of particular significance in the Middle Ages, it would not be the mid-thirteenth century, but the mid-fourteenth – when as much as half of the population of Europe was wiped out by the Black Death. The social, economic, political, moral and even cultural changes that followed the first and greatest assault of the Plague were profound. That was indeed a time of transformation.

But if the mid-thirteenth century saw less dramatic changes, it none the less stood at the culmination of several centuries of rapid development. After the Roman Empire had collapsed, Europe as a whole had experienced successive waves of invasions from lands which had never been conquered by the Romans. In the south, Roman practices, habits of thought and even institutions lingered on, if in bastard-ized forms. But in some places – England, for example – so complete had been the break with the past that an Anglo-Saxon poet could look at the ruins of Roman cities like Bath, and wonder what race of giants had inhabited them. It now no longer seems certain to historians that the Romano-British population was completely des-troyed or driven into the 'Celtic fringes' of Wales and Cornwall by the Anglo-Saxons; but if the descendants of the Romano-British survived physically, memories of that culture did not. And even where, elsewhere in Europe, clouded memories did survive, civilization seemed a very fragile thing, liable at any moment to be swamped by yet one more, and greater, wave of invaders.

In 900, the population of Europe was tiny, huddled together and scattered amid a great wilderness of forests and marshes. Trade had not entirely died out, but it was uncertain and much reduced since the fall of the Roman Empire. There was very little money; most low-level trading involved barter. Above all, although the ghost of the Roman Empire was still flitting around the European corridors of power into mod-ern times, in reality 'emperors', kings, princes and counts exercised infinitely less authority, over much smaller areas, and infinitely less firmly, than had been the case in Rome's heyday. Three hundred and fifty years later, by contrast, numbers had increased dramatically. In England, a population which may still have been under a million in 1100, by 1300 may have exceeded six million. Even six million is small by today's standards; but not by the standards of history. Not until the eighteenth century was the population to rise above this level. Historically speaking, then, it was a demographic explosion. Growth of this order was enough to act as a sharp stimu-lant to the market, leading to a sustained attack on forested and marginal lands by a land-hungry populace, encouraging trade, and prompting the development of an economy in which coin, and even substitutes like the written bond (IOU) which could be passed from hand to hand, played an ever-larger role. It led directly to a growth in government and to its centralization, as successive kings of England tried to find ways of tapping into these new volumes and types of wealth.[1]

In England, particularly, a number of factors had helped to ensure that govern-ment was comparatively centralized, well-developed and effective by 1247: the fact that William of Normandy took the throne as a conqueror in 1066; that England was physically small compared to the lands that contemporary French kings, for example, attempted to rule; that there was already in place a fairly well-developed administra-tion; and that William's followers acquired their holdings where they could, often piecemeal. The growth of royal government and comparatively rapid and successful assertion of royal authority can at least partly be explained by the ruthlessness with which William the Conqueror's youngest son, Henry I, enforced his claim to the English throne and by the absence of serious and protracted disturbances, particularly after the civil wars of the first half of the twelfth century were settled by the accession of Henry I's grandson, King Henry II, in 1154. Unaccustomed peace acted like sunshine after frost, allowing the economy to blossom.

Culturally, England may have been a bit of a backwater. It was certainly not isolated or intellectually backward. Many of its great men, including its kings, held lands across the Channel. Its scholars were educated abroad. When St Thomas à Becket's biographer, William fitzStephen, wrote his account of the saint's life and death in about the 1170s, he interlaced it with quotes (learned at secondhand, admittedly) from Horace, Ovid and Virgil. In his day, so he says, pupils at the London schools would compete on holy days at speechifying, poetry, grammar and making witty epigrams. Like scholars of all ages, they would ridicule their rivals, or even their masters – naming no names, of course.[2]

The fact that the population was rising sharply at this period and that the economy was very active produced, in the end, a society of extreme conditions. At the lowest end, peasants had to pay dear, and on their lords' terms, for what little land they could get. Some settled in the less productive uplands. Other difficult types of terrain, like cleared woodland and drained marshes, were also invaded in the search for more agricultural land. Workers came cheap, and modern economic historians have struggled to explain how those right at the bottom of the thirteenth-century heap managed to survive at all.[3] Meanwhile, the rich were becoming very rich indeed. Consequently, social divisions and differences in wealth were much more marked at this period than earlier.

Churchmen had their own use for the surplus of men, and offered them a legitimate cause in which to spend their energies. The centre, indeed the heart, of the Christian world was Jerusalem. And in the first century or two of the second millennium Christians fought successfully to establish what became known as the Latin Kingdom in the Near East (which included, at various times, much of modern Palestine and Syria). Land which had been won in the early crusades and other military expeditions then had to be defended against rival powers: above all, against the rival religious might of Islam. Although the Muslim leaders were often divided among themselves and were then prepared to ally with Christians against their co-religionists, there were times when a single sultan was able to gather large areas under his rule, presenting a serious threat to the Latin Kingdom. Defending the Latin Kingdom required considerable resources of manpower and cash, as well as organization and a degree of pacification and common purpose in the countries of origin. The insatiable demand for men and money to defend the Latin Kingdom sought to tap the resources of the Christian West at all levels, and therefore had to inspire ordinary people with the desire to secure Christ's birthplace against 'heathen' attackers.[4]

It was undoubtedly a violent age. Little more than a decade after Bethlem's foundation, dissensions between King Henry III and some of his leading barons led to an attempt by the latter to seize control of the government and, subsequently, to outright civil war. Notoriously, Henry III's final victory at Evesham in 1265 over the rebellious Simon de Montfort – his brother-in-law – was 'hideously celebrated' by the dismemberment of the dead man's body, Montfort's head, arms, genitals and feet being cut off. But the violence was mixed with religiosity. When Montfort's body was stripped in preparation for mutilation, he was found to be wearing a hair shirt.[5] Simon de Montfort was certainly not unique among his generation in combining a genuine and intellectual Christianity with martial ardour. It was the spirit of the age. King Louis of France (St Louis) was to die in the Holy Land. After Richard I, no reigning English king got round to fulfilling his vow to participate in a crusade; but they were not necessarily being hypocritical when they expressed an intention to do so. Nor was the crusading spirit confined to the great and the wealthy. Some of the early expeditions were little more than mass movements of the poor and the young, most of whom, unprepared and defenceless as they were, died miserably along the way.[6] And there is little doubt that a similar desire to protect Christ's birthplace was one of the reasons why, in 1247, the London Alderman, Simon fitzMary, decided to give some of his properties to the Bishop of Bethlehem, for the foundation of a priory, or dependent house, of the Order of Bethlehem.

The years of transformation: 1247 to 1633

Almost exactly a hundred years after the foundation of the Priory of St Mary of Bethlehem, England suffered the first onslaught of the Plague, popularly known as the Black Death. Its recurrent attacks over the next century, in particular, had profound social, economic, political and psychological effects. A population which had been growing until about 1300, by 1400 had reduced by at least a third, and quite possibly by a half. A social structure which had become very stratified even by the standards of the time, became less so, with greater social mobility and a lessening of the enormous divide between the very rich and the very poor. The economic effects were mixed. There was less demand overall, but for better-quality goods and services. Small and medium-sized towns which had grown up to serve the needs of an increasing population, withered with it. But that left the field open to the survivors, and London in particular came to dominate a much more concentrated trade network.[7]

Politically, those lower down the social order began to have the strength and the desire to improve their lot yet further. Some contemporary commentators attributed the 'Peasants' Revolt' of 1381, which seems in fact to have involved townsmen and quite prosperous individuals as well as the poorer countryfolk, to the comparatively good standard of living enjoyed by the participants.[8]

But perhaps the greatest consequence of the Black Death was psychological. In an age when it was generally believed that God intervened both directly and indirectly, through natural phenomena, to warn human beings about their conduct, a devasting epidemic like the Plague seemed clearly to be an expression of divine anger. Its occurrence could very easily be interpreted as a sign that society was rotten from the top down: 'these pestilences were purely [the product of] sin', as the fourteenth-century poet, William Langland, had his preacher, Reason, prove. It seems amusing to us now that some of Langland's contemporaries, like the chronicler John of Reading, should ascribe the coming of the Plague at least in part to the 'emptyheadedness of the English [who] began to wear useless hoods [and] extremely short garments . . . which failed to conceal their arses or their private parts'. But wanton and immoderate dress was merely one of the outward symbols of an inward flight from godliness. Moreover, the corruption was worst where it should have been entirely absent. The Church was rotten, and therefore her intercessions had failed and her flock had remained untended and vulnerable. Kings, princes and nobles were corrupt, indifferent to the miseries created by their greed and warfare, too ignoble to perform their duty of protecting the rest of society. In the words of an Italian lawyer, Gabriele de' Mussia, 'because those I appointed to be shepherds of the world have behaved towards their flocks like ravening wolves . . . I shall take a savage revenge upon them'. The family had shown itself to be a weak support, with children refusing to tend their sick parents, and parents rejecting their sick children. Social organizations had likewise proved to be unable to provide the security, shelter and support people needed during the plague years. The individual died or survived alone.[9]

The Black Death did not create individualism and egalitarianism, but it fertilized the social soil, enabling such ideas to flourish. Together with all the other more measurable effects on medieval society, the psychological consequences encouraged different ways of thinking and different aspirations. In due course, these effects in combination were to alter society profoundly. They tended to undermine whatever was orthodox or received wisdom, to raise the value of the individual as against the community, and generally to encourage the survivors of the epidemics, particularly the first great pandemic of the late 1340s, to feel rather as do those who have had 'near-death' experiences. Having 'escaped and regained the world', they viewed that world through very different eyes.

The 1340s also saw the outbreak of another chronic affliction: the wars between England and France which, although they had been going on for over a century beforehand and were to continue in a desultory fashion into the sixteenth century, have become known as the Hundred Years War. As an international political figure as well as the head of the Catholic Church, the Pope was inevitably involved in conflicts between European Christian nations. At this period, however, matters were made much more difficult by the fact that the papal court was located at Avignon, on the borders with France, and that the majority of cardinals, like successive popes, were French. By the last quarter of the fourteenth century, the effect of internal dissent and international pressure had produced a split in the Papacy (the Schism), with rival French and Italian popes. Although this state of affairs only lasted until 1418, the result of the perceived francophilia of the papal court, rising nationalism, and, later, the Schism, was that there were periods after 1340 of considerable hostility in England towards the Papacy and the international Church.[10]

The more sceptical attitudes towards the Church and organized religion generally engendered by the social changes of the later fourteenth century thus acquired a nationalistic justification. They also acquired a practical one, in that Edward III followed the example of his father and grandfather by seizing control of the 'alien priories', or religious houses dependent on a mother-house based in France. This enabled him to exploit their revenues. Unlike his predecessors, he held onto these priories for over thirty years in total, from 1337 to 1360, and again from 1369 to his death in 1377.[11]

The last two decades of the fourteenth century saw a distinct shift in attitudes towards the wars with France, at least among the King and courtiers. There is more than a touch of anti-war sentiment in the poems of John Gower, for instance: to him, the 'kyng that wolde be the worthieste, / The more he myghte our dedly werre [war] cesse'. Even those who did not want to see the wars abandoned were despondent at the inability of the English to recapture the glory days of the mid-century, and attributed it to the moral weakness of their generation: 'Synne is the cause of this gret myscheff.'[12] No doubt it was lack of success combined with war-weariness which produced these pacifist or fatalistic sentiments, because the mood changed again following the accession of Henry V in 1413. The glory days were back with a vengeance, at least for the better part of a decade.

Bethlem was considerably affected by the seizure of the alien priories, of which, as a dependent house of the Order of Bethlehem, based at Clamecy in France, it was one. It was almost certainly in the second half of the fourteenth century that Bethlem found itself a new purpose and new ways of achieving that purpose. The social and psychological upheaval provoked by the Black Death also had its effect. For Bethlem, now a hospital and beginning to specialize in the care of the insane, the peacemaking of Richard II in the 1380s and 1390s and the warmaking of Henry V in the second decade of the fifteenth century alike offered stability and a greater degree of security. Both kings saw themselves as protectors of the Church. This was, however, something of a double-edged sword, involving both an assertion of royal rights over institutions like Bethlem and active support for them against religious dissent and would-be predators. Henry V in particular was, according to Thomas Hoccleve, the 'piler [pillar] of our feith and wareyour [warrior] / Ageyn the heresies bitter galle'. He involved the Church closely in his attempts to ensure that the country at large was behind his French campaigns. The able churchmen who formed an important part of his administration seem consciously to have enhanced and exploited the high emotional state of the period to counter the intellectual criticisms made of the Church: they encouraged faithfulness in their congregations, not by philosophical argument, but by inspiring them with the beauty of holiness – enrapturing them with glittering processions, abundant incense, and wonderful music.[13]

The second major landmark in Bethlem's history occurred exactly three hundred years after its foundation, in 1547, when the City of London acquired control over its administration. Many of the long-term effects of the social and attitudinal changes encouraged by the fourteenth-century epidemics and wars were by then clearly in evidence. As far as the position of the Church was concerned, it was probably the *reactions* to novel and contentious ideas, as much as or more than the ideas themselves, which had had the greatest impact. The protection provided to the Church by earlier kings, and in particular the way that dissent had been suppressed in the fifteenth century, had rendered it much more vulnerable to criticism in the longer term than it might otherwise have been. First, the role of the King as protector of the Church had been enhanced. This protection was bought at a price: and part of that price was that the Church supported kings by providing royal servants with (usually several) remunerative positions and offices. Of twenty-six men given permission to hold London livings in addition to others (in plurality) between 1534 and 1546, eighteen were chaplains to Henry VIII or to other great ecclesiastical or lay lords. Pluralism, and the way that absent holders of livings tended to employ ill-trained and ill-paid curates in their place, was one of the abuses most strongly criticized by religious reformers. Secondly, as a result of the State's involvement in anti-heresy activities, heresy had become closely identified with treason, and there was a tendency during the fifteenth century to interpret any form of doubt, criticism or intellectual discussion as dissidence. Even using rational arguments against dissenters could leave the proponent open to accusations of heresy, as happened to Bishop Reginald Pecock of Chichester in 1457. Thirdly, the exaltation of spirituality over rationality left the Church exceptionally vulnerable to criticisms that its practices were exploiting the credulity and fear of a gullible laity when the dissenting attacks were openly renewed, in the early sixteenth century.[14]

By 1547, the year in which Henry VIII died, the Reformation of the English Church was well under way; Bethlem itself was seized for a time by the King. The Reformation was important in many ways, but to suppose that it was generally welcomed by a populace which had long grown sick of the abuses and corruption of the Catholic Church, as English historians – Anglicans, at least – once tended to do, would be mistaken. Certainly, private religion – how ordinary men and women worshipped – had changed significantly since Bethlem was founded. Private religious life was now increasingly focused on individual intercommunication with God and on practical works of charity. None the less, the Church and the communal worship of the parish remained important. In the fourteenth and fifteenth centuries, individuals in search of an early release from Purgatory had been ever less inclined to leave bequests of land or money to monasteries or other religious institutions. Instead, if they could afford to do so, they endowed temporary or perpetual chantries in which, so the founders hoped, priests prayed for the release of the founder's soul from torment. Even on the eve of the Reformation, this way of attempting to mitigate the pains of Purgatory remained popular. A 1546 survey identified well over three hundred chantry priests in London alone, and half the wills of wealthier Londoners in the early 1520s contained bequests to pay for chantry priests to sing for the soul of the testator.[15]

Probably the best evidence for the success of the Church in responding to the needs of its flock comes, oddly enough, from the hostile comments of royal Commissioners reporting back on the innumerable examples they found of what they regarded as superstitious practices and idolatry. These same reports also show clearly why a successful Church was at the same time so vulnerable to reasoned criticism: much of what had been done to accommodate the needs of worshippers, to inculcate a sense of awe and mystery, involved practices which were at best somewhat deceptive, at worst, downright fraudulent. Sir Thomas More was probably right to warn that the great strength of the dissenters lay, not in their own numbers, but in the weakness of the Church once exposed to their criticisms. It also lay, as chance would have it, in a coincidence between King Henry VIII's needs and desires, the political goals of his advisers, and some of the dissenters' aims.[16]

In 1536, the dissolution of all religious houses worth less than £200 a year was authorized by Parliament. Hospitals were neither specifically included nor exempted, and, as many were linked to other religious institutions, a number were surrendered.

London was more affected than places at a greater distance from Westminster. All of its surviving older hospitals (St Mary within Cripplegate, usually known as Elsing Spital after its founder; the 'New Hospital' of St Mary without Bishopsgate; St Thomas of Acon; St Bartholomew's; and St Anthony's) were in the Crown's hands by 1560, and of these only St Bartholomew's survived as a hospital. Even Henry VII's Savoy Hospital was dissolved, and had to be re-founded by his granddaughter Queen Mary in 1556.[17]

Between the early sixteenth century and the early seventeenth, a period of great political and religious upheaval and intellectual discovery, the overriding concern of leaders of society remained, as ever, social stability. Increasingly assertive oligarchies have been detected in almost every town in the land from the later fifteenth century onwards.[18] Kings and nobles sought to stress the God-given privileges of their status, in the face of evidence of the permeability of social structures. Perhaps it is simply the greater opportunities for recording ideas, and their greater survival rate, resulting from the use of printing, which makes the sixteenth and early seventeenth century appear a time of incessant debate and questioning, and almost paranoid reaction. But there was reason to fear the consequences of new ideas: just after the end of our period, Charles I's execution heralded the start of a radical constitutional experiment, the Commonwealth. This is the period during which the third great landmark in Bethlem's history occurred: the moment which signalled the end of the medieval Hospital and of the old ways of doing things.

NOTES

1 J. L. Bolton, *The Medieval English Economy 1150–1500* (London: Dent, 1980), ch. 2, especially Figure 2.1, 65; R. Woods, *The Population of Britain in the Nineteenth Century* (London: The Economic History Society and Macmillan Education, 1992), ch. 2, especially Table 1, 22.

2 *Norman London by William FitzStephen*, with commentary by Sir Frank Stenton, introduction by F. D. Logan (New York: Italica Press, 1990), 51.

3 For example, Christopher Dyer, *Standards of Living in the Later Middle Ages: Social Change in England, c. 1200–1520* (Cambridge, New York, Melbourne: CUP, 1989), 257.

4 See, for example, Christopher Marshall, *Warfare in the Latin East, 1192–1291* (Cambridge, New York and Melbourne: CUP, 1992).

5 Michael T. Clanchy, *England and its Rulers 1066–1272* (London: Fontana Press, paperback, 1989), 280.

6 Richard Barber, *The Two Cities: Medieval Europe 1050–1320* (London: Routledge, paperback, 1993), 119–24.

7 On the immediate impact of the Black Death from a contemporary perspective, see Henry Knighton's account in R. B. Dobson, *The Peasants' Revolt of 1381*, 2nd edn (Basingstoke: Macmillan, paperback, 1993), 59–63; for a modern analysis of its longer-term effects, see, for example, Dyer, *op. cit.* chs 5, 6, 7.

8 On causes of the 1381 revolt, see Dobson, *op. cit.* part vii, especially 370.

9 For contemporary reactions to the Black Death, see R. Horrox (ed. and trans.), *The Black Death* (Manchester and New York: Manchester University Press, paperback, 1994), especially 132–4 (on lewd dress/sin), 135 (Langland), 306–9 (the Archbishop of Canterbury's criticisms of the 'unbridled' greed of the lower clergy), 15, 128–30 (the failures of the Church and lay princes), 2–3, 30–3 (on abandonment by families and neighbours), 271 (on priests refusing to confess the dying); and for an analysis of its impact and of historians' (changing) assessment of that impact: *ibid.* 229–47.

10 John Barnie, *War in Medieval Society: Social Values and the Hundred Years War 1337–99* (London: Weidenfeld & Nicolson, 1974), 12.

11 See, for example, Peter Heath, *Church and Realm 1272–1461: Conflict and Collaboration in an Age of Crisis* (London: Fontana Press, paperback, 1988), ch. 3, especially 123–4; for the Schism, 260–1; for the seizures, 112–13.

12 *Ibid.* 109, Gerald L. Harriss, 'Introduction: The Exemplar of Kingship', in *idem* (ed.), *Henry V: The Practice of Kingship* (Gloucester: Alan Sutton Publishing, paperback, 1993), 1–29, especially 2–5; Barnie, *op. cit.* 28.

13 Harris, *op. cit.* 24; Heath, *op. cit.* 108–10, 209–22, 273–96; Jeremy Catto, 'Religious Change under Henry V', *Henry V: The Practice of Kingship*, 97–115, especially 102–5.

14 Susan Brigden, *London in the Reformation* (Oxford: Clarendon Press, 1989), 53–6; and see, for example, Robert N. Swanson, *Church and Society in Late Medieval England* (Oxford and Cambridge, Mass.: Blackwell Publishers, paperback, 1993), ch. 7, 309–61.

15 Brigden, *op. cit.* 47, 34. The wills concerned were those proved in the Prerogative Court of Canterbury.

16 *Ibid.* 289, 7–12, 82–3, 1.

17 Nicholas Orme and Margaret Webster, *The English Hospital 1070–1570* (New Haven and London: Yale University Press, 1995), 156–7, 161. By contrast with London's experience, 'most of the working hospitals and almshouses which had escaped the dissolutions of Henry VIII – a very large body . . . survived into the post-Reformation era': *ibid.* 160–1.

18 E. M. W. Tillyard, *The Elizabethan World Picture* (Harmondsworth and Victoria: Penguin, 1970), especially 26; Stephen Rigby, 'Urban Oligarchy in Late Medieval England', in John A. F. Thomson (ed.), *Towns and Townspeople in the Fifteenth Century* (Gloucester: Alan Sutton Publishing, 1988), 62–106, and the sources cited therein.

THE FOUNDATION OF THE PRIORY OF ST MARY OF BETHLEHEM

—— •◆• ——

INTRODUCTION

Gentleman. By whom was these fields [Moorfields, an expanse of marshy ground immediately to the west of the future Bethlem site] given to the citty? *Citizen*. Marry, sir, by two mayds, the only daughters of Sir *William Fines*, a knight of the Rhodes, in the time of Edward the Confessor, . . . *Mary* and *Katherine*; who . . . became two Nuns in the Monastery of Bedlem . . . The Monasterie (now ruinated) was built by their father, Sir *William Fines* . . . Likewise, here in *Bedlem*, is now scituated an hospital for the cure of distracted people, which in former times, about the yeare 1246, was founded by *Simon Fitzmarie*, one of the sheriffes of London, of the same house and kindred, naming it the priory of *Saint Marie de Bethlem*, after the elder of the two sisters.[1]

Much of this early seventeenth-century account of Bethlem's foundation is non-sense: the product of a little knowledge and a lot of guesswork. This is not surprising. Sources of evidence for London as a whole in the first half of the thirteenth century are scant. The early records of the Priory or House, later Hospital, of St Mary of Bethlem have vanished; the foundation charter survives only in a copy, embedded in the record of an early fifteenth-century visitation. The earliest London chronicles tell us something, but only about matters which seemed important to the chroniclers. To make matters worse, chroniclers had their biases. It is on the basis of hostile chronicle evidence that the character of the founder, Simon fitzMary, has been judged and his motives deduced. Almost everything we know about him comes from a London chronicle attributed to an alderman who served a few decades after fitzMary's time, Arnold fitzThedmar. In the opinion of one of its editors, this chronicle was written – or, more probably, written down in its present form – in 1274, some fifteen years after fitzMary was forced out of the city political scene.[2] The chronicler was certainly partisan, though not blindly so, in his championship of the City and its privileges, and he has been used largely uncritically by historians of London politics. On the basis of fitzThedmar's account, fitzMary has been portrayed by modern historians as a royalist trojan horse within the City's walls, prepared to allow himself to be used in Henry III's several assaults on the City's privileges and liberties.[3]

Sometimes the administrative and legal records allow one to check the accuracy of statements in the chronicles. Unfortunately, even the central records are incomplete. There is, for instance, a gap in the Curia Regis (King's Court) rolls between 1244/5 and 1248/9 which neatly encompasses the time when a contentious legal case involving fitzMary was before the King and Council. Had this record survived, it might have provided a valuable check on the reliability of the city chronicler's account. But it does not. As a result of losses like this, there are serious difficulties in reconstructing the background and activities of the Hospital's thirteenth-century founder.

It is not all doom and gloom, however. Even impressions of fitzMary's seal survive incidentally among the ancient deeds in the Public Record Office and Guildhall Library (see Plates 3.1 and 3.2). He bought and sold property, and on a couple of occasions mentioned members of his family. His activities in an official capacity brought him to public notice and record, and he also witnessed the acts of others in what was apparently a private capacity. It is true that fitzMary the man has to be reconstructed from a few bare bones of fact, with much of the skeleton missing, and fleshed out with some educated guesses. But the activity is not wasted effort. Something recognizable and of some value emerges. The result does not entirely support the chronicler's interpretation of fitzMary's career. What it does do is offer some clues as to the founder's motives in donating his lands for the establishment of the future Priory of St Mary of Bethlem.

Plate 3.1 Simon fitzMary's seal: obverse, portraying the Virgin and Child (text unclear). Reproduced by kind permission of the Dean and Chapter of St Paul's Cathedral; deposited at the Guildhall Library.

Plate 3.2 Simon fitzMary's seal: reverse, portraying a boar's head, text 'SI: FILII MARIE'. Reproduced by kind permission of the Dean and Chapter of St Paul's Cathedral; deposited at the Guildhall Library.

To understand fitzMary's motives, one needs some insight into the social and political milieu in which he lived and worked. London and its often-fraught relationship with the King, Henry III, form an influential background to fitzMary's story. But this chapter is not just about Simon fitzMary. Without his donation, Bethlem might never have been built, it is true. He may quite possibly have been toying for some time with the idea of endowing some sort of a religious institution: he seems to have had no sons, and his only daughter was apparently outlawed for her part in a murder which, although it was committed about a decade after Bethlem was founded, may merely have been the nadir of the kind of career that most fathers would prefer their daughters not to embark upon. All the same, it is unlikely, though not impossible, that the particular form the foundation took was fitzMary's idea. He was probably persuaded to make his donation by a chance meeting with the Bishop-elect of Bethlehem, an Italian called Goffredo de Prefetti, in the late autumn of 1247. De Prefetti's motives are therefore no less important a part of the story, as is the reason why he was in England in the first place.

THIRTEENTH-CENTURY LONDON

On the whole, London seems to have done well from the economic and social developments of the twelfth and thirteenth centuries. The modern image of medieval towns is of crowded, noisy, smelly places in which pedestrians were constantly at risk of having the contents of chamber-pots thrown over them. There is some truth in the image: medieval London had more in common with modern Third World towns than with First World cities. In the 1240s, its inhabitants had plenty of complaints about nuisances caused by people blocking the drains, noxious butchers' stalls, and extensions to houses which encroached into and obstructed the streets. But the very fact that they complained about their neighbours' unsanitary practices, about polluted air and about overcrowding suggests that they aspired to better things – and, no doubt, in part achieved them. By about 1250, the City had its own water-supply system, running through pipes from springs at Tyburn, to the west of the City (one conduit head stood just to the north of a property at Charing Cross, the Stone House, which Bethlem subsequently acquired). The climate, which became colder and wetter in the later Middle Ages, was still benign. William fitzStephen's London in the late twelfth century was a place in which the inhabitants were never far from gardens, trees, pastures and forests. Even in Alderman fitzMary's day, over half a century later, parts of the City may have been relatively empty and rural. The name of one relatively central street and ward, Cornhill, may preserve an earlier reality, and the marshy nature of the central and north-eastern areas may have discouraged development there for some time. Even if fitzStephen was exaggerating just a little when he claimed that 'the matrons of London are very Sabines' (models of virtue), his praise of the City as a whole was probably not entirely misplaced.[4]

By 1247, London had developed enormously, both in physical size and complexity and in its governmental organization. The great City was, in William fitzStephen's description, a busy hub of trade. Its population, like that of much of Europe, grew greatly, almost certainly reaching 70,000, and perhaps even 100,000, by the end of the thirteenth century. At that point, people may have been being driven away from their rural homes by a combination of a worsening climate, increased competition for land, and lack of employment, rather than lured to London by the realistic prospect of good conditions. But in the first half of the thirteenth century it may have been the carrot rather than the stick which drew them to the City. As trade increased and specialisms developed, so employment opportunities improved. In 1247, London had for well over a century been attracting merchants and traders from France and Germany. It already boasted a large number of distinct trades (the Weavers Company got its first charter at about the same time as the City obtained its first recorded one, in the late twelfth century). This reflected both the trend towards diversification and the growing reliance on craftsmen to produce what might otherwise have been produced at home. A hundred parish churches served its burgeoning population: though some, admittedly, were small by later standards.[5]

Politically, London had also been developing strongly in the hundred years or so before the foundation of the Priory of St Mary of Bethlem. Some of its institutions, like the great Folkmoot when all citizens met together to witness if not actually participate actively in major civic events and elections, or the Court of Husting, which had had administrative functions but gradually came to be almost entirely a court of law and record, seem to have been pre-Conquest in origin. The division of the City into some twenty-four 'wards' or areas with fixed boundaries, probably for defensive purposes, seems to have occurred shortly after the Conquest. Certainly the wards were in place by 1127 (see Figure 3.1). The aldermanic office, with (broadly

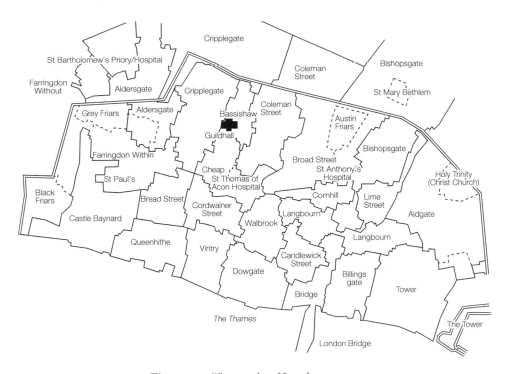

Figure 3.1 The wards of London *c.* 1127

speaking) one Alderman having responsibility for each Ward, seems to have developed at much the same time. During the twelfth and early thirteenth centuries, however, the City was steadily increasing the privileges it obtained from successive kings and was as steadily building up an independent hierarchy of government. Since the early twelfth century, the City had had the right to elect its own Sheriffs. In the first decade of the thirteenth century it was granted the right to have a Mayor.[6]

This process was not entirely smooth. Londoners tended to regard the City's privileges and liberties, once obtained, as a perpetual right. Any intervention in the conduct of civic government by the King or royal officials was much resented: as Simon fitzMary was to discover to his cost. The fact, however, was that any grant was at the King's pleasure. Any individual King could take away what he or his forebears had granted. In practice, if he was in a strong enough position, he could do so on a whim; and in theory he could do so at any stage if the City abused its rights or offended him in some way. As late as Richard II's reign, at the end of the fourteenth century, London found itself paying a very heavy price for incurring the King's displeasure. And yet the assertion of civic privilege could be very effective indeed. In 1403, two men commissioned by Chancery to conduct a visitation of the then Hospital of St Mary of Bethlem attempted to summon a jury of Londoners to inform them about alleged alienations of hospital property. The Londoners protested that they were not bound to serve on juries summoned outside the City or by external authorities, save in particular circumstances, and flatly – and successfully – refused to cooperate. The Commissioners withdrew, defeated.

The consistent efforts made by Londoners to defend and if possible extend their City's privileges and liberties, and the fact that the King and royal officials were normally keen to ensure that London did not escape royal supervision and control, quite often led to clashes. On several occasions during Henry III's reign the Mayor and Aldermen found themselves being summoned before an irate King to explain their attitude or behaviour. There were times when matters reached such a pass that the City was 'taken into the King's hands', and a warden or wardens appointed to govern it in the place of the Mayor and Aldermen until one side or the other backed down. The City was also drawn into the civil wars of the period: the barons who opposed King John are said to have replaced one London mayor with another in 1214/15, and the City was actively involved in the violent disputes between Henry III and his barons during the 1250s and 1260s.[7] It is possible that another of Simon fitzMary's motives for offering his land just outside Bishopsgate for the foundation of a priory was that he hoped to gratify King Henry by doing so. Or possibly he thought this would be a suitably grand gesture with which to set the seal to a civic career which – as he was probably already aware – would shortly be coming to an end. If so, political ambition and personal pride, as well as religious zeal, formed part of the motivation for the foundation.

THE CIRCUMSTANCES AND PUBLIC AIMS OF THE FOUNDATION

Bethlem was intended, 'not as a mad-house, but as a link between England and the Holy Land, part of a wider movement in which the cathedral church of the Nativity at Bethlehem and its bishops sought land, alms and hospitality in western Europe'.[8] The motive for the foundation appears straightforward: religious and crusading zeal. Three years earlier, the town of Bethlehem and its cathedral church, which had been recovered from the Saracens (Arabian Muslims) in 1229, had fallen to the Turks. Unlike the Saracens, the Turks appear to have inflicted considerable damage on the places they over-ran. The See of Bethlehem had also suffered considerable aliena-tions of its possessions during the episcopate of its previous Bishop, John 'Romanus'. Bishop John was removed in 1244, and was succeeded by Goffredo de Prefetti. De Prefetti seems to have spent the years following his election in attempting to recover the possessions alienated by his predecessor and to restore the financial position of his see. It seems to have been at about this time that the Order of Bethlehem developed as a distinct entity, with alms-raising as a major aim. In 1245, a mere month after de Prefetti's election, the canons of Bethlehem were granted a general protection by the Pope to enable them to seek alms in England. Then, in 1246, the Bishop-elect himself was sent as papal envoy to Scotland. From there, he travelled south to join the English court of Henry III. He remained in England for about a year. Towards the end of his stay, in September 1247, King Henry issued an unlimited protection to the 'brethren of the house of Betleem', again perhaps in connection with their alms-raising activities.[9] Exactly a month later, on 23 October, Simon fitzMary granted the Bishop and the Church of Bethlehem his lands and tenements in the parish of St Botolph's, Bishopsgate Ward, in the north-eastern suburbs of London.

It may be wrong, however, to assume that it was the difficulties faced by the Church of Bethlehem which alone prompted the foundation. The name of the founder and Bishop de Prefetti's background suggest the possibility that other influ-ences may have encouraged the two men to found this particular priory at this particular time. The first half of the thirteenth century was a time of internal as well as external struggle for the Catholic Church. Schismatic or heretic sects, like the Cathars, attracted many, including those in high places. In its developed form, Cathar-ism was a dualist creed, its followers believing that the existence of evil in a world created by a good God was explained by the fact that God had his evil mirror-image, the anti-God, Satan. As Catharism diverged more widely from heterodoxy, it came increasingly to deny the central doctrines of the Catholic Church, including the traditional teaching about Christ in the New Testament: the Incarnation (and hence Mary's motherhood of God-made-flesh), the Redemption and the Resurrection.[10]

As part of its response, the Catholic Church launched a programme of religious education and sought to involve the laity more actively than before in the defence of its dogma. In Italy, this drive was at first led by movements and organizations like the Franciscan Order of Penitence and the Society of Faith: the latter played a specifically anti-heretic role. In time, however, these were complemented and succeeded by lay confraternities. Two of the earliest were founded by an ex-Cathar, the Milanese inquisitor Peter the Martyr, in 1232 and 1244. Both these companies were devoted to Mary. This was probably deliberately done: 'As an ex-Cathar himself, Peter realized that it was possible to capitalize on the growing popularity of Mary in face of the Cathars' denial of her divine motherhood.'[11]

Apart from the fact that from 1232–3 de Prefetti helped negotiate a truce between the communes of Sienna, Orvieto and Florence, and that it was in Florence that the second of the confraternities associated with Peter the Martyr was established, there seems to be nothing to link de Prefetti closely with either the education campaign or the Marian societies. But he would certainly have been aware of the policy and of the means being used to further it. Perhaps, having encountered Sheriff fitzMary in the latter's official capacity while he was staying at Westminster, the Bishop was prompted by fitzMary's matronymic ('son of Mary') to talk to him of the need to defend not only Bethlehem from the Infidel but also Mary from heretic attacks. It may therefore be that the foundation of the Priory of St Mary of Bethlem owed something to a wish to protect the Church from internal dissent as well as to the intention to fund its fight against external enemies.

FitzMary's grant was designed to provide the physical basis of the foundation of a priory which would offer hospitality to the poor, and for the Bishop and any other members or representatives of the Order of Bethlehem when they visited England. The aim was to give the Order both a permanent home from which the English brothers could routinely seek funds for the support of the Order overseas, and a temporary base for those visiting from abroad in order to make special collections. This was probably the first 'house' of the Church of Bethlehem to be founded in England.[12]

THE FOUNDER AND HIS PERSONAL MOTIVES

FitzMary's background: family, friends, and wealth

The motives of de Prefetti were probably exactly what one would expect in the circumstances: he wanted to generate in England regular sources of income for the Order of Bethlehem and to obtain support for the crusade announced in the year of his election. What, though, of Alderman Simon fitzMary?

It would almost certainly make it easier to gain some insight into Simon fitzMary's personal or political motivations if one knew something about his family background. Was he, for example, a member of one of the dynasties which ruled London during the thirteenth century? If so, he would have started with a great advantage in civic public life. Or was he a 'self-made man'? In that case, he made his way in civic life against the odds, lacking the advantage of many of his peers: presumably he was a particularly able, fortunate or ruthless man.

The date of his birth is unknown, but he seems to have lived until 1269 at the earliest, and had reached his majority by 1228 or 1229 at the latest. So he was probably born in about 1200. Bethlem's historian, Rev. E. G. O'Donoghue, discussed the possibility that he was illegitimate, a thought suggested by the fact that he bore a matronymic. That in turn led to speculations about the possibility that his humble, or, at least, irregular origins might have contributed to fitzMary's political aims, encouraging him to develop into a champion of the 'proletariat' against the ruling dynasts.[13] What is clear is that fitzMary knew who his father was: in one of his deeds he names him as Walter of Fulham, and says that they jointly held some property in Bread Street Ward, London. As Walter did not join his son in authorizing the transaction, it is likely that he was dead by this time (the early 1230s). A witness to an earlier transaction relating to the land in Bread Street Ward was a man called Alan de Balun, probably the Alderman of that name who was serving in about 1215. FitzMary was related by blood or marriage to the Baluns, who were a substantial London family. He had a nephew called Alan Balun, although there is no evidence that the two Alans were closely connected.[14] The evidence, such as it is, gives the impression that fitzMary's father was a man of middling status, but that the family had some grander connections. Perhaps Walter's wife (Mary?) was a Balun, and their son's surname reflects her higher status.

FitzMary himself may have been married twice. His wife is called Avice in 1241 and (if the man concerned is our Simon fitzMary, which seems likely) Edith in Leicestershire records of 1262 and 1269. There is no evidence in his various deeds that he had any children. However, as was mentioned earlier, he does in fact seem to have had a daughter, Joan. We only know about Joan because she was accused of involvement in the murder of another woman's husband in 1357–8.[15]

The two families with which fitzMary seems to have been most closely associated were the Aswys and the Viels. Both were leading London families, with shrievalties and even mayoralties to their credit. In 1234, Ralph Aswy III and William Aswy, together with another man, undertook to prosecute the men alleged to have murdered their father, Ralph Aswy II. FitzMary was one of their pledges; in other words, he promised to pay a sum to the King if the Aswys failed to pursue the prosecution. At some unknown date, John Viel senior and two of his sons witnessed a deed of fitzMary's. In November 1246 fitzMary was said to have 'stood openly with Margery [Viel, John's widow]' in a controversial law suit. In so doing, he put his civic career on the line. It is possible to identify some of his other friends, too. In his foundation charter, he requested prayers for three men and three women: they were, in addition to Ralph Aswy III and his wife Dionysia, Guy de Merlaw and his wife Mathilda, and John Durant and his wife Margery. John Durant is described as a *narrator* or pleader (a lawyer who argued his client's case in law, as opposed to an attorney who simply took the client's place for the duration of the case) and was evidently a man of some standing.[16]

FitzMary does seem to have been fairly wealthy, possibly even meriting the description of 'a great landowner'. His earliest surviving property transaction is from the late 1220s, when he sold property in Cripplegate Ward (to the north of Bread Street Ward) and Westminster for 10s. This is not a particularly large sum. In the course of the next twelve years, however, fitzMary sold over £10-worth of properties or rents. To put this in some sort of perspective, in the 1240s the King ordered that all men holding property worth £20 a year were to be knighted. This is about eight times the income fitzMary would have received from the lands and rents he sold between 1228/9 and 1240/1.[17]

By the 1240s, fitzMary was more often to be found purchasing than selling property. In 1246 he made a valuable purchase, paying £20 for a property in Walbrook Ward. Two years later, he bought thirty-five acres of land and the rents of two tenements in Shoreditch. Again, he paid £20 for these properties and rents. At some stage he also acquired property in the parish of St Laurence Jewry, though its value is unknown. Unless he sold the Walbrook tenements to fund his later purchases, his investment in land and rents by the late 1240s must have amounted to at least £40, giving him an income of at least £10 a year. And of course he had, sometime before 1247, acquired the properties in Bishopsgate Ward which he granted to the Order of Bethlehem.[18]

There is no evidence of any further transactions in the 1250s, and by the 1260s he had probably left London. At any rate, he bought writs directed to the Sheriff of that county in 1262 and 1269. Unfortunately, the record does not say what the Sheriff of Leicestershire was required to do. But evidently fitzMary had some interest in that region, and it may well be that he was buying or defending the acquisition of property there.[19]

FitzMary's political career

Despite his influential friends and acquaintances, fitzMary remained just below the highest levels of civic life, never becoming Mayor, for instance, despite being an Alderman and twice serving as a Sheriff. Whether this reflected the fact that his social standing and connections were not quite good enough, or whether it was merely that his political attitudes and behaviour prevented him climbing even higher, it is unfortunately impossible to tell.

This is despite the fact that fitzMary's career was controversial and was therefore better recorded than the careers of many other Aldermen of his period. He first emerged into historical view when, according to fitzThedmar's account, as Sheriff he wasted the City's 'goods' so seriously that the receipt of the farm of the City was removed from him by the Mayor and given into the control of the Sheriffs' Clerks (the 'farm' was a fixed sum paid, in this case, to the Exchequer, the 'farmers', the Sheriffs, keeping any surplus profits they managed to make while in office). There is no way of judging how much truth there is in this story.[20] There are however reasons for suspecting that fitzThedmar might have got it slightly wrong. FitzMary was 'the King's Chamberlain of England', in 1232/3 or 1234. One possibility is that fitz-Thedmar confused criticism of fitzMary's conduct as King's Chamberlain with that concerning his conduct as Sheriff. Moreover, part of the function of the King's Chamberlain was to supervise the conduct of the Sheriffs, with whom he was associated in various inquests. The fact that fitzMary occupied these offices together for a period, holding one inquest as both King's Chamberlain and Sheriff, may well have been regarded as unsatisfactory, with the result that the Chamberlainship was taken from him.[21]

Whatever problems fitzMary may have had during his Shrievalty, he contrived to be elected Alderman of Walbrook Ward in 1237, together with Ralph Aswy III and Robert de Cornhill, said to be 'a prominent loyalist'. In view of the known connections between fitzMary and the Aswys, it is quite possible that these elections represented an increase in power by one of the City's political factions. There can certainly be no doubting the politically provocative nature of fitzMary's next move. In 1239, he obtained royal letters appointing him Sheriff for a second time. As London had for many years been electing its Sheriffs, instead of having them appointed by the King, the City refused to admit him. Henry III promptly suspended the City's liberties for three months. None the less, the immediate victory went to

London, or at least to the other party: the Aldermen in due course chose the Sheriffs, and fitzMary was not one of them.[22]

In September 1246, fitzMary finally secured a second term as Sheriff. Thus far, his career had been like the proverbial curate's egg – good in parts. He was almost certainly regarded with suspicion and hostility by some of his fellow Aldermen, but most of his actions, though controversial, had been technically correct. His enemies were eventually to get the upper hand, however. The seeds of his downfall were sown during his second Shrievalty. In the spring of 1247, a notorious case involving Margery, widow of the former Alderman, John Viel senior, was adjudged in the City's Court of Husting, at this time the main City court for trying civil (private) cases. The Viel case involved the rules applied in the City in actions for dower. City custom normally allowed the widow one-third of the late husband's possessions; more, if there were no children. In Mrs Viel's case, however, it was decided that widows to whom a specific dowry had been assigned as part of the marriage settlement were only entitled to that property, unless their late husbands had chosen to leave them more. Mrs Viel was seeking the usual third part of John Viel's goods. Under the rules as they had now been interpreted, she was evidently going to get considerably less than this. She therefore appealed to the King.

Although there is no mention of fitzMary in the passage in which fitzThedmar deals with the Viel case, a memorandum further on in the chronicle notes that he openly supported Margery. On account of this and what fitzThedmar unhelpfully describes as the 'many other wicked and detestible acts which he had secretly perpetrated against the city', he was judged to have breached conditions placed upon him in 1244 for opposing the Mayor's attempt to appoint a Sheriff for a second consecutive term, and in March 1249 he finally lost his Aldermanry.[23] There are no further references to him in the city chronicles after this date. On 22 August 1261, his property in St Lawrence Jewry was described as 'late of Simon fitzMary'. As already mentioned, he may have retired to Leicestershire.

FitzMary's character and motives

Even if fitzMary was not a financially incompetent Sheriff as fitzThedmar alleges, and even if the Mayor did not interfere in his exercise of the Shrievalty for this reason, he clearly made enemies. The surviving legal sources also suggest that he may have abused his position in a number of ways while he was Sheriff. Among the complaints made during the course of the judicial visitation (eyre) of 1244 was the allegation that fitzMary, together with one Robert de Herbintun, had seized an orphan from the widow of the boy's lawful guardian and had kept him imprisoned until he died. FitzMary and Herbintun claimed that they 'had possession' and that the boy had 'died lawfully in Robert's custody': in other words, they were claiming guardianship of the boy. Unfortunately, no outcome is recorded, but the case probably amounted to no more than a straightforward dispute over who should act as the boy's guardian, now that the man to whom his care had been committed had died.[24]

A case which looks, at first sight, even more unsavoury led to fitzMary being mentioned during an investigation in 1234 into oppressions of the London Jewish community by royal officials and others. However, in this instance fitzMary probably merely, as Sheriff, took over the custody of certain deeds and charters which had allegedly been stolen from the complainant for the duration of the dispute. There is no suggestion that he himself accepted bribes or was involved in any direct wrongdoing.[25]

The 1244 eyre also provides some evidence which needs to be taken into account when considering whether fitzMary was merely a royalist stooge. In the course of one enquiry, he offered a hundred marks (£67), pledged against all his goods, that 'the pleas of the City might be held and pleaded as they were pleaded in the time of King Richard and King John' (in other words, that the limit of precedent be set at 1189). FitzMary's offer probably saved 'all the barons', or leading men, from a corporate fine. Similarly, during his second Shrievalty, he and his fellow-Sheriff had the misfortune to incur swingeing fines of £20 each for distraining (seizing goods in order to force compliance with a court order) a woman after they had received a royal writ ordering them not to do so. Almost certainly the Sheriffs acted as they did because a case was pending against the woman in the city courts. The probability is that the City was trying to insist that actions begun in its courts should not be stayed by ones subsequently initiated in the King's Court. If so, fitzMary and his colleague were attempting to defend or assert an important civic privilege.[26]

FitzThedmar provides some evidence to show that fitzMary was keen to protect the City's customs and practices against attack, whatever the source. In 1245, the chronicler tells us, 'there arose the greatest dissension in the City through the agency of Simon FitzMary, who, hearing that the Mayor wanted to admit Nicholas Bat [the serving sheriff] for the following year', pointed out that this was forbidden by an ordinance made fifteen years previously. The Mayor managed to force the election of Bat through, despite the Aldermen's objections. It required the King's intervention to correct this piece of civic despotism. FitzMary himself was forced to resign his Aldermanry, 'out of reverence for the Mayor'(!), although he was subsequently readmitted on condition that he do nothing further 'contrary to the city's liberties'. It was his alleged breach of this condition which was used to justify his permanent dismissal from the Aldermanry in 1249.[27]

Finally, there is the Viel case. If fitzThedmar is to be believed, this was an instance of unjustified royal intervention in city affairs. Again, however, all may not be quite as it appears. Margery Viel's main champion was, according to the chronicler, one Henry de la Mare, who is spoken of as though he was simply a friend or supporter of the widow. He was in fact 'the most distinguished Surrey man in the royal service in the 13th century'. In October 1247 he had been appointed justice of the King's Court. Whether de la Mare was acting for the King or as Margery's counsel is unclear. Either way, heavy guns were being brought to bear on the City.

This does not mean that the City was being unfairly treated. In early August 1248, the Chief Justice, Henry of Bath, sat at St Martin le Grand to examine the case (undoubtedly on error; in other words, Mrs Viel was alleging a technical fault in the way that her case had been dealt with). That the case involved important principles is certain, although this does not emerge clearly from fitzThedmar's account. According to the chronicler, Henry of Bath said that the judgment itself was not false, but that the process was defective in that Margery's opponents had not been duly summoned; and that, since John Viel had made a testament, the matter was in any event subject to ecclesiastical jurisdiction. Certainly in this respect the City's defence (that Margery's opponents were on permanent standby to answer, and that the parties had consented to have the matter determined in Husting) was weak. Moreover, fitzThedmar may well have misreported Henry of Bath. The King himself described it as a 'false judgment'. Despite the chronicler's assertions, therefore, the Viel case was almost certainly not an instance of high-handed royal interference in the City's courts, but of the City attempting and failing to get away with evading the supervisory jurisdiction of the royal justices.[28]

It was while the Viel case was still being fought out, in October 1247, just after his second Shrievalty ended, that fitzMary sealed the charter granting his lands in Bishopsgate Ward for the foundation of the Priory of St Mary of Bethlehem. This endowment may possibly have overstretched his resources; by early spring 1248, his two sureties for £33 13s 4d owed to the Exchequer were seeking protection against the possibility of being distrained because of his default – although they clearly believed that he had sufficient to cover the debt himself.[29]

CONCLUSION

What does all this evidence suggest about fitzMary's background, career, personality and character, and, by extension, about his motives for founding the Priory?

As far as his financial position is concerned, the surviving deeds and fines clearly do not account for all his holdings. All the same, it is apparent that he inherited fairly valuable property, or acquired it, relatively early in life. He may also have enjoyed the income from other properties in right of his wife or wives: the Camberwell lands sold in the early 1240s may well have been his wife Avice's, since not only Simon and Avice, but also Avice's heirs, offered a guarantee to the purchaser. He may none the less have been in some financial embarrassment in the early 1230s. But if he did get into difficulties in the early years of his civic career, he seems to have recovered. By the late 1240s, he was undoubtedly a wealthy man.

On the basis of the few known facts about fitzMary's family, it does not really seem true to say of him that he was one of the London dynasts. He appears neither to have belonged to, nor founded, a city dynasty. The most that can be said, assuming that his nephew was related in some way to Alderman Balun, is that fitzMary was connected by blood or marriage to an aldermanic family. On the other hand, there seems to be no good reason to suppose that he was illegitimate, or to attribute to this circumstance his conduct in political life. As O'Donoghue himself pointed out, other factors could result in the use of the mother's name: inheritance from the mother rather than the father, for example. Several prominent Londoners of this period were known by matronyms (for example, William fitzIsabel and William fitzAlice, who were Sheriffs in 1194/5 and 1201/2 respectively). Even if fitzMary himself did not belong to one of the city dynasties, however, he moved in those circles, and he had some powerful friends to whom he appears to have been close, or, at least, loyal.

When it comes to assessing his career and motivations, much depends on fitz-Thedmar's reliability on the subject of events which had occurred some forty years before the probable date of the compilation of his chronicle, and, indeed, on his veracity. There is little doubt that fitzThedmar was sometimes accidentally or deliberately misleading. The allegation about fitzMary's financial mismanagement may be one example. The account of the Viel case, and the statement that this was merely one more instance of fitzMary's manifold wrongdoings, is certainly another. And the very fact that the statement about fitzMary's involvement in this case is misplaced in the narrative, and appears merely as a justification for his eventual dismissal, suggests that he did not so much fall as a result of the outrage generated immediately by his conduct, as that the Viel episode was used in a later political *coup* as an excuse to oust him.

Overall, therefore, if fitzMary was a royalist agent, it seems that he was so only intermittently. On two occasions, he acted to promote City interests, not the King's. Even when he behaved in ways which were considered disrespectful to the Mayor or disadvantageous to the City, he was not necessarily prompted by a desire to please the King. His attitude over the improper re-election of Sheriff Bat was justified. The Mayor was quite clearly in the wrong. FitzMary may not have been actuated by high moral principles, of course; city politics may have prompted him to oppose Bat's re-election. On the other hand, if he did indeed support Margery Viel openly, his attitude may well have been based on a mixture of personal loyalty (to the Viels) and on the strict justice of the case. There is no evidence that he benefited from it, or could have done so. Margery remained a widow to the end of her days, so he was evidently not planning to marry her.[30] Nor does it seem all that probable that fitzMary was using the case for some political end of Henry III's. This was not a case of 'royal' courts trying to poach litigation from city ones; Henry of Bath stated explicitly that jurisdiction belonged to the Church courts.

What the evidence suggests is that fitzMary was a man of uncompromising nature. If some of the things he did were to the King's advantage, others were not. He was almost certainly not simply the King's puppet. Possibly his family background prevented him from having the success in civic life which he felt he ought to have had, and he resented this. He probably was a difficult man. It is clear that he made enemies who eventually managed to destroy him as a political force. But he was not a lone wolf. He had influential friends, and he seems to have been loyal to them. If he realized, as presumably he must have done, what the reaction to his support of Margery Viel was likely to be, he was prepared to make considerable sacrifices on their behalves.

His known behaviour suggests that his motive for founding the Priory may have been genuinely religious: the product of a rather aggressive concern to do what was right. It may not be too fanciful to see in him something of the muscular Christianity that motivated his much greater contemporary and namesake, Simon de Montfort. And no doubt, as Geoffrey O'Donoghue suggested, his matronymic provided at least part of his motivation, as a devoted son of Mary.

NOTES

1 [Richard Johnson], *The Pleasant Walkes of Moore-fields: Being the Gift of Two Sisters, Now Beautified, to the Continuing Fame of this Worthy Citty* (London: Henry Gosson, 1607), 6, 13.
2 T. Stapledon (ed.), *De Antiquis Legibus Liber: Cronica Maiorum et Vicecomitum Londoniam et quedam, que contingebant temporibus illis ab anno MCLXXVIII° ad annum MCCLXXIV^m*,

Camden Society, First Series, xxxiv (1846), 7, and (in English) H. T. Riley (ed. and trans.), *Chronicles of the Mayors and Sheriffs of London AD 1189 to AD 1274 . . . [and] The French Chronicle of London, AD 1259 to AD 1343* (London: Trubner, 1863), p. i.

3 Gwynn A. Williams, *Medieval London: From Commune to Capital* (London: University of London/Athlone Press, 1963), 202–7.

4 H. M. Chew and M. Weinbaum (eds), *The London Eyre of 1244*, London Record Society, vi (1970); C. M. Barron, 'The Later Middle Ages: 1270–1520', in M. D. Lobel (ed.), *The City of London: From Prehistoric Times to c. 1520*, 2nd edn, *The British Atlas of Historic Towns*, iii (Oxford: OUP/The Historic Towns Trust, 1991), 42–56, especially 45; C. Brooke, 'The Central Middle Ages: 800–1270', *The City of London: From Prehistoric Times to c. 1520*, 30–41, especially 34; *Norman London by William FitzStephen*, with commentary by Sir Frank Stenton, introduction by F. D. Lozan (New York: Italica Press, 1990), 50.

5 Bruce M. S. Campbell, James A. Galloway, Derek Keene and Margaret Murphy, *A Medieval Capital and its Grain Supply: Agrarian Production in the London Region c. 1300*, Historical Geography Research Series, xxx (The Queen's University of Belfast/Centre for Metropolitan History, University of London, 1993), 31–2, 34–7; Brooke, *op. cit.*, 8–12; George Unwin, *The Gilds and Companies of London* (London: Methuen, 1908), 43.

6 Christopher N. L. Brooke and Gillian Keir, *London 800–1216: The Shaping of a City* (London: Secker & Warburg, 1975), 168–70; H. T. Riley (ed. and trans.), *Liber Albus: The White Book of the City of London* (London: R. Griffin, 1861), 114, 119.

7 [E. Tyrrell and N. H. Nicolas (eds)], *Chronicle of London, from 1089 to 1483 . . .* (1827; reprinted, Felinfach: Llanerch Publishers, 1995), 8.

8 Nicholas Vincent, 'Goffredo de Prefetti and the Church of Bethlehem in England', *Journal of Ecclesiastical History* (forthcoming, January 1998). We are most grateful to Dr Vincent for allowing us sight of this article, which throws considerable light on the circumstances of Bethlem's foundation. What follows, unless otherwise stated, is based on his account.

9 *Calendar of Patent Rolls, 1232–1247*, 510.

10 On Catharism and responses to it, see, for example, Malcolm Barber, *The Two Cities: Medieval Europe 1050–1320* (London and New York: Routledge, paperback, 1993), 183–92.

11 John Henderson, *Piety and Charity in Late Medieval Florence* (Oxford, New York: Clarendon Press/OUP, 1994), 27–8.

12 There is a reference from 1223 to the procurator of 'domus Sancte Marie de Bethleem in Anglia', but the meaning is probably that the Procurator, not the House, was in England: *Calendar of Patent Rolls 1216–25*, 371.

13 Edward G. O'Donoghue, *The Story of Bethlehem Hospital from its Foundation in 1247* (London: T. Fisher Unwin, 1914), 5.

14 M. S. Guiseppe, H. Jenkinson and the Reverend W. Hudson (eds), *Chertsey Abbey Cartularies, Volume II, Part I*, Surrey Record Society, xii (1958), 300–1; *ibid.* 299 and 297–8 (items 1209 and 1207); Alan Balun junior is described as 'son of William, son of Richard'; N. J. M. Kerling (ed.), *The Cartulary of St Bartholomew's Hospital: founded 1123, a Calendar* (London: St Bartholomew's/Lund Humphries, 1973), 77 and 72 (items 744 and 682).

15 PRO Surrey Feet of Fines, CP25/1/226/11 item 235; C. Roberts (ed.), *Excerpta e Rotulis Finium in Turri Londoniensi Asservatis, Henrico Tertio Regis, AD 1216–1272*, 2 volumes (London: Record Commission, 1835–6), ii, 376, 496 (it is however possible that 'Avice' and 'Edith' are variant forms of the one name); M. Weinbaum (ed.), *The London Eyre of 1276*, London Record Society, xii (1976), 25 (item 84).

16 *Calendar of Close Rolls of Henry 3, AD 1227–1231* (London: Eyre and Spottiswoode 1902), 92; *Ghall*, Ancient Deeds, MS 25121/1070; *De Antiquis Legibus Liber*, 15; PRO, Chancery, Ecclesiastical Miscellanea, C270/22, m 5; *The London Eyre of 1276*, 145, 148 (items 669 and 715). A Robert Duraunt was one of the wardens of London in 1196/7.

17 Williams, *op. cit.* 202; PRO, Ancient Deeds, C210/3160 (the date is based on an endorsement in a later hand); *Chertsey Abbey Cartularies, II, I*, 300–1; PRO, Surrey Feet of Fines, CP25/1/226/11, item 235; *Ghall*, St Paul's Ancient Deeds, MS 25121/1070; *Calendar of Close Rolls 1237–42*, 428, 434–5, etc.

18 *Ghall*, St Paul's Ancient Deeds, MS 25121/214; *Cartulary of St Bartholomew's*, 74 (item 699);

Calendar of Charter Rolls, Volume I: Henry 3, AD 1226–1257 (London, 1903), 307; PRO, Feet of Fines, London and Middlesex, CP25/1/147/15, item 275, and *Ghall*, St Paul's Ancient Deeds, MS 25121/1704; *Calendar of Charter Rolls 1257–1300*, 38.

19 *Excerpta e Rotuli Finium*, ii, 376, 496.

20 *De Antiquis Legibus Liber*, 7. There was no evident effect on the proffers, or initial payments in, made by fitzMary and his fellow-Sheriff when they were first called to account at the Exchequer; their immediate proffer against the farm was of over £52. However, this is not conclusive. His clerks may simply have done their job well: PRO, Pipe Roll, E372/78.

21 According to the London records, fitzMary was superseded as King's Chamberlain by John de Colemere sometime between late September 1233 and early September 1234. However, the Exchequer records show that Colemere succeeded Richard Reynger. Therefore fitzMary may in fact have been Reynger's deputy: *The London Eyre of 1244*, 35–6 and 37–8 (nos. 84 and 89); *Calendar of Close Rolls 1231–34*, 386; W. Kellaway, 'The Coroner in Medieval London', in A. E. J. Hollaender and W. Kellaway (eds), *Studies in London History Presented to P. E. Jones* (London: Hodder & Stoughton, 1969), 75–91, especially 76–7, 87; *Ghall*, MS 111/5 mm. 827, 817, 830. *The London Eyre of 1244*, 2–3 (item 4) and note; *ibid.* 35–6 and 37–8 (items 84 and 89).

22 Williams, *op. cit.* 203–5; *De Antiquis Legibus Liber*, 8, 7; *Calendar of Close Rolls 1237–42*, 254.

23 *De Antiquis Legibus Liber*, 15; Williams, *op. cit.* 207; *Calendar of Charter Rolls, 1257–1300*, 38.

24 *The London Eyre of 1244*, 73–4 (item 184); printed in *Liber Albus*, 95–6, under 'pleas of the 27th year [of Henry III]', i.e. 1242–3.

25 *Curia Regis Rolls of the Reign of Henry 3: vol XV: 17 to 21 Henry 3 (1233–1237)*, 257–8 (item 1110).

26 *The London Eyre of 1244*, 9–10 (item 36), and p. xx, pledge pardoned, May 1245: *Calendar of Close Rolls 1242–47*, 307; *Curia Regis Rolls, 1233–37*, 470 (item 1876) (this is a curious, even a suspicious-looking, entry, added at the end of the roll, but misplaced by ten years. Presumably a clerk at some much later date decided that the record should be amended, and mistook 'xx Henry III' for 'xxx Henry III'); *Calendar of Liberate Rolls 1245–51*, 113.

27 *De Antiquis Legibus Liber*, 10–11, 15; and see 6, for the ordinance he was quoting.

28 C. A. F. Meekings and D. Crook (eds), *The 1235 Surrey Eyre*, Surrey Record Society (2 vols, 1979), i, 220 (We are grateful to Dr Crook for this reference); *De Antiquis Legibus Liber*, 12–15; *ibid.* 12–14; *Calendar of Close Rolls 1247–51*, 79.

29 *Calendar of Close Rolls 1247–51*, 32 and 33.

30 *CLRO* MCFP 78 (Husting Roll 2, case 153), the acknowledgement in early 1260s of a bond made in favour of Margery Viel and her sister, Dionisia de Bufle.

THE DEVELOPMENT OF THE BETHLEM PRECINCT

—— ·◆· ——

INTRODUCTION

Most of what we know about the early development of Bethlem relates to its property holdings and transactions. Over the years, its precinct underwent enormous development. By the 1630s there were nearly sixty houses, a couple of them being very substantial ones, occupying between an acre and an acre and a half of space (smaller than a football pitch). The precinct had changed from an open area, in which a few buildings were dotted about, to a crowded urban plot in which every foot of ground which was not used as a thoroughfare was occupied by a house, a yard or garden, or outbuildings.

Together with the physical changes went a considerable change of character. Early Bethlem was almost certainly a quiet backwater; by the 1630s it was a busy community. The insistence by Bethlem's sixteenth- and seventeenth century Governors that the Porter should close the gates at a set hour, and thereafter only admit those with a very good reason to enter, has a Canutian air to it: the tides of time would soon sweep away the last vestiges of separateness.

DEVELOPMENT OF THE SITE TO *c.* 1400

Although Bethlem lay outside the City walls, it was inside the 'bars' or barriers which marked the City boundaries. It stood moreover beside the highway which linked the City with the Great North Road and ran on southwards to London Bridge (see Figure 4.1). It was thus well-placed for its original purpose of offering a base and accommodation for members of the Order of Bethlem when they set out on or returned from their fund-raising journeys. It was also, as it happened, a good site for a hospital, as alms could be solicited from passers-by. Later, visiting Bethlem became a popular pastime, in part at least because the Hospital was close to the first Elizabethan theatres and other sources of entertainment. In the seventeenth and eighteenth centuries, casual visitors contributed quite substantial sums to the income of the Hospital and its staff.

The general appearance of the area immediately around Bethlem is shown in

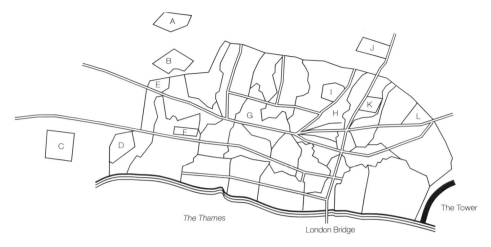

Figure 4.1 The main thoroughfares of London, *c.* 1400

Key:

A Charterhouse	G St Thomas of Acon Hospital
B St Bartholomew's Priory/Hospital	H St Anthony's Hospital
C White Friars	I Austin Friars
D Black Friars	J St Mary Bethlem
E Grey Friars	K St Helen's Priory
F St Paul's	L Holy Trinity Priory (Christ Church)

Plate 4.1. Moorfields, the large open expanse to the west, remained marshy until it was drained in the sixteenth century. Before that, Bishopsgate Without largely retained its character as a stopping-place for travellers, with 'a large Inne for the receit of travellers . . . called the *Dolphin*' directly opposite Bethlem on Bishopsgate Street and, heading northwards towards the site of the 'New Hospital' of St Mary Without Bishopsgate, 'many fair houses builded, for receipt and lodging of worshipful persons' (the 'New Hospital' was in fact older than Bethlem by a half-century, and got its misnomer when it was re-founded). Suburban wards tended to be occupied by tradesmen whose occupations were unacceptable within the City walls: butchery, trades involving fire or highly inflammable materials and processes, and the like. Bishopsgate does not however appear to have become associated with any particular trade during the medieval period, unlike neighbouring Portsoken where the bell-founders congregated. By the early seventeenth century, 'noxious' trades were certainly practised there, but the impression is that the area remained relatively under-developed commercially before then. Indeed, it seems to have been mainly a place of resort and entertainment. Access to Moorfields had been made easier by the opening up of Moorgate in the late fifteenth century, and within a century the area offered all sorts of amusements to Londoners and travellers alike, from promenades and theatres (briefly) to archery and artillery-practice grounds.

By the time the city chronicler and antiquarian John Stow was writing his *Survey* of London in the last decades of the sixteenth century, however, Bishopsgate Without was getting overcrowded. The western side of Bishopsgate Street, beyond

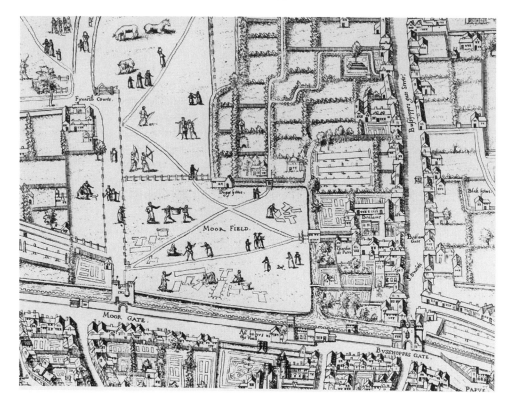

Plate 4.1 The Moorfields area: section of 'Copperplate Map', *c.* 1559. Reproduced by kind permission of the Museum of London.

Bethlem precinct, was densely packed with 'many houses ... builded with Allies backward ... [which were] too much pesterd with people ... up to the Bars'. Stow also complained about the way that houses had been built on a causeway along the north bank of the City Ditch between St Botolph's Church and Petty France, with the result that household refuse blocked the Ditch 'to the danger of empoisoning the whole city'. The failure of successive city governments to keep the City Ditch clear was a favourite theme of Stow's, but there is no reason to doubt that the problem existed.[1]

The site of the first Bethlem was directly to the north of St Botolph's Church, which itself lay a short distance outside Bishopsgate, on the west side of Bishopsgate Street. Simon fitzMary's foundation charter seems at first sight to give some indication of what exactly he was granting to the future priory: 'all that I had or might have there, in houses, gardens, orchards, fishponds, ditches, marshes, and all other appurtenances [within boundaries which stretch] in length from the king's highway [Bishopsgate Street] eastwards to the ditch to the west called depeditch, and in breadth from the lands which are Ralph Dunnyng's in the north and to the land of St Botolph's Church in the south.' Unfortunately, although the boundaries mean something, there is no guarantee that the site of the future priory contained any, let alone every one, of the features listed in the charter. The catalogue may well be no more than a catch-all.[2]

If fitzMary's plot was undeveloped when it was granted, it cannot have remained so for long. Precinct walls were probably built or erected at an early stage. Excavations carried out in 1986 to the west of the precinct have revealed the probable position of the Deep Ditch and what are described as wooden revetments or retaining walls running east to west which, it is suggested, may have marked the southern perimeter of the precinct.[3] Judging by late seventeenth-century maps of London, the precinct walls enclosed an area of about 6,000 square yards: just under 120 yards on the northern edge and just over 100 yards on the southern, with the Bishopsgate frontage and western perimeter extending for 50–60 yards. Open ground belonging to Bethlem surrounded the precinct on three sides. The property as a whole probably covered about three and a quarter acres.

The Church of St Mary of Bethlehem may well also have been built shortly after the foundation of the Priory (see Figure 4.2 for this and other, probably early, buildings). According to a mid-sixteenth-century rental, it stood near the East Gate, the main entrance to the precinct off Bishopsgate Street. A map of the same date, the Copperplate Map, and another derived from it (the 'Agas' Map, *c.* 1560–70) show in this position a tall, towerless, crenellated building with features which appear to be buttresses and three large windows. There is however also a building in a west-central position which looks like an early church tower, but without a nave. In 1403, the Bethlem Porter was occupying a ground-floor room in the Hospital's West Gate, described as being separated from the 'high altar' of the Hospital by a garden. 'High

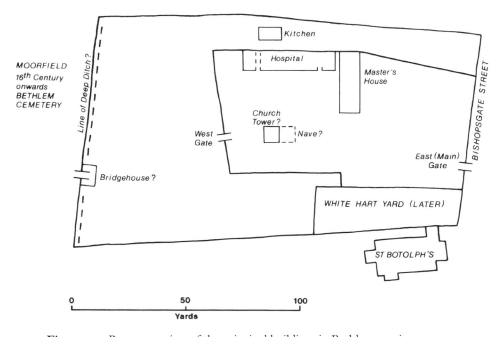

Figure 4.2 Reconstruction of the principal buildings in Bethlem precinct, *c.* 1300

altar' presumably means the Church. If so, the Church was the naveless western building. As both these buildings were referred to indifferently from the late fourteenth century onwards as chapels, it may be that confusion arose over time. By the early sixteenth century it was believed that Bethlem had begun life as a monastery, which indicates that there was considerable uncertainty by this stage over its origins. The solution to the riddle may therefore be that the westernmost building was indeed originally the Church, but that its nave was destroyed in the 1390s to make way for a churchyard which was laid out and consecrated then. By this time the Chapel had been built and could offer more spacious as well as more prestigious accommodation. As a result, it tended to be regarded, not merely as the 'Great Chapel', but also as 'Bethlem Church'.[4]

Another early building must have been some form of accommodation for the Master, the brethren, and their visitors. Possibly the Long House mentioned in later documents and shown in sixteenth- and seventeenth-century maps as forming or abutting the northern perimeter of the precinct served this purpose from the outset, or replaced an earlier building on the same site. The Master may from an early stage have occupied a separate building which stood at right angles to the Long House at its eastern end: the Master's right to the tenancy of a house in this position had been established by the sixteenth century at the latest. The East Gate must have existed from the start, though no doubt its appearance and the accommodation it offered changed over time. It seems very likely, too, that there was from the beginning a west gate allowing access to the open ground between the precinct and the Deep Ditch.

By the late fourteenth century, if not before, the precinct was being developed as a source of income. There is evidence to suggest that Bethlem accommodated quite a few individuals who were neither inmates nor 'staff': at least eight, and possibly twelve in 1403 (of whom the two women were relatives of the Master). In 1391, for example, there is a mention of 'chambers newly built between the church and chapel as soon as they shall be finished', one of which was granted to Robert Baron and his wife. Sixteenth-century maps show nothing lying directly between the Church and Chapel. Conceivably the chambers were never built, the graveyard taking their place. However, it seems more likely that the chambers planned in 1391 were built somewhere in the previously open area between the Chapel, the Churchyard and the Church, but were poorly constructed and did not survive into the sixteenth century.

If so, the 'chambers' were not the only private buildings constructed during this period. When Robert Baron died, the land he had acquired under a second grant, by now containing a room with a private parlour or bedroom over it, was let out again. Baron may also have sublet a third tenement to someone he describes only as 'Sire Hugh'. Moreover, Baron, his wife and their subtenants were almost certainly not the only private tenants in the precinct. The London fishmonger, Hugh Bartelot, who died in 1413 'within Bedlem', was probably also a tenant of the Hospital rather than an inmate, since his will was registered and proved in the London Commissary Court.[5]

The re-grant of Robert Baron's land incidentally reveals the existence of another building which was probably erected at an early stage. It describes Baron's property as lying 'on the north side of the chief kitchen of the hospital'. There is nothing to indicate where this kitchen was (other than that it was close to and somewhere to the south of 'the great garden'). Possibly, however, it was the old kitchen which stood in a yard just behind (to the north of) the Hospital building in the seventeenth century.[6]

The main focus of development between 1350 and 1400 was the new Chapel. Considerable effort and, no doubt, money, was expended on its construction. This venture led to friction with the Rector of the local parish church, St Botolph's, Bishopsgate, in 1361. A year later, the Master had to pay the Rector 13s 4d and undertake to allow him 'peaceably to enjoy' the profits of that Church, in return for which the rector withdrew his objection to the erection of the Chapel. This seems not to have resolved the situation, however. In 1364 the Master obtained a royal writ of protection, alleging that 'some evildoers try by armed force to dispute his possession of the hospital, and prevent him from completing the chapel and other buildings begun by him in the hospital'. Two years later, the project was threatened from another direction (but possibly from the same motive). The Mayor and Aldermen were persuaded to write to the Bishop of Bethlehem and one of his advisers saying that they had heard that the Bishop intended to let the Hospital to farm, and that the Master and brethren had started 'a great work of a chapel there, which work they would be unable to accomplish and carry out successfully without the charitable assistance of the mayor and aldermen and other good folk of [London]'. Despite all the opposition to the building of the Chapel, however, the work was eventually completed. By 1403, and in fact probably by the early 1380s, the Hospital rejoiced in what were then known as the Great and the Little Chapel.[7] Figure 4.3 shows the positions of the major buildings which existed by the early fifteenth century.

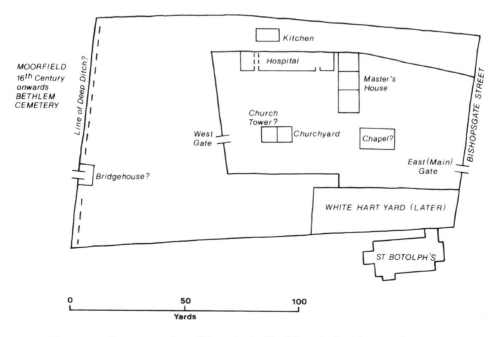

Figure 4.3 Reconstruction of the principal buildings in Bethlem precinct, *c.* 1400

DEVELOPMENT OF THE SITE, *c.* 1400–1633

All this, though tantalizing, hardly enables one to map out the precinct and its buildings with any degree of confidence. It is not until the sixteenth century that it begins to be possible to picture the area. The map of London known as the 'Copperplate Map' (see Plate 4.1), probably surveyed in the late 1550s, shows sixteen substantial buildings in addition to the old Hospital or Long House, the Church, and the Chapel. The scale of the Map at this point is about 25 inches to the mile. Just how reliable the Map is, is however open to question. The precinct was clearly not really about 100 to 120 yards square, as it appears to be on the Copperplate Map, and it seems certain that the old Hospital building did not occupy anything like as much of the northern perimeter as the Map suggests. Even more disturbingly, most of the buildings have dimensions which are multiples of a standard length and width. That the Map is to some extent inaccurate is therefore certain. On the other hand, it seems not to be entirely fanciful: certainly the northern and southern edges of the perimeter seem to be about the right length. The question therefore is whether or not the number, orientation and relative size of the buildings offer an indication of the appearance of the precinct during Elizabeth I's reign.[8]

Fortunately, it is possible to cross-check the reliability of the Copperplate Map against other evidence. A royal grant confirming the transfer of control of the Hospital to the City, made in 1555, lists all the properties involved. It also states their income value, which gives some indication of the relative size or importance of the properties. It is thus possible to make a direct and contemporaneous comparison with the Map.

The 1555 grant starts by listing four tenements, two with gardens, held for between £1 6s 8d and £2 a year. Leaving these aside for the moment, there follows 'the greate Gardincs withe a litle lodge in the same, one tenemente therunto adioyninge in the tenure of Peter DeSaylle [de Saville]. Also one Tenement with a stable under the weste gate of the said House of Bethlem . . .'. According to the Copperplate Map, to the south and south-west of the precinct lies a large garden, subdivided into plots, orchards, and a substantial walled area which on the map is described as 'Giardin di Piero'. In the north-west corner of 'Peter's Garden' is a small house, and a much more substantial house, which lies between the west gate and the south-west corner of the precinct, juts out into it. Judging by the description, it seems very likely indeed that this is a bloc formed by Peter de Saville's house, his stabling and a tenement in the west gate, and his garden with its little lodge to the west. Indeed, there is other evidence to confirm it. When the same properties were leased anew in 1561, they were described as 'the litell house or lodge sett and beinge in th'one of the said greate gardens on the *west* parte of Bethlem [emphasis added] . . . And also one tenement adioyninge the said lodge nowe or of late in the tenure of Peter Dessavaille . . .'.

The grant next mentions 'iij Tenementes withe iij Gardines to the same belonging'. These probably form the range of buildings along the southern side of the precinct. Then there is 'one great Tenement with a great yarde or voyde place, and all the Roomes over the East gate to the same Tenement belongynge'. Assuming, as seems likely, that we are being taken round the precinct in a logical order, this probably refers to the large house which, according to the Map, lies between the south-east corner of the precinct and the east gate. That this is so is proved by the 1561 lease already mentioned, which describes the same property as being 'sett and edified next unto the king's highway or streate called Bisshopsgate'.

Then there are two further houses, held at lowish rents (20s and £1 13s 4d respectively), followed by a house and garden occupied by the then Keeper (as the City-appointed Masters were known), Edward Alleyn, for £2 10s a year. The first two are probably represented on the Map by the two roofs and chimneys just visible between the Chapel/'Church' and Bishopsgate Street, immediately to the north of the main gate. The Master's House is, almost certainly, the large building abutting the east end of the old Hospital building, since in 1575 Edward Alleyn's house was described as lying between 'the said great olde chapell ther on the Southe' and another property held by one of the Queen's Yeomen of the Guard to the north.[9]

Finally, to return to the four houses which were listed first in the grant, the only remaining candidates are the four houses located between the west end of the old Hospital and the West Gate, with gardens beyond them. The grant mentions a further house and garden, let for a mere 10s a year, as lying outside the precinct itself in the parish of St Botolph's, Bishopsgate. Presumably, this is what was later described as a 'faire Tenement with a garden to it situate on the other side of the Street over against this place [opposite Bethlem]'; if so, it was a bargain.[10]

By this stage, the Hospital had acquired a house at Charing Cross, usually described as 'the Stone House', which the Master was accused in 1403 of having alienated. This probably means that it had been let out and its income appropriated by the Master, whereas the profits ought properly to have remained to the Hospital as a whole. Certainly the house was still in the Hospital's possession in 1555, when it brought in £3 a year. In fact, the Stone House had already (before 1545) been divided into three tenements, with the tenants subletting it to others. Royal Commissioners in 1632 surmised that part of it had been lost to the Hospital in the second half of the sixteenth century, in circumstances which aroused Geoffrey O'Donoghue to a positive fury of indignation.

The Commissioners' surmise was based on depositions made in the course of an Exchequer Chamber case of 1609–10. However, royal Commissioners seem almost as a matter of routine to have suspected that alienation had occurred or that property rights had not been properly protected (the same suspicion led to a confrontation between the 1403 Commissioners and the London jurors, who refused to cooperate with the Commission). It appears in fact that one of the three parcels of land concerned had belonged to Westminster Abbey since the fifteenth century at the latest, and in 1493 the third plot of land was described as 'the garden of the Mews'. The second plot was in the 1630s tenanted by the same people as the 'Mews garden', and also belonged to the Crown. So it seems that none of the properties which Bethlem's Governors, prompted presumably by the Commissioners' report, attempted to 'recover' in 1649 had ever been part of the Stone House site.[11]

Within the precinct, development continued. In 1575, a couple of builders were granted permission to redevelop two tenements on the southern side of the precinct, described as lying between Peter de Saville's house to the west and a house to the east which had been let to Mrs Margaret Johnson and her husband. The builders were also given permission to erect as many dwellings as they thought appropriate on the site of the 'greate old chapell', re-using any materials they found.[12] By this stage the 'Great Chapel' or 'Church' was clearly ruinous. It had been granted to the Parish Clerks company for their meetings in 1552, suggesting that it was then in fair order. But when in May 1568 it was proposed to let it again, the lead from its roof was reserved for the use of Bridewell (despite all the assurances that the Court of Aldermen had offered to the Bishop of London in 1556 'concernynge the repayringe of the said Churche and ornaments thereof').[13]

By the late sixteenth century the precinct was probably already looking very different from the way it had appeared in the 1550s. If the redevelopment had not yet reached the extent shown in a map in the 1650s (see Plate 4.2), it is likely that a good deal of infilling had taken place. The builders managed to fit no fewer than fourteen 'tenements and dwelling houses' in the two sites granted to them in 1575. Mrs Johnson's tenement was rebuilt by her successor as two. By the early seventeenth century, most of the centre of the precinct was probably occupied by houses and their gardens or yards. In 1618, at least ten houses were described as being in the 'Middle rowe' of Bethlem. These houses evidently stood on and between the former Church and Chapel sites.[14]

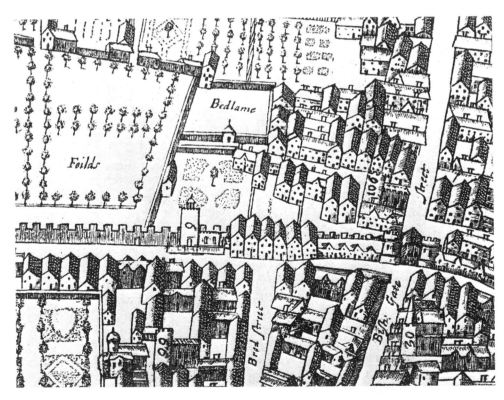

Plate 4.2 Bethlem and its vicinity: section of a map by William Faithhorne and Richard Newcourt, 1658. Reproduced by kind permission of the Museum of London.

THE 'OLD HOSPITAL' IN 1633

In 1632, we finally get a glimpse of the layout of the Hospital itself. Then 'Bethlem house wherein the poore distracted persons are kept' consisted of 'the old house' with, on the ground floor, a parlour, kitchen, two larders, 'a long entrie throughout the house' and twenty-one rooms occupied by the inmates. Upstairs were eight rooms for servants and inmates, and a long room, then derelict but being refurbished to provide eight further rooms for inmates. 'Room' at this period did not mean what it now means: rather, it was a place, space or office (as in the 'room' of an attorney in the Mayor's Court). The inmates, and indeed those who looked after them, may therefore have inhabited a single large chamber on each floor, partitioned into cubicles. Quite what the 'long entrie' was is unclear. It sounds like a corridor running the full length of the building, but might equally have gone from front to rear. The Copperplate Map shows two doorways at either end of the building, one of which certainly led to such a passage. In 1561 a tenant was granted rights of access 'through the Entrie sett and beinge on the west ende of the longe house of Bethlem' to the stables and common lavatory at the rear.

In 1632, there was also a brick house 'being newly added unto the old roomes' which contained a cellar, kitchen, hall, four chambers and a garret. This formed, or more probably formed part of, the range of buildings which ran southwards from the east end of the main Hospital, judging by a 1626 reference which stated that the Brick House was to be built to replace a 'little house next Bethlem'. In April 1632, the Privy Council had suggested that this new house, which was not yet leased out, should be used to accommodate 'suche poore lunaticks as eyther shall bee sicke or in a nearer hope of recovery'. The Bridewell Governors, who had control of Bethlem's administration and who had originally planned to use the house for this purpose, subsequently decided otherwise, despite the Privy Councillors' advice. By October, it was tenanted, if not occupied, by the Keeper (it will be recalled that the Master's House had long formed part of the same range). It is possible, of course, that the Keeper was himself using it to accommodate some of the inmates.[15]

The Copperplate Map probably gives a fair impression of the appearance of the Hospital building even in the early seventeenth century. It shows what appears to be a single-storey house, possibly with some small windows directly under the eaves, and eight windows at ground-floor level between the two doors. In 1629, the Bridewell Governors ordered that iron bars should be provided for the house and its cellar, together with casements for eight windows, six of which were to be glazed. Presumably the windows had previously been secured by shutters at night time; the window bars appear to have been a novelty.[16]

Even more promising, apparently, is a detailed description of the Hospital given in a lease of the old Bethlem site, dated 1677. The lessee undertook to redevelop 'All that ruinous and decayed building lately called the old Hospital of Bethlem', including two tenements to the east formerly occupied by the Hospital's Steward and Porter (part of the former Master's House range), and to erect new houses on the site. The site also included an area (a yard) to the north which contained 'a great chimney and barn'.

The document goes on to say that 'the same is more particularly set forth and described by a Map . . . to these presents annexed'. The annex (Plate 4.3) shows the

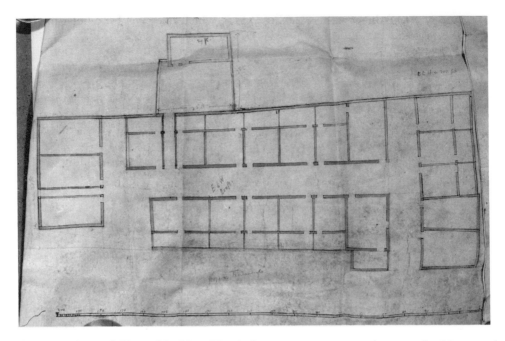

Plate 4.3 'Ground Plan of Bethlem Hospital': annex to agreement between the Mayor and Commonalty of London and William Bates, 1677. Reproduced by permission of the Bethlem Royal Hospital Archives and Museum.

ground-plan of what appear to be two long buildings running east to west. The northernmost is about one hundred and twenty feet long, the southern about ten feet shorter. There is also a range of rooms or individual houses to the east and a smaller range to the west. These measure, respectively, about 80 and about 51 feet, north–south. To the north is a walled plot with an internal wall, probably of a building; its measurements are exactly those of the yard. All but the southern building are outlined in yellow on the original.[17]

Although the plan is of the Hospital site in 1677, it is possible to work out what was likely to have existed forty or fifty years earlier. We know, for example, that in 1643 the Bridewell Governors decided to pull down 'two little tenements . . . scituate at the west end of Bethlem house . . . and ranging straight westwards with the same' in order, at last, to build a substantial extension to house the Hospital's inmates. Despite the implication that the new building would be an extension on the same east–west axis as the Hospital, in fact the site ran southwards, being 49 feet north to south and a mere 26 feet east to west. Almost certainly the western range shown in the 1677 plan is the 1643 building, even though, at around 51 by 30 feet, it is slightly larger than the two houses it replaced. In 1633, therefore, although something of roughly similar dimensions to the western range existed, it did not form part of the Hospital building. The east range, as has already been mentioned, consisted in part of the house 'builded of bricke . . . newly added unto the old roomes' in 1632; even if it was used to house inmates from 1632 onwards, which is not certain, it was undoubtedly privately occupied before that time.[18] Thus, at least until 1632, the Hospital consisted merely of the central (northern) block, which may well have been the last surviving remnant of the original Long House.

It has to be said that Geoffrey O'Donoghue saw matters differently. He took it for granted that everything on the plan was both to be included in the redevelopment and formed part of the Hospital buildings. On this basis, he proceeded to make what sense he could of what he believed was the ground-plan of old Bethlem, using the 1632 description of its layout (see Figure 4.4). He suggested that the northern building was an extension built sometime before 1662, and referred to by the Bridewell Governors in 1669 as 'that part of the hospitall house of Bethlem last built Northward'. The long southern building he took to be the original Hospital building, which, like the northern building, contained pairs of bedrooms and 'corridors'.[19]

The present Bethlem Archivist, Patricia Allderidge, long ago spotted some improbable features in all this. To begin with, the long, narrow spaces which O'Donoghue thought were 'corridors' ('C') do not connect or lead anywhere; with some being as large as five feet by twenty-five, they would have been a considerable waste of space. The 'rooms' ('D'), too, none of which interconnect, are unlikely to have housed individual inmates. The smallest is about twelve feet by fifteen. The 'porter's lodge' ('E') is over twenty feet by fifteen.

In fact, O'Donoghue probably misread the evidence. The yellow outlining on the plan may well have been intended to delineate the site available for redevelopment. The long southern building on the 1677 plan was probably the range described in the deed as Thomas Hopper's tenements. Where, then, is 'that part of the hospitall house

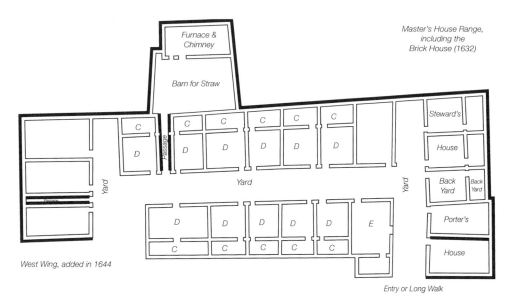

Figure 4.4 'Ground-plan of Bethlem Hospital': Geoffrey O'Donoghue's interpretation of the annex to the 1677 Agreement
Type of text used: *O'Donoghue's notes*
Additional notes
C Corridors   D Room   E Porter's Lodge
▬▬▬ (probably marking the area available for redevelopment)

of Bethlem last built Northwards', mentioned in 1669? It may in fact be the yard, with its chimney and barn, which protrudes to the north, as the 1669 entry goes on immediately to discuss the state of the 'Straw Rome' and 'the wall on the backeside of the Hospitall'. Although O'Donoghue assumed that the new construction referred to in 1669 was the same as the 'Roomes in the last new buildings' mentioned in 1663, which were to be used to house the most distracted female patients, it is more likely that the 1643 building was meant.[20]

Even if this is correct, however, it does not explain those curious groupings of 'corridors' and 'rooms' in the 1677 plan. They seem impossible to reconcile with the 1632 description of the Hospital's layout, even allowing generously for alterations meanwhile. Nor does the layout of the east wing fit the description of the 1632 Brick House. The answer may in fact be simple: this is *not* a ground-plan of the old Hospital. The indenture may be one of the several known *post hoc* grants made by the City, and merely recorded what the grantee had already done, or, at the very least, planned to do shortly. In other words, this may be the ground-plan of one-up, one-down terraced houses with narrow yards at the back.

On the basis of the 1677 ground-plan, the only parts of the original layout of the Hospital which one can feel at all confident were unchanged were the boundaries of, and the rights-of-way through, the property (identified by bold line). Intriguingly, however, late seventeenth-century maps continued to show a long building with a northern protrusion, very similar in appearance to the northern central block and yard, but about 160 feet long instead of 120 feet. In the map produced by Ogilby and Morgan at the time of the move to Moorfields, this building is shown 'double Hatch'd' in the fashion of 'Churches and Eminent Buildings' (see Plate 4.4), although the same building is not so distinguished in Morgan's map of the early 1680s (see Plate 4.5).[21] A possible explanation is that the two northernmost rooms of the eastern range (the 1632 Brick House?) were incorporated into the central block before the rest was demolished or redeveloped. The length of the building in Ogilby and Morgan's map is virtually identical to that of the central building plus the two rooms of the eastern range, as shown on the 1677 ground-plan.

This raises the possibility that, whatever redevelopment of the site took place in the late 1670s, it did not obliterate the oldest part of the Hospital. The Long House, together with the early seventeenth-century Brick House, may have survived for some while after the move to Moorfields with its external appearance, at least, intact. However, bearing in mind that the Bridewell Governors ordered several major repairs to the structure, perhaps one should not exaggerate the antiquity of what survived.[22] 'Old Bethlem' may well have been very much like grandfather's axe: still as good as new after two replacement shafts and three replacement heads.

THE CHARACTER AND ATMOSPHERE OF SIXTEENTH- AND SEVENTEENTH-CENTURY BETHLEM

Passing references to Bethlem in the late sixteenth- and early seventeenth-century records give the impression of a place which was accessible and largely indistinguishable

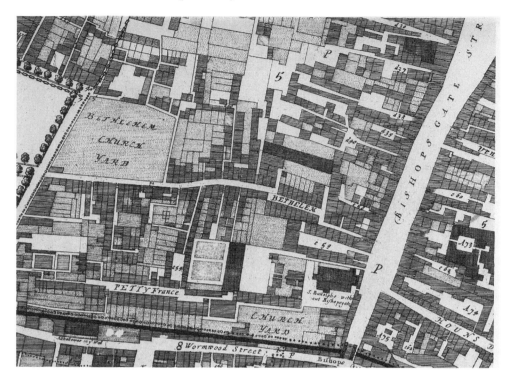

Plate 4.4 Bethlem and its vicinity: section of map by John Ogilby and William Morgan, 1677. Reproduced by kind permission of the Guildhall Library, Corporation of London.

in character from the rest of Bishopsgate. Possibly the closing of the main gates at set hours in the evening limited the amount of coming and going after nine or ten o'clock at night. Otherwise, the precinct seems to have been wide open to the population at large. A witness before the Bridewell Court in October 1579 described how he and a couple of his friends 'dogged [his sister and her lover] through Bedlem' and were eventually rewarded by finding them 'in thalley of a garden goenge to Shorditche . . . abusinge their bodyes'. In another case, a young woman testified that Mr Lee, who had slept with her in her father's house 'And promysed her ij or iij Angells [the large sum of 20s or 30s] but he gave her not', unsurprisingly proved elusive thereafter: 'last weike she sawe hym in Bedlam and he ran away into a house.'

Passers-by may have been attracted in by the fact that there was at least one inn in the precinct itself by the late sixteenth century, the Black Bull. There was also a property known 'by the sign of the Cocke' which may have been an inn, and was probably inside the precinct. By the early 1640s, a house immediately to the north-west of the main Hospital building was tenanted by a distiller who used the premises as a tavern – much to the Bridewell Governors' disapproval; when the lease came up for renewal, the tenant was forbidden to continue with this part of his trade.[23]

Other aspects of the Bethlem tenants' and visitors' conduct came to the Governors'

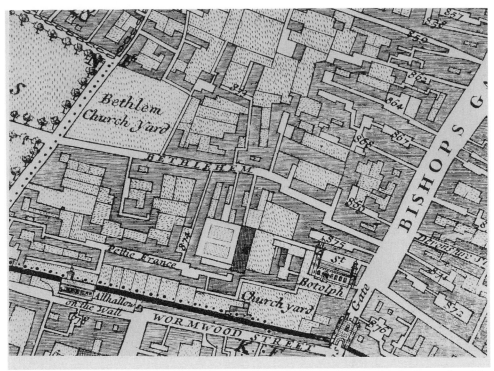

Plate 4.5 Bethlem and its vicinity: section of map by William Morgan, 1681/2. Reproduced by kind permission of the Guildhall Library, Corporation of London.

disapproving notice. In May 1578, they decided to set free Joane Medcalfe, 'a commen Bedlem harlott which of longe tyme hath ben in Bedlem', after she promised to reform her way of life. A month later, an Italian was accused before the Court of keeping his mistress (in a house) in Bethlem. In a similar vein, another Bridewell Court witness reported (one can hear her saying it) that 'Dick Comes used a had the three yonge men to agone with him to a douchewomans in bedlem this last somer'.[24]

Whether Bethlem precinct was any worse in this respect than any other city precinct of similar size and similar location, there seems to be no way of knowing. Certainly it was not just a place of entertainment. Quite a number of the precinct properties seem to have been used as industrial sites. Sometime before 1574 the Chapel was leased to a founder, and in that year the forge of 'goodwife Ventris' was let out anew, with a blacksmith as surety for the payments. The Chapel was eventually re-leased to a painter, after a mason failed for some reason to secure the tenancy. In 1619, the Bridewell Governors were concerned by the threat of fire posed by a chimney newly constructed by a hop boiler, and by the fact that the chimney stood very close to a chandler's shop. The general environment was affected by commercial activities immediately outside the precinct as well as within. In 1612, the Governors were informed that the 'garden place' at the back (to the north) of the Hospital building 'standeth full of Filth and stincking water which is verry noisome to the prisoners [inmates]'; a ditch had become clogged with the rubbish or sewage from the nearby houses of a dyer and a vintner. Probably this was industrial waste.[25]

That these activities could create public nuisances, or, at least, generate noise and pungent or offensive smells, is clear. Rapid development and infilling of the precinct of itself created problems. Public and private privy vaults left unemptied until the last minute, and the flooding or stagnant water created when new building interfered with existing drainage arrangements, must certainly have created temporary unpleasantness. However, the Bridewell Governors did try to ensure that hazards were kept to a minimum.[26] Reactive though the arrangements were, problems were dealt with once they were noticed. It would be wrong to conclude that nobody ever disposed of waste without polluting the neighbourhood, or that the medieval and early-modern precinct invariably stank of urine and rotting rubbish. Bethlem precinct may not have been a model of hygiene and civic morality, certainly by the late sixteenth century, but it was not a dungheap either.

What of the Hospital itself? One point worth stressing is that it was an open building. Raving lunatics were certainly chained up, and in some cases they were shut up too. But otherwise inmates seem to have been free to wander about the house. They may also have been able to wander about the precinct, judging by the case of Katherine Fletcher, who scandalized passers-by with her immodest behaviour in 1575 (see Chapter 10). Inhabitants of the precinct may not have been in the habit of going into the Hospital building, but they certainly had access to its immediate surroundings. In the 1560s, and probably long before that, those tenants who did not possess their own lavatories were required to traipse through 'the west end of the long house of Bethlem' to reach the 'comon Jaques' which were located behind the Hospital. Even if these tenants paid as little attention as possible to the inmates, they cannot have been entirely unaware of the conditions within. Indeed, in the late fourteenth century corrodians ('pensioners': see Chapter 6 for a discussion of these arrangements) were sometimes lodged in what were described as 'decent chambers' in the Hospital building until other accommodation was available, although this practice may have ceased once the Hospital began to take in the insane.[27]

It appears, moreover, that friends and relatives of the inmates were not only allowed to visit, but, in the case of the poor, were expected to do so in order to bring in food and other necessities. That would be in keeping with the practices found in developing countries today, and with the free access which was clearly permitted to visitors to Bethlem in the late sixteenth century and the seventeenth century. When Robert Baron and his wife were granted a corrody in the 1390s, it was agreed that they could have additional foodstuff brought in if they liked, in the same way as the poor inmates did.[28]

None of this alters the fact that Bethlem Hospital, once it started to specialize in accommodating the mad, cannot have been anything other than noisy and unpleasant. Donald Lupton wrote in the 1630s of the 'cryings, screechings, roarings, brawlings, shaking of chaines, swearings, frettings, chaffings' which made Bethlem a place liable to send a sane man mad. Lady Eleanor Davies, who was confined in Bethlem as a lunatic in the late 1630s after a period spent in prison, described the experience as being 'as it were, to exchange the grave for hell, such were the blasphemies and the noisome scents' (she was in fact kept in the Master's House, not even in the main Hospital). Even if Lupton's witty commentaries and Lady Eleanor's pathetic petition were exaggerated for effect, the fact that Bethlem tended to take particularly troubled and difficult madmen and madwomen means that there must be some truth in their accounts.[29]

CONCLUSION

Between 1247 and 1350, Bethlem precinct seems to have remained largely undeveloped. Such buildings as there were, in addition to the two main access points to the east and west and the Church, lay along or close to the northern perimeter. A few rooms may have been let out privately, but otherwise the buildings were for the use of members of the Order of Bethlem.

In the second half of the fourteenth century there is evidence of the commercial development of the precinct. Individuals were allowed to occupy rooms in the main building and to buy plots of land on which to build houses. The major construction away from the perimeter, however, was the new Chapel, which was probably completed in the early 1380s. Otherwise, building work seems to have been largely confined to the perimeter. It was probably in this period that the first of the privately tenanted houses on the western, southern and eastern sides of the precinct were built. Although it is not clear exactly what was constructed when, the whole perimeter of the precinct had been built upon by the 1550s. Some of the houses were small, but others were large properties occupied by individuals of some consequence. Like Bishopsgate Without as a whole, Bethlem precinct seems in the later fifteenth century and early sixteenth century to have been an area which attracted some fairly wealthy inhabitants.

Further rapid development in the second half of the sixteenth century altered the character of the precinct. Its whole appearance underwent a change, with considerable infilling of what had previously been the almost empty central area. Commercial rents became commonplace, and larger houses were divided up – as indeed were not-so-large houses. If Bethlem was quite a prestigious address in the 1520s, it was clearly not very prestigious at all fifty years later. By the 1630s, everything in the precinct, including the extended Hospital building, was beginning to bulge at the seams. The precinct had been transformed from a quiet, enclosed world to a lively, noisy, and probably much more stressful one.

NOTES

1 *The Survey of London: Contayning The Originall, Increase, Moderne Estate, and Government of that City ... Begunne first by the Paines and Industry of Iohn Stow, in the yeere 1598* ... (London: Elizabeth Purslow, 1633), 176, 175, 173. The Dolphin Inn belonged in the fifteenth century to John Styward or Steward, tallow-chandler, whose connection with Bethlem is discussed in the next chapter: Randall Monter-Williams, *The Tallow Chandlers of London*, 4 volumes (London: Kaye & Ward, 1970–7), iii, 37.

2 FitzMary's charter: PRO Chancery, Ecclesiastical Miscellanea, C270/22, especially mm. 5 and 4. It is transcribed and translated in, among other places, Stow's *Survey*, 173–4.

3 Museum of London, Department of Urban Archaeology Archive Catalogue ed. John Schofield, Gillian Dunn and Charlotte Harding, London, The Museum, 1987, 169.

4 M. D. Lobel (ed.), *The City of London from Prehistoric Times to c. 1520*, The British Atlas of Historic Towns, iii (Oxford: OUP/The Historic Towns Trust, 2nd edn, 1991), Maps Section, 'City of London c. 1520, Map 4'; *BRHA*, Muniment Book, fols 58, 58v; PRO C270/22, m. 3; for the eastern side being described as the 'great old Chapell', see *BRHA*, Muniment Book, fols 61–2; for Johnson, see Chapter 2; Fredson Bower (ed.), *Thomas Dekker: The Dramatic Works*, 4 volumes (Cambridge: CUP, 1953–61), ii, 100.

5 PRO C270/22, m. 3; *Calendar of Patent Rolls 1388–92*, 484; *Calendar of Patent Rolls 1401–1405*, 316 (this plot, too, was 40 by 20 feet); *Ghall* MS 9171, London Commissary Court Wills, Register 1, fol. 463v; *ibid.* Register 2, fol. 269v; PRO C270/22, m. 1. The question of who had the right to prove the testaments of precinct residents was a bone of contention, Robert Lincoln having complained bitterly to the Visitation Commissioners ten years earlier that the Commissary's activities were contrary to the rights and privileges of the hospital. The Commissioners did not answer this point, and as the wills of Bethlem tenants and chaplains continued to be proved before the Commissary, it appears that Lincoln's bid for control failed.

6 *Calendar of Patent Rolls 1401–1405*, 316; *BCGM* volume 9, fol. 45.

7 *Ghall* MS 142, 163–74, especially 164; *Ghall* MS 25121/837, St Paul's Ancient Deeds; *Calendar of Patent Rolls 1361–64*, 477; R. R. Sharpe (ed.), *Calendar of Letters from the Mayor and Corporation of the City of London c. AD 1350–1370 . . .* (London: J. C. Francis, 1885), 145–6; PRO C270/22, m. 1.

8 *A Collection of Early London Maps, 1553–1667*, introduction by John Fisher (Lympne Castle: Harry Margary/Guildhall Library, 1981).

9 *BRHA*, Muniment Book, fols 30–30v, 58, 62.

10 PRO SP 16/224 no. 21, m. 2.

11 *Report of the Commissioners . . . concerning Charities in England and Wales . . .* (32 volumes, London: W. Clowes & Sons/HMSO, 1819–40), xxxii, part vi, 478; Edward G. O'Donoghue, *The Story of Bethlehem Hospital From its Foundation in 1247* (London: T. Fisher Unwin, 1914), 114–19; Sir George Gater and Walter H. Godfrey, *Survey of London, Issued by the Joint Publishing Committee Representing The London County Council and the London Survey Committee*, xxi, *Trafalgar Square and Neighbourhood (Parish of St Martin's in the Fields, part iii)* (London 1940), published for the London County Council by Country Life, 10–13.

12 *BRHA*, Muniment Book, fols 61–4 and 50v. In 1595 Mrs Johnson's tenement was said to measure 15 feet 4 inches in length 'east to west by the street side' – which probably means on the south front, the opposite side from the precinct – and 20 feet in depth: *ibid.* fol. 91.

13 *CA Rep.* 16, fols 364v and 365; Reginald H. Adams, *The Parish Clerks of London: A History of the Worshipful Company of Parish Clerks of London* (London and Chichester: Phillimore, 1971), 30. Although the Court of Aldermen stayed the 1568 lease of the Church shortly after, unsure whether 'the same chapell may conveniently be granted by lease or not', there is no reason to suppose that the building survived in its original form for much longer. For the assurances given to the Bishop of London: *CA Rep.* 13/2, fol. 443.

14 *BRHA*, Muniment Book, fols 91 and 103v–4; *BCGM* volume 6, fols 53v–4 (where there is a reference to a house 'in the Chappell in the Middle Rowe'), 206.

15 *BRHA*, Muniment Book, fols 208, 58v; *BCGM* volume 6, fol. 423v; *Acts of the Privy Council 1630–1*, 285 (item 821); *BRHA*, Muniment Book, fol. 208; *BCGM* volume 7, fol. 69.

16 *BCGM* volume 7, fol. 137v.

17 *BRHA*, indenture of 16 March 1677 between the Mayor and Commonalty and citizens of London and William Bates, citizen and fletcher of London.

18 *BCGM* volume 9, fol. 43; *ibid.* volume 6, fol. 423v.

19 O'Donoghue, *op. cit.* 194–5 and 200–1.

20 *BCGM 1666–76*, 148v; *BCGM* (Rough Court Book) 1662–4, fol. 30v.

21 Unfortunately, late seventeenth- and early eighteenth-century mapmakers continued to rely on the work done by Morgan and his associates in the 1670s and 1680s. Not until John Rocque issued his map in 1746 does there appear to have been an extensive re-survey of the

City. By this stage, the features evident in the Morgan series of maps are no longer visible. When they disappeared, however, it is impossible to say.

22 For example, 11 December 1577, 4 December 1598, 18 July 1609, 14 October 1620, 23 April 1628, 31 July 1629, [illegible] June 1643: *BCGM* volume 3, fol. 259*v*; *ibid.* volume 4, fol. 51; *ibid.* volume 5, fol. 365*v*; *ibid.* volume 6, fol. 22; *ibid.* volume 7, fols 69, 137*v*; *ibid.* volume 9, fol. 43.

23 *BCGM* volume 3, fols 223, 429*v*, 158*v*, 160, 224; *BRHA*, Muniment Book, fol. 93; *BCGM* volume 4, fol. 18. There are also references to bowling-alleys in Bethlem by the early seventeenth century: O'Donoghue, *op. cit.* 145–6.

24 *BCGM* volume 3, fols 305*v*, 317*v*, 247*v*; *ibid.* volume 8, fol. 336*v*.

25 *BCGM* volume 2, fols 35*v*, 72*v*, 70*v*, 72; *ibid.* volume 5, fol. 198.

26 For orders to clean vaults, see: *BCGM* volume 4, fols 51*v*, 449*v*; *ibid.* volume 6, fol. 128; *ibid.* volume 7, fol. 183. For drainage problems, see: *ibid.* volume 3, fol. 288; *ibid.* volume 4, fol. 51.

27 *BRHA*, Muniment Book, fol. 58*v*; *Calendar of Patent Rolls 1388–92*, 484.

28 *Calendar of Patent Rolls 1388–92*, 484.

29 *London and the Countrey Carbonadoed and Quartred into Seuerall Characters by D. Lupton (1632)*, 2 volumes (Edinburgh: Aungervyle Society, 1883), ii, 25; *Sixth Report of the Royal Commission on Historical Manuscripts, Part i, Report and Appendix* (London: Eyre & Spottiswoode, 1877), 197; *BCGM* volume 8, fol. 133.

POLITICS AND PATRONAGE

—— ·◆· ——

INTRODUCTION

This chapter and the next are mainly about money. What appear, on the surface, to be political manoeuvres and power struggles, prove upon closer inspection to have had money as their motive. The Priory of St Mary of Bethlem was founded in order to raise money. Bethlem was seized for the King in the 1370s, and quite possibly in the 1340s as well, in order to prevent money reaching the papal court at Avignon and thence finding its way into the hands of the French. The whole purpose of Bethlem probably changed after 1350 because it was prevented from raising money for its mother-house and, in so doing, for its own support. The need to find new sources of support altered the behaviour of its Masters, who from the late fourteenth century onwards were royal clerks or other royal servants who delegated the business of administering the Hospital to laymen. Money was behind the tussles over who had the right to appoint to the Mastership (patronage) of the fourteenth-century Hospital; in the fifteenth and sixteenth centuries, patronage enabled kings and civic magistrates to reward their servants and to buy new friends at someone else's expense. It was money which provoked the very serious quarrels between the Governors of the Hospital of Bethlem and its last independent Master, Dr Helkiah or Hilkiah Crooke. Money, it could be said, ultimately led the City to opt for direct management of Bethlem, and thus to make the first move towards a more modern-looking institution.

But that is not how those involved in these various contests saw matters. To them, there was a principle involved: who had the right to the Hospital, its patronage or its revenues? Who was best-placed to ensure that it served the purpose for which it was, from the later fourteenth century onwards at any rate, intended?

WHOSE HOSPITAL IS IT, ANYWAY?

Relationships between Bethlem Hospital, the Crown and the City of London, 1247–c. 1500

To Geoffrey O'Donoghue, there was no doubt at all whose Hospital Bethlem was. 'In 1547 – to be frank – the city bought back the "custody and patronage" of the hospital which she had already acquired in 1346 in legal form and on equitable terms.' 'It is the generosity of the brigand' he added, meaning Henry VIII, 'to permit his victim to buy back his own property.'[1]

The reason O'Donoghue was so confident that the City owned the Hospital is that in 1346 letters under the common seal of London were issued, taking Bethlem 'under the patronage and protection of the mayor and aldermen of the city of London'. The letters also recorded an agreement between Mayor Richard Lacer and the Master, John Matheu 'called de Nortone', concerning 'the manner of the election of two Aldermen on St. Mathew's Day . . . in connexion with the maintenance and government of the said house'. On this basis, so O'Donoghue believed, London's governors almost immediately attempted to exercise the right of presentation to the Mastership: that, on the death of John de Nortone in 1350, the Mayor and Aldermen 'at once took the hospital into their own hands'. His reference, however, relates to an order to one of the City's Sergeants at Mace to take over either 'the house' of St Mary of Bethlem as a whole, or a specific part of it described in a preceding entry, on the death of John de Nortone, who is called 'the tenant'. There is no evidence that the City either claimed or attempted to exercise a right to present to the vacant Mastership in 1350.[2]

None the less, it made the claim at a later stage, and one can see why. The 1346 agreement does indeed give the impression that the City had assumed responsibility for, perhaps even control of, the Hospital. But appearances are probably misleading. The conflict over the right to appoint the Master of Bethlem echoes tussles between the City and the Crown for control of leper houses in the London area. In the thirteenth century the City made a vigorous attempt to claim both the advowson of the Chapel of St Giles-in-the-Fields, one of the suburban leper houses, and the right to appoint to the Mastership. On these issues, the King emerged victorious. What the City did eventually manage to assert, in 1354, was a claim to supervise St Giles's revenues. The fact that this occurred at about the same time as the Master of Bethlem commended his Hospital to the protection of London's governors suggests that the civic authorities were following a policy. The details of the arrangement with John de Nortone echo the appointment of overseers (or viewers, or supervisors) of the leper houses by the civic authorities.[3]

The order issued in 1350, on Nortone's death, was prompted by the fact that in 1346 the City had undertaken to supervise the Hospital's affairs, and in particular the administration of its revenues and properties. The City did without doubt subsequently supervise Bethlem's finances. In October 1454 the Mayor, Stephen Forster, was named in a bond by which two London citizens undertook to pay him £50 if they failed to carry out faithfully and in full an agreement made previously with the Master of Bethlem, Edward Atherton. What they had agreed with Atherton to do was to 'farm' the profits of Bethlem: in other words, they paid the Master £50 a year, and in return they made what they could from collecting the rents and from other profits arising out of the rights of the Hospital. The two men concerned, John Styward or Steward, tallow-chandler, and John Tate senior, mercer, were prominent citizens. Both served as Common Councilmen (the Common Council was the next level of civic government below the Aldermanry). Tate was Common Councilman and, from 1463 onwards, Alderman, of his home ward, Tower; Styward was Common

Councilman for Bishopsgate Ward itself in the 1450s if not earlier, and almost certainly lived there.[4]

There seems to be no evidence that the elections of Bethlem supervisors, as anticipated in the 1346 letters, were ever held. But the fact that appointments of supervisors are never recorded does not prove that such appointments never occurred. Relatively minor appointments were not always entered in the main civic records. It is, for instance, only because he was called upon to protect them in 1468 that the name of the Alderman then charged with overseeing the interests of the group of London-based alien merchants called the Hanse, Ralph Josselyn, is known.[5]

A piece of evidence which suggests that the City maintained a general oversight of the Hospital is an entry in the civic records, dated April 1436. This noted that William Mawere tailor (with a marginal note, 'Will'i Marowe') had been discharged from serving on civic juries and carrying out other civic duties by the Mayor 'owing to his constant attention to the poor mad lunatics of the Hospital of St. Mary de Bedlem without Bishopsgate'. The nature and wording of this concession is very similar to those granted to the overseers of the leper houses.[6] It could be that Mawere/Marowe was just what he appears at first sight to have been, namely an attendant. But it is quite likely that he was the man who became an Alderman in 1449, despite the fact that Alderman William Marowe was a grocer, not a tailor, by the time he reached the Bench. At least 10 per cent of fifteenth-century Aldermen changed to a more prestigious Company before achieving election, and the Tailors were considerably less prestigious than the Grocers at the time. Certainly Alderman Marowe took some interest in the Hospital. The fact that he himself left a bequest is not surprising, as he was a resident of Bishopsgate Ward at the time of his death. Somewhat more unusual is the fact that his widow also left a modest legacy to Bethlem.[7]

Whether or not the City supervised and protected the Hospital as it said it would in 1346, the question remains, why did John de Nortone seek to be taken under the City's wing? Was it a response to the royal seizure of alien priories? The fourteenth-century Masters of the Hospital of St Mary of Bethlem would have had good cause to feel anxious about the possibility that their house might suffer from anti-alien sentiment or that the revenues which were normally sent abroad might be appropriated. Bethlem was in fact seized for the King, as noted on p. 58. On the face of it, 1346 seems a curious moment for the Master to act: one would expect him to have sought the City's protection almost a decade earlier (assuming, that is, that the City was able to do anything to protect alien priories from seizure). However, in the late 1340s there occur for the first time in both civic and royal records descriptions of the Order of Bethlem as 'the order of brethren of the *knighthood* of St Mary of Bethlehem'. The Order was not in fact a military one. None the less, the myth seems to have grown up during the fourteenth century that it was one, and that it was founded during the lifetime of the famous Crusader and first ruler of Jerusalem, Godfrey de Bouillon, in the second half of the eleventh century. (This may explain why in the early sixteenth century it was believed that the 'Monastery' of Bethlem had been founded before the Conquest by Sir William Fines, a 'knight of Rhodes', and that Simon fitzMary had merely founded the Hospital.) This myth was linked by a would-be patron in 1381 to Edward III's custom of granting the patronage of Bethlem to knights. So perhaps the first of these knightly patrons had just been granted the right to present to the Mastership, and John de Nortone, who had been succeeded by John de Wilton by 1347, feared that he was about to be ousted.[8]

Without doubt, the City had its own motives for agreeing to supervise the Hospital's affairs. It could even be that the petition was not a spontaneous approach by de Nortone, but was in fact prompted by the civic authorities. If so, their aim may have been to protect the charitable support provided for particularly vulnerable groups, like lepers and lunatics, at a time when this support was reducing. Charitable provision appears to have declined considerably in the second half of the fourteenth century, partly because of reduced demand in the wake of the mid-century epidemics, but also because 'income fell, especially that which came from tithes and offerings, while expenses grew as wages and prices rose'. By the late 1380s, for instance, the leper house of St Giles was described as 'miserably depressed and in debt'.[9] The City may also have had other objects in view. Even if the Mayor and Aldermen did not delude themselves, in 1346, that they had obtained overall control of the Hospital from John de Nortone, they might well have regarded their agreement with him as a valuable foot in the door, one which could perhaps be exploited more actively by their successors.

In any event, the fact that the Hospital was taken 'under the patronage' of the City does not mean that the City obtained the patronage of the Mastership. Nor is it at all likely that the current Master was free to dispose of it in this way. Later, in 1364, the then Master, Robert Mannyel, described himself as holding the Hospital 'for life under a lease of Durand, late bishop of Bedlem, for a farm of twenty florins of Florence to be paid to the bishop and his successors'. No doubt the Bishop of Bethlehem believed that it was he who had the right of patronage. Whether, given the international political situation during Edward III's reign, he was often able to exercise that right is another question.[10]

What seems certain is that Edward III took control of Bethlem in the mid-1370s. The Hospital's muniment book contains a copy of a return to a writ *certiorari*, requiring the 'vicar' of the Hospital to state what Bethlem was worth. The copy is marginated '48 E. 3', that is, sometime between 25 January 1374 and 24 January 1375, and states that the Hospital was then 'in the king's hand' as an alien priory. Although the original writ and return do not appear to survive in the Public Record Office, there is no reason to doubt that they once existed. For some while, then, Bethlem was seized for the King. Whether this made much difference to its day-to-day life is doubtful: even the Master, if he had been appointed under a royal grant of patronage, was probably left in peaceful occupation – though perhaps with the title 'vicar' (deputy or stand-in) rather than Master. On the other hand, the seizure may well mark the point at which the Bishop of Bethlem lost his right of patronage permanently and payments to him finally and completely ceased. If so, this would no doubt have encouraged the perception, on the part of royal servants at least, that the Hospital was held from the King.[11]

Without doubt, however, there was scope for dispute and misunderstanding. The wording of the City's letters patent to John de Nortone could be, and soon was, interpreted as conveying the right of patronage to the City. In April 1381, the City appointed John Gardyner, chaplain, to be 'warden or master' of the Hospital. This was challenged immediately by one William Welles, who presented a petition to Parliament complaining that, 'whereas the king had given him the keeping of the hospital of Bedelem without Bishopsgate', the citizens of London were claiming it for themselves. Welles stated that 'the king and his ancestors had always previously presented to the hospital', adding, as mentioned earlier, that all the previous holders of the delegated right of presentment had been knights.[12] No royal grants of the right of appointment to anyone, including the three men mentioned by Welles (Sir John Darcy, Sir John Beauchamp and Sir James Audley), appear to survive from Edward III's reign. This seems on the face of it to damn Welles's claim. On the other hand, no record of any grant to Welles himself is extant either. He would have had to be impudent indeed to present a petition in Parliament claiming a recent grant which he had not received. It is highly unlikely that Welles would have made his story up. O'Donoghue speculated that a reference to one of the Hospital's patrons called 'Saudalee' in a document of 1361 was a mis-transcription for 'Daudalee', and that this in turn might be a phonetic spelling of 'De Audley'. He was correct about the mis-transcription: 'Daudalee' it is, and it is safe to assume that the modern spelling would be 'De Audley' or 'd'Audley'.[13]

Undoubtedly the youthful Richard II's advisers took the view that the patronage was the King's to grant. What the immediate outcome of Welles's petition was is uncertain. But it looks as though the City was able, in the tense circumstances of 1381, the year of the 'Peasants' Revolt', to fend him off. Almost eight years later the Mayor and Aldermen stated that their nominee of 1381, John Gardyner, occupied what they called the Keepership, and for the first time made their claim that the patronage belonged to the City. They were responding to royal writs ordering them to induct Robert Lincoln, issued in January 1389. This time the King was in a much stronger position, and the City's attempt at resistance clearly failed: Lincoln must have obtained the office almost immediately, since in 1403 he was described as having held the Mastership for about thirteen years.[14] For over a century after that, successive kings and queens exercised their right as patrons of the Hospital to appoint its Masters without any attempt at contradiction.

Towards a City Hospital, *c.* 1500–1633

Being what lawyers call an incorporeal thing and therefore immortal, the City could afford to bide its time. Moreover, its memory was almost as long-lasting as its invisible body. Early in 1504, the Court of Aldermen recollected the old claim to Bethlem, and ordered that anything in the City's records relating to the Hospital and its patronage should be produced to it at the next (Mayor's) Court day. Nothing apparently came of this, nor of a further search ordered a decade later. So the Mayor and Aldermen decided to try another tack. On 28 September 1518 it was agreed that a committee consisting of the Mayor, the Recorder (the City's senior legal officer), two Aldermen and six Common Councilmen would be 'solicitors to the kings grace and his most honorable counsell for the hospitall of Bethlem withoute Bysshoppesgate to the which the cite hath Ryght &c'. This, too, failed to achieve the desired results, perhaps because the Aldermen's insistence that London was entitled to Bethlem weakened their case by leading them to demand what, in reality, they could not prove was rightfully the City's.[15]

Almost twenty years later, in 1537, the city authorities finally accepted that they were not going to be able to talk their way into control of the Hospital. The Court of Aldermen authorized the Mayor to open negotiations with the then patron, Sir Peter Mewtys, to see whether and upon what terms he would (as the City insisted on phrasing it) 'restore the possession of the patronage of Bedlem whiche of Right belongeth to this city'. This did not produce instant results. But finally, four years later, the Mayor was able to report to his fellows that he had persuaded Mewtys to relinquish his life-interest in the Hospital's patronage for £100, and had also struck a deal with Mewtys's deputy, the mercer Thomas Scopeham.[16]

At much the same time as the City accepted the need to buy Mewtys out, it made another attempt to persuade Henry VIII to grant it four recently suppressed religious foundations, the New Hospital of St Mary without Bishopsgate, the Hospitals of St Bartholomew and St Thomas Southwark, and the 'New Abbey on Tower Hill' (the Minories, or the Abbey of Minoresses), for the benefit of its sick poor. After many delays, Henry VIII finally, in late 1546, agreed to grant the City St Bartholomew's Hospital. Included in the grant, made on 13 January 1547, was the concession of the 'custody, order and governance of [Bethlem]' and of its occupants and revenues.[17]

The wording is curious. In effect, Henry VIII seems to have granted the City, which of course could never die, the Mastership in perpetuity, subject to the King's pleasure. Why did the King give St Bartholomew's to the City, but baulk at an outright grant of the much less valuable Bethlem Hospital?

Perhaps it was simply a matter of principle, or a reaction to the City's attitude, after two centuries of conflict over the right of patronage. However, political or religious considerations – the two were at this period largely indistinguishable – may well have played a part. The Master of Bethlem from 1529 until his spectacular downfall and execution in May 1536 was George Bulleyn or Boleyn, Queen Anne's brother. Like his sister, Bulleyn was a supporter of the evangelicals, the religious reformers whose activities, led and orchestrated by that well-known London citizen, Thomas Cromwell, had already produced the break with Rome and the beginning of the Dissolution of the Monasteries. There is some evidence to suggest that Bethlem became a focus for evangelicals under Bulleyn. After his fall, the radical preacher Dr Robert Barnes tried to persuade Cromwell to support him in his bid for the Mastership (worth £40 a year, and more desirable to him than a bishopric, so Barnes said).

It is moreover possible that Bethlem had been a battleground over which the evangelicals and the conservatives had been fighting for some time. John Cavalari, the Master succeeded by Bulleyn, was a Luccan (Italian) merchant who had received papers of denization for himself and his children only in 1513, the year he obtained the Mastership. He seems an odd choice for Master: given the usual relationship between Italian merchants and English kings, one would normally suspect that the Mastership was a way of paying off royal debts. But when in 1543 Charles 'Cavallary' of St Helen's Bishopsgate (a large parish to the south-east of St Botolph's) made his last will and testament, he named as his executors another Luccan merchant, Anthony Bonvisi, and Sir Thomas More's son-in-law, William Roper. Roper had been won over by the reformers' views at one stage, but More had won him back. And Bonvisi was an ardent Catholic and perhaps More's staunchest friend from his old humanist circle, supporting him in his last days: Sir Thomas then had looked forward to seeing his old friend in Heaven, 'where no wall shall dissever us, where no porter shall keep us from talking together'. Charles Cavallary was very probably a member of John Cavalari's family, perhaps his son. While Cavalari was Master of Bethlem, More was living nearby in Crosby Place and was a member of the Skinners' Fraternity, with its links with Bethlem Chapel.

The existence of a strongly anti-reformist circle in the area may help to explain why a Harwich curate opposed to the reforms, Thomas Corthop, was to be found preaching at Bethlem in 1535. His audience, which included some prominent reformers, promptly reported him for criticizing royal policy. At the time, Corthop's words were dangerous. Yet it may well be that King Henry, once he had repudiated Anne Boleyn's influence, began to fear that Corthop was right when he said that the evangelicals 'have made and brought in such divisions and seditions among us as was never seen in the realm'. For this reason, perhaps, Dr Barnes did not get the Mastership; it went instead to Mewtys, Gentleman of the Privy Chamber, who was presumably a 'safe pair of hands'. If Bethlem was by the late 1530s associated with a religious radicalism which was itself beginning to smell of political radicalism, the King might well have been reluctant to hand it over completely to London's governors, even on his deathbed (he died on 28 January 1547).[18]

In practice, the City seems to have been left in undisturbed occupation for some time thereafter, and in the long term it managed quietly to convert control into ownership. But its title remained vulnerable for some time, and the Mayor and Aldermen clearly were conscious of that vulnerability. It was with some foreboding that a group of Aldermen who had been summoned before the Commissioners Spiritual 'for th'answerying of the Cytyes matters concernynge Bethelem and the ponyshemente of harlottes and bawdes' went to the meeting. Their relief at finding the Commissioners 'reasonably and frendely-inclynyd and mynded towardes the saide Cytye nor seakynge or covetynge to restrayne breake or infrynge any parte of [its] liberties' is patent.[19]

It is not entirely clear who 'governed' Bethlem in the early years of the City's control. There is a reference in September 1550 to the (unspecified) 'governors' of Bethlem. Despite this, initially the Court of Aldermen seems to have administered the Hospital itself. Although no record of the appointment survives, the Mayor and Aldermen probably appointed the first Keeper, Edward Alleyn; they certainly appointed his successor. (The word 'Keeper' itself indicates that Alleyn held the position equivalent to the Masters' deputies of former days, and that the City was in effect acting as the 'Master'.) They also required the City's Chamberlain to receive, dispense and account to the Court for the Hospital's revenues and expenditure, which is strong evidence in favour of central civic control.[20]

In January 1556, however, two Aldermen and the Chamberlain were ordered to check the Keeper's accounts up to Michaelmas (29 September) last. This was in preparation for a transfer of administrative control. Edward VI had just granted to the City three institutions for its poor: Christ's Hospital, which 'hath bene erected for the vertuous bringinge up of the myserable youth, and St Thomas hospitall for the relevynge of the neadye and deseased, and Bridewell for thenforcinge of the lewde and naughtie sorte to labor and worke'. Christ's was ordered to assume the 'governaunce of the saide house of Beathelem and of the keeper and other officers thereof … and Receyve theire Reaconyngs and Accomptes … and not the Chamberlayne of this Cytie'. According to the 1837 Charity Commissioners, the administration of Bethlem did not remain with the Governors of Christ's Hospital for long. The Commissioners believed that, on 27 September 1557, the Governors of the three hospitals granted to the City by Edward VI decided both to include St Bartholomew's in the administrative arrangements then being approved and also to put Bethlem under the wing of Bridewell. Bridewell, the splendid palace built for Henry VIII less than a quarter-century before, was now, rather ignominiously, a 'house of correction' for petty offenders, vagrants, and immoral persons.[21]

It is in fact doubtful whether Christ's ever actually administered Bethlem. There is no mention of Bethlem in the Christ's Hospital Court Minute books before June 1561, when a decision was taken to offer a lease of some Bethlem tenements. This decision was taken, not at a Christ's Hospital Court, but at a 'General Court' of all the city hospitals. In September 1561, the Court of Aldermen ordered the 'Comptroller General' of the Hospitals, Alderman Martin Bowes, another senior Aldermen and four Common Councilmen to take over 'the orderynge grauntynge & lettyng to ferme' of Bethlem and its lands and possessions, a responsibility they were still exercising under instructions from the Court of Aldermen until at least the following spring. On 23 September 1562, Bowes was asked to arrange for the making of a silver seal with which leases and other legal documents relating to Bethlem's property could be sealed. Four days earlier, Bowes had been tasked to produce a seal for the City's other hospitals, which was to be used indifferently for sealing the deeds of any one of them. This suggests that Bethlem was still being administered separately from the rest of the hospitals, and on a rather *ad hoc* basis, well into the 1560s.

There is indeed no evidence that the Bridewell had responsibility for Bethlem before 28 August 1574, when the Bridewell Governors agreed that John Mell, the third Keeper of Bethlem, should have 'the Romes which were letten to Mr Agare before any other at suche tyme as it is to be letten'. From that point on, it is clear that it was the Governors of Bridewell who were both supervising admissions to the Hospital and handling its revenues and property. Moreover, it was in 1579 that the Bridewell Governors appear first to have attempted to control appointments to the Keepership, when they dismissed John Mell on the grounds that he had withheld legacies left to Bethlem. Mell replied, very pertinently, that 'he was admytted to [his office] by my L maior and Court of Aldermen. And if by them he shalbe myslyked then he will be content to departe'. So it seems likely that the real point at which the Bridewell Governors assumed control of Bethlem's affairs was well after 1557; quite possibly, not much before the mid-1570s (unfortunately, there seems to be nothing in the Court of Aldermen records to indicate precisely when this happened, and the Bridewell Court of Governors Minute Books covering 1562 to 1574 do not survive).[22]

Why then did the 1837 Charity Commissioners assert so confidently that Bethlem's administration had passed to Bridewell at the General Court held on 27 September 1557? Probably because of a confusion resulting from a statement in a work published in 1836, *Memoranda, References and Documents Relating to the Royal Hospitals of the City of London*. This included a copy of the 1557 ordinances, together with the comment that disputes which had arisen over them had been resolved in 1782, when it was decided that the London Common Council would appoint forty-eight Governors, of which 'twelve shall be sent to St Bartholomew's Hospital, twelve to the united Hospitals of Bridewell and Bethlem'.[23]

The reluctance of the Mayor and Aldermen to yield their control of admission to the Bethlem Keepership, despite the fact that the Bridewell Governors seem from the outset to have controlled admissions to all the Bridewell offices, may reflect the long struggle to obtain the right to appoint to the office in the first place. The Keepership was also useful for purposes of patronage, as a way of rewarding city officers for good service. On three occasions at least the office was granted to one of the Mayor's officers or at the Mayor's request.[24]

It was none the less anomalous that the Keepership was not in the hands of the Bridewell Governors. In October 1607 the Steward of Bridewell clearly assumed that the office must be controlled by the Governors, as it was one of several positions he suggested as possible appointments for his son (the others being his own office and the Portership of Bridewell). He was too precipitate, however. The first time the Bridewell Governors were involved in choosing the Keeper was in April 1619, when Dr Helkiah Crooke was elected in a two-horse contest in a session of the Court of Governors attended by the Mayor and the Recorder. (As the other contestant, John Pirie, may well have been the Bridewell Governor of that name, the 'two-horse contest' may in fact have been no contest at all.) Crooke had laid complaints against the serving Keeper, Thomas Jenner, in the autumn of 1618, having previously petitioned King James I for the Keepership. The knowledge that the King was taking an interest in the outcome may well have prompted an unusually formal procedure, and at least the pretence of an election.[25]

If the Governors thought that they would from then on have the same sort of control over the Keeper of Bethlem as they had over the Steward of Bridewell, however, they were mistaken. Dr Crooke was a man of altogether different standing from his sixteenth- and early seventeenth-century predecessors. Clearly the City recognized this, for Crooke was required to swear to a set of articles on admission, which bound him, among other things, to be 'subiect to the direccon and controll of the Governors of this hospitall, for the time beinge and accompt to them' and to accept that he would hold office only so long as he conducted himself well. Moreover, the Governors attempted to pre-empt a long-standing source of disputes by ordering that any charitable gifts, no doubt including bequests, made to Bethlem should be delivered first to the Bridewell Treasurer before being passed to Crooke 'att the discreccon of the Governors'.[26] It took more than that to tie down a man of Crooke's calibre, however.

At first the relationship seems to have been amicable enough. Crooke was a demanding Keeper, and the Court of Governors gave in to his demands. A small committee was appointed to view the state of Bethlem House in May; a larger committee, to do the same, in June. Just over a week later, several Governors were asked to join the President at the Guildhall. The Treasurer and Clerk were to meet him beforehand, 'to acquaint him with some writings and notes for his better instruction touchyng this buisnes'. Ten days later it was agreed that 'a sluce shalbe made for the conveyance of water out of the vaulte at Bethlem'. Four days after that, 'fittinge dressers and shelves' were ordered to be installed in the kitchen at Bethlem House.[27]

Thus far, Crooke had been an 'improving' Keeper, and the Governors had obliged him. But the honeymoon period did not last for long. By November 1619, the differences between the Bridewell Governors and Crooke were sufficient to require the attention of an aldermanic committee. The Governors continued to be troubled on and off throughout 1620 over 'doctor Crooks busines'; Crooke was evidently bidding for an increase in the allowance made for inmates supported by Bridewell, despite having sworn on admission not to do so.[28]

The Governors responded by being much readier than they might otherwise have been to hear complaints against the Keeper. In April 1620, a committee was appointed to hear the complaints made by a Mr Slater about his daughter's mistreatment and abuses in general; in July, three Governors were ordered to discuss and investigate further alleged abuses. If the Governors hoped by this means to discourage Crooke from pursuing his complaints, they were disappointed. By June 1621, there was another source of disagreement. Like a number of his predecessors, Crooke did not accept that he was bound to hand over to the Bridewell Treasurer any gifts or bequests made to Bethlem, and (according to the Bridewell Clerk) 'violently averred to the Governors that hee would give noe accompt' for sums he had received from these sources. Typically, he began by trying to bring heavy guns to bear: the Bridewell Governors found themselves having to explain themselves to the Earl of Arundel, the Earl-Marshal and a Privy Councillor. The dispute was referred back to the Mayor and Aldermen, but the temperature was by now high, with the Bridewell Governors referring to the Keeper's 'scandalous peticiones'. Even when summoned again before Lord Arundel, the Governors stood firm and refused to accept that they owed Crooke the £7 he was then claiming from them.[29] Arundel appears to have been persuaded by the City's arguments, and for a time Crooke and his complaints disappeared from the records, to be replaced by a controversy over new buildings at Bethlem.[30]

No further major problems arose until towards the end of the decade, although the Governors did find themselves having to intervene in order to ensure that two Hospital servants were paid by the Keeper. In early 1628, however, an aldermanic committee was formed to consider Crooke's proposals 'concerninge some reformacion in the house of Bethelem and . . . his bill entended to be proffered to the house of Parliament'. In November 1630, the Bridewell Clerk was ordered to keep separate accounts for Bethlem and Bridewell. Less than a week later, Crooke again petitioned for an increase in the poor inmates' allowance. Although the Governors did not respond immediately, in February 1631 a visiting Bridewell committee found that there was almost no food in the Hospital and reported that 'it was complayned unto them that the poore were likely to starve'. This visit does not seem to have been ordered by the Court, and may indeed have been solicited by Crooke as part of his campaign to prove how inadequate the inmates' allowance was. In any event, the Governors merely ordered a committee headed by the Treasurer to make what improvements it thought appropriate.[31]

If the February visit was instigated by Crooke, it clearly did not achieve his aims. The following month, probably as a result, the Mayor and Aldermen found themselves facing a much more serious challenge. The Privy Council began to take an interest in the affairs of Bethlem. The Council initially reacted sympathetically to the petition presented to it by Crooke, ordering the production of an account of the Hospital's revenues from the time of Henry VIII's donation to the present time and of the Orders laid down for the Hospital in 1612. The Privy Councillors also decided to raise the poor inmates' allowance to 2s a week. At that point, Crooke probably felt that he had won.[32]

The City seems to have accepted this, and arranged for a copy of the Orders to be taken to the Council. In early May, however, the Privy Council decided to require the Mayor and Aldermen to bring in 'a more clear and ample account of their annual receipts and payments' relating to all the Royal Hospitals, Christ's 'being specially required to seek out the donation by Henry VIII [*sic*]'. This rang alarm bells, with good cause, especially given the limitations of the 1547 grant of Bethlem to the City. The Mayor and Aldermen were probably little comforted by the Privy Council's answer to their protests, that 'the purpose of the king in a suit between himself and the City regarding the right to [Bethlem] was to apply it, as his royal progenitors had done, according to the foundation'. The Council – or the King himself – was evidently keen to assert the royal rights fully.[33]

The outcome was not as Crooke would have wished it, however. The Privy Council appointed two Commissioners to examine the complaints both by and against the Keeper. The Commission reported in October, and its findings damned Crooke. The following April, an enlarged Commission reported specifically on the matters relating to the Keeper's alleged mismanagement. Crooke was found to have tendered inaccurate accounts, to have extorted fees for the admission of lunatic patients, to have sold off gifts made for the inmates' relief, and to have broken every one of the conditions upon which he was admitted to office. Finally, despite the fact that he was by now receiving an allowance per poor inmate which was nearly double that given in other Hospitals, 'the poor were in none of them so ill ordered and provided for, whilst nothing was done towards their cure'.[34]

The interventions of the Privy Council, reminders as they were of the City's potential weakness in the face of any king determined to assert his rights to the full, as Charles I had shown himself to be, almost certainly alarmed the city magistrates. In combination with the difficulties the City had had with Crooke and the fact that the semi-independent status of the Master or Keeper had quite often in the past resulted in power-struggles, they led the Mayor and Aldermen to think again about how Bethlem was to be managed. The Crooke episode seems, in fact, to have been the trigger which enabled the Governors to persuade the Mayor and Aldermen to cease treating the Keepership as a useful piece of patronage, and instead to give the Bridewell Governors the direct control over Bethlem that they had long enjoyed over Bridewell.

NOTES

1 Edward G. O'Donoghue, *The Story of Bethlehem Hospital from its Foundation in 1247* (London: T. Fisher Unwin, 1914), 113.
2 *Calendar of Letter Book F*, 154, 155; O'Donoghue, *op. cit.* 55; the editor of the City's letterbooks, Sharpe, also assumed that in 1346 the City acquired the patronage of the Hospital,

something which 'appear[ed] to have escaped the notice of Stow, Newcourt, and others':
Calendar of Letter Book F, 154, fn. 1, 163.

3 On overseers, see, for example, the oath taken on appointment by the overseers of the leper
houses of St Giles and Kingsford (described as 'masters of the lepers' in 1449): *CLRO*
Journal of the Common Council 4, fol. 168; Journal of the Common Council 5, fol. 4*v*;
Margery B. Honeybourne, *The Leper Hospitals of the London Area: With an Appendix on Some
Other Medieval Hospitals of Middlesex*, Transactions of the London and Middlesex Archaeo-
logical Society, xxi, Part i (1963), 21.

4 British Library, Harleian Charter 56. F. 48; *CLRO* MS Letterbook D, fols 70*v* and 74.

5 K. Hohlbaum *et al.* (eds), *Hansisches Urkundenbuch*, 11 volumes (Halle, Leipzig: von Duncker
& Humblot, 1876–1916), ix, 339.

6 *Calendar of Letter Book K*, 196–7; C. M. Barron, 'London and Parliament in the Lancastrian
Period', *Parliamentary History*, ix (1990), 347, and C. M. Barron, 'The Government of London
and its Relations with the Crown, 1400–1450' (Unpublished Ph.D. thesis, University of
London, 1970), ch. 5; *Calendar of Letter Book K*, 194; Honeybourne, *op. cit.* 8. It seems likely
that Alderman Marowe was the son of William Marowe of Bishopsgate Ward who died in
1432/3; if so, the family had been settled in St Botolph's parish for many years: R. R. Sharpe,
Calendar of Wills proved and enrolled in the Court of Husting, London, AD 1258-AD 1688, 2 volumes
(London: J. C. Francis, 1889–90), ii, 462, 606; PRO, PCC PROB 11/5/9.

7 P. Tucker, 'Government and Politics: London, 1461–1483' (Unpublished Ph.D. thesis, University of London, 1995), 104–6; *Calendar of Letter Book K*, 197; PRO, PCC PROB 11/5/9,
Ghall MS 9171, London Commissary Court, Register 6, fol. 63*v*.

8 For the sixteenth-century version of the foundation, see the beginning of Chapter 3. For
references to the Order of Bethlehem as a military order: *Calendar of Letterbook F*, 154, 163;
Calendar of Patent Rolls 1345–48, 357; *Calendar of Patent Rolls 1354–58*, 423. For the statement that
previous patrons had been knights, and that the foundation had been 'of the time of
Godefroy de Bulloyn': *Rotuli Parliamentorum*, iii, 128. For Bouillon: Richard Barber, *The Two
Cities: Medieval Europe 1050–1320* (London: Routledge, paperback, 1989), 123, 398, 400, 409;
Nicholas Vincent, 'Goffredo de Prefetti and the Church of Bethlehem in England', *Journal of
Ecclesiastical History* (forthcoming, January 1998).

9 Nicholas Orme and Margaret Webster, *The Medieval Hospital 1070–1570* (New Haven and
London: Yale University Press, 1995), 128–9; Honeybourne, *op. cit.* 7.

10 *Calendar of Patent Rolls 1363–64*, 477; see also *Calendar of . . . Papal Registers*, xi, 6–8.

11 *BRHA*, Muniment Book, fol. 175.

12 *Calendar of Letter Book H*, 165; *Rotuli Parliamentorum*, iii, 128.

13 O'Donoghue, *op. cit.* 49; *Calendar of Close Rolls 1339–41*, 87. In a 1339 acknowledgment of a
debt, Audley is spelt 'Daudele'.

14 *Calendar of Letter Book H*, 338; H. T. Riley (ed.), *Liber Albus: The White Book of the City of
London* (London: R. Griffin, 1861), 461.

15 *CA Rep.* 1, fols 150, 152; *CA Rep.* 2, fol. 180; *CLRO* Journal of the Common Council 11, fol.
362.

16 *CA Rep.* 10, fols 5, 229; *CA Rep.* 11, 271.

17 *CLRO* MS Letterbook P, fols 178*v*–9; *CA Rep.* 14, fols 129–9*v*; *Letters and Papers (Foreign and
Domestic), Henry VIII, 1546–7*, part ii, 416–7 (item 717 (14)). The City also asked for the four
dissolved London friaries (the Carmelite Whitefriars off Fleet Street, the Franciscan Grey-
friars (Christ's Hospital), north of St Paul's, the Dominican Blackfriars, south-west of St
Paul's, and the Augustine Austin Friars, which lay just south of Moorfields, for spiritual
sustenance and for use as 'isolation hospitals': Letterbook P, fols 179, 220*v*–1*v*; *CA Rep.* 14,
fols 129*v*–30, 216*v*.

18 Susan Brigden, *London in the Reformation* (Oxford: Clarendon Press, 1989), 127, 221, 158–9,
247; PRO, PCC PROB 11/29/22; Brigden, *op. cit.* 418, 212, 321, 420–1, 257; *Letters and Papers
(Foreign and Domestic), Henry VIII, 1536*, i, 366 (item 880); *ibid. 1535*, 364 (item 1059) (Corthop
was also accused of describing Barnes as a 'false knave and heretic'). It has been suggested
that the grant of St Bartholomew's and Bethlem to the City was prompted by the religiously
radical party which seized power on Henry VIII's death. However, the fact that the hospitals

were granted to the 'Communalty' of London is no evidence that the radicals were involved (the grant was in fact in the standard form, to the 'Mayor and Commonalty and citizens'). The grant had been agreed the previous month, and Henry VIII's conscience seems a more likely explanation for its being made more-or-less on his deathbed: Brigden, *op. cit.* 458. Bethlem seems to have retained its association with religious radicalism; a sect known as the 'Barrowists' reportedly held an 'assembly in a gardeyne house neare Bedlem, wher Iames Forester did expounde the Scriptures . . . before ther Churche was setled' during the 1590s, and the Anabaptist Samual Eaton was in 1639 buried in Bethlem Churchyard (the sixteenth-century one), attended by an estimated two hundred radicals: Champlin Burrage, *The Early English Dissenters in the Light of Recent Research (1550–1641)*, 2 volumes (Cambridge: CUP, 1912), i, 132, 145, 329–30; ii, 39, 49, 326–7.

19 *CA Rep.* 13/2, fol. 456v.

20 *CA Rep.* 12/1, fol. 260; *ibid.* 14, fol. 524; *ibid.* 12/1, fols 350, 483v; *ibid.* 13/1, fols 20, 123; *ibid.* 13/2, fol. 365.

21 *CA Rep.* 13/2, fol. 363; *Ghall* MS 12806, Christ's Hospital Minute Book volume 1, fol. 9v; *Report of the Commissioners . . . Concerning Charities in England and Wales . . .* , 32 volumes (London: W. Clowes/HMSO, 1819–40), xxxii, part vi, 290, 473, followed by O'Donoghue, *op. cit.* 123.

22 *Ghall* MS 12806, Christ's Hospital Court Minute Book volume 1, 42v; *CA Rep.* 14, fol. 524; *ibid.* fols 533, 532; *BCGM* volume 2, fol. 35v; *CA Rep.* 17, fol. 162v. For examples of 1574 leases: *BCGM* volume 2, fols 35v (3 leases), 36 (Bragge), 45; for admissions/ejections: fols 47, 47v (2 instances), 63; *ibid.* volume 3, fol. 409.

23 For 'The Order of the hospitalls of K. Henry the viijth and K. Edward the vjth . . . 1557': BL MS 288.9.4l; a nineteenth-century manuscript version: *CLRO* MS 63.5; printed in *Memoranda, References, and Documents Relating to the Royal Hospitals of the City of London . . .* (London: Arthur Taylor, 1836), and see pp. viii–ix. Neither the Orders, nor the record of the General Court held on 27 September 1557, mention Bethlem: *Ghall* MS 12806, Christ's Hospital Court Minute Book volume 1, fols 8v–10.

24 In September 1561, the Mayor's Porter, Richard Minnes, was admitted at the Mayor's request; on 14 June 1571, John Mell was granted the office *vice* the late Edward Rest, at the Mayor's request; Rowland Sleeford was in December 1579 appointed 'lovingly', this time at the Mayor's 'nomination', suggesting that the patronage of the office was by now beginning to be considered as one of the Mayor's perquisites: *CA Rep.* 14, fol. 524; *CA Rep.* 17, fol. 162v; *CA Rep.* 20, fol. 23.

25 *BCGM* volume 5, fol. 220; *ibid.* volume 6, fol. 70; *CA Rep.* 33, fol. 408 (committee set up by the Court of Aldermen to consider appropriate response to the King's letter on behalf of Crooke, 8 October 1618); *CSPD, 1611–18*, 601 (Privy Council orders an inquiry into Crooke's complaints against the present Keeper, 10 December 1618); *BCGM* volume 6, fol. 110 (election, 13 April 1619). For a full discussion of Crooke and his relationship with Bethlem, see Patricia Allderidge, 'Management and Mismanagement at Bedlam 1547–1633', in Charles Webster (ed.), *Health, Medicine and Mentality in the Sixteenth Century* (Cambridge: CUP, 1979), 141–63, esp. 154ff.

26 *BCGM* volume 6, fols 110, 110v.

27 *BCGM* volume 6, fols 124v, 125v, 126, 128, 179v; 128v.

28 *CA Rep.* 34, fol. 94v; *BCGM* volume 6, fols 144v, 156v, 164v, 167v.

29 *BCGM* volume 6, fols 183, 193; *CA Rep.* 35, fol. 201; *BCGM* volume 6, fols 234, 241, 253; *CA Rep.* 35, fols 229v–30; *ibid.* 36, fol. 172.

30 *BCGM* volume 6, fols 291, 299, 303; *CA Rep.* 37, fols [illegible, 23 January 1623], 176v.

31 *BCGM* volume 6, fol. 341; *CA Rep.* 43, fol. 100v; *BCGM* volume 7, fols 205v, 206v, 217.

32 *Acts of the Privy Council, 1630–1*, 262 (item 751); *CA Rep.* 45, fol. 216.

33 *CA Rep.* 45, fols 266–6v, 406–6v; *CA Rep.* 31/1, fols 167–9v; *CSPD, 1631–33*, 280.

34 *CSPD, 1631–33*, 424.

BETHLEM'S INCOME

—— ·◆· ——

SOURCES OF INCOME, 1247–*c.* 1350

At first sight, it seems curious that money should have lain at the root of most of the conflicts over Bethlem. Because of its original purpose, what was by the twentieth century a wealthy hospital, began life as one of the poorest. In the mid-fourteenth century, the Master and brethren of the House were said to depend on charity for their subsistence. Most of the evidence for its existence at this period comes from royal grants of protections to those whom Bethlem licensed to collect alms on its behalf.[1] By 1403, the Hospital had other resources, but the Master of the Hospital estimated its income from charitable donations – admittedly, in suspiciously round figures, and he had incentive to exaggerate – at a healthy £11 or so a year. Since both the amount and the focus of charitable giving seems to have changed after the Black Death, and of course money values shifted over time, this figure is not a reliable indicator of earlier levels of donations. What one can say is that by the early fifteenth century alms contributed about half the Hospital and Master's incomes, leaving aside the uncertain contribution made by bequests. It is therefore possible that it was largely charity which kept the Hospital going in the century after its foundation.[2]

FitzMary's Priory (after its foundation, Bethlem seems never again to have been described as a priory) had been endowed with very little land and may initially have possessed no properties which it could rent out. This modesty of endowment is reflected in the paucity of references to Bethlem in legal records by comparison with other London hospitals, for example as party to disputes over property boundaries and rents. The New Hospital of St Mary without Bishopsgate, the older sister just up the road with which Bethlem is often confused, was a much wealthier institution. Its Prior was party to six cases recorded in the City's books and rolls of pleas of the Court of Husting between 1437 and 1484, whereas the Master of St Mary of Bethlem was party to none. Likewise, the New Hospital was involved in three property actions recorded in the City's plea and memoranda rolls between 1413 and 1437, but St Mary of Bethlem is not mentioned at all.[3]

Even so, it does not follow that Bethlem was entirely dependent on charitable donations, even in the first century of its existence. Rents within the precinct may have contributed something towards the support of the Hospital and its residents from quite an early stage, if not from the very beginning. In 1346 a small tenement consisting of a 'chamber, solar [private room] and cellar within the close of the moat [precinct] of the hospital' was let out. But the evidence is scant, and may perhaps reflect how very limited was the Hospital's involvement in letting property within the precinct before the second half of the fourteenth century. The first time we know for certain that tenements, or at least rooms, were being built in order to be leased out is in the 1380s and 1390s. It may therefore be that the development of the precinct for commercial purposes did not take place until then.[4]

What we do know is that Bethlem engaged almost from the outset in property transactions which involved tenements *outside* the precinct. In 1270/1, a property on the east side of Bishopsgate Street was described as being 'bounded on the south by the tenement once of Sabrina Sake now of the master of Bedlehem'. In the late 1320s or 1330 William de Banham (described as 'procurator general of the order of Bethlehem', but probably the then Master) leased two properties to a London fishmonger, Richard Swanlond. One of these properties was known as 'de Bethlehem', but Banham himself had evidently rented it from the City.[5] Masters like Banham seem to have been engaged in an attempt to make money at a time of fast-rising population and, therefore, fast-rising rents, by subletting for a larger sum properties held long-term on a fixed rent. The property known as 'de Bethlehem' was leased to Swanland for an annual rent of £1 payable to the Hospital and £2 to the Chamber of London (the Chamber was London's main financial and accounting department). Although Swanlond was required to discharge all the rent owed to the City, Banham still reserved some part of the property for the use of himself and his brethren. So, not only was the Hospital able to use part of the property rent-free, but it also obtained an income from the tenement equivalent to 50 per cent of that charged by the City Chamber.

Another potential source of income was lending. Religious houses and persons were, throughout the Middle Ages, a major source of loans for a wide variety of individuals, from the King downwards. Like lawyers, they seem to have had money on their hands and no doubt lent at interest, despite the fact that contemporary anti-usury laws and Church teaching for much of the period tended to equate any interest-taking, not just excessive interest, with unchristian usury. Certainly the New Hospital of St Mary without Bishopsgate obtained income in this way.[6] However, there is no evidence that the fourteenth-century Masters of St Mary of Bethlem were engaged in similar financial ventures. It may well be that Bethlem's income was simply too low to generate the surplus cash needed for this type of activity.

In addition, depending on when Bethlem started to accommodate people who were not members of its parent Order, it may have derived some income in the period before 1350 from payments by inmates for their keep. Again, however, the evidence is lacking; if the Hospital earned money from this source, it seems never to have had to sue for default of payment.

SOURCES OF INCOME, *c.* 1350–1546

There is no doubt at all that the Hospital remained comparatively poor in terms of the rents it received. In 1363, the Master stated that the Hospital's rents – probably excluding his own income – amounted to no more than £1 13s. If that was true, there was a considerable improvement over the course of the following two decades. A clerical tax of 1379/80 assessed Bethlem's liability at 11s, indicating that the total revenue amounted to about £22 *per annum* (the Master's income was estimated at £10, and he paid 5s; that is, 2.5 per cent or 6d in the £). Even so, only the liability of the Hospital of St Anthony was anything like as low (16s). St Anthony's, a former Jewish synagogue at the eastern end of Broad Street, was rebuilt and expanded in the fifteenth century, but in the last decade of the fourteenth was a small hospital which specialized in treating ergotism ('St Anthony's Fire'). By contrast, the Hospitals of St Bartholomew's, St Thomas of Acon (a substantial house of the Order of St Thomas of Acre, founded at St Thomas à Becket's birthplace just off Cheapside) and the New Hospital of St Mary without Bishopsgate were all required to pay over £2, giving them an estimated annual income four times as high as that of St Mary of Bethlem. The Hospital's income was evidently very low compared to other, broadly similar, institutions, in the half-century after 1350.[7]

Indeed, by the end of the century St Mary of Bethlem's rents in London appear to have fallen back, and to have fallen markedly. A return of 1374/5 put the value of the Hospital at £4. In 1392 its rents were said to be worth a total of £3 15s, probably excluding the Master's income. By contrast, the New Hospital's rents were said to be worth over £120, excluding those reserved to the Prior. Whereas all St Mary of Bethlem's rents were within Bishopsgate Ward, and most of its income came from properties on the Hospital site itself, the New Hospital's properties were spread through over half of the City's wards. During the next decade, the situation seems if anything to have worsened slightly. A witness who testified before the commissioners at the 1403 visitation estimated the Hospital's revenues then at £4 1s 4d, including £1 from the house at Charing Cross which may have been acquired since 1392, plus £4 reserved to the Master.[8]

All this suggests that the face value of Bethlem's rents was declining in the last quarter of the fourteenth century. It could well be that the income from its modest property portfolio fell in the wake of the first onslaught of the Black Death in the middle of the fourteenth century. In addition, the building of a new Chapel probably depleted the Hospital's annual income in the second half of the century both because rents were sold for cash sums and because the Hospital presumably had to borrow a certain amount at interest as well. At some stage thereafter, however, rental income recovered. Bethlem's rents were certainly being farmed for a substantial annual sum in the fifteenth century.[9]

In the last decades of the fourteenth century the Master at least contemplated the speculative building of tenements. The incoming tenants were in effect being invited to pay for the building in return for a low-cost or rent-free lease for the term of their lives. In the end the Master may have decided to offer prospective tenants a 'self-build' scheme instead; the effect would have been much the same. In the longer term the Hospital would acquire the tenements without having to borrow at interest to fund the building of them.

The Hospital did not rely entirely on either of these forms of investment, how-ever. By the 1390s it was granting corrodies (life grants of maintenance, in this case within the Hospital – a speculation on the longevity of the purchasers somewhat similar to that made by medical and life assurers today) in some of its as yet unbuilt accommodation. The fact that corrodians were offered lodgings in the Hospital itself until the new chambers were available suggests that corrodies in general, without the element of new development included, were already a feature of the Hospital's financial practices. O'Donoghue assumed that at least one of these corrodies, that granted to Robert Baron and his wife, was made on the King's orders, and at the Hospital's costs. But the evidence is not compelling.[10]

The probability is that even the Barons' corrody and the subsequent grant of a plot on which to build was made in return either for a grant of land or, as was almost certainly the case here, a lump sum. For much of the Middle Ages, the former arrangement usually made good business sense for the establishment concerned; although that would probably not have been true in the second half of the fourteenth century. Whether or not the latter arrangement was sound financially depended on the Masters' actuarial skills, and who benefited, if the Masters calculated correctly. The practice was criticized by contemporaries on the grounds that it tended to divert surplus food and worn clothing away from the poor and towards corrodians. This was clearly true initially. Once the system was established, however, there would or should have been a balance between current corrodians, who diminished the available resources, and income from gifts and payments made by past corrodians, which increased them. In the case of the Barons, Baron himself died soon after the grant was made. However, his wife outlived him for an unknown period and was entitled to continue to hold the properties granted to the couple in Bethlem precinct until she died or the term of years expired. If indeed it was Baron's 'new place . . . that I have do [had] made be twyxen the kychen and the Gardyn' which was granted out again to corrodians in September 1400, presumably the Hospital had to buy out the remainder of the term from Mrs Baron; something which, rightly or wrongly, it judged worth doing.[11]

At first sight, the building of a new chapel seems a pointless extravagance. The Hospital had its Church, and if that was too small to serve the needs of a growing precinct, probably the nearby Church of St Botolph's could have accommodated the overflow. But appearances are deceptive. The Masters were using the Chapel as part of a positive attempt to find a further source of income through patronage. Possibly the decision of Master John de Nortone to commend the Hospital to the City of London's protection in 1346 was an early instance of this policy. But the first and most important source of support was probably the Hospitals' fourteenth-century patrons, men who had been granted the right to appoint the Master. As has already been mentioned, one of them, Sir James Audley, was described as a patron of the fourteenth-century Chapel.

The explanation for the determination of the Masters of the Hospital to complete the Chapel lies in their need to find other ways of enhancing the revenues and status of, not to mention support for, their modestly endowed and decaying institution. In 1363, the Master obtained a papal grant, effective for just over a year, offering a ten-year relaxation of penance to those who attended the Hospital's great feasts and helped with its restoration for the same period. And the reason he had to do this was twofold: first, the Christian lands in the East had effectively fallen to the Muslims at the end of the thirteenth century. Although the crusading spirit did not die for many years, support for attempts to recover the former Latin East tended to be uneven. Secondly, the wars between England and France from 1340 onwards increasingly made it both practically difficult and politically impossible for English houses, like Bethlem, to act as fund-raisers for parent Orders based in France, even in the few years when their revenues had not been appropriated for the King.[12]

An additional and potentially important source of patronage and support was the associated Fraternity of St Mary of Bethlem. This was established in 1361, at much the same time as work on the Chapel began, by the 'good people Drapers of Cornhill and other good men and women'. Almost certainly, the same motive underlay both the building of the Chapel and the founding of the Fraternity: indeed, the one enabled the other, by providing a suitable and attractive place in which the Fraternity could gather to worship. The brothers and sisters of the Fraternity were clearly wealthy, for the entry fine was set at 20s, and members were expected to pay at least 2s a year and to attend the main events of the fraternity year – in particular, the Feast of the Purification of the Blessed Virgin Mary on 2 February, but also the masses sung for dead brothers and sisters – clothed in a suit of clothes bought at their own expense. Those who fell on hard times were entitled to the substantial sum of 16½d a week, or over £3 10s a year. (As late as the 1580s the Skinners considered 6d a week sufficient to pay for a pensioner widow's support in Bethlem.) More fortunate brethren were asked to leave the Fraternity a piece of silver at their deaths. The Fraternity also raised money with the intention of buying property out of which to fund a chaplain.[13]

The connection with the Drapers Company seems not to have lasted long, but the Skinners also established a link with Bethlem at much the same time, and this was maintained. Their yeomanry (members who did not belong to the superior group entitled to wear the livery – mainly artisans and young men at the beginning of their careers) had its own Fraternity, that of the Blessed Virgin Mary or Our Lady, 'holden at Seint Mary Spitel and at Bethleem', as an early membership list puts it. The connection with Bethlem survived the absorption of the Fraternity of the Blessed Virgin Mary by the major Skinners' Fraternity, Corpus Christi, in 1472. Sir Thomas More, who lived for a time at Crosby Hall, Bishopsgate, was a member of this new Fraternity. More undoubtedly visited the Hospital building, because he describes the behaviour of one of the inmates – much more realistically than later commentators; it is by no means inconceivable that he took his friend Erasmus there too.[14]

As a 1519 letter of advertisement for the Fraternity makes clear, one of the major attractions for its brothers and sisters was the chance to share in the spiritual benefits of an institution dedicated to works of charity. Indulgences such as those granted in 1363 and again in 1389 were probably of particular importance to Bethlem. Most medieval hospitals could rely on benefactions from members of the laity who were keen to limit their time in Purgatory through the intercession of the poor, whose prayers were believed to be especially efficacious. But, although there were some physically ill people in Bethlem, they seem on the whole not to have been poor; and those who were poor seem on the whole to have been mad. The intercessions of the mad, even assuming that they could be induced to make them, were hardly likely to wing their benefactors to heavenly bliss. So Bethlem may well have had to offer that little bit more by way of access to the general benefits of a religious foundation than other hospitals.[15]

The effect of these attempts to solicit the goodwill and patronage of Londoners and other prominent people is evident in some of the legacies left to the Hospital. From 1361 onwards, bequests began to trickle in. A number of wills which left money to the 'work', 'new work' or 'fabric' of the Church or to the Chapel of Bethlem were recorded in the City's Court of Husting in the second half of the fourteenth century, beginning with that of William Brangewyn, vintner, in March 1361, the year the Fraternity was founded. Ten years later came the first of the bequests to the Fraternity itself. From the fact that gifts specifically for the Church, Chapel, or 'new work' are concentrated in the period 1361 to 1378, it seems that the fund-raising, if not the building work itself, was largely completed by 1380.[16]

The new Chapel never attracted large numbers of people to be buried there, other than its own chaplains and those who lived within the precinct, although, nearly a hundred years after it was built, the London mercer Peter Adderton preferred to be buried there rather than in his parish church, St Leonard's, Shoreditch. But bequests were sometimes substantial and from important people. In 1389, Ralph Lord Basset left £200 to pay for priests to sing for his soul in four chantries, one of which was to be at Bethlem. In 1408 the poet John Gower bequeathed sums of money to 'each sister professed, to each who is a nurse of the sick, and to every sick person' in Bethlem and three other hospitals (he recognized that not all these hospitals still had members of a religious order in them). During the fifteenth century it seems to have been normal for any Alderman who lived in Bishopsgate Ward to leave a substantial bequest to Bethlem, usually to its poor inmates. Some of London's fifteenth-century Common Councilmen were even more generous to the Hospital. The tallow-chandler John Styward – who was one of Marowe's executors, and whose own connection with Bethlem has already been noted – left £20, to be dispensed at the rate of £3 a year, and the mercer John Donne left £13 6s 8d to be spent on food, drink, linen and woollen clothing for the sick poor detained at Bethlem.[17]

Bequests from ordinary Londoners who had no particular connections with the Hospital, however, seem to have been very few and far between during the fifteenth and sixteenth centuries. Of nearly two hundred and fifty wills entered in the records of the London Consistory Court between 1492 and 1547, only two mention such bequests: one of 2s, another of 1s 4d, for food and drink for the poor inmates of Bethlem. Even Bethlem chaplains and residents seem rarely to have left legacies for the inmates, though they paid to be buried and prayed for in the Church or Chapel. In 1437, the incoming Master alleged that the neglect and damage done under previous masters was so great as to threaten 'the worship of God there, and alms and other works of piety and the succour of demented lunatics and other poor and sick persons resorting thither'. In 1446, an indulgence claimed that the rents and profits of 'the ancient almshouse . . . commonly called the hospital of St Mary of Bethleem . . . are not sufficient to support the multitude of miserable persons of both sexes dwelling there'. This was merely a continuation of the state of affairs found by the Commissioners in 1403. Their report paints a picture of a Chapel which was hardly used, adequately but sparsely decorated, its more valuable ornaments held by the Master, its senior chaplain negligent in performing his routine duties (he was imprisoned for a while in the wake of the visitation). Something had clearly gone wrong for the Chapel to be in this state within twenty-five years of its construction. Presumably the failure of the City's bid to control the Mastership had soured relations.[18]

Finally, a slightly unusual source of income was the privilege possessed by Bethlem, which was outside the jurisdiction of the Bishop of London, of marrying couples by licence and without the banns being read. This caused a certain amount of heat in Parliament in 1539, where it was portrayed as a bigamist's charter.[19] How much income the Hospital drew from this source, however, it is impossible to say.

SOURCES OF INCOME, 1547–1633

Having had to buy out the interest of Sir Peter Mewtys and his deputy, Thomas Scopeham, at considerable cost, the City soon began to look at ways of making the Hospital more profitable. In 1552, the Chamberlain was told 'to do his beste for the profett of the cytie in lettyng oute of the chapell of bethlem from yere to yere & none otherwyse'. The City had already acted to divert potential worshippers from the Chapel, having in 1551 joined those living within the precinct with the parish of St Botolph's, at a cost of £1 6s 8d a year, and pensioning off the curate at the same rate. Clearly the Mayor and Aldermen expected to get more than this by renting out or rebuilding the two sites. Lest this seem to modern eyes intolerably money-grubbing, it should be said that it was not just the income of the Hospital that the City's Governors sought to increase. In 1550, for example, they granted an additional £1 6s 8d a year for the maintenance of poor inmates, over and above the sum allowed previously.[20]

Once the City had got control of the Hospital, Bethlem began to attract property bequests. In 1575 Sir Thomas Gresham, whose father had been deeply involved in the City's attempts to acquire the City hospitals in the 1540s, bequeathed a rent-charge of £10 a year for the benefit of poor inmates, payable by the Mercers Company. A property bequest to the Mercers, Grocers, Vintners and Clothworkers in 1599 included the stipulation that £2 a year of the profits be given to the poor of Bethlem. It was on the basis of bequests such as these that the foundations of the Hospital's later fortunes were laid. On the other hand, an analysis of charitable bequests, 1570–3 and 1594–7, shows that Bethlem was mentioned only in around 3 per cent of cash bequests to City hospitals (Christ's, St Bartholomew's, St Thomas' Southwark, plus Bridewell). The value of such cash bequests as it received varied enormously. In the 1570s the value was both actually and proportionately low (£12 out of £1,310, or less than 1 per cent); in the 1590s, it was high (£141 out of £2,359, or just under 6 per cent). By contrast, the value of cash bequests and endowments left to the best-supported City Hospital, Christ's, which cared for poor and orphaned children, was £2,654 in the period 1594–7.[21]

Bethlem did, however, have other resources to draw on. Its rentals produced substantial annual sums (according to the 1632 Commissioners, £34 13s 4d in 1555, just under £50 in 1606, leaping to nearly £108 in 1622, when a particularly substantial lease expired).[22] There were several other sources of income for inmates' support. Until 1556 or perhaps until the 1570s, the Keeper was receiving an annual payment of

£1 6s 8d from the Chamber towards the 'sustentation and finding of [each of] the poor sick and distraught people' supported by the City. This was continued by Bridewell, being doubled in 1609 and again in 1631. Parishes and private maintainers paid at least part of some inmates' costs. Weekly doles of food, beer and fuel were provided by the Mayor, Sheriffs and Chamberlain, certainly by the 1630s and probably for years before that. Prominent Bishopsgate residents also regularly gave gifts in kind. Bethlem benefited from the almsgiving of inmates' friends and visitors. In the 1630s it was claimed that 'on some weekes the expence of the distracted persons that bene wholely defrayed' by doles, parish payments and alms. Moreover, from 1618 onwards the tenancies resulting from the first major phase of sixteenth-century redevelopment started to become available for re-leasing. Although property rents were by this stage subsumed into Bridewell's accounts, the fines paid by incoming tenants went directly to support Bethlem.[23]

Despite this rosy picture, Bethlem throughout the period from 1547 to the early 1630s appears to have had recurrent problems arising out of an actual or alleged shortage of funds. Bearing in mind the Bethlem rental income and the Royal Commissioners' statement about the value of other sources of income, the number of people the Hospital supported charitably seems very low. In 1598 there were only six inmates in Bethlem who were wholly dependent on the 'allowance of the house' for their basic necessities. In 1624, the Governors decided that there should never be more than twenty inmates 'for that the house is overcharged and wanteth roome there being nowe 31 att the house charge', alleging that the revenues could not support so many.[24]

One reason for the perception that Bethlem was inadequately funded is that it was not separately administered and accounted for, other than in the period 1547 to c. 1574. In the longer term, the result was that the distinction between Bethlem and Bridewell properties became blurred. The Governors talked of the Bethlem property as though it belonged to Bridewell. Perhaps 'Bridewell' was shorthand for 'Bridewell-and-Bethlem'. None the less, the fact that the Governors spent the great majority of their time dealing with the very much more sizeable population and staff of Bridewell seems to have coloured their attitude towards paying for Bethlem – an attitude which often appears grudging. Those Bethlem inmates who were too poor to maintain themselves were said to have had to rely on 'the charitable alms of the City', as the Court of Aldermen put it. In the circumstances, it is perhaps not surprising that increases in the allowances made for poor inmates at Bethlem were slow in coming and sometimes apparently had to be prised out of the Bridewell Governors.[25]

In fairness to them, however, the Governors were quick to accept in 1609 that the allowance was 'verie smale' and to agree a substantial increase. This brought Bethlem's allowance up to the level that was being granted by other city hospitals. The Bridewell Court of Governors Minute books quite regularly record payments for the upkeep of precinct property and, occasionally, the Court approved payments for major repairs to the Hospital building. Not all the rental income was therefore available to support the inmates. It was also reasonable that some income from Bethlem should be retained as a contribution towards Bridewell's administrative costs. Moreover, between 1609 and 1622, when the rental income was about £50 a year, the 'allowance of the house' stood at £2 13s 8d and the number of inmates supported by charity was rising towards its peak of thirty-one, Bethlem was probably at an advantage *vis-à-vis* Bridewell. The same will have been true after 1631, when the rental income was over £100 a year but each charitably supported inmate cost £5 6s 8d. What Bethlem suffered from as a result of its relationship with Bridewell was primarily the Governors' inattention, combined with a failure on their part to separate out the two Hospitals' revenues. This combination of factors only occasionally worked to Bethlem's advantage.

CONCLUSION

Despite its poverty and comparative obscurity, Bethlem attracted attention both because of its potential financial value and because of its international connections. These factors in combination changed its purpose and, eventually, its character markedly. For the first century after it was founded, the House of St Mary of Bethlem served the purpose for which it was intended: it supported the Order of Bethlem, offering a base for members visiting from abroad as part of a larger drive to gather alms. It also obtained licences, and sent out delegates, to collect money for its own support and for that of its parent Order. As far as one can tell, it is largely true to say that Bethlem survived on charitable donations raised in this way. It evidently made a small amount of additional income by subletting properties it rented from other organizations and institutions, but this probably merely supplemented its charitable revenues by a modest amount.

From the 1340s, social and economic changes obliged Bethlem to seek new ways of fulfilling its new aim. The effect was to open up the Hospital from about 1350 onwards. The later fourteenth-century Masters cultivated patrons, wooing both the City and prominent individuals with a fine Chapel and a new Fraternity which offered generous spiritual and social benefits. They engaged in financial speculation, selling corrodies or pensions. By the end of the century, they were attracting inwards investment by granting land to private individuals, whose property, now graced with new houses, reverted to Bethlem in due course.

Of the existence of a deliberate campaign to improve the Hospital's financial position, which lasted for most of the second half of the fourteenth century, there seems no doubt. At that period, the Masters were successful in generating both financial and moral support for Bethlem. By 1400, however, support seems to have slackened. The connection with the Drapers did not last; Bethlem received some generous bequests from prominent men who lived locally and therefore presumably were familiar with the Hospital, but it seems not to have attracted many bequests from fifteenth-century Londoners generally. Possibly this was the result of the successful assertion by Richard II in the late 1380s of his right to the patronage of the Hospital, against the rival claims of London.

If that was the reason, one would expect Londoners to have became more generous again once the City finally managed to gain control of Bethlem in early 1547. In fact, however, this did not happen, or at least not to any marked extent. Overall, Bethlem seems to have done rather worse than one would expect, even allowing for its modest size compared to the other hospitals. Possibly the habit of *not* giving to Bethlem died hard. Or perhaps we have here an example of an aspect of charitable giving which persists to this day: the fact that it is much easier to raise money for charities which support children than for those which help the mentally handicapped and ill.

The growth of London in the later sixteenth century produced another shift in Bethlem's fortunes. By the 1570s, there are signs of competition for Bethlem leases. Although the rents were by this stage going into Bridewell's coffers, larger rents usually meant larger 'entry fines', paid by incoming tenants; and these, Bethlem did receive. As the benefits of the earlier 'self-build' policies started to be reaped, and the Governors were increasingly able to force a hard bargain, Bethlem rental income more than doubled. But there were also increasing demands on Bethlem's income, ones which, for all their efforts, the Governors were ultimately unable to resist.

Social attitudes were also changing. In 1612, when laying down orders for Bethlem, the Bridewell Governors spoke sympathetically of the inmates as 'soule sicke'.[26] A new spirit was abroad, one which breathed even through Bethlem. In 1619, it was at least arguable that it was inappropriate to have as Bethlem's Keeper a man who had no medical knowledge. By the 1630s, the Privy Council referred to Bethlem's inmates, who had in the past commonly been described as 'prisoners', as 'patients'. It was not just the administrative arrangements which would be different from then on.

NOTES

1 *Calendar of Patent Rolls 1354–58*, 423; *Calendar of Patent Rolls 1290–92*, 484; *Calendar of Patent Rolls 1327–30*, 446, 511; *Calendar of Patent Rolls 1330–34*, 84, 107; *Calendar of Patent Rolls 1334–38*, 344.
2 PRO C270/22, mm. 1 and 3.
3 *CLRO* Hustings Book, fols 67 (x 2), 75, 113*v* and 126*v*; *CLRO* Hustings Common Pleas Roll 160, m. 5; *Calendar of Plea and Memoranda Rolls 1413–1437*, 25, 221 and 293.
4 *Calendar of Letter Book F*, 163, 177.
5 G. A. Hodgett, *The Cartulary of Holy Trinity Aldgate*, London Record Society, vii (1971), 166; *Calendar of Plea and Memoranda Rolls 1323–64*, 185; *Calendar of Letter Book E*, 251 (the footnote on p. 163 of the *Calendar of Letter Book F* is incorrect to identify this 'Stapelede Hall' with one in the parish of All Hallows, Barking, as the Letter Book E grant makes clear).
6 *Calendar of Close Rolls 1327–30*, 563, 570; *Calendar of Close Rolls 1330–33*, 299; *Calendar of Close Rolls 1341–43*, 104; *Calendar of Close Rolls 1349–54*, 505; *Calendar of Close Rolls 1354–60*, 203, 230; *Calendar of Close Rolls 1461–8*, 182; *A Descriptive Catalogue of Ancient Deeds [in the PRO] . . .* , 6 volumes (London: HMSO, 1890–1915), ii, part ii, 508.
7 W. H. Bliss (ed.), *Calendar of Entries in the Papal Registers . . . : Petitions to the Pope, i, AD 1342–1419* (London: HMSO/Eyre & Spottiswoode, 1896), 423; A. K. McHardy, *The Church in London 1375–92*, London Record Society, xiii (1977), 1–3.
8 *BRHA*, Muniment Book, fol. 3; McHardy, *op. cit.* 40–77; PRO C270/22, m. 3.
9 British Museum, Harleian Charter 56 F. 48 (dorse).
10 *Calendar of Patent Rolls 1388–92*, 484; Edward G. O'Donoghue, *The Story of Bethlehem Hospital from its Foundation in 1247* (London: T. Fisher Unwin, 1914), 59.
11 Barbara Harvey, *Living and Dying in England, 1100–1540: The Monastic Experience* (Oxford and New York: Clarendon Press/OUP, 1993), 179–81, 191; *Ghall* MS 9171, London Commissary Court Wills, Register 1, fol. 463*v*.

12 *Calendar of Entries in the Papal Registers: Petitions*, 423–4. In 1367, the Proctor or deputy of the 'warden' of Bethlem was accused of using forged bulls offering remission of sins in order to collect money on behalf of the Hospital: *Calendar of Patent Rolls 1367–70*, 68–9.

13 *Ghall* MS 142, 164, 166, 170, 174; J. J. Lambert (ed.), *Records of the Skinners of London, Edward I to James I* (London: Allen & Unwin, 1933), 238 and 379.

14 A. H. Johnson, *The History of the Worshipful Company of the Drapers of London*, 4 volumes (Oxford: Clarendon Press, 1914–22), i, 110; Lambert, *op. cit.*, 76, 91, 77; *The Complete Works of Sir Thomas More*, 15 volumes (New Haven: Yale University Press, 1963–86), ix, 118.

15 British Library, MS C18 E2, items 12*, 12, 13, 14; J. A. Tremlow (ed.), *Calendar of Entries in the Papal Registers. . . . : Papal Letters*, xi, *AD 1455–1464*, 6–8, especially 8. We are grateful to Dr Carole Rawcliffe for pointing out to us the particular difficulty under which a hospital which catered primarily for the mentally ill probably laboured.

16 Reginald R. Sharpe (ed.), *Calendar of Wills Proved and Enrolled in the Court of Husting, London, AD 1258–AD 1688*, 2 volumes (London: J. C. Francis, 1889–90), ii, 41, 50, 152, 153, 162, 207 (bequests to the Church/Chapel/new work, 1361–78; none of these testators seem to have been, or have been married to, Drapers or Skinners); 159, 218 (bequests to the Fraternity, 1371 and 1380, the first by a Vintner, the second by a Draper).

17 *Ghall* MS 9171, London Commissary Court Wills, Register 6, fol. 28*v* (Adderton); W. Dugdale, *The Baronage of England, or a Historical Account of the Lives and Most Notable Acts of our English Nobility . . . Before the End of King Henry the Third's Reign*, 2 volumes (London: Thomas Newcomb, 1675–6), i, 380 (Basset); Sir Nicholas H. Nicolas, *Testamenta Vetusta*, 2 volumes (London: Nichols, 1826), ii, 779; F. W. Weaver (ed.), *Somerset Medieval Wills 1383–1500*, Somerset Record Society, xvi (1901), 181, 182 (Alderman Stephen Forster); PRO, PCC PROB 11/5/9; *Ghall* MS 9171; London Commissary Court Wills, Register 6, fol. 63*v* (Alderman Marowe and his widow, Katherine); PRO, PCC PROB 11/6/24 (Alderman Sir John Crosby); PRO, PCC PROB 11/5/16 (Alderman William Gregory, a Skinner); PRO, PCC PROB 11/6/7 (Styward); PRO, PCC PROB 11/7/2 (Donne); see also PRO, PCC PROB 11/6/28 (William Blackman, tallow-chandler). For Blackman and Styward, see Randall Monter-Williams, *The Tallow Chandlers of London*, 4 volumes (London: Kaye & Ward, 1970–7), iii, 35, 37, 42.

18 Ida Darlington (ed.), *London Consistory Court Wills 1492–1547*, London Record Society, iii (1967), 23, 137. Of the fifty wills included in a selection of early ones, two (the testament of John Chelmyswyk Esquire of Shropshire (1418) and that of John Toller, London Vintner (1478)), left sums to Bethlem among other hospitals: F. J. Furnivall (ed.), *The Fifty Earliest English Wills in the Court of Probate AD 1387–1439: with a Priest's of 1454*, Early English Text Society, Old Series lxxviii (1882), 31–2, 78. Robert Baron, corrodian (pensioner), left 3s 4d apiece to the high altar and for paving the Church, asking to be buried in the chancel; the chaplain, Thomas Grene, merely required his executors to distribute the rest of his goods for the good of his soul: *Ghall* MS 9171, London Commissary Court Wills, Register 1, fol. 463*v*; *ibid.* Register 2, fol. 17; *Calendar of Patent Rolls 1436–41*, 87; H. C. Maxwell-Lyte (ed.), *The Register of Thomas Bekyngton, Bishop of Bath and Wells, 1443–1465, Part I*, Somerset Record Society, xlix (1934), 59.

19 *CSPD, 1539*, 870, 896.

20 *CA Rep.* 11, fol. 271; *ibid. CA Rep.* 13/1, fol. 20*v*; *BRHA*, Muniment Book, fol. 30; *CA Rep.* 12/2, fols 319*v*, 350; *ibid.* 12/1, fol. 260.

21 *Report of the Commissioners . . . concerning Charities in England and Wales*, 32 volumes (London: W. Clowes/HMSO, 1819–40), xxxii, part vi, 488; Ian W. Archer, *The Pursuit of Stability: Social Relations in Elizabethan London* (Cambridge, New York, etc.: CUP, 1991), 170, 176 (Christ's Hospital was however outstandingly well supported: all the other hospitals together only managed to attract £879).

22 The income generated by Bethlem rents between 1555 and 1632 is given in PRO SP16/224 no. 21, m. 3.

23 *CA Rep.* 12/1, fol. 260; *BCGM* volume 5, fol. 383*v*; *Acts of the Privy Council 1630–1*, 264; PRO SP16/224 no. 21, fols 4–5. In June 1607 the poorbox yielded £1 4s 2d, 10s of which was spent on buying new 'vessells and other necessarryes' and the rest on shirts and smocks for

the inmates; two years later, apparently the first time it had been opened since, it yielded 5s, which was again given to the poor inmates: *BCGM* volume 5, fols 197*v*, 365*v*.

24 *BCGM* volume 4, fol. 51*v*, *ibid.* volume 6, fol. 368.

25 *CA Rep.* 13/2, fol. 363. For increases, see: *BCGM* volume 5, fol. 383*v*; *Acts of the Privy Council 1630–1*, 264; *CSPD, 1633–4*, 22.

26 *CA Rep.* 31/1, fols 169–9*v*.

FROM BETHLEHEM TO BEDLAM
Changing roles and personnel

—— •◆• ——

INTRODUCTION

Between 1247 and the 1630s, Bethlem's role changed substantially. By the middle of the sixteenth century at the latest, it was regarded as a specialist hospital for the insane. The trouble is that we do not know when or how the change began. The evidence shows that it was under way by about 1400, but not for how long it had been going on. And not only do we not know for sure what kind of role Bethlem had for the first hundred and fifty years of its existence, but it is not entirely certain what kind of institution it became thereafter.

The argument made here is that substantial change came late, probably not much before 1400. Until then, Bethlem was a religious institution which continued to focus primarily on collecting and distributing alms, although by the fourteenth century the main beneficiaries, apart from the Hospital and its staff, were probably poor people who lived locally, rather than the Order of Bethlehem. As the social and political changes of the mid-fourteenth century onwards made alms-collecting more difficult, the Hospital started to concentrate ever more on the care of the sick, and in particular on the care of the mad. Typically, this happened at just the moment when other English hospitals were abandoning or cutting back this type of provision severely.

Then there is the matter of who ran this changing institution, and how. Various factors worked to impede administrative change, even once Bethlem's role was clear. What kept the Hospital in a timewarp was probably its small size relative to other city institutions and activities, and, above all, the insulating effect of a delegated administration. The existence of Keepers who were, even after 1547, semi-independent, seems to have had the effect of preserving Bethlem in a state approaching suspended animation.

FROM PRIORY TO 'MADHOUSE'

It is not known when Bethlem became a hospital in the medieval sense (a place which accommodated people other than its brethren and fellow-members of their Order), much less when it started to take in the sick and old. The earliest surviving reference which indicates that it might have cared for the sick is from 1292, when envoys of 'the bishop and brethren of St Mary's, Bethleem' were granted a protection while collecting alms 'for the poor and infirm in their hospitals', one of which, of course, may have been Bethlem.[1] However, the fact that Bethlem was routinely referred to as a hospital from the 1330s onwards is not evidence that it was no longer simply or primarily a base for alms-collectors. 'Hospital' was a word which could mean merely a place of refuge for travellers, akin to the modern 'hostel'. It would be a perfectly appropriate way of describing an institution which offered accommodation to travelling alms-collectors.

The first time we know for sure that the sick, the elderly and pensioners were being accommodated in the Hospital is in 1403. By then, such activities had been going on for several years. One witness, however, who had first known the Hospital nearly a quarter of a century before, spoke as though its work then had been focused on 'outdoor relief': collecting alms and distributing them to the non-resident poor.[2]

What Bethlem almost certainly did not do until about 1400 is look after the mad other than, perhaps, incidentally and temporarily. The 1632 Commissioners commented that it was not clear when it first 'employed to the use of distracted persons', but that the earliest reference they could find to its use for this purpose 'was in the beginninge of the Reigne of Rich: 2': in the late 1370s or early 1380s, presumably. Unfortunately they did not say where they found this, and nothing has survived which looks as though it might have been their source.[3]

For what it is worth, when the right to appoint to the Mastership of the Hospital was disputed in 1381, there was no indication that it had become in part or whole a hospital for the insane. John Stow claimed that the Stone House at Charing Cross had at one time contained 'distraught and lunatike people . . . : but it was said, that sometime a King of England, not liking such a kind of people to remaine so neere his Palace, caused them to be removed farther off, to Bethlem without Bishops gate of London, and to that Hospitall the said house of Charing Crosse doth yet remaine'.[4] On this basis, Geoffrey O'Donoghue constructed an elaborate argument in favour of 1377 as the date of the transfer. He suggested that, once the royal Mews were rebuilt, the presence nearby of a house accommodating madmen proved unacceptable to Richard II. Perhaps the youthful King did have cause to visit the Mews (which were some way from Westminster Palace, of course). However, it is also possible that one of the Masters, most probably Robert Lincoln, Master from 1389 and a royal clerk, managed to acquire the Charing Cross house as part of his attempts to increase the Hospital's endowment, and that the transfer of the inmates to Bethlem was undertaken in order to release the property for letting. It was Lincoln who was accused in 1403 of 'alienating' the property; possibly he was the first Master to have had the opportunity to do so. Certainly the evidence in favour of 1377 as the date of acquisition or transfer is not strong, and the 1632 Commissioners may simply have been mistaken. Conceivably they had in mind the report of their fifteenth-century predecessors, which recorded the presence of mad inmates at the beginning, not of Richard II's reign, but of that of his successor, Henry IV, who seized the throne in 1399.[5]

During the 1403 visitation, the Porter stated that the Hospital then contained 'six insane men & three others who were sick'. In view of Stow's tale and of the absence of any reliable evidence before the early fifteenth century that the Hospital cared for the insane, it does seem likely that it was the transfer of the Charing Cross lunatics to Bethlem in about 1400 which changed the latter from a small generalist hospital to one which would, in due course, come to specialize in the care of the insane. It was not an overnight transformation, however. The sick and old continued to be taken in for another thirty years at least.[6]

The need to provide for the care of certain types of insane person in the London area was recognized at the period. In the 1370s, a chaplain, Robert Denton, planned to create a place to care for 'poor priests and other men and women who had fallen into frenzy and lost their memories and where they could remain until they were cured and restored to sanity'.[7] None the less, it seems likely that Bethlem's change of function was, like so much else in the Hospital's early history, the product of pure chance.

The process of specialization seems to have been well under way by 1437, and may have been largely complete by the 1460s, when the care of the mad was the only function ascribed to Bethlem in a commonplace book compiled by a sometime Mayor of London. By the time the City took control of the Hospital, specialization was complete. There was still a tendency to refer to Bethlem's inmates as 'poor sick and distraught', but the City's governors had no doubt that the one essential criterion for admission was insanity. In 1553, the Court of Aldermen ordered an examination of some 'poore persons lately sente from the hospytall in Smythefelde [St Bartholomew's]' to see if they were mad or not, and, if not, 'they shalbe put owte of the said howse of bethelem'.[8]

So the Hospital's role was clear by the mid-sixteenth century. But what kind of an institution did the City gain?

It is natural to assume that any place which was founded as a religious house and was not specifically re-founded as something else at a later stage (as happened to some of the London hospitals which were suppressed by Henry V as alien priories and then founded again as almshouses) continued to be a 'religious institution' until the Dissolution of the Monasteries. But this was probably not true of Bethlem. In 1403, the only 'sister' the Hospital contained was the Master's mother, who, so her daughter claimed, would happily have worn the prescribed dress of the Order and carried out the requisite duties – had anyone asked her to do so. The longest-staying witness who testified before the Commissioners said that there had been [professed] brothers and sisters in the Hospital in Master William Tytte's time (Tytte died in 1381). By implication, that was the last time the Hospital had contained men and women who had taken their vows. There were certainly chaplains present in the precinct, but the focus of their testimonies, as of their testaments, was the Chapel, not the Hospital building.[9]

What changes, then, were prompted by the transfer of control to London? The acquisition by the City of the Royal Hospitals from Henry VIII and his son had a number of consequences beyond the obvious ones of altered administrative and financial arrangements. The very process by which London was granted its hospitals encouraged definition of their purposes and identities. Moreover, because the revenues of the four main hospitals were separately accounted for, the Hospital's Governors were keen to avoid paying for anyone who was not their responsibility. In

1624 the Bridewell Governors proposed that an inmate whom they judged to be recovered should be sent to some other hospital, 'being onely lame of his feete'.[10] This attitude seems both to have led to a desire for greater autonomy on the part of the Bridewell Governors in their capacity of overseers of Bethlem, and to have created an emphasis on the different functions of the hospitals.

On the other hand, the City tried from the outset to maintain a coherent and uniform system of administration for its hospitals. It had received St Bartholomew's, with Bethlem in the margins, in 1547; just under a decade later it was granted Christ's, St Thomas's and Bridewell. Almost immediately, Alderman Martin Bowes and his committee were ordered to get together with the Governors of Christ's, St Thomas's and Bridewell in order to produce new Ordinances for their 'good & politique governaunce'. On 27 September at the General Court held at Christ's Hospital, the Governors agreed that the Ordinances they had just approved should also apply to St Bartholomew's. A large body of Governors, sixty-six in total, was to be elected, consisting of a given number of Aldermen and Common Councilmen, and from this single body the Governors of the four hospitals were to be drawn. The respective hospitals' rules, officers, and officers' duties were modelled, *mutatis mutandis*, on the Ordinances drawn up for Christ's.[11]

The fact that Bethlem does not seem to have been subsumed into Bridewell's administration in September 1557 is important. Its distinctiveness, marked by the provision of a separate seal for Bethlem in 1562, continued even after the Bridewell Governors did eventually start to supervise its affairs. The other hospitals had their officers, headed by the Steward and Clerk, who were sworn in on admission and paid fees (salaries), and whose servants were in turn paid for by the respective hospitals once the requirement for their services was recognized. Bethlem had its Keeper. Although the record of the admission of Richard Minnes as Keeper in 1561 spoke of him receiving all the fees, profits and advantages belonging to the office, the Keeper's salary and reward (bonus) are never discussed in the Court of Aldermen or Bridewell records between then and 1633. It is highly improbable that, if the Keeper was salaried, one or other Court would not have approved an increase at some stage. And while several Keepers did battle with the Bridewell Governors over the question of their right to retain legacies left to Bethlem and over the amount of the 'house allowance' for the poor inmates, they never once asked for a rise in their own fees.[12]

In fact, something very similar to the pre-1547 arrangement appears to have continued. Since the City was now in effect the 'Master' (though Dr Crooke would not have agreed), the Keeper had no control over the Hospital's income from its properties. The 'advantages' he got were, it seems, the right to occupy, let out portions of, and accommodate paying inmates in, the Master's House, and to make what profit he could out of any difference between the Bridewell allowances plus the gifts and doles Bethlem received and the cost of maintaining the poor inmates. In the late 1390s and early 1400s, Master Lincoln's deputy, Peter Taverner, had apparently also sold ale, reared pigs, and run a boys' school. If his sixteenth- and seventeenth-century successors were not quite this entrepreneurial, they are likely none the less to have approached the Keepership with a lively spirit of private enterprise.

Because the Keeper was appointed by the Court of Aldermen (often enough, as a favour to the then Mayor), the Bridewell Governors had great difficulty in exerting any effective control over Bethlem. They were rebuffed in their early attempt to discharge one Keeper and appoint another. In 1598, they tried to discover whether they had the right to appoint the Keeper. Having failed to identify anything useful in a search of the records, they seem to have accepted the situation. They did appoint 'surveyors for Bethlem', although these men were probably mainly concerned with inspecting hospital property; and they did make visitations to the Hospital from time to time (in 1598, 1607, 1609, 1620 and 1624), criticizing maladministration and arranging to have physical defects in the structure of the building put right. There may, despite the irregularity reflected in the records, have been a formal annual visit, when the 'poor box' was opened and the money used to buy goods for the Hospital or distributed in cash or kind among the poor inmates. And Governors may have 'dropped in' individually from time to time. But it was an aldermanic committee, headed by the Comptroller of the Chamber, which inspected the Hospital in 1612 and drew up (at long last) Orders for its government. The division of authority over the Keeper enabled him to play one off against another, as John Mell did in 1579. For most purposes and for most of the time, the Keeper was in charge of Bethlem, not the Bridewell Governors. The City had inadvertently created something akin to a private madhouse which took in poor people at civic expense.[13]

THE PERSONNEL

The Priors, Masters, Wardens or Keepers

Not much is known about the early Masters or Wardens, and nothing at all about the Priors, if indeed Bethlem ever was headed by a man known as the Prior (for a list of all known Masters, Keepers or Wardens, 1247–1633, see Appendix 1). It seems likely that most men who figured in the thirteenth- and fourteenth-century records as the Bishop of Bethlehem's procurator-generals or attorneys in England were Masters of Bethlem, the Master being the most senior English brother of the Order of Bethlehem. On this basis, the earliest known Master was Thomas of Doncastre, appointed the Bishop's attorney in February 1292, who was almost certainly the same man as the 'Brother Thomas' who was 'master of the House of Bethleem' in 1293. His successor, or successor-but-one, was probably the 'Friar William de Banham, procurator-general of the Order of Bethlehem', who is mentioned in a Bethlem lease of 1330. O'Donoghue identified Brother de Banham with 'William de Banham, clerk', whose arrest was ordered in 1324 – evidently successfully, for he received a pardon for breaking out of prison at Corfe Castle in March 1327. Prison taught this bold clerk no lessons, it seems; he was accused of robbery a matter of days later. However, it looks as though he may not have pursued his riotous career for much longer: in May 1327 one John atte Church of Tibenham was pardoned for William de Banham's death. Unless this was an error, therefore, there were two William de Banhams. The future Master of Bethlem seems to have started out in the Bishop of Norwich's service, and then transferred to that of the new King, Edward III, in the late 1320s. Whether he was rewarded for this service by being appointed Master of Bethlem by the King, or whether the Bishop of Bethlehem thought it politically prudent to choose a royal clerk as his representative in England, there seems to be no way of knowing. But the appointment of a man like Banham certainly presaged later practices.[14]

Banham was probably succeeded by John [Matheu] de Nortone sometime before June 1342, for at this date 'John de Norton received the bishop of Bethlehem's attorneys by writ'. This is the man who entered into an agreement with the City of London four years later (see Chapter 5). Some of the Masters who served during Edward III's reign, or from the 1340s onwards at least, were probably the nominees of Sir John Darcy, Sir John Beauchamp, and Sir James Audley. These were the men who, according to Sir William Welles's Parliamentary petition of 1381, had been granted 'le garde' of the Hospital by Edward III. Darcy is probably John Darcy senior of Knaith, who was Steward of the King's Household in 1337, Chamberlain in 1341, and finally Constable of the Tower in 1346, and who died in May 1347. The likeliest contender among the several Edwardian John Beauchamps is a younger son of Guy, Earl of Warwick. He was a distinguished soldier, being elected Knight of the Garter in 1344; he died in late 1364. Finally, Sir James Audley is probably the 'most valiant knight' who served under Edward III's martial son, the Black Prince, and who died in 1386.[15]

Of the later fourteenth-century Masters, potentially the most interesting is William Tytte or Tuyt, who was Master by 1380, and possibly by 1367. Tytte is said to have founded the Fraternity of St Mary of Bethlem in 1361, although he was almost certainly not the Master then. He is interesting because he may possibly be the same man as William 'Tytnt', Master of Burton Lazars between about 1358 and 1373, who was at one time Master of the leper house of St Giles-in-the-Fields. The interest arises from the possibility that Tytte had spent much of his career in these hospitals, and the Masterships were not simply sinecures, as seems often to have been the case by the fifteenth century.[16]

William Tytte was probably the last of the Masters to be appointed by the Bishop of Bethlem. The Hospital appears to have been thoroughly secularized after his departure. Edward III's successors, like Edward himself, treated the patronage of the Hospital as a way of rewarding their servants. What did change from time to time was the type of person kings chose to reward. Moreover, in the late fourteenth century and the fifteenth, they no longer granted the right of patronage to others: they granted the Mastership itself. Most of these Masters were royal clerks (men in minor religious orders, who played a significant part in the royal households and 'civil service' of the period). But three of the Hospital's fifteenth-century Wardens, as they were usually known at the time, also served as physicians or surgeons to the King (John Arundell and William Hobbys) or, in the case of Thomas Deinman, to the King's mother, Lady Margaret Beaufort. Conceivably, all three men were appointed because of their medical expertise. However, it must have been very much the luck of the draw whether the Mastership of a hospital would be vacant at a time when the King was seeking ways of rewarding his physicians. The notion of royal physicians like John Arundel routinely ministering to the poor inmates of Bethlem seems far-fetched. The one possible exception is Thomas Deinman, who was appointed in June 1494. He seems to have lived in the Hospital precinct from time to time. Certainly he kept some of his belongings there and had friends and connections in the area: he had a godson in St Botolph's parish, and left one of his executors household goods, including two beds and sets of bedclothes, which were at Bethlem at the time of his death in early 1501.[17] But if Deinman was indeed an exception to the general rule, being both expert in medical matters and at least occasionally resident in the Hospital, the appointment of his successor, Matthew Baker, Esquire for the King's Body, was a reversion to the long-standing practice of rewarding royal servants with sinecures.

In general, the opportunities for fifteenth-century Masters to minister to the sick at Bethlem were probably very limited. The fact that the alleged depredations of the Porter, Peter Taverner, went unchallenged for many years in the 1390s and early 1400s suggests that Master Lincoln did not supervise his employee at all closely. Nor is there much evidence that those more closely involved with the day-to-day running of the Hospital were medically competent. Certainly sixteenth-century Keepers, such as Edward Alleyn, who may actually have lived in the precinct for the duration of their Keeperships, do not appear to have had any sort of medical training or experience. Their role was very similar to that of the Stewards of Bridewell. Indeed, in 1607 a Keeper was referred to by the Clerk of the Bridewell Court of Governors as the 'steward' of Bethlem. The fact that a serving Steward of Bridewell thought the Keepership of Bethlem roughly equivalent to the Stewardship or Portership of Bridewell tells a similar tale.[18]

Not until Helkiah (or Hilkiah) Crooke petitioned to be admitted in Thomas Jenner's stead in 1618/19 is it clear, not only that a physician like Crooke regarded some level of medical competence as a prerequisite for a Keeper, but that the Governors – perhaps reluctantly, for they were under pressure – agreed. According to the record of Crooke's election, it was the fact that Jenner was 'altogether unskilfull' which rendered him 'unfitt for the same [office]'. It seems indeed to have been enough to prove that he was guilty of 'misgoverninge and misbehavinge himselfe in the government therof', since no other offence was alleged against him. According to his biographer, Crooke was in the habit of advancing his career by pointing with 'self-righteous indignation, although not always with a clean finger', at the wrongdoing of others; Jenner may have been a perfectly competent Keeper, judged by non-medical standards.[19]

Helkiah Crooke was certainly medically trained. Yet his admission was merely the harbinger of the new thinking. In the longer term, he too treated the Keepership as a sinecure, putting in his son-in-law as his deputy. Certainly the Bridewell Governors continued to think of the Keepership as a job similar to the Steward of Bridewell's. In 1629, before events overtook them, they were quite happy to contemplate giving the Keepership of Bethlem to the son of the Bridewell Steward, John Jeweller junior, when Crooke died or resigned. It was the father's merits, not the son's medical expertise, which influenced this decision.[20]

It was however during Crooke's tenure of the Mastership that a Bethlem Surgeon was first mentioned. Bridewell was employing a surgeon on a regular basis by 1627 at the latest (although, as it happens, the first notice of this office relates to the dismissal of the incumbent, who was to be paid 10s for his last quarter's wages and was then to be 'discharged of his attendance'). Then, on 1 March 1628, the question of the fee to be paid to 'Mr Quince the Surgeon for Bethlem' was decided. Quince had evidently already done some work in the Hospital, but it seems that this was the first time that he or any other surgeon was paid a regular sum for work at Bethlem. The frequency with which surgeons at both hospitals claimed additional payment for 'doing cures', together with the modest size of their fees, indicates that the latter were retainers rather than salaries.[21]

Despite this and other evidence of increasing concern on the part of the Governors to procure expert assistance when prisoners were physically ill, there is no surviving evidence to show that men like Quince cured, or even attempted to cure, the Bethlem inmates' mental ills: if they were expected, in return for their modest retainers, to bleed the inmates as necessary (which could, according to contemporary thinking, be expected to improve their mental health), the records do not say so. Certainly neither they nor physicians appear to have been involved in assessing whether actual or potential inmates were mad. It is very rarely the case that the records state how such an assessment was made. In August 1632, however, the Bridewell Minute Book noted that a vagrant who 'seemeth distracted but answereth sensibly[?] to any questions whereof he is demanded yet it is affirmed by some of the Governors who know him that he is distracted' was retained at Bridewell 'untill the matter may . . . be decided where he shalbe kept'. In June 1633, Mary Ash was 'sett by to be examined by Mr Treasurer'. In the same month the Treasurer took the view that a woman sent to Bethlem by the Court of Sessions was 'not distracted [but, rather,] an unruly woman'. Although it is clear that there was often doubt about an individual's true mental state, ascertaining what that was remained, as it had been in the century when Bethlem was founded, something to be decided by senior members of the community on the basis of their observation of an individual's behaviour, of his or her response to questioning, and of community knowledge.[22]

The admission of a permanent, or retained, Surgeon for Bethlem was a novelty in other respects, too. The payment of Quince's salary out of 'Bridewell' income was the first time that the Governors of Bridewell accepted that they should pay wages to anyone who worked at Bethlem. The Governors probably saw no reason why it should set a precedent as far as the other staff at Bethlem were concerned. The fact was that it presaged developments which, willy-nilly, were eventually to transform the arrangements for the administration and control of the Hospital.

The introduction of the Surgeon's office was one of several such heralds of a new way of treating and looking after the insane. What went before Crooke's Keepership was very different from what developed subsequently. Eminent and interesting though a number of the medieval and early modern Masters, Wardens or Keepers of Bethlem were in their own right, their importance to the Hospital probably lay not in any medical expertise they may have had but in the influence they might bring to bear on Bethlem's behalf, and in the care with which they appointed their deputies.

The Master's deputies

It is in the lower strata of the City and Hospital hierarchies that we need to look for evidence of the sort of people who normally tended to and treated the Bethlem inmates before the 1620s. In 1403 the Hospital was effectively run by the Porter, and this state of affairs may have lasted until at least 1547. Medieval porters were not necessarily people of low status, and Robert Lincoln was not, in principle, being negligent when he delegated the running of the Hospital to its Porter. It was the Janitor or Porter of one of the City's prisons who was clearly in charge of it in 1469 when the Mayor and Aldermen were investigating allegations that one of the Sheriffs had extorted money from a prisoner. This man, identified only as 'Kesten', is quite possibly Henry Kesten, who was described as a Sheriff's Clerk in 1460. The Bethlem Porter was almost certainly not as educated and important a man as this, but he was expected to keep and produce accounts, and apparently he ran a school for boys. If Taverner employed someone else to do all this on his behalf, we are not told so. Medieval porters were certainly gatekeepers, but they were not *merely* gatekeepers.[23]

The fact that the Porter's surname was 'Taverner' and that he was accused of selling ale to the inmates at high prices may well be significant. Innkeepers of this period did quite often provide lodging and food on a semi-permanent basis: the medieval equivalent of 'meals-on-wheels' and sheltered housing for the elderly. Edward Alleyn, the first City-appointed Keeper, was an innkeeper by trade.[24] Most of his successors are of unknown status, but at least one was a city officer: Richard Minnes, appointed at the Mayor's request in 1561, was the Mayor's Porter, suggesting that this type of office continued to be regarded as offering an appropriate route into the Keepership.[25]

It was the appointment in 1619 of Dr Crooke, a considerably more prestigious and influential person than his immediate predecessors, and a man who undoubtedly saw himself more as a Master than a Keeper, which led to the emergence of a third position, that of Steward. Bridewell had long had a Steward, but there is no evidence of any such post at Bethlem before Crooke's time. In 1632 the Commissioners who reported on Bethlem referred to 'some Stewards accompts' from which they had drawn information about aspects of Bethlem's income. As there is no reason to believe that the Bridewell Steward had anything to do with Bethlem's day-to-day accounts, evidently the Steward concerned was, and had for some little while been, employed at Bethlem. Not entirely surprisingly, Crooke had delegated the day-to-day running of the Hospital, despite taking an oath to serve in person, first to Thomas Willis, earlier described as the Keeper's 'man', and then to his son-in-law Thomas Bedford.[26]

What, then, is one to make of a reference in July 1618 to 'the keeper of Bethlem and his deputy', and another in October 1620 to the 'underkeeper' of Bethlem? 'Underkeeper' or 'deputy' could be another way of describing the Porter. It is however quite possible that both Crooke and his predecessor(s) appointed deputies with the knowledge of the Court of Aldermen and the Governors, and that the stipulation in his admission oath that Crooke serve in person, not by deputy, meant no more than that he could not leave the management of the Hospital entirely to an underling. If so, 'Steward' may merely be a rather grander title, adopted by Crooke's son-in-law, for a pre-existing office.[27]

In the early fifteenth century, physical care of all the inmates may well have been provided by the Porter and his wife (judging by the terms of the corrody granted to Robert Baron and his wife, corrodians were not required to do this type of work). By the 1570s, servants employed directly by the Keeper probably looked after the wealthier or more important inmates: those who lodged in chambers in the Master's House and who were by the early seventeenth century dignified with the name of 'boarders'.[28] Arrangements to care for the inmates remained *ad hoc,* however, until the early seventeenth century, with people other than the Porter's or Keeper's servants being employed for specific tasks. In June 1578, Mrs Thomson was paid the hand-some sum of 8s a week (at a time when the allowance for the poor was 6d a week) to look after two lunatics 'in Bedlem in romes ther provided for her she to finde them diett and medsens', after impressing the Bridewell Governors with her claims of previous successes in curing the insane. In 1632, Commissioners investigating Beth-lem's affairs reported that they had found a bill relating to a suit brought in the Exchequer in 1611 or 1612 against Agnes Garland, who was presumably a relative of Thomas Garland, tenant of the former Stone House site in the 1630s. She was described as 'sometimes employed for the harbouringe of madd and distracted persons, before such time as they were removed to the new Hospitall of Bethlem withoute Bishops-gate'.[29] Quite what this means is not clear. Perhaps Mrs Garland looked after certain lunatics, possibly those inmates who could not be accommodated in the old building, until the Brick House was eventually built; and conceivably she did this at Charing Cross.[30]

Not until 1619 is one of the (in)famous 'Basketmen' mentioned in the Bridewell records: in May of that year, Dr Crooke's nomination of James Hoore was accepted by the Governors. However, the fact that this occurred before Crooke was even 'put in possession' of Bethlem indicates that it was not an innovation. In fact, in January 1606 the Mayor and Aldermen had ordered that the Basketman – evidently there was only one – should thenceforth receive a third of anything given in alms by the 'markett folkes in Cheape side'. The post was, it seems, no novelty even in 1606. It is presumably the fact that Crooke was not yet safely installed which led to him taking the unusual step of asking the Governors to approve his choice. The Keeper was still, at this date, responsible for the selection and payment of Bethlem staff.[31]

Attitudes were, however, beginning to change. In 1623, the Bridewell Governors did at least accept a responsibility for ensuring that staff *were* paid. In July of that year, the Basketmen (there were two of them by then) petitioned the Court of Governors because their wages were in arrears, and the Governors ordered that sums of money which were due to be paid to Crooke should be withheld until the Basketmen received their due. Subsequently, on 11 October, the Bridewell Treasurer was ordered to settle the debt out of a surplus from the previous quarter's 'Bill' (allocation).[32]

One position which is not mentioned in relation to Bethlem before the second quarter of the seventeenth century is that of Matron. The first reference occurs in a Privy Council order of 1630, which required the Justices of the Peace for Westmin-ster to send three insane people to Bethlem by warrant addressed to 'the Master and Matron of Bedlame'. The terminology used by the Council when referring to the Master or Keeper of Bethlem was, unfortunately, variable and is not necessarily a good indicator of the actual posts in existence.[33] None the less, it is possible that the post of Matron was first recognized formally while Crooke was Master. Bridewell had long had a Matron, an important if not always an entirely reliable member of its staff. In Bethlem, by contrast, O'Donoghue thought that 'until a later date . . . the only attendants upon [the female patients] were male keepers'. Why he thought this is not clear. It is true that the only female servants noted in the sixteenth century were those employed by the Keeper, who may well not have worked in the main house. It is also clear that Basketmen were responsible for controlling both male and female inmates, and that it was not until a relatively late date that the potential evils of allowing male attendants to work unsupervised with madwomen were recognized. None the less, it does not follow that *only* men attended the female inmates in the medieval and early modern period. O'Donoghue himself thought that the Porter's wife acted as midwife to those women who gave birth in the Hospital (though this seems to be an assumption unsupported by evidence), and it was she who held the title of Matron from the time when the details of the incumbents are first known, later in the seventeenth century, until the 1750s. The formal bestowing of a title on a post which had previously existed, but only informally, may well have occurred during Dr Crooke's tenure, just as the former Underkeeper's job may at this time have been dignified with the title of Steward.[34]

CONCLUSION

Until shortly before 1400, Bethlem seems to have remained as a base for alms-collecting. As the link with the Order of Bethlehem was interrupted and then finally broken it probably directed its surplus donations to the non-resident poor, but this activity seems to have been replaced by the provision of care for the sick by 1400. The Hospital may just possibly have been caring for a few old and sick people within fifty years of its foundation, but it was over a hundred years more before it definitely began to take in, not merely the physically ill, but also the insane. Even then, the change may have been the accidental by-product of a property-deal struck by the Master at the turn of the century, or even of the re-building of the royal Mews in the 1370s.

Once the mad had been admitted, they seem fairly rapidly to have begun to displace other sick people: naturally enough, perhaps, as it would not be surprising if the physically ill had preferred not to share their accommodation with lunatics, many of whom seem to have been physically or verbally violent. But if Bethlem was generally thought to be a madhouse as early as the 1460s, it was nearly a hundred years later before there is evidence that London's magistrates thought that *only* the mad should be admitted.

It was a very long time indeed before the staffing of Bethlem reflected the alterations in its role. There was one significant change, none the less. Professed brothers and sisters had apparently been entirely replaced by laymen and laywomen by the end of the fourteenth century: in practice, it may well be the Master's Deputy, together with any servants he chose to employ, who staffed the Hospital from then on. Initially, the Master's Deputy was the Porter. By the early sixteenth century, and quite possibly for much of the fifteenth, Masters probably appointed deputies in addition to the Porters, as Sir Peter Mewtys did. These deputies may well have made their money out of paying inmates, leaving the Porter and his wife to look after the rest.

The status of the Masters appears, at first sight, to have shifted over the centuries. In fact, however, although the terms used to describe the Master and his deputy varied and were not strictly applied, it is clear enough that the men who had been appointed either directly or indirectly by the Crown were quite prominent individuals: despite having been appointed by the City, Helkiah Crooke was in practice the last of this type. Men appointed by the Masters, or by the City for most of the time that it administered the Hospital between 1547 and 1633, were of more modest status. In practice a good many seem to have gained experience in some form of 'house management' role, or were engaged in the victualling, brewing or innkeeping trades. Even after Crooke's appointment, the Governors seem to have clung to the idea that the Keeper was essentially a house-manager, and that medical expertise was not a requirement.

Not until the early seventeenth century do specific lower offices, such as Basket-men, appear (and even then, they were not necessarily employed immediately in looking after the inmates). Likewise, not until the very end of our period are there the first signs of a move towards the paying of salaries and fees out of Bridewell funds, rather than from the Master's pocket. As a result, it is only then that specialists, such as medical experts, start to be mentioned in the Bridewell and city records. This does not mean that no specialists were employed before: merely, if they were employed, it was the Hospital Master or Keeper who arranged for them to attend, and it was he, or the inmates' families and friends, who paid. The fact that specialists and fees begin to be noted in the Bridewell Court Minute Books does however mark a change more significant than simply one of recording practice. This was the point at which the City ceased simply to supervise the provision made by others, and accepted a direct responsibility for Bethlem and its inmates.

NOTES

1 *Calendar of Patent Rolls 1290–92*, 484.

2 PRO C270/22, m. 4 (Thomas Swanton's testimony).

3 PRO SP16/224 no. 21, m. 1; *Rotuli Parliamentorum*, iii, 128.

4 *The Survey of London: Contayning The Originall, Increase, Moderne Estate, and Government of that City . . . Begunne first by the Paines and Industry of Iohn Stow, in the yeere 1598 . . .* (London: Elizabeth Purslow, 1633), 493.

5 Edward G. O'Donoghue, *The Story of Bethlehem Hospital from its Foundation in 1247* (London: T. Fisher Unwin, 1914), 69; PRO C270/22, m.3.

6 PRO C270/22, m. 3. In 1437, a Commission to inspect the Hospital, granted at the request of the incoming Master, spoke of 'the demented lunatics and other poor and sick persons resorting thither': *Calendar of Patent Rolls 1436–41*, 87.

7 *Calendar of Patent Rolls 1377–81*, 266.

8 *Calendar of Patent Rolls 1436–41*, 87; James Gairdner (ed.), *The Historical Collections of a Citizen of London in the Fifteenth Century*, Camden Society, New Series, xvii (1876), p. ix; *CA Rep.* 12/1, fol. 260 (1550); *CA Rep.* 13/1, fol. 100v (1553).

9 Carole Rawcliffe, 'The Hospitals of Later Medieval England', *Medical History*, xxviii (1984), 1–21, especially 18–21; PRO C270/22, mm. 4, 3; Ghall MS 9171, Commissary Court of London, Register 2, fol. 17.

10 *CA Rep.* 14, fols 129–9v, 129v–130, 216v; *BCGM* volume 6, fol. 386v.

11 *CLRO* MS 63.5; *Memoranda, References, and Documents relating to the Royal Hospitals of the City of London . . .* (London: Arthur Taylor, 1836), 83–107; also BL 288.9.4L.

12 *CA Rep.* 14, fol. 524.

13 *BCGM* volume 4, fols 50v, 51–2; *ibid.* volume 5, fols 197v–8, 365v; *ibid.* volume 6, fols 183, 368–9. On Crooke's appointment, his predecessor, Keeper Jenner, was ordered to arrange

for his private patients to be removed, if those maintaining them had not agreed terms with Crooke: *BCGM* 6, fol. 123.

14 *Calendar of Patent Rolls 1290–92*, 473; *Calendar of Close Rolls 1288–96*, 316; *Calendar of Early Mayor's Court Rolls 1298–1307*, 88, 113–14; *Calendar of Letterbook E*, 351; O'Donoghue, *op. cit.* 34–5; *Calendar of Patent Rolls 1324–27*, 51; *Calendar of Patent Rolls 1327–30*, 31, 79, 52; *Calendar of Patent Rolls 1321–24*, 186; *Calendar of Patent Rolls 1327–30*, 98, 303, 388.

15 Vicary Gibbs (ed.), *The Complete Peerage of England, Scotland and Ireland, Great Britain, and the United Kingdom, by G. E. C.*, 13 volumes (London: St Catherine Press, 1910), iii, 53–8, 58–60; ii, 50; i, 339–40; H. J. Hewitt, *The Organization of War under Edward III, 1338–62* (New York: Manchester University Press/Barnes & Noble, 1966), 31, 143.

16 Robert Mannyel was Master in 1364, and since Tytte founded the Fraternity as 'Brother William Tytte, brother of the Hospital', it seems virtually certain that Tytte was indeed merely a brother in 1361, becoming Master at a later date. When Tytte succeeded to the Mastership is however uncertain. Tytte's Receiver (accountant) was pardoned for failing to produce his account in 1380, and Tytte was said in 1403 to have been Master about twenty-four years previously. However, this is merely evidence that he became Master sometime before 1380. The Master ('Warden') in December 1367 was called William. It is possible therefore that Tytte succeeded Mannyel in the later 1360s: *Ghall* MS 142, 164; *Calendar of Patent Rolls 1361–64*, 477; *Calendar of Patent Rolls 1377–81*, 431 and PRO C270/22, m. 4; *Calendar of Patent Rolls 1367–70*, 68; Margery B. Honeybourne, *The Leper Hospitals of the London Area: with an Appendix on Some Other Medieval Hospitals of Middlesex*, Transactions of the London and Middlesex Archaeological Society, xxi, part i (1963), 27.

17 For the question of who appointed the fourteenth-century Masters, see Chapter 5. For later Masters: *DNB*, *sub* 'Arundell John'; *Calendar of Patent Rolls 1452–61*, 338; *Calendar of Patent Rolls 1476–85*, 166; *Calendar of Patent Rolls 1452–61*, 471; Canterbury Chapter Library, Cathedral Priory Register F, fols 25–5*v* (I am most grateful to Dr Rawcliffe, who is writing a biography of Deinman for the forthcoming edition of the *New DNB*, for a copy of this testament). Deinman also left 12d a head to the poor inmates. For the suggestion that Arundell, Hobbes and Deinman may have been among the physicians who treated Bethlem inmates, see Martha Carlin, 'Medieval English Hospitals', in L. Granshaw and R. Porter (eds), *The Hospital in History* (London: Routledge, 1989), 21–39, especially 30, something doubted by Rawcliffe, *op. cit.* 8–9, and Basil Clarke, *Mental Disorder in Earlier Britain: Exploratory Studies* (Cardiff: University of Wales Press, 1975), 80–1.

18 PRO C270/22, m. 1; *BCGM*, volume 5, fols 196*v*, 220.

19 C. D. O'Malley, 'Helkiah Crooke, M.D., F.R.C.P., 1576–1648', *Bulletin of the History of Medicine*, xlii (1968), 1–18, especially 3; *BCGM* volume 6, fol. 110.

20 *BCGM* volume 7, fol. 144*v*.

21 *BCGM* volume 7, fols 26, 61, 159, 131, 239, 287. Quince was succeeded by Edward Say, who in February 1633 received sums additional to his 40s salary because he 'attendeth the poore at Bethlem and hath done severall cures ther which deserve more allowance than his ordinary wages'; Wright's successor received 33s 4d for similar causes in the same month: *ibid.* fols 314, 315.

22 *BCGM* volume 7, fols 292, 333, 333*v*.

23 *CLRO* Journal of the Common Council 6, fol. 342.

24 *CLRO* Journal of the Common Council 7, fol. 187*v*; *ibid.* 6, fol. 342; on the overlap between barber-surgeons and ale-brewers/innkeepers: Margaret Pelling, 'Occupational Diversity: Barber-surgeons and the Trades of Norwich, 1550–1640', *Bulletin of the History of Medicine*, lvi (1982), 484–511, especially 505; on innkeepers as lodgers of the old and mentally ill, see, for example, Annie Saunier, '"Hors de sens et de mémoire": une approche de la folie au travers de quelques acts judiciaires de la fin du XIIe à la fin du XIVe siècle' in Philippe Contamine, Thierry Dutour and Bertrand Schneib (eds), *Commerce, Finances et Société (XIe-XVIe Siècles): Recueil de travaux d'Histoire médiévale offert à M. le Professeur Henri Dubois* (Centre de recherche 'Les Pouvoirs XIIIe-XVe siècles', Université de Paris-Sorbonne, 1993), 489–99, especially 490. We are grateful to Sandra Cavallo for drawing the role of victuallers and innkeepers to our attention.

25 *CA Rep.* 14, fol. 524 (Minnes); *ibid.* 17, fol. 162*v* (Mell and his predecessor); *ibid.* 24, fol. 311.

26 *BCGM* volume 7, fol. 137*v* (31 July 1629); *ibid.* volume 6, fol. 397 (2 April 1625); PRO SP16/ 224 no. 21, m. 5; *ibid.* volume 7, fols 311, 329. Possibly, too, Steward Isaac Lovell preceded or succeeded Willis, as he was described in 1634 as having not received certain sums during his time as Steward on Crooke's orders. However, he could equally have served (like acting Steward Morton, who was 'executing that place [office]' in 1635) during the 'interregnum' between Crooke's initial dismissal in 1632/3 and the moment, in 1635/6, when the City finally appointed the Steward itself: *BCGM* volume 7, fol. 281*v* (Bridewell Treasurer/ Governors ordered to report on a dispute between Lovell and a Mr Townesende, 1 June 1632); *ibid.* volume 8, fols 20, 22, 65.

27 *CA Rep.* 33, fol. 353*v*; *BCGM* volume 6, fol. 205.

28 *Calendar of Patent Rolls 1388–92*, 484; for Joane Phillippe 'servante to John Mell keper of Bedlem' (probably the same person as 'Joane ffitche servante in Bedlem house') and her fellow-servant Edward Dey, see: *BCGM* volume 3, fol. 308, 331*v*; *ibid.* volume 6, fol. 123.

29 *BCGM* volume 3, fol. 313; PRO SP16/224 no. 21, fol. 3. The deaths of two Garlands, Peter and Elizabeth, are recorded in the Churchwardens' accounts for St Martin's-in-the-Fields, the parish church of Charing Cross, in 1569: John V. Kitto (ed.), *St Martin's-in-the-Fields: The Accounts of the Churchwardens 1525–1603* (London: Simpkin Marshall Kent Hamilton, 1901), 244. For investigations ordered in late 1609 and early 1610 into the lands 'suspected to be concealed and deteyned from Bethlem', see: *BCGM* volume 5, fols 398, 417*v*.

30 Certainly the Governors were noticeably concerned about overcrowding at Bethlem during the 1620s and early 1630s. In 1624 they insisted that numbers should not rise above twenty-five, and that all admissions should be first approved by them. There were further attempts to get rid of unsuitable inmates in October 1628 and June 1631: *BCGM* volume 6, fol. 368; *ibid.* volume 7, fols 91, 231*v*.

31 *BCGM* volume 6, fol. 120*v*; *CA Rep.* 25, fol. 339.

32 *BCGM* volume 6, fols 341, 347*v*.

33 *Acts of the Privy Council 1630–1*, 108.

34 O'Donoghue, *op. cit.* 143–4.

CHAPTER EIGHT

MEDIEVAL ATTITUDES TOWARDS AND TREATMENT OF THE INSANE

—— •◆• ——

INTRODUCTION

Historians commenting on responses to the insane in medieval Europe have tended to divide into two broad camps: those who emphasize whatever is strange and repellent to modern observers in medieval attitudes; and those who view the Middle Ages as a period in which official attitudes were relatively relaxed and humane, and the treatments offered were designed to bring body and mind back into harmony.[1]

The relatively sympathetic views towards alternative medicine which now exist make it easier than it once was to envisage the possibility that some of the 'eclectic methods of psychological healing' employed in the Middle Ages worked. The medieval and early modern belief that the mad required spiritual healing before physical treatment can be interpreted as a contemporary manifestation, couched in contemporary terms, of the view, entirely defensible in modern terms, that madness has both psychological and physical dimensions, and that one must ease the suffering of the mind as well as attempting to alter the chemistry of the body.

One can however go too far in rejecting criticism of the medieval approach. If the Middle Ages operated a form of 'care in the community', it was (it will be argued here) very much a *laissez-faire*, reactive system, and sometimes the treatment madmen and madwomen received was violent and cruel, although the aim was, usually, a therapeutic one. But to say this is merely to say that human nature changes little over the centuries, even if the ways in which it expresses itself alter. Madness is capable of arousing powerful emotions in the beholder, from empathy and sympathy to revulsion and denial. How the sane regarded the insane no doubt varied as much in the Middle Ages as it does today.

Medical tracts, the range of treatments on offer and the choices made should tell us a good deal about real beliefs about insanity. Whatever was done to the mad and the idiotic was done for a reason. Even treatments which seem to us incomprehensible had their own logic. Those who used charms, for example, may have believed that they had the power to get God to act. And those who probably did not believe this, like Roger Clerk who was found guilty in 1382 of giving a man a piece of an old book wrapped in cloth of gold to hang round the neck of his sick wife, may have realized that it was the patient's belief in the efficacy of the treatment, not theirs, that mattered.[2] But the fact is that a great many insane people do not appear to have received any medical treatment at all. Therefore, in order to get some insight into contemporary attitudes in all their complexity one needs to look both inside and outside the medical treatise and the sickroom. Studying the interplay between laws, social, religious and moral rhetoric and what was actually done for and to the mad can throw some light on what contemporaries thought and felt about madness.

THE LAW AND THE INSANE

Legal theory

For almost as long as there has been something which could reasonably be described as English law, that law has had something to say about the treatment of the criminally insane.[3] The tenth-century laws of King Aethelred stated that, if someone committed an offence without willing or intending to do so, 'the case is different from that of one who offends of his own free will'. The criminally insane 'should always be entitled to clemency'. In Henry III's reign a vast compilation of legal theory and practice, known as 'Bracton', was produced. Almost everything with which the law could concern itself is mentioned in *Bracton*. The nature of law and authority is discussed, as is the nature of man; even the hermaphrodite finds a place. But even so *Bracton* does not often address the question of insanity. One of the few sections in which it is explicitly addressed is that dealing with suicide. There the author states that the madman or the idiot cannot commit a crime by killing himself, nor does he forfeit his inheritance or possessions as a penalty of a crime. The reason is that the mentally incompetent person is no more capable of committing an intentional wrong or crime than an animal, from whom he is not far removed in terms of reasoning capacity. To this is added the comment, 'That a madman is not liable is true, unless he acts under pretense of madness while enjoying lucid intervals'.[4]

By the time that Bethlem was founded, then, it was well-established legal theory that intent was necessary for the committing of a crime or personal wrong, and that the mentally incompetent, lacking reason and therefore will and intent, could not be found guilty of such acts. The only question at issue was whether or not the accused did the deed, and, if he/she did, whether he/she was mentally incompetent at the time. But it was one thing to enjoin courts to make due allowance for the mental state of wrongdoers; quite another, to set wrongdoers free to do wrong again. On this issue, the 'Laws of Henry I' say merely that '[i]nsane persons and children of like sort should be guarded and treated leniently by their parents'.

What of that much larger group of people, the quietly and uncontroversially mad and the 'natural fool'?

Although early English law had little to say on the subject of the vulnerability of the insane, the danger that the inheritances and possessions of idiots and madmen would be exploited by those who were supposed to be looking after them was certainly recognized. Indeed, the risk to the mentally impaired was even greater than that posed to another especially vulnerable group, fatherless children, because fatherless children, if they do not die, eventually reach adulthood and can then fight back. Idiots, however, never emerge from mental and legal childhood; the same is true of some lunatics.[5]

Discussions of medieval legal protection for the idiot and the lunatic usually take as their starting-point two clauses in a summary of royal prerogative (privileged) rights known as 'Prerogativa Regis'. The first of these clauses, Clause 11, placed the lifelong guardianship of all congenitally idiotic heirs to 'feudal lands' (held by military service) in the King's hands, even when the lands were held from some intermediate lord. This principle was definitely established by Edward I's reign, and it may have originated in the previous reign. In return for ensuring that the inheritance was not wasted, the King enjoyed the income of the inheritance for the idiot's lifetime, being required merely to ensure that the idiot himself was supplied with 'the necessities'. The second clause (Clause 12) stated what was to be done in the event that a feudal tenant 'happen to fail of his wit'. In this case, the King had not only to protect the inheritance, but also to ensure that the profits were used to support both the lunatic and his family 'competently'. Any surplus profits were retained for the tenant's use, should he recover.[6]

Not all idiots and perpetual lunatics who were heirs or heiresses held lands subject to 'feudal law'. Citizens of boroughs (towns granted certain rights and privileges, including jurisdiction over civil cases) could normally expect the town's magistracy to accept responsibility for protecting and determining what should happen to other vulnerable groups, like fatherless children and widows. Mary Bateson's *Borough Customs* is a comprehensive survey of medieval and early modern customary law practices, as recorded in town collections (custumals). There are two examples in *Borough Customs* which specifically relate to lunatics. The first, from Bristol, dated to 1344, states that 'concerning a lunatic, the mayor shall have his goods and chattels handed over to his next friends to keep until the man recovers his senses' and that the custodians are to ensure that he is neither harmed nor does harm to others. The second, from Hereford, dated to 1486, discusses what is to happen if someone who is not of sound mind, or idiotic, inherits some property. Such individuals are to be treated like children who risk being defrauded, 'unless they have father or mother living who claims to look after and guard them'.[7]

Legal practice

In theory, then, the law by 1247 was compassionate in its treatment of mad people. The royal right of lifelong guardianship of the born idiot was intended to protect the next heir rather than the idiot, but at least it resulted in a number of idiots' affairs being supervised and regulated. In boroughs, it looks as though the aim was to protect the idiot or lunatic against exploitation by family and the authorities alike. But did theory and practice coincide?

It is wise to be cautious about taking legal theory, as recorded in lawbooks and custumals, for practice. Certainly medieval writs and inquisitions concerning idiocy did not confine themselves to enquiring whether the person was an idiot and had been so from birth. Many inquest returns were (according to the theory behind 'Prerogativa Regis') muddling up idiots and lunatics, with individuals being described as 'idiots from birth', but also being said to be 'worse at lunations and [to rave] with madness'. However, to take 'Prerogativa Regis' as a starting-point and to judge the practice of medieval officials and jurors on the basis of compliance with its wording and distinctions is probably to give too much weight to a document which may merely have been an assertion of the 'king's view of his own rights (at every doubtful point it leans towards royal claims)', or possibly even 'a purely private work'. If 'Prerogativa Regis' was no more than one interpretation of the King's rights and obligations among several, the fact that medieval officials and inquest juries did not distinguish between congenital idiots and lunatics as they were supposed to do, according to 'Prerogativa Regis', is hardly surprising.[8]

What seems to have been of concern to the Crown during the Middle Ages was not whether an individual was a 'natural fool' or a 'lunatic', but whether the mental disability was likely to be permanent. Those royal tenants whose mental condition came to the notice of the King's officers and who were judged to be permanently impaired were treated like any other royal ward, with their possessions being 'farmed' to the highest bidder. In fact, however, royal officials sometimes failed to identify even prominent idiots. The congenital idiocy of Joan Fauconberg seems to have gone unremarked until 1463, when her husband died and she was aged nearly sixty. Conceivably the influence of her first husband's family – she had married William Nevill, son of the Earl of Westmorland by his second wife – kept the writs and escheators at bay. If so, the behaviour of royal officials in relation to the King's rights to the guardianship of idiots was quite different from their behaviour in relation to the King's rights to the wardship of heirs under age: they pursued the latter vigorously, more or less regardless of who the family was.[9]

As far as criminal lunatics were concerned, juries do seem to have brought in verdicts which recognized that idiots and lunatics were not competent as other men and women were: as in the case of the hapless idiot who in 1212 had been imprisoned 'because in his witlessness he confessed he is a thief, though in fact he is not to blame'. Although the judges were not able to acquit these people themselves, at least until the sixteenth century, they usually referred the matter to the King for a pardon. And while there is a good deal of evidence that the violently or criminally insane were confined in royal or other official prisons, 'official prisons' were few and far between, certainly until towards the end of the Middle Ages, and they were not, generally speaking, intended to hold prisoners for long periods. When madmen and madwomen committed offences which were less serious, or made a public nuisance of themselves, they were probably simply subdued and confined at home or elsewhere without any formal procedure.[10]

The fact that family members were sometimes given custody of criminal lunatics sounds less harsh to modern ears than control by the authorities, and sometimes no doubt it was. However, because those who had charge of the violent mad were responsible for their behaviour, and because of the practical difficulty of controlling such people at home, families could feel driven to treat their relatives with what seems to us to be considerable cruelty. In 1348, a man appeared in court on a charge of assault and false imprisonment, and defended himself on the grounds that he and other family members had merely acted to calm and control his relative who 'was in a mad fit and was doing great harm'. Before locking him up, the plaintiff's relatives 'chastised him and beat him with a rod'.[11] It should be said, however, that apparently cruel treatment meted out by families was probably not designed simply to subdue the mad. The perpetrators of the assault committed in 1348 may well have thought that a beating would improve the madman's mental state.

SOCIAL RESPONSES TO THE INSANE

Social attitudes

It is difficult for us to do justice to the attitudes of medieval authorities and prominent individuals towards the mad and mentally incompetent. On the one hand, one encounters many examples of what appear to be genuinely compassionate responses. Those fifteenth-century London Aldermen and Common Councilmen who left bequests to the 'poor sick people' of Bethlem not infrequently went to some lengths to try to ensure that their legacies – which, though similar in amount to those left to other hospitals, were disproportionate when one takes account of the very small size of Bethlem – were employed 'to their moost comfort and Relief'. Alderman Sir John Crosby was not especially lavish with his money, but he took pains to urge his executors to make sure that 'the distract peple being thanne within thospitall of Bedleem' should receive the bequest in whatever form was best, 'outher in redy money or in vitailles good and holsom for thaim or in other wise, necessary for thaime'. Similarly, the tallow-chandler William Blackman, who left 20s for the poor people in Bethlem, required his executors to give it in the form of 'brede and other things wherof they have moost nede'. This carefulness contrasts strongly with the way that the same men spoke about their bequests to poor patients in other London hospitals and to the inmates of the various prisons in and around the city. Apparently in these cases the testators felt that it was enough to leave it to the Priors, Masters and Wardens concerned to dole out the bequest in cash or kind, as they saw fit.[12]

On the other hand, looking at the reactions of the City's Mayor and Aldermen in the sixteenth century, when they were considering requests for the admission of mad people to Bethlem, the word which springs most readily to mind is 'resistant'. Individuals or their families and neighbours were clearly expected, if they could not look after the mentally afflicted themselves, to pay whatever they could towards the cost of their keep and care elsewhere. The Mercer John Donne, who left substantial bequests in the 1470s both to provide free medical treatment to the sick poor and to the main London hospitals, was concerned to exclude 'hearty beggars' from enjoyment of his legacy. This reflected a widespread opinion that those who could work to earn their keep should work, and those who could pay for their keep, should pay. The pauper inmates were probably expected to consign what few possessions they had to Bethlem, a practice which was common in medieval hospitals: certainly if they died there the Hospital kept whatever they had. The attempts of Master Robert Lincoln and his successors to obtain or recover the administration of the testaments of everybody, from wealthy patients to hospital chaplains and tenants, may also have been prompted by a belief that the Hospital was entitled to their goods.[13]

Moreover, although a 1446 indulgence spoke of the 'multitude of miserable persons of both sexes' living in Bethlem, the numbers of entirely indigent patients that medieval hospitals, including Bethlem, were prepared or allowed to support seem in fact to have been severely limited. It may well not be an accident that there were six insane men in Bethlem in 1403 and six pauper mad inmates there in 1598. Conceivably, it was a condition of the transfer of the Stone House at Charing Cross to Bethlem that the Hospital should continue to provide care for six poor madmen in perpetuity. It would be entirely in keeping with what one can observe of their careful control over the more well-to-do who were permitted to enter the Hospital, and over the financial terms on which they were admitted, that the sixteenth-century city fathers should have taken the view that this was both the minimum and the maximum number of pauper mad that the City should normally support. It is also possible that there was a degree of screening of patients for 'worthiness' as well as financial support. The Aldermen normally interviewed the relatives of those potential inmates who were likely to depend at least in part on City support. Perhaps they just wanted to ask about financial provision and to assess the individual's state of mind. But they may also have used the interviews to check, as tended to be the case with candidates for places in late fifteenth-century almshouses, that those admitted were 'of good governaunce and . . . fallen in poverty' – the genteel poor, in other words. This, apparently rather grudging, attitude was not a peculiarly English phenomenon: it was, for example, found equally in Italy. Nor, as it is sometimes thought, did it only emerge in the sixteenth century, when more 'Puritan' attitudes towards the moral worth of work began to be voiced. Even in the early Middle Ages, philanthropy was 'far from indiscriminate'; of Turin it has been said that 'medieval charity too was selective'.[14]

If, however, the Aldermen and the Bridewell Governors could at times be exceedingly sceptical about claims that an individual was mad and needed to be cared for at Bethlem, it does not follow that they were without compassion for men and women whom they regarded as clearly insane. In 1609, not only did the Governors order the Bridewell Clerk to provide a lunatic ex-soldier who wanted to return home to Gloucester with a pass and the usual 12d to help him on his way, but they had a whip-round among themselves and gave him an extra 2s.[15]

Social practice

The first instinct of the sane in the Middle Ages and early modern period was not to incarcerate the insane. Even the anti-social mad tended to be left alone unless they became unbearably annoying or frightening people. The ex-Bethlem man whom Sir Thomas More had 'stryped . . . tyl he waxed wery and somwhat lenger' had been having a high old time of it for some while, hanging around churches, disrupting the services and throwing the skirts of kneeling women over their heads. Similarly, William Bradye, a merchant who was sent to Bethlem on the Court of Aldermen's orders in 1551 – uncharacteristically, without any attempt on the Court's part to ensure that someone paid for his keep – had been causing considerable alarm by his 'rayling' and other 'frantyk' behaviour.[16]

As with cases of apparently brutal treatment administered by families, civic authorities were at most only partly motivated by a desire to control or punish when they ordered that madmen should be confined, chained or beaten. Sir Thomas More clearly identified in the ex-Bethlem man a malevolence or naughtiness – perhaps because the man was a heretic, although it is a response which others who have had to deal with the apparent wilfulness of a manic person will recognize. But he certainly also believed that the whipping he had administered to the man had a therapeutic value.

More's story is also of interest because, although Sir Thomas described the man as a heretic, he did not apparently contemplate returning him to Bethlem, and there is no reason to suppose that the civic authorities had sent him there in the first place. It is very doubtful whether, at this period, the Hospital was considered a suitable place in which to lock up anti-social or morally contaminating individuals who were not in fact insane.

On the other hand, More's tale does illustrate the readiness of the authorities to resort to force. Margery Kempe, the fifteenth-century Norwich mystic, who herself lost her reason temporarily after the birth of her first child, reported a number of reactions to supposed or actual madness which seem far from tolerant: the way that bystanders, assuming from her contortions that she was epileptic, 'spat at her in horror at the illness', or the treatment of a woman who also lost her wits after giving birth, and who 'was taken to a room at the furthest end of the town . . . And there she was bound hand and foot with chains of iron'.[17]

The impression given by the inquest returns that royal officials did not go out of their way to detect idiots and permanent lunatics is mirrored in the borough records. Neither customary law nor those jurisdictions which applied it paid much attention to idiots or lunatics. The London letterbooks from the early fourteenth century onwards are full of records of the arrangements made for the fatherless heirs of London citizens; there seems to be only one note of a similar arrangement being made for an idiot or a lunatic. When in 1478 Alderman John Tate senior was incapacitated through illness and 'imbecility', the Court of Aldermen arranged for Robert Tate to assume responsibility for his ward; nothing was said about making provision for the custody of his person or possessions. The one reference to an idiot (or, at least, to someone who 'was in maner an idote and had nor knew no worldly reason') in the City's plea and memoranda rolls is entirely incidental, and the woman appears to have married and lived out her days without any external intervention. In Norwich, the picture is similar. Both Mrs Kempe, during her bout of insanity, and her husband, who became senile after a blow to the head, were looked after at home without civic intervention. Attitudes did not apparently change much over the next hundred years. All three individuals (out of 2,359) who were described in a 1570 Census of the Poor in Norwich as being 'beside themselves' or 'somewhat lunatic' were 'apparently living independently'.[18]

That the authorities expected families to look after their relatives at home if at all possible does not, however, entirely explain why Bethlem's population remained low for so long. When Christ's Hospital was established as an orphanage in 1556, its Ordinances made it clear that only the destitute children of citizen fathers were to be admitted. The Governors paid to have the gates guarded against poor non-citizens who might try to bring children into the City to abandon them there in the hope of taking advantage of the new provision. It punished women caught abandoning their children severely. Yet the fact remains that it was, from July 1557 onwards, taking in babies found abandoned on stalls and doorsteps and in the streets. No doubt what made the difference was mainly the fact that lone madmen and madwomen are only relatively vulnerable, whereas abandoned babies and small children are wholly so. But it may also be that the authorities' attitude towards the care of the insane was widespread in the population at large, and that on the whole families, friends and neighbours made their own arrangements.[19]

THE MORAL DIMENSION OF INSANITY

Religious and moral attitudes

Contemporary reactions to the mentally ill included the belief that 'madness [was] a punishment inflicted by God for wrongdoing'. Sufferers, too, seem often to have accepted that they were being punished for their sins. Most famously, Margery Kempe in the fifteenth century thought she went mad after childbirth because she was unable to bring herself to confess all her sins; she regarded her particular vices as pride, envy, greed and lustfulness. Madness was a peculiarly appropriate punishment for the proud, reducing God's finest creation, thinking Man, to the level of a dumb brute.[20]

A sinful life was certainly blamed by some for the madness of the French King, Charles VI. However, this would seem, to modern eyes, a harsh or even unjustifiable explanation for the descent into insanity of King Charles's grandson, Henry VI, in 1454. Henry VI's posthumous reputation for piety bordering on saintliness seems to have replaced a reputation for simpleness in his own day, at least among his ill-wishers. But there is plenty of evidence of his religiosity. Contemporaries might possibly have judged Henry guilty of the sin of sloth: that would be one way of interpreting his reported distress when required to attend to affairs of state and preference for contemplation and prayer. In general, however, he seems to have been more free from sin than most. Henry's mental collapse may none the less have been attributed to sin, though not his own: 'for I the Lord thy God am a jealous God, and visit the sins of the fathers upon the children unto the third and fourth generation.' Not only was Henry the grandson on his mother's side of a man who had himself been mad, but his paternal grandfather, Henry IV, was a usurper; one who, according to his enemies, had been inflicted with leprosy for having the rebellious Archbishop Scrope executed. In addition, as King, Henry VI could be thought to be suffering for sins which were neither his own nor his progenitors'. According to a frequently used metaphor of the period, the King was the head of the body, the Realm of England, with the various 'estates', the knights, the merchants, the peasants, being identified with specific limbs. It was conceivable that a King's person might be visited with the consequences of divine wrath against that impersonal entity, the Realm; madness would be a fitting affliction for the 'head' of England to suffer. So Henry's illness could be interpreted as a sign of God's anger against England, not against the King himself.[21]

Some madmen and madwomen were believed to be diabolically possessed. This might or might not have resulted from weakness or sinfulness on the part of the sufferer. Sir Thomas More had no doubt that Sir Roger Wentworth's 12-year-old daughter had been 'tormented by our ghostly enemy the Devil, raving with despising and blasphemy of God'. The case-notes of the seventeenth-century clergyman and healer of insane, Richard Napier, lend some support to the argument that certain types of mad people, perhaps typically the sort of person who would now be categorized as manic-depressive, were especially likely to be regarded as possessed. These included both the very pious and the very dutiful family member. Perhaps mania allowed them to express unacceptable feelings, and their hate-filled attacks on the Church or their family and friends seemed to the observer to be inspired by a real and wilful malevolence. In a society which set a high value both on outward religious conformity and on familial obedience, this was presumably even more shocking than such behaviour would seem nowadays.[22]

Spiritual healing

With those thought to be possessed, treatment was spiritual in intent even if it took a physical form. Belief in the power of holy water to cleanse the soul meant that lunatics were not infrequently bathed or suddenly ducked in a source thought to be holy. In the case of unexpected immersions in water, the procedure may well have been influenced by the observation that shock seemed to render some lunatics more sensible, at least temporarily. Other uses of holy water included the practice of binding madmen and madwomen, sprinkling them with water from a holy source, and then leaving them to sleep.

Certain churches and saints' shrines attracted those suffering from mental ills and their friends and families. St Thomas à Becket's tomb at Canterbury was a considerable focus of pilgrimage, and saints like St Godric, also associated with Canterbury, and St William of Norwich were credited with curing the mad as well as the physically sick. At the Priory of Bromholm, Norfolk, was a portion of the True Cross which, according to the chronicler Roger of Wendover, freed the mad from the demons which possessed them. Thomas More had no doubt that Sir Roger Wentworth's daughter owed her recovery to the fact that she was taken to the shrine of the Blessed Virgin Mary at Ipswich. The tomb of Henry VI at Windsor attracted quite large numbers of mentally disturbed pilgrims; in this case, the fact that the King himself had been insane for a while presumably led to his being regarded as a particular protector of the mad. Miracle-books record how lunatics were dragged to the altars and shrines in chains, crying and shrieking, and were left to struggle against their bonds until, eventually, they became calm. Modern commentators tend to view this treatment as brutal, although the high theatricality of the events described suggests that there was a degree of 'playing to the audience' or exaggerated reporting involved. Moreover, it was not necessary for the sufferer to be dragged to the shrine. The simple act of going on pilgrimage to a holy place, either in person or by proxy, was thought capable of bringing relief to someone who was possessed.[23]

Spiritual healing played a very large part in the treatment offered to 'in-patients' in medieval institutions. At a number of early medieval hospitals, such as Canterbury Cathedral's infirmary, St Mary's, Chichester, and St Giles's, Norwich, the infirmary hall was joined to the nave of the chapel, with the chancel directly opposite. Although the sick did not always have as clear a view into the chapel as this, and although, by the fifteenth century, it seems to have become increasingly the practice to partition off the side aisles into cubicles or cells, or even 'bed-sittingrooms', liturgy remained a fundamental part of the life of the inmates in most if not all medieval hospitals and almshouses. Indeed, if benefactors' wishes were honoured in full, by the late Middle Ages the inmates of such institutions would have been spending much of their day in prayer. Those mentally ill men and women who were treated in the generalist medieval hospitals may well not have been able to enjoy as full a range of spiritual ministrations as sane patients. However, they would have benefited from the richly spiritual environment which seems to have characterized so many hospitals founded in the Middle Ages.[24]

THE RATIONALE BEHIND TREATMENTS OFFERED TO THE INSANE

Reconciling spiritual and physical treatments

The fourth Lateran Council of 1215 had commanded physicians 'before all else . . . to call for the physician of souls, so that after spiritual health has been restored to [the patients], the application of medicine may be of greater benefit'.[25] How could contemporaries have reconciled this injunction with the fact that the mad were 'soul-sick' by definition, and were often incapable of benefiting from confession, the Mass and other ministrations? If the physician had to wait until the patient was restored to spiritual health before attempting to treat the insane, was he not in effect being commanded not to treat the mad at all?

To modern eyes, it seems inevitable that medieval and early modern beliefs about the spiritual causes of mental illness would have impeded attempts to administer medical treatments. Even in the later sixteenth century, the Mayor and Aldermen could talk of consigning a woman to Bethlem 'until such time as God shall restore her to perfect memory', which gives little ground for anticipating any active human intervention. The belief that God used terrible afflictions, epidemic diseases and that most dreadful of all visitations for rational man, the loss of one's reasoning powers, as a punishment for vice, a test of faith, or a method of purging sin – Purgatory on earth – might well be expected to have discouraged attempts at physical therapy. Mrs Kempe evidently felt, at least with hindsight, that insanity was a spiritual trial which she had to undergo, a chastening experience which, by implication, it would have been wrong and presumably useless to attempt to curtail. It was not human agency or intercession, but the appearance of the Lord 'to this creature who had forsaken him' which lifted her affliction, so that 'presently the creature grew calm in her wits'.[26]

A second and very different strand in Christian belief might have impeded attempts at physical therapy. The concept of the holy maniac was an old one, but it had been given special force by the episode recounted by St Mark, when Jesus's behaviour seemed so strange to his family that they concluded that he was mad. In his translation, Erasmus reinforced this by interpreting a passage relating to the family's decision to restrain him as an attempt to bind him with chains, appropriate treatment for a raving lunatic. Consequently, '[a]ny Christian doctor treating what he took to be madness had to take great care to ensure that he was not resisting the Spirit: that he was not, that is, treating as organically or diabolically mad an enraptured lover of the Living God'. The difficulty of distinguishing between the two, particularly at a time when there was considerable social nervousness about heretical sects, was something which clearly perplexed those who encountered Mrs Kempe in her shouting or lecturing fits.[27]

The notion that madness was Godsent and purposeful and required spiritual remedies was clearly capable of resulting in a refusal to allow the illness to be treated medically. The mere difference between priests and physicians over the root cause of madness could have been enough to create an unbridgeable gulf. There is some evidence which suggests early attempts by physicians to distinguish clearly between 'proper' and magical – though not spiritual – treatments. In 1300, the Rector of St Margaret Lothbury, London, had imported a cask containing four dead wolves (Latin, *lupus*, French, *loup*) which he claimed were to be used in order to treat a skin disease or cancer called 'Le Lou'. He was handed over to the Archdeacon of London after he had admitted that neither he nor anyone he knew had the disease and that he was not a physician or a surgeon. A panel of the City's medical men had testified in the Mayor's Court that they could find no reference in their books to any illness against which wolves' flesh could be used. Possibly the priest was suspected of witchcraft rather than plain quackery or employing sympathetic medicine, but it seems likely that the medical men were using the case – had perhaps initiated it – in order to prevent the defendant treating the sick.[28]

In practice, however, no such gulf developed between medieval divines and medieval physicians. This was no doubt largely because the seventeenth-century clergyman, Napier, was merely following a well-established tradition by treating the mad. The fifteenth-century 'masters of Physik' who treated Henry VI were clerics. At the lower end of the social scale, it is very likely that the Rector of St Margaret Lothbury was a part-time 'doctor'. At all levels of society, therefore, clergymen seem to have been involved in the physical treatment of the sick (though, because the more senior clergy and those with the cure of souls – subdeacons, deacons and priests – were forbidden to burn or cut patients, they could not be surgeons).[29]

This fact alone would be enough to explain why churchmen justified treating the spiritual corruption evidenced by madness with physical medicines as well as psychological ones, and why there does not seem to have been a great deal of conflict between the spiritual and the physical ministers to the mad. The argument that God would not have equipped men with minds capable of developing medicines which could be used to treat the mad, or have created the ingredients of those medicines, had he not intended them to be used, was a compelling one to those who believed that God acted rationally. In addition, if in particular instances it was not God's will that a madman should recover as a result of physical treatment, He would find ways of making the medicines inefficacious. And of course the mad did not necessarily or predictably respond to treatment. As the preamble to the letter patent authorizing physicians and surgeons to minister to Henry VI put it, medical treatment was appropriate because:

We, by divine visitation, suffer from bodily illhealth, from which We hope to be able to be freed, if it should please Him who is the true health of all things . . . [and] because we do not wish to avoid the medicine which the Almighty created for the relief of human weaknesses . . . [30]

It was a matter, in the end, of God's will.

Medical theories

Physicians integrated spiritual and physical forms of healing by means of the theory that the divine and cosmic entities perceptible through astrology could act upon the human body to influence both its composition and its susceptibility to illness. For example, by analogy with the tides, 'the moon was thought to control the amount of blood in the veins', with the result that 'astrology inevitably became the handmaid of phlebotomy', dictating when blood could and could not be let. Lunatics, as the word suggests, were believed to be particularly affected by the moon.[31]

The dominant medical theory, throughout the medieval and early modern period, was Galenism. This was a version of the ancient belief, propounded in the *corpus* of works attributed to the father of medicine, Hippocrates, that the body consisted of four elements (earth, fire, air and water). Galen characterized the elements as having certain combinations of qualities (respectively: cold and dry, hot and dry, hot and moist, cold and moist), and associated them with four 'humours', black bile (melancholia), yellow bile (cholera), blood and phlegm.[32]

Disease occurred when the humours got out of balance. Humoral imbalances could also occur in the brain, and imbalances in the body could cause 'vapours' to rise to the brain, inducing mental disturbance. Equally, disturbances of the soul could create physical imbalances and so cause disease of either mind or body, as, for example, when a man's bad conscience made him depressed and anxious or unsettled his stomach. Even in the eighteenth century, Jonathan Swift could credit his priest, 'who is indeed an excellent Divine, and withal an able Physician', with prescribing efficacious remedies to settle the conscience, to calm an overactive mind, to cure love-sickness, or to reduce anger and thoughts of revenge. Physicians could make physical examinations (and were usually portrayed in medical treatises and in pictures of hospitals holding aloft a phial of urine, which was commonly used for just this purpose) and might use astrology to determine the cause of, and the prognosis and the treatment for, the illness.[33]

The belief that humoral imbalances underlay all illness, and that these imbalances were in turn produced by some disturbing influence, physical or mental, had considerable implications for the types of treatment employed. Depending upon the physical and astrological complexion of the patient and his or her illness, treatments were designed to purge the system of whatever was in excess. The majority of the treatments which doctors were authorized to use on Henry VI in 1454 were of this type: bowel clearers and cleansers, gargles for shifting phlegm, bloodletting in various forms, and applications of heated or heat-inducing materials to draw out impurities through the skin. But because medieval physicians treated the man as a whole, they were equally concerned to remove whatever was excessive or unbalanced in the mind. Thus Henry VI's doctors were also permitted to prescribe a range of draughts and ointments, which could be used to soothe a troubled mind, or, in Henry's case, to stimulate an excessively torpid one. They would certainly also have prescribed a daily regime designed to produce the same effect. Every aspect of the King's day, from how much sleep he was allowed and when he rose, through the types of food and drink and how much he could have, to forms of exercise (if he could be persuaded to move) and entertainment, and the interactions he was permitted or encouraged to have with others, is likely to have been worked out carefully.[34]

Many sufferers from mental illness could not have afforded the services of physicians. Whether or not the advice being offered to kings and nobles by contemporary physicians actually did percolate downwards through the barber-surgeons and assistants employed by the physicians is impossible to say, but 'do-it-yourself medical manuals' were available and were probably used by unlicensed practitioners.[35] The treatment which seems most often to have been recommended involved a change of lifestyle which, in part at least, could be copied by all but the poorest sufferer. Likewise, the kind of minor surgery offered by barber-surgeons, such as bloodletting, probably was available to all but the very poor. This type of surgery could be used, according to contemporary ideas, in treating the insane.

Some of the remedies contained in medieval medical recipe books, it is true, do not appear to have any underlying humoral justification. They may have been the result of empiricism, or perhaps just superstition or sympathetic magical beliefs, and probably belonged to an older tradition. This is obviously true of charms and magical rituals, but it may also apply to some 'simples', or herbal medicines. However, the fact that a humoral justification was not offered in relation to a particular remedy does not prove that it did not exist. A collection of recipes written, probably, in the 1440s, contains two medicines of this type. One, which was said to be effective against 'phantasma or delusions', prescribed a garland of the herb betony to be worn at night. In another, used against 'the frenzy', wild teazle was crushed to create a poultice for the head. The first may have had, or have been believed to have, a soothing effect; the second, a drawing or heat-releasing capability.[36]

CONCLUSION

As with children or the impotent old, there was in the Middle Ages an unspoken consensus about what ought to be done to look after the mad, and who ought to do it. Those who had valuable possessions undoubtedly required special measures for their protection (and 'feudal tenants' were at risk of being exploited for financial gain by the King), but otherwise their family, friends, neighbours or parish were expected to look after them without permission or other intervention by the authorities. Only if the family and neighbourhood failed in its obligations would higher authorities, often reluctantly, become involved.

In some respects it does seem to be true that the medieval and early modern period was a time of relative physical freedom for, and tolerance of, the madman.

However, 'freedom' and 'toleration' are positive words to use of states which may have had very negative aspects. There are enough references to the beating and incarceration in dismal conditions of lunatics to indicate that the practice was fairly common. Despite this fact, what medieval and early modern madmen and mad-women probably suffered from most was not official coercion and repression, but official inattention.

Attitudes generally were mixed. On the one hand, madness and afflictions like epilepsy could provoke a superstitious horror or moral condemnation. On the other, Bethlem's benefactors often displayed a tender care for the inmates' welfare which seems not simply to be a consequence of the benefactors' anxiety to minimize the time they spent in Purgatory. Treatments also varied widely, from the semi-magical, through spiritual solace, to physical and mental prescriptions that had a logic which is by no means wholly incomprehensible to us today. The fact that many insane people probably did not have access to often violently purgative physic was not necessarily a disadvantage: other aspects of medieval medical treatment, such as prescriptions relating to the sufferer's general environment and daily regime, could be adopted even by the poor. And there is some evidence that notions about the benefits of specific environments (such as quiet, dark conditions for the raving mad) had penetrated the popular consciousness: the Mayor and Aldermen of London, for example, thought they knew what would be best for Mr Bradye, ordering that he should be held in close confinement and totally *incommunicado*.

But the very fact that the Court of Aldermen felt the need to say what should happen to Bradye tells its own tale about the extent to which Bethlem was, at least in the mid-sixteenth century, applying even the most basic popular notions of an appropriate regime for the mad. If it is true to say that the insane in the Middle Ages did not always suffer from being under-physicked, it is also true to say that they can hardly ever have benefited from being neglected.

NOTES

1 For examples of the former: Penelope B. R. Doob, *Nebuchadnezzar's Children: Conventions of Madness in Middle English Literature* (New Haven and London: Yale University Press, 1974); Andrew Scull, *Museums of Madness: The Social Organization of Insanity in Nineteenth Century England* (London: Allen Lane, 1979), especially 64–6. For perceptions among historians of the Middle Ages as a period of darkness, superstition, neglect and cruelty, see, for example, Chris Philo, '"The Chaotic Spaces" of Medieval Madness: Thoughts on the English and Welsh Experience', in Mikuláš Teich, Roy Porter and Bo Gustafsson (eds), *Nature and Society in Historical Context* (Cambridge: CUP, 1996), 51–90, especially 51–2. For examples of the latter: Alan Macfarlane, *Witchcraft in Tudor and Stuart England: A Regional and Comparative Study* (London: Routledge and Kegan Paul, 1970), 183; Michael MacDonald, *Mystical Bedlam: Madness, Anxiety, and Healing in Seventeenth-Century England* (Cambridge and New York: CUP, 1989), 230–1; David Roffe and Christine Roffe, 'Madness and Care in the Community: A Medieval Perspective', *British Medical Journal*, cccxi (1995), 1708–12. For an overview of medieval attitudes towards insanity, see, for example, Ellie Phillips, 'Medieval Madness: Convention and Reality' (University of East Anglia unpublished BA thesis, 1996).
2 *Calendar of Letterbook H*, 184.

3 For what follows, unless otherwise stated, see Nigel Walker, *Crime and Insanity in England, volume 1: The Historical Perspective* (Edinburgh: Edinburgh University Press, 1968), especially 15–28.

4 G. E. Woodbine (ed.), S. E. Thorne (trans.), *Bracton, On the Laws and Customs of England*, 4 volumes (Cambridge, Mass.: The Belknap Press/Selden Society, 1968), ii, especially 23, 34, 424.

5 'Being adjudged ever to be, as it were, below full age': H. G. Richardson and G. O. Sayles (eds), *Fleta*, Selden Society, lxxii, lxxxix, ic (1955–83), ii, 178.

6 A. Luders *et al.* (eds), *Statutes of the Realm*, 11 volumes in 12 (London: George Eyre and Andrew Strahan, 1810–28), i, 226.

7 Mary Bateson, *Borough Customs*, Selden Society, xviii, xxi (1904, 1906), ii, 150, 156–7.

8 *Calendar of Inquisitions Post Mortem and Other Analogous Documents Preserved in the Public Record Office*, iv, 78–9. For discussion of the possible implications of these variations in terminology, see Frederick M. Maitland, 'The Praerogativa Regis', *English Historical Review*, vi (1891), 367–72; Richard Neugebauer, 'Treatment of the Mentally Ill in Medieval and Early Modern England: A Reappraisal', *Journal of the History of the Behavioural Sciences*, xiv (1978), 158–69; David Roffe, '"A Novel and Noteworthy Thing"? The Guardianship of Lunatics and the Crown in Medieval England' – we are most grateful to Dr Roffe for allowing us to see this article in draft form.

9 *The Complete Peerage*, v, 281–2, 285; *Calendar of Patent Rolls 1461–67*, 277.

10 Walker, *op. cit.* 19, 25.

11 J. H. Baker and S. F. C. Milsom, *Sources of English Legal History: Private Law to 1750* (London: Butterworths, paperback edn, 1986), 311–12; PRO C270/22, m. 4.

12 PRO, PCC PROB 11/6/7, m. 57; PRO, PCC PROB 11/6/24, m. 183; PRO, PCC PROB 11/6/28, m. 211*v*. This carefulness might of course indicate that the fifteenth-century Masters of Bethlem were considered particularly venal; however, the Wardens of the prisons at least were certainly not regarded as being above suspicion.

13 Carole Rawcliffe, 'The Hospitals of Later Medieval London', *Medical History*, xxviii (1984), 1–21, especially 4; Martha Carlin, 'Medieval English Hospitals', in L. Granshaw and R. Porter (eds), *The Hospital in History* (London: Routledge, 1989), 21–39, especially 30–2; PRO, PCC PROB 11/7/2; PRO C270/22 m. 3.

14 See, for example, Peregrine Horden, 'A Discipline of Relevance: the Historiography of the Later Medieval Hospital', *The Society for the Social History of Medicine*, i (1988), 359–74, especially 365–6; H. C. Maxwell-Lyte (ed.), *The Register of Thomas Bekynton, Bishop of Bath and Wells, 1443–1465 (Part I)*, Somerset Record Society, xlix, 59; Sandra Cavallo, *Charity and Power in Early Modern Italy: Benefactors and their Motives in Turin, 1541–1789* (Cambridge, New York, Melbourne: CUP, 1995), 25.

15 *BCGM* volume 5, fol. 376*v*.

16 *The Complete Works of Sir Thomas More*, 15 volumes (New Haven and London: Yale University Press, 1963–86), ix, 118 ('The Apology'); *CA Rep.* 12/2, fol. 323.

17 B. A. Windeatt (ed. and trans.), *The Book of Margery Kempe* (London, New York, etc.: Penguin Books, paperback, 1994), 33, 41–3, 143, 217–18.

18 *Calendar of Letterbook H*, 430–1 (an idiot city 'orphan' whose custody was granted to her father's executor, though she was adult); *CLRO* Journal of the Common Council 8, fol. 190 (Tate senior had been one of the 'farmers' of Bethlem's revenues in 1454: see Chapter 5); *Calendar of Plea and Memoranda Rolls of the City of London, 1458–1482*, 5; Margaret Pelling, 'Healing the Sick Poor: Social Policy and Disability in Norwich 1550–1640', *Medical History*, xxix (1985), 115–37, especially 119.

19 *Ghall* MS 12806, Christ's Hospital Court Minute Book volume 1, fols 3*v*, 4, 5*v*, 4*v*; 6, 7, 11, 11*v*, etc. In 1563, the Governors agreed to take in 'the idiot bequethed by Mrs Sympson' of Chigwell, Essex, in return for a legacy: *ibid.* volume 2, fols 13, 13*v*.

20 Doob, *op. cit.* 20–5, 41, Chapter 2; Windeatt, *op. cit.* 41, 43–5, 48–50.

21 Carole Rawcliffe, 'The Insanity of Henry VI', *The Historian*, l (1996), 8–12; Ralph Griffiths, *The Reign of King Henry the Sixth: The Exercise of Royal Authority, 1422–1461* (London: Benn, 1981), 715–40; Vivian Green, *The Madness of Kings: Personal Trauma and the Fate of Nations* (Stroud: Alan Sutton, 1994), 68 (Kempe died on 22 March); J. Stevenson (ed.), *Letters and*

Papers Illustrative of the Wars of the English in France during the Reign of Henry the Sixth, King of England, 2 volumes (Rolls Series, 1861–4), ii, part 2, 771.

22 Susan Brigden, *London and the Reformation* (Oxford: Clarendon Press, 1989), 68, 8; Michael MacDonald, *Mystical Bedlam: Madness, Anxiety and Healing in Seventeenth Century England* (Cambridge: CUP, 1989), 199–200.

23 R. C. Finucane, *Miracles and Pilgrims: Popular Beliefs in Medieval England* (London: J. M. Dent, 1977), 91–2, 107–9; Philo, *op. cit.* 70–5; Basil Clarke, *Mental Disorder in Earlier Britain: Exploratory Studies* (Cardiff: University of Wales Press, 1975), 128–30, 143, 160–1, 165; Benedicta Ward, *Miracles and the Medieval Mind: Theory, Record and Event 1000–1215* (London: Scolar Press, 1982), 45, 72–4, 80, 85–6, 89, 96; Carole Rawcliffe, *The Hospitals of Medieval Norwich* (Centre of East Anglian Studies: University of East Anglia, 1995), 141; *eadem*, '"Gret Criynge and Joly Chauntynge": Life, Death and Liturgy at St Giles's Hospital, Norwich, in the Thirteenth and Fourteenth Centuries', in Carole Rawcliffe, Roger Virgoe and Richard Wilson (eds), *Counties and Communities: Essays on East Anglian History Presented to Hassell Smith* (Centre of East Anglian Studies: University of East Anglia, forthcoming), 37–55.

24 Nicholas Orme and Margaret Webster, *The English Hospital 1070–1570* (New Haven and London: Yale University Press, 1995), 86, 88, 90, 91, 49–55; Rawcliffe, *The Hospitals of Medieval Norwich*, 110.

25 Cited in Rawcliffe, 'The Insanity of Henry VI', 9.

26 *CA Rep.* 18, fol. 24; Windeatt, *op. cit.* 42.

27 Michael A. Screech, 'Good Madness in Christendom', in W. F. Bynum, Roy Porter and Michael Shepherd (eds), *The Anatomy of Madness: Essay in the History of Psychiatry, vol. I: People and Ideas* (London: Tavistock, 1985), 25–39, especially 33–4.

28 A. H. Thomas (ed.), *Calendar of Early Mayor's Court Rolls . . . AD 1298–1307* (London, New York, etc.: CUP, 1924), 51; M. C. Pouchelle, *The Body and Surgery in the Middle Ages* (Cambridge: Polity Press/Blackwell, 1990), 168–9; *Joannes de Vigo, The Most Excellent Works of Chirurgerye, 1543* (Amsterdam and New York: De Capo Press, facsimile edn, 1968), fol. 43*v*.

29 Daniel W. Amundsen, 'The Medieval Catholic Tradition', in Ronald L. Numbers and Daniel W. Amundsen (eds), *Caring and Curing: Health and Medicine in the Western Religious Traditions* (London and New York: Macmillan, 1986), 65–107, especially 81–8; *idem*, 'Medieval Canon Law on Medical and Surgical Practice by the Clergy', *Bulletin of the History of Medicine*, lii (1978), 22–44, especially 40. Although in the sixteenth century the London-based College of Physicians tried to suppress 'quackery', it found it expedient to distinguish between 'public' and 'private' practice, and was quite unable to prevent practice by clergymen: Margaret Pelling, 'Knowledge Common and Acquired: The Education of Unlicensed Medical Practitioners in Early Modern London', in Vivian Nutton and Roy Porter (eds), *The History of Medical Education in Britain* (Amsterdam and Atlanta: Rodopi, 1995), 250–79, especially 250–1, 254–5, 253.

30 *Foedera, Conventiones, Literae . . . Accurante Thoma Rymer*, 20 volumes (London: J. Tonson, 2nd edn, 1727), 347.

31 Amundsen, *op. cit.* 94–5; Allan Chapman, 'Astrological Medicine', in Charles Webster (ed.), *Health Medicine and Mortality in the Sixteenth Century* (Cambridge and New York: CUP, 1979), 275–300, especially 293–4; Charles H. Talbot, *Medicine in Medieval England* (London: Oldbourne, 1967), 127; Paul Slack, 'Uses of Vernacular Medical Literature', in Webster, *op. cit.* 237–73, especially 265, 268, 269–70; Margaret Pelling, 'Medical Practitioners', in Webster, *op. cit.* 165–235, especially 165–6.

32 Thomas Lester Canavan, 'Madness and Enthusiasm in Burton's *Anatomy of Melancholy* and Swift's *Tale of a Tub*' (D.Phil. thesis, Columbia University, 1970), 40.

33 *Ibid.* 55, 18–19; Stanley Rubin, *Medieval English Medicine* (Newton Abbot and New York: David & Charles/Barnes & Noble Books, 1974), 191–2.

34 *Foedera, op. cit.* xi, 366; for a discussion of the mix of regime, physical medicine and surgery recommended by Bartolomeus Anglicus in 'De proprietatibus rerum', written *c.* 1230–50, see Rubin, *op. cit.* 195–200; eighty years later, Duke Philip of Mecklenburg's physicians prescribed just such a detailed regime in an attempt to alleviate his melancholy: H. C. Erik Midelfort, *Mad Princes of Renaissance Germany* (Charlottesville: University Press of Virginia, 1994), 49–51.

35 Talbot, *op. cit.* 126, 128–33 (the discussion however appears to assume that these handbooks were mainly used by 'the medical profession', presumably meaning physicians and surgeons).

36 W. R. Dawson, *A Leechbook or Collection of Medical Recipes of the Fifteenth Century* (London: Macmillan, 1934), 2–3, 123, 129; for other examples of herbs recommended in the treatment of melancholy, frenzy and lunacy: D. H. Tuke, *Chapters in the History of the Insane in the British Isles* (London: Kegan Paul Trench, 1882), 30–1.

CHAPTER NINE

INSTITUTIONAL CARE FOR THE INSANE IN MEDIEVAL AND EARLY MODERN TIMES

—— ·◆· ——

INTRODUCTION

With the possible exception of the Stone House at Charing Cross, there was no known medieval institutional provision in England before the fifteenth century specifically for the mad, though some hospitals evidently admitted the temporarily insane along with other sick people.[1] Even when Bethlem started to specialize in looking after the insane, it contained very few patients. In 1598, there were only twenty inmates, and until the 1630s at least the Bridewell Governors tried hard to keep the numbers at about this level. This poses three questions: why were individuals admitted at all?; what characterized the selected few? and what did those admitting them expect to achieve by doing so? It also invites comparisons with provision elsewhere: was the English provision of institutional care for, and treatment of, the mad atypical for its time?

The chronology of developments in European hospitals seems in fact to have varied considerably. This is immediately apparent when one compares the great Florentine hospitals of the later Middle Ages with the one broadly equivalent English institution, Henry VII's Savoy. In 1428, a tax assessment revealed that the Florentine Ospedale di Matteo was paying for two doctors, and the larger hospitals all had pharmacies by the mid-fifteenth century. The Savoy was, according to its Statutes, to be served by a pharmacist as well as a physician and a surgeon, all salaried; but it did not open its doors until about 1520. The patterns of hospital foundation, and what hospitals provided to whom, and when, differed across Europe, and by no means all regions were affected by the kind of shift of emphasis in the wake of the Black Death which so influenced charitable donations in England.[2]

There were however some marked similarities between regions, too. All over Europe, small generalist hospitals of the type so commonly encountered in medieval London were to be found. The tendency of hospitals during the later Middle Ages to abandon care of the sick and dying in favour of providing lodging for the elderly or schooling for boys, to concentrate ever more resources on their religious buildings and services, to delegate tasks to lay brethren or corrodians, and to cut back severely on 'outside relief' and beds for the poor, seems very widespread indeed. The late fourteenth-century Masters of Bethlem were doing as their peers did, when they built a fine Chapel and encouraged support for it by founding a Fraternity. Even those splendid Florentine hospitals of the late medieval period shared some of these characteristics: far more was spent on food and clothing for the patients than on medicines, and the doctors' salaries were low, suggesting that the position was regarded as a semi-charitable one, or was very much part-time.[3]

But this is of course charity in the modern sense of practical philanthropy. Much of late-medieval charity sought above all to save souls from the pains of Purgatory, not bodies from physical ills: in St John's, Cambridge, 'liturgy, not therapeutics, was the centre of its life', as it was of St Giles's, Norwich, and of many if not all hospitals which continued to be religious institutions into the fifteenth century and beyond.[4] There is a danger, however, of allowing the high survival rate of records from religious houses and of foundation charters to distort our judgment. The priorities of religious institutions and those who served in them were not necessarily the same as the priorities of kings or civic authorities. In any case, what the rules said, and what people did, were not always the same thing. Hospital staff may not have been conscientious about obliging patients to say all the prayers they were supposed to say. Practical philanthropy continued to exist, even after the Black Death. Not every late-medieval man believed that what really mattered was the health of the soul, or that clergymen were 'real doctors' even if they had not undergone a full medical training or apprenticeship. In 1434, for example, the authorities in Lyon complained about the fact that the town's physicians were not treating the sick in the hospitals as they ought to do, leaving them instead to the ministrations of 'ignorant hospital brothers, superstitious monks, empirics, or self-proclaimed sorcerers'. The Hôtel-Dieu in Paris had enjoyed the services of a surgeon and a physician in the early thirteenth century, although it was not until the late fifteenth century that it got its own pharmacy.[5]

As in England, some early-medieval general hospitals on the Continent admitted lunatics, while others barred them along with pregnant women and those suffering from sexually transmitted diseases. Attitudes generally were similar. Sixteenth-century Castilians were at one with Sir Thomas More in believing that lunatics could be 'treated by means of floggings'. The mad inmates of the Royal Hospital of Granada were, like the Bethlem inmates, suffering severely in the late sixteenth century. The larger German hospitals were, from the fourteenth century if not before, building separate 'madhouses' or providing 'madrooms'. The early fifteenth century saw the creation of hospitals specifically for the insane in Seville and Valencia. In the wider context of Europe, therefore, the fact that Bethlem seems to have begun to specialize in looking after the insane in the early fifteenth century fits a pattern: although probably more by luck than judgment. There are some other similarities. At the Paris Hôtel-Dieu, the 'fantastiques et frenetiques' were placed in 'couches closes, a deux fenestres pour veoir et donner'; they lay in ordinary beds, but were bound and rendered largely immobile. Assuming that the inmates' 'rooms' mentioned in 1632 were indeed cubicles, the layout of Bethlem Hospital, at least in the seventeenth century, echoed the arrangements in the medieval Hôtel-Dieu of Paris. As a number of other English hospitals started to provide 'cubicles' in the fifteenth century, Bethlem's internal layout may have been much the same in the late medieval period. However, it looks as though Bethlem inmates did not enjoy any routine, 'professional' medical provision until the early modern period, and in this respect the Hospital lagged behind its greater continental counterparts.[6]

TREATMENT IN BETHLEM, *c.* 1400–1633

It is to Bethlem above all that one has to look if one wants to examine the institutional care and treatment of the mad in England in medieval and early modern times; and Bethlem, unfortunately, is a hard book to read. We know nothing at all about the Hospital's role before about 1400. The most one can say is that, *if* Bethlem was taking in the sick and dying before then, it *may* have looked after them in much the same way as other religious institutions did: perhaps patients lay in the old Church nave, or in a small infirmary hall attached to it, where they would have been best-placed to benefit from the spiritual healing which was so vital to those for whom death might be very close at hand.

The situation is hardly better after 1400. Almost no evidence about the treatment of the insane in the medieval Hospital exists. What does seem likely is that the ill and insane were being accommodated in the Long House by then, and that the Porter and his wife had the main responsibility both for running the Hospital and for looking after the inmates. In these circumstances, spiritual solace may not have been readily available even to those inmates who were able to benefit consciously from it. Those who could afford to pay for some form of medical advice and physical treatment, presumably obtained it. In the case of the six lunatic men, it may be that nature was left to take her course unimpeded.

Whatever else the acquisition of Bethlem by the City in 1547 achieved, it does not seem to have altered the treatment of its inmates significantly. Spiritual healing seems to have had a low priority, with Bethlem's curate being dismissed almost at once. By 1612, the Bridewell Governors were concerned about the lack of spiritual solace for their 'soule sicke' patients. In words which contain many echoes of Robert Burton's comments about melancholy, published less than a decade later, the Governors lingered for some time on the thought that, as Bethlehem meant 'house of bread', it had been intended by the founder as a memorial of Christ's birthplace and of his bodily sacrifice; therefore it was right that the Hospital should provide for the inmates' spiritual as well as their physical sustenance and cure by encouraging 'divines', doctors of theology, as well as physicians and surgeons to attend at Bethlem.[7]

Apart from the fact that the sixteenth- and early seventeenth-century Governors quite often sent people to Bethlem 'to be cured', there is very little evidence of formal arrangements to provide anything which, even on the most generous assessment, could be termed medical help. That is not to say that inmates got no treatment at all for their physical or mental ills, or that the things that were done to them were never done with therapeutic aims. The Governors undoubtedly expected inmates to be looked after in a way that did not damage them. When the father of Elizabeth Slater, a woman transferred from Bridewell to Bethlem in August 1620, complained that 'her foote was rotten . . . for want of good looking to' a mere three weeks later, they immediately ordered a committee to investigate this and any other possible abuses. Normally, however, arrangements for treatment were left to the Bethlem staff. In

January 1631, for example, the Governors increased the amount allowed for the diet of Henry Hobson, an inmate 'whose Legg is so ulcerated that it is thought it must be cutt of[f]', but made no provision for medical treatment.[8]

Even after Dr Crooke was elected explicitly because of his medical expertise, it is not certain that much in the way of therapeutic innovations followed. He did undoubtedly try to enhance the general appearance and equipment of the kitchen, and the decision to construct a sluice for the vault may have been prompted by a desire to improve hygiene as well as to save money or effort. Possibly, too, Crooke's battle with the Governors to obtain a doubling of the payment for poor inmates was prompted, not by greed or sound business sense, but by the knowledge that the original sum was too low to provide even the most basic of diets. The fact remains that there is nothing to show that Crooke altered any existing therapeutic regime or introduced a new one. At the end of his time in office the type of food eaten by the Bethlem inmates appears to have been identical to the type of food eaten by prisoners in Bridewell, and the Royal Commission which investigated his administration declared roundly that 'nothing was done towards the cure' of the poor inmates.[9]

Some forms of medieval and early modern treatment involved what contemporaries would have regarded as therapeutic interventions, but we would not. As the story told by Sir Thomas More makes clear, Bethlem in the early sixteenth century administered 'betynge and correccyon' in an attempt to restore the wits of the raving mad. Physical constraint was also frequently practised. An indulgence issued in 1446 states plainly enough that many of the 'miserable persons dwelling there . . . are so alienated in mind and possessed of unclean spirits that they must be restrained with chains and fetters'.[10]

Constraint, solitary confinement and beatings were not the only treatment offered to patients. *Ad hoc* treatment with medicines did also occur, and occasionally the Governors of Bethlem paid for it, as when in 1578 they paid Mrs Thomson to look after two inmates, 'she to finde them diett and medesens'. Were Bethlem inmates offered any better-quality medical treatment than this? Probably not from the few medically trained men who held the masterships before the seventeenth century, for the reasons given in Chapter 5. However, there is no reason why Bethlem patients should not have been treated by less eminent medical persons. Certainly, if the Hospital's claims are to be believed, it would appear that some patients received trained medical care by the early sixteenth century. An advertisement for the Fraternity of the Blessed Mary of Bethlem written in 1519 encouraged potential brothers and sisters to join by offering them 'certain indulgences and remissions of sins' if they helped towards the support of the mentally afflicted inmates of Bethlem, 'who are there kept and nurtured with great care and diligence, and are cured by the doctor [medicus] and unceasing solicitude'.[11]

None the less, the fact remains that Bethlem did not retain medically trained men at all until the seventeenth century; and the payment to Mrs Thomson in 1578 sounds more like an arrangement designed to reward past service, or even a form of pension, rather than a regular method of providing medical care for the lunatics. It reinforces the impression that therapeutics were not a matter in which the Governors took much interest or for which there was any regular, formal provision, by them or anyone else.

NEGLECT AND ABUSE IN BETHLEM

The one fact that is widely known about Bethlem in its early days is that in 1403, at the same time as there were six mentally ill men at the hospital, its inventory listed six iron chains with attached locks and keys, four sets of manacles, six other iron chains, and two pairs of stocks. Naturally the nineteenth-century Charity Commissioners — followed by most historians since — made the connection. 'It seems probable', their report said, 'that from the first reception of lunatics into Bethlem their condition and treatment was wretched indeed.' The ironmongery inventoried in the early fifteenth century 'indicate[d] but too plainly the system then pursued'.[12]

Other evidence points to neglect as well as constraint. In August 1567 the Mayor and Aldermen of London arranged for confiscated coalsacks to be washed, stuffed and made into 'pallets' (straw mattresses) for the poor distraught people of Bethlem, many of whom were reportedly lying on bare boards. And thirty years later a civic committee reported that the Hospital was 'so loathsomily and so filthely kept [that it was] not fitt for anye man to come into'. The 1403 visitation also revealed a catalogue of wrongdoing and neglect. The Visitation Commissioners found the Porter guilty of retaining the Hospital's goods and of defrauding the poor, calculating the loss to the Hospital at £50. It is true that they made no comment about the physical conditions in which inmates were kept. But this was perhaps because they did not bother to inquire into them. Although they visited the precinct on two occasions and examined the state and contents of the Chapel, they appear not to have inspected the Hospital building itself.[13]

There is, however, some less gloomy evidence which can be set against the image which so appalled the Charity Commissioners and the conditions reported by the late sixteenth-century civic committee. A London Mayor of the mid-fifteenth century, possibly a member of the Grocers Company, spoke glowingly of Bethlem and the care it provided. Perhaps he was simply allowing civic pride to run away with him. It is, however, unlikely that he wrote in ignorance. As we have already seen, the Hospital was anything but a closed community. In any case, not all the fifteenth-century inmates were mad, and some testified before the Visitation Commissioners in 1403. Hans Riche, who had been a patient for two years, complained about the harm done to inmates by Taverner's depredations, but not about physical neglect or cruelty. Agnes Coteneys, a London woman who was brought in by her neighbours 'in order to recover her health', may or may not have been mad. Certainly once she had recovered she could recall not having received the donations made for her support. However, like Hans Riche, she did not allege that she had been mistreated in other ways.[14]

While no amount of openness would guarantee that inmates were not neglected or mistreated, it would make it less likely that prominent Londoners would be seriously misinformed about conditions in the Hospital. So, although it is possible that inmates had been lying on bare boards and wallowing in their own filth for years before the City's magistrates decided to do something about it, it is equally possible that they responded fairly promptly when conditions deteriorated. The impression one gleans from the 'Bedlam' scenes included in some early seventeenth-century plays, that the poor inmates at least had nothing but straw to lie upon, is probably incorrect. In June

1620, the Bridewell Governors ordered that the 'poores Beddes' should be replaced as they were rotten and broken, suggesting that beds for the poor were no novelty at the time. It may well also be that the 'bare boards' on which many of the pauper inmates were sleeping in 1567 were bedboards rather than floorboards. Probably it was only 'dirty' inmates, the incontinent or those who would not be kept clean, who had to put up with nothing but straw. Moreover, the Governors had their own motives for keeping at least half an eye on conditions in Bethlem: even if they had been entirely lacking in compassion for the inmates – and that is far from certain – they were undoubtedly very concerned indeed about the kind of 'slanderous reports' about Bridewell which were circulating in late 1602, alleging that the reformatory 'hathe in former tymes exacted of such prisoners as have been sent into the hospital for dyett and lodgings more then is convenyent, to the discreditt of this house'.[15]

As for the fetters and chains whose existence in the fifteenth-century inventory so shocked the Charity Commissioners, there is no doubt at all that raving lunatics were commonly chained and fettered at this period. However, whether all of the iron-mongery listed in 1403 was used on the six madmen then kept at Bethlem is another matter. The six chains and padlocks are listed straight after three chests, and may have been used to secure them; and even the stocks and manacles may have been kept in the precinct for the use of the neighbourhood as a whole. All one can safely assume is that any of the lunatics who were violent will have been physically restrained.

MISUSE AND ABUSE OF BETHLEM'S FACILITIES

Internal and external politics certainly had an impact on who was admitted to Bethlem at different periods. The acquisition of Bethlem by the City did not end the tussle between City and Crown over control of the Hospital. It seems in fact to have resulted in two conflicting outcomes. On the one hand, the hospitals generally became a potential focus of civic pride and an additional means of exercising power and influence, through patronage or benevolence. On the other, kings or their advisers seem for the first time in the 1540s to have begun to use places like Bridewell and Bethlem for their own ends. In 1545, for example, the Privy Council ordered the release of a madman who had earlier been committed to Bethlem – presumably by the Council itself – 'for certeyne lewd wordes in tyme of his frenesey spoken agaynst the Kinges Majeste', and there was a further instance of a similar nature in July 1546. The Council also sent a few individuals to Bethlem during the 1540s and 1550s simply, apparently, because they were mad. None the less, the interesting thing about the man released in 1545 is that the Privy Council acted as it did, not because the man had recovered his sanity, but because the Council was persuaded that 'there appered no malice in him'.[16] It is unfortunately not clear what would have happened had he been adjudged sane, but still malevolent: perhaps he would have been transferred to custody elsewhere – but perhaps not.

It is as though the high profile of Bethlem, resulting from the negotiations over its transfer to the City, reminded the Privy Council of the existence of this useful resource; for there are no more recorded instances of incarcerations until the 1570s, when the Council once again began sending to Bethlem those who uttered 'sedicious wordes' and (or) who seemed mad. This renewal of Council interest in Bethlem was almost certainly the product of the political unease of the period, not of greater publicity about Bethlem. It was mirrored, in the 1590s, by orders to incarcerate suspected traitors and terrorists in Bridewell and to examine them in manacles and under torture.[17]

It seems that the partial clarification of the relationship between the Crown and the City in 1547, together with the granting of control over the Hospital's administration to the latter, made it easier or more likely that abuse of Bethlem's facilities for quasi-political purposes would occur. It is none the less worth noting that the committal by the Privy Council of individuals who criticized royal government seems to have been a novelty in the 1540s. If it was done at all in the fifteenth and the first three decades of the sixteenth century, the surviving – admittedly imperfect – council records do not record the fact. There is no evidence of the committal of individuals for criticizing *civic* government before the 1590s, which may be why the despatch to Bethlem in June 1595 of a silkweaver who 'had some hard speeches concerning [the Mayor] and in dispraise of his government' resulted in a riot and the forcible release of the supposed madman.[18]

The 1540s may also have seen the first instances of the use of Bethlem as a deliberate method of general social control. There is no shortage of examples of individuals being despatched to the Hospital because they were making a great nuisance of themselves. Modern suspicions of patriarchy would certainly find something to feed on in the reasons given for the committal of some Bethlem inmates. In 1609, one of the things that persuaded the Bridewell Governors that John Croshawe was mad was that he 'cursed his father & rayled egregriouslie upon my lord maior Mr doctor Meddowes & others'. In 1617, Richard Brawell was (after some hesitation) sent to Bethlem, having been brought in to Bridewell for 'breakinge the pease and takinge wares from menes stalles and spoylinge them'. It is tempting to interpret these cases as examples of the contemporary worship of hierarchy and property, one which resulted in a belief that disrespect for one's social superiors and wanton destructiveness were so unnatural as to constitute clear evidence of mental derangement.[19]

Overall, however, the evidence suggests otherwise. The fact that an apprentice, Richard Walker, drew a rapier and waved it in his master's face does not seem to have persuaded the Governors to send him to Bethlem (even though Walker was 'supposed to be distracted'). In 1629 Anthony Droughton, who was brought into Bridewell for 'neglecting his service', would have got very short shrift had not his master intervened to save him, the Bridewell Clerk recording that 'good cause appeared to the Court why he should have been punished'. This entry is followed by the note, 'Droughton a distracted man sent to Bethlem'. What convinced the Bridewell Governors that Croshawe was mad was not his shocking disrespect for his elders and betters, but his frantic behaviour. Similarly, it was Brawell's irrational actions, not his destruction of property *per se*, which led them eventually to accept that he was out of his mind.[20]

Even if sending anti-social individuals to Bethlem did serve the secondary purpose of ridding the streets of them, social control was not the real aim. The Bethlem Governors, if not the Privy Council, clearly preferred to use Bridewell for the imprisonment of those disruptive individuals who were not mad, or whose madness was in doubt. Typical of their reaction is the treatment of Katherine Comy. Having been brought into Bridewell in April 1620 as a 'lewd counterfeite vagrant & kept at work', she was 'afterwards found to be Lunatique' and sent to Bethlem instead. As in the 1577 case of John Langton, 'a rogue fayninge hym selfe to be made', the tendency seems to have been to assume that the individual was counterfeiting madness in order to escape punishment.[21]

The fact that Bethlem inmates were routinely referred to as prisoners should not, therefore, be taken to mean anything more than that they were more-or-less rigorously confined within the house. Whatever the Privy Councillors or (perhaps just the once) the Mayor of London may have thought, Bethlem was regarded by its Governors as a place for the secure accommodation of the insane while they were being cured. And, even if it is the case that the Privy Councillors were sending some politically troublesome individuals to Bethlem for confinement rather than cure, the recorded numbers are tiny: five at most, for the whole sixteenth century (Elyott, 'gentleman', was clearly despatched in 1598 to be cured: the Council asked that he be kept 'in some convenient chamber, and . . . well used untill he shuld recover'). Nor were the Governors of Bridewell alone in preferring not to assume from the outset that a socially troublesome individual was mad. In 1598, Joseph Crich, described as a minister, was put in the Aldermanbury 'Cage' (lock-up) before his state of mind was recognized and he was sent to Bethlem as a lunatic.[22]

To judge by the Bethlem records, another modern misapprehension is the suspicion that in the past misogynistic attitudes made it likely that those women who created disturbances at home or among their neighbours would, unlike men, be locked away on the grounds that any woman who behaved in so unfeminine a fashion must be mad. While women who troubled their neighbours or the world at large might find themselves hauled before the Bridewell Governors, they were rarely sent to Bethlem: it was men, like William Bradye in 1551 or Henry Shalcrosse in 1618, whose 'rayling' was liable to result in them being labelled mad. The only recorded instance of a domestic disturbance with anything approaching a similar outcome is the 1575 case of William Trotter, summoned before the Bridewell Court 'for misvsinge of his wife and for that he counterfayted madnes & is not madde'.[23]

Nor is there much to suggest even more nefarious male practices, such as using an allegation of lunacy in order to get rid of an unruly or unwanted wife or in order to obtain control of an heiress's fortune. According to a number of eighteenth-century commentators, the misuse of private madhouses to dispose of or intimidate sane individuals was common, with 'wives and husbands trying who could first get the other to Bedlam'. However, it is unsafe to rely on this type of comment as evidence for the incidence of abuse.[24]

In Bethlem's early annals, there is one case of a man allegedly attempting to have his wife locked up in Bethlem so that he could live with his lover undisturbed, and at the same time (1574) two men were ordered to remove their wives, in one case on the grounds that she was not really mad. However, it is quite clear that the Bridewell Governors' sympathies were entirely with the woman in the first instance; and, if one or more of the other husbands was attempting to play a similar trick (which is improbable), they too got no support from the Court. There is some slight evidence that Bethlem may have occasionally served the ends of those intent on fleecing the wealthy. The only recorded instance in this period of an undoubted attempt of this type involved a man, Philip Manger, of whom it was said that Viscount Montague had left him £30 which was 'kept from him by strong hands for want of means'. Manger had been mad but had since, in the Bridewell Governors' opinion, recovered. The same visitation of 1624 may have revealed a similar abuse, this time of a mad inmate who owned considerable property but was not being maintained by anyone. Again, however, the individual was a man, John Gibbons.[25]

TYPES OF PATIENT ADMITTED

Once the City fathers had got Bethlem within their grasp, they began to receive requests and formal petitions from citizens who were anxious to secure a place at the Hospital for their insane relations or neighbours. Sometimes, too, non-Londoners who fell ill while visiting the City and therefore had no-one to care for them were sent to Bethlem. It had clearly been the practice in the early fifteenth century to take in sick people from other parts of the country. Quite a few of the past and present patients mentioned during the 1403 Visitation were not Londoners. At first sight, this seems to have been less common later. The only non-Londoner mentioned in the Court of Aldermen records (the Repertories) between 1550 and 1600 was the wife of a Norwich Worsted Weaver, who was admitted in 1554.[26] But it was not only the Mayor and Aldermen and, from the 1570s onwards, the Bridewell Governors, who controlled paying inmates' access to Bethlem. Indeed, not all admissions by the City magistrates were recorded in the civic records. There is no record in the Repertories of the admission of Mrs Brockhurste, a widow whose maintenance was paid for by the Skinners Company after it had arranged for her to be removed from her house and taken to Bethlem. It transpires that the Skinners had sought the agreement of the then Mayor, Sir Wolsey Dixey, who had presumably acted on his own authority.

The paying inmates listed in 1598 had been 'sent in' by a whole host of different persons and agencies, from their neighbours, through the Governors of the Dutch Church in London, to such luminaries as the Archbishop of Canterbury, the Lord Admiral, and Lady Stafford; not to mention the Benchers of Grays Inn. Similarly, in 1577 the Bridewell Governors agreed to keep Humphrey Whitlock in Bethlem 'as well as we can att his frends chardge for his dyet' if the Justices of the King's Bench decided to send him there as a lunatic. The records in fact suggest that any private person who was prepared to pay the full cost of an individual's maintenance could have them admitted, if the Keeper agreed. The inmates consequently continued to be a heterogeneous lot. In the late 1580s, a young man called John Saye was being maintained in the Hospital by a Mr Francis Nycolle of Hardwick, Northamptonshire, presumably under a private arrangement with the Keeper of Bethlem, to whom he was making the payments. Four of the inmates listed by the visiting Governors in 1598 were from outside London and its suburbs (Essex, Kent, Cambridge and Berkshire).[27]

Londoners who were admitted by the Mayor and Aldermen between the 1540s and the 1630s were people of quite modest if respectable status: an unnamed woman, whose friends and neighbours were, admittedly, able to pay at least the first instalment of the annual charge of £1 6s 8d for her; the son of a Carpenter; a Cook's wife from St John Street and a widow of Cordwainer Street Ward.[28] A good many of those admitted by the Bridewell Governors had been brought in initially to the Bridewell Court as vagrants or peacebreakers. The former at least were normally poor; in some cases, even their first name was unknown. The Governors were, however, prepared to admit paying inmates, too, like Robert Heathe, admitted in 1575 with John Tailor of Surrey paying for his keep, or William Cartwright, the son of a London merchant, who was admitted at his father's request and cost in 1600.[29] Those admitted by the Keeper were by definition sufficiently well-to-do not to be a charge on Bethlem, or at least they were supported by individuals or organizations with sufficient funds. Throughout the medieval and early modern period, charges and provision were basically tailored to the inmate's ability to pay. In 1403, payments ranged from £1 1s 8d a year to the equivalent of £2 12s a year. Some later 'boarders' were clearly persons of relatively high status, like Sir William Clifton, or Lord Lumley's nephew, or Lady Mary Bohun *alias* Stafford.[30]

Although it is not possible to assess the ages of the Bethlem population accurately, there is some evidence on this subject. Only one of over a hundred individuals whose details are recoverable from the Bridewell and other City records between 1550 and 1630 seems to have been a child, and not many more are likely to have been under twenty-one: John Lansdale was called a boy, but others described as sons and daughters were not necessarily young.[31] The St Botolph's burial registers give the ages at death of thirty-eight Bethlem inmates who had been admitted between the mid-1580s and 1633. Of these, one was fifteen, another, about sixteen, a third, eighteen, and a further two could have been under twenty-one on admission (13 per cent of the total at most). Five more (an additional 13 per cent) were or could have been under twenty-five. The majority of the inmates (up to 82 per cent) were twenty-five or over, however. At least 20 per cent were probably over fifty (see Table 9.1).

The surviving records of medieval and early-modern Bethlem do not suggest much of a sex bias in admissions, nor that (as one might expect) women were much more likely than men to spend their declining years in Bethlem. It is true that vagrant and elderly poor women were somewhat more likely than vagrant or elderly poor men to be sent to Bethlem: in 1598, four of the six inmates who had been sent in by the Bridewell Governors were women. It is also the case that some of these women stayed there for many years. Examples include Mother Withers, who was said to have died aged sixty-eight; Mother Palmer, doubtless also no spring chicken when she died; Mother (Anne) Cleye, who was sixty-six when she died, Jone Bromfeild and Mother (Elizabeth) Kempe, all of whom spent at least twenty years in Bethlem; and women like 'Joanne of the hospital' and 'Old Maddam', whose nicknames tell their own tale.[32] On the other hand, at any one time men were more likely than not to outnumber women among the inmates as a whole. In 1598, there were nine men and eleven women in Bethlem; in 1612, nine men and five women; in 1624, eighteen men and thirteen women. A few women certainly soldiered on in the Hospital for very many years, but others seem to have come and gone rapidly – apparently more rapidly than the men. In 1624, five of the men had been in for eighteen years or more, but the only long-staying women, Mother (Margaret) Ellis and Anne Parratt, had been in for about sixteen and fourteen years respectively. These two were exceptional among the women for the length of their stay. Nor were the only elderly residents of Bethlem female: Walter Marshall was said to be sixty-eight when he died in 1609.[33]

THE CRITERIA USED IN ADMISSIONS AND REJECTIONS

What sort of people were regarded as suitable cases for admission? Of those admitted by the Court of Aldermen, Mr Bradye was clearly a raving lunatic. The Carpenter's son was described merely as 'distraught'. The Cook's wife was admitted 'until such time as God shall restore her to perfect memory'. Widow Hallywell of Cordwainer Street Ward had 'lately become lunatic, and distraught of her wits'. Of the unnamed woman admitted in 1552 and of Widow Brockhurste's condition, nothing is said; but it required a writ and no less than four beadles to extract Mrs Brockhurste, and one John Brockhurste sold to the Skinners' Wardens 'a lock, hasps and staples to set upon the door of her room' – whether this was in order to sequester the room from which she had just been removed, or to keep her secure in Bethlem, is unfortunately not clear. Identical terminology was applied by the Bridewell Governors to those admitted by them: in 1575, Robert Heathe was said to be 'nowe Lunaticke'; in 1598, Henry Richards was described as a 'Lunaticke person', and so on. The Privy Council sent Mr Elyott to Bethlem in 1591, describing him as 'dusordered and dystracted in his wyttes . . . playing very lewd and franticke partes'. Recoveries were said to have occurred when individuals, like Thomas Dowsinge, waterman, in 1576, were 'well & in perfecte memorye'.[34]

According to the opinion recorded by John Strype in his 1720 edition of Stow's *Survey*, those judged most suitable as patients were people who were 'raving and furious, and capable of cure, or if not, yet are likely to do mischief to themselves or others, and are poor, and cannot otherwise be provided for. But for those that are only melancholic or idiots, and judged not capable of cure, these the governors think the house ought not to be burdened with.' The opinion is a late one, but it reflects a fairly constant attitude on the part of the Governors and Aldermen alike. In June 1624, the Bridewell Governors ordered a large committee to visit Bethlem and to examine 'by what warrant the persons there came in, and to discharge ideotts and others not fitt for that house'. Both then and on subsequent visitations, inmates described as 'idiots' or as 'simple' were ordered to be discharged as 'not fit to be kept'. However, pressure from parishes or families, or simple compassion, could lead to a softening of this hard line. In 1624, Robert Tedder *alias* Bennett was allowed to stay, despite being a 'simple fellow', because he 'did servise in the house', and Gabriel Shawler or Shaller, similarly described, was allowed back to Bethlem in November at the request of the parishioners of St Peter's, Paul's Wharf.[35]

Certain other forms of mental derangement or illness were evidently also considered not to be the concern of Bethlem. Those who had 'the falling sicknes' (like Humphrey Jellens in 1579) or who were 'somewhat distempered in [their] wits' (like Robert Kinge in 1606) do not appear to have been regarded as appropriate patients. Indeed, if they misbehaved themselves they were liable to be punished. Sometimes individuals were not admitted even though they were apparently regarded

Table 9.1 Ages of Bethlem inmates on admission, c. 1580–1633

Name	Admitted	Died	Age at death*	Age at entry	Source (entry)†	Source (death)‡
Willis, Edward	1629	1684	70	15	BCGM7/141v	RegStB/2/245
Whetstone, William	c. 1605	1624	35	16	BCGM6/368	RegStB/1/433
Burcott, Charles	1620	1625	23	18	BCGM6/177v	RegStB/2/436
Webster, An	>1598	1611	30	18–30		RegStB/1/370
Horsey, Percivall	>? 1612 §	1615	22	20–22		RegStB/1/382
Wallis, Ellene	>? 1612 §	1615	23	21–23		RegStB/1/382
Pounde, Susan	>1598	1608	30	21–30		RegStB/1/356
Jones, Alice ‖	>? 1612 §	1616	24	21–24	?Rep31/1/168	RegStB/1/385
Kewe, Bridget	>1598	1606	29	22–29		RegStB/1/351
Bromfeild, Rose	>1598	1606	30	22	BCGM4/51v	RegStB/1/325
Ellis, William	1617	1618¶	26	25	APC1615–7/392	RegStB/1/391
Lovelace, Mary	>? 1612 §	1616	30	27–30		RegStB/1/385
Mileay, Robert	>1612	1615	30	27–30	BCGM6/368	RegStB/1/381
Harries, Henry	>1598	1612	40	27–40		RegStB/1/372
Cartwright, William	>1600	1608	36	c. 28	BCGM4/191	RegStB/1/357
Felday, William	1624	1615	30	c. 29	BCGM6/368v	RegStB/1/435
Broadbent, Edward	>? 1612	1613	30	30		RegStB/1/375
Carter, Sara	1619	1635	47	31	BCGM6/368v	RegStB/2/23
'Welch Elizabeth'	1598	1608	46	c. 36	Rep31/1/168	RegStB/1/359
Pynfolde, William	>? 1612	1613	37	36–37		RegStB/1/375

Name					†BCGM	‡RegStB
Hamond, John	> 1614	1626	60	39–60	BCGM6/368v	RegStB/1/436
Shawler, Gabriel	c. 1604	1634	70	c. 40	BCGM6/368	RegStB/2/20
Hinde, Edward	>? 1612 §	1612	40	40		RegStB/1/374
Browne, Edmund	> 1598	1606	55	40–47	BCGM4/52	RegStB/1/352
Beste, George	>? 1612 §	1614	42	41–42		RegStB/1/378
Andrewes, Elizabeth	c. 1588	1605	60	c. 43	BCGM4/51v	RegStB/1/350
Cley, Anne	c. 1585	1607	66	c. 44	BCGM4/51v	RegStB/1/355
Baker, An	>? 1612 §	1613	44	44		RegStB/1/374
Williams, Elizabeth	1632	1636	50	46	BCGM7/289v	RegStB/2/24
Everet, Audreye	>? 1612 §	1613	47	47		RegStB/1/374
Dickenson, John	>? 1612 §	1612	54	54		RegStB/1/374
'Mother' Withers	> 1598	1609	68	58–68	BCGM6/362	RegStB/1/362
Marshall, Walter	> 1598	1609	68	58–68	BCGM6/364	RegStB/1/364
Parrett, Anne	c. 1610	1647	100	c. 63	BCGM6/386v	RegStB/2/92
Warde, John	> 1598	1602	66	63–66		RegStB/1/329
Browne, Jone	1624	1630	70	64	BCGM6/369v	RegStB/2/4
Lewes, Jone	>? 1612 §	1617	70	66–70	BCGM6/368	RegStB/1/388
Bohun, Lady Marye	> 1598	1608	140 [sic]	c. 90?		RegStB/1/357

* Age figures given in the St Botolph's registers are almost certainly estimates.
† BCGM volume and folio number (e.g. BCGM6/2), CA (Rep) volume (part) and folio numbers (e.g. Rep13/1/2), or Acts of the Privy Council, date (e.g. APC1556–8/36).
‡ Register of St Botolph's Bishopsgate, Volume number and folio number (e.g. RegStB2/123).
§ Not listed in the September 1612 visitation (CA Rep. 31/1/167–9/v), but this may only include inmates dependent on the city for their maintenance.
‖ Alice Jones may be the same person as Anne Jones, who is listed in the 1612 visitation.
¶ The only recorded suicide (by hanging) during this period.

as mad and met the normal admittance criteria. In 1562, for example, Margaret Armstrong was brought into Bridewell because she 'semed to be lunatyk and a troubler of the people', and was probably kept there. However, these apparently perverse decisions tended to occur at times when the Bridewell Governors were embarked on a policy of restricting admissions as part of a financial or political reaction: as in the 1570s and the late 1620s and early 1630s, when large numbers of 'counterfeit' lunatics were suddenly discovered.[36]

One other criterion which seems to have influenced whether or not an individual was admitted was patronage in its broadest sense. The Governors clearly regarded it as an abuse if other members of the City's magistracy, or external authorities and important individuals, sought to deposit mad relatives and servants in Bethlem at the expense of the Hospital. In the course of the 1624 visitation, they discovered that Deputy Alderman Whitwell had arranged for his niece to be admitted to the Hospital at Bethlem's charge ten weeks previously: her removal was instantly ordered. On the other hand, it is almost certainly significant that a number of Bethlem inmates had the same surname as past or future Keepers: between the 1540s and the 1630s, we find 'Mother Withers' (died, 1609), Anne Parratt (an inmate, c. 1612–24), John Lansdale ('a poore lunatique boy' admitted in 1626). It seems quite likely that Mrs Withers and Mrs Parratt were related to the Porter and Keeper of that name respectively (Humphrey Withers, who served between the 1630s and 1650s, and John Parrott, 1598–1605). John Lansdale, who was not so poor that his father could not contribute to his maintenance, may also have been a relative of Richard Lansdale, Keeper, 1605–14. Anne Parratt may perhaps have been admitted during Keeper Parrott's period of office (she was apparently sent to Bethlem on the order of the Court of Aldermen), but the other two were evidently not taken in while their namesakes were serving. If they benefited from some form of patronage, it seems likely to be the result of being members of local families or known to the Governors. This possibility is reinforced by the fact that there are a couple of examples of inmates of the same (relatively uncommon) name being admitted: Jone and Rose Bromfeild and William and Richard Whetstone. The Bromfeilds were almost certainly related, and Rose died as a parishioner of St Botolph's Bishopsgate – but not, it seems, in Bethlem Hospital.[37]

The evidence is hardly overwhelming, but it would not be altogether surprising if Bethlem tended to take in a disproportionate number of lunatics from the immediate area and if a disproportionate number of its offices were held by local people. And it would certainly not be surprising if local families with past or present members employed at Bethlem were disproportionately likely to place their mad or senile relatives there.

LENGTH OF STAY AND SURVIVAL AND RECOVERY RATES

Only two of the twenty inmates listed in 1598 had been admitted within a year of the visit; at least six had been in the Hospital eight years or longer. One had spent about twenty-five years in the place. A similar pattern has already been remarked on in relation to the inmates present in 1624, when seven of the thirty-one inmates had been in the Hospital for at least fourteen years. This suggests that a fair proportion of those admitted were not in fact curable, at least by Bethlem. It may of course be that the Keeper did not much care whether his charges were curable or not, so long as their maintainers continued to pay for their keep, and that the City found it impossible to refuse to take in even some patently incurable individuals if they were requested to admit them by a prominent person whose favour London needed to curry. But it is also possible that the assumptions which seem to have informed the admission criteria led to people who were in fact incurable being treated as though they could be cured: that it was assumed, for example, that those who had lost their wits were in principle curable, whereas those who were born idiotic or mad were not.

In any event, it is not the proportion of incurables found when one takes snapshots of Bethlem's population which matters, but the proportion of all those admitted over a period of time. Incurables stayed a disproportionate length of time, and so made up a disproportionate percentage of the population at any one moment. In the absence of anything like a complete list of admissions, the best one can do is to compare different snapshots. And what one finds then is that the turnover was quite high in the late sixteenth century and the early seventeenth, but that the system seems to have begun to clog up thereafter. That it did clog up is not surprising, given the cumulative effect of even a small number of long-stayers in a population which was under twenty for much of the period before 1620, although one wonders why this did not happen much earlier. Only one of the ten 'poor' listed in 1607 (an incomplete list) had been in Bethlem in 1598, when there were twenty inmates in all, although two had died in the Hospital in the meantime. The same person, Jone Bromfeild, was in 1612 the only surviving inmate from the 1598 list. By contrast, six of the thirteen present in 1612 were among the thirty-one inmates listed in 1624, and one had died meanwhile. Similarly, nine of the forty-four individuals despatched to Bethlem by the Bridewell Governors from 1618 onwards were there in 1624, and one who had been discharged for the second time sometime between 1621 and 1624 was readmitted in 1625.[38]

Recorded readmissions are not all that common, but that may be because it is rare to have a full picture of an individual's history. Sara Carter was certainly discharged and readmitted twice. The Governors ordered the discharge of Mary Fludd in 1620, although she was either not released or was readmitted at once, since she was said in 1624 to have been in the Hospital for about four years. The Governors' unavailing struggle to rid themselves of Gabriel Shawler or Shaller has already been mentioned. In her lengthy Bethlem career, Anne Parratt was reportedly 'divers times putt oute of the house and returned' by the Court of Aldermen or by the Mayor and Recorder. In July 1624 the Governors concluded that she was merely 'somewhat idle headed' and despatched her to the keeping of a Mrs Paulter. The following month she was readmitted, with Mr Paulter contributing a £2 down-payment and 6d a week towards her charges, which were otherwise to be defrayed by Bridewell. Mrs Parratt eventually died in Bethlem, having apparently reached the grand old age of a hundred.[39]

Not all attempts at discharge were this unsuccessful. After sixteen years in Bethlem, Margaret Ellis was pronounced cured and was sent back to her home parish. Agnes or Anne Banberry was discharged in 1610, after six months in the Hospital, and seems not have returned. However, whether these women had really recovered or were merely well enough to make it out of the precinct and stay there, there is unfortunately no way of knowing.[40]

CONCLUSION

In some respects, such as the restricted and modest institutional provision for the insane generally, medieval England resembled continental Europe. Aspects of Bethlem were also similar to the characteristics of its continental equivalents: it began specializing in looking after the insane at a time when such specialization, using a whole hospital or part of one, seems to have been becoming more common in Europe. The type of people it admitted, and the layout of the Hospital, likewise have parallels on the Continent. However, treatment and the administration of Bethlem remained on an informal, *ad hoc* basis for longer than was the case in continental hospitals serving similarly large centres of population.

On the whole, the Hospital does not appear to have been abused as a way of confining dangerous, anti-social or simply unwanted people, either by individuals or by the central or civic authorities. Administrative abuses did occur, but the main problem was, as has been said before, the inability or unwillingness of the Masters and their successor, the City of London, to maintain a close oversight of the Hospital.

Bethlem was primarily a place for keeping lunatics who were a menace to themselves or others, when nobody else would keep them safe: an asylum, in effect. Some extremely confused people were accepted, and in practice a few simpletons too, but the civic authorities tried hard to avoid this, even when these people were being fully maintained by others. Initially, perhaps simply because the demand from families and friends was not as great as it would later become, the strict admissions criteria seem to have been effective in keeping numbers down. By the beginning of the seventeenth century, however, the proportion of long-stayers seems to have risen and so, perhaps in consequence, had overall number of inmates. It may also be that the Hospital's policy of taking in the most violent and disorderly madmen and madwomen conflicted with its other aim, of accepting only curables.

NOTES

1 D. Knowles and R. N. Hadcock, *Medieval Religious Houses, England and Wales* (Harlow and London: Longman, 2nd edn, 1971), 351; Martha Carlin, 'Medieval English Hospitals', in L. Granshaw and R. Porter (eds), *The Hospital in History* (London: Routledge, 1989), 21–39, especially 33–4, 25; *The Survey of London: Contayning The Originall, Increase, Moderne Estate, and Government of that City . . . Begunne first by the Paines and Industry of Iohn Stow, in the yeere 1598 . . .* (London: Elizabeth Purslow, 1633), 452. 'A few establishments, of which St Bartholomew's hospitium in London is the best known, did certainly allow a few very disturbed patients who visited the church as a healing shrine to stay for a few days': Basil Clarke, *Mental Disorder in Earlier Britain: Exploratory Studies* (Cardiff: University of Wales Press, 1975), 83; Miri Rubin, *Charity and Community in Medieval Cambridge* (Cambridge and New York: CUP, 1987), 157; Chris Philo, 'The "Chaotic Spaces" of Medieval Madness: Thoughts on the English and Welsh Experience', in Mikuláš Teich, Roy Porter and Bo Gustafsson (eds), *Nature and Society*

in Historical Context (Cambridge: CUP, 1997), 51–90, especially 65–68 (suggesting that, despite the fact that some medieval hospital ordinances prohibited the admission of 'intolerable' patients, such as incurables, lepers, prostitutes, and the insane, hospitals were normally prepared to accept the mad).

2 John Henderson, 'The Hospitals of Late-medieval and Renaissance Florence: A Preliminary Survey', in L. Granshaw and R. Porter (eds), *The Hospital in History*, 63–92, especially 79, 75; Carole Rawcliffe, 'The Hospitals of Later Medieval London', *Medical History*, xxviii (1984), 1–21, especially 9, 20–1; Peregrine Horden, 'A Discipline of Relevance: The Historiography of the Later Medieval Hospital', *The Society for the Social History of Medicine*, i (1988), 359–74, especially 362, 365.

3 Horden, *op. cit.* 366; Henderson, *op. cit.* 79. For the early sixteenth-century Protestant Land-grave of Hesse's justification for re-founding the Hessian hospitals (that the existing religious institutions were 'sinful' and 'secularized'), see Christina Vanja, 'The Care for the Insane in the Hospitals of Hesse in the Sixteenth to the Eighteenth Centuries', in Norbert Fintzch and Robert Jütte (eds), *The Prerogative of Confinement* (Cambridge, CUP, 1997).

4 Horden, *op. cit.* 367; Carole Rawcliffe, '"Gret Criynge and Joly Chauntynge": Life, Death and Liturgy at St Giles's Hospital, Norwich, in the Thirteenth and Fourteenth Centuries', in Carole Rawcliffe, Roger Virgoe and Richard Wilson (eds), *Counties and Communities: Essays on East Anglian History Presented to Hassell Smith* (Centre of East Anglian Studies: University of East Anglia, forthcoming), 37–55.

5 Katherine Park, 'Medicine and Society in Medieval Europe, 500–1500', in Andrew Wear (ed.), *Medicine in Society: Historical Essays* (Cambridge: CUP, 1992), 59–90, especially 85–6; E. Coyecque, *L'Hôtel-Dieu de Paris*, 2 volumes (Paris: H. Champion, 1889, 1891), i, 98–100, 110 (before that, the Master had obtained drugs from local grocers).

6 Muriel Joerger, 'The Structure of the Hospital System in France in the Ancien Régime', in Robert Forster and Orest Ranum (eds), *Medicine and Society in France: Selections from the Annales: Economies, Societes, Civilizations, vi*, trans. Elborg Forster and Patricia M. Ranum (Baltimore and London: The Johns Hopkins University Press, 1980), 104–36, especially 106; L. Martz, *Poverty and Welfare in Hapsburg Spain: The Example of Toledo* (Cambridge/New York: CUP, 1983), 40, 50; George Rosen, *Madness in Society: Chapters in the Historical Sociology of Mental Illness* (London: Routledge & Kegan Paul, 1968), 139; Park, *op. cit.* 88–9; Coyecque, *op. cit.* i, 109; Nicholas Orme and Margaret Webster, *The English Hospital 1070–1570* (New Haven and London: Yale University Press, 1995), 91.

7 *CA Rep.* 31/1, fol. 169–9v; Thomas Lester Canavan, 'Madness and Enthusiasm in Burton's *Anatomy of Melancholy* and Swift's *Tale of a Tub*' (D.Phil. thesis, Columbia University, 1970), 18.

8 *BCGM* volume 6, fols 179, 183; *ibid.* volume 7, fol. 211.

9 The diet offered in Bethlem has to be deduced from the sources of gifts in kind described by Royal Commissioners in 1632 and from the brief details given by the Bridewell Governors who visited the Hospital in 1631; but it seems to have been identical in content if not amount to that provided for Bridewell's inmates: PRO SP16/224 no. 21, 4–5 (bread, beef, potage made with oatmeal, beer, confiscated meat of unspecified types), *BCGM* volume 7, fol. 217 (cheese); in January 1601, the diet of non-working Bridewell inmates consisted of 12 oz. of bread a day, $6\frac{1}{2}$ oz. of beef – replaced by cheese or butter on fast days – porridge, and a quart of beer: *ibid.* volume 4, fol. 213; *CSPD, 1633–4*, 22.

10 H. C. Maxwell-Lyte (ed.), *The Register of Thomas Bekyngton, Bishop of Bath and Wells, 1443–1465, Part I*, Somerset Record Society, xlix (1934), 59.

11 *BCGM* volume 3, fol. 322; British Library C18 E2, 'Fragmenta Antiqua . . . ', items 12*, 12, 13, 14.

12 *Report of the Charity Commissioners . . . concerning Charities in England and Wales*, 32 volumes (London: W. Clowes/HMSO, 1819–40), xxxii, part vi, 506.

13 *CA Rep.* 16, fol. 266; *Report of the Charity Commissioners . . .* , xxxii, part vi, 506; *BCGM* volume 4, fol. 51v; PRO C270/22, mm. 1, 5.

14 J. Gairdner (ed.), *The Historical Collections of a Citizen of London in the Fifteenth Century*, Camden Society, New Series, xvii (1876), ix. It is unlikely that the author or compiler of this passage was the skinner William Gregory, to whom it is usually ascribed, but he could well have been

either one of two Grocers who served as Mayor between 1468 and 1470, William Taylor and Richard Lee, Lee being the more likely candidate. The connection with the Grocers is of some interest, given that Grocers were initially involved in the provision of medicinal supplies: PRO C270/22, fol. 4.

15 *BCGM* volume 6, fol. 284*v*; *ibid.* 4, fol. 331*v*.

16 *Acts of the Privy Council 1542–7*, 388, 481, possibly also *ibid. 1552–4*, 288 (1553); *ibid. 1550–2*, 124; *ibid. 1552–4*, 72; *ibid. 1556–8*, 68.

17 *Acts of the Privy Council 1575–7*, 23, 299, xi, 88; *ibid. 1586–7*, 266; *ibid. 1591–2*, 51; *ibid. 1596–7*, 325, 374.

18 Records of the Privy Council have been published for 1386–1418 and 1422–60: Sir Harris Nicolas (ed.), *Proceedings of Ordinances of the Privy Council of England*, volumes i–vi; G. B. Harrison, *The Elizabethan Journals: Being a Record of those Things most Talked of during the Years 1591–1603* (London: Routledge & Kegan Paul, 1955), part ii, 27.

19 *BCGM* volume 5, fol. 338*v*; *ibid.* volume 6, fol. 15*v*. For an example of the modern belief that 'hostility to ordinary middle-class values [was in the past] associated instantly, automatically, with insanity, and insanity with confinement', see Max Byrd, *Visits to Bedlam: Madness and Literature in the Eighteenth Century* (Columbia, S.C.: University of South Carolina Press, 1974), 43.

20 *BCGM* volume 7, fols 57*v*, 29.

21 *BCGM* volume 6, fol. 181; *ibid.* volume 3, fol. 153.

22 *BCGM* volume 6, fol. 181; *ibid.* volume 3, fol. 153; *Acts of the Privy Council 1591–2*, 51; *BCGM* volume 4, fol. 31.

23 *BCGM* volume 1, fols 132, 181*v*; *ibid.* volume 5, fol. 425*v*; *ibid.* volume 7, fol. 80; *CA Rep. 12/2*, fol. 323; *BCGM* volume 6, fol. 184*v*. Lest it be thought that women were being discriminated against by *not* being labelled mad when they 'trobled the cytte' and the like, this also happened to men: *BCGM* volume 3, fol. 268; *Acts of the Privy Council 1630–31*, 108.

24 Byrd, *op. cit.* 42–4, 41.

25 *BCGM* volume 2, fols 47, 47*v*, 63; *ibid.* volume 6, fols 369*v*, 368*v*.

26 *CA Rep. 13/1*, fol. 123.

27 *BCGM* volume 3, fol. 256*v*; Richard Hunter and Ida Macalpine, *Three Hundred Years of Psychiatry 1535–1860: A History Presented in Selected English Texts* (London and New York: OUP, 1963), 40.

28 *CA Rep. 12/2*, fols 483*v*, 548; *ibid.* 18, fols 24–5 and 406; J. J. Lambert (ed.), *The Records of the Skinners Company of London, Edward I to James I* (London: Allen & Unwin, 1933), 238, 379; *CA Rep. 13/1*, fol. 100.

29 *BCGM* volume 6, fols 85, 232*v*. Other inmates were known only as 'Welsh Elizabeth', 'Rose', 'Hawnce [Hans]', 'Welsh Harry', 'Abraham', 'Black Will', 'Old Maddam', or 'Jone of the Hospital': *ibid.* volume 4, fol. 51*v*; *ibid.* volume 5, 197*v*; *ibid.* volume 2, fol. 126*v*; *ibid.* volume 4, fol. 191.

30 *Acts of the Privy Council 1621–23*, 449; M. S. Guiseppe (ed.), *Calendar of the Manuscripts of the Most Honorable the Marquess of Salisbury preserved at Hatfield House Hertfordshire, Part xviii (AD 1606)*, Historical Manuscripts Commission, ix (Dublin: HMSO, 1906), 470; A. W. Cornelius Hallam (ed.), *Register of St Botolph's Bishopsgate*, 3 volumes (published to subscribers, 1889–95), i, 357.

31 *BCGM* volume 6, fol. 433*v*.

32 *BCGM* volume 4, fol. 51*v*; *Register of St Botolph's Bishopsgate*, i, 362, 281, 355; *BCGM* volume 5, fol. 197*v*.

33 *BCGM* volume 4, fol. 51*v*; *CA Rep. 31/1*, fol. 168; *ibid.* volume 6, fols 368–8*v*; *Register of St Botolph's Bishopsgate*, i, 364.

34 *BCGM* volume 4, fol. 44; *Acts of the Privy Council 1591–2*, 51; *BCGM* volume 3, 54.

35 A. H. Thomas (ed.), *Calendar of Early Mayor's Court Rolls . . .* (London, New York, etc.: CUP, 1924), 155; *Report of the Commissioners . . .* , xxxii, part vi, 506; *BCGM* volume 6, fol. 368, 368*v*; *ibid.* volume 7, fol. 137*v*.

36 *BCGM* volume 3, 415*v*; *ibid.* volume 5, fol. 88*v*; *ibid.* volume 1, fol. 132; *ibid.* volume 2, fols 47, 47*v*, 98, 108*v*, 130*v*, 140*v*, *et seq.* to volume 3, 415*v*, and *ibid.* volume 7, fols 80, 100*v*, 109*v*, 115, 123*v*, 131, 137*v*, *et seq.*, to 241.

37 *Register of St Botolph's Bishopsgate*, i, 362; *CA Rep.* 31/1, fol. 168; *BCGM* volume 6, fols 386*v*, 433*v*; *ibid.* volume 4, fol. 51*v*, *Register of St Botolph's Bishopsgate*, i, 325; *CA Rep.* 31/1, fol. 168.

38 *BCGM* volume 5, fol. 197*v*; *ibid.* volume 4, fol. 51*v*; *CA Rep.* 31/1, fol. 168; *BCGM* volume 6, fols 368–8*v*, 200, 217, 260*v*, 274*v*, 278, 331*v*, 347, 368, 124, 230*v*, 390.

39 *BCGM* volume 6, fols 124, 230*v*, 390; 200, 205; *ibid.* fols 368*v*, 369*v*; *Register of St Botolph's Bishopsgate*, ii, 92.

40 *BCGM* volume 6, fols 386*v*, 389*v*; *ibid.* volume 5, fols 402, 435*v*.

IMAGES OF BEDLAM

———— •◦• ————

INTRODUCTION

It is easy to take the existence of 'Bedlam', the world gone mad, for granted. Insanely chaotic though the behaviour of some of Bethlem's inmates may have been, however, that alone would not necessarily have been enough to give 'Bedlam' its particular connotations or to make it so universal an English word for a state or even a world of mindless chaos. What was it that fixed Bethlem's *alter ego* so firmly in the popular consciousness and vocabulary – so firmly that it is much better-known today than the Hospital itself?

'A characteristic feature . . . occurring in several Jacobean and Caroline plays, is the inclusion of a scene set in "Bedlam".' Thomas Dekker included Bedlam scenes in *The Honest Whore, Part I* (1604) and *Northward Ho* (1607), co-written with John Webster. Similar scenes appeared in Webster's *The Duchess of Malfi* (1612), John Fletcher's *The Pilgrim* (c. 1621) and Thomas Middleton and William Rowley's *The Changeling* (1622). There are also references to Bedlam in a number of other plays of the same period, including Ben Jonson's *Epicoene, or The Silent Woman* (1609) and *Bartholomew Fair* (1614) and Philip Massinger's *A New Way to Pay Old Debts* (c. 1625). For some reason, the first quarter of the seventeenth century was a period in which playwrights seem first to have 'discovered' Bethlem as a dramatic resource. Both before and after that date, interest in Bedlam, apart from passing references or 'Bedlam Ballads', a rather different *genre*, was slight. It was very possibly as a result of the Jacobean playwrights' exploitation of the dramatic potential of Bethlem that the Hospital's *alter ego* developed.[1] But that is probably not the whole explanation. There seems in fact to be no one reason why 'Bedlam' developed. A conjunction of circumstances and the mentality of the times appear to offer the nearest thing to an explanation for what is, appropriately, an unfathomable riddle.

The image of Bethlem shown on the early seventeenth-century stages, and the effect this had on public attitudes towards the Hospital and its inmates, is interesting for other reasons. In view of the sparse and uninformative evidence about Bethlem staff and inmates provided by the Bridewell and City records, it is tempting to turn to the early seventeenth-century dramatists in the attempt to establish who did what in Bethlem, and to whom. Even if the playwrights were not being strictly representational when they described Bethlem in their works, they might none the less have captured the reality of the place, its atmosphere and interactions, more perfectly than a painstakingly accurate account could do.

In fact, it is suggested here, 'Bethlem' and 'Bedlam' were two quite different places. Even in *Northward Ho*, in which contemporary (seventeenth-century) characters play out their parts in contemporary Bishopsgate, Dekker and Webster were probably doing little more than exploiting the contrast between the familiarity of the context and the strangeness of the proceedings. This is, however, not to say that the Jacobean plays have nothing at all to tell us about Bethlem, or that the creation of its *alter ego* had no implications at all for the Hospital. On the contrary, the interplay, though subtle and difficult to track at this distance in time, provides a fascinating glimpse of the way in which life can be influenced by art.

THE EMERGENCE OF 'BEDLAM THE STATE'

'Bedlehem', 'Bedleem', and even 'Bedlam' are to found as variant forms of Bethlehem or Bethlem from the fourteenth century onwards. At some stage, this variant form ceased simply to be the colloquial name for the Hospital, and acquired a meaning of its own. It became both the synonym for and epitome of insane chaos: not a place merely, but a state. There is a considerable difference between describing any mad-house as a bedlam, or any mad person as a bedlamite/er, or even using the word bedlam as a synonym for madness, and employing it as a metaphor to describe an irrational world. In the first sense, Lord Hervey in 1804 wrote that 'Those virgins act a wise part Who hospitals and bedlams would explore', William Blundell in the 1670s wrote of 'A gentleman who passed as a Bedlamer', and Levinus Leminus in 1561 distinguished 'Bedlem madnesse' from other forms of insanity, such as 'losse of right witts, feeblenes of brayne, dittrye, phrensie, melancholike affections, furie and franticke fitts'. In the second sense, in the seventeenth century Michael Drayton wrote that 'This Isle is a meere Bedlam' and Abraham Cowley observed 'Thou dost . . . A Babel and a Bedlam grow.'[2]

Bedlam the state had certainly established itself in the consciousness of Englishmen by the Jacobean period. There must have been some reason why this metaphorical use of the word developed – so the evidence suggests – relatively late, probably not before 1600. Something about the physical place and its development, or about the psychology of the period during which this particular meaning developed, or both, must have contributed to the emergence of Bedlam the state. Possibly, the reverse may be true: in earlier periods, the absence of certain physical or psychological characteristics may have prevented the notion of 'Bedlam the state' gaining currency.

Picking up on a description by Chateaubriand of *Hamlet* as 'that tragedy of maniacs, that Royal Bedlam, in which every character is either crazed or criminal', Duncan Salkeld suggests a possible explanation for this phenomenon:

Bedlam scenes became popular in Renaissance drama probably because they depicted a single *locus* in which the spectacularity and strangeness of madness were contained. As a kind of theatre-space itself, a place where tragic and comic fictions of the mind were painfully lived out, Bedlam furnished dramatists with a resource of spectacular material.[3]

But that stills begs the question. *Why* did Jacobean playwrights use Bethlem in this way? Why did *they* do so, and not their predecessors or successors? Shakespeare was as fascinated by madness as anyone, but – despite Chateaubriand's perception of *Hamlet* as Bedlam writ large – neither Shakespeare nor his contemporaries used Bethlem as a theatre-within-a-theatre.

The explanation may in fact be relatively simple, and attributable to one or a combination of the physical developments in and around Bethlem Hospital. The building of the Theatre and the Curtain playhouses on the west side of Moorfields in 1576, the development of the Artillery Gardens as a place for firework displays in the sixteenth century and the relative proximity of Bishopsgate to the Tower, where the royal collection of exotic beasts was on show, produced a range of entertainments in the vicinity which of itself would have tended to encourage the idly curious to visit the Hospital, merely because it was easy to do and formed a natural extension to the round of pleasure.[4]

Possibly there was a deliberate attempt to exploit the Hospital's physical location. The Governors' criticism of the unclean state of the Hospital in 1598 could have been prompted by something more than a concern to make it less disgusting from the inmates' point of view. It was partly the fact that it was 'so loathsomily and filthely kept not fitt for any man *to come into*' (emphasis added) which exercised the visiting committee. 'Come into' might here equate to 'be admitted to', but, given that the Governors had already commented on the unfitness of the House as a dwelling, it seems more likely that what they had in mind at this point was that visitors might be put off. As, within limits, family members and friends could be relied on to continue visiting regardless, it was presumably the impact of the insanitary conditions on unrelated visitors which they had in mind. In other words, criticism of the Hospital may have been the product of the Governors' desire to encourage unrelated visitors. So one thing which may have changed between 1598 and 1632, by which time the Commissioners distinguished between 'friends of some of the distracted persons' and 'persons that come to see the House, and the prisoners', is that the Bridewell Governors had decided to increase revenues by exploiting the attraction of the Hospital as a spectacle.[5]

It is in any event not necessarily correct to assume that, because playwrights of the first half of the seventeenth century set scenes in bedlams and portrayed visits by well-to-do young men in search of diversion, this type of behaviour was common-place by 1600: much less, that it was a feature of Elizabethan social life.[6] There is little evidence that large numbers of people visited the Hospital itself for its enter-tainment or moral value in the sixteenth century: Sir Thomas More's comment that 'thou shalt in Bedleem see one laugh at the knocking of his head against a post' (1522) stands alone. As More had been Undersheriff of London, and moreover was living in Crosby Place, Bishopsgate Ward, at the time he wrote this, his familiarity with Bethlem and its inmates is not evidence that Londoners generally resorted to the Hospital. We do not, for instance, find the younger Pastons amusing themselves in the fifteenth century by popping into Bethlem, as young sprigs – and not-so-young sprigs, like Pepys and John Evelyn – did in the seventeenth century. The first undoubted reference to a real-life visit to see 'the shew of Bethlem' is from 1610, when Lord Percy spent 10s on a visit, possibly in company of 'Lady Penelope and his two sisters'.[7]

Jacobean playwrights may in fact have been unusually familiar with Bethlem, and it may have been their use of it in their plays which fostered interest in the Hospital as a place to visit casually, instead of the other way about. The fact that two of the earliest playhouses were so close by will of itself has meant that playwrights had more cause than most to be in the area of Bethlem. Possibly even more significant is the fact that the father of the actor Edward Alleyn, also called Edward, was the first City-appointed Keeper, succeeding Sir Peter Mewtys's deputy in 1546. Although Alleyn was succeeded in his turn by Richard Minnes in 1561, he still held the Master's ('Keeper's') House in 1575. Although the House had by then been divided into three and was sublet, and it is not certain that the Alleyns lived in any part of it, the family certainly continued to be parishioners of St Botolph's Bishopsgate after Alleyn had been persuaded to resign his office: Edward Alleyn junior was baptized in that church in 1566. Ben Jonson, too, was a sometime parishioner, his young son being buried in St Botolph's in 1600.[8] It is quite possible, therefore, that Alleyn's and Jonson's circles had a considerably greater acquaintance with Bethlem than most Londoners and visitors to the city.

Any or all of these circumstances might explain the familiarity of early Jacobean playwrights with Bethlem. That familiarity with Bethlem might explain the development of Bedlam as a theatre-within-a-theatre (a mirror-image or an *alter*-theatre). Late sixteenth-century literature and language abound with references to madness. Both the artificial fool, with his ability to say wise and dangerous things under the guise of talking nonsense, and the natural fool with his peculiar behaviour and utterances, were popular entertainers of the period. But bedlamites do not seem to have been much used in this role, even on the stage. To take *Lear* as an example, explicit entertainment and implicit moral instruction through the 'licensed jester' is delivered mainly by the fool and by the pretended madman, Edgar, whose existence in the wild may perhaps mean that he should be taken to represent the 'natural' fool. Towards the end of the Jacobean period, by contrast, the idea of Bethlem as an academy or school of folly, a place where 'mad-folks shall be tutors to me', became a popular one, rivalling if not displacing the fool as a source of wry commentary on the madness of the world. It may be that, as theatres developed, bedlam scenes were employed as an alternative and more flexible way of saying and doing the sort of things fools had long been doing in the semi-private arena of courts and great houses; like fools, bedlamites were quite often associated with morris dancing.[9]

Yet these explanations do not seem wholly satisfactory. Bedlam as an *alter*-theatre was merely a staging-post towards the development of Bedlam the looking-glass world or *alter*-state. For an explanation of the development of the *alter*-state, one must almost certainly look outside the theatre, and to the wider world. Natsu Hattori sees the use of Bedlam scenes in the Jacobean stage not merely as a dramatic device but as part of 'cultural perceptions of madness in society at large', and of a 'pervasive fascination with madness'. This reflected a growing fashionable preoccupation with 'melancholy', an illness which, like consumption in the nineteenth century, came to be regarded as an affliction to which the sensitive, the refined, or the intellectual individual was particularly prone: and, by extension, an illness from which the better sort of person might without indignity suffer. Yet 'melancholy' had been known for very many generations by the time it caught the interest of intellectuals and courtiers. It seems more likely that melancholy became interesting because there was an existing preoccupation with madness than that a fashionable taste for melancholy created an interest in madness generally.

The late Elizabethan and Jacobean fascination with madness was an aspect of the contemporary perception that the world itself had gone mad. As one of the characters in John Ford's *The Lovers Melancholy* says,

> I will not court the madness of the times; . . .
> When commonwealths
> Totter and reel from that nobility
> And ancient virtue which renowns the great,
> Who steer the helm of government, while mushrooms
> Grow up, and make new laws to license folly;
> Why should not I, a May-game, scorn the weight
> Of my sunk fortunes? snarl at the vices
> Which rot the land . . . ?
> This rule is certain,
> 'He that pursues his safety from the school
> Of state must learn to be a madman or a fool'.[10]

There was of course nothing new in the conceit that the world was, like Lord Byron, 'mad, bad and dangerous to know', and it remained a commonplace of later writing. None the less, there is something distinctive about the overall tone of many Jacobean plays: an unrelieved darkness, sometimes, and very often an amorality which stems not from the playwrights' exploitation of an audience's love of violence and sex, but from a sense that the world and its people are as irredeemable as they are irrational. King Lear, though maddened by suffering, remains a recognizably human character who is capable himself of learning from the fool and the real madman. What lessons do the characters or can the audience draw from *The Duchess of Malfi*?

Madness was perhaps particularly intriguing to late sixteenth- and early seventeenth-century playwrights because the apparently sharp distinction between the sane and the insane world could so easily melt. Hattori argues that there was an intimate connection in the Jacobean mind between madness and performance: it was through behaviour that madness manifested itself, and behaviour, particularly as stereotypes of 'mad behaviour' developed, was comparatively easy to mimic. Such stereotypes could readily become dramatic conventions or be counterfeited in real life by beggars. Indeed, no doubt nature sometimes imitated art, with the mentally ill soliciting assistance by exaggerating their behaviour, or modifying it in line with the responses of others. This mingling contrast highlights other contemporary themes, of 'the gap between appearances and reality, and the thin line' (often blurred to invisibility) 'between madness and sanity'.[11] Thus the mad could act as a mirror and their world as an anti-world to society. At the same time, they were part of the sane world, and the sane were part of their mad world. In short, nothing was what it appeared: an intriguing notion for a dramatist to play around with.

Many of the themes chosen by the Jacobean dramatists involved contrast and contradiction: alluding both to the might and to the vulnerability of government; to the increasing assertiveness of those who held power and to the way that dissenting views were increasingly challenging their authority; to the almost frenetic efforts made to achieve power and status and yet the irrationality and futility of attempting to do so. In pursuing these themes, the playwrights were examining and commenting upon the obsessions of their age. The sixteenth century and the early part of the seventeenth was a period when the power of the state and its intervention in areas which had once been governed by other authorities, such as the Church, seemed much greater than it had been. Although little that was thought, argued or done then was entirely new, it was pushed to new heights or greater extremes. Eternal verities had been discovered to be so much superstition: 'there were very many left puzzled, perplexed, bereft.'[12] On the other hand, 'state power' was, by modern standards, an extremely slight and fragile thing. Government was at once self-consciously assertive and conscious of its vulnerability. The majesty of monarchs, eventually elaborated into the theory of the divine right of kings, was itself a perception created in large measure by an extravagant pageant. By setting plays entirely or in part in such anarchic environments as Bedlam or Bartholomew Fair, in contrast to the courts of the mighty, or by mingling the two by importing Bedlam into a palace as Webster did in *The Duchess of Malfi*, Jacobean playwrights were able to highlight these contrasts and incongruities to their audiences in different ways and more subtly than would have been the case had they had to rely on wordplay alone. Or, as Nicholas Breton succinctly remarked in the 1630s, it was 'A Mad World, My Masters'; and its name was Bedlam.[13]

Once 'Bedlam' had become established, it took on a life of its own. Possibly it was the fact that later theatres were built further to the south, mainly on the banks of the Thames, so shifting the focus of playwrights' professional interest away from the Bishopsgate area, which led to the disappearance of Bedlam scenes from plays. Or possibly casual visiting was by the 1630s sufficiently commonplace for theatrical representations of Bethlem to be less attractive to playwrights or audiences. The real Bedlam was, perhaps, becoming too much of an entertainment in its own right; or too accessible, and hence too crowded and too full of unfashionable folk.[14]

REPRESENTATIONS OF BEDLAM AS EVIDENCE OF REALITY IN BETHLEM

What can those theatrical bedlams tell us about the real Bethlem?

It is very tempting to connect information found in the plays with evidence about Bethlem and its inhabitants: to assume, for example, that the Sweeper in Thomas Dekker's *The Honest Whore, Part I* was a forerunner of Robert Tedder, a 'simple fellow' rather than a lunatic, whose presence in the Hospital was excused by the visiting Governors in 1624 on the grounds that 'he doth servise in the house'. Perhaps, when in *Northward Ho* Dekker and Webster described what purports to be an actual visit to

Bethlem, a scene which includes a man who opens the gate to the visitors and says that he 'keeps' the madmen, together with his two deputies ('keepers'), we have here a portrait of the Keeper or Porter and two Basketmen.[15]

The temptation should however be resisted. Even on the relatively straightforward question of whether the 'keeper' had two assistants, Dekker and Webster were not necessarily good guides. At least, given that there was only one Basketman in 1607, both these assistants cannot have been Basketmen. Other possibilities suggest themselves: the Keeper, Porter (or Underkeeper) and the Basketman, perhaps? But it is equally possible, and in fact more likely, that the image of Cerberus was so familiar and apt that even those playwrights who did not explicitly compare the Bethlem Keeper and Officers to the three-headed watchdog of Hell could not resist the urge to invite the audience to make the comparison for itself.[16] Likewise, the Jacobean plays almost certainly do not show us the physical layout of the real-life Bethlem. The very fact that the visitors in *Northward Ho* walked straight into Bethlem (House, presumably) off Bishopsgate Street, and that the man who 'kept' the madmen was called Full-moone, should warn us that we are not dealing here with an entirely realistic portrait of Bethlem. When in *The Honest Whore, Part I* the Master, Father Anselmo, says of the Chapel that it 'stands hard by,/Vpon the west end of the Abbey wall', Dekker was evidently permitting himself some artistic licence: neither the Church nor the Chapel stood in that relationship to the Long House or Master's House.[17]

So plays like *Northward Ho* cannot safely be used to learn more about the staff of Bethlem or the Hospital's layout. Perhaps, however, they reveal more about the Hospital's inmates and the conditions in which they lived than the formal records do.

As far as the conditions are concerned, the answer is a mixed one. It has already been said that the impression given in *Northward Ho* that inmates had nothing but straw for bedding was almost certainly false (see Chapter 9). On the other hand, when the 'keeper', Full-moone, said that he could not allow a new inmate wood and coal for a fire, he was reflecting reality. There certainly were restrictions on the availability of fires, at least at some periods: in 1663 the Bridewell Governors ordered that henceforth only one fire should be maintained at the Hospital's charge (in the kitchen), unless visiting Governors ordered one to be lit in the parlour for themselves. This, however, merely demonstrates that there had previously been a tendency to light other fires, and the Governors did not forbid the lighting of fires if someone else paid for them. Of more relevance to Full-moone's response is the probability that, given the use of straw for 'dirty' inmates, and perhaps also as floor covering, it was too dangerous to allow inmates to have fires (braziers, presumably) in their 'rooms'.[18]

But what of the inmates themselves? Happily, the first plays to contain scenes set either in a 'Bedlam' or in Bethlem itself were written within a decade of the 1598 visitation. In *The Honest Whore, Part I* (1604), some of the characters decide to visit the local madhouse and persuade the Master, Father Anselmo, to allow them to talk to the quieter inmates. The first is a merchant, described as a 'very graue and wealthy Cittizen' who had been in the monastery for seven years, having gone mad after he lost all his possessions to pirates at sea. He is followed by two men, one of whom lost his reason after his beloved died, the other going mad as a result of an obsessive jealousy of his wife. In *Northward Ho* (1607), the mad characters are a musician who went insane after falling in love with an Italian dwarf and a prostitute who 'was frighted out of her wittes by fire'. The prostitute is particularly insistent that she was '[n]euer in bride-wel I protest, as Ime a virgin'.[19]

With the exception of the merchant, all these characters had gone mad because of some sexual or amorous deviance or mishap (the 'fire' which sent the prostitute out of her wits is undoubtedly a euphemism for syphilis). None of them seem to be particularly close to those who were actually in Bethlem in 1598, although they could perhaps have been based on earlier inmates or others like them: the merchant, Mr Bradye, or the naughtily behaved Katherine Fletcher, who in 1575 'most filthelie' ran about outside Bethlem house with her skirts hoisted up, 'shewinge her privie members' to the world at large, for example. Indeed, there was a perfect model for Dekker's prostitute, a woman called Elizabeth Rathbone, who was transferred to Bethlem from St Thomas's Hospital 'wher she was cured of the fowle disease [syphilis] and fell madd' – but this did not happen until 1624.[20]

This dissimilarity is all the more surprising, since in 1598 the inmates included Salvado Mendes, presumably a Spaniard, Constable Barwick, 'Welch Elizabeth', John Somerskall, who was supported by the Benchers of Grays Inn, and Anthony Greene, Fellow of Pembroke College, Cambridge. They all, even 'Hawnce' the Dutchman, seem so eminently suitable for caricatures. Very similar characters – the mad scholar, the insane justice, the lecherous madwoman, the Welshman mad for cheese – all appear in a single later play, Fletcher's *The Pilgrim*. But by this stage, or at least by 1624, the Bethlem inmates seem to have been a comparatively unexotic bunch.[21] Perhaps the visiting governors in 1624 failed to do justice to the inmates' peculiarities; possibly, behind the tame description of William Robertson of Hull, brother (in-law, presumably) of Mr Jackson, draper of Watling Street, there lurked an Englishman mad for ale. Or perhaps the explanation is that caricatures take time to develop, and then mature into altogether more fanciful images, so that Fletcher's characters are a distorted reflection of a much earlier reality. By the time Ned Ward was writing, at the end of the century, the stereotypes were so well-developed as to be caricatures of themselves. In this journalistic, and therefore supposedly fairly realistic account, not only is there a 'brawny Cerebus' guarding the iron-barred entrance, but the Bethlem inmates, wheeled on one by one in true dramatic style, include the commander of an army of eagles; a praiser of bread and cheese; a scholar of St John's College, Cambridge (a melancholy, musical man, naturally); one 'confined for the noble sin of drinking'; a man who spent his time trampling his conscience; a 'ranter against kingly government'; and a madwoman whose conversation was largely confined to such gems as 'blow wind blow'.[22]

Stage bedlamites, therefore, were the inhabitants of Bedlam, not Bethlem. There had of course to be some overlap between reality and fiction, in order to give the characters verisimilitude, but what the playwrights did was to exaggerate the more interesting or curious aspects of insane behaviour, or take up existing stereotypes. Indeed, far from portraying reality, they probably contributed to the creation of an unreality. For one of the things that the early seventeenth-century playwrights' interest in Bethlem in particular and in madness in general may well have done is to foster stereotypes of lunacy and give them greater currency than they would otherwise have had. Popular perceptions of what insanity was might well have fed back into and influenced reality, for example by creating stereotypical images in the minds of those assessing candidates for admission to Bethlem.

It is clear that the early-modern Governors of Bridewell found it difficult to tell who was mad and who was not. They made their pronouncements on the matter with conviction – as in 1575, when Mary Hollowell was brought into Bridewell for a second time 'for that she dothe counterfaite madnes and is not madde' – but did not necessarily stick to their guns. That same year, not only did Katherine Fletcher end up in Bethlem despite a firm statement that 'she [was] not madde', but Davy Richards, having been declared in August 'an Idle Person . . . counterfayting madnes', was none the less in the custody of the Keeper of Bethlem three months later.[23]

One case, that of Katherine Fletcher, is particularly interesting for what it may reveal about contemporary perceptions of madness. A month after the Bridewell Governors had agreed that Mrs Fletcher could stay on at Bethlem for a further month because she had nowhere else to go, she was packed off back to Barking, having, as has already been mentioned, disgraced herself by exposing herself publicly. The Governors seem to have regarded her as more bad than mad, despite the fact that she was behaving in a fashion which fitted the later stereotype of a female lunatic as one who lacked all sense of decency and self-restraint. Like the She-fool in John Fletcher's *The Pilgrim* (1621–2), who was said to be 'leacherous . . . as a she-ferret', madwomen were by then thought to be possessed of a gargantuan and untramelled sexual appetite.[24]

One possible explanation of the Bridewell Governors' failure to accept that Mrs Fletcher's rude behaviour was a sign of madness is that the 'licentious madwoman' stereotype had yet to develop. Another is that the stereotype *had* developed, or was developing, but the fact that it could be abused was already recognized. The Governors may have suspected a deliberate attempt to behave as, stereotypically, a madwoman was expected to behave. The fact is that Mrs Fletcher conducted herself in the outrageous way she did at just the moment when she was facing the probability of being expelled from Bethlem. She may very well have been hoping to avoid being sent away by persuading the sceptical Governors that she really was mad.

One effect of images of madness generally, therefore, may have been to influence how would-be inmates of Bethlem behaved. This in turn may have influenced the way that the Bridewell Governors responded to putative madmen and madwomen. The Governors' reaction to those whose disorderly conduct possibly indicated disordered wits certainly varied considerably. On the whole, it was only occasionally that they accused someone of feigning madness: it happened to one of the five pauper candidates for admission in 1519, for example. Between 1574 and 1577, however, the Bridewell Court records suggest that the Governors were very sceptical indeed about supposed lunatics: out of twelve individuals considered, eleven were adjudged to be counterfeiting. Likewise, in the period 1628 to 1630, eleven out of fourteen candidates for admission were in the Governors' opinions not mad: although they later changed their minds about one of the eleven.[25]

The Governors' scepticism in the 1570s may be explained, at least in part, by the fact that Bridewell had just assumed control of Bethlem and was engaged in a cleaning-out operation, with seven current inmates being either discharged or having the arrangements for their maintenance reviewed. The pressure on Bethlem's accommodation in the late 1620s doubtless created a reluctance to admit new inmates at this time. But there probably was more to short-lived preoccupations with 'counterfeit madmen' than this. The existence of a *corpus* of 'Bedlam Ballads' has already been mentioned. These songs typically featured a 'Tom' or 'Bess/Maudlin of Bedlam', and recounted the supposed ex-Bethlemite's tale of suffering in order to solicit alms: 'Poor Tom is very dry, one drink for charity.' Conceivably a few real ex-Bethlemites sang songs and recounted their tales. However, the ballads are sometimes polished pieces and certainly therefore artificial creations, and even more often have a tone which combines 'passive endurance . . . with a kind of taunting insurrection, indicative of a seditious underworld'. Their messages were created by and aimed at the sane.[26]

The heroes of these ballads were just the sort of counterfeit lunatics whose suspected trickery periodically so exercised the Bridewell Governors. Public concern about counterfeit beggars, particularly those who, like Anne Taylor in 1628, 'dissembleth herselfe to be distracted' and attacked anyone who refused to reward her act with money, was an aspect of a more general anxiety during the early modern period about 'vagabonds': rootless, masterless, idle people who were felt to prey upon society. In a work published in 1566, one Thomas Harman warned of 'Abram-men . . . that feign themselves to have been mad, and have been kept . . . in Bethlem . . . , and not one in twenty that ever came in prison for any such cause. Yet will they say how piteously and most extremely they have been beaten and dealt withal.' The ballads endured longer as a popular phenomenon than did the theatrical bedlams, keeping in the public mind the image of the wheedling, counterfeiting beggar. It was an image which may very well have loomed large in the minds of Bridewell's Governors at times, prompting them to see trickery where, as was perhaps the case with Thomas Jackson in 1628, there really was only 'the falling sickenesse'.[27]

CONCLUSION

Almost certainly the Bedlam scenes of Jacobean drama do not portray the reality of the contemporary Bethlem Hospital, any more than London's streets really did ring day and night to the harmonious solicitations of hawkers, as composed by Orlando Gibbons, or Elizabethan courtiers and princes spoke in the sculpted language of Shakespeare. Thomas More's poor mad fellow beating his head against the wall is one thing, the elusive mad wit of the theatrical bedlamite quite another. What the theatrical madmen say and do is largely a product of the playwrights' imaginations and their dramatic requirements. It is not reality but dramatic convention which is at issue when, as Dr Salkeld puts it, 'compelled to dance to the keeper's whip, the mad display the suppression of the naked by the force of naked power'.[28]

For a time, it seems, Bedlam scenes offered playwrights an effective and attractive means of expressing certain ideas about their world. If these scenes represent reality at all, it is in a very mannered and stereotypical way. To some extent, it is true, life may eventually have imitated art. It is possible that Bethlem inmates learned eventually that it would please their real-life audiences if they behaved in the sort of ways they had come to expect. But at most the inmates seem to have become skilful beggars, and perhaps 'put on a bit of a show' in terms of talking exaggerated nonsense or gesturing even more wildly and absurdly than they otherwise would have done. It was probably the sane, like Katherine Fletcher and the Bridewell Governors, who were most influenced by the images of 'bedlam madness'.

NOTES

1 Natsu Hattori, '"The Pleasure of your Bedlam": The Theatre of Madness in the Renaissance', *History of Psychiatry*, vi (1995), 283–308, especially 283, 293.

2 *Oxford English Dictionary*, *sub* 'bedlam'; J. William Hebel (ed.), *The Works of Michael Drayton*, 5 volumes (Oxford: Basil Blackwell, 1931–41), iii, 209; Duncan Salkeld, *Madness and Drama in the Age of Shakespeare* (Manchester and New York: Manchester University Press, 1993), 24.

3 Salkeld, *op. cit.* 88, 123.

4 Hattori, *op.cit.* 287; Henry T. Stephenson, *Shakespeare's London* (Westminster: Archibald Constable, 1905), 290–1, 295–7.

5 PRO SP16/224 no. 21, m. 5.

6 According to O'Donoghue, 'Everybody who lived in London or ever came to London visited Bethlem as a matter of course' – a large claim even by his own generous standards, and not one he attempted to substantiate: Edward G. O'Donoghue, *The Story of Bethlehem Hospital* (London: T. Fisher Unwin, 1914), 152.

7 D. O'Connor (ed.), *Sir Thomas More, Four Last Things* (London: Burns, Oates & Washbourne, 1935), 6; Stephenson, *op. cit.* 203; *Sixth Report of the Royal Commissioners on Historical Manuscripts: Part I, Report and Appendix* (London: Eyre & Spottiswoode, 1877), 229.

8 *BRHA* Muniment Book, 61–2; Stephenson, *op. cit.* 205; A. W. Cornelius Hallam (ed.), *The Registers of St Botolph, Bishopsgate London*, 3 volumes (published to subscribers, 1889–95) i, 84. Apparently William Shakespeare himself was a parishioner of St Helen's Bishopsgate (to the south of St Botolph's) in 1598, and another Elizabethan dramatist, Robert Greene, was buried in the new churchyard of Bethlem: Stephenson, *op. cit.* 205; John Heneage Jesse, *London and Its Celebrities*, 3 volumes (London: John C. Nimmo, 1901), i, 311.

9 For examples of Bedlam the school of fools and Bedlamite tutors, see Jonathan Andrews, 'Bedlam Revisited: A History of Bethlem Hospital, 1634–*c.* 1770' (Ph.D. thesis, University of London, 1991), 24–5 (citing Fletcher's *The Pilgrim* (*c.* 1621)), Robert Burton's *Anatomy of Melancholy* (1621), Middleton and Rowley's *The Changeling* (1622), Donald Lupton's *London and the Countrey Carbonadoed* (1632)); Sandra Billington, *A Social History of the Fool* (Sussex and New York: Harvester Press/St Martin's Press, 1984), 26, 32–3, 41, 43. In both *The Changeling* and *The Duchess of Malfi* one finds bedlamites dancing morris dances as a conclusion to their set pieces.

10 Hattori, *op. cit.* 283–5, 307; Havelock Ellis (ed.), *The Best Plays of John Ford* (London: Vizabelly, 1888), 14 (I, ii).

11 Hattori, *op. cit.* 307.

12 Susan Brigden, *London and the Reformation* (Oxford: Clarendon Press, 1989), 469.

13 Or, as Thomas Jordan put it in 1642, 'The world is all but madness': Billington, *op. cit.* 51. The theme of a mirror-image or topsy-turvy world was so common and strong in the mid-seventeenth century that it provided the title of a book on the period, Christopher Hill's *The World Turned Upside-Down: Radical Ideas during the English Revolution* (London: Temple Smith, 1972).

14 Although public theatres themselves may not in the early seventeenth century have been much frequented by the populace at large, because of the cost and the fact that performances were matinees and were, after 1586, confined to workdays (Monday to Saturday): Ann J. Cook, *The Privileged Playgoers of Shakespeare's London 1576–1642* (Princeton, Guildford: Princeton University Press, 1981), 8; Robert Ashton, 'Popular Entertainment and Social

Control in Later Elizabethan and Early Stuart London', *The London Journal*, ix (1983), 3–20, especially 5, 7–8.

15 Fredson Bowers (ed.), *The Dramatic Works of Thomas Dekker*, 4 volumes (Cambridge: CUP, 1953–61), ii, 458ff.; *BCGM* volume 6, fols 368, 298 (Treasurer to give Crooke a pair of shoes for Tedder).

16 For James Carkesse's later characterization of the Bethlem Porter as 'a Cerberus', see below, p. 292.

17 Bowers, *op. cit.* ii, 458, 94.

18 *Ibid.* ii, 461; *BCGM* (Rough Minute Book) 1662–64, fol. 56*v*; Robert R. Reed, *Bedlam on the Jacobean Stage* (Cambridge: Harvard University Press, 1952), 32. Reed's discussion is, however, inclined to take the evidence from the plays literally, and to read back into the early seventeenth century what is known from later periods.

19 Bowers, *op. cit.* ii, 98–102, 458–9, 461.

20 *BCGM* volume 2, fol. 140*v*; *ibid.* volume 6, fols 347, 368*v*.

21 Fredson Bowers (ed.), *The Dramatic Works in the Beaumont and Fletcher Canon*, 8 volumes (Cambridge, London, New York, etc.: CUP, 1966–92), vi, 161–6, 182–6; *BCGM* volume 6, fols 368–8*v*.

22 Arthur L. Hayward, *The London Spy: The Varieties and Vices of the Town Exposed to View, by Ned Ward* (London, Toronto, Melbourne and Sydney: Cassell, 1927), 52–5.

23 *BCGM* volume 1, fol. 181*v*, *ibid.* volume 2, fols 137, 98, 130*v*, 145, 173.

24 *BCGM* volume 2, 140*v*; Bowers, *The Dramatic Works in the Beaumont and Fletcher Canon*, vi, 162.

25 *BCGM* volume 7, fols 57*v*, 61, 68, 80, 91*v*, 100*v*, 109*v*, 115, 123*v*, 131, 141*v*, 147, 154, 190.

26 Hattori, *op. cit.* 289–93.

27 *BCGM* volume 7, fol. 80; A. V. Judges (ed.), *The Elizabethan Underworld: A Collection of Tudor and Early Stuart Tracts* . . . (London: George Routledge & Sons, 1930), 83, 86–7, 372. Bedlam Ballads remained popular throughout the seventeenth century: Hattori, *op. cit.* 290, fn. 29; *BCGM* volume 7, fol. 61.

28 Salkeld, *op. cit.* 123.

PART II

1633–1783

CHAPTER ELEVEN

BACKGROUND

———·◆·———

The disgracing of Helkiah Crooke brings down the curtain on the first act. By the early seventeenth century Bethlem had established itself as an institution. It was not just the chief – from some points of view, the *only* – receptacle for lunatics in England, but it had become a byword for lunacy itself: it was, as has been seen, both Bethlem hospital but also Bedlam, with all that that implied in terms of fame and name. The Crooke scandal reveals many of the tension-points around 1600: the relationship between the institution and its Master or Keeper was awry; the Keeper could exploit his charges; Bethlem's public image encouraged a compound vision of its inmates as lunatics, captives yet also lost souls. Bedlam had several masks: as a hospital, a bad dream of the damned, an inferno of cruelty.

During Crooke's career it remained unclear whether Bethlem was going to thrive as a valuable institution, or go down in the annals of history as a sink of corruption. On the positive side, the Crown had at least stepped in, apparently to cleanse the institution. Yet so many aspects of Stuart history show how Crown intercession could be a recipe for ruin not rescue.

It is to that wider relationship between Bethlem and the tide of affairs in Stuart and Hanoverian England that we must now turn. Bethlem must be set in the context of other institutions and ideologies: national change in politics and religion, the growth of London itself, the rise of other (and sometimes rival) receptacles for the insane, and, not least, changing attitudes and treatments of the insane.

It is no surprise that it was in London that the first English receptacle for lunatics had emerged. After all, the medieval City had become the nucleus of trade and manufactures, the focus of faith, the home of Parliament and of the Court. Throughout the Tudor and Stuart centuries, it expanded at an astonishing rate. Around 50,000 people were living there in 1500, but by the accession of Charles II in 1660 London's population had increased perhaps tenfold, and by 1800 it was already nearing a million.[1] London had become, by 1750, the largest city in Europe and probably the world – by 1820 it may have been the first 'million city' the world had seen.[2]

In the process, London became a very special sort of city. Particularly after the Restoration in 1660, the development of the West End brought its first residential quarter designed as a fashionable abode for the elite. At the same time, London became Europe's foremost financial and commercial city, supporting huge service industries and a flourishing cultural sector. People flocked to the dazzling metropolis; for some its streets seemed paved with gold, for others it was alluring because alive, a place where fashionable people could see and be seen.[3]

By 1700, London was emerging as one of the great culture cities, supporting theatres, shows, exhibitions, spectacles, coffee houses and taverns, one whose urban spaces and buoyant economy encouraged a throbbing street-life.[4] This London, graphically described by journalists like Ned Ward and artists like William Hogarth, was a haunt of faces, a city of spectators and voyeurs.[5] Bethlem played a part in making and reflecting that highly visible city. As will be discussed, it became one of the sights of London. Rebuilt on a new site in the 1670s, Bethlem was transformed into a great spectacular palace, a statement designed to display the benevolence and the solicitude of the citizens.

Yet London also grew full of ambiguities and contradictions. London suffered considerably from the Civil War, culminating in the beheading of Charles I in Whitehall in 1649. Tensions between King and Corporation, no less than between King and Parliament, had been precipitants of the great rebellion; the City sustained the Parliamentary cause throughout the war, financing it while its Puritan preachers provided spiritual cannon. During the Interregnum London became the national centre for extreme religious and political opinions that many regarded as crazy – by a nice irony, Oliver Cromwell's own porter ended up in Bethlem.[6] London was then devastated by the Great Plague of 1665 and by the Fire of 1666 (Bethlem escaped the flames).[7] The Restoration promised to heal wounds, but Court and Parliamentary politics grew more divided than ever thanks to a new 'rage of party', with violent divisions between Tory and Whig, Anglican and Dissenter.[8]

And the City's history grew physically and structurally divided, a tale of two cities, and more, split between the City of London – essentially the old Roman fortified settlement[9] – and the new West End, the fashionable aristocratic precinct, abutting onto Westminster, the centre of Parliament and the Court;[10] then, to the east of the Wall, there were the sprawling slums of the East End, living off the riches of the river; and the murky industrial waterfront south of the Thames, which, from 1815, would house Bethlem itself.[11] London's geographical contrasts point to a society increasingly split between rich and poor, patrician and plebeian, the rational and the rabble.

Bethlem had begun its career at Bishopsgate, just beyond the City walls. It moved in the 1670s to Moorfields, in a similarly liminal spot. There it was associated not just with the fortunes of the City, who supplied its Governors, but (in imagination at least) with other institutions on the verge of the City. Nearby Shoreditch had been one of the seedbeds of the Elizabethan theatre, prompting a conflation of madhouse and playhouse that was to prove long-lasting. Hard by Moorfields there also grew up Grub Street, the real and metaphorical abode of scribblers, hacks and poetasters – that new world of journalism and the media that irate contemporaries condemned as a mark of metropolitan madness – misrepresentation, fiction, speculation and imagination.[12] Hence Bethlem assumed an ambiguous place in a divided city.

Across Europe, the Baroque age of religious zeal and political turmoil culminated in an 'age of crisis', and then resolved itself in the stabilization of the *ancien régime* and the criticism of the Enlightenment. Understanding of mental derangement itself also underwent great change. The spectre of madness assumed greater prominence in the public mind. In England this was partly for political reasons. The tumults of the Civil War attracted the epithet 'madness': 'crazy' was a label bandied around and pinned upon enemies and extremists, especially so-called religious zealots and enthusiasts.[13]

Representations of madness thus became woven into a wider psychopathology and social pathology. Amongst the elite, physicians and philosophers deployed the term as a stigma: those who caused disorder were called disordered, those who created disturbance were diagnosed as disturbed. Madness became a football in Augustan culture, being kicked around in the writings of Pope, Swift and Johnson and in the caricatures of Hogarth. Those stepping out of line were increasingly vulnerable to being called mad – the fate in the eighteenth century, for example, of many Wesleyans and evangelicals.[14]

There was also a programmatic secularizing approach to madness, rejecting the old traditional notions of Divine and Diabolical madness, of madness as transcendental inspiration or bewitchment. Increasingly, madness fell under the gaze of the medical profession. The more madness was detached from an old religious culture, the more it became the subject of a specialism in itself; the mad ceased to be simply part of fallen humanity and became seen as a separate subgroup, needing help, confinement, treatment, and, not least, institutions.[15]

Nevertheless, before the Restoration, there is little evidence of moves to confine the mad, no emergence of other hospitals alongside Bethlem. Michael MacDonald's research into the practice of Shakespeare's younger contemporary, the physician-clergyman Richard Napier, confirms how rarely the mad were confined. In his dealings with thousands of disturbed folks who came to him to be healed, that Buckinghamshire clergyman would pray with them, give comfort, prescribe medicines, and proffer good counsel: he never advocated institutionalization. Throughout the seventeenth century and (though to a lesser degree) the eighteenth, the mad were typically kept at home and looked after by their families, or taken into parish care.[16] If Bethlem enjoyed something of an institutional monopoly in treating English madness and came to symbolize madness, its restraint and confinement were rather exceptional.

But there is evidence after 1660 of the slow emergence of new receptacles for the insane. These came in various forms. Some madhouses were temporary, others were permanent. Some were medical, some were run by clergy or self-styled healers; some were large, others small; some were for profit, others were charitable. The impression is of great heterogeneity and *ad hoc* solutions.[17]

We may see two trends in the development of institutions for the mad in the eighteenth century. One is the rise of charity asylums (somewhat along the lines of Bethlem) in large cities like Norwich, Manchester, Liverpool, York, Newcastle and Leicester. These institutions were funded by subscribers and managed by governors, with some honorific posts for medical men.[18] The other development – rather special to England – is the emergence of a private sector in the treatment of the mad, sometimes termed by contemporaries the 'trade in lunacy'. Individual entrepreneurs, some of them doctors (including Bethlem's own physicians), set up private lunatic asylums, often in their own homes, treating patients who might number from a handful to hundreds. Some were humane, competently managed, and therapeutically innovative; others were hellish.[19]

Their significance for our story lies in the fact that by the eighteenth century Bethlem lost its monopoly; parallel and rival institutions developed, and disparities in the way the mad were housed and treated – especially between rich and poor – began to emerge in starker relief. In 1751 St Luke's Asylum was set up just a stone's throw away from Moorfields; from then, Bethlem had to be on its mettle – and was more obviously open to criticism. With the nation increasingly perceiving an insanity problem, new ways of treating it won greater attention, with a growing number of books and pamphlets being published and madness becoming a topic of public discussion, especially with the madness of George III from 1788. In the new age of sensibility, madness might even be fashionable. From around 1750 Bethlem could no longer go its own sweet way unchallenged.[20]

Bethlem was in the public eye and would ignore public opinion at its peril. Without modernization and responsiveness, Bethlem was in grave danger of being regarded as old-fashioned, a relic of the past rather than a harbinger of the future. Exploration of such problems will occupy later chapters, and Bethlem's limping attempts to put its own house into order will be examined – moves largely overtaken by public concern and criticism that culminated in the Parliamentary Inquiry of 1815, an intrusion of the wider world of opinion and politics dealt with in Part III of this book.

How were mad people regarded in the seventeenth and eighteenth centuries? And how did such notions change? There was, of course, more than one model of madness. Image vied with counter-image, different religious and social groups had different views – medical, godly, legal, philosophical, proverbial – of what madness was and how it should be handled. It is crucial to avoid oversimplification.

Fierce debate has raged amongst historians as to how models of madness were changing in the age of reason. A pessimistic school of interpretation, typified perhaps by the French scholar, Michel Foucault, believes that the Renaissance era had entertained a passably positive view of madness – madness had had its own truth and could be associated with genius, artistic inspiration and religious revelation. In due course, however, madness came to be controlled and silenced, 'shut up' as part of the 'great confinement' instigated during the long eighteenth century. Such historians also maintain that the mad were assumed to be tantamount to wild animals. Some have stressed how the ideas of insanity changed with the 'new science' in the era of the Royal Society. Others have drawn attention to the new 'humanity' with which the mad were treated in the latter part of the eighteenth century, perhaps thanks to the beliefs of the Enlightenment. Such interpretations are not mutually exclusive – there never was a single image of the insane, nor indeed of Bethlem; notions of insanity were always contested.[21]

And that applies equally to the question of treatments. The eighteenth century brought a tendency to institutionalization. In some respects the trend towards putting lunatics behind bars confirmed notions that the mad were brutal or similar to criminals, sanctioning methods that were punitive, repressive and violent. Like nineteenth-century reformers, historians have dwelt on the manacles, chains and whips.[22] This has been portrayed as entirely consonant with the image of the insane as sub-human.

If the mad were brutal, they should be caged. Thus contemporary treatment has itself been seen as brutalizing, a matter of control, coercion and intimidation.

Doubtless such beliefs were common, and the mad were frequently badly treated. But by no means everybody held such views. Subsequent chapters will explore the beliefs of those who were running Bethlem, and the sorts of therapies there developed. Key questions will be explored. Exactly how were Bedlamites viewed? How were they treated? What philosophy underpinned Bethlem's practice? Was it one that was more honoured in the breach? Did the medical staff and the Governors make Bethlem an institution that lived up to its own ideals and philosophy, or was it permeated by that inner corruption frequently associated with the age of Walpole? These are some of the wider issues to which we now turn.[23]

EARLY MODERN BETHLEM: A HISTORY IN CAPSULE, 1633–1783

The scene reopens with Bethlem on its Bishopsgate site, a small charity catering for little more than thirty patients during the 1620s and less than fifty at mid-century. For much of the seventeenth century, in consonance with its modest size, and the rather low profile of its lunatic charges as a matter of public concern, Bethlem continued to take second place to Bridewell in its Governors' regard, as it had done since its union under Bridewell's administration in the sixteenth century. The Court of Governors' Minutes are dominated by the business of Bridewell. Governors' visitations of Bethlem were intermittent, and tended to reveal just how much the stewards, men servants (or basketmen) and maidservants of the Hospital continued to exploit their positions for peculation and profit, in the manner of former masters and keepers.

Even so, it was in this period that Bethlem began to assume many of the aspects of the more modern, medicalized institution dominant by the nineteenth century. From the 1630s, a separate medical establishment was introduced to Bethlem for the first time, with a visiting physician, surgeon and apothecary attending the patients, rather than medical care being dispensed or contracted by a lay or physician-keeper as formerly. Patients were admitted during the early part of the century in rather casual, if not mysterious circumstances, meaning that the Governors were often unaware on exactly whose warrant (if any) they were there. Subsequently, admission procedures were tightened up, with patients subjected by the 1650s to certification, and the Steward's records of patient turnover gradually being formalized by the 1680s into admission and discharge registers. By the early eighteenth century, Bethlem's affairs were being devolved more effectively onto committees, in particular on the Weekly Committee of Governors, which not only kept a tighter grip on the management of the Hospital's staff, buildings, provisioning, properties and tenants, but also vetted patients along with the Physician a week prior to their admission. From this time also, formalism in admission procedures was further assured by the standardizing of fees for patients, and the abolition of maintenance fees for curable patients.

Yet such changes also tell a story of some genuine loss of power on the part of patients' families and parishes. Prior to 1700, admission had tended to be negotiated directly by patients' friends and parishes on direct petition or application to the

Governors. Responsible parties (securities) bargained to secure maintenance, material care and even medicine and surgery at reduced rates from the Bridewell and Bethlem Court, outlining their circumstances of poverty. On the one hand, setting fees and granting regular abatements of such reinforced the Governors' sense of the charitable, sympathetic role they were performing, and graced concerns of control and extirpation with a tone of charitable beneficence. On the other hand, this pattern had the decided drawback that it often reduced admission and discharge of Bethlem patients essentially to a matter of economic exigency.

The great majority of Bethlem's patients were paupers, and from the metropolitan region, supported on (or with substantial contributions from) the poor rates, and in many ways Bethlem functioned as an adjunct to care of the sick under the Elizabethan Poor Law. Yet far from all of Bethlem's patients were poor, more than one-third tending to be supported on private means – and, even if specializing in the care of the insane poor, the Hospital should properly be characterized as a mixed institution. A substantial proportion of its patients also came from outside the City (for, after all, there were few other available institutions), especially from the home counties, but also from as far afield as Cornwall and Yorkshire, and the Hospital's catchment area clearly expanded considerably after its move to Moorfields. From 1700, however, and more especially from 1750, Bethlem began slowly to distance itself from the care of the poor, seeking, not altogether successfully at first, to privilege the admission of patients of private means and from the 'educated' classes.

Other major changes in admissions came with increased attempts by the Governors and Bethlem doctors to prioritize curable cases, involving occasional clear-outs of chronics and other unfit patients. The identification of a separate group of incurable patients, however, saw Bethlem caught up in a general counter-reaction of public sympathy for those chronically sick individuals excluded from the benefits of its own and other hospitals' charity. Indeed, inspired by a spate of charitable benefactions, Bethlem was at the forefront of a dramatic re-embracing of care of the incurable, erecting its own wards in the 1720s and 1730s for more than a hundred incurable male and female patients contemporaneously with provision for the incurably sick at metropolitan hospitals like Westminster and Guy's. The care of the incurably insane continued to be an important, if somewhat ambiguous, part of Bethlem's concerns well into the next century. In general, an enhanced effort by the Hospital and its medical staff to exert authority over the type of patients deemed suitable for admission may be discerned – and by the 1780s, a stronger element of medicalization is revealed by a decline in the number of patients discharged at the request of their families, and by heightened opposition to those who sought to remove patients or interfere in their treatment.

The treatment regime at Bethlem betrays perhaps the greatest continuity of all during the early modern period. The basic dominance of evacuative remedies – bleeding, purging and vomiting – seems to have continued virtually unchanged into the nineteenth century. Yet, as will be seen, there were periods of genuine innovation, in particular under the Physicianship of Edward Tyson, whose introduction *inter alia* of cold bathing, of a specific nurse for the physically sick, and of out-patient dispensing and a degree of material patient after-care, were forward-thinking initiatives worthy of considerable credit. Even under the Monros, certain initiatives were taken, in particular the erection of segregated infirmaries in the 1740s–60s, and the appointment of a resident apothecary and the establishment of an apothecary's shop to dispense medicines to in- and out-patients in the 1770s. From this date, in fact, it was increasingly the latter officer who undertook prime responsibility for the medical establishment and the day-to-day management of patients. Nevertheless, the inauguration in 1728 of a 26-year dynasty of Monros dominating the Hospital's Physicianship had, on the whole, meant increasing retrenchment and conservatism in Bethlem's medical regime.

Bethlem proved especially hidebound in response to the challenge represented by the foundation of the new generation of subscription lunatic asylums, and in particular to the establishment of St Luke's Hospital just across the way under the Physicianship of one of Bethlem's own Governors, William Battie. Criticisms of its antique therapeutics, of its medical regime's lack of openness (typified by its refusal to allow medical students onto its wards), received little but repudiation from the powerful majority on the Bethlem Board and from their Physician, John Monro. It took eighteen years after St Luke's ban on public visiting for Bethlem finally to accede to the weight of enlightened censure. However, as shall be seen, St Luke's was in practice not so radical a departure from the old, unreformed Bethlem as has been imagined, owing much to its predecessor, both in terms of its architectural form and in terms of its internal medical management and administrative organization. Nor did many of its ideals endure, and by the 1780s there was perhaps little distinguishing the medical care dispensed at the two establishments.

What clearly emerges is that there are many sides to the polemic surrounding the history of Bethlem. If the Hospital worked hard to promote a more flattering image of itself, visitors and others who recorded their observations about Bethlem also tended to have their own ideological axes to grind about what they had (or, indeed, had not) witnessed. Thus, while a celebratory poem allegedly written by a patient in the 1740s might claim that

> The Beds and Bedding are both warm and clean,
> Which to each Comer may be plainly seen[24]

visitors regularly reported a contrary verdict about hygiene standards. Contrariwise, although Swift and other Augustan satirists exposed 'the shit and stench' of Bethlem, the Hospital's own records reveal that its Governors were far from oblivious to the needs to keep patients 'sweete' and 'clean'. We must be careful to sift contemporary accounts as the constructions that they were.

While Bethlem has served as a paradigm of historical immutability in attitudes to and treatment of the insane, this monolithic vision of the institution's history is misleading. Considerable changes in the physical environment of Bethlem took place. Clearly, animalistic conceptions of insanity continued, to some extent, to justify keeping patients in rather squalid, stable-like conditions. Yet the environment at Bethlem and observations about it were affected by a growing divide between the foul and the fragrant, and what Corbin has termed a 'deodorising' or 'redefining [of] the intolerable' by the elite.[25] Contemporaries' and modern historians' characterizations of Bethlem as a squalid place of shit and stench, in which naked patients dabbled idly, may be partly validated by the Hospital's own records. Yet genuine ameliorations in the hygiene and in patient comfort were effected, for example, with the introduction of the Wardrobe Fund in the 1690s to outfit patients; with the standardization of Hospital clothing and bedding (at fixed prices) from the early eighteenth century, and with the banning of receipt of such materials from outside sources. Neither mechanical restraint, nor, more especially, whipping or beating, was the kind of indiscriminate feature of patients' lives at Bethlem described by modern observers. Indeed, from the mid-seventeenth century, staff were being strictly admonished not to beat or abuse patients; and even if staff fell short in their performance of Governors' standards, these standards were regularly reinforced. Segregation of the sexes was also maintained at Bethlem from (at least) early in the seventeenth century, although breaches still occurred and monitoring the situation was not made easy by the continuing and rather undermining presence of public visitors. Yet, by the 1760s, heightened awareness of the sensibilities of the insane – reflected most powerfully at Bethlem by the gradual curtailing of public visiting – is also increasingly discernible in Governors' Minutes legislating for the 'welfare' and 'comfort' of patients.

Bethlem's early and growing popularity as a resort for curious and idle visitors, out for fun or diversion, powerfully attested by the Bedlam scenes of Jacobean literature, was widened spectacularly in the 1670s with the Hospital's rebuilding at Moorfields. Indeed, that patients' liberty and therapy took a poor second place to the cosmetic concerns of spectacle and to the economic, civic and public relations interests of Bethlem's managers, was vividly reflected in the very design of the Moorfields building. Patients were not only forbidden to use the front gardens of new Bethlem, because the increase in the height of the front walls would spoil the view for visitors and passers-by, they were also, initially at least, forbidden to walk in the galleries out of anxiety that 'such persons as come to see the the said Lunatikes may goe in Danger of their Lives'.[26] New Bethlem's very gateway, crowned by the gargantuan, half-naked figures of 'melancholy and raving madness' (Plate 11.1), was itself an advert (as well as a warning) to the public of the madness that lurked within.

It was from this time, and in particular during the middle decades of the next century when visiting reached its peak, that Bethlem attained its apogee as a spectacle of scandal, in the public imagination a site of chaos and of all things mad. The well-rehearsed stories of ill-motivated abuse of patients, and of uproar and riots in galleries and cells, may certainly be corroborated. Yet the meanings of visiting the insane and the nature of patients' interactions with visitors were far more complex and varied than the simple picture of Bethlem as a human zoo would suggest. While Bedlamites were monsters, curiosities and good clean fun, they were also seen as moving exhortations to pity and sympathy, and as lessons to the mentally vulnerable, and it was clearly the latter motivations for visiting – and the fact that visiting was so profitable – that had encouraged Bethlem's Governors to sustain the practice well beyond the point at which opinion-leaders had become disenchanted.

Nor would it be fair to say that no patients benefited from visiting, for, according to their own and other contemporary testimony, the lives of many were brightened by sight and conversation with outsiders, and by the occasional present and tit-bit. Indeed, there were genuine drawbacks to the exclusion of the public. Most especially, patients lost an important link with the outside world, while their management was henceforth to proceed rather more behind closed doors, a period when the worst

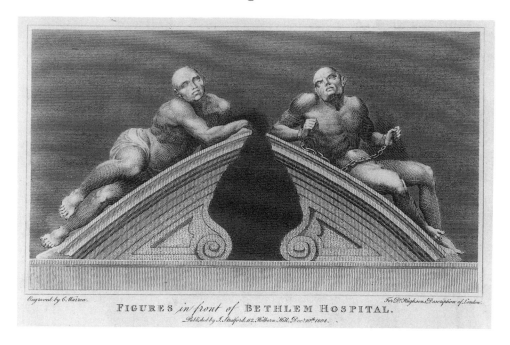

Engraved by C. Mirren.   For Dr. Hughson's Description of London.

FIGURES *in front of* BETHLEM HOSPITAL.

Published by J. Stratford, 112, Holborn Hill, Dec.10th 1808.

Plate 11.1 'Melancholy and Raving Madness', a print showing the statues attributed to Caius Gabriel Cibber: the figures are in the Bethlem Royal Hospital Archives and Museum. Reproduced by kind permission of the Wellcome Institute Library, London.

abuses seem to have been perpetrated – although, as the history of early Victorian Bethlem will demonstrate, the Hospital was never, before say 1850, far from the public eye.

Quite apart from the impact of changing sensibilities towards insanity as both disease and public spectacle, there were more practical reasons for Bethlem to close its doors to the world. By this time, benefactions and legacies had provided the Hospital with a much more secure financial footing in property, stocks and shares, its well-connected Governors and Treasurers taking real advantage of the opportunities for investment in City business and in the widening commercial, capitalist economy of the eighteenth century. Indeed, Bethlem had become increasingly self-financing, entering a new stage of independence and confidence, more secure in the belief that it could manage its own affairs.

NOTES

1 For a brief survey see Roy Porter, *London: A Social History* (London: Hamish Hamilton, 1994), chs 2–3, and the Bibliographical essay, pp. 394–5.
2 A. L. Beier and Roger Finlay (eds), *London 1500–1700. The Making of the Metropolis* (London: Longman, 1986), 168–96; E. A. Wrigley, 'A Simple Model of London's Importance in Changing English Society and Economy, 1650–1750', *Past and Present*, xxxvii (1967), 44–70; John Landers, *Death in the Metropolis: Studies in the Demographic History of London 1670–1830* (Cambridge: CUP, 1993).

3 See Roy Porter, *London: A Social History* (London: Hamish Hamilton, 1994), chs 5–7, and corresponding Bibliographical essay, pp. 395–6; M. D. George, *London Life in the Eighteenth Century* (Harmondsworth: Penguin, 1966).

4 For London as show and spectacle, see R. D. Altick, *The Shows of London: A Panoramic History of Exhibitions, 1600–1862* (Cambridge, Mass.: Belknap Press, 1978); on shops, see Dorothy Davis, *A History of Shopping* (London: Routledge & Kegan Paul, 1966); for metropolitan amusements, see M. Willson Disher, *Pleasures of London* (London: Robert Hale Limited, 1950).

5 On Hogarth's London see Roy Porter, 'Hogarth and London', in F. Ogée (ed.), *The Dumb Show. Image and Society in the Works of William Hogarth: Studies on Voltaire and the Eighteenth Century* (forthcoming), and the literature there cited.

6 Valerie Pearl, *London and the Outbreak of the Puritan Revolution. City Government and National Politics, 1625–43* (Oxford: OUP, 1961); Tai Liu, *Puritan London: A Study of Religion and Society in the City Parishes* (Newark: University of Delaware Press; London: Associated University Press, 1986).

7 On plague, see Walter G. Bell, *The Great Plague in London in 1665* (London: John Lane the Bodley Head Ltd, 1951); on the Fire, see Walter G. Bell, *The Great Fire of London in 1666*, rev. edn (London: the Bodley Head, 1951). Rebuilding is covered in Thomas F. Reddaway's *The Rebuilding of London After the Great Fire* (London: Jonathan Cape, 1940).

8 For politics and disorder see Gary Stuart De Krey, *A Fractured Society: The Politics of London in the First Age of Party 1688–1715* (Oxford: Clarendon Press, 1985); Tim Harris, *London Crowds in the Reign of Charles II: Propaganda and Politics from the Restoration until the Exclusion Crisis* (Cambridge and New York: CUP, 1987).

9 See Philip G. M. Dickson, *The Financial Revolution in England: A Study in the Development of Public Credit, 1688–1756* (London: Macmillan, 1967).

10 For the flowering of the West End, see M. C. Borer, *Mayfair: The Years of Grandeur* (London: W. H. Allen, 1975); Sir John N. Summerson, *Georgian London* (London: Barrie & Jenkins, 1970).

11 For the East End, see Michael Power, 'The Social Topography of Restoration London', in A. L. Beier and Roger Finlay (eds), *London 1500–1700: The Making of the Metropolis* (London: Longman, 1986), 199–23.

12 For the City and the theatre see R. R. Reed, *Bedlam on the Jacobean Stage* (Cambridge, Mass.: Harvard University Press, 1952); Max Byrd, *Visits to Bedlam: Madness and Literature in the Eighteenth Century* (Columbia: University of South Carolina Press, 1974).

13 Michael Heyd, *"Be Sober and Reasonable": The Critique of Enthusiasm in the Seventeenth and Early Eighteenth Centuries* (Leiden: E. J. Brill, 1995). On religion and madness, the work of Michael MacDonald is fundamental: 'Insanity and the Realities of History in Early Modern England', *Psychological Medicine*, xi (1981), 11–25; *idem*, 'Popular Beliefs about Mental Disorder in Early Modern England', in W. Eckhart and J. Geyer-Kordesch (eds), *Heilberufe und Kranke in 17 und 18 Jahrhundert* (Münster: Burgverlag, 1982), 148–73; *idem*, 'Religion, Social Change and Psychological Healing in England 1600–1800', in W. Sheils (ed.), *The Church and Healing* (Oxford: Basil Blackwell, 1982).

14 Fear of extremes and mental disorder are analysed in D. F. Bond, "'Distrust' of Imagination in English Neoclassicism', *Philological Quarterly*, xiv (1935), 54–89; *idem*, 'The Neoclassical Psychology of the Imagination', *English Literature and History*, iv (1937), 245–64.

15 For the medicalization of madness, see Akihito Suzuki, 'Mind and its Disease in Enlightenment British Medicine' (Ph.D. thesis, University of London, 1992).

16 Michael MacDonald, *Mystical Bedlam: Madness, Anxiety and Healing in Seventeenth Century England* (Cambridge: CUP, 1981); Akihito Suzuki, 'Lunacy in Seventeenth- and Eighteenth-Century England: Analysis of Quarter Sessions Records', Part I, *History of Psychiatry*, ii (1991), 437–56; Part II, iii (1992), 29–44; P. Rushton, 'Lunatics and Idiots: Mental Disability, the Community and the Poor Law in North-East England, 1600–1800', *Medical History*, xxxii (1988), 34–50.

17 For a survey, see Roy Porter, *Mind Forg'd Manacles: Madness and Psychiatry in England from Restoration to Regency* (London, Athlone Press, 1987; Penguin, 1990). For other therapeutic

institutions, see Donna T. Andrew, *Philanthropy and Police: London Charity in the Eighteenth Century* (Princeton, N.J.: Princeton University Press, 1990); Ruth K. McClure, *Coram's Children: The London Foundling Hospital in the Eighteenth Century* (New Haven, Conn.: Yale University Press, 1981).

18 See Mark Winston, 'The Bethel at Norwich: An Eighteenth-Century Hospital for Lunatics', *Medical History*, xxxviii (1994), 27–51; and Anne Digby, 'Changes in the Asylum: The Case of York, 1777–1815', *Economic History Review*, second series, xxxvii (1983), 218–39; *eadem, From York Lunatic Asylum to Bootham Park Hospital* (York: Borthwick Papers, no. 69, 1986).

19 William Llewellyn Parry-Jones, *The Trade in Lunacy: A Study of Private Madhouses in England in the Eighteenth and Nineteenth Centuries* (London: Routledge & Kegan Paul, 1971); for specific studies see L. D. Smith, 'Eighteenth-century Madhouse Practice: The Prouds of Bilston', *History of Psychiatry*, iii (1992), 45–52; *idem*, 'To Cure those Afflicted with the Disease of Insanity: Thomas Bakewell and Spring Vale Asylum', *History of Psychiatry*, iv (1993), 107–28.

20 C. N. French, *The Story of St. Luke's Hospital* (London: Heinemann Medical Books, 1951). For the King, see Richard Hunter and Ida Macalpine, *George III and the Mad-Business* (London: Allen Lane, 1969).

21 Michel Foucault, *La Folie et la Déraison: Histoire de la Folie à l'Age Classique* (Paris: Librairie Plon, 1961), trans. by Richard Howard and abridged as *Madness and Civilization: A History of Insanity in the Age of Reason* (London: Tavistock Publications, 1967). Foucault's book is evaluated in Arthur Still and Irving Velody (eds), *Rewriting the History of Madness: Studies in Foucault's 'Histoire de la Folie'* (London/New York: Routledge, 1992).

22 Andrew Scull, 'The Domestication of Madness', in Andrew Scull (ed.), *Social Order/Mental Disorder: Anglo-American Psychiatry in Historical Perspective* (London: Routledge, 1989), 54–79; and see more broadly *idem, The Most Solitary of Afflictions: Madness and Society in Britain, 1700–1900* (New Haven, Conn. and London: Yale University Press, 1993). For more 'humane' views, see Anne Digby, *Madness, Morality and Medicine. A Study of the York Retreat, 1796–1914* (Cambridge: CUP, 1985). For attempts to put the historiography of madness into perspective see Mark Micale and Roy Porter (eds), *Discovering the History of Psychiatry* (New York: OUP, 1994).

23 For the contentious image and contested state of Bethlem, see Patricia H. Allderidge, 'Bedlam: Fact or Fantasy?', in W. F. Bynum, Roy Porter and Michael Shepherd (eds), *The Anatomy of Madness*, vol. 2 (London: Tavistock, 1985), 17–33; Allan Ingram, *The Madhouse of Language: Writing and Reading Madness in the Eighteenth Century* (London/New York: Routledge, 1991).

24 *Bethlem. A Poem* (1714), in P. Allderidge, *Catalogue for Bethlem Royal Hospital Museum & Archives* (London: Bethlem Royal, 1976).

25 Alain Corbin, *The Foul and the Fragrant* (Cambridge: Harvard University Press, 1986), esp. chs 4 and 6.

26 *BCGM*, 5 May 1676, fol. 246.

CHAPTER TWELVE

'CHARITABLE PERSONS FOR EXCELLENT ENDS'

The administration and finance of Bethlem

— ·◆· —

INTRODUCTION

Bedlam as the Hogarthian house of crazy kings and bedlamite caricatures, or as the Swiftian 'Legion Club' of deranged parliamentarians is very familiar to historians of early modern madness.[1] Little, however, is known about the actual government and governance of Bethlem itself. This chapter will stress that the development of Bethlem's changing administration in this period can only be understood in relation to the development and growth of other city institutions, the Royal London Hospitals in particular. Moreover, Bethlem's complex history was deeply bound up with the wider development of the City, its government and society, as well as with that of the Crown, and with the general to-ings and fro-ings of City and court politics.

As we have seen (Chapter 5), Bethlem had been separately administered from the later sixteenth century by the joint Bridewell and Bethlem Court of Governors. While largely secularized, and freed (although not entirely) from Church politics and patronage in the arbitration of its offices and finances, it had also been a state institution – a City and a royal institution, whose Governors continued to owe allegiance to both powers. From the 1630s, despite and because of Bethlem's exposure to the scrutiny of a royal commission, Bethlem was to emerge as a City more than a royal institution, and ultimately as its own Governors' institution more than that of any other authority. As the period progressed, the Governors were to forge a rambling, often contradictory path towards autonomy and self-government. And yet, just as its image was the property of many, Bethlem could never really be the master of its own destiny. The institution was never, before the mid-nineteenth century, to be far removed from the watchful (or prying) eyes of outside authorities, many of whom were anyway as much insiders as outsiders. While Bethlem's patients became a microcosm of mad London, Bethlem's governance became a microcosm of London's governance. As we shall see, the growth of London as a corporation, and the ebbs and flows of City affairs, was intimately reflected in the way in which the Lord Mayor and the Courts of Aldermen and Common Council were able to exert a fluctuating control over the Hospital's government.

Chapter 15 will emphasize the nature of the Hospital as an architectural, cultural and political metaphor for Restoration and renewal. Restored Bethlem at Moorfields, however, also brought the Hospital to the centre stage of City political and cultural life in another way, attracting persons of distinction and influence to governorships, while concurrently granting both the City and royal authorities new opportunities for interference in the Hospital's affairs. Analogously, the Glorious Revolution of the 1680s was replicated in Bethlem (as at other City institutions) by a period of Glorious Revolution in the Hospital's own government.[2] The Court of Governors and the Hospitals which it administered became one of many major sites on which many of the leading players in the City's intersecting political, commercial and financial worlds struggled over patronage rights and over status and influence in the Hospitals' and the City's business. London's prodigious growth as a commercial and financial centre, partaking of a credit boom,[3] was to transform the way in which Bethlem and Bridewell were administered. In particular, it signalled Bethlem's emergence from its identity as an insecure, dependent charity towards an increasingly self-financing, self-determining hospital, with its finances relatively safe in capital and property investments and the metropolis's important bankers and financiers well represented on its governing courts. Concurrently, as new Bethlem was swept up in the journalistic explosion of the late seventeenth and eighteenth centuries,[4] newspapers were also becoming vital ways by which Bethlem's Governors were seeking to protect and promote the Hospital's interests, and by which they and others competed for positions within the Hospital, counterpointing their vying for positions of credit and status in the City.

THE GOVERNORS, THE CITY AND THE CROWN: BETHLEM'S GOVERNMENT

At this point it might be best to recap briefly. After Bethlem's donation from the Crown to the City in 1547, Edward VI's royal grant of Christ's, Bridewell and St Thomas's to the City dating from 1553 had formed the Mayor, Commonalty and Citizens of London into a corporate body as 'Governours of the Posessions Revenues and Goods of the same Hospitalls'.[5] This corporation was also empowered to make rules 'for the well governing of the hospitalls' and to elect officers and governors. In 1557, after a meeting at Christ's Hospital, the Hospitals (including St Bartholomew's, but apparently excluding Bethlem) were subsumed under a united government of two aldermen, as Controller-General and Treasurer, plus eight Governors. As outlined in Chapter 5, while Christ's was ordered to administer Bethlem, *de facto* the Hospitals all seem to have continued to be governed by the City. A further meeting at Christ's Hospital on St Matthew's Day in 1664 brought to an end what had been a rather unsatisfactory period of joint governorship. Governors were instead elected for each hospital, with Bethlem undergoing unification with Bridewell, London's house of correction. Henceforth, Bethlem and Bridewell were *de jure* administered by the same Court of Governors.

Concurrently, pursuant to an act of Common Council, the Court of Aldermen had drawn up (in 1557) a series of rules for the government of the four London hospitals. These rules defined *inter alia* how the Governors should be chosen, most importantly stipulating that elections should take place annually on St Matthew's Day at a General

Court in Christ's Hospital and that all new Governors were to be presented to and approved of by the Court of Aldermen. Subsequently, especially after about 1615, however, this form of confirming Governors' elections was allowed to lapse. The London Hospitals increasingly emphasized that it was in their own courts or general assemblies that Governors were chosen, the Bridewell Court, for example, ruling in 1631 'that henceforth no staffe be sent unto any new governor unlesse the same Governor be elected and chosen in an assembly or generall Courte here to be held'.[6] Lists were being sent to and confirmed at Christ's and before the city authorities without any attempt to contest or alter them. The London Hospitals thus grew increasingly accustomed to electing Governors in rather more casual, autonomous ways.[7]

This three-way split in authority over the Royal Hospitals, between the City, the Crown and the Governors themselves, was to cause repeated wrangles over their government and appointments throughout the seventeenth century. As indicated above and as Craig Rose's study has demonstrated, these wrangles broke out into full-blooded conflict during the course of the Glorious Revolution (1688) – when officers at Bethlem and Bridewell deemed disloyal to the government were displaced, only for restitutions and further displacements to take place once the political climate shifted again.[8] In fact, the Crown strove intermittently throughout the seventeenth century to make its authority over the Royal Hospitals stick. Particular attention was reserved to Bethlem, owing to the rather distinctive nature of the original charter by which mere 'custody' of the Hospital had been granted. The Crown continued to use Bethlem as a special place of detention for deranged individuals who had infringed on the royal person or property (see Chapter 19). Its authority also extended to intervening in other areas, especially the management of Bethlem's revenues and properties, and the election of its officers. In 1638, for example, Charles I confirmed in council the 'house & soyle' of the Hospital in the custody of the Mayor, Commonalty and City, as its Governors, but imposed new strictures on the ways in which Bethlem's lands and properties were to be leased. Later, when the Governors decided that Bethlem needed rebuilding at Moorfields, while cooperation was required from the City authorities, it was the Crown that had to be applied to for ultimate sanction.[9]

Only for brief periods, however, when the royal prerogative was more assured, was the Crown successful in exerting control. When in 1663, for example, John Moore attempted (via the King's letter) to secure a reversion to the Clerk's place, he was respectfully informed that reversions were against hospital 'custom and orders'. On having taken offence and 'Clapt on his hatt in the face of the Courte', furthermore, he was barred completely from future nomination.[10] The Crown succeeded in the turbulent 1680s in getting a royal commission appointed to manage the London Hospitals' affairs, which elected and confirmed governors and ensured the appointment of a number of royal candidates to hospital posts.[11] Yet this commission and its changes were short-lived. Feeling its own prerogative under threat, the Court of Aldermen had reiterated in 1682 its previous requirement that all elections of Governors for the Royal Hospitals be subject to its confirmation.[12] Simultaneously, an influential group amongst the Hospitals' own Governors were themselves struggling to enforce their rights to decide the Hospitals' affairs. The Court of Aldermen decided the election of the Bethlem Porter in 1687, while, in 1689, the Bridewell

Court pointedly rejected the application of the King's candidate for the Apothecary's post, sending a deputation to ask the Secretary of State that no further letters of recommendation be sent in future, 'but that the . . . Election . . . may be left to the Governors'.[13]

The importance of Mayoral and City authority over Bethlem and the London Hospitals cannot be stressed too highly. As the chief City magistrate, the Mayor was responsible for the committal of a wide variety of petty felons, vagrants, prostitutes and lunatics to Bridewell and Bethlem. In his capacity as the head of the Court of Aldermen and Commonalty, the Mayor was also the chief guardian of the government, property and revenues of the London Hospitals. Thus, in the 1640s, when Bethlem had grown so full that it was unable to receive a patient sent by Mayoral warrant, the ensuing investigation by the Mayor and Court of Aldermen into Bethlem's recently leased property provoked the addition of twenty extra cells for patients.[14] Business concerning Hospital leases continued to require the consent of the Mayor and Commonalty throughout the century.[15] When it came to other areas of Hospital business, however, in particular the conduct of elections, the majority in the Court of Governors had put up stern resistence to attempts by the Lord Mayor and City authorities to exert control. They ignored the Mayor's strong recommendations of a cousin as candidate for the Bridewell Portership in 1640, just as they had disregarded the Mayor's challenge in the election of the Clerk in 1626.[16] Likewise, when, in 1687, Sir William Turner had resigned as Alderman and President, the Governors were again at pains to assert their own prerogative to appoint a successor, without interference from the City – despite their own electee's attempt to uphold the City's prerogative.[17] Even more emphatically, in 1689, the Court cancelled the clause in the 'Charge' read to each newly elected Governor specifying that this was to be 'allowed by the Lord Maior and Courte of Aldermen'.[18]

With the question of prerogatives over the government of the Hospitals largely settled in the Governors' favour, the Governors were able to proceed after 1700 with their management of Bridewell and Bethlem with little direct interference from the Crown or the City.[19] Yet, some confusion and disagreement still remained. Most importantly, the rights of Common Councillors to be Governors had not always been consistently upheld, while the City had found itself becoming liable in legal proceedings concerning the Hospitals' rights and possessions. Not until 1782, however, was a comprehensive series of articles laid down by the Court of Common Council to settle these issues, confirming the right of the Common Council to appoint twelve governors to each of the four hospitals.[20] Nevertheless, the possibility of outside interference remained, and the nineteenth century was to usher in a new wave of inquiries by central government into goings on at Bethlem.

For much of this period then, Bridewell and Bethlem shared the same structure of government as that prevailing at the other three London hospitals, with the chief somewhat ceremonial position being that of President, flanked by the important posts of Treasurer, Auditor-General and Clerk. Presidencies of the London Hospitals were confined to Lord Mayors and the Aldermanry. Most of the Presidents of the united Hospitals during 1630–1770 seem to have been Lord Mayors at one time or another. Few, however, were Mayors when actually elected, and a number declined the office, typically making the excuse of business.[21] Subsequently, those aldermen who were not already presidents of hospitals or workhouses, or otherwise engaged, would be put into election, by the eighteenth century those in the Commission of Peace having priority.[22] Treasurers too were often aldermen, and occasionally Lord Mayors, common councilmen and/or MPs.[23] So too, were Auditor-Generals.[24] The top positions at the Hospitals were often held by more than one member of the same family, although rarely in succession or concurrently. During the eighteenth century, for example, two Rawlinsons served as President, two Alsops as Treasurer, and two Levetts as Auditor-General, while John Taylor was Treasurer at the same time as Joseph Taylor was Auditor-General. Selection of the higher offices at the Hospitals was not infrequently the occasion for political and social rivalries between candidates being played out – the Presidential election of 1755 being the best example and telling as to the continuing tensions between the City authorities and the Hospitals, and as to divided loyalties amongst the Governors.[25]

Despite their rather honorary role, some Presidents succeeded in stamping their authority more overtly on the business of the united hospitals. Sir William Turner, the wealthy merchant tailor and Whig magistrate, became a figure of considerable, if rather ambiguous, reputation whilst President (1669–88 and 1690–3). A onetime Lord Mayor of London (1669–70), renowned for his energy in overseeing the rebuilding of the City after the Great Fire, Turner also helped to see to Bethlem's rebuilding at Moorfields. While he was celebrated by some as a 'wise and just' administrator, and 'the City's Darling', he was notorious amongst others as a stern scourge of felons, prostitutes and beggars, they referring to his 'Flogging Spirit' – 'Whose Name to Harlots smells like Birch'.[26] Yet this, no doubt, says as much about the intensity of political differences at this time as it does about the character of his presidency. During the turbulent period of Whig reprisals and transitory Tory reversals preceding the Glorious Revolution, Turner was obliged to resign from the aldermanry and his presidency in 1688, only to resume it again in 1690 following the Whig victory.

The Treasurer took care of the Hospitals' finances, of which he was obliged to keep a regular account. He also had an important role to play in chairing Court and Committee sessions and having the casting vote in ballots in the absence of the President (and/or Lord Mayor).[27] In fact, the Treasurer was the officer who tended to be most at the centre of affairs in the Hospitals, his influential position and control over hospital finances, coupled with the extent of business he transacted presiding over small committees of governors, occasionally causing tensions with other jealous officers.[28]

The Auditor-General (presiding, from the eighteenth century, over a committee of auditor-governors) was responsible for the auditing of both hospitals' accounts, as well as the examination of the securities for the officers and patients. Rather less often than the Treasurer, he was also called upon intermittently to act as chair.[29]

The Clerk was responsible for the Hospitals' paperwork, including the drawing up, issuing and signing of warrants and bonds for the admission of patients to Bethlem; the drawing up of all the Hospitals' orders, petitions, annual accounts and agreements for leases; the issuing of summons for Courts and Committees; the copying out of lists of apprentices and governors; the writing up of the Court and Committee Minutes; and the actual receipt and recovery of hospital rents. The position was one of weighty responsibility, bringing with it a good salary and numerous perquisites, and attracted considerable competition whenever a vacancy arose, applicants by the early eighteenth century sometimes appearing in numbers over thirty at a time.[30]

For much of the seventeenth century, Bridewell and Bethlem were governed through Court of Governors meetings, which met between one and four times a month, with the aid of occasional committees. Affairs at Bethlem were overseen through a process of occasional visitations or 'views' by individual Governors and small committees of Governors, summoned for specific purposes, such as inspecting provisions, or repairs and properties. These committees were also often responsible for scrutinizing patients and staff.[31] In addition, Governors who lived close to the Hospital might also be asked to visit as often as they felt able.[32] This system left much to be desired, however, and reflected the rather inferior regard paid to the Hospital and its patients by the Governors. It tended to mean that insufficient responsibility was taken for managing Bethlem, that officers and servants were left too much to their own devices, and that abuses flourished and were little checked.

From *c.* 1700, the business of both Hospitals was increasingly devolved onto committees. The Bethlem Committee developed partially from the earlier committees for the inspection of provisions, but in particular from the building committees and other committees that were chosen from the 1670s onwards to manage the Hospital's rebuilding at Moorfields.[33] From 1677, the Bethlem Committee was composed of twenty Governors, supposed to meet fortnightly 'or oftener', with half their number being replaced every year; it was responsible for overseeing whatever was 'amisse' at Bethlem and what rules were expedient for its 'better Government'.[34] In addition, part of this committee met so as to be able to inspect hospital provisions. Initially monthly, from 1709 these ('Sub-') committees were made fortnightly, now regularly combining the viewing of provisions with vetting patient admission. Increasingly commonly they tended to meet weekly (becoming known as 'Weekly Committees'). Since the 1670s, the Bethlem Committee had been gradually expanded, so that for most of the eighteenth century it comprised forty-two Governors, elected every year with fourteen going off in rotation and with seven comprising the quorum who made up the Weekly Committee. The Committee generally only came together in its larger group as the 'Grand Committee' to deal with contracts, general financial matters and other extraordinary business. As a result of this committee management, General Court meetings were gradually restricted to very general business, elections and other more important financial and administrative matters, and although from 1736 they were supposed to be convened 'at least once in every Month' they often met less regularly.[35]

There were clearly considerable changes in the composition and size of these courts and committees over the course of the period. Reflecting the initially rather humble nature of the two institutions, little more than fifty made up the Court of Bridewell and Bethlem in the 1630s. By the 1700s, more than two hundred and seventy stood on the list of Governors, and over the next seven decades the Court felt compelled to strive to limit numbers by regularly suspending nominations for periods increasing from six months to eight years.[36] This strategy was only partially successful, however, as Governors were generally keen to retain the social privileges and rights of patronage that the office brought with it. By 1769, 325 were living, 190 of whom had the right to nominate new Governors at the next General Court.[37]

Attendance recorded at Court meetings before the 1670s ranged from less than ten to over forty, but was often lax. By the 1750s and 1760s attendance could reach peaks of well over two hundred Governors, although the average was around fifty,[38] tending to reach its apogee when elections of Governors and officers were to be decided,[39] although incomplete attendance lists mean that the real averages must have considerably exceeded this.

Court Minutes can only provide a limited impression of the role of Governors, however, and given that Bethlem's business was increasingly conducted through committees, conducted by a relatively small number of Governors, it is to these committee proceedings that we must turn. Grand Committee meetings were usually chaired by the Treasurer, with other senior officers and Governors filling in during his absences. All forty-two Governors rarely met for Grand Committee sessions, recorded attendance between 1710 and 1760 averaging between nine and sixteen. Sub-committees were generally even smaller, Governors' recorded attendance averaging between five and six during the period 1700–1720, with the Physician and Treasurer in almost constant attendance. Such patterns of committee service tended to introduce a rather more cliquish element into the running of the Hospital in the eighteenth century, with individuals, families and small groups of Governors able to exert considerable influence. Most of those officiating were the normal tradesmen and businessmen, although the professional and upper-middling sort seem to have been better represented at committees than they were at courts. Not untypically, the Bethlem Committee of 1711 included ten esquires, three common councillors, three military officers and two doctors amongst its forty-two members, and at least four seem to have been related by family. The requirement that committee membership be rotational ensured, to some extent, the sharing of committee responsibilities quite broadly across the members of the Court of Governors. Nevertheless, certain Governors and families of Governors served repeatedly on such committees over the years, encouraging their somewhat club-like atmosphere. In the 1790s, the Court attempted to further democratize attendance on committees, by reforming the system of rotation and notification, emphasizing the advantage to the Hospitals if every governor was granted 'an opportunity . . . to inform himselfe of the Business of the Hospitals'.[40]

THE GOVERNORS: WHO WERE THEY?

Who then were the Governors of Bridewell and Bethlem? And how did they conceive of their roles? What should be stressed from the outset is that far from the elite band of English aristocrats as once portrayed by Scull, their backgrounds better accord with the heterogeneous patterns of intermingling found at other contemporary medical institutions.[41] The vast majority of the Governors were recruited from the ranks of London's manufacturing and commercial classes – the craftsmen, tradesmen, retailers and businessmen who (at best) made up the City's labouring aristocracy. While many of these men were relatively prosperous in their trades and professions, and some were leading figures in City guilds and in commercial or financial houses, many were rather minor, humble figures, for whom a hospital governorship (or any number of institutional affiliations) might represent a means to bolster their social status and civic standing. A small but significant proportion of the Governors were also from the professional classes.

For example, amongst ninety-six Governors elected from September 1631 to September 1635, sixty-four were dealers and victuallers; twenty were craftsmen and semi-skilled labourers; and twelve were professionals (six scriveners, three divines, two apothecaries and one barber-surgeon). Not a single electee was from the aristocracy.

Dealers and craftsmen continued to dominate the governing courts throughout the period. However, as the London Hospitals in general grew and became more secure, self-financing and self-promoting bastions of civic virtues and influential arenas of city politics, and as Bethlem, in particular, became a larger more wealthy establishment, a markedly broader segment of the ruling, political and professional classes were attracted to positions on their Courts.

Between January 1685 and January 1695, of 108 Governors nominated for election whose occupations or titles were recorded, fifty-three were dealers and victuallers; eighteen were craftsmen or semi-skilled workers, while seventeen were professionals. At least twenty-one hailed from (or asserted) superior social backgrounds, three being knights, two being close relatives of knights, one being related to the Recorder of London, thirteen styling themselves esquires and two calling themselves gentlemen. Between March 1695 and March 1705, similar patterns are reflected amongst the 103 Governors nominated whose professions are recorded. While earls, lords and knights were prominently listed at the beginning of Court Minutes, in fact they generally made up less than 5 per cent of all those on the list of Governors. By 1800 their number had increased by between 1 or 2 per cent. Furthermore, a large number of these men came from the aldermanry, who had standing places as Governors, while attendance lists often only mentioned the most important participants.[42]

As the eighteenth century wore on there is evidence that governorship at Bridewell and Bethlem was becoming rather more of a closed shop, with lower-ranking tradesmen, craftsmen and semi-skilled labourers being elected less frequently, and MPs, landowners, city notables, the professions, financiers, lawyers, and leading tradesmen dominating the Hospitals' meetings and business. In the 1730s, the London papers were standardly speaking of new electees as 'gentlemen and eminent Tradesmen', or were emphasizing that a fair number were men 'of Quality and Distinction'.[43] Governorship was restricted to more mature males (i.e. 30 years old or above), although the order was repealed in the following decade.[44] The legal and medical professions were especially well-represented amongst the Governors, the prominence of the latter reflecting both the social aspirations of medical men and a genuine academic interest in the opportunities for observing a large group of the insane gathered together uniquely in one place. Notable amongst such Governors in the eighteenth century were a number of specialist mad-doctors, including Drs William Battie (Physician of St Luke's), elected in 1747; (Sir) Richard Blackmore, elected in 1696 (writer on nervous disorders); Nicholas Robinson (the mechanist and author of a famous treatise on spleen); Richard Mead (Physician to St Thomas's and writer on delirium and madness); and the Revd Dr Francis Willis, elected in 1789 soon after his first famous attendance of the 'mad' King George III.[45] Leading Anglican churchmen were also conspicuous figures amongst the Hospitals' Governors in this period, although such men might be as important in their roles as publicists and opinion leaders as for their professional backgrounds. They included Francis Atterbury, the Bishop of Rochester, who had been Chaplain at Bridewell (1693–1713) before his election in 1714 and had composed the new Governors' 'Charge' of 1708, as well as his friend, Jonathan Swift, satirist and Dean of St Patrick's, who was elected at the same time.[46] Conformity in religion had traditionally been highly valued by the Bridewell and Bethlem Governors. It was reflected in their choices of Ministers and other officers for the Hospitals, and was impressed on all Governors by the 'antient custome' of requiring two, by turns, to attend divine service at the Bridewell Chapel every Sunday.[47] William Hogarth was also made a Governor of the Hospitals in 1752.[48]

The election of Governors required a nomination from an existing Governor.[49] Encouraged by this system of nomination, governorships tended intimately to reflect family and business relationships. For example, of ninety-nine nominees recorded in 1776, at least fourteen were from the families of the recommending Governors.[50] Nominations also tended to specify the addresses of nominees, clearly important for reassuring the Court of Governors that prospective members came from the right kind of areas.[51]

Sometimes, governorships were conferred as a mark of recognition and respect for individuals who had attained a particular social status.[52] Aldermen and certain common councillors were *de jure* elected governors of the City Hospitals during their periods of office, and sheriffs too were almost automatic choices as Governors.[53] Wardens and Masters of the London Companies were similarly virtually automatic Governors, as were the City Chamberlain and the Recorder of London.[54] Indeed, the governing court was in part a microcosm of City political and commercial life.

The professional and occupational backgrounds of Governors were often called into play to expedite the business of the Hospitals. Governors as fellow parishioners, relatives, employers, associates and acquaintances of patients and their friends, frequently interposed in recommending and securing admissions, or in negotiating maintenance fees and arrears.[55] Lawyer-governors counselled on the procurement of legacies, benefactions, maintenance fees and rent arrears; medical-governors on the quality of medicines and the erection of an apothecary's shop or dispensary; brewer-governors on the erection of a brewhouse at Bethlem; and victualler-governors on provisions.[56] While the servant classes were normally debarred from officiating as Governors by their inferior social status, higher-ranking officers not uncommonly consolidated an elevated social ranking through election as a Hospital Governor – for example, Tennison, the Archbishop of Canterbury's Steward, elected in 1700.[57] Some exploited their governorships to procure contracts for the supply of provisions – however partisanship on the part of the Court was mitigated by its determination to secure supplies of appropriate quantity and quality.[58] Others seem to have used their governorships to engineer election to office. When the Minister's place fell vacant in 1676, for example, the Court declared 'that such Governors . . . that are willing that any friend or acquaintance of theirs should be putt into nominacon and preach for the same place' should present their names to the next court.[59] William Kinleside had been a Governor for sixteen years when elected Treasurer in 1768.[60] Governors also often prevailed over other candidates in attaining posts as Stewards of Bridewell and

Bethlem. Although some were subsequently obliged to lay down their staffs, by the eighteenth century being a Hospital officer was no longer a bar to holding a governorship and not until 1743 were officers prohibited from nominating others as Governors.[61] Despite the barring of medical officers from being Governors in 1678, this order was subsequently rescinded and, for much of the period, Bethlem and Bridewell's medical staff were generally elected as Governors.[62] While this ensured a degree of loyalty it also furthered the 'jobs for the boys' atmosphere in which Hospital business and the medical establishment were too frequently conducted (see Chapter 16).

Governors had to be citizens of London. They might be freemen or unfreemen, although the former tended to predominate over the latter and were apt to claim seniority. Pecking orders amongst Governors were vital and the source of considerable negotiation, political interest, length of service and social status being the major determinants – the latter criterion distinguishing one group of governors from the rest in seniority as 'the Gentlemen of the Long Robe' (Aldermen were distinguished as 'of the grey robe').[63]

Of course, not all those nominated as Governors were elected to office, some dying and a few others being deemed unsuitable. Election was not automatic, nominations requiring confirmation. The Court attempted intermittently to place governorships under closer scrutiny, from 1673 stipulating a month for nominations to be considered.[64] Exceptionally, those elected as Governors even declined the charge, the plasterer, William Alice, for example, deciding in 1632 that his 'leisure time' would not allow him the luxury of attending the office[65] – a sign perhaps of how exacting of their time service as a governor might be, or alternatively of the casual, hobby-like way others accepted the undertaking. In the seventeenth century, the Court attempted to ensure that the schedules of its busy members did not prevent them from regularly attending, restricting Court days to Fridays (or Wednesdays) and requiring that Governors arrive before 8 a.m. 'that they may goe hence to the Exchange and about their owne Occacions'.[66] While governorships were, to a large extent, honorary and ceremonial in function, periodic attendance at general courts and on important election days was seen as rather more essential, and occasionally the Court assembled to strike off Governors who had failed sufficiently to attend.[67]

Hospital governorships were also purchasable, either via benefactions, or through a specific donation of £100 (or more), the latter custom becoming particularly established around 1750 (helped on, no doubt, by the growth of subscription hospitals).[68] For much of the period governorships had granted holders the possibility of negotiating other financially lucrative privileges and offices within the Hospitals, but gradually these opportunities were curtailed by the Court – in line with general, if rather inconsistent, moves in early modern institutions to restrict the licence for corruption and conflicting interests that their management had often furnished. As Chapter 14 outlines, while governorships at Bridewell and Bethlem had been a means for the Hospitals' existing or prospective tenants to help to secure their interests[69] (whereas tenants who were 'mere stranger[s] to the Governors', or 'never cometh to Church', could expect rather less sympathy),[70] such preferential bargaining was subsequently banned.[71] In 1755 Governors were also prohibited from being involved in contracting to supply the Hospitals with provisions, and in building work for the Hospitals.[72]

What motivated individuals to become governors, then, and how did they conceive of their functions? Hospitals in this period provided the focus for a wide range of mixed and often competing interests.[73] Hospital governorship conveyed a social cachet, as well as material benefits. Service as a Governor also emphasized an individual's standing as a good citizen, appreciative of his civic duties. While election was often a result of and was reflective of the importance of patronage in the attainment of public office, employment and social status, it was also itself a means to establish and cement familial, business, political and other useful associations. Election of officers was a vital way in which patronage might be dispensed and inter-personal links built up by Governors. The amount of fuss over procedures in elections and the frequency with which 'heats and misunderstandings' seem to have arisen during them are clear signs of how fiercely such interests were fought over, hospital elections mirroring the factionalism and dogged electioneering so much in evidence in contemporary Parliamentary elections.[74]

Some Governors were also motivated by more spiritual feelings of beneficence, charity and humanitarianism – seeing themselves as in the service of God and of more metaphysical virtues – that responsibility over institutions for the needy, the disorderly and the lunatic signified.[75] Concurrently, they regarded their office as one of serving the interests of the Hospitals as public charities, as well as serving the greater good of the City.[76] The weight and honour of office as a Governor was communicated in the conveyance of a green staff of office to every newly elected governor, as well as by the wearing of gowns or cloaks of office, which were employed at court and ceremonial occasions.[77] It was also underlined by the Governors' Charge read to each individual on his election, which described the office as 'a Station of great trust & influence & will provide you many opportunities of promoting God's Glory and the Good of your fellow Creatures'. Here, in addition, the charitable nature of the Hospitals' functions was impressed on the Governor, who was called upon to undertake 'the distribution of the revenues designed by Charitable persons for . . . Excellent Ends' and was

> earnestly desired to discharge your duty . . . in such a conscientious Regard as that you may appear with joy at the Judgment Seat of Christ where a particular account will be taken of all the offices of Charity . . . and a particular reward conferred on those who have with fidelity and Zeal performed them.[78]

However, one should not underestimate other concerns with public order, the extirpation of vice and the reformation of manners and morals, also associated with provision for the insane – presumably rendered all the more acute by the Governors' combined oversight of both the Bethlem lunatics and the flotsam and jetsam of Bridewell. The Governors' Charge defined the Hospitals' ends as 'Employing idle and Vagrant and correcting lewd and disorderly persons . . . Educating Poor Children in honest Trades and . . . cureing needy deplorable Lunaticks'. Not all Governors took their positions so seriously. Indeed, they sometimes showed themselves thoroughly unsuitable for office by bringing down disrepute on the Hospitals. In 1639, for example, some unnamed Governors were suspended for being frequently drunk at Court meetings.[79]

THE POLITICS OF THE GOVERNORS

It would be wrong to portray the Bridewell and Bethlem Governors as a unified, homogeneous grouping. Rivalries between royal and City authorities over control and patronage of the Hospitals, alongside the Governors' own increasing efforts at self-determination, were reflected by divided loyalties within the Governors' own ranks. The obtaining, holding and conduct of public office was frequently a source and site of scandal and faction in this period, as competing individuals and groups struggled for political supremacy and for patronage rights. Hospitals also strove to be protective of their public image, and their Governors sometimes appear more concerned about the manner in which criticisms of Hospital policies and the transaction of Hospital business were expressed, than whether they were valid or not. Criticisms were apt to raise considerable umbrage if publicized abroad. Complaints from outsiders could be dismissed as ill-informed and *infra dig*, while those emerging from members of the Governors' own ranks exposed the complainant to accusations of disloyalty and partisanship.

Such issues help to explain why the Governors of Bridewell and Bethlem were so slow to react to public criticisms of the practice of visiting lunatics (See Chapter 13), and why sometimes they appear slack in addressing alleged abuses. The treatment of the Governor, Sir William Bolton, when serving as a member of the building committee responsible for supervising the erection of New Bethlem in the 1670s, exemplifies these issues very well, and illustrates how divided Governors' loyalties might be. In 1674, when Bolton (most vociferously, amongst a group of Governors) criticized the materials and workmanship in the new building, a special committee of Governors, surveyors and builders not only vindicated the workmen and building committee, but persuaded the Court to pass a verdict of censure on Bolton, declaring his 'Reflections' 'false and scandalous' and his 'ends' 'private and sinister'.[80] However, the Court seems to have been just as worried about Bolton having 'blaze[d] the same [criticisms] abroad' as about the accuracy of his charges. Indeed, 120 years later, a published report on the condition of Bethlem declared a rather contemptuous (if slightly anachronistic) judgment on the original workmanship and materials used in the Moorfields building.[81] No doubt, as much as it was about either good workmanship or loyalty to the Hospitals' interests, this conflict was also about the old rivalries between the politics of City and Court factions. A champion of City government and former Lord Mayor (1666–7), who had tactfully defended the City interest against the royal prerogative on a number of occasions, Bolton was also well represented at the Royal Court and regarded as a good servant of the Crown. Within six months of being censured he was restored to his governorship through the interest he enjoyed with the King.

Midway through the next century, a detailed series of complaints from another concerned (but anonymous) observer were also dismissed by the Court of Governors.[82] In this instance the complainant had attempted to blackmail the Court into remedying the 'Irregularitys' he identified by threatening to publish them in the press 'since printing is become so fashionable'. His allegations concerning Bethlem focused on corruption and exploitation by staff, public visiting, and the consumption of alcohol, and plainly indicate that he was an insider, well-informed about the

Hospitals – probably being a disaffected Governor. His complaints that money was extorted from patients' friends when they came to deliver or collect bedding; that 'the Holyday behaviour in that Hospital' was 'a Nuisance to the Inhabitants & a scandal to passengers'; and that 'large Quantitys of strong Liquor' were 'carried in daily which gives great offence to all who observe it', suggest a rather puritanical bias. Yet they were reiterated by a number of others who criticized Bethlem's management, and clearly had more than a kernel of truth. Moreover, the response of the Bethlem Committee, endorsed by the Court of Governors, can at best be seen as rather complacent, and at worst as something of a whitewash. To the first, it was objected that servants' fees from visitors amounted to 'a penny only' – but literary evidence and rebukes to servants in the Court's own minutes suggest that profiteering was endemic at Bethlem. To the second, the Governors defended the adequacy of their existing precautions of having the Porter elected as a constable and denied 'that any complaint has ever been made by any of the Neighbours or others concerning this matter', ignoring mounting diatribes against public visiting. To the last, they replied that alcohol was mostly ordered for medicinal purposes and that neither servants nor patients 'are suffered to drink to excess', and yet drunkenness amongst servants was hardly a rare source of reprimand in Court Minutes. The Governors were capable of thorough investigation and amendment of abuses at Bethlem, although they were regularly confronted with problems that were inveterate and emphasize the gap between the sensibilities of the elite and of their servants. Yet they were also increasingly out of touch with public opinion as to how lunatics should be treated and how a public institution should be run. They were thus disposed to treat dispersions on their own management lightly, not merely for the sake of retaining public support and keeping up appearances, but also because they were simply slow to perceive that anything was seriously wrong.

This chapter began by stressing the close relationship between the London Hospitals and the way in which they were governed. Initiatives in one hospital frequently brought about changes or responses in others. Individuals commonly served as governors of more than one hospital, and elections and patronage within them was often contested by the same individuals. Yet there were also important differences between the Hospitals, which considerably reflected the particularism and 'rage of party' of City politics, as well as differing views as to charity and medicine. While during the late seventeenth century, Bridewell and Bethlem had been presided over by a group of Whigs, headed by Sir William Turner as President and Daniel Baker as Treasurer, the overall composition of the Court of Governors was increasingly weighted the other way. By the second or third decade of the eighteenth century, Bethlem (and St Bartholomew's) were well known as Tory establishments, their governing Courts and Committees being decidedly biased in favour of Tory politics and politicians, and High Church Anglicanism.[83] By contrast, St Thomas's was generally regarded as a Whig establishment. The election of officers at the London Hospitals was often determined along political lines. By the 1720s and 1730s, aldermen from the Tory wards of Farringdon, Queenhithe and Aldersgate, for example, dominated Bridewell and Bethlem's top posts as Presidents, Treasurers and Auditor-Generals.

Particularly prominent amongst the Bridewell and Bethlem Governors in the Augustan era was the Rawlinson family, well-known Jacobite-Tories: Sir Thomas

(1647–1708) serving as President (1705–8); Thomas (1681–1725), his eldest son, the Oxford bibliophile, as an enthusiastic Governor from 1706; and Dr Richard (1690–1755), his fourth son, the scholar and non-juring bishop, as perhaps the most active of the three as a governor during the half century from 1713. The accession to the Presidency of the Alderman, Walter Rawlinson Esquire, in 1773, who continued to serve until 1779, illustrates the continuing association of the family with the Hospitals.[84] Nevertheless, like most City institutions, with a large and powerful group of Whigs also represented at the Court and struggling for supremacy, political differences were rarely clearly manifested in actual policy decisions. Alongside committed Tories – like Sir John Hynde Cotton; Sir Richard Grosvenor; Sir Robert Abdy, and Henry Hoar Esquire – stood Whig publicists like Sir Richard Blackmore MD, and solid Whig MPs like Sir Philip Yorke and William Pitt Esquire.[85]

Bridewell and Bethlem's Toryism is well reflected in its championing by that bastion of the 'country interest' and the Tory press, the *London Evening Post* – lambasted by its critics as 'a Jacobite paper'[86] – which proved a great promoter of the Hospitals' interests from the 1720s. Arraigned against it were the *Public Advertiser* (sympathetic to dissenters) and the Whig *Daily Journal*, both of which papers were apt to comment disparagingly on the activities of the majority on the Hospitals' Court of Governors.

THE 'POORE MEANES' OF CHARITY: GOVERNORS, BENEFACTORS AND FINANCE

Although Bridewell and Bethlem were not subscription hospitals, they were heavily reliant on charitable donations to finance themselves – during the seventeenth century, such making up over a third of Bethlem's income. The importance of the Hospitals' identities as charities and the degree of their dependency on charity to finance themselves was vigorously expressed in the Spital Sermons delivered on behalf of all the London Hospitals every Easter. These services, involving grandiose congregations and processions composed of the Lord Mayor and other city dignitaries, as well as the Hospitals' Governors, officers, apprentices and school children, were organized to act as direct appeals to public charity, as well as cementing the group fellowship of the London Hospitals and their proponents. Each hospital designed its own specific 'report', advertising its work and appealing for funds, and these were delivered and printed every year in conjunction with sermons composed by preachers commissioned for the purpose. The distribution list for the Spital Sermons drawn up in 1784 presents us with a revealing view of the influential circles in city and court politics where the Governors were seeking and obtaining support and patronage by this time.[87] Apart from every Governor, copies were sent to the Presidents and Treasurers of the other Royal Hospitals, as well as of Guy's and St Luke's; to the peers and peeresses of Britain; to all MPs, judges and common councillors; to the Directors of the Bank South Sea and East India Companies; to the College of Physicians, the Doctors of Civil Law, the King's Council, Sergeants at Law and other Sergeants, and the Masters in Chancery; to the Bankers of the City of London and Westminster, and to the editors of the various city magazines.

Not surprisingly, benefactors were especially well-represented on the governing courts of Bridewell and Bethlem – many having donated money as Governors or else being appointed Governors as a result of their (or their relations') benefactions and legacies. In 1690, the merchant William Lethieullier was made a Governor after presenting a legacy of £100 to Bridewell and Bethlem from his deceased brother, an Alderman and former Governor, Sir Christopher Lethieullier.[88] Apart from being benefactors themselves, furthermore, Governors were often instrumental in persuading relations, friends and associates to donate – the Governor, Marmaduke Alington, for example, being entrusted with £200 for Bethlem in 1738 by an anonymous lady.[89]

A number of surveys have recently redrawn our picture of charitable giving as it defined the identity of early modern hospitals, emphasizing the changing, multifaceted nature of charity, as well as the mixed nexus of motives according to which benefactors signalled their interest and support.[90] Beside the impetus of a governorship (not, of course, open to female benefactors), there was a multiplicity of other incentives for those who gave large amounts to the Hospitals – for example, storing up gold in heaven; establishing social cachet with one's peers; and signalling and solidifying familial, societal, political and commercial loyalties.[91] Those who could afford to do so were under a degree of social expectation to give generously to charity, if they were to be acknowledged as 'persons of quality' and 'enlightenment' – their charitable works often being cited whilst they lived, as well as posthumously. Charity represented key ground on which the reputation of many families stood. As at other contemporary hospitals and public institutions, at Bethlem and Bridewell too there was the added attraction of entry into a charitable roll of merit, benefactors having their own names displayed publicly and for posterity in tables hung up at the Hospitals.[92] Conspicuous outward display was of considerable importance in gaining social recognition, both of worthy causes and of charitable acts. Spectacle and charity were deeply bound up with each other, and the Governors of Bridewell and Bethlem proved stalwart defenders of the view that charity and its objects required the medium of spectacle in order to be fully appreciated.

By the mid-eighteenth century, however, increasing criticism is discernible. Sustained complaints about public visiting at Bethlem arose at a time when more and more benefactors were seeking anonymity for their charitable donations.[93] Typical of this new critique of charity is an article in *The World* of 1756, that same magazine that had earlier censured Bethlem's show of lunatics. Commenting on the 'long tablets' of benefactors in 'one of our famous hospitals', the editors launched into an extensive attack on 'ridiculous . . . ostentatious' charity, which (it was alleged) arose out of selfish and vain motives, often sacrificing family interest for the glorification of personal largesse. 'There is no such thing' as posthumous charity, it was announced, and the tide was clearly turning against such, posthumous giving having fallen into substantial decline by the 1790s.[94]

Criticism emerged, furthermore, not only from outsiders but from within the Governors' own ranks, and moreover from rival charities which began to run, or were set up, on contrary principles. When, in 1752, the rather grandiose and expensive entertainments that had traditionally been conducted by the Governors at Easter or on St Matthew's Day were exposed to criticism and a motion, from Dr Richard Rawlinson, to have them discontinued, the majority threw the same out of Court.[95] Commenting on the vote, the loyal *London Evening Post* put the politics of this particular view of charity quite plainly. It asserted that 'these feasts are really for the grandeur and dignity of the city' and for 'the Encouragement of the Social Virtues', emphasizing that they 'were honour'd with Nobility and Persons of Distinction' and casting aspersions on 'the mean methods made use of by the rival charities lately set up by generous and disinterested Persons'.[96] Despite the Governors' doggedness, however, their policies were growing steadily more out of step with those at new charities like St George's Hospital, and St Luke's, and with polite sensibilities which sought more feeling, but more discreet, ways to express their charitable nature.

While the public glow of charity remained an important motivation for many benefactors in this period, more practically, through their gifts, benefactors were able to secure a degree of extra privilege and power within the institutions themselves – including, for example, influence over patients' admissions. Often such legacies were themselves the means of effecting or bolstering initiatives in the care and treatment of patients at Bethlem. Part of the Governor and Baronet Sir John Crispe's benefaction to the Hospitals in 1702 went towards the establishment of the Wardrobe Fund at Bethlem. Donations by others to the incurables of Bethlem in the 1720s inspired the establishment of incurables wards at the Hospital, with expansions of this provision in subsequent years also funded primarily by charity.[97] In the 1740s, £100 from an anonymous lady donor 'for . . . such Patients as happen to fall sick of a Feavor or other Distempers' (conveyed via the Governor, John Markham, an established London apothecary), sparked off the establishment of Bethlem's first infirmary.[98] Such initiatives highlight the significance of Bethlem's identity as a charity in this period, and the close relationship between charity and medicine emphasized in numerous other recent studies.[99]

Partly as a result of such benefactions and legacies, both Hospitals grew increasingly financially self-sufficient. Bethlem in particular, after its magnificent rebuilding at Moorfields, attracted more and more support from the public and from its own Governors. Many of these gifts came in the form of annuities, bonds and lands. Benefactors themselves were increasingly prone to ensuring greater posterity and security for their gifts and the Hospitals' revenues by specifying that they should be spent in such ways, while the Treasurers and Court of Governors were also at pains to convert financial donations into similarly long-term forms of capital interest and investment.[100] The gift of extensive lands in Lincolnshire to Bethlem and the incurables by Edward Barkham in the 1730s was a particularly rich one, and the Lincolnshire estate continued to be an important source of revenue for the Hospital until its sale in 1918.[101]

In earlier times, Bethlem had clearly suffered considerably, both administratively and financially, as an indirect result of its modest size and its subordination to Bridewell in the minds of its Governors and patrons. Bethlem had not even been included alongside Bridewell in the Spital Sermons until the 1640s, and during the early part of the century accounting had become so confused between the Hospitals that sums of Bethlem's money had been mistakenly laid out for Bridewell. Benefactors, too, seem to have been prone to conceiving that Bethlem was actually reliant on Bridewell for its funding, and that a gift to the former was also a gift to the latter. The Governors were at some pains in their first Spital reports on Bethlem to correct this view.[102] From the late 1660s, however, the relationship between the Hospitals became more equal, helped by the holding of court sessions at Bethlem after Bridewell had been damaged during the 1666 Fire of London, by Bethlem's rebuilding, and by the separation of the two Hospitals' accounts.[103] During the seventeenth century, the Governors had also tended to pursue a rather short-sighted policy regarding letting Hospital properties, meaning that net income suffered from depreciating rents. Exercising their continuing sway over the Royal Hospitals in the 1630s, the King and Privy Council forbade the Governors to 'take or grant long Leases at small Rents or give away the money belonging to the poore', and restricted the leasing of Bethlem's land and property to twenty-one years, without reversion, with half the yearly value reserved for rent.[104] The Governors also took measures to expedite the quicker recovery of leases, so that they might be renewed on better terms; to see the satisfaction of rent arrears, and to ensure the proper occupancy and upkeep of the Hospitals' houses and lands.[105] By 1700, the policy of long-term letting was largely discredited, and wiser investment decisions succeeded in placing both hospitals on a firmer financial footing.[106]

Benefiting from their close relationship with the City and its established companies, the Hospitals also increased their revenues by lending money at profitable rates of interest. At the beginning of the eighteenth century, Bethlem, for example, lent £1,500 to the Merchant Taylors Companies at an interest of 5 per cent per annum, taking good advantage of the new credit economy.[107] Not all investments proved so sound, nevertheless, the Hospitals being amongst many losers when the South Sea Bubble burst in the 1720s.[108] In the seventeenth century, poor management of the accounts had also left a number of Treasurers, Clerks and Stewards in debt.[109] During the following century, however, Treasurers and other officers clearly benefited from the increased prosperity of the Hospitals, with their activities more closely guarded from the mistakes in the management of hospital revenues made by their predecessors. While the annual account of Bethlem still fell well below that of Bridewell on occasion during the eighteenth century, this was, by and large, when the Governors had embarked on expensive new building programmes at the former.[110]

NOTES

1 William Hogarth, 'A Rake's Progress' (1735); Jonathan Swift, 'A Character, Panegyric, and Description of the Legion Club,' in Harold Williams (ed.), *The Poems of Jonathan Swift*, 3 volumes (Oxford: Clarendon, 1937; 3rd edn, 1966), iii, 827–39.

2 Craig M. Rose, 'Politics at the London Royal Hospitals, 1683–92', in Lindsay Granshaw and Roy Porter (eds), *The Hospital in History* (London and New York: Routledge, 1989), 123–48; *idem*, 'Politics, Religion and Charity in Augustan London, 1680–1720' (Cambridge: Ph.D. thesis, 1989). Rose did not include Bridewell and Bethlem in his admirable survey.

3 See Philip G. M. Dickson, *The Financial Revolution in England: A Study in the Development of Public Credit, 1688–1756* (London: Macmillan, 1967).

4 See Jeremy Black, *The English Press in the Eighteenth Century* (London: Croom Helm, 1986); Pat Rogers, *Grub Street: Studies in a Subculture* (London: Methuen, 1972).

5 These grants were made through several charters and letters patent dated *13 Jan., 38 Hen. VIII* and *26 June, 6 Ed. VI*.

6 *BCGM*, 15 Sept. 1631, fol. 240. However, election might still require the approval of all four hospitals, via their Treasurers; see *ibid.* 18 Aug. 1648, 9 June and 22 Aug. 1649, 9 Sept. 1663, fols 355, 386, 395, 66.

7 For the above account, see esp. *CLRO CA Rep.* 95, 10 March 1691, fols 233–234*b*. See, also, *ibid. Rep.* 83, fol. 114*b*, 143*b* and 222; *Rep.* 86, fol. 71*b*; *Rep.* 87, fols 70*b*, 86*b*, 248*b*; *Rep.* 94, fols 37–8; *Rep.* 95, fols 231*b*, 236, 284*b*; *BCGM*, 14 June 1782, fols 50–5.

8 Rose, 'Politics at the London Royal Hospitals'; *idem*, 'Politics, Religion and Charity in Augustan London'.

9 *BCGM*, 18 April, 8 and 30 May, 25 Sept., 9 Oct. 1674, 10 Sept. 1675, 26 May, 9 June 1676, 30 March 1677, fols 632, 637–8, 650, 37, 45–6, 174, 251, 255, 363; 4 Sept., 30 Oct. 1674, fols 3, 32, 59–60.

10 *Ibid.* 28 Aug. and 9 Sept. 1663, fols 64–5, 67.

11 For the Royal Commission for the Visitation of City Hospitals, see e.g. *CLRO CA Rep.* 95, fol. 324*b*; *CLRO*, Small MS, Box 27, no. 14, Exemplification of appointment of a Royal Commission for visiting Hospitals, 18 Aug. 1691; *CLRO* Misc. MS 58.26, 7 and 18 Dec. 1683, 22 Jan., 19 Feb., 1 March, 6 May and 1 Nov. 1684, 15 Dec. 1685, 15 June and 27 Nov. 1686, 10 Feb. 1687, 9 and 14 Feb., 5 April, 8 May and 20 Sept. 1688.

12 For the Court of Alderman's order of 9 Feb. 1682 and its enaction, see e.g. *BCGM*, 10 Feb. and 2 Oct. 1682, fols 280 and 336.

13 *Ibid.* 19 Dec. 1684, 11 Dec. 1685, 4 Feb. and 4 March 1687, 19 April 1689, fols 28, 121, 225, 235–6, 392–3.

14 *Ibid.* [illegible] July 1647, fol. 313. According to long-standing charitable Mayoral and Shrieval grants, Bethlem also received an allowance of free beer from the City, and the Clerks of the London markets were obliged to send in bread and meat gratis. *Ibid.* e.g. 1 Feb. 1644, 17 May 1667, 3 June 1668, 22 Oct. 1675, fols 91, 45, 97, 186.

15 *Ibid.* 23 Dec. 1641, 21 Oct. 1642, 2 and 16 June, 7 July, 25 Aug., 10 Nov. 1643, 17 April 1646, fols 363–4, 2, 43–6, 51, 61, 77, 258–9.

16 *Ibid.*, 2 March 1626 and 1 Aug. 1640, fols 21 and 301–2.

17 After Sir James Smyth's election, he initially declined to serve unless the Court present him to the Lord Mayor and Aldermen for their approbation, but a deputation from the Governors acquainted him that they had a right to elect their own President. See, *ibid.* 14 Nov., 7 Dec. 1688, 4 and 9 July 1689, fols 336, 338, 419 and 426.

18 *Ibid.* 5 April 1689, fol. 387.

19 In 1704, the Court reiterated that it was the Bridewell Committee, rather than the City authorities, who should approve all those nominated as Governors, and this was generally how elections proceeded in future; *ibid.* 17 Aug. 1704, fol. 212.

20 See Court of Common Council order dated 30 May 1782 reproduced in *BCGM*, 14 June 1782, fols 50–62, and *ibid.* 30 April 1783, 17 July and 27 Nov. 1788, fols 95–6, 302, for actual election of the twelve Governors.

21 Sir John Wollaston, for example, declined his Presidency of Bridewell and Bethlem after accepting that of Christ's in 1649; *ibid.* 26 Oct. 1649., fol. 401.

22 *Ibid.* e.g. 9 July 1689, 10 March 1721, 5 Aug. 1725, fols 426, 453, 59.

23 For example, Deputy John Withers (1631–7); Deputy Robert Edwards (1641–3); Deputy Gethin (1654–73); Colonel (later Alderman and Sir) John Cass (1709–14); Deputy John Taylor (1714–29); Robert Alsop Esquire (1729–37), an ex-Sheriff, and Alderman of Queenhithe Ward, and his son, also Robert Alsop (1750–55), an alderman and Lord Mayor (1751–2); and Alderman Richard Clark Esquire, Treasurer during the 1780s, when he was also elected to the Mayoralty.

24 For example, of nine elected during 1629–78, eight were aldermen and one was a common councillor.

25 For the public storm provoked when a junior alderman was nominated after an unusual meeting of Governors organized at a Cheapside tavern to elect a successor to the deceased President, William Benn, and the passionate objections it aroused from dissenting aldermen and Governors, in particular from the allies of the then Treasurer and former Lord Mayor, Robert Alsop; see *BCGM*, 25 Sept. 1755, fol. 198; *LEP*, nos. 4332, 4333, 4343, 4350, 14–16 and 16–19 Aug., 9–11 and 25–27 Sept. 1755; *Public Advertiser*, nos. 6501, 6502, 6503, 6534, 6535, 18 and 20 Aug., 8, 9, 22 and 26 Sept. 1755; *Gazetteer*, 16 Aug. 1755.

26 For Sir William Turner, see e.g. *BCGM*, 1669–93, *passim* and esp. 22 Oct. 1669, 14 Nov. 1688, 28 Aug. 1690, 17 March 1693, fols 170, 336, 74–5, 30.

27 For the Treasurer's duties, see e.g. *ibid.* 4 May 1737, fols 434–5.

28 See e.g. *ibid.* 13 and 18 Dec. 1639, fols 272–4, *re* the accusations of John Jeweller, the dismissed Bridewell Steward, against the government of the Hospitals, including the charge that 'the Treasurer [Withers] and 2 or 3 others . . . dawbe over things'.

29 For the Auditor-General's and auditors' duties, see e.g. *ibid.* 18 March 1709, 17 April 1713, 10 Aug. 1717, 27 March and 14 Aug. 1735, 28 Jan. 1736, fols 468, 700, 272, 342, 351–2, 370.

30 See e.g. the election of 9 May 1707, *ibid.* fols 349–51, when there were thirty-two applicants. For the Clerk's perks and duties, see *ibid.* e.g. 10 Oct. 1636, 29 Sept. 1704, 2 May 1707, 27 March 1735, 7 Feb. 1760, fols 95–6, 221–2, 343, 332.

31 For these committees and views, see *ibid.* e.g. 15 March 1633, 9 July 1647, 17 Dec. 1656, 13 May 1659, fols 289, 312, 310, 779, 88.

32 *Ibid.* 16 May 1655, fol. 702.

33 *Ibid.* e.g. 9 and 16 Feb., 30 March 1677, fols 331–2, 336–7, 356, 361.

34 *Ibid.* 16 Feb. and 30 March 1677, 11 Jan. 1678, 11 Nov. 1692, fols 336, 356, 361, 450, 206.

35 For this account of the development of committees, see *ibid.* e.g. 6 Nov. 1702, 25 Feb. 1709, 27 March 1724, 28 Jan. 1736, fols 119, 465, 32, 370; *BSCM, passim; BGCM, passim* and esp. volume for 1792–1802, which contains list of standing rules for the Bethlem Committee.

36 This policy of electing Governors only to suspend nominations was practised from 1707 well into the 1780s, although exceptions were made. Not until 1785 were Governors once again permitted to nominate at any general court. See *BCGM*, e.g. 19 May 1707, 26 June 1713, 2 Oct. 1724, 2 July 1730, 27 Feb. 1740 6 June 1755, 17 Feb., 28 April and 23 June 1785, fols 350–1, 4, 421–2, 193–4, 426–7, 378–85, 173–6, 184–7, 194–5.

37 *Ibid.* 22 Dec. 1768, 2 March, 27 April and 29 June 1769, fols 236, 242, 253–5, 263.

38 For high attendances on ordinary Court days in the 1740s, see *ibid.* e.g. 8 Oct. 1742 and 22 May 1751, fols 163–4 and 1–2, when 102 and 145 respectively are listed as attending the Court.

39 *Ibid.* 10 Sept. 1708, 8 Feb. 1758, fols 439–40, 278–9.

40 While these reforms may have democratized the Hospitals' management, they may also have intensified problems of lack of continuity in oversight; see *ibid.* 2 Feb. 1796, fols 55–7.

41 Andrew T. Scull, *Museums of Madness* (London: Allen Lane, 1979), 74; Patricia H. Allderidge, 'Bedlam: Fact or Fantasy?', in W. F. Bynum, Roy Porter and Michael Shepherd (eds), *The Anatomy of Madness: Essays in the History of Psychiatry*, 3 volumes (London and New York: Tavistock/Routledge, 1985–8), ii (1985), 24–46, 24; Donna T. Andrew, *Philanthropy and Police: London Charity in the Eighteenth Century* (Princeton, N.J.: Princeton University Press, 1989).

42 See e.g. *BCGM*, 9 May 1707, fol. 349, where of thirty-three listed as attending, sixteen are knights (one being President and eleven being aldermen), but 270 Governors voted on the Clerk's election at the same court.

43 *The Old Whig: or the Consistent Protestant*, no. 109, 7 April 1737; *LEP*, no. 3197, 28–30 April 1748.

44 Made in 1743, all of these orders were upheld by a narrow vote in 1749. The age limit was repealed in 1754, despite a subsequent motion from a number of Governors that it should be reconsidered. See *BCGM*, 8 July 1743, 29 April and 2 Dec. 1748, 9 Jan. 1749, 17 Jan. 1752, 16 Jan. and 11 April 1754, fols 194, 360, 389, 393, 32–3, 134, 139; *LEP*, no. 3785, 21–23 Jan. 1752.

45 For the nomination and election of these Governors, see *BCGM*, 4 Dec. 1696, 18 June 1742, 27 March and 6 June 1755, 16 July 1789 and 13 June 1793, fols 60, 149, 175–6, 183–5.

46 For Atterbury and Swift, see *ibid.* 4 Oct. 1693, 9 Dec. 1698, 23 Jan. 1708, 19 and 26 June 1713, 26 Feb. 1714, 25 Feb. 1715, fols 285, 230, 396, 710, 1–2, 43, 117.

47 *Ibid.* 27 April 1659, 29 Nov. 1678, 9 May 1679, fols 131, 61, 84.

48 *Ibid.* 26 Feb. 1752, fol. 40; *LEP*, no. 3820, 11–14 April 1752.

49 Stressing the importance of this role, the Court decided in 1693 that Governors nominating any individual (if present) should stand by them at the Court meeting when they were to receive their 'Charge'. Nomination rights were restricted in 1748 to those Governors who were present at Court and had served the office of Steward of the Election Feast. *Ibid.* 22 Sept. 1693 and 29 April 1748, fols 283 and 358.

50 Box 'D' in *BRHA*, item 9.

51 Joseph Reeve was ordered a Governors' staff in 1677 as thanks for his council about hospital lands at Leicestershire, while Captain Perry received the same in 1679 having got Bethlem excused from the hearth tax assessment. *BCGM*, 9 Aug. 1677 and 5 Dec. 1679, fols 411 and 118.

52 For example, the son-in-law of the Recorder of London in 1685; the son of Sir Thomas Chambers in 1690; the Dukes of Beaufort in 1710 and 1745, and Arthur Onslow, Speaker of the House of Commons in 1745; *ibid.* 11 Sept. 1685, 21 Aug. 1690, 7 Feb. and 3 Aug. 1710, 13 Oct. 1743, 10 April and 17 May 1745, 18 July 1750, fols 99, 71, 526, 568, 200, 253, 259, 454.

53 On aldermen serving as Governors, being too preoccupied, old or sick; see e.g. *ibid.* 18 May 1748, fol. 364.

54 *Re* election of Company Wardens and Masters, Chamberlains and Recorders of London, as Governors, see *ibid.* e.g. 10 Jan. 1644, 11 July 1655, 20 Jan. 1669, 18 Jan. 1695, 21 June 1751 and 31 Jan. 1783, fols 87, 710, 8, 76, 84 and 423.

55 *Ibid.* e.g. 5 July 1633, 17 June and 7 Oct. 1635, 2 Sept. 1641, 15 Feb. 1642, fols 334, 50, 63, 346, 370; see Chapter 18.

56 *BCGM*, 14 April, 10 May and 6 Oct. 1643, 5 Feb. 1706, 23 June 1737, 12 April and 16 May 1750, 26 March 1752, fols 32, 39, 70, 287, 438, 444, 446 and 55.

57 See, also, cases of Richard Belmy, the King's Upholsterer, nominated in 1691; and Robert Streeter, the King's Sergeant Painter, nominated in 1700; *ibid.* 7 Aug. 1674, 8 April 1691, 12 July and 9 Aug. 1700, fols 26, 117, 387 and 392.

58 For example, Braham Smith (an active Governor and member of the Bethlem Committee) and his son, Banks, were successively cheesemongers in the period 1700–1720, but the latter's services were dispensed with after repeated complaints about his butter and cheese.

59 *BCGM*, 13 Oct. 1676, fol. 293.

60 *Ibid.* 17 Jan. 1752 and 16 June 1768, fols 32–4 and 205; *LEP*, no. 3800, 25–27 Feb. 1752.

61 *Re* Stewards as Governors, see cases of Matthew Benson (required 'To Lay down his Staff'), Walter Acton, Charles Cotton and Robert Waite. *Ibid.* 22 Jan. 1647, 21 July 1648, 20 Jan. 1716, 8 July 1743, 18 May 1748, 26 Feb. and 12 March 1752, 20 Dec. 1759, fols 290, 352, 188–9, 194, 365, 46, 51, 327; *LEP*, no. 3817, 4–7 April 1752.

62 For elections of medical officers as Governors, see *ibid.* 13 Aug. 1672, 15 Feb. and 15 March 1678, 15 May 1747, 29 April and 14 Oct. 1748, 9 March 1769, 26 July 1770, 17 Feb. and 28 April 1785, fols 433, 7, 15, 323, 360, 378–86, 247, 303, 173–6, 184–7.

63 *Ibid.* e.g. 23 Nov. 1716, 2 May 1739, 27 Jan. 1742, fols 245–6, 47, 135. *Re* priority according to length of service, or 'antiquity', see *ibid.* e.g. 27 Sept. 1640, 12 July 1677 and 15 Oct. 1686, fols 312, 401, 200.

64 *Ibid.* 7 Nov. 1673, fols 580. *Re* Governors as freemen or unfreemen, see *ibid.* 22 Sept. 1705, fol. 271.

65 *Ibid.* 19 Oct. 1632, fol. 299. For other declinations/resignations, see *ibid.* 4 Nov. 1668, 12 Sept. 1712, 25 Jan. 1776, fols 115, 664, 504–5.

66 *Ibid.* 22 Sept. 1641, fol. 350.

67 *Re* Governors being ousted who had 'left the house'; were 'thought fitt not to continue in the table of Governors'; and who refused to make 'Bien venues according to antient custome', or (as latterly defined) to serve as Stewards at Election Day feasts, see *ibid.* e.g. 19 Oct. 1632, 3 Aug. 1688, 30 July 1714, 14 July 1737, 29 April and 18 May 1748, fols 299, 319, 68, 443, 358, 364.

68 See, e.g., gifts of Dr James Monro and the Lord Windsor on becoming Governors; *ibid.* 15 July 1747, 19 Feb. 1748, fols 330, 353.

69 *Ibid.* 29 Jan. 1640, fol. 279.

70 *Re* Governors as tenants, see, e.g., Deputy Tutchin's lease, *ibid.* 9 Feb. 1659, fol. 100.

71 *Ibid.* e.g. 17 April 1644, fol. 106.

72 See *ibid.* 30 April 1651 and 20 Nov. 1685, fols 497 and 116.

73 Sandra Cavallo, 'Charity, Power and Patronage in 18th Century Italian Hospitals,' in Lindsay Granshaw and Roy Porter (eds), *The Hospital in History* (London and New York: Routledge, 1989), 93–122.

74 The manner in which elections were conducted was subjected to a sweeping review and reform in 1737, single ballots replacing double or multiple ballots, and every aspect of the procedure being carefully regulated. For these and other adjustments to electoral procedures, see *ibid.* 4 May and 23 June 1737, 27 Nov. 1741, 1 Oct. 1742, fols 435, 439, 120, 163.

75 David Owen, *English Philanthropy, 1660–1960* (Cambridge, Mass.: Belknap Press, 1964).

76 See *BCGM*, 10 Nov. 1652, fol. 575, where Treasurer Isaacson is reminded of his responsibilities 'for the Good of the . . . hospitalls & the service of the Citty of London'.

77 Green staffs were delivered to newly elected Governors by the Bridewell Steward, who was occasionally accompanied by one or more existing Governors. See, e.g., *ibid.* 15 Feb. 1678, fol. 7. For Governors' cloaks and gowns, see *ibid.* 2 Sept. 1641, 4 Sept. 1650, fols 346, 461.

78 For the charge read to every Governor, see, e.g., *ibid.* 5 April 1689 and 19 Dec. 1707, fols 387 and 392; *CLRO CA Rep.*, 95, fol. 235; *LEP*, no. 3817, 4–7 April 1752.

79 *BCGM*, 15 and 25 Oct. 1639, fols 267 and 269.

80 For the following discussion of this episode involving Bolton, see *ibid.* 27 Nov. and 4 Dec. 1674, 23 Dec. 1674, 31 March, 16 and 30 April, and 19 May 1675, 4 July 1679; fols 71, 75–6, 81, 115, 120, 125, 129 and 96.

81 See *ibid.* 28 May and 29 June 1791, 14 March 1792, fols 24, 26–42, 47; *Report respecting the present State and Condition of Bethlem Hospital* (London: J. Richardson, 1800), 3–14.

82 For these complaints and the Governors' response to them, see *BCGM*, 27 Jan., 11 Feb., 12 March 1742, fols 135, 138, 141.

83 See the *LEP*'s coverage of the Presidential vacancy of 1737 at Bartholomew's, *re* its support of aldermen 'in the COUNTRY INTEREST'. *LEP*, nos. 1561, 1565 and 1567, 15–17 and 24–26 Nov., and 29 Nov.–1 Dec. 1737.

84 For the Rawlinsons at Bridewell and Bethlem, see *BCGM*, e.g., 22 Sept. 1705, 13 March 1706, 13 Aug. 1713, 13 May 1715, 23 June 1732, 27 Jan. 1742, 16 May 1750, 11 Feb. 1773, fols 271, 288–9, 10–12, 135, 286, 135, 446, 383. See, also, *DNB*, 331–5; *LEP*, 6–8 April 1755.

85 For the election of these and other Tory and Whig Governors, see *BCGM*, e.g. 4 Sept. 1696, 12 Nov. 1725, 18 Feb. 1726, 28 Sept. 1727, 26 July 1728, 18 July 1729, 22 Dec. 1757, 30 July 1761, fols 60, 66, 80, 136, 157, 181, 273, 384.

86 *LEP*, e.g., no. 3648, 7–9 March 1751, letter from 'Tom Tar'.

87 Thomas Bowen, *An Historical Account of the Origin, Progress, and Present State of Bethlem Hospital* (London: For the Governors, 1784); *BCGM*, 30 April and 22 Nov. 1783, fols 98–115, 126.

88 *BCGM*, 31 Oct. 1690, 2 Dec. 1715, 13 Jan. 1716, fols 87, 166, 182. For other legacies to Bethlem, see e.g. *ibid.* 13 Oct. 1743, 1 Nov. and 19 Dec. 1750, 27 Nov. 1783, fols 200, 468 and 471, 125, 131; *LEP*, nos. 3596, 3633, 3646 and 3694, 6–8 Nov. 1750, 31 Jan.–2 Feb., 2–5 March and 20–22 June 1751.

89 *BCGM*, 20 July 1738, fol. 27.

90 See especially, Amanda Berry, 'Charity, Patronage and Medical Men: Philanthropy and Provincial Hospitals (D. Phil. thesis, University of Oxford, 1995); Ann Borsay, 'Cash and Conscience,' *Social History of Medicine*, iv (1991), 207–30.

91 Ann Borsay, 'Persons of Honour and Reputation', *Medical History*, xxxv (1991), 281–94.

92 For these and other refs to benefactors' tables, see *BCGM*, e.g., 7 March 1679, 20 Oct 1693, 11 May and 14 Sept. 1694, 29 Sept. 1704, 2 Dec. 1748, fols 76, 294, 344, 383, 223, 389; BGCM, 14 March 1753 and 26 Jan. 1754, in *BSCM*, fols 341, 392.

93 For anonymous benefactions to Bethlem, see *BCGM*, e.g. 4 Jan. 1682, 27 July 1738, 30 July

1741, 30 April 1789, fols 274, 108, 336, 581; *LEP*, nos. 3643 and 3708, 23–26 Feb. and 23–25 July 1751.

94 *The World*, no. 180, 1 April 1756, 1019–24.

95 *BCGM*, 26 March 1752, fol. 55.

96 *LEP*, no. 3820, 11–14 April 1752. In the seventeenth century, such banquets and similar 'bienvenues' had been justified in rather more flowery terms: 'for the preservacion & continuance of loveing meetings & Amity amongst the Governors'; *BCGM*, 20 Aug. 1629, fol. 305.

97 *BCGM*, 8 May 1702, 4 Aug. 1720, fols 81, 429. For numerous other gifts to the Bethlem incurables of amounts ranging between £50 and £600, see *ibid.* 10 March 1721, 18 Oct. 1723, 28 May 1752, 5 Aug. 1784, 28 Jan. 1790, fols 447, 23, 63–4, 155–6, 349–50. For more on provision for incurables at Bethlem and elsewhere, see Chapter 18, this volume; Jonathan Andrews, 'The Lot of the "Incurably" Insane in Enlightenment England', *18th Century Life*, xii (1988), 1–18; Cavallo, 'Charity, Power and Patronage', 102–10.

98 *BCGM*, 30 July and 9 Sept. 1741, 12 March 1742, fols 108, 111, 141.

99 See Jonathan Andrews, '"Hardly a Hospital, but a Charity for Pauper Lunatics"?: Therapeutics at Bethlem in the Seventeenth and Eighteenth Centuries', in Jonathan Barry and Colin Jones (eds), *Medicine and Charity Before the Welfare State* (London and New York: Routledge, 1991), 63–82; Roy Porter, 'The Gift Relation: Philanthropy and Provincial Hospitals in Eighteenth-Century England', in Lindsay Granshaw and Roy Porter (eds), *The Hospital in History* (London and New York: Routledge, 1989), 149–78.

100 For gifts of annuities, stock and lands, see e.g. *BCGM*, 24 Oct. 1707, 23 Nov. 1716, 18 July 1723, 12 Jan. 1738 and 2 Dec. 1784, fols 379–80, 243–4, 19, 3, 166. For purchases of annuities, see e.g. *ibid.* 4 April 1751, fol. 495.

101 *Re* the Lincolnshire estate and Barkham's legacy, see *ibid.* 18 July 1738, 19 Nov. 1741, 22 June 1750, 4 April 1751, 30 Nov. 1769, 21 Nov. 1770, fols 438, 24, 115–16, 450, 494, 278–9, 317–18.

102 See *ibid.* e.g. 24 March 1643, 15 March, 5 and 17 April 1644, fols 27, 98 and 100–2.

103 In 1630, the Court ordered that henceforth the accounts of Bethlem 'be constantly kepte by itselfe distincke and aparte from Bridewells accompts': *ibid.* 13 Nov. 1630, fol. 205. For the translation of Court meetings to Bethlem, see *ibid.* 28 Sept. 1666, fol. 5.

104 *Ibid.* 2 and 11 April 1638, 18 Sept. 1639, fols 133, 174, 262.

105 *Ibid.* e.g. 23 Aug. 1644, 18 Feb. 1648, (Audit) 11 and 18 May 1658, 23 March 1659, fols 142, 337–8, 869, 872, 120.

106 Although, in fact, by the second half of the seventeenth century, the Governors were already ignoring former royal orders, and were agreeing leases for thirty-one years and more. See *ibid.* e.g. 7 Oct. 1681, fols 260–1.

107 *Ibid.* e.g. 25 July 1718, fol. 353. *Re* other sums lent, e.g. to the Chamber of London, see *ibid.* 20 Jan. 1642, 366. *Re* the role of other institutions as integral parts of urban financial structures, see e.g. Cavallo, *op. cit.* 109–10.

108 For legacies and other money invested by Bethlem in South Sea stock, see *BCGM*, e.g. 4 Aug. 1720, 7 April 1737 and 21 Nov. 1782, fols 429, 432 and 71–4.

109 See *ibid.* e.g. 20 Jan. 1642, 9 July 1656, 20 March 1668 and 29 July 1715, fols 360, 760–1, 88 and 148.

110 During the 1740s–60s, Bethlem's balance of accounts was on average over twice that of Bridewell's. By the 1780s, however, Bethlem's expenses were regularly exceeding its income, the arrears requiring to be made up by Bridewell's funds; *ibid.*, e.g., 2 July 1760, 30 April 1783 and 28 April 1784, fols 340–1, 87–8 and 134–5.

CHAPTER THIRTEEN

VISITING

————— •❖• —————

Londonwas widely portrayed as a suitable site for Bethlem, because it was depicted as a crazed, chaotic city.[1] Mad London formed the stage set for Alexander Pope's *Dunciad*, for Hogarth's satires upon human vice and folly, for Samuel Johnson's Juvenalian poem, *London*, and for the journalist Ned Ward's *The London Spy*. Recounting a visit to Bedlam, Ward reported such 'drumming of doors, ranting, holloaing, singing and rattling, that I could think of nothing but Don Quevedo's vision, where the damn'd broke loose, and put Hell in an uproar'.[2]

As Ward's write-up reveals, members of the public could visit Bethlem; indeed, it was a pastime that was actually encouraged. Amongst contemporary critics and later historians, the fact that Bethlem served as one of the shows of London is taken as symptomatic of its scandal: it was deliberately putting the Other on show, a blatant form of voyeurism – as depicted by Hogarth in the final scene of his *The Rake's Progress*, where two visiting ladies of fashion – or perhaps courtesans – appear, one, with fan coyly raised, the other conspiratorially whispering in her ear and clutching her arm, before the cell of a naked 'mad monarch' patient (see Plate 13.1). As zoo and freakshow, Bethlem could be exploited to emblematize a cosmology of madness, in which the inmate was regarded as a beast or monster.[3] In such a reading, the curtailing of visiting in 1770 represents a belated humanizing of the madman, a progress from animal to patient. In broad terms, this paradigm is persuasive, but there is more to visiting Bethlem than meets the eye.

Visiting Bethlem was a real phenomenon and not merely a popular cultural trope. In 1681 the Governors took note of 'the greate quantity of persons that come daily to see the said Lunatickes'.[4] Numbers must have been rising, because Bethlem had recently moved to its palatial new Moorfields building, designed as a public showpiece. In 1689, Thomas Tryon railed in his *A Treatise of Dreams and Visions* against the 'Swarms of People' resorting to the Hospital, especially on public holidays.[5] In 1753 a correspondent of *The World* magazine estimated 'one hundred people at least' visiting Bethlem at a time in Easter week.[6] However, there is no evidence to support the claim of modern historians like Michael MacDonald that some 96,000 people passed through the gates per year. That figure has been arrived at thanks to dubious projections from the quantity of money placed in the 'poor's box' (see Plate 13.2).[7] Computations of the annual totals and seasonality of poor's box takings in the eighteenth

Plate 13.1 Scene viii from *A Rake's Progress* by William Hogarth (1735), set in Bethlem. Reproduced by kind permission of the Wellcome Institute Library, London.

Plate 13.2 Replicas of the poor's boxes (*c.* 1676) which stood inside Bethlem's entrance for donations from visitors. Reproduced by permission of the Bethlem Royal Hospital Archives and Museum. (Originals in the Wellcome Collection, Science Museum, London.)

century may, indeed, be taken as evidence of a large number of visitors (see Figures 13.1, 13.2, 13.3). Around £400 was finding its way into the box in a good year; if every visitor dropped a penny in, that might suggest towards 100,000 visitors. But we have little idea how much anyone donated; wealthier or more charitable visitors evidently left far more, Lord Percy giving 10s in 1610, and the Prince of Wales 5 guineas in 1735.[8] Tenants of Bethlem also customarily made donations to the poor's box on securing leases and other bargains with the Governors.

Nor must we forget that a fair proportion of visitors were patients' relatives, friends and sureties, who contributed towards the creature comforts of patients by furnishing them with food, drink, money, clothes, furniture, books, paper, ink and pens. During his confinement in the 1670s, James Carkesse received a host of such gifts from visitors. On visiting in 1786, the German novelist Sophie von la Roche found Margaret Nicholson, George III's would-be assassin, writing and reading Shakespeare, and also an unnamed man 'in the lowest cell, with books all around him'.[9]

Sightseers – of an approved kind – were positively courted by the Governors. The ideal visitor was the 'person of quality', who came to the Hospital with the intention

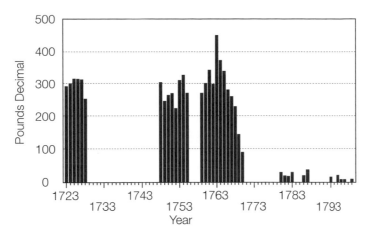

Figure 13.1 Annual poor's box takings, 1723–99, as a guide to incidence of visiting
Sources: Derived from *BSCM, BCGM* and *BSA*, 1723–8 and 1748–70

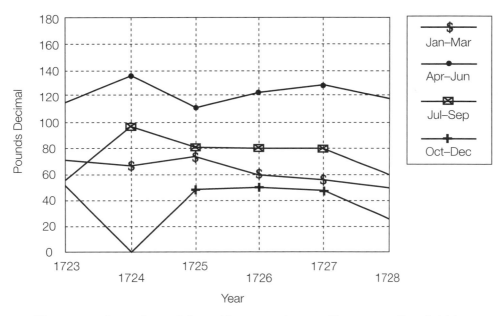

Figure 13.2 Quarterly poor's box takings, 1723–8, as a guide to seasonality of visiting
Source: Derived from *BSCM*, 1723–8

of doing 'the poore Lunatiques' good '& releiving them'.[10] Such 'people of note and quallitie' who were given particular access by the rules, were defined in accordance with elite notions of morality and benevolence, and with Bethlem's charitable status.[11] That the educated and wealthy comprised a fair proportion of visitors to the Hospital is suggested by their letters and diaries. By contrast, those coming to Bethlem for 'idle' or mischievous purposes were regarded by the Governors as visitors under false 'pretence', with 'no Business' being in the Hospital.[12]

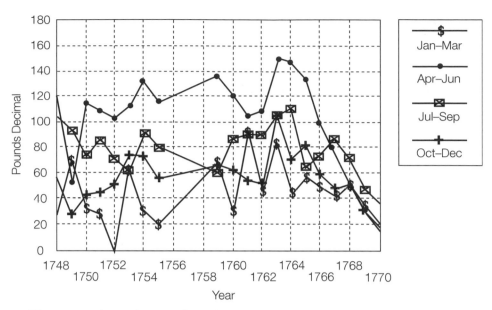

Figure 13.3 Quarterly poor's box takings, 1748–70, as a guide to seasonality of visiting
Sources: Derived from *BSCM*, *BCGM* and *BSA*, 1748–70

The insane were to be shown off to the better sort as an appeal to piety and charity; an inscription on the poor's box prayed that visitors should 'remember the poore Lunaticks'.[13] Visitors were not only exhorted to give donations, but exhibiting the insane might also elicit benefactions and legacies. The enactment of 'show' and 'spectacle' was built into the dynamics of charity at large and was far from confined to Bethlem. The desirability of seeing an 'assembly of objects ... proper to excite ... charity and compassion', was widely emphasized.[14] Spital sermons, processions and congregations held on thanksgiving days and other special occasions on behalf of the capital's hospitals and charity schools involved dignitaries, Governors, staff and poor children themselves. Impressed by pomp, the Augustans extended such spectacles as never before, confident that they were 'pleasing to God and man';[15] similar displays took place at the Foundling Hospital and the Magdalen Hospital for Penitent Prostitutes. Bethlem was far from the only institution to give the public freedom of access so as to generate good will. Ned Ward also visited Bridewell, Newgate, Ludgate, the Poultry Compter, St Bartholomew's, Christ's and St Thomas's.[16] Visitors admitted to Christ's Hospital were able to observe the children eating supper. The London Smallpox Hospital was conscious of breaking with traditions in the 1760s, when apologizing to the public for being forced to 'forbid Strangers to visit' its patients and hoping 'that the Affection or Curiosity of particular Persons will not be offended'.[17] The pleasure gardens and other London sights experienced similar problems to Bethlem with the influx of visitors, and at similar times.[18]

Besides the fund-raising function, the insane were displayed as a didactic spectacle, and it was 'a desire for instruction' that was supposed to bring the 'feeling' visitor to the hospital.[19] Not merely 'Objects of Charity', Bedlamites served as object lessons, living exemplars of the wages of vice and indulgence. In an account of a visit to Bethlem published in *The World* (1753), there was said to be no

> better lesson [to] be taught us in any part of the globe than in this school of misery. Here we may see the mighty reasoners of the earth, below even the insects that crawl upon it; and from so humbling a sight we may learn to moderate our pride, and to keep those passions within bounds, which if too much indulged, would drive Reason from her seat, and level us with the wretches of this unhappy mansion.[20]

The utter degradation of the mad, their atavism, their mockery of the natural order, were meant to impress the minds and hearts of sincere visitors. Madness as the beast within operated as both leveller and admonition to keep baser instincts in check.

Rather than the 'good mania'[21] of the Classical and Christian traditions, Bedlamites served to illustrate the punitive madness of providential theology. Conceived as a school of folly, Bedlam was presented as a mirror for the follies of its visitants and of mankind in general: the 'desperate Caitifes' in Bethlem demonstrated how strong was 'the Divell . . . to Delude', how 'easily' were 'men . . . to be drawne', and what inevitably befell those who 'dare make a mocke of judgment'.[22] The hand of judgment continued to figure in the annual Spital sermons, which mingled edification with fund-raising. The Bethlem mad were represented as defacing 'the Image' of their 'Maker', and preachers looked to 'Divine Providence' for their relief. In 1681, for example, Edward Stillingfleet, Dean of St Paul's, King's chaplain and later Bishop of Worcester, instructed his congregation to count their blessings for their 'Reason and Understanding' and to 'pity the poor Creatures [in Bethlem] whom God had deprived of it', remembering 'How easily, how justly, how suddenly may God cast you into their condition.'[23] His sentiments were echoed by John Gilbert, Bishop of Llandaff. Referring to the hordes visiting the Hospital during the same Easter, he asked 'is it possible any rational Creature should look on such moving Objects as these as an unconcern'd spectator?'[24]

That last word is, of course, fraught with resonance. The idea of seeing for oneself was part of Enlightenment pedagogy. Magazines and periodicals like the aptly named *Spectator* aimed to unite entertainment with instruction for its readers, so as to 'make . . . their Diversion useful'. The approved pastime of visiting Bethlem was ideally suited to these ends, that journal poignantly recalling the beneficial effects of 'the actual View and Survey of outward Objects', and aiming to turn every reader into a real or virtual spectator.[25]

'Philanthropus', a correspondent to *The Guardian* in 1713, similarly spoke of having 'rambled about the galleries at Bedlam . . . for an hour' and having 'thoroughly reflected' on what he 'beheld'.[26] Caius Cibber's figures of 'Melancholy and Raving Madness', displayed on top of the gateway of new Bethlem, were evidently carved with the same object in mind, as warnings and advertisements of the madness lurking within — within Bethlem, within everyone. 'Seeing the insane' was portrayed as an instructive experience, and a sight of Bethlem might be recommended as a peculiarly effective deterrent to the wayward inclinations of children.[27] In 1709, Richard Steele personally took three young brothers, to whom he was (significantly) guardian, 'to show 'em . . . *Bedlam*' and other sights; the exemplary quality of Lockian psychology is made clear by Steele's justifying his visit on the grounds that 'such places . . . strike forcibly on the Fancy' of 'raw minds'.[28]

To illustrate the madness of pride, Steele cited a consultation with 'the Collegiates of *Moorfields*', where 'Benefit' was 'reaped' from a view of the 'Duchesses . . . Earls . . . Heathen Gods . . . Emperor . . . Prophet . . . Duke . . . and Lady Mayoress' to be found amongst the deluded patients.[29] An old lesson – passion conceived as a cause of madness, and madness as warning – belonged, of course, to classical moral theories. It was invested with new significance by Lockian psychology and enlightened utilitarianism:

> I was resolved to guard myself against a Passion which makes such Havock in the Brain, and produces so much Disorder in the Imagination. For this Reason, I have endeavoured to keep down the secret Swellings of Resentment, and stifle the very first suggestions of self-esteem; to establish my Mind in Tranquility, and over-value nothing in my own, or in another's Possession.[30]

Seventeenth-century philosophy had stressed sight as the gates of perception and understanding, and the peculiarly forceful operation of 'an outward object' on the mind or imagination.[31] While, on the one hand, pointing to the power of objects to distort sensory impressions by their imprint and thus cause insanity, the new philosophy encouraged Enlightenment faith in the ability to mould perceptions. Thus, seeing the insane could be advocated with enthusiasm as a formative spectacle for the developing mind.

Visiting Bethlem was meant to serve as a moral experience through turning the mirror. Standard Bedlamite parables ran and ran, elaborated with each telling. Take the tale of the 'young man' or 'Bristol apprentice', who asked a 'madman' in Bethlem the reasons for his committal; the patient refused to divulge them; the apprentice abused him; and the Bedlamite answered with 'calm disdain' that he had been locked away 'for the loss of that which God Almighty never gave you'. First recorded in 1761 by 'Benevolus', a correspondent to the *London Chronicle*, this episode was embellished three years later in newspapers in both city and country.[32]

Instructive literature often embroidered the theme of Bethlem as the microcosm of Britain. Visits to Bethlem turning the mirror of madness onto society transformed patients into familiar public caricatures, such as the Welshman mad for cheese, the crazed speculator, the mad politician (like Charles James Fox), the war-mongering general, the megalomaniac emperor, the enthusiast, the Ophelia or the love-sick melancholic.[33] To some, the prevalence of such caricatures in representations of Bethlem may seem to manifest the distance rather than the proximity of the observer from the observed. Indeed, when reporting on the standard menu of characters at Bethlem, the spectator seems more aware of models of what he should be seeing than able to respond independently to the actual presence of the patient. Yet this would tend to ignore the extent to which experience is generally mediated by stereotypes, to underestimate the significance of such models in terms of the way contemporaries understood madness, and to underplay the impact of the didactic spectacle of madness on early modern society. The meaning and humour of such inversions proved resilient. For example, James Boswell shared Johnson's joke, when visiting Bethlem in 1775, by turning the mirror from a 'very furious' patient 'beating his straw', to the 'cruelties' of the Duke of Cumberland at and after the battle of Culloden.[34] As late as 1794 – twenty-four years after visiting had been curtailed – the cartoonist Richard Newton still drew the resemblance between the passions of its patients, staring through the grates of their cell doors, and those of the grimacing visitors observing them. The scopophilic spectator of Newton's print could hardly escape his own connection with insanity.[35]

Literary devices for equating or identifying visitors with the insane, and portrayal of visitors as 'yet lower' than the 'brutes' they observed,[36] were obviously ambiguous, because, while ostensibly moralizing, they did little to raise the image of Bedlamites themselves. For many, moreover, madness was still to be viewed, as Foucault emphasized, 'on the other side of bars', where reason 'would not compromise itself by too close a resemblance'.[37] Indeed, visiting Bedlam was promoted by many insofar as in showing insanity, its symptoms and causes, people might shore themselves up against its threat. In this way, the divide between madness and reason, between the follies of the crazy and the sobriety of the enlightened might be reinforced. The popularity in this period of Stoic philosophy also tended to bolster this perspective. It was according to this tradition that Steele and other writers portrayed themselves as moral censors on the Roman model, using polemic to clap up 'whole Packs of Delinquents . . . in kennels' and more than imaginary Bedlams.[38] Stoicism 'recommended' actively 'making comparisons' to stave off 'melancholy and . . . gloomy thoughts', and that 'by . . . observation of the miseries of others . . . fortitude is strengthened, and the mind is brought to a more extensive knowledge of her powers'.[39] Likewise, 'the sufferer' was to be put 'in mind of heavier pressures, and more excruciating calamities, than those of which he himself has reason to complain', the better to endure his own.[40] Thus Johnson and Boswell conceived familiarizing themselves with the spectacle of madness as a duty strengthening that 'firmness' and 'Steadiness of Mind' espoused by the Stoics, while Steele stressed the 'Benefit' gleaned from his visit to Bethlem in terms of 'establish[ing] my Mind in Tranquility'.[41] Emphasizing a stiff upper lip in the face of trials and tribulations, however, was also apt to discourage sympathy for those who failed in this resolve. Indeed, moralists, in their determination to reconcile their readers to the experience of living,[42] might render those who succumbed and actually became mad as all the more to be pilloried for their weaknesses. Lockian psychology, too, could underline the culpability of the insane by emphasizing man's innate capacity to submit imagination and passion to judgment. It was on this account that men like Johnson tended to regard the madness of 'many . . . people' as 'their fault'.[43] At the same time as empathizing with the plight of the insane, Augustan satirists were encouraged to ridicule and stigmatize the singular and the crazy as beyond the pale.

Nevertheless, Foucault overestimated the aloofness of the classical response to madness. It is simply untenable to assert that 'reason no longer felt any relation to [madness]'[44] in this period. In many respects, Augustans experienced madness more often and at closer proximity than their forebears. Furthermore, the majority of those who deployed visits to Bethlem for moral and literary effects were concerned less with real madness than with what they deemed to be the more curable and condemnable luxuries and vices of the outside world.

If contemporaries felt no relation to madness, why did so many delight in donning the mask of madness, turning themselves fleetingly into licensed fools, claiming freedom to criticize while pre-empting and disarming criticism? Swift indulged in the role of the mad narrator, Boswell in that of the hypochondriac, and Fielding and others penned magazine columns from fictitious Moorfields addresses.[45] Ned Ward's visit drew on the proverbial moral of 'Truth' flying to Bethlem 'for sanctuary', alluding to the 'privlege[d]' position of inmates free to speak their minds. He reported one of the Bedlamites supposedly:

> holding forth with much vehemence against Kingly government. I told him he deserv'd to be hang'd for talking of treason. 'Now,' says he, 'you're a fool, for we madmen have as much privilege of speaking our minds as an ignorant dictator when he spews out his nonsense to a whole parish . . . you may talk what you will, and nobody will call you in question for it. Truth is persecuted everywhere abroad, and flies thither for sanctuary, where she sits as safe as a knave in a church, or a whore in a nunnery. I can use her as I please and that's more than you dare to.'[46]

For the likes of Johnson and Boswell, visiting Bethlem was properly a moral duty, painful and distressing, yet pointing useful lessons – indeed one especially pertinent for those who, like that pair, believed themselves prone to mental disorder.[47] Boswell spoke of Bethlem and its twin, St Luke's, as 'receptacles' where one might 'contemplate human nature in ruins'. Likewise, 'Philanthropus', *The Guardian* correspondent, emphasized the food for thought provided by the 'lamentable objects' he saw. Zealous spectators could make a conscious and solemn habit of taking 'a walk of mortification, and pass[ing] a whole day in making myself profitably sad', by visiting Bethlem and 'the [other] hospitals about . . . [the] city'.[48]

It would be presumptuous to deny the genuine compassion that such spectators felt when gazing at the insane in Bethlem. Humanity, pity and charity were considered essential emotions of the enlightened towards the insane and other objects of tenderness. On viewing Bethlem's patients in 1710, Steele confessed to being 'very sensibly touched with Compassion towards these miserable People; and indeed, extremely mortified to see Human Nature capable of being thus disfigured'.[49] Even before the arrival of the 'Age of Sensibility', to be 'unmoved with the calamities of others' was regarded as 'monstrous', and he who had the support of his reason could be seen as 'in the same class of natural necessity with him that wants a support'.[50]

Visiting Bedlam could thus be advocated as an instructive experience for thoughtful heads and tender hearts. Yet the majority of visitors were not 'persons of quality'; and we can assume that even those who were, were not drawn solely out of duty and compassion, nor even by the calls of Enlightenment pedagogy. The chief enticement was entertainment, the *frisson* of the freakshow. Visitors were primarily sightseers, for whom Bethlem was 'a rare Diversion'.[51] A trip to Bedlam served as comic diversion in Jacobean drama – in *The Changeling* (1622), Isabella asks Lollio, the keeper, to 'Afford me then the pleasure of your bedlam'; and Bethlem remained an obvious choice for contemporaries seeking, like James Yonge, the Plymouth surgeon, in 1678, to 'divert' themselves 'with all that was curious in London'.[52]

Londoners and tourists alike flocked to Bethlem as one of the wonders of the city. The Hospital was, typically, just one stop on a Cook's tour of sights that could include the Tower, Westminster Abbey, the Zoo, the Waterworks, London Bridge, the Exchange, Whitehall, the China Houses, the theatres and the gardens of London, as well as Moorfields. In George Farquhar's *Love and a Bottle* (1697), Mackmode, an Irishman visiting London, 'longs', 'of all the Rarities of the Town', 'to see nothing more than the Poets [i.e. Poets' Corner, in Westminster Abbey] and *Bedlam*'.[53] However inhumane the spectacle of madness was later to appear to polite society, formerly it might be considered 'barbarous *not* to have let' a young lady down from the country to 'see the Tower, the abby, and Bedlam, and two or three plays'.[54]

In 1610, Lord Percy and company 'saw the lions, the shew of Bethlem, the places where the prince was created, and the fireworks at the Artillery Gardens'.[55] The diarist John Evelyn in 1657 'step'd in to Bedlame' out of curiosity, expecting to see something 'extraordinarie'.[56] In 1669, Samuel Pepys sent his cousin's children, down from Cambridge for a fortnight, 'to see Bedlam' as their first treat on an itinerary embracing shopping, dancing, dining, the theatre and Westminster Abbey.[57] Nicholas Blundell, a Lancashire gentleman, 'walked to Bedlom' on his first visit to London in 1703, and returned on at least two subsequent occasions to show his wife and daughters.[58]

Curiosity was a standard motive for visiting: sightseers typically spoke of Bethlem's patients as 'curiosities' or 'remarkable characters'.[59] Often they were drawn by famous patients. Notorious curiosities included Cromwell's Porter, Daniel; the playwright, Nathaniel Lee; the naval office clerk, James Carkesse; and, in a later age, the attempted regicide, Margaret Nicholson, all star attractions. The German traveller von Uffenbach visited in 1710, having heard of a patient 'who is said to have crowed all day long like a cock'.[60]

Visitors were often quite frank about the 'delight' Bethlem afforded. Writing to the *London Chronicle* in 1761, 'Benevolus' related the answer of a lady visitor of whom he had asked whether she could have obtained 'any degree of pleasure' from visiting Bethlem:

> Oh yes, replied she with a smile, I assure you I was highly entertained; I met with some very amusing objects; and I heard a great many excellent stories; and was prodigiously delighted with the humour of the mad folks.[61]

Ned Ward and his companion apparently scoured the hospital in an unashamed search for 'remarkable figure[s] worth our observing', starting up conversations solely 'to divert' and 'entertain' themselves with patients' 'frenzical extravagancies' and 'whimsical vagaries'. Tom Brown's description of Bethlem in *Amusements Serious and Comical* as 'but one entire Amusement' was in much the same vein.[62] Guides like *Les Délices d'Angleterre* (1707), and *Travels in London* (1710) similarly presented Bethlem in 'pleasant' fashion to foreigners, who flocked in to be amused by the 'tomfoolery' of the patients.[63] William Hutton, a Birmingham businessman in town in 1749, claimed to have 'never [been] out of the way of entertainment', specifying a trip to Bethlem where he had 'met with a variety of curious anecdotes' and 'found conversation with a multitude of characters'.[64]

The way the rabble element amongst visitors obtained their entertainment and treated the patients was often vicious in the extreme. Many were said to turn up with this in mind 'merely', as a correspondent to *The Gentleman's Magazine* declared in 1748, 'to mock at the nakedness of human nature, and make themselves merry'.[65] The most graphic account of this sport was given by Thomas Tryon in his *A Treatise of Dreams and Visions* (1689). Visitors were admitted indiscriminately, he complained, permitted to stay 'for several hours (almost all day long)', making so much 'noise' that the patients 'can never be at any quiet'. Young and 'Drunken' visitors, he claimed, delighted in interrogating patients with no end of 'vain' and 'impertinent Questions' – such as 'what are you here for? How long have you been here?' – purely to incense the patients and give themselves a feast of 'Laughing and Hooting' at the 'Raving . . . Cursing and Swearing' they provoked. Such behaviour evidently involved a good deal of youthful exhibitionism and high-jinks, visitors aping the role of tour-guides, according to Tryon, 'going along from one Apartment to the other, and Crying out; This Woman is in for Love; That man for Jealousie; He has Over-studied himself, and the Like'.[66]

Tryon's observations are supported by numerous other testimonies. In 1723, Hildebrand Jacob denounced the 'unseasonable Mirth' of 'the noisy Crowd' of visitors or 'gaping Fools . . . who joy to see/Man fallen from his native Dignity'.[67] Visiting the playwright, Nat Lee, confined in Bethlem in 1684, William Wycherley condemned the entertainment of his 'Gaping Audience', expressing his censure in verse:

> And now, the Rabble to thee does resort
> That thy Want of Wits may be their Sport.[68]

Of course we must not take accounts at face value: the antics of the plebs are recorded through the prejudices of their betters. These accounts were polemical in aim, displaying greater disdain towards the thronging spectators than the mad themselves. The Georgian elite was seeking to drive a wedge between patrician and plebeian culture, condemning the conduct of the crowd and withdrawing from entertainments and recreations they once had shared.[69]

Rather as with rising elite disquiet over the rowdy spectacle of public executions, growing unease was being expressed towards undesirable implications of visiting Bethlem.[70] Abraham Cowley recorded in the mid-seventeenth century that his own visits 'wrought so contrary an effect' on him that he 'always returned, not onely Melancholy, but ev'n sick with the sight!'[71] As sensibilities grew more refined, the fun went out of seeing the insane. The new sentiments of the Age of Sensibility robbed visiting Bethlem of its humour, replacing the ribaldry of a Brown or Ward with the tears of a 'Man of Feeling'.[72] Genteel visitors now looked at patients less as a commentary on the madness of 'sane' society than as figures of distress in their own right. The curious visitor gave way to the man or woman of sentiment, and from searching out the most entertaining or brutish of the inmates, spectators now concentrated on the most moving. While, before the mid-eighteenth century, there had been nothing more remarkable or amusing than Bedlam and its inmates, there was subsequently 'nothing so affecting'.[73] When John Taylor visited the actor Samuel Reddish in the 1780s, he did not poke fun or point a moral, but 'soothed' him over the humiliation which had provoked his mental collapse.[74] The educated elite now condemned not merely the raucous pleasure of the rabble, but 'any mind' that could derive 'delight' or 'any degree of pleasure' from visiting Bethlem. It was now being declared 'impossible' for anyone 'tolerably civilised' to derive pleasure in this way.[75] A polarization of opinion came about: those who denounced showing off the insane also commonly denounced public executions, cruel sports and so forth, while those, like Samuel Johnson, who valued keeping insanity in view, often approved of public executions – recall his rage at the almost simultaneous ending of Tyburn hangings in 1783: 'the age is running mad after innovation.'[76]

A growing recognition of the sensibilities of the afflicted and those less well endowed by nature, created new empathy with the plight of the mad. The mad were ceasing to be 'creatures' and were becoming 'fellow creatures'.[77] It was no mere coincidence that Thomas Tryon, one of the first to revile making 'a *show*' of Bedlamites as 'very Undecent [and] Inhumane', was a Dissenter, a vegetarian and the author of 'an enlightened plea for the more human treatment of negro slaves'.[78] Others too, like 'Benevolus' of the *London Chronicle*, had grown increasingly aware of the connection between cruelty to insects and animals, cruelty to children, cruelty to the insane, and a brutalized society.[79] Visiting Bedlam was increasingly seen as bad for the visitors.

Growing disgust at the spectacle of madness thus involved expression of tender compassion for the plight of abused patients. Above all, the turn of the tide against visiting arose from the new sensibilities of polite culture. For the man of feeling, the face of madness was now almost too terrible to be shown. From the early eighteenth century there are signs of a growing repugnance for the sight of the 'Lunatick' and the 'Ideot': 'We should . . . throw a veil', it was said, 'upon those unhappy Instances of human Nature, who seem to breathe without the Direction of Reason and Understanding.'[80] A note of squeamishness enters accounts of visiting Bethlem, a growing aversion to 'exhibit' those 'in circumstances of the most pityable infirmity'.[81] 'The distresses' of the mad 'afflict' the new man of feeling 'too much to incline [him] . . . to be a spectator of them'.[82] While deigning to visit Bethlem in 1786, the German novelist, Sophie von la Roche, confessed to 'a horror of such establishments, where my heart would be torn at the sight of so much anguish, and seized with an aversion to those in authority'.[83] By the 1770s, the polite were increasingly 'withdrawing to hide insanity'. On hearing of the mad exploits of his nephew, Lord Orford, in 1778, Horace Walpole declared, 'What a humiliation, to know he is thus exposing himself.'[84] Late eighteenth-century medical treatises are suffused with similar expressions of sensibility. Outlining the symptomatology of 'melancholia', William Pargeter for example expostulated: '*This* is most horrible indeed; and those who have once experienced such a spectacle, I am confident, will never wish it a second time.'[85]

Changing public attitudes forced the hands of Bethlem's Governors. There is no reason to suppose they initially had any qualms about public visiting: it brought in useful income, and the tips kept badly paid staff happy; it gratified civic pride, showing off one of the City's noblest edifices; and it served as a public exemplar. But the Governors became aware of abuses and felt obliged to tackle them. There were persistent complaints of prostitutes and thieves infiltrating the ranks of visitors. And visitors themselves exploited the patients by getting them drunk, while hucksters hawked 'Nutts Cake [and] . . . fruite' to the patients and visitors, contributing to the fairground atmosphere.[86] From time to time, the Governors issued prohibitions against such activities, and repeatedly instructed the servants to put them into effect.

They also sought to curtail improper kinds of visiting. After anonymous complaints in 1650, the Governors somewhat unrealistically required the Porter to discriminate between well-intentioned and ill-motivated visitors, and to expel loiterers.[87] Some, it was alleged, derived gratification from gazing at the nakedness of patients, females in particular. The 1677 rules for Moorfields state that 'noe Lunaticke that lyeth naked or that be in a course of cure be seene by any [visitor] . . . without the Consent of the Physitian'.[88] Further orders followed against the exposure of 'the Nakednesse and Sufferings of the Patients . . .to Strangers', indicating not only that the ruling was being neglected, but also that the Governors were at least as much concerned with *spectators'* sense of propriety and the Hospital's image, as with patients' modesty.[89] To prevent sexual contact between visitors and women patients, the Steward was to take particular care 'on the Women's side', and the Matron to be equally diligent in confining 'Woman Patients as are Lewdly Given' and in barring visitors from them unless 'in Company with one of the Gallery Maids'.[90]

Some, like Tryon, complained of the long hours of visiting and its unsupervised nature, and their complaints are confirmed by Court Minutes. Visitors were largely left to their own devices, leading to reports that visitors could 'lurk' or idle away 'the Interim houres', free to 'practise' whatever 'jest' or 'knavery' might suit their whim.[91] In 1650, Sunday visiting was banned, while the ban was made total in 1657, and extended to festival days.[92] The Governors also imposed mandatory time limits. From 1663, the Porter was instructed (reiterating an earlier order) to ensure that the Hospital gates were shut at 7 p.m. in Autumn and Winter, and 9 p.m. in Spring and Summer, and to allow no-one 'to come into the hospitall after . . . those respective houres'.[93]

The cases of Cromwell's Porter, Daniel, and Richard Stafford, the Jacobite, whose friends and devotees maintained regular contact with them, illustrate, however, the difficulty of restricting access to patients, despite orders to the contrary from the Board of Greencloth. For at least six of the eight months Stafford was incarcerated, 'a great Concourse of people' was allowed 'daily [to] resort' to him, and he was permitted to preach to them, was supplied with writing materials by them and able to issue a stream of 'Pamphlets and Libels' deemed 'treasonable' by the Board, through his cell window which directly overlooked the street.[94] Similarly, according to the Reverend Charles Leslie, the basketman who had the charge of the lower southern gallery where Daniel was confined, did nothing about the 'Persons' (mostly 'Women') who 'often come . . . to hear him Preach', and who 'wou'd sit many hours under his Window, with great signs of Devotion', turning the pages of 'their Bibles' to Daniel's 'Quotations'. Open access to Bethlem continued to grant the insane a voice, indeed perhaps amplified it.[95]

Things were changing by the mid-eighteenth century. John Wesley, George Whitefield and other Methodist preachers were, by their own accounts, effectually barred from Bethlem, out of fears they would aggravate patients' conditions. Although able to correspond with one such devotee, Joseph Periam, confined during the late 1730s, Whitefield reported 'there was an order given, that neither I, or any of his friends, should be permitted to come unto him'.[96] Likewise, Wesley described having just begun an interview with 'a young woman in Bedlam' he was visiting in 1750, when he was informed 'that "None of these preachers were to come there"', 'for fear', commented Wesley sardonically, 'of making them [the patients] mad'.[97] *Bethlem A Poem. By A Patient* (see Plate 13.3), dated May 1744 and sold to visitors for 3d, reflects the Governors' antipathy for the 'pernicious Doctrines' of Methodism.[98]

One method used to keep order was appointing the Porter to the constabulary, a move intended not only to curb the activities of visiting thieves but 'to prevent disturbances' in general 'at Holliday times'.[99] Then, in 1764, it was openly acknowledged by the Committee 'that great Riots and Disorders have been Committed in this Hospital during the Holidays' – revealing how out of control holiday-makers had become. At Easter 1764 the Steward was ordered to provide 'four Constables and also four Stout Fellows as Assistants in each Gallery . . . to Suppress any Riots or Disorders that might happen'. Two years later, visiting on the three succeeding days after Easter, Whitsunday and Christmas day, was banned altogether – notice was to be printed in four public newspapers and posted 'upon the Pillars of this Hospital'; the outer gates and front windows were to be kept locked and shut; and the staff were instructed to 'attend their duty diligently during these three Holydays' – all such directions clearly conjure up the kind of holiday siege to which the Hospital had evidently been subjected. The gradual curtailment of visiting in the 1760s was partly a reaction to the disenchantment of the educated public, but it was also an internal response to the problems posed by disorderly visitors.[100]

The old era of unrestricted visits finally came to an end in 1770, with the introduction of the ticket system, after which visitors were permitted entrance only on production of a ticket signed by a Governor. Clearly historians like Scull have been partially right to see general visiting as only permissible in an age when the mad were conceived of as bestial and insensible, and the madhouse as something of a human zoo.[101] Yet, while the end of visiting was an outcome of elite pressure and enlightened sensibility, the story is more nuanced than this account would allow. If the new men and women of feeling were more aware of the feelings and welfare of the mad, there was a squeamishness at the heart of such reactions that threatened to shut madness more firmly away. Visiting must also be understood in the context of Bethlem's evolution as a charity, as well as of the classical meaning of spectacle. The Hospital's enduring dependency on the goodwill and liberality of its benefactors had rendered public access to Bethlem economically expedient, while charity had long utilized the exhortatory power involved in the display of sickness and want. By 1770 the Hospital was financially self-sufficient, and the curtailing of visiting signals the Hospital's increasing capacity for self-definition. Indubitably, it was late in coming. Despite critiques by observers from the 1740s, and the establishment of rival institutions which disowned the policy, the Bethlem Governors proved hidebound.

Ticket-only visiting served as a social filter. In 1779 access had further to be restricted to four persons per ticket, on the discovery of 'great Numbers of Persons' visiting the Hospital on single tickets.[102] The exclusion of the visitor in the age of sensibility was an act expressive of the full complexity of Enlightenment motives. Patients were to be protected from the voyeur and the lecher, and the baser instincts of the herd were to be curbed through suppressing a popular sport. Once the elite chose to withdraw from the habit of visiting, there was no longer any good reason to keep the practice going.

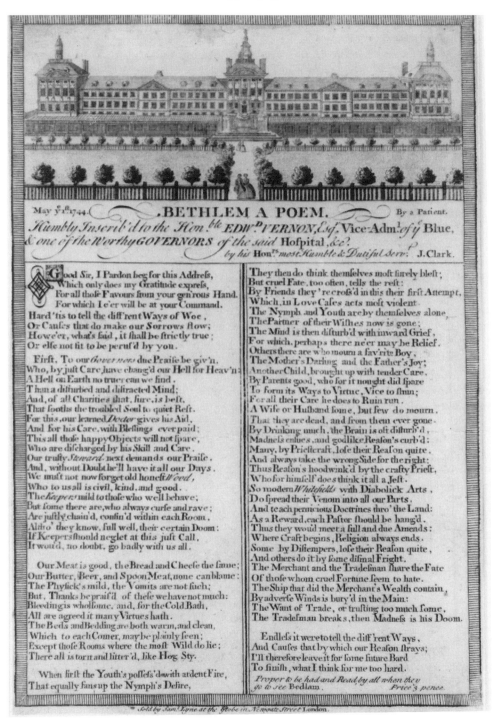

Plate 13.3 Broadsheet sold to visitors in the 1740s. Reproduced by permission of the Bethlem Royal Hospital Archives and Museum.

The Governors congratulated themselves that exclusion was for the patients' good. 'A general Admission of Visitors', according to Boyer's Spital Sermon (1789), had 'from its first Institution ... been found prejudicial and inconvenient to the Patients'.[103] Visiting, alleged the Revd Thomas Bowen, 'tended to disturb the tranquillity of the patients'.[104] It is at least arguable, however, that the termination of general visiting did no good to the patients: behind locked doors, they had more to fear from the depredations of the staff than previously from the public. It is probably no accident that the worst scandals, as in the case of James Norris and perhaps that of James Tilly Matthews, occurred after 1770.[105] The main patient complaint narrative protesting against ill-treatment by staff – Urbane Metcalf's *The Interior of Bethlehem Hospital* – dates from 1818.[106]

After 1770, patients were subject to a considerable degree of isolation from their friends and the outside world. A year previously, the Governors had ordered that female patients' friends should only be permitted to see them in the committee room, attended by the nurse, and during normal visiting hours, unless the visit was authorized by the physician.[107] Subsequently, friends had their visits further limited or entirely banned in individual cases; some patients were confined to their cells on visiting days; while, from 1780, after a violent incident, ex-incurables were excluded from admission as visitors to Bethlem.[108] By 1815, visiting had been restricted to Mondays only, while at other hospitals like St Luke's, where friends and relations were limited to just 'half an Hour' at a time from 1790, visiting was even more tightly curtailed.[109] Of course, decisions to restrict visits were generally taken in the declared interests of patients themselves; yet while patients may have been better protected from ill-motivated visitors, such benefits were offset by patients' loss of intimacy with caring family and friends.

The mingling of patients with the public had its benefits. Our main surviving narrative from a patient's own mouth of his encounters with visitors to Bethlem is that of James Carkesse, and it is one of unqualified approval. In his series of poems entitled *Lucida Intervalla* (1679), composed during confinement at Finsbury Madhouse and at Bethlem between 1676 and 1677, Carkesse relates being visited at Bethlem by at least fourteen persons, only three of whom he designates as 'friends', the others evidently being spectators. The reliability of Carkesse's text is, of course, debatable, and his claims to attention from the Quality have led some to suspect his visitors were merely products of his delusions of grandeur. Yet Carkesse is honest enough to describe the Duke of Monmouth's visit, without pretending that the Duke visited *him*; and however problematic, his account provides an authentic enough insight into what the patient felt about his environment.[110]

To his visitors, Carkesse responds with pleasure and gratitude, dedicating one or two poems to each. Seven are inspired by the generous gifts he receives from his visitors, comprising money, food, clothing, furniture and writing materials. His poems show how the articulate patient could wheedle considerable privileges out of visitors. Apart from the material rewards of visiting, his poems reveal the rapture a patient might experience at the appearance of visitors of the opposite sex, and the 'Extasie' he could feel at the visit of a dignitary, like the Duke of Grafton. It is not the conduct of the general public of which Carkesse complains, quite the reverse: the one question he records being asked by a visitor is not insulting, but 'kindly' – the Duke inquiring 'How he did' – while others, judging by their gifts, had asked him what he needed. Likewise, Cromwell's Porter, according to James Yonge, had 'begged' a Bible from the King 'when his Majesty came to visit the place'.[111]

Of course both Carkesse and Daniel were exceptional patients, and may have received a superior class of visitor. Yet it was far from exceptional for run-of-the-mill patients to beg and receive money and favours from visitors. Bedlamites evidently played to the gallery, putting on a 'show' in return for attention, ha'pence and food. Some patients even made items for sale to visitors in the hospital. Sophie von la Roche purchased 'a little basket of plaited straw' 'from one poor, melancholy creature', who ran off to hoard her money in her cell.[112]

The Governors' Minutes confirm that patients grew skilled at begging and at interacting with visitors. The literary stereotype of a spectator conducted around Bedlam by a 'decent looking chap', only to discover that he was in reality a patient, is grounded in fact.[113] In 1727, a patient was found to have shown visitors up to 'the chequer' (the basketman 'having forgot to Lock ye door'), and to have taken a fee for so doing. Keys even seem also to have been entrusted to patients on occasion, and as late as the 1760s patients were still being permitted by staff to 'Walk Idle up and down the House Shewing it to Strangers and begging Money'.[114]

The history of visits to Bethlem queries some aspects of Foucault's reading of the 'great confinement'. He was without doubt right to stress certain features of the hardening of attitudes towards madness during the 'long eighteenth century' and to draw attention to growing policies of confinement. But in so far as he was arguing that the mad were shut away in this period, that inference does not apply to Bethlem. Rather than being sequestrated, the mad were put on show there. Far from lunatics being taken out of circulation and shut up, they became a spectacle in what was, till 1770, a quite astonishingly permeable institution. Far from being silenced, the Bedlamites became loquacious.[115]

Visiting was wound down after 1770, bringing down an iron curtain between reason and unreason. But that is almost at the close of the period Foucault termed the great confinement. And what happened in 1770 was not the shutting away of the mad, but the locking out of the sane. And that was not for the sort of reasons Foucault adduces – turning madness into pure negativity – but in some measure to protect the mad, and, more so, to protect the sensibilities of civilized society in a manner that better corresponds to the explanatory categories adduced by Norbert Elias's notion of a 'civilizing process'.

Something fundamental had altered. And yet it would be misleading to suggest that the spectacle of madness came to an abrupt end. However hostile (certain) members of polite society had become to putting madness on show, on a smaller, more formalized and 'domesticated' scale, visiting the insane continued. Crowds still gathered around the bizarre, the mad and the foolish in squares and market places, families and physicians occasionally devising elaborate ruses to avoid the prying eyes of the masses, while the popularity of anecdotal collections of Bedlamites and other odd characters endured well into the nineteenth century.[116]

NOTES

1 For the sights of London see Roy Porter, *London: A Social History* (London: Hamish Hamilton, 1994; Penguin books, 1996), ch. 7. For the culture of early modern madness see Michael V. DePorte, *Nightmares and Hobby Horses: Swift, Sterne, and Augustan Ideas of Madness* (San Marino, Calif.: Huntingdon Library, 1974). For fuller referencing see Jonathan Andrews, 'A History of Bethlem Hospital, *c.* 1634–*c.* 1770' (Ph.D. thesis, University of London, 1991), which forms the basis of this and the following chapters.

2 Ned Ward, *The London Spy*, edited by K. Fenwick (London: Folio Society, 1955), 48–50.

3 J. Kromm, 'Studies in the Iconography of Madness, 1600–1900' (Ph.D. diss., Emory University, 1984); Peter Wagner, 'The Satire on Doctors in Hogarth's Graphic Works', in Marie Mulvey Roberts and Roy Porter (eds), *Literature and Medicine During the Eighteenth Century* (London and New York: Routledge, 1993), 200–25; Andrew Scull, 'The Domestication of Madness', *Medical History*, xxvii (1983), 233–48.

4 *BCGM*, 22 April 1681, fol. 217.

5 Thomas Tryon, *A Treatise of Dreams and Visions*, 2nd edn (London: T. Sowle, 1695), 290.

6 See *The World*, no. xxiii, 7 June 1753, 138. Michael MacDonald, *Mystical Bedlam: Madness, Anxiety and Healing in Seventeenth Century England* (Cambridge: CUP, 1981), 122.

7 See Patricia Allderidge, 'Bedlam: Fact or Fantasy?' in W. F. Bynum, Roy Porter and Michael Shepherd (eds), *The Anatomy of Madness: Essays in the History of Psychiatry*, 2 volumes, (London and New York: Tavistock, 1985), ii, 17–33.

8 Edward G. O'Donoghue, *The Story of Bethlehem Hospital from its Foundation in 1247* (London: T. Fisher Unwin, 1914), 405; *Sixth Report of the Royal Commissioners on Historical Manuscripts: Part I, Report and Appendix* (London: Eyre & Spottiswoode, 1877); *London Evening Post* (henceforth *LEP*), no. 1239, 25–28 Oct. 1735.

9 For Peg Nicholson, see Claire Williams (ed.), *Sophie in London* (London: Jonathan Cape, 1933), 169–70.

10 *BCGM*, 21 June 1637 and 4 September 1650, fols 127, 462–3 and *passim*.

11 *Ibid.* 4 Sept. 1650 and 11 August 1669, fols 462–3 and 289.

12 For instance, Samuel Pepys, *The Diary of Samuel Pepys*, 11 vols, edited by R. Latham and W. Matthews (London: Bell & Hyman, 1970–83); E. S. De Beer (ed.), *The Diary of John Evelyn*, 6 volumes (Oxford: OUP, 1955).

13 *BCGM*, 25 February 1709, fol. 465.

14 See *The Guardian*, no. 105, 11 July 1713.

15 *Ibid.*; R. K. McClure, *Coram's Children: The London Foundling Hospital in the Eighteenth Century* (New Haven, Conn.: Yale University Press, 1981); Richard Altick, *The Shows of London* (Cambridge, Mass.: The Belknap Press of Harvard University Press, 1978).

16 Ward, *op. cit.*.

17 W. H. Quarrell and Margaret Mare (eds), *London in 1710. From the travels of Zacharias Conrad von Uffenbach* (London: Faber & Faber, 1934), 86–8; *London Chronicle*, 18 April 1757; *BCGM*, 30 April 1680, fol. 148; *An Account of the Rise, Progress, & State of the Hospitals for relieving Poor People afflicted with the Small-Pox, & for Inoculation; from its First Institution* (London: H. Woodfall, 1764), 34.

18 W. Wroth and A. E. Wroth, *The London Pleasure Gardens of the Eighteenth Century* (abr., Hamden: Archon Books, 1979; 1st edn, 1896); J. G. Southworth, *Vauxhall Gardens. A Chapter in the Social History of England* (New York: Columbia University Press, 1941); Altick, *op. cit.* 94–6.

19 See *The World*, no. 23, 7 June 1753, 138.

20 *Ibid.*

21 M. A. Screech, *Erasmus: Ecstasy and the Praise of Folly* (London: Penguin/Peregrine, 1988; orig. Duckworth, 1980); *idem*, 'Good Mania in Christendom', in W. F. Bynum, Roy Porter and Michael Shepherd (eds), The *Anatomy of Madness: Essays in the History of Psychiatry* (London and New York: Tavistock, 1985), i, 25–39.

22 Donald Lupton, *London and the Countrey Carbonadoed and Quantied into severall Characters* (London: N. Okes, 1632), 74–8.

23 Edward Stillingfleet, *Protestant Charity. A Sermon Preached at S. Sepulchres Church, on Tuesday in Easter Week, A.D. 1681* (London: M. Flesher for Henry Mortlock, 1681), 28 and 47.

24 Gilbert declared: 'That reason which they have lost, should excite us to shew our Thankfulness to God for the Continuance of this Blessing to ourselves, by contributing all in our Power towards restoring, in these most deplorable objects of our Compassion, that Faculty which stamps upon us all the Image of God': John Gilbert, *A Sermon Preached before . . . in Easter Week 1743* (London: Printed for J. and H. Pemberton, 1743).

25 Addison quite consciously chose the title *Spectator* for his magazine, and constantly reiterated his concern 'that his Reader becomes a kind of Spectator, and feels in himself all the variety of Passions, which are correspondent to the several Parts of the Relation'; *Spectator*, no. 420 (2 July 1712), 574.

26 *The Guardian*, no. 79 (11 June 1713), 313.

27 Sander L. Gilman, *Seeing the Insane: A Cultural History of Madness and Art in the Western World* (New York: Wiley, in association with Brunner-Mazel, 1982).

28 *Tatler*, no. 30 (18 June 1708), 223–4.

29 *Tatler*, no. 127 (31 January 1710), 242–3.

30 *Ibid.* 223–5.

31 See John Locke, *An Essay on Human Understanding*, revised edn, ed. John W. Yolton (London: J. M. Dent, 1965), 306–14.

32 W. S. Lewis (ed.), *Horace Walpole's Correspondence*, 48 volumes (New Haven: Yale University Press, 1954), xxxviii, letter dated 29 Oct. 1764, 453; *London Chronicle*, 21–23 May 1761, 491. See also parable of Bedlam blacksmith in *The Universal Spectator*, no. 317 (1734), 2; *The Gentleman's Magazine* (henceforth *GM*), 4 (1734), 596.

33 See Christopher Hill, *The World Turned Upside Down: Radical Ideas during the English Revolution* (London: Temple Smith, 1972), 223–7, 306; Roy Porter, *Mind Forg'd Manacles: Madness and Psychiatry in England from Restoration to Regency* (London: Athlone Press, 1987; Penguin, 1990), 25–31; Gilman, *op. cit.* 56–7; Max Byrd, *Visits to Bedlam: Madness and Literature in the Eighteenth Century* (Columbia: University of South Carolina Press, 1974).

34 James Boswell, *Life of Johnson*, ed. R. W. Chapman (Oxford: OUP, 1980), 635.

35 Gilman, *op. cit.* 56–7.

36 *GM*, 18 (May 1748), 199.

37 Michel Foucault, *Folie et Déraison: Histoire de la Folie à L'Age Classique* (Paris: Librairie Plon, 1961), trans. and abridged by Richard Howard as *Madness and Civilisation: A History of Insanity in the Age of Reason* (New York: Random House, 1965), 70.

38 *Tatler*, nos. 125 and 162 (26 January and 26 April 1710), 234–8 and 402–5.

39 *Rambler*, no. 52 (15 Sept. 1750), 222–5.

40 *Ibid.*

41 *Ibid.*; James Boswell, *The Hypochondriac*, ed. Margery Bailey (Stanford: Stanford University Press, 1928), Sept. 1778, 197; *Tatler*, no. 125 (31 January 1710), 244.

42 *Rambler*, no. 52 (15 Sept. 1750) 225; *Spectator*, nos. 438 and 576 (23 July 1712 and 4 August 1714) 39–42 and 569–71.

43 Boswell, *Life of Johnson*, 1226.

44 Foucault, *op. cit.* 88.

45 Jonathan Swift, 'A Tale of a Tub', in Kathleen Williams (ed.), *A Tale of a Tub and other Satires* (London: J. M. Dent, 1975); idem, *A Serious and Useful Scheme To make an Hospital for Incurables. Of Universal Benefit to all His Majesty's Subjects* (London: J. Roberts, 1733), 14; Henry Fielding, *The Covent Garden Journal* (henceforth, *CGJ*), nos. 35 and 62 (2 May and 16 September 1752), 210–14 and 332–4.

46 Ward, *op. cit.* 54.

47 A. M. Ingram, *Boswell's Creative Gloom* (London: Macmillan, 1982); Roy Porter, 'The Hunger of Imagination: Approaching Samuel Johnson's Melancholy', in W. F. Bynum, Roy Porter and M. Shepherd (eds), *The Anatomy of Madness: Essays in the History of Psychiatry*, 2 volumes (London: Tavistock, 1985), i, 63–88.

48 Boswell, *Hypochondriac*, i (Sept. 1778), 197; *Rambler*, no. 52 (15 September 1750), 222–5; *Guardian*, no. 79 (11 June 1713), 312–13.

49 *Tatler*, nos. 125 and 162 (26 January and 26 April 1710), 235 and 402–5.

50 *Guardian*, no. 79 (11 June 1713), 314–15.

51 Tryon, *op. cit.* 292.

52 Thomas Middleton and William Rowley, *The Changeling*, 1622 edn, ed. N. W. Bawcutt, III, iii, l.21, 45; F. N. L. Poynter (ed.), *The Journal of James Yonge* (London: Longmans, 1963), 158–9; Natsu Hattori '"The pleasure of your Bedlam"; The Theatre of Madness in the Renaissance', *History of Psychiatry*, vi (1995), 283–308; Robert R. Reed, *Bedlam on the Jacobean Stage* (Cambridge, Mass.: Harvard University Press, 1952).

53 George Farquhar, *Love and a Bottle* (London, 1697/8), in Shirley Strum Kenny (ed.), *The Works of George Farquhar*, 2 volumes (Oxford: Clarendon, 1988), i, 3–112, II, ii, lines 346–8.

54 Fielding, *CGJ*, no. 54 (1752), 294.

55 See *Sixth Report of the Royal Commissioners on Historical Manuscripts* (note 8); O'Donoghue, *op. cit.* 405.

56 De Beer, *op. cit.* iii, 21 April 1657, 191; Boswell, *Life of Johnson*, 8 May 1775, 635.

57 Pepys, *op. cit.* ix, 19 February 1669, 454. This was six years prior to Pepys's election on 18 June 1765 as Governor of Bridewell and Bethlem, at the nomination of his friend, the Bethlem Physician, Thomas Allen.

58 J. J. Bagley (ed.), *The Great Diurnal of Nicholas Blundell of Little Cosby, Lancashire* (1702–28), 3 volumes (Liverpool, London and Prescot: The Record Society of Lancs and Cheshire, 1968–72), i, 8 May 1703, 35; ii, 31 Aug. 1717, 208; iii, 19 August 1723, 113.

59 See, e.g., William Hutton, *The Life of William Hutton, published by his daughter, Catherine Hutton* (London: Printed for Baldwin, Cradock & Joy, 1816), 71; Ward, *op. cit.* 52–5; Thomas Browne, *Amusements Serious and Comical* (London: Printed for John Nutt, 1700), 35.

60 Quarrell and Mare, *op. cit.* 51–2. For patients making animal and bird noises, see *The Changeling*, III, iii, lines 190–8, 54.

61 *London Chronicle*, 21–3 May 1761, 491.

62 Ward, *op. cit.*, 51–5; Browne, *Amusements*, iii, 35–8.

63 Quarrell and Mare, *op. cit.* 51–2; J. Beeverell, *Les Délices de la Grande Bretagne* (Leiden: P. vander Aa, 1707).

64 Hutton, *op. cit.* 71.

65 *GM*, xviii (May 1748), 199.

66 Tryon, *op. cit.* 288–93.

67 Hildebrand Jacob, *Bedlam. A Poem* (London: Printed for W. Lewis and Tho. Edlin, 1723), 13.

68 William Wycherley, *To NATH. LEE in Bethlem . . .* , in *The Works of the Ingenious Mr William Wycherley* (ed.), Montague Summers (London: Printed for B. Tooke, 1924), iii, 233–7, 235.

69 Peter Burke, *Popular Culture in Early Modern Europe* (London: Maurice Temple Smith, 1978); Norbert Elias, *The Civilizing Process*, vol. 1, *The History of Manners* (New York: Pantheon, 1978); vol. 2, *Power and Civility* (New York: Pantheon, 1982); vol. 3, *The Court Society* (New York: Pantheon, 1983).

70 V. A. C. Gatrell, *The Hanging Tree: Execution and the English People 1770–1868* (Oxford: OUP, 1994); Pieter Spierenburg, *The Spectacle of Suffering: Executions and the Evolution of Repression: From a Preindustrial Metropolis to the European Experience* (Cambridge: CUP, 1984).

71 Abraham Cowley, *Several Discourses by Way of Essays in Verse and Prose in The Works of Mr Abraham Cowley* (London: Henry Herringman, 1668), ed. H. C. Minelin (1904), essay 8, 'The Dangers of an Honest Man in Much Company', 93–4.

72 Janet Todd, *Sensibility: An Introduction* (London: Methuen, 1986); John Mullan, *Sentiment and Sociability. The Language of Feeling in the Eighteenth Century* (Oxford: Clarendon, 1988); Everett Zimmermann, 'Fragments of History and *The Man of Feeling*; from Richard Bentley to Walter Scott', in *Eighteenth Century Studies*, xxiii (1990), 283–300; F. J. Barker-Benfield, *The Culture of Sensibility: Sex and Society in Eighteenth Century Britain* (Chicago: University of Chicago Press, 1992); Henry Mackenzie, *The Man of Feeling* (Oxford: OUP, 1970; 1st edn, 1771).

73 *The World*, no. 23 (7 June 1753) 137–8.

74 John Taylor, *Records of My Life*, 2 volumes (London: Edward Bull, 1832), i, 49.

75 *London Chronicle*, 21–23 May 1761, 491.

76 G. B. Hill (ed.), *Boswell's Life of Johnson*, 6 volumes (New York: Harper, 1891), iv, 217.

77 *Guardian*, no. 79 (11 June 1713), 314–15; *GM*, xviii (May 1748), 199.

78 Tryon, *op. cit.* 288–93; *idem*, *A Treatise on Cleanness in Meats and Drinks* (London: L. Curtis, 1682); *idem*, *Friendly Advice to the Gentlemen Planters of the East and West Indies* (London: Andrew Sowle, 1684).

79 *London Chronicle*, 21–23 May 1761, 491.

80 *Tatler*, no. 40 (12 July 1709), 289.

81 *GM*, xviii (1748), 199.

82 *The World*, no. 23 (7 June 1753), 137.

83 Claire Williams, *op. cit.* 166.

84 Walpole, *Correspondence*, letter dated 9 April 1778, 332.

85 W. Pargeter, *Observations on Maniacal Disorders*, ed. Stanley Jackson (London: Routledge, 1988; 1st edn, Reading: for the author, 1792), 39.

86 *BCGM*, 30 March 1677, fol. 358.

87 *Ibid.* 4 Sept. 1650, fols 462–3.

88 *Ibid.* 30 March 1677, fol. 358.

89 *Ibid.* 31 January and 14 March 1690, fols 18 and 31.

90 *Ibid.*

91 *Ibid.* 4 Sept. 1650, fols 462–3; Tryon, *Dreams*.

92 *BCGM*, 4 Sept. 1650 and 12 June 1657, fols 462–3 and 817.

93 *Ibid.* 21 January 1663, fol. 31.

94 For refs and fuller discussion of Stafford's case see Chapter 18.

95 Charles Leslie, *The Snake in the Grass* (London: Charles Browne, 1696), lxxxviii–xcii. Leslie's anecdote is possibly entirely fictitious of course, being designed merely in accordance with his grand scheme of stigmatizing the Quakers as mad.

96 W. Wale (ed.), *George Whitefield's Journals: to which is prefixed his 'Short Account' and 'Further Account'* (London: Henry J. Drane, 1905), 261–7, and *George Whitefield's Letters. For the period 1734–42* (Edinburgh: The Banner of Truth Trust, 1976), letters 13, and 295, 497, 273.

97 Nehemiah Curnock (ed.), *The Journal of the Reverend John Wesley*, 2 volumes (London: Epworth Press, 1938), ii, 22 February 1750.

98 Railing against the 'Whitefields' and the 'pernicious Doctrines' of Methodism, the patient-poet alleged that their 'Priestcraft' made men mad, and that their pastors deserved to 'be hang'd'; *Bethlem A Poem. By a Patient* (London: *s.n.*, 1744). The original is in *BRHA*.

99 *BCGM*, 12 March 1742, fol. 175.

100 *BSCM*, 21 April 1664.

101 Andrew T. Scull, *The Most Solitary of Afflictions. Madness and Society in Britain, 1700–1900* (New Haven and London: Yale University Press, 1993); *idem*, *Social Order/Mental Disorder: Anglo-American Psychiatry in Historical Perspective* (London: Routledge, 1989).

102 *BCGM*, 7 July and 22 October 1708, fols 424 and 446.

103 Revd James Boyer, *A Psalm of Thanksgiving . . . [and] A true Report of the great Number of . . . Poor People maintained in the several Hospital . . .* (London: Charles Rivington, 1789).

104 T. Bowen, *An Historical Account of the Origin, Progress and Present State of Bethlem Hospital* (London: for the author, 1783), 111.

105 Roy Porter (ed.), *John Haslam: Illustrations of Madness* (London: Routledge, 1988; 1st edn, 1810).

106 Urbane Metcalf, *The Interior of Bethlehem Hospital* (London: by the Author, 1818).

107 *BCGM*, 27 April 1769, fol. 250.

108 For example, *BSCM*, 28 Oct. 1780, 12 July 1781, 1 June 1782, 28 May 1785 and 29 March 1800, cases of Richard Hyde, Peter Pattinson, Thomas Thomas and Jane Gibbs.

109 House of Commons, *Reports from the Committee on Madhouses in England* (London: House of Commons, 1815–16); *St Luke's Hospital General Committee Minutes*, 7 April 1790.

110 James Carkesse, *Lucida Intervalla: Containing Divers Miscellaneous Poems*, ed. M. V. DePorte (Los Angeles: University of California Press, 1979; 1st edn, London: 1679).

111 *Ibid.* 24; Poynter, *op. cit.* 158.

112 Claire Williams, *op. cit.* 170.

113 See e.g. Mackenzie, *op. cit.* 30–2. See also Jonathan Andrews, '"In her Vapours . . . [or] in her Madness"? Mrs Clerke's Case: An Early Eighteenth Century Psychiatric Controversy', *History of Psychiatry*, i (1990), 125–44, *re* daily deceiving of visitors by Bedlamites.

114 *BSCM*, 12 May 1727, fols 11–12; *BCGM*, 20 June 1765, fol. 11.

115 For evaluations of Foucault's interpretation, see Arthur Still and Irving Velody (eds), *Rewriting the History of Madness: Studies in Foucault's 'Histoire de la Folie'* (London and New York: Routledge, 1992).

116 See, e.g., Anon., *Sketches in Bedlam: or Characteristic Traits of Insanity. By a Constant Observer* (London: Sherwood, Jones 1823); George Man Burrows, *An Inquiry into Certain Errors Relative to Insanity* (London: Underwood, 1820); Andrew Scull, 'The Domestication of Madness'; *idem*, *The Most Solitary of Afflictions*.

'THE DISCIPLINE OF THE HOUSE'

Environment, management and architecture

———— •◆• ————

INTRODUCTION

Early modern Bethlem attracted a negative public image which was exploited by later reformers and became passed down into conventional historical judgment. 'Bedlam' has often thus been portrayed as the epitome of squalor, characterized by naked, starved and abused patients, dabbling in their own excrement, languishing in dark cells, sleeping on straw, constantly in chains and subject to lashings.[1] As recently as 1982 one historian declared:

> Bedlam (or Bethlem) was ... a wretched place ... The records show that patients were beaten, starved and manacled, and for months at a time they were placed in filthy dungeons, with no light or clothing; they were given only excrement-sodden straw on which to lie. Amputations of the toes and fingers of patients, due to frostbite, were not uncommon.[2]

Bethlem has all too readily been conflated with the satirical image of 'Bedlam', and scholars have accepted the verdict of the 1815/16 Parliamentary Madhouses Committee inquiry as if it were a blanket indictment of the entire span of the Hospital's history. Certainly, by modern standards Bethlem was brutal, cold, dark, slummy and filthy, but that is hardly a useful historical yardstick. Just how squalid were conditions at Bethlem by comparison with conditions for the poor, insane and sick elsewhere? In what ways did the Bethlem environment change over time? These are the pertinent questions.

Historians have moreover tended to take the polemics of nineteenth-century reformers too much at face value; for instance, Charles Dickens's verdict that 'coercion ... chains, straw, filthy solitude, darkness, and starvation ... spinning in whirligigs, corporal punishment, gagging', etc. were standard issue in a medical regime for which 'nothing was too widely extravagant, nothing too monstrously cruel to be prescribed'.[3] A recent historian's claim 'that madmen were chained, whipped, menaced, and half starved in asylums in the eighteenth century', and that this was a result of the public exhibition of the insane and of the advocacy of such treatment by 'many a treatise on the management of the mad' echoes the reformers' verdicts.[4] Yet such descriptions misrepresent the Bethlem regime and its shortcomings.[5]

BEDDING AND CLOTHING

Let us test aspects of the stereotype of Bedlam against what the records show: how faithful a reflection of reality is the popular image of the naked Bedlamite? It is almost impossible to know exactly how many patients were unclothed or bedded on straw, but it was certainly at some times a large proportion.[6]

Patients' securities were required by their bonds to provide or pay for patients' clothes and bedding, on top of their weekly maintenance fees. During the seventeenth century, however, the poverty of most patients and of the parishes and families supporting them meant that this provision was often inadequate. While the charity occasionally supplied the deficit, such assistance was *ad hoc*, and clothes and bedding were often dispensed belatedly, when patients had 'been waiting for an indeterminate time in [a] . . . state of dire and obvious necessity'.[7]

Beds and bedding were sparse at old Bethlem, yet far from every patient was left to languish upon straw. Humphrey Withers, Bethlem Porter (1633–54), had a supply of 'bedding and Linnen and other household stuffe', which he dispensed. That the Governors agreed in 1637 to recompense him with as much as £10, in consequence of these articles having been 'worne out & spoyld by the prisoners in Bethlem', suggests his supply was not inconsiderable. A fair number of patients were provided with beds at the Hospital's expense, for in 1676 all 'the old Bedsteads . . . for the Lunatikes' were removed to new Bethlem.[8] Despite the more than doubling of the Hospital's capacity by the move to Moorfields, initially only twenty-one extra beds were bought. Combined with those salvaged from the old building, these could barely have catered for half of the patient population.[9] It was generally only a minority of special cases – those committed to Bethlem by royal, governmental or mayoral authority, or those apprehended as vagrants without friends or other means of support – who were provided with bedding, clothing and other relief at the Hospital's charge.[10] Besides the new beds provided for patients in 1676, twelve such charity patients were also bought a 'rug' (i.e. coverlet).[11] There is no mention of sheets being provided before the eighteenth century.

Provision of clothing at old Bethlem was better organized and more generous. The Steward was enjoined to inform the Treasurer of any 'need' of 'clothing linen shoes stockings coats and gownes' and was to supply the lack.[12] From 1645 a Committee of Governors, selected from amongst those employed in the cloth trade, was appointed every year 'to give advice & assistance' to the Stewards of both Bethlem and Bridewell 'in buying and providing of [clothing etc.] . . . and other necessaryes for the said hospitalls'.[13] With the move to Moorfields, this function was assumed by the Bethlem Sub-Committee.[14] As with bedding, clothing was provided by the Governors almost exclusively for those 'poore Lunatiques . . . which have noe friends to take care of them'.[15] Most was ordered during August–December, to preserve patients from the worst inclemencies of the weather. The policy of 'winter clothes' was common to contemporary poor relief.[16]

It would be a mistake to hold the Bethlem administration solely accountable for failure to furnish patients with adequate bedding or clothing, for this was viewed as the responsibility of parishes and friends.[17] Letters admonishing sureties of their obligations to supply patients with clothing were sent by the Steward.[18] When in 1664 four London and Middlesex parishes 'refused to buy clothes' for their parishioners, they were warned that, unless they did so, the patients would be discharged. After a month, only Wapping persisted in its refusal, and its churchwardens were allowed just eight more days' grace before their parishioner was to be delivered to them.[19]

Benefactors were appreciative of the hardships endured by patients exposed to winter cold. In 1652, the Court of Governors devised a five-year plan whereby five lunatics admitted 'out of the poorest parishes aboute London shal bee cloathed yearely betweene the first of November & the five & twentieth of December att the direccon of the Treasurer', so as to reassure 'a Gentleman freind' of the Treasurer's that his intended donation of £30 would indeed reach the 'poore Lunatikes'.[20] Similar legacies given during the period 1690–2 'for Cloths for the poore Lunatikes' inspired the Governors to convert a cell into 'a repository or wardrobe' for the clothing of neglected patients.[21] Subsequent benefactions from 'Charitable persons' and Governors over the next three years augmented 'the Wardrobe Fund' to a running total of £300, while a legacy in 1697 of £60 from the Bethlem Apothecary, William Dickenson, was also applied to the wardrobe. This initiative is itself, however, a measure of how serious a problem 'the Nakedness and [resultant] Sufferings of the Patients' had been and of the mixed motives that underlay the Governors' new-found appreciation. Though concerned that 'Patients have suffered very much from want' of clothes, the Governors were anxious about the 'considerable extraordinary charge in Phisick and Surgerye' the Hospital had incurred and the exposure of its 'Honour and Reputacion . . . to Strangers'. Yet the real failure, as the Governors alleged, had been on the part of patients' friends and parishes not fulfilling their bonds, despite 'the care . . . taken by the Officers in applying to the Securitye[s] for Cloths'.[22]

Provision clearly improved following the move to Moorfields.[23] Tending to supply patients with clothes and bill sureties retrospectively, the Hospital was not infrequently forced to let sureties off their clothing debts, as in 1712 when more than £87 of arrears were cancelled by the Committee.[24] Bethlem's clothing provision was not confined to patients under cure. In 1768, the Steward was instructed by the Committee to 'provide all the Incurable Women Patients in this Hospital with Two Aprons in Case their friends do not provide the same'.[25] (Evidently, proper attire was regarded as more important for female patients.)[26] Part of the Hospital's after-care comprised furnishing apparel to patients on discharge, and Tyson's Gift (see Chapter 18) consolidated this into a much more extensive relief system after 1708.

By Thomas Weston's Stewardship (1713–34), all patients' bedding and the great majority of their clothing was being furnished by the Steward, at fixed prices.[27] Comparing Bethlem Court orders from the mid-eighteenth century, detailing standard outfits and prices of bedding and clothing, with seventeenth-century orders for the outfitting of charity patients shows significant improvements in provision at Bethlem and yet how traditional outfitting had remained.[28] It would be unreasonable to expect a hospital in those times to provide a great deal more. Indeed, a Bethlem outfit compares quite favourably in prices and range with provision at other contemporary institutions for the sick-poor. In the 1750s the Steward was required to submit a weekly account of all the apparel and bedding he had supplied and of what necessaries were still 'wanting for the respective Patients the ensuing Week', and was to make an inspection every Friday to check what patients lacked.[29]

Nevertheless, the Governors were often more worried about economy than comfort, and when in the 1770s it was discovered that servants were destroying the bedding of discharged curables the Committee ruled that in future such should be vetted by the Steward so that it might be appropriated to supply lack amongst the incurables – ensuring second-hand provision for chronic patients.[30] Yet it was only 'wet' and manic cases, prone to destroying their clothing or bedding, who were *supposed* to be confined without clothes (or with only a 'blanket gown' to cover them – hence the label 'blanket patients') and bedded on straw as a matter of policy. Given the cost of such items, it is not surprising that, confronted with patients like the pensioner, widow Davies, transferred to Bethlem from Bridewell in 1638 so 'distracted [that she] . . . doth teare her cloathes off her backe', Governors, staff and patients' friends preferred to deprive them altogether.[31] Equally, it would be foolish to be shocked by patients kept Houyhnhnm-like on straw, which was a perfectly normal kind of bedding at the time – not just for the mad, but for the sick and vagrants.[32] Straw was not only cheap, it was considered hygienic, permitting urine to drain through to the bottom of patients' cribs rather than soak into sheets and mattresses.[33] Yet, by the latter eighteenth century at least, most patients lay on sheeted beds rather than straw, in 1780 the Steward calculating that out of a total capacity of 281 patients only 61 (22 per cent) 'will be Patients who lye in Straw' and that all others required 'Sheeted Beds'.[34]

Governors and staff were far from oblivious to the need for cleanliness and hygiene. The reason given by the Hospital for its later decision to supply all bedding itself and to cease receiving it from securities was 'to prevent Buggs being brought in bedding to the Hospital'.[35] It was on the same account that Thomas Weston (Steward, 1713–34), had 'refused to suffer' any 'Apparell . . . to be taken in' when sent by patients' friends, furnishing all himself. His obstinacy where clothing was concerned had been resented by some securities, who were put to expense. After his death the Governors restored the 'liberty' of 'the friends of the Patients . . . to [so] provide'.[36]

Rats, too, plagued both the Bishopsgate and Moorfields buildings. Prevailing animalistic conceptions of insanity and the proverbial affinity of the insane with vermin, typified by Poor Tom in King Lear, for whom 'mice and rats . . . Have been food for seven long year',[37] may have bred apathy to their presence. It was not until 1777 that the Governors recognized 'that the Numbers of Rats infesting this Hospital are a great Detriment as well as a Nusance', and took any action to combat the problem. The discreet advertisement placed in the press, which appealed for 'Any Person to Undertake the Clearing of *a Large Building* . . . from rats', in an obvious attempt to shield the Hospital from public aspersion, offers a clue to the Governors' general unwillingness to come clean about conditions.[38]

Yet bugs and rats were endemic to contemporary buildings – most city hospitals and even the royal family had their own bug-destroyers and rat-catchers.[39] Neither were the Governors and staff altogether neglectful of patients' reactions. The Bethlem Physician, Thomas Allen, 'Sent *Catmore* [i.e. a cat] in to Relieve' Carkesse from the '*Rats* and *Mice*' that 'swarm[ed]' in his cell at Allen's Finsbury Madhouse; James Norris was also given a cat.[40]

From 1771, patients discharged from Bethlem 'either Sick or Incurable' were required first to 'be Stripped and Examined' to ensure that they 'be sent out from the

Hospital clean and free from Vermin' – although the Governors were, perhaps, more concerned about projecting a clean image of the Hospital than about the health of their charges.[41] The hiring in the 1770s and 1780s of a bug-destroyer and a rat-catcher ('to attend once a Week or oftner') might be interpreted as timely acts of modernization, in line with the calls of contemporary hygienists and initiatives taken at other hospitals.[42] Such extermination methods were not very successful. When the Surveyors reported in 1791, they found 'The Bed-places in the Cells . . . a harbor for Rats and other Vermin and . . . in such a state as to endanger the Health of the Patients.'[43]

Enhanced concern for hygiene is a feature of the management of Bethlem in the latter eighteenth century, mirrored in other contemporary hospitals, and can be seen as an aspect of medicalization. Prior to the 1770s, patients had been left to defend themselves against lice and rats; the growing appreciation of the sensibility of the insane and of the advantages of subjecting them to a medical regime gave new priority to hygiene. In 1793, the medical officers for the first time advised the Governors upon the type of clothing for patients that 'might be . . . more conducive to their health and Cleanliness'.[44] Bryan Crowther, the Surgeon, was even entrusted to design 'such a Dress as he may think proper', although the inadequacy of patients' 'blanket-gowns' was still to be a subject of censure in the 1815/16 Madhouses Committee inquiry.[45] The extension of the Hospital's responsibility for outfitting also served to impose external conformity.

KEEPING 'THE POORE LUNATIQUES SWEET AND CLEANE'

Just how dirty and unhygienic, then, had Bethlem and its patients previously been? When the Governors visited in 1598, they found that 'the sayd house' had been left in such a state 'by the Keeper for that it is so loathsomly and filthely kept', that it was 'not fitt for anye mann to come into the sayd howse', let alone 'to dwell in'.[46] Indeed, there is very little evidence that staff maintained, or even that the Board required, a very high standard of cleanliness at old Bethlem. The primitive water supply there, comprising a single wooden cistern in the backyard, from which servants had to transport water by buckets, hardly helped. In 1657 this was found insufficient and was replaced by a larger structure 'to keepe water for the use of the poore Lunatiques'.[47] Following the establishment of the New River Water Company in the early seventeenth century, supplying the City with water from a reservoir in Islington, the Treasurer was ordered to act quickly to obtain a constant supply of 'the New river water'. But it was the Hospital's neighbours, not the Governors, who in 1663 took the initiative in 'bringing New River Water into the . . . precinct'.[48]

Although continent patients seem to have had access to a 'house of easement' (i.e. latrine), and 'a new vault and house of easement' were included in the 1644 extension, patients were largely reliant on 'piss-pots', and the Bishopsgate building appears to have been served by only a couple of vaults.[49] Of course, standards of personal hygiene in the wider world were far from high. However, the fact that contemporaries bothered to record instances of urinating and defecating openly in the streets or, like

Samuel Pepys, in their own fireplaces (for servants to clear up), suggests that real standards existed even if they were being abused. The widening rift between the foul and the fragant may well have been exaggerated. Nevertheless, it seems significant that it was not until the Augustan age – when, alongside growing disdain for the odours of poverty, scented handkerchiefs and wigs became *à la mode* attire – that we begin to hear much of contemporaries turning away and stopping their noses at the sight and smell of the Bedlamites.[50]

While the Bethlem Board was keen to ensure the removal of 'filth' from the precinct, there appears to have been more tolerance of dirt within the Hospital itself, where the rudimentary water supply and lack of latrines, combined with many incontinent patients, meant low levels of cleanliness. The Court of Governors Minutes document patients' tendency to throw 'filth & Excrement' and other 'noysome things' 'into the yards', and to dislodge the tiles outside their windows, in a way that confirms the Swiftian notion of Bethlem as a filthy hospital, where patients were left to 'dabble in their dung'.[51] Whether one interprets such acts as protests against the indignities of confinement[52] or merely as symptomatic of the extremes of alienation, it was not until the 1670s that the Governors attempted to do something about this habit. The placing of tarred boards 'under the Dormers' and the installing of wire linings into patients' windows may, partially, have achieved the desired effect.[53] However, the Governors were often as concerned about exterior cleanliness as about hygiene and seemliness in patients' cells, ruling in 1765, for example, that 'rags Straw' and 'other Nastiness' thrust by patients through the wires of their windows, should be removed, and windows henceforth kept 'light' and free of matter 'which shall look unseemly to the streets'.[54]

The complaints of patients like the Jacobite, Richard Stafford, accustomed to a better class of accommodation, that they were put 'down into a low, dark, narrow and stinking Room', suggest that conditions at new Bethlem were mean and unhygienic. But patients who were well-connected or well-behaved might be promoted to a better-furnished cell. James Carkesse described his rise to a higher 'degree' at the 'University' of Bethlem:

> Among the common *Herd* at first he's enter'd
> After into a Room, with windows ventur'd[55]

Special or private cases lodged in the Steward's house at old Bethlem, like Lady Eleanor Davies, were certainly catered for in greater comfort.

Water supply and waste disposal were somewhat improved at new Bethlem, where staff and patients had the use of cisterns on every gallery, except the upper floor.[56] 'Seats for Easement' with cisterns and sewer outlets attached were located in the yards at either end of the Hospital and in the stove rooms. Latrines seem to have been more adequate at Moorfields, and the Governors were more responsive to the need to extend this provision.[57] In 1766, however, the Steward paid 7s 6d for '15 Days Laboures Cleaning ye Necessarys both Men & Women', a Herculean labour which rather than recommending the hospital's hygienic standards suggests how bad things had become.[58]

The lack of cisterns at the top of the house (or pumps to supply them) was a serious inconvenience. On inspecting Bethlem in the 1780s, the philanthropist and prison reformer John Howard remarked upon the absence of any 'water [supply] in the upper floor' and on the inadequate number and 'very offensive' state of the vaults.[59] Bethlem suffered by comparison with St Luke's, where Howard found 'many cisterns on the top of the house' and 'in each gallery . . . a vault'.[60] Two years after the publication of Howard's account, a Committee of Surveyors condemned the 'bad state' of the privies,[61] though it was another six years before steps were taken to amend their 'bad construction'.[62]

In fact, the Moorfields building had altogether been constructed in undue haste, dogged by shoddy workmanship, and by 1800 the building had become extremely dilapidated.[63] Conditions were even worse, however, at many other hospitals and prisons in early modern Europe. Tenon's description of his visit to the Hôtel Dieu in the 1780s recounts a disgusting catalogue of decay, stench and filth, at a hospital which catered for nearly six hundred patients with just five lavatory seats.[64]

At both Bethlem buildings, however, visitors and patients complained of 'noisome' stenches. Old Bethlem was built over a regularly blocked common sewer, while new Bethlem suffered from subsidence upon the site of the old city ditch, used as a dump for rubbish and waste.[65] James Tilly Matthews, in Bethlem from 1797 to 1814, felt assailed by all kinds of 'putrid effluvia', although, clearly, not all of these emanated from the Hospital itself.[66] Smells from the sewers continued to be a source of offence. The repellant 'odours of incarceration' were almost universal to early modern institutions.[67]

When the German, Conrad Zacharius von Uffenbach, paid a visit to Bethlem in 1710, he concurred with Swift, finding that the Hospital 'is kept in a rather slovenly manner'.[68] Patients were not simply left, however (as Swift put it) to 'stare and stink together'.[69] As early as 1684, the new matron was instructed 'that shee must be carefull and diligent to see that the poore Lunatikes there be kept sweet and clean'.[70] Servants acknowledged well enough, as in 1736, that they were required to clean all parts of the Hospital, to help clothe the patients and to help 'to Wash . . . [and] Iron the Linnen of all the Patients'.[71] Much of the laundering, however, was done by 'the poor patients friends' themselves, who attended 'to bring clean, or take away foul Linnen from them in Bethlem'.[72] The employment of laundry women by the 1760s must, however, have improved the cleanliness of both clothing and bedding.[73]

There was a hard core at Bethlem of what Governors and staff referred to as 'wet', 'dirty' or 'highly irritated' patients, for whom it was generally accepted little could be done by way of cleanliness and comfort. Conditions for those, protected from the cold by (at most) a single blanket gown, chained singly to their straw beds or collectively against the tables, forms or walls of the warming or 'side rooms', were assuredly squalid in the extreme. The methods used to deal with incontinent and destructive patients tended towards accepting bad habits as ineradicable.[74] John Monro expressed resignation to the insensibility of patients whom he witnessed 'for months (I may say years) together, not suffering even a rag of cloaths on [them] . . . lying in straw . . . without shewing any signs of discontent'.[75] Many patients had a history of tearing their own clothes.[76]

Wet or destructive patients were not the majority, however, nor is there any evidence that even these patients 'were given only excrement-sodden straw'.[77] If Strype's claim in 1720 (on Tyson's authority), that 'they are every Day provided with fresh and clean Straw', seems like wishful thinking, the reality was probably some-where between these two extremes.[78] At the 1815/16 inquiry, the Steward claimed that straw was removed whenever wet, while the Matron testified that straw was changed 'every other day, but if it is wet at all, it is changed every day'. After grilling, however, both admitted that it was only the 'top [or wet] straw' which was changed daily, the rest being changed at most once a week.[79]

Awareness of the need for cleanliness intensified in the half century prior to 1815. Enhanced concern with hygiene is especially apparent in the additions made to the duties of Bethlem officers and servants in 1765. The Steward was required by stand-ing order to make a thrice-weekly morning inspection of the cells, galleries and chequers, while the Matron was to examine the female patients every morning to ensure that they had been properly 'Shifted and Sheeted' by the maids. Every Wednesday, the Matron was also 'to Observe the Washer Women' and make sure that patients' linen was being 'Boiled . . . and Washed in proper Suds'.[80]

Cleaning began at Bethlem first thing in the morning. 'Dirty patients' were to be moved 'from one Cell to another' to 'Wash their Dirty Cells', although, in practice, they were often chained up in the stove rooms or in bed. Officers and servants were enjoined to take 'great care in removeing old Straw and providing Fresh', changing it whenever it was 'Damp or Dirty'.[81]

It was not until after mid-century that the patients were officially required to be washed and men shaved three times a week; that a 'clean round Towell' was allowed 'each Gallery every day'; that longer-lasting hard soap was substituted for the soft soap formerly ordered, and that the Committee regularly went round the house inspecting it for cleanliness.[82] In earlier times, patients had been shaved just once a fortnight and washed when staff or visiting governors conceived a need.[83]

Visiting Bethlem around 1770, the Frenchman, Grosley, found the females' parlour (or convalescents' room) 'full of women of various ages . . . wearing rather clean linen and camisoles . . . about to take tea together'. On the male side, however, he still encountered a gallery 'in each' of the 'large cells' in which a patient 'was lying chained up in his bed', at least one (if not most) of whom was 'in a state of almost complete nudity'.[84] In 1784, Sophie von la Roche eulogized the Hospital. She found its rooms so 'sound, spacious [and] clean' that she wished that 'every good, honest worker and wage-earner and their families' in her native Germany might have it so good![85] The environment of Bethlem had not altered radically over the fourteen years separating these accounts, of course, and it was the rose of sensibility tinting Sophie's spectacles that probably made the real difference.

Yet other observers also testified to the comparatively clean and wholesome provi-sion. Jacques Cambry, the author of *De Londres et ses environs* (1788), found Bethlem revealed 'a cleanliness, hardly conceivable unless seen'.[86] Standards at French hos-pitals may well have been inferior, and the comments of natives upon the environ-ment of Bethlem offer a more immediately reliable context than those of foreigners. Despite judging Bethlem in 1789 inferior to St Luke's and in need of whitewashing, John Howard nevertheless deemed its 'two hundred and seventy rooms . . . quite clean and not offensive'.[87] Finally, whereas members of the 1815/16 Committee deplored the filthy, uncomfortable conditions in the Hospital's side rooms, they did not find 'the rest of the house . . . particularly deficient in cleanliness', and judged 'the apartments in general ... to be clean, and the patients who were not confined tolerably comfortable'.[88]

LIGHT, AIR AND HEAT

The stock depiction of Bethlem as a dark, close, festering place also requires revision. For one thing, confinement in darkened rooms had long been considered therapeutic in cases of lunacy,[89] and as late as 1766 there was a 'Dark Cell' at the Hospital. The conversion of this cell, together with one adjoining, into a sitting room 'for the Conveniency of the Patients' signifies the decline of such theories in the wake of a growing appreciation of the sensibility of the mad to creature comforts and a civilized environment.[90]

The Governors had been sensitive since the seventeenth century to the need for light and ventilation. Five additional dormers had been installed into the upper south side of the Bishopsgate building in 1663.[91] Whereas the old house had gradually become submerged by encroaching buildings, the Governors went to some lengths to prevent this happening at Moorfields.[92] Contemporary prints and drawings of the Hospital show a prodigious allowance of space for light and air and the largeness of the windows on the first two storeys (see Chapter 15). Observers described its rooms as 'spacious and bright', its galleries as 'thoroughly well lit' and its 'fine gardens' as places where patients 'enjoy fresh air and recreate themselves amongst trees, flowers and plants'.[93] The Hospital's provision of light, air, cleanliness and exercise, and its wainscoted rooms and open doors, were especially admired by foreign visitors.[94] In 1765, 'the upper doors' of isolated patients' cells were required, by standing order, to be opened to ensure 'the Circulation of fresh Air'. The Bethlem administration had long been appreciative of the putative benefits of fresh air. Those 'well enough' were 'permitted to walke the Yards there in the day tyme', as a means to 'take the aire in order to aid their Recovery'.[95] A policy of leaves of absence for convalescents was also designed to afford them the benefit of country air.[96]

While there was only a single yard at old Bethlem (entailing obvious segregation problems) until the expansion of 1643/4 added another, the space allotted was far greater at Moorfields, where separate yards for both sexes at either end of the Hospital comprised grass and gravel plots of 120 feet each.[97] By 1719, benches were added for patients.[98] But patients were forbidden to walk in the front yard and gardens of new Bethlem,[99] which was designed for show. The addition, however, of the incurables wards in the 1720s and 1730s, and, around mid-century, of the infirmary, the apothecary's house and shop and other buildings considerably reduced the airing grounds. By 1815, they were actually being described as 'small' by a member of the Madhouses Committee, besides being 'damp ... and encumbered with rubbish'.[100]

Patients were over-exposed to the elements. The winter cold and damp was a constant plaint of patients. James Carkesse grumbled of being 'opprest with cold' and heartily thanked a Mr Stackhouse who had presented him with a periwig, vital to keep his '*Noddle*' warm'.[101] The cold was partly the result of harsh economics, but also of a mind-set in classical attitudes which urged the '*sedative* power' of cold upon the insane while denying their sensibility to its 'bad effects'. Theories of the dangers of over-heating the brain remained popular.[102] But the Bethlem Governors and contemporaries in general were not completely oblivious to the sensibility of the insane to the cold. The installation of shutters to cell windows; improvements in clothing and bedding; the introduction of caps into the standard Bethlem outfit, and the use of the 'hot Bath' for restoring patients' limbs when 'numbed', were all measures taken to combat Jack Frost.[103]

The two warming-rooms at old Bethlem originally contained unguarded fires, and their replacement in 1675 by stoves fenced in 'with Iron Barrs' was undoubtedly a salutary initiative. Indeed, it was these rooms which evolved into the 'stove rooms' and ultimately 'sitting rooms' for patients in new Bethlem.[104] As late as 1663, fires appear to have been maintained only in the kitchen or where the Governors convened.[105] At Moorfields, possibly out of misplaced frugality, the Hospital reverted to a system of 'grates' and persisted with it for over three decades, despite risks of injury, before installing stoves again 'for the better and safer accomodateing the Patients'.[106] Within four years of this alteration, the Committee declared the stove-rooms too small. Their enlargement and alteration 'for ye Conveniency of ye patients' demonstrates that the Governors did not simply ignore inmates' needs. Moreover, from the 1760s these rooms began to be seen as more than simply warming-rooms, gradually taking on a more therapeutic and recreational function, as parlours where convalescents might associate and take tea together.[107] Governors never sought to justify patients' exposure to cold by leaning on theories of the insensibility of the mad.

Patients' bodily health clearly suffered from cold and damp. Carkesse complained of 'stiff' joints 'as if grown old', 'for want of Fire' at the Hospital,[108] and the Governors themselves spoke of 'Phisick and surgerye' needing to be applied to patients lacking clothes and presumably suffering from exposure.[109] Patients' susceptibility to the mortification of feet and hands plainly owed a great deal to their prolonged subjection to cold, mechanical restraint and inactivity, obstructing healthy circulation. The Governors did not confront this problem until January 1778, when servants were instructed by the Court (on the recommendation of John Monro, Bethlem Physician, and the Sub-Committee) 'That the Feet of every Patient in Chains or Straw be Carefully Examined, well rubb'd and covered with Flannell ... every Night and Morning during the Winter Season and if Necessary that immediate Notice be given to the Surgeon.'[110]

DIET: FEEDING AND STARVING THE POOR LUNATICS

In early Stuart times patients were poorly fed. Under the keepership of Crooke, provision had reached such a nadir that, on visiting the house in 1631, two Governors found the patients 'likely to starve'.[111] The Privy Council Commissioners in the next year found that victuals and beer were sold to patients by the exploitative Steward; that patients without money often simply went without; and that the Steward appropriated the choicest morsels for his own use.[112] Jacobean literature paints a similar picture of starving Bedlamites.[113] Besides staff dishonesty, part of the problem in feeding the poor was the Steward's dependency upon the Keeper for money; the Hospital's dependence upon gifts in kind, sent in from the Mayor, and the lack of direct supervision of provisionment by the Governors.[114]

From 1635, the Steward was made directly responsible to the Governors for his management of the provisions, yet the next two decades proved little greater comfort to the patients, who continued to suffer from the extortion of Stewards and inferior staff.[115] Bethlem continued to rely upon gifts in kind from City markets to feed its inmates until the move to Moorfields.[116] Supplies were variable and intermittent, while disputes with suppliers might delay or halt their delivery.[117]

Embezzlement and wastage of provisions by staff continued to deprive patients of their rightful portions.[118] Yet prosperity meant that the pantry and buttery grew better stocked. The earlier scenes of starvation were not repeated, and patients were much better fed in 1800 than in 1600, John Howard declaring in 1789 that the bread, butter, cheese and beer were 'very good'.[119] The Madhouses Committee of 1815/16 found little wrong with the diet, though inmates like Urbane Metcalf were still protesting that much of it was simply not reaching the patients.[120]

Diet at Bethlem must be seen in the context of contemporary theories of bodily operation in sickness and health. Humoral medicine defined the body as a fragile balance of vital fluids and highlighted bad diet as 'the mother of diseases'. Cure of madness was believed to be dependent upon restoring this balance, via evacuations and a disciplined dietary regimen, countering repletion with depletion, intemperance with a 'low' diet. Depriving the proverbial crazy Welshman of cheese and the mad Englishman of malt was a stock therapy for insane cravings.[121]

No diet sheet exists for old Bethlem, a further indication of the inferior attention given to its affairs by the Bridewell Governors.[122] But patients were evidently fed on a basic ration of bread, beef (or mutton),[123] oatmeal or milk pottage, butter, cheese and beer. They were sustained on a very simple, lowering diet, with perhaps three meat days each week, and were fed just 'twice a day' (missing breakfast).[124] To modern eyes this regimen appears inadequate in nutritional balance and lacking in vitamins (especially vitamin C), since it was wholly wanting in fresh fruit and vegetables – even the 'fruite' found 'growing on the trees' at Bethlem in 1645 was 'sold for the best advantage of the said hospitall' rather than given to its inmates.[125] Regimen, however, was in accordance with the advice given for the cure of madness by contemporary authorities.[126]

And the Governors did make some efforts to ensure the quality of patients' food, by, for example, instructing the Steward that 'beofe oatmeale & salt … shalbee bought at the best hand and not of any Chaundler or Huckster'.[127] But it is not until later that we find evidence of them beginning regularly to reject poor quality consumables or listening to patients' complaints. In 1667, the 'broken Beere usually fetched from the Lord Mayor and Sheriffes' was, for the first time, declared 'not fitt to be given to the Lunatikes'.[128]

The Governors were confident that their new diet plan devised in 1677 for Moorfields would both be 'sufficient for their Supporte and maintenance and much more conduce to their Recovery then the former Dyett given unto them',[129] having it publicly displayed in the Hospital, alongside other standing orders, for visitors' perusal.[130] As the first extant for Bethlem, this diet sheet is worth summarizing:

Diet for New Bethlem (1677)

Sundays, Tuesdays and Thursdays: Meat Days

Dinners:

　　Boiled meat (mutton or veal on Tuesdays, but otherwise beef)

　　Broth

　　Piece of bread

Suppers:

　　Remaining broth, reheated as a mess

　　Bread

Mondays, Wednesdays and Fridays: Dairy, 'Meagre' or 'Banyan' Days

Dinners:

　　Bread

　　Cheese or butter

Suppers:

　　Milk pottage

　　Other pottage

　　Bread

(Except Mondays, when water gruel or pease pottage were to be alternatives to milk and other pottage)

Saturdays: Dairy, 'Meagre' or 'Banyan' Day

Dinners:

　　Pease pottage

　　Other pottage

　　Rice milk

Suppers:

　　Bread

　　Cheese or butter

In addition, 'fruite may be given unto them that is most seasonable'.

What was missing from the Governors' outline of course was beer. This was invariably 'small beer'; i.e. very weak and diluted, so as to act as a lubricant and digestive, rather than the intoxicant to which insanity was often attributed by contemporaries.[131] Bills amounting to over £200 for beer supplied to Bethlem by 1728, and nearly £400 by 1747,[132] suggest that, however weak, large quantities were consumed.[133]

The basic 'therapeutic' structure of the diet, with three meat days alternating with four meagre days, continued unchanged. The only other positive alterations appear to have been the introduction of veal as an alternative to mutton on Tuesdays, 'pease pottage' instead of oatmeal or milk pottage, and the allowance of 'fruite' in season.[134]

Vegetables and fruit can still have been only occasional items,[135] and patients clearly did not receive the vitamins they required, though stewards' accounts reveal that, from at least the early eighteenth century, 'codlins' (i.e. cooking-apples) were provided every August 'for ye Patients'.[136]

The establishment in 1677 of a committee of Governors responsible rotationally every month for inspecting provisions and ensuring they were 'duely and rightly expended among the . . . Lunatikes' had evidently improved the management of patients' diet.[137] The Grand and Sub-Committee Minutes and Stewards' Accounts give a vivid account of this management. The frequency with which provisions were found deficient in quality, quantity and value suggests suppliers fobbed the Hospital off with inferior produce. For example, during the five years between 1714 and 1719 the beef was judged neither 'good' nor 'wholesome'; the beer was deemed 'not . . . fitt to drink'; while the cheese was declared 'Considerably worse than the hospital used to be served with'. Most contemporary hospitals had problems with their suppliers, however, while the fact that so many deficiencies were discovered may reflect increased vigilance by the Governors.[138]

A few further changes were also made in the diet. The addition of 'Turnipps & Carrotts' to meat days in 1730, and the subsequent provision of 'a better sort of small beer', perhaps went some way towards diminishing patients' proneness to scurvy and 'fluxes'.[139] The accounts also record that patients were treated with mince pies, with, possibly, plum pudding at Christmas, and veal at Easter and Whitsun, even if pancakes and fritters on Shrove Tuesday, hot cross buns, bacon, plum pudding and strong beer at Easter and Whitsun, and Christmas buns and strong beer, were all reserved for servants.[140] By the 1720s, 'Furmity' (i.e. frumenty) was adding spice to patients' meals, while, in 1761, veal was established on the menu 'during the Season' ('from Lady-Day to Michaelmas').[141] Butter instead of cheese on 'banyan days' was also allowed as a privilege to 'twelve out of each gallery, in their turn . . . if they prefer it'.[142] By the early nineteenth century, potatoes added starch to patients' diet,[143] and the quantities permitted had substantially increased.

Breakfasts were introduced, and by the 1780s patients also received 8 oz. of meat on every meat day, and 'a pint of small beer' and 8 oz. of bread at every dinner and supper.[144] In the 1780s patients consumed, on the four 'meagre days', 'for breakfast . . . a large bason of water-gruel' and 2 oz. of bread; for dinner a quart of milk pottage, 7 oz. of bread, 2 oz. of cheese and a quart of beer; and for supper, 7 oz. of bread and 2 oz. of cheese. On the three 'meat days', patients had 'for breakfast water-gruel'; 'for dinner', 8 oz. of meat 'after being dressed', 7 oz. of bread, about 1 lb. of potatoes and a quart 'of table beer'. The nutritional value was still inadequate, yet other contemporary institutions were rarely much better.

Special diets were allowed at both Bethlem and Bridewell in the event of bodily sickness, to fortify and replenish the constitution. When, in 1631, a male patient's leg had become 'so ulcerated' that amputation was considered necessary, it was recognized that 'his diett therefore must be bettered', and the Governors agreed to allow his sister 2s 4d per week to provide.[145] With the appointment of a nurse in 1692, specifically to help those 'who cannot help themselves with their Dyett', the care of the (physically) sick and sick diet became part of the Hospital's provision. By the early eighteenth century, sick patients under the Nurse's care were receiving special orders of 'Wine', 'Rum', 'Oyle', 'Sage', 'Fowl', 'Oat cakes' and 'Fish'.[146] From the 1780s, a list of patients 'on the sick list' was to be hung up 'in the Cutting Room', so that staff might know which were entitled to sick diet, and servants were being instructed to ensure that patients 'Confined' to their galleries were properly fed, with their food cut up for them.[147]

EXERCISE, RECREATION AND OCCUPATION

Exercise and occupation were standardly recommended as salutary and therapeutic in early modern times.[148] By the time of the Madhouses Committee inquiry, however, one of the Hospital's own servants was affirming that there were 'no occupations' and 'no amusements' available for patients 'other than walking in the green yard[s], whenever it is fine', and a single pack of cards provided by the Apothecary.[149] That Committee found, in general, that 'wet patients' and any others 'who were inclined to lie a-bed, were allowed to do so', because found 'less troublesome'.[150] The policy was evidently, in part, a way of coping with understaffing.

Walking in the airing-grounds or galleries was not the only form of occupation, however. Cooperative convalescent patients were employed as helpers about the house. References to working patients are sparse before the eighteenth century, but Stewards' Accounts and Committee Minutes after 1700 reveal rewards and privileges for labouring patients who were recompensed in money and alcohol for a wide variety of services, from 'Leavelling the Yard' to 'Screening Ash's'. Patients might even be appointed as helpers by the medical staff, like the one in 1796 'permitted to assist the Cook' and 'allowed a pint of Porter a day',[151] and exceptionally patients were even employed and rewarded for helping to capture escapees.[152]

The policy of employing patients perhaps owed something to Bethlem's joint governorship with Bridewell, but it was more a consequence of under-staffing rather than a means of therapy. During the 1750s and 1760s the Governors had ruled attempting to ensure that every maidservant had 'a proper Number of such hands as are fit for Work to assist her'.[153] The Governors, however, had plainly grown more concerned about employing patients as time went on. The gendered nature of Court orders, which also required that all unoccupied and 'Capable' females should be employed 'at their Needle', instead of letting them 'Walk Idle up and down the House', and that 'low Spirited or . . . Mopish' females be turfed out of their cells and the Physician acquainted of malingerers,[154] suggests a new identification of idleness (especially amongst females) as unhealthy. Such evidence may also show how pecking orders might be established, or how easily occupation became exploitation. Metcalf related how patients were bribed or coerced into becoming 'bullies' or 'drudges' by servants keen to ease their attendance and labour.[155] All this, nevertheless, is far removed from the view offered by historians like Doerner and Foucault that labour was 'the essential justification of confinement' in this period. On the other hand, in emphasizing how Bethlem's 'anarchy' was 'based' on 'idleness and dissipation', others like Donnelly seem to have erred in the other direction, and failed to appreciate how 'the therapeutic rationales of labour' developed by reformers also relied on exaggerating old Bethlem's apathy and disorder.[156]

Apart from employment, inmates might in addition be permitted a limited number of recreations, in particular, books, writing materials and even newspapers, while the gradual addition of patients' sitting-rooms encouraged patients to socialize.[157] When Sophie von la Roche visited the Hospital in the 1780s, she 'saw some of the quieter patients . . . sewing', others reading and writing, 'and others sitting together', and claimed that these patients were 'gladly allowed to make friends and be sociable'.[158] The Steward's Accounts record the purchase of a 'Sett of Skittles for Patients' in 1773, while six years later he was ordered to buy two more sets.[159]

'A REGIME OF UNDIFFERENTIATED RESTRAINT AND FEAR'?

The statement in this heading represents one historical view of the environment of the early modern asylum.[160] Certainly the abuse of restraint was adjudged one of the worst features of the Bethlem regime by the Madhouses Committee, and there can be no quarrel with its judgment that restraint was deployed 'much beyond what is necessary'.[161] It would be a mistake, however, automatically to project backwards and accept the Committee's assessment as conclusive proof of the regime's perennial brutality. Not least, general expectations were changing: Enlightened ideas, heightened sensibilities and Evangelicalism were joining by 1800 to condemn a casual use of violence and coercion once taken for granted.

When, around 1770, Grosley witnessed 'a whole gallery of large cells in Bedlam . . . in each [of which] . . . a poor wretch was lying chained up in his bed', he expressed neither surprise nor disapproval. Indeed, when one of these patients, 'having rid himself of his chains . . . leapt upon the back of one of [his] . . . conductors', Grosley admired the authoritarian way he was taken 'by the arm, and led . . . back to his room', appreciating the conductor as 'precisely his quarter master'.[162] Sixteen years later, Sophie von la Roche saw 'the forethought and humanity' of Bethlem as 'exemplified' in the manner of restraint: chains had been replaced by the 'strong-jacket', which, she claimed, obviated the tendency of 'chains or straps to rub sores if [patients] . . . made frenzied gestures', rendering the insane 'harmless without having to suffer'.[163] She relied for her account, however, as much on her guide (probably John Gozna, the resident Apothecary), as on her own observations, and her impressionability is evident.

In fact, despite Gozna's espousal of it, practical experience with the strait-jacket convinced others of its inferiority to traditional mechanical restraint. Within a decade of Sophie's visit, after the succession of John Haslam as Apothecary (1792), the Hospital reverted 'by degrees' to its old system of manacles and leg-locks. Haslam opposed the strait-waistcoat as constricting: it was uncomfortably hot and provoking of perspiration, it disabled movement of the arms, hands and fingers, prevented the patient from relieving irritation, and inhibited attention to 'personal cleanliness'.[164] Thomas Monro and most other witnesses at the 1815/16 inquiry, however, considered 'a strait-waistcoat a much better thing than irons'. Monro's testimony suggests that the employment of irons was justified more on the basis of rank and economy than on medical grounds; and that they were suitable only for the pauper insane 'in a hospital [where] there is no possibility of having servants enough to watch a great number of persons'.[165]

Strait-waistcoats seem to have been employed first in private madhouses and adopted by public hospitals only towards the latter part of the century. The Stewards' Accounts reveal that during the 1760s the Hospital was still very much reliant on 'Legg Lock[s]' and 'HandCuffs'.[166] It was not until the 1770s that purchase of 'strait Waistcoats' was mentioned,[167] presumably introduced on the initiative of John Gozna, appointed Apothecary in 1772.[168] Even then, handcuffs and chains were abandoned only gradually. Continuing to be used in the Infirmary,[169] they were also used on 'the ferocious maniac' and on some incurables, who the medical statistician, William Black, declared (on Gozna's authority) were to be 'kept as wild beasts, constantly in fetters'.[170] This seems a clear indication of the inveteracy of animalistic conceptions of the insane and of prolonged and terrific modes of restraint. That sixty leg-locks and a dozen handcuffs were purchased by the Steward[171] within the space of just two years during the 1760s, also suggests that restraint had been widely employed on the Hospital's two hundred and sixty or so patients by its skeleton nursing staff of ten or eleven. The extent to which Bethlem was placed at the disposal of the public must also have necessitated exceptional levels of confinement, compelling or encouraging staff to restrain or seclude patients considered apt to endanger or annoy visitors. Yet foreign visitors accepted the type and extent of restraint at Bethlem as necessary. Like Grosley fifty years later, De Saussure found 'a corridor' of 'cells' in which 'most of' the patients were 'chained', describing these 'maniacs' as 'dangerous . . . and terrible to behold', while observing that 'many inoffensive madmen walk in the big gallery'.[172] In 1788, another French visitor admired the 'open doors' and other freedoms from 'bolts' and 'bars' permitted 'the poor creatures there [who] are not chained up in dark cellars' but allowed to 'exercise' in 'long airy corridors'.[173] Referring to the 1770s and 1780s, William Black claimed that 'by far the great majority of Patients . . . walk peaceably along the long wards', and that only 'a very small number even of the Incurables' were 'constantly' chained. A very large proportion of patients, nevertheless, seem to have been subjected to the temporary intimidation of irons, strait-waistcoats and solitary confinement.[174] The Hospital's prioritization of 'dangerous' or 'mischievous' cases, particularly after the establishment of the incurables' wards, must also have encouraged a high degree of restraint.[175]

Medical opinion was mixed. Thomas Willis had no doubts that madness 'requires . . . bonds';[176] on the other hand, Richard Mead advised restraint only for 'those who are outragious'; and it was Mead's view, rather than Willis's, which prevailed at Bethlem.[177] Like Mead, the Bethlem Physicians Richard Hale and James Monro preferred to rely on dosing rather than restraint, Hale being praised by his successor for 'dealing with . . . furious . . . maniacs . . . not so much . . . with chains and bars, as by sedating them'.[178] Around 1800 John Haslam viewed restraint primarily as a means to prevent 'the most violent' patients 'from doing mischief to themselves' or others.[179] It was thus justified more as an expedient or a necessity than a cure.

The Governors' Minutes seldom record instances of restraint. The case of Edward Purcell, however, confined in old Bethlem on a royal warrant from 1672 to 1674, provides a rare concrete instance.[180] In August 1673, Purcell was 'found to be a wild desperate & dangerous person' and ordered 'kept in chaines & locked upp to prevent danger of fire & hurting the persons of the Officers there', i.e. as a last resort. Eight months previously, however, Purcell had been declared 'cured & recovered of his Lunacy', and the Hospital had made three successive applications for his discharge. The refusal of the Privy Council to discharge him at the end of May 1673, 'but rather to allow the house somewhat towards his keeping there', suggests some excuse for Purcell's 'wild' and 'desperate' behaviour. In February, following another certificate of recovery from Dr Thomas Allen and a petition for his discharge, the Court ordered 'that the Chaine be taken off Edward Purcells Leg', and provided he behave himself that he 'have the Like Liberty as others there have'. Although this marked the end of his restraint, it was not the end of his confinement, and the punitive nature of restraint in this instance is undeniable. All the same, Purcell's restraint was registered as exceptional by the Governors, and lasted no longer than six months – a much more realistic measure of the customary duration of restraint than the much more notorious years endured by James Norris at the end of the next century.

Visitors like Sophie von la Roche commented on the relative freedoms allowed the attempted regicide Margaret Nicholson and others, they being liberally supplied with reading and writing materials.[181] Yet, following her admission in 1786, Nicholson was 'confined in her Cell by a chain' for a year, and secluded from all visitors unaccompanied by a Governor for five years, before she was allowed the liberty of the house by the Committee.[182] Nor, even for apparently milder cases, was restraint always only a last resort. Chains were imposed as a matter of course on many patients on their admission. In 1617, the anabaptist, William Ellis, was ordered kept 'safe . . . in chaynes' at Bethlem by the Privy Council, while during the 1670s, James Carkesse was chained from the first at both Finsbury and Bethlem,[183] resenting this as one of many oppressive torments designed to break his resistance.[184] Contemporary physicians conceived their roles in curing the insane in terms of gaining ascendancy over the patient: imposing order and commanding obedience by words, actions and their very demeanour. Hence restraint was often a tool of subjugation. Carkesse represented his own treatment in terms which typify this 'terrific' therapeutic ethos as essentially a struggle of authority, in which cure required submission.

Restraint was generally envisaged by contemporaries as the just deserts of, and the appropriate response to, raving lunacy. The putative patient-poet of 1744 penned lines which reveal how physical constraint dominated expectations about the treatment of the insane:

> The *Keepers* mild to those who well behave;
> But some there are, who always curse and rave;
> Are justly chain'd, confin'd within each Room
> Altho' they know, full well, their certain Doom:
> If Keepers should neglect at this just Call,
> It wou'd, no doubt, go badly with us all.[185]

Thomas Monro's evidence before the 1815/16 Committee that 'gentlemen . . . were unlikely to be chained'[186] made a distinction between his private and his public practice, but the discrimination at Bethlem was primarily one of behaviour, not rank. Alexander Cruden was peculiarly qualified to judge, having already experienced during the 1730s and 1740s a spell in both Bethnal Green madhouse and in Bethlem itself. Yet, although he bitterly denounced the 'severe' management received in the former at the hands of the Bethlem Physician, James Monro, his aggrieved narrative betrays a good deal of partisanship. His prolonged restraint by 'handcuffs', 'Iron Fetters, Chains and Cords', the strait-waistcoat and ultimately by being 'chained night and day' to 'the bedstead' over nine weeks and six days was essentially the doing of his keepers, rather than Monro. In fact, on the doctor's four visits, Cruden was actually 'unchained', once even being, 'by Dr. Monro's advice, allowed . . . to walk in the garden'.[187]

Restraint at Bethlem was likewise, by and large, left to the keepers. Only in special cases did the Court itself order a patient to be chained. It was not until 1779 that staff were instructed to acquaint the Steward 'immediately' it was 'Necessary to confine any Patients by Chains or otherwise', and only in 1792 were staff required to inform the Apothecary whenever a patient was restrained and of the reasons for it.[188] Obviously, lack of accountability in previous times had left its imposition open to abuse, while the findings of the 1815/16 Madhouses Committee suggest that such rulings continued to provide limited protection for patients. The policy followed at Bethlem and encapsulated by Haslam's dictum that 'when a patient has misbehaved, [the attendant] should confine him immediately', was too often a licence for punishment.[189] The judgment, however, that Bethlem's was 'a regime of undifferentiated restraint and fear'[190] gives a rather distorted impression of the average experiences of its patients. Furthermore, heed should be paid to Showalter's observation, that 'mad-doctors were not cruelly inventing torments for their patients, but applying traditional methods and remedies'.[191]

ENVIRONMENT AND TENANTS

The importance of the role of Bethlem's tenants in shaping the Hospital has rarely been appreciated. Much of the Court of Governors' Minutes are taken up by dealings with the tenants of Bridewell and Bethlem. Both hospitals were considerably reliant for their incomes upon rents and other revenue from tenants, who (as outlined in Chapter 12) might also be benefactors and suppliers, securities for patients, members of staff or even Governors, while many of the workmen employed on the Hospital buildings were tenants or neighbours.[192] In 1651, the Court forbade the granting of any lease of property or land belonging to the Hospitals to any Governor or officer, but this meant very little in practice. It was only in 1685 that tenants of the London hospitals were barred from election as Governors.'[193]

Bethlem was the antithesis of a Goffmanesque 'total institution', a self-contained, self-administering environment, cut off from the outside world; or of the Foucauldian paradigm of radical sequestration. Neighbours resided at such proximity that patients could hurl masonry or other objects through their windows or into their backyards. The Governors were keen to prevent 'the Lunatiques doe[ing] . . . any damage to any of the neighbours',[194] a theme regularly encountered in their Minutes. The need to bolster Hospital funds by ensuring its property was earning rent encouraged the Governors to grant long-term leases, with minimal restrictions.[195] Partly as a consequence of this policy and of Bethlem's expansion in the 1640s, the Bishopsgate house was soon hemmed-in and encroached upon by neighbouring properties.

Despite the Governors' preoccupation with neighbours and tenants, they were seldom permitted to take precedence over the interests of patients. Revenues from tenants were regularly spoken of as 'for the use' or 'benefit of the Lunatikes'. Although this was also a rhetorical device, legitimizing administrative policy as disinterested charity, there was a genuine connection between the Hospital's rent-roll and expenditure for the benefit of patients, the expense of Bethlem's expansion in the 1640s being partly justified and offset by profits from Hospital leases.[196] Where conflicts of interest did arise, as when tenants went to erect chimneys on their properties, the Bethlem Board consistently ruled in patients' favour.[197] Interdicts imposed upon tenants converting Hospital property into taverns or victualling houses were designed with the same ends in mind: to preserve a salubrious environment for Bethlem's inmates.[198] These efforts were somewhat belated, however, for the Bishopsgate building was already surrounded by a lively group of taverns.

The paramountcy accorded patients' interests over those of Hospital tenants was rather more explicit at Moorfields. For example, the application of Coleman Street Ward in the 1760s for land on which to erect a watch-house was rejected on medical officers' advice that patients needed 'Quiet' for recovery and would 'be greatly Affected and prejudiced by the Noise', and also because the Governors were worried about the risk of fire to a hospital with unglazed windows and 'Patients lying upon Straw'.[199] The Board was quite prepared to rent out basement space beneath the Moorfields buildings as warehouses, yet it was a policy justified in so far as it would 'increase the revvenue of the said hospitall for the keeping and mainteyning the poore Lunatiques'. It was also on condition that the leaseholder 'put noe goods into the warehouse that may be offensive to the Lunatiques or [a fire hazard]' (doubtless they had the Great Fire of 1666 in mind). Nevertheless, since pepper, potash, beer, victuals, fruit and tobacco were all stored under patients' cells, it is questionable what exactly the Governors considered 'offensive'.[200] Furthermore, the excavation of cellar space in pursuit of profit caused severe subsidence of the Hospital's walls and floors, and in 1800 a printed report on the condition of Bethlem declared that this meant that 'there is not one of the floors which are *level*, nor any of the walls *upright*'.[201] Indeed, by this time Hooke's 'palace' was not only dilapidated, it was falling down.

SEGREGATION, SEX AND SEXUAL ABUSE

Bethlem was also sharply criticized in the 1815/16 Madhouses Committee inquiry over deficiencies in its segregation of the sexes, and its total lack of segregation between 'patients who are outrageous' and 'those who are quiet', and also between the incontinent and the 'cleanly'.[202]

Prior to the 1640s, there was no segregation whatsoever, beyond simply confining patients in their cells. The Privy Council issued a directive to the Governors in 1631 that 'a new house next adjoyning unto the Hospitall which is yet voyd without a tennaunt . . . bee ymployed for the use of such poore lunaticks as eyther shall bee sicke or in a nearer hope of recovery',[203] but the Governors seem to have done nothing about it. With the addition of an extra wing in 1644–5, however, a building committee of six Governors made the remarkable recommendation, anticipating the concerns of the Madhouses Committee nearly two hundred years later, 'that itt wil bee necessary to keepe the distracted people in Bethlem which are most quiett & orderly in the new building of that hospital and those that are most unquiett in the old building'.[204] The proposal was 'approved of & confirmed by the Courte', and the innovative nature of this differentiation deserves recognition.

This initiative was taken over a decade before any structural or regulatory separation of the sexes was attempted. In practice, no formal action was taken until the 1650s by the Court of Governors to prevent the mingling of male and female patients and keepers. Since the 1630s, the custom had been for the Porter's wife and maid servant to 'be helpfull to the woemen',[205] while the Porter and basketmen concentrated on the men; but male patients and members of staff still enjoyed unregulated access to female patients.

In 1657 the Bethlem Court explicitly ruled 'that the men and women there bee kept asunder'.[206] The method subsequently arrived at, however, seriously compromised the effectiveness of the former distinction. Henceforth, 'twenty such of the distracted woemen as are most ... outragious' were to be housed in the new building.[207] Thus the therapeutic/classificatory division of 1645 had been partially abandoned in preference for a gender divide.

In practice, however, a basic, informal division seems to have been implemented and perpetuated at the Moorfields building from the 1670s, by keeping the more violent cases on the upper floors.[208] Convalescents were also partially separated by being permitted to walk the galleries and airing yards, and through the provision of sitting rooms. This arrangement was, however, rather unregulated and inadequate. With the addition of cells in the Hospital's basement storey towards the century's end, violent and dirty patients were, vice versa, being relegated downwards. In the next century, Urbane Metcalf's exposure of the ill-motivated pretexts by which poor, weak and uncooperative patients were got down into the basement by staff indicates that this form of segregation was far from therapeutic.[209] Officially, Bethlem seems to have abandoned all attempts at diagnostic segregation by this time. Before the Commons Inquiry of 1815 Haslam asserted 'we know of no distinction of patients', while the Bethlem Matron was admitting that, due to the Hospital's structure, separation of 'the noisy from the quiet' was 'impossible'.[210]

Gender segregation, however, was rather more efficiently imposed. Shortly after the Restoration, the Governors sought to consolidate their policy of imposing sexual propriety by ordering the hiring of a matron.[211] In fact, the experiment of unmarried matrons was to last just twenty months, both appointees being discharged, and the Governors returning to their former reliance on the Porter's wife.[212] At Moorfields male patients were originally lodged in the lower galleries and females in the upper, the Governors ruling that they were not to 'lodge promiscuously together'.[213] In 1681, nevertheless, it emerged that two basketmen, Edward Langdale and William Jones, had been allowed free access to the female patients and had impregnated two of them. The Board's belated discovery of these abuses is rather revealing. While on 30 March the Governors claimed (with an ironic choice of phrase) to be 'very sencible of the great miscarriages lately com[m]itted in . . . Bethlem', they were only cognizant of the abuses of 'one of the beadles or basketmen' – not both – while Mary Loveland and Esther Smyth were already, respectively, six and three months pregnant. Langdale and Jones were 'expelled'.[214]

The Governors also directed that two locks be installed on the doors to women's cells and that the Matron be entrusted with one of the keys. As an additional precaution, in 1681 cells were to be locked 'every night and every Sunday', and not opened in the mornings until the Matron 'or some of the maid servants are there present', while no male servant was to be allowed a key to any of the cells of naked females. The plain implication is that female patients, whether naked or sparsely clothed, had been exploited by male staff, and this throws into sharper relief the Governors' anxiety that visitors be excluded from female patients until shifted.

Despite the Governors' resolutions, further breaches of segregation and embarrassing pregnancies amongst patients followed.[215] The cause of such was partially attributable to faults in the Hospital's design. Soon after 1676, Bethlem had adopted an east–west division between males and females, no doubt necessitated by rising numbers. Yet 'Iron Rayles' were not ordered erected in the galleries until June 1689 'to keepe the Lunatike men and the Lunatike woemen assunder' – probably on the initiative of the energetic Edward Tyson.[216] The Governors had initially contemplated making this structural partition in the galleries when new Bethlem was first being constructed, but they had preferred to forbid patients 'to walke in the Galloryes' and to sustain the admiration and safety of visitors than to 'hinder the Grandieur & Prospect of the said Galleryes'; another sign of how the cosmetics of charity took precedence over the interests of patients.[217]

A strict gender division was also sought in the building of the new wings for incurable patients from 1723. In 1729, a year after the first wing for male incurables had been opened at Bethlem's east end, the 'Iron Grills in the middle of the second Gallery' were removed to 'the Stairs head' so that twelve of the fifty new cells could be cloistered off for female incurables.[218] Symmetrical segregation was restored to the Hospital from 1733, with the addition of a complementary west wing for fifty such females and the return of the grilles to their former position.[219] The Infirmary constructed in the 1740s similarly preserved separation between the sexes.[220]

What is particularly striking in the language of the Governors' rulings concerning segregation is a heightened anxiety about the libido of female patients. Indeed, it is only 'such of the Women Patients as are Lewdly Given', whom the Governors specifically ordered 'Confined to their Cells'.[221]

CONCLUSION

The 'dominant images' of the treatment of the insane in this period, modern historians have argued, are 'whips, chains, depletion and degradation . . . the loss of the mad person's very humanness', with the 'constant accompaniments' of 'shit, straw, and stench'.[222] The reality of the Bethlem patients' environment, however, was more complex and less degrading than this would suggest. The nature of confinement was considerably dependent on their behaviour and their relations with staff. Nor was

Bethlem a monolith, or as resistant to reforms as some have portrayed it. While many patients went naked, were bedded on straw and half-starved, the majority were provided with sheeted beds, adequate apparel and sufficient (if slender) meals. Indeed, patients' clothing, bedding and diet were neither as poor nor as distinct from that on offer at other contemporary institutions as historians have assumed. Patients certainly suffered grievously from cold, unhygienic and rather brutal conditions. Indubitably, they were often, particularly in the seventeenth century, deprived of food, clothing and bedding. They received little exercise, and even the engagement of patients in occupations about the house arose less as therapy than to supplement staffing. Throughout the period, patients were subject to prolonged and frequently unprovoked, if not simply callous, periods of mechanical restraint, and coerced by staff into obeisance, dejection or outright revolt. The nature and persistence of such treatment reflect the vigour of the prevailing cosmology of madness, and medical theory might be the licence for even rougher practices.[223] But this explanation is not sufficient to explain overall responses to the insane. Often the squalor and brutality of conditions at Bethlem arose simply from the failure of its administration and staff to meet its own ideals.

NOTES

1 Max Byrd, *Visits to Bedlam: Madness and Literature in the Eighteenth Century* (Columbia: University of South Carolina Press, 1974), ch. 3, esp. 85 and note to plate 6. Byrd refers to 'the . . . squalor of Bedlam', and to Yahoos dabbling in their dung 'like the inmates of Bedlam'. For fuller referencing see Jonathan Andrews, 'Bedlam Revisited: A History of Bethlem Hospital, *c.* 1634–*c.* 1770' (Ph.D. thesis, University of London, 1991), which forms the basis of this and the following chapters.

2 Beatrice Saunders, *Our Ancestors of the Eighteenth Century* (Sussex: The Book Guild, 1982), 31.

3 Charles Dickens, 'A Curious Dance Round a Curious Tree', in Harry Stone (ed.), *The Uncollected Writings of Charles Dickens: Household Words, 1850–59* (London: Allen Lane, 1969), ii, 382. The passage is quoted to illustrate the point in Andrew Scull, *Social Order/Mental Disorder: Anglo-American Psychiatry in Historical Perspective* (London: Routledge, 1989), 127 and note 22.

4 Andrew Scull, *Museums of Madness: The Social Organization of Insanity in Nineteenth-Century England* (London: Allen Lane; New York: St Martin's Press, 1979), 63; *idem, Social Order/ Mental Disorder*, 51.

5 Scull, *Social Order/Mental Disorder*, 51; and idem, *Museums*, 63.

6 See Patricia H. Allderidge, 'Management and Mismanagement at Bedlam, 1547–1633', in Charles Webster (ed.), *Health, Medicine and Mortality in the Sixteenth Century* (Cambridge: CUP, 1979), 141–64, 150.

7 *Ibid.* 154.

8 *BCGM*, 22 March 1676, fol. 235. Staff were forbidden 'to dispose of any of' these beds, until they had been removed and inspected by the Committee.

9 Just fifteen new bedsteads were ordered 'with all expedition for the Lunatikes . . . before their Removall'; another six were ordered three months later. See *ibid.* 21 July and 13 Oct. 1676, fols 277 and 293.

10 See Chapter 18, this volume.

11 *BCGM*, 13 Oct. 1676, fol. 293.

12 *Ibid.* 4 Nov. 1635 and 23 Oct. 1643, fols 66 and 74.

13 See *ibid.* e.g. 10 Sept. 1645, 21 Nov. 1645, 9 Sept. 1646, undated Court meeting sometime

between 13 Nov. and 18 Dec. 1646, 31 Aug. 1647, 25 Aug. 1648, 26 Nov. 1658, 25 Nov. 1663 and 13 Sept. 1676, fols 215, 228, 274, 284, 317, 358, 80, 80 and 290.

14 See, e.g., *ibid.* 13 Sept. 1676, 24 May 1689 and 29 Nov. 1695, fols 404, 290 and 17.

15 Even charity patients were rarely furnished with bedding. For the clothing of such patients, see e.g. *ibid.* 16 Dec. 1664, 28 Sept. and 19 Dec. 1666, 11 Sept. 1667.

16 See e.g. *Ghall* MSS 4215/2, case of Henry Marshall, supported at Bethlem and Hoxton during 1743–54, esp. fol. 181, 15 Oct. 1751, 'Cloaths for Henry Marshall for Winter 10/11'.

17 See, e.g., *BCGM*, 27 Feb. 1691, fol. 105.

18 See *ibid.* 10 Feb. and 16 March 1664, 24 Oct. 1679, 27 Feb. 1691 and 29 Nov. 1695, fols 90, 93, 112, 105 and 16–17.

19 *Ibid.* 10 Feb. and 16 March 1664, fols 90 and 93.

20 *Ibid.* 26 Nov. 1652, fol. 581.

21 See *ibid.* 31 Jan. and 14 March 1690, 22 April and 11 Nov. 1692, 2 June 1693, 15 March 1695, 29 Nov. 1695, 26 Nov. 1697, 10 and 17 Oct. 1701, fols 81, 31, 170, 206, 247–8, 476, 16–17, 150, 38 and 41.

22 *Ibid.* 29 Nov. 1695, fols 16–17.

23 Patients unprovided with clothes were supplied out of the Wardrobe. As before, clothing was issued by the Steward, at the direction of the Bethlem Committee.

24 *BCGM*, 7 Nov. 1712, fol. 678.

25 *BSCM*, 16 Jan. 1768.

26 For attitudes in Victorian asylums, see e.g. Elaine Showalter, *The Female Malady: Women, Madness, and English Culture, 1830–1980* (New York: Pantheon Press, 1986; London: Virago, 1987), 84–5.

27 See *BCGM*, 22 Jan. 1734, fols 324–5.

28 See e.g. *ibid.* 10 Sept. 1645, 9 Sept. 1646, 31 Aug. 1647, 16 Dec. 1664, 19 July 1749, fols 215, 274, 317, 125. Seventeenth-century orders concerning men's clothing mention 'Gownes Coates Shirts & Smockes' or 'shift[s], 'Capp[s]' or 'hatts', 'Shooes Stockings', and 'Woollen and Linnen Cloth'. In 1749, patients were to be provided with a bed, bolster, rug, blanket and sheets, while clothing consisted, for men, of coat, breeches, shirt, shoes, stockings and cap, and, for women, of baize gown, petticoat, shift, shoes, stockings, cap and handkerchief.

29 *BSCM*, 26 June 1756 and 26 March 1757, fols 2 and 8.

30 *Bethlem Incurables Sub-Committee Minutes* (henceforth, *BISCM*), 16 Jan. 1779. See also *BSCM*, 9 Nov. 1793, fol. 178, where thirty blankets on the brink of being disposed of are ordered inspected by the Committee.

31 *BCGM*, 2 Aug. 1638, fol. 193.

32 *Ibid.* 9 Dec. 1698.

33 The *Annual Register* recommended 'the use of straw' in all metropolitan hospitals on these grounds: *AR* (1764), 71. Rye straw supplied to Bethlem was supposed to be 'sweete' (i.e. clean) and free of weeds, and remained cheap, at 15s per load (i.e. 36 trusses/lb.), for at least the duration of the period 1643–1716. See *BCGM*, 2 June 1643, 21 June 1650 and 22 Jan 1734 fols 42, 446 and 324, and *BSCM*, 27 March 1713 and 14 Jan. 1716, fols 117 and 248.

34 *BSCM*, 29 Jan. 1780.

35 *BCGM*, 22 Jan. 1734 and 18 May 1748, fols 324–5 and 365.

36 See *ibid.* 19 July 1749, fol. 410. See, also, *BSCM*, 2 May 1761, fol. 29; *BGCM* in *BSCM*, 24 March 1762, fol. 377.

37 *King Lear*, III, iv, lines 130–40.

38 See *BSCM*, 17 May 1777.

39 See Roy Porter, *English Society in the Eighteenth Century* (Harmondsworth: Penguin, 1982), 33; J. Woodward, *To Do The Sick No Harm: A Study of the British Voluntary Hospital System to 1875* (London and Boston: Routledge & Kegan Paul, 1974), 101.

40 See James Carkesse, *Lucida Intervalla: Containing Divers Miscellaneous Poems*, ed. M. V. DePorte (Los Angeles: University of California Press, 1979), 13; *Madhouses Committee Reports*, 1815, 1st Report, 89.

41 *BSCM*, 21 Dec. 1771.

42 The first rat-catcher appointed to Bethlem was Alexander Ballendine, hired in 1777 on a salary of 3 guineas p/q. Robert Roberts of Great Montague Court, Little Britain, was the first bug-destroyer, appointed in 1786, on a salary of 3 guineas per annum, to keep the beds of both patients and staff 'clear of Bugs'. See *ibid.* 17 and 31 May 1777, 6 June and 19 Sept. 1778 and 29 April 1786.

43 *BCGM*, 29 June 1791, fol. 29.

44 It was patients' 'flannel Gowns' which were objected to by Thomas Monro and Bryan Crowther. See *BSCM*, 16 Nov. 1793, fol. 178.

45 See esp. 1st Report, 11–12.

46 *BCGM*, 4 Dec. 1598, fol. 52; Allderidge, *op. cit.* 153.

47 *BCGM*, 23 Sept. and 20 Nov. 1657, fols 828 and 836.

48 *Ibid.* 25 Aug. and 22 Sept. 1669, fols 155 and 166.

49 See *Ibid.* 29 Feb. 1644, fol. 96, the first reference to the instalment of a vault and latrine at Bethlem during the period.

50 See Lawrence Stone, *The Family, Sex and Marriage in England, 1500–1800* (London: Weidenfeld & Nicolson, 1977), 62–3, 113–14, 171 and 304; Mark Jenner, 'Early Modern English Conceptions of "Cleanliness" and "Dirt" as Reflected in the Environmental Regulation of London *c.* 1530–*c.* 1700' (Oxford, D.Phil., 1991), and Alain Corbin, *The Foul and the Fragrant: Odor and the French Social Imagination* (Leamington Spa, Hamburg and New York: Berg, 1986) on odour as one of the major facets of 'the world we have lost'.

51 *BCGM*, 18 Aug. 1671 and 18 Sept. 1672, fols 334 and 445.

52 Prisoners in contemporary (and indeed present-day) prisons have made almost identical demonstrations of protest. In the 1777 Newgate riot, for example, 'all the windows and casements were demolished and thrown down into the square'. See *AR*, 1777, 196.

53 Although the Board directed that these gratings be set up in 1671, no action was taken for over a year, when the Court was obliged to repeat its instruction. See note 51.

54 *BCGM*, 20 June 1765, fol. 133.

55 Carkesse, *op. cit.* 50.

56 At least one of these cisterns was not installed until 1685, nine years after the patients had been transferred to Moorfields.

57 For mention of the installation and repair of 'Boghouse[s]', cisterns and sewers, see e.g. *BSCM*, 26 Nov. 1715, 24 March, 7 April 17 May 1716, 26 July 1754, 25 Oct. 1777, fols 203, 215, 217, 222, 486. See *BCGM*, 3 and 17 July 1685, fols 89 and 94.

58 *BSA*, 26 July–2 Aug. 1766.

59 John Howard, *An Account of the Present State of the Prisons, Houses of Correction, and Hospitals in London and Westminster* . . . (London: Proclamation Society, 1789), 33; *idem, An Account of the Principal Lazarettos in Europe* (Warrington: William Eyres, 1789), 33, 139.

60 Howard, *An Account of . . . Prisons*, 34.

61 In fact, the poor state of the privies had originally been reported and ordered amended in 1790. See *BGCM*, 28 Aug. 1790 and 29 June 1791, fols 19 and 29.

62 The walls were ordered demolished, the drains cleaned and a well sunk for supplying a reservoir for the use of the new privies in 1796, after Thomas Monro had opined 'that the health of Patients would be much less likely to suffer if an improvement were made in the Privies & by an additional supply of water'. See *ibid.* 19 Feb. 1793, 20 Sept. 1796 and 3 Feb. and 10 May 1797, fols 5, 66, 70 and 75; also *BSCM*, 20 Aug. 1796.

63 A published survey concluded, *inter alia*, that, 'the materials, with which all the original walls . . . were constructed, are bad', and that 'the first and largest part of the structure was hurried'. See *Report Respecting the Present State and Condition of Bethlem Hospital* (London: J. Richardson, 1800), 3–14.

64 See Corbin, *op. cit.* 52; Jacques-René Tenon, *Mémoires sur les hôpitaux de Paris* (Paris: De l'inprimerie de Ph.-D. Pierres, 1788), 208.

65 See *Report Respecting . . . Bethlem* (note 63), 4.

66 Matthews's description of this effluvia suggests Schneiderian First Rank symptoms of schizophrenia, but it also indicates patients' peculiar sensitivity to the stench of the

Hospital when locked up in the confines of their cells. See John Haslam, *Illustrations of Madness* (1810), ed. Roy Porter (London and New York: Routledge, 1988), xxxii and 28; Robert Howard, unpublished paper, 'Air-Looms, Pneumatic Chemistry, and Magnetic Mind-Control: First Rank Schizophrenic Symptoms in John Haslam's Account of James Tilly Matthews'.

67 See Corbin, *op. cit.*, esp. 49–53.

68 W. H. Quarrell and Margaret Mare (eds), *London in 1710. From the Travels of Z. C. von Uffenbach* (London: Faber & Faber, 1934), 51; see also John Dryden, 'The Medal. A Satyre Against Sedition' (1682), in James Kingsley (ed.), *The Poems of John Dryden* (Oxford: OUP, 1958), 261, l. 285: 'A Heav'n, like *Bedlam*, slovenly and sad.'

69 Jonathan Swift, 'A Character, Panegyric and Description of the Legion Club', in H. Williams (ed.), *The Poems of Jonathan Swift*, 3 volumes (Oxford: Clarendon Press, 1937), iii, 827–39.

70 *BCGM*, 2 May 1684, fol. 421.

71 *Ibid.* 30 March 1677 and May 1736, fols 356–61, 379, 388 and 391–2.

72 *Ibid.* 27 Jan. 1742, fol. 135.

73 See *ibid.* 20 June 1765, fol. 135.

74 See Edward Hare, 'Old Familiar Faces: Some Aspects of the Asylum Era in Britain', in R. M. Murray and T. H. Turner (eds), *Lectures on the History of Psychiatry. The Squibb Series* (London: Gaskell, 1990), 96.

75 John Monro, *Remarks on Dr. Battie's Treatise on Madness*, reprinted with introduction by Richard Hunter and Ida Macalpine (London: Dawsons, 1962; 1st edn London: Clarke, 1758), 6.

76 Indeed, this qualifies Hare's point that permitting patients to wear their own clothes 'constituted a powerful reason for not tearing them' (Hare, *op. cit.*), although Bethlem issue clothing would have been coarse and uncomfortable, and may have been seen as demeaning by some patients.

77 Saunders, *op. cit.* 31.

78 John Strype, *A Survey of the Cities of London & Westminster . . . Written at First . . . by John Stow* (London: A. Churchill, 1720), i, 195.

79 *Report from the Madhouses Committee, 1st Report*, 36 and 60.

80 *BCGM*, 24 April and 20 June 1765, 126 and 132–7.

81 That is, soon after 6 a.m. in summer and 7 a.m. in winter.

82 Soap had been used at Bethlem since the early seventeenth century. In 1642 the Porter was quizzed by the Court as to why 'soe much soape was spent at Bethlem' and answered that there were simply more patients. By 1785 8 lb. of soap was being provided every week for the Hospital's use. See *BCGM*, 29 April 1642, fol. 382; *BSCM*, 17 and 24 Sept. 1785, 20 June 1795, 25 July 1812.

83 See *BCGM*, 22 Dec. 1768, fol. 238, where patients are ordered to be shaved once a week.

84 Pierre Jean Grosley, *Londres* (Lausanne: *S.N.*, 1770), ii, 12–13.

85 Clare Williams (ed. and trans.), *Sophie in London, 1786, Being the Diary of Sophie v. La Roche* (London: Jonathan Cape, 1933), 166–71.

86 Jacques Cambray, *De Londres et de ses environs* (Amsterdam: *S.N.*, 1788), ii, 12–13; Edward G. O'Donoghue, *The Story of Bethlehem Hospital* (London: T. Fisher Unwin, 1914), 283.

87 Howard, *Lazarettos*, 139–41. In fact, Bethlem had been whitewashed about ten years before Howard's survey.

88. *Select Committe on Madhouses, 1st Report*, 1815, 150–2; *3rd Report*, 1815, 175.

89 See, e.g., Bartholomaeus Anglicus, *De Proprietatibus Rerum* (London: in aedibus Thomae Bertheleti, 1535), fols 31–2, 'The medycyne is – that in the begynnynge . . . he be well kepte or bounde in a darke place'; cited in Richard Hunter and Ida Macalpine, *Three Hundred Years of Psychiatry: 1535–1860* (London: OUP, 1963), 3.

90 See *BSCM*, 15 Nov. 1766.

91 *BCGM*, 17 Oct. and 4 Nov. 1663, fols 71 and 75–6.

92 *Ibid.* 8 and 16 May 1674, fol. 638, 642. Bethlem was not only to be rebuilt 'more large', but was also to be removed to 'a more convenient place'.

93 Williams *op. cit.* 166–7.

94 'The poor creatures . . . are not chained up in dark cellars, stretched on damp ground, nor reclining on cold paving stones . . . The doors are open, their rooms wainscoted, and long airy corridors give them a chance of exercise.' See Cambry, *op. cit.* ii, 12–13, quoted in O'Donoghue, *op. cit.* 282–3.

95 *BCGM*, 23 Oct. 1674 and 5 May 1676, and Bethlem Committee report, dated 16 Oct. 1674, fols 52, 55 and 246; *The Royal Magazine*, v, Aug. 1761, 60; Strype *op. cit.*

96 *BCGM*, 10 Sept. and 3 Dec. 1675, 5 May 1676, 24 May and 28 June 1689, fols 174, 199–200, 246, 404 and 416. See, also, Strype *op. cit.* 195.

97 For the yards at old Bethlem, see *BCGM*, 2 June 1643, fols 43–4. For those at new Bethlem, see *ibid.* 23 Oct 1674, fol. 52.

98 See *BSCM*, 16 May 1719, fol. 45.

99 *BCGM*, 23 Oct. 1674, fol. 52.

100 See evidence of William Smith, *Select Committe on Madhouses, 2nd Report*, 1815, 152.

101 Carkesse, *op. cit.* 28 and 49.

102 See, e.g., W. Pargeter, *Observations on Maniacal Disorders*, ed. Stanley Jackson (London: Routledge, 1988; 1st edn Reading: for the author, 1792), 8, 95; Scull, *Social Order/Mental Disorder*, 57.

103 See this chapter, and Strype *op. cit.* 195.

104 *Ibid.*; *BCGM*, e.g. 3 Dec. 1675 and 20 June 1765, fols 199 and 135; Howard, *Lazarettos*, 139.

105 *BCGM*, 3 July 1663, fol. 57.

106 *BSCM*, 21 Oct. 1710.

107 In 1714–15, the Court rejected a plan for removing the stove rooms to the east and west ends of the Hospital. By 1766 patients were using a former servant's room as a warming-room, and two more rooms were added for patients' convenience. *Ibid.* 15 June 1714, 10 May, 7 July and 26 Nov. 1715, 16 May 1719, 15 Nov. 1766, 30 Oct. 1778, fols 160, 191, 203, 45 and 228; *BCGM*, 25 June 1714, 13 May and 7 Oct. 1715, and 28 Feb. 1793, fols 62, 135 and 155.

108 Carkesse, *op. cit.* 28.

109 *BCGM*, 29 Nov. 1695, fol. 17.

110 See *BSCM*, 17 Jan. 1778, 25 Feb. 1778.

111 Middleton and Watts 'found that the poore there had noe victualls, but some smale scrapps'. That the patients 'were likely to starve' was not only their own judgment, but was actually 'complained unto them', presumably by the Steward Willis. See *BCGM*, 18 Feb. 1631, fol. 217; Alldderidge, *op. cit.* 161.

112 See Allderidge, *op. cit.* 161–2; PRO, *State Papers Domestic 16*, 224, no. 21 and 237, no. 5.

113 See, e.g., Dekker, *The Honest Whore*, Part 1, V, ii, lines 232–4.

114 See Allderidge, *op. cit.* 161.

115 See O'Donoghue, *op. cit.* 177–8.

116 The marshall's men were paid 40s each for their deliveries on Lord Mayor's Day, 1635; while the sheriffs and the clerks of the markets received 30s each for their deliveries from the City markets.

117 In 1644, the Clerk of Leadenhall Market demanded an increase in his gratuity, alleging that 'hee hath sent more bread & meate to Bethlem then the Clarks of other marketts or his predecessors have done'; sheriff Fowke's officer's allowance was ceased entirely as he 'giveth nothing to Bethlem'; *BCGM*, 1 Feb. 1644, fol. 91.

118 See Chapter 17, 'Provisions and Peculation'.

119 Howard, *Lazarettos*, 33.

120 Urbane Metcalf, *The Interior of Bethlehem Hospital* (London: the Author, 1818), 5–6, 14–15.

121 See, e.g., Robert Burton, *The Anatomy of Melancholy*, eds D. Floyd and P. Jordan-Smith (New York: Tudor Publishing Company, 1948; 1st edn, London: H. Cripps, 1621), part 1, sect. 2, 146–55; part 2, sect. 2, 304–13; part 3, sect. 2, 505; part 3, sect. 2, 586.

122 For the diet at Bridewell, see *BCGM*, 7 May 1667, fol. 304.

123 For mutton, see, e.g., *BCGM*, 5 Jan. 1672 and 30 March 1677, fols 368 and 360.

124 *Ibid.* 21 April 1653, 27 July 1655, 17 Dec. 1656, fols 604, 712, 779. See also 3 July 1663, fol. 56.

125 *Ibid.* 21 July 1645, fol. 205. Contrast this with the ideals of self-sufficient, productive, working communities, represented by the management of nineteenth-century asylums.

126 Burton, *op. cit.* part 2, sect. 2, 307–10.

127 *Ibid.* 307.

128 *BCGM*, 4 Nov. 1635 and 23 Oct. 1643, fols 74 and 66.

129 *Ibid.* 17 May 1667, fol. 45.

130 *Ibid.* 30 March 1677, fols 360–1.

131 While old Bethlem had a large beer cellar, the Moorfields building was equipped with both a large and a small beer cellar. The drawing of beer was restricted in 1765 to an hour at dinner and half an hour at supper. See *ibid.* 30 March 1677, 20 June 1765, fols 359, 133–7; *BSCM*, 10 Oct. 1724, fol. 214; *BGCM* in *BSCM*, 22 Jan. 1780, 15 Sept. 1785.

132 *BSCM*, 6 April 1728 and 17 Jan. 1747, fols 41 and 1.

133 When planning the erection of a 'brewhouse' at the Hospital in 1752, the Grand Committee estimated that a storage capacity of ninety-seven barrels would be required, suggesting over a third of a barrel per patient, or rather that much was being consumed by staff. *BGCM* in *BSCM*, 15 April 1752, fol. 290.

134 Fruit seems to have returned into favour in the medical treatises of the later seventeenth century; e.g. Tryon, *A Treatise on Cleanness in Meats and Drinks* (London: Printed for the Author, 1682).

135 Along with other rich food stuffs, fruit was forbidden to be given to patients by visitors at the same juncture.

136 Purchases of 3 or 4 bushels, or of 800 codlings, could not have gone very far between 150 patients. See *BSA*, e.g. 3–10 Aug. 1724, 8–15 Aug. 1725, 21–8 Aug. 1726. Codlings were still being given to patients in August during the 1780s. See e.g. *BSCM*, 4 August 1781, when 'all the Patients' in the Hospital were ordered 'Codlings and Milk'.

137 *BCGM*, 30 March 1677, fol. 361.

138 *Ibid.*, e.g. 21 March 1750, 20 July 1753, 2 Oct. 1780, fols 168–9 and 360; *BSCM*, 23 Oct. and 11 Dec. 1714, 18 and 25 July 1719, 22 March 1755, fols 171, 174–5, 50–1 and 455.

139 *BSCM*, 26 Sept. 1730, fol. 145; T. Bowen, *An Historical Account of the Origin, Progress and Present State of Bethlem Hospital* (London: For the Governors, 1783), 10, note; also William Black, *A Dissertation on Insanity* (London: Ridgway, 1810), 28; Hunter and Macalpine, *op. cit.* 647. Bowen stated, however, that 'vegetables' and better beer had only 'lately [been] allowed'.

140 *BSA*, e.g. 23 Feb.–2 March 1723, 'Making Pancakes 3/9'; 6–13 Feb. 1725, 'Lard Eggs & Apples for Fritters 4/6'; 20–27 March 1726, 'Buns & Ale for ye Servts 3/6'; 7–14 Jan. 1727, 'A Legg Veal for Twelf Night'; 4–11 April 1724, 'fruit for Easter puddings 2/7 Bacon 2/-'; 9–16 April 1726, 'Bacon, Eggs, Plumbs & Beer for Easter day 6/8'; 28 May–4 June 1726, 'Plumbs Bacon Eggs & spice for ye Servts 6/8'; 9–16 Jan. 1725, 'Ale for ye Servts on Xmas day 1/-'. Entries which, by their quantities, evidently denote items for patients, include: 11–18 Jan. 1724, '160 Mince Pyes Each 6d £4'; 23–30 Jan. 1773, 'Paid 320 minced Pyes at Christmas £8'; 14–17 May 1726, '19 Stone 3 lb of Veale for Easter Monday . . . £2 11/8'; 28 May–4 June 1726, the same 'for Whit Monday . . . £2 8/9'; 15–22 Dec. 1764, 'Fruit &c for Pottage & Puddings £4 5/3'.

141 *Ibid.* 8–15 May 1725; *BSCM*, 4 April 1761 and *BCGM*, 6 May 1636, fol. 391; Bowen, *op. cit.* 10.

142 Bowen, *op. cit.* 10–11.

143 See *Select Committee on Madhouses, 1st Report*, 1815, 37.

144 Bowen, *op. cit.* 10–11; Howard, *Lazarettos*, 33.

145 See *BCGM*, 14 Jan. 1631, fol. 211.

146 *BSA*, 7–14 April 1722; 19–26 Jan., 6–13 April, 20–27 July, 28 Sept.–5 Oct. and 21–28 Dec. 1723; 14–21 March 1724; 9–16 Jan. 1725; 12–19 March 1726; 11–18 Nov. 1727. See also *BCGM*, 20 June 1765, fols 133–7; *BCGM* in *BSCM*, 15 Sept. 1785.

147 *BGCM* in *BSCM*, 15 Sept. 1785; *BSCM*, 25 Feb. 1786.

148 See, e.g., Thomas Willis, *The Practice of Physick* (London: Dring, Harper & Leigh, 1684), 194; John Moore, *Of Religious Melancholy. A Sermon Preach'd before the Queen* (London: Printed for William Rogers, 1692); Richard Mead, *Medical Precepts and Cautions* (London: J. Brindley, 1751), 100–1.

149 *1st Report*, 1816, 92.

150 See *1st Report*, 1815, 12, 35, 40, 58; *1st Report*, 1816, 55; and *Report of the Commissioners Enquiring Concerning Charities* (London: House of Commons, 1837), 514.

151 See *BSA*, e.g. 22–9 July and 11–18 Nov. 1727; 9–16 March 1728, 7–14 June 1729; 14–21 Jan. 11–18 Feb., 10–17 March and 7–14 April 1764; 26 April–3 May and 30 Aug.–6 Sept. 1766; 27 March–3 April, 14–21 Aug., 2–9 and 9–16 Oct. 1773; *BSCM*, 19 June 1756, 7 Oct. 1769 and 31 Dec. 1796. See, also, Jonathan Andrews, '"Hardly a Hospital, But a Charity for Pauper Lunatics"?: Therapeutics at Bethlem in the Seventeenth and Eighteenth Centuries', in Jonathan Barry and Colin Jones (eds), *Medicine and Charity Before the Welfare State* (London and New York: Routledge, 1991), 63–81.

152 *BSA*, 5–12 and 12–19 Jan. 1765; *BSCM*, 12 Jan. 1765.

153 See Chapter 17; *BSCM*, 19 June 1756, fol. 1; *BCGM*, 20 June 1765, fol. 135.

154 *BCGM*, 20 June 1765, fol. 135.

155 Metcalf, *op. cit.* 8 and 10.

156 Klaus Doerner, *Madmen and the Bourgeoisie. A Social History of Insanity and Psychiatry* (Oxford: Basil Blackwell, 1981), 35, 51; Michel Foucault, *Madness and Civilization: A History of Insanity in the Age of Reason* (London: Tavistock Publications, 1967), ch. ii, 38–64 and ch. viii, 230–4; M. Donnelly, *Managing the Mind. A Study of Medical Psychology in Early Nineteenth-Century Britain* (London: Tavistock, 1983), 36.

157 For newspapers, see *BSA*, e.g. 24 March–7 April and 22–29 Sept. 1764. That only 7d was spent on papers each week, however, may suggest that they were purchased for staff, not for patients.

158 Williams, *op. cit.* 167–9. See, also, *BSA*, e.g. 30 March–6 April 1766, which record purchase of 'Newspapers . . . at 7d per Week', for fifty weeks.

159 *BSA*, 24 April–1 May 1773; *BSCM*, 17 July 1779.

160 Scull, *Social Order/Mental Disorder*, 76.

161 See *1st Report*, 1815, 12–13, 16, 38, 40, 42, 58–60, 62–7, 82–90, 95–8, 106, 108, 132; *2nd Report*, 150–2; *3rd Report*, 175–7; *1st Report*, 1816, 38–44, 47, 50, 55–7, 90–2.

162 Grosley, *op. cit.* vol. ii,

163 Williams, *op. cit.* 167–8.

164 1815, *1st Report*, 62–3; John Haslam, *Observations on Madness and Melancholy*, 2nd edn (London: John Callow, 1809), 289.

165 1815, *1st Report*, 96.

166 *BSA*, 16–23 June 1764. *Re* strait-waistcoats at private madhouses, see e.g. Alexander Cruden, *The London Citizen Exceedingly Injured* (London: For the Author, 1739), title page and 8.

167 *BSA*, 30 Jan.–6 Feb. and 27 March–3 April 1773.

168 *BCGM*, 9 July 1772, fols 359–60.

169 *BSA*, e.g. 5–12 June 1773; 'Paid Chains for the Infirmary 6/8'.

170 See William Black, *A Dissertation on Insanity: Illustrated with Tables and Extracted from Between Two and Three Thousand Cases in Bedlam* (London 1810), 13–14; Hunter and Macalpine, *op. cit.* 644–7; *BSCM*, 15 Sept. 1785 and 21 Jan. 1786.

171 *BSA*, 16–23 June 1764; '4 Dozen of Men & Womens Legg Lock £66/-'; 24–31 May 1766; '1 Dozen leg Locks at 33/-. 1 Doz HandCuffs 30/- . . . [total] £3 3/-'. The lengthy description of smith's work needing to be done at Bethlem in 1791, contained in a voluminous surveyor's report of necessary repairs, evokes a rather gruesome picture of the standard degree of confinement: 'To take off all the Locks Latches Catches Bolts Bars Hinges and Grates that are found bad and decayed and replace and make good with new and to provide and fix on proper Strap Irons with Chains and Staples where they may be wanted to compleat all the New Bed Steads and bed places and to take off and repair and refix the old Straps Chains &c to fix new Stay braces straps and irons as shall be directed.' See *BGCM*, 29 June 1791, fols 34–5.

172 Madame Van Muyden (ed. and trans.), *A Foreign View of England in the Reigns of George I. & George II. The Letters of Monsieur César de Saussure to his Family* (London: John Murray, 1902), 93.

173 Cambray, *op. cit.*, quoted in O'Donoghue, *op. cit.* 282–3.

174 Black, *op. cit.* 13–14; Hunter and Macalpine, *op. cit.* 646. In 1790, a maidservant was dismissed 'particularly' for 'omitting to secure the Patients in their Cells at Night', reflecting the importance attached by the governing board to matters of security, although this often simply seems to have entailed locking their doors. See *BSCM*, 2 Oct. 1790.

175 See e.g. Chapter 18; *BCGM*, 15 Nov. 1723, 12 July 1728, fols 25, 153, 63; and Jonathan Andrews, 'The Lot of the "incurably" insane in enlightenment England', *Eighteenth Century Life*, 12, (February 1988), i, 1–18.

176 Willis, *op. cit.* 206.

177 Richard Mead, *Medica Sacra*, in *The Medical Works of Richard Mead* (London: Hitch & Hawes, 1762), 623.

178 See Jonathan Andrews, 'A Respectable Mad-doctor? Dr Richard Hale FRS, 1670–1728', *Notes & Records of the Royal Society of London*, xliv (1990), 169–203, 185; James Monro, *Oratio Anniversaria in Theatro Collegii Regalis Medicorum Londinensium; ex Harvaei Instituto* (London: G. Strahan, 1737), 22.

179 John Haslam, *Observations on Madness*, 289–90; Hunter and Macalpine, *op. cit.* 635.

180 For this discussion, see *BCGM*, 22 Jan., 25 March, 23 April, 28 May, 17 July and 7 Aug. 1673, and 11 Feb. 1674, fols 474, 491, 498, 509, 527, 548, 612 and 615, and Chapter 6, this volume.

181 See Williams *op. cit.* 167–9, and also *Sketches in Bedlam* (London: Sherwood, Jones, 1823), for an inside view of Nicholson and other patients.

182 See *BSCM*, 12 Aug. and 2 Sept. 1786, 3 Feb., 14 April and 11 Aug. 1787, 12 March 1791, no fol. no. and fol. 5.

183 See *Acts of the Privy Council, 1616–17*, 25 and 29 Nov. and 21 Dec. 1617, 387–9 and 392–3.

184. Carkesse, *op. cit.* 6, 12, 22–3, 36.

185 *Ibid.* 12, 39, 52.

186 *Bedlam. A Poem* (1744), reproduced in Patricia Allderidge, *Catalogue to Bethlem Royal Hospital Museum* (London: Bethlem Royal Hospital, 1976); original in *BRHA*.

187 Alexander Cruden, *The Adventures of Alexander the Corrector* (London: Printed for the author and sold by Richard Baldwin, 1754); *idem, The London Citizen Exceedingly Injured* (London: For the Author, 1738); *BAR*, fol. 184. Cruden was in Bethlem from 17 Dec. 1743 until 3 March 1744, but mysteriously failed to mention his few months there in his subsequent writings.

188 See *BSCM*, 13 March 1779 and 'General Orders for Bethlem Hospital' attached as an appendix to Bowen's *Historical Account* (see note 139), and the *Report of the [Governors'] Select Committee of Enquiry* (London: Thomas Parker, 1792), no. ix, 51.

189 Haslam, *Observations on Madness*, 123.

190 Scull, *Social Order/Mental Disorder*, 76.

191 Showalter, *op. cit.* 31.

192 For example, Richard Tyler, who supplied Bethlem with beer in the 1640s, was paying the Hospital rent for his dwelling house, two large rooms and a pump-house in the Hospital precinct. See *BCGM*, 30 Jan. 1646, 29 Feb. 1656 and 21 Jan. 1659, fols 239–40, 740 and 90, and Chapters 12 (pp. 156–77) and 17 ('Recruitment').

193 *Ibid.* 30 April 1651 and 20 Nov. 1685, fols 493 and 116.

194 *Ibid.* 18 Aug. 1671, 18 Sept 1672, 9 Aug. 1678, fols 337, 445 and 41, and above.

195 See Chapter 12.

196 *BCGM*, 2 June 1643, fol. 44.

197 *Ibid.* Oct. 1647, fol. 320: landlords' property; 19 Dec. 1666, fol. 27; 6 July and 3 Sept. 1686, fols 185 and 192; *BSCM*, 12 May 1711, fol. 53.

198 See *BCGM*, e.g. 2 June 1641, fol. 336.

199 *Ibid.* 21 Oct. 1762 and 27 Jan. 1763, fols 42 and 46.

200 These warehouses were normally advertised when vacant in the city newspapers. Governors were rarely the leaseholders.

201 *Report Respecting the . . . Condition of Bethlem* (note 63).
202 See *Select Committee on Madhouses*, summary report, dated 11 July 1815, 4; *1st Report*, 1815, 11, 16, 25, 27, 31, 34–6, 40, 76–7, 79, 91, 93, 102–3, 105, 107, 118, 125 and 129.
203 *Acts of the Privy Council*, ed. John Roche Dosent (London: HMSO, 1964), *2/40, 821*, 6 April 1631, 285.
204 *BCGM*, 21 July 1645, fol. 205.
205 See *ibid.* 3 July 1663, fol. 56.
206 *Ibid.* 12 June 1657, fol. 817.
207 When exactly this initiative was taken is not clear. When it is first mentioned in the surviving Minutes, during 1663, the women patients have plainly already been separated, for the Court directs that they are 'still' to be 'kept in the Roomes in the last new buildings'. Segregation of the sexes may have been imposed soon after June 1657, or more likely sometime during August 1659–July 1662, for which period no minutes are extant. See *ibid.* 21 Jan. 1663, fol. 31.
208 For eighteenth-century references to separate quartering of violent cases, see e.g. Van Muyden, *op. cit.* 93; Henry Mackenzie, *The Man of Feeling* (Oxford: OUP, 1970; 1st edn 1771), 30.
209 Metcalf, *op. cit.*
210 *1st Report*, 1815, 58 and 90.
211 *BCGM*, 21 Jan., 11 Feb. and 1 April 1663, fols 31, 36 and 43.
212 The Governors were openly doubting the merits (not to say expense) of this office of matron just six months after its creation, although they were to persist with the experiment for another fourteen months and the Porter's wife was subsequently to assume the same title and function. See *BCGM*, 11 Feb., 1 April and 3 July 1663, and 23 Sept. 1664, fols 36, 43, 56 and 114, and Chapter 5.
213 *BCGM*, 21 July 1676, fol. 276.
214 For this incident and the ensuing discussion, see *ibid.* 10 Dec. 1680, 30 March, 15 and 22 April, 5 Aug., 1 and 23 Sept. 1681, fols 190, 209, 213, 216, 218, 241 and 258.
215 *Ibid.* 25 Oct. and 8 Nov. 1689, fols 451–2 and 458.
216 See *ibid.* 10 and 24 May, and 28 June 1689, fols 398, 404–5 and 416.
217 The Governors had been particularly anxious that the iron bars of the partition should 'hardly be discovered by any person in the said Gallery', although, once erected, the ground floor bar gates were not ordered discreetly concealed behind wooden screens until 1788. See *ibid.* 23 Oct. 1674, 10 Sept. 1675, 3 Dec. 1675 and 5 May 1676, fols 53, 174, 199–200 and 246; *BSCM*, 31 May 1788.
218 See *BCGM*, 9 Oct. 1729, fol. 187. Indeed, it is this wing, and not the one subsequently added to the Hospital in the 1730s, which Hogarth chose to depict in his *Rake's Progress*.
219 *Ibid.* 28 June, 13 July, 2 Aug. and 18 Oct. 1733, 11 Feb. 1736, fols 309, 311, 315, 318 and 376.
220 *Ibid.* 17 Feb. 1742, 8 Aug. 1753, fol. 120; *BGCM* in *BSCM*, 3 May, 20 June, 20 July and 24 Aug. 1753, fols 137, 347, 355, 360 and 366; *BSCM*, 11 Oct. 1753, fol. 375.
221 See *BCGM*, 20 June 1765, fol. 137; also Chapter 11.
222 Scull, *Social Order/Mental Disorder*, 56.
223 John Wesley, *Primitive Physic*, cited in Roy Porter, *Mind Forg'd Manacles: Madness and Psychiatry in England from Restoration to Regency* (London: Athlone Press, 1987; Penguin, 1990), 30.

THE ARCHITECTURE OF BETHLEM AT MOORFIELDS

———— •◆• ————

Christine Stevenson

Bethlem's move in 1676 to the building designed by Robert Hooke (1635–1703) inaugurated great changes for the Hospital. Its size permitted expansion; its magnificence, expansiveness – that is, a new dignity among London's charitable institutions and international renown. Bethlem became one of the sights of London, its more than five hundred feet of façade facing Moorfields illustrated in at least thirty-six tourist guides and topographical books published in 1681 and after (see Plate 15.1). Among London's hospitals, only Chelsea and Greenwich would be pictured more often.[1] References to visits there abound, and Bethlem's significance as a cultural nexus, the place where England questioned not just its own socio-political sanity (or lack of it) but the relations between body and soul, imagination and memory, has been the subject of sophisticated modern exegesis.[2] Like the Bastille or Newgate, Bethlem at Moorfields has achieved emblematic status sufficient to dematerialize it, to turn it into something more or less than a building. We however know less about this building than is generally assumed: Hooke's Bethlem remains mysterious in several respects. This chapter describes its construction, and its receptions: the celebrations, condemnations, and its influence.

EVOKING A PALACE

Poems about new buildings were virtually unknown in England before 1660. The Restoration provided a powerful stimulus to celebrations of new constructions, concrete emblems of political and religious 're-edification', the moral rebuilding of England, after the instabilities of the Interregnum.[3] The Fire in 1666 gave urgency to a symbolic logic under which London was ceaselessly figured as rising again, phoenix-like, salamander-like, under the wise superintendence of the restored monarchy.

In the half-century after 1676, Hooke's Bethlem attracted as many poems as any other building.[4] There was not much competition: Charles was not the builder his panegyrists claimed, and no undertaking escaped the effects of the plague and the Fire on the supply of labour and materials. After Edward Jarman's Royal Exchange

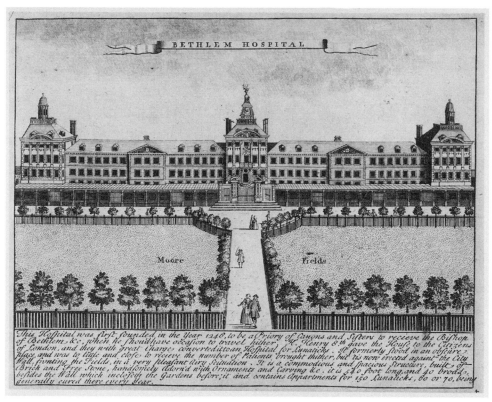

Plate 15.1 'Bethlem Hospital', from *British Views* (*c.* 1723), inexpensive popular prints published by John Bowles which appeared with 'Particular accounts'; this one gives an overall length of 540 feet for Bethlem, after the 1720 Stow edition. Reproduced by kind permission of the Wellcome Institute Library, London.

(1667–71) and Christopher Wren's Custom House (1669–71), Bethlem was London's first great public construction in half a century, one surpassing the other two in size, stylishness, ornament and, not least, superb siting. It was moreover dedicated to charity and not to the commerce that, however celebrated, was not (quite) a cardinal Christian virtue. England had seen no new hospital on that scale since the completion of the Savoy, off the Strand, 160 years earlier in 1519; with Bethlem it could boast a challenge to the palatial hospitals of Italy and France.[5] Finally, for a hardened seventeenth-century versifier, trained in the art of what was called 'metaphysical' paradox, a palace for lunatics was irresistible.

Bethlehems Beauty (1676), the first and most informative of the poems about Bethlem at Moorfields, is an anonymous broadsheet licensed for publication two and a half weeks after the Hospital opened there:

> So Brave, so Neat, so Sweet it does appear,
> Makes one Half-Madd to be a Lodger there . . .
>
> (lines 35–6)[6]

The danger such sweetness presented to the stability of passers-by was compounded for Bethlem's inhabitants (that lunatics imagined themselves to have been born to high estate was already proverbial):

> And those pour Souls, whose Crazed Brains advance
> Their roving Fancies to the Extravagance
> Of being Princes, needs must think it True,
> When they shall such a Towering Pallace view.
>
> (lines 37–40)

The poem was written in the light of the late sixteenth- and earlier seventeenth-century 'Bedlamite' ballads, which differed inasmuch as they were written as if by former inmates of the old and humbler hospital at Bishopsgate. In them, bombast and humility were artfully mixed along with nonsensically exotic geographical and mythological allusion. The lyrics were clever in their appeal to the listener, who sifts through delusion to discern pathetic reality at the core. When Mad Tom sings of the 'lordly lofts of Bedlam' we know that what we see, in our mind's eye, is not what poor Tom sees.[7]

If discovering Bethlem at Bishopsgate as grand was a sure sign of craziness, what happened when the Hospital *became* grand, at Moorfields? At the simplest and most durable level was more-or-less *faux-naïf* speculation as to precisely who was, or should be, inside it or out. The 'London Spy' Ned Ward (1667–1731) claimed in 1699 that 'I conceiv'd it to be my Lord Mayor's Palace, for I could not imagine so stately a structure could be design'd for any Quality inferior', even as Thomas Brown (1663–1704) announced that:

> *Bedlam* is a pleasant Piece, that it is, and abounds with Amusements; the first of which is the building so stately a Fabrick for Persons wholly unsensible of the Beauty and Use of it: The Outside is a perfect Mockery to the Inside, and Admits of two Amusing Queries, Whether the Persons that ordered the Building of it, or those that inhabit it, were the maddest?[8]

The joke was nourished by the perverse pride Londoners would come to take in the grubbiness of their palaces, compared to their new charitable buildings. A century later they were still delightedly reporting that foreigners reckoned the latter to be 'more fitted, by their grandeur and extent, for the residences of kings' while the palaces looked like pauper hospitals; Hooke's Bethlem was (in 1815) described as having been 'for many years the only building which looked like a palace in London'.[9]

More subtle are the extravagances that extended the conceit, begun in *Bethlehems Beauty*, about the delusions actually induced by the new building. One lunatic really succumbed, or pretended to. James Carkesse's 'Miscellaneous Poems written at Finsbury and Bethlem', the ambiguously titled *Lucida Intervalla* (1679), made witty use of Bethlem's delusional grandeur, describing his transfer there from the Finsbury madhouse as a military triumph: 'This, moving towards my *Palace*, was my *course*.'[10] In *Bedlam* (1723), by Hildebrand Jacob (1693–1739), the inmates are similarly over-excited by giant pilasters:

> Magnific to their wild, delighted Eyes
> Peruvian Roofs, and Parian Columns rise;
> Beneath their Thrones the Nile and Ganges meet,
> And waft unbounded Riches to their Feet. . . [11]

But meanwhile John Rutter described how at *Bethlem Hospital* (1717),

> The curious Eye observes Proportion just,
> And all the Rules of Art, cornice and fr[i]eze,
> Adorning Pilasters Entablature,
> With Festoons; Ornament enough or more,
> Than may seem fit for the ill-fated Plight
> Of those, who dwell therein, distracted Men.[12]

And in 1733 Thomas Fitzgerald's 'Bedlam' settled down to a portentous contrast between the peace of Moorfields, where for a millennium the Roman Wall had lain ruined but serene, safe against military aggression, and the din that raged within its great civil ornament.

> Where proud Augusta, blest with long Repose,
> Her ancient Wall and ruin'd Bulwark shows;
> Close by a verdant Plain, with graceful Height,
> A stately Fabric rises to the Sight.
> Yet, though its Parts all elegantly shine,
> And sweet proportion crowns the whole Designe;
>
> *
>
> Far other Views than these within appear,
> And Woe and Horror dwell for ever here.
> For ever from the echoing Roofs rebounds,
> A dreadful Din of heterogenous Sounds; . . . [13]

Fitzgerald used the paradox propelling earlier accounts of the building, that of the palace for pauper lunatics. Here, however, it is entirely sinister, as Hooke's 'sweet' and 'stately' façade becomes a screen, or a mask that is also a muffler, obscuring and silencing the grief and fear within. Fitzgerald intended us to understand sincerity in his praise of the beauty (however superficial) of the building; this is what gives his image its force. The idea of Bethlem as a mask must be taken seriously, for echoes of it survive today;[14] it reappears at the end of this chapter, which will first describe Hooke's building and how it came into being.

BUILDING THE 'SUBURB WONDER'

In early 1674, the Bethlem and Bridewell Court of Governors decided:

> that the Hospitall House of Bethlem is very old weake & ruinous and to[o] small & streight for keepeing the greater numb[e]r of Lunatikes as are therein att p[re]sent and more are often needfull to be sent thither.[15]

On 8 April, the Court determined to petition for the King's approval for a new building, a step that necessarily involved the Committee for City Lands, that 'pack of Knaves'[16] (as he called them) to which Robert Hooke, a City Surveyor since October 1666, was responsible.

In 1674 Hooke was still at his most creative as an experimental philosopher and deviser of scientific instruments;[17] it is for this work that he is today remembered. Most of his wide acquaintance, however, knew him as 'Mr Hooke the Surveyor', which is what the Bethlem Governors called him (at least in their Minute books).[18] Any distinction is anachronistic: for Hooke, the Surveyorship was a professional mathematical practice[19] (Christopher Wren [1632–1723] had reached architecture by the same route) alongside other, less remunerative positions as Gresham Professor, Cutlerian Lecturer, and Curator at the Royal Society. 'Architect' was a word not yet in general use and anyway the old title seems more apt. Hooke's *Diary* leaves the impression of a man perpetually roving around London, meeting craftsmen, committees, and Royal Society colleagues, inspecting and above all discoursing. Experimental philosophy merged into architecture, and together emerged in the talk, very often with his friend and relation (by marriage) Wren. In February 1675 they 'discoursed much', and Wren told him 'of an excellent way for a Gallery &c.': this was probably for Bethlem, but the *Diary*'s charm is its crazed terseness, and we will never know.[20] Hooke was the logical choice for Bethlem: of all the architects involved with the City's reconstruction he was, after Wren, the most active and the most prominent. He had originally been a City (as opposed to royal) nominee to the work of reconstructing London; new Bethlem was emphatically a City project, and he was already supervising Bridewell's rebuilding after the Fire. Hooke first talked about it with Sir William Turner (d. 1693), President of Bethlem and Bridewell, later credited with being the driving force behind the rebuilding.[21] When he formally inspected the site a few months later it was in the company of Turner and Sir Thomas Player (d. 1686), a recent Governor and Chamberlain of London.[22]

On 3 July 1674 Hooke attended the meeting of the Court, where he presented 'Twoe Plotts', that is drawings, for the

> New House for Lunatikes intended to be erected betweene Moorgate and the Posterne next London Wall where there wilbe ground enough for One Hundred & Twenty Roomes for the Lunatikes & Officers being about Fower Hundred & Twenty foote long.

He was asked 'to make a Modell thereof in pas[te]board', and to bring it along with his estimate of the building cost to the Court's next meeting. (This was an age that preferred three- over two-dimensional representations of architectural projects.)[23] The Minutes for the meeting of 11 July 1674 record the Governors' decision that the new Bethlem 'be [a] single building and not double', evidently on the basis of the model which, like most of the drawings for Bethlem, is now lost.[24]

This was the single most important decision to be made about the Moorfields building. 'Double building' meant a double-pile building; that is, one divided by a spine wall (or sometimes corridor) to form two 'piles' or ranges of rooms.[25] Bethlem was to be a single pile, one row of rooms (plus galleries), the type that Roger North (1653–1734) would characterize in his treatise *Of Building* (c. 1698) as 'fit for

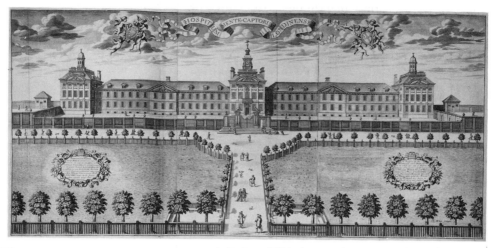

Plate 15.2 'Hospitium Mente-Captorum'. Robert White's very large engraving of Bethlem (1677) was not for sale, but later impressions of it are known, perhaps because the Governors gave the plates to the Hospital Clerk 'to make the best Advantage hee can thereof'. Reproduced by kind permission of the Guildhall Library, Corporation of London.

a colledge or hospitall, to be devided into cells, and chambers independent of each other'.[26] Houses of any pretension, traditionally single piles, were in the 1670s increasingly being built as more economical and convenient double piles and with an ingenuity appropriate to a genius of scientific instrumentation, Hooke's houses for Ralph Montagu in Bloomsbury (1675–9), Lord Conway at Ragley, Warwickshire (1679–83), and for Sir William Jones at Ramsbury, Wiltshire (c. 1680–3) actively explored the potential of the new type.[27] Bethlem's single-pile plan, on the other hand, would permit the great length of façade, the direct lighting of the galleries, and claims to be made for the building's openness to the healthful air of Moorfields.

Hooke's friend Edward Tyson (1650–1708), Bethlem Physician from 1684, later explained for the benefit of John Strype's great new edition of Stow's *Survey of the Cities of London and Westminster* (1720), that 'though the Structure be so large and magnificent, yet by the great Application that was made in hastning the Building, 'twas finished the next Year'. The claim also featured on an inscription in the entrance hall, and indeed on the engraving by Robert White (see Plate 15.2) that the Governors commissioned for themselves; later London guides, which drew heavily on the *Survey*, repeated it throughout the eighteenth century.[28] The boast was misleading. Much work, including the digging for the foundations, had preceded the official starting date in April 1675 and much remained after the King's inaugural visit on 29 August 1676.[29] Speed of construction, also claimed for London's rebuilding after the Fire, had since antiquity been a conventional sign for architectural magnificence, understandably when every project was vulnerable to the weather, and to fluctuations in supplies of currency, materials, and manpower. Yet Bethlem's construction was impressively fast work by any standard, and the effect of the great range rising over

Moorfields, of the 'Suburb Wonder' (*Bethlehems Beauty*, line 30), must have seemed particularly miraculous in a London starved for new architecture after civil war and a calamitous fire. The boast of speed was always matched by that of expense. Bethlem cost £17,000, a sum that was not in fact excessive (Hooke's Monument to the Fire [1671–7], which accommodated no-one, cost almost as much)[30] but which was sufficient to render its patients, as Edward Hatton put it in his *New View of London* (1708), 'great Objects of Charity'.[31]

A Committee of about twenty-two Governors took care of construction. On 23 October 1674, its first three reports were read into the Court Minutes. After November 1674, it began keeping its own minute book, preparatory to its complete independence four months later, when the Court desired only to be kept appraised of costs.[32] Because the Committee's book no longer exists, we now lose sight of the close deliberations. The first three reports are almost entirely about the wall to surround the new Bethlem, which was conceived and described in terms that demonstrate unequivocally that the building was there to be seen.[33]

Every eighteenth-century topographical compiler would, after the 1720 *Survey*, repeat the measure of Bethlem's walls: 680 feet long, 70 feet deep.[34] They rivalled the stretch of the ancient London Wall that then ran 714 feet west from Moorgate, nine feet away from the south front of the hospital, and which 'in some measure, acts as a screen' to it, as the antiquarian and topographical artist John Thomas Smith (1766–1833) wrote in 1815.[35] One of his etched views of the *Ancient Topography of London* shows 'Parts of London-Wall and Bethlem Hospital' (see Plate 15.3). It is a useful picture: aside from the small sketch on William Morgan's map of 1682, prints of Bethlem are invariably of the north front, towards Moorfields.[36] It shows part of one of the huge chimney-stacks, dormer windows, the cornice, and beneath it the grilled windows of the cells. From one of these windows a small hand, holding a windmill toy on a stick, emerges to be dwarfed by the massiveness of the masonry, ancient and modern.

This was the wall to Bethlem's back. On each side began the new wall, which the Committee discussed in two parts. At each end of the building were to be yards 'reserved for the use and benefitt' of the inmates (men to the east, women to the west, it would later be decided), where they could 'walk and take the aire in order to their Recovery'. Here the wall would be fourteen feet high, with a 'Coping . . . intended to p[re]vent the Escape of Lunatikes'. The front wall to the north of the Hospital, however, would be no more than *eight* feet high so that the 'Grace & Ornament of the said intended Building may better appeare towards Morefeilds' to the north; this would be high enough, simply because the inmates would not be allowed 'to walk in the yard' at the front.

Three points emerge, in embryo, from these, the first recorded discussions about Bethlem: the idea that the provision of exercise yards, or more specifically the air of the yards, would promote the recovery of the inmates; the importance of the view from Moorfields, one of the largest open spaces in London and a popular place of resort; and the evident refusal even to consider the possibility of allowing inmates access to the front yard, too. The last two have, logically enough, been linked by historians who have at this point seen the freedom of the inmates sacrificed to the 'Grace & Ornament' of the building.[37] However, distinguishing between the two is

Plate 15.3 'Parts of London-Wall and Bethlem Hospital'. An etching from John Thomas Smith's *Ancient Topography of London* (1815). Reproduced by kind permission of the Wellcome Institute Library, London.

also useful. The Governors were inordinately anxious to preserve the view of Bethlem from the north; but they also conceived of the Hospital (in a way explained below), as a kind of large household in which the inmates were analogous to junior servants. Hooke's colleague Roger Pratt (1620–85) explained around 1660 that a house should be 'so contrived . . . that the ordinary servants may never publicly appear' in the course of their duties.[38]

From a distance, Bethlem's beauty would be assured by the relative lowness of the front walls. For the benefit of those closer to the building (whose 'Ornament & Beauty' is the formula at this point in the Minutes), six apertures would be introduced into the walls in the form of 'open Iron Grates . . . made the breadth of Tenne foote

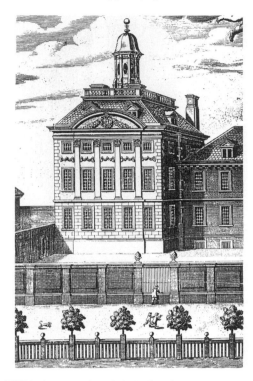

Plate 15.4 A detail of White's engraving (1677) showing a man peering through one of the 'transparent windows' in the Bethlem Wall. Reproduced by kind permission of the Guildhall Library, Corporation of London.

att the least in such Three convenient places' on each side of the entrance gate. In 1660 Roger Pratt had, charmingly, called such devices 'transparent windows'; he associated them with grand Continental houses, where they were admitted into court-yard walls to permit views of 'beautiful objects' outside the court: 'gardens, woods, walks, fountains, statues, etc.'[39] At Bethlem, of course, they were there so people could look *in*. Topped with stone pineapples (which themselves would occupy an inordinate amount of the Governors' attention) they are clearly visible on Robert White's print, which shows a man taking advantage of one (see Plate 15.4). The entrance 'Gateway or Passage', it was decided at the same time, would consist of stone piers enclosing iron gates, with everyday entrances on either side; they are also shown in use on the White print, which provides not only a record of the building, but a guide to looking at it.

The most famous and durable emblems of Bethlem, the statues that came to rest on the broken pediment on the gate piers (see Plates 11.1 and 15.6), are nowhere mentioned in the Court Minutes. Now in the museum of Bethlem Royal Hospital, they are attributed to Caius Gabriel Cibber (1630–1700), and have been identified as representing 'raving' and 'melancholy' lunatic, at least since 1740.[40] In 1813 John Carter (1748–1817) published a close description of the exterior of Bethlem, whose demolition had already begun;[41] significantly, he was anxious only for the fate of the

Plate 15.5 'Bethlem Hospital', *c.* 1747 by Edward Haytley (fl. 1746–61), one of a set prepared for the Foundling Hospital, shows how the entrance gates and wall had been altered. Reproduced by kind permission of the Thomas Coram Foundation and the Bridgeman Art Library, London.

statues, invariably admired, as he explained, by local and foreign visitors alike. They were probably more effective than the sight of real, living and breathing lunatics in arousing pity;[42] their power as works of art was augmented by the stories and associations that grew around them. Oliver Cromwell's porter Daniel, for example, a big man whose fervent religiosity led him to Bethlem around 1656, was supposedly the model for chained frenzy; the story would have appealed to those who believed that enthusiasts should be locked up. William Hogarth (1697–1764) borrowed the figure and its pose for his instrumentally influential depiction of the *Rake in Bedlam* (see Plate 13.1), who is mercifully insensible to the shame of his nakedness.[43] Cibber's nudes, which, it is important to note, *are* beautiful by the standards of the day and of the previous two millennia, contributed to an eighteenth-century symbolic logic by which lunacy was a soulless condition, and lunatics persons who, however beautiful to look at, are lifeless clay. It was a logic readily extendible to the building itself.[44]

Beyond the wall, strollers in Moorfields saw an enormous structure, over 500 feet long. (Eighteenth-century reports of Bethlem's overall length are inconsistent.)[45] That great length was organized by stone-fronted pavilions, two at each end and the tallest in the centre, and between them brick wings one storey lower. Each of these five parts was separately roofed, very prominently on the pavilions. Since the mid-sixteenth century, French architects had been accustomed to turn the steep roof pitches demanded by their climate (then colder and snowier) to dramatic advantage; this exploitation is one of the key distinctions between French and Italian architectural classicism. Along with the grand house in Bloomsbury that Hooke designed for the notably francophile Ralph Montagu, begun a few months later, Bethlem stood, by virtue of its pavilions and their roofings, as an outstanding example of French influence on English architecture. The story that it was actually modelled on a French building, the Louvre (or alternately, the Tuileries) in Paris is a myth, though

A View of the Hospital of Bethlehem. Vûe de l'Hôpital de Bethlehem.

Plate 15.6 'A View of the Hospital of Bethlehem', a mid-eighteenth-century engraving showing the new wings for 'incurables'. Reproduced by kind permission of the Wellcome Institute Library, London.

one that began as early as 1700, with Thomas Brown: he used the Louvre to make some overwrought venereal- ('French') disease jokes about Bethlem.[46]

The pavilions broke forward slightly under segmental (curved) pediments with their shields and wreaths; below each stood four Corinthian pilasters. Carved swags separated the second- and attic-storey windows. The latter was a Dutch device that reminds us that it was Amsterdam, a Protestant, hostile, and inordinately prosperous harbour city, that stood as the model for London's rebuilders;[47] and more specifically that it was Amsterdam's Dolhuys, a much smaller and architecturally less pretentious establishment, that none the less offered the precedent for a free-standing asylum building.[48] The Corinthian order must have raised knowledgeable eyebrows: it was more ornately carved and therefore more expensive than Ionic, Doric, or Tuscan; not just the grandest but the most licentious of the classical orders in its associations.[49] The central pavilion, more ornate than those at the sides, had the 'highly enriched' main door, on whose cornice rested an iron balcony; between door-opening and cornice was what John Carter called a 'very elegant horizontal oval window . . . , surrounded with laurel wreath, and a festoon of drapery, flower, and fruit' and what, on White's print, looks like a lion skin.[50] Its pediment boasted the royal arms; above was a larger cupola, with a clock, something deeply impressive in itself. The 1720 edition of Stow's *Survey* of London describes, in weirdly Biblical cadences, how 'in the Building, the Architecture is good. It hath a large Cupolo with a gilded Ball, and a Vane at the Top of it, and a Clock within, and three fair Dials without.'[51]

240

Another sign of grandeur was provided by roofs that even Carter, an experienced architectural journalist, would later have difficulty in describing, for in 1813 the type was no longer common in England: a 'kind of pedimented roof . . . , stopped by a large square balustrade[d] gallery.'[52] On these rested octagonal cupolas, with vanes. The balustraded platforms were a wonderful fashion of the day and Hooke's Montagu House and Pratt's earlier Coleshill House, Berkshire (begun *c.* 1657) and Clarendon House, Piccadilly (1664) all had them: the idea was to afford a place 'From whence the many pleasant Landskips round / May be with Ease and with Delight survey'd', and perhaps to have a drink.[53] Even if never used (as they surely were not at Bethlem) they still evoked splendid privilege.

The Court Minute book refers to the pavilions as the 'three ornamentall fronts', the 'three highbuildings', the 'three high ornamentall buildings'.[54] Part of this interest, predictably, lay in their cost, though nothing seems to have been denied to Hooke, or the Committee. Thus, while the cost of the 'Cubiloes' (or 'Lanthornes') and the balustraded 'platformes' induced cold feet at the relatively late stage of September 1675, their construction was soon approved.[55] Two months earlier, the pavilions had prompted one of the most teasing references in Hooke's *Diary*, for 19 July 1675: 'Committee at Bedlam orderd all stone front. A great Huff with treasurer and Chase. At the Rose spent 5sh. on Chase.'[56] The choice was between stone dressings against cheaper brick, as the linking wings between the pavilions were made, and stone.[57] The Committee's meeting was huffy, requiring five shillings' worth of placation from Hooke, a careful man.[58] Four days later the Governors ordered that the 'Three ornamentall fronts of the Building shalbe carryed w[i]th stone only & not w[i]th Bricke and Stone.'[59] 'Stone only' was a manifestly luxurious choice; once made, the pavilions were indeed 'ornamentall' and so the Minutes began to describe them. Like the brick walls had, and the galleries would, for a while the pavilions were, in the Governors' deliberations, carrying the weight of the building's overall 'Grace & Ornament'.

At a time when English architecture was embarking upon one of the most imaginative and vigorous periods in its history, Bethlem would have intrigued connoisseurs. The diary of John Evelyn, who knew something about architecture, conveys the excitement: on 18 April 1678 he 'went to see new Bedlam Hospital, magnificently built, & most sweetely placed in Morefields, since the dreadfull fire'.[60] Its style was also unfamiliar in the capital, and unfamiliarly sophisticated in the handling of its varied parts. Around 1695 North commended Bethlem (along with Wren's Chelsea, whose design had been influenced by Hooke's hospital) for the way its vertical and horizontal breaks pre-empted monotony: so 'long a range could not well be better distributed to give the whole a grace, and take off the fastidiousness of its length'.[61] ('Fastidiousness' here has the old meaning of 'tedium'.) The only comparable buildings in London then would have been Hooke's Montagu House, built at the same time; and the house in Piccadilly that Pratt designed for Edward Hyde, First Earl of Clarendon (1664–7).[62] These two houses, in what was becoming the West End, and one lunatic asylum in the City were similar in their strong projections and recessions, emphasized with quoins, along long fronts. They had floors of roughly equal heights above half-basements; high roofs with dormers, and above them balustraded platforms with cupolas. Bethlem's articulation with an order, and a

Corinthian order at that, made it the grandest of all by one, not unimportant, standard.

New Bethlem, usually called the 'Hospitall House' in the Court Minutes, was nothing more or less than that. It boasted modern status indicators – the wall with its 'transparent windows' and handsome gate, the clock, the turrets, the roof platforms, and the stone fronts with their pilasters and figurative carving – that together were more imposing than any other house then in London. It remains to finish the comparison by explaining Bethlem's plan, which was in equal parts archaic and entirely up to date by domestic standards.

INSIDE BETHLEM

Bethlem had one public entrance, on the north or Moorfields side.[63] After climbing the semicircular steps, visitors entered a hall via a narrow passage. On the right of the passage, to the north, was the Steward's room and on the left the 'committee room' used to examine patients upon admission and discharge. At the back of the hall, stairs (whose well was, like the hall itself, adorned with tablets bearing benefactors' names) led up to the first-floor lobby. The Governors' room, with the balcony visible in pictures of the building, was at the front of the first floor.[64] On each side of the hall on the ground floor, and the lobby on the first, were iron grilles with gates in them. Beyond these on the north side stretched the galleries, lit by the casements that gave this façade a high window-to-wall ratio. (Hooke, who may have been the inventor of the new sash type of window, was installing them at the College of Physicians and Montagu House, in 1673–5, but the windows in Bethlem's linking wings do not seem to have been sashes.)[65] Eighteenth-century topographical guides always gave the length of the galleries in full, without reference to the iron grilles or the central lobbies. In this they took their cue from the description in the 1720 edition of Stow's *Survey*:

> The inside consists chiefly of Two Galleries, one over the other, each 193 Yards long, 13 Foot high, and 16 Foot broad; not including the Cells for the Patients, which are 12 Foot deep.[66]

Bethlem was in this way described as a shell around two galleries, one on top of the other, running the full length of the building. The length given in the *Survey*, 579 feet, is too long for an overall length for the building of 540 feet (a figure also often encountered: see Plate 15.1), though one guide guilelessly gave both in 1761.[67] Relative unanimity began to dissolve when Bowen's 1783 *Historical Account* gave a gallery length of 321 feet; the French doctor Jacques Tenon (1724–1816) in 1787 and Smith in 1815 recorded similar figures.[68] Bethlem's length had not, however, been drastically overstated for half a century; rather, as Smith made clear, the gallery had been redefined in a change accompanying its translation into 'ward'.[69] It was now the space on each side of the central stairs (that is, two to a floor); the 300-foot-plus length is accounted for if the galleries were taken as including their direct continuations in the new wings (see Plate 15.6) added between 1723 and 1735 for the accommodation of 'incurably mad mischievous and ungovernable' patients, but not counting the new parts projecting north, perpendicular to the old block. The evidence suggests that the

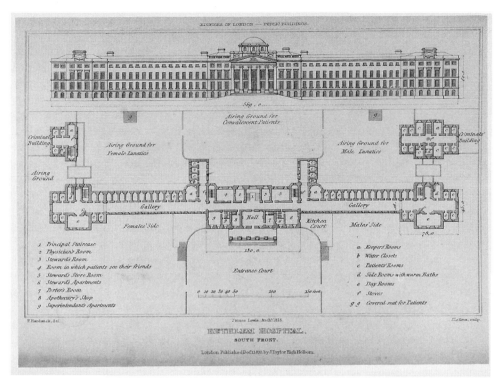

Plate 15.7 'Bethlem Hospital, South Front. James Lewis Arch. 1815'. The plan signals an appeal to architects and 'connoisseurs' in the *Illustrations of the Public Buildings of London* (1825–8) edited by John Britton and Augustus Pugin, but it is, in fact, the north front. Reproduced by kind permission of the Wellcome Institute Library, London.

original galleries were indeed in the area of 579 feet long, and Hooke's building a bit longer overall.[70]

At the back of the galleries on both floors, facing south to London Wall and the City beyond, were the individual cells for the lunatics, thirty-eight on each side of each gallery, Tenon counted, probably including those in the extension. John Howard recorded the cells' dimensions as 12 feet by 8 feet 10 inches and 12 feet 10 inches high, which gave him no grounds for complaint; he objected to the lack of a chapel (as he always did) and noted (as everyone did) the noise.[71] Appalling acoustics was the building's single great fault, something perhaps indirectly acknowledged in the architect's own, rather striking observation, made to the Royal Society in 1689, that 'Lunaticks . . . cannot obtain that, which should, and in all Probability would, cure them, and that is a profound and quiet Sleep.'[72] The inmates' sleep was also discouraged by the failure to glaze their cell windows; 150 years later this would be justified as obviating the 'disagreeable effluvias . . . peculiar to all Madhouses'.[73]

Cells lined *both* sides of the eighteenth-century wings (nine each side of each wing, Tenon wrote); this was more economical of space, but abandoned an arrangement powerfully celebrated for its healthfulness when the original building had opened (as explained below; William Hogarth's Rake (see Plate 13.1) was incurable, and is shown in one of the new wings).[74] With other rooms 'for the safer sort of patients', wrote

Smith in 1815, installed in the attic (alongside, or perhaps in place of some of the 'commodious apartments for the porter, matron, nurse, and servants' noted in the 1720 *Survey*) Bethlem could hold 275 people by 1783.[75] Below stairs, in the raised cellar, were storage areas, whose arrangement mapped those of the galleries and cells above, and 'all necessary Offices for keeping and dressing the provisions, for washing, and other Necessaries belonging to so large a Family'.[76]

As this phrase suggests, Bethlem was, like other residential institutions in Northern Europe, figured as a family, the central cultural model for the 'proper way of life';[77] 'family' in the old sense, that is an entire household, including servants and others not blood-related to the owner, but quite possibly gentlefolk. Such 'families' had long been shrinking, and even disappearing, in England, a change reflected in new and more compact domestic plans, the double piles – but the English were nothing if not respectful of the old social organization. It had survived, as Roger North described in 1698, in very grand, quasi-royal households, and in such institutions as almshouses and university colleges, which also maintained the old, single-pile plan-type: apartments permitting independence for adults who shared the house, linked by external walkways and stairs.[78] North's way of understanding public buildings as throwbacks to what he called the 'antique order' of English houses, suggests that it is worth pursuing houses a little more, in the hope of filling some of the blank spaces in our mental plan of the hospital.

Visiting Roger Pratt's Coleshill, Berkshire, Celia Fiennes (1662–1741) described what she called a 'gallery' running through the attic storey 'all through the house and on each side severall garret roomes for servants furnished very neate'. In 1660 Pratt had written that 'garrets should be parted, the mens quarter from the womens' and we can assume that Coleshill's, and Bethlem's, servants were divided, male and female, on either side of the building.[79] Not so Bethlem's patients, for men were at first placed on the ground floor and women above.[80] This was obviously inconvenient for the use of the exercise yards: it would have required escorting some patients the full length of the building, unless men and women took the air in shifts (which seems unlikely) or together (impossible). The arrangement was probably understood as temporary; in any case the patients were soon rearranged on an east–west division (men to the east, and women to the west, or on the left as we face the façade).

The entrance hall and stairs, after 1689 separated from the patients' cells by gratings, served only the Hospital's visitors and staff, perhaps just senior staff. (In 1708 Hatton apologized for not listing every benefactor's name recorded on the tablets hanging in the hall, but the light was too dim; it was however 'the only proper place they could be exposed to publick view . . . and at the same time *secured from the distracted People*'.[81]) Backstairs on each side of the building must have led down from the garrets to the galleries, and then to the yards, as they did at the next Bethlem (see Plates 15.7 and 15.10), designed by James Lewis (*c.* 1751–1820), whose plan did not radically depart from the old.[82] In this respect, Bethlem's plan was up to date by domestic standards; backstairs had only just appeared in English houses and Hooke would design a wildly elaborate set for Ragley Hall a couple of years after Bethlem opened. It was again Roger Pratt, Hooke's former colleague on the City rebuilding committee, who had systematized a planning device self-evidently advantageous to the new, more compact houses whose owners were increasingly conscious of family

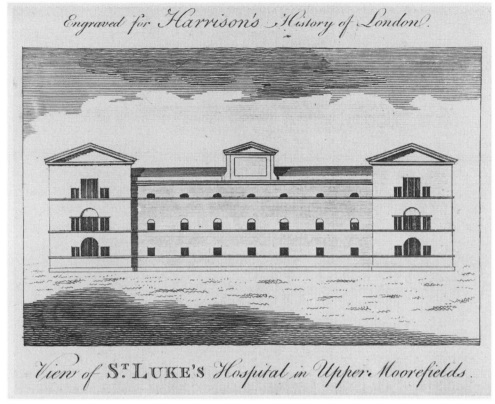

Plate 15.8 'View of St. Luke's Hospital in Upper Moorefields'. The first St Luke's, designed by George Dance the Elder, engraved for the 1775 *New and Universal History* compiled by the pseudonymous 'Walter Harrison'. Reproduced by kind permission of the Wellcome Institute Library, London.

privacy, and the needs to separate domestic functions and to reinforce social divisions. These changes were also associated with the advent of compact, double-pile domestic plans and the disappearance of great halls and long galleries, the glories of older and more sprawling houses.[83]

Sometime in the fifteenth century, English domestic galleries, the 'long galleries' familiar from visits to, for example, Hardwick Hall and Sudbury Hall in Derbyshire, originated as 'covered walks, sometimes roofed but open on one side, sometimes completely enclosed'.[84] Physicians emphasized the importance of regular exercise to physical and mental health and galleries soon became spaces in which to walk in bad weather. Many had pictures, something to look at while strolling (whence the modern meaning of the word); the diversion they offered contributed to the psychological healthfulness of the activity.[85] 'This is a room', wrote North, 'for no other use but pastime and health.' He knew that modern, compact houses were increasingly omitting them; Sudbury Hall's, which like Bethlem's was finished in 1676, was one of the last of the old type.[86] The length of a gallery had been a simple and powerful

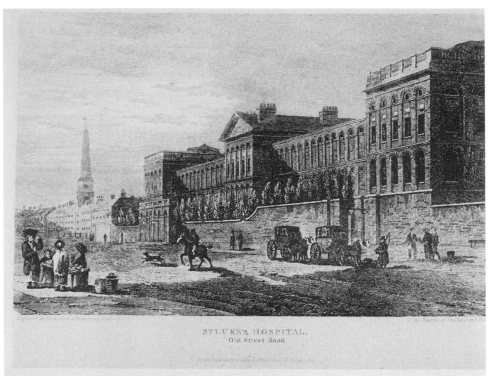

Plate 15.9 'St Luke's Hospital, Old Street Road'. George Dance the Younger's building, engraved by R. Sands (1815) after T. H. Shepherd, for *The Beauties of England and Wales*. The raking perspective makes the resemblance to Lewis's Bethlem (Plate 15.10) apparent: they had a common source in Hooke's building. Reproduced by kind permission of the Wellcome Institute Library, London.

index of prestige and some were very long: that at the Bridewell Palace, for example, around 200 feet.[87] If calculated at their full length, Bethlem's were the longest in England.[88]

North suggested that galleries were particularly useful when entertaining guests of the 'middle' sort, as it pleased them and was convenient for the host.[89] Galleries were one of the things that casual visitors to great houses, whose numbers were increasing, might hope to see, and the longer and fuller of pictures the better.[90] In a pre-Freudian slip, Hooke referred to the 'Bedlam *picture gallery*' in his *Diary*.[91] The anonymous author of *Bethlehems Beauty* evoked the visual exhaustion that results from tourism: 'Since, *Strangers* that Survey the *Galleries* / Find the *Vast Length* wearies their Travelling eyes ... ' (lines 41–2). In general this poem, the first to be published about the building, communicates with some ingenuity (not least of rhyme: 'galleries' is tricky) what any lover of Hooke's Bethlem might then have wanted to say about it, including the boast that it was one of the *architectural* sights of London.

Casual visitors came to Bethlem to see the lunatics as people today visit Hardwick Hall to see its famous collection of tapestries, and for the same reasons: instruction, pleasure, and because everyone else is doing it. A few however visit Hardwick Hall to see the building, and in particular, perhaps, its gallery (160 feet long). Perhaps at Hooke's Bethlem, amid the tapestries, we have lost sight of the galleries (over 550 feet long). Bethlem's Governors were building, among other things, an instant 'stately home', at once private and public, domestic and monumental. Hence their anxiety that the view of what the Minutes call the 'long' galleries[92] should be unimpeded, as explained below; and the clear allusion in *Bethlehems Beauty*, a poem uniquely well-informed about the building, to its tourist appeal. (See Chapter 12.)

There is no reason to doubt that, once planned, the galleries were intended for the use of the patients. On 3 December 1675, the Governors received the Committee's report on the partitions to be put into the galleries to keep 'the distracted men from the distracted women': around eight feet high, to consist of iron bars, each two inches broad and a quarter of an inch thick, at six-inch intervals. Such an arrangement was, unsurprisingly, considered to be sufficiently strong.[93] The Governors had already decided that the galleries would 'be continued and remaine intire the whole length w[i]thout any partition',[94] but this did not preclude the iron grates, which did not count as partitions in this purely visual context. This, the Governors' original understanding of the building, would eventually be perpetuated by Tyson's account in Strype's 1720 edition of Stow. However, trouble loomed. When the form of the grates was specified at the meeting, it was noted that they would 'hardly be discovered by any person that shalbe in the said Galleryes'.[95] And, on 20 April 1676, several Committee reports were read, and everything approved,

> excepting the Iron open Grates to be made and placed in the long Galleryes of the new Hospitall of Bethlem w[hi]ch was excepted against by severall Governors here p[re]sent because they consider the same will obscure the Grandeur and Prospect of the said Galleryes.

A wooden model of the grates was ordered to be put in one of the galleries, so the entire Court could visit the site and decide.[96] When on 5 May this experiment was recorded as showing that the grates would indeed 'hinder the Grandeur & Prospect of the said Galleryes', the resulting decision – to forbid patients recreational use of the galleries – was attended by two neatly tendentious reversals. '[T]here is no occasion for any such Grates *if* the Lunatikes . . . be not permitted to walk in the Galleryes'; 'such persons as come to see the said Lunatikes may goe in great danger of their Lives *if* the said Lunatikes should be suffered to walke in the same Galleryes'.[97] However, they could walk in the yards to each side of the building, being taken there and back from their cells. The Governors then got down to the equally serious business of considering whether the royal arms, in the central pediment, were not in fact too small. The grates were not installed until June 1689; they were perhaps prompted by the pregnancy of one patient (see Chapter 14).[98] They did not, after all, interfere with the impact of the galleries, whose great length continued to be carefully itemized in the London guidebooks following the example of John Strype's account, which also describes how patients 'that are fit for it, at Convenient Hours, have liberty to walk in the long Galleries, which are large and noble'.[99]

Galleries, a venerable type, were novel in this context, but the context of a lunatic asylum was unprecedented. Italian hospitals and lazarettos had private rooms behind what sixteenth- and seventeenth-century English travellers sometimes called 'galleries'[100] – that is, roofed passageways open to a courtyard, a form also found at English almshouses. Unlike these, Bethlem's galleries were self-contained, for security: it was, on the other hand, that very closure which turned them into the splendid rooms that they were. They were spaces both attractive and attractions, literally 'recreational'. That conception moreover embraced another healthful quality whose appreciation at Bethlem we know its Governors encouraged.

In 1708 Edward Hatton emphasized Bethlem's spaciousness to show the salubrity of the institution, whose Governors provided every inmate with a 'Room in a good Air, proper Physick, and Diet gratis'.[101] The Hospital's great front, which stretched like a screen between Lower Moorfields and London Wall and the City beyond, was permitted by a building of great length and shallowness, extraordinarily and extravagantly proportioned. Certainly, Bethlem's Governors were anxious to make a show, but palatial effect could have been achieved without quite so many bricks.[102] If the proportions were dictated by the site, it was a very happy accident: the plan of Hooke's building not only determined the next century and a half of English asylum design, it was immediately and pointedly celebrated as offering accommodation for lunatics that was spacious, airy, and light.

When, in May 1674, the Bethlem Governors agreed that the Lord Mayor and Aldermen of London should be 'acquainted' with the 'great necessity' of a new building, it was with reference to the agreement, with the Committee for City lands, of a site 'for health and Aire'.[103] The good air of Moorfields provided a refrain in early descriptions of the building: the 'sweet' placement Evelyn noted; and, more publicly, the Stow edition's ominous evocation of the Hospital's former location ('an obscure and close Place, near unto many common Sewers') and Hatton's explicit comparison of the constrained and 'ruinous' accommodation at Bishopsgate with the Moorfields site, a 'situation much more commodious as to Air, &c.'.[104] The most extraordinary celebration of that air came from the anonymous *Bethlehems Beauty* (1676), which offers a striking (and prescient) vision of unmediated healing by a perfectly ventilated building:

> Th' Approaching Air, in every gentle Breeze,
> Is *Fan'd* and *Winnow'd* through the neighbouring *Trees*,
> And comes so *Pure*, the *Spirits* to Refine,
> As if th' wise Governours had a Designe
> That should alone, without *Physick* Restore
> Those whom *Gross Vapours* discompos'd before; . . .
>
> (lines 46–51)

The Bethlem Governors would claim a high 'cured and discharged' rate implicitly on behalf of the building and the pure air it admitted.

In 1676 air was self-evidently desirable, in quantity and in movement, in a hospital. 'Good' or 'excellent' air featured in the printed advertisements for suburban madhouses then.[105] Air had for years been the subject of investigation by Hooke and his colleagues at the Royal Society. In ways related to both kinds of scientific, or would-be scientific production, air also had a powerfully metaphorical part to play in celebrations of the rebuilding of the City.[106] In 1669, for example, the poem *Londons Resurrection . . . Humbly Presented to His Most Sacred Majesty* by Simon Ford (*c.* 1619–99) contrasted pre- and post-Fire London. Once the place 'Where *obscure Lanes* obscurer Facts did hide: / And *Pests* by being straitned, spread more wide', now the sunlight admitted to new, wider streets revealed any '*skulking Sinners*'; 'And *transient Air* infectious steams shall chase'.[107] The scouring of London's streets by light and air, permitted by the King's surveillance of the work of reconstruction, would flush out infectious steams and skulking sinners.

Or perhaps skulking steams and infectious sinners. Charles's return had been identified as, literally, providential.[108] Imaginative reconstruction of what had happened in England before then did not hesitate to call on metaphors of lunacy, and specifically religious lunacy: 'Madness the Pulpit, Faction seiz'd the Throne' wrote John Dryden in his celebratory *Astraea Redux* of 1660.[109] Religious enthusiasm was still 'explosive, a divisive, frightening phenomenon to many moderates' in 1660; the threat sectarianism presented to the stability of the Restoration permeated political discussion for decades thereafter. And, to return full circle in this constellation of political mythmaking and laden natural-philosophical imagery, that sort of lunacy was commonly figured as a sort of 'cloudy confusion'[110] to be dispelled, of course, by the light and air of divinely constituted authority. Hooke's Bethlem was a manifestation of Restoration.

The galleries were sometimes later called 'wards', which suggests that some Bethlem officers were concerned, perhaps unconsciously, to substitute general-hospital for domestic connotations; but the older and more precise word remained

Plate 15.10 'New Bethlem Hospital, St. George's Fields'. Drawn by the great Thomas H. Shepherd (1793–1864) and steel-engraved by James Tingle (fl. 1830–60) for the *Metropolitan Improvements or: London in the nineteenth century*, edited by James Elmes (1782–1862) and published 1827–30. Reproduced by kind permission of the Wellcome Institute Library, London.

current at Lewis's building (see Plate 15.7) and was used at others (Plate 15.10).[111] Circulation spaces that could be used as day rooms became the device that defined what was long the most important asylum plan type in England.[112] The first (and best-studied) of Bethlem's progeny was in fact Irish, St Patrick's in Dublin, founded with a legacy from the former Bethlem Governor Jonathan Swift, and built 1749–53 to designs by George Semple.[113] It is not just St Patrick's cell–gallery configuration (though its galleries were at right angles to the central block, to make a U-shape) but also documents recording its planning which make it clear that Bethlem was the model, down to the dimensions of the cells.

Virtually nothing is known about the first St Luke's Hospital (Plate 15.8), built beside an old foundry in Windmill Street, Upper Moorfields by George Dance the Elder (1695–1768) in 1751. Like its successor in Old Street Road (1782–9) it offered individual cells for its patients.[114] No plans exist of it, but when an open competition for rebuilding St Luke's was announced in 1778 several architects, including the young James Lewis and John Soane, submitted designs that have survived; in Soane's two sets, the galleries meet the geometry of neo-classicism to tremendous effect, as curved cell-wings swoop round semi-circular courtyards.[115] In the event, the elder Dance's son George the Younger (1741–1825) got the commission and adhered to the century-old formula: like Hooke's building, St Luke's Old Street Road (Plate 15.9) was organized around three pavilions with lower linking wings and, internally, by what Jacques Tenon called *galeries* on each of three floors.[116] Tenon was well briefed at St Luke's by its intelligent and widely travelled architect, and his account is clear that it had six galleries, not three. They were not, in other words, reckoned as running across the building, though the iron grilles used there, as at Bethlem, were apparently designed to present no obstacle to the view.[117] Where Dance the Younger's St Luke's, the first asylum comparable in size to Bethlem, differed was in placing some cells on both sides of the galleries, as had been done in the 'incurables' wings at Moorfields. This economy would often be followed at nineteenth-century asylums, where complaints of oppressive gloom followed.[118] 'Le public n'entre point dans cet hôpital', Tenon wrote in his journal.[119] The hospital's opening had, however, been delayed at the end of 1786, as the Governors decided to make the patients wait three weeks in the old building while they proudly invited the public into the new.[120]

James Lewis was appointed Surveyor to Bridewell and Bethlem in 1793. He was one of the adjudicators (along with Dance the Younger) of the competition advertised in July 1810, after the demolition of the hospital at Moorfields, which went on for years, had already begun. Lewis's pupil William Lochner (*c.* 1780–1861) won the competition, but Lewis was instructed to take the best features of the three premiated designs and incorporate them into his own. This was approved in 1811 and he contracted for three million yellow stock bricks that year; the foundation stone was laid 18 April 1812 and the hospital ready for 122 patients, brought over in hackney coaches from Moorfields, in August 1815.[121] The debt to Bethlem at Moorfields is apparent on the plan (Plate 15.7), though equally evident is design with attention to the possibility of future expansion, impossible at the old and relatively constricted site where Hooke's building stood as a single pavilion.[122] Its ultimate significance to later hospital design may reside in its influence, via Wren and the eighteenth-century English naval hospitals, on pavilion planning.

Meanwhile John Aikin's (1747–1822) *Thoughts on Hospitals* (1771), a rare eighteenth-century attempt to prescribe a plan-type for general hospitals, simply recommended Bethlem: 'the best plan would seem to be, a range of cells or small rooms opening into a wide airy gallery, having a brisk circulation of air through it.' A foe of the 'impropriety and cruelty' of casual asylum-visiting, Aikin, however, felt obliged to name Greenwich as his model, though its double-pile wards did not fit the description.[123] Not for the last time, Bethlem's administrative inadequacies forbade acknowledgement of the building.

REPRESENTING BETHLEM

The Governors' concern with how their building be viewed had extended to its visual representations. On 24 January 1677, Treasurer Ducane, a prominent member of the Building Committee, was asked to bring the 'platt' of the Hospital to the next Court,

> that the same may be examined whether itt be done w[i]th the greatest exactness and if the same be approved of by the Courte that then a Print thereof may be made att the Charge of this Hospitall[.]

This print was to serve, at least in part, as a confirmation of the pleasures of proprietorship. A copy was presented to every Governor,[124] as well as to the King and his brother the Duke of York. Enormous pains were taken over the great three-plate engraving made by Robert White for £40 by the Governors, who insisted on checking the first pulls for accuracy; at the same time they resolved to enter with Stationers' Hall that

> noe person be p[er]mitted to ingrave a platt or print of the said Hospitall in respect care is taken by the Governors of this Hospitall that a print thereof shall be made in the most exacte manner.[125]

On 30 March 1677 Hooke intervened with an extremely significant suggestion. He informed the Governors that

> itt is very necessary that a ground plott of the said Hospitall should be made w[i]th a large Scale in one of the Vacancyes of the said plott that so the whole contrivance of the said Building may be plainely seene

- seen, that is, on the authorized engraving of the hospital, which was of course to show its great north front to Moorfields. On one of the 'vacancies' of Moorfields, as depicted in the print, Hooke would have a floorplan of the building; he assured the Court that engraving the plan would cost no more than engraving the grass of the field.

> And that an Inscript[i]on be putt thereon w[hi]ch hee [Hooke] promises to make to show the severall Conveniences of the same Building . . .

'Contrivance' and 'convenience' did not, in the seventeenth century, refer to gadgets or trivialities. We will, however, never know precisely what they were at Hooke's Bethlem, for the plan was never printed and none seems to survive.[126]

Bethlem, one might say, remained a façade in its literary and visual representations, and that came to be conceived as at best a tawdry screen, Ned Ward's 'ostentatious piece of vanity';[127] at worst as an obscenity in its denial of the inmates' experience behind it. There is no single resolution for the paradox described at the beginning of this chapter, of 'Bethlem's beauty'. Most fundamental to understanding it is the Governors' conception of Hooke's building as the home of an ancient Christian charity, one all the more noble because its recipients could not be grateful nor, indeed, comprehend the nobility of the building.[128] In this way, Bethlem's appearance did not violate decorum, the principle that ever since antiquity had held that the 'form and style of a building should be suited to its use and the station of its proprietor'.[129] It was, however, asking a great deal of observers to see it (as the last defender of the old interpretation, Thomas Bowen, put it in 1783) as an 'illustrious monument of [to] British charity', a 'friendly mansion' of 'becoming magnificence'[130] and not as the weirdly stylish home of lunacy incarnate. Bethlem at Moorfields has collapsed under a great weight of symbolic meaning. The task here has been to restore some literal and figurative depth to a complex and, on its own terms, singularly successful building; successful, rather, in all but one respect. The most genuinely affecting description of it was not written by one of the sprightly foreigners, harrowed men of feeling, or earnest Spital-sermonizers whose essays are described elsewhere in this volume, but rather by James Lewis, the Hospital Surveyor scenting a big commission.

Hooke's Bethlem had not been built as quickly as the Governors claimed, but there is no doubt that it was built too fast,[131] as Lewis reported in 1800 and subsequently. Such of the Bethlem Governors as were 'in the architectural line' assisted him in his inspection of the fabric and they found that,

> In the *Mechanisms* of the structure, it is evidently of the most artless kind, put together without any tye or connexion between the two front walls, except at the base of the triangle of the roof

– nothing aside from the tie-beams, in other words, actually joined the front to the back. No floor was level, no wall upright.[132] Piers in the cellars had been thinned to make more warehouse space for commercial rental; the foundations were anyway completely inadequate. In an age fond of comparing the mentally ill to ruined buildings,[133] what did you do with a ruined lunatic asylum? Lewis and his colleagues described a building itself mad, or certainly unsound; 'melancholy' and 'incurable'.

ACKNOWLEDGEMENT

The research for this chapter, and for my article 'Robert Hooke's Bethlem' (see note 14) upon which it is based in part, was made possible by a Research Leave Award from the British Academy.

NOTES

1 Bernard Adams, *London Illustrated 1604–1851: A Survey and Index of Topographical Books and their Plates* (London: The Library Association, 1983) lists book illustrations by subject; several prints sold singly showed Bethlem, too.

2 Michael DePorte, *Nightmares and Hobbyhorses: Swift, Sterne and Augustan Ideas of Madness* (San Marino, Calif.: Huntington Library, 1974); Max Byrd, *Visits to Bedlam: Madness and Literature in the Eighteenth Century* (Columbia, S.C.: University of South Carolina Press, 1974).

3 Nicholas Jose has shown how the language of monuments permeated *The Idea of Restoration in English Literature 1660–71* (London: Macmillan, 1984), 36–37, 55–7: Mark Jenner's excellent 'The Politics of London Air: John Evelyn's *Fumifugium* [1661] and the Restoration', *Historical Journal*, xxxviii (1995), 535–51 places the rhetorical convention in a context important to Bethlem at Moorfields.

4 See Robert Arnold Aubin, *Topographical Poetry in XVIII-century England* (New York: Modern Language Association of America, 1936): Bethlem was, as a subject, rivalled only by the Exchange and St Paul's Cathedral.

5 Edward Chaney, '"Philanthropy in Italy": English Observations on Italian Hospitals, 1545–1789', in Thomas Riis (ed.), *Aspects of Poverty in Early Modern Europe* (Alphen aan den Rijn: Sijthoff, 1981), 207. See also J. D. Alsop, 'Some Notes on Seventeenth-Century Continental Hospitals', *British Library Journal*, vii (Spring 1981), 70–4.

6 *Bethlehems Beauty, London's Charity, and the Cities Glory, a Panegyrical Poem on that Magnificent Structure Lately Erected in Moorfields, Vulgarly called New Bedlam. Humbly Addressed to the Honourable Master, Governours, and Other Noble Benefactors of that Most Splendid and Useful Hospital* is reprinted in Robert Arnold Aubin (ed.), *London in Flames, London in Glory: Poems on the Fire and Rebuilding of London 1666–1709* (New Brunswick, N.J.: Rutgers University Press, 1943), 245–8 as anonymous.

7 'From the Hagg and Hungry Goblin', first known from a manuscript of 1615; a selection of the songs was published with an astute introduction by Robert Graves in Jack Lindsay (ed.), *Loving Mad Tom: Bedlamite Verses of the XVI and XVII Centuries* (Welwyn Garden City: Seven Dials Press, 1969; first edn 1927).

8 Paul Hyland (ed.), *The London Spy* (East Lansing, Mich.: Colleagues Press, 1993; first printed 1699), 54; Thomas Brown, *Amusements Serious and Comical, Calculated for the Meridian of London*, 7th edn, published as *The Third Volume of the Works of Mr. Thomas Brown* (London: Edward Midwinter, 1730; first edn 1700), 29.

9 [Thomas Faulkner], *An Historical and Descriptive Account of the Royal Hospital . . . at Chelsea* (London: T. Faulkner, 1805), 46; John Thomas Smith, *Ancient Topography of London* (London: J. M'Creery, published and sold by the proprietor, John Thomas Smith, 1815), 32: Carlton House was a lodging-house by contrast and St James's 'a place of confinement'.

10 Michael V. DePorte (ed.), *Lucida Intervalla*, Augustan Reprint Society 195–6 (Los Angeles: Clark Memorial Library, University of California Los Angeles, 1979), 22, from 'Jackstraws Progress'.

11 Hildebrand Jacob, *Bedlam, A Poem* (London: W. Lewis & Thomas Edlin, 1723), 5.

12 [John Rutter], *Bethlem Hospital. A Poem in Blank Verse* (London: E. Smith, 1717), 4.

13 Thomas Fitzgerald, 'Bedlam' (1733), in Thomas Wintour (ed.), *Poems on Several Occasions* (Oxford 1781), lines 1–6, 9–12.

14 Christine Stevenson, 'Robert Hooke's Bethlem', *Journal of the Society of Architectural Historians*, lv (1996), 253. Much material below is taken from this article, which benefited greatly from the advice of the *Journal*'s editor, Professor Nicholas Adams.

15 *BCGM*, 23 January 1674. This passage is taken from Patricia Allderidge's précis of the books; for help with the Bethlem archives I am very grateful to her, as well as to Jonathan Andrews. Allderidge has elsewhere suggested that the fact that the Court of Governors was forced to hold its meetings at Bishopsgate after the Fire, instead of the more spacious Bridewell, which had suffered great damage, may also have prompted this perception of weakness and ruin: *Cibber's Figures from the Gates of Bedlam*, Victoria & Albert Museum Masterpieces 14 (London: Victoria & Albert Museum, 1977).

16 H. W. Robinson and Walter Adams (eds), *The Diary of Robert Hooke, 1672–1680* (London: Taylor & Francis, 1935), 7 July 1674, 111.

17 J. A. Bennett, 'Robert Hooke as Mechanic and Natural Philosopher', *Notes and Records of the Royal Society*, xxxv (1980), 34.

18 M. I. Batten, 'The Architecture of Robert Hooke', *The Walpole Society*, xxv (1936–7), 83–113 is the best account of the subject.

19 Bennett, *op. cit.* 38.

20 *Diary of Robert Hooke*, 27 February and 5 June 1675, 150, 163. See Margaret Whinney and Oliver Millar, *English Art 1625–1714* (Oxford: Clarendon Press, 1957), 206–7, 210–11, 216 for what Wren learned from Hooke, an influence which Kerry Downes has extended to the healthful planning of Wren's hospitals: Bethlem 'set new standards for the admission of light and air into institutional buildings': *The Architecture of Wren*, 2nd edn (Redhedge, 1988), 84.

21 *Diary of Robert Hooke*, 14 April 1674, 96. Turner was also a prominent Merchant Taylor, and Hooke was working regularly for the Company in this period: Batten, *op. cit.* 90–1.

22 He 'set out Morefield for Bethlehem'. *Diary of Robert Hooke*, 28 September 1674, 123.

23 *BCGM*, 3 July 1674, fol. 9; *Diary of Robert Hooke*, 10 and 11 July 1674, 112. Roger Davis the joiner made the model. See notes from 1660 on architectural models in R. T. Gunther (ed.), *The Architecture of Sir Roger Pratt . . . from his Note-books* (Oxford: Oxford University Press for the editor, 1928), 22–3.

24 *BCGM*, 11 July 1674, fols 15–16. A drawing for Bethlem attributed to Hooke for one end pavilion is in the British Library (Add. MSS 5238; it is reproduced in Hooke's *Diary* edition [see note 16]), and two more are in the Gough collection of the Bodleian Library, Oxford.

25 Stevenson, *op. cit.* 257.

26 Howard Colvin and John Newman (eds), *Of Building: Roger North's Writings on Architecture* (Oxford: OUP, 1981), 32.

27 For Montagu House, see Kerry Downes, *English Baroque Architecture* (London: Zwemmer, 1966), 57–8 and pl. 133; Fritz-Eugen Keller, 'Christian Eltester's Drawings of Roger Pratt's Clarendon House and Robert Hooke's Montague [*sic*] House', *Burlington Magazine*, cxxxviii (1986), 732–7. For Ragley Hall, see Batten, *op. cit.* 97–103, and Mark Girouard, *Life in the English Country House* (New Haven and London: Yale University Press, 1978), 135–6, with a plan.

28 John Strype (ed.), *A Survey of the Cities of London and Westminster . . .* , 2 volumes (London: A. Churchill and others, 1720), i, 192, in which Tyson's account is acknowledged; Adams, *op. cit.* xv describes the general dependency of later 'Surveys' and 'Histories' on this edition.

29 The Hospital was not reported finished to the Court of Governors until 9 February 1677 (*BCGM*, fol. 332); see also Batten, *op. cit.* 91–2. Hooke mentioned Charles II's visit in his *Diary*, 248. Four years had been allowed for: *BCGM*, 25 September 1674, fol. 37.

30 Bethlem's cost is from Stow as edited by Strype, who presumably had it from Tyson (*Survey*, i, 192). The Monument cost £14,500, according to H. W. Robinson, 'Robert Hooke as a Surveyor and Architect', *Notes and Records of the Royal Society*, vi (1949), 52. Bridewell's post-Fire reconstruction, which Hooke began in 1671, cost £12,000; the Royal (military) Hospital, Kilmainham, near Dublin (begun 1680), £23,559; and Chelsea Hospital £152,000 to build, furnish, and landscape 1681–1702: for references see Stevenson, *op. cit.* 270, n. 47.

31 [Edward Hatton], *A New View of London; Or, An Ample Account of that City*, 2 volumes (London, R. Chiswell and others, 1708), ii, 732.

32 *BCGM*, for 6 November 1674 and 5 February 1675; from Patricia Allderidge's précis.

33 Following from *BCGM* for 23 October 1674, beginning fol. 48: the Committee's reports for 13, 16, and 20 October 1674.

34 Strype, *op. cit.* i, 192.

35 Smith, *op. cit.* 32.

36 *London &c. Actually Survey'd* (repr. Lympne, Kent: Harry Margery and The Guildhall Library, 1977); the detail is reproduced in Stevenson, *op cit.* 253.

37 The Governors were 'much more concerned with "the Grace and Ornament of the . . . Building" than with the patients' exercise or any other therapeutic purpose'. Jonathan Andrews, 'Bedlam Revisited: A History of Bethlem Hospital, *c.* 1634–*c.* 1770' (Ph.D. thesis, University of London, 1991), 174 as quoted (in agreement) by Andrew Scull, *The Most Solitary of Afflictions: Madness and Society in Britain, 1700–1900* (New Haven and London: Yale University Press, 1993), 22; and see Chapter 14 here.

38 Quoted Girouard, *op.cit.* 138.

39 Gunther, *op. cit.* 25–6.

40 Thomas Bowen, *An Historical Account of the Rise, Progress and Present State of Bethlem Hospital* . . . (London: For the Governors 1783), 5, quotes Cibber's son Colley's autobiography of 1740.

41 [John Carter], 'Architectural Innovation No. CLXX', *Gentleman's Magazine*, new series, lxxxiii, part 1 (January 1813), 36–8.

42 Allderidge, *op.cit.*

43 Sander L. Gilman, *Seeing the Insane: A Cultural History of Madness and Art in the Western World* . . . (New York: John Wiley & Sons, 1982), 54–6 and John M. MacGregor, *The Discovery of the Art of the Insane* (Princeton, N.J.: Princeton University Press, 1989), 13–21, discuss Hogarth's image and provide evidence for its definitiveness; the handful of later pictures purporting to show Bethlem are crude copies or else show no architecture at all, and the *Tale of a Tub* illustration from 1710, reproduced in both books, cannot show Bethlem, which had no wards.

44 Stevenson, *op. cit.* 267; that this was a myth, or at least requires more careful distinctions to be drawn between lunacy and lunatics is suggested by the accounts in Chapter 13 ('Visiting') here, about the repugnance inspired by Bethlem's patients.

45 Five hundred and forty feet was the statistic repeated most often (see Plate 15.1); the first to be given in print, Hatton's '528 feet', was the most conservative: *New View of London*, ii, 731.

46 Brown, *op. cit.* 29–30; Stevenson, *op. cit.* 254.

47 Batten, *op. cit.* 88; and Whinney and Miller, *op. cit.* 207 comment on the swags, and Hooke's interest in Dutch architecture. England was at war with the United Provinces during the Commonwealth, and again from 1665–7 and 1672–4.

48 Dieter Jetter's survey *Grundzüge der Geschichte des Irrenhauses* (Darmstadt: Wissenschaftliche Buchgesellschaft, 1981) reckons Hooke's Bethlem as the third purpose-built asylum, after one in Valencia (1409, destroyed 1512 and not replaced) and Amsterdam's Dolhuys, built 1562 and steadily enlarged to contain about forty cells by 1792 – a 'place for mad persons & fooles, like our Bethleem', according to John Evelyn, in 1641: E. S. de Beer (ed.), *The Diary of John Evelyn*, 6 volumes (Oxford: Clarendon Press, 1955), *c.* 21 August 1641, ii, 45. This building, which John Howard described as a rectangular cloister, whose covered walks were separated from the central 'garden' by partly walled-up arcades, deserves investigation in connection with Hooke's Bethlem: *The State of the Prisons in England and Wales, with Preliminary Observations, and an Account of some Foreign Prisons* (Warrington: W. Eyres; London: T. Cadell & N. Conant, 1777), 128. Allderidge, *op. cit.* and Gilman, *op. cit.* 19–20, 49 incidentally illustrate three Dutch carvings of mad persons from the period, comparable to Cibber's.

49 Hence Robert Dodsley's suggestion, in 1761, that the Tuscan (so plain that it was scarcely used) would have been more appropriate for Bethlem: *London and its Environs Described. Containing an Account of Whatever is Most Remarkable for Grandeur, Elegance, Curiosity or Use*, 6 volumes (London: R. & J. Dodsley, 1761), i, 297.

50 Carter, *op. cit.* 36.

51 Strype, *op. cit.* i, 192.

52 'Carter, *op. cit.* 36.

53 John Clerk of Eldin's 'The Country House' (late 1720s) is quoted by James Macaulay, *The Classical Country House in Scotland 1660–1800* (London: Faber, 1987), 171.

54 *BCGM*, 23 July 1675, fol. 153; 10 September 1675, fol. 173; 24 September 1675, fol. 177.

55 *Ibid.* 10 September 1675, fol. 173; 24 September 1675, fol. 177. Their final form was only

then being worked out: Hooke's Diary is filled with references to 'draughts' of the turrets at this point; the British Library drawing (see note 24) shows turrets, but no balustrades.

56 *Diary of Robert Hooke*, 170: John Chase, the King's Apothecary, was an active member of the Building Committee.

57 Oddly, all the prints show seventeen windows in the linking wings, but Haytley's painting (Plate 15.5) shows fifteen and the reliable Carter (*op. cit.* 37) counted the same.

58 Shapin was moved to refer to the 'carefree generosity of an Edinburgh accountant' in this connection: Steven Shapin, 'Who was Robert Hooke?', in Michael Hunter and Simon Schaffer (eds), *Robert Hooke: New Studies* (Woodbridge, Suffolk: Boydell, 1989), 273.

59 *BCGM*, 23 July 1675, fol. 153.

60 *Diary of John Evelyn*, iv, 133–4.

61 Colvin and Newman, *op. cit.* 61 n. (from a preliminary manuscript).

62 Illustrated in Downes, *English Baroque Architecture*, pl. 133 and fig. 24 (Montagu House) and pl. 127 (Clarendon House); see also Keller, *op. cit.*

63 Among the 1677 Court orders was the stipulation that the back gate to London Wall was always to be kept shut 'except extraordinary Occasions of bringing in Beer, &c.' and that no-one 'shall come to see the Lunaticks that way'. Quoted in Strype *op. cit.* i, 193. Edward O'Donoghue, *The Story of Bethlehem Hospital from its Foundation in 1247* (London: T. Fisher Unwin, 1914) synthesized the available descriptions of Bethlem's interior: the best are those in Strype's *Survey* edition of 1720; Bowen, *op. cit.*; John Howard, *An Account of the Principal Lazarettos in Europe* . . . (London: T. Cadell and others, 1789); and Smith *op. cit.* They can now be supplemented with the travel diary (first published 1992) of Jacques Tenon, who visited England in 1787 to gather information useful to hospital design: Jacques Carré (ed.), *Journal d'Observations sur les principaux hôpitaux et sur quelques prisons d'Angleterre*, Publications de la Faculté des Lettres et Sciences humaines de l'Université Blaise-Pascal 37 (Clermont-Ferrand 1992).

64 See Smith, *op. cit.* 34.

65 H. J. Louw, 'The Origin of the Sash-Window', *Architectural History*, xxvi (1983), 65, 69.

66 Strype, *op. cit.* i, 193. This account of the building, identifiable by the '193 yard' reckoning of the galleries' length, was the basis for topographical compilers until 1775 (the *New and Universal History* by the pseudonymous 'Walter Harrison'), at least.

67 Dodsley, *op. cit.* i, 296, 298; by some aberration 'A Tour through the Cities of London and Westminster, and the Parts Adjacent to these Populous Cities', *Royal Magazine* v (August 1761), 59–61 more or less a reprinting of Dodsley, gives the galleries' length as 1,179 feet.

68 Carré, *op. cit.*: Tenon's *Journal* (in 1787) gives 51 *toises* 1 *pied*, or 327 feet (calculating one *toise* as 1.95 metres, and a French foot as 0.33 metres); Smith gives 330 feet (*op. cit.* 35).

69 Smith explained that he was not counting the 'additional wings' when giving his gallery length: see previous note. Bowen, *op. cit.* 9: the 'wards are spacious and airy'; Smith, *op. cit.* 34: the iron gates open 'into the galleries, or wards for the patients'.

70 In 1720 the Strype edition of Stow's *Survey* gave a total of 136 cells, noting that some more had 'lately' been finished to bring the total to 150 ('lately' might mean anything; Strype spent at least seventeen years collecting material). If each cell was 8 feet wide (the width Bowen gave in 1783; he was the first to specify the cell dimensions) that would mean an original cell-range length (assuming the cells were equally distributed among the four sides of the two galleries) of 8 feet × 34 cells = 272 feet, or 544 feet worth of cells down the entire length of the building, a figure which does not include dividing walls and the central stairwell. This sounds right for an original gallery length (calculated the way it was in the Stow edition) of 193 yards.

71 Howard, *Account of the Principal Lazarettos*, 139.

72 Richard Hunter and Ida Macalpine, *Three Hundred Years of Psychiatry 1535–1860: A History Presented in Selected English Texts* (London: OUP, 1963), 220: he was recommending the therapeutic use of marijuana.

73 Ida Darlington, *The Survey of London: St. George's Fields* xxv (London: London County Council, 1955), 78: in response to a complaint by the Select Committee of the House of Commons the Deputy Surveyor advanced this argument, but the windows were glazed in

1816. Cell windows at St Luke's Old Street were unglazed at the time of William Tuke's visit in 1812: Scull, *op. cit.* 65–6.

74 O'Donoghue, *op. cit.* 244–6.

75 According to Bowen, *op. cit.* 9.

76 Strype *op. cit.* i, 193.

77 Continental prisons and workhouses had since the sixteenth century been run as 'complex households': Pieter Spierenburg, 'Prisoners and Beggars: Quantitative Data on Imprisonment in Holland and Hamburg, 1597–1752', *Historical Social Research* xv, part 4 (1990), 35. This model must not be confused with the 'self-consciously domestic' environments created for early nineteenth-century British asylums: Andrew Scull, 'The Domestication of Madness', *Medical History*, xxvii (1983), 246–7.

78 Colvin and Newman, *op. cit.* 68–9, 32.

79 Gunther, *op. cit.* 28; Christopher Morris (ed.), *The Journeys of Celia Fiennes* (London: Cresset, 1947), 24–5; compare Rosalys Coope, 'The "Long Gallery": Its Origins, Development, Use and Decoration', *Architectural History*, xxix (1986), 55.

80 *BCGM*, 21 July 1676, fol. 276.

81 Hatton, *op. cit.* ii, 732; emphasis added.

82 For the resemblances between the buildings see Patricia Allderidge, *The Bethlem Historical Museum: Catalogue* (n.p., 1976), 8, and O'Donoghue, *op. cit.* 209; the Governors ordered on 26 July 1676 that the men and women were 'not to be suffered to lodge promiscuously' (*ibid.* 210).

83 John Bold, 'Privacy and the Plan', in John Bold and Edward Chaney (eds), *English Architecture Public and Private: Essays for Kerry Downes* (London and Rio Grande: Hambledon, 1993): 107–19; Colin Platt, *The Great Rebuildings of Tudor and Stuart England: Revolutions in Architectural Taste* (London: UCL Press, 1994).

84 Girouard, *op. cit.* 100–2.

85 Compare Robert Burton, *The Anatomy of Melancholy*, ed. Holbrook Jackson, 3 volumes (London: J. M. Dent, 1932; first edn 1621), ii, 86–7 on the pleasure of mental exercise within doors, 'so fit and proper to expel idleness and melancholy'.

86 For this 'very conservative feature', see Nikolaus Pevsner, *Derbyshire*, 2nd edn, revised Elizabeth Williamson (Harmondsworth: Penguin, 1986), 334.

87 Destroyed in the Fire, it had anyway long been partitioned into shops: Edward O'Donoghue, *Bridewell Hospital: Palace, Prison, Schools*, vol. 2, *1603–1929* (London: John Lane The Bodley Head, 1929), 146, 148, 151.

88 Coope, *op. cit.* 51 offers some useful comparisons, without of course reckoning Bethlem's in them.

89 *Ibid.* 59, 60; and p. 45 for evidence for fifteenth- and sixteenth-century 'corridor galleries' used as similarly 'useful "socially neutral" ground'.

90 For this phenomenon, see Adrian Tinniswood, *A History of Country House Visiting* (Oxford: Basil Blackwell for the National Trust, 1989).

91 *Diary of Robert Hooke*, 28 April 1676, 228.

92 Admittedly, Coope concluded that the phrase 'long gallery' would remain fluid in its application until the second half of the eighteenth century: Rosalys Coope, 'The Gallery in England: Names and Meanings', *Design and Practice in British Architecture: Studies in Architectural History Presented to Howard Colvin*, *Architectural History*, xxvii (1984), 449, 450.

93 *BCGM*, 3 December 1675, fol. 199.

94 *Ibid.* 10 September 1675, fol. 174.

95 *Ibid.* 3 December 1675, fol. 199.

96 *Ibid.* 20 April 1676, fol. 243.

97 *Ibid.* 5 May 1676, fol. 246; compare Andrews, *op. cit.* 211.

98 See also Andrews, *op. cit.* 230–4.

99 Strype, *op. cit.* i, 196.

100 Chaney, *op. cit.* 204, 205; Stevenson, *op. cit.* 264–5.

101 Hatton, *op. cit.* ii, 747–8.

102 Even assuming it was 540 × 40 feet and not longer; see note 45.

103 *BCGM*, 8 May 1674, fol. 638; 16 May 1674, fol. 642. See also Andrews, *op. cit.* 170–81.

104 *Diary of John Evelyn*, iv, 133–4; Strype *op. cit.* i, 192; Hatton, *op. cit.* ii, 731.

105 See Hunter and Macalpine, *op. cit.*, 199 for John Archer's description (1673) of how he could 'place [patients] in an excellent Air nere the City, fit for that purpose.'

106 See Steven Shapin and Simon Schaffer, *Leviathan and the Air Pump: Hobbes, Boyle, and the Experimental Life* (Princeton, N.J.: Princeton University Press, 1985) for the Royal Society's function in the Restoration and specifically in the face of enthusiasm's 'radical individualism in knowledge'.

107 In Aubin, *London in Flames*, 134–50: lines 519–20, 523–4.

108 Jose, *op. cit.* 33–5.

109 *Ibid.* 60.

110 *Ibid.* 14, 15.

111 See note 69.

112 Thomas A. Markus, *Buildings and Power: Freedom and Control in the Origin of Modern Building Types* (London and New York: Routledge, 1993), 130: the gallery (as distinct from the circulation corridor) 'was almost exclusive to [asylums in] English-speaking countries'. See also Andrew Scull, 'A Convenient Place to Get Rid of Inconvenient People: The Victorian Lunatic Asylum', in Anthony D. King (ed.), *Buildings and Society: Essays on the Social Development of the Built Environment* (London: Routledge & Kegan Paul, 1980), 53.

113 Elizabeth Malcolm, *Swift's Hospital: A History of St Patrick's Hospital, Dublin, 1746–1989* (Dublin: Gill & Macmillan, 1989) is excellent for architecture.

114 C. N. French, *The Story of St Luke's Hospital* (London: William Heinemann, 1951), 9–13.

115 The competition was won by James Gandon: Pierre de la Ruffinière du Prey, *John Soane: The Making of an Architect* (Chicago, 1982), ch. 3, 'Architecture for Madness: The St Luke's Competition'. None of the plans illustrated by du Prey show cells on both sides of the galleries. Contract drawings for the second St Luke's are in Sir John Soane's Museum.

116 Carré, *op. cit.* 43–9 for St Luke's; Harold D. Kalman, 'The Architecture of George Dance the Younger' (Ph.D., Princeton University, 1971, Ann Arbor: University Microfilms, 1972), 104–10 is brief but useful on St Luke's appearance.

117 See the account from 1904 quoted by French, *op. cit.* 37: '"The wards are shut off from the central portion by thick upright iron bars and heavy iron gates which afford a complete view of their whole length on each side."'

118 Scull, 'The Victorian Lunatic Asylum', 52–3.

119 Carré *op. cit.* 42.

120 French, *op. cit.* 30.

121 These details are taken from Darlington, *op. cit.* 76–8; Howard Colvin, *A Biographical Dictionary of British Architects 1600–1840*, 3rd edn (New Haven and London: Yale University Press, 1995), s.v. 'James Lewis', corrects Darlington on the identity of the competition winner.

122 Lewis remarked that the 'general plan, and the internal economy of its parts' meant that Hooke's building 'cannot be improved or altered': *Proceedings of the Committee and Reports from Surveyors, Respecting the State of Bethlem Hospital, in the years 1800, 1803 and 1804* (London: H Bryer, 1805), 14.

123 John Aikin, *Thoughts on Hospitals* (London: Joseph Johnson, 1771), 20; 'The absolute necessity of a separate room or cell [in asylums] for every patient is very apparent; and it would seem needless to inculcate in the humane, the very great impropriety and cruelty of allowing the poor unhappy sufferers [in asylums] to become spectacles for the brutal curiosity of the populace', 71.

124 'And that every one of the Governors have one of the same Prints delivered unto them w[i]thout any Charge unto them': for 24 January 1677, from Patricia Allderidge's précis.

125 *BCGM*, for 30 March 1677, fol. 364.

126 Though both the Court Minutes and his Diary seem to suggest that Hooke got his way: *ibid.* 30 March 1677, fol. 367; *Diary of Robert Hooke*, 6 April 1677, 284.

127 Hyland, *op. cit.* 54. Ned Ward's sarcasm is often quoted; only Byrd, *op. cit.* 24 has pointed out

that it might be interpreted as a reworking of the old theme that poverty is what the poor must get.

128 Stevenson, *op. cit.* 266.

129 John Archer, 'Character in English Architectural Design', *Eighteenth Century Studies*, xii (1979), 354.

130 Bowen, *op. cit.* 5.

131 Andrews, *op. cit.* 161, describes the Governor Sir William Bolton's criticism of the site as damp and subsiding in late 1674 and early 1675.

132 *Proceedings of the Committee*, 'Appendix': 'Survey of Bethlem Hospital, November and December, 1799', 10, 13.

133 See the suggestive passages quoted from a play (1714) and poem (1807) by Allan Ingram, *The Madhouse of Language: Reading and Writing Madness in the Eighteenth Century* (London/New York: Routledge, 1991), 86, 102–3; and William Pargeter, *Observations on Maniacal Disorders*, ed. Stanley W. Jackson (London and New York: Routledge, 1988; first edn 1792), 2–3: the madman 'retains indeed the outward figure of the human species, but like the ruins of a once magnificent edifice, it only serves to remind us of his former dignity, and fill us with gloomy reflections for the loss of it'.

CHAPTER SIXTEEN

MEDICINE, MEDICAL OFFICERS AND THERAPEUTICS

———— •✦• ————

INTRODUCTION

The great defect of pre-modern Bethlem, it has been said, was indifference to its patients and its failure to develop new and effective treatments. From the physician-keepership of Helkiah Crooke to the physicianship of Thomas Monro (1792–1816), disgraced and not elected after the public revelations of the Madhouses Committee inquiry (1815–16), its medical regime has been pictured in a dismal light.[1] There is much truth in these criticisms, but it is also important to avoid anachronistic judgments. For instance, apparent proof of 'apathy' has been the failure of its physicians to publish on insanity until John Monro was forced into print in 1758 by William Battie's criticisms.[2] Yet it was exceptional for physicians in general in this period to publish the fruits of their hospital experience.[3] Prior to the 1750s, the majority of those writing about treatments for the insane were private practitioners, without hospital practice, quacks or clergymen. Indeed, until then, the fact that Bethlem physicians did not write books about their experiences was not a matter on which aspersions were cast.

Historians have drawn attention to Bethlem's stubborn response to the foundation of St Luke's and to the salvos of its physician, William Battie, against Bethlem's medical regime, and to the damning evidence of the Madhouses Committee inquiry. But the Battie/Monro controversy was more complex than is sometimes represented; and in the preceding century Bethlem had been, in some respects, a scene of vitality and innovation.

It is true that Bethlem's medical officers remained committed into the nineteenth century to traditional depleting and antiphlogistic remedies. But not all treatments were hidebound, or applied as indiscriminately as has been alleged; nor was Bethlem wholly insulated from wider initiatives taking place in medical care, and in some areas the Hospital was actually a pioneer. Despite their characterization as negligent absentees, the majority of Bethlem's practitioners were conscientious, and allowance must be made for the honorary, charitable basis on which medical officers were employed at Bethlem and other hospitals. If Bethlem's officers were preoccupied with private practice, they were little different in this respect from other hospital doctors.

APPOINTMENTS, PATRONAGE, SALARIES AND CONDITIONS OF SERVICE

Helkiah Crooke, Keeper-Physician from 1619–32, was the first physician appointed to Bethlem. His supplanting of the lay Keeper, Thomas Jenner, after complaints, *inter alia*, that Jenner was 'unskilful in the practice of medicine', marks early recognition of the need for professional medical attendance. Yet in the conditions of service to which Crooke subscribed on his appointment, there is no sign that medical attention was one of the Keeper's express duties,[4] and the inmates were not yet referred to by the Governors as 'patients' but simply as 'the poore' or even as 'prisoners'.

Early incumbents had received the Mastership of Bethlem as a reward of royal favour, and, after 1547, the Keepership was in the City's gift. The Masters and Keepers of Bethlem had probably regarded the office rather in the manner of a sinecure. Crooke's appointment, as a royal nominee, signalled a renewal of ancient Crown claims. Whatever the likely benefits of the separation of the administration of Bethlem from Bridewell advocated in Crooke's 1619 petition to the King, his proposal plainly accorded with both his own and the royal concern to wrest control away from the Bridewell Governors and out of the hands of the City notables.[5] His dismissal was the turning-point between the old and new administration,[6] marking the inauguration of a medical establishment on the model already prevailing at other royal hospitals. Consisting of three medical officers elected by the Court of Governors – a physician, surgeon and apothecary – this establishment long remained unchanged. The temptation to pit medicine against profit-making was no longer to be encouraged by a system of entrusting patients' treatment to a keeper/physician reimbursed via the submission of bills and a per capita maintenance allowance for each patient. Henceforth, a succession of salaried physicians attended Bethlem, with a very minor role in the receipt of patients' fees and Hospital revenues. After Crooke, Bethlem's practitioners emerged unsullied at least from the former taint of profiteering.

Royal patronage continued to exert a significant influence in the election of Physicians, nullified temporarily during the Protectorate and finally after the Glorious Revolution. Othewell Meverall (Physician 1634–48) and Thomas Allen (Physician 1667–84) had both been royal physicians prior to their appointment.[7] Indeed Meverall continued to give assistance to Charles I during the Civil War.[8] Edward Tyson (Physician 1684–1708) was appointed by order of the Royal Commission for Regulating the Several Hospitals in London, which supervised elections at the five royal hospitals, Tyson having been recommended to the Commissioners 'by his Majestye' via a royal *mandamus*.[9] Thomas Nurse (Physician 1648–67), appointed during the Protectorate, was the only physician elected at this time without a Court connection.

Even so, the Governors were moderately successful in handling royal interference. In 1665 Thomas Allen attempted to sue for royal favour by devoting an entire work to a eulogy of 'his sacred Majesty'. *XEIPEΞOKH. The Excellency or Handy-Work of the Royal Hand*, signed 'T.A. M.D.' and attributed to Allen, is an unedifying 'account of cures wrought by the touch of the King's hand', which makes no bones about the author's 'Ambition . . . to invoke your Highnesse's Patronage'.[10] His supplication fell on deaf ears, for the King's nominee was Richard Francklin, then assistant physician to St Bartholomew's. Despite such canvassing, however, the Governors came out in favour of Allen and of their own right to govern their hospital.[11] The Lord Mayor, Sir William Bolton, made circumspect excuses for the Governors' assertion of their prerogative, explaining politely but firmly that while 'all due respects [were] paid to the King's letter', Allen 'had made his way before' and was 'Better knowen then ordnary to ye governors'.[12]

Royal will certainly prevailed, on the other hand, in the election of Edward Tyson after Allen's death, although the situation may have been confused by the presence of two royal nominees. An anonymous obituary claimed that it was through the 'Interest' 'at Court' of 'the Lord Keeper [Francis] North', who 'was the Doctor's hearty Friend', that Tyson had procured his royal writ. The same source also attested that Charles Goodall, a Fellow and future President of the College of Physicians, also obtained a *mandamus* for the Bethlem post 'by the Sollicitation of his Friends', and that he and Tyson 'acted in that station [for some time] conjointly', until Tyson 'at last bought out the other'.[13] The Hospital's Minutes give no backing to this story. Whatever the case, medical posts were plainly decided by interest before talent, but this is not to say that physicians' credentials were insignificant. An Oxbridge education was a virtual prerequisite, Cambridge graduates giving way to Oxonians from the 1680s, as might be expected with Tories dominating the Governors' ranks.

Affiliation with the College of Physicians was also important for applicants. Six of the ten physicians appointed in this period (Crooke, Meverall, Allen, Tyson, and John and Thomas Monro) had become Candidates of the College prior to their appointments. Allen, Tyson and Thomas Monro had been elected Fellows, while Meverall had been Censor on four occasions and Anatomy Reader before being selected for Bethlem.

The foundation of the Royal Society in 1660 provided physicians with an additional platform for corporate identity and visibility. Three successive Bethlem Physicians (Allen, Tyson and Hale) were quick to seize the opportunities membership offered. Tyson was particularly active, establishing a reputation as a comparative anatomist, serving on the Council and being made Anatomy Curator (1683), before he was appointed Physician to Bridewell and Bethlem in 1684.[14] Richard Hale also went about acquiring the right credentials prior to his appointment to Bethlem, courting recognition of the Royal Society via his anatomical research; and it was evidently his friendships with established physicians, Edward Tyson his Bethlem predecessor in particular, which helped him prevail in the 1708 election.[15]

How secondary paper qualifications might be in determining election to the physicianship is suggested by the superior calibre of many of those whose candidacy failed to gain the support of the assembled Governors. The number and quality of these candidates also indicates how hotly elections were contested, especially during the times of political turmoil in the late Stuart era. Although the appointments of Crooke, Meverall and Tyson were essentially determined by outside authorities, the elections won by Nurse (1648), Allen (1667) and James Monro (1728) were contested by a total of twenty doctors.[16] Judged strictly on medical experience and credentials, neither Nurse, Allen, Hale nor Monro was the obvious choice. Indeed, when Monro was elected in 1728, inaugurating 125 years of dynastic domination by the Monro family, the opposition was first-class. It included four physicians relatively well-established in the contemporary medical world, two of whom already occupied physicianships at other institutions. Richard Tyson (1680–1750) the runner-up, was not only Physician to St Bartholomew's (1725–50), but was a Fellow (1718), Registrar (1723–35) and Censor (1718, 1728) of the College, and had been the favourite nephew of the former Bridewell and Bethlem Physicians, Edward Tyson and Richard Hale.[17] Charles Bale, who got through to the second ballot, was FRCP (1719), Censor (1723) and Physician to the Charterhouse (1725–30); William Rutty (1687–1730) was Censor (1723), Secretary to the Royal Society (1727–30) and had published *A Treatise on the Urinary Passages* (1726). Sir Richard Manningham was already renowned by 1728 for his practice as accoucheur; he had been made FRS in 1720, knighted in 1721 and was celebrated for his exposure in 1726 of the fraud of Mary Toft, the pretended 'rabbit breeder'.[18]

James Monro (Plate 16.1), however, was far from unknown – he had been involved in one of the first pioneering experiments in smallpox inoculation.[19] He was also the second son of the Jacobite, Alexander Monro DD (d. 1715?), Principal of Edinburgh University.[20] The slur of paternal Jacobitism continued to be visited upon the Monros, James being condemned as 'a Jacobite' by his private patient, Alexander Cruden, while his son John was censured by Horace Mann as one of 'the Jacobites abroad', frequenting the Pretender's Court when in Italy.[21] In the event, the Monros displayed no signs of disaffection to the Hanoverian regime, James Monro being an active supporter of High Church Anglicanism. Given the strength of the Tory presence on the Bridewell and Bethlem Court of Governors, the Monros' domination of the Hospital's physicianship appears less surprising.[22]

It was not unusual for sons to succeed to their fathers' practices, and family interest played a decisive part in the allocation of offices at many medical and other institutions.[23] Four nepotistic generations of Monros at Bethlem – unprecedented in the annals of English hospitals – undoubtedly imparted a stultifying therapeutic conservatism. But each proved his worth to the Governors as an assistant to his father prior to appointment as sole physician. John's years after 1741 studying medicine in Europe as a Radcliffe travelling-fellow would have equipped him well;[24] making himself known to the Governors by regular attendance at Courts and Committees, he was the natural choice to assist his ailing father in 1751 and to replace him on his death the following year.

Nepotism was also rife in the appointment of surgeons, three sons succeeding their fathers to the post between 1656 and 1815. Between them, the Higgses, Wheelers and Crowthers provided the inmates of both Hospitals with surgical attention for a total of 130 years. Like the Monros, however, the junior members of the partnership proved themselves through serving quasi-apprenticeships at the Hospitals, and the Governors plainly put their trust in tried service and experience. The aged Edmund Higgs submitted the petition by virtue of which his son, Jeremy, succeeded him in 1656, yet there was little reason for the Governors to object to a candidate who had 'been free of the Company of Chirurgeons about fowerteene yeares', had 'Assisted his father in the said imployment' and was 'well experienced therein'.[25] Charles Wheeler (Surgeon 1741–61) and Bryan Crowther (1789–1815), also succeeded their fathers.[26] Like Higgs, Wheeler had not only 'served his Apprenticeship' under his father at Bridewell and Bethlem, but had 'ever since [i.e. from 1729]

Plate 16.1 James Monro, Physician to Bethlem (1728–52), oil on canvas by John Michael Williams, 1747. Photograph courtesy of Bethlem Royal Hospital Archives and Museum.

attended the patients in the said Hospitals', while his brother and cousin had served apprenticeships there too.[27] Though, as William Battie was to complain, the Governors and medical officers failed to make any formal provision for medical students on the wards, various junior surgeons and apothecaries had been broken in at the Hospital.

The majority of physicians, surgeons and apothecaries elected to Bethlem received their training outside the Hospital, however, and elections tended to be hotly contested.[28] There was an average of five candidates for each election to the post of Surgeon between 1643 and 1789, while for the Apothecary's place, applicants between 1656 and 1772 averaged eight, although numbers dwindled after 1750.[29]

No Apothecary succeeded to his post directly by nepotism. Whereas most took on apprentices, only Jeremy Lester (Apothecary 1678–85) and William Dickenson (1689–96) had served their apprenticeships at Bridewell and Bethlem, and succeeded to the post largely on that account.[30] Obviously, not just medical families and outside authorities, but Governors and benefactors often had their own fish to fry in trying to swing the election of particular men. Yet such appointments were not made lightly. Lester had not only 'made and prepared physicke for the poore Lunatikes . . . for about nine yeares . . . during the age and weaknes of Mr. James' when elected, but was 'well reported of by severall Governors . . . to have been very dilligent and carefull about the said Lunatikes'. Likewise, when Lester's nephew, John, substituted for him during his sickness, the Governors were careful to ensure through his examination by the Committee and apothecary-governor that 'he bee capable'.[31]

Just as the will of the Governors and the City interest tended to prevail over that of the Crown in the appointment of physicians, royal patronage was rarely influential in the election of Apothecaries and Surgeons. It was only during the politically charged 1680s that the Crown succeeded in getting a nominee as Apothecary appointed to Bridewell and Bethlem.[32] John Pelling was admitted Apothecary in 1685 after being recommended by the King.[33] Four years later, however, the hackles of City notables and Hospital Governors were raised when the King attempted to get another of his candidates, Charles Watts, admitted and his letter was rebuffed.[34]

ATTENDANCE AND SALARIES

Bethlem Physicians have commonly been censured for absenteeism and apathy, and the conduct of Helkiah Crooke at the beginning of the period and of Thomas Monro at the end corroborates this charge. Crooke was found by the Royal Commissioners in 1632 to have turned up only on quarter days, and then only to submit his bills.[35] Thomas Monro confessed before the 1815/16 Madhouses Committee that, although attending Bethlem 'about three times a week', he did 'not always go through the Hospital', and he never examined all the patients but only those the Apothecary recommended. Indeed to mitigate his culpability for mismanagement, he actually emphasized how 'very seldom' he was there – and one of the keepers testified that Monro's attendance was even less regular than the doctor had claimed.[36]

Yet while Bethlem Physicians certainly saw their posts as rather ceremonial, this was partly encouraged by the terms of their contracts which mirrored the requirements of medical attendance at other contemporary hospitals.[37] Physicians were appointed merely in a visiting or part-time capacity, and hospital posts were sought as means to an end, a path to prestige: rewards came primarily from private practice. The Bethlem Physicianship paid a nominal salary of twenty marks (i.e. £26 13s 4d) per annum, which impressed upon its holders the honorary nature of their position.[38] Physic and surgery were looked upon very much as part of the charitable relief offered by hospitals. When Henry Levett filled in as physician at Bethlem in 1708 and was rewarded by the Governors with ten guineas, his donation of the money 'towards buying Cloths' for the patients accorded with this charitable ethos. Likewise, when in 1751 the Governors elected John Monro 'joint Physician' 'without Salary', the comment of the *London Evening Post* that this was 'an Honour sufficient ... to counter-balance any Salary', squared with such expectations.[39] From the 1650s, the Physician's salary was supplemented by regular annual gratuities, and although these were increased fivefold between 1652 and 1708, for the seven subsequent decades they stayed fixed at £50 per annum. Indeed, the salaries of Bethlem's medical officers remained substantially below those at other London hospitals throughout the period, no doubt a reflection of the lower status of attendance on lunatics. Small wonder, then, that the Monros were preoccupied with their private practice.

Surgeons and Apothecaries served the Hospitals initially without any salary or gratuity, being recompensed solely via bills they periodically submitted for attendance.[40] It was a payment system cumbersome and open to abuse; medical officers were led to submit exorbitant bills. The Apothecary, James James, was suspended on this account in 1672, while John Pelling and William Dickenson were likewise in trouble for the same reason in the 1680s and 1690s.[41] The Court attempted to regulate the practice by checking the Apothecary's bills against the Physician's prescription book and, from the 1670s, subjecting them to regular audit.[42] James attempted to reclaim his place by offering to charge just 'Twelve pence a potion', and succeeded in being reinstated.[43]

The great expense and 'Embezzlement of Medicines' continued to be a problem at Bethlem,[44] but another decade passed before any effective economy measure was taken. The construction of an apothecary's shop in 1750/1 and the election of a resident salaried Apothecary went a considerable way towards achieving the desired end.[45] Henceforth the Apothecary was to receive £80 per annum, with coals, candles, soap and house provisions, and was required 'to deliver a List to the Committee every Saturday of all Medicines necessary for the Shop'.[46]

For surgery, payment procedures were rather more elaborate, the Surgeon being required to await the approval of the Physician and Apothecary (or Governors) before performing any operation, so that they might verify its necessity and agree a fee.[47] A divided responsibility was recognized for the payment of surgery bills; the Hospitals paid for surgery on any wound sustained after a patient's admission, but the patients' sureties were expected to pay for the rest. The expense provoked the Governors to rule in 1645 that a patient's sureties were bound to defray 'the Charges of all kinds of Surgery to bee applyed to him'.[48] While, even so, the majority of surgery continued to be performed free of charge, occasionally sureties were forced to meet their obligations. Opposition forced the Governors in 1749/50 to reconsider the equity of this clause in bonds, but after consultation through committee and interviewing the Surgeon it was upheld.[49] It was only in 1761 – significantly nine years after the opening of St Luke's, where all surgery was gratis – that the Governors finally abolished this clause and compensated the Surgeon with an extra £10 on top of his salary.[50]

As with the Apothecaries, all three Surgeons attending Bethlem and Bridewell between 1634 and 1669 were apt to submit 'immoderate' bills.[51] Only after the move to Moorfields was the Surgeon allowed a salary 'for all surgery worke to be done in and about the poore Lunatikes'. From 1679 he was to receive '£4 every quarter . . . over and above the charge of letting them blood and makeing issues', for which he received a per capita allowance of 12d.[52] Two further raises and a gratuity of £20 per annum brought his wages to a level five times the former rate, a clear incentive to more conscientious attendance. But the Governors' failure to raise the Surgeon's salary for over fifty years after 1710, and a raise of only ten guineas in 1775 may, however, have had the opposite effect.[53]

Medical officers who regarded their posts as essentially a charitable office, whose duties were divided between Bridewell and Bethlem, and whose bills were regularly queried by the Governors, were unlikely, perhaps, to provide a regular and thorough attendance on Bethlem's lunatics. Allegations of absenteeism have often been made, with some truth, but it is by no means clear how often the medical staff were supposed to attend. At no stage prior to the mid-eighteenth century do the Governors appear to have stipulated the frequency of attendance. Crooke had merely been required to serve in person, rather than via a proxy, itself indicative of the liability of his predecessors to absenteeism. With the introduction of certification in the 1650s, physicians were obliged by Court order to preside over every patient's admission and discharge. It was not, however, until the re-siting at Moorfields that inspecting applicants for admission became a weekly duty of the Physician and Bethlem Sub-Committee, which, by the eighteenth century, convened for two hours every Saturday morning.[54] Sub-Committee Minutes from September 1709 onwards reveal that both Richard Hale and James Monro attended virtually every meeting. By the 1730s at least, the Physician was also visiting the Hospital on Mondays and Wednesdays, when he was furnished with 'an Account of the . . . Patients' by the Porter, Nurse and presumably the Matron.[55]

The same attendance rate was sustained by the Monros for much of the remainder of the period.[56] From the mid-eighteenth century, the bulk of the responsibility for medical attention devolved onto the Apothecary, who was required to be resident and to 'Attend [in person, or by a servant proxy] at Bethlem Hospital once every day in the Week except Sunday and oftner if need be'.[57] In attending Bethlem on Mondays and Wednesdays, but rarely on Committee days, Thomas Monro had in fact substantially been fulfilling what was demanded of him by the Court of Governors.[58] It took a public inquiry to expose the inadequacies of that requirement, and to compel the Governors to replace Monro with the dual physicianship floated earlier. According to the *London Evening Post*, on the death of Richard Hale in 1728 the Governors had proposed, owing to 'the Increase' of their patients, to appoint 'two Physicians', 'the one for Men, and the other for Women', and Sir Richard Manningham was to 'stand Candidate for the latter' (a suggestion no doubt encouraged by his gynaecological experience).[59] Nothing came of this, however, nor indeed of other proposals 'for a Trinaty of Physicians', or 'a joint Physician'.[60] Despite rising patient numbers a single physician continued to preside over both Hospitals. It was only for brief interludes and due to the frailty of the acting physician (and his own interests in securing a possible succession) that the Hospitals were afforded the assistance of an extra physician, and even then, it was simply Monro junior who deputized.

It is unclear exactly how often the Apothecary was required to attend, though the size of their bills suggests attendance was regular. It was not until 1750, however (nine years after the Apothecary, William Elderton, had failed to answer a summons to attend a Bridewell apprentice), that the Governors inquired into 'the Attendance given by the present Apothecary'.[61] As even the Hospitals' staunchest advocate, the *London Evening Post*, admitted in 1751, the Apothecary's duties had 'for many Years past ... been much neglected'. Elderton's replacement by a resident Apothecary (John Winder) required to attend Bethlem at least once a day, six days a week, was a clear acknowledgment of the need for change.[62] Indeed, however blimpish was the Hospital's reaction to the challenge represented by St Luke's foundation in 1751, its adoption of a resident Apothecary and apothecary shop on the model originated at St Bartholomew's indicates that it was not unresponsive to all outside initiatives in medical care.[63] The demand for residency and the new requirement that the Apothecary be unmarried were, however, allowed to lapse during John Haslam's tenure (Haslam resided at his house in Islington by 1815 and his wife substituted temporarily as Matron in 1799), but there is no doubt that he attended Bethlem regularly.[64] The practice of occasional attendance meant that medical staff were reliant on the information of the Hospital's servants regarding the condition, behaviour and needs of patients.[65]

Little was specified respecting the Surgeon's attendance. While instructed early in the seventeenth century to 'performe the businesses and cures in his owne person', some surgeons performed their duties partly through their assistants.[66] The size of bills suggests that the Surgeon also attended quite regularly. The need for surgery at both Hospitals had increased to such a degree by the early eighteenth century that John Wheeler claimed to have 'given constant daily attendance at one or other of ye hospitals'.[67] When medical officers were absent or unavailable, their service was sometimes fulfilled by the hire of other, non-elected practitioners living nearby.[68] The rather haphazard state of medical attention at Bethlem, the openness of the Hospital's environment and the extent to which patients' friends might interfere in their care, are all indicated by an account given by the apothecary, Cromwell Mortimer, of how, visiting an inmate there in 1742 at a relative's request, he was at liberty to try out his evacuant pills on the patient.[69]

Absenteeism was certainly a problem, and the Court was at times lax in ensuring medical attendance. On the death or during the sickness of medical staff, the Governors were only intermittently careful to arrange promptly for a replacement.[70] In 1761, during the vacancy of the Surgeon's place, the Apothecary, John Winder, was instructed to 'Apply to the Surgeons of Saint Bartholomew's requesting their Assistance' 'if any Accidents shou'd happen to any of the Patients'.[71] The Surgeon, Jeremy Higgs, and the Apothecary, James James, were dealt with very firmly in 1672, however, when they were found to have gone AWOL and employed unauthorized servants to attend in their place. Both were suspended and petitions for replacements were received before they were restored on promising to mend their ways.[72]

The inadequacies of medical provision were aggravated by Bethlem's union with Bridewell.[73] By the early eighteenth century, the Surgeon's business had increased to such a degree that the Court was obliged to allow him a separate salary for Bridewell, as increasingly it had been Bridewell rather than Bethlem which demanded the Surgeon's 'frequent attendance'.[74]

The vast majority of Physicians' and Surgeons' time was spent outside the Hospitals, servants occasionally encountering problems obtaining medical assistance. Despite its appeal as a charitable and civic duty, carrying some professional prestige, hospital attendance was secondary to, while also helping to drum up, private practice.[75] Indeed, profiting from Bethlem's virtual monopoly in the care and treatment of the insane, Physicians gained a large private practice in a field that inevitably took up a great deal of time. They were not simply sought after for house-calls on the vapourish relatives of the elite, or to attend the private madhouses multiplying in the capital, but were themselves madhouse proprietors. Helkiah Crooke ministered to private patients in his own home; Othewell Meverall attended clients like John Evelyn's mother, 'who died of a malignant feavor' proceeding 'from griefe' upon the loss of a number of children.[76] Thomas Allen presided at Finsbury Madhouse, where James Carkesse was first confined, and exploited his Bethlem position by milking-off for his own house the wealthier patients – or transferring them to Bethlem when, like Carkesse, they proved stubborn or ran out of money. Indeed, Carkesse reviled Allen as avaricious, alleging that he 'both *Bedlams* does haunt, like the *Louse*'.[77] Edward Tyson and Richard Hale both amassed wealthy practices outside Bethlem, gaining reputations as mad-doctors and being deferred to by other general physicians in diagnosing and treating the mad.[78] Only in Allen's case did Bethlem's Governors take issue with the impinging of the Physician's private on his public practice. Being 'informed' in 1680 'that Dr. Allen hath severall Lunatike persons under his Care that are not sent to the hospitall of Bethlem for their Cure', the Governors demanded periodic written accounts of the names, settlements and current lodgings of all these and future patients.[79]

The Monros especially, as proprietors of madhouses in Hackney and Clerkenwell and visiting physicians to many others (e.g. Bethnal Green and Chelsea), established an unprecedented insanity business. A casebook detailing John Monro's attendance on patients at Brooke House, Hackney, during 1766, mentions one hundred cases.[80] The Monros' fees were far from modest. Joseph Girdler, Sergeant-at-law of the Inner Temple, complained to Lord Fermanagh in 1733 of his father's estate being 'ready to be Devour'd by the mad Doctors', 'Dr. [James] Monroe alone demanding for himself and assistants about £130 though we think not a Quarter could be due or deserved'.[81] According to Cruden, both James and John Monro were grasping, although, despite John Monro receiving half a guinea a visit and making twenty guineas per annum from his attendance at Duffield's two madhouses, such fees were by no means exceptional amongst the metropolitan medical elite.[82]

The wills and bequests left by the medical officers of Bridewell and Bethlem attest the lucrativeness of their trade in lunacy.[83] Othewell Meverall was wealthy enough to leave his daughter £666 13s 4d.[84] Thomas Nurse's will and codicil details pecuniary bequests of over £2,000, besides land in Leicestershire.[85] Edward Tyson was reported to have died 'worth about thirty Thousand pounds',[86] and his meticulous will lists stock alone of nearly £9,000 and annuities totalling £400 per annum; Richard Hale died worth something in the region of £100,000.[87] John Monro recorded legacies and sums already given his family totalling £12,500, besides wealthy leasehold estate and property in Clerkenwell and Clapton (including Brook House). Indeed, he made detailed provision to ensure the continuance of his private madhouse under his sons, expecting his 'Business' and the Clapton estates to bring in an annual profit of well over £500.[88]

Alongside wealth, other responsibilities and honours within medical colleges and societies mark the wider success of Bethlem's medical officers. Bethlem's Physicians were prominent at the College of Physicians, only Nurse, Tyson and James Monro failing to assume higher office there.[89] Allen, Tyson and Hale were all active in the Royal Society. Allen was elected to Council in 1678/9. Tyson served on the Council ten times; conducting anatomical experiments, producing a remarkable number of studies in comparative anatomy, and serving on numerous committees.[90] Plainly, Bethlem's physicians were men of some public visibility.

THERAPY OR NEGLECT?

Bethlem has been accused of therapeutic conservatism, and it has been suggested that the institution did not even pretend to cure its inmates.[91] But there was more to Bethlem's medical regime than that. For one thing, there is no doubt that the Governors and medical officers believed it was their business to cure. When Thomas Nurse was elected Physician in 1648 it was explicitly 'for cure of the poore Lunatiques', and the Hospital advertised itself repeatedly as 'for keeping & curing distracted persons'.[92] Patients, indeed, very occasionally left tokens of their gratitude for their cure: William Cooling bequeathed £40 to Bethlem on his death around 1683 after being 'cured'.[93] A letter from the parents of another patient, John Dickenson, thanking the Apothecary, John Gozna, and the Committee, 'for the great Care our Son has received', was read by the Committee in 1792.[94] The Governors employed to dramatic rhetorical effect the production of another grateful patient, displaying his prayer for the mad, carved on a gilded plaque, in the Hospital's examining room.[95] The reality behind the rhetoric was rather different, yet it is false to state that Bethlem did not even claim to cure its patients.

Most medical officers were hard-working enough to satisfy the Governors. Physicians were regularly rewarded from the 1650s with gratuities in consideration of their 'extraordinary care and paynes'. It was during the physicianship of Thomas Nurse that certification was introduced at Bethlem, and Nurse is regularly to be found working with the Sub-Committee to identify and eject those patients deemed to be 'Idiotts', 'not Lunatike' or otherwise 'unfit to be kept at the hospital' (see Chapter 18). His work was continued by Thomas Allen. During the suspension in 1672 of the Apothecary James, the Governors declared themselves 'well satisfied of the Integrity and fidelity of Doctor Allen', and commended him for despatching the Apothecary's business during the latter's suspension,[96] the Court electing him Governor five months later.[97] Allen was, beyond doubt, energetically involved in the Hospitals' affairs. He was one of the first to discuss the plans for the new Moorfields building with the architect,[98] and in 1677 was appointed a member of the new rotational committee.[99] Edward Tyson's physicianship was a time of therapeutic initiative and optimism, the doctor inspiring various improvements, including the appointment of the first nurse, the establishment of the Wardrobe Fund, the introduction of cold and warm bathing, and the inauguration of after-care with a relief fund for discharged patients commonly known as 'Tyson's Gift'. Richard Hale consolidated his work and was instrumental in the establishment of the incurables' wards.[100]

Yet, like the Monros subsequently, Allen, Tyson and Hale all had clashes with individual patients which show them in a different light.[101] In his treatment of James Carkesse at his own Finsbury madhouse and at Bethlem, Allen won a poor press from his patient. Refusing to certify Carkesse as recovered until he ceased writing the poetry which so mercilessly lampooned his medical practice, it is not insignificant that Carkesse was one of the few patients discharged from Bethlem on his own petition. Allen may have been prejudiced against Carkesse's case by his own friendship with Samuel Pepys, for, prior to Carkesse's confinement, Pepys – who was made a Governor at Allen's nomination, becoming an active member of the Court – had been Carkesse's declared 'rival' and enemy at the Navy Office.[102]

There was beyond doubt a strong vein of conservatism in the Bethlem medical regime, and the scholarly activity of Bethlem Physicians was preoccupied with anatomical rather than 'psychiatric' study.[103] Thomas Allen was a 'passionate' defender of 'Galenicall physic' against those 'Iatrochemists' who espoused chemical medicines.[104] John Monro reacted with complacent pessimism against the upbeat challenges issued by William Battie at St Luke's to Bethlem's traditional therapeutics. Half a century later, Thomas Monro incriminated himself and his methods of treatment in confessing before a Parliamentary Committee that he merely followed the prescriptions of his father, despite believing they were virtually nugatory. Yet conservatism could lead physicians to be quite protective of their patients. Despite the heady enthusiasm of the Royal Society for novel animal-to-man blood-transfusion experiments as a means of curing insanity, efforts by its leading fellows to persuade their new member, Thomas Allen, 'to try it upon some mad person in . . . Bethlem' met his resistance.[105]

A certain amount of investigation of insanity was pursued by Bethlem's physicians. Both Allen and Tyson conducted numerous post-mortem examinations on patients and other cases. Richard Wiseman, Sargeant-surgeon to Charles I, published an account of a post-mortem conducted by Allen on a Bethlem patient in 1676, while a 'Roome . . . for Doctor Allen . . . to open the Bodyes of Lunatickes' was part of the plans for the Moorfields building.[106] Edward Tyson used post-mortem findings to cast doubt upon the correlation some physicians were attempting to establish between petrifaction of the pineal gland and fatuity.[107] In a letter to Dr Robert Plot in 1681, Tyson described how he had 'made a new dissection of the Braine different from Dr. Willis', and his findings were subsequently published in Samuel Collins's *System of Anatomy*.[108] Allen communicated an account to the Royal Society 'of the loss of part of a man's brain without any prejudice to the patient', and Tyson published papers on post-mortems of an infant and an adult born with malformations of the brain.[109] From at least 1765, there was certainly a mortuary (the 'Bone House' or 'Dead House') at the Hospital, where such examinations would probably have been performed, as they later were by the Surgeon, Bryan Crowther, and the Apothecary, John Haslam.[110] The anatomical studies of Bethlem Physicians made little contribution to their hospital practices, yet comparative anatomy was an important initiative in an age preoccupied with the riddle of human rationality and with unravelling what exactly distinguished mankind from the brute creation.

Not all Bethlem's remedies were old-fashioned. Bathing was certainly not a new therapy when it was introduced to Bethlem in the 1680s, yet this was a time of rediscovered enthusiasm for the benefits of hydro therapy, with the publication of treatises by Sir John Floyer and others.[111] In 1702, Floyer cited an allegedly successful experiment of Tyson's on a suicidal patient as a vindication for the utility of cold baths 'in curing madness'. John Strype described, more or less in Tyson's own words, the therapeutic rationale behind the treatment:

> In the Heat of the Weather, a very convenient Bathing Place, to cool and wash them, and is of great Service in airing their Lunacy; and it is easily made a hot Bath for restoring their Limbs when numbed, or cleansing and preserving them from Scurvey, or other cutaneous Distempers.[112]

By the nineteenth century, however, Bethlem's baths were admitted 'to be in a very inconvenient situation indeed'.[113] Staff testified to the Madhouses Committee that 'no warm bath' existed.[114] Yet Hospital records make it clear that bathing was practised at Bethlem for much of the eighteenth century.[115] Bethlem's Physicians remained convinced of its virtues, John Monro believing that 'cold bathing . . . has in general an excellent effect'.[116] Practitioners were not always entirely in agreement, however, on how it should be used. Tyson recommended it for the suicidal; Monro favoured it for the withdrawn, melancholy patient.[117] At the end of the eighteenth century, hydrotherapy was further elaborated when Thomas Monro provided a douche, or 'Shower bath', considering 'that it would be much for the benefit of the Patients'.[118] By 1815 bathing had become so routine at Bethlem that it was generally applied from 'July to the setting-in of the cold weather', the only discrimination being between patients who 'would' or 'would not bear it'.[119]

It is primarily upon the Monros that the blame must rest for Bethlem's poor reputation. Very few accounts of the attendance given by them on their patients survive, and those that do pertain largely to their private practice. Such accounts do little credit to the Monros or their methods. Alexander Cruden, attended privately by both James and John on different occasions over the course of fifteen years, presents a particularly damning assessment of the medical attention he received at their hands. Yet many of Cruden's charges appear prejudiced if not paranoid. For example, Cruden's interpretation of the exclusion of visitors without Monro's written approval as a conspiratorial attempt to silence him and prevent his escape. In fact, a conviction in the need for complete authority over patients and the therapeutic values of isolation seems to have been standard policy for the Monros in private practice (although reflecting poorly on their tolerance of public visiting at Bethlem).[120] Some families were clearly very pleased by their treatment. Horace Walpole seems to have been highly satisfied with John Monro's attendance on his nephew, Lord Orford. Henry Roberts was helped out sympathetically by both James Monro and by the Apothecary and Governor, John Markham, when striving to gain liberty from a Canterbury madhouse, while William Belcher praised Thomas Monro as 'a man of feeling' and 'understanding' for assistance in getting him out of Hackney madhouse.[121] Yet this would only go to confirm the impression that the Monros were more concerned with, and maintained considerably higher standards in, their private than their public practice.

There is little sign that James Monro was very involved in the various initiatives of the twenty-five years he officiated at Bethlem: the addition of the female incurables wing from 1733–5; the establishment of an infirmary in the 1740s, or the review of medicinal aid which culminated in the erection of the Apothecary's shop and the appointment of a resident apothecary. His presence or opinion is rarely mentioned in the Governors' Minutes, excluding the routine business of admitting and discharging patients.[122]

John Monro appears more dedicated than his father. Indeed, he partially engineered a gradual extension of the Physician's authority over the running of the Hospital and its occupants. He advised at numerous Courts and Committees, including those which directed the construction of an infirmary in 1763; which introduced sweeping reforms to the standing rules and orders governing the ancillary staff in 1765; which abolished servants' gratuities and curtailed public visiting in 1769/70; which established new guidelines for the Apothecary in 1772, and which added cells for both curables and incurables.[123] Often, indeed, he took part in these meetings in conjunction with William Battie, Physician to St Luke's, an indication that the differences between the two that erupted in 1758 were neither extreme nor permanent.

For their part, Bethlem's resident Apothecaries seem to have acquitted themselves well. In the 1780s Sophie von la Roche gave a glowing if rose-tinted account of the Apothecary John Gozna and John Monro, both of whom she characterized as men of superior 'feeling' and 'humanity', Gozna refraining from using 'the cruel expressions "fool" or "madman"' and implementing Monro's 'institute[s]' to tend all patients with 'affectionate care'.[124] Gozna was sufficiently energetic to keep a detailed 'private register of all the patients', comprising 'a concise abstract of the sexes, ages, causes, prominent features, cures, relapses, discharges, deaths &c', and to entrust it to the physician William Black, for use in the first quantitative study in England of the causes of insanity.[125]

Signs of neglect for the surgical needs of patients are not common. A shadow of suspicion is cast by the case of Henry Hobson in the 1630s, whose leg was allowed to become 'soe Ulcerated' that amputation was required, just a month after the Surgeon, William Wright's, dismissal; while in the 1690s Christopher Talmon complained of the expense he had been put to in providing medicines for patients 'left in a very ill condicion at the late Surgeons [Jeremy Higgs] death'.[126] Yet the majority of Surgeons seem to have been hard-working. They regularly complained of the multiplying numbers of patients and the smallness of their salaries. Yet, while John Wheeler claimed to have 'annually blooded about a thousand in & out patients belonging to both hospitals; & found Medicines plasters & Ligatures at his own charge', he also claimed to have 'cured near a hundred every year of Ulcers Fractures Mortifications &c'.[127] The Physician Richard Hale confirmed that Wheeler 'hath given constant attendance & hath done many Chirurgicall operations & cured more patients on extraordinary accidents of Mortifications Ulcers & other Sores than formerly has been done', and he was rewarded with an annual gratuity.[128]

The appointment of a nurse on Tyson's recommendation to look after all patients 'as shall happen to be ill of other distempers besides lunacy and such who cannot helpe themselves with their Dyett', was one of a number of initiatives which extended the Hospital's provision for bodily ailments.[129] The Steward's Accounts present a running journal of the special attention the nurse gave to the physically sick.[130] The establishment of an infirmary in 1741/2 at the instigation of John Markham, a Governor and Apothecary, and the addition of a second infirmary in 1753, enabled a degree of segregation of the sick, and offers further evidence of Bethlem responding to wider modernizations in hospital care.[131] However, infirmary provision remained inadequate, and clearly inferior to the detached infirmary accommodation available in other hospitals like St Luke's. At the 1815 Madhouses Committee inquiry staff admitted that the infirmaries were apt to be overcrowded and were amongst the foulest rooms in the building.[132]

The Governors and medical officers were quite conscientious in ensuring that patients with infectious diseases were refused admission or were transferred to the appropriate hospital.[133] Those with minor physical ailments, on the other hand, were freely admitted and attended to.[134] Staff did not always examine patients properly on admission, however, both because they failed to detect 'Wounds or Sores' on patients' bodies, and because 'Friends Neglect[ed] to give Notice'. It was not until 1778 that, in an effort to combat this, patients were instructed to be 'stripped and examined' by servants on admission 'in the presence of their Friends' and the Surgeon informed immediately if necesssary.[135] Smallpox was a considerable scourge, and the Governors and officers were rather slow in taking preventative and quarantining measures. Sufferers were placed under the care of the nurse, yet there is little indication of diseased patients being isolated in their cells, or of any other quarantine procedure, nor of inoculation being employed. Untold 'Numbers of Patients' (whose causes of death are rarely unrecorded in admission registers) had 'Annually Die[d] . . . of the Small Pox' at Bethlem. Despite the founding in 1746 of the London Smallpox Hospital, it was only in the 1770s that a subscription from the Bethlem Governors enabled poxed patients to be transferred.[136]

Medical treatment at Bethlem has been especially criticized for the indiscriminate and violent way in which it was applied. The routine method of dosing is suggested by the lack of any mention in the Governors' Minutes of the precise nature of medicines administered.[137] 'Certain days were fixed for . . . medical operations'; medicines were applied to most patients virtually without distinction and only during the spring and summer; while incurables received practically no medical treatment whatsoever.[138] A 1741 poem, allegedly penned by a patient, claimed that

> The Physick's mild, the Vomits are not such;
> But, Thanks be praised of them we have not much:
> Blooding is wholesome, and for the Cold Bath,
> All are agreed it many Virtues hath.[139]

But most patients who expressed an opinion gave a contrary assessment. In the 1670s Carkesse poured contempt on the '*Purges, Vomits,* and *Bleeding*' he received under Allen at Finsbury Madhouse and Bethlem, and Cruden later denounced the 'common Prescriptions of a Bethlemetical Doctor' he was subjected to under James and John Monro. Carkesse regarded Allen's 'Phisick' as worse than 'all *darkness, chains,* and *keepers* blows'. For such patients, their medicine was 'Hellish' or 'Mad *Physick*' and the practitioners who attended them merely 'Mad-Quack[s]'.[140]

Indeed, it is little wonder patients rejected contemporary physic as 'poison', when its operation was often so painful and debilitating, involving voiding from the bowels, vomiting, scarification, sores and bruises. Carkesse complained that Allen did not even deign 'to feel his *Pulse*' before drenching him, had visited him only 'once' 'in a Month' and had no idea 'how my Mad *Physick* has wrought'; Cruden similarly alleged that James Monro prescribed for him 'six days before he had seen him', and had not even inquired 'about the operation of his physick'.[141] Likewise, James Monro apparently prescribed 'without asking any questions' after merely examining another young man's tongue.[142] Furthermore, the bleedings and blisters were allegedly administered so liberally as to enervate patients to the point where not only their health, but their lives, were endangered.[143]

At Bethlem, medicine was often administered by staff and rarely, it seems, under the direct supervision of medical officers. The result must inevitably have been that it was sometimes doled out in a punitive or even brutal manner. Not until 1772 was the Apothecary required to 'attend the Administration of the Vomits and the Purges on the Days appointed for them and see they are properly Administred to the Patients'.[144] The evangelical George Whitefield's account of how Joseph Periam was treated, when 'unwilling' to take his medicine by staff who harboured no small antipathy for religious dissenters is not untypical: 'four or five took hold of him, cursed him most heartily, put a key in his mouth, threw him upon the bed, and said . . . "You are one of Whitefield's gang".'[145] One must, however, recognize the bias in such accounts: Methodists were openly hostile to the Bethlem regime, dominated as it was by a staunchly Anglican governing court.[146]

Dosages were not always uniform. The Governors instructed Thomas Allen, on his election in 1667, to 'be careful to see and speake with every Lunatike before hee prescribeth any physicke for him from tyme to tyme'.[147] And some attention was paid to individual needs. By 1700, on being examined by the Physician and Sub-Committee, patients were regularly being rejected or discharged if deemed 'too weak to undergo a Course of Physick'. And the early Sub-Committee Minutes, extant from 1709, provide a record of this policy in action.[148] The fact that patients had to be discharged for fear that they 'will dye in a short time if they are continued' equally indicates just how depleting 'physicking' could be.[149]

Patients' treatment was not solely under the care of Hospital staff, being partially negotiated with relatives and other obligors. For example, Periam's father, having initially agreed to discharge him provided Monro and the Committee agreed, subsequently vacillated wondering if it would be better for him 'to stay the summer, and to take physic twice a week, fearing a relapse'.[150] Relapse had long been recognized as a problem. Under the guidance of Tyson, the Hospital's rather *ad hoc* relapse policy was coordinated into a coherent provision, with the establishment of a facility for 'out-patients physic'. On Tyson's advice that 'patients who have been Cured of their Lunacys in . . . Bethlem being poore and not able to procure themselves a little necessary Phisick at the Spring and fall of the yeare for want thereof many . . . have relapsed . . . and become Patients again . . . to the [Hospital's] great Charge', the Governors made arrangements for them, on 'Applicacon to the weekly Committee', to obtain 'Phisick' at Hospital expense.[151] Tyson himself procured a first instalment of £50 'for Phisick & Medicines' from an anonymous benefactor. Out-patients became a standard and significant part of the relief that Bethlem offered.[152] Another clause in Tyson's will gave the Physician and Committee discretionary power to allow any patient discharged 'cured' and 'known to be very poor and unprovided for', with 'a sume of money not exceeding 40/- . . . towards their present subsistence or finding them Cloths' – subsequently dispensed to patients at Bethlem as 'Tyson's Gift'.[153]

Bethlem thus increasingly recognized a continuing responsibility towards after-care, gradually extending a guarantee of readmission to former patients discharged 'cured', should they relapse and reapply.[154] Incurables admitted from 1728 were exclusively supposed to be 'such Patients as have been in Bethlem Hospital', and 'by Tryall' and 'examination' 'appear . . . incurably mad mischievous and ungovernable'.[155] Incurables who had recovered but subsequently relapsed were, from 1772, given 'precedence' over 'any other patient on the [waiting] List'.[156]

Despite such developments, medicinally the Bethlem regime remained staunchly conservative. Yet in bleeding, vomiting, purging and blistering patients the medical officers of Bethlem were following approved practice and doing what they thought best.[157] Indeed it is occasionally their innovations that appear most fearsome. At the beginning of the nineteenth century, the Apothecary, John Haslam, alluding to the forced-dosing procedure employed, observed with some pride how he had developed a new model for a feeding-key which always achieved the desired end with much less damage to the patient's teeth.[158] And it might be argued that the true problem with Bethlem medicine was not so much the overdosing of patients, as that, as one servant put it in 1816, 'they have very little physic given them' either 'for their corporeal or mental diseases'.[159] In other words, there was little attempt to pioneer new therapies. In the 1750s John Monro's reaction to Battie's criticisms of evacuative and 'shock' therapies was negative and complacent.

Here it is worth briefly examining the significance of the altercation between William Battie, who inspired the founding in 1751 of St Luke's Asylum, and John Monro, in the wake of the publication in 1758 of Battie's *A Treatise on Madness* and Monro's response, *Remarks on Dr. Battie's Treatise on Madness*, appearing in the same year.[160] Battie characterized Bethlem (and by implication the regime of the recently deceased James Monro) as antiquated, negligent and wedded to a therapeutics that was harsh, indiscriminate, ineffectual and pessimistic. Battie presented himself (and by implication St Luke's) as just the opposite: scientific, innovative and hopeful. He suggested that if Bethlem's routine purges and vomits were abandoned, and his own preferred system of 'management' were adopted, most cases could be cured.

Monro rebutted these charges in a polemical manner. But careful reading of his *Remarks* show that he was not simply a blind reactionary. Monro himself gave clear outlines on the 'management' of the insane. While emphasizing the need for obedience and of gaining authority, he stressed that the mad should be 'talked to kindly' and 'used with the greatest tenderness and affection.' Going on the attack, he criticized Battie for the irrationality of some of the arguments he employed and his metaphysical posturing.[161] He denied that vomiting was either shocking, violent or useless, and was of one mind with Battie that medicaments should not be applied 'indiscriminately' or 'too strong', and that evacuation should be 'determined by the constitution of the patient'.[162]

Battie himself, according to Monro, espoused old doctrines of his own, for instance the antique therapeutic doctrine of substituting one extreme sensation for its opposite, especially employing fear to cast out anger.[163] Monro also liked to present himself as, in some respects, more genuinely optimistic than Battie. Whereas Battie pronounced 'Original Madness . . . incurable by art', Monro claimed that '*hereditary* complaints . . . are often treated with success', and accused Battie of extending the boundaries of incurability with his definition of '*original* madness'.[164]

Overall, however, Monro was clearly stung by Battie into an intemperate rejoinder, allowing himself and Bethlem to appear to set their face, Canute-like, against the tides of change in denying the importance of studying aetiology and of any nosology of mental illness, and in dismissing the utility of theorizing on the nature of insanity.[165] His pronouncement that 'very little of real use can be said concerning [madness]' proved nihilistic and out of tune with an ensuing century of debate about the subject.[166] While Battie cited the more modern investigations of Locke, Sydenham, Willis, Stahl and Mead, Monro harked back to the hoary wisdom of classical authors to establish his points. Suggesting he might present the 'metaphysical enquiries' of Battie 'as prize questions . . . to the academicians of *Bethlem*', Monro's politically incorrect joke at the expense of his patients casts a poor light on his own regard for them.[167]

Monro fell back upon 'evacuation' as 'the most adequate and constant cure' of madness.[168] While Battie stressed the dangers of 'rougher cathartics, emetics', etc., impeached 'vomits' as 'shocking', and advised a period of respite between each course of medicines, Monro unashamedly countered (echoing earlier writers like Nicholas Robinson) that cures were often protracted by physicians' timidity in dosing.[169] Both made reference to experience in treating the insane, but for Monro madness could 'be understood no otherwise than by personal observation'.[170] This claim sat uneasily with Bethlem's failure to admit medical students. More concerned with upholding the authority of the mad-doctor, Monro seemed to be averse to granting opportunities to other practitioners.[171] Indeed, he denied that writing a handbook for students (as Battie conceived his *Treatise*) would have any use.[172]

The Battie/Monro dispute is just one dimension, of course, of the wider reaction of the Bethlem administration to the foundation of St Luke's, a reaction negative in the extreme. Rather than prompting its Governors and officers to any fundamental reforms or review of their medical regime, the challenges issued by St Luke's provoked nothing more than another addition of cells at Bethlem.[173] The reasonable enough observation contained in inaugural appeals for funds for St Luke's that, while 'a noble Charity', Bethlem was unable to receive every needy applicant was dismissed by the *London Evening Post*, Bethlem's mouthpiece, as the complaint of 'ill-wishers'.[174] Instead of regarding St Luke's (as its promoters invited them to) as a supplement to Bethlem, the Governors did little but snipe at the initiatives of an upstart, attempting to nullify its challenge initially by referring to it as 'new Bethlem'. In his rejoinder, John Monro was responding for the Bethlem Governors themselves, who had apparently urged him to reply. A Governor of Bethlem since 1742, Battie's defection to St Luke's and criticisms of the Bethlem administration must have appeared to the Bethlem Court as a betrayal. In this light, the intransigence of Bethlem's Governors and officers is less surprising.

St Luke's was both a tangible and an ideological rebuke to Bethlem. One aim of its foundation was the object of improving contemporary knowledge and treatment of insanity by granting trainee doctors the opportunity of first-hand study on its wards.[175] Nor was it only the example of St Luke's that Bethlem was ignoring, for five other London hospitals had already opened to students.[176] The plain façade of St Luke's just across the way at Moorfields was a stark contrast to the classical opulence and old notions of spectacle enshrined in Bethlem. As outlined in Chapter 12, the expensive Easter entertainments enjoyed by the Governors of Bridewell and Bethlem on the funds of the charity were seen by an increasingly influential lobby (in particular those of a utilitarian and Dissenting religious bent), as a vain show and a waste – they were banned at St Luke's. Indeed, this mid-century controversy must be recognized as a struggle between two divergent conceptions: the older classical view, where public show was a crucial accompaniment of charity, demonstrating its extent and efficacy; and a renovated puritan and utilitarian ideology, which favoured a more understated, anonymous charity, and had closer links with family virtues.

The revolution represented by St Luke's and Battie can, however, be exaggerated. St Luke's relied as much on the example and practices of Bethlem as it was a departure from them. Cold bathing, cupping, purging, mechanical restraint and other traditional remedies criticized by Battie were all widely employed at the former.[177] Classifications and procedures adopted at St Luke's were considerably modelled on existing arrangements at Bethlem.[178] The 'resident apothecary' Hunter and Macalpine thought 'created' at Bethlem in 1772 'after the example of St Luke's, 1766', was in fact introduced at Bethlem in 1751, the relationship between the Hospitals being quite the opposite.[179] Architecturally, as Chapter 15 demonstrates, St Luke's layout of two segregated wings with connecting galleries was substantially in accord with Bethlem's design.[180] Not all was scissors against stone. There was also some cooperation between the Hospitals, for example, in 1777 when they combined to repudiate allegations made in the press about ill-treatment of patients by servants, while in 1783 Thomas Bowen spoke of both being 'engaged in the same good work', with the same objectives.[181]

Such was also papering over the cracks, however. Significant differences and frictions remained. John Monro's antipathy towards Battie was even carried over into his private casebook.[182] The very year (1765) St Luke's appointed a nurse for sick patients emphasizing how 'absolutely necessary' it was, Bethlem abolished the position as a separate office, and while St Luke's refused to accept old, 'uncured' cases from Bethlem, Bethlem proudly touted its willingness to accept those from its rival.[183] The two institutions began and continued as rivals, and appeared as such in the 1815/16 Madhouses inquiry, which was much kinder to St Luke's than Bethlem. St Luke's was no new Bethlem, even if medical students walked the wards there for only a few years, while Bethlem set itself stubbornly against following St Luke's.

CONCLUSION

There was somewhat more to Bethlem than a 'scene of stagnation and unassailed tradition'.[184] The introduction of cold-bathing in the 1680s; the post-mortem investigations carried out; the attendance of a nurse; the arrangements made for after-care; the erection of wards for the 'incurably' insane, and the establishment of a resident Apothecary, demonstrate that the Bethlem medical regime was for much of the time in touch with innovations in hospital care.[185] While the attendance of Bethlem's medical officers was at best casual and at worst inadequate, they were contracted to serve the Hospital in a visiting capacity only, in accordance with the charitable ethos informing medical attendance at early modern hospitals. Given the large private practice of the Monros, Cruden's comment about James Monro that his patients were 'too many to be well minded by one man' serves as an accurate assessment for the entire family's Bethlem attendance.[186] Ultimately, it is the surviving testimonies of their patients which primarily indict the medical officers of Bethlem as aloof and uninterested, and which condemn their therapeutics as routine and coercive to the point of cruelty.

NOTES

1 Roy Porter, *Mind Forg'd Manacles: Madness and Psychiatry in England from Restoration to Regency* (London: Athlone Press, 1987; paperback edition, Penguin, 1990); Denis Leigh, *The Historical Development of British Psychiatry* (Oxford: Pergamon, 1961); Andrew Scull, *The Most Solitary of Afflictions. Madness and Society in Britain, 1700–1900* (New Haven, Conn. and London: Yale University Press, 1993). For further detail and references, see Jonathan Andrews, 'Bedlam Revisited: A History of Bethlem Hospital *c.* 1634–*c.* 1770' (Ph.D. diss., London University, 1991).

2 Porter, *op. cit.* 128.

3 W. F. Bynum, 'Physicians, Hospitals and Career Structures in Eighteenth-century London', in W. F. Bynum and Roy Porter (eds), *William Hunter and the Eighteenth-Century Medical World* (Cambridge: CUP, 1985), 105–28.

4 Patricia H. Allderidge, 'Management and Mismanagement at Bedlam, 1547–1633', in Charles Webster (ed.), *Health, Medicine and Mortality in the Sixteenth Century* (Cambridge: CUP, 1979), 163.

5 Placing Bethlem solely under the custody of a physician/keeper may have seen it degenerate into little more than a private madhouse, at the disposal of royal patronage. James I had been primarily concerned to restore the royal prerogative over Bethlem which he (rightly) conceived had been undermined by the union with Bridewell. See Charles O'Malley, 'Helkiah Crooke. MD, FRCP, 1576–1648', *Bulletin of the History of Medicine*, xlii (1968), 13–14.

6 Allderidge, *op. cit.* 155.

7 See Daniel Oxenbridge, *General Observations and Prescriptions in the Practice of Physick. On several persons of Quality, &c. By an Eminent London Physician. Who was Contemporary with Dr. Gifford, Dr. Ridgeley, Dr. Meveral, Dr Andrews & Sir Theodore Mayerne, Physicians in Ordinary to King James and King Charles the first* (London: W. Mears, 1715); Thomas Allen *XEIPEΞOKE. The Excellency or Handy-Work of the Royal Hand*, by 'T[homas] A[llen] M.D.' (London: William Godbid, 1665), esp. 'Epistle Dedicatory'.

8 See Baldwin Hamey, *Bustorum Aliquot Reliquiae* (Latin MS, Royal College of Physicians), and William Munk, *The Roll of the Royal College of Physicians of London*, 2 volumes (London: Longman, Green, Longman & Roberts, 1861), 173–4.

9 See *BCGM*, 19 Dec. 1684, fol. 28; *CLRO* Misc. MSS 58.26, 1 Nov. 1684. Crooke, too, had been elected in accordance with a royal *mandamus*, with the additional support of testimonials from other Court worthies. See Allderidge, *op. cit.* 154–7.

10 Allen, *op. cit.*

11 *BCGM*, 12 and 26 June 1667, fols 49, 51 and 52; *PRO SP* 29/206, fols 103–4 and *SP* 29/207, fol. 13; *CSPD*, vol. ccvi, 103–4 and ccvii, 13, 216 and 231.

12 See note 11.

13 *A Compleat History of Europe*, David Jones (London: Printed for Henry Rhodes, John Nicholson and Andrew Bell, 1708), 404–9, repr. as 'An Account of the Life and Writings of Dr. Edward Tyson', *European Magazine and London Review*, 16 (July–Dec.: 1789), 241–3.

14 For Tyson and the Royal Society, see Michael Hunter, *The Royal Society and its Fellows 1660–1700. The Morphology of an Early Scientific Institution* (Chalfont St Giles: The British Society for the History of Science, 1982), 220. For further background, see M. F. Ashley Montagu, *Edward Tyson M.D. F.R.S. 1650–1708 and the Rise of Comparative Anatomy in England* (Philadelphia: The American Philosophical Society, 1943).

15 See Jonathan Andrews, 'A Respectable Mad-Doctor? The Career of Dr. Richard Hale (1670–1728), F.R.S., F.R.C.P. Physician to Bethlehem Hospital', *Notes and Records of the Royal Society of London*, xliv (1990), 172–3, and *Royal Society Copy Journal Books, passim*, 1679–1708.

16 Nurse prevailed over four opponents in 1648; Allen over six in 1667, and James Monro over seven opponents in 1728. Unfortunately, the number of candidates contesting the 1708 election, won by Hale, is not given in the Governors' Minutes. See *BCGM*, 13 April 1619, 21 July 1648, 26 June 1667, 19 Dec. 1684, 10 Sept. 1708 and 9 Oct. 1728, fols 110, 352, 53, 28, 439 and 163; also Andrews, 'A Respectable Mad-Doctor', 172.

17 See Andrews, 'A Respectable Mad-Doctor', 173 and n. 25.

18 Manningham may have suffered from the inferior status accorded man-midwifery. See *The Daily Journal*, no. 2411, 30 Sept. 1728; *LEP*, no. 126, 26–8 Sept. 1728; Munk, *op. cit.* ii, 68, 74–5, 110; Sir Richard Manningham, *Exact Diary of What Was Observ'd During a Close Attendance Upon Mary Toft the Pretended Rabbit Breeder* (London: Fletcher, Gyles & Roberts, 1726).

19 See letters from Claudius Amyand to James Jurin; from James Monro to Jurin; from Lady Percival to Amyand, and from Amyand to Jurin; dated, respectively, 26 March 1726, 14 April 1726, 6 Aug. and 26 Aug. 1725, in 'Inoculation Letters & Papers', in *Royal Society Library*, fols 319–22 and 328–31.

20 James was entered eight years later as a Snell Exhibitioner at Balliol College, Oxford, where he graduated AB, 1703; MA, 1708; MB, 1709 and MD, 1722. See Munk, *op. cit.* 113–14; Admission Book of Balliol College.

21 See Alexander Cruden, *Mr. Cruden Greatly Injured* (London: By the Author, 1739), 24; *idem, The Adventures of Alexander the Corrector* (London: By the Author, 1754), part i, 23; W. S. Lewis (ed.), *Horace Walpole's Correspondence*, 48 volumes (New Haven: Yale University Press, 1954), vol. 19, letters from Horace Mann to Walpole dated 4 and 18 Jan. 1746 and 16 May 1747, 191, 196 and 400.

22 See *Daily Journal*, no. 2452, 16 Nov. 1728; Chapter 12.

23 See, e.g., G. Holmes, *Augustan England: Professions, State & Society* (London: George Allen & Unwin, 1982), 217.

24 Lewis, *op. cit.*; Munk, *op. cit.* 183–4. For John's attendance, e.g. at twelve Sub-Committee meetings during 1748, see *BCGM* and *BSCM, passim* for 1748.

25 See *BCGM*, 10 June 1669, fol. 144, *Ghall* MS 5265/1, Register of Admissions to the Freedom of the Worshipful Company of Barber Surgeons, 1522–1664, fols 76 and 112.

26 See *BCGM*, 11 Dec. 1741 and 5 Feb. 1789, fols 126 and 325.

27. *Ibid.* 16 May 1734, fol. 327; *Ghall* MS 5265/1, Register of Admissions to the Freedom of the Worshipful Company of Barber Surgeons, 1665–1704 and 1707–32, fols 43, 146 and 188; MS5266/1, Barber Surgeons Apprenticeships Bindings, 1673–1707 and 1707–25, fols 302, 134, 326 and 336.

28 Samuel Sambrooke (Surgeon 1632–43) qualified under William Martin on 3 Dec. 1611; John Meredith (Surgeon 1643–56) qualified under Edwin Ingolsby on 26 Jan. 1635; Christopher Talman (Surgeon 1693–1708), son of Gus/William Talman of Westminster, gent., was apprenticed initially with Thomas Devonish on 10 March 1674 and subsequently with Thomas Barker, under whom he was admitted free on 5 June 1681; Richard Blackstone (Surgeon 1708–14) qualified under Edward Green on 3 Dec. 1700; Henry Wentworth (Surgeon 1761–9) qualified under William Singleton on 3 Oct. 1732. See *Ghall* MS 5255/1 and 5266/1.

29 For each election of an Apothecary from 1751 and of a Surgeon from 1741 there was an average of three candidates.

30 No apothecary was succeeded by his son or seems even to have been related to any former incumbent.

31. *BCGM*, 15 March 1678, 5 Dec. 1683, 31 Jan., 15 Feb, 21 March and 18 April 1684, and 20 Nov. 1685, fols 15, 396–7, 403, 407–8, 414–15, 417, 116.

32 See Chapter 12.

33 See *BCGM*, 11 Dec. 1685, fol. 121; *CLRO* Misc. MSS 58.26, 15 Dec. 1685.

34 *BCGM*, 19 April 1689, fols 392–3; Chapter 12.

35 See Allderidge, *op. cit.* 163; E. G. O'Donoghue, *The Story of Bethlehem Hospital from its Foundation in 1247* (London: T. Fisher Unwin, 1914), 167; *PRO SP* 16/237, no. 5.

36 John Blackburn alleged that Monro generally attended just twice a week (including Committee days), 'going round the Hospital' only once in 'more than a month': *Select Committee on Madhouses* (London: House of Commons, 1815–16), *1st Report*, 1815, 92, 94–5; *2nd Report*, 1816, 92–3.

37 Porter, *op. cit.* 128.

38 The first mention in the Court Minutes of any fee paid a Bethlem Physician is not until the election of Thomas Nurse, on 21 July 1648, but the 'forty marks per annum' he was granted – higher than his successors, because it seems to have excluded the yearly gratuity paid them – is already 'the accustomed fee', and must have been received by Meverall before him. See *BCGM*, fol. 312. For regular records of salaries paid, see *Bethlem Auditors' Accounts*, 1708–68.

39 *BCGM*, 24 Sept. and 22 Oct. 1708, fols 440 and 446; *LEP*, no. 3706, 18–20 July 1751.

40 With the exception of a brief period during 1629–37, when surgeons received a token fee of £2 per annum; *BCGM*, 23 Dec. 1629, 6 July 1632, 18 Sept. 1637, 29 March 1651 and 24 Oct. 1656, fols 159, 287, 139, 487 and 770.

41 See esp. *ibid.* 5 Jan., 7 Feb., 29 March and 4 April 1672, 11 Jan. 1689, 10 and 24 May 1689, 11 April 1690, fols 367–8, 371–2, 382–3, 390, 353, 398, 405 and 36.

42 See, e.g., *ibid.* 19 Dec. 1645, 18 Dec. 1646, 24 Dec. 1647, 6 July 1649, 6 Dec. 1672, fols 232, 286, 328, 390 and 465.

43 *Ibid.* 7 Feb. and 29 March 1672, fols 371 and 382–3.

44 See e.g. *ibid.* 5 Dec. 1718, fol. 369, where the Bridewell Committee reports that the Apothecary's bills for the past year had been very high, but the Physician confirmed that they were reasonable.

45 For example, *ibid.* 12 April, 16 May, 1 Nov. and 19 Dec. 1750, 1 Feb., 4 April and 22 May 1751, 25 May 1753, fols, 125, 444, 446–7, 467, 476, 480–1, 493, 6 and 114. Auditors' accounts for the 1760s reveal that expenses on supplies of medicines normally amounted to less than £150; see *Bethlem Auditors' Accounts*, 1708–9 and 1759–68.

46 In fact, this latter stipulation was not mentioned until 1772, but presumably had been operating in practice since 1751. See *BCGM*, 25 June 1772, fol. 359.

47 See e.g., *ibid.* 24 May and 5 June 1644, 28 March 1645, 23 Nov. 1649, 24 Oct. 1656 and 19 Feb. 1674, fols 118, 123, 189, 408, 769 and 616.

48 *Ibid.* 8 Feb. 1645, fol. 176.

49 *Ibid.* 22 Dec. 1749 and 2 Feb. 1750, fols 430 and 434; *BSCM*, 3 March 1716, fol. 212; *BGCM* in *BSCM*, 31 Jan. 1750, fol. 160.

50 *BSCM*, 28 Oct. 1761, fol. 387.

51 *BCGM*, 3 March 1643, 5 June 1644, 9 July and 24 Oct. 1656, and 26 Feb. 1658, fols 18, 23, 760, 770–1 and 851.

52 *Ibid.* 10 July 1679 and 19 Dec. 1694, fols 98 and 415. Parish records make it clear that 1s was the standard rate practitioners charged for bleeding in this period.

53 For the Surgeon's salary post 1694, see *ibid.* 4 and 18 Feb. 1715, 10 Jan. and 14 Feb. 1718, 22 June 1775, 5 Feb. 1789, fols 106, 115, 319, 324 and 471–81; *BSB*, 1777–1815; *Bwell/GCM*, 1738–47, *passim*.

54 Originally, the twenty-strong Bethlem Committee was only 'to meete once a fortnight or oftener as to them [its members] shall seem meete' at new Bethlem. See Chapter 12, and *BCGM*, 16 Feb., 30 March 1677, 3 July 1685, 6 Nov. 1702, 25 Feb. 1709, fols 336–7, 356, 361, 89, 119 and 465, and *BSCM, passim*.

55 Unlike the Porter and Nurse, the Matron did not include this duty in the list of those she 'apprehended' to belong to her office (indeed, she mentioned only two duties). One

assumes, however, that the doctor received accounts of ordinary women patients, as well as of male patients and of those sick patients under the Nurse's care. See *BCGM*, 6 May 1736, fol. 391.

56 John and Thomas Monro may seem to have attended the meetings of the Bethlem committees much less often. Yet the minutes of actual admissions were separated at the back of Sub-Committee books after about mid-century. Even a cursory examination of these minutes demonstrates that one of the Monros continued to preside over almost every admission to Bethlem.

57 See, e.g., *BCGM*, 10 Feb., 7 July, 4 Aug. and 20 Oct. 1643, 24 Oct. 1656, 3 June 1685, fols 15, 31, 56, 72, 771, 76, *re* outside surgeons and others treating and taking care of sick Bridewell apprentices. For Bethlem, see, e.g., *ibid.* 7 Nov. 1645, fol. 226. Significantly, instances are mostly restricted to the seventeenth century, medical practice being more tightly regulated as the period progressed.

58 *Ibid.* 12 June 1657, fol. 817.

59 *LEP*, no. 130, 5–8 Oct. 1728. No mention is made of this alleged plan in the Minutes.

60 *BCGM*, 21 June 1751 and 24 Nov. 1752, fols 9 and 91; *LEP*, nos. 3694, 3706 and 3708, 20–2 June and 23–5 July 1751.

61 See, e.g. *BCGM*, 20 March 1696, 25 Feb. 1715, fols 32, 117; *BSCM*, 11 July 1795; *BGCM*, 22 Sept. 1795, fol. 51.

62 *BCGM*, 16 May 1750 and 1 Feb. 1751, fols 46, 480 and 359; note 60; and *BSCM*, 26 Sept. 1761. Gozna, Winder's replacement, had to attend even more often, 'every Morning . . . or oftener if necessary'; *BCGM*, 9 July 1772, fol. 359.

63 For this discussion, see *BCGM*, 12 April, 16 May, 1 Nov. and 19 Dec. 1750, 1 Feb., 4 April and 22 May 1751, and 25 May 1753, fols 125, 444, 446–7, 467, 476, 480–1, 493, 6 and 114; *BGCM* in *BSCM*, 5 Dec. 1750 fol. 211; *BwellGCM*, 8 May 1750; *LEP*, nos. 3596, 3614, 3633, 3639, 3643, 3650, 3658, 3660 and 3682, 6–8 Nov. and 18–20 Dec. 1750, 31 Jan.–2 Feb., 14–16 and 23–6 Feb., 12–14 March, 30 March–2 April, 4–6 April and 21–3 May 1751. Not until 1772, however, did Bethlem follow the advice of Bartholomew's and the *LEP* that the Apothecary should serve alone 'without Incumbrance of Family'; *BCGM*, 25 June 1772, fol. 359.

64 *BGCM*, 30 Jan. 1799; *Madhouses Committee Reports, 1st Report*, 1815, 61.

65 See, e.g., Thomas Bowen, *An Historical Account of the Rise, Progress and Present State of Bethlem Hospital* . . . (London: for the Governors 1783), 11.

66 *BCGM*, 23 Dec. 1629, 6 July 1632, 3 March 1643 and 12 Nov. 1656, fols 159, 287, 18 and 773.

67 *Ibid.* 10 Jan. and 14 Feb. 1718, fols 319 and 324.

68 *Ibid.* e.g., 7 Nov. 1645, fol. 226.

69 See Cromwell Mortimer, *An Address to the Publick* (London: C. Davis, 1745), 28, cited in Porter, *op. cit.* 184–5.

70 Indeed, 'the necessity', as emphasized in 1696, 'of Chooseing another person to succeed . . . with all convenient speed' was rarely acknowledged by the Governors. See *BCGM*, 20 March 1696 and 25 Feb. 1715, fols 32 and 117; *BSCM*, 11 July 1795; *BGCM*, 22 Sept. 1795, fol. 51.

71 *BSCM*, 26 Sept. 1761.

72 *BCGM*, 5 Jan., 7 Feb., 29 March and 4 April 1672, fols 367–8, 371–2, 382–3 and 390. James had also got into trouble over his bills at this juncture.

73 Partly in reaction to Bethlem's history, St Luke's had, of course, rejected the idea that the Hospital ought to be annexed to another existing institution. See C. N. French, *The Story of St. Luke's Hospital 1750–1948* (London: William Heinemann, 1951).

74 The £60 salary allowed the Surgeon from 1710 comprised £30 for each Hospital, although an earlier request seems to have been refused. *BCGM*, 23 May 1690, 13 Feb. 1691, 4 and 18 Feb. 1715, and 10 Jan. 1718, fols 48, 102, 106, 115 and 319.

75 See *ibid.* e.g., 11 Dec. 1741, fol. 125; Holmes, *op. cit.* 226; Bynum, *op.cit.*

76 O'Malley, *op. cit.*; Alldridge, *op. cit.*; E. S. de Beer (ed.), *The Diary of John Evelyn*, 6 volumes (Oxford: Clarendon Press, 1955), ii, 13–14.

77 James Carkesse, *Lucida Intervalla: Containing Divers Miscellaneous Poems,* edited by M. V. DePorte (Los Angeles: University of California Press, 1979), 9. Allen also received parochial cases at Finsbury, charging roughly double the Bethlem rate at 8s p/w. See, e.g., the case of Thomas Stevenson of St Bride, *Ghall* MS 6552/1, 29 Oct. 1671–April 1672; Richard Hunter and Ida Macalpine, *Three Hundred Years of Psychiatry 1535–1860: A History Presented in Selected English Texts* (London: OUP, 1963), 199 and 214–15.

78 See Andrews, 'A Respectable Mad-Doctor'; Daniel Defoe, *A Review of the State of the English Nation,* nos. 69, 82 and 89, 8 June, 9 and 25 July, 1706, 277–80, 327 and 353–6.

79 *BCGM,* 6 Feb. 1680, fol. 128.

80 The MS of Monro's casebook is in the possession of Dr F. J. G. Jefferiss, himself a distant relative of the family. We are grateful for his assistance.

81 Margaret Marie Verney (ed.), *Verney Letters of the Eighteenth Century from the MSS at Claydon House,* 2 volumes (London: Ernest Benn, 1930), ii, 202. Others amongst James Monro's wealthy private clients were Lord Galloway and John Newport, son of the 3rd Earl of Bradford. John Monro's clientele included Lady Dorothy Child and Sir Charles Hanbury Williams.

82 Cruden, *Adventures,* i, 22; ii, 21–2.

83 For Physicians' wills, see *PRO PROB:* 11/205, q.n. 127, fols 161–2 (Meverall); 11/324, q.n. 82 (Nurse); 11/502, q.n. 176, fols 333–5 (Tyson); 11/625, q.n. 291, fols 60–2 (Hale); 11/798, q.n. 302, fols 250–1 (James Monro); 11/1213, q.n. 32, fols 266–8 (John Monro). For Surgeons' wills/administrations, see *ibid.* 11/254, q.n. 149, fol. 357 (Meredith); 11/500, q.n. 74, fol. 239 (Talman); 6/91, fol. 108/215 (Blackstone); 11/714, q.n. 369, fols 325–6 (John Wheeler); 11/1174, q.n. 18, fols 143–4 (Richard Crowther). For Apothecaries wills/administrations, see *ibid.* 11/252, q.n. 18, fols 136–8 (Yardley); 11/356, fols 194–5 (James); 11/395, q.n. 53, fol. 52 (Pelling); 11/430, q.n. 29, fols 224–5 (Dickenson); 6/92, fols 10–11/20–1 (Adams); 11/815, fol. 20 (Elderton).

84 Meverall had a residence in Chertsey, Herts, which he left to his wife, Catherine. His 'whole library' and unspecified landed estate were bequeathed to his eldest son, Othewell.

85 Nurse's codicil reveals that his son, George, had since the writing of his will, married and had a child 'by the daughter of Mr. Winstanley', a governor of Bridewell and Bethlem, 'Expressly against my Command', but the doctor was magnanimous enough to leave the child £50. He left all his books to his son, Richard.

86 See Thomas Hearne, *Remarks and Collections,* 11 volumes (Oxford: Oxford Historical Society, 1885–1921), ii, 124.

87 See Andrews, 'A Respectable Mad-Doctor'.

88 It was out of these profits that the Monro sons were required to allow their mother a £500 annuity. John had also been a good friend of Jonathan Miles and his family, the proprietors of Hoxton madhouse, as were his son Thomas and John Haslam, the Bethlem Apothecary, after him, a large number of patients being passed from one institution to the other. For Miles, see *RO PROB* 11/984, fol. 193; *Madhouses Committee Report,* 1815, *1st Report,* 30; *3rd Report,* 171–4.

89 Crooke was Censor five times (1627–31) and Anatomy Reader (1629); Meverall was Censor eight times (1624, 1626–7, 1632, 1637–40), Elect (1639), Registrar (1638 and 1640), Anatomy Reader (1628), President (1641–4), Treasurer (1645), and Consilarius (1645–7); Allen was Censor thrice (1674, 1679 and 1682); Tyson was Censor only once, in 1694, being penalized as one of a minority of physicians and Fellows who supported the apothecaries in their battle against the College's plans for a dispensary. Hale was Censor thrice (1718–19 and 1724) and Harveian Orator (1724); James Monro was merely Harveian Orator (1737), and John Monro was Censor seven times (1754, 1759, 1763, 1768, 1772, 1778 and 1785) and Harveian Orator (1757).

90 For the involvement of Bethlem Physicians with the Royal Society, see e.g. Thomas Birch, *The History of the Royal Society* (London: A. Millar, 1756–7); Ashley Montagu, *op. cit.;* Andrews, 'A Respectable Mad-Doctor'.

91 For a qualified rebuttal, see Jonathan Andrews, '"Hardly a Hospital, but a Charity for Pauper Lunatics"?: Therapeutics at Bethlem in the Seventeenth and Eighteenth Centuries',

in Jonathan Barry and Colin Jones (eds), *Medicine and Charity Before the Welfare State* (London and New York: Routledge, 1991), 63–81.

92 *BCGM*, 21 July 1648, fol. 352; Spital Sermons, termed *Psalms of thanksgiving . . .* and *True report . . .* , listed in Andrews, 'Bedlam Revisited', 283, note 166, and 582–3.

93 See *BCGM*, 14 March 1683, fol 358.

94 *BSCM*, 1 Dec. 1792, fol. 105.

95 See John Thomas Smith, *Ancient Topography of London* (London: J. M'Creery, published and sold by the proprietor, John Thomas Smith, 1815), 34.

96 *BCGM*, 5 Jan., 7 Feb. and 29 March 1672, fols 367–8, 371 and 382–3.

97 *Ibid.* 13 Aug. 1672, fol. 433.

98 H. W. Robinson and W. Adams (eds), *The Diary of Robert Hooke (1672–1680)* (London: Taylor & Francis, 1935): 14 April 1674; 'With Dr. Allen at Bedlam. View'd Moorfields for new Bedlam. Drew up report for him'. Hooke's diary suggests how active Allen was in the project and that the two were on friendly terms, Hooke even taking advice on his diet from Allen.

99 See *BCGM*, 16 Feb. and 30 March 1677, fols 336 and 356–61.

100 See Andrews, 'A Respectable Mad-Doctor'.

101 For more on Hale and Tyson's controversial private attendance, see Jonathan Andrews, '"In her Vapours . . . [or] in her Madness"? Mrs Clerke's Case: an Early Eighteenth Century Psychiatric Controversy', *History of Psychiatry*, i, 1 (1990), 125–44; for Allen's treatment of James Carkesse, see the latter's *Lucida Intervalla*.

102 See *BCGM*, esp. 18 June 1675, 21 July 1676, 2 March 1677, fols 138–9, 277 and 346; R. Latham and W. Matthews (eds), *The Diary of Samuel Pepys*, 11 volumes (London: Bell & Hyman, 1983), esp. vols vi–viii. Another Pepys, Henry, also became a member of the Court in 1675; see *BCGM*, 16 July 1675, fol. 145.

103 See e.g. Thomas Allen, 'An Exact Narrative Of an Hermaphrodite now in London', *Philosophical Transactions*, ii (10 Feb. 1668), 624; Andrews, 'A Respectable Mad-Doctor'.

104 Allen was overheard in a coffee-house by his old university chum, Pepys, inveighing against 'a Couple of Apothecarys' on the matter; see *Diary*, vol. iv, 3 and 11 Nov. 1663, 361–2 and 378; vol. vii, 1 April 1666, 87.

105 *Roy. Soc. Copy Journal Books*, iii, 11–12, 15, 36 and 39; Birch, *op. cit.* (ref. 90), ii, 202, 204 and 214–16; iii, 356.

106 William Wiseman, *Several Chirurgical Treaties* (London: Norton & Maycock, 1686), Book I, 132. Wiseman was appointed a governor of Bethlem in 1678 and was, also, alongside Allen, amongst the first members of the new rotational committee for Bethlem.

107 After Descartes had posited the location of the seat of the soul or 'anima rationalis' as the pineal gland, Willis suggested that the condition and size of these parts directly corresponded to the brutishness of the particular creature. See, e.g., Thomas Willis, *Two Discourses Concerning the Soul of Brutes* (London: Dring, Harper & Leigh, 1683).

108 Tyson had been friendly with Plot since their College days. See R. T. Gunther (ed.), *Early Science in Oxford* (London: Dawsons, 1937; reprinted, 1968), vol. xii, 3.

109 Tyson was clearly interested in brain function throughout the animal kingdom. See Birch, *op. cit.* ii, 252–3; Royal Society of London, *Philosophical Transactions*, vol. 19 (1683), 533–7.

110 *BCGM*, 20 June 1765, fols 136–7; *BSCM*, 29 Jan. 1780 and 24 April 1790; *CLRO MS Comp. City Lands Plan 303*; Bryan Crowther, *Practical Remarks on Insanity: to which is Added, a Commentary on the Dissection of the Brains of Maniacs; with some Account of Diseases Incident to the Insane* (London: Thomas Underwood, 1811); and John Haslam, *Observations on Insanity: with Practical Remarks on the Disease and an Account of the Morbid Appearances on Dissection* (London: John Callow, 1798), 36–133.

111 For bathing at Bethlem, see esp. *BCGM*, 7 July 1687, 29 June 1688, 24 May and 28 June 1689, fols 249, 312 and 416. For water therapy, see Edward Baynard and John Floyer, *Psychrolousia: Or the History of Cold Bathing Both Ancient and Modern in Two Parts*, 2nd edn (London: Sam Smith & Benj Walford, 1706).

112 John Strype, *A Survey of the Cities of London and Westminster . . . Written at First . . . by John Stow . . .* (London: A. Churchill, 1720), 195.

113 *Madhouses Committee Reports*, 1815, *1st Report*, 60.

114 *Ibid.* 39, 60, 94.

115 *BSCM*, e.g. 13 May 1710, 19 and 26 March 1757, 25 Oct. 1777, 7 Feb. 1778 and 6 May 1780, fols 20 and 6–7. John Howard mentioned only cold-bathing facilities for both sexes at Bethlem on his visit there in the 1780s, yet there was certainly a hot bath for male patients as late as 1778. See John Howard, *An Account of the Principal Lazarettos in Europe* (London: T. Cadell, 1789), 139.

116 John Monro, *Remarks on Dr. Battie's Treatise on Madness* (London: John Clarke, 1758), 52.

117 See e.g. *ibid.*; John Floyer, *Enquiry into the Right Use and Abuses of the Cold and Temperate Baths in England* (London: R. Clavel, 1697), 104–5; Edward Baynard, *History of Cold-Bathing*, 5th edn (London: W. & J. Innys, 1722), 142–3.

118 *BSCM*, 20 Jan. 1798.

119 *Madhouses Committee Reports*, 1815, *1st Report*, 94 and 103.

120 Cruden, *Mr. Cruden Greatly Injured*, 2 and 4.

121 Lewis, *op. cit.*: vol. 12, 95; vol. 24, 316, 367 and 372; vol. 34, 47; vol. 36, 118, 335–6 and vol. 42, 355–6; *The Sufferings and Death of Henry Roberts Esquire*, trans. Paul de St Pierre (Dublin 1748), 52 and 54; Porter, *op. cit.* 112–13; Hunter and Macalpine, *op. cit.* 373–5; William Belcher, *Address to Humanity* (London: Allen & West, 1796), 1–4.

122 See e.g. *BCGM*, 12 March 1742, fol. 141, for an exception.

123 *Ibid.* 8 Aug. 1763, 20 June 1765, 27 April 1769, 25 June and 9 July 1772, 5 Aug. 1784, fols 118–20, 132–7, 248–50, 349, 359–60 and 155–6.

124 Clare Williams (ed.), *Sophie in London, 1786, Being the Diary of Sophie v. La Roche* (London: Jonathan Cape, 1933), 167–71.

125 William Black, *A Dissertation on Insanity* (London: Ridgway, 1810).

126 BCGM, 3 Dec. 1630, 14 Jan. 1631 and 19 Dec. 1694, fols 208, 211 and 415.

127 *Ibid.* 10 Jan. 1718, fols 319.

128 *Ibid.* 14 Feb. 1718, fol. 324.

129 *Ibid.* 16 Dec. 1692, 13 and 27 Jan. 1693, 15 March 1700, fols 213, 217, 219 and 356; *BSCM*, *passim*.

130 See *BSA*, 5–12 Dec. 1724, and *passim*.

131 See *BCGM*, 30 July and 9 Sept. 1741, 17 Feb., 12 March and 8 Aug. 1753, fols 108, 111, 137, 141 and 120; *BSCM*, 11 Oct. 1753, fol. 375, 7 and 14 Feb. and 17 Oct. 1778, 23 Jan. 1779; *LEP*, no. 2230, 23–5 Feb. 1742; *Madhouses Committee Report*, 1815, *1st Report*, 36; *SLHCM*, 9 Nov. 1764; *SLGCM*, 6 Oct. 1754, 6 Feb. 1771, fol. 195.

132 *Madhouses Committee Report*, 1815, *1st Report*, 36; *SLHCM*, 9 Nov. 1764; *SLGCM*, 6 Oct. 1764, 6 Feb. 1771, fol. 195.

133 For example, the case of Robert Porter suffering from 'the foule disease' [i.e., VD] and ordered discharged to his friends 'for his maintenance & cure of his disease', in 1656; for this and other examples, see *BCGM*, 13 Jan. 1649, 7 May 1656, fols 370, 749–50; *BAR*, fol. 27. *BSCM*, 23 June 1711, 23 June 1716, fols 58, 224.

134 For example, the case of Abigail James; *BCGM*, 27 May 1663, fols 48 and 50.

135 *BSCM*, 19 Sept. 1778.

136 *Ibid.* 30 May 1778, 5 June 1779 and 28 Oct. 1780; *BSA*, 10–17 April and 15–22 May 1731, fols 482 and 487; Peter Razzell, *The Conquest of Smallpox* (Firle: Caliban, 1977); from 1769 St Luke's made provision for the nursing of patients with smallpox 'out of the House' and ordered that the friends of any patient with smallpox be notified. Patients were not sent to the London Smallpox Hospital, however, until the later 1770s. *SLHCM*, 19 May, 6 June and 15 Dec. 1769 and 22 May 1772.

137 In 1679 appears the first reference to the Surgeon's standard duty 'of letting them [the patients'] blood"; *BCGM*, 10 July 1679, fol. 98.

138 Bowen, *op. cit.* 11; *Madhouses Committee Report*, 11 July 1815, *Summary Report*, 4; 1815, *1st Report*, esp. 15, 26, 42, 93, 95, 99–100, 103, 105, 107; 1816, *1st Report*, 39, 41, 47–9; Jonathan Andrews, 'The Lot of the "Incurably" Insane in Enlightenment England', *Eighteenth Century Life*, xii (1988), 1–18.

139 See *Bethlem. A Poem* (1744), in Patricia H. Allderidge, *Catalogue to Bethlem Royal Hospital Museum* (London: Bethlem Royal Hospital, 1976).

140 For this discussion, see Carkesse, *op. cit.* esp. 9, 12, 14–15, 20, 23, 30, 32, 39–40, 52, 62; Cruden, *Adventures*; idem, *The London-Citizen Exceedingly Injur'd: or a British Inquisition Display'd* (London: The Author, 1738); idem, *Mr. Cruden Greatly Injured*.

141 Carkesse, *op. cit.* 14; Cruden, *London-Citizen*, 16 and 23.

142 Nehemiah Curnock (ed.), *The Journal of the Reverend John Wesley* (London: Epworth Press, 1938), vol. ii, 52.

143 *Ibid.* Wesley alleged that, on Monro's orders, this man, Peter Shaw, was 'blooded . . . largely, confined . . . to a dark room, and . . . a strong blister [put] on each of his arms, [and] . . . over his head'; that treatment was sustained 'for six weeks' entirely 'in vain' and that Shaw was left 'so weak he could not stand alone'.

144 *BCGM*, 25 June 1772, fol. 359.

145 W. Wale (ed.), *Whitefield's Journals* (London: H. J. Drane, 1905), 256.

146 Porter, *op. cit.* esp. 62–81.

147 *BCGM*, 26 June 1667, fol. 53.

148 See e.g. *BSCM*, 23 June 1711, 7 Nov. 1713, 17 Sept. and 3 Dec. 1715, 30 June 1716, 20 July and 24 Aug. 1717, 10 May 1718, 17 Jan. 1719 and 30 Nov. 1723, fols 58, 137, 198, 204, 225, 264, 267, 13, 34 and 189.

149 *Ibid.* e.g. 23 June 1711 and 1 Nov. 1729, fols 58 and 29. John Monro was appreciative in his *Remarks* of the need to keep patients' strength up and not to carry depletion 'beyond the patient's strength' (*op. cit.* 39 and 57).

150 Wale, *op. cit.* 264.

151 *BCGM*, 26 April 1700, fols 366–7.

152 See e.g. *ibid.* 10 Jan. 1718, fol. 319; *BSCM*, 1 Jan. 1726, fol. 252; Bowen, *op. cit.* 14.

153 *BCGM*, 3 Sept. 1708, fol. 436.

154 See e.g. *ibid.* 29 July 1692, fols 189–90, case of Elizabeth Long.

155 *Ibid.* 12 July 1728 and 19 July 1739, fols 153 and 63; Bowen, *op. cit.* 13, and Andrews, 'Incurably Insane'.

156 See, e.g., *BSCM*, 18 Jan. and 22 Feb. 1772.

157 See e.g. Haslam, *op. cit.* 316; George Cheyne, *The English Malady; or a Treatise of Nervous Diseases of All Kinds* (London: G. Strahan, 1733); repr. edited by Roy Porter (London: Tavistock, Routledge, 1991), 198; William Battie, *A Treatise on Madness* (London: J. Whitson & B. White, 1758), 36, 47, 63 and 99.

158 Haslam, *op. cit.* 316–20.

159 *Madhouses Committee Reports*, 1816, *First Report*, 92.

160 For this controversy, see William Battie, *op. cit.*, and Monro, *op. cit.* Both have conveniently been reprinted with an introduction by R. Hunter and I. Macalpine (London: Dawsons, 1962). For further discussion see Akihito Suzuki, 'Mind and its Disease in Enlightenment British Medicine' (Ph.D. thesis, University of London, 1992), and Roy Porter, *op. cit.*.

161 See Battie, *op. cit.* 6, 70; Monro, *op. cit.* 16–19, 25, 28, 34–5, 49.

162 Both Cheyne and Battie, however, expressed much deeper reservations about bleeding; Battie, *op. cit.* 94, 96; Monro, *op. cit.* 50, 52, 55, 57; Cheyne, *op. cit.* 207.

163 Battie, *op. cit.* 84–5; Monro, *op. cit.* 38, 45.

164 Battie, *op. cit.* 59, 67; compare Monro, *op. cit.* 24–5.

165 Battie's stress on divining the aetiology of madness as a starting-point for cure is a constant theme of his *Treatise*; see esp. 73, 88. This was translated into practice at St Luke's, where unlike Bethlem, standard admission forms required from the certifying practitioner an account of the 'state of the Patient's Case' and 'of the Methods (if any) used to obtain a Cure'. See the book in St Luke's, Woodside, archives, entitled, 'Considerations Upon the Usefulness', 14. For Monro's scepticism see his *Remarks*, 15, 21–3, 33–4.

166 Monro, *op. cit.* opening 'Advertisement', 21–3; Battie, *op. cit.* 21.

167 Monro, *op. cit.* 50–1.

168 Battie, *op. cit.* 75–7, 97–9; Monro, *op. cit.* 50–1.

169 Battie, *op. cit.* 41–58, 61–2; Monro, *op. cit.* 20–34, esp. 33–4. See, also, Bryan Robinson,

Observations on the Virtues and Operations of Medicines (London: J. Nourse, 1752), 145. Monro surprisingly failed to cite the work of the Bethlem Governor, Nicholas Robinson, *A Treatise of the Spleen, Vapours, and Hypochondriack Melancholy . . .* (London: A. Bettesworth, W. Innys and C. Rivington, 1729), see esp. 399–402. For Nicholas Robinson's election as a governor, see *BCGM*, 27 March 1755, fol. 175.

170 Monro, *op. cit.* 36.
171 *Ibid.* 35–6.
172 *Ibid.* 55.
173 Significantly, the proposal of the Governors to extend the Hospital by a further fifty-two cells was made by the Bethlem Grand Committee just three weeks after the 'Considerations upon the usefulness and necessity of establishing' St Luke's, which refers to the want of space at Bethlem, had been ordered to be printed by its Governors (10 Oct. 1750).
174 See *LEP*, nos. 3621, 3625 and 3650, 3–5 and 12–15 Jan., and 12–15 March 1751.
175 As early as July 1750, the press was reporting that the 'Design' for a 'new Receptacle for Madmen' was intended 'to breed up more young Physicians in the Cases of Lunacy'. See *LEP*, no. 3543, 7–10 July 1750.
176 Holmes, *op. cit.* 183.
177 *SLHCM*, e.g. 30 Jan. 1767, 12 Feb. 1773.
178 *Ibid.* 14 Sept. 1759, 7 March 1760, 27 May 1774; *SLGCM*, 6 Oct. 1764, 1 Aug. 1770, 7 Jan. 1778; *LEP*, no. 3708, 23–5 July 1751.
179 Hunter and Macalpine, 'Introduction' to their edn of Battie's *Treatise* and Monro's *Remarks*, 10.
180 Michael Donnelly, *Managing the Mind. A Study of Medical Psychology in Early Nineteenth-Century Britain* (London: Tavistock, 1983), 53–4 and 167, note 3. See also Chapter 15.
181 *SLGCM*, 22 Oct. 1777; *Morning Post*, 14 Oct. 1777; Bowen, *op. cit.* 8 (note).
182 Monro observed about one patient 'once before . . . attended by Dr. Battie to little purpose'; *Casebook*, 4–5.
183 Bowen, *op. cit.* 13.
184 Hunter and Macalpine, 'Introduction' to their edn of Battie's *Treatise* and Monro's *Remarks*, 9.
185 See Andrews, 'Incurably Insane'.
186 Cruden, *London-Citizen*, 53.

CHAPTER SEVENTEEN

THE RULE OF 'SKY-COLOUR'D COATS'

Inferior officers and servants

——— •◆• ———

INTRODUCTION

In early modern Bethlem the inferior officers and keepers were in much closer personal contact to the patient population than the Governors or medical staff. They shared the patients' environment, and were required to submit to an analogous form of confinement, residing, eating and sleeping within the Hospital walls. They caught the same diseases and were often buried in the same graveyards. It was not doctors or administrators who ruled the roost and determined the tone of patients' lives; rather, it was, in James Carkesse's words, 'th'Azure of [the] sky-colour'd Coats' of the attendants.[1] The inferior officers, servants and nurses tended to be reviled by contemporaries, however, and have been condemned or ignored by historians. Bethlem's officers and servants have received a particularly bad press, accused by contemporaries and historians alike of beating, starving, fleecing and abusing those under their care. Indeed, 'Bedlamite nurses' have generally appeared as the most notorious of all madhouse keepers.[2] Interactions between staff and patients were rather more complex than this paradigm of neglect and abuse would suggest.

RECRUITMENT AND STATUS: OFFICERS

The dismissal of Helkiah Crooke in 1633 marked a break at Bethlem, not just in the separation of the physicianship from the keepership, but in the Governors' assertion of their prerogative to choose their own staff. Crooke was the last in a line of old masters, the last royal nominee to receive custody of Bethlem as a dispensation of royal favour. The office of Keeper, making his own private profits, was dispensed with in favour of salaried Stewards and Porters. Stewards or Underkeepers under Crooke and before[3] had normally applied for reimbursement of their disbursements and accounted for their receipts directly to the Keeper/Master.[4] Prior to 1633, the appointment of the Steward and Porter had largely been left to the Master/Keeper – in 1633 Crooke, for example, had installed his own son-in-law, Thomas Bedford, as Steward, while Bedford's predecessor or predecessors appear to have been Crooke's choices, not the Governors'. The Crooke scandal led them to reject the policy of reversions, as other London hospitals were striving to do.[5] As usual, the initiative was taken first at Bridewell, where reversions were abolished in 1632.[6] In practice, however, this ruling was instituted for Bethlem officers as well. All appointed to inferior offices at Bethlem from 1636 (with one exception) were subjected to free elections before the Court of Governors.[7]

The Stewardship was ranked alongside the post of Bridewell Clerk. Its holders hoped it would prove lucrative, but four of the six who served Bethlem between 1636 and 1690 were to die in debt to the Hospital, although this had less to do with the hazards of the office than with the profligacy of its occupants.[8] The size of the security required from them was a recognition of the need for hefty insurance against the large sums of money passing through the Steward's hands. From 1690, as a result of the improvidence and dishonesty of the Stewards, the security for the office was augmented to the huge sum of £500.[9]

The Bethlem Stewardship was hotly contested,[10] and the desirability of the post is demonstrated by the numbers and standing of those applying for it. For the eight elections between 1635 and 1700, there was an average of almost six petitioners for each vacancy, although falling to fewer than four as election procedure tightened during the subsequent seventy years.[11] The only condition was that candidates be freemen (i.e. citizens) of London.[12] The vast majority of successful applicants came from London's retail cloth trade. Richard Langley and Thomas Hodges were both drapers; George Foye, a merchant taylor; Matthew Benson, a broderer (embroiderer); Thomas Yates, a haberdasher, and William Godbed, a weaver.[13]

Elections were held by a ballot of assembled governors. Family interest played a part, but pure nepotism is rarely in evidence. Although the sons of Bethlem's inferior officers were occasionally candidates to succeed their fathers (and might work as assistants),[14] there is only one instance of direct nepotism.[15] Richard Langley, 'the dishonest Steward'[16] and the most troublesome occupant of the office throughout the Hospital's history, owed his election in 1636 partly to his father's social standing.[17] Indeed, Langley's Stewardship highlights the negative influence of interest. The Governors were encouraged to retain Langley, in the face of his misdemeanours and embezzling, out of anxiety that his father would be 'utterly disgraced and undone' if they fired him.[18]

Inferior offices seem to have been filled, not just at Bethlem but at most London hospitals, more on the basis of favour than merit, and to have been enjoyed virtually as tenureships.[19] An officer was customarily appointed conditionally, 'soe long as he demeaneth himselfe well', yet this proviso was rarely exacting. Only one of Bethlem's Stewards and Porters between 1633 and 1800 was discharged for misdemeanours.[20] Applicants for the Stewardship were not infrequently decayed citizens, who had either fallen on hard times through misfortunes of trade or were simply too old to continue their former occupations. Both Stewards and Porters normally died in office, assuming office late in life.[21]

In the eighteenth century there are signs that Bethlem Stewards were being drawn from a somewhat better class than their predecessors and that elections were increasingly closed affairs. Both William Birch, Steward 1734–48, and Thomas Hodges, who succeeded him (1748–65), were Common Councilmen for the ward of Farringdon Within.[22] In the fractious political atmosphere of the 1730s and 1740s, hospital elections had also become rather more politicized. Farringdon was a notorious Tory stronghold, and so a likely source of supply of staff for Bridewell/Bethlem (and St Bartholomew's). Election of both superior and inferior officers could raise considerable passions and dissensions in the ranks of the voting Governors. Several Governors refused to accept the result in the 1734 election, demanding that a poll be conducted before Birch was confirmed as victor.[23] By mid-century, candidates for offices at Bethlem and other London hospitals were placing adverts in the press lobbying support. Both Hodges and Cooke published adverts in 1748, detailing their credentials and integrity, although neither would have applied for the post but for the collapse of their businesses.[24] By this time, nevertheless, the office came with considerable benefits, the Steward enjoying a generous Hospital house comprising ten rooms, furniture worth over £130 and a shed for his horse and chaise, and permission to deploy three servants to assist him.[25]

Porters were recruited from rather more modest backgrounds. Nine of the fourteen men obtaining the portership between 1633 and 1777 were promoted from inferior posts at either Bethlem or Bridewell. One had formerly been a barber; seven had been basketmen; two had been Bridewell beadles, and one had been a Bridewell Artsmaster, in charge of the sieve-makers.[26] Promotional appointments had the advantage that appointees were often already familiar with the Hospital, but it discouraged competitive elections and fostered collusive relations between porters and servants.

During the seventeenth century, appointments were hotly contested. For at least five of the six elections between 1633 and 1700 there was an average of between three and four candidates, while only three of those elected were promoted from inferior positions in the Hospitals.[27] For the seven elections between 1700 and 1774, when promotion was almost invariably the rule, there was an average of only two candidates for each election.[28]

Despite the (seeming) greater competitiveness of seventeenth-century elections, Porters appear to have been drawn from lowlier ranks than later. That in the latter eighteenth century three of those elected as Porter (Richard Wright, William Dodd and William Nixon) were Governors suggests a rise in the office's status.[29] All these had formerly been basketmen, however, and were far from members of the governing elite. Yet a significant rise in both their status and prosperity is also argued by the fact that seventeenth-century officers' wills detail bequests of pounds and shillings, while later stewards and porters were disposing of hundreds, or thousands, of pounds.[30]

Matrons were invariably, until 1752 (and except for a brief period between 1663 and 1664, when the Governors experimented by seeking to appoint 'a discreete careful & single woemen' from outside the Hospital), the wives of the Bethlem Porter. This arrangement suited the Court because it was both cheap (the Matron was unsalaried until 1694, apart from the 1663–4 spell) and convenient. On the other hand, it limited the extent of disciplinary proceedings against the Porter and Matron. Matrons generally survived their husbands, and were replaced by the incoming Porter's wife.[31]

The death of Rachel Wood in 1752 brought the line of Matrons-cum-Porters'-wives at Bethlem to an end. Two of the next three Matrons were the wives of the

Steward, elected like male officers on their own petitions but without opposition. The other appointee was the Nurse, Mary Spencer, whose succession when the offices of Matron and Nurse were amalgamated in 1765 marked another attempt by the Court to economize.[32] Following her death in 1793, a special committee of Governors, prompted by recognition of the Matron's 'highly important and necessary' role, laid down, for the first time, detailed qualifications for the post. Returning to its seventeenth-century commitment to an unmarried Matron, the Court specified that the Matron should be between 32 and 40 years of age; 'of a good moral Character'; 'Strong Active and healthy'; and able to 'bear confinement and . . . not subject to lowness of Spirits'.[33]

RECRUITMENT AND STATUS: SERVANTS

Information concerning servants is much less forthcoming. Evidence is particularly scant during the eighteenth century, when hiring and firing had devolved entirely onto the Bethlem Committee, whose minutes merely register appointments. Servants' recruitment was a very casual affair. Before the 1630s, the Keeper seems to have been given more or less a free hand to provide the servants he deemed necessary.[34] Subsequently, the Steward, Porter and Matron (and on one occasion basketmen themselves) were normally made responsible for procuring servants.[35] While the Bethlem Steward and Matron had long enjoyed sway over servant recruitment and dismissal, it was not until 1765 that the 'Hiring' and 'Discharging' of the gallery maids was established by Court order in the Matron's hand, subject to the 'Consent' of the Committee.[36]

In the seventeenth century, appointments still ordinarily received formal confirmation from the Court, and (more rarely) a vetting from the Steward or Treasurer. In theory, those presented might be deemed unfit,[37] but in practice servants were seldom appointed with any examination before 1677. This was made a condition of admittance only in the rules devised for the new Moorfields building, when the Committee was required to examine the suitability of every prospective servant.[38] There are one or two instances, in the 1650s, of basketmen being admitted 'uppon triall'.[39] It was not until 1654 that servants, as well as officers, came up for election annually before retaining their places. The court rulings of 1654 and 1677 were clearly designed to tighten up staff scrutiny. In fact, between 1675 and 1693, basketmen were appointed after an examination before the Court, rather than before the Committee – the first and only period during which there was more than one candidate for each vacancy.[40] Subsequently, until 1701, five of the eight basketmen were confirmed in their places by the Court only after a trial period.[41] But there is not a single reference in the Governors' Minutes to a servant being rejected after a probationary examination, and for much of the eighteenth century there is little evidence that probationary periods were being imposed at all upon servants. Not until 1781, a week after the discharge of a male keeper for selling the clothes of a deceased patient to another, did the Sub-Committee rule that 'no person be Appointed a Servant . . . without a Month's previous Trial'. This was extended to two months in the next year.[42]

By the latter eighteenth century there was plainly a more elaborate pecking-order amongst Bethlem staff, with assistant basketmen seeking promotion to junior, or women's, basketman, junior basketmen promotable to senior basketmen, and senior to the office of Porter, and with a similar arrangement prevailing for maids and their assistants.[43] Further insurance of proper conduct had been sought from 1677 by demanding that every new recruit procure security of £40 'for his honest and faithfull discharge of his said Service'.[44] Such conditions did little to restrain basketmen from misconduct, however, and not once do the Governors appear to have sued the securities of a discharged servant. Before 1677, the sole condition of service for menservants and maidservants was that they must not be or become married or have children.[45] The Governors were determined to avoid the situation whereby the families of deceased servants became a financial burden, while their presence was also liable to involve unavoidable distractions from servants' attendance. Yet even this narrow definition of suitability was not absolute. Francis Wood, William Jones, William Whetstone (or Whetham) and Richard Miles (or Mills) were all elected as basketmen despite being married.

Servants were also recruited on the recommendation of Governors, benefactors and others connected with the hospitals. William Whetstone was 'recommended by Ellis Crispe Esq', a very active Governor; Joseph Arnold was admitted on 'severall Governors now present Giveing this Court a good Character of the Peticioner to his fidelity'; while William Jones's appointment was endorsed by the bricklayer to the united hospitals.[46] Yet such references were by no means a reliable guarantee, and all these recommended basketmen were discharged from Bethlem as totally unfit for service.[47]

James Carkesse's comments are pertinent here. In his striking contemporaneous description of the Bethlem Porter and servants as a single Cerberus, with one head (Matthews) and 'three tails' (Jones, Langdale and Whetstone), Whetstone is the tail with 'no sting', which causes 'the Monster' to 'rail'.[48] Soon after his appointment, Whetstone had been found to be 'unfit' for service because 'aged [and] weakely', and married besides, while Jones, one of two basketmen described by Carkesse as rather brutal, was discharged after nine years' service because of sexual abuse of female patients. Despite their bias, Carkesse's poems, juxtaposing the feeble Whetstone against the 'fierce' and obsequious tails of his colleagues, which 'wag only, and on their Master fawn', offer a convincing perspective on both the qualities and the frailties of Bethlem servants, and are suggestive as to what their superior officers might require. Physical prowess, an authoritarian demeanour and obedience to superiors were evidently prized.

Very little can be gleaned from the Governors' Minutes concerning the social origins of servants recruited, although undoubtedly they were very humble, and roughly on a par with most patients and with low-ranking domestic servants outside the Hospital. What records survive of their former employments suggest that basketmen were primarily drawn from the ranks of small craftsmen and tradesmen, and ex-apprentices, and were rarely already in service let alone experienced in the care of the insane. Surviving receipts for servants' wages, signed with marks, suggest that (as with staff at St Luke's) a large number were illiterate.[49] It is likely that a better class of basketman had begun to be attracted to the Hospital by the 1760s and 1770s, when their salaries were augmented to a level thirteen times their previous rate.[50] In the

1750s and 1760s, basketmen were for the first time wealthy enough to have their wills registered.[51]

Even less may be ascertained about the recruitment and backgrounds of the maidservants; in the seventeenth century, maidservants are rarely even named.[52] Only once is there any evidence that they were appointed on recommendations or that they contested their posts with other candidates. Some were wives or relations of basketmen, and one was a former Matron.[53] Women might also be presented as maidservants to Bethlem at parish expense, in the same way that paupers were removed as burdens on the rates and provided with a livelihood by being put out to domestic service. The churchwardens of Allhallows Lombard Street paid 12s in 1764/5 to get Sarah Fitch 'admitted a Nurse in Bethlehem Hospital', and the fact that she was in receipt of parochial relief four years later seems indicative of the rather lowly origins of Bethlem's female servants.[54]

During the eighteenth century, the Governors relaxed their former preference for single servants, although evidently being stricter in this matter with female servants.[55] The espousal of staff with patients appears to have been a rare occurrence at Bethlem, but the occasional inter-marriage, alongside the more frequent marriages between staff, suggests how much the lives of staff were conditioned by their environment.[56] Furthermore, marital and other familial relations constitute a significant channel via which staff were often recruited, and may help to explain the somewhat conspiratorial way in which they often abused their service.[57]

The recruitment of the Nurse, cook or 'cook maid', laundry maids and assistant servants, seems to have been little different to that for other Bethlem servants. Elizabeth Clashby, the first Nurse appointed to Bethlem (in 1693), far from the 'trained nurse' described by Denis Leigh, was simply promoted from the position of maidservant, being regarded as 'an experienced and able person about the Lunaticks'.[58] All of Clashby's successors were recruited from outside the Hospital. While nurses were originally supposed to be single, by mid-century appointees were all married, and, after Clashby, there is no record of nurses undergoing a probationary period of service.[59]

SALARIES, PERKS AND GRATUITIES

The rather poor standards of recruitment at Bethlem, the inferior quality of nursing and the low level of staff salaries were clearly all connected with each other. With servants' wages remaining at the same meagre levels of between £2 and £5 10s for 130 years from 1635 to 1765, it is hardly surprising that much of their energy was devoted to petty profiteering and embezzling.[60] Neither is it remarkable that Bethlem's servants were drawn from the poorer classes, nor that 'Bedlamite nurses' were regarded with contempt. In 1645, the sisters of St Bartholomew's were already being paid nearly £3 more than Bethlem basketmen; sisters and nurses at Guy's in 1725 earned over six and five times the wages of Bethlem maids. Bethlem staff were paid substantially less than Bridewell's.[61] The Bethlem Matron was unsalaried for almost the entirety of the period 1635–93, sharing her husband's wages. The Porter's own wages remained unchanged for 130 years. In 1725, the Porter of Guy's was being paid more than three times as much as the Bethlem Porter, while Guy's Matron received five times as much as Bethlem's.

This disparity began to be redressed only in the 1760s and 1770s, with the curtailment of visiting, when basketmen's wages were raised to £10 per annum and maidservants' wages to £8 per annum, and four years later, to £20 and £14 per annum respectively. Likewise, the Matron's salary was, for the first time, raised above that of the Porter's (whose role as supervisor of visitors and of the Hospital doors was being steadily reduced), to £24 in 1765 and to £40 in 1769.

Clearly, the Porter and servants had been highly reliant on visitors' tips to supplement their incomes. In 1676 and 1677, servants' box takings had already reached figures in excess of £20 and £30, affording the Porter and Matron as much as an extra £11 between them; the basketmen another £5 each; and the maidservants another £3.50 each, on top of their wages. By 1750, staff portions from the servants' box must have rivalled their salaries.[62]

The inadequacy of staff wages is indicated by the frequency with which staff petitioned for, and were refused, a raise.[63] By 1735, the Porter and servants had become accustomed to bolster their wages by charging a fee of 9s, plus another 5s to the servants' box, on every patient's admission.[64] While the Governors abolished these fees, instead of increasing staff salaries out of Hospital funds, just four months later they re-imposed a more specific charge of 10s to the servants' box for parochial admissions. In the face of predictable evasion 'by the parish Officers', however, the fee was soon converted into a universal 'contribution' from patients' friends, at the admitting Committee's discretion, but 'not exceeding 10s'.[65] Moreover, judging from the Governors' calculations of the numbers of patients admitted between 1752 and 1758, the Porter, Matron and servants could make almost £100 per annum between them, simply from patients' admission.[66]

The best comparison for salaries at Bethlem is St Luke's. Established as a reforming rival, St Luke's also, initially at least, offered superior wages. Staff were forbidden to accept 'any Fee, Gratuity or Reward' from anyone dealing with, or entering, the Hospital, on pain of dismissal.[67] Not until the 1760s were servants' salaries at Bethlem brought into line and their perks and gratuities abolished (except for the money they received from the servants' box).[68] Subsequently, however, both servants' and assistant servants' wages at Bethlem strikingly surpassed those at St Luke's. By 1809, Thomas Dunstan, Master of St Luke's (and a former Bethlem servant), was blaming low wages for his great difficulty in obtaining 'proper persons to do the service of the house'.[69] The Bethlem Matron was consistently paid more than the Matron at St Luke's, and from 1765–90 the differential was more than double.[70] While Bethlem servants' wages remained uniformly low until the 1760s, the Bethlem Steward was comparatively rather well paid. With a salary of £50, bolstered from 1653–68 by a gratuity of £10, the Stewardship was a considerable prize. Besides his salary, he also seems to have been expected to make 'reasonable profit' from the friends of patients he furnished with clothing and bedding.[71]

Salaries, perks and gratuities were not the only rewards of service for Bethlem staff. As at other London hospitals, employment also entailed lodging quarters, furniture, meals, clothing, bedding, (occasionally) coals and even medical treatment, provided at the Charity's expense. The Steward and Porter were furnished with their own houses, adjoining each other in the Hospital.[72] In addition to the standard outfit of clothing, the Porter's blue coat of office was also renewed, and the basketmen provided with coats, and occasionally breeches, every Easter.[73] One can speak of a uniform for Bethlem staff only at the Moorfields building. In 1675, basketmen's coats were made from material of 'a sad muske colour', possibly to compensate for the grubby nature of their work. From 1676, their coats were fashioned to conform with those of the Bridewell Beadles and with the grandeur of New Bethlem – in blue (the colour of charity), with silver badges depicting the Hospital arms on the sleeves. Likewise, the Porter's gown was to be lined with blue and his authority advertised to visitors and servants by providing him with 'a good large staffe' with the Hospital arms engraved on its silver tip.[74] Employees also received a generous portion of provisions and the Matron and maidservant or cook maid shared the profits of 'the kitchen Stuff'.[75] Additionally, staff supplemented their income by performing extra duties about the Hospital, or even by outside employment. For a brief period in the early seventeenth century, basketmen were rewarded with a few extra shillings for warning Hospital tenants to pay their rents, while it was expected that the Bethlem Steward would 'attend . . . other business or Employment'.[76] In the 1680s the Porter, Matron, and a basketman were running victualling-houses at the same time as serving at the Hospital, meaning grievous neglect of their duties. The Matron, in particular, had been 'constantly attending' at the Bull Alehouse, nearby old Bethlem.[77] Given that the property was in the Hospital's possession, it is surprising that the Porter had ever been permitted to enjoy the lease.[78]

NUMBERS

So long as Bethlem remained on its Bishopsgate site, rarely holding more than fifty patients, staffing was, in numerical terms, quite adequate. With resiting at Moorfields, however, with the addition of one hundred cells for male and female incurables (1725–35), and with the less spectacular extension during the 1750s, the attendants–patients ratio deteriorated to less than half, and latterly, less than one-fifth, of its previous level, when at other hospitals it was improving. The Court was lax in recognizing the worsening situation. Rather than supplementing staffing, seven years after the construction of a new wing of twenty cells in 1644 the Governors actually contemplated reducing staff by amalgamating the offices of Steward and Porter in 'one man'.[79] More remarkably, in 1681, five years after the Hospital's capacity had been more than doubled, the Court resolved to restrict the number of basketmen to two.[80] The Governors ultimately decided against both these motions, acknowledging not only 'the greate number of Lunatikes in the . . . hospitall' but also 'the great quantity of . . . dayly [visitors]'.[81] Moreover, as a clear response to the enlargement of Bethlem in 1675/6, and the need for a division of the sexes in the new building, an additional maidservant was appointed in 1677 and in 1681.[82] In 1693, a 'nurse' was also recruited.[83]

Even three new resident members of staff might be regarded as insufficient to cope with so substantial an increase in capacity. And the Governors' failure to appreciate the mounting demands upon their staff after 1728, when the patient population was doubled again and public visiting peaked, is also striking. The one hundred incurables were catered for without the addition of a single member of staff. Even when twenty more cells were installed from 1751–3, and the Governors considered employing a number of extra servants and a 'proper person to Attend at the Iron-gates of the Womens Ward' to ensure segregation, it was decided to persist with the same staff quota, relying on a basketman stationed 'on the Womans side' to prevent mingling.[84]

Servants relied increasingly on patient-workers to supply the deficiency of their numbers, an arrangement (as Urbane Metcalf's account of life at Bethlem around 1800 indicates) fraught with problems of favouritism, frictions, exploitation and inefficiency.[85] Only in 1769, for instance, did the Governors recognize that the use of patients to serve meals had caused 'great inconvenience', agreeing to add another two assistant basketmen to the staff to take this duty out of patients' hands.[86]

DUTIES

The 'medical' duties of staff are sketched in other chapters, so the following will be mostly confined to their more 'domestic' responsibilities. The Steward's duties were laid down in detail in the 1635 set of nine articles.[87] Crooke had refused to concede accountability to the Governors, and this was the issue most prominent in the articles. The new Steward was primarily responsible for receipts and payments for the Hospital, comprising legacies and donations, charges towards patients' maintenance, provisions, clothing, bedding and other necessaries. He was required to keep a daily account of all such receipts and disbursements and to submit his account for weekly scrutiny at the Bridewell Court Sessions. In addition, he was responsible for ensuring an adequate supply of provisions. He was supposed to check the pantry and buttery each morning and to examine the patients' clothing, either supplying the lack or notifying patients' sureties so to do. The Governors instructed him from which tradesmen provisions should be bought. Echoing articles undertaken by Crooke, while also in reaction to Crooke's abuse of them, the new Steward's articles forbade him any claim to the Hospital's income.[88]

As part of his responsibility for patients' fees, he was also required to write letters to patients' sureties demanding payment, or notifying them of patients' deaths, recovery or material needs, and was obliged to visit sureties direct.[89] With the Porter, he was also supposed to oversee the servants, a role consolidated in 1699 when he was formally appointed as 'Supervisor' of the inferior staff.[90] After 1732, when the bulk of provisions were delivered on a contractual basis, the Steward was required to check the quantity and quality of all such provision. He was in sole charge of the admission registers and of entering all patient details. With the multiplication of patients, and of the types of admission record required to be kept, this and other of the Steward's duties became increasingly onerous.

Not until 1765, when the duties of staff were radically extended following a Grand Committee report, did therapeutic considerations and patients' comfort assume an explicit part in the Steward's responsibilities.[91] Henceforth, his duties were to include thrice-weekly checking that galleries and cells were 'kept clean and neat'; that naked or 'physicked' patients were 'kept properly Confined' and their cells ventilated, and that their cell windows were kept light and free from obstructions. He was also placed more in control of the patients' clothing. He was to ensure that the coals were sufficient, and to notify the Committee of any repairs needed. Most of the other duties stipulated in the 1765 list concern the Steward's management of provisions, including counting 'the pieces of meat before they are put into the Pot'.

A good deal of the Steward's duties were performed in collaboration with the Porter, and relied on affable relations. The Porter too was required to keep an account of moneys given, and provisions delivered, at the Hospital door.[92] With the Steward, he was responsible for the Hospital provisions. He was supposed to help with the apportioning of food and, from 1677, was placed in sole charge of the buttery key.[93] The Porter's primary function, of course, was to attend the Hospital doors, and to account for whatever entered or left the Hospital – visitors, staff, patients and provisions. Yet his duties were much more varied than this. Very occasionally, he might be instructed to deliver patients to their friends, or to perform other duties increasingly reserved to the Steward and servants.[94]

The Matron's role was initially extremely limited, and entailed little more than that of a superior domestic servant, supervising a single maidservant in laundering and cooking, and the care of female patients. Both she and the Porter were also to assist (alongside the servants) with the bathing and bleeding, respectively, of female and male patients. The Matron's function became explicitly segregative only after 1663. With the addition of another two maids after 1677, however, her supervisory station was substantially augmented.

From 1765, the Matron was granted a supervisory role over the female wards, virtually equivalent to that exercised by the Steward over males. She was henceforth to make daily inspections to ensure that women patients were 'regularly Shifted and Sheeted'; to keep accounts of patients' linen and to check every Wednesday that it was properly washed, and to take care that patients were kept clean and their 'Straw . . . changed when Damp or Dirty'. She was to ensure that the stove-room fire was punctually lit and the designated patients removed there in good time; that the 'low Spirited and Mopish be Obliged to get up', ejected and locked out of their cells; that the 'Lewdly given be Confined' and allowed visitors solely under chaperonage by a maidservant; and that the sick were properly cared for and removed to the infirmary if necessary; and she was to acquaint the Physician whenever any patient took to their bed 'without particular Sickness'. Finally, she was to ensure that patients who were 'Capable' were employed rather than 'Idle'.[95]

Menservants and maidservants, along with assisting patients, were the dogsbodies of the workforce. Their manifold duties included 'dressing' (i.e. cooking), 'cutting out' (i.e. dividing into bowls) and serving patients' meals; cleaning the Hospital and patients' bodies, cells and clothing; conducting visitors; 'shifting' (i.e. dressing) patients; restraining unruly patients and quelling disorders when they arose; assisting in barbering, bleeding and bathing; administering physic; fetching provisions; delivering patients to their sureties, and taking various other messages as instructed by the Committee, Treasurer, Clerk or Steward. Basketmen alone were asked to deliver

Hospital correspondence and attend on Committees, while maidservants were also excluded from the actual apportioning of food and drink.

Maids were more widely employed in domestic chores. They were required to clean the Committee Rooms and other areas in the centre of the house, and to perform laundry work. The shifting of (incapable) female patients, however, seems to have been relieved from the maids, following the appointment of a Nurse.[96] By 1736, basketmen took turns in being in charge of the beer and its distribution from the Hospital cellar. In 1765, these duties were entrusted to the newly created office of assistant basketman, who was also given charge of the Hospital's coals.[97]

Governors and medical staff were, of course, very much reliant on the testimony of inferior officers and servants for information about the condition of patients and the physical state of the Hospital. Lay staff frequently testified to the recovery or continued insanity of their charges, and their opinions were not uninfluential. As the Governors' management of affairs became increasingly more direct, and as the advice of medical staff exerted an increasing sway on patients' lives, the consultative role of inferior attendants was also augmented and formalized. By 1736, the Porter was required 'to attend and assist the Doctor Mondays and Wednesdays to give him an Account of the Men Patients', just as the Nurse was obliged to inform the Physician of the condition of the sick.[98]

RESIDENCE AND ABSENTEEISM

Between 1635 and 1677, Bethlem was attended by a lay staff of seven, comprising a Steward, Porter, Matron, three basketmen and a single maidservant. All were normally required to be resident and were provided with accommodation within the Hospital. At the Bishopsgate building, the houses of the Steward and Porter were located adjacent to each other, at the entrance of the Hospital, the proximity of which was to arouse much friction between the two during the 1630s.[99] Servants lodged in garrets situated above stairs, over the building's second and top storey.[100] In the planning of the Moorfields building, the City surveyor, Robert Hooke, was carefully instructed by the Governors to make servants' rooms 'convenient' for preventing

> Dainger that may happen among the lunatikes themselves when they are permitted to walke the yards there in the day tyme and alsoe that they be ready to prevent or suppresse any miscarriage that may happen by the said Lunatikes in the night tyme.[101]

Security and quelling disorder were the priorities here.

In the Steward's case, residence was something of a novel stipulation, arising out of a growing awareness of the necessity for constant attendance.[102] Ordinarily, the Governors permitted staff to reside outside the Hospital only in exceptional cases. Richard Langley was ordered 'to settle himselfe in Bethlem house' immediately on his election, but George Foye, his successor, was allowed to continue in his own house because it was 'neere unto the hospitall', and the Steward's house was in need of repair.[103] Residence somewhat contradicted the practical demands of the Steward's service, since he was frequently ordered to attend sureties direct to obtain arrears for patients, or secure patients' removal from the Hospital; to appear before other courts concerning charges for patients, and to enquire about town for details of patients' settlements.[104] The Steward's absences posed real problems, however, since servants' misdemeanours must have gone undetected while he was outside on business.[105]

Obvious instances of absenteeism were more conspicuous amongst the Porter, Matron and servants, who had fewer pretexts to be abroad. Amongst the duties of Bethlem basketmen, solely those of delivering letters, fetching and carrying provisions and warning tenants would involve them leaving the house. The Governors, in fact, did all they could to restrict servants to their responsibilities within the Hospital, insisting that 'their personal Attendance is required both day and night'.[106] Staff frequently had other ideas, and the Governors strove doggedly to rectify the absenteeism and neglect of servants fond of tippling in taverns.

Before mid-century, nothing beyond a severe warning seems to have been done to prevent staff going AWOL. In 1652, on pain of summary dismissal, officers and servants were forbidden to depart from Bethlem after 7 p.m. during Autumn/Winter, or after 9 p.m. during Spring/Summer, unless on business.[107] Yet within five years this rule was already being flouted by the maidservant, Elizabeth Withers, the Porter being directed not to 'suffer [her] ... to goe abroad unlesse upon necessary iust occacion'.[108]

Judging by the Court and Committee Minutes, absenteeism was rarely discovered during the eighteenth century, but much went on. According to Metcalf, the 'supineness' of the medical staff, and 'the weakness of the steward' allowed keepers a free rein to neglect their service.[109] One keeper (Rodbird), he alleged, was a lazy, negligent absentee, present in his gallery for only three hours a day; another (Blackburn) observed his place 'almost [as] a sinecure', spending more time over 'the care of his birds and ... cage making', than in the Hospital. Male servants played cards for hours at a time, while bribing patients to act as lookouts for the approach of Officers, whereas the Matron and maidservants devoted time to a private patient at the expense of their duties.

GENERAL RECORD OF SERVICE AND CONDUCT

There is much in the Governors' Minutes to confirm the traditional account of low standards of nursing, and of exploitative and neglectful servants. The same abuses occurred again and again, despite repeated orders and exhortations. The misappropriation of funds, misuse of provisions and negligence of sixteenth-century masters/keepers and their deputies finds a more explicit reflection in later complaints against stewards, porters, matrons, basketmen and maidservants. Under the governorship of Bridewell, Bethlem suffered a lack of thorough supervision, the product of an unwieldy administration with too many commitments and too little time, which too often left staff to their own devices. The Court Books testify that most of the Governors' business was taken up with affairs at Bridewell or with tenants. The Governors were often lenient with misconduct. For example, 'the dishonest Steward', Richard Langley, was repeatedly rebuked and twice suspended during his eight years of office for persistent forgery of his accounts, embezzlement, drunkenness and obstreperousness.

One must be careful, however, not to exaggerate the grimness of the reality. Members of staff were occasionally long-serving and rewarded for good service. With the institution of a weekly Committee for Bethlem at the end of the seventeenth century, and of a Grand Committee dealing with the affairs of both Hospitals, the disciplining of staff was settled with more alacrity outside the Court forum, although the dramatic growth of the Hospital from the 1670s still allowed staff plenty of scope for abuse.

Basketmen were found guilty of misdemeanours and discharged with especial regularity throughout the period. Between 1633 and 1700 over one-third (fifteen) of the forty-three mentioned in hospital records were discharged from their posts (although in fourteen cases the outcome of service is unknown). Less than a quarter (ten) are recorded to have died in office, only one is said to have resigned and four to have been promoted. Their poor quality of service is partially reflected in their average length of service, the mean being about five and a half years, and over half serving for less than three years. Only slight improvement is discernible in the eighteenth century, when basketmen's average length of service between 1700 and 1777 increases to over six years, over one-third serving for under three years. Only one-fifth (seven) have been identified who were dismissed, while one-seventh (five) were promoted, and deaths and resignations accounted for two-ninths (eight), although the fates of nearly half (sixteen) are unknown. While there is less information available concerning maidservants' service, the general impression is that female staff behaved better and served longer. Indeed, amongst five appointees during 1756–60 the average length of service was eleven years, while both laundry women appointed in 1777 enjoyed their posts for over fourteen years and were rewarded for satisfactory conduct. Amongst the officers, their records of service are (at face value) rather more impressive. Of five nurses and fifteen Matrons employed at Bethlem between 1633 and 1798 only two of the latter received their marching orders from the Governors, and their average length of service was at least sixteen years. Similarly, amongst fourteen Porters and sixteen Stewards, only one Porter was sacked by the Court, and only two Stewards failed (due to sickness and temporary appointment) to serve until their deaths. Despite these apparently rather favourable figures concerning staff employment, a great deal of muddy water lay under the surface, staff tending to avail themselves of considerable leeway for abuses.

KEEPING ORDER: MANAGING AND ABUSING PATIENTS

How true, then, is the standard image of Bethlem staff as cruel and brutish tormentors, tyrannizing patients, enforcing their authority with the whip at the slightest provocation?[110] The literary evidence is certainly overwhelming. From Middleton and Rowley's keeper, Lollio, whose management of the insane was relied on by the 'poison' of the whip and the maxim 'Abuse 'em . . . and then you use 'em kindly', to

Swift's *Legion Club* keeper, with his 'Scorpion rods', Bethlem attendants are portrayed as sadistic circus-tamers, who regarded and treated patients as animals.[111]

It must be remembered that the efficacy of beating the mad had remained medical orthodoxy since Antiquity, and harsh treatment was advocated as salutary in some of the most influential medical treatises. For Thomas Willis, writing in 1672, curing the mad 'requires threatnings, bonds, or strokes' and keeping them 'in awe'; over a century later, William Cullen espoused the same principles of fear and punishment, regarding it as generally 'necessary . . . to inspire them [maniacs] with the awe and dread of those who are to be constantly near them . . . even by stripes and blows'.[112]

Yet beating, whipping and otherwise abusing the insane were far less widespread or orthodox at early modern Bethlem than some historians have assumed. While many a Poor Tom was 'whipped from tithing to tithing, and stock-punished and imprisoned',[113] as the harsh Vagrancy Acts of the sixteenth century commanded, whipping the mad and sick was declining by 1650.[114] Even before vagrant lunatics were exempted from whipping by the 1714 Act,[115] a cursory examination of the Court of Governors' Minutes, or correlation of surviving parochial pass warrants, constables' books and parish officers' accounts reveals that most mad/sick vagrants were already being excused from the customary whipping, and even relieved with a few pence, on account of their afflicted state.[116]

Contemporaneously with the decline and eventual abolition of statutory flogging of mad vagrants, medical practitioners too were displaying disenchantment with punitive measures.[117] Richard Mead dismissed 'torments and stripes' 'or other rough treatment' as 'not necessary . . . to bring them into order', 'even [for] the most frantic and mischievous'.[118] Richard Hale, Bethlem Physician (1708–28) and a friend of Mead's, gained something of a reputation for his gentle methods in treating patients.[119] By 1758, John Monro, Bethlem Physician (1751–92), could confidently declare theories concerning the salutary effects of 'beating' to be 'deservedly exploded . . . as unnecessary, cruel, and pernicious', disputing William Battie's assertion of the utility of 'bodily pain' and 'fear' in the treatment of the insane.[120]

Long before, neither the beating nor the whipping of the mad was countenanced, let alone advocated, by Bethlem's Governors. In fact, there is barely a scrap of evidence, beyond literary testimony, that whips were employed at the Hospital.[121] Lunacy was generally regarded by the Governors as an exculpation for crimes and misdemeanours. When bothersome individuals like Marie Williams were brought before courts at Bridewell or elsewhere and were found 'somewhat distracted', they were standardly either 'delivered' or confined, and 'the cause' dismissed as 'not deserving punishment'.[122] Bethlem's Governors saw punishment as counterproductive when dealing with 'distempered brayne[s]'. It would rather 'be an occasion to put him [a frenzied man] quite out of his witts'.[123]

As early as 1646, Bethlem officers and servants were forbidden either to 'give any blowes . . . to the Madd folkes', or even to use 'any . . . ill language' towards them, upon pain of dismissal.[124] Thirty years later, it was ordained as one of the standing rules for staff at the new Moorfields building 'that none of the Officers or Servants shall att any time beate or abuse any of the Lunatickes . . . neither shall offer any force unto them'.[125]

The effect of the latter order was somewhat mitigated by the qualifying clause: 'but uppon absolute necessity for the better Government of the said hospitall Lunatikes', underlining that in some cases, at least, 'force' was fully countenanced. Nevertheless, the pronouncements of the Bethlem Governors are emphatically at variance with the traditional view of Bethlem tortures. The Governors' ideals, on the other hand, were often at odds with the inclinations of staff to observe them, and the necessity for such rulings itself meant that staff needed telling. The Steward, Richard Langley and his wife had certainly 'used yll words to the [patient] Lady [Eleanor Davies]', the notorious prophetess. Her billeting in their house during the late 1630s was, understandably, greatly resented by the obstreperous couple, so much so that they claimed, in an ultimately successful attempt to persuade the Governors to remove her, she had 'used all the meanes she could to escape'.[126]

Outsiders patently believed that flogging was normal at Bethlem. Parliament sent the blasphemer, John Taylor, to Bethlem with the instruction that he be confined on 'bread and water and such due bodily Correcon as may conduce to his Recovery', but the Bethlem Court did not sanction such treatment. Indeed, on the Physician finding Taylor sane, he was directed to inform the Clerk of Parliament not only of the patient's 'Disposition', but 'that there is noe punishment for any kept in Bethlem'.[127] In 1720, more than a decade before Swift deployed Bedlam imagery to appeal for the 'daily' lashing of 'mad' Irish politicians, Strype was pronouncing, on the authority of Edward Tyson, that 'there is nothing of violence suffered to be offered to any of the Patients, but they are treated with all the Care and Tenderness imaginable'.[128]

There is remarkably little evidence in the Governors' Minutes that staff were ever found guilty of physically assaulting patients. The only recorded autopsy conducted on a patient who died in suspicious circumstances concluded that she had died of 'naturall' causes.[129] Although the Bethlem Porter Humphrey Withers was accused by a Katherine Goodfellow of 'abuses . . . done to [the patient] Bridget Martyn' in 1647, he was exonerated by the Court, after 'inquiring of the Servants of the house', and Goodfellow dismissed as 'a woeman crazed in her braine & neither knowing nor careing what shee saith of any one', although this episode may simply reflect how difficult it was to make such accusations stick.[130]

The few surviving testimonies of patients themselves, supported by literary depictions, suggest that a rhetorical veil covers a welter of sins. Both James Carkesse and Urbane Metcalf speak of beatings and of the callous nature of staff conduct.[131] Metcalf recounts gruesome experiences of cruelties practised for years by staff upon patients without detection, alleging that the Porter and every male keeper indulged in beating and tormenting, or got other patients to 'bully' for them; and that the officers were anyway too weak, supine or cruel to put a stop to this treatment. What lends credence to Metcalf's testimony is his admission that he was personally 'treated with great civility'. Carkesse likewise spoke of the 'keepers blows' and 'Tyranny' he endured at Bethlem.[132] However, Metcalf's view of staff/patient relations (dating from 1818) cannot be taken as an accurate reflection of the situation at Bethlem before 1800, let alone before 1770 once the public was virtually excluded, while Carkesse's account may well have been exaggerated and prejudiced by disaffection. It was certainly coloured by his hostility to the very fact of being treated as if he was insane – in particular, being threatened, chained, kept in darkness and having physic poured or forced down his throat by staff. Furthermore, to maintain that Bethlem had a peculiar pre-minence as a site of cruelty towards the mad would tend to ignore the standard nature of such treatment in early modern institutions and to disregard the host of similar allegations foisted on private madhouses (where patients' treatment was subject in a much more limited way to public scrutiny) and on other public asylums.

The primary duties of servants were keeping order amongst, and restraining and administering physic to, patients. Inevitably, they encountered resistance and used some degree of coercion.[133] Staff were encouraged to think of their role at Bethlem as one of both ruling and caring for the insane.[134] While the Governors, through their spokesman, Thomas Bowen, the Bridewell Chaplain, were still striving in 1783 to contradict the 'most injurious notion' that Bethlem patients 'are beaten, and . . . ill treated', exceptions were still made 'in cases of self-defence' and the Governors could do little, otherwise, than 'strictly enjoin' their staff to the contrary.[135] Likewise, despite emphasizing the need for 'the greatest tenderness and affection' in managing the insane and declaring that attendants should never 'be suffered to behave otherwise', John Monro was rather pessimistic that it was really 'possible to prevent' ill treatment by staff.[136]

Often the Governors' Minutes are simply not explicit about the nature of staff misconduct once discovered. What is one to make, for example, of the discharge of the basketman, Anthony Dadsworth, in 1652, for unspecified 'abusive carriages and misbehaviour', just a year and a half after the Porter and servants had been admonished for alehouse tippling, embezzlement and absenteeism?[137] Or what of the discharge of the basketman, Roland Woolly in 1675 as 'a person of evill fame and of a dishonest Conversacon', the very year after he had been 'wounded by a Lunaticke' so as to require medicine and surgery?[138] Plainly, violence occurred and might proceed from both directions. When the Steward, Richard Langley, and his wife had committed 'abuses in words blowes assaults & fowle carriages' against the Porter, Humphrey Withers, how much worse may they have treated the patients?[139]

Staff were certainly found guilty of sexually abusing patients. In the 1680s, the basketmen Edward Langden/Langdale and William Jones were both discharged for this offence, the former for having made a patient pregnant and the latter for his complicity in the same (or another patient's) abuse.[140] While the Porter was pointedly reprimanded for his own and his wife's (the Matron) negligence in this affair, and informed in 1681 'that this Courte is very sencible of the greate miscarriages lately committed in . . . Bethlem', in fact the Governors were at that time aware of the abuses of only 'one of the . . . basketmen' and this was all rather late in the day.[141] The Governors were rather slow in ensuring that segregation of female patients, both from staff and visitors, was strictly maintained at the Hospital, and the need to repeat the order implied the suspicion of abuse. If, however, the abuse of patients by Bethlem staff was much more common than the Governors were aware, or were apt to recognize, it was also rarer than the popular image of the Hospital has suggested.

PROVISIONS AND PECULATION: EMBEZZLEMENT, EXTORTION AND DRUNKENNESS

Much more prevalent and easier to detect than the physical abuse of patients were embezzlement and inebriation. Amongst 'divers abuses lately complayned of against them' in 1651, the servants and Porter (the previously exonerated Withers) were found guilty of 'curring provisions to Alehouses & abiding there to tiple & disorder themselves & neglect their service & [of] staying out late in the evening'.[142] The Steward's 1635 articles demonstrate that this was far from the first time that provisions had been diverted by staff, an abuse continuing to figure in the standing orders and rulings of the Governors.[143] During the 1630s, the Steward, Richard Langley, and his wife, were also found guilty of carousing, of frequently returning 'home both together very farre gone in drinke and that at 11 and 12 of Clocke at night';[144] while, throughout the 1630s and 1640s, Langley was persistently stealing provisions and falsifying his accounts. Obviously, such conduct also had grave implications concerning neglect and ill-treatment of patients. The Langleys were not only 'very unquiet uncivell and ungoverned people' ('especiall[y] . . . Mrs Langley'), but also 'very much disturbe the Lady Davies who is prisoner in their house and all their neighbours neare adioyning'.[145] The Steward, Porter and their wives were admonished again in 1641 for 'being drunke' and foul-mouthed towards each other, while basketmen received repeated admonishments concerning drunken and disorderly behaviour in the 1640s, 1650s and 1660s.[146] This endemic problem was not helped by the Governors' lenience in disciplining offenders. Abuses tended to be dealt with first and foremost as a matter of moral and social disobedience and disloyalty to the governing patriarchy itself – often forgivable on special pleading to governor-patrons and if sufficient deference, regret and promise of amendment were shown – rather than as infringements of patients' entitlements or threats to patients' health. John Batt's dismissal in 1654 'for his drunkenness' was, however, immediate and unceremonious, occurring just over a month after his admission.[147]

The unique and drastic measure proposed in 1657 for correcting the conduct of Elizabeth Withers, the maidservant and widowed former matron (and possibly, during 1655 and 1662, a patient herself), may also be explained by her propensity towards alehouses.[148] She had not only been gadding about town with no legitimate pretext and returning late, but had not been behaving 'herselfe in [an] orderly manner'. Upon any future disorderliness, the Porter was instructed to 'locke her upp in one of the roomes appointed for Lunatique persons there'. If 'the widow Withers' had, indeed, been a patient, the remedy prescribed is more comprehensible. Whether Mrs Withers was merely drunk, insane or half-sane, this recourse was clearly designed to shock her back into her senses. It may also be that two basketmen dismissed at the same Court for 'being rude and disorderly persons' had accompanied her on her jaunts.[149] It was servants' conduct respecting visitors, however, which particularly concerned the Court. Drunkenness and related abuses as reasons for disciplining staff virtually disappear from the Governors' Minutes from the late seventeenth century, but this has more to do with the delegation of Court business onto Committees of Governors and the hiatuses of the Committee Minutes than with any radical improvement. Indeed, the intake and conveyance of alcohol continued as an occasional feature in complaints to the Governors and their own rulings well into the next century.[150]

Misappropriation of provisions was an even more prevalent feature of Hospital life. In the 1630s and 1640s inferior officers were convicted of widespread abuses. The delivery of produce from the City markets and elsewhere to Bethlem was a prime target for theft.[151] The Withers (the Porter and his wife) were accused by the Langleys (the Steward and Matron) of extorting money from patients for bread and of selling 'the house Sewett' to a chandler, and were found 'faultie' by the Court, while Langley was himself recurrently convicted by the Court of embezzling Hospital food and funds.[152] Langley not only falsified every one of his provision bills for the Michaelmas quarter in 1637/8 but sought to mitigate his guilt by admitting to having stolen only the occasional 'marrowbone or a piece of Beefe'.[153] Langley's Stewardship illustrates the considerable scope for embezzlement within Bethlem's primitive system of accounting and surveillance.

Richard Langley was far from the only improvident Steward. Thomas Lewis quit Bethlem in 1648 only to end up in Ludgate prison in the Hospital's debt to the tune of £30 for provisions, plus another £40 in maintenance fees, while his three successors also perished in a state of arrears.[154] John Carter was culpable for charging 'immoderate prizes [prices] for beoffe mutton [and] ... meale'.[155] The continual plundering of the buttery provoked the Court, in 1652, to order the installation of two locks to its door and to divide custody of the two keys between the Steward and Porter, so that provisions could be removed only in the presence of them both 'or [if sick] of some trusty person or persons'.[156] The introduction of scales into the hospital to check the weight of incoming stores and the appointing of the Treasurer and Governors as weekly overseers of provisions also went a limited way towards reforming abuses, and the further requirement that receipts be presented and inspected for every bill proved a lasting and effective reform.[157] Early in the eighteenth century, the Matron and Cook were found to be gleaning the fat from patients' food and selling it as kitchen stuff, and continued to be caught abusing their privileges despite the Governors' abolition of the perk.[158] Staff were also regularly rebuked throughout the period for simple wastage of provisions.[159] Yet accounting and distribution of provisions does seem to have become more regular once subject to the oversight of the Bethlem Committee from the early eighteenth century, while the introduction in 1732 of contractual agreements with suppliers at fixed prices clearly helped in tightening up the economy and scrutiny of supplies, suppliers having formerly been apt to deliver provisions deficient in quality and quantity.[160]

Not all abused their trusts and managed hospital provisions dishonestly, however. Stewards were occasionally rewarded with gratuities for their 'care dilligence and fidelity'.[161] Henry White (Steward 1778–85) was a particularly efficient officer. The architect of considerable savings in the expense of patients' sheets, he was handsomely praised and recompensed for his services by the Court.[162] Yet abuses remained rather inveterate, and the nature of, and alterations to, the standing duties of officers and staff in 1677, 1736, 1765, 1769 and 1785 do more to suggest the endurance of wastage, pilfering, extortion and inefficiency in the management of provisions, than to inspire confidence in the effectiveness of reforms.[163] While staff were forbidden repeatedly 'to Sell or Retail any Thing whatever to any of the

Patients', a fair number were plainly running a lively trade doing just that.[164] Despite attempts at greater stringency over such practices, the Governors had to endure the embarrassment in 1777 of a member of their own ranks, Thomas Horne, having drawn whatever he desired from the buttery for about six months with the connivance of the Steward, Rashfield.[165]

CONCLUSION

Ultimately, the conclusion is inescapable that, as Metcalf put it at the beginning of the nineteenth century, while the standing or 'printed rules' of the Hospital were 'good' in 'principle', they were 'departed from' in practice by the staff.[166] His allegation, however, that 'the keepers do just as they please' is exaggerated. The ideals expressed in the rhetoric and rulings of Court and Committee meetings were, assuredly, greatly in advance of their implementation. Yet wayward staff were regularly reprimanded or dismissed, and there is considerable evidence of qualified success on the part of the Governors in bringing the staff under control. Indeed a comparison between the procedural vacuum and casual visitations of the early seventeenth century, and the procedural maze and Committee-centred *dirigisme* of the latter eighteenth century, indicates that house management had made progress in efficiency. The majority of visitors and other outsiders denounced the brutishness and corruption of Bethlem's inferior staff, and even foreign visitors, who complimented the general management of the Hospital, missed what they perceived as the kindness and humanity of the Catholic nursing sisters of continental hospitals.[167] Yet not all observers depicted 'Bedlamite nurses' so negatively. Teresia Constantia Phillips, writing in the late 1740s, represented the female keeper of her anti-heroine 'Peggy' (committed to Bethlem by her parents as a melancholic) in a much softer light, as dutiful, attentive, and instrumental in recovery.[168]

The story of recruitment and conduct at Bethlem continued, however, to underline the difficulties of finding reliable staff and of effectively overseeing their behaviour. The Governors' bark was generally worse than their bite. Ultimately, the overwhelmingly negative assessments of contemporary visitors to the Hospital are difficult to dispute. Again and again visitors castigated staff brutality, and there is little evidence to contradict the general impression that it was 'terrific' discipline rather than considerate care which epitomized treatment of patients by staff at Bethlem.

NOTES

1 James Carkesse, *Lucida Intervalla: Containing Divers Miscellaneous Poems*, ed. M. V. DePorte (Los Angeles: University of California Press, 1979; 1st edn, London: 1679), 34 and *passim*; Urbane Metcalf, *The Interior of Bethlehem Hospital* (London: By the Author, 1818). For further detail and references, see Jonathan Andrews, 'A history of Bethlem Hospital *c.* 1634–*c.* 1770', (Ph.D. dissertation, London University, 1991).

2 For this phrase, see *Mrs Clark's Case* (London: J. Roberts, 1718), cited in Jonathan Andrews, '"In her Vapours . . . [or] in her Madness"? Mrs Clerke's Case: an Early Eighteenth Century Psychiatric Controversy', *History of Psychiatry*, i, 1 (1990), 137. For nineteenth-century

asylum nursing, see e.g. L. D. Smith, 'Behind Closed Doors; Lunatic Asylum Keepers, 1800–1860', *Social History of Medicine,* i (1988), 301 28; Anne Digby, *Madness, Morality and Medicine. A Study of the York Retreat 1796–1914* (Cambridge: CUP, 1985), 140–70; M. Carpenter, 'Asylum Nursing Before 1914: A Chapter in the History of Labour', in C. Davies (ed.), *Rewriting Nursing History* (London: Croom Helm, 1980).

3 See Chapter 7, where Crooke's Stewards are discussed.

4 *BCGM,* 3 and 17 Dec. 1634, and 11 Aug. 1635, fols 20, 22 and 56*v.*

5 In 1635, the Governors required that John Jeweller junior renounce his 1629 grant of the reversion of either the Keepership of Bethlem or the Clerkship of Bridewell as a condition of his standing for election as Steward of Bethlem. When, however, he subsequently refused to find securities for his performance of the latter office he was debarred from taking it up or standing ever again for election; *ibid.* 25 Sept. 1629, 21 Oct., 4 and 8 Nov., and 28 Dec. 1635 and 20 Jan. 1636, fols 144*v*, 65–7, 69, 73 and 77–8.

6 *Ibid.* 19 Oct. 1632, fol. 299.

7 The exception was Francis Wood, elected as Porter by the Court of Aldermen during the constitutional crisis of 1687/8, although even he had, initially, been presented (with one other candidate) by the Governors themselves. See *Ibid.* 4 Feb. and 4 March 1687, fols 225 and 227.

8 The debtor Stewards were Richard Langley, Thomas Lewis, William Godbed (or Godbid) and John Carter, who held the office 1636–44, 1647–8, 1658–63 and 1663–90, respectively.

9 *BCGM,* 19 Dec. 1690, fol. 94.

10 Jeweller was so keen for the post that, despite his disqualification in 1635, he re-applied on the vacancies of 1644 and 1647. See *ibid.* 1 Feb. 1644, fol. 88.

11 Forty-five candidates in all are recorded in the Court Minutes, although ranging from as few as two to as many as fourteen.

12 Robert Sole, though calling himself a 'Gent', was disqualified from the election of 1 Feb. 1644, because he did not meet this condition; *BCGM,* fol. 88.

13 The occupations/status of failed candidates, where given or deducible, tells a similar story. Twelve worked in the retail/manufacture of clothing (two drapers, two broderers, two merchant taylors, two haberdashers, two cordwainers, a mercer and a girdler); three worked in the retail/manufacture of food (two grocers and a mercer); and so forth. See *ibid.* 9 Feb. 1644, fol. 93 and *passim.*

14 Although, in the seventeenth century, the Governors attempted to eliminate children from the Hospital, they had limited success; see *ibid.* 28 April 1643, 30 March 1677, 25 May and 15 June 1758, fols 35, 360, 284 and 286.

15 That is, Hannah Matthews, Matron 1684–7, who succeeded her mother Millicent, Matron 1663–4. Henry Carter, son of the deceased Steward, John, was a failed applicant in 1690, as was Robert Yates, son of the deceased Steward, Thomas, in 1713. See *ibid.* 19 Dec. 1690 and 19 June 1713, fols 94 and 710, and *PCC PROB* 11/532, fol. 388, where Robert is sole executor of Thomas Yates's will.

16 As he was appropriately named by E. G. O'Donoghue, *The Story of Bethlehem Hospital from its Foundation in 1247* (London: T. Fisher Unwin, 1914), 177–8.

17 *BCGM,* 28 Feb. 1638, fol. 166. This seems to have been John Langley of St Peter Cornhill, London.

18 *Ibid.*

19 For example, Nathaniel Woolfreys was 58 when elected Steward of St Bartholomew's, and served until his death twenty years later in 1748; others like John Ashton (d. 1765), Steward of Christ's for many years, held office until so aged and infirm they were forced to retire. *LEP,* nos. 3200 and 5824.

20 This was William Dodd, discharged in 1774.

21 Twelve out of thirteen Stewards (1636–1785) died in office; seven served for under ten years; for Porters, the proportion during 1633–74 was ten out of eleven, six of whom served for under ten years and five of whom lasted less than five years.

22 See *LEP,* nos. 956, 961–4, 3190, 3197–8, 3200–1, 3203–5; *Read's Weekly Journal or British Gazetteer,* nos. 461–2, and *BCGM,* 22 Jan. 1734 and 18 May 1748, fols 324–5 and 365.

23 The loser was Christopher Blackett, possibly related to Sir Walter Blackett, Tory MP for Newcastle upon Tyne from 1734 to 1777.

24 Hodges was related to Capt. Benjamin Hodges, the Bethlem Governor, and James Hodges, 'tory bookseller and Half Moon [Club] habitué'. His ad. was half a page in length and even notified the Governors of the date, time and place of the oncoming election. Cooke was related to the Governor George Cooke, moderate Tory MP for Tregony and for Middlesex. Like Cooke, Charles Cotton begged the Court's 'Vote and Interest' by advertisement for the Bridewell Stewardship in 1752, detailing how he had 'been more than Twenty Years a Governor', but lost to Robert Waite, a draper and Governor for over sixteen years. See *LEP*, nos. 956, 961–4, 3190, 3197–8, 3200–1, 3203–5 and 3817; *Read's Weekly Journal or British Gazetteer*, nos. 461–2; L. Colley, *In Defiance of Oligarchy. The Tory Party 1714–60* (Cambridge: CUP, 1982), 40, 158, 164, 173, 258, 260, 270 and 280; and *BCGM*, 22 Jan. 1734, 18 May 1748 and 8 April 1752, fols 324–5, 365 and 59–60.

25 See inventory of the household furniture of the late Henry White, dated 19 Sept. 1785, which details furniture worth £135 4s, in Box 'D', in *BRHA* and *BSCM*, 15 Dec. 1781 and 15 Sept. 1785.

26 Francis Wood had served as both basketman and beadle, and John Wood as both basketman and barber.

27 As many basketmen were failed candidates as were successful in this period. The basketman, Thomas Cooke, was a failed candidate in 1657; likewise, Edward Lloyd in 1663.

28 Only two of the seven elected as Porters, Humphrey Pooler and Benjamin Brockden, were not already in inferior posts at either Hospital.

29 All three are recorded in the Court Minutes as obliged 'to lay down his staff'. See *BCGM*, 5 Aug. 1762, 25 July 1765, 1 Aug. 1771, 7 July 1788 and 16 July 1789, fols 35, 144, 339, 302 and 343.

30 At least one seventeenth-century Porter (Hopkins) and two eighteenth-century Porters (Wood and Wright) also referred to themselves as 'Gentlemen'. Wood's enormous pecuniary bequests, totalling £2,405, with, in addition, three messuages/tenements, seem rather exceptional, however. The will of Richard Wright reveals the Porter's friendship with the well-known and very wealthy keeper of Hoxton Madhouse, Jonathan Miles, who was made joint administrator of a trust for the upbringing of Wood's youngest sons. Indeed, Wright was probably related to the notorious keeper of Bethnal Green madhouse, Matthew Wright. He seems a good example of the rather shady links established in the trade in lunacy. For references to wills, see Jonathan Andrews, 'Bedlam Revisited: A History of Bethlem Hospital, *c.* 1600–*c.* 1750' (Ph.D. thesis, University of London, 1991), 339.

31 See, e.g., the case of Gartwright Wood, *BCGM*, 25 Feb. 1709, fol. 465.

32 See *ibid.* 20 June 1765, fol. 135. Spencer replaced Diana Hodges, who was, nevertheless, permitted to retain her former salary until her death in 1784. For Diana Hodges's will see *PRO PROB* 11/1085, q.n. 596, fols 162–3.

33 *BCGM*, 31 Jan. 1793.

34 Crooke's two basketmen, Anthony Stanley and Ferdinand Catlin, were kept on at the Hospital by the Governors after Crooke's dismissal.

35 In 1641, the basketmen John Pewtris and Richard Browne were 'appoynted to get an honest paynefull man to helpe them a while' during the sickness of a third, Ferdinand Catlin. See *BCGM*, 22 September 1641 and 11 Feb. 1663, fols 350 and 36.

36 *Ibid.*, 20 June 1765, fol. 135. The Matron was from 1765 to be 'Absolute Mistress' of this responsibility.

37 The Court instructed the Treasurer in 1663 either to appoint the three servants presented by the Steward and Porter, or to provide 'such others as he shall thinke more fitt'; *ibid.* 21 Jan. 1663, fol. 31.

38 *Ibid.* 30 March 1677, fol. 357.

39 *Ibid.* (illegible) June 1656 and 27 July 1655, fols 758 and 713; cases of Andrew Sapster and Thomas Franke. Sapster's trial was to last for, at most, three weeks, the Steward being ordered to 'certify' to 'the next court of his carriage and behavior there'.

40 *Ibid.* 12 Jan. 1654, 8 Oct. 1675, 30 March 1677, 27 March and 12 April 1678, 4 July 1679, 15 April and 6 May 1681, 6 Oct. 1682 and 2 June 1693, fols 638, 182–3, 357, 16, 21, 95, 213, 220, 333 and 247.

41 These eight were Richard Mills, William Cornet, Richard Peach, Joseph Arnold, William Cartwright, Moses Ransome, Stephen Siveler and John Baker. See *ibid.* 2 June 1693, 2 March 1694, 28 June 1695, 28 Feb. 1696, 26 Feb. and 26 Nov. 1697, and 12 April and 8 Nov. 1700; fols 247, 324, 458, 29, 96, 151, 363 and 409; and Box D1, in *BRHA*, where Cartwright signed for receipt of a gratuity, 1 April 1698, the only reference found to his service during this time.

42 *BSCM*, 6 and 13 Jan. 1781 and 6 April 1782.

43 See, e.g., *BCGM*, 20 June 1765, fol. 136, where the new assistant basketman was given the right 'for his better Encouragement . . . [to] Succeed the Junior Basketman'.

44 *Ibid.* 30 March 1677, fol. 357. The next five basketmen elected, nevertheless, do not seem to have been asked for any security.

45 For example, see *ibid.* 16 May 1655, fol. 702, *re* 'the orders of that house [that] noe married man ought to bee a servant there'.

46 *Ibid.* 4 June 1679 and 26 Feb. 1697, fols 91 and 96.

47 *Ibid.* 29 March 1672, 24 May and 4 June 1679, 28 June 1695, 28 Feb. 1696 and 18 June 1697, fols 382, 88, 91, 468, 29 and 117.

48 Carkesse, *op. cit.* esp. poems entitled 'Jackstraw's Progress', 'The Founder's Intention' and 'The Mistake', 21–3, 52 and 62.

49 See 'Box D' in Bethlem archives, and C. N. French, *The Story of St Luke's Hospital* (London: Heinemann Medical Books, 1951), 20–1.

50 See 'Salaries', pp. 293–5.

51 That is, at the Prerogative Court of Canterbury, where all testators were required to be worth £40. See, e.g., wills of Thomas Wright, William Hart, Anthony Cockrum and Edward Davies; *PRO PROB* 11/820, 11/819, 11/835, and 11/903, q.ns. 24, 315, 34 and 230.

52 Only six maidservants are mentioned between 1633 and 1700, and the first of these remains entirely anonymous.

53 *BCGM*, 31 July 1657, fol. 822; *BSCM*, 24 Dec. 1791, fol. 47; *Steward's Accounts*, 1763–74; *BSB*.

54 *Ghall* MS 4051/2. 'Nurse' probably means maidservant.

55 *BSCM*, 31 Dec. 1708, fol. 10.

56 *BAR*; Hannah Hollis, of St Mary, Lambeth, in Surrey, had been admitted as a patient on 8 Oct. 1737 and was discharged on 22 April 1738, having married James Grayson, basketman, six days before. Only three marriages amongst staff are mentioned in the minutes, *c.* 1633–1777.

57 Just how nepotistic minor appointments to Bethlem were is by no means easy to substantiate. Amongst the basketmen, Nathaniel and Thomas Freckleton, serving in the 1640s and 1650s, were probably brothers; Francis Wood, basketman, beadle and finally Porter, from 1672 until his death in 1709, was possibly the father of John Wood, basketman from at least 1709, barber from 1718, and Porter from 1724 until his death in 1753, and of Christopher Wood, basketman from at least 1713 until his discharge in 1716. Richard Wright, basketman from at least 1735 until 1753, and Porter from 1753 until his death in 1765, was probably related to Thomas Wright, basketman from 1751 until his death in 1755, and to Sarah Wright, nurse from 1718 until her discharge (?) in 1727 and latterly (according to Alexander Cruden), the wife of Matthew Wright, keeper of Bethnal Green madhouse. Thomas Wright may himself have been the cousin of William Morgan, whom he succeeded as basketman (for his aunt, mentioned in his will, was an Elizabeth Morgan); Edward Davi(e)s, basketman from *c.* 1762 until his death in 1764, was possibly related to Reynold Davi(e)s, basketman 1766–74, Porter 1774–7(?), and to Edward Davi(e)s, assistant, cook and basketman from *c.* 1783 until the early nineteenth century; Thomas Dunstan, basketman (and assistant basketman) 1774–81 and subsequently renowned head-keeper of St Luke's, was probably related to Edward Dunstan, cook and basketman in the early 1780s; Anne Nixon, laundry woman from *c.* 1777 until at least 1790, was probably wife of William Nixon,

assistant, basketman and porter, over the period 1767–93 (?), just as Mary Davi(e)s, bar gates servant and laundry woman from 1769 until at least 1790, was wife of Reynold Davi(e)s; Jane Hughes, maidservant by 1754, may have been related to John Hughes, Steward 1765–70; Hannah Matthews, Matron 1684–7, succeeded her mother, Millicent Matthews, to the post.

58 *BCGM*, 27 Jan. 1693, fol. 220; Denis Leigh, *The Historical Development of British Psychiatry*, vol. 1 (Oxford: Pergamon, 1961), 2; *BSCM*, 1727–70.

59 *BSCM*, 18 and 25 Jan. 1718, fols 2–3. In Clashby's case, probation lasted a year, being a singular imposition designed to evaluate the utility of the newly created post; *ibid.* 27 Jan. 1693, fol. 220.

60 This stagnation of Hospital wages occurred in a period (1630–1730) when, according to some historians, 'real wages doubled' across the board. See E. A. Wrigley and R. S. Schofield, *The Population History of England 1541–1871* (Cambridge: CUP, 1981), Appendix 9, 638–44.

61 See e.g. H. C. Cameron, *Mr. Guy's Hospital, 1726–1948* (London: Longmans & Green, 1972); *Guy's Court of Committees Minutes*; V. C. Medvei and J. L. Thornton (eds), *The Royal Hospital of Saint Bartholomew, 1232–1975* (London: St Bartholomew's Hospital Medical College, 1974). In 1710 Bridewell Beadles received more than three times the salary of Bethlem basketmen/beadles.

62 In 1752, with the escalation of visitors to the Hospital, a basketman's share was £9 6s, indicating a total of £64 16s. See *BCGM*, e.g. 31 July 1657, 3 July 1663, 20 Oct. 1676, 16 Feb. 1677 and 12 April 1678, fols 822, 57, 297–8, 377 and 21; *BSCM*, 11 July 1752 and 20 June 1753, fols 304 and 355.

63 For example, for basketmen's petitions see *BCGM*, 7 March 1684, 10 April 1685, 30 April 1686, 4 March 1687 and 28 March 1690, fols 411, 67, 162, 231, 33; for Stewards', see 24 Sept. 1662, 15 Jan. 1692, 5 May 1699, fols 14, 162 and 262.

64 See *ibid.* 16 May 1734, 27 March 1735, 21 Aug. 1635, fols 327, 343 and 359, and *BGCM* in *BSCM*, 25 March 1735 and 16 July 1735, fols 312 and 326–7.

65 *BCGM*, 13 Nov. 1735, fol. 364, and *BGCM* in *BSCM*, 8 Oct. 1735, fol. 342.

66 For these figures, see *BGCM*, 3 July 1759, fol. 220.

67 See rule xxx, in General 'Rules and Orders', dated 26 June 1751, in book of foundation orders at St Luke's Woodside, fol. 11; also reproduced in French, *op. cit.* 192.

68 See *BCGM*, 20 June 1765 and 27 April 1769, fols 138 and 249–50.

69 As a result, the Governors agreed to raise menservants' wages from £21 to £25 and womenservants' wages from £18 to £20 – a level well below that offered at Bethlem. See French, *op. cit.* 45.

70 Elizabeth Hindsley was appointed in 1772 at £15 per annum plus £5 gratuity per annum as the first Assistant Matron to St Luke's, after a six-month trial.

71 See *BCGM*, 19 July 1749, fol. 410, and Chapter 14.

72 Initially, the Steward was required to pay rent for his house 'adioyning the hospitall'.

73 Until 1678, the Porter was allowed 15s, and the basketmen given material for, or actually ordered, these coats. Subsequently, all their coats were made for them at the Hospital's direction.

74 Formerly the Porter's gown had been lined with bay. See *BCGM*, 22 Oct. 1662, 2 July 1675 and 21 July 1676, fols 19, 143 and 276. In 1658, Bridewell beadles had been ordered to wear their blue coats at every meeting of the Governors, on pain of losing their clothing allowance if not their very places, an indication of the mounting importance attached by the Governors to the cosmetics of charity.

75 See *ibid.* 31 July 1657, fol. 822.

76 See, e.g., *BCGM*, 9 Oct. 1640, 26 Jan. 1644, 28 Feb. 1663, 15 Jan. 1692, 19 Jan. 1694, 8 Feb. 1695, 3 July 1696, 26 Feb. 1697, 7 Jan. 1698 and 5 May 1699, fols 316, 88, 39, 162, 314, 426, 46, 94, 158 and 262.

77 *Ibid*, 18 Nov. 1681 and 15 March 1689, fols 268 and 380.

78 For the Hospital's grant of this and other leases (of Bridewell properties) to Matthews, see *ibid.* 15 Sept., 6 Oct. and 24 Nov. 1670 and 17 Feb. 1671, fols 227, 229, 250 and 275–6. See

also 24 March 1727, 9 Oct. 1729 and 2 July 1730, fols 121, 187 and 217, when Edward Howard, executor of the deceased lessee, Martha Phillips, was allowed to succeed to the Bull's lease.

79 *Ibid.* 27 May 1651, fols 496–7.

80 *Ibid.* 30 March and 15 April 1681, fols 209 and 213.

81 BCGM, 27 May 1651 and 22 April 1681, fols 497 and 216–17.

82 *Ibid.* 16 Feb. and 30 March 1677, fols 337 and 360; where 'the Twoe maid-servants of the said hospitall' are referred to for the first time.

83 *Ibid.* 16 Dec. 1692 and 27 Jan. 1693, fols 213 and 220.

84 See *ibid.* 22 May and 21 June 1751, and 20 June 1765, fols 5, 9 and 137; BGCM, 27 April 1751, 3 May, 20 June, 20 July, 24 Aug. and 11 Oct. 1753 in BSCM, fols 243, 347, 355, 360, 366 and 375.

85 Metcalf, *op. cit.*

86 BSCM, 7 Oct. 1769.

87 BCGM, 4 Nov. 1635, fols 66–7. See, also, *ibid.* 23 Oct. 1643, fols 74–5, for the renewal of Langley's bond to perform the same articles and their reiteration in the Court Minutes.

88 See 1619 articles, no. 2; Patricia H. Allderidge, 'Management and Mismanagement at Bedlam, 1547–1633', in Charles Webster (ed.), *Health, Medicine and Mortality in the Sixteenth Century* (Cambridge: CUP, 1979), 157 and 161–3. Crooke had, in fact, refused to admit any patient without a fee of between 10s and 20s, regardless of their warrants.

89 Securities were often difficult to persuade and the Steward forced to write repeatedly before payment was received, or legal action taken. See e.g. BCGM, 15 March 1700, fol. 357.

90 *Ibid.* 11 Aug. 1699, fol. 288.

91 *Ibid.* 20 June 1765, fols 133–4.

92 See, e.g., the Steward's 1635 articles which mention the Porter's book. The Steward's account of fees taken each day was to include moneys taken at the Hospital door by the Porter, and he was supposed to consult the Porter concerning any lack in the provisions of the house.

93 BCGM, 30 March 1677, fol. 359. By 1736, the Porter alone was responsible for the apportioning of meat on two of the Hospital's three meat days; *ibid.* 6 May 1736, fol. 391.

94 See e.g. *Ibid.* 21 Oct. 1657, 26 Oct. 1666, fols 831, 13; BSCM, 16 March and 23 April 1726, fols 256 and 260.

95 BCGM, 20 June 1765, fols 135–6.

96 *Ibid.* 6 May 1736, fol. 391.

97 *Ibid.* 6 May 1736 and 20 June 1765, fols 391 and 136.

98 *Ibid.* 6 May 1736, fol. 391.

99 See *ibid.* 20 Dec. 1636, 28 Feb. and 21 June 1637, fols 100, 165–6 and 125–7.

100 This is part supposition, based upon the few existing drawings of the original building, on the customary practice in lodging domestic servants and on specifications in the Court Minutes for the extra wing added to Bethlem in 1643/4. BCGM, 2 June 1643, fols 43–4.

101 *Ibid.* 23 Oct 1674, fol. 55, report of Bethlem Committee, dated 16 Oct. 1674.

102 For example, the Court ordered in 1635 'that whosoever be elected to the Steward's place of Bethlem should have his dwelling house there'; BCGM, 21 Oct. 1635, fol. 65.

103 *Ibid.* 4 March 1636, and 18 and 24 May 1644, fols 81, 114 and 116–17.

104 For these duties, see e.g. *ibid.* 19 Jan. and 20 Oct. 1670, 28 May, 15 and 29 Aug. 1673, and 2 Oct. 1674, fols 181, 235–6, 509, 553, 558 and 41.

105 *Ibid.* 11 Aug. 1699, fol. 288.

106 In 1672, e.g., the Court (with apparent success) took measures to obtain immunity for Bethlem servants from diverting obligations of parochial office. *Ibid.* 21 June 1672, fols 406–7.

107 *Ibid.* 24 Sept. 1652, fol. 567.

108 *Ibid.* 2 Sept. 1657, fol. 825.

109 Metcalf, *op. cit.*

110 Max Byrd, *Visits to Bedlam: Madness and Literature in the Eighteenth Century* (Columbia: University of South Carolina Press, 1974), 91; Andrew Scull, *Museums of Madness: The Social Organization of Insanity in Nineteenth-Century England* (London: Allen Lane, 1979), 62–6.

111 William Rowley and Thomas Middleton, *The Changeling* (London: written 1622; printed for Humphrey Moseley, 1653), edited by N. W. Bawcutt, IV, iii, 46–7 and *passim*; Jonathan Swift, 'A Character, Panegyric and Description of the Legion Club' (1736), in H. Williams (ed.), *The Poems of Jonathan Swift*, 3 vols (Oxford: Clarendon Press, 1937), iii, 153–8:

> Lash them daily, lash them duly
> Though 'tis hopeless to reclaim them
> Scorpion rods, perhaps, may tame them.

See, also, Henry Mackenzie, *Man of Feeling*, edited by Brian Vickers (London: Oxford and New York, 1967; London: 1771), 30, *re* the Bethlem attendant who displayed the patients to visitors in the manner 'of those who keep wild beasts for a shew'.

112 Thomas Willis, *De Anima Brutorum* (Amstelodami: Johannem Blaeu, 1672), trans. by Samuel Pordage as *Two Discourses Concerning the Soul of Brutes* (London: Dring, Harper & Leigh, 1683), 206–7; William Cullen, *First Lines in the Practice of Physic*, 4 volumes (Edinburgh: W. Creech, 1777–84), 4th edn, vol. iii, 141–3; R. Hunter and I. Macalpine, *Three Hundred Years of Psychiatry, 1535–1860* (London: OUP, 1963), 191 and 478.

113 Shakespeare, *King Lear*, III, iv, 135–7. See also *The Ballad of Poor Tom of Bedlam*, cited in O'Donoghue, *op. cit.* 137, which speaks of 'whips ding-dong'.

114 For whipping under the 1531 Poor Law and the Vagrancy Acts of 1572 and 1597, see *Statutes, III. 329, IV. i. 591, ii. 899*; A. L. Beier, *Masterless Men. The Vagrancy Problem in England, 1560–1640* (London: Methuen, 1985), 159; Sir Thomas More, *The Apologye of Syr T. More, Knygt* (London: W. Rastell, 1533), fols 197–8; Hunter and Macalpine, *op. cit.* 5–6; Geoffrey Taylor, *The Problem of Poverty, 1660–1834* (Harlow: Longmans, 1969), 53–4.

115 For Vagrancy Act of 1714, see *12 Anne, c. 23*; Hunter and Macalpine, *op. cit.* 299–301.

116 See Chapters 18 and 19. *Re* immunity of sick from punishment, see also *BCGM*, 13 Dec. 1639, fol. 272; case of falling sickness.

117 *Pace* Scull, *op. cit.* 63.

118 Richard Mead, *Medical Precepts and Cautions* (1751), trans. by Thomas Stack (London: J. Brindley, 1751), ch. iii, 98; *idem, Medica Sacra*, in *The Medical Works of Richard Mead* (London: Hitch & Hawes, 1762), ix, 623. In the former work, however, Mead still compared the behaviour of the maniac to that of a 'wild beast' who needed 'to be tied down, & even beat, to prevent his doing mischief to himself or others': 74.

119 See J. Andrews, 'A Respectable Mad-Doctor? Dr Richard Hale, F.R.S. (1670–1728)', in *Notes and Records of the Royal Society of London*, xliv (1990), 169–203.

120 John Monro, *Remarks on Dr. Battie's Treatise on Madness*, 38 and 47; William Battie, *A Treatise on Madness*, 84–5, both cited from the edition edited by R. Hunter and I. Macalpine (London: Dawsons, 1962).

121 There is no mention of the use or purchase of whips or rods in any of the archival material, not even in the Stewards' Accounts.

122 *BCGM*, 11 March 1635, fol. 35.

123 See the case of John Jeweller, discharged from the office of Bridewell Steward in 1633 and (definitively) in 1635, for falsifying his accounts and slandering the Court and its officers; *ibid.* 1 and 27 March 1633, 31 Oct. and 17 Dec. 1634, 2 and 16 Feb., 7 and 9 March 1635, and 13 Dec. 1639, fols 317, 322–4, 16, 21, 25–7, 29–30, 32–4 and 272–4.

124 *Ibid.* 18 July 1646, fol. 270.

125 *Ibid.* 30 March 1677, fols 358–9.

126 See *ibid.* 16 Aug. 1637, fol. 134. For more on her case, see this volume, esp. Chapter 19.

127 Latin warrant/letter dated 14 May 1675 from John Browne, Clerk of Parliament, with English translation, at back of 1666–74 Court Book, and *BCGM*, 19 May 1675, fols 129–30, for response.

128 See Swift, *op. cit.* iii, 827–39; John Strype, *A Survey of the Cities of London & Westminster . . . Written at First . . . by John Stow* (London: A. Churchill, 1720), i, 196.

129 *BCGM*, 11 Feb. 1674, fol. 613. Two examinations were in fact conducted by the City Coroner, one on the body of Elizabeth Soe, alias Jackson, a lunatic who had been sent to Bethlem from Newgate, and the other on John Robotham, formerly a prisoner at Bridewell.

130 *Ibid.* 24 Dec. 1647, fol. 329.

131 Carkesse, *op. cit.*; Metcalf, *op. cit.*

132 Carkesse (*op. cit.* 14–15, 39, 52 and 62) alleged even worse ill-treatment behind the closed doors of the Bethlem Physician Thomas Allen's Finsbury madhouse.

133 For the importance of such duties, see e.g. *BCGM*, 16 Oct. 1674, fol. 55.

134 On her appointment as Matron in 1663, Jane Johnson was told 'to looke to and take care of the distracted woemen', and to summon one or more of 'the Menservants . . . [when] shee cannott rule any distracted woeman herselfe'; *ibid.* 1 April 1663, fol. 43.

135 Thomas Bowen, *An Historical Account of the Rise, Progress and Present State of Bethlem Hospital* . . . (London: For the Governors, 1783), 12.

136 Monro, *op. cit.* 38.

137 *BCGM*, 27 May 1651, 6 and 20 Oct. 1652, fols 496, 569 and 572, and Chapter 11.

138 The Apothecary's bill for Woolly's treatment was not paid for over sixteen months after the first mention of his injury. This is the only recorded instance in the Minutes of a member of staff being seriously injured by a patient; *BCGM*, 20 May 1674, 10 Sept. and 8 Oct. 1675, fols 645, 174 and 182.

139 See *ibid.* 21 June 1637, fol. 126.

140 *Ibid.* 8 March 1672, 12 April 1678, 30 March, 15 April and 5 Aug. 1681, fols 376, 18, 21, 216 and 241.

141 *Ibid.* 30 March 1681, fol. 209.

142 *Ibid.* 27 May 1651, fol. 496.

143 *Ibid.* 4 Nov. 1635 and 23 Oct. 1643, fols 66–7 and 74–5.

144 *Ibid.* 28 Feb. 1638, fols 165–6.

145 *Ibid.* 28 Feb. 1638, fol. 165.

146 See *ibid.* e.g. 3 Dec. 1641, (?) Nov. 1644, 4 Oct. 1645, 21 Jan., 11 Feb., 3 July and 28 Aug. 1663, fols 359, 156, 217, 30–1, 35, 56–7 and 63.

147 *Ibid.* 4 Oct. 1654, fol. 676.

148 For the ensuing discussion, see *ibid.* 4 April 1655, 31 July and 26 Nov. 1657, and 3 Sept. 1662, fols 698, 822, 835 and 9. Withers is, however, a common name, and it seems unlikely that the servant and the patient are one and the same.

149 *Ibid.* 2 Sept. 1657, fol. 825.

150 For example, complaints of Walter Pryse and 1765 rulings; *ibid.* 27 Jan. and 12 March 1742 and 20 June 1765, fols 135, 141 and 133. Inebriation amongst staff was certainly a cause for concern in the 1815–16 Commons Inquiry into Madhouses: *Madhouses Committee Reports, 1st Report* (1815), 85–6, 99, 104 and 106; *1st Report* (1815), 92.

151 See *BCGM*, 21 June 1637, fol. 126, when the Porter and servants are ordered to show the Steward, every day, what provision has been delivered from the markets or otherwise, a clear pointer to the nature of the maidservants' gossip concerning the former.

152 *Ibid.* 28 April 1643, fols 35–6.

153 Langley was also found guilty of illicitly subletting rooms in his house. For these abuses, see *BCGM*, 9 Feb. and 2 April 1638, 25 Oct. 1639, 18 Dec. 1640, 29 April 1642, 28 April, 2 June, 4 and 25 Aug., 12 Sept., 6 and 23 Oct., and 15 Dec. 1643, and 26 Jan. and 29 Feb. 1644, fols 162, 172–3, 269, 322, 381–2, 34–6, 42–3, 56, 61, 65–6, 70, 74–5, 82–3, 88–9 and 95.

154 *Ibid.* 24 Feb. 1649, fol 378.

155 *BCGM*, 3 Jan. 1672, fol. 368.

156 *Ibid.* 19 Aug. 1652, fol. 561. The repetition of this order, soon after Godbed's election as Steward, however, suggests that it had fallen into neglect; *ibid.* 24 Sept. 1658, fol. 70.

157 *Ibid.* e.g. 16 June 1637, 9 Feb., 2 April, 17 Oct. and 13 Dec. 1638, 28 July and 3 Dec. 1641, 15 Dec. 1643, 4 March and 28 July 1648, 8 Sept. 1652, 3 July 1663 and 30 March 1677, fols 126, 162, 172–3, 182, 203, 216, 231, 343, 359, 82–3, 340, 354, 564, 56–7 and 359–61.

158 *Ibid.* 31 July 1657, 4 Aug. 1709 and 20 June 1765, fols 822, 500, 133 and 137. *BSCM*, 30 Aug. 1712, 24 Sept. 1715, 17 March 1716, 15 Dec. 1759 and 31 Dec. 1796, fols 98, 199, 214 and 249.

159 *BCGM*, e.g. 19 Aug. 1652 and 27 May 1751, fols 561 and 496.

160 *Ibid.* 23 June 1732 and 21 June and 30 Nov. 1739, fols 286, 50 and 65; *BGCM* in *BSCM*, fols 197 and 213–15.

161 See rewards to Foye and Benson: *BCGM*, 12 March 1647, 21 April 1653, 27 July 1655, 17 Dec. 1656 and 26 Nov. 1658, fols 297, 604, 712, 779 and 80.

162 *Ibid.* e.g. 15 Nov. 1781, 21 Nov. 1782, 27 Nov. 1783 and 2 Dec. 1784, fols 19–20, 70, 124–5 and 165; *BSCM*, 29 Jan. 1780 and 19 July 1783; and Journal of Richard Clark, *Ghall* MS 3385, part ii, 23 Aug. 1785.

163 *BCGM*, 30 March 1677, 6 May 1736, 20 June 1765 and 27 April 1769, fols 359–60, 391–2, 133, 135–7 and 250; *BGCM*, 15 Sept. 1785, in *BSCM*.

164 *BCGM*, 20 June 1765 and 27 April 1769, fols 137 and 250; *BGCM* in *BSCM*, 15 Sept. 1785; Metcalf, *op. cit.*.

165 *BCGM*, 1 Oct. 1777; O'Donoghue, *op. cit.* 264; *Gentleman's Magazine*, vol. xlvii, 26 Sept. and 1 Oct. 1777, 459 and 503, and note.

166 Metcalf, *op. cit.* 4.

167 See Jacques Cambry, *De Londres et ses environs* (Amsterdam, 1788).

168 *An Apology for the Conduct of Mrs T. C. Phillips* (London: For the Author, 1748–9), 71–89.

ADMISSION AND DISCHARGE

— ·◆· —

INTRODUCTION

Patients have long been the 'hidden dimension' in institutional histories, viewed as little more than administrative problems or as anonymous statistics. Their stories are not easy to resurrect from the records. This chapter attempts to discover who Bethlem's patients were – and also to determine what sort of patients Bethlem was attempting to serve.

Bethlem's admission practices involved an evolving interplay of procedures designed to distinguish proper patients. Admission depended upon the poverty of patients and their securities. This set the charitable tenor of the provision. But significant gradations in status, occupation and wealth characterized the Hospital's clientele, and much was personal and negotiable. Indeed, an aura of privilege was attached to reception of patients, as is evident from the mounting waiting-list, the need to obtain a Governor's nomination, and the increasing discrimination exercised over the course of the period.

This chapter explores the wider aspects of admissions. It examines patients' geographical origins, locating settlement information in the broader context of parochial relief. It shows the difficulties of enforcing settlement obligations and the expense of maintaining the insane. It stresses the acceptance of a responsibility to cater for the poor insane, and the legal and administrative resources the Hospital possessed to enforce these obligations. Ambiguities in the Hospital's efforts to distinguish suitable 'objects of Charity' will be examined, along with the evolution of diagnostic criteria. Bethlem prioritized cases designated as 'dangerous', and some investigation of what the 'danger' of the insane signified for contemporaries will also be attempted. In addition, the Hospital's commitment to short-stay, 'curable' cases will be demonstrated, as will its enhanced recognition from the early eighteenth century of the need to provide for chronic or incurable cases.

Bethlem claimed a cure-rate of over two-thirds, but the final sections of this chapter assess the darker reality of the Hospital's record behind the rosy rhetoric. Examination of the after-life of patients indicates but limited therapeutic achievements. Rarely is evidence found that discharged patients fully recovered or were capable of resuming their former lives. Nevertheless, given the inadequacies of

Plate 18.1 Engraving by Bernard Lens and John Sturt of the interior of Bethlem, showing patients as caricatures. Published in the 5th edition of *A Tale of a Tub* (London, 1710) by Jonathan Swift. Reproduced by permission of the Bethlem Royal Hospital Archives and Museum.

alternative provision, Bethlem was performing no mean service to localities in offering affordable provision for difficult individuals. Finally, discussing mortality at Bethlem, it will be shown that while not one of the 'gateways to death' envisaged by some historians, its declining mortality rates are partially a rather cosmetic outcome of a policy of excluding and discharging debilitated and moribund patients.

RELIEVING THE POOR INSANE OR UNBURDENING THEIR FRIENDS?

Like other early modern hospitals, Bethlem functioned as a charity, reliant on public goodwill and benefactions. Patients were received, maintained and treated only if deemed 'fitt obiects of Charity'. In Bethlem's case, they were supposed to be both 'poor and mad'. Obviously, both designations are profoundly problematic, but the Hospital's Governors and officers tried to uphold those two basic requirements, and were increasingly choosy about whom to support.

Bethlem was first and foremost an institution for the *poor* insane. The majority were supported on the poor rate and committed by parish officers; in lesser but significant numbers, they were poor individuals, provided for by friends, relatives or their own meagre funds, too poor to afford private care but not poor enough to qualify for parish relief. As a Royal and a City Hospital, Bethlem also received insane individuals committed by order of government in its widest sense (royal, Parliamentary, church and municipal) and by courts of law; or recommended by other civic hospitals, boards and companies. This last class formed a motley collection of poor criminals and disturbers of the peace, vagrants, pensioners and the lower ranks of the military (see Chapter 19). For much of the period, the Hospital's administrators referred to patients as 'the poore' or 'the poore Lunatikes', while provision for them was spoken of as charitable 'relief', of which medicine, diet, lodging, maintenance fees and even cure itself were conceived of as a part. From the 1630s, parochial and private patients were admitted on petitions detailing the circumstances of their poverty. It was primarily on these grounds that assessment was agreed of the weekly charge for patients and of the bond requiring securities to fulfil certain conditions for their maintenance and removal.

Each patient, except those for whom an institution stood as guarantor, was required to have two 'sufficient' sureties resident within, or in the suburbs of, London, who signed the bond and acted as insurance for the Hospital. Fees for patients' support were seen as merely contributions 'towards the charge of keeping', signifying that the charity would supply the remainder. Securities might pay anything from nothing to 8s per week. The standard (and highest) charge for much of the period, however, was 5s, subject to a sustained policy of 'abatements'.[1] Until the standardizing of maintenance fees at the turn of the eighteenth century, securities spent much energy bargaining with Governors, and outlining their circumstances of poverty to achieve affordable rates. Bethlem's Governors conceived their role as succouring both the 'very poore' families and 'overburthened' parishes of the insane, as well as the 'poore decayed ... distracted' individuals themselves. Lunatics (curables and incurables) or relations with means of their own were required to contribute, and if those means were deemed sufficient for a patient to be maintained elsewhere, patients were ordinarily barred from admission.[2] The policy of excluding moneyed patients was largely self-enforcing, few wealthier families preferring Bethlem to private care.

The policy of abatements underlines Bethlem's charitable orientation. Over one hundred and fifty abatements of patients' weekly fees, ranging from 6d to the whole amount, are recorded as granted in the Governors' Minutes between 1640 and 1677, and after the move to Moorfields abatements rose to over ten a year. Securities who fell into arrears also quite frequently had their debts cancelled or mitigated. The sympathetic and paternalistic spirit of this relief is evident in the tenor of orders 'commiserating' the 'sad condicion' of patients and their securities 'decayed' in their 'estates'.[3]

In 1701, the top weekly fee was reduced to 2s 6d, while from 1703, it was abolished altogether, the Court ruling that 'all Lunaticks of what condicion or quality so ever that shalbee thought fitt to bee received into the . . . hospitall . . . shall bee kept . . . uppon the Charity thereof as to all things except clothes' (and bedding, surgery, and removal or burial expenses).[4] This sweeping dispensation emphasizes the intimate relationship between medical care and charity. It was attributed by the Court to the augmentation of the Hospital's annual revenue 'by the charitable benevolence of severall worthy benefactors', and was granted in the hope that it 'will bee a greate Inducement to all well disposed Christians to Contribute to soe good a worke'. While incurables, supported from 1728, were not included in this dispensation, the same ethos was to inspire the Governors in 1738 to reduce the standard maintenance fees for incurables also, from 5s to 2s 6d per week.[5]

There were severe limits to Bethlem's charity of course, and as the period wore on its administrators began to deviate from their earlier commitment to relief of the poorest sort. Bethlem's relief did not normally extend to providing for the clothing, bedding, transportation or burial of its patients, nor always to surgery. In 1674, with the Governors feeling the expense of the Hospital's rebuilding at Moorfields (for which they were forced to borrow heavily), mitigations of fees ceased altogether. Abatements were resumed again a few years later, but a ceiling of 4s was imposed on the weekly fees of 'Country' parishes. Thereafter abatements were restricted to patients who had remained over six months, while parishes were barred absolutely from receiving abatements for the remainder of the century, being regarded as better able to afford to provide. New penalties were also levied to deter securities from failing to collect patients once ordered discharged, while the appeal to poor families and parishes of provision for incurables established at Bethlem in the 1720s was somewhat mitigated by rather prohibitive deposits demanded for each admission.[6] Old prejudices against parochial admissions were subsequently reinforced: from 1735 parishes alone were obliged to deposit 10s in the servants' box for every parishioner admitted, and were later required to pay extra for bedding. By mid-century, the Governors made it explicit in their rulings that patients supported by their friends should be preferred as admissions to parochial cases.[7] However, parochial patients continued to outnumber private cases at Bethlem, despite its Governors' attempt to embourgeoise provision (mirrored in the same period by St Luke's increasing preference for 'the middling sort' of patient). The Governors were still doubting in the 1790s that patients, like Stephen Whitchurch, 'in Possession of a clear Income of £35

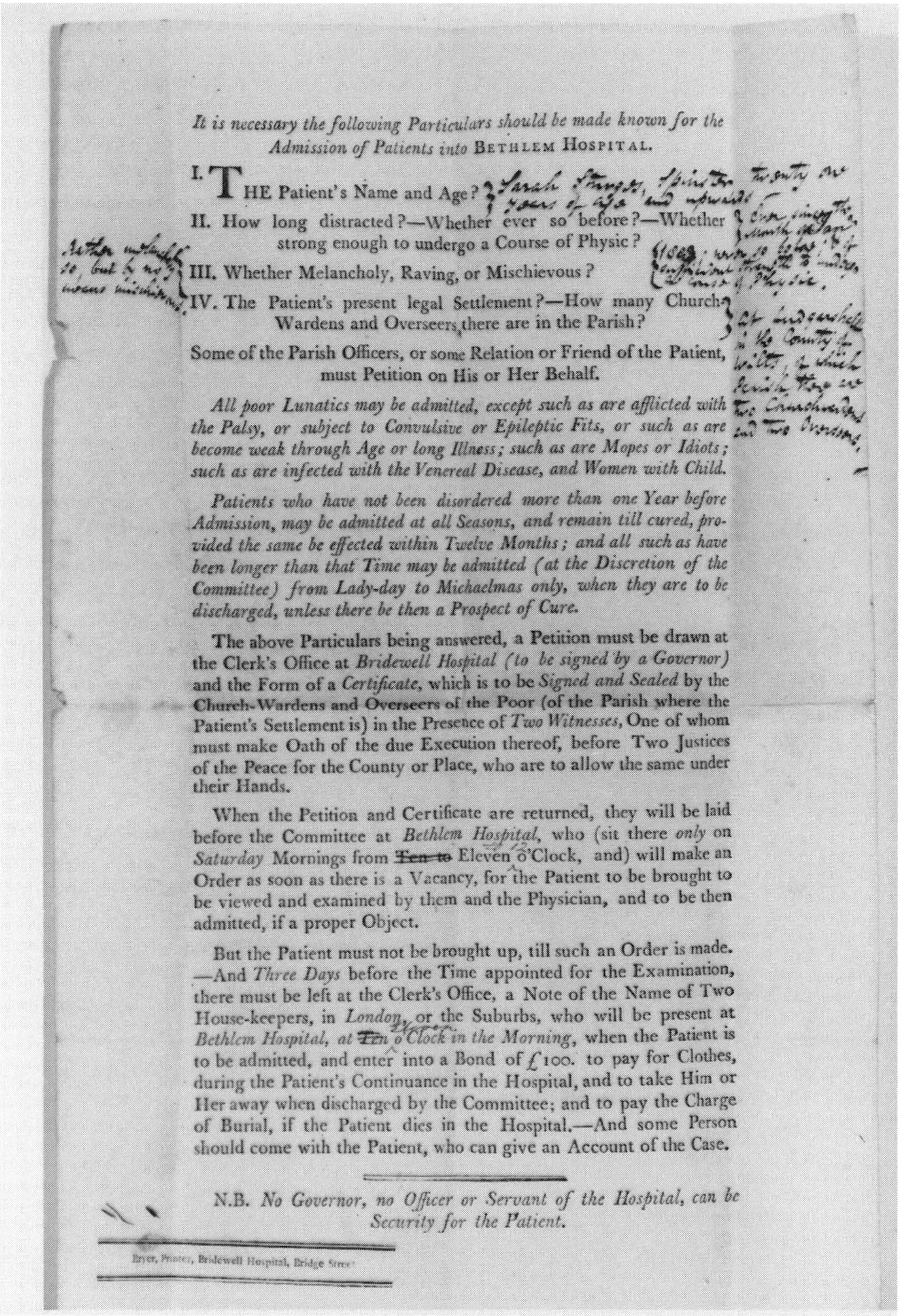

It is necessary the following Particulars should be made known for the Admission of Patients into BETHLEM HOSPITAL.

I. THE Patient's Name and Age?

II. How long distracted?—Whether ever so before?—Whether strong enough to undergo a Course of Physic?

III. Whether Melancholy, Raving, or Mischievous?

IV. The Patient's present legal Settlement?—How many Church Wardens and Overseers there are in the Parish?

Some of the Parish Officers, or some Relation or Friend of the Patient, must Petition on His or Her Behalf.

All poor Lunatics may be admitted, except such as are afflicted with the Palsy, or subject to Convulsive or Epileptic Fits, or such as are become weak through Age or long Illness; such as are Mopes or Idiots; such as are infected with the Venereal Disease, and Women with Child.

Patients who have not been disordered more than one Year before Admission, may be admitted at all Seasons, and remain till cured, provided the same be effected within Twelve Months; and all such as have been longer than that Time may be admitted (at the Discretion of the Committee) from Lady-day to Michaelmas only, when they are to be discharged, unless there be then a Prospect of Cure.

The above Particulars being answered, a Petition must be drawn at the Clerk's Office at *Bridewell Hospital (to be signed by a Governor)* and the Form of a *Certificate,* which is to be *Signed and Sealed* by the Church-Wardens and Overseers of the Poor (of the Parish where the Patient's Settlement is) in the Presence of *Two Witnesses,* One of whom must make Oath of the due Execution thereof, before Two Justices of the Peace for the County or Place, who are to allow the same under their Hands.

When the Petition and Certificate are returned, they will be laid before the Committee at *Bethlem Hospital,* who (sit there *only* on *Saturday* Mornings from ~~Ten to~~ Eleven o'Clock, and) will make an Order as soon as there is a Vacancy, for the Patient to be brought to be viewed and examined by them and the Physician, and to be then admitted, if a proper Object.

But the Patient must not be brought up, till such an Order is made. —And *Three Days* before the Time appointed for the Examination, there must be left at the Clerk's Office, a Note of the Name of Two House-keepers, in *London,* or the Suburbs, who will be present at *Bethlem Hospital,* at ~~Ten~~ o'Clock in the Morning, when the Patient is to be admitted, and enter into a Bond of £100. to pay for Clothes, during the Patient's Continuance in the Hospital, and to take Him or Her away when discharged by the Committee; and to pay the Charge of Burial, if the Patient dies in the Hospital.—And some Person should come with the Patient, who can give an Account of the Case.

N.B. *No Governor, no Officer or Servant of the Hospital, can be Security for the Patient.*

Bryer, Printer, Bridewell Hospital, Bridge Street.

Plate 18.2 Instructions for admission, 1804. Reproduced by permission of the Bethlem Royal Hospital Archives and Museum.

a Year', were 'proper object[s] of this Charity'.[8] It was not until the mid-nineteenth century that Bethlem truly relinquished, in a gradual way, its traditional responsibility for the pauper insane, shunting them off to the new generation of private and county asylums.[9]

Admission registers, which do not begin to record patients' occupations regularly until the mid-eighteenth century, emphasize that it was the poorer classes – apprentices, journeymen, labourers, mariners, pensioners, common soldiers and sailors, vagrants, craftsmen, minor tradesmen, semi-skilled workers and ancillary workers – who comprised the vast majority of those supported. The Hospital failed to record regularly the occupations of female patients, a symptom of their status as dependants. About half the inmates were maintained solely by their parishes, while many were supported on the charity of public boards and institutions. Incurables Admission Registers demonstrate that parochial patients continued to make up nearly 60 per cent of incurables admissions.

There were none the less considerable gradations of wealth and class amongst admissions. Patients privately supported clearly had access to incomes which placed them above the poverty line. At least a quarter of those admitted between 1640 and 1680 were maintained privately, and others were maintained by their friends with financial assistance from various public, parochial and municipal authorities, and from the Hospital itself. Amongst incurables supported between 1735 and 1800, private patients consistently comprised over one-third of the total incurable patient population.

Some patients were only part of the way towards financial dependency, qualifying only for a contribution from their parishes towards the weekly fee. That the largest single occupational/social status category amongst admissions between 1694 and 1719 is that of 'gentleman', accounting for over 11 per cent of those recorded, indicates that a fair proportion of patients hailed from less humble backgrounds – although, it must be stressed, in only a quarter of male cases is the occupation known. The presence of five vintners, two victuallers, three surgeons, a public notary, a Navy lieutenant, three mercers, eight clerks and three apothecaries amongst these patients, and of a barber surgeon, a doctor, three brokers, two hatters, two silversmiths and two victuallers, amongst the relatives/friends of patients admitted in the same period, also suggests that a fair number of admissions came from the middling sort. Similarly, between 1640 and 1680, one finds five 'gentlemen', two landowners, a vintner, a victualler, a haberdasher and a clerk of the royal poultry; and amongst supporting relatives/friends, there were eight haberdashers, four merchant taylors, three 'gentlemen', a merchant and a cheesemonger. Some of those patients committed by Government to Bethlem were well above the status of paupers, including the prophetess, Lady Eleanor Davies, supported by the Privy Council; the dramatist, Nathaniel Lee, supported privately and by the Board of Greencloth; a 'Captain White', and the Reverend Joseph Ward, also supported by the Board of Greencloth.[10] George Lyth, in Bethlem for eight months during 1710, had been proprietor of Lyth's, or St Dunstan's, coffee-house. Governors of the Hospitals themselves, like Captain Clarke, plainly thought enough of the care at Bethlem to have their own friends and relations admitted on occasion.[11] Between 1733 and 1794 at least twelve Bethlem patients underwent Commissions of Lunacy, demonstrating that they were possessed of substantial estates, although some were discharged as a result.[12]

Dominated by London merchants, tradesmen, craftsmen and citizens, the Court of Governors was appreciative of the numerous hazards to the business of patients and their securities, and also of the significance in mental illness of hardship and loss. There are constant references in the Minutes to securities whose 'Estate and Trade' had 'decayed'; who had been afflicted by 'the deadnes/lowness/decay' of trade' or the 'hardness of the times'; who had 'nothing in the world . . . save what they Earne' by their 'trade', 'Industry' or 'dayly Labor'; and to patients who had 'wasted & consumed' their estates. These testify to the importance the Court attached to the virtues and adversities of the world of work, and its recognition of the knife-edge between capacity and failure.[13] A similar compassionate regard was taken in Sessions proceedings concerning impoverishment and economic reversals in cases of lunacy. A typical example is the case of Lewis Powell, a Whitechapel silk-throwster, who was admitted to Bethlem at the request of his wife, Mary, at a weekly charge of just 2s 6d, after 'by unhappy losses faileing in his Estate & becomeing Lunatike', and whose support was directed by Sessions to be taken over by the parish, after Mary had been robbed and beset by creditors.[14]

The Governing Court clearly listened to hard-luck stories, but was also swayed by peculiar biases, tending to dispense its favour to particular groups, such as 'the industrious poor', respectable citizens, and dutiful soldiers and sailors, and at particular times, as when extending charity to certain Puritans during the Protectorate.[15] For example, Mary Reade was admitted in 1654 at a weekly charge of just 2s 6d, her father, Simon Grover, being a 'an aged decayed citizen'.[16] Likewise, William Parr (Parre) was admitted to Bethlem in 1642 at a charge of only 1s per week, on a recommendation from the Lord Mayor that he was a citizen and girdler, had been a shopkeeper for over fifteen years, and had 'noe meanes left' either 'to mainteyne' his family, or 'for the recovery of his sences', and on the Governors granting substantial 'consideration' to 'his distressed estate'.[17] Little wonder either, when so many of the Governors were themselves involved in the cloth trade, that the Court lent a sympathetic ear to cases like that of Robert Bundy in 1697, a London clothworker who was not only supporting his sister, Denise, in Bethlem out of 'kindnesse', but was maintaining his own family and his Mother and had experienced 'Losses' in his trade 'to the value of £300'.[18] Such cases emphasize the extent to which insanity was regarded both as, in itself, a natural, although deplorable, consequence of calamity, and also as bringing a burdensome calamity down upon distressed families. The Court was well-disposed to those who had experienced 'great losses by fire' or other misfortune, granting mitigations for patients after the Great Fire of London.[19] Indeed, the frequency with which lunacy was ascribed to, or associated with, calamity – something well reflected in contemporary literature, from Burton to Smollett – has been underestimated. In his 'Table of the Causes of Insanity', compiled from the notebooks of the Bethlem Apothecary, John Gozna, on the basis of admissions to Bethlem during 1772–87, William Black presented 'Misfortunes, Troubles, Disappointments [and] Grief' as by far the most common cause of insanity, accounting for almost a quarter of all known causes.[20]

Occasionally the sympathy of the Governors for patients and their families was rather more explicit, as in 1709 when Mary Heath was admitted as 'an Object of great Compassion and young and lately deprived of her senses'. Similarly, in 1672, an abatement was granted in the case of Ann Urring, 'a young maiden' and her mother Joan, 'a poore Minister's Widdow' with no means beyond 'what she getteth by her hard Labour and the Charity of good people', on the 'Courte commiserating the sad condicon both of Mother and Daughter'.[21]

Petitions submitted to the Court also indicate sympathy amongst patients' securities for the circumstances of the insane, some claiming to have undertaken to provide out of 'pity' to them 'as neighbours', or out of 'kindnesses' and 'charity' to their friendless and penurious condition.[22] Obviously, however, petitioners were keen to emphasize their own as well as the patient's indigence, and their own charitable disposition, so as to strike a good maintenance bargain. It might also be asked who it was – patients or their securities – that Bethlem's Governors were primarily relieving, the patient often being only indirectly referred to in the admission process. Just as patients' mental or physical conditions were rarely referred to in admission proceedings, it seems also often to have been more a matter of economic expediency that provoked Governors to discharge patients, and securities' decisions to request patients' removal or refuse to support them any longer, than concerns over the health and welfare of patients.

The Governors' Minutes testify to the burden the insane represented to their friends and parishes. Just how burdensome a load the insane might be and how much their support might depend on economic matters is exemplified by the case of Christopher Symmonds of St Dionis parish. After his admission to Bethlem for the fifth time in 1664, the parish resolved to help meet the arrears of his maintenance by sending a delegation of the churchwardens and 'some of the Ancients' to the Hospital to 'Speake with' him and force him to assign his mortgaged lease of a house which they had repossessed for this purpose. If Symmonds agreed, 'they should enlarge him', but if he refused they were 'to aquaint him that he is to remain there upon his own Charge'.[23] Symmonds was indeed discharged and his lease assigned.

PRIVILEGE AND PATRONAGE: RECOMMENDING PATIENTS TO BETHLEM

There was a strong element of privilege attached to the reception of patients. They were frequently admitted at concessionary rates, or had their fees abated, on the recommendations of Governors, officers, benefactors, notables, or other institutions and authorities. In 1679, Sarah Turner, for example, was allowed to 'be continued in . . . Bethlem for her cure', and had her arrears remitted and her weekly fee halved 'att the request of Captaine Perry' (who was in good odour, 'haveing beene instrumentall in haveing the hospitall . . . excused from paying any hearth money').[24] Sarah Derrington of Essex was admitted in 1652 'att the request of Mr Yardley', the Apothecary, he 'promising to give her all her phisicke freely without any charge to the said hospitall', while Mary Burrows was admitted gratis in 1693 on being 'Recommended' to the President by John Johns, a Governor and benefactor.[25] Besides nominating patients for admission, Governors also regularly testified to the accuracy of information offered before the Court on behalf of patients and their securities, often being connected with them through employment, public office or property ownership in the same parishes. Petitions before Sessions occasionally detail how patients' friends had 'obteyned favour to gett [them] . . . into the hospitall of Bethlem'.[26] Admission was by no means automatic, requiring not only the nomination of Governors but 'expedition' for the officials who administered such admissions, from JPs and the Bethlem Treasurer and Clerk, down to the Steward and underservants.[27] This was partially the old story of institutional corruption, and an outcome of shortage of space. With 320 'incurable' patients on the waiting-list by 1770, little more than a quarter of whom obtained admission; and with almost two-thirds of those admitted forced to wait between five and nine years for their admissions, patients were competing for places. By the 1780s, there were 200 patients every year on the waiting-list.[28] Although, by the second half of the century, patients were admitted according to rotation, some were occasionally permitted to jump the queue.

On the other hand, this factor of privilege was rather circumscribed, and tended to belong less to patients themselves than to those suing for their admissions. Recommendations from notables were often motivated more by concern to get rid of bothersome presences than by charity or thoughts of benefiting the patient. While in 1642, for example, a group of earls petitioned successfully for the admission of a Charterhouse pensioner, Tobias Hume, their avowed motivation was to nullify the 'dainger' in him 'goeing abroad of doinge hurt by pressinge uppon severall honourable Parsonages and others and useinge disorderly blasphemous and distempered behaviour both in words & Accions'.[29]

SETTLEMENT: WHERE DID PATIENTS COME FROM?

Bethlem was predominantly a local institution, serving London and Middlesex and their environs. Between 1640 and 1680, 74 per cent of cases whose settlement is known came from London or Middlesex. Patients with settlements in the Home Counties (Berkshire, Buckinghamshire, Essex, Hertfordshire, Kent and Surrey) comprised a further 19 per cent of all cases in which settlement is known. Only 7 per cent of known cases had their settlements beyond the Home Counties (see Figure 18.1).

Much militated against admission of patients from the regions. Higher rates tended to be set for such patients,[30] and logistical difficulties and expenses were also a discouragement. While messengers might be sent to local parishes and families to inform them of a vacancy,[31] this was much more difficult in the case of those living far away. Drawn-out admission procedures, which by the eighteenth century required that patients be viewed a week prior to admission, could further deter country parishes and families from conveying an insane member to the capital when there was a chance their admission might be refused. Then there was the necessity of finding two securities resident within the City or twenty miles of it[32] to become bound for the patient, and of procuring some recommendation from the Governors, no mean task for strangers. With 37 per cent of patients' settlements unknown, however, it is

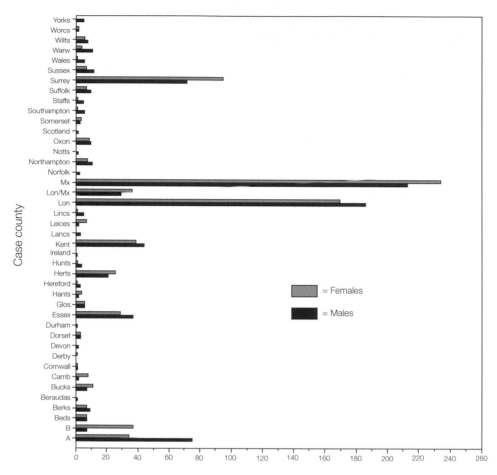

Figure 18.1 Patients' settlements, for each distinct case, 1694–1718.
Key: A = unknown; B = only relatives given

questionable how reliable figures gathered from the Court Minutes of the old Hospital (admission registers not being extant until 1683) can be as guides to the patient population. The provincial insane were probably better represented at Bethlem than is documented.

The settlements of 1858 patients and their friends between 1694 and 1718 show that while the majority (between 52 and 54 per cent) hailed from London and Middlesex, an impressive proportion (between 23 and 25 per cent of males and females) had settlements in the Home Counties, while a significant number (*c.* 16 per cent of men and 12 per cent of women) had settlements in the outlying counties. With the spectacular expansion of the Hospital after 1677, its catchment area evidently also widened. Bethlem was henceforth to function as a national institution, taking in patients from Cornwall to Yorkshire. Given its monopoly as a hospital specializing in the care of lunatics, it is easy to explain why Bethlem attracted clients from far afield.

Patients with provincial settlements were better represented on the incurables wards, where they comprised the majority of those admitted. Over 57 per cent of those 805 patients admitted during 1728–88 whose settlements are known hailed from outside London and Middlesex, over 25 per cent having settlements more than 100 km outside.[33] As some historians of medical care under the Old Poor Law have emphasized, provincial parishes were quite prepared to pay the considerable expenses necessary to get troublesome insane individuals admitted to Bethlem.[34] Standardly this would involve payments for persons travelling with applicants, tending to their needs and restraining them from escape; the costs of food and lodging for the party while on the road, or while applying for admission; paying perquisites to servants and fees to hospital officials; and paying the waggoner for journeys to and from London both when the patient was first examined and when subsequently admitted.

One should not, however, draw too close a correlation between patients' settlements and the Hospital's catchment area. A large proportion of patients with provincial settlements had clearly been living or working in the metropolis (or both). The Poor Law was partly designed to immobilize the poor, but that was more hope than reality, and, not surprisingly, those disordered in their wits became vagrants, and vagrants often became mentally odd.[35] The 1662 form of settlement certificates, which carried the enabling clause 'to save the parish harmless', licensed parish officers to remove the bearer forthwith, 'if likely to become chargeable'. Parish records show that the insane were not infrequently shunted on removal orders from one parish to another, in effect passing the buck. The 1697 Act, which stipulated that certificate holders could not be removed *until* they became a charge on the rates, only partially combated this tendency. Many patients were admitted to Bethlem weeks or months after they had been passed from another parish, indicating how vulnerable to committal were those individuals whose ties with their families or localities had been loosened.[36] Typical cases, like those of Alice Walker and Mary Taylor who were both fortuitously reclaimed by family members from Bridewell where they had been sent as lunatics, also suggest how important were family and community ties in preventing (or aiding) the committal of the insane. The former had been found 'wandring' in a 'distracted' condition, and her sister was obliged to promise 'to keepe her from wandring' in future, while the latter had escaped from the house 'by the neglect' of her husband's Servants and had likewise been apprehended 'in the streets'.[37] Institutional and parochial authorities were faced with real problems in enforcing settlement obligations, not only because of the unwelcome financial burden the insane might entail, but also due to their very liability to vagrancy, so that they were frequently committed to Bethlem without anyone who might identify them.[38] Lunatics were often admitted to Bethlem as a temporary measure, until it could be discovered where they were 'borne or last lawfully settled'.[39]

The proceedings of the Court of Governors in so far as they concerned lunatics were largely taken up with negotiations and disputes over settlements, maintenance fees and arrears. These were often long drawn-out affairs, liable to delay discharge. Relatives might seek to escape obligations towards the insane, either by their incapacity, or by flight, or by proving the existence of other, closer kin. Yet the Hospital was generally successful (with the help of Sessions and other authorities) in compelling securities to cough up. For example, as only the brother-in-law of

Elizabeth Hazeler, Matthew Heydon was not legally bound to support her in Bethlem, yet once he entered into a bond, Heydon found it very difficult to free himself from the obligation. Despite having tried desperately during 1667/8 to do so, and despite his position as servant to an Alderman, he was still made to meet 83 per cent of his debt.[40] In such disputes, nevertheless, the patient was often the loser, Hazeler being forced to linger in Bethlem for an extra two months before recourse to Sessions compelled the parish where she had formerly worked to provide.

By the eighteenth century, as admission procedures were formalized, patients were rarely being admitted without their settlement being established and a bond sealed. In 1752 it was made a standing order that no patients be viewed for admission 'untill a Petition and a proper Certificate of . . . Settlement' was presented. Exceptions, as in the cases of foreign patients and peripatetics who had no settlements in England, amounted to a mere handful, and were only admitted on the additional security of a £100 bond.[41]

'ADMITTING AND KEEPING THE POORE LUNATIKES'

How else did the Hospital decide which patients were 'fitt obiects of Charity'? Examination of patients on admission was by no means a formal requirement. Before the 1630s, the Governors had been happy to leave affairs largely to the Keeper, and neglect and indiscriminate reception of patients had greeted the Governors on their rare visits.[42] One such visit in 1624 revealed eleven patients 'not fitt to bee kepte'; three of them were variously described as merely 'Idiot', 'simple' or 'something idle headed' and were to be removed; three were suffering only from 'physical' ailments and were ordered sent 'to some other hospital'; and the rest were either sufficiently recovered – or had not been paid for – and were to be returned from whence they came.[43] While indicative of the negligence of official oversight of Bethlem at this time, such clear-outs also testify to the basic exclusion criteria evolving at the Hospital. The Governors were especially concerned because Bethlem was overcrowded, and having demanded to 'see the warrants' as to how such patients 'were taken in', they ruled that patient numbers should henceforth not exceed twenty-five and that patients should not be admitted without a Governors' warrant. Their efforts were, however, only partially successful. In 1629 the Court directed the discharge of a further three patients found 'onely . . . idiote' and twenty years later was ordering another 'view' of Bethlem to determine 'what people . . . are fitt to be discharged, itt being reported that many of them are rather Idiotte then Lunatiques'.[44]

Such differentiations were standard. A legal distinction had long been established between idiocy and lunacy, yet the distinction was liable to collapse in practice. Parish records also register this same flux in the use of terms like 'natural', 'fool' and 'crackbrained'.[45] Ambiguities in contemporary definitions should not, however, be exaggerated. Both the Hospital's own records and indeed the records of parishes and Quarter Sessions suggest that, on the whole, the idiotic and the foolish were being identified and responded to in ways often quite distinct from the lunatic and distracted, and that contemporaries knew what they meant by such distinctions. It was the latter who were generally recognized as appropriate for madhouses like Bethlem, while the former tended to be contained within their own families, and only to emerge as a problem for the family or parish on the death of supporting family members.[46]

The precise methods employed to determine whether an individual was idiotic or mad require a certain amount of supposition. Interrogation was the accepted way, although physiognomic differences might also be emphasized. In contemporary legal compendiums, parochial records and commissions or other proceedings regarding idiocy/lunacy, however, it was the judgment that idiocy was congenital or born with one and a permanent affliction, while lunacy was acquired and potentially remedial, which appears to have provided the most consistent grounds for differentiation. The ability of the insane to experience 'lucid intervals' or temporary remissions gave further grounds for distinctions. Theoretical distinctions were clarified by Locke's 1690 formulation (the madman reasons, but reasons wrongly; the idiot cannot reason), although there is limited evidence that this greatly influenced actual practice.[47] Nevertheless, the Minutes of the Bethlem Sub-Committee and the Hospital's admission registers show that 'idiots' were invariably rejected or discharged, while the paucity of such cases in the eighteenth century is indicative of a relatively rigidly imposed exclusion policy.[48]

Admission not only of 'idiotts' but also of 'sottish people which are noe Lunatikes' provoked the Governors in 1653 to introduce a requirement of certification to the Hospital. Henceforth, 'noe Lunatike' was supposed to be 'taken into . . . Bethlem . . . unles the Doctor . . . first finde & reporte such person to bee a Lunatike'.[49] The Hospital's efforts to exclude 'idiots' and 'sots' manifests a curative intention. Demands on space also encouraged the Governors to restrict admission to those deemed curable, or else to those considered 'dangerous to be abroad'. With a capacity until 1645 for no more than twenty-five patients, and only around fifty thereafter, old Bethlem was habitually full.[50] While the Governors exercised much greater control over admissions after Crooke's dismissal, they were required to repeat their former order (of 1629) in 1646, that 'noe Lunatique person' be admitted 'without a Warrant from the President or Treasurer'.[51]

Common law had long sanctioned the confinement of the insane,[52] yet the lack of large-scale provision for the insane at Bethlem or anywhere else meant that the majority of those spoken of as 'crack-brayned', etc. and brought before the criminal proceedings of the Bridewell Court of Governors, Sessions and other courts, were discharged and passed back to their places of settlement. Bethlem's union with Bridewell and the diagnostic difficulties inherent in defining the mentally ill entailed a considerable blurring of the boundaries between the bad and the mad. The insane were sometimes admitted to Bridewell until further inquiry might be made into their mental states and/or settlements,[53] or until a vacancy arose at Bethlem. Parish officers were disposed to support this expedient rather than take an insane individual back home. Sometimes such admissions had distinctly punitive overtones. In the 1630s, Thomas More was removed to Bethlem as insane only after a month in Bridewell where he had been sent by the Privy Council to 'be dayly sett on worke & well whipped in case he refuses', while two 'crackbrayned' men were ordered 'sett at worke' at Bridewell, despite (and perhaps because) of family testimony that one was 'very weak headed & did not worke in his trade since St. James tide last'.[54] Patients who had apparently recovered but refused to leave Bethlem, or to show themselves willing to labour, might also be sent to Bridewell, the Governors (like most contemporary authorities) having little truck with work-shy individuals.[55]

The cases of the recidivists William Landy and Anne Bassett, repeatedly in and out of Bethlem and Bridewell, illustrate the ambivalence in the provision offered by the two institutions and the coercive, street-cleaning tendencies of policies towards the insane.[56] Committed for the third time to Bethlem around 1673 on the authority of the King's Bench, and certified for the third time as recovered by the Physician, Landy's discharge was authorized by the judiciary 'if hee be not dangerous abroad' and he was given 5s by the Governors 'to beare his Charges to his friends in the Country'. Landy had other ideas, refusing to return to the country and remaining bothersome 'abroad'. He had formerly told the Physician in poignant terms, 'that hee had noe place to goe to but the hospitall of Bethlem'. Landy was then consigned to hard labour at Bridewell, the Court having finally lost patience with him and judged him a malingerer. Although the Governors doubted whether he was 'mad or pretends himselfe to be mad', they concluded the latter and that he was quite 'able to Labour for his Liveing'. In general they were at a loss to know how to deal with him. His presence in Bethlem for at least another two spells, during 1697–1703 and 1704–9, indicates that the Governors' strategies were unsuccessful. Anne Bassett was similarly at both institutions at least twice during 1647–55. Arrested in 1647 as 'idle' and 'disorderly', Bassett seems to have determined her committal to Bethlem as 'distracted' by having 'abused the [Bridewell] Court'. When apprehended by a constable two years later for stealing a handkerchief, however, despite being adjudged 'Crasy' she was sent to Bridewell, while in 1655 an Anne Bassett was one of three prisoners transferred to Bethlem from Bridewell having been arrested by a different constable.

Bethlem was often the last resort for families with a lunatic, as in the case of John Norton, committed in 1667 only after his parents had died and after his brother had lost most of his estate in the Great Fire and been 'forced to become a journeyman' to maintain his seven children and brother, and after John had himself 'become very unruly'.[57] The sister of James James sought his admission to Bethlem in 1781, because she was 'unable to Support the Expence of Maintaining him in a Private Madhouse'.[58] For some patients themselves, especially those from more polite circles, like Alexander Cruden, however detestable private madhouses were, the alternative fate of being transferred to a public madhouse like Bethlem might appear worse 'than Death',[59] although (as suggested in earlier chapters) the idea of Bethlem must often have been worse than the reality.

Many patients had wits enough about them to confess themselves insane when brought before the authorities at Bridewell and elsewhere. The frequency with which individuals appeared before the Governors 'feigneing' themselves 'to be mad' to evade punishment, and the persistent problem of Tom o' Bedlam beggars who tramped the highways with fake brass plates, badges or other licences claiming to be collecting to meet arrears for their keeping at Bethlem, or to be 'Out Patients', strained the Governors' patience and lent a suspicious tone to their treatment of recidivists.[60] The Governors attempted on more than one occasion to correct the slur to the charity imprinted by such imposters on the public imagination.

Particularly during the seventeenth century, it was lay persons who were the prima facie arbiters of mental illness, initially identifying the mad and instigating proceedings.[61] The Governors were very much dependent on prior assessments by friends, parishioners and others in making a judgment as to their mental health. Despite the introduction of medical certification around mid-century, it was only slowly and partially that authority over this matter was ceded to the Hospital's medical officers. Certification involved the Physician in both a visual and verbal exchange with patients. Thomas Allen, for example, was not just told to 'be careful to see and speake with every Lunatike before hee prescribeth any physicke for him'; he was also ordered to discover whether patients were 'Lunatike or noe', 'uppon sight of & conferrance with' them.[62]

In practice, the Physician was certifying patients as 'recovered' and 'fitt to be discharged' from the 1640s, yet such examinations were far from regular or even requisite,[63] and not until 1664 was certification by the Physician introduced as a statutory requirement for discharge.[64] This helps to explain why patients were not infrequently permitted to linger in Bethlem when it was evident to staff that they had recovered. The only standing rule governing discharge was that it required the authority of the President, Treasurer or twelve of the Governors.[65] Seldom does this ruling appear to have been rigidly upheld, however. From the 1650s, the Court began to demand that the Steward present to them a regular account of patients admitted and discharged, with dates, as also of the warrants by which they were admitted and the names of patients' sureties. From 1663 'A booke' of such was ordered to be 'kept', and this developed into the admission (and discharge) registers which survive from 1683.[66] From 1681 the Governors demanded that discharge certificates issued by the Physician should be delivered to the Court, and that every patient be brought before the Court for scrutiny prior to discharge, although by the century's end this function had been subsumed under the Weekly Committee's competence and discharge subsequently required the authority of only three governors.[67]

Many patients were rejected or discharged from Bethlem having been certified as 'not Lunatike'.[68] Increasing discrimination over admissions during the eighteenth century is evident from Committee Minutes, which, for example, document the rejection of eighty-two patients between 1709 and 1728 for a range of reasons besides 'sanity'. Patients were also rejected and discharged 'too weak' or 'unable to take Physick', if 'Mopish' or 'Paralytic', for reasons of chronicity and old age, or because suffering from 'fits' or 'convulsions' – all considered to render patients unlikely to be cured. Patients were also excluded if liable to cause the Hospital extra expense or to place other patients under severe threat of infection, as in the case of those suffering from venereal disease.

Such rejections reflect the heightening of the Governors' emphasis on the reception of 'curable' cases, something discernible at Bethlem (as at St Thomas's and St Bartholomew's) from as early as the 1680s. Concerted efforts commenced at that time to expel long-stay patients and those considered 'incurable', by the more regular and vigilant viewing of patients prior to admission, by penalizing those securities who failed to collect discharged patients and by periodic clear-outs.[69] 'Incurables' were re-embraced as suitable objects for hospital care from the 1720s,[70] in a rather ambiguous, face-saving attempt by the Hospital to counter criticism of the limits of its charity, and to attribute therapeutic failure to the inveterate nature of mental disease.[71]

The notion that Bethlem served primarily as a long-term warehouse is, however, misconceived. Most patients were short-stay. Even before the establishment of incurables wards, patients were being admitted for little more than a year, if remaining uncured, from which time they were liable to be discharged as incurable. Computations of the lengths of stay of curables between 1694 and 1718 (see Table 18.1), and between 1728 and 1770 (before their readmission as incurables), demonstrate that the great majority remained less than two years and that the Hospital was quite stringent in imposing its ceiling. After 1750, patients insane for more than a year were being rejected from admission (as curables) to the Hospital, exceptions being made only on the Physicians' and Committee's discretion and being confined to admission during the putatively healthier spring and summer months.[72]

Table 18.1 Duration of stay of male and female patients at
Bethlem, 1694–1718

Years	Numbers		
	Males	*Females*	*Totals*
0–1	608	506	1,114
1–2	136	155	291
2–3	75	80	155
3–5	51	82	133
5–10	60	64	124
10–15	13	11	24
15–20	2	2	4
20–30	2	0	2
30–40	1	0	1
Totals	948	900	1,848

The emphasis was on rapid turnover, on targeting limited resources where they were deemed to be most efficacious (i.e. on the 'curable' and 'dangerous') and on the virtues of early treatment. Patients were supposed to be supported at Bethlem only so long as they remained in a condition (mental and economic) that made it impossible for them to be supported elsewhere. During the seventeenth century in particular, they were commonly ordered discharged if 'conceived not now so Lunatique' or 'soe unruly but that they may bee kept in any other place as well as here'. Bethlem strove (not altogether successfully or consistently) to prioritize acute and 'dangerous' cases, stressing the need to make space for 'others whoe are distracted Lunatique & dangerous abroad'.[73] Such a policy was apt, neverthless, to give the Hospital more of the character of a detention centre. Although by the mid-seventeenth century the Governors ceased to identify their charges at Bethlem as 'prisoners', parish officers were still at the century's end referring to Bethlem as a 'Hospitall or Prison'.[74] The hope of security was clearly paramount in persuading many country parishes to meet the expense of sending an insane individual to London.[75]

The tradition that Bethlem received 'dangerous' cases was recognized by contemporaries.[76] Towards the end of the seventeenth century, efforts were intensified to exclude those designated merely 'mopish' or 'melancholic', and even when incurables' wards were set up in the eighteenth century, only 'mischievous and ungovernable' cases, or those adjudged 'outrageous and likely to do mischief to themselves and others', were supposed to be admitted, whilst 'mopes' were barred.[77] Bethlem still, however, continued to support a significant number of cases deemed innocuous. Black found that of 1,972 patients admitted between 1772 and 1787, only 38 per cent were 'Mischievous', only 16 per cent had 'Attempted Suicide' and only 1 per cent had 'Committed Murders' (making 55 per cent putatively dangerously insane), while 45 per cent had been admitted as 'Not Mischievous'.[78] A similar impression of a majority of 'dangerous' cases, but a large proportion of the more innocuous, is offered by petitions for admission in the Bethlem archives. Amongst ninety-eight covering the period 1763–1803 (see Table 18.2), 57 per cent record that applicants were 'Raving',

Table 18.2 Description of applicants for admission to Bethlem, 1763–1803

Description	Number*
Melancholy	22
Raving, furious, bad	56
Melancholy and raving	8
Mischievous	59
Not mischievous	39
Hysterical fits and laughter	1
Suicidal	4

* Derived from 98 extant petitions for admission

'bad' or 'furious'; 60 per cent that patients were 'Mischievous'; and only 40 per cent that patients were 'not Mischievous' and 22 per cent that patients were 'Melancholy'. Petitioners may have been encouraged to exaggerate the unruliness of the insane so as to try to ensure their reception. Developments at Bethlem must furthermore be seen in the context of vagrancy and lunacy legislation, which also reflect this emphasis on security in confinement, instructing authorities that it was those who 'are furiously Mad, and dangerous to be permitted to go Abroad' who should 'be Apprehended, and kept safely Locked up'.[79]

Concerns with security and cure were not mutually exclusive, of course, and tended to be accorded more or less equal weight in petitions for patients' admissions. Cure seems to have figured more prominently as a motivation for confining the insane in the petitions of families than it does in those from parishes and parochial or public bodies. Indeed, it was private securities who more often claimed to have made their own unavailing efforts to cure patients before resorting to Bethlem, or petitioned to the effect that penury prevented them 'from procuring proper Advice' for their insane friends and relatives.[80] Parish officers on the other hand tended more frequently to stress pragmatic concerns with economy and safety in their dealings with Bethlem over patients. Nevertheless, other institutions also gave cure a high priority in their applications for patients' reception, the Sick and Wounded Board, for example, emphasizing the curative objective in almost every case of those mad sailors it sent to Bethlem. Spital Sermons on behalf of the London Hospitals stressed that Bethlem was both 'for keeping and curing distracted persons'.[81]

As a result of the pressure on space and the looseness of the criteria governing discharge, rarely did patients' families or friends experience much opposition if they desired to remove a patient before recovery. Discharge was often negotiated with and instigated by their securities, or even with patients themselves. The admission registers and Sub-Committee Minutes are replete with instances of a patient being discharged 'at the request of friends', family, sureties or parish, while during the seventeenth century patients were sometimes even discharged at their 'owne request'.[82] Contrariwise, discharge was occasionally enforced by the Hospital in opposition to the wishes of a patient's securities, as in the case of James Carkesse, liberated on his own petition in 1678, 'severall of his relacions being . . . present and not able to satisfye this Courte That hee is not void or discomposed of his sences'.[83]

Even those still regarded as 'dangerous abroad' might be discharged if their securities asked it, although in such cases the Hospital was normally careful to issue an admonishment to ensure that the patient was provided for and 'restrained from doing any hurt'.[84] On occasion, the Court might be more coercive in its concern with public safety and patients' cure (and the recovery of arrears), as in the case of Margaret Rawson. Refusing to discharge Rawson for over a year (1689–90), the Governors finally insisted that her security seal a new bond guaranteeing 'not to permitt' the patient 'to wander about the streetes but to use what meanes hee can for her Cure or to put her into . . . Bethlem againe', before agreeing to her discharge.[85] Discharge was generally delayed in the event of outstanding arrears.[86] Furthermore, the discharge of those patients committed by order of Government or some other external authority normally required the consent of that authority.[87]

As time went on, the administration grew more insistent on its own judgments and dismissive of alternative suggestions, so that the intervention of patients' representatives began to be conceived as interference. The Hospital's medical officers began to exert increasing sway over policies governing admission and discharge. As the freedom of access formerly enjoyed by patients' friends was restricted, securities were increasingly required to demand the release of patients, and the Physician and Committee became more emphatic in their advice. By the later eighteenth century, Hospital records register the disapproval felt when patients were 'taken out against the advice of the Committee', but also that they might be barred (as a result) from readmission, and that, if deemed dangerous, they might be refused discharge altogether. The appearance of such cases suggests the intensifying of areas of conflict over discharge between patients' securities and Hospital policy, and a narrowing of the avenues of negotiation with patients' representatives. An overall decline in the number of patients removed at the request of friends between 1750 and 1775, however, may indicate a heightened preparedness on the part of patients' friends to defer to the judgment of officials regarding discharge.

THE 'DANGER' OF THE INSANE

If, as detailed above, Bethlem tended to prioritize admission of the 'dangerous' insane, it is important to analyse what was meant by 'dangerous', and what distinguished those confined at Bethlem or other institutions from the majority of lunatics retained in the community. In the case of individuals deemed a danger to themselves or suicidal, committal was more straightforward, usually following an attempt or threat to commit suicide. There is little trace in the Bethlem Minutes of punitive responses to suicidal cases. More often the emphasis was on prevention, as in the case of an anonymous 'poore distracted weoman' who had 'lately wandred up and downe the ... parish [of St Botolph Billingsgate] and like to have drowned herselfe last night in the Thames', admitted to Bethlem on the 'applicacion' of a Governor 'and other Inhabitants'.[88] William Peares/Piercey, 'who Cutt his throat' in the parish of St Botolph Bishopsgate in 1707 was treated with remarkable sympathy; the parish officers hired a surgeon to heal his throat, paid a nurse 3s per week 'for looking to' him, relieved him with 5s 'in order to goe to Kent', and settled a bill of £2 'for [his] lodgeing and diett' at the Dolphin Inn.[89] Suicide or its attempt did not necessarily imply insanity in this period, as some of those brought before the Court of Governors for this reason who were 'past' or dealt with otherwise than being sent to Bethlem indicate. Yet, later cases, such as a cook from the ship 'Victory', whose attempt to hang himself was conceived of by the naval authorities as 'Proof of the Frenzy of his Mind' and sufficient cause for his conveyance to Bethlem, indicate that, as MacDonald has argued, suicide increasingly assumed the ineluctable taint of insanity as the period wore on.[90] Often, however, attempts at self-harm were not sufficient on their own to precipitate a committal, and were part of a long history of violent behaviour – revealing considerable preparedness on the part of poor families to contain the problems posed by the insane within the home. For the family of Catherine Gary/Gazy, for example, admitted to Bethlem in 1765 having 'been distracted for 7 years' and 'in her first melancholy Fit ... cut her Throat and ... severall Times since, alarmed her Husband & Neighbours with apprehensions of her doing herself, her children & them Mischief', Bethlem seems to have been the last resort.[91]

With those thought dangerous to others, the matter was rather more complicated, but it was primarily when the insane were conceived as a threat to life or property that they seem to have been hospitalized. Though wards for the criminally insane were not established until the nineteenth century, many patients had attempted or committed some violent act. Yet dangerousness might simply mean that the insane were at large, beyond domestic restraint, and it was often mere vagrancy and civil disorders which brought insane individuals to the authorities' attention. Anne Read of Burford, Oxford, for example, petitioned the Governors for the admission of her son John in 1674, informing them that he had abandoned 'his Service' as a journeyman to a London mercer, and returned to 'the Countrey', where he was 'running about in A daingerous condicion shee haveing noe meanes to keepe him within doores'.[92] Such 'mental vagrancy'[93] went far beyond the loss of control signified by the ordinary vagrant in flouting life-supporting ties with families, neighbourhoods and wider society, and vagrancy was itself acquiring an increasingly irrational and threatening aspect to established society during this period. The wandering of lunatics was seen as unpredictable, their relinquishment of work contrary to self-interest and to the interests of their dependants and the community. Many of the insane brought before Bridewell and the metropolitan Sessions had been rounded up by constables and other local officers, found 'vagrant and lurkeing' or 'taken in the watch', abroad in the wrong places, or at the wrong times (night-time especially).[94] While a degree of sympathy for such cases found 'lying under stalls' is occasionally discernible, more frequently they seem to have been treated as 'annoyances' or 'nuisances'. Their committal was in essence street-cleaning, and keeping public rights of way free from obstructions and protecting respectable citizens from the pestering of the idle was a vigorous concern of early modern legislation.[95]

Property was, of course, of paramount importance in this period definitive of rate-paying and the franchise. Little wonder then that arson or its threat was a particularly common charge against those lunatics appearing before the Court of Governors and Sessions. The insane were not merely apprehended or admitted to Bethlem 'for threatening to burne houses' or 'for wishing the Cittie on fire', but often seem to have gone through with their threats, as did Elizabeth Tarleton, committed in 1656, having 'sett fire last night on faggotts dangerously'.[96] The prominence of arson in committal proceedings must also owe something to the large number of buildings constructed out of wood and to the fact that it was written large in the test cases on which common law governing the detention of lunatics was based.[97] The wanton destruction of property appeared as particularly irrational to contemporaries, representing an assault on the material basis of social status, and, for poorer families, on the very stuff of subsistence and security, marking out the offender as at odds with household and social identities and values. Items of conspicuous consumption, such as windows and furniture, wherein was symbolized contemporaries' prosperity and *locus standi*, were invested with especial meaning, and it was not merely the vulnerability of such items as a target for the estranged that made damage to them figure in a significant number of cases committed to Bethlem. A lunatic porter, Henry Bates, for example, was sent to Bethlem at considerable trouble and expense by his parish in 1693 only after he had upset a number of respectable 'Inhabitants . . . by breakeing their windows And Afronteing every one that passed him'.[98]

Destruction of one's own property was even less comprehensible, and more replete with fearsome signification. Dress was likewise important as a symbol of social status and civilization; those who tore or cast off their own clothing abnegated that status. Nakedness and dishevelled attire were heavily associated with lunacy.[99] Widow Davies was thus deemed dangerously insane and transferred from Bridewell to Bethlem in 1638 because she 'doth teare her cloathes off her backe and soe misuse those that come about her'.[100] Lunatics who destroyed their clothing were conceived as reducing themselves to the condition of beasts, stripping themselves of decency and the cloak of reason, while naked, bestial lunacy was often depicted as indistinguishable from sexual wantonness. Nakedness was a powerful and damaging affront, an outward display of infirmity that should be hidden, provoking shock and embarrassment, for the insane were not just 'exposing themselves', as their kith and kin often complained, they were exposing their families as well. Patients were occasionally those who had damaged the actual buildings in which they had previously been lodged, and Bethlem sometimes served as a more secure holding facility for individuals who could not be managed in former places of confinement. Lunatics were not only committed to Bethlem for damaging property; they were also frequently admitted having been caught stealing, but insane thieves were generally more likely to end up in Bridewell or prison.[101]

The power of mere words to distinguish the insane and to connote threat in this period must also be emphasized. It figured prominently in committals, with petitions by the later eighteenth century standardly recording whether patients were 'raving' or not. As will be further elaborated in the next chapter, it was sometimes more important who, rather than how, individuals slandered. The hierarchical structure of early modern society allowed little scope for those who abused that hierarchy and, either by words or deed, gave offence above their station. Many contemporaries were committed believing that they were the Emperor, the King, the Queen, etc., or for troubling the high and mighty. Those disturbing their family, neighbours or ordinary citizens were, predictably, much more common, however, than those who harassed the governing classes. The frequency with which patients committed to Bethlem were deemed to have threatened the 'neighbourhood', or abused 'the neighbours' is a striking feature of the Governors' Minutes, and of the dealings of Sessions and parish officers with the insane. Offence to hierarchies was more commonly caused on the lower levels of domestic and working life. Unruly apprentices and fractious servants, for example, being liable to be charged with madness or viciousness for flouting the authority of their masters and mistresses, had been strongly represented amongst committals.[102] Patients had often been local nuisances and noisy disturbers of the peace. Katherine Scudamore, for example, was sent to Bethlem in 1685 on 'committing many disturbances amongst the neighbours to their terror and affrightment', and Thomasin Withers was dealt with in the same way in 1682 'for being a continueall Disturber of her neighbours and threatening to fire the house of one John Preston and being an idle person' but 'distracted'.[103] Loss of patience as a motivation for the committal of the insane seems to have become especially prominent in Bethlem committals after the Restoration, typified by the case of Dr Richard Burd who complained of being 'forced to get' Margaret Hebb readmitted to Bethlem, she having 'continued to vex and trouble the peticioner in a most insupportable manner'.[104]

By the eighteenth century, contemporaries were being even more explicit about the 'nuisance' the behaviour of the insane caused them. Just as in Spital Sermons, clerics like Andrew Snape and Robert Moss recommended Bridewell for vagrants of all kinds, others saw Bethlem as 'that Pest House of the Head' or, like Jonathan Swift, envisaged hospitals as receptacles to lock away society's pests.[105] Jacob Beezley was arrested on Christmas Day 1755 and 'Committed to the London Workhouse' 'till the [next] Meeting of the Governors of Bethlem', because his parish 'could by no other means get rid of him', being described as 'a Vagrant and Lunatick', who had

for a long time before been a publick Nusance to the ... Parish by constantly attending Divine Service as well on Sundays as other Days at prayer time and very often Obstructed the publick Service by talking to the Minister and otherwise misbehaving in a very indecent Manner.[106]

Likewise, those who threatened domestic harmony were also liable to be regarded as dangerously insane and to require confinement. This could be understood in terms of patriarchy, so that children and wives who upset that harmony were more liable to be deemed mad or vicious, and carted off to Bethlem or to prison, and fathers and husbands faced with the disobedience of their domestic inferiors might be treated with sympathy by male authorities. In 1680, for example, the Board of Greencloth committed Thomas Whittmore, Yeoman of the King's Pantry, to Bethlem on the complaint of his wife, Mary, that he was distracted and had attempted suicide 'severall times'. When, however, 'on further examinacion of the matter', 'it appeared' that Whittmore was 'not Lunatick but only discontented & melancholy, by reason of his . . . Wife's disorderly course of life', all sympathy was transferred to the husband who was immediately 'released'.[107] On the other hand, patriarchy was but one (by no means uncontestable) constituent of household integrity, and husbands whose insanity involved a similar neglect of their roles as breadwinners, or disregard of their natural bonds of affection to wives, parents and children, might also find themselves being committed by their friends and dependants.

As the work of Peter Linebaugh and others on 'excarceration' has helped to suggest,[108] the kinds of patients not sent to Bethlem also suggest something about what sort of individuals were seen as more threatening or more in need of confinement by early modern society. Parish and hospital records reveal that neither the very old nor the very young were apt to be supported at Bethlem. The senile, the anile, the demented and the doddering tended to be supported by their families or by outdoor relief with parish nurses, or else in almshouses and workhouses, as even more so were the young mentally disabled.[109] There was scant incentive for parishes and families to go to the trouble and expense of getting such individuals (adjudged more manageable and more innocuous) admitted to Bethlem. Computations of the ages of admissions to Bethlem after the 1760s (when ages are more consistently recorded) confirm that while roughly only between 1 and 7 per cent of admissions were under 20, and only 11 or 12 per cent were over 50, the great majority were in the prime of life between 20 and 40.[110]

RELIGION AND LUNACY

The mentally disordered had long been recognized as afflicted by God and restored to their understanding only according to God's will; they were often spoken of as 'innocents' or 'naturals', and associated with the holy and the elemental. Essentially, however, the insane were conceived by definition as divorced from God's blessing, closer to the damned than the holy. Such beliefs informed contemporary mentalities and exerted considerable force in the proceedings of legal and administrative bodies. Royal licences authorizing collections on behalf of the poor maintained at the royal hospitals pleaded on behalf of those 'stryken by the hande of God . . . untyle God caule them to his marcy or to their wyttes agayne'.[111]

At least since the Reformation, Bethlem's patients had traditionally received no formal pastoral care. Religious instruction was introduced for the Hospital's inmates in 1677 at the instigation of the new Bethlem Committee, plainly influenced by the feelings of renewal arising out of the Hospital's spectacular resiting at Moorfields.[112] From 1677 to 1713, Bridewell Chaplains were allowed an additional £20 per annum 'to give . . . seasonable Instruccion to any of the said Lunaticks', and were supposed to attend Bethlem 'three or fower tymes a weeke' for this purpose.

The Committee's original idea had been for a separate, salaried pastor, resident at Bethlem. Yet the majority on the Court were moderate Anglicans, suspicious of zeal, and pessimistic regarding the possible benefit that the insane might receive from religious counsel. The Court rejected the Committee's proposal on the grounds that the Hospital was 'yett in debt', that there was no precedent for it, and 'that If any of the Lunaticks kept in the said hospital be capable to receive Instruccion they are not soe fitt to be kept there'. The Governors preferred to save money and preserve orthodoxy by employing the Bridewell Minister, who was ordered to confine his discourse to convalescents or those patients 'in their Intervalls'.[113] Even for these patients, however, this form of divine dispensation was soon permitted to lapse, being officially abolished in 1713, 'the Committee not finding there is any occasion for such attendance'. Henceforth, no Bethlem patient was recognized by the Governors as 'capable of receiveing [religious] instruccion'.[114]

There was even less sympathy in eighteenth-century Bethlem for the role of religion in patients' lives, or for interpretations of insanity as an affliction of the conscience. The intervention of preachers into the lives of the mentally unstable was increasingly viewed as a provocation. As Quakers and other evangelicals took on the role of visiting the mad, sick and criminal, Bethlem closed its ranks against the claims of religious inspiration. Far from capable of receiving and benefiting from religious instruction, the mad of Bethlem were seen as those whose weak minds had been or could be unhinged by exposure to religion. While religious radicalism and evangelism encouraged followers to give vent to transports of devotion, traditional Anglicanism stressed moderation, and individuals who had created uproar in church services, or who, like the poet, Kit Smart, disturbed family and neighbours by praying at the top of their voices, became conspicuous amongst Bethlem admissions.

Humble tradesmen and craftsmen who claimed to have seen the light and appointed themselves God's prophets were increasingly seen as vainglorious and deluded. Edward Osburne, for example, a weaver sent to Bethlem in 1700 by the Board of Greencloth, had not only 'been for some time very troublesome to his Majestie', 'but . . . also impudently assumes the habit of a minister'.[115] This is not to say that during the earlier seventeenth century too, especially during the uncompromising orthodoxy of the Laudian period, that individuals claiming divine inspiration or disrupting church services were not frequently declared mad enthusiasts or vicious reprobates. From the notorious bigamist, Richard Farnham, who re-enacted Christ's entry to Jerusalem and was sent to Bethlem by Archbishop Laud; the Lady Eleanor Davies, who assailed nobility and royalty with prophesies of doom from the Book of Daniel; to the 'crased' Peter Delight, committed by the Lord Mayor for 'making proclamacions' and tumult 'in the streets', drawing attention to himself with a fife and drummer boy, the 1630s were a particularly intolerant time for rival claims of religious inspiration.[116] The campaign against enthusiasm was already under way,[117] but it was only from the late seventeenth century that significant numbers of such enthusiasts began to be confined.[118] According to William Black, tabulating information provided to him by the Bethlem Apothecary, John Gozna, 'Religion and Methodism' were, by the late eighteenth century, the fourth most common cause of insanity, accounting for over 10 per cent of all cases.[119]

RESULTS OF ADMISSION: CURE, DISCHARGE AND RELAPSE; RHETORIC AND REALITY

At face value the outcomes of admissions contradict the negative impression of Bethlem's record held by some historians. In nine annual reports from 1681–1705, Bethlem claimed a cure rate of between 57 per cent and 82 per cent of the patients admitted over the same period, or between 31 per cent and 63 per cent of the total patient population. These figures give mean percentage cure rates of 71 per cent and 34 per cent respectively. In 1682, the Court of Governors' Minutes recorded the discharge of forty 'recovered' patients, or about 66 per cent of the number admitted, and 34 per cent of the average patient population. Computing the results of all 1,858 admissions to Bethlem as recorded in the registers during the period 1694–1718, demonstrates a similarly high rate of discharge, at 80 per cent.

Only limited conclusions can be drawn, however, from the numbers of patients discharged. While only 25 per cent (sixteen men and thirteen women) of 118 patients (sixty men and fifty-eight women) in the Hospital during 1683 are known to have been discharged, in 1702 this proportion had increased to 61 per cent (43 men and 42 women) of the 139 patients being supported (seventy-five men and sixty-four women). Yet this had little to do with any improvement in patients' recovery rates, being explained by the administration's increased efforts to exclude chronics and other cases deemed unfit.[120] Moreover, Spital reports calculated patients 'Cured and Discharged' cumulatively, without distinguishing the proportion discharged uncured, effectively counting each discharge as a cure. Nor do the Hospital's admission registers allow any such distinction to be made before 1750, failing until the late 1730s to record the condition in which patients were discharged, and failing before the 1750s consistently to record this information. Spital reports went on failing to distinguish between those cured and those discharged, so as to sustain public confidence.[121] More realistically, the Bethlem Apothecary, John Haslam, claimed that of 8,874 patients (4,832 women and 4,042 men) admitted to Bethlem between 1748 and 1794, only 29 per cent (2,557) 'recovered' or 'were discharged cured'.[122]

Patients' recovery, of course, frequently proved only a temporary remission, and neither did Bethlem's annual reports take into account relapses or readmissions. Black estimated that between 1772 and 1787 only 32 per cent of those discharged were 'cured', while 58 per cent of these patients relapsed; indicating that at most just 14 per cent can be said to have recovered and sustained their recoveries.[123] The Apothecary, John Haslam, found that of 389 patients admitted to the Hospital during the two years 1796 and 1797, fifty-three, or just over 13 per cent, were readmissions.[124]

BETHLEM'S RECORD, ACCORDING TO PARISH RECORDS

Parish records provide a rather negative impression of the Hospital's success as a curative establishment. They provide evidence in very few cases that the parish poor committed to Bethlem were discharged fully recovered, or remained well for long. For example, of thirteen St Botolph Bishopsgate paupers admitted between 1636 and 1676, at least two died; at least five were discharged; while the outcome of six admissions was unrecorded. At least four of those 'discharged' were, however, discharged in an unhealthy condition, two perishing within a year of their discharge, one within three years, while the last died still suffering from 'frenzy' after being kept by a parishioner and his wife for a year and a half. Of twenty-eight such parishioners received at the Hospital between 1676 and 1721, twenty-four are known to have been discharged, only three to have died, while one case remains undetermined. Of those discharged, at least eleven were discharged incurable or rapidly relapsed; and only two may confidently be said to have sustained recoveries, although thirteen outcomes are unknown. Likewise, of fifteen patients admitted from St Dunstan in the West between 1700 and 1730 three perished in Bethlem, while thirteen were discharged. Of eight of the latter (seven being private cases) nothing else is heard; one escaped; two were discharged incurable, one of whom was sent to a madhouse, while the other was nursed in the parish and then at Lambeth until her death; one was rich enough to be supported elsewhere, and died two months later under the care of a Hampstead nurse; the last, having been admitted and discharged five times over an eighteen-year period simply disappears from the parochial accounts.

Bethlem's record regarding the poor insane of St Stephen Coleman Street and St Dionis Backchurch is little better, and the results of admissions from six other London parishes surveyed tell a similarly grim if incomplete story. The majority of parochial patients admitted to Bethlem probably failed to leave the Hospital in a condition able to resume their ordinary lives and livelihoods. Indeed, only a minority may have been committed primarily for their 'cure'. Parish records do register cure as an objective of the admission and support of patients in Bethlem, but only very rarely.[125] That parochial relief seldom extended to providing medical assistance for insane parishioners prior or subsequent to their admission to Bethlem, or indeed for the majority of mad inhabitants never admitted to the Hospital, also suggests that curative concerns had a low priority. While most mad parishioners received lodging, diet and nursing at parish expense, a minority only were provided with medical attention. However, while it was not until 1744 that parishes were made legally responsible not only for restraining and maintaining pauper lunatics, but also for 'curing such Person during such Restraint',[126] there were considerable local and temporal variations in preparedness to provide therapeutic aid. Some parishes were prepared to spend considerable amounts on procuring treatment for patients prior to admission to Bethlem, no doubt hoping to preclude such and keep costs at a minimum – as when Coleman Street expended £1 5s on Jeremy Tucker being nursed, washed, bled and 'physicked', or when Allhallows the Great ordered John Burton 'put under the care of a Physician till he can be admitted into Bethlehem Hospital', and kept in 'a proper place' on 'the best Terms . . . for his Diett Physick &c'.[127]

Providing for lunatics was extremely expensive and troublesome, and Bethlem was probably sought after first and foremost for the charitable rates at which it offered secure detention, rather than for its therapeutic assistance. In the seventeenth century, the majority of the insane were retained in their localities, with their families or parish nurses. During the eighteenth century, considerably more insane parishioners were being maintained in institutional care, at Bethlem and other hospitals, at private madhouses and at workhouses. Amongst the private madhouses, Hoxton and Bethnal Green were particularly popular, being the largest and cheapest, although others, including those at White Cross Alley, Moorfields; Finsbury; Hackney; Dog Row, Mile End New Town and Newington were used in a more limited way. St Botolph Bishopsgate alone used at least four private houses for its insane parishioners prior to 1720.[128] Parish records reveal that for parishes and the poorest families at least the provision of private madhouses was generally a temporary or exigency measure, until admission was obtained, or in the event of exclusion or discharge from Bethlem and other public hospitals. Other authorities too, like the Sick and Wounded Board, used Bethnal Green and other madhouses mainly (if not solely) as a second choice to Bethlem. Bethlem's profile as a specialist institution for the most difficult and dangerous cases meant that violent and destructive cases rejected or expelled from contemporary workhouses, prisons and indeed private madhouses were also frequently transferred to Bethlem.[129] Indeed, the extent of the service the Hospital was performing – given the lack of much alternative provision – in taking in the least desirable cases may have been underestimated.

MORTALITY AND LUNACY

Prior to 1683 it is difficult to estimate the mortality of the Hospital's patient population. It is not until after the Hospital's resiting at Moorfields, however, and some years after Thomas Tymes had received the dubious honour of being recorded in St Stephen's Coleman Street's burial registers as 'ye first Lunatick in new Bedlam Buryed', that any reliable impression can be gained.[130] These burial registers record the deaths of only forty-three lunatics in Bethlem during the period 1680–90, and eighty-nine from 1690–4. Only from the 1690s do they appear to record almost every patient's burial.

Bethlem's admission registers record that from 1694–1718, out of a total of 1,841 admissions of which the result is known, 355, or over 19 per cent, were to end with the death of the patient in Bethlem.[131] This represents a particularly high proportion, although the death of an average of about fourteen patients a year denotes only about 11 per cent of the patient population, and this appears to have been no worse, if not marginally better, than mortality at the county asylums founded in the early nineteenth century. The 6–9 per cent differentials found indicating higher mortality amongst males roughly accords with patterns concerning contemporaneous hospital deaths elsewhere.[132]

Mortality declined at Bethlem during the eighteenth century. Spital reports sampled between 1681 and 1775 record a steady decline from an initial average of 29 per cent of admissions to just 9 per cent by the period's end, and are confirmed by

Black's calculation of a mortality rate of just 8 per cent of admissions with a result during the period 1772–87.[133] Suicide appears to have been remarkably exceptional as a cause of death, given that one of the major criteria of eligibility for admission throughout the period was being 'dangerous', or having attempted 'mischief', towards oneself or others. Possibly suicides sometimes went unrecorded in admission registers.

CONCLUSION

The Hospital served a broad array of functions and needs beyond the carceral. The records testify to the nuisance and burden the pauper insane constituted for local inhabitants; a main object of committing patients to Bethlem was clearly the expulsion and confinement of bothersome and threatening presences within the family and neighbourhood. Yet the sources also document a strong element of compassion for the afflicted, and a significant concern with their cure. Not just any mad person was admitted to Bethlem. An increasingly sophisticated array of conditions and exclusions attempted to restrict eligibility to those deemed dangerous and curable. The need for applicants to satisfy these conditions and (in most cases) to obtain a governor's nomination; a continual shortage of space; and the Hospital's commitment to a rapid turnover of 'curable' cases, meant that the great majority of patients were short-stay. Admission was often sued for and conferred, especially in the seventeenth century, as something of a privilege – if, clearly, an ambiguous one.

Bethlem did more for its public and its paying clients than for its patients. Historians have underestimated the value of the service Bethlem was performing in furnishing affordable provision for poor families and parishes bereft of sufficient means to provide themselves, when alternative facilities were so limited and so expensive. While families of means preferred to purchase superior living conditions at private madhouses, parishes and families lacking such purchasing power tended to lodge insane members at private madhouses only if failing, or awaiting, to obtain a vacancy at Bethlem or at some other equally cheap public hospital.

NOTES

1 *BCGM*, e.g. 16 Nov. 1653, 3 Feb. 1654, 16 Jan. 1656, fols 629, 641 and 729. For further detail and references, see Jonathan Andrews, 'A History of Bethlem Hospital *c.* 1634–*c.* 1770' (Ph.D. diss., London University, 1991).
2 For moneyed patients forced to contribute or discharged from Bethlem, see *BCGM*, e.g. 16 June 1682, 24 July 1691, 6 May 1698, fols 308, 134, 182–3; *BSCM*, e.g. 22 Sept. 1759, 17 Sept. 1763, 5 May 1770 and 8 Nov. 1783.
3 *BCGM*, e.g. 28 Oct. 1653, 26 July 1654, 6 Aug. 1656 and 9 Feb. 1683, fols 627, 668, 763 and 350; cases of Benjamin Hide, supported by his father, Benjamin; Holmes, supported by his father, Walter Holmes ('a poore Minister'); Mary Wilkinson, supported by her aunt, Martha Boutha, and Elizabeth Hall, supported by Margaret Hall.
4 *Ibid.* 11 April 1701 and 6 Nov. 1702, fols 439–40 and 119.
5 Rising prices forced the Governors, in 1789, to restore the original fee of 5s a week for incurables.

6   *BCGM*, 30 May, 11 and 29 July 1674, 30 April and 30 July 1675, 2 April, 14 May and 23 July 1680, 17 Aug. 1681, 4 Sept. 1702, 9 Oct. 1729, fols 648, 15, 23, 135, 146, 153, 161–2, 244, 109, 192.

7   *Ibid.* 16 May 1734, 29 Jan., 27 March and 13 Nov. 1735, fols 327, 339, 343 and 364; also Chapter 14, this volume; Thomas Bowen, *An Historical Account of the Origin, Progress and Present State of Bethlem Hospital* (London: For the Governors, 1783), 13–14; *BCGM* in *BSCM*, 7 June 1751, fol. 243, and *BCGM*, 21 June 1751, fol. 9. See, also, Jonathan Andrews, 'The Lot of the Incurably Insane in Enlightenment England', *Eighteenth Century Life*, xii (1988), 1–18.

8   C. N. French, *The Story of St. Luke's Hospital 1750–1948* (London: William Heinemann, 1951); *BSCM*, 6 June 1795.

9   This policy later met with much disdain and opposition from the Corporation of London and the Poor Law authorities of the City Unions, keen to carry on using Bethlem and avoid the expense of erecting the City of London Lunatic Asylum. *CLRO*, MS 188.1 and 2.

10 *Ghall* MS 4515/1; *BCGM*, 2 June 1641, 28 May 1644, 21 April 1648, 20 April 1659, 30 June 1671, fols 336, 114, 344, 127 and 315.

11 For Lyth, see *Ghall* MS 2968/7, 3 Oct. 1710 to 3 Feb. 1711; 3016/3, fol. 126; *BAR*, fol. 167. Clarke had his brother admitted to Bethlem sometime before Sept. 1682: *BCGM*, 1 and 22 Sept. 1682, 326 and 328.

12 See *BAR* and *BIAR*; *PRO* MS C211 2/98 and 140, 5/95, 7/57, 10/35, 11/67, 18/7, 22/29, 23/118, 25/21, 26/9 and 27/78.

13 *BCGM*, e.g. 18 Aug. 1643, 2 Jan. 1668, 3 Nov. 1671, 15 March and 9 Aug. 1682, 28 Nov. and 19 Dec. 1690 and 6 Dec. 1700, fols 287, 319, 24–5, 252, 287, 319, 91 and 418; cases of Emma Kitchenman, William Marshall, Thomas Bishop, Thomas Almond, Abraham Byard (Byward), Thomas Sutton, Rachel Franks and Ann Stone.

14 *GLRO SM* 42, 27 Feb. 1673.

15 See *BCGM*, e.g. 24 Sept. 1651, 8 Sept. 1653, 2 Sept. and 21 Oct. 1657, fols 510, 599, 825 and 831, *re* privileges extended to sailor/soldiers who had served Parliament, and their wives. Contrast entry in *ibid.* 27 July 1655, fol. 710: 'in the second yeare of Oliver's usurpacion'. *Re* favours to those in Crown's service, see, e.g., *ibid.* 28 Sept. 1666, 4 July 1690 and 30 April 1697, fols 8, 62 and 107.

16 *Ibid.* 3 Feb. 1654, fol. 640.

17 *Ibid.* 30 Sept. 1642, fol. 411.

18 *Ibid.* 12 March 1697, fol. 99. See also, e.g., case of Thomas Wattee, 'a poore decayed citizen' admitted in 1656; *ibid.* 16 Jan. and 17 Dec. 1656, fols 729 and 778.

19 *Ibid.* e.g. 14 Sept., 19 Dec. 1666, 25 Jan., 26 April, 10 July and 16 Oct. 1667, fols 3, 26, 30, 41, 54 and 62; *GLRO SM* 26, 12 Oct. 1667; cases of John Felgate, Thomas Beasely, Elizabeth Hazeler, John Felgate, Mary Sharpe and John Norton.

20 William Black, *A Dissertation on Insanity* (London: Ridgway, 1810), 18–19.

21 *BSCM*, 1 Oct. 1709, fol. 3; *BCGM*, 22 Nov. 1672, fol. 459. For similar cases, see *BCGM*, e.g. 4 April 1672, 22 Jan. 1675 and 9 Feb. 1683, fols 386, 92 and 350–1.

22 *BCFM*, e.g., 10 June 1669, 19 and 28 Nov. 1673, 12 March 1697, 1 April 1698, 3 Nov. 1699 and 12 April 1700, fols 145, 587, 591, 99, 177, 321 and 363; *GLRO SM* 44, 8 Dec. 1673; cases of Thomas Almond, Sarah Wyatt, Denise (Dennis) Bundy, Daniel Bull, Edward Cook and Mary Dolling.

23 See *Ghall* MS 4216/1, fols 205 and 207; 4215/1, 1664–6 accounts; *BCGM*, 23 Nov. and 16 Dec. 1664, fols 119 and 125.

24 *BCGM*, 5 Dec. 1679, fol. 118.

25 *Ibid.* 10 Nov. 1652 and 2 June 1693, fols 574 and 247–8.

26 For example, *GLRO SM* 42, 27 Feb. 1673, case of Mary and Lewis Powell.

27 For Governors' connections with patients, see *BCGM*, e.g. 21 June 1678, 24 July 1691 and 8 Nov. 1700, fols 34, 133 and 408.

28 Bowen, *op. cit.* 7.

29 *BCGM*, 27 May 1642, fol. 385.

30 Those cases for whom the highest weekly fees of between 6s and 8s were charged were almost invariably from outside London.

31 See, e.g., *Ghall* MS 2968/7, 22 June 1710; 4525/10, fol. 153, 2 and 3 Nov. 1688; 4525/18, fol. 124, 24 Nov. 1697, and 4525/23, fols 135–6, 11 March 1703; cases of Elizabeth Pearson of St Dunstan in the West, and Abraham Byard, Elizabeth Teare and Elizabeth Gibson, of St Botolph Bishopsgate.

32 Securities were required to be worth at least £40 initially, but, by the latter seventeenth century, this requirement had been raised to at least £100.

33 Sixty-eight cases (i.e. over 8 per cent of those known) had settlements more than 200 km from the metropolitan area.

34 See, e.g., A. Fessler, 'The Management of Lunacy in Seventeenth Century England. An Investigation of Quarter Session Records', *Proceedings of the Royal Society of Medicine*, ixl (1989), 901–7; E. G. Thomas, 'The Old Poor Law and Medicine', *Medical History*, xxiv (1980), 1–19; Peter Rushton, 'Lunatics and Idiots: Mental Disability, the Community and the Poor Law in North-East England, 1600–1800', *Medical History*, xxxii (1988), 34–50; Joan Lane, 'The Provincial Medical Practitioner and his Services to the Poor, 1750–1800', *Bulletin of the Society of the Social History of Medicine*, xxviii (1981), 10–14; Hilary Marland, *Medicine and Society in Wakefield and Huddersfield* (Cambridge: CUP, 1987), 64; Akihito Suzuki, 'Lunacy in Seventeenth- and Eighteenth-century England: Analysis of Quarter Sessions Records. Parts I & II', *History of Psychiatry*, ii (1991), 437–56 and iii (1992), 29–44.

35 See A. L. Beier, *Masterless Men: The Vagrancy Problem in England 1560–1640* (London: Methuen, 1985); Geoffrey Taylor, *The Problem of Poverty 1680–1834* (Harlow: Longman, 1969).

36 See, e.g., cases of Thomas Slannard, passed two weeks before his admission to Bethlem in 1719; Judith Rayner, passed ten weeks before her admission in 1725, and John Whetstone, passed a month prior to his admission in 1756; *Ghall* MS 4215/1, 1719–20 and 22 March 1725–9; 11280/1, vouchers dated 8 May and 24 Nov. 1725; 11280/4, voucher dated 8 July 1757; 11280A/5, pass warrants dated 23 July 1719, 3 March 1724/5; 4220/1, 8 Aug. 1719.

37 *BCGM*, 20 Jan. 1669 and 5 Jan. 1672, fols 123 and 367.

38 See, e.g., case of Pierce Bonest, admitted to Bethlem on 27 Aug. 1692, as 'a Person refusing to tell his name'. See *BAR*, and *GLRO CA Rep.* 146, 13 July 1742, fol. 309.

39 For example, cases of David Lewis and Susan Wallis; *BCGM*, 10 June 1653, 6 May and 25 Nov. 1663, 16 Dec. 1664, 28 Sept. 1666, 11 Sept. 1667, 25 Nov. 1668, 22 Oct. 1669, 3 Nov. 1670, 7 Sept. 1671 and 10 Oct. 1672, fols 617, 45, 47, 76, 79, 125, 9, 60, 117, 171, 240, 338 and 449; *GLRO SM* 41, 14 Oct. 1672.

40 For Hazeler's case, see *BCGM*, 25 Jan., 29 March, 28 Aug. and 16 Oct. 1667, 5 Feb., 20 May and 3 June 1668, fols 30, 38, 59, 62, 66, 82, 94 and 96; *GLRO SM* 23, 8 Nov. 1667; *GLRO SM* 24, 11 Dec. 1667.

41 *BCGM*, 17 July 1752, 22 Dec. 1757, 7 Jan. 1762, 24 April 1765 and 26 April 1781, fols 69, 272, 4, 128 and 9, cases of Ann Arthur, a former French prisoner; Elizabeth Slous, from Jersey; Thomas Hayly, an Irishman; and James James, an Edinburgh-born pedlar.

42 Patricia H. Allderidge, 'Management and Mismanagement at Bedlam, 1547–1633', in Charles Webster (ed.), *Health, Medicine and Mortality in the Sixteenth Century* (Cambridge: CUP, 1979), 141–64.

43 *Ibid.* 152–3; *BCGM*, 1624, fol. 368.

44 *BCGM*, 31 July 1629, fol. 137.

45 See, e.g., St Botolph Bishopsgate cases, Elizabeth/Betty Ratcliffe; described in the church-warden accounts as a 'Lunatick' with three children when passed to the parish, but subsequently as 'fooleish', and on regular poor relief from 1691–8 (at least); *Ghall* MS 4525/13, fols 61 and 75; 4525/14, fols 55, 65, 72, 81, 88–107; 4525/15, fols 52–101; 4525/16, fols 59 and 61; 4525/19, fols 84, 87, 90 and 102.

46 See Jonathan Andrews, 'Identifying and Providing for the Mentally Disabled in Early Modern London', in Anne Digby and David Wright (eds), *Historical Perspectives on People with Learning Disabilities* (London: Routledge, 1996), and *idem*, 'The Definition, Epistemology and Socio-cultural History of Idiocy in Early Modern England', forthcoming in *History of Psychiatry*.

47 See Richard Hunter and Ida Macalpine, *Three Hundred Years of Psychiatry: 1535–1860* (London: OUP, 1963), 121, 521, 236–8, 434–6. For eighteenth-century legal distinctions between idiocy and lunacy, see e.g. Nigel Walker, *Crime and Insanity in England* (Edinburgh: Edinburgh University Press, 1969), 56; Sir William Blackstone, *Commentaries on the Laws of England*, 4 volumes (Oxford: Clarendon, 1765–9), i, 292–5 and iv, 20–26.

48 For the discharge/rejection of idiots in the eighteenth century, see, e.g., *BSCM*, 5 Oct. 1734, 5 Oct. 1751, fols 296 and 261, cases of Elizabeth Ford, Judith Hanson.

49 *BCGM*, 16 Nov. 1653, fol. 629.

50 See Allderidge, *op. cit.* 158; *BCGM*, 1624, fol. 368.

51 *BCGM*, 29 May 1646, fol. 266.

52 See Patricia Allderidge, 'Hospitals, Madhouses and Asylums: Cycles in the Care of the Insane', in R. M. Murray and T. H. Turner (eds), *Lectures on the History of Psychiatry. The Squibb Series* (London: Gaskell, 1990), 28–46.

53 See, e.g., case of Anthony Drayton, *BCGM*, 21 Feb. 1645, fol. 177.

54 *Ibid.* 21 Nov. and 20 Dec. 1638, fols 211 and 217; *PRO PCR* 2/46, 9 Oct. and 5 Nov. 1636, fol. 426.

55 For example, cases of John Blackwell, Susan Newell and William Toote/Lets, *BCGM*, 13 and 27 Jan., 24 Feb., 16 March, (?) May and 9 June 1649, and 20 Jan. and 10 Feb. 1664, fols 370, 374, 376, 380, 384, 386, 88 and 90.

56 For Landy, see *ibid.* 19 Nov. 1673, 19 Feb., 18 April, 8 May and 2 Oct. 1674, 18 June 1675, 9 Aug. 1678, 1 July 1681, 28 July and 1 Sept. 1682, and 9 Sept. 1704; fols 587, 618–19, 630, 637, 137, 41, 236, 315, 326 and 216; *BAR*, fols 231, 51; *PRO LS* 13/172, fol. 37. For Anne Bassett, see *BCGM*, 16 April 1647, 10 Aug. 1649 and 13 June 1655, fols 301, 392 and 704.

57 *GLRO SM* 26, 12 Oct. 1667.

58 *BCGM*, 26 April 1781, fol. 9. See also *ibid.* 23 June 1785, fols 220–1, case of Henry Finlayson and wife, and *BGCM*, 28 Aug. 1798, fols 17–19, case of Jane Lufkin.

59 For this discussion, see Alexander Cruden, *Mr. Cruden Greatly Injured* (London: Printed for A. Injured and sold by the pamphlet sellers of London and Westminster, 1740), i, 27–8; *idem*, *The London Citizen Exceedingly Injured* (London: For the Author, 1739), 5, 27–34; *idem*, *The Adventures of Alexander the Corrector* (London: By the Author, 1754), i, 34–7; iii, 7.

60 William Scavenger was sent to Bridewell in 1673 as 'a Lewd Vagrant man wandring about the Streetes . . . by the Name of Tom A Bedlam'. For this and other such cases, see *BCGM*, e.g., 28 Jan. 1657, 25 March and 7 May 1673, 21 Oct. 1692, 24 July 1754, 7 March and 23 May 1764, fols 783, 497, 501, 201, 150, 71 and 79.

61 See Michael MacDonald, *Mystical Bedlam. Madness, Anxiety and Healing in Seventeenth Century England* (Cambridge: CUP, 1981); *idem*, 'Popular Beliefs about Mental Disorder in Early Modern England', in W. Eckhart and J. Geyer-Kordesch (eds), *Heilberufe und Kranke in 17 und 18 Jahrhundert* (Münster: Burgverlag, 1982), 148–73.

62 *BCGM*, e.g., 26 June 1667, 19 Feb. and 25 March 1673, fols 53, 485 and 492, cases of William Oliver and Richard Burwill.

63 See, *ibid.* e.g., 11 March and 1 April 1642, 24 March 1643, 13 Jan. 1649, fols 374–5, 27 and 370.

64 *Ibid.* 23 Sept. 1664, fol. 114.

65 See, e.g., *ibid.* 30 Sept. 1642, 29 Jan. 1651, fols 411, 484, cases of William Parre and William Everard, and bonds in Box 'D', *BRHA*.

66 See *BCGM*, 10 Nov. 1658 and 3 July 1663, fols 75–6 and 56.

67 *Ibid.* 1 July and 2 Nov. 1681, fols 236 and 267. For recovered patients appearing before the Court, see *ibid.* e.g. 15 March and 7 April 1682, fols 287, 293.

68 See, e.g., cases of Samuel Kendricke, John Kempton, James Smyth, Alice Clarke, John Syms, Richard Tillear; *ibid.* 7 May 1656, 11 Sept. 1667, 16 June 1680 and 30 April 1703, fols 751, 60, 155 and 144.

69 *Ibid.* 17 Aug. 1681, 11 April 1701, 4 Sept., 6 and 20 Nov. 1702, fols 236, 244, 440, 109, 119, 123; *BSCM*, *passim*, but esp. 13 Oct. 1711, 10 May 1712, 30 Jan. 1714, 9 April 1715, fols 69, 87, 143, 184.

70 See Andrews, 'Incurably Insane'.

71 *Ibid.*; Jonathan Swift, *A Serious and Useful Scheme to Make an Hospital for Incurables* (London: J. Roberts, 1733).

72 Applicants' representatives were required to provide a statement as to the duration of the insanity of those they proposed. See, e.g., *BSCM*, 1 Nov. 1760, 4 March 1769, fols 329, 346.

73 *BCGM*, e.g., 27 June 1638, 11 March 1642, 5 Dec. 1645, 12 June 1667, 11 July 1674, fols 186, 375, 229, 49 and 15.

74 See orders for payment of Johanna Sanbache's gift to Bethlem, in *Ghall* MS 6552/1, e.g., 13 May 1664, 17 Oct. 1677; 6554/2, 1694–5 account.

75 See, e.g., Marland, *op. cit.* 64 and note 46, where it is argued that it was the 'more dangerous' cases who were sent to Bethlem and other metropolitan madhouses.

76 See Donald Lupton, *London and the Countrey Carbonadoed* (London: N. Okes, 1632), ch. 19, 77–8: 'hee that keepes the House may be sayd to live among wilde Creatures. It's thought many are kept here, not so much in hope of recovery, as to keepe them from further and more desperate Inconveniences'; John Strype, *A Survey of the Cities of London and Westminister written at First . . . by John Stow* (London: A. Churchill, 1720), 194–5.

77 See, e.g., *BCGM*, 17 Aug. 1681, 12 July 1728 and 30 Nov. 1739, fols 153, 63 and 244; *BAR*; *BLAR*; *BSCM*, e.g., 13 Nov. 1773 and 29 Nov. 1783.

78 Black, *op. cit.* 18.

79 *An Act . . . For Reducing the Laws relating to Rogues, Vagabonds, Sturdy Beggars, and Vagrants . . . 1714, 12 Anne, c. 23; 17 Geo. II, c. 5*; Hunter and Macalpine, *op. cit.* 299–301.

80 See, e.g., *BCGM*, 29 Jan. 1651, fol. 487, case of John Read; eighteenth-century petitions in Box 'D' in *BHRA*, especially those on behalf of Ann Carvill (Oct. 1780) and Daniel Gardiner (April 1775).

81 For sailors, see, e.g., cases of Thomas Marshall (1692), Ciferon Hill (1696), John Henworth (1697), Daniel Weston (1703), Samuel Griffin (1708), Francis Mallin (1708) and Roger Purdie (1710), in *BAR*, fols 156, 222, 234, 35, 113, 132 and 9; *PRO Kew* ADM. 99/4, 27 July 1703; 99/10, 27 Feb. 1711. See also *A True Report . . .* (London 1656).

82 See, e.g., *BCGM*, 1 Oct. 1634, 11 March and 1 April 1642, 18 Nov. 1681, 4 Jan. 1682, fols 14, 374, 375, 268 and 274, cases of Jervice Blande, James Whitall and Anne Kingston.

83 *Ibid.* 29 Nov. 1678, fol. 64. See James Carkesse, *Lucida Intervalla* (London: The Author, 1679), edited by M. V. DePorte (Los Angeles: University of California Press, 1979), 38, where Carkesse boasts of cheating 'my Shrewish Wife and her Relations' of 'their End' in sending him 'successively to be Tam'd' to Finsbury and Bethlem, having 'grown fiercer' instead.

84 See, e.g., case of Thomas Wattee, whose parish was allowed, on paying the arrears, to reclaim him from Bethlem in 1654, but was 'admonished to take care that he may bee kept from doeing any hurte hereafter'; *BCGM*, 24 May 1654, fol. 657.

85 Rawson's surety, Francis Berry, had clearly been more concerned about the expense of her maintenance than her cure. Having fallen into arrears and repeatedly petitioned for Rawson's discharge and some mitigation of his fees from Jan. 1689 (although she was 'not recovered'), Berry was forced firstly to settle his arrears by the Governors, and then was persuaded 'to continue her some tyme longer' by the carrot of an abatement.

86 See, e.g., *BCGM*, 12 Sept. 1673, 7 Nov. 1684, fols 560, 20, cases of Adam Hooker, Anne Parker.

87 See esp. Chapter 19, this volume.

88 *BCGM*, 15 April 1681, fol. 213. See also *Ghall* MS 4525/14, fol. 132, case of Grissell Lawnder of Bishopsgate.

89 *Ghall* MS 4525/28, fols 151–3, 163.

90 Michael MacDonald and T. R. Murphy, *Sleepless Souls. Suicide in Early Modern England* (Oxford: Clarendon Press, 1990); MacDonald, 'The Inner Side of Wisdom: Suicide in Early Modern England', *Psychological Medicine*, vii (1977), 565–82; case of Alice Bradley, *BCGM*, 27 Sept. 1676, fol. 287. For the naval cook, see *PRO Kew* ADM. 99/17, fol. 281.

91 Letter and petition dated *c.* 16 Nov. 1765 in Box 'D' in *BRHA*.

92 *BCGM*, 7 Aug. 1674, fol. 25.

93 MacDonald, 'Popular Beliefs', 155.

94 See, e.g., *BCGM*, 10 Nov. 1643, 29 Feb. 1644, 19 Jan. and 2 March 1653, 4 Feb. and 27 Oct. 1676, 7 Sept. 1683, 1 July 1726, fols 76, 94, 587, 597, 769–70, 217, 278, 299, 92; *GLRO CA Rep*. 154, 24 April 1750, fols 252–3.

95 Mark Jenner, 'Early Modern English Conceptions of "Cleanliness" and "Dirt" as Reflected in the Environmental Regulation of London *c*. 1530–*c*. 1700' (Oxford, D.Phil., 1991)

96 See *BCGM*, e.g. 17 April 1644, 31 March 1652, 15 Feb. 1656, 16 June 1682, fols 101, 307, 539, 736 and 307.

97 See Allderidge, 'Hospitals, Madhouses and Asylums'.

98 For early modern notions of insanity linked to property, see MacDonald, 'Popular Beliefs', 154. For Bates, see *Ghall* MS 4525/14, fols 98–101, 133–5; 4525/15, fols 91, 94–100, 128 and 198; 951/2, 1692–4 churchwardens' accounts; and 2836/2, 19 March 1693; *GLRO SM* 63, 5 May 1693 and London Sessions Papers for 1693; *BAR*, fol. 4.

99 MacDonald, 'Popular Beliefs', 154–5.

100 *BCGM*, 22 Aug. 1638, fol. 193. See also case of Joseph Read, a 9-year-old boy, described as 'very mischievous will not wear any Cloaths', and admitted to Bethlem at the request of his father in 1776; *ibid*. 12 Dec. 1776, fol. 545.

101 See, e.g., cases of Joseph Price, a silk-stocking knitter, arrested and committed to Bethlem in 1699 after stealing the lining out of the churchwarden's pew, although originally delivered back to his parish on 'makeing Good the damage done'. *Ibid*. 10 Aug. 1649, 27 Jan. 1699 and 24 Nov. 1709, fols 392, 237 and 517; *BAR*, fols 261 and 162; *Ghall* MS 6522/3, 26 Nov. 1709–14 July 1711; 6552/4, fol. 193, 235–6; *BIAR*.

102 See, e.g., cases of Thomas Leadman and Henry Crispe, *BCGM*, 10 Feb. 1664, 23 Dec. 1670, 19 Jan. and 16 June 1671, fols 89, 92, 256–7, 266 and 310.

103 *GLRO SM* 55, 27 April 1685; *BCGM*, 16 June 1682, fol. 307.

104 *BCGM*, 18 Dec. 1696 and 12 Feb. 1697, fols 81 and 91.

105 R. Moss, *A Sermon Preached . . . at St. Sepulchre* (London: R. Sare & J. Tonson, 1706), 24–5; A. Snape, *A Sermon Preached . . . at St. Bride . . .* (London: R. Sare, 1707; 2nd edn, London: C. Bowyer, 1731), 14–17; Swift, *op. cit*.

106 *GLRO CA Rep*. 60, fols 74–6, 20 Jan 1756.

107 *PRO LS*. 13/104, fol. 111.

108 Peter Linebaugh, *The London Hanged* (London: Allen Lane, 1991).

109 Rushton, *op. cit*.; Fessler, *op. cit*.; Suzuki, *op. cit*.

110 See, e.g., John Haslam, *Observations on Insanity* (London: Printed for F. & C. Rivington, 1798), 112.

111 See W. A. Bewes, *Church Briefs* (London: Black, 1896), cited in E. G. O'Donoghue, *The Story of Bethlehem Hospital from its Foundation in 1247* (London: T. Fisher Unwin, 1914), 124.

112 For the ensuing discussion, see *BCGM*, 30 March and 20 June 1677, 10 July 1679, 17 Aug. 1681, 7 April 1682, fols 362, 389–90, 98, 244, 294.

113 Likewise, in applying an anonymous donation of £100 'for the instructing of [patients] . . . in God's Service', it was not the 'raving' or chronically insane, but 'those . . . whoe uppon any degree of recovery are capable thereof'; or, 'that are soe far recovered to there [*sic*] former sences as shalbe capable to receive any benefit thereby', who were meant, by both benefactor and Governors, to be so relieved. See *ibid*. 20 Jan. 1682, fol. 277.

114 *Ibid*. 26 June 1713, fols 1–2.

115 *BAR*, 1700. For MacDonald's arguments concerning the intensifying campaign against religious enthusiasm after the Restoration, see, e.g., 'Insanity and the Realities of History in Early Modern England', in R. M. Murray and T. H. Turner (eds), *Lectures on the History of Psychiatry. The Squibb Series* (London: Gaskell, 1990), 60–77.

116 See *BCGM*, 22 Oct. 1634, 16 Aug. 1637, 3 Jan., 28 Feb. and 27 June 1638, 11 March 1642, fols 15, 134, 154, 165, 186 and 374; *PRO PC* 2/47, fols 26–7, 49, 175, 262, 335; 2/48, 21 Feb. 1638, fol. 619; 2/49, 25 April and 27 June 1638, fols 123 and 296; 2/50, 12 July 1639, 6 Sept. 1640, fols 509, 717.

117 See, e.g., [T. Heywood], *A True Discourse of the Two infamous upstart Prophets, Richard Farnham*

Weaver of White-Chappell, & John Bull Weaver of Saint Botolph Algate, now Prisoners, the One in Newgate, and the Other in Bridewell: with Their Examinations and Opinions Taken from their Owne Mouthes . . . (London: T. Lambert, 1636).

118 See MacDonald, 'Insanity and the Realities of History in Early Modern England'.

119 Black, *op. cit.* 18–19.

120 *BAR*, fols 1–12.

121 Figures from five Spital reports covering admissions during 1739–58 would suggest that 71 per cent of those whose admissions had a result in this period were 'Cured and Discharged', or 55 per cent of the average yearly patient population; see reports dated 1740, 1741, 1743, 1750 and 1759.

122 According to Haslam (*op. cit.* 108–9 and 111–12), the age of patients admitted to the Hospital had a profound significance on the likelihood of their recovery: 'insane persons recover in proportion to their youth.'

123 Black, *op. cit.* 18–19; Hunter and Macalpine, *op. cit.* 646. Black also seems to have included relapses prior to admission in his totals.

124 See Haslam, *op. cit.* 109.

125 For cases in which this objective or function is recorded, see, e.g., those of Elizabeth Hackett, of St Bride and George Lyth, of St Dunstans in the West; *Ghall* MS 6552/2, 9 May 1695; 3016/3, fol. 126.

126 *12 Anne, c. 23* and *17 Geo II, c. 5*; Hunter and Macalpine, *op. cit.* 299–301.

127 *Ghall* MS 4457/5, 24 March–13 Aug. 1720, 30 May 1729 and 2 Feb. 1737; 819/2, fol. 162.

128 Churchwardens' accounts from the 1770s reveal that, subsequently, Bishopsgate, like most city parishes, was to rely on Bethnal Green and Hoxton primarily for such provision.

129 For the Sick and Wounded Board's use of madhouses and Bethlem, see e.g. *PRO Kew* ADM. 99/16, 24 Dec. 1742, 3 Jan. 1743; 19/18, part 4, 18 July 1744, cases of William Cook and John Williamson. For workhouses' exclusions of lunatics, see *Ghall* MS 4501; 11280A/4. See also case of John Bewley, *LEP*, nos. 5829 and 5846, 9–12 March and 18–20 April 1765.

130 Tymes was buried on 2 August 1676; see *Ghall* MS 449/2.

131 We are grateful to Rosemary Weinstein for making her own arithmetic available regarding burials in the Coleman Street registers. Figures from 1694 onwards are derived from admission registers verified (where possible) by these burial registers.

132 See, e.g., Anne Digby, *Madness, Morality and Medicine. A Study of the York Retreat, 1796–1914* (Cambridge: CUP, 1985), 225; Charlotte MacKenzie, 'Social Factors in the Admission, Discharge and Continuing Stay of Patients at Ticehurst Asylum 1845–1917', in W. F. Bynum, Roy Porter and Michael Shepherd (eds), *The Anatomy of Madness* (London: Tavistock, 1985), ii, 150; T. R. Forbes, 'By What Disease or Causality: The Changing Face of Death in London', in C. Webster (ed.), *Health, Medicine and Mortality*, 130. For urban mortality, see P. J. Corfield, *The Impact of English Towns* (Oxford: OUP, 1982), 109–23.

133 Black, *op. cit.* 27–8; Hunter and Macalpine, *op. cit.* 647; Spital reports 1681–1705, 1739–68 and 1772–5.

THE POLITICS OF COMMITTAL TO EARLY MODERN BETHLEM

—— ·•· ——

INTRODUCTION

Much attention has recently been paid to the political aspects of definitions of insanity and the incarceration of the mad – the political 'abuse' of psychiatry, past and present. Michel Foucault particularly emphasized the mixed nature of the French institutions of the 'classical age', in which the insane were routinely locked away alongside vagrants, whores, felons, dissenters and idiots in *l'hôpital général* and at a host of other hospitals, *maisons de santé* and prisons.[1] It has been noted that 'it was standard Old Regime practice for one party who wanted another removed from the scene for whatever nefarious reason to obtain a *lettre de cachet* from the Crown authorizing incarceration on grounds of lunacy'.[2] Lax admission policies meant that individuals continued to be 'unjustly imprisoned',[3] and it was only later that French hospital administrators began to object to 'arbitrary or repressive imprisonment'.[4] In the post-revolutionary period too, close ties continued to exist between emergent French psychiatry and the central state bureaucracy. What was the situation on the other side of the Channel?

Links between central authority and madness were somewhat different in England. English institutions were largely 'voluntary' or private establishments, set up by benefactors and subscribers, and removed from direct state supervision.[5] The eighteenth century was distinguished by its free 'trade in lunacy',[6] and there is little evidence in legal and administrative records of the kinds of politicized definitions of insanity common in France. One major explanation for these differences lies in the radically different nature of the state bureaucracies in the two kingdoms. The governance of post-Restoration England was typified by a devolved localism that made for heterogeneity; by contrast, lunacy administration in France has usually been characterized as part of a large, centralized bureaucracy.[7]

Nevertheless, the political aspects of British institutions must not be ignored. As previous chapters have underlined, the Royal Hospitals of London were profoundly affected by the violent political upheavals of the 1680s and 1690s: the Exclusion Crisis, the turbulent reign of James II and the Glorious Revolution.[8] Such institutions were intermittently engaged in a struggle for autonomy, frustrated in their desire for self-government and regularly locking horns with both the Crown and the City over questions of income, patronage and appointments. In this light, the political and social nature of confinement at Bethlem needs to be explored more thoroughly. When was it that lunacy 'overstepped the bounds of the politically endurable'?[9] How far, in drawing up and policing those bounds, was lunacy itself being politicized?

BETHLEM AS AN ARM OF STATE

Chapter 12, in particular, has demonstrated how Bethlem was a City and also a Crown institution, owing allegiance to both arms of government. Part of this dual loyalty was a virtual obligation to receive patients sent by both the royal and the City authorities. It was due to its ancient relationship with these authorities that it was Bethlem which took into custody attempted regicides such as Margaret Nicholson and James Hadfield under George III. Bethlem also received numerous other cases committed by royal authority, or by the House of Lords, the Privy Council and High Commission. In addition, it became the main receptacle for mad and disorderly individuals who came under the aegis of a new body set up to oversee the royal household, the Board of Green Cloth, a branch of the Lord Steward's Department, as well as for those deemed mentally unfit for service in the Army and Navy. Large numbers of patients were sent by the Sick and Wounded Seaman's Office and by the War Office. In addition, Bethlem regularly received patients committed by the Lord Mayor, the Court of Aldermen, the Court of Common Council and the London and Middlesex Sessions. It is in these cases, sent by the major external authorities, that the political implications of confinement are most apparent.

'LEWDE WORDES IN TYME OF FRENSEY': EARLY POLITICAL LIMITS TO SPEAKING ONE'S MIND

Christopher Hill has emphasized the ostensible tolerance for the mad in political circles in England during the first half of the seventeenth century.[10] State papers, Privy Council records and the Minutes of the Bridewell and Bethlem Court of Governors confirm that there was a resilient tradition of immunity for the mad, and underline the frequency with which madness was actually accepted as an excuse for offences, even ones of a highly political nature. For example, when John Watson's complaints against the Bishop of London in 1579 were declared baseless on the ground that Watson was *non compos mentis*, the Star Chamber decided that imprisonment 'might further distracte him', and left Watson's future care to the Bishop's discretion.[11]

It was not always easy for the authorities to determine whether an offender was mad or not. In addition, there was no standard, legal procedure for certification, and this contributed to confusion in official policies towards the insane. In any case, those engaged in radical political and religious writings availed themselves of the great scope for appeals to folly and playing the fool. Aping madness was one way for dissenters and protesters to gain an exculpatory licence for their unorthodoxies. The Erasmian tradition of praising folly was very durable.[12]

Nevertheless, folly was double-edged, and many individuals were sent to Bethlem by the Government upon slandering or questioning the Establishment. Bethlem had long been used as a receptacle for unruliness by the central and City government. One Elizabethan journal described how on 5 June 1595:

> a certain citizen, being a silkweaver, came to the Lord Mayor's house, using some hard speeches concerning him and in dispraise of his government. The Lord Mayor said he was mad and so committed him to Bedlam as a madman, but not having his officers about him sent him thither by some of his own servants; but without Bishopsgate he was rescued by prentices and divers other to the number of two or three hundred persons.[13]

Tolerance of lunacy was clearly breached when lunacy transcended the individual and the private, and entered the public sphere. Above all it was when railers, agitators and prophets gained active adherents that they began to assume a dangerous aspect. Bartholomew Helston, according to one diarist, went about town in 1607 'giving himself forth to be Queen Mary's son', and was 'oftentimes gathering people about him'. When apprehended, he was adjudged of 'a seditious disposition' rather than lunatic, and went to Bridewell. The choice subsequently placed before Lord Salisbury, however, was 'whether he remain in Bridewell or be sent to Bedlam', the Bridewell Governors having evidently found his behaviour clashed with the orderliness of their house.[14] Cases like Helston's highlight the possible political recourse to Bethlem as an alternative place for the incarceration of individuals who had transgressed against the established order. As late as 1672 the Privy Council could still refer to Bethlem's inmates as 'prisoners'.[15]

Rounding up those who, like Helston, 'went abroad' causing public tumults constituted part of social policing. Many such individuals had also infringed the vagrancy laws, and were a threat by being 'at large', free of any familial or parochial supervision, and their disorderly conduct was thus apt to impinge upon regular society. In 1630 the Privy Council issued a warrant to the Westminster JPs for the arrest and committal to Bethlem of 'certaine persons who run up and downe the streetes and doe much harme, being either distracted or els counterfeictes, and therefore not to be suffered to have their liberties to range', specifically naming a 'King Robert', 'Doctor Owen' and 'Mistris Vaughan'.[16] Mary Davies found herself in Bethlem in 1676 because she had 'frequented' Whitehall Palace 'for some space of time' and was 'much distracted', but also because 'she hath noe certaine abode'.[17] Hence she was cut off from the parochial or familial support that might have vouchsafed that she would no longer constitute a threat to royalty. The vagrancy of the insane was especially dangerous when it encroached directly on the security of the ruling classes.[18]

STATE COMMITTALS, THE BOARD OF GREEN CLOTH AND OTHER CENTRAL AUTHORITIES

It is in the Board of Green Cloth's dealings with Bethlem that the political nature of confinement appears at its most emphatic. This Board, which carried authority over the territory known as 'the verge of the Court' – that is, twelve miles of wherever the

Court was sitting – sent forty-one patients to Bethlem between 1670 and 1750. The Board's dealings with offenders inevitably had political implications. There were few more highly sensitive political arenas than the court, and offences committed within the bounds of the 'verge' were invested with political threat.

Merely intruding onto royal property carried an element of risk. In at least seventeen of the forty-one cases, 'intrusion' was specified as one of the offences. There was naturally a heightened sense of trespass where royalty was concerned. Royal palaces, royal parks and other areas frequented by the royal family were open to the public and hence insecure;[19] while the power and person of the monarch were peculiarly on show within the public sphere. Self-appointed correctors of the public morals, like the one-time Bedlamite Alexander Cruden, might even gain an audience with, and kiss the hand of, the monarch.[20] A royal touch was held to cure scrofula ('the King's Evil'), while petitioning the monarch or his ministers was a standard form of obtaining redress. Hence the royal palaces and parks might be beset by throngs of people waving petitions, or waiting for a sight or a touch of majesty.

Violence or its threat also seems to have precipitated Board of Green Cloth committals to Bethlem. Six cases were accused of threatening violence or actual physical assault. In a significant number of instances, furthermore, the description 'troublesome' was used in the Board's minutes and warrants. When Deborah Lydall was committed to Bethlem in 1677, it was not her frequent trespassing and 'severall disorders' in St James's Park that provoked the Board to act, but the specific fact that she 'tooke a Stone offering to throw it at the Queene' – and the distracted nature of 'her whole Carriage and deportment'.[21] Similarly, Richard Harris had been a 'frequent' intruder and 'committed several disorders' in St James's Park, and had 'long ... shewed himselfe ... distracted', before the act of 'throwing an Orange at the King' in 1678 provoked his incarceration in Bethlem.[22]

The Board of Green Cloth also dealt with disorders and verbal transgressions within or close by the royal household. While often taking the form of essentially inter-personal disputes, mutinous words from a royal footman, or a violent altercation between a royal servant and a lieutenant of the Tower could also have worrying political ramifications. The Board was understandably anxious about seditious utterances or actions inside the royal household. Catherine Edwards, servant to the Duchess of Richmond and living in Whitehall Palace, was admitted to Bethlem in 1679 having 'been guilty of many disorders contrary to the good Government of his Majesties Household'.[23] Two years earlier, Nicholas Valiant, one of the King's Footmen-in-Ordinary, had also been admitted to Bethlem at the King's 'express command', having 'been guilty of many disorders' and 'for a long time shewed himselfe to be a person distracted & voyd of right understanding'. More especially, Valiant had 'of late uttered treasonable words saying he had rather kill the King then my Lord of Pembrook'.[24]

Madness was identified by the language people spoke. Imprudent or passionate words, whether blasphemous or disrespectful of royalty, were readily deemed treasonable or threatening to the established order. Individuals 'speakeing daingerous words', or cursing the name of the King were regularly arraigned before justices.[25] Such individuals commonly appear in the minutes of the Bridewell and Bethlem

Governors, and in the proceedings of the Privy Council, the Board of Green Cloth and other courts. They had often been apprehended for simple civil disorders and vagrancy, as part of the ordinary policing of the streets. James Williams, for example, admitted to Bethlem in 1662, had been detained 'for being a disorderly person & causeing tumults in the streetes', but went on to compound his offence before the Bridewell Court by 'uttering here this day wicked & seditious words concerning the Kings Majestye'.[26] Military authorities were, not surprisingly, particularly intolerant of insubordination and disaffected words against any superior, let alone the sovereign. Slandering royalty, even in jest, was liable to land men on a charge, and might be the cause of expulsion from a military hospital and the loss of a military pension.[27]

Of course, expressions of disaffection were not necessarily taken as signs of madness. Apparently sane individuals sent to the Bridewell and Bethlem Governors by the Green Cloth for scandalous words more often received a whipping or a brief period of custody at Bridewell, before their deliverance.[28] The power of mere gestures and deportment to convey clear socio-political messages, outraging norms of etiquette and hierarchy and identifying individuals as irrational, should not be underestimated. The authorities sought to distinguish political deviancy from lunacy and to respond appropriately. For most individuals discussed so far, committal was politicized primarily because their transgressions took place in a political arena, or touched upon establishment figures. These cases must be distinguished from others confined primarily for political reasons.

KEEPING THE INSANE CLOSE: SPECIAL INSTRUCTIONS FOR STATE COMMITTALS

Bodies like the Board of Green Cloth and the Privy Council thus sent persistent nuisances to Bethlem. But they also occasionally issued special instructions to impose an extra degree of confinement upon such patients, or to deprive them of any voice or audience for their words. The Privy Council warrant committing William Ellis (who had 'expressed . . . scandulous wordes against his Majestie's person') in 1617, ordered that he be kept 'safe their in chaynes until farther order'.[29] A more explicit warrant committing Richard Day in 1639 ordered that no-one be permitted 'to have Access unto him or to speake with him, but in the presence of his keeper'.[30] In 1673, a warrant from the Secretary of State ordered the Bethlem Porter not only 'to lock up Dun . . . a Person in his Custody', but 'not to Suffer him to be seen or spoken to by any person in his room. And when it should be thought fit to suffer him to walk out, that no body be permitted to talk with him.'[31]

Security was generally important to Bethlem, but it loomed particularly large in state committals. In the late seventeenth century, even when warrants from the Board of Green Cloth instructed that patients be treated 'in the usual manner', it was also specified or assumed that this entailed patients being 'secured'.[32] Confinement, furthermore, did not only tend to be more severe for state committals; its length and character might depend on the individual's capacity for moral reformation. When Richard Farnham had wound up in Bethlem at the command of Archbishop Laud and the High Commission, it was ordered that he be kept in close confinement. He was granted 'the Liberty usually afforded to others in that house' only once the Hospital's officers had sued for it and testified that he 'did not appear either by words or gestures to be madd or Lunatique'.[33] Farnham was still in Bethlem a year and a half after being declared sane, when the Hospital petitioned the Archbishop directly, pleading lack of space for other lunatics and that Farnham was 'not . . . soe Lunatique as still to [need to] continue there'.[34] Even then, he was not to gain his liberation. After the next year saw his acquittal on the charge of bigamy, in July 1639 he was sent to Bridewell – another example of the two institutions' symbiotic relationship.

MADMAN OR POLITICO-RELIGIOUS DISSENTER? THE CASE OF RICHARD STAFFORD

Perhaps the most explicit example of the use of Bethlem to silence politico-religious dissent is the case of Richard Stafford. The second son of John Stafford of Thornbury, Gloucester, the grandson of William Stafford, a moderate parliamentarian pamphleteer, and the nephew of Sir John Stafford, Constable of Bristol Castle, Stafford (1663–1703) undoubtedly came from respectable and wealthy stock. His family was prominent amongst the Gloucestershire gentry, owning Marlwood Park in Thornbury, and Richard was able on his death to dispose of land and property mortgaged to the value of £500.

Educated for the bar, Stafford soon found himself paying more attention to divinity, in which he became a voracious autodidact, taking the Old Testament in particular to heart. His upbringing led him to radical Protestant dissent.[35] His entry into print reads like a personal creed of faith, with plain, ingenuous instructions on how happiness was to be achieved by following God's commands. Yet Stafford was also a devout monarchist, firmly convinced of the divine right of kings.

With the Glorious Revolution (1688–9) bringing about the exile of the Roman Catholic James II and the succession of his daughter Mary II and his Dutch son-in-law William III, Stafford launched into much more dangerous waters. Convinced not only that William's enthronement was against God's law but of his own divinely appointed mission, Stafford published tract after tract saying just that and declaring himself a Scribe of Jesus Christ. His writings gained the support of Jacobite publicists. Bold in distributing his pamphlets around Westminster, Stafford was to find himself twice arrested and dealt with as a sane offender – before being finally judged insane and sent to Bethlem.

Bringing out the first of his anti-government pamphlets on 4 January 1690,[36] he was indicted and confined in Newgate for a week. On publishing another two pamphlets and delivering them to Commons members in the following April (having already left two letters on the backstairs at Whitehall),[37] his punishment was more severe.[38] He suffered another four weeks' detention in the custody of the Sergeant-at-Arms, had his chamber searched and was handed over to his father's safe-keeping in Gloucester. A year and a half later, once he had published several more tracts and returned to London to distribute them around the Queen's Court, he was dispatched to Bethlem in November 1691, where he was to remain for nearly eight months. The reasons for his committal specified in the warrant were being 'distracted' and 'very troublesome to their Majesties at Kensington By Dispersing Books & Pamphlets full of Enthusiasme and Sedition'.[39] There can be few other cases where the political motivations for incarcerating an individual as insane appear more overt, or where the insanity stigma served so effectively to discredit and silence dissent.

Stafford's pamphlets certainly contain signs of peculiarity of character, being deeply self-referential, obsessive, and increasingly full of delusive hubris and contradiction. Yet by contrast with the tracts of Lady Eleanor Davies, there was nothing intellectually incoherent about his writings. Complaining bitterly about the illegality and unconstitutional nature of William's accession, Stafford gave quite lucid and impressive expression to a widely felt outrage against the Glorious Revolution: 'In the late Revolution of putting down one King, and setting up another ... they have actually departed from that Established and fixed Order of Things he [God] hath set up', he declared in his 1690 *A Supplemental Tract of Government*,[40] it was an affair that 'makes Protestantism stink'.[41] This hardly surprisingly landed him in Newgate. Yet the pamphlet, if intemperate, contains no signs of insanity, and neither do Stafford's two subsequent productions, repeating condemnations of 'Popery and Arbitrary Government'.[42]

In his *Apology*, published soon after his second period of confinement and the year before his committal to Bethlem, Stafford shows he was already aware of a campaign to identify him as a lunatic, which he condemned as an attempt to discredit him. 'A malicious and false imputation may be cast and endeavoured to be fastened on anyone', he declared, six months prior to being sent to Bethlem:

> And also, what is a little new or unusual, or doth somewhat exceed common apprehension, may seem to the vulgar sort, yea, and be called by them madness; but this is so trivial, that it is sufficient answer only to take notice of such an Ignorant Calumny.[43]

His remarks on how insanity had thus been manipulated, and his devices to turn the mirror on his accusers, show Stafford was capable of considerable insight and composure. In fact, he was developing an old theme, adumbrated in his very first publication, *Of Happiness* (1689). 'Distraction and Restlessness of mind', he there stated in a long digression, 'do pass in the World for pure Melancholy. It is an Aspersion cast upon sincere Religion [that] ... All Thoughts of God ... are by the Ignorant and Ungodly thus esteemed.'[44] He emphasized the positive, scriptural definition of melancholy as synonymous with sorrow; through melancholy the Holy Spirit might act on the conscience. Melancholy was to be prized as a legitimate way of knowing God, of entering into his guidance and experiencing the 'regrets of Conscience'. Apparently he was already feeling the brunt of that vigorous campaign against 'enthusiasm' in politics and religion so distinctive of post-Restoration orthodoxy.[45]

Stafford was one of a small minority of individuals sent to Bethlem whose transgressions took the explicit form of politico-religious dissent. It was only gradually that the Government seems to have determined that he was mad. And it could be said that Stafford's *Apology* presents some signals of mental deterioration. His assertion 'I speak nothing of my self, but from his Word only', and its preface by a detailed account of his own education and attainment of credentials 'at the School of Prophets', was one of a number of extravagancies. By claiming to be a divine messenger, he may well have been compensating somewhat for the 'personal Deformity and Lameness' which he blamed in the *Apology*, amongst other things, for his being called mad.[46] Stafford was treated seriously enough, however, to be responded to quite candidly and without any slur of insanity by the Government publicist, Edward Stephens. Replying in his *Apology*, Stephens devoted an entire pamphlet to the self-elected scribe.[47]

Significantly, it was not Stafford's opinions themselves which Stephens deemed so 'extraordinary and rare' – it was the very popularity of Stafford's opinions that was most worrying the Government. What was exceptional was 'the Zeal . . . he . . . shewed . . . for what he thought to be true', so much so that it could be dismissed as bizarre (or as Stephens put it, 'it could not deserve to be taken notice of in print').[48] Stafford's last production before his committal involved a few additions to his previous *Things Plain and Weighty*; it contributed nothing noticeably madder than his previous works. Yet Stafford's awareness was even more acute, in these works, that his ambition to 'blow the unjust Possessors out of the Throne' through his words, 'might be lookt upon' not only as savouring 'of high Self-conceit or rank Enthusiasm' but even as 'like the . . . droppings forth of Mad Men'.[49] At no stage did he attempt to conceal his activities or identity. If he was clearly, therefore, no ordinary plotter, what else could he have been but a fool or madman?[50]

Stafford continued to publish even during his confinement at Bethlem, and it is the strategy adopted by the Government towards him during this time which most of all underlines how the Hospital could be used (if not very effectively) for political repression. Just a week after Stafford's committal, the Green Cloth were informed that 'many persons do frequently resort to him'. Fearing he would resume 'his former evill practices, and be incouraged to write and publish more of his treasonable Books and Papers', they instructed the Governors to withhold all writing materials from him, unless he was writing to his father or close friends and the letter had been perused by the Governors.[51] The Government's main concern, then, in keeping Stafford in Bethlem was silencing his troublesome dissent. Never in its communications with the Hospital did the Green Cloth express any concern about Stafford's recovery. What was plainly most important to the Government was the 'seditious', 'treasonable' and 'scandalous' nature of his writings.

Five months later, however, the Board was informed 'that a great Concourse of people' was still seeing Stafford, and hearing him 'preach and Scandalously reflect on ye Government'. Moreover, these people were providing him with pen and ink, were receiving his productions through his cell window, and were carrying them to the printers. Furthermore, claimed the Green Cloth, these 'Pamphletts & Libells' were 'more full of Treason & Sedition then those for which we Sent him to your Hospitall'.

The Government thus attempted to use Bethlem for political quarantine or the muzzling of madness. Stafford's words were dangerous and needed to be quelled, not because they were insane but because they expressed a radical disaffection that won adherents and inflamed popular dissent. Ultimately, it mattered less whether the Government believed Stafford really was mad than that he could be (and, indeed, was being) taken seriously by others. While the members of the Green Cloth recognized that they depended on Bethlem's Governors to enforce their orders, their comment that 'we must leave the further Care of suppressing these infamous Practices, to you who are ye Governours of ye Place' was a clear rebuke and allowed the Governors little space for objection. On the other hand, it was ultimately impossible to use Bethlem like the Bicêtre in Paris, to silence political dissidence, given the Hospital's identity as a public resort and the unregulated and open nature of its environment as part of the public sphere. Devotees of Daniel, Cromwell's canting porter, in Bethlem during the 1640s, also seem to have been allowed such ready access to him: by means of his cell window they were able to follow his Bible readings. Bethlem was no 'total institution'.[52]

And, under the circumstances, it may be argued that Stafford was still treated with remarkable leniency. Despite a forced recantation, he continued to publish his dissenting opinions and to escape further punishment.[53] Subsequent criticism from some that Stafford had perjured himself by his publications since his release from Bethlem provoked the over-sensitive scribe to respond with a further vindicating pamphlet.[54]

Cases like this raise questions about the nature of power in defining insanity. How far was 'madness' just a scapegoating stigma?[55] The words of the dramatist, Nathaniel Lee, who, after being sent to Bethlem by his family and supported there by the Green Cloth, declared 'They said I was mad; and I said they were mad; damn them they outvoted me', put the politics of this view in a nutshell.[56] Stafford had been saying something very similar when he described how 'the multitude' labelled the righteous mad, and when he told the Government, after his release: 'what ye lately did to me, was . . . only Gotten Power, and the Will of Men. It was so done meerly because ye were stronger; and it could be so done.'[57] The question was about where exactly authority resided. For Stafford, Lee and others who took the Bible to their hearts, the ultimate authority was God's word, interpreted by the godly.

ORDERING THE CARE AND CURE OF THE INSANE: POLITICAL TOLERANCE FOR PERSISTENT NUISANCES?

Stafford's case is unusual, however, for comparatively few of Bethlem's patients were committed with special instructions from outside authorities for their closer detention. And such instructions were more common in the seventeenth century than later, when Bethlem's administration and medical officers were more successful in asserting their control over admissions. Yet even in the seventeenth century, the Board of Green Cloth, the Privy Council and other bodies generally left it to the Hospital to 'take care of [patients] in the same manner as is usual'. Nor were these authorities concerned only with detention. Occasionally, the Board and other authorities even stipulated that individuals had been sent to be 'cured' at Bethlem. Even when committing recidivists, the Board of Green Cloth might request that the individual 'be put into a way of recovery'.

Nor should one see 'political' committals to Bethlem in too conspiratorial a light. Many of those committed by outside authorities carried a long record of incursions and disorders, whether in connection with City notables or with royal property. And it is worth stressing the inadequacies of the legal machinery available to deal with persistent offenders. The authorities had few convenient options open to them, and confinement was often the last of these. This may make it less surprising that confinement was often meted out in a language suffused with the ideology of deterrence. That trespassers onto royal property and other politically charged detainees who wound up in Bethlem were often guilty of numerous transgressions suggests a modicum of tolerance, even in the most sensitive of places. By no means all those committing disorders within the verge were sent to Bethlem – they were a rather incorrigible minority.

That the mad were, however, quite often confused with the bad manifests ambiguities in Government policies towards offenders. It suggests that, while irrationality might itself exonerate offences, to affront the highest authorities could itself be perceived as innately irrational. Nevertheless, the majority of those guilty of such offences were charged with civil offences, and in very few cases is there evidence that any suspicion of madness was attached to the nature of the crime itself. If confinement was imposed, the sentence tended to be a brief spell in Bridewell, or in prison. Cases like William Glaseborough, sent to Tuthill Fields Bridewell 'to be punished' after apprehension as 'a Sturdy Beggar and Vagabond', and Elizabeth Gibbs, who spent sixteen days there for 'often' intruding into the King's palace after which she was discharged to her parish,[58] are much more typical of the Government's policing activities, than those sent to Bethlem.

OBJECTIONS TO POLITICAL COMMITTALS

Bethlem had little option but to admit patients sent to it by authorities like the Privy Council and Board of Green Cloth – a fact well illustrated by the customary wording of some warrants: 'will be acceptable service to the King.'[59] On the other hand, the Hospital had its own admission criteria, which the Governors were not averse to citing when rejecting or discharging patients. Indeed, most public bodies, even the Board of Green Cloth, acknowledged at times that admission depended on whether 'upon Examination he appear a fit Object'.[60] After the Restoration, and especially at times when the royal prerogative was less assured, authorities had to be rather more deferential to both the City and the Hospital authorities when seeking an individual's admission.

On some rare occasions, the Governors objected in quite categorical terms to the billeting of unsuitable cases.[61] The case of John Taylor (mentioned in a previous chapter), who in 1675 was 'conceived to be distracted' and conveyed to Bethlem by the House of Lords, is especially illustrative here.[62] Originally sent to Guildford Gaol 'for uttering Blasphemous Words', described as 'tend[ing] immediately to the Destruction of all Religion & Government', he was subsequently tried by the House of Lords. Just a few days after his committal to Bethlem, however, Taylor was declared quite sane by the Bethlem Physician, Thomas Allen, who was then ordered by the Court of Governors to acquaint the Clerk of Parliament with this fact in no uncertain terms, informing the Clerk not only 'what hee conceiveth [Taylor's] ... Disposition to be' (i.e. highly culpable), but moreover 'that there is noe punishment for any kept in Bethlem'.

The Governors had evidently taken umbrage at the tone of the Lords' warrant, which had ordered the Keeper not only to take custody of Taylor but to see that he was 'kept there with bread and water and such due bodily Correccon as may conduce to his Recovery from the Madnes wherewith hee seemes to be possessed'. Plainly even the Lords had not been convinced that Taylor was insane, having also stipulated that if he 'shall not prove to be mad but persist in the said blasphemyes', he was 'to be delivered to be proceeded against according to the Law'. Yet the implication that recovery from madness would mean the end of Taylor's blasphemy, or even that Taylor was committed to be cured of his blaspheming, suggests that lunacy was here politicized.

In this as in most instances, Parliament was clearly recognizing that Bethlem was primarily a place for the cure of the insane, but it was also attempting to ensure that Taylor received punishment for blasphemy. While Bethlem refused to perform the latter role, it assisted Parliament and served to endorse Taylor's conviction and punishment for felony, by identifying him as bad rather than mad. Indeed, the Governors even offered Parliament suggestions as to how Taylor should be dealt with, asking whether he should either be sent 'to Newgate' to await prosecution 'for blasphemy', or 'to Bridewell to be kept att hard Labour'. While Bethlem was clearly not a 'mixed' institution in the sense of French hospitals like the Bicêtre, there were evidently times when its boundaries were rather hazy.

CONTINUITIES AND DISCONTINUITIES

The treatment of cases like Richard Stafford in the seventeenth century may be compared to that of other political deviants a century later, for whom there seems to have been rather less tolerance. Alexander Hatton, apprehended 'in the Apartments of His Majesty's Palace at St. James's ... behaving in such a manner as to give suspicion that he had some ill Design' and ordered 'into Confinement' by the Board of Green Cloth, remained in Bethlem until his death in 1765.[63] Thomas Stone, too, sent to Bethlem in 1787 by the Secretary of State, died there in 1805, having had his fate sealed not only by the Physician's examination, but also by the King personally perusing the letters he continued to write whilst in confinement.[64]

The case of James Tilly Matthews, who was locked away for nearly twenty years in Bethlem after some deranged remarks in the gallery of the House of Commons, is the best illustration of how times had changed. That Matthews continued to be perceived as dangerous to the Government, despite numerous medically endorsed attempts to free him, and no direct evidence of any violent propensities, suggests that it grew more difficult for such individuals to obtain their liberty. Matthews's writings, too, were exploited as evidence to justify his continued incarceration. All such individuals were transferred to the incurables wards, the provision of which after 1728 furthered the tendency of certain patients to remain in Bethlem for the rest of their lives.[65]

Of course, there are still many significant signs of continuities between seventeenth- and eighteenth-century treatment of insane offenders, who were often dealt with leniently, receiving exculpation for their crimes, even if of a highly political nature. Although arraigned and confined in Newgate in 1790 for throwing a stone at the royal coach, John Frith was subsequently declared 'unfit to plead by reason of insanity' and was freed from gaol on condition of security being given 'that he should be confined in some proper place as a lunatic, or in some other manner taken care of'.[66] Throughout the period, there was an effort in state committals to communicate a sense of the gracious and forgiving nature of monarchy in dealing with the insane. It is not surprising that Margaret Nicholson, given the seriousness of her crime in attempting to assassinate George III, was confined in Bethlem for life, spending her first year there in chains at the Government's command. Subsequently, however, she seems to have been treated quite leniently. She was personally enquired after by the King, permitted after a year in confinement to have the same freedom as ordinary patients, and allowed to receive visitors.[67]

CONCLUSION

The extent to which lunacy was politicized in early modern England has been underestimated. A significant number of individuals were incarcerated as lunatics first and foremost by reason of the political threat they were deemed to pose. Bethlem clearly operated as a state institution, not only receiving politically dangerous individuals but subjecting them to a more extreme form of confinement at the behest of the royal and civic authorities. There was plainly a considerable element of ambivalence in distinguishing between those fit for Bethlem and those fit for prison or the house of correction, a conclusion well illustrated by the relationship between Bridewell and Bethlem.

Nevertheless, political motivations predominated only in a minority of cases. Even when politics did figure in committal, this was seldom sufficient alone to get a patient admitted to Bethlem. Outside authorities tended to respect the peculiar competence of the Hospital for the insane, and seem to have striven to reserve committals to it to those conceived to be truly mad.

NOTES

1 Michel Foucault, *Madness and Civilisation: A History of Insanity in the Age of Reason* (London: Tavistock, 1967), originally published as *Histoire de la Folie* (Paris: Librairie Plon, 1961), esp. ch. viii, 224–5, 234–40. For further discussion and documentation, see Jonathan Andrews, 'The Politics of Committal to Early Modern Bethlem', in Roy Porter (ed.), *Medicine in the Enlightenment* (Amsterdam: Rodopi, 1995), 6–63.

2 Jan Goldstein, *Console and Classify. The French Psychiatric Profession in the Nineteenth Century* (Cambridge: CUP, 1987), 107. Erwin H. Ackerknecht, 'Political Prisoners in French Mental Institutions before 1789, During the Revolution, and under Napoleon I', *Medical History*, xix (1975), 250–5.

3 Colin Jones, 'The Treatment of the Insane in Eighteenth and Early Nineteenth-Century Montpellier. A Contribution to the Prehistory of the Lunatic Asylum in Provincial France', *Medical History*, xxiv (1980), 381–2.

4 *Ibid.* 377.

5 Roy Porter, *Mind-Forg'd Manacles. A History of Madness in England from the Restoration to the Regency* (London: The Athlone Press, 1987), esp. 113–14; and *idem*, 'Foucault's Great Confinement', *History of the Human Sciences*, iii (1990), 47–54, reprinted in A. Still and I. Velody (eds), *Rewriting the History of Madness* (London: Routledge, 1992), 119–25. The whole volume is relevant.

6 William Llewellyn Parry-Jones, *The Trade in Lunacy. A Study of Private Madhouses in England in the Eighteenth and Nineteenth Centuries* (London: Routledge & Kegan Paul, 1971).

7 Akihito Suzuki, 'Lunacy in Seventeenth- and Eighteenth-century England: Analysis of Quarter Sessions Records', Parts I and II, *History of Psychiatry*, ii (1991), 437–56, and iii (1992), 29–44; A. Fessler, 'The Management of Lunacy in Seventeenth Century England: An Investigation of Quarter-Sessions Records', *Proceedings of the Royal Society of Medicine*, xlix (1956), 901–7; Peter Rushton, 'Lunatics and Idiots: Mental Disability, the Community and the Poor Law in North-east England 1600–1800', *Medical History*, xxxii (1988), 34–50.

8 Craig Rose, 'Politics at the London Royal Hospitals, 1683–92', in L. Granshaw and Roy Porter (eds), *The Hospital in History* (London and New York: Routledge, 1989), 123–48; *idem*, 'Politics, Religion and Charity in Augustan London, 1680–1720' (University of Cambridge Ph.D. thesis, 1989).

9 Christopher Hill, *The World Turned Upside-Down: Radical Ideas During the English Revolution* (Harmondsworth: Penguin, 1978), 223–4.

10 *Ibid.* 223–4; Christopher Hill, *Change and Continuity in Seventeenth-Century England*, revised edn (New Haven and London: Yale University Press, 1991), esp. 48–77, 270–1, 316–19; *idem* and Michael Shepherd, 'The Case of Arise Evans: A Historico-psychiatric Study', *Psychological Medicine*, vi (1976), 351–8.

11 *Acts of the Privy Council*, xi (1578–80), 284.

12 M. A. Screech, *Erasmus: Esctasy and the Praise of Folly* (London: Penguin/Peregrine, 1988; orig. Duckworth, 1980); *idem*, 'Good Madness in Christendom', in W. F. Bynum, Roy Porter and Michael Shepherd (eds), *The Anatomy of Madness*, vol. 1 (London: Tavistock, 1985), 25–39; Sandra Billington, *A Social History of the Fool* (Brighton: Harvester Press, 1984); E. Welsford, *The Fool: His Social and Literary History* (London: Faber & Faber, 1935).

13 G. B. Harrison, *The Elizabethan Journals. Being a Record of the Things Most Talked of During the Years 1591–1603* (London: Routledge, 1939; revised edn of 1928 edn), 27.

14 See G. B. Harrison, *A Second Jacobean Journal. Being a Record of Those Things Most Talked of During the Years 1607 to 1610* (London: Routledge & Kegan Paul, 1958), 41, 9 July 1607.

15 *PRO SP* 44/31, 28 March 1672, fol. 86.

16 *Acts of the Privy Council (PRO PCR* 2/40), 10 Nov. 1630, 108; A. L. Beier, *Masterless Men: The Vagrancy Problem in England 1560–1640* (London: Methuen, 1987).

17 *PRO LS* 13/104, fol. 79; *BCGM*, 1 July 1676, fol. 277.

18 *Acts of the Privy Council* (1625–6), 15 April 1626, 432.

19 See e.g. *PRO LS* 13/86, fol. 51; *LS* 13/105, fols 66, 68; *LS* 13/115, fol. 116; *LS* 13/172, fol. 91; *LS* 13/173, fols 106–7. Recent social historians have stressed how the masses still rubbed shoulders with the elite in early modern society. See Peter Burke, *Popular Culture in Early Modern Europe* (Aldershot: Wildwood House Ltd, 1988).

20 See *BAR*, fol. 184, 17 Dec. 1743; Alexander Cruden, *The Adventures of Alexander the Corrector* (London: Printed for the Author, 1754); *The Gentleman's Magazine*, xxiv (1761), 601.

21 *PRO LS* 13/104, 16 Aug. 1677, fol. 89.

22 *PRO LS* 13/104, 12 Jan. 1678, fol. 94.

23 *PRO LS* 13/104, 8 July 1678 and 17 April 1679, fols 98 and 105.

24 *PRO LS* 13/104, 4 Dec. 1677, fol. 90.

25 Allan Ingram, *The Madhouse of Language. Writing and Reading Madness in the Eighteenth Century* (London: Routledge, 1992).

26 *BCGM*, fol. 17, 22 Oct. 1662.

27 *PRO Kew ADM.* 67/124, 14 and 17 Dec. 1733, fols 86–8; *ADM.* 67/125, 7 Nov. 1737, fols 59–60.

28 Henry Horwitz (ed.), *The Parliamentary Diary of Narcissus Luttrell 1691–1693* (Oxford: Clarendon Press, 1972), 10 Dec. 1692, 307–8.

29 *Acts of the Privy Council* (1616–17), 21 Dec. 1617, 392–3.

30 *PRO PC* 2/50, 28 July and 12 Aug. 1639, fols 546 and 594.

31 *PRO SP* 44/28, 7 Oct. 1673, fol. 92; *CSPD*, Car. II, 1673, 571.

32 For example, cases of Peter Massey, Deborah Lyddall and Nicholas Valiant, *PRO LS* 13/104, 29 Sept. 1675, 16 Aug. and 4 Dec. 1677, fols 73 and 89–90.

33 *PRO PCR* II, 26 Jan. 1637, fol. 537.

34 *BCGM*, 20 June 1638, fol. 186.

35 Biographical information about Stafford, and the chronology of his writings and periods of confinement, may be pieced together from his publications. See Richard Stafford, *A Clear Apology* (London 1691). See also the wills of Richard Stafford and John Stafford, Gloucs. Records Office; Anthony A. Wood, *Athenae Oxonienses* (New York and London: Johnson Reprint Corporation, 1967), iv, 781–2; Joseph Foster, *Alumni Oxonienses* (Oxford and London: Parker & Co., 1891), 1405; *DNB*, liii, 459.

36 Richard Stafford, *A Supplemental Tract of Government, To Be Annexed unto the Book of Happiness and c, Chapter 3 Circa page 147. Which may be applied to all Nations; But is now particularly referred to the Consideration of the Lords and Commons assembled in the present Parliament at Westminster, 4 Jan., 1690* (London 1690). See also his *Of Happiness: Wherein it is Fully and Particularly Manifested, that the greatest Happiness of this Life consisteth in the Fear of God and keeping his Commandments in Opposition to the Pleasures of Sin, or the pretended conveniency of Disobedience* (London: 1689).

37 Richard Stafford, *Things Plain and Weighty, Referred Unto the Consideration of both Houses of Parliament, 25 March 1690* (reprinted, with additions, London: 1691); *idem, A Copy of Two Letters left on the Back-Stairs at Whitehall, Jan. 26, 1690* (London: 1690), and *idem, The Case of Richard Stafford humbly offered to both Houses of Parliament* (London: 1690).

38 Richard Stafford, *A Short Printed Petition to the Knights, Citizens and Burgesses in Parliament assembled. Delivered to them whilst I was their Prisoner under the Custody of the Seargeant at Arms* (London: 1691), and *idem, A Short Remonstrance of Richard Stafford unto the Parliament of England, upon their not receiving and hearing of his Testimony, but shutting him up in Prison for the same* (London: 1691).

39 *PRO LS* 13/105, fol. 69; *BAR*, letter dated 4 Nov. 1691, fol. 140.

40 Stafford, *A Supplemental Tract*, 1; *idem, Things Plain and Weighty*, 9.

41 *Ibid.*

42 Stafford, *Things Plain and Weighty*, 11–12.

43 Stafford's *Apology*, 25. For background on religion, politics and Protestant dissenters during this period, see Tim Harris, Paul Seaward and Mark Goldie (eds), *The Politics of Religion in Restoration England* (Oxford: Basil Blackwell, 1990); Tim Harris, *Politics Under the Later Stuarts: Party Conflict in a Divided Society 1660–1715* (London and New York: Longman, 1993); Douglas R. Lacey, *Dissent and Parliamentary Politics in England, 1661–1689: A Study in the Perpetuation and Tempering of Parliamentarianism* (New Brunswick: Rutgers University Press, 1969); Richard L. Greaves, *Enemies Under His Feet. Radicals and Nonconformists in Britain, 1664–1677* (Stanford: Stanford University Press, 1990); Geoffrey Holmes, *Politics, Religion and Society in England, 1679–1742* (London and Ronceverte: The Hambledon Press, 1986).

44 Stafford, *Of Happiness*, 657.

45 Michael MacDonald, *Mystical Bedlam: Madness, Anxiety and Healing in Seventeenth Century England* (Cambridge: CUP, 1981); *idem*, 'Popular Beliefs About Mental Disorder in Early Modern England', in Wolfgang Eckhart and Johanna Geyer-Kordesch (eds), *Münstersche Beiträge zur Geschichte und Theorie der Medizin* (Munster: Burgverlag, 1982), 148–73; *idem*, 'Lunatics and the State in Georgian England', in *Social History of Medicine*, ii (1989), 299–314.

46 Stafford, *Apology*, 15–16.

47 Edward Stephens, *An Apology for Mr. Richard Stafford, with an Admonition to Him and Other Honest Mistaken People* (London: 1690).

48 Following his discharge from Bethlem, and clearly bearing a whole host of grudges against his persecutors, Stafford was to blame a Mr Robert Stephens for the refusal of 'several Printers' to publish his works: Richard Stafford, *Because that to many People, I have seemed to falsify my Word and Promise, which I made on being discharged out of Bethlehem Hospital . . .* (n.d., c. 1693), 3.

49 Stafford, *The Truth which God hath shewn* (London: 1691), Preface.

50 See his *Apology*, 13, where Stafford describes ordering his petition to be printed and given to Commons members, 'though I knew before this was contrary to Custom and Usage'.

51 *PRO LS* 13/105, fol. 70, 11 Nov. 1691. According to the diary of Narcissus Luttrell, within another fortnight Stafford had managed to get some more of his productions as far as the Speaker of the House of Commons. On the Speaker taking notice in the House of 'a packet of seditious papers', asserted Luttrell, it was recommended that the President of Bridewell and Bethlem, Sir William Turner, be asked to ensure that Stafford be deprived of pen, ink and paper 'to prevent his writing such scandalous papers'; Horwitz, *op. cit.* 25 Nov. 1691, 38; Wood, *op. cit.* iv, 782.

52 Irving Goffman, *Asylums* (New York: Anchor Books, 1961).

53 Amongst Stafford's publications subsequent to his discharge were *To the Right Honourable Daniel Earl of Nottingham Principal Secretary of State, and To the other members of the Privy Council Richard Stafford, a Scribe of Jesus Christ, sendeth Greeting* (n.d., *c.* 1692); *Some Thoughts Concerning The Life to Come: With a Brief Account Of the State of Religion, As it is now in the World* (London: 1693); *Because that to many People . . .* (n.d., *c.* 1693), and *A Scribe . . .* (n.d., *c.* 1693). In his *The Mystery of Iniquity somewhat laid open . . .* (1692), Stafford spoke of being imprisoned 'four times' (p. 10), while in his last *Testimony* (p.1), he claimed to have been 'imprisoned . . . five times'.

54 Stafford, *Because that to many People.*

55 Porter, *op. cit.* 2.

56 *Ibid.* Although Lee was not a state committal, once his independent means of support had been exhausted, he was subsequently supported in Bethlem by the Green Cloth, presumably because, as writer to the King's Players, he was counted as a quasi-member of the Royal Household.

57 Stafford, *To the Right Honourable Daniel*, 3.

58 *PRO LS* 13/87, discharge warrants dated 10 June and 6 Nov. 1687. See also case of George Bells, discharged on 23 March 1688.

59 For example, *PRO LS* 13/105, fol. 134; *BAR*, 15 July 1686, 25 Aug. 1688, 12 Feb. 1690, cases of the soldiers John Greene, James Walker and Eric Prenson.

60 *PRO LS* 13/177, fol. 98.

61 See, e.g., *PRO SP* 44/31, fol. 86; *SP* 29/361, no. 94; and *SP* 44/31, fol. 132, *re* the appointments of the Bethlem Apothecary in 1672 and the Bridewell Minister in 1674.

62 For Taylor's case, see *BCGM*, 19 May 1675, fol. 129, and warrant dated 14 May 1675 at end of same Court Book; House of Lords Journals, xii, 691, 700–1; xiii, 18–19, 26; *House of Lords RO, Braye MS. 3*, fol. 396.

63 *PRO LS* 13/179, fol. 17; *BSCM*, 3 Aug. 1762; *BAR* and *BIAR*.

64 *BSCM*, 27 Sept. 1788.

65 Jonathan Andrews, 'Bedlam Revisited: A History of Bethlem Hospital *c.* 1634–*c.* 1770.' (Ph.D. diss., London University, 1990).

66 Ida Macalpine and Richard Hunter, *George III and the Mad-Business* (London: Pimlico, 1991; orig. Allen Lane, 1969), 313; G. D. Collinson, *A Treatise on the Law Concerning Idiots, Lunatics, and Other Persons Considered Non Compotes Mentis* (London: Reed, 1812), vol. i, 502–3.

67 *BSCM*, 12 Aug. and 2 Sept. 1786, 3 Feb., 14 April and 11 Aug. 1787, 12 March 1791.

PART III

1783–1900

ENCOMIUM

Bethlem, charity and the first history of the Hospital

—— •◆• ——

The first history of Bethlem, described by its author as 'an illustrious monument of British charity', appeared in 1783. This was near the beginning of a decade of unprecedented transformation in the history of England and Europe, which saw the rise of new nation-states and social, urban and industrial change in Britain. In psychiatry, the history came ten years before the legendary event where Philippe Pinel (1745–1826) in revolution-torn France supposedly liberated the insane at the Bicêtre, where he was the Physician-in-Chief, by throwing off their chains.[1] While there are few facts to support this claim, with the story assuming mythical status in the history of psychiatry, developments in psychiatry at the turn of the nineteenth century had important implications for the treatment of patients and attitudes towards their care.[2] Although the event was noted at Bethlem, the 1783 *Historical Account of the Origin, Progress and Present State of Bethlem Hospital* had little to say about treatment. It was designed to serve another purpose that had little to do with medicine and everything to do with the late eighteenth-century charity.

Caius Gabriel Cibber's grim pair of statues, 'Raving and Melancholy Madness', were chosen for the frontispiece, and were unmistakably English in style and purpose. The history was dedicated to the Right Worshipful Brass Crosby, President from 1782 to 1793; the Worshipful Richard Clark, Treasurer and then Lord Mayor in 1784; Henry Cranke, Auditor-General; and the Governors of the Hospitals of Bridewell and Bethlem. Considered as a history, the sixteen-page presentation written by Thomas Bowen, the Reader and Schoolmaster at Bridewell Hospital, was cursory, lacking in depth, and in one main point erroneous. Although its author was a Fellow of St John's College, Oxford, it was not designed to satisfy scholarly appetites. Above all it was a panegyric, an appeal for 'alms', and Bowen referred explicitly to 'that active spirit of humanity, and rational benevolence which peculiarly adorns the British name'.[3] The Governors ordered the *Account* to be distributed 'in such a manner, as may tend most effectually to promote the Interests of that excellent Charity'. John Woodhouse, the Clerk, duly sent the *Account* to every Governor, members of both Houses of Parliament, and to a large number of bankers and editors. He was tailoring his market to those who could afford to give and would be inclined to do so by building on existing sympathies. Bethlem was, after all, well represented in Parliament and in the City, from where it continued to draw most of its Governors.

At a time when new voluntary societies were clamouring for support, the Governors took an innovative approach for a traditional organization. They avoided a public appeal or the other approaches to charitable fund-raising that were later to be criticized and prepared what amounted to a historical prospectus and a defence of Bethlem.[4] The Governors borrowed from the private madhouses whose physicians were publishing small books or pamphlets that made considerable claims for the author's success. This was seen as an effective way of 'drumming up trade and attracting clients'.[5] Bethlem had a different purpose in mind and the style and language were coloured by this aim. When the Hospital needed charitable funds for the new buildings at St George's Fields, and in 1928 to cover the cost of rebuilding, another approach was adopted that reflected changing attitudes to how money should be raised. None the less, given that its purpose was to raise money, the *Account* is informative in several respects, casting light on the Hospital's routines and efforts to counter criticism and present a positive image. It therefore demands more careful textual examination than it has previously received.

A HISTORY AND AN APPEAL

The *Account* asserted the close relationship between Bethlem and Bridewell that had been built up since the sixteenth century (see Chapters 5 and 12) with both institutions sharing the same Court and governance, which they were to do until 1948 (see Chapter 31). Here Bowen drew on Bridewell more than Bethlem. He was working from within the Bridewell world, a world of 'correction', and he was to become its Chaplain. Over a hundred years later Geoffrey O'Donoghue, another Chaplain although this time of Bethlem, was to publish his more scholarly history to serve a different purpose.[6] Only later did Bowen become a Governor of Bethlem. Yet where Bridewells had been established in different parts of the country, there was only one Bethlem.[7] The profit-oriented 'trade in lunacy', as part of the wider growth of service industries in Georgian England, was producing a growing number of private madhouses mostly concentrated around Hoxton and Chelsea in London.[8] Voluntary effort and humanitarian feelings were also encouraging the creation of new charitable mental hospitals across the country.[9] Whereas these institutions borrowed some features from Bethlem, or claimed to be the antithesis, the Hospital could still claim to be unique, if no longer alone in the 1780s.

Once the relationship between Bridewell and Bethlem had been established the *Account* went on to stress the two institutions' direct relationship with the City of London. It was a relationship that involved London's livery companies, regular providers of charity, from several of whom Bethlem benefited. The *Account* made clear that Bethlem was now a City institution. Bowen noted that 'it is most probable that the City of London had felt great inconvenience from the want of a proper receptacle for these unhappy objects, who were afflicted by the most deplorable malady incident on the human frame'. He mentioned that Stephen Gennings, 'a merchant-taylor', had left £40 towards the purchase of the patronage of Bethlem and that the Mayor and Commonalty had 'taken some steps to procure it'.[10] The City had entered the story of Bethlem, therefore, before the Crown had confirmed its privileges. In

1547, given the President's imprisonment in 1770 for boldly defending the City's liberties while Lord Mayor, it was felt to be important to stress this point. Differences had also arisen over management of the Royal Hospitals (St Bartholomew's, Christ's Hospital, St Thomas's, Bridewell and Bethlem). A settlement had been reached only the year before the *Account* was written with a compromise that allowed for the admission of twelve members of the Common Council of the City to sit on the Court of each of the Royal Hospitals. Bowen therefore described the City of London, which had grown substantially in size and wealth during the eighteenth century, as 'wealthy and munificent'. Indeed, he wrote of a 'HAPPY UNION' between City and Crown and hoped that this would in the future operate 'to the relief of the distressed poor'.[11] In an appeal for funds this was a careful piece of political manipulation to show Bethlem as a proud manifestation of civic spirit and achievement. Other institutions and hospitals were making similar claims. As previous chapters have shown, this had not always been the case. Only in a footnote did Bowen refer to any differences between the Common Council of the City and the Royal Hospitals.[12]

In well-balanced eighteenth-century prose, the *Account* stressed the role of charitable giving that allowed private donors 'the pleasing sensations of benevolence'. Before 1632 there had been no record of the full extent of such giving, but the 'manifest utility' of Bethlem had encouraged donors 'to attend to the security of those members, who through the visitation of God, were become dangerous to the community'. Care of the insane was one of many good causes dependent on the financial support of the benevolent public, given the faith in a minimal state.[13] Until the twentieth century, charity was seen as 'the most wholesome and reliable remedy for the nation's ills'. Philanthropy was ubiquitous; an integral part of civil society. Charity in the eighteenth century was in fashion, although anxiety was frequently expressed about whether it was being directed into the right channels or came from the desired impulses. Families at every social level commonly assigned part of their income to charitable causes, although the reasons behind such actions have been hotly debated by historians.[14] Where the Governors could draw on the posthumous benevolence of previous centuries through its endowments, such means of giving were moving out of fashion. The nature of charity was changing at the end of the eighteenth century to favour subscriptions and donations. Benevolence was cast as an agent of 'national regeneration', aiding the development of character and reforming the minds and morals of the labouring poor.[15] It became 'the acceptable face of the new commercial society, defusing the political and moral tensions thrown up by a changing economic order'.[16] 'Private charity', Bowen generalized,

> may not perhaps excite and animate others so much as public benefactions, but it affords the strongest recommendation of an institution which it favours. He who conceals his good deeds cannot possibly be influenced by any other than the purest motives.

New charities were being established for every social and moral problem (imagined or real) to build on this surge in donations and subscriptions. In London the largest voluntary organizations being formed were a new breed of hospitals like the Westminster in 1719, Guy's in 1721 and the Middlesex in 1745. A hospital boom occurred in the eighteenth century and these new institutions adopted the structure and methods of contemporary voluntary organizations rather than the old royal hospitals. Voluntary hospitals were shown as a vehicle for a form of practical benevolence free of sectarian associations that appealed to Georgian ideas of benevolence. They built on the new conspicuous and self-congratulatory form of philanthropy prevalent.[17] By the time Bowen was writing there were no fewer than seven general hospitals in London.[18] However, Bethlem, already over six hundred years old, was not part of this movement and did not attempt to borrow the new organizational structures or fund-raising activities. With no 'subscriber democracy' and no need for subscriptions, the Governors were trying to attract donations and legacies by cashing in on the rising support for philanthropy, and medical charity in particular.[19] Bowen was trying to show that the Hospital was a fit and proper object for benevolence and appealed to the many multi-layered sentiments that lay behind philanthropy.

In true Enlightenment fashion, the last sentence of the *Account* proclaimed the need through giving to 'LESSEN THE EVILS OF HUMANITY'.[20] 'Humanity' was a key word in the current European vocabulary, and within the language of fund-raising it was a term frequently repeated to play on philanthropic sentiments. Any organization that wanted to raise money from the benevolent public had to claim that it was a benefit to society. Bowen did this partly by pointing to the number of curable cases in the Hospital, praising the care provided. He sought to highlight Bethlem's utility without mentioning specific cases. Mercantilism still shaped much economic theory in the eighteenth century, and any charity that could prove that it returned people to 'health' and work had a powerful claim.[21] It was to become a standard feature of hospital fund-raising in the nineteenth century for institutions to flaunt their statistics to produce similar results.[22] Bowen therefore carefully pointed to

> the number of patients in the house, who are supposed capable of being relieved, commonly amounts to about ONE HUNDRED AND SEVENTY, and of these, it has been found upon an average, that nearly two out of three are restored to their understanding.

This was an impressive record. John Haslam, the Apothecary, in his *Observations on Insanity*, however, claimed that the average number of patients discharged cured was closer to 35 per cent for the period 1784 to 1794.[23] With no access to such figures, Bowen resorted to making claims he could not justify to present a better image of the Hospital. Playing on charitable sensibilities, he extolled the work of the Hospital: 'How glorious then would be the work! How comprehensive the charity, that should contribute to increase the establishment for incurables.'[24]

Bethlem's nature and history, however, provided a barrier to the unhindered flow of charity into the Hospital. Bowen dealt with these matters carefully. Despite the obvious growth in philanthropy, mental illness was not a popular cause, while the Hospital had the Bedlam image to contend with. The *Account* tried to get around this by presenting a positive view of the treatment offered in the Hospital. In an age of heightened sensibility, reflected in books with titles like *The Man of Feeling* (1771), a much read novel by Henry Mackenzie, cruelty was condemned in most of its forms.[25] Bowen showed that patients were treated kindly, manipulating growing humanitarian feelings and changing attitudes to the insane, in certain circles at least.[26] Bethlem's medieval origins (see Chapter 2) were seen as providing more of a problem. At a time of intense anti-papal feeling it was important to distance the Hospital from Catholicism. Three years before Bowen's history was prepared, London had been disturbed by the anti-papal Gordon Riots and rioters had set fire to the Roman Catholic chapel in Moorfields. This was too close for comfort for the Governors, especially as 'riots' had broken out inside Bethlem in 1764. While they could be compared with the 'riots' inside Newgate Prison in 1777, the street riots of 1780 were both on a bigger scale and near enough to Bethlem for the glare of the flames to be seen by its inmates.[27] Within the history therefore, there was a strong protestant bias and the medieval history of Bethlem was written off disparagingly. Simon fitzMary's initiative in 1247 was referred to, but his founding of a religious house was described as being influenced by the 'prevailing superstition of the age'. The history of the Hospital, as Bowen understood it, began three hundred years later with the 'seizure' of Bethlem by Henry VIII in 1547. Any indication that Bethlem had been a Catholic institution would have damaged the very object of the *Account* and limited the amount of money raised. In Bowen's perspective 'judicious benevolence' could only flow freely after the destruction of 'the vast fabric of papal superstition in England', and it was only then that the Mayor, Commonalty and Citizens of London converted Bethlem into 'an hospital for the care of lunatics'. There was no reference to any earlier care of lunatics or to the 'vast fabric' of medieval charity that had been destroyed by the Reformation. However, drawing on John Stow's 1598 *Survey of London*, Bowen did note that the Hospital had received several legacies before 1547 – indeed before the Henrician Reformation – to aid the poor diseased in their minds. He described how the letters patent granted in 1552 to John Whitehead, Proctor to the Hospital of Bethlem, had allowed Whitehead 'to solicit donations within the counties of Lincoln and Cambridge, the City of London, and the Isle of Ely', although he did not refer specifically to the clause in Sir Thomas Gresham's will bequeathing a rent-charge of £10 a year to Bethlem.[28] Fund-raising was Bowen's main preoccupation and dictated what he put into his *Account* and what he left out.

OBJECT OF THE APPEAL

The *Account* did not just point to Bridewell and Bethlem's management and relationship with the City. It had a purpose to serve. Partly this was to provide a history, but it was also to describe the Hospital. Bowen praised late seventeenth-century enterprise and extolled the building of the new hospital at Moorfields:

> never were expense and trouble better bestowed . . . Whether we consider the becoming magnificence of the building, the commodious arrangement of the interior apartments, or the effectual relief which it reaches out to the poor objects whom it shelters [he liked the term 'poor objects'], we may safely pronounce, that it is not to be parallelled [*sic*] in the whole world.[29]

He noted, as others had done before him, that the wards or galleries were 'spacious' and 'airy'. The word 'galleries' had imposing architectural associations: the word 'ward' was part of the vocabulary of the Hospital just as the word 'cell' was part of the vocabulary of the prison. It was the word 'cell', however, which was used most at Bethlem. There were 275 of them, Bowen noted, each measuring twelve feet six inches by eight feet.[30] Georgian Bethlem was not overcrowded, with each patient having a cell, an architectural feature that remained at Bethlem where other asylums moved towards wards. Bethlem's building, Bowen went on to explain, had been extended in 1723 and 1736 when two new wings were added to provide accommodation for 'incurables', 'those forlorn beings, of whose return to the comforts of a sound mind there were no hopes'.[31] Support for the department came from Edward Barkham's gift of land in Lincolnshire in the 1730s to support 'poor incurable lunatics' held in Bethlem.[32] This had doubled the Hospital's capacity, making it a large establishment by eighteenth-century standards. The Manchester Asylum (founded in 1766) had twenty-two cells; Bethel Hospital, Norwich provided care for between twenty and thirty patients.[33] This was getting close to the object of the appeal. The incurable department was for 100 patients, 'fifty of each sex, who enjoy every advantage which their deplorable state can admit'. In addition, there were 150 curable cases in the wards, and Bowen suggested that two-thirds of these would be discharged cured.[34]

It was to provide further accommodation for the 'incurables' that funds were being sought. In Europe this was a popular cause for charity, with benefactors in Turin endowing beds often as an insurance policy for their elderly servants.[35] In Britain, however, incurables were not a popular cause. Hospitals, concerned with producing statistics that made them look good, had elaborate stipulations that discouraged the admission of incurable patients. County asylums did not begin to appear on a national scale until after the 1808 County Asylums Act, the need for which emerged out of the prison reform movement, and there was little accommodation in work-houses.[36] At Guy's a ward for chronic lunatics had been established in 1728, but while Spital Sermons continued to stress the need to provide care for 'Incurable Lunatiks', few institutions catered for their needs.[37] Once state asylums began to be opened they quickly filled with these patients.[38] Bethlem had previously excluded such patients, but with the building of the incurable wings it was able to take its patients discharged as incurable and readmit them. The Hospital only took its own incurables however. Bowen concentrated on those 'whose disorder no medicine can reach', using emotive language in an attempt to touch even the most hard-hearted. 'Instances of longevity were frequent in insane persons', he observed, and the burden on their families was therefore disproportionately great, especially as Bethlem had a long waiting-list, up to seven years, before an incurable could be readmitted. 'Oeconomy' was requisite in 'humble life' and a family faced with maintaining an incurable lunatic confronted 'a severe struggle . . . between necessity and pity, between natural affec-tion and the pride of honest industry'. The Hospital was projected not only as a means to relieve the suffering of the individual but also of the family and parish. These concerns were to become important in the nineteenth-century debate over welfare. Moreover, Bethlem was shown to be meeting the interests of all, not just of the burdened family, by providing a place where 'the frantic maniac, and the despond-ing lunatic' could be 'secured from doing violence to themselves, and others'. In an institution that did not offer contributors physical benefits for their gift, like the admission of a certain number of patients for a donation, Bethlem had to find other ways to reward the benevolent.[39] Attitudes to madness were gradually changing, but for the public fear and stigma continued to surround mental illness.[40] These sentiments took much longer to subside and Bowen was clearly playing on these concerns. Already 'many have appropriated their benefactions solely to the incurables'.[41]

A POSITIVE VIEW OF TREATMENT

The last part of the *Account* was devoted to the present, to the management of Bethlem and its daily routines. The 'conduct and management' of Bethlem, Bowen explained, was 'entrusted' to a Committee of forty-two Governors for 'the regulation of such other matters, as may concern the ease, welfare, and convenience, of so large a family'. The choice of the word 'family' is interesting. The image recurs later in the *Account* when Bowen stressed that 'the members of this family are regarded with that lenity which their situation claims'.[42] Managing Bethlem was conceived of in this way, in terms of a 'household'. The term 'family' was to be taken up by other asylums that wanted to show that they treated their patients in a very different way from the regime associated with Bethlem.[43] It became a metaphor for care and important in the language of moral restraint, where the patient was freed from chains but placed under a system of moral management.[44] Here doctors were seen as the fathers in institutions where the patients were often treated like children. Bowen was already sensitive to the connotations of the word, but unlike later moral-restraint enthusiasts he used it mainly in a rhetorical sense as a device to defend Bethlem. He chose 'family' deliberately to 'contradict a most injurious notion', that had been adopted

> chiefly indeed by that class of people, who are most prone to form prejudices against eleemosynary institutions, which is that the patients in Bethlem Hospital are beaten, and in other respects ill-treated in order to compel them to submit to the necessary operations.

Bowen was trying to create an image of the Hospital that would counter criticism and the Bedlam reputation, while at the same time evoke the sympathy of the charitable public.

There was some truth to Bowen's exaggerated claims. As early as 1646, before the move to Moorfields, Bethlem officers and servants had been forbidden not merely to 'give any blowes to the Madd folkes there' but to employ any 'ill language' towards them on pain of dismissal.[45] The duties of the basketmen and gallery maids had been revised in 1778. It was in the knowledge of such rules that Bowen reiterated that 'no servant' was allowed 'so to wanton an abuse of the authority that is given him'. In addition, it was explained that the previous practice where the public had been able to view patients in Bethlem had been stopped in 1770.[46] There was no attempt to treat the fact as an important event or assess its financial consequences (see Chapter 13).[47] It was strictly enjoined that a patient should never be struck except in self-defence. Bowen felt it 'scarce necessary to assert, that the unhappy patients enjoy the ablest assistance administered with the greatest humanity'.[48] This was to contrast sharply with the behaviour of the staff Urbane Metcalf wrote about in 1818 and the report of the 1815 Select Committee which found considerable cause for concern. It must be remembered that in 1783 Bowen was trying to raise money for Bethlem. For instance, he neglected to mention that problems were still being encountered with absentee staff. In 1785 it was necessary for the Governors to forbid resident staff to sleep outside the Hospital without permission. This did not solve the problem.

Whereas Bowen exemplified Bethlem's kindness, there was little detail about the actual treatments used. Bowen did refer to 'proper medical operations' and to hot and cold bath treatments that had been used since the 1740s. The insistence that John Monro, the second in the Monro dynasty of physicians at the Hospital established with James Monro in 1728, had placed on 'the management requisite' for dealing with the insane was 'never to be learned but from observation' was not, however, a point alluded to. Nor was Monro's belief that it was 'disingenuous to perplex mankind with points that must for ever remain darkly intricate and uncertain'. No mention was made of the regime of purging and vomiting that Monro practised, or that patients continued to be restrained. Although Tuke and other supporters of moral restraint criticized such modes of treatment, including 'the enormous catalogue of powders, extracts, juleps, electuaries, draughts and epitherms', Bethlem was not unusual.[49] Other institutions used similar methods, despite the growing faith in moral methods of management. The general principles of 'antiphlogistic' medicine, which was designed to deplete the system, was seen as an acceptable way of lowering turbulent spirits. Bowen ignored this as such concerns were not fitting for an appeal. Instead, he referred to a special 'best of all worlds' claim made for Bethlem:

> In short, such is the comfortable subsistence, kind treatment, and able medical aid, which the patients here meet with, that many, who are intimately acquainted with the conduct of the house, have declared that if ever God should be pleased to visit them with insanity, BETHLEM HOSPITAL is the place into which they would wish to be admitted.[50]

In a footnote, Bowen added that 'the patients themselves are often known to prefer Bethlem to private mad-houses', although it was not pointed out that Monro ran a private madhouse, Brooke House, in Hackney. Bowen went on to note the 'known humanity and attention of the officers of the house'. He added that if this was not itself 'a sufficient security' for the patients being well treated, 'the frequent inspection which the Hospital undergoes from a large proportion of the Governors would at once invalidate the suspicion that has been mentioned'.[51]

Bowen's claims were not to stand the test of inspection from outside (see Chapter 23). For his own part he was content to put his trust in authority, backed by experience, confident that the quality of management depended on

> the prudence and information of persons of different habits of life, respectable citizens who are engaged in, or have retired from business, gentlemen of the medical profession, and others of independent fortune, whose leisure or benevolence may lead them to attend.[52]

The implication was that the charitable had to do the same. It was an important claim to make, given concerns about corruption that had emerged in the eighteenth century, while it asserted Bethlem's clear philanthropic nature and matched statements made by other voluntary organizations which relied on similar people to run them.[53]

With William Battie's attack on Bethlem's style of management and the therapeutic regime, John Monro had come under increased criticism.[54] It was therefore felt to be important to defend the Hospital's record and treatment, and to clear up misconceptions.[55] While Monro had published his forthright rejoinder to Battie, Bowen still found it necessary thirty years later to reassure the public that all was well at Bethlem and that the patients were treated kindly. Bowen did, however, make one long reference – in a footnote – to St Luke's, the institution that Battie had founded in 1751 and with which Bethlem was often contrasted. It was not the differences between the approaches of Battie at St Luke's and Monro at Bethlem that dominated, but the misconceptions that had persisted after Battie had resigned his place at St Luke's in 1774.[56] Bowen was at pains to point out that a 'mistaken notion had gone forth into the world' that Bethlem and St Luke's were 'connected' and that St Luke's received incurables discharged by Bethlem. The Bethlem Steward, in consequence, had often received letters from 'persons of educational credit' who desired to know when people discharged as incurable 'would be sent to St Luke's'. To prevent this, the *Account* explained that where 'the Governors, Officers and Friends of each charity are totally separate and distinct', both hospitals were in fact 'engaged in the same good work, [had] the same object in view, the restoration of reason to the distracted' and 'both admitted a limited number of incurables'.[57] It was important for this to be said, and Bowen said it clearly.

THE PRESENT: ROUTINE AND MANAGEMENT

Bowen did not only set out to provide a sanitized history full of praise for the Hospital and its Governors to help their attempts to increased charitable support. He also provided a snapshot of Bethlem's routine and admission procedure in the 1780s. Part of the aim was to provide information to potential contributors to explain how Bethlem worked.

Bowen described the Hospital's routine briefly but systematically: 'the cells are visited every morning by servants of the house' who went on to make a report to the resident Apothecary, named as John Gozna, who carried out his rounds at about eight each morning 'to inspect them himself and to give such orders and directions as may be necessary'. He carefully explained that there were 'certain rooms' with 'comfortable fires' and 'to prevent mischief . . . [they were] defended by large guard-irons'. In addition, there were 'large adjoining court-yards' where inmates could walk in summer. Airing courts were to become a common architectural feature of asylum design.[58] Throughout the Hospital, it was revealed, patients could indulge in 'such diversions as are deemed not improper to quiet their spirits, and compose the agitation of their minds'. The image was a homely one to contrast with the conditions attributed to Bethlem and those found in other institutions for the care and treatment of the poor. All this was general. On food, however, Bowen offered ample detail of the diet that had recently been 'liberalised' by the introduction of fresh vegetables and 'a better sort of small beer':

> The constant breakfast allotted the patients throughout the year, is water-gruel, with bread, butter and salt. They have meat for dinner three days in a week.

Beef is the Sunday's fare; mutton is their Tuesday's dinner, and they have veal on Thursdays, but the last only from Lady-Day to Michaelmas; during the winter months, mutton or pork is substituted in it's [*sic*] place. They have also a sufficient quantity of broth; and that every indulgence, which economy permits, may be given to the poor patients, on the meat days one gallery [there were five galleries in all] is always gratified with roast meat. The quantity of solid meat, besides vegetables and a pint of small beer, allowed each individual, is eight ounces. On the days in which they have no meat, and which are called banyan days, they have milk pottage or rice-milk, with bread and cheese. Their constant supper is bread and cheese, with a pint of small beer; and twelve out of each gallery have butter if they prefer it.

'Apparel' received as much detailed attention from Bowen as food. It was explained, presumably for those wanting to send patients to Bethlem, that clothes could be provided by friends, but if this was not done they were 'furnished by the Steward on the orders of the weekly committee'.[59] There were other elements of guidance, some of them repeating, even in the same words, what John Strype, bringing Stow up to date, had written of Bethlem and its procedures in 1720.[60] It was explained that on the admission of a patient, a ticket was delivered which authorized the bearer to come to the Hospital, 'on Mondays and Wednesdays, between the hours of ten and twelve' to visit. Restrictions on visiting were to remain in force into the twentieth century.[61]

Admission was 'attended with very little difficulty' provided that a Governor's recommendation was presented and that certificates of the would-be patient's parish settlement were available. There were happily forms for this purpose from the 1780s, obtainable from the Clerk's office, a sign of a modernized approach to entry. The new voluntary hospitals adopted similar procedures. Bethlem was a national charity open to lunatics from the whole kingdom, though each applicant was interviewed by a special committee and the Physicians. It was stressed that no person would be excluded from Bethlem who had been discharged uncured from any other lunatic hospital. This was later to change when the nature of the patients altered under Charles Hood (see Chapter 26). Only 'mopes, persons afflicted with the palsy, or subject to convulsive or epileptic fits, and such as are become weak through age, or long illness' were not admitted. There were old distinctions here that were to remain important in the later history of Bethlem. Upon admission one requirement was that two housekeepers 'residing in or near London' should enter into a bond to take a patient away when discharged by the Committee, and to pay the expense of clothing and, in case of death, burial – stipulations common to many voluntary hospitals.[62] If 'the lunatic' was sent by a parish, or by any other public body, the sum of £3 4s had to be paid for bedding, but if he was placed there by friends, Bowen explained that the Hospital, 'anxious to lighten their burthen', would reduce the sum to 'two pounds five shillings and sixpence'. When an incurable patient was settled in the house, the sum of half-a-crown a week was to be paid by his friends or by the parish that he lived in. The new charitable asylums had similar practices where they admitted paying and pauper patients, using the former to fund the care of the latter. At Bethlem from 1733 to 1800 between 35 and 39 per cent of the patients were private. Attempts were made to provide a rapid turnover of patients to prevent the institution from silting-up. The 'care of the Governors' did not cease on discharge. The patient was 'interrogated as to the treatment he has received, and, if he has cause of complaint, could be required to declare it.' Every patient discharged was encouraged to apply to the medical officer

> who gives him such advice and medicines as are proper to prevent a relapse, and if it should appear that his circumstances are particularly distressing, the Treasurer and Physician possess a discretionary power to relieve him with a small sum of money at his departure.[63]

This was still a feature of the rules until the 1920s.

The inclusion of such abundant detail demonstrates further that Bowen was trying to create a good image of the Hospital and to provide a guide, especially as he numbered among the intended readers of his *Account*, sponsors of possible patients, including the Governors themselves.

CONCLUSION

Bethlem was to be criticized more than once in the future – not so much because of its procedures and the underlying rules on which they were based, but because of its failure to follow them. Much of the criticism concerning divergences or gaps between regulations and practice was attributable to lack of resources, human and financial. This was outside Bowen's remit, as were 'scandals' in the treatment of lunatics that were being spotlighted in private madhouses in the two decades before the *Account* appeared.[64] Many of them were producing tempting advertisements far more eulogistic than Bowen's history, given that the 1774 Act for Regulating Private Madhouses made them subject to inspection by a five-man Commission of the Royal College of Physicians. As a public charitable hospital Bethlem was outside the inspection system, which in any case lacked sanctions to enforce the Commissioners' findings.[65] Inevitably, therefore, what happened in secrecy inside the Hospital would be compared with what was being said about other places from which the veil of secrecy had been removed. Bethlem was losing its monopoly as the only institution in England for the care of the insane. As concern for the fate of the insane grew during the 1780s and 1790s, attention was bound to turn increasingly to the metropolis. These were decades when the Press, always interested in Bethlem, became increasingly active, supplementing the role of essayists and pamphleteers. Cruelty of all kinds was under attack, not least in prisons. The appeal to humanity pointed to the task of redefining inhumanity.

Half a century after it appeared, Bowen's *Account* was described by the Charity Commissioners as nothing more than 'a panegyric' or 'an eulogium' on the history of Bethlem. It threw 'no light', they complained, and felt that it was based on 'a very superficial acquaintance with the subject'.[66] Geoffrey O'Donoghue, chaplain from 1892 to 1930, was just as scathing about Bowen on different grounds in his *Story of Bethlehem Hospital*. He felt 'the author had not the faintest idea that Bethlem had been engaged in its present work since 1377 at least'. O'Donoghue admitted, however, that Bowen's book 'appears to have benefited the funds very considerably'.[67] That was its purpose. New funds for the incurables were raised and the Hospital's endowments increased. Money was attracted from the City livery companies, particularly from the Mercers' and Grocers' Companies, and from the Hospital's Governors and officers. Bethlem's income improved as a result, but there was still cause for concern in 1792.[68]

Bowen's *Account*, despite its obvious fund-raising nature, was not entirely a eulogistic sketch of the institution he served. Others reflected his assessment of the Hospital. In 1788, one French visitor allowed into Bethlem could not only compare it favourably with hospitals in his own country but praise it in terms not dissimilar to those of Bowen:

> I stayed for some time in Bedlam. The poor creatures there are not chained up in dark cellars, stretched on damp ground, nor reclining on cold paving stones . . . no bolts, no bars. The doors are open, their rooms wainscoted, and long airy corridors give them a chance of exercise. A cleanliness, hardly conceivable unless seen reigns in their hospital.[69]

Three years earlier, the Inspector-General of French Hospitals, Jean Colombier, had stated of conditions in his own country that

> thousands of lunatics are locked up in [French] prisons without anyone even thinking of administering the slightest remedy. The half-mad are mingled with those who are totally deranged, those who rage with those who are quiet; some are in chains, while others are free in their prison. Finally, unless nature comes to their aid by curing them, the duration of their misery is life-long, for unfortunately the illness does not improve but only grows worse.[70]

Another French visitor to Bethlem before the 1789 Revolution, Jacques Tenon, was impressed by the very existence of Bethlem. He also provided details of its architecture and design, comparing it in 1787 with other hospitals.[71] Tenon belonged to the *ancien régime*. Those who came to investigate Bethlem in the early nineteenth century belonged to a new tradition, one inspired by Pinel in France, the work of the Quaker York Retreat, and an evangelical reformism. They subscribed to a different view of how mental illness should be treated that conflicted with practices at Bethlem at a time of increasing incarceration of the insane. This was to prove more controversial and far-reaching in its implications than Bethlem had been before it ceased to be a place of public spectacle in 1770.[72] When the *Account* was written, changes had already started to be made. Two years before, Richard Clarke had been appointed Treasurer and was responsible for its publication. He was to remain Treasurer until 1836. In 1792 Thomas Monro succeeded his father as Resident Physician, and a still more important internal change was made in 1795 when John Haslam became Apothecary. Haslam believed in a slightly different approach to treatment. He continued to support bleeding and purging, but started to turn against vomiting, cold baths, blisters on the head and the use of opium. Haslam espoused moral management and was keen to talk to patients and increase their confidence.[73] Given such ideas, he dismissed the whirling or spinning treatments, practices that were adopted at other institutions. Haslam figured prominently in Pinel's *Traité Medico-philosophique sur la Manie*, published in 1801. His career at Bethlem was to end in dismissal in 1816. Pinel was to go from success to success, and his name remains a household name in psychiatry. In any explanation of the fates of the two men, both the historiography of Bethlem (and of the Bicêtre) and the historiography of psychiatry converge.

NOTES

1 See Dora Weiner, '"*Le geste de Pinel*": The History of a Psychiatric Myth', in Mark Micale and Roy Porter (eds), *Discovering the History of Psychiatry* (Oxford and New York: OUP, 1994), 232–47; *idem*, 'Health and Mental Health in the Thought of Philippe Pinel', in Charles Rosenberg (ed.), *Healing and History: Essays for George Rosen* (Kent and New York: Dawson, 1979), 59–85; while the topic of the myth has been explored in J. Gortais, 'Le rôle du mythe de Pinel dans l'organisation et le fonctionnement de la psychiatrie du 19eme siècle', *Psychanalyse à l'université*, iv (1979), 197–244.

2 Much has been written on moral restraint from varying angles. Historians have tried to see it as a product of the emergence of moral humane ideas in the eighteenth century, a challenge to medical control, or a means to assert a new form of Foucaultdian control over the insane. See, for example, Anne Digby, 'Moral Treatment at the Retreat', in W. F. Bynum, Roy Porter and Michael Shepherd (eds), *Anatomy of Madness* (London: Tavistock Press, 1985), vol. ii, 52–72; Anne Digby, *Madness, Morality and Medicine: A Study of the York Retreat* (New York: CUP, 1985); Roy Porter, 'Was There a Moral Therapy in the Eighteenth Century?', *Lychnos* (1981), 12–26; Nancy Tomes, 'The Great Restraint Controversy' in W. F. Bynum, Roy Porter and Michael Shepherd (eds), *Anatomy of Madness* (London: Tavistock Press, 1988), vol. iii, 190–225; Andrew Scull, 'Moral Restraint Reconsidered' in *idem*, *Madhouses, Mad-Doctors and Madmen* (Philadelphia: University of Pennsylvania, 1981), 105–20.

3 Thomas Bowen, *An Historical Account of the Origin, Progress, and Present State of Bethlem Hospital, founded by Henry the Eighth, for the Cure of Lunatics, and Enlarged by Subsequent Benefactors, for the Reception and Maintenance of Incurables* (London: For the Governors 1783), 16; for the statues see Chapter 15.

4 See R. J. Morris, 'Clubs, Societies and Associations', in F. M. L. Thompson (ed.), *Cambridge Social History of Britain* (Cambridge: CUP, 1990), vol. iii, 395–443, who shows that voluntary organizations grew rapidly from the mid-eighteenth century as a major social response to the problems posed by change and complexity; Keir Waddington, 'Finance, Philanthropy and the Hospital' (unpublished Ph.D. Thesis, University of London, 1995), ch. 2.

5 Andrew Scull, *The Most Solitary of Afflictions: Madness and Society in Britain, 1700–1900* (New Haven and London: Yale University Press, 1993), 20.

6 Edward G. O'Donoghue, Chaplain of Bethlem Hospital from 1892 to 1930 followed up his *Story of Bethlehem Hospital from its Foundation in 1247* (London: T. Fisher Unwin, 1914) with *Bridewell Hospital Palace, Prisons, Schools*, 2 volumes (London: J. Hane, 1923 and 1929)

7 Bridewells in the late eighteenth century were not only for vagrants and beggars, but also provided houses of confinement for the more dangerous lunatics: see Akihito Suzuki, 'Lunacy in Seventeenth and Eighteenth Century England', *History of Psychiatry*, iii (1992), 29–44.

8 See William L. Parry Jones, *The Trade in Lunacy, A Study of Private Madhouses in England in the Eighteenth and Nineteenth Centuries* (London: Routledge, 1972). When new legislation licensed private madhouses in 1774 there were sixteen licensed metropolitan houses, although non-registration was common.

9 The York Retreat, analysed by Digby, *op. cit.*, and St Luke's (see C. N. French, *The Story of St. Luke's Hospital* (London: Heinemann, 1951), were among these new charitable asylums, with the Bethel Hospital in Norwich, founded in 1713, being the oldest.

10 In 1837 the Charity Commissioners claimed that there was no outside authority for Stow's statement. The Commissioners argued that 'the will had been searched for without effect in

the Prerogative Court of Canterbury, the Consistory Courts of London and the Mayor's Court': F. O. Martin, *The Report of the Commissioners for Enquiry into Charities for 1837* (London: 1837), 472.

11 See M. D. George, *London Life in the Eighteenth Century* 3rd edn (London: LSE, 1959); Roy Porter, *London: A Social History* (London: Hamish Hamilton, 1994), esp. ch. 6; George Rudé, *Hanoverian London, 1714–1808* (London: Secker & Warburg, 1971); and P. Langford, *A Polite and Commercial People, 1727–1783* (London: Guild Publishing, 1989).

12 Bowen, *op. cit.* 16.

13 See B. K. Gray, *A History of English Philanthropy* (London: P. S. King & Son, 1905); David Owen, *English Philanthropy, 1660–1960* (Harvard: Harvard University Press, 1965); Donna Andrew, *Philanthropy and Police: London Charity in the Eighteenth Century* (Princeton, N.J.: Princeton University Press, 1989); while Pat Thane, 'Government and Society in England and Wales, 1750–1914', in Thompson, *op. cit.* pp. 1–62, discusses the idea of a minimal state.

14 Frank Prochaska, 'Philanthropy', in Thompson *op. cit.* 357. Philanthropy has frequently been labelled an instrument of social control or a method of class domination, a view held by historians like Gareth Stedman Jones, *Outcast London* (Oxford: OUP, 1971) or more recently by R. J. Morris, *Class, Sect and Party: The Making of the British Middle Class, Leeds 1820–50* (London: Macmillan, 1979) and R. Trainor, *Black Country Elites: The Exercise of Authority in an Industrial Area* (Oxford: OUP, 1993). Their work counters the more sympathetic treatment of philanthropy by Frank Prochaska, *Women and Philanthropy in Nineteenth Century England* (Oxford: Clarendon Press, 1980), who believes, as earlier historians did, that humanitarianism continued to play an important role in giving. Where philanthropy might be motivated by ideas of class hegemony or social control, it is arguable that this was only one part of the motivation that encouraged benevolent action: see Keir Waddington, '"Grasping Gratitude": Hospitals and Charity in Late-Victorian London', in Martin Daunton (ed.), *Charity, Self-Interest and Welfare in the English Past* (London: UCL Press, 1996), 181–202.

15 Andrew, *op. cit.*

16 Ann Borsay, '"Persons of Honour and Reputation": The Voluntary Hospital in the Age of Corruption', *Medical History*, xxxv (1991), 1–15.

17 Roy Porter, 'The Gift Relationship', in Roy Porter and Lindsay Granshaw (eds), *The Hospital in History* (London: Routledge, 1990), 149–78.

18 *The Medical Register for the Year 1783*. For the voluntary hospital movement see Brian Abel Smith, *The Hospitals 1800–1948* (London: Heinemann, 1964); W. H. McMenemey, 'The Hospital Movement of the Eighteenth Century and its Development', in F. N. L. Poynter (ed.), *Evolution of Hospitals in Britain* (London: Pitman, 1968), or for London, Geoffrey Rivett, *Development of the London Hospital System 1823–1982* (London: OUP, 1986).

19 Morris uses the term to denote a system of voluntary organization management where one subscriber, one vote was the general rule and membership was limited to those who contributed: Morris, *Class, Sect and Party*, 184. This was not the case at Bethlem and Bridewell which had an administrative structure similar to that of the other Royal Hospitals.

20 Bowen, *op. cit.* 16.

21 Ann Borsay, 'Cash and Conscience: Financing the General Hospital at Bath', *Social History of Medicine*, iv (1991), 215; Andrew, *op. cit.* 22–4.

22 See Waddington, 'Finance, Philanthropy and the Hospital'; J. Woodward, *To Do the Sick No Harm* (London: Routledge, 1974).

23 See John Haslam, *Observations on Insanity* (London: Rivington, 1798), 112.

24 Bowen, *op. cit.* 6, 14–15.

25 Henry Mackenzie, *The Man of Feeling* (London: Cadell, 1771).

26 In the treatment of the insane, practices often lagged behind the rhetoric as the investigations of the early nineteenth century were to show.

27 When the riots were over, Horace Walpole would have sent Lord George Gordon, their ringleader, to Bethlem rather than to the Tower: J. P. de Castro, *The Gordon Riots* (London: OUP, 1926); George Rudé, *Paris and London in the Eighteenth Century* (London: Collins, 1970); J. Brewer and J. Styles (eds), *An Ungovernable People: The British and Their Law in the Seventeenth and Eighteenth Centuries* (London: Hutchinson, 1980).

28 Bowen, *op. cit.* 3; *The Report of the Commissioners*, 291.

29 Bowen, *op.cit.* 5. For a discussion of the Moorfield's building and the influential role it played, see Chapter 15.

30 Bowen, *op. cit.* 9.

31 See Jonathan Andrews, 'The Lot of the "Incurably" Insane in Enlightenment England', *Eighteenth Century Life*, xii (1988), 17.

32 Edward Barkham had been baptized in 1673 in Kelstern in North Lincolnshire, and although little is known about his early life he travelled as a 'free merchant' on an East India Company ship, working for the company in Sumatra, returning to England by 1714. Wainfleet on the Lincolnshire coast passed to him through complicated means in 1718 from his great-great-grandfather, citizen and leatherseller of London and Lord Mayor in 1621–2. Edward now started to live the life of a county gentleman, finally dying childless in 1733. His will provided for his wife and godson, and for the poor of Wainfleet, but practically all his estate was left to Bethlem to provide for the care of incurables, an object of concern for Barkham. Edward's relations tried to obstruct the will, but it passed to Bethlem in 1735 and estates in Lincolnshire remained the property of the Hospital until 1919: *Bethlem & Maudsley Gazette* (March 1959), 23–6.

33 Scull, *The Most Solitary of Afflictions*, 18.

34 Bowen, *op. cit.* 6, 14–15.

35 See Sandra Cavallo, 'Charity, Power and Patronage in Eighteenth-Century Italian Hospitals', in Roy Porter and Lindsay Granshaw, *The Hospital in History* (London: Routledge, 1990), 93–122.

36 Kathleen Jones, *Asylums and After* (London: Athlone, 1993), 33–4.

37 Michael Donnelly, *Managing the Mind: A Study of Medical Psychology in Early Nineteenth-Century Britain* (London: Tavistock, 1983), 6.

38 Scull, *The Most Solitary of Afflictions*, 269–76.

39 For the benefits associated with voluntary hospitals see Waddington, 'Finance, Philanthropy and the Hospital', Chapter 2; Lindsay Granshaw, 'The Rise of the Modern Hospital in Britain', in Andrew Wear (ed.), *Medicine in Society* (Cambridge: CUP, 1994), 201.

40 See Roy Porter, *Mind-Forg'd Manacles, A History of Madness in England from the Reformation to the Regency* (London: Athlone, 1987).

41 Bowen, *op. cit.* 8.

42 *Ibid.* 10, 12.

43 Samuel Tuke, *A Description of the Retreat* (London: S. Tuke, 1813); Digby, *Madness, Morality and Medicine*, 147.

44 See note 2.

45 Court of Governors, 18 July 1646, fol. 270; Patricia Allderidge, 'Bedlam, Fact or Fantasy', in W. F. Bynum, Roy Porter and Michael Shepherd (eds), *Anatomy of Madness*, vol. iii (London: Tavistock Press, 1988), 17–33.

46 M. Byrd, *Visits to Bethlem: Madness and Literature in the Eighteenth Century* (Columbia: University of Carolina Press, 1974), and *idem*, 'Bedlam and Parnassus', in G. Levine (ed.), *One Culture: Essays in Science and Literature* (Madison, Wis.: University of Wisconsin Press, 1987), which covers 'the long-eighteenth century'.

47 Bowen, *op.cit.* 12.

48 *Ibid.* 10.

49 S. Tuke, *op. cit.* 123.

50 Bowen, *op. cit.* 12.

51 *Ibid.* 9.

52 *Ibid.*

53 Borsay, *op. cit.* 281–2.

54 See Chapter 16.

55 Ironically, Battie himself, who has been seen as one of the original pioneers of Tukean moral therapy, continued to emphasis the use of 'bodily pain' and fear in the treatment of the insane: Scull, *The Most Solitary of Afflictions*, 62.

56 W. Rawes, *A Short History of St. Luke's Hospital* (London: n.s., 1901); French, *op. cit.*; Porter,

Mind-Forg'd Manacles, especially 317; William Battie, *A Treatise on Madness* (London: J. Whitson & B. White, 1758) and John Monro, *Remarks on Dr. Battie's Treatise on Madness*, with an introduction by Richard Hunter and Ida Macalpine (London: Dawsons, 1962, reprint of 1758 edn); and O'Donoghue, *op. cit.* 415.

57 Bowen, *op. cit.* 8.

58 See Jeremy Taylor, *Hospital and Asylum Architecture in England 1840–1914: Building for Health Care* (London: Mansell, 1991), 133–60.

59 Bowen, *op. cit.* 10, 14.

60 See J. Strype, *A Survey of the Cities of London and Westminster . . . Written at First in the year MDXCVIII By John Stow . . . Corrected, Improved and Very Much Enlarged . . . to the Present Time* (London: A. Churchill, 1720).

61 Bowen, *op. cit.* 12.

62 See Woodward, *op. cit.*

63 Bowen, *op. cit.* 14.

64 Parry Jones, *op. cit.*; B. Faulkner, *Observations on the General and Improper Treatment of Insanity* (London 1790); and Porter, *Mind-Forg'd Manacles*, 129–55. For an early account of a scandal in a private madhouse see the *Gentleman's Magazine*, January 1763. For a fictional description comparing private madhouses with the Bastille, see T. Smollett, *The Life and Adventures of Sir Lancelot Greaves* (London and New York: OUP, 1973 edn), 190.

65 Richard Hunter and Ida Macalpine, *Three Hundred Years of Psychiatry, 1535–1860* (London: OUP, 1963), 452–4; Charlotte MacKenzie, *Psychiatry for the Rich: A History of Ticehurst Private Asylum* (London: Routledge, 1992), 9–11.

66 Martin, *op. cit.* 507. See also *Memoranda, References and Documents relating to the Royal Hospitals of the City of London* (London: For the Governors, 1836).

67 O'Donoghue, *op. cit.* 278.

68 1792 Select Committee Report.

69 Cited in O'Donoghue, *op. cit.* 282–3.

70 Cited in R. Somelaigne, *Les Pionniers de la Psychiatrie Française avant et après Pinel* (Paris: Baillière, 1930), vol. i, 85.

71 For a modern edition of Tenon's travel diaries see J. Carré (ed.), *Journal d'Observations sur les Principaux Hôpitaux et sur Quelques Prisons d'Angleterre* (Paris: Claremont-Ferrand, 1992).

72 For the controversy and for the special place of Britain in relation to it see Roy Porter, 'Madness and Society in England: The Historiography Reconsidered', *Studies in History*, vol. iii (New Delhi and London, 1987); Michel Foucault, *La Folie et la Déraison: Histoire de la Folie à l'Age Classique* (Paris: Plon, 1961), translated and abridged as *Madness and Civilisation: A History of Lunacy in the Age of Reason* (New York: Pantheon Books, 1965); the review of the English translation by R. D. Laing in *The New Statesman*, 16 June 1967; A. Still and I. Velody (eds), *Rewriting the History of Madness: Studies in Foucault's Histoire de la Folie* (London: Routledge, 1992); George Rosen, *Madness and Society: Chapters in the Historical Sociology of Mental Illness* (London: Routledge, 1968); and Andrew Scull (ed.), *Madhouses, Mad Doctors and Madmen* (Philadelphia: University of Philadelphia Press, 1981).

73 See John Haslam, *Illustrations of Madness*, with an introduction by Roy Porter (London: Routledge, 1988), xxviii.

CHAPTER TWENTY-ONE

FACT AND FANCY

——— •◆• ———

Within less than a decade of the publication of Thomas Bowen's *Historical Account of the Origin, Progress and Present State of Bethlem Hospital* in 1783, it became evident that all was not well with Bethlem.[1] Nor had it been in 1783. In the *Account* an exaggerated and positive image of the Hospital was presented. Bowen's history was designed to help raise funds from the City and benevolent public for the care of the hundred or so incurables in Bethlem, but no indication was given as to the real reason why such charity was needed. Using a common vocabulary of fund-raising, the Hospital and care of incurables were presented as a worthy cause. This in itself was supposed to justify support.[2] However, given the nature of the *Account*, it was not possible to explain why funds were urgently needed. No mention was made therefore of the fact that Bethlem and Bridewell were facing a financial crisis.

Bethlem's poor financial situation had been brought about nine years earlier when the Treasurer, William Kinleside, who had been in office since 1774, had been adjudged bankrupt. The Governors had lost £6,000 of the Bridewell and Bethlem's funds in the process. To cover the gap in income, borrowing had become necessary and the debts and interest generated constituted a new burden. At the same time, prices were rising, particularly the price of provisions, and so were wages given the inflationary effect of the Revolutionary wars with France and marked fluctuations in harvests.[3] Most serious of all, the heavy maintenance costs of the Moorfields building, which were eventually to lead to its abandonment and the building of a new hospital in Southwark (see Chapter 22), forced the Governors to review all their obligations. In response they appointed their own committee of inquiry in 1792 to investigate.

REASSURING THE CHARITABLE: THE 1792 SELECT COMMITTEE AND IMAGES OF THE HOSPITAL

The 1792 Select Committee of Inquiry was established to review every aspect of Bethlem's management. It started with the finances and went on to consider the Hospital's standing rules and daily management. The Committee was 'embarrassed' to discover lax record-keeping and poor accounting that made an assessment of the financial situation difficult. For the 'Incurable Fund', established with Edward Barkham's benefaction in the 1730s and central to the fund-raising purpose of the *Account*, it was found that it was difficult to determine its present or projected income from charitable donations.[4] This was particularly disconcerting because in 1789 it had been decided to increase the incurable charges. As a result, all incurable patients admitted after Michaelmas Day 1790 were now charged 2s a week for their maintenance and those paid for by parishes 5s (instead of 2s 6d).[5] Inflation countered these changes and in 1812 it was necessary to transfer £7,000 from the general account to the Incurables' Fund.

The Committee went on to find that the accounts were 'imperfect . . . extremely obscure and defective'. The Governors could not entirely blame Kinleside. He had been discharged and struck off the list of Governors, but problems had existed before he was appointed Treasurer. The Committee found that there had been a 'total want of books of legacies and benefactions' over the previous forty years in 'utter disregard of an express standing order'.[6] The embarrassment of the Committee arose from their recognition that it was the 'peculiarly sacred and inviolate duty, of the Governors to record faithfully all the bequests and donations which were specifically limited to any Particular branch of the charities'. It was 'decidedly of the opinion' that 'the Fund for the Incurables' should be kept completely separate.[7] The Committee spent a considerable amount of time extracting items relating to the revenues of Bethlem from the Court Books and Cash Books to provide an accurate picture of the Hospital's finances. In addition, the post of the Lincolnshire Receiver, who had handled the receipts from the properties sustaining the Incurables' Fund, was discontinued. As an act of kindness, the Governors decided that only when 'the worthy Possessor retires' that his 'House should then be let' to increase income. To fulfil the receiver's role a new office was created. Now a bailiff, 'residing contiguous to these Estates', was appointed on a small salary to 'superintend their Management' and collect the rents.[8] The aim was to ensure that the property was administered more closely. When it became clear that these measures were not sufficient, further financial controls were introduced. In the general revision of the rules governing Bethlem's management in 1802 (see pp. 384–7), the Treasurer's financial duties were extended. He was instructed to report on 'all legacies and benefactions' and to 'keep a regular Cash Book for both Hospitals' stating what legacies and benefactions had been received since the last meeting. To prevent fraud, he was also required to give 'a compleat and satisfactory Security for £3000'.[9] Sound financial accounting and strict regulation of the Treasurer's duties were necessary to guarantee public trust.[10]

Given Bridewell and Bethlem's financial situation, economy now became a byword in the administration. The 1792 Special Committee did not need to state explicitly that there should be 'a strict oeconomy constantly observed in dispensing the revenues of the Charities'. Aware that the Hospital still needed funds, savings were made. In 1793 when the duties of the officers were being revised, it was decided that the Clerk's salary should be reduced to £200. Because 'the other emoluments incident to his situation' were considerable it was felt that he should have 'no Perquisites whatsoever from the Hospitals or an Allowance for a House'. There was no corresponding reduction in his duties. To prevent problems from arising, the existing Clerk was allowed to remain on the existing terms. The 1792 Committee also recommended that 'no repairs, works and purchases or projects' costing more than £200 should be undertaken without the agreement of two-thirds of the Governors present at two successive General Courts. 'All orders whatsoever' were to be issued in writing to the respective workmen, who were expected to issue vouchers for their accounts. These were to be checked by daily entries in 'the proper books to be kept for that purpose by the Stewards and Porters at both Hospitals'.[11] 'Oeconomy' and order went together. A careful check continued to be made on expenditure. Limits were set on the Steward and Matron's provision allowances. Allowances for them (and for the Barber) for extra meat and fish at Easter, Whitsuntide and Christmas were ended in 1802. 'All Newspapers, except one' were cancelled, which was to be produced 'for the use of the Committee every Saturday Morning'. The Governors themselves were not exempt. In 1802 it was decided that 'coffee and Toast usually ordered for the Governors on committee days be in future discontinued'.[12] Economy was a powerful concept in hospital administration. It was important in increasing the claims of voluntary organizations for support, countering concerns about corruption prevalent in Georgian society.

Bowen's *Account* had increased the amount of charitable support Bethlem received, but the 1792 Committee showed that there were problems with the internal administration of the Hospital.[13] A better system of accounting and money-saving schemes were attempts to solve this problem. It also might be seen as a way of reassuring the charitable public and potential benefactors given the durability of the Bedlam image. The closure of the Hospital to sightseers, and the *Account*, had not ended Bethlem's association with Bedlam. This was only to come in the twentieth century.[14] At the turn of the nineteenth century, the Governors still had to confront a Hogarthian image of Bethlem. In 1733 an anonymous poet, encouraging fancy, could still speak of the Hospital in terms of its Bedlam imagery:

> For other views than these within appear
> And Woe and Horror dwell forever here;
> Forever from the echoing roofs rebound
> A dreadful Din of heterogeneous sounds.
> From this, from that from every quarter rise
> Loud shouts and sullen groans and doleful cries . . .
> Within the Chambers which this Dome contains
> In all her 'frantic' forms Distraction reigns . . .
> Rattling his chains, the wretch all raving lies
> And roars and fumes, and Earth and heaven defies.[15]

There were similar stereotyped images in a Gillray cartoon of 1789 that showed Edmund Burke, heavily fettered to the floor, presumably in Bethlem, having his head shaved.[16] No matter what the Governors did these images did not disappear. They only seemed to be confirmed by Urbane Metcalf, a hawker by occupation, who wrote about Bethlem after his discharge in his threepenny pamphlet, *The Interior of Bethlehem Hospital*, published in 1818.[17]

Visitors to Bethlem in the first decade of the nineteenth century were often impressed by what they saw, but many continued to express reservations that helped confirm accepted stereotypes. The Viennese Johann Peter Frank, who visited many European hospitals in 1802, found that the Hospital did not compare favourably in cleanliness with several other English asylums.[18] He went on to condemn the treatment meted out by John Haslam (see Chapter 23), the Apothecary, who appeared not to be taking account of the trends towards non-restraint encouraged by Pinel, Tuke and the York Retreat.[19] Bethlem was later to be attacked for its methods of treating patients (see Chapter 23), but visitors also identified problems with the fabric of the Hospital. The Hospital was cold and damp and in need of considerable renovations and repairs. Mortality rates were high, although resolute efforts were being made to keep the Hospital cleaner than it had been in the middle years of the eighteenth century. It was around the time that Bowen was writing that a bug-destroyer and a rat-catcher were appointed. The former took up his post in 1777 (paid 8 guineas per annum from 1778) and Robert Roberts who was appointed to the second post (paid 3 guineas per annum) in 1786. They had a difficult task. In 1791 the Surveyor reported that conditions in the Hospital were 'in such a state as to endanger the Health of the patients'.[20] Image did not entirely match reality, and there was still certainly much substance that could be found to support negative claims.

Given the images of Bethlem, its reputation, and Bowen's *Account*, it is difficult to separate fact from fancy in the late eighteenth century. The 1815 House of Commons Select Committee investigating madhouses and Metcalf's pamphlet only seemed to confirm in retrospect that Bethlem represented all that was bad in the management of the insane. Efforts, however, had been made before 1815 to improve the situation in the Hospital. The 1792 Committee's suggestions were important in the Governors' efforts to stimulate charity, but they had wider implications for how Bethlem was administered.

REFORMING MANAGEMENT

The 1792 inquiry did not just deal with Bethlem's financial management in an attempt to create the impression that the Hospital was a well-managed and publicly accountable institution. The Governors clearly recognized that other reforms were needed throughout the administration. The 1792 Committee acknowledged that rules and orders had not been kept up to date. It therefore recommended revision. The Governors considered it necessary to republish the Hospital's rules and orders, along with lists of the duties of Bethlem's officers. In 1793 they presented a new set of rules for the Hospital and its staff.[21] Firm as these were, there was a need to examine them again in 1800, suggesting that they were not all being observed. The task of drafting a new version, which ran to 47 pages and appeared in 1802, was left to a Joint House and Bethlem Committee appointed in 1800. However, this still did not solve the problems facing Bethlem.[22]

The instructions given to each Governor on appointment took the form of a solemn charge read to them on admission by the Bridewell Chaplain, Bowen, and his successors. They looked back to the 'original orders' for the Royal Hospitals compiled in 1557:

Sir, you have been elected and are admitted a Governor of the Royal Hospitals of Bridewell and Bethlem, a station of great honour and trust, which will afford you many opportunities of promoting the glory of God and the welfare of your fellow creatures; for in those Hospitals a provision is made for employing and correcting idle, vagrant and disorderly persons, and educating your children in honest trades, and also for maintaining and curing needy and deplorable lunatics. The distribution of the revenues designed by royal bounty, and many charitable persons, for those truly noble and excellent purposes is now committed to your care. And you are hereby solemnly required and earnestly requested to discharge your duty in this behalf with such conscientious regard, that you may appear with joy at the judgement seat of Christ, when a particular account will be taken of all the Offices of Charity, in which we have abounded towards our poor brethren ... In confidence that you will diligently attend this good work, you are now admitted a Governor ...

To discharge such obligations demanded time and in the first instance knowledge of procedures, and clearly different Governors responded in different ways. Scull has argued that these Governors were predominately 'aristocratic' and gave respectability to the institution.[23] This, as Patricia Allderidge has shown, was clearly not the case. Of the 414 Governors named in 1818 only twenty-one were members of the aristocracy. Other hospitals in London and in the provinces in the late eighteenth century were also not dominated by the gentry as some have assumed.[24] With the City of London's Court of the Common Council able to nominate twelve Governors, City interests were strongly represented and a large portion of the Governors continued to be drawn from the City and the Alderman class.

When in 1800 it was decided to prepare a report on the *Standing Rules and Orders*, there was a need to clarify the situation in an attempt to provide an accurate indication of the Governors' duties and responsibilities. After two years of revision, the 1802 Court Book began by explaining how the changes were to affect those running the Hospital and pointed to the new weekly timetable. Every Governor, of whom there were 414 in 1818, was entitled to attend the Court, which met quarterly.[25] The unwieldy nature of Court had required an administrative streamlining with managerial responsibility transferred to the General Committee.[26] The Court remained Bethlem's ultimate executive authority, but from the General Committee's creation in 1737 management had effectively devolved to a smaller elected committee.[27] In 1802 the importance of the General Committee was recognized. Governors were informed that it was 'one responsible and effective committee ... to conduct the affairs of these Hospitals'. It now met regularly at Bridewell on the first Wednesday of each month except during January, August and September. The timetable was not inflexible: extraordinary meetings to discuss emergency issues could be called by the President or Treasurer. Six of the General Committee's members were replaced annually by ballot.[28] With no subscribing body these new members were drawn from the existing Court.[29] In case of emergency 'by death or resignation', the Court could nominate a substitute who would serve for the same period of time as the Governor whose place he filled. The system was designed partly to ensure a degree of continuity so that some members of the General Committee were familiar with the Hospital's administration and partly to prevent criticism that management was not democratic. The latter aim was wholly effective. In practice the administration passed to a small active group, a characteristic common to many voluntary organizations and true of Bethlem's management throughout the twentieth century.[30]

In the revision of the 1793 rules, the place of the President and Treasurer as heads of the administrative structure was emphasized. The President was 'Chief Ruler and Governor', as he had been of Bridewell since 1557. Presidents were drawn from those holding the post of Lord Mayor. This retained the administrative link with the City of London, although Governors were also elected from the Court of the Common Council. Whereas Presidents had considerable influence, most of the administrative work in Bridewell and Bethlem fell to the Treasurer. The Treasurer was considered 'next in rank to the President' and, in a change from 1793, he was expected to reside at Bridewell. He was to attend all meetings, hire all servants at Bethlem and generally 'to inspect, direct, and superintend the affairs and management' both of Bethlem and Bridewell. Given the importance of the post and the possibilities of corruption, no 'Officer or Servant of either Hospital' was permitted 'to perform the Duties of the Office by Deputy'.[31] Both sets of rules ensured that the Treasurer was the main executive officer for the Hospitals.

These arrangements covered the general management of Bridewell and Bethlem. To run the two institutions, a further administrative subdivision occurred to delegate authority to small subcommittees that would have more direct contact with the daily running of Bridewell and Bethlem. Three subcommittees, each reporting through the General Committee to the Court existed: an Audit Subcommittee that would examine the accounts of both Bethlem and Bridewell every three months and prepare an annual statement each March; a Prison (Bridewell) Subcommittee; and a Bethlem Subcommittee, open to all Governors and meeting at Bethlem each Saturday at eleven. The Bethlem Subcommittee, as with the other subcommittees, had a quorum of at least three, and the proceedings of each Committee were minuted and read to the Committee 'previous to their breaking up'. Governors could choose their months of attendance, but one had to be in summer, the other in winter. The aim of giving the Governors a choice was to ensure a higher level of attendance and to spread the work across the governing body. Their task would be 'to admit and discharge patients, to inspect those in the house, to examine provisions, audit weekly bills and despatch any ordinary and unusual business'.[32] It was not resolved until February 1803 that the Steward should make out and deliver to the President before meetings a 'correct list of all the incurable patients with their ward places, dates of their respective admissions, the names of their sureties or nearest relatives and the places of their abode or the parishes to which they belonged'.[33] A serious attempt was being made to improve what would now be called the database of the Hospital. This was a financial measure to help ensure that Bethlem's income was maintained.

The Bethlem Subcommittee did not have undisputed control of the Hospital or its management. This was to occur only in the twentieth century.[34] It was subservient to the General Committee and to the Court. Both regularly intervened in its decisions. In 1802, for example, the Court refused to confirm a suggestion that the Steward,

Peter Alavoine, should be given a gratuity of £50.[35] This was to save money. It also reflected Alavoine's junior status in the Hospital as he had succeeded a treasured and greatly experienced Steward, Henry White, who had served since 1778.[36] However, with membership drawn from the main governing body, those on the Bethlem Sub-committee were represented at other levels in the Hospitals' management. This extended Bethlem's influence, but Bridewell, estate management and City politics continued to take up a large part of the Governors' time.

Bridewell and Bethlem's administrative structure was not unique. A corresponding system of management existed at other Royal and voluntary hospitals as a way of ensuring that administration did not become too cumbersome. At Bridewell and Bethlem, however, managerial subdivision had occurred earlier. This reflected a situation where two different institutions were administered by the same governing body. In other respects, Bethlem and Bridewell were run like other voluntary organizations, although their management was not as open.[37] Such an administration had little to do with asylum management, reflecting Bethlem's charitable origins.

NEW DUTIES FOR OLD POSTS: REVISION OF SERVANTS' RULES

At the same time as the rules and orders of the Hospital were being considered for revision, an effort was made to amend and republish the duties of the Hospital's officers. The 1792 Committee prepared the way for detailed statements concerning duties and salaries of the staff when it recommended that in future on the vacancy of 'any Officer or Servant' a report should be prepared for the Court, including a statement of 'the necessity of such officers or servants'.[38] Further revisions were needed in 1800 in an attempt to ensure that the rules were being observed.

The regulations prepared in 1793 and 1802 allowed for shifts in duties, reductions in salaries, and the abolition of particular offices like that of Auditor-General, a post felt to be 'merely honorary and unnecessary'. This was a cost-saving measure. Other changes were to promote efficient and diligent service. Certain rules governed the entire staff and remained unaltered in the 1802 version. The 1782 inquiry recommended 'that all the Officers and Servants of these Hospitals' should have 'fixed and liberal salaries, suited to their services, to be paid quarterly by the Treasurer; and that all perquisites and emoluments of every kind be avoided and discouraged'. The Governors agreed. By paying staff well they hoped to avoid the previous problems with fraud and theft. To prevent financial impropriety staff were not allowed to 'give or receive a Fee, Christmas-box, or other perquisite, to or from any tradesman or workman, who serves or works for either of the Hospitals, or from any patient or prisoner, or from any persons visiting the patients or prisons. If found guilty, he or she be forthwith discharged'.[39] Other hospitals had identical rules in an effort to limit corruption, although Governors themselves were often accused of using their connections to ensure profitable contracts or to secure patronage. At Bethlem, similar stipulations were repeated in further revisions and remained in force into the twentieth century. Throughout, emphasis was now placed not on qualifications for positions – these were not usually prescribed – but on responsibilities, sole and shared. The administration was, however, strictly divided between medical and domestic spheres.

The Steward was listed first among the servants. His duties were described in considerable detail; one rule even stipulated that he was to check the 'number the pieces of meat before they are put into the pot'. In general terms he was 'to supervise all the Servants of the House', who were initially appointed for 'a trial of two months'. Work was arduous, especially for the Porter. He had to be 'on his station from six in the morning till seven in the evening during the summer, and from seven to five in the winter, and not on any pretence to quit his station at the door'. Nurses were still called Basketmen and Gallery Maids in a language peculiar to Bethlem. The division in name did not match the sexual segregation in the wards, with Basketmen, assisted by the Gallery Maids, working with both male and female patients. Like attendants in other asylums they worked long hours that were identical to the Porter's.[40] No hours were stipulated for the Barber who was considered last in the rules. He was, however, to shave the patients and Servants 'once a week or oftener, if so directed by the Steward'. In theory the management of the servants was strict.[41] Practice, as the 1815 House of Commons inquiry revealed, was different.[42]

On the medical side, the opportunity was taken to reconsider the role of the Matron given that Mary Spencer, who had been Matron since 1765, had died in 1793. The Court, advised by a special committee, specified after Spencer's death that the new Matron should be aged between 32 and 40 years. This was because in 1791 it was felt that Spencer was 'greatly advanced in years and extremely infirm' and unable to discharge her duties properly. More attention was now paid to the character of the Matron. The Governors through their rules were looking for a woman 'of a good moral Character'; 'strong, active and healthy'; and able to 'bear confinement and . . . not [be] subject to lowness of Spirits'. As in the seventeenth century, she was to be unmarried.[43] Little else was changed in revision, with the rules largely matching those devised in 1765. Emphasis was still placed on the cleanliness of the patients, but this was also matched with greater concern for their care. The Matron was required 'to go round the House every day on the Women's side before ten o'clock, but on Tuesday before nine, and to see that the linen and sheets of the Patients are regularly changed as they ought to be'.[44] Her duties included taking care of those who were 'low-spirited, or inclined to be mopish'. This was to be through pressure to make them 'quit their cells' when the doors would be locked so 'that they may not return to their beds'. It was a role later taken over by the nurses. It was the Matron's responsibility 'to hire [and discharge] the Gallery Maids with the approbation of the Treasurer and Committee'.[45] Here was a clearly defined Matron's post and other asylums were later to adopt regulations that to some extent mirrored those used in Georgian Bethlem. The new rules assigned the Matron considerable authority over the Basketmen and Gallery Maids and ensured that she was a major force in the patients' lives. The Matron was clearly shown to be in charge of the domestic management of the patients.

In July 1795 there was a similar but still more detailed redefinition of the Apothecary's role and qualifications after John Haslam was appointed to succeed John Gozna, who had filled the post since 1772.[46] Haslam had been born in 1764 and was educated largely at St Bartholomew's Hospital and Edinburgh University. Autocratic and evasive, he did not always create a good impression.[47] Given the strategic significance of Haslam's career at Bethlem and his support of moral management, it is easy to underestimate Gozna's impact. Gozna did, however, make a contribution to William Black's 'mental arithmetic', which culminated in his *Dissertation on Insanity* and drew on 'between two and three thousand cases in Bedlam'.[48] Haslam's work was more carefully controlled by the Governors in an effort to promote a higher standard of care for the patients. The position of Apothecary was 'slightly ambiguous'. His job was to attend to the general health of the patients and was roughly equivalent of a resident medical officer. He was part of a three-man medical team, but with the dubious support of visiting Physician (Monro) and a mad surgeon (Bryan Crowther), Haslam was the main medical authority in Bethlem, although he lacked any formal basis for this role.[49]

Haslam's salary was set at about £300 at a time when few other medical officers in London were paid for their institutional work.[50] Consequently, he was expected to reside 'in the house provided for him' at Bethlem 'clear of taxes and cost of repairs' and 'not to absent himself one day without leave of the Bethlem Committee or the President or Treasurer'. Haslam was required to devote his entire attention to the Hospital 'and not to follow any other business'. The Governors defined the Apothecary's post in largely medical terms that went beyond the 'special care that all the Druggs and Medicines are of the best kind and are not wasted or applied to any other purpose than the true object of the Charities'. Although subordinate to the Physician, Haslam had 'to give Advice and Medicines to any of the resident Officers or Servants of either hospital' and 'direct the Keepers in their management of the Patients during the absence of the Physicians'. This was a formidable remit. Given Monro's role as visiting Physician, it placed considerable responsibility on Haslam. He was expected 'to visit the Patients in Bethlem Hospital regularly every morning or oftener if necessary and [to] report to the Physicians any neglect he may observe in the management of the Patients'.[51] Overall therapy increasingly devolved to him, leading Haslam to develop his own ideas on mental illness and treatment.[52]

By comparison, the Physician's duties were more ceremonial. He was paid a salary of £100 and was required to attend the weekly Bethlem Subcommittee at which admissions and discharges were settled. The Physician was to examine and prescribe for the patients every Monday and Wednesday, inform the Governors of any neglect and abuse, and suggest 'such reforms as he may think necessary'.[53] From the rules it was clear that it was the Apothecary who was expected to conduct most of the medical work at Bethlem.

Rules were one thing, practice was something different. The 1815 House of Commons inquiry revealed glaring irregularities in Bethlem's management.[54] Evidence was also to reveal that Monro had not fulfilled his duties.[55] The Governors may have been able to make and revise the rules to promote the care of the patients, but they had problems ensuring that they were enforced. This was to prove a major problem for the Hospital.

THE NOTABLE AND THE UNKNOWN: PATIENTS IN LATE EIGHTEENTH- AND EARLY NINETEENTH-CENTURY BETHLEM

The rules had been modified to improve the Hospital's finances and management. They had also been changed to improve the treatment extended to the patients. In the 1802 rules those relating to patients took numerical precedence over those relating to officers and servants. Haslam was attracted to the ideas of moral management if not non-restraint, but the Governors did not define the type of treatment practised in the Hospital.[56] However, to remove abuse by the staff they did order that 'No Patient' was to be confined in chains 'without the previous knowledge and approbation of the Apothecary, nor released from such confinement without his consent'.[57] How patients responded to these rules is hard to determine. Indeed, patients themselves are difficult to quantify.

Notable and interesting cases like the attempted regicides Nicholson and Hadfield (discussed on pp. 390–2) emerge from the case notes. In admitting these patients, Bethlem built on a tradition of receiving those dangerous to the King or country sent to it by the Board of the Green Cloth.[58] Geoffrey O'Donoghue wrote about these patients in his *The Story of Bethlehem Hospital*, but also provided information on other cases.[59] The two cases he dwelt on were those of Hannah Snell and Elizabeth Catlett. The former, admitted in 1791, had disguised herself as a man and fought as a soldier in India where she was wounded. She died in the Hospital 'of senile decay' on 8 February 1792 at the age of 69. Elizabeth Catlett was the niece of the converted Evangelical clergyman John Newton, who before his conversion had been a slave trader and 'blasphemer'. She was admitted as a free patient in 1801, remaining in Bethlem for nearly a year before returning to her uncle. While she was in the Hospital, Newton was said to have walked past one of its windows waiting for a prearranged signal that she was well. O'Donoghue drew a familiar moral from this romantic tale: 'take courage, dear hearts! Elizabeth Catlett became her bright useful self again, and many dark clouds, if not all, will yet reveal a silver lining.'[60] Other cases included Bannister Truelock, a man with a mission, who had been admitted in December 1800 on the basis of a letter from the Duke of Portland. He believed that he was a great prophet named Saturn, or even the Messiah. On 1 July 1816 Thomas Monro, Bethlem's physician and the third in the Monro dynasty, wrote of Truelock that he was 'perfectly quiet and always occupied at his trade of shoemaking'. Truelock allegedly persuaded James Hadfield (see pp. 391–2) to shoot George III by preaching 'that our Saviour's second advent, and the dissolution of all human things were at hand'.[61] He had an insight into his own condition and acknowledged that his religious views were preventing his discharge, although he considered them perfectly orthodox. The author of *Sketches in Bedlam* (1823) described Truelock as hating the New Testament, but, leaving religion aside, considered him 'cool, steady and deliberate in all his actions, cleanly in his person, and regular and decent in his apartment'.[62]

Margaret (or Peg) Nicholson attracted far more attention, especially from contemporaries. From Stockton-on-Tees, she had spent much of her life in service to upper-class families. After an affair with a valet, Nicholson found herself in much reduced circumstances and made a living from plain needlework. Already showing signs of delusion, in August 1786 she drew up a petition to George III:

> as the King was alighting from his chariot at the garden entrance of St. James's, a woman, very decently dressed, in the act of presenting a petition, which His Majesty was receiving with great condescension, struck a concealed knife at his breast; which happily he avoided by drawing back. As she was making a second thrust, one of the yeomen caught her arm, and, at the same instant, one of the King's footmen wrenched the knife from her hand. The King, with great temper and fortitude, exclaimed, 'I am not hurt; take care of the poor woman; do not hurt her'.[63]

Forty years later Nicholson claimed it was a mistake. At the time she noted that she had contemplated 'Regicide [for] about a week'. In her testimony she claimed that 'the crown was hers; she wanted nothing but her right; that she had great property; that if she had not her right, England would be drowned in blood for a thousand generations'. Nicholson was arrested and presented to the Board of Green Cloth that day where she was examined by Monro, who was uncertain about her sanity. A week later the Privy Council judged her disordered.[64] There was no trial or suggestion that she should be hanged for High Treason, and she was sent to Bethlem.[65] Lord Sidney of the Privy Council instructed the Governors to 'cause the most strict and proper care to be taken of her' and she was subsequently confined to her cell. On the intervention of George III in 1787 she was transferred to the incurable wing, but it was not until 1791 that it was decided that Nicholson no longer needed to be confined. Transferred to the female incurable department, she was rewarded for her willingness to work. Snuff was her favourite luxury. She seldom spoke and had lost her sense of hearing, 'nor would the discharge of a cannon at her ear in the least disturb her'. At the age of 82, after thirty-six years in the Hospital, 'she had contracted a singular aversion to bread, and never can be induced to eat any'. Despite this, she showed no sign of insanity in 1823 beyond an occasional irritability. Nicholson remained in the incurable wing until her death at the age of 94. Throughout she enjoyed 'a good state of health, is regular, cleanly and attentive to her little concerns, and is desirous to render herself useful'.[66]

Another attempted regicide, James Hadfield, was also sent to Bethlem, but his case had more significance for the treatment of those judged to be criminally insane. Hadfield was made famous for his attack on George III in 1800. During the wars against France following the French Revolution (1789), Hadfield had been injured at the Battle of Lincelles (1793), while serving as one of the Duke of York's bodyguards, and received severe wounds to the head that damaged his brain.[67] He was subsequently discharged from the army on the grounds of insanity. Hadfield took up silversmithing in London, where he was influenced by a chance meeting with the Pentecostal Truelock who convinced him that if George III was killed all obstacles to the Messiah's return would be removed. Already suffering delusions about the imminent end of the world, Hadfield readily believed that he was God's chosen instrument. After attempting to kill his son in 1800 on what he felt was the command of God, he believed he had to sacrifice himself to save mankind. Unwilling to commit suicide, he 'wished that by the appearance of crime his life might be taken away from him by others'.[68] To achieve this, Hadfield went to Drury Lane Theatre on 15 May 1800 armed with a pistol. Once inside the theatre:

> His Majesty had scarcely entered the box, when in the act of bowing with his usual condescension to the audience, a pistol was fired by Hadfield who sat in the pit . . . The ball struck the roof of the royal box, just at the moment when the Queen and Princess were entering. His Majesty with great presence of mind, waved his hands as a signal to dissuade the royal party from making their immediate appearance, and instantly standing erect, raised his right hand to his breast and continued bowing for some minutes . . .[69]

He had failed to hit his target by twelve inches. This was the most notorious attempt on the King's life. Hadfield was immediately arrested, but his trial for High Treason was halted when the defence lawyer, Thomas Erskine, 'the brightest ornament of which the English bar can boast', convinced the court that Hadfield was a religious maniac and incurably insane after the wounds he had received.[70] Erskine introduced the concept of delusion into the courts; no longer need the accused be totally mad or totally without memory.[71] A verdict of 'not guilty: he being under the influence of Insanity at the time the act was committed' was returned, and Hadfield was subsequently sent to Bethlem.[72] It was not the first time an insanity plea had been used, but it did lead to an immediate change in the law. Hadfield's case had a tremendous impact. According to the author of *Medical Jurisprudence: On Madness* (1800) it was 'one of the most momentous cases on which a jury was ever impanelled'.[73] With a verdict of 'not guilty', Hadfield could be released as a man dangerous to his family and probably to the King, or illegally detained. Under these circumstances, Parliament rushed through the 'Act for the safe custody of insane persons charged with offenses' and gave it retrospective powers.[74] The Act allowed Hadfield's safe custody and created a new category of detainees named 'criminal lunatics', a term subsequently considered wholly undesirable but not removed until the 1930s.

Hadfield was sent to Bethlem like Nicholson and others deemed dangerous to Crown and country before him. He remained in the Hospital until his escape in 1802, when he made it as far as Dover before being arrested.[75] After spending fourteen years in Newgate prison he was returned to Bethlem and placed in the criminal lunatics' wing shortly after it opened. Writing in 1823, James Smyth (keeper) described Hadfield as symptom-free, but inclined to find fault. At Bethlem, he was allowed some freedom and kept birds and cats, while he also sold poems, spending the money on tobacco.[76] In 1833 the Governors bought Hadfield a wig, presumably to cover up the wounds to his head. After his death in 1841, the autopsy revealed that his injuries had caused considerable damage.

Other patients proved less notable and attracted little attention, and are therefore harder to determine. There are no annual figures of the numbers of patients in Bethlem for the period 1783 to 1814. However, there had been little change since the late sixteenth century. Haslam noted that between 1748 and 1794, 4,832 women and 4,042 men were admitted, with 1,664 patients admitted between 1784 and 1794. He suggested that women continued to predominate at Bethlem, and historians have seen a similar preponderance of women in admissions.[77] Some general impressions can be made. Most patients at the end of the eighteenth century were in the 20–50 age range, with few patients admitted under the age of 20.[78] Social class was mixed. That at least twelve patients underwent Commissions of Lunacy between 1733 and 1794 suggests that not all patients were paupers. Those subject to a Commission came from wealthy estates and it is possible to identify a significant number of patients of gentlemanly origins, although this does not rule out that they could be poor.[79] Among the patients for the 1790s, Haslam numbered the raving, the melancholy, those of 'liberal education', 'good scholars', and those prone to 'habitual intoxication'.[80] None the less, unlike private institutions such as Ticehurst, the majority of patients continued to come from the pauper class.[81] The extant petitions give a further indication of the type of patients admitted. The classifications used at Bethlem were clumsy. Governors and staff seemed far more concerned with patient behaviour than with the symptoms of their illness. This was not surprising. Bethlem frequently received the most dangerous cases in London and such cases presented serious management problems. By far more petitions (twenty-five) survive from 1789 than from any other year. The totals between 1783 and 1802 produce the pattern shown in Table 21.1.

Table 21.1 Causes of admission, 1783–1802

Symptom	Number
Melancholy	14
Raving	34
Melancholy and raving	2
Mischievous	17

Source: Petitions, 1783–1802

There is more detail for the incurables where records for the deaths and discharges and settlements exist. Of these, 59 per cent between 1776 and 1800 were referred by public institutions, with 35 per cent of the securities being family or friends.[82] Most incurables came from outside London. Twenty came from London and ten from Middlesex, while eight came from Surrey, seven from Oxfordshire, five from Essex and four from Hertfordshire and Gloucestershire. Wales sent two and Cornwall one.[83] This was a similar distribution to the period 1728 to 1788 (see Chapter 18). Bethlem had a national role to play, like the York Retreat in its treatment of Quakers, but also like the Retreat this was to come under attack during the nineteenth century with the growth of county and borough asylums that created competing institutions for the care of pauper patients.[84] Under these conditions the type of patients admitted to Bethlem from the mid-nineteenth century changed through a conscious policy pursued by the Physician Charles Hood (see Chapter 26).

AIMS AND EFFECTS

The 1792 Select Committee promoted reform and consolidation. Bethlem was affected at all levels, although the initial aim had been to investigate the financial position of the Hospital. Reform followed in an attempt to define the rules and orders and tighten up the regulations. The aim was to encourage a greater degree of financial accountability to help increase the charitable public's confidence in the institution and counter images that Bethlem was Bedlam in every sense of the word. Some success was achieved, at least on paper. Attention was paid to the structure of the administration that was defined in clearer terms to guide those running Bridewell and Bethlem. The principles of care were reaffirmed to remind the staff how they should treat patients and of their duties to the Hospital. However, two sets of revisions (in 1793 and in 1802) were needed. This suggests that although the Governors were committed to economy and a set of management principles their ideas were harder to translate into practice at the day-to-day level. As Kathleen Jones notes, 'the good intentions of the Governors were often frustrated ... '.[85] Problems of the past continued to emerge. Content to draw up regulations, they seemed unable to ensure that they were enforced. Monitoring of discipline was left to the staff. As the 1815 House of Commons inquiry was to expose, this was not enough.

NOTES

1 Thomas Bowen, *An Historical Account of the Origin, Progress, and Present State of Bethlem Hospital, founded by Henry the Eighth, for the Cure of Lunatics, and Enlarged by Subsequent Benefactors, for the Reception and Maintenance of Incurables* (London: For the Governors, 1783).

2 See Chapter 20.

3 See D. H. Aldcroft and P. Fearon (eds), *British Economic Fluctuations, 1790–1939* (London: Macmillan, 1972); W. G. Hoskins, 'Harvest Fluctuations and English Economic History', *Agricultural History Review*, xvi (1968), 15–31.

4 1792 Select Committee Report.

5 Bethlem Grand Committee, 25 April, 11 July, 21 November 1789.

6 1792 Select Committee Report.

7 *Ibid.*

8 Court of Governors, 28 February 1793.

9 *Standing Rules of Orders for the Governors of the Royal Hospitals of Bridewell and Bethlem with the Duties of the Governors and of the several officers and servants* (London: 1802), 15–17.

10 These practices were widespread in voluntary hospitals: see Ann Borsay, '"Persons of Honour and Reputation": The Voluntary Hospital in the Age of Corruption', *Medical History*, xxxv (1991), 281–94.

11 Bethlem Subcommittee, 28 February 1793.

12 *Ibid.* 6 October 1802.

13 See Chapter 20, pp. 369–71.

14 See Chapter 28, pp. 539–41.

15 Cited in D. H. Tuke, *Chapters in the History of the Insane in the British Isles* (London: Kegan Paul, 1882), 75.

16 The cartoon is reproduced in Edward O'Donoghue, *The Story of the Bethlehem Hospital from its Foundation in 1247* (London: T. Fisher Unwin, 1914), 19.

17 Urbane Metcalf, *The Interior of Bethlehem Hospital, Humbly Addressed to His Royal Highness the Duke of Sussex and to the Other Governors* (London: For the Author, 1818).

18 J. Frank, *Reise nach Paris, London und einem grossen Theile des übrigen Englands und Schottlands* (Vienna: Camesina, 1804), quoted in O. M. Marx, 'Descriptions of Psychiatric Care in Some Hospitals during the First Half of the Nineteenth Century', a paper read at the 39th Annual meeting of the American Association for the History of Medicine, May 1966.

19 See Chapter 20, p. 365; Anne Digby, *Madness, Morality and Medicine: A Study of the York Retreat* (New York: CUP, 1985).

20 Report by Henry Holland, 27 June 1791; Court of Governors, 22 July 1791.

21 Court of Governors, 28 February 1793.

22 See Chapter 23.

23 Andrew Scull, *Museums of Madness* (London: Allen Lane, 1979), 74.

24 Patricia Allderidge, 'Bedlam: Fact or Fantasy?', in W. F. Bynum, Roy Porter and Michael Shepherd (eds), *The Anatomy of Madness* (London: Tavistock, 1985), vol. ii, 24. Roy Porter, 'The Gift Relation', in Lindsey Granshaw and Roy Porter (eds), *The Hospital in History* (London: Routledge, 1989), 158–60, has criticized the view that voluntary hospitals depended primarily on the middle classes. Ann Borsay, 'Cash and Conscience: Financing the General Hospital at Bath', *Social History of Medicine*, iv (1991), 208, and Mary Fissell, 'The Physic of Charity: Health and Welfare in the West County' (unpublished Ph.D. Thesis, University of Pennsylvania, 1988), 96, have argued against this view, and certainly the government of Bethlem matched the latter pattern.

25 *A List of the Governors of the Royal Hospitals of Bridewell and Bethlem* (London: For the Governors, 1818).

26 Court of Governors, 13 May, 7 July, 3 November 1802.

27 Allderidge, *op. cit.* 17–33.

28 Court of Governors, 13 May, 7 July, 3 November 1802.

29 See R. J. Morris, 'Voluntary Societies and British Urban Elites, 1780–1850', *Historical Journal*, xxvi (1983), 95–118.

30 See Keir Waddington, 'Finance, Philanthropy and the Hospital' (unpublished Ph.D. Thesis, University of London, 1995), ch. 5; Brian Abel Smith, *The Hospitals 1800–1948* (London: Heinemann, 1964).

31 *Standing Rules of Orders*, 15–17.

32 Court of Governors, 13 May, 7 July, 3 November 1802.

33 *Ibid.* 9 February 1803.

34 See Chapter 31.

35 Court of Governors, 8 January 1803.

36 Diary of Richard Clark, *Ghall* MS 3385, 31 August, 5, 15, 16, 23 September 1785.

37 Waddington, 'Finance, Philanthropy and the Hospital', Chapter 5.

38 Court of Governors, 28 February 1793.

39 *Ibid.*

40 Digby, *op. cit.* 141–4.

41 *Standing Rules of Orders.*

42 House of Commons, *Report of the Select Committee on Madhouses* (London: 1815).

43 Court of Governors, 31 January 1793.

44 At the York Retreat and other asylums a similar emphasis was placed on cleanliness in the rules: Digby, *op. cit.* 145.

45 Rule VIII, *Standing Rules of Orders.*

46 Court of Governors, 16 July 1795.

47 John Haslam, *Illustrations of Madness*, with an introduction by Roy Porter (London: Routledge, 1988), xxvi; Richard Hunter and Ida Macalpine, 'John Haslam: His Will and His Daughter', *Medical History*, vi (1962), 22–6.

48 W. D. Black, *A Dissertation on Insanity: Illustrated with Tables Extracted From Between Two and Three Thousand Cases in Bedlam* (London: Ridgway, 1810).

49 Haslam, *op. cit.* xxv.

50 See Anne Digby, *Making a Medical Living: Doctors and Patients in the English Market for Medicine, 1720–1911* (Cambridge: CUP, 1994) for the economics of the medical profession.

51 *Report of the Select Committee on Madhouses*, 35–6.

52 See John Haslam, *Observations on Insanity* (London: F. & C. Rivington, 1798); *idem, Illustrations of Madness*; *idem, Sound Mind* (London: Longman, 1819) or *idem, On the Nature of Thought* (London: Longman, 1835). Historians of psychiatry have credited Haslam with giving the first precise clinical accounts of general paralysis and of schizophrenia,

although he himself strongly distrusted psychiatrists' claims that they could comprehend madness.

53 Court of Governors, 16 November 1793.

54 *Report of the Select Committee on Madhouses*, 37.

55 *Ibid.* 35–6.

56 Haslam, *Illustrations of Madness*, xxviii.

57 *Standing Rules of Orders.*

58 See Chapter 19.

59 O'Donoghue, *op.cit.*.

60 *Ibid.* 278–81; 287–9.

61 Cited in Roy Porter, *Mind-Forg'd Manacles: A History of Madness in England from the Restoration to the Regency* (London: Penguin, 1990), 116.

62 *Sketches in Bedlam* (London: Sherwood, Jones & Co., 1823), 19–27; 255–8; 263–5.

63 *Ibid.*

64 For the process of Nicholson's committal to Bethlem, see Richard Hunter and Ida Macalpine, *George III and the Mad-Business* (London: Pimlico, 1993), 310–13.

65 Patricia Allderidge, 'Criminal Insanity: Bethlem to Broadmoor', *Proceedings of the Royal Society of Medicine*, lxvii (1974), 897–904, especially 898.

66 Cited in David Russell, *Scenes from Bedlam* (London: Baillière Tindall, 1996), 107.

67 Allderidge, 'Criminal Insanity', 898.

68 Richard Hunter and Ida Macalpine, *Three Hundred Years of Psychiatry* (London: OUP, 1963), 572.

69 Cited in Russell, *op. cit.* 109.

70 Allderidge, 'Criminal Insanity', 898.

71 Joel Eigen, 'Intentionality and Insanity: What the Eighteenth-Century Juror Heard', in W. F. Bynum, Roy Porter and Michael Shepherd (eds), *The Anatomy of Madness* (London: Tavistock Press, 1985), vol. ii, 41.

72 Henry Rollin, 'Forensic Psychiatry in England', in Hugh Freeman and German Berrios (eds), *150 Years of British Psychiatry: The Aftermath* (London: Athlone, 1996), 246.

73 Cited in Hunter and Macalpine, *George III*, 326. They argued that the development of county asylums under the 1808 Wynn's Act owed 'their existence in no small measure to Hadfield's crime' (p. 318).

74 House of Commons, *Report of the Select Committee on Criminal Lunatics* (London 1807).

75 Hadfield was followed by other attempted regicides, including Edward Oxford, who had discharged two pistols at Queen Victoria in 1840, and Daniel McNaughten, who had shot and killed Edward Drummond in 1843, mistaking him for Sir Robert Peel, prime minister: see Nigel Walker, *Crime and Insanity in England*, vol. i (Edinburgh: Edinburgh University Press, 1968).

76 *Sketches in Bedlam.*

77 John Haslam, *Observations of Insanity*, 108, 112; see Elaine Showalter, *The Female Malady: Women, Madness, and English Culture 1830–1980* (London: Virago, 1987).

78 See Haslam, *Observations of Insanity*, 112.

79 Andrew Scull, *The Most Solitary of Afflictions: Madness and Society in Britain, 1700–1900* (New Haven, Conn. and London: Yale University Press, 1993), 112.

80 Haslam, *Observations of Insanity*, 21, 24.

81 Charlotte MacKenzie, *Psychiatry for the Rich: A History of Ticehurst Private Asylum 1792–1917* (London: Routledge, 1992).

82 Jonathan Andrews, 'Bedlam Revisited: A History of Bethlem Hospital *c.* 1634–*c.* 1770' (unpublished Ph.D. thesis, University of London, 1991), 508.

83 Incurables Admissions Register.

84 Digby, *Madness, Morality and Medicine*, 178. For the growth of asylums see Scull, *op. cit.*, and Kathleen Jones, *Asylum and After* (London: Athlone, 1993).

85 Jones, *op. cit.* 10.

A CHANGE OF SCENE
Bethlem's move to Southwark

———— •◆• ————

The 'new Bethlem' at Moorfields, designed by the City Surveyor and experimental philosopher Robert Hooke, had since its opening in 1676 been described as 'grand', 'beautiful' and 'noble'.[1] In 1815, when the building was already being demolished, one writer felt that for many years it had been 'the only building that looked like a palace in London'.[2] Bethlem at Moorfields with its long, impressive façade became one of the sights of London. More than a century after its opening, Thomas Bowen in his eulogistic *Historical Account of the Origin, Progress and Present State of Bethlem Hospital*, quoted such earlier descriptions, but did nothing to qualify them.[3] Already, however, there were signs that the very fabric of the building was decaying. John Howard, the prison reformer, had visited Bethlem during his investigation of European hospitals and asylums and passed a dismal verdict. He was disturbed by the lack of suitable classification for the patients, and particularly the absence of physical separation of the 'calm and quiet' from 'the noisy and turbulent'. He pointed to structural problems and noted the absence of any water supply on the upper floor and the offensive state of the vaults.[4] By 1800 it was obvious that many of the floors in the building were uneven, that its roof leaked, and that some of its walls were not upright.

From the 1790s onwards, the Governors increasingly turned their attention to the state of the Hospital. Under the weight of evidence produced that the building was old and unsuitable, that Moorfields was no longer an ideal site, and that at the very least expensive renovations were needed, a decision was made to move Bethlem to a new home. This was to be the Hospital's third incarnation, although the new building at St George's Fields, Southwark still owed much to Hooke's seventeenth-century design.

AN OLD AND DECAYING BUILDING

Two years after Howard's *An Account of the Principal Lazarettos of Europe* appeared, with its criticisms of Bethlem, the Governors were presented with a full report on the poor state of the Moorfields building. This started the slow process of rebuilding. In July 1790 the Court of Governors were informed that 'very extensive repairs are wanting and necessary to be done at Bethlem'. After a year's investigation, the Surveyor, Henry Holland, provided a fourteen-page report with plans, giving a long list of faults that began with the roofs, dormer windows, gutters, parapets, turrets and chimney stacks and ended with the privies.[5] Holland's report only confirmed what Howard had noted earlier.

Holland presented his report amidst plans to extend the accommodation Bethlem provided. The Governors had wanted to convert the cellars, occupied by the brewers Messrs. Calvert and Company, into cells for six patients to provide additional accommodation.[6] Before Holland's report had been discussed, they had already informed the brewers that they had to leave the building 'by Lady Day'. Holland suggested that this would require 'considerable repairs' to make the cellars 'open, airy and wholesome', while they 'want nearly all new windows'. Holland went on to describe the poor condition of the Hospital. He explained that the walls at the east end were 'so decayed as to be insecure'. In addition, Holland had found that 'the whole of the wood and ironwork wants painting and the plastering repairing and whitewashing'. This had not been done 'for fifteen years', suggesting neglect by the Governors, although this was probably connected to the funding problems facing Bridewell and Bethlem from the 1780s. Holland went on to build on concerns about the cleanliness of the building, suggesting that they were 'endanger[ing] the health of the patients'.[7] The Governors were appalled. In 1786 they had appointed a rat-catcher and in 1793 and 1802 they were to revise the regulations again, stressing the import-ance of keeping the patients clean and healthy.[8] This proved a constant concern among the Governors and encouraged them to act.

At the end of his report, Holland estimated the cost of repairing and improving Bethlem at £8,660 and explained that the work would take at least five years.[9] The Treasurer was alarmed at the cost. He insisted that all work on the Hospital should be suspended until the Select Committee of Inquiry into Bethlem's finances had reported.[10] In November 1792, however, the Bethlem Grand Committee, with a remit to improve the Hospital, recommended in face of increasing complaints that the existing building should be repaired 'in a substantial manner' but not rebuilt.[11] The Court, already anxious about the state of the Hospital's finances, agreed.[12] On the grounds of economy, the amount allocated for repairs was paltry and insufficient to undertake all the work Holland had insisted was necessary. The Governors allowed only £1,070 to be spent in 1793 and £1,483 in the following year.[13] Pressure mounted, largely from the Physician Thomas Monro, the third in the Monro dynasty, throughout the 1790s to improve Bethlem's sanitation. He wanted the privies improved and a new well to provide an additional supply of water.[14] All this involved additional expense.

The amount allocated did little to improve the situation. By 1799 it had become clear to the Governors that the money spent on improvements and repairs since 1793 had not achieved the desired result. In many ways, at a time of increasing economies and rising costs, it had been money wasted because many of the problems identified by Holland in 1791 remained. In the spring of 1799 a motion was therefore carried in the Court, requiring James Lewis, Holland's successor, 'to consider the present condi-tion of the buildings' and report back his opinion 'together with the probable annual expense of keeping the same in repair'. Those Governors who were 'of the archi-tectural line' were asked to help him.[15] Lewis (1751–1820) from South Wales, like all the Hospital's Surveyors, was an architect before being appointed in 1793. He had worked mainly on designing and remodelling houses, although he had submitted designs for the new St Luke's Hospital in 1778 and, in the same year as he was appointed as Surveyor, submitted plans 'for the uniform and gradual rebuilding of [Christ's] hospital'. It was probably on the merit of these last two designs, with their strong classical bias, and because he was Surveyor to Christ's Hospital and to the Mercers' Company, that he was employed.[16] The Governors, aware of his abilities, were not, however, as yet calling for a new hospital. Despite the increase in attention to the state of the buildings, they still envisaged that repairs could be made.

Lewis gladly accepted the assistance of qualified Governors and quickly prepared a fourteen-page *Report Respecting the Present State and Condition of Bethlem Hospital* which dispelled any remaining complacency amongst the Governors.[17] Lewis explained that in 1800 he had examined 'the whole of the building from end to end, and from the foundations to the roofs', including those places 'where the eye could not reach'. Based on this survey and his professional standing, he felt confident about his findings. Lewis's conclusions were plain:

> I am clearly of opinion, that the present condition of the *Buildings*, is not in such a state as to warrant any other *repair* to be made thereto, than to preserve it, with the common care and attention, by such works as may be requisite; . . . To do more would be unwise and improvident in the highest degree. The parts defective, and to be rendered *stout* for duration, are so extensive and intermixed with others; that not only great expense, but danger will be derived therefrom, which, of itself must be foreseen and prevented.[18]

The *Report* left the Governors with little room for doubt that action was urgently needed. Bethlem was shown to be 'dreary, low and melancholy' with an 'ill-contrived' interior and insufficient accommodation to match the increasing number of patients seeking admission.[19] Lewis went on to note that:

> The present building is not formed in point of convenience and a proper connection of all its parts, for the business to be done in the readiest manner, and with the fewest officers and servants possible; for it is to be lamented, that in many of these last respects, it is incurable.[20]

Lewis had chosen his words carefully and used the rhetoric of the Hospital. Few adjectives would have carried more impact. Lewis was unable to offer any estimate of the cost, although he was aware that 'wrong directed expenditure' would be completely misguided.[21] To prevent this, he was implying that funds would be better spent rebuilding Bethlem on a new site.

The *Report* explained why problems had arisen with the Moorfields building. This removed the blame from the current governing body and placed it squarely on the construction, not on Hooke's original design. From the beginning the palace of 1676 had been a house that could not stand. The parcel of land on which it had been built had included part of 'the Town Ditch', which had gradually been filled in with rubbish. This had not served as a sound base for a building with a façade over 500 feet long, while no effort had been made to ensure how the 'requisite stability' could be secured. Lewis noted that when Hooke's building was under construction, the builders had worked with 'more haste than provident wisdom'. They merely dug into the soil 'about four feet' to provide the 'cellar story [*sic*]'. In addition, 'the brickwork was set down, on the surface of the soil, a few inches below the present floor'. There was no indication that any foundation had been laid. Lewis was of the opinion that the materials used had been 'bad', and 'want of skill, or attention' were obvious 'in the carpentry of the walls and floors, below the roofs; there being no bond, or tyes, between the several parts'. He did note that a few iron tyes had been introduced later, but these 'had fallen short of their purpose'. In conclusion, Lewis felt that the roofs were too heavy and the walls 'neither sound, upright nor level'. What had been praised since the late seventeenth century as magnificent was now seen as the product of 'improvident dispatch'.[22] Above all, Bethlem was a palace that had been built too fast. Nothing was said, however, of the many changes (which included the extension of the Hospital through the addition of two incurable wings in 1723 and 1736) that had been made to Hooke's design during the eighteenth century.

Lewis's *Report* provided the Governors with damning evidence on the state of the Hospital. Yet it merely added to what Henry Holland had described in 1791. It illustrated that the attempts made at repairing Bethlem between 1793 and 1799 had proved unsuccessful and implied that the money had been poorly spent at a time when the Governors were economizing in other areas. Pressure to find a solution and to move was increasing.

BUILD? BUILD!

The Governors were shocked by Lewis's devastating *Report*. The Court, feeling that it was unable to decide the matter, given its unwieldy size and breadth of representation, passed the issue to a small Special House Committee, which was appointed in April 1801. After nearly seven months of deliberation, the Committee recommended that Bethlem should be moved to a new site.[23] This was the first proposal made by the Governors that recognized that the Moorfields' building could not be economically repaired. Now discussion focused on the possibility of moving Bethlem, rather than purely on the need to renovate the Hospital. There was a positive side to the House Committee's proposal. While the House Committee was meeting, the City of London was preparing plans to alter Moorfields as part of a general scheme to make 'improvements' to the area from the Royal Exchange and the Bank of England to Finsbury Square. Given this information, the House Committee felt that the need to move could be made into an asset. It concluded that 'having considered the value of the ground on which the Hospital stands . . . and also the value of the materials of the said hospital', it was 'of the opinion that it was desirable and would ultimately be beneficial to remove the Hospital to another situation'.[24] Whereas the House Committee had voted unanimously, the Court had other concerns. It was deeply worried about Bridewell and Bethlem's finances and was subsequently willing to confirm everything in the House Committee's report 'except such parts of them relating to the expediency of rebuilding Bethlem Hospital'.[25] These were, of course, the most important parts. The Court felt that economy was more important than a new building, which would only prove expensive, especially as charities seen to be extravagant or wasting their resources on fund-raising or ceremony were increasingly under attack. In the Hospital an impasse was produced by the need to move and the desire to save money.

Rumours arose of what was happening in the Hospital. In 1802 the *Monthly Review* reported that 'according to a new City plan for building on Moorfields', Bethlem was to be pulled down and re-erected on a more convenient site near Islington.[26] The site the *Monthly Review* was referring to was Gossey Fields, which belonged to the Drapers' Company.[27] Islington was the first City suburb to be built up in the eighteenth century. On high ground, it had a 'magnificent panorama' and was considered a healthy area with clean air.[28] The idea that an asylum should be located in 'an Airy and Healthy Situation, with a good supply of Water' was incorporated into legislation under the Wynn's Act of 1808 (see p. 404).[29] A clean and healthy environment was seen as central to hospital design and location throughout the nineteenth century.[30] Covering just under seven acres, the Governors themselves felt the site presented a 'most eligible spot' for a new hospital.[31] Sympathy for the need to move was increasing. Between 1802 and 1803 the Court began to soften its resolve. Lewis was called upon again to give advice and reiterated the views expressed in his 1800 *Report*. He added that while there was no immediate danger to the patients, 'the various parts' of Bethlem were in 'a decaying and crippled state'. Under the weight of evidence, the Court resolved unanimously in 1803 to buy Gossey Fields.[32] Notwithstanding this resolution, the costs involved continued to deter the Governors. It was not until the spring of 1804, after yet another report from Lewis, that practical steps were taken to raise a fund to 'aid and ultimately discharge' the expense of erecting a new building'.[33] A clear decision had finally been made after thirteen years of investigation, reports and deliberation. To achieve this, Bethlem was again considering an appeal to the charitable public.

Meanwhile, there were decisions to make about where the inmates should be moved pending rebuilding. The London Hospital in Whitechapel was approached to house the women inmates. Although it had several empty wards, the London refused to do so after 'mature' consideration, despite Bethlem's offer that it would provide the medical staff and servants. 'Receiving lunatics at the House', the medical staff at the London argued, would be a 'complete subversion of the principles upon which this Hospital is established'.[34] The London had been founded as a voluntary hospital for the care of the sick poor. Its admission criteria did not include the mentally ill and unlike Guy's, which had its own wing for the incurably insane, it had no facilities for the care of this type of patient.[35] It seems a strange decision for the Governors to have approached the London Hospital, although they were probably motivated by an awareness that the Hospital had spare capacity. Other resolutions were passed now that it had been decided to move to a new site. The condition of Hooke's building revealed by Lewis persuaded the Governors in 1804 to restrict admissions to those on the waiting list.[36] This ensured that the number of patients in the Hospital was gradually reduced. Between 1800 and 1814 the number of patients fell from 266 to 119, a necessity given that sections of the building became completely uninhabitable and were demolished.[37]

A PROBLEM OF MONEY; A PROBLEM OF LOCATION

It was not until after a Building Committee had been appointed in 1805 that Lewis was asked to prepare plans for a completely new building. At the same time, the Court ordered that advertisements should be placed in the national press and 'inserted in the London and provincial newspapers from time to time'. Bethlem was staking its claim to being a national charity. The aim was 'for the purpose of informing the public of the necessity of rebuilding Bethlem Hospital and of soliciting their contributions in aid of that benevolent purpose'. The names of subscribers were to be read out by the Clerk at every Court meeting.[38] A charitable appeal was the most direct way of raising money from the benevolent public. It allowed a voluntary organization to raise a large amount in a relatively short time. Here the press became an important vehicle for fund-raising where the aim was to reach the largest possible audience at a local and national level.[39] Voluntary societies readily adopted this fund-raising measure and wearied the public with their constant appeals for support.[40] Unlike Bethlem, however, they published the list of subscribers in an attempt to stimulate others to contribute and to reward those that had. Metropolitan hospital administrators seemed consumed with a mania to build and invariably linked these appeals to the need to provide new buildings. Here charity was crucial. Most hospitals lacked the resources needed to fund rebuilding, which itself placed an intolerable strain on the institution.[41] Bethlem was trying to avoid a similar situation. The Governors were virtually forced into providing a new building by the condition of the old. They therefore did not want to strain an already fragile financial situation.

However, the Governors decided not to rely on charity alone. The Court therefore decided that Parliament should be approached for a grant. In return the Governors agreed to make permanent provision in any new building for disturbed soldiers and sailors, 'the mental wreckage of the French Wars'.[42] Such a source of funding was not available to other London hospitals. They defended their charitable nature and violently resisted any suggestion that funds should be sought from the state. Bethlem proved more flexible. It was already used to receiving limited indirect state funding through the admission of patients from state institutions and the Board of the Green Cloth.[43] The Governors' approach was rewarded. In 1806, the House of Commons responded by voting to give £10,000 towards the appeal.

Problems, however, were beginning to emerge with the Gossey Fields site. While the Government's appropriation to Bethlem was being discussed in the House of Lords, the original lease for the Moorfields site was investigated. It was found that a clause in the 1674 lease had specified that the site at Moorfields would revert to the City of London if the Governors did not keep a hospital standing on it. It was impossible for the Hospital to retain the Moorfields site for revenue purposes if it moved to a different place. This was a major stumbling-block. The Governors could not therefore buy a new site and pay for it with the revenue from the old. This made the economics of the contemplated transfer impossible: Bethlem did not have enough money, even with the appeal, to fund an entirely new purchase. The only solution was to exchange the Moorfields site for another piece of land. However, the Drapers' Company was unwilling to reinvest in land. Urgently the Governors sought other sites. In vain they explored Ball's Pond in Clerkenwell and the district at the back of the Foundling Hospital.[44] Attention finally focused in June 1807 on a City-owned site in St George's Fields, Southwark. The land was held by a Mr Hedger under the City of London's Bridge House Estates and the lease was due to revert to the Corporation of London on Lady Day 1810.[45] The Treasurer and President were immediately interested.

Southwark, on the south of the Thames, was a swampy, overcrowded and pre-dominately poor part of London.[46] When the cholera epidemics hit London in 1832 and 1847, it was felt that the poisonous gas that caused the epidemic lay particularly heavily over Southwark.[47] By the late nineteenth century, half the population in the borough were considered below the poverty line. The area was industrialized, with Southwark and neighbouring Lambeth having the highest number of smoke-consuming furnaces in London.[48] A chaotic jumble of small houses and alleys, it had the world's largest hop markets, while Lambeth was dominated by its potteries and engineering works.[49]

The site itself, roughly triangular in shape, consisted of a ground plot of nearly twelve acres. On the road frontage there were houses.[50] Part of St George's Fields had been occupied by the School for the Indigent Blind; on another the house and pleasure gardens of the Dog and Duck tavern had been situated. The tavern had an interesting eighteenth-century history. Along with Bethlem, it had provided a diversion for visitors to London. For a time it had been a spa, and Samuel Johnson, who figures prominently in histories of 'madness', had advised Mrs Thrale to take the waters there.[51] By the end of the eighteenth century, the Dog and Duck building had become a mill for making bread out of potato flour. The building was finally pulled down in 1813.[52] St George's Fields and Southwark were hardly an ideal location, but this did not dull the Governors' enthusiasm. Desperate for a suitable site, the problems with Southwark and St George's Fields were overlooked.

Before the swampy Southwark site was acquired by Bethlem there was further argument about trust powers, property rights, revenues and expenditures. With both St George's Fields and the Moorfields estate owned by the City, a way out from the dilemma of the 1674 lease became possible. With the sanction of Parliament, the City exchanged part of the land that belonged to it in St George's Fields for the whole of the Moorfields land and allowed Bethlem to have the benefit of the unexpired portion of the lease.[53] Negotiations took nearly three years and were finally settled in 1810. In the process no money had been exchanged. It was now possible for the Governors to go ahead with rebuilding.

CRIMINAL LUNATICS

Before the final assent for the transfer of the lease had been given by Parliament, a largely unexpected development occurred. In June 1808 an Address from the House of Commons was presented to the King praying that 'he would be pleased to give directions that a separate prison might be erected' for the confinement of criminal lunatics. Bethlem was suggested in 1810 as the obvious choice and the Governors were approached.[54]

Interest in the 'state of the Criminal and Pauper lunatics' had been generated in 1806 when Sir George Onesiphorus Paul, an admirer of Jeremy Bentham's utilitarian philosophy and a prison reformer in the Howard mould, wrote a letter to the Secretary of State about their care. Paul recognized that the law relating to the criminally insane was manifestly unjust. He felt that 'the antipathies and reigning conceits of a madman' rarely required 'a perpetual confinement'.[55] After James Hadfield's attempted regicide in 1800 (see pp. 391–2), legislation had been rushed through Parliament to provide for the disposal of those judged criminally insane. In the troubled circumstances of the 1790s, with war and revolution across the Channel and with domestic cases arising like those of Hadfield and Truelock, there seemed a need for clear-cut rules of provision for insane criminals. Hadfield's case and the resulting legislation created a new category of offenders, the 'criminal lunatic'.[56] The 1800 Act applied only to persons tried for treason, murder and felony. It allowed a court to order such persons 'to be kept in strict custody, in such place and manner as to the Court should seem fit, until His Majesty's Pleasure be known'. The Act had not directed, however, where different classes of criminal lunatics would be housed or how (if at all) they might be released. Paul recognized that the 1800 Act amounted to a life sentence that was either spent in a county gaol, a lunatic asylum, or, for a few, in Bethlem. He proposed that special wards should be set aside in 'extensive and independent Institutions'.[57] There was a clear need for a new type of institution.

Paul's letter provided sufficient evidence for the creation of a House of Commons Select Committee in 1807, set up shortly after the establishment of Charles James Fox's Ministry of All the Talents.[58] The Committee agreed with Paul that 'to confine such persons in a common gaol is equally destructive of all possibility of the recovery of the insane and of the security and comfort of the other prisoners'.[59] At the time, there was also a move to publicize and improve the conditions under which the insane were kept. The new asylums that Paul referred to were created by Charles Williams-Wynn's (a member of the 1807 Select Committee) Act of 1808. The Act 'for the better Care and Maintenance of Lunatics, being Paupers or Criminals, in England' empowered, but did not oblige, counties to set up asylums where both lunatics and criminals could be housed. The new county asylums, of which the first was built at Bedford in 1809–1812, owed their existence to the problem of what to do with 'this unfortunate class in an increasingly enlightened age'.[60] The Committee had, however, also recommended the building of a separate asylum for criminal lunatics to serve the entire county and operate under regulations made by the Home Secretary.[61] If there was to be a national centre, Bethlem seemed the obvious place.

Two years after the 1808 Act, the Governors of Bethlem were approached by Lord Sidmouth, Secretary of State for the Home Department.[62] He asked whether it would 'be consistent with the Plan' for a new hospital if a portion of it were to be set apart for 'the special accommodation of Criminal Lunatics'. Lord Liverpool's Tory government was aware that the Governors were planning to provide a new building in St George's Fields and hoped to use the opportunity to further its (and the 1807 Select Committee's) aims. It felt that the provision of a criminal lunatics' wing at Bethlem would be a 'great advantage', arguing that it made sense to have 'buildings allotted similar purposes and requiring the same species of superintendence' placed 'in the neighbourhood of each other'.[63] It was a proposition that was to be questioned in the future. The Governors, although aware that Bethlem already received criminal lunatics from the Privy Council and the Courts under the 1800 Act, hesitated before accepting. They expressed some 'apprehension' and asked for more information. The Governors speculated – although this had not been stated in the original letter – that the approach related to the 1808 Act 'for the better … maintenance of Lunatics being Paupers or Criminals'. The Secretary of State promised Bethlem that the Government wished to pursue negotiations not according to the 1808 Act but to the 'Parliamentary Address of June'.

Bethlem's Governors were not reassured. They worried that by agreeing to the proposals they would become subject to inspection under the 1808 Act. The Governors were at first uncertain who would pay for the new wing and negotiations proved protracted.[64] Indeed, they instructed the President and Treasurer to have a meeting with the Secretary of State to clarify the Government's policy. Unable to see the Secretary of State, they did receive new guarantees, backed by the Law Officers of the Crown, that there would be no interference with their 'control and management' of Bethlem.[65] The Secretary of State went on to inform them that while he expected the numbers of criminal lunatics to average around fifty, accommodation would be provided for sixty. This was to be for forty-five men and fifteen women in two self-contained blocks with their own exercise yards at the back of the new hospital.[66] This had been thought to be a generous estimate. At the time, Bethlem contained twenty men and twelve women judged criminally insane, and the new wings were not intended to hold all criminal lunatics in the county, 'only those who could not be safely left to the county asylums'.[67] Bethlem, in return for providing facilities and care, would receive direct state funding. The Government agreed to pay for the new wing and, once built, provide 'such a sum for each patient as shall be equivalent to the maintenance, management and clothing of each'. Medical care was to be supplied by the Hospital but paid for by the state, although an 'Inspector of Criminal Lunatics' was appointed to act on the Government's behalf.[68] Now certain that the Government would not intervene in the Hospital's management, the Governors expressed themselves 'satisfied' with the proposed arrangement.[69] An agreement was finally reached in 1814. The Governors had total control over what was built, although a limit of £19,800 was set for the two 'criminal' blocks, which were added to the plans and opened in 1816.[70] One of the first patients transferred was Hadfield. This was the first purpose-built establishment for those judged criminally insane in England. It quickly proved to be too small.

PLANNING A NEW BETHLEM

While negotiations were underway with the City of London over St George's Fields and with the Government for a criminal lunatics' wing, the Governors decided to press ahead with planning a new hospital. Lewis had been called on in 1805 to present his plans for rebuilding, but in the summer of 1810 it was decided that an advertisement should be placed in *The Times* offering premiums of £200, £100 and £50 for the best three designs for a 'new Bethlem'.[71] There were over thirty competitors. One was of particular interest: he was the contentious Bethlem inmate, James Tilly Matthews.

Matthews was a London tea-broker of Welsh and Huguenot descent. Little is known about his early life, but in the 1790s he became increasingly anxious about the deterioration of Anglo-French relations given the outbreak of Revolution in France. Matthews, along with David Williams, a Welsh radical, started discussions (that he regarded as official missions) from 1792 with French Girondin revolutionaries to promote peace. At first the French took Matthews seriously and regarded his demands as authentic, given their desire to secure peace, but the peculiar way in which he conducted his mission and his outrageously grandiose use of language lost him credibility.[72] With the fall of the Girondins, he had been arrested in Paris in 1793 and held in prison there on suspicion that he was a spy until 1796 when he returned to England. During his imprisonment, Matthews had become disturbed, convinced of plots and persecution, although he was already showing signs of paranoia and instability in 1793. Believing that he had unique inside knowledge of the motives of the leading French revolutionaries, he set out on his return to England to convey it to the authorities and wrote two letters to Lord Liverpool, whom he considered the right person to inform. When he had received no reply to the first letter, he described Liverpool as 'a most diabolical Traitor', and later in the letter he declared himself 'to be at open war with you . . . and with all those your partners or Apostles in craft and treason'. Matthews also predicted, correctly, that 'you may succeed in imposing upon the world that I am insane'.[73] With little response, he proceeded to the gallery of the House of Commons where he harangued the Government for 'traitorous venality'.[74] The act brought him before the Privy Council who sent him from a secure workhouse at Tothill Fields to Bethlem in January 1797. After a year he was transferred to the incurable wing.

In 1809 his relatives pressed for his release on the grounds that he was sane and that the damp conditions in the Hospital were damaging his health.[75] Throughout, Matthews protested his sanity. The medical staff were convinced that this was not true and John Haslam, the Apothecary, was moved to write *Illustrations of Madness* (1810) to prove the point. Haslam and the Physician, Thomas Monro, felt that Matthews was suffering from political delusions, although others felt him to be 'philosophical' and only delusional in his discussion of the 'Air Loom'. Haslam explained in *Illustrations of Madness* that Matthews believed 'a gang of villains, profoundly skilled in pneumatic chemistry' lived near Moorfields and tormented him by means of an 'Air Loom', 'a diabolical machine emitting rays which possess his mind'. The effluvia emitted by the 'Air Loom' can be straightforwardly explained: Matthews was not the only patient to be sensitive to the stench of the Hospital by night. He also alleged that the gang used mind control and torture, and felt that the French had used magnetic and mesmeric strategies from the beginning of the war against England.[76] While in gaol, Matthews had become interested in the fashionable magnetic theories and practices of Franz Anton Mesmer and recent developments in other scientific thought, including chemistry.[77] Such ideas probably influenced his delusions, but he was clearly insane with his delusional system so encapsulated that no medical examination could fail to demonstrate any symptoms of madness. A retrospective diagnosis has considered that Matthews was schizophrenic.[78] Matthews's release was not granted, on the grounds that he was dangerous to King and country.

Matthews became a *cause célèbre*. His case was later used against Bethlem and Haslam in the 1815 inquiry, which led to Haslam not being re-elected in 1816.[79] At the Hospital, however, he had been allowed a room in 1809 by the Governors and was offered special privileges. Matthews learnt engraving and technical drawing.[80] Well aware of the defects of the building where he was kept, Matthews presented his own carefully drawn and illustrated plans for the new Bethlem in a 46-page dossier of explanations with nine plans. The Governors did not take Matthews's designs seriously, but they presented him with £30 for his efforts in an act of genuine benevolence and to keep his relatives quiet. Although Matthews continued to present plans in an attempt to influence Lewis, he did not see the new Bethlem built. On health grounds he was transferred in 1814 to Fox's London House Asylum in Hackney where he died in 1815.[81]

Matthews's designs were not one of the three selected on 30 January 1811 when the three adjudicators (Lewis, George Dance the younger (1741–1825) who had designed St Luke's Hospital in 1778, and, best known of the three, the architect S. P. Cockerel) made their award.[82] Lewis's pupil William Lochner (*c.* 1780–1861) won the competition. The second prize went to J. A. and G. S. Repton, and the third to John Dotchen.[83] None of the designs was adopted however. Instead, Lewis was instructed to incorporate the best features in a new design of his own. The Governors gave their approval in 1811 and work started in the following year.

Bethlem was one of the few mental hospitals being constructed at the time. Wynn's Act had provided for new county asylums, but between 1808 and 1846 only seventeen were opened. At the same time as Bethlem was being built, work had nearly been completed on the Bedford (1809–1812) and the Nottingham (1810–1812) asylums.[84] Few guidelines were given as to design, but they were originally intended for a small number of patients and no more than a maximum of 300. Bethlem was well within this limit. Later asylums were greatly to exceed this.[85] Lewis designed a well-planned but slightly 'barrack-like building' inspired by the classical tradition.[86] The new Bethlem looked back to the old Moorfields building. Lochner's winning design had been influenced by St Luke's, which in turn had inspired by Hooke. The influence persisted in Lewis's plan, especially given that the two buildings were similar in size and presentation. The new building, however, was plainer and less ornamented. It borrowed elements from the classic revival style, which aimed to add the expression of Rome's weight and majesty to true Greek restraint. Classical revival exemplified a belief in simplicity and pure geometric forms seen in buildings like University College London (1825–7) and the British Museum (1823–46). Summerson felt it was 'a cold expressionless style'.[87] Other early nineteenth-century asylums followed classical lines. At Lincoln, the asylum (1820) had a three-storey central building with a giant Ionic portico and two-storey lateral wings. The Oxford Asylum (1821–6) used a pedimented centre administration block.[88] How much these buildings owed to Lewis's plan is uncertain. The new Bethlem combined classical elements with a plan that borrowed from Hooke's influential design.[89] However, Lewis allowed for the possibility of subsidiary buildings and future expansion that had been impossible at Moorfields.

Lewis's Bethlem consisted of two wings of three storeys divided by a central block. In total it was 580 feet long and ran parallel to Lambeth Road. The western wing was allocated to female patients; the eastern to males. A higher degree of classification was included. Rooms for 'uncleanly patients' were in the basement so that the straw on which they slept could be easily changed.[90] The wards were in galleries as at Moorfields. There was a pool on the east side and the Governors contemplated using it for drawing water, not as strange an idea as it might seem since, after all, the Dog and Duck had offered the facilities of a spa.[91] More ominously there was an open sewer, not to be covered over until 1849.[92] The one and a half acre kitchen garden, along with the pigsty and carpenter's shop, was at the back.

The basement galleries, with passages, were known as Number 1. They included keepers' and nurses' rooms (with fireplaces) as well as inmates' sleeping and dining rooms. One passage led into the criminals' wing, completed in 1816 (see pp. 403–5). There was only one water closet, a sink, and cold baths.[93] There were also 'coal and straw places'. On the ground floor there were other galleries, known as Number 2. Bath rooms and pump (or washing) rooms were included in a pattern that repeated the basement design. This was copied on the first and second floors, with galleries Number 3 and Number 4. In the central block there was a small gallery, with partitioned sleeping rooms, for female incurable patients. This was a world where large parts were hidden from view, and it was a world where there were backstairs as there had been at Moorfields. In the criminal lunatics' department, some inmates were housed in 'cages', divided by iron rods or wires, with sleeping rooms adjacent, allowing them to be separated from each other without being locked up in their sleeping rooms.[94]

The Moorfields pattern was repeated not only in the wings but also in the centre block where there were offices, official quarters, and basement rooms for stores, although at Moorfields the central block consisted of little more than a lobby. This served to separate the male from the female quarters. Lewis created an imposing, if somewhat gloomy, portico of six Ionic columns, raised on a flight of steps. In the tympanum was a relief of the Royal Arms. Underneath it was the erroneous reference '*Henrico VIII, Rege Fundatum Vicium Largitas Perfecit*' (In the Reign of Henry VIII the munificence of the citizens completed this Foundation). This had cost the Governors 130 guineas. Given the concern for economy, a saving had been made and the original estimate of £500 for Portland stone had been rejected. Originally, there was a low cupola above the central portico. In 1812, the Admiralty had complained that the building was interrupting the telegraph between the Admiralty and West Square. The Admiralty wanted an intermediate transmittor on the roof.[95] The Governors took the matter seriously and consulted the staff. 'Strong objections' were raised because any instrument would disturb the patients and interrupt the domestic routine of the Hospital.[96] The cupola was removed in 1844/5 by the addition of a copper-covered dome designed by the architect, Sydney Smirke.[97] According to one writer in *Under the Dome*, it 'gave character to a long featureless building'. This had been built to enlarge the chapel underneath for 220 worshippers to take account of the growth of the Hospital.[98] When the Hospital was being built, the Governors had sought the advice of John Bacon, the sculptor, about where to site Cibber's statutes of Raving and Melancholy Madness. He advised that they should not be placed on the pediment as initially decided. Instead the statues were placed in the entrance hall, offering a disconcerting welcome to visitors.

OPENING AND ENLARGING

The foundation stone of the new building was laid on 18 April 1812 by Sir Richard Carr Glyn, the President, who had succeeded Crosby, in the presence of the Treasurer, Richard Clarke, the Lord Mayor, Sheriffs and Governors. Work began – in war-time – soon afterwards.[99] It took longer to build than Hooke's Bethlem, but work was completed in 1815, the year when the long wars against Revolutionary and Napoleonic France ended. The new building had cost £122,572, with £72,819 0s 6d raised from Parliamentary grants, £5,405 from public bodies, £5,709 from private donations and the rest from the Hospital's funds. Francis Offley Martin, reporting for the Charity Commission on Bethlem in 1836, saw this as excessive. He noted 'it is submitted, after an attentive consideration of the subject, that sufficient regard has not been paid to economy in the management of these charities'.[100]

On 24 August 1815 one hundred and twenty-two patients were carried in Hackney coaches across London to their new quarters. According to Darlington

> they must have suffered acute discomfort during their first winter; the system for warming by steam was installed only in the basement storey and the windows in the upper storeys were not glazed so that the sleeping cells were either exposed to the full blast of cold air or were completely darkened.[101]

The medical staff shared this assessment, reporting that there was damp in the basement and trouble in the galleries because of the hot air system. The 1815 Select Committee had expressed similar concerns. It visited the new Hospital before the inmates had moved there from Moorfields. In addition to complaining about the unglazed windows, the Committee felt the windows were too high for the patients to be able to see out, although their height was defended on the grounds that outsiders should not be able to pry in. They noted that there were no flues for carrying warm air through the building to the lower galleries on the basement floor. The construction of the privies was thought to be objectionable, and there was only one privy on each of the upper galleries and one in the criminal wing. Whereas the Governors wanted to use four acres of the site for profit, the Select Committee disagreed. It felt the land should be used to benefit the patients in providing space both for exercise and employment.[102] The Governors defended the unglazed windows on the grounds that this allowed ventilation to prevent a build up of 'the disagreeable effluvias peculiar to all madhouses'.[103] They were, however, glazed in 1816.

Bethlem did not remain static. Expansion had always been intended, but this had been postponed on financial grounds. However, expansion became necessary with increased admissions, which quickly led to overcrowding in the wards. Additional buildings were added in the 1830s, although in 1835 the Governors had resolved that it was not expedient to enlarge the Hospital.[104] In the same year an additional vacant parcel of land fronting the Hospital was acquired and a sum of £300 was paid to the Trustees of the Surrey and Sussex Turnpike in order to alter the road. At the same time the criminal lunatics' wing, already overcrowded, was extended to take a further thirty men. The new buildings were designed by Smirke, the new Surveyor. Lewis had resigned on the grounds of ill-health in 1817. Smirke, brother of the architect Robert Smirke, who had designed the British Museum, had won several medals at the Royal

Academy and was Surveyor to the Inner Temple and to the Duchy of Lancaster and, when appointed, had just finished the Conservative Club in St James's Street. Like Lewis and his brother he was committed to a classical style and at Bethlem provided accommodation for another 166 patients. 'Honoured by his appointment', Smirke explained that he had chosen a different mode of enlargement from that conceived by Lewis to prevent the new building being dark. It had been Lewis's intention, Smirke surmised, to enlarge by 'carrying out lofty wings, behind, at right angles with the main central building'. This, he felt, would destroy the present cheerfulness of the rooms. Smirke argued that

> The space between the two wings would never have the sun upon it except about mid-day. There would be so much dampness thus occasioned on all these grounds, as well as on the lower stories of the whole buildings, as would not fail to be prejudicial to the present healthy character of the hospital.[105]

He proposed extending in this direction by adding a range of low buildings and to gain the necessary extra accommodation by extending the existing front of the main building eastward and westward. This increased the Hospital's capacity to 364 patients. Smirke left the administration block with an unhindered view of the gardens. This greatly improved the appearance of the façade, and when Smirke added his dome he gave a grandeur to the new Bethlem that it had lacked in 1815.[106]

The foundation stone of Smirke's extension was laid by Sir Peter Laurie, then President and a keen supporter of schemes for social improvement, on 26 July 1838 at a more expensive inauguration ceremony than that which had taken place in 1812.[107] One feature was a public breakfast which, as the Charity Commissioners meticulously recorded, cost £44 8s. This was used to raise money for the building, a new variation on an old practice of holding charity dinners.[108] Another was a benediction by the Archbishop of Canterbury. Below the foundation stone a box was deposited containing a coronation medal and a complete set of coins of the young Queen Victoria. The Commissioners, who disapproved of the timing of the venture, also noted that the circulation of a printed version of Laurie's speech cost £140 9s. They added tartly that 'however valuable and interesting the matter contained in it' might be, 'the propriety of disbursing so large a sum for the purpose seems questionable, and the same remark applied to the entertainment itself'. Their main complaint, however, for once cautiously expressed, was that the decision to add new buildings 'on the eve of the publication of a Parliamentary Report . . . may, perhaps, be thought somewhat premature'.[109] The same might have been said in 1814 or 1815. Bethlem's move did not symbolize the end of an era. In some ways, this was to come with the 1815 Select Committee, which revealed that despite efforts to provide a new Hospital much remained wrong with Bethlem. The Select Committee and the reforms which followed will form the subject of the next chapters.

NOTES

1 See Chapter 15, and Christine Stevenson, 'Robert Hooke's Bethlem', *Journal of the Society of Architectural Historians*, lv (1996), 252–73.

2 John Thomas Smith, *Ancient Topography of London* (London: J. M'Creery, published and sold by the proprietor, John Thomas Smith, 1815), 32.

3 See Chapter 20; Thomas Bowen, *An Historical Account of the Origin, Progress, and Present State of Bethlem Hospital, founded by Henry the Eighth, for the Cure of Lunatics, and Enlarged by Subsequent Benefactors, for the Reception and Maintenance of Incurables* (London: For the Governors, 1783), 5.

4 John Howard, *An Account of the Principal Lazarettos of Europe* (London: Cadell, 1789).

5 Report by Henry Holland: Bethlem Grand Committee, 29 June 1791.

6 *Ibid.*

7 *Ibid.*

8 Court of Governors, 28 February 1793; *Standing Rules of Orders for the Governors of the Royal Hospitals of Bridewell and Bethlem with the Duties of the Governors and of the several officers and servants* (London 1802)

9 Report by Henry Holland.

10 Bethlem Grand Committee, 17 March 1792; see Chapter 21.

11 *Ibid.* 27 November 1792.

12 Court of Governors, 29 November 1792.

13 *Ibid.* 28 February 1793, 15 March 1794.

14 Bethlem Grand Committee, 20 September 1796; 3 February, 10 May 1797.

15 Court of Governors, 25 April 1799.

16 Howard Colvin, *A Biographical Dictionary of British Architects 1600–1840* (New Haven and London: Yale University Press, 1995), 614–16.

17 *Report Respecting the Present State and Condition of Bethlem Hospital* (London: For the Governors, 1800).

18 *Ibid.*.

19 David Russell, *Scenes from Bedlam* (London: Baillière Tindall, 1996), 11.

20 *Report Respecting the Present State and Condition of Bethlem Hospital.*

21 *Ibid.*.

22 *Ibid.* 4–5.

23 Court of Governors, 30 April and 12 November 1801.

24 Special House Committee, 12 November 1801.

25 Court of Governors, 26 November 1801.

26 Cited in Edward Walford, *Old and New London* (London: Cassell, Peter & Galpin, 1873–6), vol. vi, 352.

27 Court of Assistants of the Drapers' Company, 3 March 1803.

28 Roy Porter, *London: A Social History* (London: Penguin, 1994), 122. It was only in the twentieth century that slum clearance was seen as necessary in Islington: see Jim Yelling, 'The Metropolitan Slum', in S. Martin Gaskell (ed.), *Slums* (Leicester: Leicester University Press, 1990), 201.

29 Kathleen Jones, *Asylums and After* (London: Athlone, 1993), 37.

30 A healthy environment was elevated into a matter of considerable design importance for hospitals and asylums in the nineteenth century and incorporated in the pavilion plan: see Jeremy Taylor, *Hospital and Asylum Architecture in England 1840–1914: Buildings for Health Care* (London: Mansell, 1991).

31 Court of Governors, 11 May 1804.

32 *Ibid.* 16 March and 21 April 1803.

33 *Ibid.* 7 March; 12 April and 11 May 1804.

34 Letter from the Secretary of the London Hospital to Bethlem, 10 July 1804, enclosing a copy of the Hospital's minute: see A. E. Clark-Kennedy, *The London* (London: Pitman, 1962), vol. i, 196.

35 See H. C. Cameron, *Mr Guy's Hospital* (London: Longmans, 1954), 71–2.

36 Court of Governors, 4 July 1804.

37 Andrew Scull, *The Most Solitary of Afflictions: Madness and Society in Britain, 1700–1900* (New Haven, Conn. and London: Yale University Press, 1993), 112.

38 Court of Governors, 25 July 1805.

39 Frank Prochaska, *Women and Philanthropy in Nineteenth-Century England* (Oxford: Clarendon Press, 1980), 39; Keir Waddington, 'Finance, Philanthropy and the Hospital' (unpublished Ph.D. Thesis, University of London, 1995), 66–7.

40 This was not just a phenomenon of the concentration of voluntary societies in London: see N. Evans, 'Urbanisation, Elite Attitudes and Philanthropy: Cardiff 1850–1914', *International Review of Social History*, xxvii (1982), 308. For hospital fund-raising see Waddington, 'Finance, Philanthropy and the Hospital', or *idem*, '"Grasping Gratitude": Hospitals and Charity in Late-Victorian London', in Martin Daunton (ed.), *Charity, Self-Interest and Welfare in the English Past* (London: UCL Press, 1996), 181–202.

41 See Waddington, 'Finance, Philanthropy and the Hospital', 149–56, for the nineteenth century.

42 Edward G. O'Donoghue, *The Story of the Bethlehem Hospital from its Foundation in 1247* (London: T. Fisher Unwin, 1914), 290. Unlike later psychiatric casualties of war little historical attention has been paid to this group, with interest mainly focusing on shell-shock and the First World War: see M. Stone, 'Shellshock and the Psychologists', in W. F. Bynum, R. Porter and M. Shepherd (eds), *The Anatomy of Madness* (London: Tavistock Press, 1985), vol. ii, 242ff., and H. Merskcy, 'Shell-Shock', in German Berrios and Hugh Freeman (eds), *150 Years of British Psychiatry, 1841–1991* (London: Gaskell, 1991), 245–67, or Sydney Brandon, 'LMF in Bomber Command 1939–1945', in Hugh Freeman and German Berrios (eds), *150 Years of British Psychiatry, 1841–1991: The Aftermath* (London: Athlone, 1996), 119–29.

43 See Chapter 19.

44 O'Donoghue, *op. cit.* 290.

45 Ida Darlington, *The Survey of London: St. George's Fields*, xxv (London: LCC, 1955), 77.

46 Ken Young and Patricia Garside, *Metropolitan London: Politics and Urban Change 1837–1891* (London: Edward Arnold, 1982), 195; C. R. Martin, *Slums and Slummers* (London: Bale & Co., 1935), 28.

47 A. S. Wohl, *The Eternal Slum* (London: Edward Arnold, 1977), 16.

48 A. S. Wohl, *Endangered Lives* (London: Methuen, 1984), 393.

49 P. Waller, *Town, City and Nation* (Oxford: OUP, 1983), 42.

50 Darlington, *op. cit.* 77.

51 Bruce Redford (ed.), *The Letters of Samuel Johnson*, vol. iv (Oxford: Clarendon Press, 1994), 245–5.

52 O'Donoghue, *op. cit.* 299; *Under the Dome* (1898), 6.

53 Court of Governors, 6 July 1809.

54 Patricia Allderidge, 'Why was McNaughton Sent to Bethlem', in D. J. West and A. Walk (eds), *Daniel McNaughton: His Trial and the Aftermath* (London: Gaskell, 1977), 197.

55 Ida Macalpine and Richard Hunter, *George III and the Mad-Business* (London: Pimlico, 1991), 318.

56 Henry R. Rollin, 'Forensic Psychiatry in England', in Hugh Freeman and German Berrios (eds), *150 Years of British Psychiatry: The Aftermath* (London: Athlone, 1996), 247.

57 Cited in Macalpine and Hunter, *op. cit.* 318.

58 Jones, *op. cit.* 35.

59 Cited in Nigel Walker and Sarah McCabe, *Crime and Insanity in England: New Solutions and New Problems* (Edinburgh: University of Edinburgh, 1973), vol. ii, 3.

60 Macalpine and Hunter, *op. cit.* 318.

61 Walker and McCabe, *op. cit.* 3.

62 Richard Hunter and Ida Macalpine, *Three Hundred Years of British Psychiatry* (London: OUP, 1963), 10.

63 F. O. Martin, *The Report of the Commissioners for Enquiry into Charities for 1837* (London: 1837), 504.

64 Patricia Allderidge, 'Criminal Insanity: Bethlem to Broadmoor', *Proceedings of the Royal Society of Medicine*, lxvii (1974), 899.

65 Walker and McCabe, *op. cit.* 3.

66 Allderidge, 'Criminal Insanity', 899.

67 Walker and McCabe, *op. cit.* 4.

68 Letter from Beckett to Poynder, 5 January 1811; Court of Governors, 6 March 1811.

69 General Court, 6 March 1811.

70 The cost of the new wings exceeded the amount allocated by £5,344; the Government, having forced the issue, were not in a position to argue: Walker and McCabe, *op. cit.* 3.

71 *The Times*, 3 July 1810.

72 D. Williams, 'The Missions of David Williams and James Tilly Matthews to England', *English Historical Review*, lii (1938), 651–68; Robert Howard, 'James Tilly Matthews in London and Paris 1793: His First Peace Mission – In His Own Words', *History of Psychiatry*, ii (1991), 53–69.

73 John Haslam, *Illustrations of Madness*, with an introduction by Roy Porter (London: Routledge, 1988), xv–xxiv.

74 *Hansard*, H. of C., vol. xxxii, 27 May 1795 to 2 March 1797, 1440–94.

75 Haslam, *op. cit.* xv–xxiv.

76 *Ibid.* xxxii–iv.

77 Mesmer graduated from Vienna in 1766 and moved to Paris in 1779 where he published his *Mémoire sur la découverte du magnétisme animal*. An investigation of his work by a committee which included Benjamin Franklin and Antoine Lavoisier led him to leave Paris, but it did not curb interest in mesmerism. The report of the investigation was translated anonymously into English. For the later story of mesmerism and its place in the history of psychiatry, see Hunter and Macalpine, *Three Hundred Years of British Psychiatry*, 480–6.

78 Howard, 'James Tilly Matthews', 69; P. K. Carpenter, 'Description of Schizophrenia in the Psychiatry of Georgian Britain', *Comprehensive Psychiatry*, xxx (1989), 332–8.

79 See Chapter 23, *First Report of the Select Committee on Madhouses*.

80 Court of Governors, 30 December 1809.

81 Court of Governors, 11 August 1814; Denis Leigh, *Historical Development of British Psychiatry* (Oxford: Pergamon, 1961), vol. i, 134ff.

82 Dance had used a similar formula to Hooke's Bethlem for St Luke's, organizing the Hospital around three pavilions with lower linking wings: see Harold D. Kalman, 'The Architecture of George Dance the Younger' (unpublished Ph.D. Thesis, Princeton University, 1971), 104–10.

83 St George's Fields Building Records, BR/SGF/2. This corrects Darlington, *op. cit.* 76–8, who stated that E. John Gandy of 21 New Street, Charing Cross, a member of an architectural family, was the winner of the competition.

84 Taylor, *op. cit.* 134.

85 See Scull, *op. cit.* 267–84; 335–8.

86 Colvin, *op. cit.* 615.

87 John Summerson, *Architecture in Britian* (London: Penguin, 1969), 275.

88 Taylor, *op. cit.* 134.

89 See Chapter 15.

90 Darlington, *op. cit.* 77.

91 O'Donoghue, *op. cit.* 299.

92 Court of Governors, 1849.

93 *First Report of the Select Committee on Madhouses*, 6.

94 F. O. Martin, *An Account of Bethlem Hospital Abridged from the Report of the Late Charity Commissioners* (London: Groombridge, 1853).

95 Bethlem Building Committee, 30 September 1812.

96 *Ibid.* 28 October 1812.

97 Darlington, *op. cit.* 79.

98 *Under the Dome*, June 1930, 26; Russell, *op. cit.* 11.

99 St George's Building Records: BR/SGF/2.

100 Martin, *Report of the Commissioners for Enquiry into Charities for 1837*, 572.

101 Darlington, *op. cit.* 79.

102 *Observations made by Members of the Committee on a Visit to the New Bethlehem Hospital in St. George's Fields.*

103 Cited in Darlington, *op. cit.* 78.
104 General Committee, 27 April 1835.
105 Report of Sydney Smirke, 29 January 1838.
106 Darlington, *op. cit.* 79.
107 P. Laurie, *A Narrative of the Proceedings at the Laying of the First Stone of the New Buildings at Bethlem Hospital* (London: 1838).
108 See Waddington, 'Finance, Philanthropy and the Hospital', chs 2 and 3.
109 *Report of the Commissioners*, 506.

ATTACK

Bethlem and the 1815 Select Committee

—— •◆• ——

The 1815 House of Commons Select Committee on Madhouses, looking at Bethlem from outside, revealed clearly that the attempts between 1783 and 1814 by the Governors to strengthen Bethlem's organization had proved ineffectual. From the vantage point of Westminster not of the City of London, the Select Committee produced an influential report that was the antithesis of Thomas Bowen's 1783 *Historical Account of the Origin, Progress and Present State of Bethlem Hospital*.[1] No longer was Bethlem singled out for praise. Now it appeared to represent all that was bad in the management and institutional care of the insane.

The 1815 Committee was very different from its predecessor, the 1807 Select Committee on the State of Criminal and Pauper Lunatics, although it included several of its members.[2] The 1807 Select Committee had produced permissive legislation that created a new type of institution: the county asylum. The 1815 Committee deliberated for longer but produced no immediate national reform. It met over almost two years and surveyed treatment in charity asylums, county asylums, private madhouses, and Poor-Law workhouses. According to the historian Joan Busfield, 'it attempted the first detailed investigation of lunatics'.[3] With forty-one witnesses, it provided a mass of information from the medical profession, madhouse keepers, magistrates, and those interested in reforming the care of the insane. Reformers were uncertain what they wanted to achieve, but the focus throughout 'was on the conditions endured by those insane confined in institutions, with no effort being made to gather comparable data on lunatics in the community'.[4] The emphasis was produced largely by the overriding concerns of those who had called for the Select Committee. They built on the shocking conditions Godfrey Higgins had exposed at the York Asylum and Edward Wakefield at Bethlem. Scandal was to drive much of the lunacy reform movement during the nineteenth century and helped legitimize its aims with the public. Rich in detail, the 1815 Select Committee report therefore reflected largely moral concerns, many of which were to be aired in the future.

The 1815 Select Committee, set up in April, went on to produce between May and July three reports, including a detailed report on Bethlem. In effect this was a total attack on the Hospital's practices and personnel. Reappointed in 1816, the Select Committee followed up these reports with a further report on 'private mad-houses' that had been the subject of generally ineffective legislation in 1774.[5] No national legislation followed however. Bills dealing with private madhouses and the authority to inspect them went through the House of Commons in 1816, 1817 and 1819, only to be rejected in the House of Lords. It was in the House of Lords that Eldon, the Lord Chancellor, made the supreme and much-quoted anti-reform statement: 'there could not be a more false humanity than an over-humanity with regard to persons afflicted with insanity.'[6] Like most other Select Committees, with which it has seldom been compared, it begged as many questions as it answered. The Committee's impact was striking but initially limited. Only later were its recommendations implemented. If Bethlem thereafter was never quite the same again, it was not radically remodelled as the most committed reforming Members of Parliament desired.

CURRENT OF REFORM

The 1815 Select Committee was set against a background of new responses to the treatment and management of mental illness that had emerged in the late eighteenth and early nineteenth centuries. Histories of psychiatry have focused on this period, seeing it as a watershed, and have readily identified the same landmarks. For Scull, the years around 1800 marked a 'paradigm switch', with others considering that events before merely formed part of a prehistory for later developments.[7] Social and medical attitudes towards the insane gradually altered during the eighteenth century. Bethlem was to be projected as the antithesis. Peter McCandless has argued that 'there was a growing sympathy with the lunatics' situation. People began to look upon them as sick human beings in need of help rather than as abandoned by God'. However, he also believed that this was joined with a growing fear of the insane that sought to keep them under control, out of view, and in an institution.[8] George III's madness helped focus public debate.[9] It showed that even a king, and by extension a nation, could be susceptible. Initially George reinforced the image of 'frantic' insanity when, according to the Prince of Wales, he had seized his son by the collar and pushed him against the wall 'with some violence'. However, the image softened as news spread of the controversial treatment of the King by Francis Willis. In the words of Countess Harcourt this 'showed that the most exalted station did not wholly exempt the sufferer from . . . stupid and inhuman usage'.[10] There was a stirring of compassion, a quality that the King himself displayed. George III's recovery in 1789 and his subsequent relapses, further helped soften the language relating to insanity, if not always its images. George III disappeared totally from public view in 1810 until his death ten years later, five years after the defeat of Napoleon. Doctors were forced to confront mental illness, dragging 'the mad-business . . . out of obscurity and ill-repute into the limelight'.[11]

A changing view of madness required a different approach to how it should be treated. This was epitomized by the non-restraint movement and moves to moral management.[12] These ideas did not suddenly emerge in the eighteenth century.[13] They had a gradual evolution and did not universally characterize treatment. Restraint was still used extensively and the non-restraint movement did not triumph in Britain until the 1840s and 1850s.[14] No 'moral manager' dismissed physical coercion. Medical writers, even those in apparent disagreement like William Battie and Bethlem's John Monro, could agree that where the insane needed to be managed they also at times needed to be manacled.[15] However, by 1800 a clear canon, building on Enlightenment thought, existed where control was not to be provided by restraint but from within the patient. The new ideal, eagerly embraced by reformers, was that the insane were to be returned to health by a system of rewards and punishments. A routine was established that incorporated the value of self-discipline. Madness was no longer to be tamed, but re-educated. Scull sees the emergence of a different way of controlling the insane that reflected the values of the urban bourgeoisie, but argues that claims for moral management were often 'absurdly over optimistic'.[16] In the new rationale, the Quaker York Retreat, opened in 1796, became a symbol of what was seen to be an 'enlightened' way of treating the insane.[17] Treatment at Bethlem was to be sharply contrasted with this new approach.

With social and medical attitudes changing, pressure mounted for reform. Alarm was also generated by the conditions under which the mad, the poor, and the convicted were kept. The public image of Georgian madhouses invoked 'the strongest emotions of horror and alarm'.[18] Complaints mounted, producing reluctant and ineffectual intervention by the Government through the 1774 Madhouses Act. This was little more than a token gesture, and did not satisfy reformers who were arguing for new institutions, better conditions, and further regulation of existing madhouses.[19] Interest was heightened in 1800 after James Hadfield's attempted assassination of George III (see Chapter 21). Now the problem of the care of the violent insane was added to the agenda, and Parliament's response seemed to create more problems than it solved. Pressure mounted, mostly from Sir George Onesiphorus Paul, Benthamite, prison reformer and frustrated Gloucester High-Sheriff, to find alternative solutions. The outcome was the 1807 Select Committee.[20]

The 1807 Committee went beyond its original remit of looking into the procedures for dealing with the pauper and criminal insane.[21] It informed the House of Commons that charity asylums (and here it lumped together St Luke's, Bethlem and the York Retreat) were a 'great success' and argued for similar state-funded institutions.[22] An asylum solution was embraced with little questioning in the 1808 Wynn's Act.[23] Early reformers lacked any real idea of 'what sort of institution they ought to set up, how it was to be run, or why it should ameliorate the condition of the insane'. They therefore suggested that the proposed institutions should be modelled on the voluntary asylums that the same reformers were to attack later.[24] Limited in scope to the creation of county asylums and permissive in character, the 1808 Act none the less broke new ground. Although the county asylums were largely an extension of the voluntary asylum movement and were uneven in their development, the Act had closely involved local authorities in the care of the insane and established a precedent by committing public funds.[25] The 1808 Act was preceded by a statistical survey, pioneering but patchy and inaccurate, of the number of pauper and criminal lunatics in different parts of the country carried out by (later Sir) Andrew Halliday.[26] Just as significant, it referred to favourable 'public opinion' as a motive force behind reform.

Public feeling was further stirred following the publication in 1813 of Samuel Tuke's *Description of the Retreat* in York. Tuke's *Description* was favourably reviewed by Sydney Smith in the *Edinburgh Review*, bringing the Retreat increased national attention and publicizing the perceived virtues of moral management and non-restraint.[27] Moral therapy was shown to be a general, pragmatic approach which recognized that the mad were sensitive and should be treated with kindness and discipline. This contrasted in the public mind with how other institutions dealt with their patients. For reformers, the Retreat appeared 'a practical realization of their own half-formulated ideas'.[28] Scandals at Bethlem and the York Asylum in 1813 and 1814 added fuel to these ideas and provided a new cause for unity and action.

A SMALL AND FAMILIAR GROUP OF REFORMERS

The reformers, who had become active while the future site of a new Bethlem was being debated in the 1800s, belonged to both sides of the House of Commons.[29] They shared an enthusiasm for social reform and had other 'good causes' in mind besides the 'improvement of the condition of lunatics'. Reformers were strongly influenced by competing Evangelical and Benthamite ideas. Both rejected 'cosmic Toryism' against a background of agricultural and industrial change.[30] The lunacy reform movement contained leading apostles of the two philosophies.[31]

Evangelicalism provided 'a useful and timely ethic for the emerging middle class'.[32] Working from a doctrine of religious conversion and Christian love around the 'lay saints' and William Wilberforce's 'Clapham sect', they sought to moralize the individual. It was a religion of duty and social responsibility.[33] Their activism had a special intensity because it served both personal and social ends. Evangelicals could not ignore the suffering of their neighbours, especially since their neighbours were made in the image of God and had an immortal soul.[34] The plight of the insane therefore created considerable interest. Benthamites, following the ideas of Jeremy Bentham, opposed hereditary privilege and were committed to the idea of good government to promote social reform. For them, the role of central government was to aid local initiative through advice and investigation. They wanted to shift the emphasis from the individual to the 'centrality of social rules and policy' in providing institutional mechanisms 'to uncover as well as to eliminate social evils'.[35] Benthamites aimed to moralize society and government to promote a Utilitarian philosophy of the greatest happiness of the greatest number.[36] Their ideas helped shape legislation, at least until the 1880s. Bentham had viewed criminals in similar terms to the insane: both were 'persons of unsound mind' who lacked the self-discipline to control their passions.[37] Both needed to be controlled, and Benthamites were closely involved in prison and lunacy reform. The idea of morality and the need for reform provided common ground. Whereas Evangelicals pitied the conditions under which the insane were held, Benthamites felt that they should be kept under constant surveillance but realized that the public had a responsibility for this care and treatment. For both, the current system of care was unsuitable.

Conditions in early nineteenth-century asylums provided a common arena for action. Working from different directions, reformers believed that as the individual could not opt out of the conditions found in asylums, the state should intervene to regulate, investigate and improve. This helped legitimize state intervention and overcome *laissez-faire* attitudes and hostility to central government interference.[38] The lunacy reform movement consequently owed much to Evangelical humanitarianism and the Benthamite emphasis on expertise and efficiency.[39] In 1815, however, it was moral pressure, public indignation, and the weight of evidence that promoted reform, especially at Bethlem, which was to escape legislative control until 1853.

Lunacy reform hinged on a comparatively small group of activists. Edward Wakefield who investigated Bethlem in 1814 was one of their number. It was these men who took up the issue and attacked the Hospital. In many cases they had worked together on other issues or were friends, even relations. Family connections proved strong. The Whig Samuel Whitbread was a relative of John Howard, the prison reformer, and shared his interest in prison reform.[40] Whitbread had also proved his credentials by being largely responsible for founding the Bedford County Asylum in 1812, the second asylum to be opened after the 1808 Act.[41] The reformers were also familiar with each other through the causes they had championed. Samuel Romilly, like George Rose and others, was deeply attached to law reforms.[42] Whitbread, Rose and Wilberforce had also worked together in 1809 when they introduced the first comprehensive legalization for charitable trust reform.[43] Common ground was also found in Poor Law, prison and factory reform. Many had been involved in the 1807 Select Committee, either as members or as witnesses. Rose, Charles Williams-Wynn, Charles Shaw-Lefevre and Whitbread had all sat on the 1807 Committee.[44] Some were even familiar with Bethlem. Chief amongst them was Lord Robert Seymour, younger son of the first Marquis of Hertford. He was a Governor of Bethlem and went on to become the Vice-Chairman of the 1815 Select Committee. Their interest in reform had not declined with the 1808 Act, and the reformers quickly took up the Parliamentary cause again in 1813. Information provided by Wakefield about Bethlem added further fuel to the demands for another Select Committee. The new campaign was started by Higgins in York.

SCANDALS AT YORK

A few months before the publication of Tuke's *Description of the Retreat*, Godfrey Higgins, a quiet local Yorkshire magistrate and archaeologist, received information concerning a pauper inmate he had sent to the York Asylum. History was repeating itself. When it was founded in 1777 as a voluntary organization supported by subscription, the York Asylum had received a favourable press, even from Paul. Abuses, however, were revealed in 1790 after the death of Hannah Mills, a melancholic Quaker from Leeds. Information at the time was hard to secure, but there was enough suspicion to promote action. Mills's death and the response within the Quaker community inspired the founding of the Tuke's York Retreat.[45] In 1813 despite the secrecy of Dr Best, the physician, evidence was provided that pointed to startling abuses.[46] There was a curious link between the Asylum and Bethlem in that Bethlem's Treasurer reported to the General Meeting in October 1812 that two Bethlem servants, Mr and Mrs King, had been invited to take charge of York Asylum.[47] Comparisons between York and Bethlem were clearly drawn.

In 1813, Higgins had sent William Vickers (or Vicars) to the asylums in a good physical condition after he was brought before him on an assault charges. In October

Vickers's wife appeared before Higgins with an application for poor relief, claiming that her husband had been ill-treated.[48] No such claims were made against Bethlem until the 1850s. Higgins investigated and found the allegations to be true.[49] He published a statement in the *York Herald*, but this was met with a denial from Best that was accepted by the Governors. They felt Vickers had been treated with 'all possible care, attention and humanity'.[50] Higgins was not satisfied with this statement. Fired by the publication of Tuke's *Description*, he began a full-scale investigation. At first he was unsuccessful at securing information, and a similar problem was encountered by Wakefield at Bethlem. By cooperating with the Tukes and with several other magistrates who were prepared to become Governors of the Asylum, Higgins forced an official investigation. The 'old Governors, if not outvoted, were certainly outflanked' and were furious.[51]

Higgins's investigation

> provided evidence of wrongdoing on a massive scale: maltreatment of the patients extending to rape and murder; forging of records to hide deaths among the inmates; an extraordinarily widespread use of chains and other forms of mechanical restraint; massive embezzlement of funds; and conditions of utter filth and neglect.[52]

A furious press and pamphlet war followed in which the *York Herald* took a major role, keeping the public and the reformers informed of what was happening. The case was constantly kept before the public, and pressure mounted for reform at a local and national level. Before the investigative committee could convene, the Asylum caught fire in December 1813, perhaps to cover up 'vital evidence'.[53] The damage was estimated at £2,392 and four patients were killed. The secretive Best argued that this was caused by sparks falling down a chimney and setting fire to 'some flocks'.[54] Higgins was not convinced and investigated nine weeks after he had launched his first attack. He found that a building designed for fifty-four patients now had 103, creating overcrowded conditions.[55] Higgins found cells hidden from public view that made him instantly vomit, and he discovered thirteen women in a cell eight feet square.[56] Conditions at Bethlem were not to compare with this. Despite the weight of evidence, Best and the Governors sought to deny the accusations, claiming that Higgins was launching merely a personal attack on Best. They denied everything and went on the defensive, but finally conceded defeat in August 1814. All the servants were dismissed, new staff were appointed and a different constitution was adopted. Best was asked to resign and Tuke took over the reorganization.[57] A similar fate was to befall Bethlem's Apothecary John Haslam.

With Best's dismissal and reform, the scandal had ended at York, but the lunacy reform movement enthusiastically took up the cause in a national campaign. They could not have hoped for a better example of what they were fighting against. Higgins expressed to the press the hope that 'the public will never rest until the Augean stable is swept clean from top to bottom'.[58] Reformers agreed and York became a *'cause célèbre* of the House of Commons Committee'.[59] Events at Bethlem were to add another example.

The ancient institution of Bethlem fell within the Parliamentary investigation because another Quaker philanthropist, Edward Wakefield, a land agent and one of the leaders of the lunacy reform movement, chose to visit the Hospital and investigate conditions there in April 1814. Though inspired by Higgins's and Tuke's descriptions of the Retreat, unlike Higgins Wakefield thought in terms of a reform movement, national in scope, not an offending local institution. Yet there were similarities in the process of intervention. In York, Higgins had at first concentrated on the treatment of one man, William Vickers. In London, Wakefield also focused largely (though not exclusively) on one inmate, James Norris.[60] Both had the spotlight placed on them. So too did those individuals who were deemed responsible for their maltreatment. The 1815 Select Committee, given its composition, had no doubt about the likely verdicts. It was geared for action, and there were victims to be called to the sacrifice.

WAKEFIELD AND REVELATIONS AT BETHLEM

In 1783 Bowen had commented that visiting 'tended to disturb the tranquillity of the patients'. Six years later in one of the annual Spital Sermons the preacher, somewhat revising history, had gone so far as to proclaim that 'a general Admission of Visitors had from its first institution ... been found prejudicial and inconvenient to the patients'.[61] Now it was a single visitor committed to lunacy reform who disturbed the tranquillity of Bethlem, armed at first with a written order from a Governor. Wakefield knew of the scandals in the York Asylum, and he had already initiated a scheme to create a new institution in London managed along the lines of the York Retreat. A committee formed to push forward his scheme deemed it necessary to examine the existing provisions for London's insane at Bethlem, St Luke's and Guy's Hospital.[62] The conditions this committee found when it investigated Bethlem, combined with the evidence from York, reopened debate on lunacy reform at a national level. Aware of the difficulties Higgins initially had at gaining access to the York Asylum, Wakefield was not entirely surprised to find that there were barriers to his admission to Bethlem. Since 1770, visiting had been restricted and the Governors were concerned to defend the Hospital's image. Although Wakefield had a letter from a Governor, he was told by Peter Alavoine, the Steward, that a resolution of twenty years' standing (there was talk of a meeting called to decide upon this in the City of London) had been revived to prevent any persons seeing the Hospital without a Governor present. Unwisely, but doubtless under instruction, Alavoine also told Wakefield that without the consent of the Clerk, John Poynder, he could not see a printed list of Governors. When Wakefield sent his own clerk to Poynder's office, he was still not given a list. The Governors were already on the defensive. Poynder was vigilantly watching the progress of a planned bill for regulating madhouses and it was hoped that the restrictions would discourage all but the most persistent visitors.[63] At the very time the Governors were appealing to Parliament and the public for funds to support the rebuilding of Bethlem at St George's Fields, they did not want adverse publicity. Wakefield, however, was committed to the cause of lunacy reform. He went on the attack and secured a Governor's invitation to visit the Hospital.

Wakefield told the House of Commons Select Committee that he had first visited Bethlem, on what was to be one of many visits, on 25 April 1814.[64] At the time the

Hospital had not moved from Moorfields to the new building at St George's Field, Southwark, which was not opened until the following year. The building Wakefield visited had been condemned as unsuitable since 1791 and much of it was in a poor condition, largely empty or derelict.[65] With the new Bethlem almost complete, the Moorfields building was hardly in a condition to create a favourable impression, but Wakefield discovered that it was not just the physical state of the Hospital that was at fault. As already mentioned, despite the fact that Wakefield was 'introduced' by an official Governor, Alderman Cox, Alavoine cut short this first visit. Wakefield was not put off. He returned in the company of others on 2 May. This time he was introduced by Robert Calvert, another Governor, and accompanied by Charles Western, a Member of Parliament.[66]

On his second visit he was

> attended by the Steward of the Hospital and likewise by a female Keeper, . . . [and] first proceeded to visit the Women's galleries; one of the sick rooms contained about ten patients, each chained by one arm or leg to the wall; the chain allowing them merely to stand up by the bench or form fixed to the wall, or to sit down on it. The nakedness of each was covered by a blanket-gown only . . . Even the feet were naked.

Wakefield passed from the Bethlem scene to its *dramatis personae*. In a side room 'one female . . . chained, was an object remarkably striking; she mentioned her maiden and married names, and stated that she had been a teacher of languages. The keepers described her as a very accomplished lady, mistress of languages and corroborated her account of herself'. This was regarded as particularly shocking given her class. The treatment of paupers under appalling conditions was one thing, the care of an intelligent woman obviously from the middle class was quite another and was used to provoke outage. Wakefield chose his language and examples carefully to create the maximum impression of horror. He made a moving appeal to the Committee:

> The Committee can hardly imagine a human being in a more degraded and brutalizing situation than that in which I found this female, who held a coherent conversation with us, and was, of course, fully sensible of the mental and bodily condition of those wretched beings, who, equally without clothing, were closely chained to the same wall with herself.

The sense of moral outrage was immensely powerful and was used frequently to shame institutions into action. There were similar sights in the side room of the male wing. Here six patients were found chained close to a wall, five handcuffed, and one, 'very noisy', locked to the wall by the right arm as well as by the right leg.[67] Henry Grey Bennet, a member of the Select Committee, in his evidence confirmed Wakefield's assessment having 'visited Bethlem some years ago'. He explained that he was 'then very much struck with the condition in which the patients were; there appeared to me the greatest coercion in general use; numbers were chained to the wall, fastened to benches and tables, and many of the patients were . . . in a state of nudity'.[68] Wakefield and Bennet agreed that all the patients were 'very cold'.[69] The Select Committee were also to criticize the new Hospital in Southwark shortly after its opening for its unglazed windows and cold wards.[70] The medical staff were aware of the problem. Haslam had noted in 1809 that the mad were not, as commonly believed, insensitive to the cold.[71] Wakefield, however, did not make the link. He preferred to use inflammatory language and compare the room he visited to a dog-kennel.[72] In the seventeenth and eighteenth centuries, the mad had been compared to 'mad dogs, or ravenous wolves'.[73] Wakefield was clearly playing on this image to contrast it with new views of insanity and its treatment.

Wakefield was particularly outraged by the way that patients were mixed together: 'from the patients not being classed, some appear objects of resentment to the others; we saw a quiet civil man, a soldier, a native of Poland, brutally attacked by another soldier'. Identical sights were reported on the female side. With one female patient, Wakefield unhesitatingly affirmed 'that confinement with patients in whom she was compelled to witness the most disgusting idiocy, and the most terrifying distraction of the human intellect, was injudicious and improper'. This the keepers informed him was not unusual: 'there were no means of separating these men except by locking one up in solitary confinement.'[74] Howard had identified the need for better classification at Bethlem in 1789, and the medical profession increasingly agreed that classification was an important part of treatment.[75] The Governors and John Lewis, the Hospital's Surveyor, had recognized this fact and designed the new Bethlem accordingly.[76] It is uncertain whether Wakefield was aware of this, but with the new Hospital not opening until the following year, he focused his attack on Bethlem at Moorfields. Wakefield shared Howard's concern and considered the mixing of patients of different kinds, irrespective of their condition or diseases, as morally wrong.

Patients were asked in both wings whether the visit had been 'inconvenient or unpleasant'. Wakefield told the Select Committee that in the female wing all 'joined in saying, No; but that the visit of a friend was always pleasant'.[77] The men were as glad to have seen their visitors as the women were. Indeed, all patients liked to be in contact with the outside world. Wakefield explained that 'the end window towards Fore-street was the chief source of entertainment to all patients: they seemed greatly to enjoy the sight of the people walking and to derive great pleasure from our visit'.[78] This was shown to be the patients' only distraction. It was only when the Hospital was expanded in the 1830s that workshops were added to provide limited occupation, although airing courts were included in the new Hospital.[79] Wakefield doubtless knew that at the York Retreat women visitors, three or four at a time, were regularly bringing to the female inmates 'the softened voice of tender sympathy'.[80] Nothing like this was attempted at Bethlem. Wakefield was trying to show that the regime in the Hospital was backward and that the patients were kept under poor conditions, treated almost like animals instead of with kindness. In all cases he chose his evidence carefully.

Bethlem, however, was later shown not to be unique. The use of restraint was still widespread as noted above. Conditions similar to Bethlem and York could be found elsewhere, even in institutions that had attracted praise. Whereas historians have considered St Luke's to be better than Bethlem or the York Asylum, Wakefield went on to illustrate that the institution was overcrowded and that patients were chained to their beds, nearly naked and clad in rags.[81] The Tukes had already pointed to these conditions in 1812.[82] St Luke's was not cited as another example of an institution requiring reform. These facts were overlooked mainly because Shaw-Lefevre and Whitbread, members of the Select Committee, were also Governors of St Luke's. No-one, not even Seymour, wanted to defend Bethlem.

Having painted a broad picture of the female and male wings, Wakefield narrowed his focus. He and the lunacy reform movement exploited the conditions under which Norris was held at Bethlem. Norris's treatment was held to epitomize all that was wrong with Bethlem. Wakefield found Norris, an American Marine admitted on 1 February 1800 via the Office for Sick and Wounded Seamen, in the incurable wing where he had been transferred a year after admission. Wakefield did not note this.[83] It was explained that Norris was 55 years old and had been 'confined about 14 years', although there was some doubt about the accuracy of the statement. He was found restrained in a carefully constructed piece of apparatus (see Plate 23.1):

> he was fastened by a long chain, which passing through a partition, enabled the keeper by going into the next cell, to draw him close to the wall at pleasure; that to prevent this, Norris muffled the chain with straw, so as to hinder its passing through the wall; that he afterwards was confined in the manner we saw him, namely a stout iron ring was rivetted round his neck, from which a short chain passed to a ring made to slide upwards or downwards on an upright massive iron bar, more than six feet high, inserted into the wall. Round his body a strong iron bar about two inches wide was rivetted; on each side the bar was a circular projection, which being fashioned to and inclosing each of his arms, pinioned them close to his sides. This waist bar was secured by two similar bars which, passing over his shoulders, were rivetted to the waist bar both before and behind. The iron ring round his neck was connected to the bars on his shoulders, by a double link. From each of these bars another short chain passed to the ring on the upright iron bar.

The harness had been in place since June 1804. The description continued to show that Norris could hardly move, given that the chains were 'only twelve inches long'. Wakefield explained that 'unnecessary restraint' had been 'inflicted on this unfortunate man'.[84] The keepers admitted that he had been restrained in this fashion – night and day – for the past nine years. This was a particularly dramatic example of restraint.

On a further unauthorized visit to Bethlem on 7 June 1814, Wakefield and the group with him discovered that all the male patients who were naked and chained to their beds in their cells were being 'punished for their behaviour'. This only seemed to confirm their fears about Norris. On this occasion they took with them an artist, G. Arnold, who sketched Norris in chains. This was engraved by George Cruickshank and was widely publicized, becoming powerful propaganda for the lunacy reform movement. Appalled by what he found and determined to promote reform, Wakefield approached the Governors to allow a group of Members of Parliament to visit. By then, however, the irons on Norris's body had been removed, and the length of the chain from his neck had been doubled.[85] There had been other signs of improvement too in the light of Wakefield's intervention (see below). When asked by a member of the Select Committee whether there were many complaints of ill-treatment then, Wakefield replied that he had heard none. However, he attributed

Plate 23.1 James Norris, mistakenly called William in the press. Reproduced by permission of the Bethlem Royal Hospital Archives and Museum.

Norris's death from tuberculosis on 26 February 1815 to 'the state of confinement in which he was held'.[86]

Wakefield did not treat Norris's case as unique, or seek to discover more of Norris, considered by his keepers as the most violent and dangerous patient that Bethlem had ever admitted.[87] He and the Committee were blinded by the fact that Norris did not appear manic and 'on each day that we saw him he discoursed coolly, and gave rational and deliberate answers to the questions put to him'.[88] Norris's case suggested otherwise. He had murderously attacked his keeper, William Hawkins, and had bitten the finger off a patient named Thompson.[89] With small wrists normal manacles were unsuitable, as they slipped off, and a strait-jacket would have proved impractical, making the apparatus he was confined in necessary to prevent further violent incidents. In addition, Norris was considered cunning and exceptionally strong.[90] Nor did Wakefield learn, as Haslam mentioned in his evidence, that Norris, 'chained up no better than a beast', amused himself by playing with his 'pet cat', although the cat had the dual purpose of keeping vermin at bay. He also kept himself occupied by reading books and newspapers.[91] The Governors were later to argue that the confinement was far from cruel, indeed, that it was kind.[92]

Not every member of the Select Committee agreed with Wakefield's assessment. Bennet presented a conflicting view of Norris's case in his evidence. He felt that Norris had been treated 'like a Christian, and that he felt himself quite comfortable'.[93] However, it was Wakefield's view that was accepted, and Bennet's was the only dissenting voice. The Select Committee found it all too easy to believe that Norris's treatment was evidence of Bethlem's barbarity.[94] A second name, that of James Tilly Matthews (see Chapter 22), which soon came to the forefront, only seemed to confirm their opinion. Unlike Norris, Matthews's case was not unknown. Haslam had already published a book on the case in 1810 in which he collected an anthology of Matthews's terrifying images, details of which he had often communicated to the Governors. The book, *Illustrations of Madness*, set out to 'exhibit' what Haslam called 'a Singular Case of Insanity' along with 'a No Less Remarkable Difference of Medical Opinion'. Dealing at length as it did with a single individual, this was the first work of its kind, although Haslam had a limited agenda, merely seeking to show and not explain. There was no doubt amongst Bethlem's medical staff that Matthews was insane.[95] Matthews's case was more complicated than that of Norris. For Wakefield:

> Mr. Matthews was a very unfit person for confinement in Bethlem without ink pen, ink, or paper, the use of knife or fork, any place to which he could retire by himself, and shut up of a night from the time of locking up till the next morning.

Matthews was recognized inside Bethlem as 'a man of considerable accomplishments'. Wakefield felt that he possessed 'great learning' and 'evidently had never kept such society as that in which he was confined for so many years'. Wakefield conceded, however, that Matthews had been moved from the common gallery, 'where he had frequently been chained to his bed', to a room of his own. In 1813 the Governors had even considered the possibility of at last discharging him on the grounds of ill-health. While in Bethlem, Matthews had plenty of ink, pen and paper and had been given help in his efforts to learn more about drawing, which he used to good effect in preparing plans for the new Hospital in 1812. Such images contrast with some of the representations produced by the Select Committee, showing a different side to Bethlem.[96] Matthews was discharged from the Hospital and transferred to Fox's asylum in Hackney before the Select Committee visited Bethlem.[97]

It is interesting that in attacking Bethlem for its treatment of Norris and Matthews (and Wakefield never suggested that they were very different cases) he did not mention why the two men were in Bethlem. Norris, as noted, was exceptionally violent. Matthews for all his 'gentleness', had been confined in Bethlem on the orders of the Secretary of State, having threatened to destroy the King and Government.[98] Much of the language Wakefield employed was old. In his attack he included images of nakedness, bestiality and cruelty, precisely the images that Bowen had tried to cast aside in 1783.[99] However, Wakefield's appeal was humanitarian. He pressed the view that the wretched, unable to help themselves, should be saved from torment and tyranny. Here was a combination of Evangelical humanitarianism and Benthamite doctrine. In spotlighting cases, Wakefield knew how to be selective as well as comprehensive. He also knew how to communicate, and published extracts from the *Report of the Select Committee* along with 'remarks' of his own under the pseudonym 'Philanthropus'.[100] Wakefield and the group of MPs, armed with firsthand experience and evidence from Bethlem and York, 'pressed for a Parliamentary investigation in madhouses and charity asylums'.[101] This was all that was needed for the Select Committee to be appointed in 1815.

THE DAMNING EVIDENCE OF THE 1815 SELECT COMMITTEE

The chronology of the last years in the lives of Norris and Matthews fitted into and influenced the chronology of the whole lunacy reform movement. So too did the building of a new Bethlem, which sought to solve many of the environmental problems attributed to the Hospital.[102] Two months elapsed between Wakefield's first visit to Bethlem and the visit of the group of MPs who saw Norris with his chains but without his irons. One year elapsed between Wakefield's first visit and the setting up of the Parliamentary Select Committee. These intervals were long enough for the Governors to appoint an inquiry to investigate the actions of their officers and to take action in an attempt to avoid criticism and keep control.

The Governors were able to instigate limited reforms before the MPs visited Bethlem. Between April and June Alavoine was replaced as Steward by George Wallet, who had previously been superintendent of a private madhouse run by Rees in Hackney; a new Matron, Elizabeth Forbes, was appointed and the old Matron pensioned off.[103] This, it was hoped, would solve some of the problems, which were not blamed on the management but on individual officers. When the Select Committee delivered its final verdict, a similar approach was adopted. Other changes had been made. Bennet explained that when he had visited Bethlem in May 'the change that had taken place in the appearance of the Patients of the Hospital' was most striking. He told the Committee that on the men's side 'no man was chained to the wall; only one was in bed, and he was ill; the Patients were mostly walking about in the

Gallery and the whole Hospital was clean and sweet'. On the women's side, where he was accompanied by the new Matron, there was an equally impressive change.[104] Forbes had 'obtained clothes for the women, freed those who were not violent, had them washed and cut their hair'.[105] Such limited reform was not enough. The Governors, after their inquiry, convinced themselves that they had done all they could and that Wakefield's charges were without foundation. They even argued that Bethlem was as good as, if not better than, any other English asylum.[106] However, after the Hospital's own officers were called before the Select Committee extensive changes were introduced. It was the evidence of staff, chiefly the medical staff who 'broke ranks and began to incriminate each other', which led to the change of regime.[107] What happened at Westminster was less dramatic.

When the new Steward gave his evidence to the Committee, he stated (inconsistently) that he had been elected in January 1815.[108] Wallet answered all questions economically and prudently. He confirmed Wakefield's evidence about how patients were mixed together. Wallet went on to note that if 'cleanly patients' were exposed to the intrusion of others the noise and disturbance would 'considerably retard' their cure. However, he also suggested that the move to St George's Fields would involve improvement. For him, the new Hospital was intended 'to put the bad patients into the basement storey, and the convalescents on the other floors'. The last questions put to Wallet concerned medical treatment. Although this was not 'his Department', he readily provided information that revealed that Thomas Monro, the third in the Monro dynasty, rarely attended the Hospital. Wallet defended Haslam's record, which Monro was later to use to blame Haslam for the therapeutic problems at Bethlem. When asked the question: 'how often does Dr. Monro attend?', however, Wallet replied 'I believe but seldom; but my associations are so numerous, that I may be out of the way when he comes. I hear he has not been round the house but once these three months.'[109] Other staff were to confirm Wallet's statements.

Evidence from the staff confirmed that Bethlem was cold and understaffed with only four keepers for 123 patients, that patients were bled regularly, and that other details Wakefield had provided were correct.[110] If this was not enough to damn the Hospital in the eyes of the Select Committee, further evidence was provided by Haslam and Monro. Both faced a hostile cross-examination that forced them to be evasive and self-contradictory. At times they were even found to be lying. As witnesses they were damaging to each other, although both blamed the dead Crowther for the worst abuses. This, however, did nothing to rescue Bethlem's reputation. Haslam, for instance, claimed that for ten years Crowther was 'mad himself, and almost continually drunk' and often 'so insane as to have a strait waistcoat'. Appallingly for a member of the College of Surgeons 'his hand was not obedient to his will'.[111] Monro stated incorrectly that 'the method of Norris's confinement' had been 'at the discretion' of Haslam, as had the selection of those patients to be bled, purged, or bathed.[112] He clearly distanced himself from the treatment used at Bethlem and laid the blame squarely on Haslam. The Governors were later to agree.

There was little disagreement between Monro and Haslam on the efficacy of the modes of medical treatment followed in the Hospital. Nor would there have been had Crowther been alive to give evidence. Drunk and insane or not, he had written in his 1811 treatise that cold baths were useful and that regular bleeding of curable patients in June and July had produced results. 'Having bled a hundred and fifty patients at one time', he had 'never found it requisite to adopt any other method of security against haemorrhage than that of sending the patient back to his accustomed confinement'.[113] Crowther's approach was not discordant with much of the writing about medical treatment at this time. He was more frank, however, than some of his colleagues.

Monro himself, Harveian Orator of the Royal College of Physicians in 1799, was more conspicuous for his graces than for his frankness. At ease in society and a connoisseur of the arts, he was sure that practices at Bethlem were necessarily different from practices elsewhere, not least in his own private madhouse, Brooke House, Hackney.[114] When questioned, Monro informed the Committee:

> *Would you treat a private individual patient in your own house in the same way as has been described in respect of Bethlem?* – No certainly not.
> *What is the difference of management?* – In Bethlem, the restraint is by chains, there is no such thing as chains in my house.
> *What are your objections to chains and fetters as a mode of restraint?* – They are fit only for pauper lunatics: if a gentleman was put in irons, he would not like it.[115]

Monro, who admitted that he had kept no records, agreed that on his visits to Bethlem 'about three times a week' he did not always 'go through the Hospital'. He had a room where he sent for patients, but did not see all of them. Monro admitted to therapeutic bankruptcy and showed that 'treatment amounted to little more than an automatic, indiscriminate spring blood-letting and purge'.[116] He confessed that his treatments were merely those inherited from his father John Monro, although he admitted that 'the disease is not cured by medicine'.[117] As far as restraint was concerned, Monro showed that it was used extensively at Bethlem, although he asserted that personally he preferred other methods than those used in the Hospital.[118] The testimony Monro gave offered nothing that defended Bethlem. Instead, it helped confirm what the Select Committee already wanted to believe.

For his part, Haslam stood by everything that he had said concerning Matthews, and claimed correctly that his advice concerning Norris had been overruled. It had been his intention to confine him in two rooms, but the Governors had told him that Norris should be chained, as he was to be in 1804.[119] Speaking generally, Haslam criticized dependence on strait-jackets and made it clear that he preferred irons and chains.[120] He supported the view that restraint was important at Bethlem, but argued that it was used with greater frequency at other asylums.[121] Haslam defended bleeding, the employment of half a dozen types of emetics, and the use of cathartic medicines weekly 'until Michaelmas and a period of physicking from mid-May to the end of September'. He added that the patients who objected to the taking of medicines did so because they did not see themselves as ill. Under these conditions, they either had to be forced or have their medicines concealed in broth or gruel.[122] Haslam was supported by Monro. No medicines were used in the winter seasons because the Hospital was 'so excessively cold that it [was] not thought proper'. When asked whether the medical treatment offered took account of 'the particular circumstances of each patient's case', Monro replied tersely that 'of course they [the patients] do not take medicine if they are not in a fit situation to take it'.[123] Here was a very different regime from the one Tuke described at the York Retreat.

The terse replies of Monro and the lengthy but sometimes arrogant replies of Haslam irritated the Select Committee. Other witnesses confirmed their statements, but those from outside the Hospital were hostile, determined to paint Bethlem in a bad light. For example, John Weir, the Inspector of Naval Hospitals, who was to criticize private madhouses, attacked Bethlem. Considering that the medical establishment was too small, 'even if they were to pay a strict and exclusive attention to the 148 patients committed to their charge', he felt that what treatment was provided in the Hospital was wrong. Having learnt of

> the indiscriminate system of bleeding and purging in the spring months . . . [and] from having observed patients lying perfectly naked and covered up within straw; from [the evidence of] their mixing the mild and frantic patients together, and others being unnecessarily loaded with chains . . .

he had reached the opinion that the medical treatment was 'injudicious' and that 'uncalled for severity' was practised.[124] This was the sort of statement the Select Committee wanted to hear. Urbane Metcalf, a hawker by occupation, provided further evidence in 1818 in his threepenny pamphlet, *The Interior of Bethlem Hospital Displayed*, that seemed only to confirm these findings.[125] Metcalf had been considered a troublemaker while he was an inmate in the Hospital from 1805 to 1806, and had been confined to his room, but had escaped. In 1813 he reported back to the Steward who detained him for a few days, waiting for advice from the Secretary of State, who ordered his release. Metcalf returned to Bethlem in 1817 on the basis of a letter from Lord Sidmouth, the Home Secretary, but was discharged in the year when his pamphlet appeared.[126]

Metcalf presented an extremely unfavourable insider's portrait of Bethlem, but never claimed that he had been unlawfully detained: he had made claims of his own to be the heir to the lawful King of Denmark, claims that he dropped just before his discharge. Nor did he allege in his pamphlet that any persecution had been directed at him personally. Instead, he attacked the system, as William Cobbett was attacking the political system. Bethlem, he declared, was operated from top to bottom solely in the interests of the physicians and staff, many of the latter 'cruel, unjust and drunken'; others corrupt profiteers. The patients were neglected and were left to fend for themselves. There was an abuse of power by the keepers who got willing patients to bully their fellow inmates. Deaths were hushed up.[127] Having spent the first part of his second spell at Bethlem in the Incurables' Gallery, Metcalf was very carefully watched and there were obvious discrepancies between his pamphlet and what the Steward and his keepers thought of him.[128] His opinions were published after Bethlem had been subjected to intense public scrutiny, but they related to a formative period when Bethlem was out of public view.

Throughout, the Select Committee evidence was provided that was used to confirm what others felt to be true. Reformers wanted to believe that Bethlem was a backward institution that took no account of recent developments in psychiatry. They heard nothing that contradicted them. Bethlem's staff condemned themselves and the institution, pointing to grave abuses and mismanagement. The Hospital was attacked from all sides and appeared to epitomize everything that the lunacy reformers were struggling against. The public were appalled, bombarded with information on the plight of the insane by newspapers and journals. All seemed to agree with Thomas Bakewell that the 'general treatment of the insane is incontestably wrong; it is an outrage to the present state of knowledge, to the best feelings of enlightened humanity, and to national policy'.[129] The Governors were forced to act. At first in an investigation of the Norris case they defended Bethlem's record. They asserted that every attention had been 'paid in the Hospital to the cleanliness, health, and comfort of the patients ... and that every degree of indulgence consistent with the security of the patients and the safety of those employed has been observed'. Here was a totally different view of Bethlem.[130] However, once the Governors had received the Select Committee's *First Report* a different approach was taken.

THE WAY FORWARD

Having savaged Bethlem, the 1815 Select Committee went on to discuss conditions in other charitable hospitals and in private madhouses. When it was reappointed the following year, it went on to provide further damning evidence that suggested conditions at other asylums matched those at York and Bethlem. York had initiated the debate, Bethlem propelled it onto the national stage, and the Committee's subsequent investigation suggested that abuses were endemic through the entire asylum system. At the end, the Committee had uncovered a mass of evidence that pointed to neglect, maltreatment, and appalling conditions. The lunacy reformers felt vindicated. They were convinced about what needed to be done: the provision of a system of state-funded asylums, and a system of inspection. The result, as noted, was less impressive. Bills to achieve this failed to pass and further investigations were needed before the proposed system was set up.[131] More success, however, was encountered at Bethlem.

The Select Committee prompted immediate and then more extensive reforms inside the Hospital. With Crowther dead, and Haslam and Monro not reappointed, new officers were appointed. Bethlem had not survived the 1815 Select Committee. The treatment of Norris and Matthews was used against the Hospital. However, as noted above, their cases had a different side that showed that Bethlem was not entirely the heartless institution others wanted to claim. This was not brought out in the Select Committee. The evidence presented showed that considerable faults existed at every level: with the new building, with the medical regime, and with the management. Reform was the only answer.

NOTES

1 See Chapter 20; Thomas Bowen, *An Historical Account of the Origin, Progress, and Present State of Bethlem Hospital, founded by Henry the Eighth, for the Cure of Lunatics, and Enlarged by Subsequent Benefactors, for the Reception and Maintenance of Incurables* (London: For the Governors, 1783).

2 See House of Commons, *Select Committee on the State of Criminal and Pauper Lunatics* (London: 1807).

3 Joan Busfield, *Managing Madness: Changing Ideas and Practice* (London: Hutchinson, 1986), 243.

4 Andrew Scull, *The Most Solitary of Afflictions: Madness and Society in Britain, 1700–1900* (New Haven, Conn. and London: Yale University Press, 1993),

5 Kathleen Jones, *Lunacy, Law and Conscience* (London: Routledge, 1955), 108–11.

6 *Hansard*, H. of C. vol. lx, first series, 1819, col. 1345.

7 Andrew Scull, *Museums of Madness* (London: Allen Lane, 1979) or Roy Porter, *Mind-Forg'd Manacles: A History of Madness in England from the Restoration to the Regency* (London: Penguin, 1990), 3–5, for a discussion of this issue.

8 Peter McCandless, 'Insanity and Society: A Study of the English Lunacy Reform Movement, 1815–1870' (unpublished Ph.D. Thesis, University of Wisconsin, 1974), 57.

9 For George III's mental illness see Ida Macalpine and Richard Hunter, *George III and the Mad-Business* (London: Pimlico, 1993).

10 Cited in J. H. Jesse, *Memoirs of the Life and Reign of George III* (London: Tinsley Brothers, 1867), vol. iii, 257.

11 Macalpine and Hunter, *op. cit.* xi.

12 Almost every history of psychiatry has noted the importance of moral restraint. See for example: Scull, *The Most Solitary of Afflictions*, 96–110; Busfield, *op. cit.* 190–224; Porter, *op. cit.* 206–28. Also Nancy Tomes, 'The Great Restraint Controversy', in W. F. Bynum, Roy Porter and Michael Shepherd (eds), *Anatomy of Madness* (London: Tavistock Press, 1988), vol. iii, 190–225; Andrew Scull, 'Moral Restraint Reconsidered', in *idem, Madhouses, Mad-Doctors and Madmen* (Philadelphia: University of Pennsylvannia, 1981), 105–20.

13 See Roy Porter, 'Was There a Moral Therapy in the Eighteenth Century?', *Lychnos* (1981), 12–26.

14 Tomes, *op. cit.* 190–225; Phil Fennell, *Treatment without Consent: Law, Psychiatry and the Treatment of Mentally Disordered People since 1845* (London: Routledge, 1995), 24–36, although he also argues that the triumph was incomplete.

15 See William Battie, *A Treatise on Madness* (London: Whiston & White, 1758); John Monro, *Remarks on Dr. Battie's Treatise on Madness* (London: Clarke, 1758).

16 Scull, *The Most Solitary of Afflictions*, 110.

17 See Anne Digby, *Madness, Morality and Medicine: A Study of the York Retreat* (New York: CUP, 1985); *eadem*, 'Moral Treatment at the Retreat', in W. F. Bynum, Roy Porter and Michael Shepherd (eds), *Anatomy of Madness* (London: Tavistock Press, 1985), vol. ii, 52–72.

18 William Pargeter, *Observations on Maniacal Disorders* (Reading: For the Author, 1792), 123.

19 Busfield, *op. cit.* 239.

20 On Paul, see Alexander Walk, 'Gloucester and the Beginnings of the RMPA', *Journal of Mental Science*, cvii (1961), 603–32; Michael Ignatieff, *A Just Measure of Pain* (London: Macmillan, 1978), 98–109.

21 See Richard Hunter and Ida Macalpine, *Three Hundred Years of Psychiatry* (London: OUP, 1969), 621–6; Michael Donnelly, *Managing the Mind* (London: Tavistock Press, 1983), 21–2.

22 *Report of the Select Committee on Criminal and Pauper Lunatics*, 6.

23 Busfield, *op. cit.* 241–2.

24 Scull, *The Most Solitary of Afflictions*, 90.

25 Busfield, *op. cit.* 242. By 1828 only nine counties had constructed new asylums under the Act: Donnelly, *op. cit.* 23.

26 In Andrew Halliday, *A General View of Lunatics and Lunatic Asylums in Britain and Ireland* (London: T. Underwood, 1828), he described himself (p. 74) as driven by 'a desire to do all the good I could in my humble sphere'. He was then Domestic Physician to the Duke of Clarence, later William IV.

27 *Edinburgh Review*, xxiii (1814), 189–98; See Digby, *op. cit.* note 17 above, for Tuke's work at the Retreat.

28 Scull, *The Most Solitary of Afflictions*, 98, 110.

29 For Bethlem's rebuilding see Chapter 22.

30 Kathleen Jones, *Asylums and After* (London: Athlone, 1993), 33.

31 Scull, *The Most Solitary of Afflictions*, 84–6.

32 See I. Bradley, *The Call to Seriousness: The Evangelical Impact on the Victorians* (London: Cape, 1976), 145, 157; S. Meacham, 'The Evangelical Inheritance', *Journal of British Studies*, iii (1963/4), 88–104.

33 Frank Prochaska, *Women and Philanthropy in Nineteenth-Century England* (Oxford: Clarendon Press, 1980), 8–17.

34 Brian Harrison, 'Philanthropy and the Victorians', *Victorian Studies*, ix (1966), 358.

35 Scull, *The Most Solitary of Afflictions*, 86.

36 Harold Perkin, *The Origins of Modern English Society 1789–1880* (London: Routledge, 1969), 269–82.

37 Cited in Ignatieff, *op. cit.* 66.

38 See Pat Thane, 'Government and Society in England and Wales 1750–1914', in F. M. L. Thompson (ed.), *Cambridge Social History of Britain 1750–1950*, iii (Cambridge: CUP, 1990), vol. iii, 33.

39 Scull, *The Most Solitary of Afflictions*, 84–6.

40 Whitbread was later considered 'of deranged mind' and committed suicide during the House of Commons inquiry in 1815. Howard had followed up his influential investigation into conditions of prisons with a further investigation of Europe's 'lazarettos'. During this he had visited Bethlem at Moorfields and criticized the building and its amenities: see Chapter 22, pp. 397–400; John Howard, *An Account of the Principal Lazarettos of Europe* (London: Cadell, 1789), 39.

41 *Dictionary of National Biography* (London: Elder & Co. 1909), 24–8.

42 *Ibid.*

43 Richard Tompson, *The Charity Commission and the Age of Reform* (London: Routledge, 1979), 90.

44 See *Select Committee on the State of Criminal and Pauper Lunatics, op. cit.*

45 Digby, *op. cit.*

46 Jones, *Asylums and After*, 43.

47 General Committee, October 1812.

48 Godfrey Higgins, *A Letter to the Right Honourable Earl Fitzwilliam respecting the Investigation which has lately taken place into the Abuses at the York Lunatic Asylum* (Doncaster: Sheardown, 1814), 8.

49 Cited in Jones, *Asylums and After*, 44.

50 Higgins, *op. cit.* 10.

51 Jones, *Asylums and After*, 44; Jonathan Gray, *A History of the York Lunatic Asylum* (York: Hargrove, 1815), 34.

52 Scull, *The Most Solitary of Afflictions*, 111.

53 Porter, *Mind Forg'd Manacles*, 135.

54 Higgins, *op. cit* 13.

55 Jones, *Asylums and After*, 43.

56 See House of Commons, *First Report of the Select Committee on Madhouses in England* (London 1815), 4–5.

57 Jones, *Asylums and After*, 47–8.

58 *Ibid.* 46.

59 Porter, *Mind Forg'd Manacles*, 135.

60 There is confusion about Norris's name. In Bethlem's case-notes he was named as 'James Norris', not 'William' as shown in the widely circulated drawing of Norris or in the 1815 Select Committee; his name was reported by Wakefield as 'William Norris': *First Report of the Select Committee on Madhouses*, 12.

61 Bowen, *op. cit.*; M. Byrd, *Visits to Bethlem: Madness and Literature in the Eighteenth Century* (Columbia: University of Carolina Press, 1974).

62 Scull, *The Most Solitary of Afflictions*, 122.

63 *First Report of the Select Committee on Madhouses*, 13.

64 *Ibid.* 11.
65 See Chapter 22.
66 *First Report of the Select Committee on Madhouses*, 11.
67 *Ibid.*.
68 *Second Report of the Select Committee on Madhouses*,150.
69 *First Report of the Select Committee on Madhouses*, 11.
70 *Ibid.* 6.
71 See John Haslam, *Observations on Madness* (London: Rivington, 1809).
72 *First Report of the Select Committee on Madhouses*, 11.
73 Cited in Scull, *The Most Solitary of Afflictions*, 57.
74 *First Report of the Select Committee on Madhouses*, 11–12.
75 See Howard, *op. cit.* 39.
76 Ida Darlington, *The Survey of London: St. George's Fields*, xxv (London: LCC, 1955), 77–8.
77 *First Report of the Select Committee on Madhouses*, 11.
78 *Ibid.* 12.
79 Darlington, *op. cit.* 79.
80 Evidence of William Tuke: *Report of the Select Committee on Madhouses*: see C. Cappe, *On the desirableness and utility of ladies visiting the female wards of hospitals and lunatic asylums* (York: Wilson, 1817).
81 Jones, *Asylums and After*, 96–8; *First Report of the Select Committee on Madhouses*, 16–17.
82 D. H. Tuke, *Chapters in the History of the Insane in the British Isles* (London: Kegan Paul, 1882), 89–90.
83 Patricia Allderidge, 'Bedlam: Fact or Fantasy?', in W. F. Bynum, Roy Porter and Michael Shepherd (eds), *The Anatomy of Madness* (London: Tavistock, 1985), vol. ii, 25.
84 *First Report of the Select Committee on Madhouses*, 12.
85 *Ibid.*
86 *Ibid.* 13.
87 Others on the Select Committee shared Wakefield's opinion, while historians have used it to show that Bethlem used an outdated treatment regime without seeing Norris's case as unique: see Scull, *Museums of Madness*, 64–6.
88 *First Report of the Select Committee on Madhouses*, 12.
89 David Russell, *Scenes from Bedlam* (London: Baillière Tindall, 1996), 20.
90 Allderidge, *op. cit.* 25.
91 *First Report of the Select Committee on Madhouses*, 89.
92 See *Report from the Committee of Governors of Bethlem Hospital in the General Court Appointed to Inquiry into the Case of James Norris* (London: For the Governors, 1815).
93 *First Report of the Select Committee on Madhouses*, 150.
94 *Ibid.* 83–104.
95 See John Haslam, *Illustrations of Madness*, with an introduction by Roy Porter (London: Routledge, 1988), xv–xxiv.
96 *First Report of the Select Committee on Madhouses*, 13–14.
97 Haslam, *op. cit.* xxxviii.
98 *Ibid.* xv–xxiv.
99 See Chapter 20; Bowen, *op. cit.*.
100 *Medical and Physical Journal*, xxxii (August 1814), 122–8.
101 Scull, *The Most Solitary of Afflictions*, 114.
102 See Chapter 22.
103 *First Report of the Select Committee on Madhouses*, 13.
104 *Second Report of the Select Committee on Madhouses*, 150.
105 Jones, *Asylums and After*, 50.
106 *Report from the Committee of Governors of Bethlem Hospital in the Case of James Norris*.
107 Porter, *Mind Forg'd Manacles*, 125.
108 *First Report of the Select Committee on Madhouses*, 35.
109 *Ibid.* 36.
110 *Ibid.* 36–7.

111 *Hansard*, H. of C., vol xxxiv, first series, 1816, col. 426; *First Report of the Select Committee on Madhouses*, 109.

112 *Ibid.* 93–101.

113 See Bryan Crowther, *Practical Remarks on Insanity* (London: T. Underwood, 1811).

114 He was a patron of J. M. W. Turner and of many other artists: Scull, *The Most Solitary of Afflictions*, 112.

115 *First Report of the Select Committee on Madhouses*, 95.

116 Porter, *Mind Forg'd Manacles*, 125.

117 *First Report of the Select Committee on Madhouses*, 93.

118 *Ibid.* 96.

119 *Ibid.* 65.

120 *Ibid.* 62.

121 *Ibid.*

122 *Ibid.*

123 *Ibid.*

124 *Ibid.* 42.

125 Urbane Metcalf, *The Interior of Bethlem Hospital Displayed* (London: By the Author, 1818).

126 George Tuthill, *Case Books*.

127 Metcalf, *op. cit.*.

128 Cited in D. A. Peterson, *A Mad People's History of Madness* (Pittsburg: University of Pittsburg Press, 1982), 76.

129 Thomas Bakewell, *State of Madhouses* (Stafford: C. Chester, 1815), 7.

130 *First Report of the Select Committee on Madhouses*, 201.

131 See Scull, *The Most Solitary of Afflictions*, 122–65; Jones, *Asylums and After*, 55–92; Busfield, *op. cit.* 243–5.

BETHLEM AND REFORM

——— ·◆· ———

The 1815 Select Committee and the move to St George's Fields were seen by contemporaries as dividing 'former' and present' times for Bethlem.[1] When Francis Offley Martin investigated the Hospital in 1836 for the recently founded Charity Commission he concluded that much had changed in the intervening years.[2] He made a full survey of Bethlem as part of a thirty-nine-volume national survey of England's endowed charities to promote reorganization. Replete with statistics and backed by copious appendices, the report noted that:

> The house is kept scrupulously clean, the galleries and sleeping-rooms being swept out every morning, and scoured all over at least twice a week. On the basement the floors are of stone, and in the sleeping-rooms slope towards a grate for purposes of drainage. When used by dirty patients they are scrubbed daily, and on the female side are also washed over with a solution of lime and water, by which a cleanly and cheerful appearance is preserved. The practice has been discontinued on the male side, in consequence of a belief that the urine of the patients is absorbed by the lime or pipe-clay, and bad smells retained by it. The house is whitewashed throughout once every year . . . [3]

Martin had no reason to offer a favourable view of the Hospital, and the 1828 Select Committee into private madhouses equally considered that Bethlem was 'new Bedlam', without the scandals of the old. When the Duke and Duchess of York and the Duke of Gloucester visited in 1817 they expressed 'the highest satisfaction . . . in the accommodation and treatment of the patients'. This was a marked contrast to the conditions Edward Wakefield, the Quaker philanthropist who had first brought the situation at Bethlem to light in 1814, had revealed in his statements to the Select Committee.[4] It also presented a favourable picture of Bethlem when compared with conditions in working-class homes, workhouses, or other asylums. The *Report on the Sanitary Condition of the Labouring Classes* revealed a picture of damp and disease-ridden hovels where people were worse off than animals.[5] Even at the purpose-built Colney Hatch asylum, for example, conditions could deteriorate. Here patients slept on the floor or were kept in side rooms for weeks at a time, and the asylum was overcrowded and understaffed.[6] Martin accounted for the differences at the Hospital entirely in terms of the impact of outside investigation: 'but for the inquiry of the committee of

1814–15 the horrors which then existed unknown in the heart of the metropolis might, it is possible, have still prevailed.'[7]

However, Martin's report showed that problems remained behind the 'scrupulous cleanliness which prevails throughout the house, the decent attire of the patients, and the unexpectedly small number of those under restraint'. He felt that 'on an attentive consideration of the subject . . . it is submitted that there is still room for considerable improvement'. Problems were blamed on 'the construction of the building'.[8] Criticisms contained in the Charity Commission's report did not alter the conclusion. They felt that the Governors had tried to carry out substantial reforms to improve the management, address the appalling conditions exposed in 1815, and solve the problems that continued to arise, especially in the administration. It was an ongoing process that was not entirely successful.

AN UNSUCCESSFUL PACKAGE OF IMMEDIATE REFORMS: MANAGEMENT CHANGES AND FINANCIAL SCANDAL

Immediately after the Select Committee had printed its first report, a copy was sent to every Governor. This, as Andrew Scull notes, 'was a scarcely veiled suggestion that the . . . [Governors] should reconsider their earlier actions'.[9] Pressure was exerted by the lunacy reform movement, the public, and the press, and this had already produced limited reform at Bethlem before the report's publication. In light of the evidence presented by Wakefield and others, complaints were heard in 1816 inside Bethlem concerning 'the internal superintendence of the Hospital'. A desire for reform mounted inside the Hospital and a report into the internal administration was called for by Alderman Atkins in February 1816.[10] The Governors agreed, and Atkins was asked to chair it. This was before the Governors had been invited to inspect the Select Committee's *Report* in April. On this occasion, the internal inquiry centred not on treatment, the issue that had disturbed the outside world, but on accounting and costing. Similar concerns had been expressed in 1792 to improve Bethlem's image.[11]

Atkins's Committee presented detailed suggestions, most of which aimed to reassure the public. To increase the amount of information available about the Hospital, the Governors decided to end the secrecy and instructed the Physician to prepare regular annual reports. These were to be written each winter in December and January, beginning in 1817. In 1819, the Governors voted that these reports should in future be inserted in three daily London papers.[12] It was not until 1843, however, that the first printed and published *General Report of the Royal Hospitals of Bridewell and Bethlem and of the House of Occupations* was produced. Voluntary hospitals had regularly published reports since the eighteenth century and Bethlem borrowed the style and tone (which was essentially self-congratulatory) from these. The *General Report* included the existing Physician reports and provided detailed statistics. The Governors felt that 'although singly they might not be safe guides, in the aggregate they would enable the inquirer to test his opinions on many points with considerable accuracy'.[13]

According to the radical medical journal the *Lancet*, the decision to publish was taken to break the 'absurd secrecy' which had surrounded the Hospital.[14] Bethlem had been excluded from the 1828 Madhouse Act, which enlarged the inspectorate for private madhouses in London. Neither was it part of the 'Doomsday book of all that concerns institutions for the insane . . .' produced after Ashley (later the seventh Earl of Shaftesbury), the chairman of the Metropolitan Lunacy Commissioners, had ordered a national tour of inspection in 1842 (see Chapter 25).[15] Reformers, keen to implement Benthamite bureaucratic controls on asylum practice, were concerned that Bethlem was still a closed institution. They compared the Hospital with other asylums and not with the Royal Hospitals, which had comparable administrative structures. Reformers put pressure on Bethlem's Governors to change at a time when other institutions were being encouraged to provide reports. Bethlem was shown to be closed and autocratic and comparisons were made with the new, rationalized and progressive Hanwell. Similar attacks had been made on William Ellis's work at Hanwell, which had been under Clitherow's guidance. Reformers at Hanwell, with their enthusiasm for non-restraint, were trying to make a point that had a large personal dimension. Differences were fought out in the pages of the *Lancet*, and the journal adopted its own stance in favour of the reformers. It approved of the decision to publish reports and suggested that until now the quarterly Physicians' reports had been read aloud to 'the scanty audiences assembled at the quarterly Courts' and had subsequently been 'consigned to oblivion'.[16] Now at least they would be public. One member of the governing body, however, claimed that whatever might be said about the new publicity, 'any attempt [on the part of the patient] to speak to the Committee or visitors in any but flattering terms of the place is immediately suppressed . . . The utmost diligence is exercised to prevent any letters from going out or from coming in.'[17] Secrecy still prevailed.

Along with increasing the information available to the Governors, the 1816 Atkins Committee addressed the Hospital's finance once it became evident that problems existed with the accounting procedures. The Committee agreed that the Steward's weekly account book should be kept regularly (as laid down in the 1802 rules) and presented to the Bethlem Subcommittee or Treasurer.[18] It revealed that the account was in arrears and this was blamed on the 'indisposition' of the Steward. Consequently, the Committee suggested that economies had to be made. It agreed that 'all meat instead of being roasted should in future be baked out of the Hospital'. The supply of soap and candles was restricted to the Steward and Matron.[19] To promote more careful regulation, the Steward's provision book was to be audited at each meeting of the Bethlem Subcommittee, which was also expected to have inspected provisions and 'occasionally visited the galleries'.[20] In addition, attention was turned to the 'conduct of the servants'. This raised more basic issues of management. Evidence before the Select Committee asserted that they had been 'absenting themselves at their own pleasure'. The Governors found that this claim was unfounded, although it was concerned about the amount of leave allowed and imposed restrictions. Under a new ruling, 'no Servant of the Hospital [was] to be out of the Hospital on any occasion after nine o'clock'. To ensure that staff remained in Bethlem during work-time, the Steward was instructed to keep the kitchen door locked, while the basement gallery doors were to be 'constantly locked at two o'clock' and the keys handed to the Steward and Matron.[21] Having covered all these matters, the Atkins Committee concluded that the Standing Rules and Orders of the Hospital together with the Regulations adopted this day will with the assistance of the Treasurer and weekly Sub-committee be found sufficient for the good government of the Hospital and that the creation of any new Officer will be unnecessary.[22]

The aim was not realized.

The accounting procedures established in 1816, and those of 1793 and 1802, did not prove effective.[23] This was not immediately clear and only emerged in 1835 after the Treasurer, Thomas Coles, had been compelled to resign. For all the Governors' deliberations and attempts to monitor the Hospital's finances, Bethlem continued to be haunted by problems of embezzlement. In his report, Martin took account of one financial scandal that shortly before his visit had loomed larger in the affairs of Bethlem than either the 'management' of the patients or the 'medicine' offered to them.

In 1835 Coles was forced to resign after it was discovered that large sums of the Hospital's funds had gone missing.[24] A special committee was appointed to investigate. In 1802, it had been decided that the Treasurer should report on 'all legacies and benefactions' and 'keep a regular Cash Book for both Hospitals'.[25] Coles had not done this. The Committee also found that it had been Coles's practice to retain a large balance in hand and to keep Hospital moneys mixed up with his own at the bankers. He claimed that the cash books presented were not his, despite having his name on the front. In Coles's mind 'every shilling of the money has been paid according to your orders'.[26] He blamed everything on the late Receiver and Accountant, Bolton Hudson, who had succeeded his father in this post in 1820. Hudson had embezzled £10,000 by adjusting returns from the Hospital's Lincolnshire estates the year before and had fled to France. Certainly Coles's deeds were only brought to light because of Hudson's actions, but it was clear that he was not innocent.

In March 1836 Coles, having resigned in December 1835, wrote to the Governors from Calais where he had taken his wife and seven dependent children (he had ten overall).[27] He explained that his flight had become necessary because of 'the great injustice to my family and friends' that the Governors had done to him by issuing a fiat for bankruptcy, an action they had started in November 1835.[28] Coles stated that his decision had been motivated by a desire to place himself 'beyond the reach of any hostile proceedings', believing that the action would do Bethlem no good.[29] He felt that his forced resignation had been sufficient punishment and had seriously damaged the good character he had built up over the previous thirty years. He did admit, however, to certain irregular financial practices to cover his and his son's (William Coles) dealings concerning a legacy. It is not certain where Coles travelled on to as no further letters were received.[30] The letter was somewhat pathetic, but did not sway the Governors who continued to press their legal action only to find that because Coles had not engaged in an act of trade he was not covered by bankruptcy. The matter appears to have been dropped here as far as Coles was concerned, but his sureties were pursued to recover some of the money.[31]

Following their investigation, the Governors opened a new bank account at Messrs Glyn, Halifax, Mills and Company, and ordered the new Treasurer, Ralph Price, to pay all dividends, legacies, benefactions or 'other moneys' into the account when they arrived. A new full-time Accountant was appointed to assist him. Martin did not approve of the new arrangement:

> It seems doubtful whether the changes made in the duties of the Treasurer and of the Accountant in consequence of the detection of the late frauds and defalcations, were altogether judicious. The losses sustained by the Hospitals are to be attributed, not to the constitution of those offices but to the loose and unsatisfactory manner in which the accounts were audited and the monthly balances ascertained.

He felt it would have been wiser to have paid a 'liberal fee' to an Accountant from outside Bethlem. Instead, not only had the special Committee refused to 'cast reflections' on the integrity of its officers, but the Court had provided the accountant with a house, and stables had been built 'expressly for him'.[32] The Charity Commission, concerned with how endowed charities were using their funds, viewed this as an extravagance. They criticized Bethlem and worried that there was still considerable room for mismanagement and fraud. Concern was raised about the attendance of the Governors. Of the forty-one Governors mentioned, seventeen had attended only once. The Treasurer headed the list with forty attendances, while the average at meetings was six. Much was to be made in later reports of inadequate attendance. Once more it appeared that the Hospital's rules and practices did not always converge, allowing the same problems to recur. This suggested that the Governors had insufficient control of Bethlem's management and its officers and that the Hospital was not run according to the rules.

REFORM OF THE MEDICAL STAFF

The publication of the Select Committee's report and pressure from its chairman brought changes to Bethlem's medical staff and regime. The Apothecary, John Haslam, and the Physician, Thomas Monro, had provided the most damning evidence to the Select Committee. Under pressure from George Rose, chair of the Select Committee, the Governors appointed a special committee to consider Monro's and Haslam's future. Rose had 'intimated his wish that the medical officers should not be reelected'.[33] The Court of Governors had been on the verge of re-electing Haslam and Monro (a point often overlooked by historians) and no candidates opposed them.[34] This was common practice at Bethlem if the Governors were satisfied with an officer's work. With pressure from Rose, who had forwarded the Select Committee's evidence, the Court of Governors decided to postpone the decision and asked Haslam and Monro to present a written defence of their conduct.[35] Outside interference altered the Governors' actions if not their minds. Monro and Haslam pointed out that the Governors had previously defended them when they investigated the case of James Norris (see Chapter 23), which had been used as clear evidence that the Hospital was barbaric.[36] The Governors, this time to defend themselves, adopted a different course.

Haslam had survived an attack on his reputation by Bryan Crowther, the recently deceased surgeon whom he considered mad. Crowther had erroneously claimed that

Haslam was engaged in private practice without the Governors' consent, but he did not survive the aftermath of the Select Committee. Norris's and James Tilly Matthews's cases (for the latter, see Chapter 22) were used against him.[37] In the 'witch-hunt to find a scapegoat for the scandalous revelations', the Governors were forced to focus on him. To prove the claims, the Governors produced documents from Matthews, written before his death, which accused Haslam of malpractice. Haslam's defence, which did not try to conceal the problems at Bethlem, if only to distance him from them, was insufficient. The Governors were not in a position to accept it and reluctantly voted that Haslam should not be re-elected.[38] In effect he was dismissed. Haslam correctly noted that he had been 'sacrificed to public clamour and party spirit'.[39] He immediately set about rescuing his career, selling his library, buying an MD from Marischal College, Aberdeen, and establishing himself as a physician.

Monro was in some ways more fortunate. At the Committee, he defended himself by blaming 'the crowded state of the hospital'. He went on to argue that he knew no better treatments than the ones he had practised.[40] The Governors were not sympathetic and also decided that he should not be re-elected.[41] This was little more than a tactical concession, as they agreed to appoint his son Edward Thomas Monro as his replacement, ensuring the continuation of the Monro dynasty. To appease a group among the Governors over the appointment of another Monro, a second physician was appointed despite opposition in the General Committee.[42] Suggestions were even being made that if Bethlem exceeded more than 150 patients, a third physician should be appointed.[43] This was already being discussed before Thomas Monro was not re-elected.[44] With two Physicians the duties were split, with one expected to attend the Hospital on Wednesdays and Saturdays at one; the other on Mondays and Thursdays at ten. They were also required to attend when necessary.[45] There was a division of labour between the two doctors, although each patient was considered under the 'peculiar care' of one or the other, without reference to any other 'officer of the establishment'.[46]

To fill the new post, George Leman Tuthill (1772–1835) was elected. Tuthill was also a physician at the Westminster Hospital and a lecturer for the Royal College of Physicians. Educated at Cambridge and having spent time in Paris, he continued his interests in general medicine while at Bethlem and was a classical scholar and good chemist.[47] Although he had a cold exterior and was always straightforward, it was felt that his 'kind, and humane attentions are ministered . . . with the most invincible patience'.[48] Interested in statistics, he kept the Governors acquainted in his annual *Medical Reports* of what was happening in the Hospital. Monro was less informative. He did, however, visit Bethlem more regularly than his father (see Chapter 23) but regularly withdrew younger attendants to care for his single patients. Edward Monro usually spent 'about one hour and a quarter, and sometimes much longer' in the Hospital when necessary, but in 1830 he confessed that he had only been at the Hospital in the evening once in fourteen years and admitted that he knew nothing of the interior of the Apothecary's shop.[49] Even when his reports were 'prepared by the Steward', Monro preferred to reassure the Governors that the Hospital was 'in a flourishing condition and avails itself of every kind of treatment calculated to promote the comfort and restoration of its patients'.[50] Tuthill was himself not above flattering the Governors, but he always had a purpose in mind. The Governors appreciated his concern and when he died in 1835 they expressed 'deep regret and unfeigned sorrow'.[51]

Haslam's replacement, Edward Wright, proved more troublesome. On his appointment in 1819 as Apothecary, Wright was given new powers of superintendence and was ordered to visit the Hospital daily. Trained in Edinburgh, he was more qualified than Haslam on his appointment and was a zealous proponent of phrenology. Wright was more concerned with dissecting skulls than with dispensing medicines: the latter task he sometimes delegated, sometimes apparently delayed. One of the many foreign visitors to Bethlem, Wilhelm Horn, wrote briskly of Wright in the late 1820s that he did not 'treat the patients actively as he believed in phrenology'.[52] That was not how Wright saw himself. As President of the Phrenological Society of London, he was at the centre of a group of people who considered themselves in the forefront of scientific thinking about insanity. Phrenology came to dominate psychiatric thought between the 1820s and 1840s. Leading psychiatrists believed there was a clear rationale behind the ideas and used them to suggest that environmental change could be used to improve man's innate faculties.[53] Wright, however, was chiefly interested in phrenology's physiological division of the brain for locating organic changes in the mentally ill.[54] He felt that phrenology was the answer to Haslam's claim in 1817 that the definition of insanity had so far been fruitless. Like Haslam, Wright believed that insanity could be understood only through a study of the brain's functions.[55] Such views contradicted those held by Tuthill, who adopted a more managerial approach to the patients. Agreement between the two was therefore strained and Wright frequently attacked Tuthill's methods, especially in 1830 when he was dismissed.[56]

Wright was enthusiastically praised by the anonymous author of *Sketches in Bedlam* as a man who 'performs all the duties of his situation, arduous as they are, with diligence and regularity'. Because of this praise, authorship has often been attributed to Wright himself.[57] Despite the praise, the Governors found it necessary to dismiss him in 1830. Martin referred tartly but obliquely to the scandal behind the dismissal. He argued that 'the supervision of the Governors was not sufficient to prevent the gross misconduct of the late Apothecary' who, on his removal in the year 1831, was rewarded with a donation of £200.[58] One scandal would have been enough for Bethlem; two were difficult to overlook. Wright denied misconduct, but it was successfully claimed that he had performed his work drunk and had sexually interfered with a female attendant. At the time, only the former charge was pressed.

Wright argued his defence in a long verbatim account, based on shorthand notes, which he himself reprinted at his own expense. It presented Bethlem in no better light than it did the Apothecary.[59] Wright's account brought out again the weaknesses of the 'medical department', the uneasy role of the Matron who (along with many of the staff) was clearly suspicious of Wright, the unreliability of the keepers, and how rules were constantly broken. Wright objected to employment of patients on Sundays, the absence of the keepers from the galleries and the administration of food and medicines.[60] He defended himself by arguing that rather than a 'sot and a drunkard', he was a 'gentleman', incapable of 'impropriety'.[61] It is clear that Wright's phrenological ideas and work in the Hospital's 'dead house' was used against him.

When questioned, many of the keepers had no idea of why he spent so much time in the 'dead house':

Q. Do you know what his occupation has been there?
A. Smoking; and opening and taking off the heads of the dead patients occasionally.
Q. State to the gentlemen what you mean by taking off heads; for what purpose – for examination, or for taking away or what?
A. They are frequently put into pans, what we used to call pickling pans, and allowed to lie there till the skin or flesh got off; and I suppose they were taken away after that.

To David King, a keeper in the Criminal Wing, the whole procedure was 'altogether indecent and improper'.[62] The horror was not surprising. In 1828 Burke and Hare's body-snatching in Edinburgh had been sensationalized in the press, arousing concern about how the dead were used by doctors and anatomists. Revulsion greeted the news and doctors were viewed with suspicion. Dissection was feared. The presentation of a bill to Parliament in 1828, which proposed that those dying in Poor Law institutions should be used for dissection where it been previously only applied to the bodies of criminals, aroused further concern and generated considerable debate. Two years after Wright was dismissed, the Anatomy Act was passed which regulated the use of corpses from Poor Law institutions for dissection.[63] This was the background against which Wright's actions were discussed. Monro defended Wright, believing that he was 'a man of very good abilities in his profession'.[64] To confirm Monro's testimony, Wright called on some of his medical friends from outside Bethlem as expert witnesses. They included Henry James Cholmeley, who had been a Physician at Guy's Hospital for twenty-six years, and William Byam Wilmot, Physician to the South London Dispensary, who had been present with Wright on many occasions when he had removed a skull-cap.

Whether Wright was guilty of the charges brought against him, he could not deny that, against the rules, he had failed to keep an Apothecary's Case Book. The books, he tried to explain, had been in arrears when he took over in March 1819.[65] Wright's defence was not accepted by the Governors. Colonel Clitherow, an Evangelical lay Metropolitan Lunacy Commissioner and influential in the establishment and early administration of Hanwell Asylum, believed him to be 'a degraded character, unfit for the association of gentlemen' and that his conduct had been 'so bad, or infamous, that no gentleman could grant me his support'. Clitherow wanted to defend Bethlem's reputation, advising Wright after the first investigation in August that he should resign 'on or before Thursday next, at two o'clock . . . This step had become necessary on account of the high character the Hospital has attained'.[66] The second investigation in October was a mere formality. The Governors had already decided that Wright was guilty and the Clerk reported to the Bethlem Subcommittee in November that the Court of Governors had decided to dismiss Wright. He refused to accept his dismissal until after the minutes of the last Court meeting had been confirmed.

Immediate changes were instigated. Tuthill informed the Governors that now the examination of patients after death would be made by the Surgeon and that he should leave a written statement concerning the examination to be inserted by the Apothecary in the case book. However, they saw no reason for the Surgeon to keep a written record of all the living patients in the Hospital as he might attend.[67] Bethlem proved a responsive institution, but usually after problems had arisen.

To improve the medical administration, the Physicians' duties were revised in 1843. Criticism had mounted on the division of the two physicians' visiting times and responsibilities. A Belgian physician, attracted to Bethlem by its elegance, expressed his disappointment in 1841 because

> there are in each ward patients under the care of one of the physicians and quite unknown to the other. I have seen Dr. Monro stand in the ward with a list in his hand and do a roll-call of his own patients, whom he was unable to tell from those belonging to his colleague. This is such an absurd and pernicious system that one can only hope it will soon be altered.[68]

In response, the Governors decided that 'one of the Physicians should attend once every day to visit the patients, and that they both meet at the Hospital one day in the week, in order that they may consult on any care requiring their joint opinion'.[69] The 1851 inquiry by the Lunacy Commissioners showed that this was not the case (see Chapter 24).

Under the new rules Physicians were allowed 'to receive any number of pupils', provided that 'no more than four' accompanied them on visits to the patients. This had been suggested in 1816, but nothing had come of the proposals.[70] The Charity Commissioners had pressed for this in 1837:

> the reception of a larger but still limited number of pupils seems desirable, together with the delivery of lectures. Means would be thus afforded for instruction in a branch of medical education now greatly if not altogether neglected in this country. No difficulty could be found in securing a proper attention to the feelings of patients and of their friends, by forbidding the publication of names, and by screening from observation all females whose cases involve considerations of delicacy. More disturbance is probably now occasioned by visitors than would be caused by the regular attendance of a small number of well-conducted young men.

Bethlem offered the advantage of a supply of insane patients in 'the earliest stages . . . where every case offers the fullest and most accurate data for their investigation'.[71] The measure was pressed by John Webster, an active and progressive Governor, who persuaded the Governors to support his idea in the face of considerable opposition. Bethlem was not the first asylum to admit students. St Luke's Hospital under William Battie had admitted students in 1753, but the decision was rescinded in 1803 and lectures were not restarted until 1843.[72] It was Bethlem's example and Morison's lecturing (see below) that doubtless encouraged St Luke's to readmit students in 1843. In 1842, John Conolly, made famous by his publicity for the non-restraint movement, had started to admit students at Hanwell and strongly urged that asylums should provide practical instruction.[73] With an eye to what was happening at progressive Hanwell, especially given that Morison and Peter Laurie were on the Hanwell Asylum committee, Bethlem followed.[74] However, formal training was not introduced until the late nineteenth century, although the London medical schools did run courses on phrenology. Asylum doctors were expected to learn on the job.[75] Bethlem therefore was one of the first mental hospitals to admit students, but it was not until the 1920s that a formal medical school was founded. The interest in education reflected the enthusiasm that (Sir) Alexander Morison, Tuthill's replacement, showed in this issue.[76]

Morison was interested in careful observation and, like Tuthill, provided the Governors with detailed statistics. He was the first Physician to be appointed to Bethlem who believed enthusiastically in the importance of teaching 'insanity' to medical students and wrote one of the first psychiatric textbooks. Yet he was 'sidelined by contemporaries largely because he did not accept the prevailing nineteenth-century institutional response to insanity'.[77] Interested in physiognomy, he was strongly influenced by Pinel and Esquirol. A leading advocate of the inauguration of a university chair devoted to the study of insanity, Morison had given his first course of lectures in 1823 under the patronage of the Duke of York. These were repeated annually in the University of Edinburgh for eight years and Morison continued lecturing when he moved to Bethlem in 1836.[78] Out of these grew his *Outline of Lectures on Mental Disease* (1825), which ran to five editions. Morison was also active as Treasurer of the 'Society for Improving the Conditions of the Insane', where he worked with the philanthropist and lunacy reformer Lord Ashley. It set out to further the 'subject of insanity' by holding meetings at which papers were read.[79] Morison consistently encouraged a greater facility of admission to the wards by students and the training of nurses.

A change in medical staff meant an alteration in Bethlem's medical regime. Thomas Monro did not follow his father's blind faith in family traditions. Tuthill and Morison had a more progressive approach that increasingly came to focus on the ideas of moral management and non-restraint, although Morison was critical of a full non-restraint policy. Support was found among some of the Governors, with Clitherow energetic in helping William Ellis at Hanwell establish a regime similar to that operating at the York Retreat. Even Wright espoused views that were seen to be in the forefront of psychiatric thought. This influenced the medical regime. Under Tuthill and Morison, Bethlem was brought in line with the practices being adopted at other asylums. However, the Hospital continued to be attacked. John Adams, a Middlesex magistrate and involved with Morison on the Hanwell Asylum committee, of which Morison was also a member, had a vendetta against Morison given his criticisms of full non-restraint.[80] Others joined the attack. Here a contradiction existed. The Hospital's image and reputation, the evidence presented in 1815, and attacks in the medical press, has prevented Bethlem from being seen as progressive. In some areas this was true. Traditional practices were maintained, but in other areas Bethlem was not the backward institution rooted in traditional therapies and mistreating its patients that many wanted to believe. Between 1815 and 1851 it was very much an institution of its time, full of contradictions and trying to adopt new psychiatric ideas.

A NEW MEDICAL REGIME

Considerable differences in approach existed between the two Physicians and Apothecary, but they could all agree on one issue: the role of religion in Bethlem. When the need to appoint a Chaplain for Bethlem was raised in 1816 by W. H. Burgess, a Governor committed to the value of religious instruction, Tuthill and Monro were adamant that religion was an 'auxiliary to cure' which was 'merely consolatory to the sufferings' of the incurable.[81] Burgess was an Evangelical and the idea that patients' souls needed to be ministered to as well as their minds was a powerful idea. This drew on a religious dissenting tradition of religious healing.[82] The Governors appointed a committee to investigate. It found that in other asylums a 'positive good has been proved to have resulted in many instances'.[83] Religion was a powerful force in nineteenth-century society. On these grounds the Chaplain of Bridewell, Henry Budd, was invited to revive 'the ancient practice' at Bethlem of offering 'religious consolation' to inmates on an experimental basis.[84] Advised by the Physicians which patients were 'in their opinion, capable of receiving religious instruction', Budd reported that he had never before 'witnessed a more eager attention, or greater decency of deportment in any audience, nor an address attended with a more willing acceptance'. Services were held on Wednesdays and Fridays, and on average twenty-four patients attended. The Chaplain's task was not always easy: at one service one man made so many loud interruptions and 'ludicrous gesticulations' that it was decided that 'no Patient should be admitted as a member of the congregation' with whom the Chaplain 'had not previously conversed'. However, Budd was not given a free hand. The Governors were opposed to any sermon that dealt with mental illness and they tried to control what was preached.[85]

After a year, Budd delivered his report. Monro and Tuthill supported the importance of religion, but were sceptical about its value in an asylum. Their attitude revealed the ongoing tension between religion and medicine and the role of the lay and professional healer. Tuthill was concerned that not all patients were suitable to receive religious instruction, given the nature of their illness. He was adamant that 'attendance on religious worship' was 'not a mode of curing insanity', believing it tended 'to retard rather than to promote recovery'.[86] The Apothecary agreed with this conclusion. While having witnessed 'with the greatest pleasure . . . the orderly conduct and attention' of the Bethlem congregation, 'the apparent beneficial results cease as soon as the assembly is dissolved'.[87] The keepers, however, felt that where services 'interfered with the cleaning on the Wednesday' they otherwise presented no trouble. Budd defended himself, arguing the value of his work with the patients and explaining that Sunday services would be beneficial both to staff and patients. The Governors supported their medical staff. The Bethlem Subcommittee resolved in March 1818 that prayers should continue, but that the Chaplain should only administer 'the same privately to such of [the patients] as shall in the discretion of the Physicians be deemed capable of deriving benefit'. This approach was confirmed in May when it was agreed that the Chaplain should confine himself to private advice and to a reading of prayers on Sunday mornings.[88] Permission was also granted to Catholic priests to attend, although 'persons who profess[ed] wild or frantic doctrines' were excluded to prevent the patients being disturbed.[89] Tuthill and Monro supported the decision, although Tuthill asserted that religious instruction should be restricted to 'recovering patients'. Permission to attend services was prized by the patients and it was considered 'a step towards convalescence'.[90]

After the appointment of a Chaplain, Tuthill and Monro had asserted their control over treatment, resisting lay influence. The Governors had accepted their views. However, the approach that Tuthill advocated was different from that championed by his predecessors. In line with the Governors' instructions that use of restraint should be modified (see pp. 451–54), Tuthill devoted much of his prose, which was usually more to the point, more lucid and persuasive than that of Monro, to rethinking a way of handling the patients. There was a definite shift in treatment at Bethlem after 1815, and in 1823 an apologist for the Hospital wrote that 'the good effects of . . . mild treatment have done wonders'.[91]

In his first report, Tuthill concentrated on the new building. He suggested 'improvements' in the buildings and airing grounds and drew attention to the need to find employment for the patients.[92] Twelve years later, he was still asking for the kitchen garden to be enclosed, a precondition of providing employment. Galen had suggested that employment was nature's best physician and at the end of the eighteenth century Pinel and Esquirol in France and Tuke in York were all advocating the therapeutic value of work.[93] Tuke preferred work that was accompanied by considerable bodily action, with employment being a means to help patients restrain themselves.[94] Work became an important tenet in the moral therapy ideology and it was believed to exert a moral influence, inculcating patients with the principles of self-discipline. Occupation as a form of treatment was supported in 1827 in the Report of the Select Committee on Pauper Lunatics. John Conolly asserted in 1847 that work provided a distraction from the monotony of asylum life and Bethlem's Governors were inclined to agree.[95] Tuthill shared these ideas and sought to introduce work into Bethlem's medical regime. His emphasis remained important in the Hospital. Work was increasingly used as a therapeutic tool in asylums and by the 1860s visitors were impressed how empty wards were during the daytime. At Bethlem, Tuthill believed that the Hospital should by 'actual experiment' give 'positive evidence on the effects of garden labour' on inmates. The project, supported by Monro, had been 'repeatedly submitted' to the Governors, but little was done until 1829 due to procrastination on the part of the Commissioners of Sewers, who were not prepared to deal adequately with an open sewer on Bethlem's site until 1849.[96] In 1828 Tuthill appealed directly to the Governing body:

> Under these circumstances I would enquire whether some of the Governors of this Charity who from their wealth and station in society enjoy the greatest influence in the City of London could not be prevailed upon to confer with the Commissioners of Sewers upon the subject so that the difficulties and delays might be effectively removed.[97]

It was to this pointed appeal that the sixth Earl of Shaftesbury (Lord Ashley's father) responded with indispensable support, and 'garden labour' was 'in action' by the end of the year. Wright did not support Tuthill's efforts. He protested that he frequently saw his patients in the airing courts and not inside the buildings.[98] Complaints were still being articulated in 1841 and the Steward, to cope with the work involved, pressed for additional servants and workshop premises.[99]

Under Tuthill and Morison, patients 'capable of employment' were set to work as soon as possible about 'the ordinary business of the house', in assisting the keepers in making the beds, washing and cleaning the wooden bowls and trenchers used at meal times, scouring, washing and sweeping the galleries.[100] Work was highly gendered, with the female patients performing the 'ordinary needlework of the house' which in 1850 amounted to 2,046 separate items. Male patients were employed in such tasks as gardening and bricklaying.[101] By 1851 the average number employed was 246, a high proportion of the number of patients in Bethlem.[102] The widespread use of patient labour was common to many hospitals. During the nineteenth century, asylum industries were rapidly developed and this had a profound effect on the relationship between staff and patients and reduced the institutional running costs.[103] The Governors did not adopt this approach, at least in their rhetoric. They argued that work was not

> a source of profit, or even of remuneration, in a pecuniary point of view, although under the judicious superintendence of Mr. Nicolls [the Steward], a considerable amount of labour has been performed by the patients in white-washing and painting, by which a very considerable outlay has been saved both at the Hospital and at the House of Occupations.

The 1843 *General Report* recognized 'the advantages of providing employment for the insane'. However, the Governors admitted that difficulties existed in extending the use of employment because Bethlem did not possess 'extensive Gardens and grounds which a metropolitan hospital cannot have'.[104] Eleven workshops were added in the 1830s when the Hospital was expanded.

Incentives were given to patients to encourage them. Those employed in household work received a small daily allowance of bread and cheese and small-beer, 'by way of luncheon', and the Matron provided 'some few little luxuries, such as barley-sugar and fruit'. About 1s 4d per week was spent by the Steward on tobacco for the men, which was given to them 'where the Physicians do not disapprove of it', as 'an inducement to go to work'. Persuasion rather than coercion was felt to be more successful, given that work was designed to aid recovery.[105] Responsible work was often an important component in discharge and there is no evidence to support the view that the most able workers had their discharges postponed. The medical staff, however, felt that employment was not the only solution. They argued that it was only 'an auxiliary to the other curative means of the Hospital'. It was rudimentary occupational therapy to distract the mind, 'a means of withdrawing [the patients'] attention from their own distempered ideas, and of alleviating the monotony of their confinement'.[106]

There was recreation as well as work. For Anne Digby, this was a trivialization of moral therapy that was widely adopted throughout English asylums.[107] Sport and recreation were to become central to the asylum regime, providing a major attraction for staff. Attempts to encourage more recreation at Bethlem were started shortly after the 1815 Select Committee had delivered its report. Other asylums did not pursue a similar course until much later.[108] In 1819, the Governors agreed that the Steward should provide 'a foot ball [*sic*] and a few battledores and shuttlecocks for the patients'. By 1836 some of the men played outdoors at 'ball, trap-ball, leap-frog, cricket and other games', while inside patients amused themselves with cards and dominoes. Female patients were encouraged to dance together in the evenings. The Governors felt that 'music might be introduced with advantage into the house, and that a musical clock or self-acting piano-forte would be a source of gratification and enjoyment, melancholy and mopish patients being frequently greatly revived by the sound of music'.[109] A pianoforte was not bought until the early 1840s, but the Governors argued that it proved a 'source of great gratification', not only to those patients who could play but also to those who could not. More sophisticated methods were to be developed later. Patients regularly expressed their 'gratitude for this attention to their comforts'.[110] However, 'great discrimination' was exercised. Patients who conducted themselves quietly 'when not at work or in the airing grounds', were always given access to the attendants' rooms, 'where, except in hot weather, a comfortable fire [was] provided'. The 'riotous and noisy' were excluded.[111]

There was a note of pride as well as of perseverance in Tuthill's reports which suggested that Bethlem had quickly regained more than its confidence after the 1815 Select Committee. In 1820, he referred to 'the constant commendations of every Visitor' and informed the Governors that 'he did not find a single observing traveller' who did not compare Bethlem favourably with other asylums.[112] In 1828, when the Middlesex magistrates proposed to build a county asylum, Tuthill suggested that 'the Hospital of Bethlem should be a pattern which in every respect the magistrates of Middlesex may delight to follow'.[113] Hanwell did not borrow from Bethlem.[114] Instead, the architect William Alderson was influenced by Samuel Tuke, and Hanwell was built around a large U-shaped court of two-storey brick buildings with octagonal pavilions at the centre and at the ends.[115] Other asylums did borrow from Bethlem. This was in management rather than style. The creation of new county asylums under the 1808 Act saw physicians being sent to Bethlem and the York Retreat to learn.[116] In 1824, Miss Leeds, the Matron at Bodmin asylum, obtained leave to visit the Hospital in 1824 'to learn the mode of conducting business here'.[117] Bethlem could be a model in many senses. Tuthill and the Governors, proud of their institution and confident about the care it offered, certainly believed it should be used as such.

Tuthill quickly stressed the need to classify patients. Wakefield had felt it morally wrong that patients in the Hospital were lumped together irrespective of their condition or disease. For him and the lunacy reform movement this was morally and clinically wrong. Tuthill, with the aid of Monro, introduced immediate changes. Classification was more topographical than medical. In the new building at St George's Fields (see Plate 24.1), patients were 'distributed into three classes'. The 'furious and mischievous and those who have no regard to cleanliness' were confined to the basement. Ordinary patients on their admission and patients 'promoted' from the basement were housed on the first floor, and patients 'who are most advanced towards recovery' were kept on the second floor.[118] The remaining galleries were used for incurables. Here the number of patients was restricted to twenty-five men and forty women. The upper gallery was used for ordinary incurable patients, while the violent and dirty patients, both curable and incurable, were placed in the basement. In the female wing the extra gallery No. 5 gave greater scope for classification, and the aged or quiet patients were placed there.[119] There was a certain fluidity in this arrangement that took account of improvements in patients' condition and patients

Plate 24.1 Anonymous watercolour of Bethlem Hospital at St George's Fields, Southwark in the 1850s. Figures in front of the building are the Physician-Superintendent, Charles Hood, and his eldest son. Reproduced by permission of the Bethlem Royal Archives and Museum.

were moved between wards.[120] However, the arrangements were not perfect. Martin reported that

> persons of the class belonging to one gallery in which all the beds are occupied, are obliged frequently to sleep in another, returning to their own in the day-time. It sometimes happens, that patients belonging to the upper galleries are compelled by their infirmities to pass the night in the basement, while, on the other hand, some who sleep in the upper galleries are placed in the basement in the day.[121]

Classification was still not ideal by 1850. The *General Report* for that year noted that 'at present the tranquil classes are intermixed with the excited of their fellow patients, whose restless habits must militate against, not only their comfort, but their cure'.[122] The Governors believed that the situation was better than a 'casual observer' might have concluded. They argued that 'the intercourse of the patients with each other under the existing regulations' was 'found beneficial'.[123] The medical staff agreed, but still pressed for a higher degree of classification.

Greater emphasis was placed on the early admission of patients. Lunacy reformers stressed the value of early treatment, suggesting that if asylums did not cure it was essentially because patients were not sent to them quickly enough. The remedy was to build more asylums, a factor that came to influence the 1845 Lunacy Act. Bethlem used the same argument for its own purpose. In his 1829 *Report*, Tuthill thanked the Governors for having agreed to admit 'recent cases' into the Hospital, which had been suggested in an earlier report.[124] These held the highest chance of recovery. Between 16 December 1826 and 25 December 1828, 145 patients had been admitted whose malady had 'not exceeded the duration of one month'. Bethlem was to continue to place considerable emphasis on the early treatment of mental illness. Tuthill recognized that these patients had a greater likelihood of recovery, allowing the Hospital to treat a higher number of patients. In the first two years, his assessment was proved correct. Of the 145 patients admitted, fifty-six had been 'discharged well' and only sixteen had been discharged as 'improper objects'. Unlike the county and borough asylums founded under the 1845 Lunacy Act, Bethlem could avoid admitting large numbers of incurables, preventing the Hospital from becoming overcrowded.

The Governors' appreciation of Tuthill's work was not surprising: most of the alterations made to Bethlem's medical regime were inspired by him. Despite the changes, Wright could still point in 1830 to the heavily locked doors, back stairs, candles and clanging bells.[125] Neither were observers from outside the Hospital convinced that substantial improvements had been made. In 1827 Alexander Halliday, a physician who did much to collect national statistics of insanity and to emphasise its extent and character, noted that whereas Bethlem was 'now well conducted and the patients are humanely and judiciously treated',

> it has still too much of the leaven of the dark ages in its constitution and too rigid a system of quackery is maintained in regard to its being seen and visited by respectable strangers, and there is too little space for exercise and employment for it ever to prove an efficient hospital.[126]

Wright was insistent, however, that 'no cruelty is inflicted' and that there was no 'use of Terror in the Treatment of the Insane'.[127] Although defensive, Wright's assertion was a clear recognition that the foundation of treatment had changed since the 1815 Select Committee's report. Patients were now returned to health by other means more in line with the ideas expressed by the moral therapy movement.

LESS RESTRAINT, NOT NON-RESTRAINT

Traditional practices continued to be used in asylums. Staff at Lancaster asylum still bled patients in the 1830s to reduce excitement.[128] Warm and cold baths were used extensively, and Bethlem shared this enthusiasm for hydrotherapy. Drugs were still employed, but not to the same degree as before. In 1836, it was usual at Bethlem to administer an aperient powder ('calomel, gr.iii or rhubarb, gr.xvii') to each patient on the night of admission, unless contrary directions were received from the Physician. Both Tuthill and Monro believed that this was necessary because 'constipation appears to be a frequent concomitant of insanity'. For this reason attendants in each gallery were provided with a bottle of salts and senna, which were 'administered in case of stoppage'.[129] Meanwhile, Bethlem did not abandon restraint, although enthusiasm was modified and its use considerably reduced under Tuthill and Morison. Until Conolly's appointment at Hanwell even the York Retreat used limited restraint, with 13 per cent of the patients secluded in 1845.[130] Reformers latched onto moral therapy and non-restraint, particularly after the successes at Wakefield, Lincoln and Hanwell, using it to support their claims for public asylums to eliminate the horrors of the old madhouse regime. Conolly's publicity at Hanwell, which showed that these methods worked even in the largest pauper asylum, gave widespread recognition to these ideas. Doctors increasingly adopted these methods, especially as it did not mean a reduction in discipline. They merged them with the ideas of moral management, but slow progress was made until the 1840s. In the mid-1840s only five county asylums had abandoned mechanical restraint, by 1854 it was twenty-seven.[131] Bethlem had released some of its patients from their 'fetters' after the 1815 Select Committee, but although the use of restraint declined, the medical staff showed no desire to advance from such a point towards the more controversial goal of non-restraint. For Martin this was partly a consequence of the new building, which did not allow new methods to be adopted as fully as they might have been.[132]

Witnesses before the Select Committee had expressed concern about the use of mechanical restraint in Bethlem. This was contrasted with conditions in other asylums, and essentially the York Retreat, where a moral management ethic prevailed.[133] To address this, the 1816 Atkins Committee raised the question of whether the Steward and Matron should exercise their own judgment in putting patients in or out of irons. George Wallet, the Steward, asserted that he had never done so. Elizabeth Forbes, the newly appointed Matron responsible for the release of the female patients from their 'fetters' in 1815, directed servants 'when necessary to put on handcuffs which she occasionally ordered both to be put on and taken off as she consider[ed] necessary'. She added that Haslam had not interfered with her method of restraint except in the case of the belt, which he disapproved of. The Governors concluded that there was 'so great a difference of opinion existing on the subject that the Committee was unable to form any correct conclusion respecting it'. Haslam informed the Governors that in his absence the servants had put 'patients in irons and he considered it necessary that they should have the power of doing so'. He was certain that he had never known 'the liberty' to be abused. The Committee resolved that 'on the absence of the Apothecary from the Hospital with leave the Steward and Matron in their respective departments have the power of confining or releasing patients, reporting to him the circumstances on his return'.[134] In July 1816 the Governors, in direct response to the complaints about excessive restraint, resolved that 'no patients of Bethlem be kept in constant restraint for more than eight days without consultation with the Physicians'.[135] So that they had a clear picture of the amount of restraint used in the Hospital, Wallet was instructed to provide details 'distinguishing the mode of such restraint in each case'.[136] In addition, the Physicians' case books were also to be inspected. The Governors were attempting to impose greater controls on the medical staff and modify Bethlem's previous enthusiasm for restraint.

In 1836, Martin was told 'that every possible endeavour' was made 'to dispense with personal coercion'. Patients were now released when staff considered it necessary 'for their own safety and that of the other lunatics'. Violent cases were sometimes confined to their beds by iron chains. Patients in the criminal wing, however, were restrained only when they became violent, unless it was felt that there was a danger of suicide or escape.[137] Besides these methods, Bethlem used stuffed and padded chairs 'to prevent the patients from injuring themselves', with a movable board or table, placed in front locked onto the frame. These patients were designated in the reports as 'in their beds', a description that in the words of the Charity

Commission was 'calculated to mislead those who read the reports without inspecting the house'. Similar methods were used at other asylums. At Ticehurst, for example, straps and loose sleeves were employed in the 1850s. Here such restraint was used to break 'damaging' patterns of behaviour.[138] Staff at Bethlem shared a comparable view.

By 1836 the number restrained was small: fifty-five male patients had been restrained among the curable and incurable patients.[139] These figures were not entirely accurate. On investigation, the Charity Commission found that in the weekly reports it 'occasionally happen[ed]', possibly by error, that a patient whose name had not been entered in the previous report was reported 'as before'.[140] This was unsatisfactory. By 1843 the number restrained had fallen dramatically, and in 1851 the Governors proudly proclaimed 'only four patients had been placed under any mechanical restraint in the course of the year' and two of these rose from 'surgical necessity'.[141] This was not so at other asylums. At Lancaster, for example, in the 1840s 'physical restraint was in general use'.[142] In their 1843 *General Report*, the Bethlem Governors explained that the 'Hospital set the example in this country of liberating lunatics from personal restraint' in 1816 when Forbes had freed many patients from their 'fetters'.[143] They were trying to mimic Pinel's claim in France and usurp Gardiner Hill's work at the Lincoln asylum, Conolly's at Hanwell and the interest they were generating in non-restraint.[144] Such a clear statement aimed to show that Bethlem was a modern institution. Monro and Morison, however, were reluctant to abandon restraint completely.

There was a consequence to this reduction. In proportion 'as the personal restraint of the patients is diminished, the vigilance of the attendants is increased'. A night watch had been established by 1843 at a similar time as one was established at Hanwell.[145] 'Night clocks', or 'tell-tales', were installed to ensure that any neglect by an attendant in their 'respective rounds at the stated hours during the night' was immediately detected.[146] To provided better care a premium was placed on the quality and number of attendants. Advocates of moral restraint saw this as crucial and believed the successful pursuit of 'moral principles' depended on the personal qualities of those caring for the patients. Bethlem's Governors agreed. To bring the Hospital in line with other institutions, the title of 'keeper' was changed to 'attendant', a move that reflected a change in function. The language was now increasingly one of care not confinement. The Governors believed that in the new medical regime 'too much care' could not be taken in the selection of attendants, arguing that their 'wages and comforts should be on a liberal scale' to ensure high quality.[147] They recognized that poor pay and working conditions were largely responsible for the failure of asylums to attract good staff. This was a problem in all asylums where work was mainly limited to cleaning, bed-making, dressing patients, serving meals and supervising the patients.[148] With no formal training until the late nineteenth century there was little chance of improvement. At Bethlem, the number of attendants was increased from twenty-one to twenty-five, with a similar growth in the number of female attendants from eleven to sixteen.[149] Staff–patient ratios had risen from 1:12 in 1836 to 1:20 in 1842. This was high in comparison to other institutions. When Colney Hatch was opened in 1851 it had a staff–patient ratio of 1:13, and Bethlem only caught up under Charles Hood's guidance (see Chapter 26). It was not until the 1880s that Bethlem reached similar staffing levels to those found at the York Retreat.[150] By 1851 the number of staff had fallen again as the Governors' initial enthusiasm declined. There were now twenty male keepers with the highest paid £60, the lowest £11 per annum. On the female side, there were nineteen female attendants, with the salaries ranging between £25 and £14. Attendants were also given a suit of clothes and a hat as well as board and lodging.[151] Female salaries were in line with those offered at other asylums, but for the attendants the salaries were high even by mid-nineteenth-century standards. At the York Retreat, for example, attendants were paid between £18 and £30 per annum, and at Lancaster an 'upper nurse' in 1841 was likely to earn between £10 and £12.[152] This made the hospital an attractive place to work, at least financially, although as the 1851 investigation revealed (see Chapter 25) it did not solve the problems of care or promote high standards.

The changes at Bethlem did not make the Hospital unusual. If anything they brought the Hospital into line with practices being adopted at other asylums in the 1840s.[153] However, there was a difference between the rules, the rhetoric, and the substance. Bethlem could still be accused of mistreating its patients in 1851/2, where seven years earlier it was felt that county asylums were 'extremely well-conducted'.[154]

ADMISSIONS AND LIFE IN THE HOSPITAL

Changes were also made in Bethlem's routine, admission procedure and the type of patients admitted. Here Bethlem was moving from the care of the poor towards an increased emphasis on those ill-suited by class to enter the county and borough asylums. In his *Report*, Martin showed that the admissions procedure had been formalized, but at the same time 'greatly simplified' since 1815. 'Poor lunatics' were admitted 'at all seasons of the year' and were 'provided with every thing necessary for their complete recovery'. However, a provision was added which asserted that assistance could only be given if recovery could be 'effected within twelve months from the time of arrival'. This was a formal recognition of an established practice, but exceptions were made. Patients who gave hope of recovery, even if they had been in the Hospital for more than a year, were permitted to remain. Petitions for patients had to be sent by 'as near a relation of the lunatic as possible [or] in default of such relation, then some friend of the patient or officer of the parish in which such patient resides'. If 'the parties' did not happen to know any Governor, the signature of one would be supplied when the petition was read.[155]

Restrictions were placed on the type of patients admitted. No patient would be treated if they had been insane for more than twelve months, as were those who had been discharged uncured from another asylum. A clear class barrier was placed on admissions that emphasized Bethlem's charitable nature. The rules stipulated that 'those lunatics who are possessed of property sufficient for their decent support in a private asylum' would not be admitted.[156] These patients were expected to pay for their care at private institutions like Ticehurst.[157] Other restrictions were enforced. Pregnant women, 'lunatics in a state of idiocy, afflicted with palsy, or with epileptic or convulsive fits', 'lunatics having the venereal disease or the itch', and those blind 'or so weakened by age or by disease as to require the attendance of a nurse, or to threaten the speedy dissolution of life', or 'so lame as to require the assistance of a crutch or a wooden leg' were all excluded.[158] Voluntary hospitals imposed similar restrictions. At Bethlem, these rules were enforced. In 1820 the Marquess of Salisbury had tried and failed to have a patient with a crutch admitted to Bethlem. Although he was a Governor, the Bethlem Subcommittee informed him they 'were of opinion that it could not be acceded to'.[159] These restrictions were to be severely criticized in the future, but the Charity Commission recognized that they were 'intended to extend the sphere of utility of the hospital, by preventing the reception of persons whose cure is improbable, or whose infirmities would cause them to engross too large a share of the attention of the keepers or nurses'.[160] Admission to a county asylum was less restricted and regulated.

After the petition and certificates had been filled in and signed, they were passed over to the Steward. On the following Friday the case was considered by the Governors who required 'some one who was really acquainted with the circumstances of the patient, as also with the other facts', to attend to give any further information that might be required. This was not necessary if the applicant resided more than ten miles from London if the petition was accompanied by an 'account from the officiating parish minister of the patient's station and circumstances in life', with a letter from a medical practitioner containing a full statement of the patient's case. If the decision was taken to admit and there was a vacancy, the patient would be admitted on the following Friday 'at the hour of ten precisely'. Punctuality was essential because the Physicians were required to see and report upon every case before the meeting of the Bethlem Subcommittee at eleven.[161] There were variations in the number of petitions admitted from month to month (for 1836, see Table 24.1).

Table 24.1 Admissions for 1836

Month	Petitions presented	Petitions approved	Petitions postponed	No attendance	Petitions rejected
January	23	22	1	0	0
February	21	19	2	0	0
March	20	17	2	1	0
April	35	31	4	0	0
May	31	28	2	0	1
June	34	29	1	0	4
July	41	35	5	0	1
August	19	15	2	0	2
September	25	20	4	1	0
October	23	23	0	0	0
November	19	17	2	0	0
December	20	17	3	0	0
Total	311	273	28	2	8

Source: *Report of the Commissioners*

In 1851 344 curable patients had been admitted, 60.7 per cent of whom were female, reflecting a national trend that lasted into the twentieth century where more women than men were admitted into asylums.[162] This was twenty-six more than the preceding year but 'considerably more than the usual average of the number discharged cured'.[163] The Governors were trying to show that Bethlem was a successful institution with a high cure rate, a situation encouraged by the move to admit early, rather than chronic, cases.

Each part of the patient's day was carefully controlled. Patients rose at six in the summer and seven in winter with breakfast served at eight; dinner at one; tea at five and 'ordinary bed-time' at eight. Patients in the different galleries took their meals in company. These were sent up in portions on wooden trenchers. The meat was divided by the nurses, and the patients themselves were 'only intrusted with implements made of bone'. For Martin the 'cheerful appearance' of the meals at Hanwell and at Nottingham had provided a 'striking contrast to the gloom of a dinner at Bethlem'.[164] There had been some discussion in 1822 as to whether earthenware should be substituted, but it had been decided that it was 'not expedient'.[165] Knives and forks were finally introduced in 1851 and crockery was provided instead of wooden platters and bowls. This change alone must have improved the reception of the dietary, which even the Matron felt should be extended. There was one powerful sanction to make patients eat. If they refused their food, the Apothecary administered it to them 'by means of a stomach pump'.[166] Force-feeding was an accepted asylum practice, and Haslam had earlier described the process. This was something to be feared.

At night, patients were locked in their rooms and their clothes were removed. Security remained vital at day and night. Attendants slept on the ward to provide constant attendance. This was common in asylums.[167] One attendant was placed in the servants' hall located in the centre of the building to provide a watch throughout the night. It was he who supplied 'the wants of those male patients who required nocturnal attendance', although staff were 'frequently disturbed at night by the patients, particularly those recently admitted'.[168] Visiting was strictly controlled and was subject to the 'approbation of the medical officer'. Each visitor was instructed to 'avoid all irritating topics', and only 'fruit, biscuits, a little tobacco or snuff, and trifling presents of that nature' were allowed into Bethlem. Visitors were even searched to prevent any dangerous objects reaching the patients. Despite the restrictions, visits were usually anticipated with much pleasure. Patients faced further constraints on the mail they received. All letters had to be read by the Matron or Apothecary and those thought likely to 'cause agitation which might retard recovery, or aggravate the disorder' were suppressed until they could be 'safely communicated'. News of death and other unpleasant circumstances was broken gradually.[169] In all circumstances it was felt necessary to protect the patients and to remove any influence that was likely to hinder their care. A common asylum culture was to develop during the nineteenth century with the growth of county and borough asylums.[170] Bethlem already had much of the basis of this by the 1840s.

Attempts were made to promote the comfort and care of the patients, at least in the rules. This was the asylum's chief function during the nineteenth century, with doctors able to do little for the insane. The patients, 'especially those who [had] been long in the Hospital', were grateful for these efforts.[171] By 1851 numerous 'indulgences' had been introduced. For the Governors these included fireplaces in the dining room and a better diet. Above all, gas started to be used in 1850 for lighting, making the premises more cheerful. A new window in the basement had made 'the female side . . . much more agreeable'.[172] The view that Bethlem was at least trying to improve conditions contrasts with what the Lunacy Commission reported in 1852. However, it might be argued that the Hospital had substantial problems to overcome in 1815. Although improvements were made, these were relative to conditions in the new county asylums and what the recently established Lunacy Commission, prejudiced against Bethlem and with their own agenda, believed to be suitable.

After the 1815 Select Committee more emphasis was placed on providing clothing 'with a view to the warmth of the extremities'. All patients were given flannel drawers, with flannel waistcoats for the men. Care was taken to prevent 'any eccentricity in dress, and to render the appearance of every patient as rational as well as decent as it may be possible'. Conformity was the key and essential to discipline. All patients were made the same. The amount spent was not large: between 1828 and 1837 on average £94 per annum, less than £1 per annum for each person, was spent on clothing. Considerable emphasis was placed on cleanliness. Patients deemed 'capable' were required to wash and comb themselves daily; others were washed and combed by their attendants. 'Dirty patients' were cleaned 'whenever occasion require[d] it', and the Steward and Matron, not the Physicians, decided when warm or cold baths were used, 'except where prohibited by the Physicians'. Those patients confined to bed were shifted every two or three days to a different room, so that 'every article of furniture about them [could] be thoroughly cleansed and purified, and the room whitewashed'.[173] All linen was washed regularly and destruction of blankets was 'exceedingly great'. 'Under ordinary circumstances', the sheets of the female patients were changed once a week, those of the men every fortnight. The basement patients did not use sheets, but slept between blankets placed upon loose straw which was moved daily.[174]

An emphasis on cleanliness and isolation of sick patients in their rooms ensured that the outbreak of infectious diseases at Bethlem was controlled. The Charity Commission considered that most were healthy, and those received 'in a weakly state' usually improved after admission. Typhus was rare and no case of cholera was reported at Bethlem during the 1832 epidemic. Great precautions were taken to prevent cholera and the Hospital's dietary was changed to include meat every day. However, Bethlem was not entirely free of disease. In 1836/7 there was a severe influenza outbreak and almost every patient who died before June 1837 was found to have diseased lungs.[175]

The 1843 *General Report* provides a clear indication of the type of patients admitted. It identified 'a class of patients . . . unable from reduced pecuniary circumstances, to purchase the comforts and assistance of experienced medical advice, or to pay for residence in a private asylum, and yet above the class entitled to the benefits of a county pauper asylum'.[176] In 1851, thirteen of the male curable patients were clerks, the biggest occupational group. There were also ten carpenters, a musician, a pianoforte-maker, an artist, an architect, a tutor, a medical student, two publicans and two clergymen.[177] The 1843 *Report* showed that Bethlem was already 'greatly favour-[ing] the admission of persons in a superior class of life to that perhaps contemplated in the original foundation'. The Governors supported this move by arguing that: 'when the ample provision which is now made by parishes in the counties of Middlesex, Surrey and Kent, for lunatic patients entitled to parochial relief, is considered, it must be conceded that the Bethlem Subcommittee have exercised a sound and judicious discretion in this respect'. A move to admit a different type of patient was enough to support the Governors' claims that 'more real charity is displayed in giving the temporary succour of this Hospital to such a class of patients as above enumerated' than before. The *Report* went on to explain that Bethlem was now for those who are 'struggling to maintain themselves in respectability by mental or bodily exertion, than in admitting those who are entitled to parochial relief'.[178] The Hospital was carving out a new role for itself, given the growth of county asylums after 1808 and the 1845 Lunacy Act, which ensured the development of a national system of state asylums. At Bethlem, the trend towards more middle-class patients was to continue throughout the century (see Chapter 26), with further shifts in policy.

CONCLUSION

All this looked and sounded good, suggesting that reforms had been made. However, the Charity Commission in 1837 had already posed a dangerous question that continued to be asked with increasing frequency. 'It may be questioned', Martin wrote, 'whether the exemption of Bethlem from visitation under the Acts 9 Geo.IV.c.40, and 2 and 3 Wil.IV,c.107, is in any way beneficial'. The reason that he gave was only one of many that were advanced:

> The small number of the medical officers, and the total absence of a medical school, the physicians being only permitted to take two pupils, and in fact rarely receiving any, seems to render an effective visitation particularly desirable. In general hospitals the presence of rival practitioners, their success depending upon their reputation, and their practice closely watched by numerous classes of intelligent pupils, has no small effect in promoting the advancement of medicine and surgery, and in securing the good treatment of the patients. At Bethlem there is no such stimulus to exertion . . .

Martin felt that the closed nature of the Hospital prevented 'the present system of conciliation and kindness from being pushed to its full extent, and thus retard the attainment of those improvements which are still attainable'. There was a warning here. The Commission suggested that 'the present weekly visits of the Committee seem calculated rather to prevent abuses on the part of the keepers and inferior officers, and to guard against uncleanliness and bad food, than to further . . . improvements in . . . medical science'.[179] Wright's misconduct and dismissal implied that the supervision of the Governors was still insufficient. Were there still any abuses to be discovered?

NOTES

1 See Chapters 22 and 23; see House of Commons, *First Report of the Select Committee on Madhouses in England* (London, 1815).

2 For the Charity Commission see Richard Tompson, *The Charity Commission and the Age of Reform* (London: Routledge, 1979).

3 F. O. Martin, *The Report of the Commissioners for Enquiry into Charities for 1837* (London: 1837), 518.

4 *Sketches in Bedlam* (London: Sherwood, Jones & Co., 1823), 293; see Chapter 23, pp. 421–7.

5 Kathleen Jones, 'The Culture of the Mental Hospital', in German Berrios and Hugh Freeman (eds), *150 Years of British Psychiatry* (London: Gaskell, 1991), 17.

6 Richard Hunter and Ida Macalpine, *Psychiatry for the Poor: 1851 Colney Hatch Asylum – Friern Hospital 1973: A Medical and Social History* (London: Dawson, 1974), 87.

7 Martin, *op. cit.*.

8 *Ibid.* 568.

9 Andrew Scull, *The Most Solitary of Afflictions: Madness and Society in Britain, 1700–1900* (New Haven, Conn. and London: Yale University Press, 1993), 117–18.

10 Court of Governors, 10 February 1816.

11 See Chapter 21.

12 General Committee, 5 May 1819.

13 *1843 General Report of the Royal Hospitals of Bridewell and Bethlem and of the House of Occupations*, 59.

14 *Lancet* (1840–1), 315.

15 Cited in Michael Donnelly, *Managing the Mind* (London: Tavistock Press, 1983), 27.

16 *Lancet* (1840–1), 447.

17 *Ibid.* 2 (1840–1), 449.

18 *Standing Rules of Orders for the Governors of the Royal Hospitals of Bridewell and Bethlem with the Duties of the Governors and of the several officers and servants* (London: For the Governors, 1802).

19 Court of Governors, 10 February 1816.

20 Martin, *op. cit.*.

21 Court of Governors, 10 February 1816.

22 Martin, *op. cit.*.

23 See Chapter 21.

24 Court of Governors, 26 June and 4 December 1835.

25 *Standing Rules of Orders*, 15–17.

26 Court of Governors, 18 January 1836.

27 *Ibid.* 4 December 1845.

28 *Ibid.* 20 November 1835.

29 *Ibid.* 21 March 1836.

30 *Ibid.* 18 January 1836.

31 *Ibid.* 5 April 1836.

32 Martin, *op. cit.* 574.

33 Cited in Ida Macalpine and Richard Hunter, *George III and the Mad-Business* (London: Pimlico, 1991), 343.

34 See for example, Scull, *op. cit.* 118, for overlooking this point.

35 Court of Governors, 30 April 1816.

36 *Report from the Committee of Governors of Bethlem Hospital in the General Court Appointed to Inquiry into the Case of James Norris* (London: For the Governors, 1815).

37 See John Haslam, *Illustrations of Madness*, with an introduction by Roy Porter (London: Routledge, 1988), xxxix.

38 Court of Governors, 5 May 1816.

39 Cited in Haslam, *op. cit.* xxxix.

40 Thomas Monro, *Observations of Dr Thomas Monro upon the Evidence taken before the Committee of the Hon. House of Commons for Regulating Madhouses* (London: Bridewell, 1816).

41 Court of Governors, 5 May 1816.

42 Richard Hunter and Ida Macalpine, *Three Hundred Years of Psychiatry* (London: OUP, 1963), 758.

43 Court of Governors, 3 May 1816.

44 General Committee, 13 April 1816; Court of Governors, 17 April 1816.

45 General Committee, 10 May 1816.

46 Martin, *op. cit.* 525–6.

47 *Gentleman's Magazine,* July 1833.

48 *Sketches in Bedlam.*

49 Martin, *op. cit.* 525–6; *Minutes of Evidence taken by the Committee appointed to inquire into the charges inferred against Dr. Wright and his Answer* (London: By the Author, 1830), 47.

50 Edward Monro, *Medical Report,* 25 January 1926.

51 Court of Governors, 10 April 1835.

52 W. Horn, *Reise durch Deutschland, Ungarn, Holland, Italien, Frankreich, Grossbritannien und Irland,* (Berlin: Enslin, 1831), vol. iii, 149.

53 See Hunter and Macalpine, *Three Hundred Years of Psychiatry,* 819. Sir William Ellis, first Resident Medical Superintendent at Wakefield and Middlesex County Asylum, was one leading figure who found phrenology stimulating. See Roger Cooter, 'Phrenology and British Alienists, *c* 1825–1845', in Andrew Scull (ed.), *Madhouses, Mad-Doctors and Madmen* (Philadelphia: University of Pennsylvania Press, 1981), 58–104.

54 *Ibid.* 62.

55 John Haslam, *Medical Jurisprudence* (London: Hunter, 1817), 62.

56 *Minutes of Evidence.*

57 *Sketches in Bedlam.*

58 Martin, *op. cit.*

59 *Minutes of Evidence.* In his reprinted version Wright printed the words 'his Answer' in larger typeface than 'the Charges'.

60 Court of Governors, 26 November 1829.

61 *Minutes of Evidence,* 17.

62 *Ibid.* 31–2.

63 See Ruth Richardson, 'Trading Assassins and the Licensing of Anatomy', in Roger French and Andrew Wear (eds), *British Medicine in an Age of Reform* (London: Routledge, 1991), 75–91; also *idem, Death, Dissection and the Destitute* (London: Harmondsworth, 1989).

64 *Minutes of Evidence,* 46, 49, 52.

65 *Ibid.* 68.

66 *Ibid.*

67 General Committee, 4 November 1830.

68 C. Crommelinck, *Rapport sur les Hopitaux d'Aliénés de l'Angleterre, la France et de l'Allemagne* (Courtrai: Imperimerie de Jaspin, 1842), 31. Crommelinck's 272-page report is quoted by Alexander Walk, 'Some Aspects of the "Moral Treatment" of the Insane up to 1854', *Journal of Mental Science* 100 (1954), 807–37.

69 *1843 General Report,* 57.

70 General Committee, 13 April 1816.

71 Martin, *op. cit.* 565.

72 See C. N. French, *The Story of St. Luke's Hospital* (London: Heinemann, 1951).

73 Akihito Suzuki, 'The Politics and Ideology of Non-Restraint: The Case of Hanwell Asylum', *Medical History,* xxxix (1995), 1–17, and Andrew Scull, 'A Victorian Alienist', in W. F. Bynum, Roy Porter and Michael Shepherd (eds), *Anatomy of Madness* (London: Tavistock Press, 1985), vol. ii, 103–50 for Conolly; Hunter and Macalpine, *Three Hundred Years of Psychiatry,* 769–70.

74 Suzuki, *op. cit.* 10.

75 John Crammer, 'Training and Education in British Psychiatry, 1770–1970', in Hugh Freeman and German Berrios (eds), *150 Years of British Psychiatry: The Aftermath* (London: Athlone, 1996), 212–13.

76 For Morison see Nick Hervey, ' Sir Alexander Morison, 1779–1886: Treating the Mad

Outside Asylum Walls', in Andrew Scull, Charlotte MacKenzie and Nick Hervey (eds), *Masters of Bedlam: The Transformation of the Mad-Doctoring Trade* (Princeton: Princeton University Press, 1996), 123–60.

77 Allan Beveridge, 'On the Origins of Psychiatric Thought', in Hugh Freeman and German Berrios (eds), *150 Years of British Psychiatry: The Aftermath* (London: Athlone, 1996), 349.

78 Alexander Morison, *Outline of Lectures on Mental Disease* (Edinburgh, 1825); *idem, Cases of Mental Disease with practical Observations . . . for the use of Students* (London, 1828), and N. Hervey, 'A Slavish Bowing Down: The Lunacy Commission and the Psychiatric Profession, 1845–60', in W. F. Bynum, Roy Porter and Michael Shepherd (eds), *The Anatomy of Madness*, (London: Tavistock Press, 1985), vol. ii, 215–16.

79 Hunter and Macalpine, *Three Hundred Years of Psychiatry*, 915.

80 *Lancet*, 2 (1840–1), 315–16, 447–8, 664–6, 761–3; *The Times*, 29 October 1941, 7.

81 *Report of the Special Committee Appointed by a General Court to Examine Witnesses and Collect Information on the Expediency of Appointing a Chaplain to Bethlem Hospital* (London: For the Governors, 1817), 32.

82 Scull, *The Most Solitary of Afflictions*, 98.

83 *Report of the Special Committee*, 11ff.

84 Court of Governors, 3 July and 16 July 1816.

85 *Report of the Special Committee*, 24ff.

86 *Ibid.* 32–40.

87 *Ibid.* 41–2.

88 Court of Governors, 6 May 1818.

89 Martin, *op. cit.* 531.

90 *Ibid.*

91 *Sketches in Bedlam.*

92 George Tuthill, *Medical Report* (1816).

93 Douglas Bennet, 'Work and Occupation of the Mentally Ill', in Hugh Freeman and German Berrios (eds), *150 Years of British Psychiatry: The Aftermath* (London: Athlone, 1996), 193.

94 See Samuel Tuke, *Description of the Retreat* (York: S. Tuke, 1813).

95 House of Commons, *Report of Select Committee on Pauper Lunatics in the County of Middlesex* (London 1827); John Conolly, *The Construction and Government of Lunatic Asylums and Hospitals for the Insane* (London: J. Churchill, 1847).

96 Court of Governors, 1849.

97 Tuthill, *Medical Report*, 28 January 1928.

98 *Minutes of Evidence.*

99 Bethlem Subcommittee, 27 November 1848.

100 Martin, *op. cit.*

101 *Ibid.; 1851 General Report*, 71.

102 *1851 General Report*, 71.

103 Mick Carpenter, 'Asylum Nursing before 1914', in Celia Davies (ed.), *Rewriting Nursing History* (London: Croom Helm, 1980), 123–46.

104 *1843 General Report.*

105 *Ibid.*

106 *Ibid.* 40–1.

107 Anne Digby, 'The Changing Profile of a Nineteenth-Century Asylum', *Psychological Medicine*, xiv (1984), 746.

108 For example, at Lancaster a programme of entertainments was only introduced in the 1840s: John Walton, 'The Treatment of Pauper Lunatics in Victorian England', in Andrew Scull (ed.), *Madhouses, Mad-Doctors and Madmen* (Philadelphia: University of Pennsylvania, 1981), 173.

109 Martin, *op. cit.* 526.

110 *1843 General Report*, 43–4.

111 Martin, *op. cit.* 526.

112 Tuthill, *Medical Report* (1819).

113 Tuthill, *Medical Report*, 29 January 1828.
114 *Ibid.*
115 Jeremy Taylor, *Hospital and Asylum Architecture in England 1840–1914: Buildings for Health Care* (London: Mansell, 1991), 135.
116 Jones, *op. cit.* 19.
117 Bethlem Subcommittee, 19 August 1824.
118 Martin, *op. cit.* 525.
119 *Ibid.* 534.
120 *Ibid.* 525.
121 *Ibid.*
122 *1851 General Report*, 51.
123 Martin, *op. cit.* 525.
124 Tuthill, *Medical Report* (1829).
125 *Minutes of Evidence.*
126 Andrew Halliday, *A General View of Lunatics and Lunatic Asylums in Britain and Ireland* (London: T. Underwood, 1828).
127 Court of Governors, 26 November 1829.
128 Walton, *op. cit.* 172.
129 Martin, *op. cit.* 525–6.
130 Anne Digby, *Madness, Morality and Medicine: A Study of the York Retreat 1796–1914* (Cambridge: CUP, 1985), 82; Suzuki, *op. cit.*
131 Walton, *op. cit.* 168.
132 Martin, *op. cit.* 568.
133 See Digby, *Madness, Morality and Medicine.*
134 Court of Governors, 10 February 1816.
135 *Ibid.* 17 July 1816.
136 *Ibid.* 10 February 1816.
137 Martin, *op. cit.* 568.
138 Charlotte MacKenzie, *Psychiatry for the Rich: A History of Ticehurst Private Asylum 1792–1917* (London: Routledge, 1992), 142–3.
139 Martin, *op. cit.* 527.
140 *Ibid.*
141 *1851 General Report.*
142 Walton, *op. cit.* 171.
143 *1843 General Report*, 51.
144 Scull, *The Most Solitary of Afflictions*, 228–9; Suzuki, *op. cit.*
145 E. Santos and E. Stainbrook, 'A History of Psychiatric Nursing in the Nineteenth Century', *Journal of the History of Medicine and Allied Sciences*, iv (1949), 48–73.
146 *1843 General Report*, 52.
147 *Ibid.* 51.
148 See Carpenter, *op. cit.* 123–46.
149 *1843 General Report*, 52.
150 Hunter and Macalpine, *Psychiatry for the Poor*, 92; David Russell, *Scenes from Bedlam* (London: Baillière Tindall, 1996), 42–3.
151 *1851 General Report.*
152 Digby, *Madness, Morality and Medicine*, 144.
153 See Carpenter, *op. cit.* 122–46.
154 Cited in Jones, *op. cit.* 20.
155 Martin, *op. cit.* 521.
156 *Ibid..*
157 See MacKenzie, *op. cit.*
158 Martin, *op. cit.* 521.
159 Bethlem Subcommittee, 6 January 1820.
160 Martin, *op. cit.* 523.
161 *Ibid.*

162 See Elaine Showalter, *The Female Malady: Women, Madness, and English Culture 1830–1980* (London: Virago, 1987).

163 *1850 General Report*

164 Martin, *op. cit.* 565.

165 General Committee, 28 November and 3 December 1822.

166 Martin, *op. cit.* 531.

167 Carpenter, *op. cit.* 133.

168 Martin, *op. cit.* 527.

169 *Ibid.* 532.

170 See Jones, *op. cit.* 16–28.

171 *1843 General Report*, 44.

172 *1851 General Report*, 71.

173 Martin, *op. cit.* 530.

174 *Ibid.*

175 *Ibid.* 532.

176 *1843 General Report*, 3–4.

177 *1851 General Report*, 67.

178 *1843 General Report*, 52.

179 Martin, *op. cit.*

CHAPTER TWENTY-FIVE

INVESTIGATION

——— •◆• ———

Zealous mid-Victorians loved to bring 'evils' to light, usually through 'scandals'. In the 1850s public opinion, stirred by a lively press, focused on a wide range of institutional and governmental 'abuses'. The rhetoric could be overpowering. John Charles Bucknill prefaced his *The Care of the Insane and Their Legal Control* (1880) with a quotation from Tennyson: 'watch what main currents draw the years.' He suggested that the strongest had been 'the reform of domestic institutions ... judged to be inadequate in their working to the humanity, or justice, or economy of the age'.[1] The lunacy reform movement was part of this process. More than the mere passage of time was involved, with reform produced through an interaction of professional and public interests, a point Bucknill did not note. Bucknill himself had no high regard for Bethlem or for those who managed it, viewing the criminal lunatics' department in 1854 as little more than a 'receptacle'.[2] The Hospital was not the utopian asylum that reformers dreamed of. It remained a closed institution, free from inspection until 1851 when after an absence of over thirty years it re-entered the lunacy reform story. When Bethlem was finally included in the national system of investigation (see pp. 480–1), an administration was revealed that, if not the subject of horror, was viewed as scandalous, especially given the changes that had been made between 1816 and 1851 (see Chapter 24). From 1852, a new regime was ushered in that marked a real change in attitude and style, although this did not mean that the Hospital ceased to be controversial.

THE LUNACY REFORM MOVEMENT, INSPECTION AND SECRECY AT BETHLEM

The lunacy reform movement had not been defeated with the unsuccessful efforts to secure legislation after the 1815 Select Committee. In 1827 another Parliamentary committee, largely motivated by the elderly Lord Robert Seymour, a member of the 1815 Committee and Bethlem Governor, and assisted by the young Lord Ashley (later the seventh Earl of Shaftesbury) renewed interest in asylum reform.[3] The cause was again pauper lunatics. Focusing on London's private madhouses, it revealed a pattern of abuse, maltreatment and neglect. The Committee asserted that such conditions were not atypical.[4] Legislation was carefully framed and resulted in the 1828 County Asylums Act, which required local magistrates to present annual reports to the Home Office (Bethlem only produced its first *General Report* in 1843), and the 1828 Madhouse Act.[5] Edward Monro, Bethlem's Physician, and other private madhouse owners campaigned vigorously but unsuccessfully against the Act.[6] Bethlem itself had spent £885 between 1814 and 1828 battling against lunacy bills with more success. This was motivated not by concerns over what inspection might reveal, but by a genuine antipathy to the growth of central government.[7] Although the emphasis now shifted to county asylums, the Madhouse Act had important implications, even though it was only a partial success for the lunacy reform movement. It replaced the inspection of the Royal College of Physicians, that had been created by the 1774 Madhouse Act, with a metropolitan Lunacy Commission of twenty members.[8] The new inspectorate, which was modelled on Benthamite principles, only applied to private asylums.[9] Bethlem, after pushing through an exemption clause, along with county asylums, was excluded.

Although critical of the new Commission, many in the lunacy reform movement secured posts as lay Commissioners where their Evangelical approach antagonized their medical colleagues.[10] The Commission was beset with organizational difficulties, but, learning by experience, it revealed a further catalogue of abuses. Its main aim was 'to spread knowledge of good practices and encourage higher standards'.[11] Success was claimed in ending these new abuses, but further Parliamentary investigations pointed to widespread administrative irregularities and defects in county asylums.[12] Reform was obviously still needed in the asylum system. However, reformers, now grouped around Ashley, and respectable asylum doctors continued to feel that an institutional response to insanity was the best solution. Emphasis was placed on the possibilities of moral reform. Throughout the model was the Quaker York Retreat where the contrast with conditions associated with traditional madhouses and with Bethlem in 1815 (see Chapter 23) was marked.[13] Both doctors and reformers were extremely effective in popularizing their views. A strong utopian view of what asylums should be emerged, epitomized by W. A. F. Browne in *What Asylums Were, Are, and Ought to Be* (1837).[14] Empirical counter-arguments were overlooked, although critics continued to be hostile to institutionalism.[15]

Driven by its faith in institutionalization and with the metropolitan Lunacy Commission showing through its periodic reports that frequent inspection could promote change, the lunacy reform movement forged ahead in the early 1840s. The Metropolitan Commissioners successfully pressed for temporary powers in 1842 to carry out a full inspection of all asylums and workhouses in England and Wales. Bethlem was the only asylum not included, although the publication of its first *General Report* in 1843 did allow the public to draw some comparisons. The 1842 Act produced a burst of activity in asylums as they sought to rectify obvious problems.[16] The Metropolitan Commissioners found that 'the asylums thus brought before our view exhibit instances of about every degree of merit and defect'.[17] Ashley was not good at analysing information, but the weight of evidence proved sufficient. Asylums under the Commissioners' jurisdiction came out well, strengthening the case for inspection. There were enough extreme cases to press an argument for change.[18] The evidence put forward by the lunacy reform movement and the Commissioners convinced both sides of the House of Commons. Ashley translated 'sentiment into action'.[19] Informed opinion moved in favour of creating more asylums to promote early treatment and a national inspectorate. Two bills were presented to secure these measures. The first, the 1845 Lunatics Act (8 and 9 Vict. *c.* 100) established a permanent national Lunacy Commission with powers to inspect all asylums. Its remit was similar to that of the Metropolitan Commissioners, and involved not only inspection but also licensing and reporting. The Act also introduced a new form of certification for admission, and all institutions covered by the Act were required to keep an admissions book and one detailing the use of restraint.[20] The second Act (8 and 9 Vict. *c.* 126) made compulsory the erection of county and borough asylums. New asylums were built at a time when 'the principles of "moral treatment" were in the ascendant', ensuring that they imperfectly incorporated such views.[21] At first the Commission dealt with administrative matters, but increasingly it turned its attention to treatment. Ashley shared Tuke's and John Conolly's views and the Commissioners seemed preoccupied with the extent of restraint, reflecting the interest shown by lunacy reforms in the James Norris case at Bethlem in 1815 (see Chapter 23).[22] The reformers had appeared to triumph. However, the weakness of the former inspectorate was maintained. Commissioners continued to be selected 'whose long acquaintance with private practice and traditional forms of care undermined the board's standing as an independent and impartial authority'.[23] The Lunacy Commission was frequently criticized and continued to fight lengthy battles with local magistrates and institutions imbued with a distrust of centralization to secure the aims of national legislation.

For Bethlem the 1845 Act was a repeat of the 1828 Act. The *Lancet* believed that the Hospital's continued exemption from inspection ensured that Bethlem had largely escaped independent judgment. This was blamed on the Hospital's connection to the City of London, an object of scorn for the journal's founder, Thomas Wakley.[24] It explained that among the 'blemishes' of the 1845 Act, 'the most reprehensible, the most unconstitutional, the most pregnant with the dangerous abuses, was the surreptitious exemption of Bethlem from the operations of the Act'.[25] For most charity asylums proposals for a Lunacy Commission were viewed with a suspicion that owed much to the dislike of central government. Bethlem's exemption clause had been struck out in the House of Commons, but was reinstated without debate in the Lords. The Hospital had a considerable lobby in Parliament: in 1845 there were at least nineteen Governors in the House of Commons and thirteen in the Lords.[26] Doubtless the presence of a state-sponsored criminal lunatics' department at Bethlem from 1816 (see Chapter 22) had been in part responsible for the exemption. The Hospital was the only asylum to be so favoured. The *Lancet* felt this was a matter of public interest and constantly called for more information about the Hospital and its inclusion in the national system of inspection.[27] Such journalistic comment influenced Parliament.

However, it was neither a journalist, a 'mad doctor', nor the Governors of a partially reformed Bethlem who propelled the process of public investigation of the Hospital in 1851. It was the patients, 'persons who felt that they had a just cause of complaint' against it. They approached the Lunacy Commissioners with the help of the Alleged Lunatic's Friend Society, some of whom had already sought opportunities to intervene. In 1847 the Lunacy Commissioners had tried to enter the Hospital and in 1848 another application had been withdrawn on the grounds of insufficient evidence. A further request had been dropped in April 1851 on the same grounds (see pp. 467–8). Unlike Edwin Chadwick at the Board of Health, Ashley was always prepared to compromise, to wait for an opportunity; and complaints from patients in 1851 provided an ideal excuse. For Ashley 'the Commission's entry into Bethlem . . . was symbolic of a lifelong struggle with his father'. The latter had actively opposed the lunacy reformers and was a Governor of Bethlem. Ironically the invitation to investigate came ten days after his death.[28] With Bethlem excluded from the 1845 Act, the Commissioners had to obtain the special authority of Sir George Grey, Home Secretary under Sir Robert Peel, to make an investigation.[29] The Evangelical and paternalistic Grey was himself interested in lunacy reform, having served as a Metropolitan Commissioner. He proved an uncertain, but important ally for the Commissioners.[30] For the *Lancet*, 'the facts, or the heavier suspicions which could move the Commissioners to take so extraordinary a step' demonstrated the gravity of the case as much as the 'impolicy' of exempting Bethlem from the ordinary jurisdiction 'appointed by the law to watch over the insane'.[31] The Hospital was once more exposed to public inspection, although this time for the last time.

COMPLAINTS OF ILL-TREATMENT

The Lunacy Commissioners had become increasingly interested in Bethlem throughout 1851, with more and more patients complaining about ill-treatment. They were already certain what they would find in the Hospital and were prejudiced against it. However, when the Treasurer, J. Johnson, inspected Bethlem in May 1851, the month when the Great Exhibition opened in Hyde Park, he found everything in 'good order'. The Commissioners were not so certain, and a month later they paid their first official visit.

Complaints from patients had been received in 1847 and 1848, and concern about abuse had already been raised and investigated in April 1851. A letter of complaint had been sent from T. J. Hyson, the father of a patient, to Bethlem's President, Sir Peter Laurie. In polite and respectful tones, Hyson claimed 'a case of either cruelty or wanton neglect, in which my Poor Girl (our only child) has fallen a sacrifice caused by or through the neglect of one of the Female Nurses or Keepers'. Shortly after his daughter (Hannah) had been admitted, Hyson and his wife had become anxious, and when informed that 'bad symptoms had appeared' they immediately went to the Hospital:

> What our feelings were I hardly can tell, my Poor Girl could not stand, and was a complete Idiot. But, sir, what was my horror when called up stairs by her Mother and others, when they had undressed her to put her to bed, her body, her legs, and her arms has above 20 wounds and lacerations on them, 2 also on her face; her bones ready to start through the skin, how caused or inflicted no one who has seen her but wish and desire to know.

Hyson had no doubt 'ere these lines reach you my Poor Girl will be in her Coffin, but that shall not prevent your satisfying yourself as to the truth of my statement'. Four days after the receipt of this letter, the Governors asked Alexander Morison as Physician and William Lawrence as Surgeon to examine the state of Hannah's body. They carried out a post-mortem along with William Wood, the Apothecary, and in the presence of independent 'medical attendants' and Hyson. All present signed certificates stating that Hannah's death was caused by 'General Paralysis', that her body was emaciated, and that the bruises on it were not caused by ill usage. It was explained that Hannah had been in 'a violent state for two or three weeks before death', and that a 'slight scratch' on her face had been reported to Morison and Edward Thomas Monro, the Physicians. The certificate ended with the words 'there was no evidence that [Hannah] had sustained any injury which could in any way have hastened her death'. The Governors felt vindicated. From this they concluded that 'the charge of cruelty against the Keepers had not been made out'. The distraught Hyson, still demanding 'justice', was not satisfied. In a series of letters he asked for written copies of the evidence and a rehearing, which was agreed to by the Governors. Unfortunately Hyson was unable to attend because of 'indisposition' and did not suggest any new date. By then the matter was in a sense out of his hands. It had become public. In May 1851, Hyson had written to Johnson stating that he had 'refrained from giving any publicity to the affair and whatever may have appeared in the Public Journals' had not been his 'doings in any way'.[32] The *Lancet*, however, believed that it was largely to Hyson that the public owed their debt for revealing the abuses at Bethlem.[33]

It was not the case of Hannah Hyson that generated most publicity in 1851 but that of Ann Morley. She had been admitted on 6 October 1850 and was discharged two-and-a-half months later on 27 December. Soon after her discharge, Ann was admitted to Northampton Lunatic Asylum where the Admissions Officer, Dr Nesbitt, found her 'in a most deplorable condition'. He informed the Lunacy Commissioners that her

> system was so enfeebled that she was unable to sit up, she had prolapsus of the *uterus* and *anus* with great mucous discharges and suffered severely from *tenesmus*. Her lower extremities were livid and *oedemalous* and their motions paralysed. On the hips and *nates* were a great many abrasions of the surface; varying in size.

Nesbitt attributed these to straw. He went on to report that 'on different parts of her body' she had 'copper coloured eruptions. She was quite unconscious of the calls of nature and her urine and faeces passed under her.' Having described her grim condition, Nesbitt reported that Ann was made comfortable at Northampton, where she was given medicine and a generous diet. Ann immediately started to improve and was 'grateful for the attention'.

With recovery, Ann started to complain about her treatment at Bethlem. Her sister claimed that within a few days of admission, Ann had been given a black eye, presumably by a nurse. Other accusations of mistreatment followed. Ann spoke of being placed in the basement, where she was expected to sleep on straw in the cold. Her nurse, apparently known to the patients as 'Black Sall', although this was hotly denied, was seen as cruel. It was reported that on one night Ann had her 'quilt' removed and she spent the night exposed. On another she was given a shower bath, while on a third night she was made to stand in a wash-tub despite being seriously ill. Nurses were apparently in the habit of addressing her in abusive terms. When she left Bethlem, Ann was emaciated and suffered from severe back pains, a result of her having to sleep on the floor. Nesbitt accepted these statements at face value because he felt Ann was 'remarkable for truthfulness and more desirous of burying in oblivion that part of her life spent in Bethlem'.[34] There was a clash of medical evidence here, however (as there was not in the case of Hannah Hyson). The Lunacy Commissioners, with what appeared to be a premeditated plan of action, used Ann's case as their reason for intervening.

INVESTIGATION

According to Hervey, 'from the outset the Commission observed only the barest decencies'.[35] Four Commissioners (Dr John Robert Hume, Bryan Waller Proctor, William George Campbell and Samuel Gaskell who had been appointed to the Commission two years earlier) visited Bethlem on 28 June.[36] With Gaskell at their head it was not a group likely to return a favourable verdict. However, the letter announcing the visit only arrived the day after it had occurred. As the Governors were keen to establish later, it only entitled the Commissioner to visit – not to start an inquiry. This was overlooked and the Lunacy Commission launched an immediate investigation that was to last six months. No indication was given how many visits had been made. Evidence was presented on nine different days. It was simply explained that the investigation had been 'extended and prolonged on account of fresh evidence having been from time to time tendered for our consideration, and by the fact that the testimony given upon one or more occasions rendered it expedient to pursue further some particular branch of the enquiry'. There was no statement of how the search for extra evidence had been pursued. The names were given, however, of the twenty-seven witnesses examined, beginning with Johnson, although initials were used for inmates examined and for their relatives. Evidence was heard from every level of the Hospital's administration, and all the staff were questioned.[37]

The final report was finished in February 1852 and presented to Parliament in December. No attempt was made to attack particular individuals as had been done in 1815.[38] The Governors were not provided with convenient scapegoats as they had been with John Haslam and Thomas Monro. Instead, the Commission focused on management. Their overriding purpose was to emphasize that Bethlem was poorly managed even by the standards they had set themselves.[39] The Commission did not deviate from this view, concerned as it was to paint the Hospital black. Ashley took a leading role. The investigation was not conducted in such a manner that the twelve conclusions reached were adequately substantiated, even if the final points were essentially correct. The Governors were not wrong therefore in condemning 'the unusual and, as they consider, the objectionable manner' in which the Commissioners had conducted their enquiry. In their *Observations*, they made several highly relevant points on this mode of procedure. No communication was made to them of 'the existence of any complaint on the nature of the charges which were to be answered . . . previously to such an enquiry being instituted'. No-one was allowed to represent the Governors at the inquiry, so they were not in a position to respond to any charges made until afterwards. When giving evidence witnesses connected with Bethlem were not informed that any specific complaint existed or was under investigation. Witnesses were not permitted to see their evidence before it was printed or to correct errors that arose from 'hasty examination' or 'the mistakes of the shorthand writer and of transcription'. This was not common practice for a Select Committee. Leading questions were used to good effect to solicit the information the Commissioners wanted. For example:

> *Q.2718*, If you were asked the question where should you say the fault was to be found principally: in what department? *A*. The fault is to be found with Dr. Wood.
> *Q.2719*, You think that he is indolent and careless? *A*. Yes.
> *Q.2720*, And he does not take sufficient trouble, you think? *A*. no.
> *Q.2721*, he does not keep the Attendants in sufficient order? *A*. Yes that is what it is.[40]

These were put to William Marson, a disgruntled former employee of Bethlem who had left 'because the money was so small: and the treatment I received was very bad indeed'. Hearsay and inference were accepted, but only when it presented Bethlem in a poor light. Bethlem's Governors argued that the Commissioners should have

> observed the course followed by every impartial tribune, viz to communicate to any person whose conduct is the subject of enquiry the specific charge against him, and to afford him the full opportunity of [responding to] it in the presence of those who make it.[41]

For the Hospital the *ex parte* nature of the investigation was 'in contravention of the first principle of justice', although the Governors did not assert that the Commissioners had been motivated by 'any desire to act unjustly or [and there was a sting here] to create a prejudice against the only institution exempted from their jurisdiction'.[42] Such dubious tactics were shown to contrast with the Governors' willingness to cooperate. Throughout the investigation, they afforded 'every facility' to enable the Commissioners to pursue their inquiry.[43] As far as the Governors were concerned they had nothing to hide. However, concerned to avoid a repetition of 1815, they consistently denied the charges made against them and presented their own published reply to the allegations.

Nesbitt spoke of the horrors of Ann's 'system'. The Commissioners, on the basis of his and other evidence, wrote of the horrors of the Bethlem system. They considered that her case was not exceptional. It was argued that all the female patients in the basement were 'dirty and refractory' and that they slept naked, in spite of the bitter cold, in cots filled with straw covered by a blanket. For the sake of warmth they crept under the straw, which, being rough and sharp and dirty, caused them to develop sores and scabies on their bodies. The Commissioners had no doubt that they were roughly treated. Because they were dirty, they were only washed down with cold water and a mop was used.[44] These were shocking allegations. In the course of questioning, the Matron, Wood, Monro and Morison all denied knowledge of these conditions. Monro himself viewed such conditions as appalling. This in itself was taken as evidence of 'culpable laxity' prevailing in 'the internal supervision of the hospital'.[45] It was clear that the rules and practice were very different. The Commissioners built their case around this to support their overriding argument that Bethlem was in need of reform and regular outside inspection.

The medical staff in their defence claimed that everything was left to the Treasurer, who was resolutely defended throughout the investigations by the Governors. The Commissioners themselves described his duties as 'very extensive'. Officers and other staff resident at Bethlem appeared 'to be in a great measure under his control', although in the Commissioners' opinion he had delegated too much power to the Matron. According to the rules, the Treasurer was to superintend the affairs of the Hospital 'both as to its attendants and details', but had no power to interfere with the medical officers or Matron 'except as an individual member of the Board', or to rescind existing rules except in cases of emergency. On one occasion, however, he had delegated to the Matron 'the very important power of classifying, employing and generally managing and arranging the female patients, without reporting such alteration to the Committee, or obtaining their sanction thereto'.[46] This, the Commissioners felt, was injudicious. They favoured a doctor in control. For them, it seemed a weakness of the system that neither Johnson nor the other members of the Bethlem Subcommittee ever visited the Hospital at night. Nor did they ever see patients unaccompanied ('regrettably' in the opinion of the Commissioners) by an attendant. The patients had no opportunity, therefore, of making complaints. Nor were any written records made of their visits 'and the particular matters observed calling for reprehension, inquiry, or amendment'. It was a fact that Monro and Morison visited Bethlem for an hour or two only four times a week.[47] Bethlem had already been criticized in 1843 for inadequate visiting and had sought to redefine the Physicians' duties. New rules stipulated that 'one of the Physicians should attend once every day to visit the patients, and that they both meet at the Hospital one day in the week, in order that they may consult on any care requiring their joint opinion'.[48] The Commission showed that this had not been so and added that they had 'no means of ascertaining' how far the Physicians had 'made themselves acquainted with neglect or abuses', except in relation to particular cases like that of Ann Morley.[49] Under questioning, Monro declared that he did not inspect the beds and clothing every time he saw the patients, although he did try to reassure the Commissioners that if he found anything wrong he put it right. Monro admitted that he did not often look inside the beds or go to the Hospital at night.[50] It was clear that neither Monro nor Morison prescribed for all their patients or signed 'such case-books as are required to be kept by the Rules and Orders'.[51] The Commissioners took a serious view of such actions, especially as records generally provided their only means of assessing practice.[52]

Wood came in for substantial criticism. Evidence suggested that the same problems had continued to recur after the 1815 Select Committee. The Commission reported that 'by far the greater portion of the medical treatment of the patients' devolved to the Apothecary. Monro and Morison even argued that Wood was not up to the task. Consequently, it appeared that 'his own peculiar duties [were] neglected'. Similar concerns had been expressed in 1815 about Haslam, but in 1851 the condemnation went further. The Commissioners argued that Wood neglected to keep his accounts, rarely visited the wards at night, and only occasionally saw the female wards.

In their view this left far too much responsibility to the Matron, Henrietta Hunter, daughter of Haslam.[53] Hunter faced 217 questions that included every aspect of her duties and the running of the Hospital. She denied every accusation of ill-treatment, but the Commissioners agreed that she had been negligent, contradicting Monro and Morison's earlier assessment that Hunter worked with 'unwearied kindness'.[54] The Commissioners were unprepared to believe that Hunter was unaware of the fifteen female patients who slept naked in the basement, and when she assured the Commissioners that this was not true they could only attribute her answer to 'the fact of her never seeing these patients after their being placed in their beds at night'.[55] For an officer who was supposed to be in charge of these cases this was deplorable. When the attendants were questioned, it became evident that contrary to the rules the supervision exercised over them was 'lax and superficial'. 'Entirely unjustifiable' practices prevailed in the wards, although the number of patients restrained had been dramatically reduced under George Tuthill and Morison in line with the non-restraint movement (see Chapter 24). The Commissioners were, however, uncertain in the absence of medical records 'to what extent these abuses may have prevailed in the Hospital in former times', although they felt that they were now 'sufficiently clear'.[56] No mention was made of the fact that restraint had been reduced and no effort was made to compare Bethlem to other asylums. If this had been done, Bethlem would not have appeared so backward, but this was not the aim of the Lunacy Commission.

The most serious point about the deficiencies of the system made by the Commissioners concerned the special responsibility of Bethlem to 'treat' and 'cure' the insane, a responsibility that derived from its 'peculiar character'.[57] Restrictions were placed on admissions that the Charity Commission had felt in 1837 were designed to ensure that time was not wasted on nursing patients at the expense of others.[58] The Lunacy Commission, with a different agenda, disagreed. It felt that patients were 'picked' on medical grounds, and in social terms 'comparatively few of them' had earned their livelihood by manual or daily labour'. Bethlem was attacked for having a 'great majority' of its patients 'accustomed to observe the proprieties, and [were] fully capable of appreciating the comforts of civilised society'. For the Commissioners such patients were expected to be treated in a private asylum. This was seen to be against Bethlem's purpose as a charitable hospital. The Commissioners were obviously concerned that the Hospital was trying to provide a semblance of private care for the middle classes.[59] Their assessment was not wrong. Facing competition from the new county and borough asylums, Bethlem from 1843 onwards was redefining the type of patient it admitted (see Chapter 24). It argued that state asylums provided care for the poor, leaving the middle classes in an unfavourable position. To solve this, the Governors rationalized that they could offer care for this group while retaining the Hospital's charitable nature.[60] This contrasted with the role the Commissioners believed Bethlem should play.

The Commissioners traced the main problems to the established system of absentee Physicians – leading Monro and Morison to dispute and to attack their findings – and, even more pointedly, to confused and divided responsibilities. They listed twelve conclusions at the end of their *Report*. Five dealt with individual cases. For all five, which included Morley and Hyson, it was asserted that they had been 'subjected to harsh and improper usage from the attendants', neglect by 'the medical and other officers of the institution', and conditions that either placed their lives in 'peril' or 'materially injured . . . bodily health'. From these individual cases, the Commissioners turned to the deficiencies in Bethlem's management. The *Report* concluded that the Bethlem Subcommittee was

> of too fluctuating and uncertain a character; that the duties imposed on the members thereof are too much of a formal kind, and that their investigations into the well-being and comfort of the patients, and the practical working of the institution, are insufficient and are nowhere properly recorded.

Johnson's action over the classification of the female patients was condemned. All the medical staff were accused of performing their duties 'imperfectly'. The Commissioners asserted that 'the Rules and Orders of the hospital, as at present existing, are not well understood; that they tend to produce confusion and mistakes, and should be revised and amended'. Even more worrying for the Commissioners was that the records had not been properly kept. Here Bethlem was shown to be on the verge of breaking the law. Finally, the Commissioners reported that they were 'of opinion that the management and condition of Bethlehem Hospital are in many material respects most unsatisfactory, both in reference to the purposes for which it was founded, and the very large funds by which it is maintained'.[61]

These were sweeping as well as shocking indictments. The Secretary of State sent the *Report* to Laurie on 21 February 1852 and expected an immediate response. There had been no such allegations concerning individuals confined to Bethlem since 1815, but on this occasion even more than then it was not only the conduct of the medical staff and attendants that was attacked but the actions (or lack of them) of the Treasurer and Governors. Only the Steward was left unmentioned. Moreover, it was not only the Governors as a whole who were blamed, but the Bethlem Subcommittee. The allegations relating to the Governors, the Bethlem Subcommittee and Johnson carried considerable force. Those relating to Monro and Morison were treated as unfair. The Governors went on the defensive.

THE GOVERNORS' DEFENCE

The Lunacy Commissioners handled the *Report* in the same manner as they had dealt with the investigation. Given the seriousness of the allegations, the Governors had decided that the *Report* needed to be circulated throughout the Hospital before a reply could be made. They had therefore arranged for it to be printed, only to be told by the Secretary of State (at the behest of the Commissioners) that they could not distribute the printed copies without his sanction. To complicate matters, there had been a change of government in 1852, and the new Secretary of State, Spencer Walpole, did not give his permission to distribute the printed copies until 2 April 1852, and then only on condition that it was transmitted 'in the strictest confidence to the Members of the committee'. The medical staff and others who had been accused by the Commissioners were not included. It was not until 25 June 1852 that permission was secured from Walpole to show the *Report* to the Hospital's officers. This was 'upon condition that such copies *are not made use of* for any purpose except that of preparing answers by the officers to the statements made in the Report'.

Once the *Report* had been received, the Governors made their own inquiry. They responded to the Lunacy Commissioners with *Bethlem Hospital, The Observations of the Governors upon the Report of the Commissioners in Lunacy*, which was presented on 29 November 1852. In it they stated clearly that 'few things are more easy than to excite a cry of cruelty against the management of a lunatic asylum, and few more difficult to disprove'. The Governors acknowledged that in such circumstances the truth was hard to find, but complained that the Commissioners had not helped in determining what this was. After dealing with the procedural problems of the investigation a detailed reply was offered to each of the twelve charges made against the Hospital. Individual cases were dealt with at length. It was explained that two of the patients covered had been 'restored to reason by means of the treatment received in the Hospital'. Over Elinor Webb and Mary Isabella W. it was argued that there was no evidence to show 'that the mode of ill treatment alleged had, at any time existed, as a practice in the Hospital'. In Hannah Hyson's case, the medical evidence presented at her post-mortem was used to demonstrate that Hannah had died, not because of her treatment but of 'a disease of the brain' that had commenced before her admission into Bethlem.[62] The Governors felt that this was irrefutable evidence to counter the Commissioner's claims.

Considerable attention was devoted to the most important case of alleged mis-treatment, that of Ann Morley. At the time, the Governors had blamed her condition on arrival at Northampton largely on the effects of the long journey.[63] After the *Report* they argued that testimony had been presented that was totally ignored. Ann's sister had not explained, as Monro and Johnson knew, that one reason for removing her from Bethlem had nothing to do with the treatment she had received. It had been to get her to sign 'a legal document' that the Hospital felt she could not sign while uncured in their institution. Johnson stated that he would not consent 'on any consideration, to allow her to sign any document, the object being to obtain money for her through such signature; and her friends suggested it would be better to remove her, and take apartments' to procure one.[64] Given concerns about wrongful confinement, the Governors were trying to appeal to popular worries and show that they had acted responsibly.[65]

The evidence in the fifth case ('a strong muscular man') was dismissed. The Governors showed that the chief witness, John Welsh, who had been 'the only person' to speak of specific cruelties, had arrived at Bethlem in August 1851 on trial as an attendant. At the end of two months' probation he had been allowed to stay on for a further trial period, after which he was reported as unsuitable and left on 7 November. Welsh had complained about his treatment and demanded to be appointed 'as of right'. The Bethlem Subcommittee refused to support his claim, declaring that Welsh had 'expressed his determination of going somewhere else, and seeing if he could not get justice there', a remark that was treated by the Subcommittee as 'clear proof of his unfitness'.[66] Others who presented evidence on this case were also shown to be unfriendly to Bethlem. Disgruntled ex-employees were prominent among the witnesses. Some of these were considered 'very illiterate, and of the humblest grade in society, and whose recollection of the subject matter of the evidence must be leavened and perverted by their unsound state when their impressions were formed'. For the Governors this was enough to show that the evidence against the Hospital had not always been the truth.

The Governors were positive in their observations concerning visiting, although they stated cautiously that despite the visiting rules 'it appears that in some cases permission has been refused without medical authority'. 'It is impossible', they added, 'to lay down any inflexible rules for visiting patients, as their medical condition may be such, when the visiting day arrives, as to render it absolutely necessary to prevent an interview.' In general, visiting was very different from the practice pursued in the eighteenth century. Visiting was permitted four days a week, a fact the Governors claimed somewhat disingenuously 'was inconsistent with a system of ill-treatment'. Inspection was supposed to achieve the same purpose. The Visitors' Book contained

> a series of unvarying testimony, especially by the late Earl of Shaftesbury as to the scrupulous cleanliness and good order of the patients, the kindness exhib-ited towards them, and the judicious arrangements made for their employment and amusement to an extent seldom equalled, and still more rarely surpassed, in any Institution of a similar description.[67]

Indeed, when the Duke and Duchess of York and the Duke of Gloucester visited in 1817 they expressed 'the highest satisfaction . . . in the accommodation and treatment of the patients'.[68] Such an appeal was not likely to win over Ashley, who was hostile to his father. The Governors were protesting too much. They were on safer ground, given the attitudes of 1851, in saying that they frowned on night visiting. The Com-missioners themselves clearly viewed it as 'a delicate part of their authority'. In 1847, when they inspected over four hundred asylums, they visited only one at night. Bethlem's Governors explained in terms reminiscent of those used by the Commis-sioners that visiting by 'night is not only open to great abuse, but might expose those who would attempt to carry it into execution to accusations by patients on their discharge, or by their friends and relations'. It was 'certain', they added, that 'unless the Governors assume the actual duties of the officers and servants, and live them-selves in the wards of the Hospital, that it is not possible to ensure, in every instance . . . strict observance of rules.'[69] This was precisely what the Commissioners felt was wrong with Bethlem.

Other points were raised about the Hospital's management. It was argued that the Treasurer had not deprived the resident Medical Officer of 'the power of classifying and employing the female patients inasmuch as these duties remained vested in the Physicians'. In addition, the Governors strongly defended the role of the Bethlem Subcommittee, reserving much of their sarcasm to the contrast of their own situation as unpaid servants of a charity with the 'interested' situation of their 'salaried' inquisi-tors. The Lunacy Commissioners had reported their 'opinion' that the Bethlem Sub-committee was of 'too fluctuating and uncertain a character'. The Governors responded by showing that the attendance of the Commissioners during this 'import-ant investigation' had certainly been of 'a fluctuating and uncertain character'. No single Commissioner heard more than half the evidence, and the nine meetings held during the investigation were presided over by three different Chairmen.[70] The Governors felt that double standards were clearly in operation.

Attention was also turned to allegations of maltreatment. Elinor Webb, 'a violent, abusive, dirty and mischievous' patient, had claimed that patients had been washed with a mop. No other witness corroborated her statement, and Elinor informed the Commissioner that she did not even speak from personal experience. The Governors felt that this was enough to dismiss the claim. Other accusations of ill-treatment were handled in a different fashion. Here the Governors tried to invoke current psychiatric thought to show that Bethlem used practices that were little different from those adopted elsewhere. They argued that the use of straw, properly covered with blankets, was not unsuitable. If anything it was shown as a hygienic measure. It had medical defenders in France and Britain, and the Commissioners of Lunacy themselves had observed in 1844 that 'many lunatics are not only sickly, but so filthy in their habits that they nearly frustrate all efforts to keep them clean; and can only be allowed to sleep upon straw or other bedding which may be thrown away or washed every day'.[71] Having scored this point, the Governors did concede that too many females had been placed in bed without 'a proper supply of night gowns'. They justified the absence of an infirmary on the grounds that the whole of Bethlem 'is an infirmary', but added that even though sick patients were best treated in their own rooms, the provision of 'additional accommodation for the sick' was almost completed.[72]

This capacity to defend vigorously before going on to show that change was already in hand was characteristic of many of the Governors' observations, which were just as inconsistent as the Commissioners' findings. Thus, they defended the role of the Treasurer as manager, but went on to explain that they had already made fundamental changes in Bethlem's administration. They also admitted that there were discrepancies between rule and observance, disapproving of the imperfect manner in which the case books had been kept 'in disregard of the explicit terms of the judicious regulations made by them for this purpose'.[73] They even dared to quote Francis Offley Martin, who had investigated the Hospital for the Charity Commission in 1836.[74] He had found 'room for considerable improvement' and the Governors argued that it had been proof of their willingness 'to profit by any suggestions, that not only have most of the improvements suggested by Mr. Commissioner Martin been adopted, but many other ameliorations introduced of a very important and costly character'.[75] Among them was the diminution of restraint and the increase of employment (see Chapter 24), although this had already been started under Tuthill. The Governors wanted to believe that they had made these improvements, not *in consequence* of the *Report*, but *concurrently* with it. Between 1815 and 1851, Bethlem had carried out moderate reforms, but only the Governors appeared to realize this.

Having defended themselves with such eloquence, the Governors wisely abstained from offering 'any lengthened reference to the Remarks' in the *Report* received from Monro, Morison or Hunter. Monro and Morison prepared their own defence. Wood, who chose not to write to defend himself, bore the brunt of the attack, a point Monro and Morison underlined. They showed no professional solidarity, except in their first joint letter. 'Nearly the whole of the treatment (medical as well as moral) and much of the business of general supervision are at present thrown upon Dr. Wood', Morison told the Governors bluntly, and he was clearly not up to the job.[76] The various comments made by them, with Morison voicing his grievances in the press, showed that both were disturbed by the Governors' lack of faith in them.[77]

Monro's evidence was particularly revealing in that it took so much for granted about 'traditional' attitudes and obligations. After thirty-six years of 'unremitting attendance', he was deeply attached to Bethlem. He blamed the system not himself, informing the Governors that he found it absolutely impossible to be 'cognizant of anything which may take place in their absence'. Monro argued that the Physicians' duties were of 'quite another character, and their standing in society did not admit of so large an apportionment of time as seems to have been contemplated by some'. He complained that it had never been required of him to act as 'a sort of general officer' or to master the details of each inmate's affairs. For Monro the new system appeared

> to incline to that hardworking attention to minute particulars which has never hitherto characterised the mental physician exercising a high profession in a liberal manner; and if the duties of a future medical officer are to be so minute and extensive, and so laborious, he must, indeed, be of a very different grade and calibre from all physicians who have heretofore exercised this high calling.

This was not for him. Monro looked to the Governors, who had long given the Physicians their 'approbation', to vindicate his professional integrity. He reserved the main point immediately in question for a postscript:

> As regards the evidence respecting A.M. I must state that I am very much shocked at its contents if true. I can only hope that the patient had a morbidly sensitive view of what really occurred; but if anything approaching this was the case, I should be among the first to see the necessity of thorough reform and correction of the past in all these details. At the same time I repeat that this department was clearly as distinct from my sphere as that of the architect or cook.[78]

It was a shocking punch-line.

Morison by contrast countered each charge. He added as an appendix a paper he had written in 1844 on the 'Causes of Mental Diseases, as forming part of the Curriculum of National Education' and an account of his experience at Bethlem between 1836 and 1841, which he had printed as a paper at his own expense. He noted Martin's comments in his *Report*:

> The duration of Dr. Morison's visits is from one to four hours or upwards. The curable, incurable, and criminal receive an equal share of attention, depending on the circumstances of each individual case; the patients are visited by him individually, every one of them being considered his own peculiar case, without reference to any other public officer of the establishment.

Since that period, Morison added, his attendance had 'considerably increased'.[79] This account was generally corroborated. In his evidence, the Steward stated that he had known Morison 'in an emergency' to sleep in the Hospital at his request and 'perhaps at Dr. Wood's too'. Morison went on to demonstrate how he had done far more than was formally required. By regulations agreed in 1848 he had been required to attend four times in a week. In fact he had exceeded the number required by 135 attendances. Moreover, he had always written notes on the history of his patients in his private case book so he could consider them 'at my leisure at home'. He felt

477

assertions of dereliction of duty made by the Commissioners could not be substantiated. It was evident to Morison therefore that 'there appear[ed] to be an *animus*
pervading the Report of anything but a liberal and impartial description'.

The *Lancet* was not impressed either by Monro and Morison or by the Governors'
Observations. The journal blamed everything on the absence of inspection.[80] It did not
believe that they constituted 'a calm dispassionate explanation or refutation of the
charges brought against their mismanagement', but were 'a series of angry and
unbecoming reflections upon the motives and conduct of those on whom devolved
the painful duty of detecting and exposing their delinquencies'. The *Lancet* explained
that the *Observations* was nothing more than 'a sinister design to detract from the
presumed impartiality of their judges'. It did, however, agree that the mode of
enquiry had been wrong.

> It is undoubtedly repulsive to the spirit of our institutions to conduct investiga-
> tions concerning grave charges against corporate bodies or individuals in
> secrecy . . . It is to be regretted that neither the Governors nor the medical
> officers were permitted to be present, in person, or by counsel, during the
> inquiry; they ought to have had the opportunity of cross-examining the
> witnesses.

The *Lancet* went on to point out contradictions in the Governors' own approach. The
journal asserted that 'at one moment we find them defending and commending the
practices and regulations condemned by the Report' and 'at the next we find them
assuming credit to themselves for having reformed those practices they had condemned'. It believed that 'the reappearance of MR. MARTIN, with a compendious
epitome of his blue-book under his arm, is an apparition as unexpected as
unwelcome'.[81] The *Lancet* wanted an end to Bethlem's exemption and expressed
vehemently that it had no confidence in the Governors.[82]

The *Lancet* was just as unfriendly to Morison and Monro. For the Journal, 'the
Physicians to Bethlehem Hospital had long held positions not less advantageous to
themselves than important to the community'. They had now proved themselves to
be 'quasi-physicians'. Monro's 'lofty' opinions were described as obsolete and had
placed him in a position where, while the Governors might sympathize with him,
they could no longer protect him.[83] Morison's replies were 'more commonplace'
and even the *Lancet*, faced with his account of his busy timetable, was forced to
exonerate him of the charge of inadequate attendance. However, he had not dis-
proved to their satisfaction the more serious charge of condoning 'abuse', 'neglect'
and 'ill treatment'.[84] The press joined the *Lancet* in condemnation. One writer in the
Journal of Psychological Medicine noted that the 'accusations of systematic cruelties,
violence, and neglect' and the subsequent 'disclosures' had shocked the 'professional and public mind'.[85] From this vantage point Bethlem was a 'model asylum'
only in the sense that it was 'a model of the asylum of half a century ago; a
warning model, set up . . . to strengthen our admiration of what is good by the
hideous exhibition of evil'.[86] He felt that Bethlem 'as an institution for the insane is
three hundred and fifty years too old'.[87] Others were all too willing to agree. For some,
nothing had really changed between 1815 and 1851, except the first names of the
two Monros who in each case were only nominally in charge. The fact that little had

apparently altered, convinced outsiders that something was radically wrong with Bethlem's government. Pressure increased for a more stringent system of external supervision.

AFTERMATH

The *Report* was delivered in confidence to the Governors in February 1852 accompanied by a letter requesting their 'attention to the alleged defects in the management of the Hospital' and expressing 'Sir George Grey's hope that measures [would] be adopted without delay for remedying such defects'.[88] What the Lunacy Commissioners required was clear, and the Governors responded at the same time as they were preparing their *Observations*. Reform took two forms: internal changes to provide a better system of medical administration and modification of existing legalization to include Bethlem.

Internal reform came first. Management changes were made, but the most significant alterations were made in the medical regime. The Commissioners had recommended that in future the Governors should make the principal 'Medical Officer' the 'paramount authority within the Hospital and be responsible for the whole of its management'.[89] They praised the appointment of medical superintendents mainly because it provided someone who could be held accountable for abuse.[90] Similar practices were adopted at county and borough asylums, providing asylum doctors with a professional base.[91] The Governors and Morison had already accepted such an arrangement, which implied *inter alia* that the principal medical officer 'should be subject to no authority' except that of the Bethlem Subcommittee. In their *Observations*, the Governors announced that they had already made changes along these lines.[92] A new Resident Medical Superintendent was appointed. This was Charles Hood and, as is noted in Chapter 26, he presided over a further period of reform.[93] It was within this context that the Governors expressed 'regret' that Monro and Morison had not 'favoured them with more extensive information respecting the particular cases'.[94] They added, making Monro not Morison their chief sacrificial victim, that Monro's remarks to the Commissioners, sent to them after the Governors had changed the system, 'proved the propriety' of what they had done. Neither Morison nor Monro was impressed, but they were made Consulting Physicians. Wood was equally dissatisfied, but with his colleagues against him he decided to tender his resignation, which the Governors accepted.[95] When Morison resigned in April 1853 they gave him an annual pension of £150.[96] They believed that the 'discharge of his duties [had] been at all times characterized by an industrious and kind attention to the patients'.[97] The *Lancet* was not impressed.[98]

Outside Bethlem a different timetable was adopted, although the need for reform was also pushed. The revelations stirred some members of the Court of Common Council of the City of London to seek a further investigation of Bethlem. On 10 March 1852, William Gilpin moved a resolution that the Court should appoint its own Committee to carry out an 'inquiry into the present and recent management at Bethlehem with particular reference to the treatment of patients there'.[99] For them the Hospital was still very much a City institution, although many believed that it was acting too late. The spirit of the resolution was applauded by some of Bethlem's Governors who wanted to end the secrecy and condemnation surrounding the Hospital, but on the intervention of Alderman Anderton the motion was withdrawn. Anderton told the Council that in future Bethlem no longer wished the exemption clause to apply. He explained that its Governors were 'most desirous that the Hospital should be visited as other places of confinement were, if it were for no other reason than that of preventing the repetition of such calumnies as had been vented against them'. This was a practical and unavoidable stance and a move being pressed for by the Lunacy Commissioners and public opinion. For the *Lancet*, the Governors' newly expressed desire, while welcome, was simply a sign that they had been forced 'to concur with a seeming grace in what they [were] unable to prevent'.[100]

The question of the Common Council's proceedings was raised in the House of Commons by Sir Benjamin Hall, MP for Marylebone, who in 1854 was to become President of the short-lived and controversial General Board of Health. He asked the Government whether any further report on Bethlem would be presented and if the Hospital's exemption would stand. He was told by Henry Fitzroy, Under-Secretary for the Home Department, that a clause had been introduced into a Lunacy Bill placing Bethlem on 'the same footing' as other 'establishments for the care and treatment of lunatics'.[101] For the *Lancet*, less sure than Fitzroy about the likelihood of the bill's passing, this was still not good enough.[102] The bill did pass, however, on 12 August 1853. The need to include the Hospital in the national system of inspection was widely recognized, but other measures were implemented. Here Bethlem was influential. Given the poor record-keeping in the Hospital, the Act required medical officers to make a special note of all patients under restraint and the reasons for it. Similar records were to be kept on medical treatment.[103] According to Fennell, the 1853 Act 'completed the system of regulation which was to persist for the life of the Lunacy Commission'.[104] An old issue was settled and any sense of secrecy was now dispelled. Bethlem, independent though it remained in its governance, was treated, at least as far as inspection was concerned, as part of a national system.

At the end of the 'Bethlem affair' nothing was entirely cleared up as far as individuals were concerned. Motives remained in dispute. Monro continued as Consulting Physician within the new regime. Some continued to be unhappy with the outcome. For Joseph Williams, an Edinburgh-educated London doctor and author of a volume, *Insanity, its Causes, Prevention and Cure* (1852), the Commissioners in Lunacy had not gone far enough. For him

> the mortality at Bethlem has indeed been great; greater by far than meets the public eye! Dying patients are discharged to die at home! and thus the registry of 'deaths' is smaller than it should be; and it must never be forgotten that all the patients received in bethlem are picked cases.[105]

Debates in the press continued. The inquiry had terminated in convicting the officials and servants of the asylum of shameful neglect, and was unreserved in its condemnation of the whole system of government and management as inefficient and mischievous. Bethlem was shown again to be a 'scandal' to the public and 'a foul blot' on 'the character of the profession'.[106] The ultimate outcome, with changes made inside Bethlem and the end of its exemption from the 1845 Act, was to satisfy the

Commissioners. However, they 'soured relations' with the Governors.[107] Under the 1853 amending Act the Lunacy Commissions were now given power after November 1853 to inspect Bethlem as regularly as they inspected other asylums.[108] Equally important, the Governors themselves introduced a new pattern of organization inside the Hospital that conformed to the pattern the Commissioners knew best and always recommended. New rules were devised for the staff. Under Charles Hood a new system was ushered in that was supported by the Lunacy Commissions, although they continued to frown on Bethlem's location in Southwark. Bethlem had passed its nadir.

NOTES

1 J. C. Bucknill, *The Care of the Insane and Their Legal Control* (London: R. Clay & Taylor, 1880), 1.

2 J. C. Bucknill, *Unsoundness of Mind in Relation to the Criminal Act* (London: Highley, 1854), 119.

3 Seymour was the only survivor of the 1815 Select Committee: Andrew Scull, *The Most Solitary of Afflictions: Madness and Society in Britain, 1700–1900* (New Haven, Conn. and London: Yale University Press, 1993), 126. For Shaftesbury, see Geoffrey Finlayson, *The Seventh Earl of Shaftesbury 1801–1885* (London: Methuen, 1981).

4 House of Commons, *Report on Pauper Lunatics in the County of Middlesex* (London: 1827).

5 *1843 General Report of the Royal Hospitals of Bridewell and Bethlem and of the House of Occupations*; Kathleen Jones, *Asylums and After* (London: Athlone, 1993), 59.

6 See Nick Hervey, 'A Slavish Bowing Down: The Lunacy Commission and the Psychiatric Profession', in W. F. Bynum, Roy Porter and Michael Shepherd (eds), *Anatomy of Madness* (London: Tavistock Press, 1985), vol. ii, 101, 120.

7 F. O. Martin, *An Account of Bethlem Hospital: Abridged from the Report of the Late Charity Commissioners* (London: 1853).

8 Jones, *op. cit.* 59.

9 Following Benthamite principles, other bodies were being formed in the early Victorian period that aimed to promote inspection and reform. These included the Factory inspectors, Poor Law Commissioners, and Chadwick's Board of Health, but according to Nick Hervey, 'The Lunacy Commission 1845–1860' (unpublished Ph.D., University of Bristol, 1987), 3–4, where these other bodies matched O. MacDonagh, *Early Victorian Government 1830–1870* (London: Weidenfield & Nicolson, 1977) thesis, the Lunacy Commission did not, especially as it was protected from political interest and interference.

10 Hervey, 'A Slavish Bowing Down', 101–3.

11 Jones, *op. cit.* 76.

12 For example, see House of Commons, *Report from the Select Committee on Hereford Lunatic Asylum, with Minutes of Evidence* (London 1839).

13 See Anne Digby, *Madness, Morality and Medicine: A Study of the York Retreat 1796–1914* (Cambridge: CUP, 1985).

14 W. A. F. Browne, *What Asylums Were, Are, and Ought to Be* (Edinburgh: Black, 1837).

15 Scull, *op. cit.* 132–46.

16 See John Walton, 'The Treatment of Pauper Lunatics in Victorian England', in Andrew Scull (ed.), *Madhouses, Mad-Doctors and Madmen* (Philadelphia: University of Pennsylvania, 1981), 171.

17 Cited in Scull, *The Most Solitary of Afflictions*, 161.

18 See *Report of the Metropolitan Commissioners in Lunacy to the Lord Chancellor* (London: Bradbury & Evans, 1844).

19 Jones, *op. cit.* 87.

20 *Ibid.* 90–1.

21 Walton, *op. cit.* 168.

22 Hervey, 'The Lunacy Commission', 220. For Conolly, see Akihito Suzuki, 'The Politics and Ideology of Non-Restraint: The Case of Hanwell Asylum', *Medical History*, xxxix (1995), 1–17.

23 Hervey, 'A Slavish Bowing Down', 104.

24 See Samuel Squire Spriggs, *Life and Times of Thomas Wakley* (London: Longmans, Green and Co., 1897).

25 *Lancet*, 1 (1852), 546.

26 1845 Names of Governors Book.

27 *Lancet*, 1 (1852), 546.

28 Hervey, 'The Lunacy Commission', 425.

29 Order of 13 June 1851.

30 Hervey, 'The Lunacy Commission', 284.

31 *Lancet*, 1 (1852).

32 Bethlem Subcommittee, 25 April 1851.

33 *Lancet*, 2 (1852), 336.

34 Letter from the Lunacy Commissioners, 3 July 1851; General Committee, 4 July 1851.

35 Hervey, 'The Lunacy Commission', 426.

36 Hume was engaged in private practice, having been Inspector-General of Hospitals between 1818 and 1821; Proctor was a minor poet and barrister who mostly practised at conveyancing; Campbell was a convinced churchman and barrister for whom the Earl of Argyle, his uncle, had secured various pasts; Gaskell had been superintendent at Lancaster Moor Asylum where he had carried out a non-restraint policy, and was a keen supporter of employment and training. It was believed that he was a very 'minute' inspector of asylums: Hervey, 'The Lunacy Commission', vol. ii, 125–7.

37 *Report and Evidence of the Lunacy Commission to the Home Secretary on Bethlehem Hospital* (London: 1852). It was contained in the *Seventh Annual Report of the Lunacy Commissioners* (1852–3).

38 See Chapter 23; House of Commons, *First Report of the Select Committee on Madhouses in England* (London: 1815).

39 *Seventh Annual Report of the Lunacy Commissioners* (1852–3), 25–6.

40 'Observations of Governors', *PP*, 1852–3, xlix, 125.

41 *Ibid.* xiv.

42 *Ibid.*

43 *Report and Evidence of the Lunacy Commission.*

44 PRO File MH50/5, Kew, Minute Books of the Lunacy Commission, April 1851–August 1852.

45 *Report and Evidence of the Lunacy Commission*, 14.

46 *Ibid.* 4.

47 *Ibid.* 5.

48 *1843 General Report*, 57.

49 *Report and Evidence of the Lunacy Commission*, 5.

50 *Ibid.* 32–5.

51 *Ibid.* 5.

52 Phil Fennell, *Treatment Without Consent: Law, Psychiatry and the Treatment of Mentally Disordered People Since 1845* (London: Routledge, 1996), 17.

53 *Report and Evidence of the Lunacy Commission*, 8.

54 *1845 General Report.*

55 *Report and Evidence of the Lunacy Commission*, 8.

56 *Ibid.*.

57 *Ibid.* 11ff.

58 F. O. Martin, *The Report of the Commissioners for Enquiry into Charities for 1837* (London 1837), 523.

59 *Report and Evidence of the Lunacy Commission*, 11ff.

60 See *1843 General Report*, 3–4.
61 *Report and Evidence of the Lunacy Commission*, 32–5.
62 'Observations of Governors'.
63 Bethlem Subcommittee, 4 July 1951.
64 'Observations of Governors'.
65 See Peter McCandless, 'Liberty and Lunacy: The Victorians and Wrongful Confinement', in Andrew Scull (ed.), *Madhouse, Mad-Doctors and Madmen* (Philadelphia: University of Pennsylvania, 1881), 339–62.
66 'Observations of Governors', xviii.
67 *Ibid.* ix.
68 *Sketches in Bedlam* (London: Sherwood, Jones & Co, 1823), 293.
69 'Observations of Governors'.
70 *Ibid.*
71 *Ibid.* xvii.
72 *Ibid.* xliii.
73 *Ibid.* xlix–xlxiii.
74 See *Report of the Commissioners*.
75 'Observations of Governors', xvii.
76 Court of Governors, 30 April 1852.
77 *Journal of Psychological Medicine*, vi (1852), 86.
78 *Report and Evidence of the Lunacy Commissioners*.
79 *Ibid.*
80 *Lancet*, 2 (1852), 336.
81 *Lancet*, 1 (1853), 16.
82 *Lancet*, 2 (1852), 2.
83 *Lancet*, 1 (1853), 61.
84 *Ibid.* 62.
85 *Journal of Psychological Medicine*, vi (1853), 83.
86 *Ibid.* 104.
87 *Ibid.* 105.
88 Letter from Waddington, 21 February 1852.
89 *Report and Evidence of the Lunacy Commissioners*, 16.
90 Fennell, *op. cit.* 18.
91 See Scull, *The Most Solitary of Afflictions*.
92 'Observations of Governors'.
93 Court of Governors, 12 June 1852.
94 'Observations of Governors'.
95 *Lancet*, 2 (1852), 66.
96 Court of Governors, 4 April 1853.
97 *Ibid.*
98 *Lancet*, 1 (1853), 370.
99 *Ibid.* 274.
100 *Ibid.*
101 *Hansard*, H. of C., first series, 11 March 1853, col. 32.
102 *Ibid.* 3 May 1853, col. 1227.
103 The Lunatics Act 1853, 16 and 17 Vict., *c.* 96, s. 90.
104 Fennell, *op. cit.* 22.
105 J. Williams, *The Lunacy Question – or the Lunatic Benefited and Protected* (London: 1852), 33–7.
106 *Journal of Psychological Medicine*, vi (1852), 83–113.
107 Hervey, 'The Lunacy Commission', 427.
108 *Lancet*, 2 (1853), 358.

CLASSIFYING AND CONSOLING

——— ·•· ———

Viewed from Victorian perspectives, the main agent of transformation at Bethlem was (Sir) William Charles Hood, the Hospital's first Resident Physician-Superintendent, appointed in 1852. For Geoffrey O'Donoghue, Bethlem's Chaplain and author of *The History of the Bethlehem Hospital*, it was Hood who advanced Bethlem 'from the grub to the chrysalis' and brought it 'into line with more modern sentiments and requirements'.[1] Hunter and Macalpine have equally seen a 'transformation' at Bethlem from 1852.[2] David Russell believes that under Hood the Hospital experienced a 'golden age', with the new Resident Physician-Superintendent throwing himself energetically into reforming the medical administration and introducing non-restraint.[3] Masters agrees. In the 1850s, 'the outward signs of restraint disappeared, bowls, skittles and other games were introduced' and parties were held.[4] In 1947, Duncan Whittaker, Bethlem's assistant physician, felt that even in the 1940s the medical system was a direct continuation from the 1850s. Hood's name and achievement lived on at Bethlem. When the day ward was closed and a psycho-therapeutic community was established in the old recreation hall in the 1970s, it was named the Charles Hood Unit, a name that was felt to be particularly appropriate given the 'emphasis he placed upon . . . moral treatment'.[5]

Hood's appointment has been perceived as a break with the past, an end of the old regime. If Bethlem was not able to avoid controversy after 1852 (see Chapter 27), under Hood it ceased to be the object of scandal and Parliamentary inquiry, and started to acquire a new reputation as a hospital rather than as an ill-governed, out-moded charitable madhouse for pauper lunatics. Between 1852 and his death in 1870, Hood, as Resident Physician and then Treasurer, instigated several far-reaching reforms. He was pivotal, but in some areas he was not as innovative as some have wanted to claim. In terms of the use of restraint and limited occupational therapy, and over the nature of the patients admitted, he accelerated changes made before 1852 under George Tuthill and Alexander Morison (see Chapter 24). Hood made the medical regime more acceptable to the Lunacy Commissioners and the Governors. Most of all, he was something new and different and unassociated with the period before 1852, although he had been a Governor since 1849. There is no cause to dismiss Hood's achievements or the changes he made, but his appointment did not mark a revolution.

THE NEW RESIDENT PHYSICIAN-SUPERINTENDENT

It was at a special Court of Governors held in June 1852, in the thick of the argument between Governors and Lunacy Commissioners (see Chapter 25) and two months after the Governors had decided to change the medical administration, that Hood was elected.[6] The Lunacy Commissioners had suggested in a footnote to their scathing *Report* on the Hospital that a new medical officer should be appointed as the 'paramount authority'.[7] It was an attempt to move control of Bethlem's medical administration from the Treasurer, whom the Commissioners saw as the main executive authority, to a medical officer. The Commissioners wanted doctors to be in control of the asylum. They had developed a model set of rules for asylum management that placed the medical superintendent in supreme power, answerable only to the visiting committee.[8] For the Commissioners this meant that there was one person responsible. Under this system, the asylum became a fief for the emerging psychiatric profession.[9] County and borough asylums followed this pattern, and in the 1830s almost all public mental hospitals had a resident medical director. Bethlem was slow to follow, but in 1851 the Governors, aware that change was necessary, agreed to the Commissioners' suggestions. Instead of a visiting committee, the new Resident Physician-Superintendent was to be answerable to the Bethlem Subcommittee. Considerable authority was vested in the position. In 1854 stress was placed in the rules on the control of the Physician, insisting that regular inspections were made. The appointment marked a change in Bethlem's medical administration, but it was not until 1865 that the title of Apothecary was to disappear to be replaced by Assistant Resident Physician. At the same time it was also specified that the Physician-Superintendent had to be a Doctor of Medicine and a fellow or member of the Royal College of Physicians.[10]

The word 'Resident' was crucial. Both John Haslam and William Wood, as Apothecaries, had effectively been the resident medical officer during their respective appointments, although Haslam had not spent all his time in the Hospital after he had moved to Islington.[11] The Physicians (Thomas Monro, Edward Thomas Monro, Tuthill and Morison) were only required to visit the Hospital on certain days and evidence presented in 1815 and 1851 showed that the Monros were not always attentive (see Chapters 23 and 25). A resident medical officer was the solution to this problem to ensure that continuous attendance was provided, although the *Lancet* had to admit that Morison had spent considerable time in Bethlem.[12] What was now deemed to have been an abuse was corrected by the new appointment. Hood took over his post in the autumn of 1852 amidst complaints from the *Lancet* about his mode of election.[13]

However, there was a significant element of continuity. The Monro dynasty ended in 1855 when Edward Thomas Monro resigned on health grounds, but when Hood was absent the Governors called Monro in as a *locum*. Hood had himself been a Governor, since 1849, and between 1849 and 1851 he seemed curiously not to be aware of the defects in the Hospital's administration. In 1855, he was proud to describe Bethlem as enjoying 'the distinction of being one of the oldest charitable institutions for the reception of the insane in Europe'.[14] Hood was to serve on the

Plate 26.1 Dr (later Sir) William Charles Hood, first resident physician superintendent of Bethlem (1852–62), by Charles Fréchon, Paris 1851. Reproduced by permission of the Bethlem Royal Hospital Archives and Museum.

spot for ten years until he became a Lord Chancellor's Visitor for the Insane in 1862. This was not the end of his connection with Bethlem. He was elected Treasurer in June 1868 and served both on the Estates Subcommittee and on the Bethlem Subcommittee.

Hood was born in 1824, not far from Bethlem. The son of a south London doctor, he was educated at Trinity College, Dublin. He had worked at Guy's Hospital before becoming Resident Physician at Colney Hatch Asylum, which had been purpose-built for the Middlesex magistrates in 1851 and was proclaimed as Europe's 'most modern asylum', housing 1,250 patients.[15] He was appointed with J. G. Davey and was in charge of the male department. Neither remained at the asylum for long. At Colney Hatch, Hood provided a strict system of classification and established a ward for juvenile boys and exercise classes. Like 'all progressive physicians of the day he prided himself on managing the disturbed without physical restraint and without gross methods of "depletion"'.[16] He introduced similar measures at Bethlem. George Sala, a journalist from the *Illustrated London News*, on his visit to the Hospital in October 1859, showed Hood to be almost saintly. Sala explained that 'he comes to soothe and heal; and we all know that he is on his Master's business, that he is doing that which shall be done to him on the great day of reckoning'.[17] No praise seemed enough for his work at Bethlem. The religious imagery was not accidental: Hood was known to invoke the blessings of God on the Hospital.[18] Hood was a specialist who without difficulty found his place in the medical establishment and contributed to the literature on the statistics of insanity and on criminal lunatics. Statistics were of prime importance to him and he provided detailed figures for Bethlem in the *General Reports* during his ten years at the Hospital. Hood was knighted in July 1868, but he died relatively young two years later at the Treasurer's house in Bridewell. Despite his work at Colney Hatch and Bethlem, he did not reach the pages of the *Dictionary of National Biography*. For O'Donoghue, Hood's 'incessant work' had undermined 'a constitution naturally robust and vigorous'.[19] The cause of death was pleurisy.

Hood had firm views on the causes of mental illness that drew heavily on James Cowles Prichard's ideas and nosographies of insanity that 'bewildered and impressed the average layman'.[20] The presentation of Hood's views was part of a defence of medical hegemony in the asylum. Rejecting a distinction between 'predisposing' and 'exciting causes', he divided causation into 'moral' and 'physical'. In his attempts to classify, he drew on existing psychiatric thought to link cause and effect. Intemperance, for instance, was a 'physical agent' that gave rise to insanity, although he admitted that most intemperate persons avoided it. Hood adopted a hereditarian approach to explain 'the diversity of results brought about by the same or very similar external agencies'. For him there was nothing 'mysterious' about the 'hereditary tendency to insanity'.[21] Other asylum doctors agreed, with alienists pointing to defective heredity as an important aetiological influence that inclined the weak to madness.

Neither did Hood see much room for debate 'that insanity is due more to moral than to physical causes'. This was an important area of interest for asylum doctors in the 1840s who were keen to illustrate that insanity had a somatic interpretation.[22] Bethlem's Surgeon, William Lawrence, had been a proponent of these ideas, believing that 'arguments, syllogisms, discourses, sermons, have never yet restored any patient'.[23] Morison was equally of the opinion that mental disorders were a physical phenomenon.[24] Lawrence went on to argue that 'the moral pharmacopoeia is quite inefficient'.[25] The stress on somatic causes was in line with developments in Victorian medicine, with asylum doctors attempting to demonstrate that there was a clear mental physiology.[26] Practice was often different from this theorizing and little evidence could be found that proved that insanity had a somatic origin.[27]

Hood had deduced as much. He adopted a different approach and one that later Resident Physicians were not to follow with any great enthusiasm (see Chapter 27). Convinced of the merits of moral management, Hood tried to explain that 'moral' causes were important. However, no mention was made of 'moral insanity', which Prichard had defined in 1835 as 'madness consisting in a morbid perversion of the natural feelings affections, inclinations, temper habits, moral dispositions, and natural impulses, without any remarkable disorder or defect of the interest or knowing and reasoning facilities'.[28] Nor did Hood cut himself off from the rest of the profession and abandon a medical approach that gave alienists a rationale for their medical credentials. He believed that treatment was best secured through a combination of moral and medical means, arguing that Bethlem's case notes showed that the number of 'moral' cases was double that of the 'physical cases' in male patients.[29] Here 'moral' was synonymous with psychological factors. Little acknowledgment was given to the growing body of opinion in the 1850s that mental illness was a product of hypothetical disorders of the vascular system and inflammation in the brain. Hood was on less certain ground with the female patients and returned to a highly gendered view of women and how they were influenced by their biology. Victorian asylum doctors were generally indifferent to the context of women's mental illness and focused on biology and life cycle, which was seen fraught with potential disasters. Menstruation was thought particularly disruptive to the female brain and predisposed women to insanity. This provided an important rationale for explaining why more women than men were admitted to asylums.[30] Hood shared a similar approach. In women, he placed considerable emphasis on 'uterine disturbances' and ovarian disorders.[31]

In studying Bethlem's statistics, Hood found moral causes to be responsible for 35.7 per cent of all mental illness and believed that the chances of recovery in the moral cases were 20 per cent higher, although he was prepared to admit that the cause was unknown in a third of all cases.[32] From this evidence, he concluded that insanity had a substantial moral dimension, an attitude that fitted with nineteenth-century concerns about character. Given this perspective, Hood dealt superficially with physical causes. Here, Hood believed that if more were known of 'the real history of the patients', it might account for still more cases than his statistics suggested. However, 'anxiety and distress' were the influences that stood out for him.[33] Later psychiatrists, even the gloomy Henry Maudsley, were to reject such attempts to differentiate insanity, and studies of case notes at other asylums show that 'a systematic nosology fell into disuse'.[34]

Throughout his time at Bethlem, Hood, while insisting on his professional responsibility, tried to involve the Governors more directly in the responsibility of managing Bethlem. Here he echoed the concerns of the Lunacy Commissioners and the *Lancet*. To keep the Governors informed of his actions he not only provided detailed figures, but also established a weekly journal that was read regularly by the Bethlem Subcommittee. In his *Reports* he constantly reminded the Governors that Bethlem was a noble charity and one of the oldest institutions for the care of the insane in Europe. Hood was partially successful in generating interest. When he delivered his first course of *Lectures on the Nature and Treatment of Insanity* in 1855 several Governors attended. That gratified him, although the small attendance of medical students remained a matter of concern. Over the Hospital's management and the changes needed, Hood and the Governors agreed. This gave the former considerable freedom to reform Bethlem. Between 1852 and 1879, the Governors did not need to assert their authority and press for change because Hood was willingly proposing alterations and improvements that fulfilled their aims and met the Lunacy Commissioners' concerns. This is what the Lunacy Commissioners had envisaged by a 'paramount authority'; but no Physician-Superintendent was to have such authority after Hood, as the Governors reasserted themselves.

REFORMING BETHLEM AND NON-RESTRAINT

Guided by his experiences at Colney Hatch, Hood immediately set about reforming the Hospital. As the first Physician-Superintendent, 'he tackled his task of introducing change with alacrity, producing a programme of physical alternations and organisational improvements that would contribute to the "moral and hygienic welfare of the patients"'.[35] Hood's *General Report* for 1855, prepared after he had become familiar with the routines of Bethlem and had set about changing some of them, spoke of 'the humane and enlightened principles which now guide us in the moral and medical treatment of insanity'. He anticipated that 'we may therefore look forward to many improvements being yet introduced into our present system of management'.[36]

Hood had struck a new note from the start. He maintained that 'the study of mental disease is now recognised to be a distinct and legitimate branch of medical science'.[37] He wanted Bethlem to become 'a place open to whatever the medical facility wished to know'.[38] Here 'the pupil has the opportunity of studying all the different forms of insanity, and that too in the early state of the disease. Here he may dismiss book-taught theories, and learn to appreciate the value of facts as they appear visibly before him.'[39] Hood could be confident that Bethlem would present the right image. One of the first things he did was to change the keys of his kingdom. In April 1853, he recommended that the locks should be altered to reduce the number of keys in the custody of each attendant.[40] Under Tuthill and Morison the Governors had been encouraged to attend to the comfort of the patients, and this was continued under Hood. For example, in December 1852 a magic lantern was installed for the amusement of the patients, and a year later, 'at the recommendation of the Physician', the Bethlem Subcommittee decided that a supply of apples, oranges, 'plain plumb cakes and negus' should be placed 'at the discretion of the Resident Physician' as Christmas treats for the patients.[41] There was a symbolic air to these changes as there was to be in much that Hood did.

When the Lunacy Commissioners made their first official visit after Bethlem's exemption order had been removed in 1853, they were impressed by what Hood had managed to achieve in such a short time.[42] The four Commissioners who visited described themselves as 'satisfied with the general cleanliness of the wards and with the condition and character of the furniture and bedding', which appeared to them 'good and comfortable'. In addition, new windows had been installed. They observed also that 'books, prints, birds and other means of amusement had been placed in the wards', contributing 'materially to the cheerfulness of the place'.[43] They promised more detailed inspections later. In 1861, on a further inspection, they praised Bethlem where in 1851 they had heaped scorn:

> the Patients on the Curable and Incurable List at the time of our visit yesterday, were, without exception, tranquil and orderly, and their personal condition was satisfactory. The Dinner, which we saw served, was of excellent quality, and ample in quantity. The Wards and Rooms generally, and the Beds and Bedding throughout, were clean, and in their usual good order. The ordinary Galleries are enlivened by a great variety of subjects of interest, which the Patients appear fully to appreciate. We have much satisfaction that the Patients of both sexes expressed themselves in terms of gratitude for their kind treatment.[44]

Bethlem in 1861, it would appear, could not have been more different from the institution it was shown to be in 1851 (see Plates 26.2 and 26.3).

That the character of the Hospital had changed was reflected by other visitors to Bethlem. Half-way through the Hood years, Henry Morley paid a tribute to the Hospital in a memorable, if sentimental, anonymous article, 'The Star of Bethlehem',

Plate 26.2 Women's ward in 1860, engraving published in the *Illustrated London News*, 24 March 1860. Reproduced by permission of the Bethlem Royal Hospital Archives and Museum.

which appeared in Charles Dickens's magazine *Household Words*.[45] St Luke's Hospital had been given the same treatment in 1852.[46] Dickens, who often described 'mental disease' in his novels, had met Hood before the article was written and told him that it was 'an honest tribute to your merit'. Morley described Bethlem's origins and drew attention to the fact that after the 1851 investigation the Governors, 'in a liberal and earnest spirit', had been working to make good past 'errors', 'aided by a new Superintendent at once thoughtful and energetic'. It was explained that the Governors 'now lead where once they used to lag upon the road'. Everything was found to be of a high standard. The generous diet was praised:

> In one cool room we found a nest of plates containing gooseberry pie, which had been deposited there by their women, simply because the room was cool and the day hot. If there be two ideas that never before came into association in our minds they are gooseberry-pie and Bedlam.

Wine was included with the meals. As the main symbol of transformation Morley selected the 'large well glazed windows with the glass set in light iron frames'. Sunshine now came in 'even tenfold' and gave life 'to the flowers in the wards' and 'sets the birds singing in their aviaries'. In every sense, the readers were informed that 'light has been let into Bethlem'.[47] Work on the windows had, however, started before Hood's appointment, although he had ordered that the massive iron bars on the windows should be removed, rooms carpeted, and armchairs and sofas provided. All this was magical for O'Donoghue.[48] There were other symbols in 'The Star of

Plate 26.3 Men's ward in 1860, engraving published in the *Illustrated London News*, 31 March 1860. Reproduced by permission of the Bethlem Royal Hospital Archives and Museum.

Bethlehem'. On his visit to Bethlem, Morley had seen Hood's children playing on the grass with some of the inmates: one of them was a little boy who looked like 'an embodiment of the good spirit that had made its way into the hospital'. Everywhere that Morley went he found 'birds, flowers, books, statuettes and pictures'.[49] Some doctors, however, were sceptical of the effect. John Charles Bucknill, no fan of Bethlem, mocked Hood's love for flowers and birds in 1857:

> If a few caged pigeons and captured linnets are more able to interest the patients at Bethlem, than to remind them of their own loss of liberty, what interest would not these patients derive from hearing the free songs of the lark and the blackbird when he sings at his best in the hawthorn tree.[50]

Hood adopted a different approach and provided more than flowers. There were chess boards, draught boards, and a billiard room. When it was cold, there were open fires.[51] Sala was impressed by the artistic ornamentation of the wards when he visited the Hospital two years later.[52] In 1868 further improvements were made and some rooms were wallpapered. Refinements continued, and in the twentieth century Bethlem was frequently compared to a first-class hotel (see Chapter 29).

Most of Hood's efforts, however, were directed at providing a suitable environment for 'impoverished middle-class patients' that he sought to attract into Bethlem. Since 1843 efforts had been made to encourage the admission of middle-class patients, but Hood accelerated this process explaining to the Governors in 1856 'that the time had now come to throw the hospital open to a higher and more educated class of people'.[53] It was a practical suggestion given that with the growing number of county and borough asylums admissions to Bethlem had been falling. County authorities were now increasingly accommodating their pauper lunatics in their own purpose-built asylums, not in the Hospital. An increasing class segregation between institutions developed after 1845. According to Len Smith, 'private patients were moved out of county asylums and paupers were removed from private asylums'.[54] This left Bethlem in an anomalous position providing care for the group in between. The Governors had accepted this position in 1857 and it was no coincidence that 'The Star of Bethlehem' appeared in the same year. The point was not lost on the author: 'thousands of middle-class homes contain nothing so pretty as a ward in Bedlam.'[55] Morley confirmed the new trend. Bethlem, he asserted, was not for the poor, who could take advantage of the new county and borough asylums. Neither was it for the rich. Instead it was a place for the 'educated working class' and middle classes like clerks, book-keepers, surveyors, governesses who had 'broken down', surgeons who had become afflicted by insanity and become 'helpless men', 'authors checked by sudden failing of the mind when bread is being earned for wife and children'.[56] There would be some incurables, whose needs were met from the incurable fund, and the criminal lunatics who would remain at Bethlem until 1863 (see pp. 502–6).[57] However, patients were not being offered safe harbour, but cure. This followed in three cases out of five, and, 'if uncured', patients were returned to their friends 'at the expiration of a twelvemonth'.[58] Such eulogistic praise was welcomed by Hood and the Governors in their concerted efforts to attract middle-class patients.

It was not just the character and conditions in the Hospital that Hood improved, it was also the treatment. Tuthill and Morison had not advocated a non-restraint ideology but they had reduced the amount of restraint practised at Bethlem (see Chapter 24). Hood took their interests further and made the reduction of restraint to a minimum central to the Hospital's medical approach. Other asylums, encouraged by the reforming Lunacy Commission, were adopting the same course following the examples set by Lincoln and Hanwell. This gave dramatic proof that the doctor had superior powers in managing the mad. Between the 1840s and 1880s non-restraint was a powerful force shaping asylums, although the implementation was neither complete nor consistent. It became a crusade, a means by which doctors asserted their control – although it was not an issue without its controversies.[59] By the 1870s asylums were seen to be using restraint only in exceptional circumstances. For some this was seen as 'the continuation and completion of the progressive and humanitarian effort that Pinel and the York Retreat' had started in the 1790s, while revisionist historians have seen it as a tactic to boost the status of asylum doctors.[60] Pinel was the hero for Hood as he was for the Seventh Earl of Shaftesbury, philanthropist and chair of the Lunacy Commissioners. In 1855, Hood explained:

> If the enlightened views of Pinel had not been adopted, and fairly tested at various public establishments, the possibility of managing violent lunatics, without imposing upon them the least mechanical restraint, would still be disputed, and the proposition denounced as utopian and impracticable.[61]

At Hanwell the 'success' of non-restraint in the 1840s made Conolly a national and international hero and gave asylum doctors a humanitarian halo.[62] Conolly proved to be the right man in the right place. His reforming zeal and moderate Whiggism appealed to the Middlesex magistrates, keen to encourage a revision of asylum management. Hood was placed in a similar position at Bethlem. Like Conolly, he was favoured by the Governors' new attitude to reform, but he was less 'embarrassingly incompetent' at providing moral therapy.[63] Hood felt that the days were past when 'the skill and experience of the physicians was thought to be less important than the watchful care of the matron or steward'. 'Experience', not knowledge, had decided against the expediency of the loss of blood in insanity. Even 'moderate measures', like leeching or cupping, were now for Hood 'seldom necessary', and seclusion in padded rooms was preferable to physical restraint.[64] Hood put his trust in the 'non-restraint' system, 'which, with some few exceptions, is, I believe, adopted in all the best conducted Asylums in the Kingdom'. Like all Victorian alienists, Hood continued to see a role for emetics and purgatives and advocated the use of opium and other drugs as a form of chemical restraint. Morphine was used at night to help the patients sleep. However, doctors were forced 'to fall back on their one remaining claim to expertise, their knowledge of moral treatment', given the large gap between the claims of cure and the actual results.[65]

In his first detailed *General Report*, Hood explained to the Governors how patients were treated and drew comparisons with previous practices. He offered his comments in what he called 'plain, unaffected language' and treated the Governors in a different fashion from outside critics, particularly journalists, to whose unpalatable rhetoric they had by then become accustomed. Hood broke with custom in referring briefly to the 'general principles which we here observe in the management of the insane, whether curable or incurable'. He explained that

> Every patient, on admission, is placed under immediate active medical treatment, although it may be very true, and the fact is confirmed by daily experience, that in some cases judicious moral treatment is of more avail in the cure of the disease than the exhibition of any kind of medicine. In the majority of cases, however, it is necessary to combine medical with moral treatment; and here I have the satisfaction of stating that the 'Non-Restraint System' continues to be unreservedly adopted in this Hospital, and as far as my experience has gone, it has been attended with considerable success.[66]

A more domestic environment, with more attendants to help control the insane was the result. The number of attendants rose from seventeen in 1842 to forty in 1863, providing a staff–patient ratio of 1:8 that brought Bethlem in line with other institutions. After 1853 the female nurses were under the authority of the Matron; the male nurses, with the appointment of the first Head Attendant (Charles Neville), under his authority. Neville was paid £17 less than the Matron and the post of Head Attendant never achieved the same status. In the rules more stress was placed on the qualities of the attendants, although increasingly this gave way to regimentation.[67] The regime was designed to encourage normative behaviour. As Bethlem was a small institution in comparison to the mammoth county and borough asylums being built for 1,000 patients or more, such methods were seen by Hood as highly successful. By the 1850s every textbook and asylum was professing to be using these methods.[68]

To stress how treatment had changed, Hood compared two cases, one from 1808, the other from 1853. The patient admitted in 1808 had been sent from Bridewell and after twelve months was placed in with the 'incurables'. Here her violent nature, blamed on intemperance, made it necessary to have her chained for eight years to a bed of straw with no covering or apparel. Hood illustrated that much had altered by 1853. It was explained that M.C. was 'a powerful, muscular, woman' who had been admitted in 'a state of violent raging excitement'. It had been necessary 'to impose upon her the restraint of a straitjacket', but on admission the mechanical restraint was removed and after a warm bath she was given two grains of 'the acetate of morphia' and placed on a bed in a padded room. Once in Bethlem:

> She continued noisy for an hour or two, and then became quieter, but the attendant who looked at her every half hour always found her sleepless. The following day she continued tranquil, but when addressed, responded with an oath or obscene expression. She was ordered one grain and a half of acetate of morphia. The third day she continued quiet and sullen, but permitted the nurse to dress her and place her in a chair in the day-room with the other patients. Her bowels not having been relieved, she was ordered one drop of croton oil on a lump of sugar. Within four hours after her bowels were acted upon she resumed her natural demeanour, and asked for employment. The following day [the fourth], she continued tranquil and rational rather shrinking from conversation; and being a little feverish was ordered 'henbane', with a saline. From that day she speedily became convalescent, and was discharged cured, November 11, 1853, having been a patient in the Hospital, 42 days.[69]

Hood observed that 'other cases' of 'a similar description' could be extracted from the case books. Nothing could be clearer. The 1870 *Annual Report* showed that between 1851 and 1870 no restraint had been employed, although seclusion in padded cells was used to isolate and control difficult patients.[70] The padding in the rooms was rigid and Hood acknowledged that prolonged confinement could have a damaging effect. Seclusion was not considered a form of restraint. Other asylums could boast a similar record. Seclusion became common, along with other methods of physical restraint that were not initially defined as mechanical.[71] For Bethlem the use of seclusion was to create problems in the 1870s and 1880s, and once Hood had left restraint began to emerge again in the Hospital.

In line with the principles of moral therapy, Hood placed considerable emphasis on the system of occupation and recreation first set up at Bethlem under Tuthill (see Chapter 24). Conolly equally linked work with non-restraint, although he advocated strict discipline.[72] Hood, like his predecessors, felt that work tended 'to divert the mind from its delusions, and which rouse and invigorate the healthy exercise of its reflecting faculties'. He did not dismiss the financial benefits for the Hospital, but considered the improvement to the patients' 'mental and bodily state of health' as the most important factor. For Hood, who obviously believed in the gospel of work, it was 'lamentable to see strong and healthy men, in the prime of life, idling away their time from morning till night, lounging listlessly about the wards, doing nothing'.[73]

There was no doubt in his mind that occupation and recreation had a curative tendency:

> Recreation, whatever be the kind of amusement, [was] only another term for mental employment, and judiciously promoted, cheers the mind, and excites a healthy tone of feeling. Hence some of the patients during the year were permitted to walk out, under the care of nurses and proper attendants, which was esteemed a great indulgence, and had perceptibly a good effect. Four of the male patients, who were, however, not fit to be discharged, were allowed to spend a day at Kew, another day they went by steam-boat to the Nore; and conducted themselves well, under the charge of careful attendants.

During 1855 for example, patients had visited many different public places, among them the National Gallery, the Crystal Palace, Marlborough House, the Zoological Gardens and the Smithfield Cattle Show.[74] Evening activities of dancing and singing were supplemented with Bible classes. Poetry reading was introduced in 1863. However, privileges were only awarded to patients gradually. Hood assessed whether a patient was suitable for an excursion by observing 'their enjoyment and quiet demeanour when first taken for a walk round the garden'. In true moral management fashion, he felt that 'if we can succeed in giving a patient the impression that we repose confidence in him, if we can make him sensible of the importance of keeping his *parole d'honneur*, we are greatly improving his mental state'.[75] Recovery was to be through self-discipline and control.

To promote the medical regime, Hood aimed for 'proper classification'. This was a subject that perhaps interested him most and had greatly disturbed earlier critics of Bethlem from John Howard, the prison reformer, onwards.[76] A topographical classification had been attempted, but the restrictions of the building at St George's Fields had not allowed this to take place to full effect.[77] Hood tried a new approach. On reception patients were now separated into categories. He felt that 'it is evident that the homicidal and the suicidal, the maniacal and melancholic, the noisy and the dirty must be separated from those who are tranquil, cleanly, well disposed, and perhaps only partially insane, or under some harmless delusion'. Hood knew when he was appointed that to make such separation possible changes to the buildings were necessary. These were made gradually and convalescent patients were finally able to spend part of their recovery at Witley House from 1870 onwards (see p. 501).

MEASURING BETHLEM

Metaphors from nature, like 'grub to chrysalis', came less naturally to Hood than meticulous statistical calculations: it was entirely fitting that his Bethlem career culminated in the Treasurership. Classification was one of the main 'modern' preoccupations of the mid-century: as Sala of the *Illustrated London News*, an articulate interpreter of what was 'modern', put it in 1859, 'subdivision, classification, and elaboration are . . . distinguishing characteristics of the present era of civilisation'.[78] Hood was in step with the times, therefore, when he prepared and published statistical tables for Bethlem. He believed these would lead the way in securing 'a uniform plan' of compilation and presentation, not only throughout Britain but in other parts of the world. The Lunacy Commissioners in their investigation had been appalled by the lack of detailed records and statistics in the Hospital in 1851.[79] Now Hood promised that Bethlem could produce statistics of a model kind.

Hood had the highest hopes of statistical standardization. He believed that 'information', until now 'scattered, vague, and consequently unsatisfactory', could 'by its uniformity, be capable of compilation'. For him this would 'assist in forming our diagnosis, prognosis, and many valuable, because practical, lessons, for our treatment of the Insane'.[80] The Bethlem statistics for fifteen years, beginning in 1846, were collected by Hood and presented in book form in 1862 with tables devised according to the plan that he had laid down in 1855.[81] By 1860 he felt that the form he had devised 'might with propriety be looked upon as a fitting model or basis for such a uniform system of Asylum Statistics as are required'.[82] One of his reviewers in 1855 had described figures as 'stubborn things'. Like facts 'they plead with a force of their own, neither requiring the sophistry of words nor the skilful arguments of a logician, yet often refuting the propositions of reasoners, and withal not to be gainsaid'.[83] Hood agreed, but viewed them not as some advertisement for the Hospital but as 'useful sources of practical information'.[84] None the less, most of the facts that Hood assembled were set out in separate tables rather than integrated with any degree of statistical sophistication.

Hood's statistics provided an indication of the type of patients being admitted into Bethlem while he was Physician-Superintendent.[85] The main changes were made in the class of patients admitted. Here Hood again continued the work of Tuthill and Morison and placed greater emphasis on the need to treat more middle-class patients. Indeed many of Hood's reforms, as noted above, were designed to make the Hospital a more attractive environment for such patients who expected higher standards. Hood believed that Bethlem should concentrate on 'the poor, though educated, insane of the middle class'.[86] In his 1859 *Report*, he singled out 'Clergymen, Medical Men, Clerks and Mechanics'. Hood argued that 'to each of these the association in a County Asylum would have been painful', while admission to Bethlem would allow them to return 'to their families, their neighbourhood, and their occupation, with their small savings untouched, their social pride unabashed, their gratitude unalloyed'.[87] One reviewer of Hood's *Statistics of Insanity, Embracing a Report of Bethlem Hospital from 1846 to 1860 Inclusive* (1862) took up the point: 'it was not possible from Hood's tables to determine the extent to which Bethlem was still used for the treatment of patients for whom the county asylum would be more suitable', but the reviewer agreed that Bethlem 'ought to be the great middle-class asylum in the country'.[88] Increasingly, this idea was accepted outside the Hospital. In 1863 Conolly argued:

> Among all the charities for the relief of suffering and privation, it is remarkable that there is yet no adequate provision, in any English Asylum or institution, for the insane of the middle classes. To a certain extent, relief is afforded at Bethlehem . . . It is on the middle classes of society that the calamities incidental to madness fall the most severely; they depend for existence on the continued power of being industrious; if the mind fails, that power is lost, and all the evils of poverty gradually surround them.

Conolly complained about the 'restrictions' in operation at Bethlem, but he did point to a clear role for the Hospital that Hood and the Governors were keen to adopt.

In this context the Law Officers of the City of London made an important statement in 1859. They confirmed that 'nothing can be done either by application to the Court of Chancery or the Charity Commissioners, or otherwise, to obtain any power of compelling the Governors of Bethlem Hospital to admit pauper lunatics'. A year earlier the Court of Common Council had set up a special committee to ascertain the number of pauper lunatics in London and to report 'whether the government and funds of Bridewell and Bethlem are administered in accordance with their original intent, and to enquire [if] the erection of a [new] pauper lunatic asylum is necessary'. Now, according to the officers, the Governors had the right not to admit pauper lunatics at all.

On the 'social condition of the male patients' between 1856 and 1860, Hood chose to arrange his tables hierarchically, heading patients 'according to their social position'. Clergymen came top in a small group of 'members of the learned professions'. Ten had been admitted over fifteen years. Three lawyers came second, nine medical men third, and two students last.[89] Hood considered that 'the mental and bodily fatigue to which a large proportion of the medical profession are exposed' not only shortened life duration but affected their mental health 'very seriously'. Schoolmasters were too often placed in an unsatisfactory social position, which tended 'to fret and irritate their minds', while musicians, 'more excitable than the majority of the population', were in the opposite danger, 'being flattered in that society where they are constantly welcomed'. This professional group formed 6.2 per cent of admissions, but when joined with those engaged in 'commerce' and 'members of other professions' those in the middle classes might be numbered at 42.5 per cent. Of this group clerks represented 13.5 per cent of patients.[90] Such figures suggest a middle-class bias and that Bethlem was attracting patients who would not want to enter a county asylum but did not have a suitable income to pay for private care or treatment at home with a nurse or attendant. The remainder of the patients, if not of the pauper classes, were from the working classes and still formed the majority of admissions. Bethlem, given its charitable status, could not avoid taking these patients without appearing churlish and arousing opposition from the Charity Commission. Indoor manufacturers, of which there were twenty-seven, were classified above those working in sedentary occupations (including clothworkers, saddlers, shoemakers). These were higher than the non-sedentary occupations (bakers, carpenters, painters and upholsterers) and people in outdoor pursuits. Servants, public and private (thirteen) came last. Hood clearly had a hierarchical view.[91]

Further distinctions can be made. Hood observed that Bethlem was not exceptional in admitting more women than men: 2,258 had been admitted over the previous fifteen years against 1,410 men.[92] Similar figures were recorded in 1869 when a journalist for *Tinsley's Magazine* noted that most of the female patients were 'governesses and the wives of badly paid clerks'.[93] Women proved prominent in asylum populations. For a recent historian this sexual ratio reflected both medical and non-medical factors. Increasingly the role of the patient was seen as female; the role of the doctor as male.[94] Sexes were strictly segregated at the Hospital and they had different experiences of the institution. Work and routines were highly gendered and patients mixed only at the monthly ball held in the ballroom built in 1838. This event was strictly controlled and only the best behaved patients could attend. At Bethlem, less success was encountered in promoting cure among its female patients, forcing them to enter other institutions after their discharge. Hood gave no explanations for these figures, although he still felt there was 'reason for congratulation' as 'the aggregate experience of the 100 years . . . reports the cures at 43.45 per cent and the deaths as 7.53 per cent'.[95]

Hood was more certain on the positive effects of urbanization. In the mid-Victorian period cities came to be viewed in a more favourable light, a change that was linked to economic progress as the initial shock of rapid urbanization passed. Reform and sanitary improvements offered the chance of a healthy, peaceful environment while the rural ideal retreated and the city's spokesmen became more self-assured. For the writer James Done cities were 'the centres and theatres of human ambition'.[96] Hood shared this optimism. He believed that 'the general voice of experience in favour of the idea that insanity is less likely to originate in the large towns than in the country' was confirmed by Bethlem's figures. Out of 3,668 patients admitted between 1846 and 1860, 2,059 were from the provinces and only 1,609 from London and 'the immediate neighbourhood'.[97] One reviewer showed that Hood was on uncertain ground here with more patients admitted from London than the provinces between 1855 and 1860. 'It speaks well for an institution', the reviewer concluded, 'that it is most used by the district in which it is best known, since any important change in the reputation of Bethlem as a hospital for the insane, would be much more fully and speedily known in London than in the provinces.' Bethlem clearly still had a national role to play, but with county asylums being established this was to decline during the late nineteenth century. Gradually the number of patients from London increased as alternatives to the Hospital were founded and enlarged.

PRESSURE TO MOVE

A bitter controversy erupted around Bethlem in 1863. The issue surrounded the Hospital's location in St George's Fields. Complaints had been raised by the Charity Commissioners and others about Bethlem's location in Southwark, but it was Conolly who wrote to the Lunacy Commissioners in 1863 explaining that the subject had 'no doubt already attracted their attention'.[98] 'It seems hardly necessary', Conolly began,

> to allude to the advantages of a country situation for Lunatic Asylums; they are numerous and unquestionable, and obvious to all who know of anything of the insane, and who have ever reflected on the requirements of Hospitals for their prevention and cure.

He mentioned 'good food' and 'cleanliness' as important in an asylum, but did not allude to the fact that standards in Hood's Bethlem were greatly superior to conditions in county and borough asylums. Neither did he note that many of the relatives of the metropolitan insane would not find it easy to visit them far from their homes. Conolly's main message was that the Governors should emulate their predecessors and move the Hospital. He was a firm advocate of siting asylums in rural locations and had provided a careful analysis of asylum design in his influential *Construction and Government of Lunatic Asylums* (1847). His ideas had been applied to large asylums, but he firmly believed that in all cases the external aspect should be cheerful, surrounded by grounds and farms.[99] Bethlem lacked this, while other asylums were increasingly being designed along the lines proposed by Conolly.[100] Conolly was not alone in his proposals. Bucknill had equally supported such a rural location in 1857, and, mocking Hood, noted that

> if birds, flowers, and pictures influence beneficially and genially the mind and temper of the patient in the corridors of the hospital in Lambeth Marsh, what rich and fruitful influences might not be expected from the garden and the field, from the rich meadow and the cheerful hill-side, from the domestic animals with whom even madmen form friendships, and from the free creatures who attend him delight ... It is known that insane persons derive the utmost pleasure and benefit from freedom and country air.[101]

Conolly pressed the Governors of Bethlem to act urgently. He argued that they should admit patients suffering for 'general paralysis' and, having changed the rules, they should create 'a new Bethlem' in the country, 'judiciously situated and planned'. Conolly believed that 'in this charitable age' money would be forthcoming. He appealed to the Lunacy Commissioners for their support, a remark not calculated to appeal to the Governors.

Conolly's arguments sounded completely disinterested. He was well-known for his lucid advocacy of fresh country air (and walks) as a mode of dealing with the insane. However, there were interests at stake. On 21 April 1863 the General Court of St Thomas's Hospital, wishing to move their hospital to the St George's Fields site, made an approach to Bethlem offering two alternative proposals. The hospital was being forced to move after the Charing Cross Railway Company had successfully applied for permission from Parliament to build a line that would cut across the north-west corner of the hospital garden. The Company offered to pay for a new north wing, which would be made unusable by the railway. Compensation was received but St Thomas's found itself in need of a new site.[102] Bethlem was one of seven sites under consideration.[103] St Thomas's, in its desperate search for a new permanent home, was therefore prepared either to build a new Bethlem 'at a cost not exceeding £150,000, including the site' following a design of their own Surveyor, or pay Bethlem the sum of £150,000 for the Governors to carry out the work. Three days later plans and drawings were sent to the Bethlem Governors with the hope that no time would be lost.[104]

At first prospects seemed favourable. On 20 February 1863 the Court of Governors had discussed St Thomas's move to the Bethlem site and on the motion of Alderman Phillips it had decided to go ahead with negotiations 'to ascertain whether it be possible to arrange terms'. Now, however, there was almost unanimous opposition in Bethlem. Hood believed that Bethlem, being a London institution, should stay where it was. He judged that from 'a sanitary point of view, the salubrity of the situation' could not be doubted. The Hospital was seen as 'well ventilated, dry and warm' with 'the healthiness of the day and sleeping rooms' unquestionable. Such arguments were cited by most of the Governors. Once the terms suggested by St Thomas's were received, the Governors decided to reject them. At a meeting on 8 May 1863 they voted that 'no proposal for the exchange of sites can be entertained which is not based on an agreement that the whole of the cost of the removal of Bethlehem Hospital is to be borne by the Governors of St. Thomas's Hospital'.[105] This decision was duly put in writing to St Thomas's. The Clerk added that what the Governors would consider as an equivalent for their present premises would probably cost a great deal more than the sum 'which the Governors of St. Thomas's would feel themselves at liberty to give, or which would be permitted either by the Court of Chancery or by Parliament to be given'.[106]

The Lunacy Commissioners supported St Thomas's proposal, expressing the hope that the 'protracted negotiations which have so long occupied the attention of both these important and wealthy charities would ere this have eventuated in an arrangement' beneficial to both. The same point was made in most sections of the press, including *The Times*, the *Lancet* and the *Journal of Mental Science*. For *The Times*, Bethlem had 'repelled with positive rudeness' all overtures to bring about a 'settlement' and had demanded 'absolute discretion to buy an estate, erect an asylum of indefinite size, and indulge in any architectural freaks which might please their own taste . . . at the sole cost of St. Thomas's'.[107] It felt that 'it was monstrous . . . that thirty or forty Governors out of the 200 or 250 on the list should have the decision left to them'.[108] Prejudice was running high against Bethlem. The language of the Commissioners was less dramatic but equally forceful. A month after the Governors had voted on the issue, a letter from the Commissioners to Sir George Grey, Secretary of State for the Home Department, was forwarded to the Hospital and published in the *Lancet*. It urged them 'to carefully consider the subject of the unfitness of the present site and buildings of Bethlehem Hospital for the purposes of the institution, and not allow the opportunity now offered of removing the site to a suitable locality to escape'. The Commissioners were forthright and asserted that

> the large funds at the disposal of the Governors confer upon them almost unprecedented means of improving the care and treatment of the insane, and consequently impose upon them, in an especial manner, the duty and responsibility of applying these funds in the manner best calculated to promote and extend the objects and benefits of the institution, which cannot be done upon the present site.

They argued that charitable purposes should be paramount. Strongly influenced by Conolly the Commissioners advised Grey 'that the site of Bethlem Hospital . . . in the centre of a dense and rapidly increasing population, is most unsuited to the due medical care and treatment of the insane, for whose sole benefit the administration of its ample property and income is intrusted to the Governors'.[109] The Commissioners were confident that 'the general aspect of the hospital externally and internally . . . cannot but exercise a depressing influence upon the inmates, whose means of outdoor exercise are so limited and inadequate'.[110] What was needed was exactly what Conolly proposed. Similar concerns were to be repeated in the 1920s over the Hospital's fourth move to Monks Orchard (see Chapter 29). Ironically what was wrong for Bethlem was shown to be suitable for St Thomas's. The *Lancet* had dismissed the 'outdated sanitary ideas of the Governors' in favour of a central site. The same standards were not applied to Bethlem.[111]

On 16 June 1863, a deputation consisting of representatives of eight South London parishes, with a population of more than half a million people, was received by Shaftesbury. They urged that two 'public sister institutions' should reach an agreement on the lines suggested by St Thomas's, especially as a central location would help 'poor people with broken limbs and severe diseases'. Shaftesbury told them that he was interested only in what happened to Bethlem, but decided to act. He instructed the Clerk of the House of Lords to present the Governors with a list of questions. Details were required 'of the amount of the revenues during the last ten years administered by the Governors' to be laid before the House along with details of the sums received from Parliamentary payments. Demands were also made of the average number of patients, the number of Governors, and the number of special meetings held since January 1863 'in reference to the removal of Bethlem Hospital and the number of Governors present on each occasion'.[112] Details were sent, but the Court held firm. Despite pressure from Shaftesbury, Conolly, the press, and St Thomas's, the Governors refused to bow to pressure. Bethlem stayed where it was and St Thomas's started protracted negotiations over the Stangate site, an area reclaimed from the Thames by the Metropolitan Board of Works.[113]

This was not the end of the story. Further pressure for the Hospital to move was applied in 1865 by the Charity Commission. Francis Offley Martin had again been instructed to visit Bethlem, and he repeated the suggestions made by Conolly.[114] Martin had recently visited Brentwood, where the asylum had pleased him very much. He believed that the Governors should build a hospital after that style for about £64,000. The Governors quickly explained that this would not be enough. The medical staff claimed that Bethlem was 'handsome' and the site 'healthy', arguing that the patients were happier here than if they were 'cultivating cabbages at Hanwell'. They drew on evidence from distinguished foreign physicians who had 'admitted' that Bethlem was the best institution of its kind and 'in several respects superior to those in other countries'. The Lunacy Commissioners again joined the fray, arguing that the London Corporation had led the way in building a new hospital near Dartford for the insane poor of the city, 'which was a good example to imitate'. The Governors were not convinced; they were more interested in Martin's suggestion for 'an institution in the country in connection with Bethlem Hospital'. This had already been tried 'to a small extent', with eight patients at a time sent to the seaside. The first had gone to the seaside in 1863 and in 1867 fifty patients spent two weeks in Brighton. However, the Governors recognized the merit of the proposal. A decision was made that a 'branch Establishment be provided in the country for the temporary reception of such of the patients as the Resident Physician of the Hospital may consider likely to be benefitted by the change'. The General Committee immediately set about finding a site. A rural site in Surrey at Witley was secured and the first patients moved there for fourteen days in September 1870. The Bethlem Subcommittee visited them in their first week and was 'glad to report' that they found the patients in excellent health and 'much enjoying the change'.[115] The Lunacy Commissioners agreed.[116] They did not give up hope, however, of moving the entire Hospital, but in 1869 they realized that at present we fear there is little prospect of this great charity being removed to a more favourable locality where with a building of modern construction and the large funds at the disposal of the Governors, it might take its proper position as one of the most important English institutions for the insane.[117]

This was to happen over fifty years later when a hospital was built that brought widespread acclaim to Bethlem (see Chapter 29).

FROM BETHLEM TO BROADMOOR

One important change was made in 1864, a change that Shaftesbury, without any pressure from outside, had advocated since 1852.[118] This was the move of the criminal lunatics' department, established at Bethlem in 1816, from the Hospital to a purpose-built asylum.[119]

When Hood arrived at Bethlem in 1852 he could do little more than lament the conditions in the criminal lunatics' department. Here he was responsible for more than a hundred of the country's 436 criminal lunatics. Hood was therefore well placed to make suggestions, the most prominent of which was that minor offenders should be placed in special wards in county and borough asylums.[120] Hood was critical of the unusual position where 'under plea of Not Guilty' a prisoner could 'allege that he did not commit the offence for which he is charged, and that when he did commit it he was unsound of mind'. He also criticized the manner by which insanity was established by prosecution and defence setting conflicting medical opinions against one another.[121] At Bethlem, Hood found the department in a deplorable condition. Accommodation for less dangerous patients had been provided at Fisherton House Asylum, Salisbury in 1849, but Bethlem's department, despite accommodation being doubled in 1838 when the Hospital was enlarged to hold 364 patients, was still overcrowded.[122] For the majority, conditions were plainly inadequate and outdated. According to Allderidge, 'it was almost impossible to provide employment or diversion for the inmates, and the only pastimes readily available were fives and running in the exercise yard, and knitting and reading in the crepuscular galleries'.[123]

Hood shared the Lunacy Commissioners concerns, complaining in 1855 of the difficulties and dangers consequent on the presence of 'powerful, daring and dangerous criminals' in the Hospital, and called for more security. However, he also worked to improve conditions and treatment. His hands, however, were tied by the prison-like construction of the building. Hood sought permission from the Lunacy Commissioners to make improvements. At first he encountered opposition because the Commissioners were convinced of the need to provide a separate state asylum. In 1857, he cleared one of the ordinary wards and turned it into a ward for forty of the 'better class' of criminal patients.[124] A library was also provided. In 1858, he applied to the Secretary of State for leave to take some of the female criminal lunatics for 'an occasional walk beyond the bounds of the Hospital'.[125] Improvements did little to make conditions better. In 1857, the *Quarterly Review* noted:

> These dens, for we can call them by no softer name, are the only remaining representatives of old Bedlam. They consist of dismal arched corridors, feebly

lit at either end by a single window in double irons, and divided in the middle by gratings more like those which enclose the fiercer carnivora at the Zoological Gardens than anything we have elsewhere seen employed for the detention of afflicted humanity.[126]

What was needed was a new purpose-built asylum.

At first, Hood had been in favour of keeping the department at Bethlem, but quickly was convinced that it would best be moved to another institution. It was the Lunacy Commissioners who revived the idea voiced in 1807 for a separate state asylum for criminal lunatics. They believed that county and borough asylums were unsuitable for the task.[127] At the same time that Hood was appointed, the idea was beginning to be taken seriously. Possible sites were investigated during the 1850s.[128] Hood objected to these proposals in 1854, believing that a single asylum would be more like a prison than a curative establishment, while it would be cheaper to leave the criminal lunatics in Bethlem.[129] His objections did not count for much, and the Home Office started looking for possible sites. Two years later the Government confirmed that the criminal lunatics at Bethlem would be moved to a new hospital for 600 inmates.[130] Problems were encountered in securing legislation to found an asylum in the country at Broadmoor.[131] The site matched concerns about the curative powers of clean air, but the institution was built along the lines of a prison by Sir Joshua Jebb, the former military engineer who had been responsible for Pentonville.[132] By now Hood was frustrated with the criminal lunatics' department at Bethlem and abandoned his opposition. He wrote to the Lunacy Commissioners in 1860 suggesting that the classification of criminal lunatics at Bethlem had been impossible and now advocated a separate asylum.[133] If nothing Hood was a pragmatist.

Broadmoor Asylum was opened for women patients in 1863 and in May nineteen of the twenty female patients were transferred. The men followed in 1864, the first batch leaving in February, with batches of eight or nine leaving by railway once or twice a week. Among them was the painter Richard Dadd (see below). One of the last was Edward Oxford (see pp. 505–6). All 112 patients arrived at Broadmoor without injury to themselves or others. The Governors sent a bill to the Home Office for the thirty new and eighty-three partially worn suits the patients had taken with them to Broadmoor. In addition, they immediately set about demolishing the criminal buildings.[134]

The criminal lunatics' wing (see Chapter 22) had provided a home for some of Bethlem's most notable patients. For example, the witty Jonathan Martin had been sent to the Hospital in 1829 for trying to set fire to York Minster. At his trial his friends tried to convince the court that he was sane, while his enemies testified that he had always been mad.[135] Daniel McNaughton, who had shot and killed Edward Drummond in 1843 in mistake for Sir Robert Peel in the belief that he was persecuted by the Tories, was also sent to Bethlem. Much has been written on McNaughton and his trial that established a set of criteria against which criminal insanity was measured, but other figures also prove of historical interest.[136]

Dadd (see Plate 26.4) had been transferred from Maidstone Gaol to Bethlem's Criminal Lunatic Department on 22 August 1844. Born in 1817 in Chatham, he had become the subject of sensational headlines in 1843 after the 'insane killing of his

Plate 26.4 Richard Dadd at work on *Oberon and Titania, c.* 1856. Reproduced by permission of Bethlem Royal Hospital Archives and Museum.

father'.[137] He was admitted to Bethlem as a criminal lunatic, a move that halted his public artistic career but did not end his work. Dadd had started to draw seriously at the age of thirteen and worked hard to enter the Royal Academy Schools in London, which he did in 1837. At the Royal Academy, he stood out at the centre of a circle of young artists and won several prizes. He was admired for his draughtsmanship and started exhibiting from the first year of his studies, drawing inspiration from Shakespeare. In 1842, Dadd was recommended to travel round the Middle East with Sir Thomas Phillips to provide a collection of paintings.[138] The trip, which took him and Phillips to Venice, Greece and Egypt, greatly affected Dadd. In Egypt, he started to exhibit symptoms of mental illness, complaining of 'nervous depression', which others blamed on sunstroke.[139] Throughout the return journey, Dadd suffered increasingly from delusions that he was being pursued by spirits. In Rome he started to be taken over by irrational impulses that dominated the rest of his life. On his return, his actions became unpredictable and occasionally violent. He was now watchful and suspicious, obsessed with Egyptian mythology. Increasingly he believed that he was being persecuted by the devil's minions and that voices were influencing him in his own mission to rid the world of the devil. His landlady became afraid of his bizarre behaviour, although Dadd's father persistently claimed that there was nothing wrong with his son despite the advice of Alexander Sutherland, physician at St Luke's, who advised that Dadd should be restrained. Shortly after Sutherland had been consulted, Dadd called on his father and suggested a walk in the country near Cobham to help him clear his mind. On the walk Dadd repeatedly stabbed his father with a spring knife he had brought along for the purpose, convinced that his father was the devil. He immediately made his escape to France where he was arrested after attacking a complete stranger. On arrest Dadd freely recounted his activities in Cobham and was committed to an asylum without trial. Although his family wanted him to remain in France, the Home Secretary had him extradited and committal proceedings were undertaken at Rochester and Maidstone. At these appearances it was evident that Dadd was insane. After spending two weeks in Maidstone Gaol, where he alternated between calm and frenzied violence, he was committed to the criminal lunatics' wing at Bethlem.

After his admission Dadd ceased to attract public attention, although during his time at the Hospital and then at Broadmoor, he continued to paint. Despite improvements throughout the main Hospital, little had been done to the criminal lunatics' wing. Here patients were encouraged to occupy themselves, and Dadd was prompted in his painting by the staff. At Bethlem, he developed his talent, producing, in Allderidge's view, works of 'incredible delicacy and beauty' that might have allowed him to escape from the conditions he lived under.[140] Hood took an interest in his work, noting in 1854 that Dadd, despite his continuing deluded and violent state, 'was a very sensible and agreeable companion. He showed in conversation, a mind well educated and thoroughly informed in all the particulars of his profession'.[141] Another person on the Bethlem staff who helped Dadd was George Henry Haydon, Hood's new Steward, who passed on some of Dadd's paintings to admirers in the outside world. Hood acquired some too, and no fewer than thirty-four Dadd paintings were sold after Hood's death. Morison also tried to secure drawings in 1856 and sent £5 to Dadd, to be told by the Treasurer that 'we must not allow any more of Dadd's drawings to leave the Hospital'.[142] Two of his most important works (*Oberon and Titania* and *The Fairy Feller's Master-stroke*) were painted for and given to Hood and Haydon. Dadd benefited from improvements in conditions at Bethlem under Hood. He was transferred to the converted ordinary ward with its flowers and ornamentation in 1857. William Michael Rossetti, who visited Bethlem in 1863, described him as 'working in a large airy room'. Here Dadd, in more pleasant surroundings, started to paint watercolour landscapes, until he was transferred to Broadmoor where he remained until his death in 1886 under conditions that had been designed to give 'inmates' more freedom within the perimeter.[143]

Oxford's attempt on Queen Victoria in 1840 had a different background from Dadd's act. Of the attempted shootings of Victoria, Oxford's (where he discharged two pistols while she took the air on Constitution Hill) was the most notorious.[144] As a young man of eighteen, he was aware of what he was doing, which as the law stood would have been enough to sentence him to death. In his notebooks he describes how he was to be an instrument in a plot by an imagined secret society and bought the pistols to this effect. When it came to the trial, Oxford's youth inspired compassion, while the pointlessness of the attack raised doubts about whether the pistols were loaded. At his trial, lay witnesses testified to Oxford's abnormal behaviour, whilst 'a veritable bevy of distinguished medical witnesses lent their support'.[145] His friends claimed that he was odd and irresponsible and Conolly, building on a science of phrenology that claimed to be both scientific and somatic, argued that Oxford's head suggested an imperfect development of the brain.[146] Here the medical witnesses added little to the case and failed to distinguish themselves. On the evidence, Oxford was considered 'not guilty by reason of insanity' and was sent as a criminal lunatic to Bethlem. At the Hospital any indication that he was insane did not appear, casting doubt on the medical witnesses at his trial. After fourteen years in the Hospital, he became a skilled linguist, mastering French, German and Italian, and learned to play the violin. He also became an accomplished knitter, carpenter and house painter.[147] Oxford, like Dadd, was transferred to Broadmoor, from which he was discharged in 1868 on the proviso that he emigrated to Australia. Here he changed his name to Freeman, a good choice.[148]

To those 'who had endured the narrow constraint of Bethlem's prison blocks, the move to Broadmoor with its terraces . . . and views across the Berkshire Downs, must have seemed almost like a release'.[149] According to Hunter and Macalpine, 'when the last criminal lunatic was transferred to Broadmoor in 1864 Bethlem broke its last link with the past and became a hospital for patients of a superior class'.[150]

BEYOND HOOD

Hood's achievements in encouraging non-restraint and rudimentary occupational therapy were successful. Under him the Hospital appeared to change, in line with the practices adopted at other asylums. This was exactly what the lunacy reform movement and the Lunacy Commission, seeking conformity to their accepted norms of treatment and administration, wanted. No-one seemed prepared to admit that Hood was carrying through reforms and practices already started under his predecessors. Against this apparent success, the number of recoveries fell by 6 per cent between the 1840s and 1860s even though 'a more humane and scientific mode of treatment' had been adopted, although it remained higher than the cure rate boasted at Ticehurst and the York Retreat.[151] Not everything was as it seemed. In the changes introduced much depended on Hood's enthusiasm and control. Between 1868 and 1870 he continued to influence Bethlem as Treasurer, and when he died in 1870 policies were to change and new practices were adopted that Hood would have opposed. Seclusion increased from 1868 and mechanical restraint was reintroduced in 1871. Bethlem, however, now had a new and growing reputation as a hospital for the middle classes and this was enhanced during the rest of the nineteenth century. In this sense Hood's legacy lived on.

NOTES

1 Edward G. O'Donoghue, *The Story of Bethlehem Hospital from its Foundation in 1247* (London: T. Fisher Unwin, 1914), 353.

2 Richard Hunter and Ida MacAlpine, *Psychiatry for the Poor, 1851 Colney Hatch Asylum, Friern Hospital, 1973: A Medical and Social History* (Folkestone: Dawson, 1974), 73.

3 David Russell, *Scenes from Bedlam* (London: Baillière Tindall, 1996), 151–2.

4 Anthony Masters, *Bedlam* (London: Michael Joseph, 1977), 160.

5 Board of Governors, 4 October 1971; MEC Presented Papers: 4 January 1973, ECD 205/72.

6 Court of Governors, 12 June 1852.

7 *Report and Evidence of the Lunacy Commission to the Home Secretary on Bethlehem Hospital* (London: 1852), 16.

8 W. Rees Thomas, 'The Unwilling Patients', *Journal of Mental Science*, xlix (1953), 191–201.

9 W. F. Bynum, Roy Porter and Michael Shepherd (eds), *Anatomy of Madness* (London: Routledge, 1988), vol. iii, 7.

10 General Court, 18 December 1865.

11 John Haslam, *Illustrations of Madness*, with an introduction by Roy Porter (London: Routledge, 1988), xxiv.

12 *Lancet*, 1 (1853), 62.

13 *Lancet*, 2 (1852), 60.

14 *General Report of the Royal Hospitals of Bridewell and Bethlem and of the House of Occupations for the year Ending 31st December 1855.*

15 Cited in Jeremy Taylor, *Hospital and Asylum Architecture in England 1840–1914: Buildings for Health Care* (London: Mansell, 1991), 138. For Colney Hatch, see Hunter and MacAlpine, *op. cit.*

16 Hunter and Macalpine, *op. cit.* 72–3.

17 *Illustrated London News*, 24 March 1860.

18 Russell, *op. cit.* 152.

19 O'Donoghue, *op.cit.* 416.

20 Andrew Scull, *The Most Solitary of Afflictions: Madness and Society in Britain, 1700–1900* (New Haven, Conn. and London: Yale University Press, 1993), 207.

21 William Charles Hood, *Statistics of Insanity, Embracing a Report of Bethlem Hospital from 1846 to 1860 Inclusive* (London: Batten, 1862), 60.

22 Scull, *op. cit.* 217–18.

23 William Lawrence, *Lectures on Physiology, Zoology and the Natural History of Man, Delivered at the Royal College of Surgeons* (London: Callow, 1819), 112.

24 Alexander Morison, *Outlines of Lectures on the Nature, Cause, and Treatment of Insanity*, 4th edn (London: Longman, Green, Brown & Longman, 1848), 422–3.

25 Lawrence, *op. cit.* 112.

26 Michael Clark, 'The Rejection of Psychological Approaches to Mental Disorder in Late Nineteenth Century British Psychiatry', in Andrew Scull (ed.), *Madhouses, Mad-Doctors, and Madmen* (Philadelphia: University of Pennsylvania, 1981), 271–313.

27 Scull, *The Most Solitary of Afflictions*, 239.

28 Cited in H. Sass and S. Herpertz, 'Personality Disorder', in German Berrios and Roy Porter (eds), *A History of Clinical Psychiatry: The Origins and History of Psychiatric Disorders* (London: Athlone, 1995), 635.

29 Hood, *op. cit.* 55.

30 Elaine Showalter, 'Victorian Women and Insanity', *Victorian Studies*, xxiii (1979), 169, 170.

31 Hood, *op. cit.* 56.

32 *Ibid.* 57.

33 *Ibid.* 69.

34 Anne Digby, *Madness, Morality and Medicine: A Study of the York Retreat 1796–1914* (Cambridge: CUP, 1985), 137; Trevor Turner, 'Rich and the Mad in Victorian England', *Psychological Medicine*, xix (1989), 43; Scull, *The Most Solitary of Afflictions*, 345.

35 Russell, *op. cit.* 151.
36 *1855 General Report.*
37 *Ibid.* 41–2.
38 Russell, *op. cit.* 151.
39 *1855 General Report,* 41–2.
40 Bethlem Subcommittee, April 1853.
41 *Ibid.* 17 December 1852 and December 1853.
42 Bethlem had been added to their register on 11 November 1853: *Lancet,* 2 (1853), 358.
43 *8th Annual Report of the Lunacy Commissioners* (1853– 4).
44 Cited in Russell, *op. cit.* 155.
45 *Household Words,* xvi (1857), 145–50.
46 *Ibid,* x (1852).
47 *Household Words,* xvi (1857), 145–50.
48 O'Donoghue, *op. cit.* 354.
49 *Household Words,* xvi (1857), 145–50.
50 *Journal of Mental Science,* July 1857.
51 *Household Words,* xvi (1857), 145–50.
52 *Illustrated London News,* 24 March 1860.
53 O'Donoghue, *op. cit.* 353.
54 See L. Smith, '"Levelled to the Same Common Standard?" Social Class in the Lunatic Asylum, 1780–1860', in Owen Ashton, Robert Fyson and Stephen Roberts (eds), *Duty of Discontent: Essays for Dorothy Thompson* (London: Mansell, 1996), 142–66, 161.
55 *Household Words,* xvi (1857), 145–50.
56 *Ibid.*
57 Dickens himself had a special interest in 'incurables' of all kinds. He spoke at charity dinners for the recently founded (1854) Royal Hospital for Incurables in 1856 and 1857: K. J. Fielding, *The Speeches of Charles Dickens* (Oxford: Clarendon Press, 1960), 222, 232.
58 *Household Words.*
59 Nancy Tomes, 'The Great Restraint Controversy', in W. F. Bynum, Roy Porter and Michael Shepherd (eds), *Anatomy of Madness* (London: Tavistock Press, 1988), vol. iii, 194; Phil Fennell, *Treatment Without Consent: Law, Psychiatry and the Treatment of Mentally Disordered People Since 1845* (London: Routledge, 1996), 24–36.
60 Akihito Suzuki, 'The Politics and Ideology of Non-Restraint: The Case of Hanwell Asylum', *Medical History,* xxxix (1995), 1.
61 *1855 General Report.*
62 Suzuki, *op. cit.* 2; see Andrew Scull, 'A Victorian Alienist', in W. F. Bynum, Roy Porter and Michael Shepherd (eds), *Anatomy of Madness* (London: Tavistock Press, 1985), vol. ii, 103–50.
63 Suzuki, *op. cit.* 14.
64 Hood, *op. cit.* 104ff.
65 Scull, *The Most Solitary of Afflictions,* 244.
66 *1855 General Report,* 45.
67 Russell, *op. cit.* 42–3, 93–4.
68 Michael Fears, 'Therapeutic Optimism and the Treatment of the Insane', in R. Dingwall *et al., Health Care and Health Knowledge* (London: Croom Helm, 1977), 66–84.
69 *1855 General Report.*
70 *1870 Annual Report of the Bethlem Royal Hospital,* 42.
71 Fennell, *op. cit.* 32–36.
72 Suzuki, *op. cit.* 10–13.
73 *1855 General Report.* Hood's approach had been advocated earlier: see Charles Pearson, 'Letter on the proposed Legislative Enactment in Reference to the Criminal Lunatics', *The Journal of Psychological Medicine',* i (1848), 182.
74 *1855 General Report.*
75 Hood, *op. cit.* 7.

76 See Chapter 22, and John Howard, *An Account of the Principal Lazarettos of Europe* (London: Cadell, 1789).

77 F. O. Martin, *The Report of the Commissioners for Enquiry into Charities for 1837* (London: 1837), 568.

78 G. A. Sala, *Gaslight and Daylight* (London: 1859), 218–19.

79 *Report and Evidence of the Lunacy Commission*, 5.

80 *1855 General Report*, 41.

81 See William Charles Hood, *Statistics of Insanity, A Decennial Report of Bethlem Hospital from 1846 to 1855* (London: Batten, 1856); idem, *Statistics of Insanity, Embracing a Report of Bethlem Hospital from 1846 to 1860 Inclusive* (London: Batten, 1862).

82 *1860 General Report*, 33.

83 *Journal of Mental Science*, iii (1857), 216.

84 R. J. Dunghison, 'Statistics of Insanity in the United States of America', *North American Medico-Chirurgical Review*, July 1860.

85 For a comparison of admissions, see Charlotte MacKenzie, 'Social Factors in the Admission, Discharge and Continuity of Stay of Patients at Ticehurst Asylum', in W. F. Bynum, Roy Porter and Michael Shepherd (eds), *Anatomy of Madness* (London: Tavistock Press, 1985), vol ii, 147–74, and Digby, *op. cit.*

86 Hood, *Statistics of Insanity, Embracing a Report of Bethlem Hospital*, 51.

87 *1859 General Report*.

88 *Ibid.* 40; *Journal of Mental Science* (October 1862).

89 Hood, *Statistics of Insanity, Embracing a Report of Bethlem Hospital*, 31–4.

90 *Ibid.* 31–2.

91 *Ibid.* 32–4.

92 *Ibid.* 15.

93 *Tinsley's Magazine*, iii (1869), 462.

94 Showalter, *op. cit.* 163, 165.

95 Hood, *Statistics of Insanity, Embracing a Report of Bethlem Hospital*, 15. When Hood's successor, Dr Helps, used the Bethlem comparative statistics in a spirit of congratulation he was sharply attacked in the *Asylum Journal* by Dr C. L. Robertson.

96 James Done, *The Need of Christianity to Cities* (London: 1844).

97 Hood, *Statistics of Insanity, Embracing a Report of Bethlem Hospital*, 60.

98 This letter is quoted in the Appendix of the *Seventeenth Report of the Commissioners in Lunacy* (1863).

99 John Conolly, *Construction and Government of Lunatic Asylums* (London: J. Churchill, 1847), 14.

100 Taylor, *op. cit* 135.

101 *Journal of Mental Science*, July 1857.

102 For St Thomas's, see Lindsay Granshaw, 'St. Thomas's Hospital, London 1850–1900' (unpublished Ph.D. Thesis, Bryn Mawr College, 1981).

103 E. M. McInnes, *St. Thomas's Hospital* (London: George Allen & Unwin, 1963), 109.

104 Letters from Robert Wainwright, Clerk of St Thomas's, to H. M. Jefferson, Clerk of Bethlem, 24 April 1863: Resolution of the Grand Committee of St Thomas's Hospital, 21 April 1863.

105 Court of Governors, 20 February and 8 May 1863.

106 *Journal of Mental Science*, July 1863.

107 *The Times*, 1 June 1863.

108 *Ibid.* 17 June 1863.

109 *Lancet*, 1 (1863), 697.

110 Copies of Spring Rice's letter and the letter from H. Waddington, Grey's chief civil servant, to the Governors were printed in a *Return to an Address of the Honourable The House of Commons*, 10 June 1863.

111 *Lancet*, 2 (1862), 364.

112 Court of Governors, 13 July 1863.

113 Geoffrey Rivett, *Development of the London Hospital System 1823–1982* (London: OUP, 1986), 100–1.

114 *Report of the Committee of the Royal Hospitals of Bridewell and Bethlehem submitted by F.O. Martin Esq.; Inspector of Charities as worthy of the consideration of the Governors, and on the Observations of Drs. Hood and Helps, the late and present Chief Resident Physicians of the Hospital, agreed to at the General Court of Governors held on the 30th of January* (London: 1865).

115 Bethlem Subcommittee, 9 September and 30 September 1870.

116 *25th Report of the Commissioners in Lunacy* (1871).

117 *23rd Report of the Commissioners in Lunacy* (1868–9).

118 Geoffrey Finlayson, *The Seventh Earl of Shaftesbury 1801–1885* (London: Methuen, 1981), 415.

119 For the establishment of the criminal lunatics department, see Chapter 22, pp. 403–5.

120 Richard Hunter and Ida Macalpine, *Three Hundred Years of Psychiatry* (London: OUP, 1963), 1020.

121 William Charles Hood, *Criminal Lunatics* (London: 1860).

122 Peter Laurie, *A Narrative of the Proceedings at the Laying of the First Stone of the New Buildings at Bethlem Hospital* (London: J. T. Norris, for the Governors, 1838).

123 Patricia Allderidge, 'Why was McNaughton Sent to Bethlem?', in D. J. West and A. Walk (eds), *Daniel McNaughton: His Trial and Aftermath* (London: Gaskell, 1977), 110.

124 *Ibid.*

125 Bethlem Subcommittee, 11 January 1858.

126 *Quarterly Review* (1857), 36.

127 Nick Hervey, 'The Lunacy Commission 1845–1860' (unpublished Ph.D. Thesis, University of Bristol, 1987), 288.

128 Nigel Walker and Sarah McCabe, *Crime and Insanity in England: New Solutions and New Problems* (Edinburgh: University of Edinburgh, 1973), vol. ii, 8.

129 William Charles Hood, *Suggestions for the Future Provision for Criminal Lunatics* (London: J. Churchill, 1954).

130 For Broadmoor, see Ralph Partridge, *Broadmoor: A History of Criminal Lunacy and its Problems* (London: Chatto and Windus, 1953).

131 Hervey, *op. cit.* 291.

132 Walker and McCabe, *op. cit.* 9.

133 *Ibid.*

134 Allderidge, *op. cit.* 111–12.

135 Patricia Allderidge, 'Criminal Insanity: Bethlem to Broadmoor', *Proceedings of the Royal Society of Medicine* (1974), lxvii, 903.

136 For McNaughton, see West and Walk, *op. cit.*; Henry Rollin, 'Forensic Psychiatry in England', in Hugh Freeman and German Berrios (eds), *150 Years of British Psychiatry: The Aftermath* (London: Athlone, 1996), 248–55; R. Smith, *Trial by Medicine: Insanity and Responsibility in Victorian Trials* (Edinburgh: Edinburgh University Press, 1981).

137 See Patricia Allderidge, *The Late Richard Dadd, 1817–1886* (London: Tate Gallery, 1974) for Richard Dadd's life, or Isaure de Saint Pierre, *Richard Dadd: His Journals* (Henley: Aidan Ellis, 1984) for a fictional account.

138 Russell, *op. cit.* 112.

139 Allderidge, *The Late Richard Dadd*, 21.

140 *Ibid.* 28.

141 Cited in *ibid.* 30.

142 *Ibid.* 35.

143 *Ibid.* 31–3 for Dadd's time at Broadmoor, where he continued to paint.

144 Allderidge, 'Criminal Insanity', 901.

145 Rollin, *op. cit.* 247.

146 See Roger Cooter, 'Phrenology and British Alienists, *c.* 1825–1845', in Andrew Scull (ed.), *Madhouses, Mad-Doctors and Madmen* (Philadelphia: University of Pennsylvania Press, 1981), 58–104.

147 Allderidge, 'Criminal Insanity', 901.

148 Rollin, *op. cit.* 247.

149 Allderidge, 'Criminal Insanity', 904.

150 Hunter and Macalpine, *Three Hundred Years of Psychiatry*, 1020.
151 *Lancet*, 1 (1863), 307; MacKenzie, *op. cit.* 151; Digby, *op. cit.* Scull argues that in county asylums the 'cure' was 26 per cent, at Bethlem it was close to 50 per cent: Andrew Scull, *Museums of Madness* (London: Allen Lane, 1979), 208, and see J. Walton, 'Casting out and Bringing Back in Victorian England', in W. F. Bynum, Roy Porter and Michael Shepherd (eds), *Anatomy of Madness* (London: Tavistock Press, 1985), vol. ii, 132–46.

CHAPTER TWENTY-SEVEN

A VICTORIAN INSTITUTION

——— •◆• ———

In his 1858 annual report William Charles Hood, Bethlem's first Resident Physician-Superintendent, informed the Governors that 'the events of the year 1858 have been but the history of 1857'. He added that he sincerely prayed that 'the same harmony may exist among officers, patients, and servants, during the year 1859'.[1] There had been a symbolic change in 1858 when the Cibber statues, curtained (except on committee days), were moved to the South Kensington Museum, and there was a further change a generation later in 1888 when they moved yet again to the Guildhall Crypt museum. The City of London had reclaimed them.[2] Bethlem appeared a very different institution from the one that had been investigated in 1815.

CONTINUING INVESTIGATION AND FURTHER IMPROVEMENTS

The Commissioners of Lunacy were in a position to test Hood's prayers and those of his successors. The situation had altered since 1851. Bethlem could no longer be accused of secrecy. In his own report for 1881, the Resident Physician-Superintendent stated unequivocally that there was now no attempt 'to hide either from the lay or the medical mind, anything which was being done from within its walls'.[3] He might have added that since 1868 the Commissioners' Reports had been bound with the *General Report*, and in 1898 it was to be decided to lay them before the Court of Governors. The Bethlem Subcommittee was confident about what the Commissioners would find.[4]

In most years the Commissioners contributed to the harmony of the Hospital, praising the medical staff and Governors for the work that had been conducted in the previous year. In 1877 they wrote approvingly:

> As we passed through the wards we observed, generally, great order and tranquillity, and no one was under restraint or in seclusion ... This is a most creditable circumstance and could only have been arrived at by the maintenance of the very adequate and skilful staff of attendants we are glad still to find here.[5]

Neither of the two Lunacy Commissioners who signed the report of 1877 had been a Commissioner when Bethlem was investigated in 1851. The two formal visits a year by the Lunacy Commissioner to the main Hospital, and to the convalescent home in Surrey, repeatedly reported that Bethlem was in 'excellent order, and its state very creditable to those engaged in its management'.[6] Praise was frequent, but not universal. In 1893 the Commissioners were concerned that the wards at Bethlem were not in 'such high order' as those in 'many other Hospitals' and lacked 'many of the objects of interest which we think so conducive to the recovery of patients; and we are sorry to see that this truly royal charity is thus lagging in the rear of the march of progress'.[7] Such criticism did not last long.

However, it was the word 'again' in the 1877 *Report* that stands out. Repeatedly the Commissioners judged that the Hospital's environment had been improved since 1851. When George Savage was appointed Resident Physician-Superintendent in 1878 he felt that the Hospital had been modernized. Looking back after ten years at Bethlem he noted:

> it remained for me to suggest to the Governors, from time to time, such improvements and alterations as yet seemed to be wanting, in order to turn what had already been done to the best account. This also embraced the taking into occupation of the Convalescent Establishment at Witley, a responsibility which the force of circumstances has left with me.

Changes in the night watch meant that by the 1870s patients were visited twice nightly, while those on a special list were visited every hour. The installation of additional hot-water heating extended the number of rooms that could be used, and a racquet court had been added.[8] By 1876 the female wards were heated by hot-water pipes, the bathroom walls were covered with glazed white tiles and it had been proposed to fit all the lavatories with marble. One alteration that was made in the bathrooms was that the double-seated toilets were replaced with single ones.[9] While Savage was Resident Physician 'an air of domesticity and cheerfulness' prevailed. The power of the lights in wards was doubled, and there was an attack on the damp with the deep well having been made 'impervious to surface water'. Paid labour replaced the labour of criminal convicts now housed in Broadmoor. In the 1880s reports were still being received that Bethlem 'generally is in good order'. Improvements continued to be made in 1886; the 'work of cleaning and decoration was in progress' when the Commissioners visited, although this had resulted in 'a certain degree of confusion'.[10] By 1896, some of the single bedrooms had been plastered and 'a considerable amount of painting had been done in different wards'. More work was 'in progress'.[11]

Other visitors passed a similar verdict. In an investigation of English asylums in the late 1870s Bethlem emerged well when compared with the large county asylums and St Luke's with which it continued to be directly associated. Both Bethlem and St Luke's were 'charities', but whereas Bethlem was rich, St Luke's was poor. Both were judged to be 'singularly ill adapted for the residence of large bodies of patients, whatever their malady'. For the Hospital this was not so much of a problem as the Governors had no intention of mimicking the large county and borough asylums with which it was being compared. However, the general appearance of their inmates was 'indicative of comfort and content'. The treatment at Bethlem was deemed to be better organized than it was at St Luke's. The investigator approved of the policy that was being followed in the Hospital of 'reliev[ing] the sufferings of those a little above the level of pauperism'.[12] He devoted most of his attention to Bethlem as a centre of care for the insane, praising in particular the detailed medical appendices that had been produced at Bethlem in 1873 and 1874. It was felt that

> even recognising, as we do, the necessity of receiving a certain proportion of quiet and tractable cases to facilitate the control of more turbulent inmates . . . an institution like Bethlem has not the excuse of a need for 'quiet' cases to eke out a scanty attendance.

The paid officers 'were sufficiently numerous and . . . of a class superior in point of efficiency' for this task.[13] The diets were judged 'generous', so generous indeed that the investigator demanded 'more adequate and suitable bodily exercise to promote nutrition and obviate the consequences of proportionate excess'.[14]

The Governors were responsive to the problems the Commissioners detected, but not always as quickly as the Commissioners wanted. Problems were identified with the food for the attendants in 1889. Attendants cooked their own dinners and 'breakfast extras' for the patients in the wards, thereby not only taking up time in 'culinary work' that should have been devoted to patients' care', but requiring the keeping of fires in the wards all the year round. This was unacceptable to the Commissioners. They also complained that attendants and nurses had their food served 'either cooked or raw at their own option'. This was seen as 'objectionable' and 'very unusual in Asylums at the present day' for food to be provided uncooked.[15] The Commissioners were still complaining in 1899 that mess rooms had not yet been introduced for the attendants, although they felt sure that 'the subject will not be forgotten'.[16] In 1886 complaints were made that an 'alteration of the upper galleries to form a supervision dormitory' should have been carried out the year before. Some other problems were occasionally detected. The Commissioners were concerned about the presence of 'sewer gas' in the wards and recommended that 'a general reconstruction of the sewage of the Hospital would no doubt be desirable, but probably a very costly operation not unattended, possibly, by danger'.[17] However, in 1896 the Commissioners recognized that 'nothing short of reconstruction' could make the Hospital more satisfactory.[18] Similar concerns were to be repeated with more force in the 1920s (see Chapter 29).

The limited range and style of the Commissioners' comments suggest that the role of the Commissioners had not substantially altered by the end of the century. They 'had developed a *modus operandi* that . . . encouraged an unhealthy adherence to the Moloch of administrative perfectibility'.[19] None the less, they were preoccupied with 'superintendence'. This was recognised in the conclusion of their 1878 *Report*: 'we desire to record our opinion that this institution maintains its high character for efficiency and usefulness and continues to reflect great credit on the management of Dr. Williams'.[20] It was an incomplete judgment, however, for one subject which did figure in Commissioners' Reports was the use of restraint. Bethlem was still under review. Like all asylums, it was constantly under pressure from the Lunacy Commissioners to modify its practices and make improvements.

CONTINUITY

A close relationship continued to exist between Bethlem and its sister organization. In 1860 a significant change had been made to the name of the Bethlem/Bridewell charity. The 'House of Occupation', which had been moved next to Bethlem in 1828, was rechristened 'King Edward's Schools'. Such a change of title was a significant step in the creation of a Victorian institution. Edward Rudge, the Chaplain and Superintendent of the Schools, felt that the alteration symbolized the Schools becoming 'not a local, but in every sense a national one'. At the same time, Bethlem was becoming more of a London institution, not only in terms of its management but also through the patients it admitted. Connections between the two institutions were maintained, however. The annual reports of the Schools, one for boys, the other for girls, were bound with the Bethlem reports. They shared the same system of government and links with the City of London, with some of the City Governors being even more prominent at school events than in Bethlem activities. When in 1870 Bethlem created its 'Convalescent Establishment' at Witley, the Schools quickly followed. Annual cricket matches were played there between Schools and Hospital.[21]

In an investigation of asylums in England and Wales, an outside observer felt that Bethlem was now in 'excellent hands'. The only institution described in comparable terms was the West Riding Asylum at Wakefield directed by James Crichton-Browne.[22] At Bethlem these 'excellent hands' worked within a management structure where there were clear continuities. The Court of Governors continued to run both institutions, although the General Committee conducted most of the work and delegated the running of the Hospital to the Bethlem Subcommittee and the administration of the Schools to the King Edward Schools Subcommittee. Continuity was also assured through those playing a conspicuous part in the management. Family connections were prominent while there was continuity in office holding and commitment to the charity as was shown by the Copelands.[23] Colonel James Alfred Copeland, Treasurer since 1885, was to take over again in 1900 after four years of forced retirement through ill health, serving until 1920. Copeland was born 'a puny child' in April 1837, but he managed to outlive his nine other siblings. He entered his father's china business in 1855 and from 1860 was regarded as an authority on china, glass and earthenware, negotiating the treaty of commerce with France with Richard Cobden. He had become a Governor of Bethlem in 1865 through his father, William Taylor Copeland, Alderman of Bishopsgate and Lord Mayor in 1835, who had been a Governor since 1861 and President from 1861 to 1868. Likewise, the new President in 1897, Sir George Faudel-Phillips, came from a prominent City Jewish family that had supported Bethlem for more than a generation. Continuity of commitment was taken for granted. Thus, Sydney Smirke was made a Governor in 1870 when he ceased to be Surveyor and Architect, a post which he had held for thirty years. Some Governors were singled out for particular praise more than others. For example, George Savage, the Resident Physician-Superintendent, recorded in 1884 that 'hundreds of kind deeds were done' by J. J. Miles, 'to patients and officers which he, last of all men, would have mentioned'.[24]

Continuity was also provided by George Henry Haydon until his retirement as Steward in 1889. He was responsible for much of the harmony that Hood and the

Lunacy Commissioners detected at Bethlem. Haydon had been appointed in 1853, having served for more than three years under John Charles Bucknill, an opponent of the Hospital, at the Devon County Asylum. At Bethlem he held office alongside a variety of Resident Physicians. Percy Smith, one of them, described him as 'a man above reproach, a sportsman, an artist and a friend'.[25] O'Donoghue hoped that future historians would find time and place for a 'little biography of him'.[26] The son of a naval purser, Haydon had had an adventurous life before joining Bucknill. He had been apprenticed to an architect, and had left England for *Australia Felix* where he explored the land around Melbourne when the first settlement there consisted of a cluster of huts on the Yarra River. On his return to England he joined Bucknill, not only at the Devon County Asylum but in the Volunteer movement, being one of the first to enrol in the First Devon Rifle Volunteers. Haydon moved in artistic circles and was a friend of George Cruickshank, John Leech and Charles Keene, and some of his own sketches were reproduced in *Punch*. He was also a great reader, telling Hack Tuke that he turned to J. G. Whittier when he was 'tempted to take sour views of men and things'. Haydon died 'of apoplexy' after only a few hours' illness on 9 November 1891, two years after leaving Bethlem.[27]

Similar continuity was seen in the medical staff, who formed a close-knit community (see Chapter 32). Savage was the best-known outside Bethlem of the Hospital's Resident Physician-Superintendents, who where men left in large measure to discharge their medical responsibilities and tasks of superintendence by themselves. There were five Resident Physicians between the resignation of Hood in 1862 and the end of the century. Their annual reports, changing from time to time in format, provide the best introduction to Bethlem as a Victorian institution. The first of the Physicians in line, William Helps, held his post for only three years, dying in office in 1865. He was followed by William Rhys Williams (1865–78); Savage (1878–88); R. Percy Smith (1888–98), and Theophilus Hyslop, appointed in 1898, who was to serve until 1910.

There was remarkable professional coherence in this line of descent, broken only by the death of Helps. Rhys Williams had worked alongside Helps and in 1878 resigned, having been selected by the Lord Chancellor to serve as a Commissioner in Lunacy. Hood had also resigned from his post to become a Lord Chancellor's Visitor for the Insane in 1862. Before his appointment, Savage had worked closely with Rhys Williams for six years as his Assistant Medical Officer and knew from experience how 'onerous' the duties of the Resident Physician were.[28] Savage's place as Assistant Medical Officer was taken by Ramsden Wood. He had formerly been a clinical student at the Hospital and had worked with both Rhys Williams and Savage.[29] Alone among Bethlem doctors, Wood resigned his post to emigrate to Queensland, Australia. Percy Smith followed Savage's career pattern in the Hospital, as did Hyslop who had first been a student at Bethlem before working as the Assistant Resident Physician. When Smith retired in 1898 it was Hyslop who replaced him. The line of succession was clear and continued throughout the first half of the twentieth century.

The junior and senior medical staff did not work alone, or devote their entire time to treating the patients. In addition some clinical teaching and lecturing was conducted, building on a tradition established under Alexander Morison in the 1830s. Terminology had changed. In 1888 Percy Smith suggested that the Resident Student should be replaced by that of Clinical Assistant. The change was designed to reflect the fact that students were carrying out a large amount of clinical work under the direction of the medical officers and were a 'most valuable addition to the staff'. Moreover, the term 'clinical assistant' was that usually applied to men holding similar positions in other hospitals and asylums.[30] By the end of the nineteenth century, lectures were being given in the Hospital to students from Guy's Hospital and Charing Cross Hospital, while Dr Rayner, a former Assistant Resident Physician who resigned in 1872, continued to lecture at Bethlem to students from St Thomas's. The Hospital had become increasingly proud of its role as a teaching institution. Rhys Williams had aimed 'to maintain the reputation of the Hospital as a school for the study of mental diseases'. He believed that observing patients was as important as listening to lectures, and, whatever difficulties were present in admitting medical students into a lunatic asylum, Rhys Williams argued that 'the experience of the last few years' at Bethlem had 'clearly demonstrated that most valuable instruction may be imparted with a minimum of annoyance or injury to the patients'.[31] Savage planned to extend teaching by adding a library and pathological museum. Some success was encountered when the first examinations for the Medico-Psychological Association were held in the Hospital in 1886.[32] As the oldest asylum in Britain it was expected that Bethlem had much to offer.

A SOCIAL LIFE FOR THE PATIENTS

Discipline and order were prized as much as harmony in late Victorian Bethlem, but within the rhetoric it was notions of the 'home' that were stressed. The language of home was used alike by Governors, Resident Physicians and Lunacy Commissioners. When in 1878 the hours of rising and going to bed were changed from six in the morning and eight in the evening to seven and nine, respectively, this was justified as being 'more in harmony with home habits'.[33] Three years later, Savage described as his 'constant aim' that of making Bethlem 'more and more home-like and comfortable'.[34] He reiterated the point in 1886:

> the great endeavour of the staff is that patients should feel 'at home' in Bethlem, and that they should be willing if they feel illness returning to come back once more, of their own free will, and submit themselves for voluntary treatment.[35]

There was an element of rhetoric in the way in which defence of the home was presented, especially as doctors believed that 'one object of an Asylum' should be to remove patients from 'old surroundings, changing as much as possible the . . . direction of thoughts'.[36] For this reason it is necessary to look more closely at the institutional aspects of the Hospital; the attempt to create a place with a life and an ethos of its own.

Goffman has cast the spotlight on this aspect of asylums (and other confining institutions) in the United States. He illustrates both the 'disculturation' of patients placed there for a long period and the making of what he calls an 'attendant culture' for patients who were there for long or short periods. This included 'work therapy' –

along with the wide range of 'moral' substitutes for physical 'restraint'. He also drew attention to the role of the 'house organ' that drew a circle around an institution.[37] Bethlem does not quite fit into Goffman's twentieth-century pattern, but it made much of its own particular life and ethos and set out to express it through its own 'house organ', *Under the Dome*, a magazine produced by the staff with contributions from the patients. It had been preceded in 1875 by *The Star of Bethlehem*, which initially had a life of only seven weeks before reappearing in 1879.[38] When *Under the Dome* first appeared in December 1889 one copy of it was 'circulated' on each 'side of the House'. Much of the early material consisted of 'literary loot', scraps from other newspapers and periodicals. Yet it included an 'Answers to Correspondents' column and light verses (some by the Chaplain), and occasional illustrations. Grumbles too were recorded in *Under the Dome*. For example, it expressed complaints about the making and serving of tea in the Hospital and the effect of the removal of a coal box from the gallery, which was said to have served as a 'comfortable seat'. Most of these complaints did not smack of discontent. The magazine provoked a rival, *Over the Dome*, edited by 'M', a clever journalist and artist, who denounced the editor of *Under the Dome* as a 'midget'. 'It was a sham fight', however, 'which injured nobody . . . an excellent advertisement, increasing the sales of both papers.'[39] 'M' went on to write articles for *Under the Dome* on life in Bethlem.

Supported by the Governors, who provided the funding to produce the magazine, and by the medical staff (Percy Smith had suggested the name and was active in its production), *Under the Dome* pointed to both continuity and change in the Hospital, not only in personnel but in forms of employment and entertainment. 'Novelties' were much prized, like the 'limelight dissolving lantern lecture' with seventy-two slides on ancient Rome, made possible by 'Messrs. Newton the well known opticians near Temple Bar'.[40] Books also provided a welcome distraction, with many donated by the Governors and staff. A large number were added to the library in 1896, including J. P. Allen's *Building Construction*, Defoe's *Robinson Crusoe*, Charlotte M. Yonge's *Daisy Chain*, and J. R. Green's *History of the English People*. Three-decker novels, once popular, were now treated as 'antediluvian' and banished from circulation to the Gallery Libraries.[41] Distraction had its benefits. One patient wrote that 'time passes so rapidly, the sharpest impressions fade so easily, that it is hard to catch the right note in the music of the past'. For him it was the band, directed by C. M. Wilson, one of the Steward's clerks, and started in 1891 which had changed most. The band had quickly become an institution at Bethlem as it did in many county and borough asylums. So too had the dances, although they had been disturbed by influenza which seemed 'to entirely destroy dancing energy'. The biggest institution of all, however, was the Christmas tree 'from which nearly every patient and attendant received some present'. It was the Governors who subscribed individually to this. There was talk then of a Bethlem 'season', a well-established annual round which in 1892 began with a 'smoking concert' on 24 October.[42]

More than literary endeavour or the Christmas trees, music was in constant demand in the Hospital. In the Bethlem regime it took many forms, both vocal and instrumental. Percy Smith was a regular violoncello concert performer, and the versatile Hyslop frequently conducted. He played the violin and was sometimes a soloist on 'the Saxe-horn'. Young resident Physicians and medical students were expected to take part, and occasionally staff would perform a pantomime. In 1895 *Aladdin* was a great success with Hyslop's wife as Princess Badyoulbadour, 'her first appearance on the Bethlem boards'.[43] Each medical family was expected to get involved and much was made of the 'family spirit' seen to be pervasive throughout the entire institution. The family was conceived of as 'our large family under the dome'.[44] Once it was described as a 'merry family'.[45] Doctors appeared with their wives on the stage, sometimes with their own families – for example, 'Dr. and Mrs. Savage, accompanied by Miss Savage and Master Harold Savage'.[46] For Savage such entertainments were valuable, 'not only for good done at the time, but for the good service they do in rousing patients to prepare for them; and they are good as leaving memories which take the patient's attention from himself'.[47] Tuthill, Morison and Hood had all expressed the same rationale, and entertainments were seen as central to Bethlem's therapeutic regime.

PAYING PATIENTS

Savage was particularly proud of the fact, as he put it in his 1881 *Report*, that 'by careful selection of cases on application' the 'class of patients' admitted had become distinctly higher, 'that is, the patients have been members of the poor educated middle classes'. By the late 1870s, the changes instigated by George Tuthill and Alexander Morison and furthered by Hood had taken full effect. Bethlem was becoming increasingly a middle-class institution. This was recognized by visitors to the Hospital and by Savage. For him 'the improved tone of the patients is most seen in the male galleries where very many poor professional men have been admitted'.[48] In response, Savage suggested that the basis of admission should be altered to recognize this fact. In 1880 he raised the question of payment. There were large numbers of unoccupied beds on the male side 'for which sufficient numbers of suitable patients are never to be found'. Since the permanent charges of running the Hospital were nearly the same whatever the numbers resident, there was a built-in financial difficulty. This was accentuated by a fall in the income of the Charity as a result of 'the great depression in agriculture' that had led the Governors to reduce rents in some cases by as much as 20 per cent.[49] Paying patients would allow the Hospital to be 'kept full' and the accounts to remain solvent. However, there was another and quite different argument in favour of admitting paying patients: 'other Hospitals are doing the same, and are by this means extending their spheres of usefulness'.

In 1881 'the whole matter' was under the careful consideration of the Governors. Savage felt that 'I have only to speak from the Medical Superintendent's point of view, and I consider that it will be a useful addition to this Hospital.'[50] He accompanied the Treasurer when he had met with the Charity Commissioners in 1881 to test their views on paying patients. The Charity Commissioners had informed Bethlem that a scheme should be presented for approval.[51] The Governors suggested that fifty patients a year could be admitted as paying patients to the free beds in the Hospital. Approval from the Commissioners was secured, but only on a five-year basis and the Governors had to reapply after this period.[52]

The first paying patients, who were promised the same treatment 'in every respect' as ordinary 'non-paying patients', were admitted on 9 August 1882. They paid two guineas a week, but bonds and the £100 deposit, which had normally been required for all patients, were dispensed with. Instead agreements were drafted and new admission forms prepared.[53] For paying patients certificates were required from a minister of religion or some other 'person of respectability'. All medical certificates had to be signed by the Resident Physician. Bond requirements for other patients were also reduced in 1883 from £100 to £10. At the same time, friends of new patients were allowed to deposit £10 with the Steward instead of entering into a bond.[54]

STATISTICS AND TREATMENT

Hood's interest in statistical analysis was continued at Bethlem, but only in a half-hearted manner. For two successive years the *Annual Reports* included an appendix dealing largely with cases and written by Rhys Williams, with help from George Savage. There was no suggestion, however, that he was dealing with the cases he was studying in any significantly different way from that followed by John Haslam, Apothecary, earlier in the century.[55] Savage himself was later to express a common concern among asylum doctors, that 'at present each layman thinks he is as good a judge of insanity as a doctor, and this is not a very absurd idea when so many doctors have no more real knowledge of insanity than the laymen'.[56] Rhys Williams drew distinctions between 'melancholia' and 'mania' and was keenly interested in pulse rates, while he used the word 'neuroses', if with little confidence.[57] His strongest point was common sense. In his *Report* for 1872, Rhys Williams pointed to the statistical tables as 'a gratifying proof that our endeavours have been crowned with success'. He added, however, that he was abstaining from recording any special cases, although 'many most interesting in a medical point of view' had been under treatment.[58] In the following year he included an appendix that did just this. In the main, Rhys Williams described himself as 'quite aware that the statistics for a single year are not of much value', but in turning to case studies in the appendix he explained that Bethlem had great advantages for obtaining correct histories because the staff always examined the nearest relatives, although this presented problems in determining 'hereditary taint, and as to the supposed cause'.[59] The reference to 'hereditary taint' showed the way in which Rhys Williams's mind was working. A year later in the appendix to the 1874 *General Report*, he placed even more stress on heredity, believing that it was 'the legacy that each of us owes to his progenitors'.[60] These concerns were regularly repeated. Rhys Williams went on to comment that 'it is a sufficiently acknowledged fact that insanity is hereditary, but it is a fact often difficult to get at'. It was noted that on the female side there were forty out of 119 patients with a distinct history of others in their families suffering mentally. There were twenty-six out of eighty-two on the male side. For Bethlem's medical staff these were striking statistics. The conclusion, however, was unclear. For Rhys Williams and Savage 'we refrain from drawing any conclusion from the statistics above, as we should prefer to have much more extended tables to work with'.[61] Confidence was to increase. Rhys Williams, Percy Smith, Savage and Hyslop shared asylum doctors' concerns with heredity. Savage and Hyslop were particularly vociferous and spoke widely to professional and lay audiences on this issue. Ideas of heredity provided a common link between their understandings of mental illness, helping to shape their attitudes to treatment.

In his later reports, Rhys Williams paid more attention to trying to trace the relationship between insanity and other diseases. Here he attempted to link influenza, rheumatic fever, scarlet fever and syphilis to mental illness. Rhys Williams's approach was more in line with other asylum doctors than Hood's ideas. Less emphasis was placed on 'moral' causes and more attention was focused on the physical or somatic causes. Here Rhys Williams shared a common understanding of causation. That insanity had mainly physical origins was a basic article of faith for British psychiatrists in the late nineteenth century.[62] Savage was later to call repeatedly for a reclassification of mental disorders on scientific lines that had a clear etiological and somatic basis.[63] Here was a concern to find the true origins of madness. In his 1874 *Report*, Rhys Williams noted that 'we have had one or two cases in which without any direct history, we have been obliged to own that there was strong evidence for syphilis having something to do with the disease'.[64] 'Drink' figured more prominently than in 1873, but Rhys Williams was at pains to criticize 'the bias so common to alienists, of considering everything that is not commonplace as insanity'.[65] There were also sections of this appendix on obstruction of the bowels and on artificial feeding: 'only two cases required continuous feeding, and both these refused food for religious reasons.'[66] Rhys Williams and later Resident Physicians were firmly convinced by somatic views.

According to the *Lancet*, treatment offered in the various institutions the writer visited was dealing almost exclusively with 'symptoms rather than with morbid conditions'. Variations of treatment reflected fashion, not understanding. In general, there were 'no new remedies or modes of relief or cure' which could be 'recommended with confidence'.[67] There was, however, a tendency to try new drugs and the *Lancet* believed that there was a need for 'manly' physicians.[68] Bethlem tried all the new fashions in treatment with varying degrees of success.

In 1873 Rhys Williams started to place more emphasis on treatment in his reports. He noted that experiments with 'galvanism' had been made and pointed to the increased use of the sphygmograph, an instrument of 'greater precision and delicacy' than any used before. Attention was also turned to chemical trials with conium and digitalis.[69] He claimed little success in relation to the experiments with galvanism. One woman patient, who had broken her arm and had had it 'united badly owing to her maniacal condition', benefited physically from the application of continuous current to her withered forearm, but 'there was no mental improvement'. Galvanism was used too 'in a case of obstinate constipation, but with little effect', and the same result followed when the treatment was applied to a patient with melancholia and 'great sexual irritability'. In this case the patient's acne was cured, but Rhys Williams detected no mental improvement. Other patients 'seemed to improve up to a certain point, as they did after shower baths, but the results were temporary'. Whatever patients may have felt about these new modes of treatment, Rhys Williams felt little better than they must have done: 'I must own that I considered as much [achieved] was due to the moral influence, and the repeated assurance that the galvanizing was done to cure them, as to the galvanism itself.'[70] He was more confident about the sphygmograph. According to the 1873 *Report*, it had 'once or twice called our attention to the heart where it might otherwise have been overlooked'. Meanwhile feelings of unease were engendered following efforts to trace the effects of digitalis and conium.[71] In 1874 several acute cases on the female side were quieter when given conium in doses of 'three drachms' every four hours. They remained in bed instead of 'tearing their clothes or knocking their bedroom door'. Another female patient, who had spent two-thirds of her time in seclusion 'in consequence of her terrific fury and blasphemy', now got 'nervous if her medicine be discontinued'.[72] Rhys Williams felt that 'undoubtedly you can quiet patients with either; but I regret to say that the ultimate cure does not seem hastened'.[73] This was the first time such details had been set out in an annual report. In many asylums, this was exactly what such chemical forms of treatment were used for.

The new drugs treatments were initially treated with caution at Bethlem. In 1878 Savage raised concerns in the *Journal of Mental Science* about the use and abuse of chloral, an issue that had been generating interest since the early 1870s. Chloral was used extensively in asylums, but Savage pointed to the dangers of such chemical restraint in 1879, believing that the treatment produced as much mental illness as it was supposed to alleviate. He felt it to be a prominent cause of ill-health and declared that chloral was often used as a form of restraint in violent cases rather than as a treatment.[74] Chloral continued to be used at Bethlem along with antimony, digitalis and conium to quieten patients. Savage, however, was more supportive of the use of hyoscyamine. The drug was used in a similar manner to chloral, but Savage did not believe it raised problems with poisoning. At the same time as he attacked chloral, Savage wrote an article supporting the use of hyoscyamine, a poisonous alkaloid that was used mainly as a sedative. He found the drug an excellent means of 'quiet restraint in violent and dangerous cases'. In the Hospital he administered hyos-cyamine regularly, secreting it into patients' food and drink. When it was needed in a large dose it was injected. In the 1870s and 1880s case notes show that violent and manic patients were given the drug. Savage used the drug not as a punishment but as a corrective, recording in the case notes that patients having been given the drug were afraid of its administration – an effect that quietened them. He believed that the drug shocked the system, although he did not consider its use curative in any sense. Instead, he believed in a regime of generous diet, hygiene and tonics.[75] Savage also believed that patients should be allowed to leave the Hospital on parole and expressed more 'confidence in letting patients go *en parole* in a city' than he would have in a 'wild district'.[76] In his opinion 'some of the patients were brought back, not improved, but hardly ever worse for the change'.[77] He advocated a mixed therapeutic regime with no slavish adherence to non-restraint or chemical restraint.

The issue of chemical restraint attracted increasing attention from the medical profession and Lunacy Commissioners in the late 1870s as it came to characterize many of the treatments used in asylums.[78] Concern did not reduce use. These methods were used with increasing frequency in late Victorian Bethlem. Savage's successors became increasingly convinced about the value of such drug treatments, and a vogue was established for sedatives and stimulants that persisted until the 1930s.

Rhys Williams had little to write about the conventional forms of 'restraint', although he recorded that 'only one or two cases [had] required forcible feeding' and that stomach pumps had been used, 'more rapid, and less distressing' than other devices.[79] In their own report on the year 1873 the Lunacy Commissioners saw no patient in seclusion or under restraint as they passed through the wards. There was no entry of restraint in the medical records, but seclusion had been employed on eleven occasions with two males and on 224 occasions with fourteen females. This gives a false impression. Of the incidence of seclusion on the female side, 163 of these were 'applicable to one patient' who was subject to 'attacks of excitement' and often passed a week or more at a time in her own room.[80] Three years later a patient committed suicide while in seclusion. The case attracted the attention of the Lunacy Commission, but despite the patient not being visited during the night the Commissions were uncritical, noting that 'even if he had been visited, the suicide might not have been earlier discovered, as he had covered himself up with sheets'.[81] When another suicide occurred in seclusion in 1880 the Commissioners merely recommended that the need for frequent visitation should be stressed in writing.[82] Seclusion was viewed as an acceptable alternative to mechanical restraint. The *Lancet* felt the system employed at Bethlem was 'eminently direct and rational'.[83]

Opinions changed in the 1880s over the issue of restraint. From the 1870s onwards more asylum doctors were beginning to become pessimistic about the number of chronic patients in asylums. Increasingly it was felt that a coercive regime was needed to address this problem. This created problems with those who continued to believe in the non-restraint ideology espoused by John Conolly. The medical regime at Bethlem was influenced by these changes. From Hood's death in 1870 restraint had been gradually increased at Bethlem. The first recorded incident in the Hospital was only a year after Hood's departure. Other asylums could point to a similar increase where restraint had previously been abandoned.[84] However, it was not until 1888 that an argument about the over-use of restraint at Bethlem threatened to tarnish the 'worldwide reputation' Hood had acquired, both in his 'devotion to the work of the Hospital' and in his 'advancement of the knowledge and study of insanity'.[85] He had only just resigned to take up a successful private practice that was to include Virginia Woolf.[86] It also had implications for Bethlem. Savage's successor used the word 'eminence' to describe the position Savage had reached, a somewhat dangerous word to apply to Victorians. Certainly the position changed in this and in other respects in the ten years after 1888.

Savage had himself written to the *Lancet* in 1888 defending the use of 'mechanical restraint'. He detailed the mechanical means used at Bethlem. These included 'soft gloves', fastened by a strap around the wrist with a screw button; 'strong dresses' made out of stout linen or wool, keeping the hands enclosed in the padded extremities of the dress; 'side-arm dresses' worn at night, which prevented the patient, who was free to walk, from using his hands to injure or destroy. Here Savage was concerned about masturbation and self-mutilation. In addition, he detailed the use of 'wet and dry packs', commonly used to attach a patient to his or her bed when they became manically excited. A belt attached to the elbows was also employed in one case to prevent the patient from 'injuring himself by picking and rubbing'. Strait-jackets and handcuffs were not used, and patients were kept quiet by heavy dosing of sedatives. Savage staunchly defended his use of such devices on the grounds that 'every physician with experience has the right to private judgement in the treatment of his cases'. He added, however, that one of the main purposes was to allow more 'liberty' to patients in other respects. For example, patients wearing soft gloves were 'really granted liberty by means of the slight restraint put upon them'. Savage noted:

> I feel that if on the one hand I can grant more freedom by using one form of mechanical restraint, while on the other I can induce rest and quiet, leading to rewarding by another method of control, I should be wanting in courage if I refrained from the use of those means simply because similar means in other times have been abused. As my profession has not reached the point of having fixed principles we must be chiefly directed by experience.[87]

He drew extensively on other writers and quoted remarks made by a close friend, Yellowlees, medical superintendent at Gartnavel asylum, and Thomas Clouston of Edinburgh, which supported his own stance. They had figured in addresses to the Medico-Psychological Association at Edinburgh in November 1887 which had been reprinted in the *Journal of Mental Science*. Clouston had said that 'in some exceptional cases ... restraint was the only remedy, the most humane resource and the most scientific application of the principle of modern brain therapeutics'. Savage added that the Lunacy Commissioners in Scotland did not require the use of padded gloves to be reported as restraint.[88] Percy Smith, Savage's successor, unequivocally associated himself with these views, quoting several cases of patients requiring restraint.[89]

Savage's article was a response to an article published in *The Times* by Charles Bucknill, an old friend of Conolly and a Governor of Bethlem. Bucknill had been concerned about the increase in restraint in the Hospital, but unable to receive a satisfactory reply from the Governors or from the Lunacy Commissioners, he wrote to *The Times*. In his article, Bucknill complained that Savage had revived the use of restraint and believed that the reasons cited had been insufficient.[90] As shown by his *Lancet* article, Savage was unrepentant and stressed that he was not governed by any previous dogma of non-restraint, arguing that treatment should be flexible. He regretted that the matter had been raised in the press, but apart from one letter he preferred to carry out the discussion in the pages of the medical press. Bucknill's letter was embarrassing not only for the Governors but also for the Lunacy Commission, who had visited Bethlem in August 1888. At the time, they had found that patients 'generally spoke well of their treatment', but recorded that 'the amount of mechanical restraint employed has certainly been very considerable'. This included two female patients who had been 'dry packed' at intervals during forty-two days, while eight men and six women had been put into side-arm dresses, 'chiefly at night', for an aggregate of 644 and 203 hours respectively. In their report, the Commissioners explained that:

> We cannot judge how far it was expedient in individual cases, but we cannot either condemn it as being bad treatment. We would only remark that it should be used with judgement, and in no case without occasional interruptions to ascertain if the patient can be managed without it.

In defence of Bethlem, they concluded that the fact could not be overlooked that 'the admissions here of acute cases are very numerous, many needing control, which may be more humanely applied by mechanical than by manual means'.[91] Rhys Williams was the medical commissioner and he accepted Savage's judgment. Savage later went on to claim that it was not because of the number of violent patients who had been admitted that restraint had been used but largely to free Bethlem from the doctrine of non-restraint practised by Hood.[92] He went on to defend the use of certain defined forms of restraint as permissible, asserting that it should only be used 'by direct medical order'.[93]

Bucknill's letter provoked controversy in the daily and medical press. While the debate raged in the press, the Lunacy Commission became more critical of the use of restraint at Bethlem. For Commissioners the night staff was too small and the supervision inadequate. They noted that 'the use of mechanical restraint to prevent attempts at suicide' might be 'largely reduced', as had been found 'practicable in other Asylums', if there were better continuous supervision. The Commissioners had seen the devices used and while they believed that soft locked gloves were acceptable, 'side-arm dresses' were not. They hoped that some other shape of dress could be introduced 'should it in future be necessary to resort to restraint of this nature'. The medical staff took note and the Commissioners were pleased to report that under Percy Smith 'improvements' had been made in February 1889 and in the months leading up to their second visit in September 1889. 'Restraint by the "side-arm" dress, which was unfavourably commented upon by us at our last visit, has been employed in the case of two patients only.'[94] In his 1889 Report, Percy Smith quoted the national report of the Commissioners, which had noted their disapproval of any 'resort to any form of mechanical restraint with a view to economy of attendants, or simply to prevent destruction of dress or bedding' but which had gone on to look less critically at 'the particular case of Bethlem'. In Smith's judgment 'the question of the supposed unjustifiable use of restraint had been allowed to subside'.[95]

Asylum doctors formed themselves into camps, although Savage – having sparked the debate – did not participate. As Conolly's disciples died, there were fewer members of the medical profession willing unequivocally to defend non-restraint. The Lunacy Commissioners' response was to note that where restraint was discouraged it was not forbidden, pointing to a general consensus that a moderate use of restraint was acceptable. The issue became bound up with the debates in the 1880s over the need for new lunacy legislation, although it was never firmly settled.[96]

NEW LUNACY LEGISLATION

Percy Smith's *Report* for 1890 dealt at length with the impact of the 1890 Lunacy Act.[97] The consolidating 1890 Act, which embodied alterations in the Lunacy laws made by the Lunacy Laws Amendment Act of 1889, came into force on 1 May and introduced a form of certification that attracted considerable comment and provoked ongoing debate. Percy Smith, like many in the medical profession, was strongly opposed to the clauses in it requiring private patients in public or private asylums to be 'detained' there for more than seven days only on their holding a reception order signed by a Magistrate, County Court Judge or a Justice of Peace specially appointed under the Act. The belief that it was necessary for individuals deemed insane to be protected by statute from unlawful detention, central to the Act, had been expressed in Parliament for decades, even at the time of the passing of the Act of 1845, but had been challenged by Shaftesbury.[98] Percy Smith played on attitudes expressed by the Lunacy Commissioners and quoted from their *44th Report*:

> The views of our Board and those of our late Chairman, the Earl of Shaftesbury, as to the expediency of this change, notwithstanding that it had been recommended by a Select Committee of the House of Commons in 1878, were made known to your Lordship, and to your Lordship's predecessors in office . . . We hope . . . that the change (in which also is involved a more complicated and difficult procedure for obtaining the order) may not lead to the results we fear, namely the placing of an impediment in the way of early treatment, so important for the care of insanity, and the withdrawal from official cognizance and supervision of many insane persons.

A substantial body of Parliamentary and press opinion outside had, however, rejected these views. They saw greater danger in the possibility of detention in asylums of people who were not insane than in delaying treatment for those who manifestly were. Percy Smith felt forced to ask again as a doctor why 'a Justice of the Peace, who although specially appointed . . . may have had very little or no experience of mental disease, can override the opinions of physicians of great experience'. For him 'it may well be asked whether there was any necessity to erect this barrier of a judicial enquiry in the way of the admission of persons suffering from so painful a disease'.[99] Percy Smith was expressing views commonly held by the profession on an Act that Kathleen Jones has seen as a 'triumph of legalism'.[100]

A year earlier, the Court of Governors had appointed a Committee of Governors and medical staff to consider the proposed legislation's effect on Bethlem's rules and orders.[101] There were 342 clauses in the Act and one of its implications was that almost twenty new forms had to be devised and filled in. For Percy Smith

> This most radical change in the working of the Lunacy Law will entail considerable additional work on the medical officers and probably diminish, correspondingly, the amount of time they can devote to the medical care and treatment of the patients. Whether the new procedure will not hamper seriously the early treatment of the cases remains to be proved; but in many respects the new Act appears to be cumbersome and difficult to work.[102]

The Lunacy Commissioners were also aware of the implications. In 1890 they recognized that 'recent legislation has added much to the work of the Medical Superintendent'.[103] It was not just the increased workload and the alteration in Bethlem's practices that were worrying for Percy Smith. He condemned a provision in the 1890 Act that mechanical restraint should be used only for medical or surgical reasons or to prevent the lunatic from injuring himself/herself or others. The new Act also stipulated that in each case of use a certificate had to be signed by one of the medical officers stating the means used, the duration of use, and the reasons for it.[104]

Percy Smith was less concerned about the fate of the 'very old destructive patient' than he was about the overworked Medical Superintendent. He noted that:

For many years it has been the aim and object of the Hospital Authorities that the chief medical officer should be really a Resident Physician, that is that he should be actively and personally concerned in the treatment of the patients, and of late a great deal has been said about the encouragement of what is called the 'Hospital Spirit' in institutions for the Insane. It is, therefore, a serious matter that the Act makes the Resident Physician more of a 'manager' [the new and objectionable term used throughout the Act] and less of a medical man.[105]

To overcome this, Percy Smith called for the appointment of an additional Assistant Medical Officer. Without such an appointment it would be impossible, he argued, for the work of the Hospital to be maintained 'in full efficiency'. The Lunacy Commissioners had recognized this and the Governors responded, creating an additional post of Assistant Medical Officer at a salary not exceeding £150.[106] With the matter resolved to Percy Smith's satisfaction, less attention was paid to the rules presented by the Lunacy Commissioners that made illegal the use of 'certain dresses which both my predecessor and myself had found to be of the greatest value in the treatment of some of the very acute cases admitted to this Hospital'.[107] However, the issue re-emerged in 1898 when Percy Smith expressed his anxiety that nothing more should be added to the 'already crushing routine entailed by the existing law'.[108] Bethlem throughout the twentieth century was to remain sceptical about the value of new lunacy legalization.

END OF A CENTURY

Bethlem ended the nineteenth century on a successful note. In the 1899 *Report* prepared by Hyslop a 50 per cent recovery rate was alluded to, a figure that was marginally higher than the recovery rate between 1864 and 1899. The *Report* also proudly proclaimed that the Recreation Hall, opened by the Duke of Cambridge and newly painted, had been in constant use. Dances and theatrical entertainments were now given on a regular basis and 'the Annual Burlesque', presented by staff in 1899, was considered 'a conspicuous success'. In addition, the band had played efficiently at all the various entertainments and dances and O'Donoghue's Sunday evening services were greatly appreciated.[109] The Lunacy Commissioners were equally satisfied. They felt that 'the Hospital was in good order throughout'.[110]

There were points of concern. In 1896 financial anxiety increased in the Hospital after the Surveyor had reported that an outlay of nearly £8,000 was necessary further to improve the heating and ventilation of the Hospital. Increasingly problems were to be found with the St George's Fields building, forcing the Governors to move Bethlem to its final home at Monks Orchard in 1930 (see Chapter 29). A Special Committee set up to examine his report would not give permission for such a large expenditure. A second survey was called for, and an expenditure of only £1,941 was allowed. There was a similar note of caution when the Treasurer was requested in the same year to write a circular letter to every Governor saying that a special fund was necessary to defray the cost of furnishing the new

Recreation Hall so that the expense would not fall on the general funds of charity.[111] The need for economy was constantly to be expressed throughout the twentieth century.

Despite caution, improvement continued. In 1901, when *Under the Dome* completed its tenth year in print, the billiard room was redecorated and there was far more use of electric light, an innovation first proposed in 1883.[112] The Commissioners' Report for 1902 was almost perfunctory: 'we have not witnessed much excitement in the wards.'[113] None the less, this was the year when it was decided to spend up to £450 on installing a telephone system 'of a domestic character' linking offices and wards.[114] The Governors were also prepared to spend more money on the nursing staff. Staff–patient ratios had continued to rise, reaching 1:3 by 1901, making Bethlem a well-staffed, but small institution, although the female nurses had only been given a nurses' style uniform in 1891 at a cost of £3 each.[115] Comparisons were difficult, with most county and borough asylums dwarfing the Hospital in size. However, to ensure that these wage rates were fixed at the right level, the Governors looked in 1902 to the rates of pay offered by the London County Council. Determined as they were to attract nurses of a high quality, the Governors were prepared to be generous. A new scale pushed the Hospital ahead and extra lodging allowances were paid to nursing staff 'to meet the advance in the price of rent, rates and taxes'.[116] Treatments had changed and more was expected of the staff, increasing the need for better qualified nurses. Wages remained low in comparison to those in many other occupations, but Bethlem now offered its nursing staff one of the highest salaries in London for attendants in an asylum.

By now Bethlem was an Edwardian not a Victorian institution. Queen Victoria's passing was mourned in the Hospital in 1902, but flares were lit to illuminate the dome to mark Edward's coronation.[117] Victoria was not forgotten. In 1904, when the wards were to be named, the first two on the male side were to be called Edward and Albert, and on the female side Victoria and Alexandra.[118]

NOTES

1 *General Reports of the Royal Hospitals of Bridewell and Bethlem and of the House of Occupations, 1858*, 39.
2 Edward G. O'Donoghue, *The Story of Bethlehem Hospital from its Foundation in 1247* (London: T. Fisher Unwin, 1914), 401. Court of Governors, 29 June 1888. The statues were moved to Guildhall on 26 November 1888 after the Library Committee of the City of London had given its approval.
3 *1881 General Report*, 48.
4 Court of Governors, 27 July 1868 and 27 June 1898.
5 *1877 General Report*, 41; *32nd Report of the Commissioners in Lunacy* (1877).
6 *1876 General Report*; *31st Report of the Commissioners in Lunacy* (1876).
7 *1893 General Report*, 65.
8 David Russell, *Scenes from Bedlam* (London: Baillière Tindall, 1996), 157.
9 *1876 General Report*; *31st Report of the Commissioners in Lunacy* (1876).
10 *1886 General Report*, 50–5.
11 *1896 General Report*, 51.
12 *The Care and Cure of the Insane* (London: Hardwicke & Bogue, 1877), 274. The Report was

dated 31 March 1877. The author further observed 'It is strange that the social value of this enterprise does not command the support that it deserves.'

13 *Ibid.* 276–7.

14 *Ibid.* 280.

15 *1889 General Report*, 53, 51.

16 *1899 General Report*, 38–9.

17 *1886 General Report*, 50–5.

18 A year earlier the Commissioners had concluded that 'the question of a General Recreation Hall, which might also be an associated dining room', was 'not likely to be easily solved': *ibid.* 51. Plans had been considered in 1894: *1894 General Report*, 55.

19 Nick Hervey, 'A Slavish Bowing Down: the Lunacy Commissioners and the Psychiatric Profession, 1845–60', in W. F. Bynum, Roy Porter and Michael Shepherd (eds), *The Anatomy of Madness* (London: Tavistock Press, 1985), vol. ii, 119.

20 *32nd Report of the Commissioners in Lunacy* (1878).

21 *Under the Dome* (1893), 26–8.

22 *Care and Cure of the Insane*, 299.

23 *Under the Dome*, 25 March, 13–19.

24 *1898 General Report*, 35.

25 *Ibid.* 43.

26 O'Donoghue, *op. cit.* 416.

27 *Under the Dome*, March 1892.

28 Bethlem Subcommittee, 26 April 1869. In 1870 the salary of the Resident Physician was raised by £150 per annum: *ibid.* 30 May 1870.

29 *Ibid.* 3 June 1878.

30 *1888 General Report*, 45.

31 *1877 General Report*, 36–7.

32 *1886 General Report*, 43–4.

33 *1878 General Report*, 32.

34 *1881 General Report*, 33.

35 *1886 General Report*, 41, 43.

36 *1883 General Report*, 36.

37 E. Goffman, *Asylums: Essays on the Social Situation of Mental Patients and Other Inmates* (New York, 1961 edn), 95.

38 *Under the Dome* (1906), 123–5. This was not the first asylum house magazine. In Edinburgh, the *Morningside Mirror* had appeared as early as 1845.

39 *Ibid.* new series, vol. 37, no. 154, June–Sept. 1930. This was the final number of *Under the Dome* which appeared as the Hospital was moving to Monks Orchard.

40 *Ibid.* (1894), 38.

41 *Ibid.* (1896), 199.

42 *Ibid.* (1892), 22–3. In *ibid.* (1894), 36, the Christmas tree was described as a fixture. There was no tree in 1895, however, because of the illness of the people who worked to decorate it: *ibid.* (1895), 15.

43 *Ibid.* (1895), 85.

44 *Ibid.* (1893), 38.

45 *Ibid.* (1897), 29.

46 *Ibid.* (1894), 36.

47 *1882 General Report*, 40.

48 *1881 General Report*, 38.

49 Court of Governors, 27 February 1882.

50 *1881 General Report*, 38–9.

51 Bethlem Subcommittee, 30 January 1882; General Committee, 27 February 1882.

52 The period was extended in 1887: General Committee, 26 September 1887. Female patients were added, with the approval of the Commissioners in the same year: Court of Governors, 28 November 1887.

53 Bethlem Subcommittee, 10 January 1887.

54 *Ibid.* 9 May 1883; General Committee, 25 June 1883.

55 See John Haslam, *Illustrations of Madness*, with an introduction by Roy Porter (London: Routledge, 1988).

56 *1886 General Report*, 44.

57 *1874 General Report*, 94.

58 *1872 General Report*, 32.

59 *1873 General Report*, 77.

60 *1874 General Report*, 85.

61 *Ibid.* 84–5.

62 Michael Clark, 'The Rejection of Psychological Approaches to Mental Disorder in Late Nineteenth Century British Psychiatry', in Andrew Scull (ed.), *Madhouses, Mad-Doctors and Madmen* (Philadelphia: University of Pennsylvania Press, 1981), 271–313.

63 George Savage, *Insanity and Allied Neurosis* (London: Cassells, 1884).

64 *1874 General Report*, 102.

65 *Ibid.* 82.

66 *Ibid.* 113.

67 *Care and Cure of the Insane.*

68 *Ibid.* 114.

69 *1873 General Report.*

70 *Ibid.* 81.

71 *Ibid.*

72 *1874 General Report.*

73 *Ibid.*

74 *Journal of Mental Science*, xxv (1879), 4–8.

75 *Ibid.* xxviii (1881), 8.

76 *1882 General Report*, 39.

77 *1880 General Report*, 36.

78 Phil Fennell, *Treatment Without Consent: Law, Psychiatry and the Treatment of Mentally Disordered People Since 1845* (London: Routledge, 1996), 41–2.

79 *1873 General Report*, 105.

80 *27th Report of the Commissioners in Lunacy* (1873).

81 *1876 General Report*, 33–4.

82 Cited in Fennell, *op. cit.* 35.

83 *Cure and Care of the Insane*, vii.

84 Fennell, *op. cit.*

85 *1888 General Report*, 34.

86 See S. Trombley, *'All that Summer She was Mad': Virginia Woolf and Her Doctors* (London: Junction Books, 1981).

87 *1889 General Report*, 390–4; *Lancet*, 2 (1888).

88 *1888 General Report*, 41.

89 *Ibid.* 43.

90 *The Times*, 22 August 1888, 6.

91 *42nd Report of the Commissioners in Lunacy* (1888).

92 Fennell, *op. cit.* 50.

93 *1888 General Report*, 40.

94 *43rd Report of the Commissioners in Lunacy* (1889).

95 *1889 General Report*, 34.

96 Fennell, *op. cit.* 52–4.

97 For the 1890 Act, see C. Unsworth, *The Politics of Mental Health Legislation* (Oxford: Clarendon, 1987); Kathleen Jones, *Asylums and After: A Revised History of the Mental Health Service, From the Early Eighteenth Century to the 1990s* (London: Athlone Press, 1993), 93–111; Andrew Scull, *The Most Solitary of Afflictions: Madness and Society in Britain, 1700–1900* (New Haven, Conn. and London: Yale University Press, 1993).

98 Concern on unlawful confinement was prominent in the nineteenth century, see Peter McCandless, 'Liberty and Lunacy: The Victorians and Wrongful Confinement', in Andrew

Scull (ed.), *Madhouse, Mad-Doctors and Madmen* (Philadelphia: University of Pennsylvania Press, 1981), 339–62.

99 *1890 General Report*, 48–9.
100 Jones, *op. cit.* 107–11.
101 Bethlem Subcommittee, 25 November 1889.
102 *1890 General Report*, 44–5.
103 Bethlem Subcommittee, 24 November 1890.
104 *1890 General Report*.
105 *Ibid.*
106 General Committee, 26 January 1891.
107 *1895 General Report*, 31.
108 *1898 General Report*, 41.
109 *1899 General Report*, 25–35.
110 *53rd Report of the Commissioners in Lunacy* (1899), 42.
111 General Committee, 29 June and 14 September 1896.
112 Bethlem Subcommittee, 12 September 1883. In 1884 it was decided that the electric lighting of the Hospital should 'not be adopted at present': *ibid.* 16 January 1884.
113 *56th Report of the Commissioners in Lunacy* (1902), 48.
114 General Committee, 28 April 1902.
115 Russell, *op. cit.* 43.
116 Bethlem Subcommittee, 16 January 1901.
117 *Under the Dome* (1930), 35.
118 *Ibid.* 7 December 1904.

Part IV

1900 TO THE PRESENT

BETHLEM AND THE TWENTIETH CENTURY

———— •◦• ————

No society can stand still over time, but in some periods change was more rapid than others. This is the case of the twentieth century. The period from 1900 to the present has attracted all manner of labels from the 'people's century' to Eric Hobsbawm's 'age of extremes'.[1] Nationally and internationally the twentieth century has seen great upheavals, ideological struggles, revolution and rapid development, but also continued famine, disease and decline. It has borne witness to two world wars that left continental Europe scarred, the Holocaust, a Cold War that frequently threatened to plunge the world into global nuclear war, the positive and negative results of nationalism, and the prospect of European union. For the philosopher Isaiah Berlin it has been 'the most terrible century in Western history'. Others have claimed that it has been marked by increasing secularization and material progress based on science and technology, where medicine has made striking advances. In every sphere, the twentieth century has brought considerable change in an age of contradictions. Looking back across the years, 1900 appears to be a very long way away, making the twentieth century hard to define. Hobsbawm explained that 'nobody can write the history of the twentieth century like that of any other era'.[2]

In 1900 London, according to Paul Johnson,

> was the world's capital city three times over – in political terms as the fulcrum of the British Empire, in commercial terms as the centre of banking and finance with sterling the dominant international currency, and in industrial terms as the largest port in the largest trading nation in the world.[3]

London fascinated contemporaries. Its continued urban expansion was seen by the author Arthur Sherwell in 1901 as 'a great hungry sea, which flows on and on', driven by railway development, slum clearance, suburban growth and the London County Council's (LCC) leadership.[4] From this high point in 1900, the twentieth century has been characterized as a period of decline for Britain through the loss of the Empire into the 'sick man of Europe'. By global standards, London ceased to be unique in terms of size as other world cities grew faster and bigger. At the same time, however, the twentieth century saw enormous improvements in the average standard of living, technological advance, and labour-saving devices unthought of at the time of Queen

Victoria's death in 1901. Britain broke away from the firm class and gender divisions of the late nineteenth century, although women gained the vote only in 1918 and it was not until after the Second World War that working-class children received an education beyond the age of fourteen. Politically the period saw the rise of the Labour Party, although it also witnessed the interwar growth of Oswald Mosley's British Union of Fascists and declining trade union power. Culturally, the strains of the First World War relaxed rigid social protocols, and a more 'ebullient night-life' emerged in London.[5] Nightclubs developed and sexual inhibitions relaxed. The unifying effect of the Second World War, although often exaggerated, engendered further social transformation, loosening hierarchies and snobberies. Economically, the average Briton had a real income 3.3 times higher in 1989 than in 1913, and life expectancy rose so that more people were living past 65. The expansion of the welfare system, at least until the 1980s, provided a growing safety net where access to pensions, unemployment benefit, housing and health was extended into the post-1945 welfare state, increasing the role of the state.[6] This must be set against growing unemployment and economic insecurity, the return of severe cyclical slumps, and stark inequalities of wealth facing society in the 1990s.

Where Britain's growth was good in comparison to previous centuries, it was not so respectable in contrast to the economic performance of other European countries or America. While Britain gradually fell down the international league table, internally the picture has been mixed. Some industries like mining suffered devastating long-term decline, impoverishing industrial regions and creating high unemployment. Other traditional areas like agriculture became more mechanized and achieved higher productivity. The service sector expanded rapidly and the increase in white-collar jobs created greater opportunities for social mobility. New industries linked to the growing mass-market were developed like the car and aeronautical sectors, which then went into decline.[7] Within this there have been considerable short-term variations, particularly during the interwar period when Britain faced a slump immediately after the First World War and then again in the 1930s in response to the 1929 Wall Street Crash.

Economic improvement encouraged the growth of a consumer society where less was spent on food and more on non-essentials. Department stores appeared following the Debenham's (opened in 1909) and Selfridge's mould. Shops multiplied and Britain's fashion and music industry flourished in the swinging Sixties, bringing the mini-skirt and the Beatles. Housing improved, especially in London under the LCC's interwar housing developments, with all post-1919 housing having electricity, a bathroom and an inside toilet.[8] Rising relative affluence allowed more time and space for leisure, which was then slowly commercialized, a process that ultimately led to the package holiday. The internal-combustion engine replaced horse-drawn vehicles, hailing a revolution for many. In London the development of the underground with electrification made horse-drawn and steam-driven transport obsolete.[9] Nineteen fifty-eight saw the opening of Britain's first motorway and the first parking meter in London, pointing to the start of mass motoring and the problems that widespread car ownership were to bring. The growth of mass communications and the silicon chip fostered further revolutions, effectively shortening distances. The distractions of the Edwardian dance halls gave way to the excitement of black-and-white films. In the 1930s, Odeon and Gaumont cinemas provided new diversions that in London stimulated the growth of popular eating-places, while television in the 1950s and the British Broadcasting Corporation started to bring popular culture directly into people's homes. The rapid spread of television ownership contributed further to the development of a common culture and a fascination with soap-operas.[10] All this has been at a price. Some have complained that the twentieth century has also brought a less cohesive society with communities weakened by urbanization, increased geographical mobility, slum clearance, immigration and a retreat into selfish individualism.

TWENTIETH-CENTURY BETHLEM

Bethlem entered the twentieth century as a reformed institution that was based on a mix of private and charitable enterprise. No longer was it the place that had dominated portraits of lunacy in the eighteenth century. Nor was it the early nineteenth-century institution that had been seen as a symbol of all that had been mad and bad in the management of the insane. Reality was always more complex than such generalizations suggest, as past chapters have shown, but Bethlem had passed its nadir after the 1852 inquiry. 'Removed largely from the public eye', the Hospital developed away from the public limelight.[11] Throughout the twentieth century, the Governors struggled to maintain Bethlem's autonomy. Although influenced by the developments of the period, adding telephones, buying cars and adopting new thera-peutic practices, the Hospital tried to remain aloof, at least until 1948. The Governors appeared uninterested about what was happening in the wider world unless it had an immediate impact on their buildings, endowments, patients or staff.

Much had changed under Smirke's dome since the mid-nineteenth century. William Charles Hood's reforms had cast Bethlem anew (see Chapter 26), although he built on earlier work by George Tuthill and Sir Alexander Morison (see Chapter 24). What had previously been a charitable hospital became a small semi-private institution of 200 beds largely for the educated middle classes in a 'presumably curable condition'. The number of free patients fell dramatically as the Governors sought to attract those unwilling to enter county and borough mental hospitals but prepared to pay Bethlem's modest charges. Patients were well cared for and the Governors did everything to promote their comfort. Many confused Bethlem with an expensive private hospital or hotel. Room could still be found for complaint: a major issue of 1928 was that 'lemonade and other refreshing drinks' were in short supply during the hot summer.[12] Paying patients proved hard to satisfy, placing new strains on an administration that strove to avoid extravagance. Gradually the Hospital was modernized, electric lighting and new heating installed, and new windows added. The opening of Witley House as a convalescent home in Surrey in 1870, the completion of a new recreation hall in 1896, the provision of an X-ray department in 1920 and a new operating theatre in 1923, extended treatment.[13] Structural problems were encountered in the 1920s with the nineteenth-century building proving expensive to maintain, old-fashioned in design, and unsuitable given its location in poor and increasingly congested Southwark. The move to Monks Orchard in 1930, a semi-rural site in Beckenham, Kent, remedied these problems (see Chapter 29). Those running the Hospital have not found it necessary to move since, although substantial changes have been made and new buildings added.

Where Bethlem was unable to escape the common culture of a mental hospital that psychiatric ideas on how patients should be managed and treated encouraged, it did prove a pioneer. The 1930 hospital, built in a villa style on 240 acres of parkland, was widely seen to be in the vanguard of mental hospital design. In other areas Bethlem led and was not the backwater that some have assumed. It was one of the first mental hospitals to encourage the admission of voluntary patients, long before the 1930 Mental Treatment Act became law (see Chapter 33). Bethlem also opened the first purely psychiatric outpatient department in London (see Chapter 29), initially led in the adoption of Freudian ideas, and developed a leading psychological department that went on to help establish behavioural therapy (see Chapter 34). These developments, however, did not guarantee Bethlem a permanent place in the forefront of psychiatry. Throughout the twentieth century, Bethlem has proved both a trail-blazer and a reluctant follower of developments elsewhere.

Important changes occurred to Bethlem's administration and nature between 1900 and 1994, with the Governors forced to abandon the voluntary ethic they had relied on for so long and to adopt a new structure as part of a national health service. The First and Second World Wars created anxiety in the Hospital and concern for the patients, but brought no immediate change or the need to evacuate. Where Bethlem made preparations for 'the safeguarding of those for whom the Governors are responsible', most of these proved unnecessary until 1944.[14] 'Total War' did create problems. Rationing encouraged petty pilfering and complaints from patients, along with staff shortages as many left to fight the war or enter war work. All hospitals experienced these problems, but Bethlem, by virtue of its suburban location, was spared the horrors and devastation of the 'Blitz'. Where 49,000 died in London with 80 per cent of the housing stock damaged and a further 20 per cent rendered uninhabitable, Bethlem was physically unscathed until 1944 when three V-1 rockets hit the Hospital, damaging every building. After nearly seven hundred years, Bethlem now faced the real possibility of closure. The Governors urgently put together emergency financial measures and started repairs in earnest.

Both London and Bethlem had survived the war, confident they could rebuild. Both encountered immediate difficulties, with London facing extensive bomb damage and overwhelming housing problems. For Bethlem, the immediate post-war period presented a new danger that threatened to be more damaging than bombing (see Chapter 30). The National Health Service (NHS), with its promises of a free and comprehensive health service available to all, was not greeted with enthusiasm by the Governors.[15] In its proposals they saw that Bethlem's independence would be ended, its endowments appropriated, and its management passed from the Governors to a regional board. To avoid this, Bethlem courted the LCC's Maudsley Hospital, which had the teaching status the Hospital needed to ensure its continued self-government. Bethlem was considered a real prize by the Maudsley. With the Maudsley facing its own post-war problems, it valued the opportunities Bethlem's site offered and its dowry of over 'a million pounds'.[16] Apart from lengthy discussions over the size of the dairy herd and the name, the planning of the merger went smoothly. Each institution gained what it wanted in the creation of what locally became known as the

Joint Hospital (see Chapter 30). Bethlem swapped Bridewell for the Maudsley and the Institute of Psychiatry. The new partnership, however, was not always ideal. Tensions quickly emerged, with most of the money being used to fund developments at the Maudsley. Until the 1960s Bethlem was considered the lesser partner in a marriage that had been purely for convenience (see Chapter 31).

Economic decline in London, as industries and services moved out of the capital and unemployment spiralled in the 1970s, was not matched by decline at Bethlem. The merger was successful. Encouraged by the Maudsley's therapeutic dynamism and research at the Institute of Psychiatry, the Joint Hospital expanded, taking over psychiatric services in Camberwell in the 1970s. New units were added, creating new challenges for the Hospital and its staff, which simultaneously changed the type of patient admitted (see Chapter 33). After 1948 Bethlem continued to prove that it was a flexible, adaptive institution, if sometimes reluctant to change. As part of Britain's only psychiatric teaching hospital, Bethlem found itself in a privileged position in the new NHS. The new status protected it from national reorganization until 1982 when the Joint Hospital became a Special Health Authority (SHA) and ultimately a NHS trust in 1994 (see Chapters 31 and 35). The Hospital adapted itself to the shifting demands of the health service and the changing ideas on how healthcare should be delivered, allowing it to grow where other psychiatric hospitals were being closed and patients moved into the community.

BETHLEM NOT BEDLAM

This has not been the image with which the Hospital has been associated. Bethlem, throughout its long history, has found it hard to escape its popular image and historians are now those primarily responsible for keeping it alive.[17] Bethlem has all too often been characterized by what happened to it in the seventeenth, eighteenth or nineteenth centuries. In the popular imagination, however, where Bethlem could never be entirely free of the Bedlam image, in the twentieth century the image itself gradually lost its associations with the Hospital. In the 1920s the term 'Bedlam' continued to exist 'in the dictionary and world of journalism'; by the 1930s the press no longer referred to Bethlem as Bedlam.[18] Little was now said about the Hospital's colourful past. In a society facing new scandals and problems there seemed little need to demonize an aged asylum where other institutions provided plenty of scope for censure. Bethlem consequently moved out of the public consciousness and metaphorical language so that by the late twentieth century, while many may associate Bedlam with chaos, few link the term to the Hospital in its present or historical sense.

How did this transformation occur? Bethlem's Governors found the Bedlam reputation counter-productive and set about trying to invent a new image. Here the Governors created a paradox. They wanted to withdraw Bethlem from public attention and simultaneously publicize the Hospital. A tension existed between these two aims. On the one hand visiting was controlled and few journalists were encouraged to see the wards.[19] On the other, visits from professional organizations like the British Medical Association and the Medico-Psychological Association were encouraged to publicize the facilities. The Governors were successful in limiting publicity they did not control. According to the *Daily Telegraph* in 1920, a warm supporter of the Hospital after Sir George Faudel-Phillips, President between 1896 and 1912, married Helen, daughter of Lord Burnham the owner of the newspaper, 'it is strange how little one reads of Bethlem'.[20] With over 60 per cent of the income from landed estates and investments, the Governors had no need to court benevolence or justify their actions to cautious ratepayers. The result was that when unwelcome publicity did occur the Governors were keen to threaten libel action. Concern could be taken to extremes: in 1906 they threatened to sue a former patient, a Mr R— of Holloway. The reason the Governors cited was that he had made curtains depicting his treatment that reflected badly on Bethlem and they unsuccessfully demanded they be removed.[21] After 1948 the Joint Hospital remained sensitive to its image. In 1974 the solicitor commented that 'it is a sound rule for the hospital that publicity is not to be courted', but this was not always possible.[22] The opening of the Interim Medium Secure Unit at Bethlem in 1980 was preceded by discussions with local residents to allay fears.[23] Jimmy Savile OBE, television presenter, was invited to open the unit, an event that, despite the bad weather, was regarded as 'a most successful exercise in public relations'.[24] Doubt remained about the value of such exercises. New concerns emerged in the 1990s. The SHA became aware that it needed an 'External Relations policy' to improve its image. This was seen as particularly important in attracting outside funding and NHS contracts given the dictates of the Thatcherite internal market (see Chapter 35).[25]

Before 1948 the Governors attempted to counter what others were saying about Bethlem by manufacturing a new image. The aim was partly to attract students to Bethlem's ailing medical school (see Chapter 30), but mainly to encourage the admission of voluntary and paying patients. In the rhetoric the Hospital's history was not ignored. Through an act of selective amnesia, Bethlem's past was modified so that it had little to do with Bedlam. No mention was made of the previous scandals. This was left to the quirky chaplain, Geoffrey O'Donoghue, in his pageant *The Story of Bethlehem Hospital from its Foundation in 1247*.[26] Later, the Governors did not entirely approve of the book, feeling that it was morbid, though in 1914 they widely distributed it.[27] In the self-conscious publicity, the Hospital's history became a liturgy of dates that stressed the institution's age and its associations with advances in psychiatry. Later attempts to research Bethlem's history received more support and an archive was established in 1969. With the Hospital's seven hundred and fiftieth anniversary in 1997 and a change in the corporate name to 'The Maudsley' in 1991, Bethlem's past became an important asset.

In their public statements, the Governors presented a positive view of the Hospital. Bethlem's scientific nature was emphasized and the 'considerable pains to keep abreast of . . . modern methods'.[28] It was carefully explained that 'the word "Bethlem", rather than stigmatising an individual, conveys the hall mark of hopefulness and curability'. The Governors hoped that the Hospital would become 'a Mecca to all those who make the study of diseases of the nervous system their life's work'.[29] No mention was made of the work or research undertaken and any description of Bethlem's day-to-day therapeutic routine was avoided. The move to Monks Orchard allowed the Governors to be more confident about the reputation they were trying to foster (see Chapter 29). It helped to 'for ever eliminate the taint of "Bedlam"'.[30]

Suburban Bethlem could easily be seen as entirely different from the Hospital's earlier incarnations. From the planning of the new hospital the Governors made a concerted effort to break with the past. The *British Medical Journal* informed its readers that the Governors had insisted that 'the old contraction of the name of the hospital to "Bedlam" should be avoided'. It added that 'the old unfortunate associations of Bethlem ... only give greater significance to the new Bethlem, incorporating as it does the most progressive and humane psychiatric ideas'.[31] The 1928 building appeal set the tone of the new rhetoric. It was felt that 'with the completion of the new building, everything that science and experience have taught us shall be employed to the fullest degree for the benefit both of those who suffer and those who strive to relieve them'. Everything was viewed as modern, where 'an incomparable reputation second to none for the skill in treatment and material care [was] lavished upon the patients'.[32] The Governors were keen to have the view accepted that Bethlem was 'in the front ranks of the field of psychological medicine'.[33] The medical staff, with an eye to their own private practices, were eager to support this view. John Porter-Phillips, Physician-Superintendent from 1914 to 1944, became an active campaigner and strove to have the slogan 'Bethlem means *curable*' adopted.[34] It was a view the Governors wholeheartedly embraced and the *British Medical Journal* accepted.[35] After 1948 it became less important to assert this rhetoric. Bethlem's connection to the Maudsley and the Institute of Psychiatry allowed the Governors to feel that they had an intrinsic claim to modernity and there was less need to stress the issue.

A CENTURY OF CHANGE?

Bethlem in 1994, when it became part of the Bethlem and Maudsley NHS Trust, was, unsurprisingly, a very different institution to the one that had mourned the death of Queen Victoria. Important continuities remained however, especially over the administration of the Hospital's extensive endowments. Little has been said about psychiatric institutions in the twentieth century, and even less about Bethlem. Where this was partly a result of the Governors' policy to control publicity, it was also because the Hospital's twentieth-century history was seen as less interesting than other periods. As the remaining chapters hope to show by bringing Bethlem's history up to 1994, this is clearly not so.

NOTES

1 Eric Hobsbawm, *Age of Extremes* (London: Michael Joseph, 1994).
2 *Ibid.*, ix.
3 Paul Johnson, 'Introduction', in Paul Johnson (ed.), *Twentieth-Century Britain: Economic, Social and Cultural Change* (London and New York: Longman, 1994), 1.
4 Cited in Roy Porter, *London: A Social History* (London: Hamish Hamilton, 1994), 306.
5 *Ibid.*, 324.
6 A. B. Atkinson, 'A National Minimum', in T. and D. Wilson (eds), *The State and Social Welfare* (London: Longman, 1991), 121–42.

7 See Sidney Pollard, *Development of the British Economy 1914–1990* (London: Edward Arnold, 1992) for the most comprehensive single-volume economic history.

8 John Burnett, *A Social History of Housing* (London: Routledge, 1993) or Alan Jackson, *Semi-Detached London* (London: Allen & Unwin, 1973).

9 See T. Barker and R. Robbins, *A History of London Transport*, vol. ii (London: Allen & Unwin, 1974).

10 Johnson, *op. cit.* 10–12.

11 *Daily Telegraph*, 15 October 1920, 5.

12 General Correspondence: Letter from Porter-Phillips, 27 July 1928.

13 *Souvenir of Bethlem Hospital (c. 1924)*, 11–12.

14 1939/40 Treasurer's Report.

15 For the creation of the NHS see Charles Webster, *Problems of Health Care: The National Health Service Before 1957* (London: HMSO, 1988).

16 William Sargant, *The Unquiet Mind* (London: Heinemann, 1967), 141.

17 See Chapter 1; for a historiographical discussion see Jonathan Andrews, 'Bedlam Revisited: A History of the Bethlem Hospital *c.* 1634–*c.* 1770' (unpublished Ph.D. Thesis, University of London, 1991), 1–10.

18 *Pamphlet for the Opening of the X-Ray Department* (1920), 10.

19 In 1923 all visitors were requested to ask for written permission from the Physician-Superintendent. This, however, did not include those visiting friends or relations in the hospital: Bethlem Subcommittee, 24 January 1923.

20 *Daily Telegraph*, 15 October 1920, 5.

21 Bethlem Subcommittee, 28 February 1906.

22 MEC Presented Papers: 7 November 1974, ECD 121/74.

23 Board of Governors, 4 October 1971 and 14 January 1980.

24 *Ibid.* 8 September 1980.

25 MEC Presented Papers: 6 December 1990, ECD 108/90.

26 Edward O'Donoghue, *The Story of Bethlehem Hospital from its Foundation in 1247* (London: T. Fisher Unwin, 1914).

27 General Correspondence: Letter to Porter-Phillips, 21 July 1936.

28 *1913 Bethlem Annual Report*, 9.

29 *Souvenir of Bethlem Hospital*, 11–12.

30 Medical Committee, 7 January 1925.

31 *BMJ*, 2 (1930), 74.

32 *City Press*, 3 March 1928, 5.

33 *1935 Bethlem Annual Report*, 14.

34 General Correspondence: Letter from Hamilton, 2 March 1946.

35 *BMJ*, 1 (1947), 935.

A NEW EDEN
Bethlem's move to Monks Orchard

———— •◆• ————

Marked variations existed between mental hospitals in the first half of the twentieth century. Private institutions like Ticehurst in Sussex and Holloway Sanatorium in Virginia Water offered a 'civilised and calming environment' with high standards of care.[1] In county and borough asylums much depended on the character of the local administration, medical superintendent, and funds available, but generally they offered mass care in drab surroundings for all those who could not afford to pay. At the London County Council's (LCC) Colney Hatch Asylum in the 1930s, fifty to sixty patients shared a toilet and all available bed space was used, creating cramped and insanitary conditions.[2] Other county asylums could point to similar problems, and the Board of Control constantly complained of overcrowding. Bethlem, as a registered hospital, had an altogether different environment. Under Charles Hood's nineteenth-century reforms (see Chapter 26) conditions had improved. In the early decades of the twentieth century, the Governors optimistically believed that the Hospital 'rather than stigmatising an individual, conveys the hallmark of hopefulness and curability'.[3] In every respect, Bethlem was seen as the antithesis of the inhuman conditions Montagu Lomax attacked in *The Experiences of an Asylum Doctor*, an almost model mental hospital.[4]

Few visitors not connected to the patients now flocked to Bethlem's wards, but those journalists who did wrote enthusiastically. According to the *London Argus* in 1904:

> the arrangements are not so much those of an asylum or a hospital as of a *first-class hotel or a hydro* [emphasis added]. The wards are furnished with comfort and even luxury, and as you pass through them and take note of the artistically disposed settees and easy chairs, and of the charming floral embellishments of the tables you might, but for the presence of the silent, watchful attendants, think that you had made a mistake in the building you had entered.[5]

Vicki Hayward, a young probationary nurse in 1928, shared this view. She felt that 'entering the wards was rather like stepping into a hotel reception'.[6] Wards were long (see Plates 29.1 and 29.2), although somewhat dark with a heavy style of furniture, and the sitting rooms and galleries 'generally warm and comfortable'.[7] Pictures, newspapers, books and even 'plants and birds and fishes' were everywhere. More

Plate 29.1 Women's ward in the early twentieth century. Reproduced by permission of the Bethlem Royal Hospital Archives and Museum.

attention was paid to the 'beauty and ornamentation' in the female wards; a common feature in mental hospitals.[8] 'The whole atmosphere', wrote the *Daily Press* in 1921, 'is that of the club rather than that of the asylum'.[9] Patients were encouraged to read or use the grounds for bowls, cricket and tennis, but a strict regime was still in operation and doors remained firmly locked. Everywhere that one *Evening Standard* reporter went he found that patients 'were protected against their own madness'. With surprise, however, he concluded that 'Bedlam is for cure and not for detention, and that the kindness and comfort are the master method.'[10] Patients responded well to this environment. 'Not a few spoke favourably' to visitors about the 'care they had received', with many mistaking Bethlem for a private hospital or country house.[11]

NEED FOR A NEW HOSPITAL

Bethlem's hotel-like conditions, however, hid a structure that was becoming increasingly ill-suited to changing ideas about the treatment of mental illness. The Board of Control informed the Governors in 1915 that Bethlem 'in some respects' was 'not entirely keeping pace with modern requirements'. This was blamed not on the enthusiasm of the staff or Governors, but on the building.[12] Criticisms mounted. In 1921 an inquiry for the *Daily Telegraph* into the state of England's asylums criticized

Plate 29.2 Men's ward in the early twentieth century. Reproduced by permission of the Bethlem Royal Hospital Archives and Museum.

Bethlem's buildings.[13] These views were shared within the Hospital. For Lionel Faudel-Phillips, the recently appointed Treasurer, this became an obsession. He was convinced that Bethlem was 'a totally inadequate and unsuitable place for the care and treatment of the mentally ill'. He dreamed of a 'fitter and lighter Bethlem', a desire shared by Sir Charles Wakefield of Wakefield & Co., the producer of Castrol oil, city luminary and the Hospital's President.[14] They felt the only way this could be achieved was to move Bethlem to a new greenfield site and rebuild.

Initially, Faudel-Phillips and Wakefield did not inform the Governors of their intentions, preferring to sound out opinion outside the Hospital first. The City of London's Bridge House Estate Committee, which held Bethlem's lease, was approached in 1922. At first the Committee was uncertain, but suggested that when a new site was found the existing lease for St George's Fields could be transferred. Their proposal would create a repetition of Bethlem's earlier moves (see Chapters 15 and 23).[15] It was only in October 1923, after lengthy consideration, that Faudel-Phillips finally took the Governors 'into his confidence'. Earlier in the year he had hinted that an important scheme was about to be discussed. In the Hospital's close administrative community many must already have suspected Faudel-Phillips's intentions. He finally informed the Governors that because of the problems facing the Hospital it was necessary to rebuild in rural surroundings within easy access of London. The Governors in response appointed a 'strong committee' to investigate.[16]

The Committee took a year to investigate before it presented its findings. It confirmed Faudel-Phillips's recommendations and provided detailed information on the need for a new hospital.[17] The Committee estimated that between 1911 and 1924 £6,000 had been spent annually on maintenance repairs, which increasingly required wards to be closed, while the sanitary arrangements remained unsatisfactory despite improvements in 1903.[18] Similar concerns had been expressed before Bethlem's rebuilding at Southwark.[19] Any move to a greenfield site, the Committee believed, would lead to an integrated hospital, allowing the convalescent home in Surrey to be closed and sold. It was estimated that this would save approximately £10,000 a year in rates, travel and maintenance. Against these financial considerations, medical reasons were added. A prime concern was the 'old fashioned lay-out', which was seen to be hampering effective treatment and recreation. The Committee argued that the buildings did not promote the proper classification of patients and lacked the facilities for the early treatment of acute cases, the need for which had been stressed before the First World War.[20] This was hardly surprising. The layout had been modelled on Robert Hooke's seventeenth-century building, which John Howard had claimed in 1789 to be ill-suited to proper classification.[21] Faudel-Phillips had already summarized these problems in 1923 and added that

> the ground available for the exercise of patients . . . is inadequate in which to provide the many interesting and helpful means of outdoor treatment which should be available particularly for those early cases of disorder, which of course present the most hopeful features.

At a basic level, Bethlem required more land, modernization, and a nurses' home. The accommodation of nurses in the wards, where their rooms were interspersed with the patients', was no longer seen as suitable, especially when the rooms for the night-nurses were no more than cubicles in a partitioned corridor.[22] It was estimated that even if £100,000 were spent modernizing the old building, the Governors would 'still have a Hospital which by reason of its situation would not meet all the proper needs of the Patients'.[23] The only solution was to move.

John Porter-Phillips, the dapper Physician-Superintendent, and Alfred Cheston, the Hospital's surveyor, added further reasons. Porter-Phillips saw that Southwark had become an unsuitable location due to 'climatic conditions'.[24] Cheston agreed that smog was prevalent and pointed to further problems. In his opinion, Bethlem was 'overhoused and under-sited'.[25] By the twentieth century, St George's Fields had become an area for the displaced poor, pushed together in overcrowded conditions and, according to Charles Booth the social surveyor, at 'the centre of the greatest mass of poverty and low life in London'.[26] Southwark had become one of the most overcrowded boroughs in London, 'a chaotic jumble of narrow streets, alleys and courts, interspersed with large business premises'.[27] Added to this was a growing transport problem. The road junction at the Elephant and Castle retained the quality Charles Dickens had seen when he called it a 'ganglion of roads'. It was 'one of the worst traffic bottlenecks in south London' and plans to improve the road layout invariably floundered.[28] The extension of the underground (now the Bakerloo Line) between Lambeth North and Elephant and Castle kept patients 'awake at night by the drilling of a shaft in the hospital grounds'. When tunnelling had finished and trains started to run they felt like a 'miniature earthquake' in the wards, further disturbing Bethlem's calm.[29] Porter-Phillips and Cheston had overestimated the problems of smog, but for a hospital for the educated middle classes Southwark was not an ideal location.[30]

Bethlem was a respectable and neatly gardened enclave in the midst of poverty, overcrowding, and traffic congestion. However, the Governors now agreed that its very building was failing to meet the high standards expected. With little outside pressure, they realized that a change was needed. The late 1920s was a period of development and improvement in registered mental and voluntary hospitals.[31] The new Bethlem was part of these changes. The medical profession had long advocated the need to move mental hospitals to semi-rural locations to take advantage of the healthier conditions and room for outdoor recreation. General hospitals were also being encouraged to relocate to reduce the overcrowding of medical institutions in central London and to match the changing distribution of the population. Bethlem had been slow to heed these calls, but once the Governors had decided to move they were enthusiastically embraced. Cheston summed up the benefits:

> a great saving should be effected in a new building by reason of reduction in repairs and upkeep, while the treatment of patients, their accommodation and recreational facilities would be provided on modern lines in more healthy, peaceful and less depressing conditions, and separate residences could be provided for the resident Medical Staff.[32]

Instead of an architectural competition being held, the witty conversationalist Charles Elcock, of the London firm Messrs Elcock & Sutcliffe, was appointed. Cheston, himself a member of the RIBA and with the experience of designing buildings for Westminster Bank and Fullers brewing company, was instructed to assist him. Elcock had been chosen because he had 'exceptional experience in the erection of modern hospitals', designing hospitals in Manchester and Harrogate in 1925 and a radiological department in Wolverhampton.[33] These successes brought him further hospital contracts and he became an expert on hospital construction, working closely with the medical profession. There was an additional reason. Faudel-Phillips, as Mayor of Hertford and from a family active in the region's administration, was aware of Elcock's work as consulting architect for Hertfordshire County Council for whom he had recently designed Hertford City Hospital.[34]

The decision to move was greeted outside the Hospital with approval. *The Times* felt that relocation 'to a fresher and more cheerful site will be in accordance with the traditions of the charity ... an attempt to gain for such persons the inestimable blessings of quiet and repose and surroundings likely to restore health and strength'.[35] Journalists confirmed that an institution that wanted to be in the forefront of psychiatry could no longer be housed in Southwark in a building that was over a hundred years old.

THE OLD AND NEW SITE

The decision to move was made with relative ease, but a suitable site took longer to find. Faudel-Phillips apologized in 1924 that 'a further twelve months should have passed without my being in a position to call the Committee together for the consideration of a draft scheme'.[36] Shortly afterwards, he was approached by an estate agent about the Monks Orchard Estate, four months before it was due to be auctioned. Faudel-Phillips expressed immediate interest on the Governors' behalf in the 334-acre semi-rural estate near Eden Park, Kent, ten miles from Charing Cross. Originally called Park Farm Estate, it had been renamed Wickham Park in the 1830s and finally became Monks Orchard in the 1850s when it was taken over by Lewis Loyd, of the banking firm Jones Loyd & Co. Loyd had taken the name from Monks Orchard Wood, named after the Monk family who had owned land in the parishes of Addington, Beckenham and West Wickham, and not after any religious connection. The Loyd family finally moved from the estate in 1911 having built two new mansions, one of which, Monks Orchard House, was completed in 1854. The estate was leased to a local builder, and then in 1913 to Arthur Preston, an engineer from Deptford. When Preston died in 1920, Frederick Loyd decided to sell. Most of the adjoining properties were sold in 1920, but the Monks Orchard Estate, along with two other neighbouring properties, remained unsold and was put on the market in 1924.[37]

Monks Orchard matched the requirements Arthur Kenyon had identified in 'The Hospital and the Garden City' for an ideal hospital located on an open green site, shielded by trees.[38] For the Governors it seemed ideal, allowing land for development and recreation. Cheston agreed, believing that it offered 'every facility for the development of a magnificent Hospital' and informed the Governors that the asking price of £35,000 was reasonable.[39] An offer was made, but not every member of the governing body was convinced, many having a sentimental attachment to the old buildings. Faudel-Phillips was insistent, convincing the waverers that a rural location would be beneficial. It was understood that both the Board of Control and the Bridge House Estate Committee would consent, the latter agreeing to transfer the lease. However, the Charity Commission was unenthusiastic and insisted that Parliamentary approval was needed.[40] The Governors accepted the suggestion, but went ahead with the purchase. The estate was bought complete with the two old mansions. At the time it was felt that these could be used in the new hospital, though only the farm was eventually incorporated to provide milk, food and limited occupational therapy. The purchase was greeted by a burst of mutual praise, but it was recognized as Faudel-Phillips's 'great work'.[41]

Considerable interest was shown in Bethlem's existing site once the Governors had formally decided to move to Monks Orchard. The Metropolitan Public Gardens Association considered that it was 'an important lung of London', expressing concern about the site's future.[42] It was widely recognized that the local residents, in a part of London where few open spaces existed, had come to appreciate Bethlem's fine lawns.[43] The Ministry of Health, the LCC and Southwark Borough Council all wanted to preserve the Hospital as an open space and were prepared to resist the bill unless a park was provided. The suggestion was made at a time when increased attention was being paid to the need for parks in London to provide a healthier urban environment.[44] Initially the Governors offered to give five acres to the public, but the Charity Commission objected.[45] The collapse of Bethlem's offer jeopardized the bill and the move. It was realized that the Southwark site, which Cheston had conservatively estimated to be worth £150,000, would play an important part in funding any new hospital.[46] The Governors had not expected any opposition and now the future of the move was uncertain.

The situation was saved by Viscount Rothermere. Rothermere was the brother of Viscount Northcliffe and, since his brother's death, head of the Amalgamated Press, owner of the *Daily Mail*.[47] He offered £155,000 for the site and proposed to turn it into a fourteen-acre park for children in memory of his mother, Geraldine Mary Harmsworth. The Governors immediately accepted and local representatives were delighted.[48] Rothermere's purchase was not an uncharacteristic act of benevolence. He had made several large donations and had a long-standing interest in the Foundling Hospital. Constraints on finance and pressure for housing ensured that philanthropists like Rothermere continued to play an important role in providing London with parks, where in other cities municipal councils took an active role.[49] Rothermere's offer removed opposition to Bethlem's Bill, which received the royal assent on 15 July 1926. The City, on the advice of the Bridge House Estates Committee, transferred the existing agreement, leasing Monks Orchard to Bethlem for the 749 years remaining on the 1674 lease on a peppercorn rent of six shillings.[50] Possession of Monks Orchard, however, could not be obtained until 1927, and with Rothermere taking occupation of the old site in 1930 a clear timetable for action existed.

PLANNING

In 1924 Wakefield proudly proclaimed that the aim was to create a hospital that lacked 'nothing known to the human mind which would in any way ameliorate the conditions and tend towards the cure' of the mentally ill.[51] Planning, however, was not the straightforward implementation of these ideas. Where work continued as normal at the old hospital, planning and then construction and furnishing came to dominate meetings. Nothing could be done between 1923 and 1930 without some reference to the move, which was given priority over all other considerations.

John Conolly, in *The Construction and Government of Lunatic Asylums*, had stressed in 1847 the importance of the physical environment in the treatment of mental illness.[52] Porter-Phillips shared his assessment. 'Bethlem', he asserted, 'should not only be "up-to-date", but even "beyond date" and give a definite lead in the development of an ultra modern type of buildings for the treatment of the mentally afflicted.' Sir Frederick Willis, chairman of the Board of Control, agreed and gave his full support. In his first report, Porter-Phillips explained his ideas, which became the basis for development. Planning had to be governed by three basic patient classifications: badly conducted, well conducted, and convalescent. To achieve this he recommended the adoption of ten separate single-storey blocks. He rejected the 'ultra modern Cottage Hospital type of building' because it did not offer the 'atmosphere of dignity' that Bethlem needed. Porter-Phillips imagined a large, spacious design that the vernacular cottage type, built with a mix of rural and domestic elements and associated with rural districts, did not provide. Instead he favoured the villa system with blocks for administration, occupational therapy, refractory patients, convalescent patients, treatment and research, along with a nurses' home, chapel, reception hospital, mortuary, workshops and a laundry.[53] Witley House, the Hospital's convalescent home in Surrey, could therefore be closed and all patients treated on one site. Elcock, interested in the villa principle, encouraged Porter-Phillips. The Governors agreed, but rejected single-storey blocks as too expensive, despite their obvious benefits in reducing opportunities for suicide.[54] At a later point they added an isolation hospital to the design, given the frequency of infectious diseases among patients.

The villa system gave Bethlem 'an opportunity of making a great leap forward'.[55] It represented a break with earlier attitudes to asylum design, although their use had been advocated in 1809.[56] During the rapid growth in asylum building in the mid-nineteenth century the 'corridor' design had dominated, with long façades and pavilion blocks. In the 1880s there was a move to separate blocks to promote better patient classification with the 'broad-arrow' plan. At Bexley (1898) and Horton Asylum (1902) separate villas were introduced, but they formed only a small part of the design. County asylums, built on a ward principle for a large number of poor patients, were obviously unsuitable models for the new Bethlem. Neither was inspiration found in other psychiatric institutions. The Governors wanted a modern institution with separate research laboratories, not the gothic county-mansion-cum-convalescent-home that private institutions offered.[57] The pavilion plan, which had become the main model for hospital development, was unsuitable because it did not promote the desired classification of patients, while the new compact multi-storey blocks were felt to be unnecessary given the land available. The villa system, which had more in common with the separate ward blocks found in tuberculosis sanatoriums, provided what the Governors and Porter-Phillips were looking for.[58] It allowed the development of a small compact institution with landscaped grounds where separate blocks could be built for different functions. Porter Phillips argued that the villa system would allow 'patients suffering from the early phases of mental illness' to be 'spared the distress which may result from association with those in the more acute stages'.[59] Classification was built into the design. Runwell mental hospital in Essex, also designed by Elcock, was the only other psychiatric institution in the interwar period that followed this plan. However, where it was built for over a thousand patients, Bethlem was initially to care for three hundred.[60] By adopting the villa system, Elcock and Porter-Phillips distanced the new hospital from both the county asylums and private institutions, making Bethlem unique.

Planning was a protracted affair. Careful attention was paid to every detail from the avoidance of sharp corners in the wards to the provision of a shelf in the rooms so patients could display their 'small belongings'.[61] Wakefield and Faudel-Phillips were committed to a modern design, but their enthusiasm was not shared by other Governors who remained dedicated to Bethlem's Victorian atmosphere. Disagreement became integral to the planning process. Each change or suggestion required new plans, which were then fully discussed and submitted to the staff for their approval. This continual process of consultation aroused criticism, forcing Faudel-Phillips to explain that if 'our progress has been slow it will, I hope, be proved that a little time expended on a clear understanding in the initial stages makes for rapid progress when we come to the actual arrangement'.[62] No-one was entirely satisfied and debates became acrimonious in December 1926 when some Governors expressed fundamental disagreements. Faudel-Phillips and Elcock were persuasive.[63] Elcock was convinced of the merit of his plans and Faudel-Phillips was determined to quash any criticism and forge ahead.

It was not simply a matter of agreeing the plans within the administration. The Board of Control expected to have an important influence, especially as it was interested in encouraging the type of hospital the Governors wanted to build. Lomax's accusations and the Royal Commission that investigated them, made the Board more sensitive.[64] Dr Hubert Bond, president of the Medico-Psychological Association (MPA), and Kirkland, the Board of Control's architect, visited Bethlem for the Board of Control on several occasions between 1926 and 1927. Bond and Kirkland were particularly concerned about the size and expense of the blocks. They clearly implied that the Governors had not really thought out what they wanted.[65] Faudel-Phillips resented Kirkland's manner and put his faith in Elcock and Cheston. He kept Willis at the Board of Control informed of developments, who in return advised him what criticisms should be accepted to secure the Board's approval. Faudel-Phillips constantly urged upon Willis 'the necessity of getting to work as soon as possible', but he did his best to agree, asking Elcock to modify the size of the corridors and treatment rooms.[66] Bond and Kirkland found almost every aspect of the Hospital 'unusually large' and were alarmed that the estimated expenditure per bed was £2,000, a concern shared by the Charity Commission.[67] There were grounds for complaint. Bethlem's expenditure per bed was high in comparison to the £1,500 other hospitals had been prepared to spend. At points Faudel-Phillips and Wakefield shared the Charity Commission's worries. Expenditure had spiralled from the original estimate of £300,000 to £495,000, though partly this was blamed on the 1926 general strike's impact on labour costs.[68] Economies were made and the estimate was finally lowered to £430,000. Last-minute modifications continued until April 1928. The Governors seemed increasingly concerned to save money rather than build the 'magnificent Hospital' initially intended. With the tender awarded to Messrs Arnold & Sons, Elcock finally insisted on 27 April that deliberations had to stop because the builders needed to start work if the Hospital was to be completed on time. The Governors reluctantly agreed, leaving fifteen months to build the new hospital (see Plate 29.3).[69]

Much had been changed in the planning. Four main blocks provided the ward accommodation: two for quiet patients divided by sex, one for excited patients, and one for convalescent. These differed from other mental hospitals by providing single-room accommodation, though several four- and five-bed wards were built for 'special purposes'. Porter-Phillips's original idea of ten blocks had been expanded to provide a lodge, separate kitchen and stores, and to take account of the existing farm on the estate. Considerable attention had been given to the Treatment and Research Unit. The effect was an 'exceptionally modern and well-equipped building' with an operating theatre and accommodation for hydrotherapy, psychotherapy, dental and electrical treatment, and a central pharmacy. Accommodation for the junior medical staff, along with the offices and a board room, was located in the Administration Block. The matron's house was removed in favour of her accommodation with the nurses, though separate houses were built for the senior medical staff. To meet the needs of the married male nurses staff houses with a 'parlour, large kitchen, scullery, three or four bedrooms, bathroom, etc.' had been added.[70] Their inclusion created

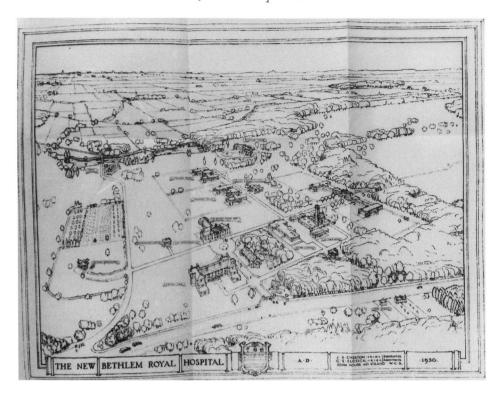

Plate 29.3 Plan of the new hospital at Monks Orchard from a brochure produced for the opening in 1930 and distributed by the Governors to the guests. Reproduced by permission of the Bethlem Royal Hospital Archives and Museum.

considerable tension given Porter-Phillips's habit of making 'last moment fresh criticisms and new suggestions'.[71] His attitude was characteristic of the entire development. Last-minute problems were discovered with Monks Orchard House, which was found to be full of dry-rot and consigned to demolition. The aim had been to use this for the nurses' home but instead a new nurses' home in the 'approved modern style' had to be included in the plans. Here Bethlem was ahead of many other institutions with the move to provide separate nurses' accommodation still in its early stages in 1946. The convalescent block, which Porter-Phillips had successfully defended in April in the face of financial restrictions, was built on the site.[72]

Finance played an important part in shaping the layout. An effort was made to balance the Board of Control's requirements with the Governors' ambitions, but cuts had been unavoidable. The chapel was saved only by a large donation from Lady Wakefield, the President's homely wife. To reduce expenditure it had been necessary 'to rely for architectural effect on compact planning and to allow the masses of the buildings to tell rather than to emphasise architectural details'.[73] The style produced was neither art deco nor *avant garde*. It hinted at a mixture of Georgian and Swedish, with elements of Bauhaus in a 'simple and dignified' style. In line with contemporary psychiatric thought on the benefits of open-air treatment, verandas were incorporated to allow patients to sit out in 'suitable weather'. Elcock went on to pioneer such veranda wards in other hospitals. To save money he was persuaded to cut the number of beds from 300 to 250 and reduce the size of the recreation hall. Plans for an isolation block and a lecture theatre were also dropped, along with the use of Portland stone in preference to the cheaper French stone. Blocks were scaled down and their location changed. The Governors had not, however, sacrificed 'the personal comfort of the patients', which was seen as considerably better than 'the accommodation afforded in other mental hospitals'.[74] Small extravagances were allowed. The stained glass in the chapel's windows was produced by Messrs William Morris & Company and Axminster carpets were used throughout.[75] Bethlem had to maintain its hotel-like atmosphere.

Cheston and Elcock's final plans received enthusiastic reviews. The *Architect & Building News* felt that the design is 'from a technical point of view, well in advance of current practice, and should provide many new ideas in mental hospital planning'.[76] The *British Medical Journal* welcomed Bethlem's change of 'habitat', so that 'greater space and purer air may add still more to its scientific value'. The new hospital would align Bethlem with the most advanced psychiatric thinking expressed by the Royal Commission on Lunacy and Mental Disorders and 'add to the comfort of the patients'. It would appear that the Governors had left nothing 'undone to render it psychiatrically efficient in every sense of the word, and that the highest aims of modern treatment and the dissemination of knowledge of psychological medicine will be amply fulfilled'. The *Journal* looked forward to the opening of the new hospital as a 'milestone in psychiatric history'.[77]

Elcock's insistence that the plans be finalized, ensured that the foundation stone was ready to be laid in July 1928 and the Duke of Connaught was invited to conduct the ceremony. However, he was unable to attend and delegated the task to his son, Prince Arthur of Connaught, chairman of the Middlesex Hospital. In his speech thanking him, Wakefield noted that 'with the completion of the new building, everything that science and experience have taught us shall be employed to the fullest degree for the benefit both of those who suffer and those who strive to relieve them'.[78] By August an army of workmen had descended on the site, clearing trees and demolishing the old Georgian mansion. Roads were planned and a railway was constructed to carry materials around the site. Meetings now reflected the Governors' excitement that work had finally started.

FUNDING THE MOVE

When the new hospital was discussed in 1924, it was estimated that £300,000 could be raised through the sale of property, mineral rights in Kent, Witley House and other unspecified investments. The aim was to sell part of the endowments but not reduce revenue. Rothermere's purchase of the old site and the sale of the buildings would provide additional income. However, by October 1926 the estimated expenditure had already risen above this and other financial measures now had to be considered, the first of which was a public appeal. The Charity Commission was cautious, fearing that it might damage other hospitals' fund-raising. Instead, it recommended that expenditure should be lowered by £1,000 per patient to bring the cost down to the original estimate.[79] The Governors ignored the suggestion. Some concern was expressed that other hospitals were launching appeals and it was therefore initially decided to postpone the announcement 'to allow the work of the new Hospital to be well under way before taking this step'.[80] However, with an urgent need for funds the decision was quickly reversed. The Governors were aware that 'every pound we can collect against our capital expenditure will have the effect of increasing our charitable effort'.[81] The appeal was launched in February 1928 by Sir Charles Batho, Lord Mayor of London, from the steps of Mansion House. The *Daily Telegraph* commented that 'for the first time within living memory ... [Bethlem] is appealing for funds'. Certainly no-one alive remembered the Hospital's similar efforts in 1812 when an appeal was organized to fund the move to St George's Fields.[82]

In their official press statement, the Governors hoped that

> the interest which has so recently been displayed towards this branch of medicine may be translated into a warm response from men and women of affluence in support of this Royal and Ancient Foundation, which has for so many centuries administered to the mentally afflicted.[83]

Privately they were apprehensive. Bethlem unsuccessfully tried to borrow the voluntary hospitals' fund-raising tactics.[84] The appeal was widely advertised and numerous letters were sent to London's leading philanthropists, City Livery Companies and businesses. A morbid interest developed in bequest announcements in anticipation of securing legacies, but the Governors had little success. London's benevolent economy was a highly competitive market. Bethlem's appeal came at a time when several well-known hospitals were launching appeals even though the public had been exhausted five years earlier by the Combined Hospitals Appeal. These other institutions had considerable fund-raising experience and knew how to pick the pockets of the philanthropic public. With no tradition of fund-raising, Bethlem found it hard to stimulate charitable feelings. The Governors' concern about Bethlem's image had led them to eschew publicity and this damaged their ability to raise funds.[85] The Hospital had no recent tradition of charitable support to draw on to counter this. Bethlem's very nature added to these problems. Popular images of Bedlam did not evoke sympathy and mental health was not a fashionable charitable concern, arousing suspicion rather than understanding. Faudel-Phillips was quick to recognize this, pointing to the 'ignorance and lack of material and moral sympathy the public had for any form of mental illness'.[86] In the public mind, mental hospitals, no matter what their credentials, were associated with local authorities and the Poor Law and did not need charity. In addition, it was widely believed that Bethlem was not in need of money. These problems and the nature of London's benevolent economy worked against Bethlem's appeal, limiting the amount of money it could raise. Donations did not come flooding in as expected. By February 1930, £48,067 14s had been raised; in the following year the fund had reached the unimpressive figure of £50,396 11s.[87] Each Governor contributed at least £52 10s, but most outside donations rarely exceeded ten guineas. Those connected to the Hospital, including the contractors, gave the largest amounts. Wakefield headed the list from the start with a donation of £25,000, stipulating that the money had to be used to fund the science and treatment block, confirming his earlier support for scientific treatment. To honour this, the Governors decided to name the block the 'Sir Charles Wakefield of Hythe Science and Treatment Laboratories'. Other large donations followed. Wakefield's wife gave £5,000 for the chapel, which was named after her. Lady Cooper contributed the same amount to build the recreation hall, which became 'The Sir Edward Cooper Recreation Hall' in memory of her husband who had been a City Alderman and a Governor of the Hospital.[88]

The poor performance of the appeal forced the Governors to adopt other strategies. Plans were modified to promote savings, but this did not solve the problem. Other solutions were suggested. One idea was to build twelve private suites that could be charged at a higher rate. The Charity Commission took exception to the idea, believing that it would create problems with income tax, and with only twelve suites they questioned the practical benefit. A bargain was struck. The Commission accepted a permanent scheme where paying patients would be charged a higher fee of five guineas. In return the Governors 'agreed not to proceed further with the proposed Special Suites'.[89] To increase income, land was set aside to sell to builders for speculative housing projects once opposition from the Bridge House Estates Committee had been overcome. The Charity Commission gave its approval out of a desire to prevent Bethlem running up unnecessary debts.[90] Cheston tried to ensure that the estate was developed to its full potential. He was adamant that all houses on the Hospital's property should be for middle-class occupants who were likely to pay a higher rent.[91] The situation, however, remained problematic. The sale of land was slow and fraught, especially as the area was only beginning to be developed with 'no shops, no houses or buses before 1932'.[92] Even when combined with higher charges to patients the income needed was not generated. More drastic measures were put forward. Faudel-Phillips even suggested that it might be necessary to sell additional endowed property.[93] The concern that this would limit future revenue was shared by the Charity Commission, which insisted that any capital sold had to be repaid through a sinking fund.[94] Ultimately, with the original investments identified for sale performing poorly, this was necessary, creating a series of annual deficits lasting into the mid-1930s.

CLOSING OUTPATIENTS

Financial concerns not only affected planning, but also existing services. The outpatient department became the main casualty even before the transfer to Monks Orchard. Porter-Phillips had first suggested the need for an outpatient department in April 1917, building on the 1914 MPA report that had recommended the need for more clinics where patients could attend voluntarily. He put forward his ideas at a time when the medical profession was increasing its support for early treatment and outpatient clinics, given wartime experiences and the growing interest in psychotherapy. Similarly the Board of Control was recommending the creation of such departments, but Porter-Phillips was not trying to provide a service for ex-servicemen suffering from shell-shock.[95] Instead he felt that Bethlem could not afford to be left behind where other hospitals – by which he meant the LCC's Maudsley Hospital – were founding similar departments.[96] An outpatient department was shown as part of a 'progressive policy' that would allow Bethlem to retain its 'high status'. Porter-Phillips optimistically argued that it would allow 'early diagnosis of abnormal nervous and mental retardation' leading to 'a complete eradication of the causative factor' in mental illness.[97] The Governors agreed. With the Royal South London Dispensary giving up its lease of Bethlem's property at 52 Lambeth Road it was decided that an outpatient department could be established. After protracted negotiations, in which Porter-Phillips became increasingly dissatisfied, the department was finally opened as the Hospital for Nervous Diseases in August 1918.[98] The name was chosen in the belief that by separating the department from the main hospital patients would not be discouraged by Bethlem's previous reputation.

Table 29.1 Hospital for Nervous Diseases: admissions, 1920–7

Year	Patients	New patients	Attendances
1920	583	—	3,009
1921	651	—	3,088
1922	—	323	3,864
1923	—	267	4,432
1924	—	240	4,253
1925	—	331	4,227
1926	—	290	3,154
1927	—	132	1,888

Source: Annual Reports, 1920–7

The department was seen as a 'landmark' and proved highly successful.[99] In the first two months nearly a hundred patients attended and admissions continued to rise (see Table 29.1). Bethlem built on provincial experiences. Although not as pioneering as St Thomas's Hospital, which had treated psychiatric patients in its outpatient department since the 1890s, Bethlem's department was the first to be established at a London mental hospital and quickly won acclaim. The University of London was impressed, feeling that it was 'fitted up in an excellent manner'.[100] Professor Robertson of Edinburgh's Morningside Hospital was of the 'definite opinion that certainly nowhere else in this country did I see better work done or a better system organised'.[101] The department's success was not enough to save it. In 1927 the Medical Committee recommended that the department be closed, a view sanctioned by the Governors in June.[102] The Board of Control regretted the decision, noting that the department had done much good work and strongly urged that arrangements should be made with other hospitals to provide a similar facility. The idea was rejected by the Governors as impractical. The medical staff were not informed of the decision until July.[103] It was immediately discussed by Alfred Tredgold, Danvers-Atkinson and Cecil Charles Worster-Drought, all leading members of the psychiatric profession. Tredgold, a controversial specialist on the treatment of mental deficiency, saw the decision as 'a serious backward step'.[104] He defended the department:

the whole tendency of modern medicine is to remove the stigma of Insanity, by breaking down the artificial barrier which has so long existed between the different forms of disease and disorders of the nervous system. In regard to this, Bethlem has been to the fore in establishing an outpatients' department which admitted all types of neurological and borderland mental conditions.[105]

Bethlem could only lose by such a decision, surrendering any reputation it had. Porter-Phillips was aware that there was 'a very general dislike' of 'attending the Out Patients Department of a Mental Hospital', but felt that the department had brought Bethlem into 'the front line with other mental hospitals'.[106] The psychiatric community agreed, but these arguments were not enough. Faudel-Phillips, more concerned with Monks Orchard and quickly 'bored with the whole incident', noted that 'there is, unfortunately, always a tendency for the medical administration side of the Hospital to be unprepared with arguments and data when far-reaching discussion [*sic*] have to be raised and all sorts of crises dealt with'.[107] He was not convinced by any of the doctors' arguments, or by a petition from the patients.[108] The Governors' decision remained unaltered and from October 1927 the department was gradually stripped and the equipment transferred to the main hospital.[109]

Why had the decision been made? An investigation by the Medical Committee revealed that the department, located between two large general hospitals, was failing to attract suitable cases.[110] Porter-Phillips reluctantly agreed, claiming that most of those attending had a prior history of treatment. This was clearly against the department's objectives. More importantly, economic considerations were at work. The financial demands of the new hospital created a need for savings. Faudel-Phillips identified the department as an 'accessory to treatment' and deemed it unnecessary.[111] From its opening it had been a financial burden, and although its closure would save only an estimated £500 a year its buildings could be leased to increase income.[112] Porter-Phillips was aware that the department had never been a financial success, even after charges had been introduced in 1921. 'As you know', Faudel-Phillips informed him, 'Bethlem's financial effort is limited and the need for conservation of our resources at the present moment is so desirable' that this overrode all arguments to keep the department open.[113] Danvers-Atkinson's accusation that the decision was made on purely financial grounds, however, was strenuously denied.[114]

The closing of the outpatient department saw the conflict of two different concerns. The medical staff could not present an effective argument to justify the department's continuation. Disappointed with the department, given its failure to meet their expectations, the Governors needed the resources it was felt to be draining. In the light of the move, where no similar venture could be provided given Monks Orchard's distance from London, the Governors' decision appeared a rational one. However, it came at a time when other hospitals were starting to develop outpatient clinics, encouraged by the 1930 Mental Treatment Act and pressure from the Board of Control. Outpatient clinics were seen as the main vehicle through which early treatment could be provided, avoiding the stigma of institutional care. In 1930 there were twenty-five outpatient centres, by 1935 this had risen to 162.[115] Outpatient care became the most dynamic sector of institutional mental health provision in the 1930s, and here Bethlem was going in the opposite direction. In closing the department and in making no effort to fund a similar venture elsewhere, the medical staff's fears were eventually realized. The effect, as shown in Chapter 30, had an important bearing on Bethlem's development. There was no forward planning in 1927, or even suggestion of the problems to come, allowing the financial needs of the new hospital to override all other concerns.

BUILDING AND OPENING

Building progressed rapidly and by 1929 serious attention was turned to the names of the new blocks. Originally it was suggested that they should be called Chestnut, Beech, Pinewood and Broomwood, but this was seen as 'somewhat commonplace and suburban'.[116] Porter-Phillips was anxious that the names should pay 'tribute to those who have played a prominent part in the evolution of this great foundation'. Faudel-Phillips agreed, and Porter-Phillips recommended: Barkham, Fitzmary, Wakefield, Witley and Connaught.[117] All were historically justified and, except Witley which was offered on grounds of pure sentiment, marked some of Bethlem's major benefactors. John Worsfold, the efficient secretary, did not consider these entirely suitable. He felt that Barkham was too 'suggestive of a mental home' and explained that Wakefield was being used for the science and treatment block. Worsfold had, however, accepted Porter-Phillips's suggestion about using Bethlem's history and after studying Geoffrey O'Donoghue's *The Story of the Bethlehem Hospital* proposed: Fitzmary, Gresham, Edmanson, Bowes, and Tyson.[118] Edward Edmanson had donated Garlinge's Farm in 1695 and Sir Martin Bowes had been a broker between Bethlem and Henry VIII during his mayoralty in 1545. Tyson, after Edward Tyson, was O'Donoghue's 'devoted physician' between 1684 and 1708. Worsfold was particularly attached to the name 'Gresham' and originally intended Monks Orchard Road to be called Gresham Avenue. Worsfold's misreading of O'Donoghue gave the impression that Sir Richard Gresham had been petitioner to Henry VIII for the grant of Bethlem to the City. This was clearly erroneous. With the Governors unable to decide, Faudel-Phillips stepped in and named the blocks Gresham and Fitzmary for quiet patients, Tyson for excited, and Witley for convalescent.[119]

During construction Faudel-Phillips, Elcock, Cheston and Porter-Phillips made regular visits to Monks Orchard and increasingly made all the decisions. Their aim was 'that the happy combination of the residences and the surrounding grounds may negate, as far as possible, the atmosphere inevitably connected with Hospital life'.[120] Great attention was therefore paid to the grounds and ward decorations. Each block was carefully arranged so that it faced 'ornamental gardens with wide expanses of turf, giving ample space for exercise'. In the wards 'a homely and comfortable air' was the guiding principle, with particular emphasis placed on 'ample lavatory and bath accommodation'. Sunshine yellow was used to stimulate patients in Gresham and Fitzmary, while 'sunny day rooms', with billiard rooms for male patients and writing rooms for female patients, were added to encourage the 'associated life of the patients'.[121] In the convalescents' unit more was done to eliminate the feeling of a mental hospital to help return patients to a 'normal' life. Some old furniture was transferred, but the move was seen as an ideal opportunity to refurnish Bethlem with

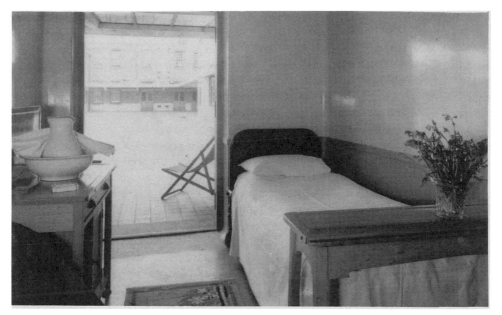

Plate 29.4 Interior of one of the single rooms. Reproduced by permission of the Bethlem Royal Hospital Archives and Museum.

furniture of a 'modern labour saving design' (Plate 29.4).[122] In the nurses' home 'nothing that is for their comfort or recreation appears to have been forgotten', and separate dining and recreation rooms were provided for the nurses and maids. Faudel-Phillips saw in the new Hospital a testament to the hard work and 'devotion to duty and genuine interest shown by everybody employed by the Governors'.[123]

The Governors' enthusiasm was reflected outside. In the national, medical and architectural press the new Bethlem was widely praised. The *Builder* explained that it was built 'on the latest and most scientific principles ... to encourage rapid improvement in the health of the patients'. It was anticipated 'that the new and up-to-date appliances for treatment and research will make the study of psychological medicine available to a large body of students'. Rebuilding had not been in vain, as the *Builder* went on to note that conditions in the new hospital were better than in many other hospitals.[124] A report prepared by the Board of Control visitors in 1931 congratulated the Governors

> on their courage and to express our conviction from all we have seen at our visit to-day that this new Bethlem will maintain its former great traditions and by the steady pursuit of its high aims will enhance still further its value and its fame.[125]

Two years later, the Board applauded 'the spacious outlook from the rooms and verandas and the wide aspect of the gardens [which had been] well calculated to mitigate the idea of confinement so often present in the distressed minds of patients'.[126] The *Journal of Mental Science* held a similar opinion. It compared the level of comfort at Monks Orchard to a 'good private house', and was impressed with the facilities for recreation and the 'ample toilet and bath accommodation'.[127]

Faudel-Phillips became anxious in 1930 to open the new hospital. Patients had been discharged from February 1930 and by the end of May Bethlem had been emptied. With no work being undertaken at the old hospital, Committee meetings were suspended and in July 1930 Faudel-Phillips started pressing Porter-Phillips to speed up the transfer of staff.[128] Porter-Phillips could do little and was himself complaining about the contractors, whose continued work at Monks Orchard was slowing the transfer.[129] Ironically preparations for the grand opening in July ensured that the new hospital was not finished on time. The new Bethlem was not officially opened until 9 July, though much of Monks Orchard remained a building site and Monks Orchard Road a cinder track. Nearly a thousand guests arrived by special trains, with Queen Mary as the honoured guest (see Plate 29.5). On the ten-mile drive to Monks Orchard she was cheered by children and spent almost an hour inspecting the Hospital in the 'blazing sunshine', making suggestions as she went.[130] As a result full-length mirrors were included in the nurses' rooms.[131] The press, though seemingly confused about the Queen's dress, with each paper reporting a different colour, widely recognized that Bethlem was entering a new era. To mark the occasion, the Queen planted a tree, once an additional six feet of red carpet had been found so she

Plate 29.5 Queen Mary at the opening of the new Hospital, 9 July 1930, with Charles Wakefield, President, Lionel Faudel-Phillips, Treasurer, and John Porter-Phillips, Physician-Superintendent. Reproduced by permission of the Bethlem Royal Hospital Archives and Museum.

could reach the designated spot. In return Cheston presented her with an antique Chinese ivory opium vase, which Queen Mary was known to have wanted, instead of the usual golden key. The opening ceremony was deliberately kept short due to the weather. Between the pink and blue hydrangeas in the marquee, large blocks of ice were placed to keep the room cool. In his speech, the Lord Mayor recognized that Faudel-Phillips and Wakefield were primarily responsible for 'this great step forward in the history of this Royal and ancient Hospital'. Arthur Greenwood, the Minister of Health, saw in the Queen's visit yet another example of her interest in the good of the people and hoped that it would encourage other mental hospitals.[132]

Bethlem, however, was still not ready to admit patients. The final preparations were fraught with problems and the Board of Control threatened to withhold the Hospital's status until many were solved. The toll had been too much for Cheston. Suffering from the strain of planning, his health had been deteriorating since 1926 and he was taken ill with septic pneumonia eight days after the opening. Cheston had brought 'his knowledge of the administration and actual detailed needs of the staff and the patients' to the planning of the new hospital.[133] Dying on 24 July, he did not see the first eight patients admitted on 20 October, although even at this date work had not been completed. Despite some blocks remaining unfinished, a sense of optimism prevailed. It was anticipated that once all the units were open admissions would increase, but continuing problems with the contractors ensured that the male wing of Tyson was not finished until 1931.

The Governors were pleased with their new hospital, feeling that it offered 'a warm welcome to all those who may desire the helpful hand of rest and cure'.[134] Porter-Phillips agreed and saw that the new Bethlem presented 'wonderful opportunities for the care and treatment of patients which can be regarded as second to none'.[135] Not all were as enthusiastic. With a firm sense of nostalgia for the old building, complaints quickly emerged. On arrival many nurses were critical about the absence of wash-stands in their rooms.[136] By October, Faudel-Phillips could point to the 'somewhat continuous complaints'. Porter-Phillips tried to explain that this was nothing more than constructive criticism, but Faudel-Phillips was not convinced and felt forced to remind the staff that the 'new hospital . . . is the finest of its type in the world'. Faudel-Phillips had invested much in the new hospital and was not prepared to have it criticized. In a fit of pique, he declared that 'he expected to have from the officers of the Hospital loyal and efficient service in both word and deed' and if any member of staff was not prepared to give this he would accept their resignation, as he felt such actions 'strike at the very foundations of the good work to be done in the Hospital'.[137] The staff stopped complaining.

When the final approximate costing was received in September 1930 (see Table 29.2), Elcock estimated that the new hospital would cost £509,595. By this point £447,917 had been raised. Faudel-Phillips was confident that the rest would follow and reassured the Governors that they had 'the largest possible value for money'.[138] As a short-term measure, £75,000 was borrowed. To raise extra money even unclaimed 'personal effects' of former patients were sold. Porter-Phillips was instructed to 'give particular attention to cases from which payment to the Hospital is forthcoming, as at this early stage it is particularly desirable to place the Hospital revenue on a sound footing without delay'.[139] By December 1932 the Finance and

Table 29.2 Sources of income for the new Hospital

	Receipts			Owed	
	£	s	d	£	s
Donations	45,693	6	0	2,570	00
Lambeth site	50,811	5	0	106,000	00
Furniture and equipment sold	908	18	1	500	00
Interest	19,185	11	9	—	
Sale of stock	103,961	12	0	—	
Monks Orchard development	21,205	13	6	22,089	00
Freehold disposals	51,624	12	6	13,586	15
Mineral rights	3,280	4	1	—	
Sundries	3,377	5	10	—	
Total	300,048	8	9	144,745	15

Source: Special Committee, 24 September 1930

Estates Subcommittee put a final figure on the total expenditure. At £537,779 3s 8d, the new hospital had cost far more than originally anticipated. It left the Governors the task of replacing £108,016 5s 5d from the property they had sold and £148,961 from the sale of investments. The Charity Commission was sympathetic, but pressed for payments to a sinking fund to recoup the Hospital's endowments.[140] Financial concerns now came to dominate meetings and the Governors became more interested in expenditure and the need for profit. The 1929 Wall Street Crash and the following depression of the 1930s added to these problems. Indirectly the cost of the move shifted the emphasis further away from charitable provision and closer to the needs of a private institution.

AFTER-EFFECTS

Bethlem had survived its third move, but a price had been paid. By the time the Imperial War Museum had moved from its cramped location in South Kensington to Bethlem's former buildings in Southwark, problems had started to emerge. Monks Orchard provided Bethlem with immense opportunities, but these were imperfectly realized and during building corners had been cut and provision scaled down. A legacy of financial problems resulted. The new Hospital was praised for its innovative design, but there had been no attempt to plan for the future. Predicted savings did not materialize and staff remained dissatisfied. The Hospital's new semi-rural location made recruitment difficult and in some ways damaged Bethlem's position. The move was a mixed blessing. It provided a thoroughly modern hospital, but sowed the seeds of problems that would lead to changes in the very nature of the institution.

NOTES

1 Charlotte MacKenzie, *Psychiatry for the Rich: A History of Ticehurst Private Asylum 1792–1917* (London: Routledge, 1992), 42.

2 Richard Hunter and Ida Macalpine, *Psychiatry for the Poor: 1851 Colney Hatch Asylum – Friern Hospital 1973* (London: Dawson, 1974), 147–148.

3 *Souvenir of Bethlem Hospital* (*c.* 1924), 6.

4 Montagu Lomax, *Experiences of an Asylum Doctor* (London: Allen & Unwin, 1921); *Daily Telegraph*, 12 September 1921, 7.

5 *London Argus*, 15 October 1904, 27–8.

6 *Inter Nos*, January 1980, 4.

7 *1920 Bethlem Annual Report*, 22.

8 *Evening Standard*, 15 May 1912.

9 *Daily Press*, 29 July 1921.

10 *Evening Standard*, 15 May 1912.

11 *1906 Bethlem Annual Report*, 53.

12 *1915 Bethlem Annual Report*, 20.

13 *Daily Telegraph*, 12 September 1921, 7.

14 Court of Governors, 29 June 1931.

15 Monks Orchard Correspondence: Letter from Still, 4 June 1923.

16 General Committee, 8 October 1923.

17 *Ibid.* 14 October 1924.

18 Special Committee, 29 September 1924.

19 *Proceedings of the Committee, and Reports from Surveyors, respecting the state of Bethlem Hospital in the years 1800, 1803, and 1804* (London: Bryer, 1805).

20 Special Committee, 11 January 1924.

21 John Howard, *An Account of Principal Lazarettos in Europe* (London: Cadell, 1789), 139. Also, see Chapter 22.

22 *Inter Nos*, January 1980, 4.

23 Special Committee, 11 January 1924.

24 *Ibid.* 17 January 1924.

25 *Ibid.* 29 September 1924.

26 Charles Booth, *Life and Labour of the People in London* (London: Macmillan, 1902), vol. iv, 18.

27 Ken Young and Patricia Garside, *Metropolitan London: Politics and Urban Change 1837–1891* (London: Edward Arnold, 1982), 195; C. R. Martin, *Slums and Slummers* (London: Bale & Co., 1935), 28.

28 Howard Roberts (ed.), *Survey of London* (London: LCC, 1955), vol. xxv, 46.

29 *Bethlem & Maudsley Gazette*, June 1959, 21.

30 See H. Berstein, 'The Mysterious Disappearance of Edwardian London Fog', *London Journal*, i (1975), 189–206.

31 For example, the Middlesex Hospital was rebuilt from 1923 and a major block was added to the National Hospital for Nervous Diseases: Geoffrey Rivett, *Development of the London Hospital System* (Oxford: OUP, 1986), 217–18.

32 Special Committee, 29 September 1924.

33 General Committee, 8 February 1926.

34 *Financial Times*, 15 October 1929, 10.

35 *The Times*, 25 September 1924, 9.

36 1924 Treasurer's Report.

37 *Bethlem & Maudsley Gazette*, March and July 1957.

38 *Hospital Gazette*, 26 (1929), 76–7.

39 General Committee, 14 October 1924.

40 Monks Orchard Correspondence: Summary of Proceedings, 10 February 1926.

41 Court of Governors, 24 November 1924.

42 General Correspondence: Letter from the Metropolitan Public Gardens Association, 19 November 1923.

43 *The Times*, 24 June 1925, 13.
44 See Gordon Cherry, *Evolution of British Town Planning* (Leighton Buzzard: Leonard Hill, 1974); Mervyn Meller, *Raymond Unwin: Garden Cities and Town Planning* (Leicester: Leicester University Press, 1992), 189–209.
45 General Committee, 9 October 1925.
46 *The Times*, 29 April 1927, 16.
47 See obituary in *The Times*, 27 November 1940, 7.
48 *Daily Mail*, 5 March 1926, 13.
49 Helen Meller, *Leisure and the Changing City 1870–1914* (London: Routledge, 1976), 117–18.
50 Monks Orchard Correspondence: Letter from Worsfold to Still, 23 June 1931.
51 *Daily Telegraph*, 23 December 1924, 12.
52 John Conolly, *The Construction and Government of Lunatic Asylums* (London: Churchill, 1847), 1–2.
53 Special Committee, 2 February 1926.
54 *Ibid.*
55 *Ibid.* 26 February 1926.
56 Robert Reid, *Observations on the Structure of Hospitals for the Treatment of Lunatics* (Edinburgh: James Ballantyne, 1809).
57 Jeremy Taylor, *Hospital and Asylum Architecture in England 1840–1914: Building for Health Care* (London: Mansell, 1991), 133–59.
58 See L. Bryder, *Beyond the Magic Mountain* (Oxford: OUP, 1988).
59 *1930 Bethlem Annual Report*, 17.
60 Kathleen Jones, *Asylums and After* (London: Athlone Press, 1993), 138.
61 Special Committee, 24 May 1927.
62 1925/6 Treasurer's Report.
63 Monks Orchard Correspondence: Letter to Faudel-Phillips, 3 December 1926.
64 See Phil Fennell, *Treatment without Consent: Law, Psychiatry and the Treatment of Mentally Disordered People Since 1845* (London: Routledge, 1996), 108–19.
65 Monks Orchard Correspondence: Letter from the Board of Control, 4 June 1926.
66 *Ibid.*: Letter from Faudel-Phillips to Worsfold, 28 July 1927.
67 Special Committee, 14 July 1927.
68 *Ibid.* 18 February 1927.
69 *Ibid.* 11 April 1928.
70 *Bethlem Royal Hospital: Projected Buildings* (1927), 2–12.
71 Memorandum from Worsfold, 2 February 1928.
72 *Projected Buildings*, 10; Special Committee, 29 December 1927.
73 *Description of the New Bethlem Hospital.*
74 *Hospital Brochure* (1930), 4.
75 Special Committee, 3 February 1931.
76 *Architect & Building News*, 2 (1930), 71.
77 *BMJ*, 1 (1927), 1018.
78 *Croydon Times*, 14 July 1928, 1.
79 Charity Commission Papers: Letter from the Charity Commission, 23 May 1927.
80 Monks Orchard Correspondence: Meeting with Wakefield, 7 February 1928.
81 *Ibid.*: Letter from Worsfold to Faudel-Phillips, 27 January 1927.
82 *Daily Telegraph*, 28 February 1928, 10.
83 *City Press*, 3 March 1928, 5.
84 For charitable fund-raising, see Keir Waddington, 'Finance, Philanthropy and the Hospital: Metropolitan Hospitals 1850–1898' (unpublished Ph.D Thesis, University of London, 1995), ch. 3.
85 See Chapter 28, pp. 539–41.
86 *Morning Post*, 6 July 1928, 6.
87 Court of Governors, 24 February 1931.
88 *Daily Chronicle*, 28 February 1928, 5.
89 Special Committee, 11 July 1927.

90 General Committee, 11 June 1928.

91 Court of Governors, 25 June 1928 and 25 November 1929.

92 *Bethlem & Maudsley Gazette* (1974), 14.

93 Court of Governors, 30 April 1928.

94 Audit Committee, 25 October 1929.

95 *1917 Board of Control Annual Report*, 5; M. Stone, 'Shellshock and the Psychologists', in W. F. Bynum, Roy Porter and Michael Shepherd (eds), *Anatomy of Madness* (London: Tavistock, 1985), vol. ii, 246.

96 Outpatient Department Papers: Report on the Proposed Establishment of an Outpatient Department, 4 April 1917.

97 *1917 Bethlem Annual Report*, 8–9.

98 Outpatient Department Papers: Letter from Porter-Phillips to Hood, 14 April 1919.

99 *1917 Bethlem Annual Report*, 8–9.

100 Medical Subcommittee, 6 April 1927.

101 Outpatient Department Papers: Letter from Robertson, 10 December 1927.

102 Court of Governors, 27 June 1927.

103 Outpatient Department Papers: Letter from Worsfold, 11 July 1927.

104 Medical Subcommittee, 29 September 1927.

105 Outpatient Department Papers: Letter from Tredgold to Worsfold, 26 July 1927.

106 Medical Subcommittee, 6 April 1927; Outpatient Department Papers: Letter from Porter-Phillips to Worsfold, 4 October 1927.

107 Outpatient Department Papers: Letter from Faudel-Phillips to Worsfold, 30 July 1927.

108 *Ibid.*: Letter from Worsfold, 25 November 1927.

109 *Ibid.* 6 October 1927.

110 Court of Governors, 25 April 1921.

111 Outpatient Department Papers: Letter from Worsfold to Board of Control, 29 June 1927.

112 1937/8 Treasurer's Report.

113 Monks Orchard Correspondence: Letter from Faudel-Phillips to Porter-Phillips, 14 March 1927.

114 Outpatient Department Papers: Letter from Danvers-Atkinson to Porter-Phillips, 22 July 1927.

115 *1935 Board of Control Annual Report*, 37.

116 General Correspondence: Letter from Worsfold, 20 November 1929.

117 *Ibid.*: Letter from Porter-Phillips, 25 November 1929.

118 *Ibid.*: Letter from Worsfold, 2 December 1929.

119 Edmanson and Bowes were not entirely rejected, but were used to name two avenues on Bethlem's Westbrook Estate in Westgate-on-Sea shortly after the new Hospital opened.

120 1930/1 Treasurer's Reports.

121 Special Committee, 5 March 1930; *Hospital Brochure*, 4.

122 Special Committee, 12 June 1929.

123 1930/1 Treasurer's Reports.

124 *Builder*, 3 October 1930, 563.

125 Visitors' Book, 1931–48.

126 *1933 Bethlem Annual Report*, 16.

127 *JMS*, 77 (1931), 288–91.

128 General Correspondence: Letter from Worsfold to Porter-Phillips, 11 July 1930.

129 1929/30 Physician-Superintendent's Report.

130 *Daily Mail*, 10 July 1930, 7.

131 Vicki Hayward, 'Bethlem in the 1930s' (Unpublished Paper, 1982), 1.

132 *City Press*, 11 July 1930, 11.

133 *Under the Dome*, June–September 1930, 54–8.

134 *1929 Bethlem Annual Report*, 21.

135 General Correspondence: Letter from Porter-Phillips to Faudel-Phillips, 6 July 1931.

136 *Ibid.* 15 January 1930.

137 House Committee, 18 October 1930.

138 Special Committee, 24 September 1930.
139 House Committee, 3 September 1930.
140 Finance & Estates Subcommittee, 9 December 1932.

NEW BEGINNINGS
The merger of Bethlem and the Maudsley

——— •◆• ———

etween the move and the outbreak of the Second World War in 1939, Bethlem settled into suburban life. Considerable developments were seen in terms of treatment that encouraged a new sense of optimism (see Chapter 34). The outward appearance, however, was one of calm. No new building projects were undertaken, but the grounds were gradually developed. The onset of war did not immediately disturb the Hospital. Bethlem emerged from the conflict damaged but not defeated. It was more fortunate than many other London hospitals, on which the German air-raids seemed focused.[1] Here the Hospital's location proved an advantage. Already in the suburbs, there was no need to evacuate Bethlem. The Hospital did not have to assume a new function through the reception of civilian or military casualties. Neither did it become part of the Emergency Medical Service (EMS), which had been established to provide and coordinate wartime medical care.[2] The Governors' contribution to the war effort was largely voluntary, but Bethlem could not escape the effects of 'total war'. Rationing limited the supply of food. Despite the Hospital's prize-winning flower beds being turned into vegetable plots and efforts to follow the national trend and 'dig for Victory', patients resented restrictions.[3] More complaints were raised over the fact that both staff and patients had to sleep on straw mattresses in the cellars during air-raids, a practice that had not been seen at Bethlem since the early nineteenth century. Admissions fell, as did income, and the Governors found it harder to retain nursing and medical staff given the demands of the EMS and the prospect of higher wages elsewhere. By careful management it was not necessary to close a ward until 1942, although treatment was restricted. Throughout the war a perennial sense of anxiety prevailed and in all departments staff and patients were expected to show a Dunkirk spirit.

The situation changed dramatically in July 1944 when German V-1 rockets brought havoc to London. V-1s gave no warning and in the summer of 1944 an estimated 2,350 fell on London, killing more than 5,000. It seemed that many were targeted directly at London's hospitals.[4] Having escaped the worst of the Blitz, three V-1 rockets landed in the grounds of Monks Orchard in July and August. Miraculously no-one was injured, but 'the widespread effect of the blast was intense'.[5] Every unit was damaged and Wakefield, Gresham and the Chapel reduced to shells. After the first attack, Bethlem was left with 107 beds and patients were evacuated. The

Governors discussed the possibility of closing the Hospital, but a series of emergency financial measures, and help from the Ministry of Works, ensured that Bethlem had nearly returned to normal by 1946.

This was the situation in 1947 when the Hospital came to celebrate its seven-hundredth anniversary. The main focus of the jubilee was a special day of celebrations, complete with a garden party and Founder's Day service. The anniversary was brought forward from October to June in the hope that those invited would be better able to attend and to take advantage of the summer weather. Repair work on the war damage was rushed so that all the buildings could be opened for inspection.[6] Queen Mary, Bethlem's President since 1941, was invited as the guest of honour and she readily accepted. No expense was spared, despite earlier doubts that not enough money was available to meet the cost of repairing the bomb damage. The celebrations saw an important gathering of those involved in hospital and mental health administration, although Aneurin Bevan, Labour's Minister of Health, was unable to attend. Poor weather did not deter the 700 guests, and few seemed concerned that Queen Mary wore a similar outfit – and certainly the same shoes – to the one she had worn to the opening of the new Hospital.[7]

Beneath the public optimism and show of the celebrations a pensive mood prevailed. While Sir Arthur Rucker, of the Ministry of Health, enthusiastically related that Bethlem was 'still in the forefront of medical treatment and psychiatric science', not all were as sanguine.[8] The passing of the 1946 National Health Service (NHS) Act promised dramatic changes in the structure and organization of healthcare, creating anxiety at Bethlem.[9] Sir George Wilkinson, Vice-President since 1941, explained to the audience that mental hospitals faced immense opportunities under the NHS, but he expressed concern that every effort should be made to hold onto the old in the new.[10] It was a direct reference to Bethlem's uncertain position. The concern was not surprising. For Bethlem the NHS represented a threat and many Governors feared the worst. Where the Hospital had weathered a conflict that had left many bereaved, injured and homeless, other challenges were faced in the immediate post-war period that changed the very nature of the Hospital and led to the creation of a new institution.

THE NHS THREAT

Bethlem's Governors had ignored the wartime debates on reconstruction in which plans for a national health service were seen as central to the post-war collectivist welfare system.[11] For Henry Willink, Conservative Minister of Health in 1944, such changes were 'the biggest single advance ever made in this country in the sphere of public health'.[12] At Bethlem, the Governors believed that the discussions and the proposed legislation had no bearing on the Hospital. Their initial view was confirmed after meetings in 1943 between the Ministry of Health, the British Medical Association (BMA) and representatives from the voluntary hospitals and local authorities. Based on these discussions, the Minister of Health stated that any new national service would exclude provision for mental health.[13] Even when the 1944 White Paper reversed this decision, Bethlem remained uninterested, consumed with the problems of repairing its war damage. The White Paper announced that the mental health services would be included in the new scheme. This was the embodiment of the ideas expressed by the 1924–6 Royal Commission that had pointed to the need for closer links between the treatment of physical and mental illness. Deliberations between the Medico-Psychological Association (MPA), the Psychological Section of the BMA and the Royal College of Physicians confirmed this view. The MPA stressed that there was a strong argument for treating psychiatry in the same manner as other branches of medicine.[14] Kathleen Jones has argued that such a policy had clear advantages. It would raise the psychiatric services' status, end the artificial divorce between mental and physical illness and increase the resources available, helping to reduce the stigma that still surrounded mental illness. However, there were disadvantages. The new service held the potential of shifting the patient between the doctor, hospital and health board, breaking any continuity of care. For Jones the 'dilemma was absolute', and 'in the circumstances the decision to proceed with full integration, even at the cost of administrative trichotomy, was a wise one'.[15]

When Aneurin Bevan circulated his proposals as the new Labour Minister of Health in January 1946 they had a mixed reception. Unlike the 1944 White Paper, Bevan resolutely asserted that all hospitals would be nationalized and brought under the Ministry of Health. For him it was 'an outrage' that mental hospitals had been isolated from the general hospital service.[16] Most mental hospitals, already administered by local government, remained quiet, but the highly vocal voluntary hospitals quickly made their opinions clear. Over the proposed NHS there was hardly the consensus that some have seen.[17] Those voluntary institutions represented by the British Hospitals Association saw in Bevan's scheme the 'mass murder of the hospitals', while the London teaching hospitals discerned some merit in the proposals. The royal hospitals were 'horrified' and complained about the uncertain future of their governors and the status of their endowments, which collectively represented approximately £300 million before the war.[18] Voluntary hospitals, with a long tradition of resisting pressure to cooperate, clung to their independence. Bethlem adopted a similar attitude. The Governor Edmund Stone and John Hamilton, the new Physician-Superintendent, were instructed to attend a meeting of the recently inaugurated Association of Registered Hospitals as observers to discuss the bill. The Governors were still uncertain about what would happen under the proposed legislation and initially decided not to dictate any general policy.[19] However, before the Association's next meeting, they agreed to adopt a more assertive policy and resist the bill.[20]

The main body of the bill contained few references to mental illness, except that the mental health service would form part of a national comprehensive service. When the appointed day for the creation of the NHS came, the Ministry of Health would assume responsibility for the administration of all mental hospitals, although the Board of Control would continue as a separate body. It was anticipated that this would bring unity to the mental health field.[21] Local authorities acquired wide but permissive powers in 'prevention, care and after-care', which included the initial care and removal of patients to a hospital.[22] The bill outlined a fundamental change in hospital administration. Hospitals were to be brought under the authority of a Regional Hospital Board; the old governing bodies either being integrated, or removed and replaced by a new management structure.[23] Bethlem's Governors rightly saw a threat to their autonomy. The NHS would end the Hospital's charitable status, remove its Governors, appropriate its endowments, and replace its management. For Bethlem, this would end seven centuries of independent development, placing the Hospital on the same footing as a county asylum. The Governors wanted to avoid this at all costs and refused to allow the Hospital to be swallowed by a region with no tradition of personal service. Bethlem was not the only institution to fear remote centralization. The London County Council (LCC) deplored the situation, and even those who accepted the new service wanted to maintain initiative at the hospital level.[24]

Bevan's proposals left room for manoeuvre. Fresh negotiations followed and in the final drafting of the 1946 Act concessions were made.[25] The King Edward's Hospital Fund for London and Sir George Aylwen, of the London Voluntary Hospitals Committee, had pressed Bevan over the teaching hospitals' existing boards and endowments.[26] The summary of the Act revealed Bevan had taken notice of their arguments. Although not given total autonomy, teaching hospitals were to be self-governing. Under the Act, they were freed from RHB control and given a degree of independence under a board of governors appointed by the Ministry of Health. The board would include members nominated 'by the University, the Regional Board . . . and the senior staff of the hospital itself'.[27] Several of the existing Governors would be reappointed. A further concession was made over their endowments. To promote teaching and research, teaching hospitals were treated differently and were allowed to maintain their endowments and have their debts paid.[28] In other hospitals the Act ensured that endowments would pass to a central fund so they could be distributed to reflect 'the actual needs of each rather than the largely accidental effect of past benefactions'. Both measures were designed to win the teaching hospitals and their influential consultants over to Bevan's ideas to ease the acceptance of the Act. At St Thomas's Hospital one doctor noted that had the 'hospital the power to decide its own fate in a national health service, it could hardly have chosen better'.[29] Many in teaching hospitals agreed. This was vitally important for Bethlem. For the Governors these concessions offered an opportunity to maintain their independence. However, they faced an important stumbling block. In 1946 the University of London had withdrawn Bethlem's status as a school of the university.[30] No longer a teaching hospital, Bethlem was deprived of a privileged position in the proposed NHS, and the Governors felt they could only lose unless changes were made. For an institution that had always stressed its leading role in psychiatric medicine, how had this situation come about?

THE MEDICAL SCHOOL, THE MAUDSLEY, AND THE REPERCUSSIONS OF THE MOVE TO MONKS ORCHARD

The main problem rested with Bethlem's medical school. Despite the support Theophilus Hyslop gave to medical education as president of the BMA's psychological medicine section and as a member of the MPA's education committee, his interest did not translate into practical measures while he was Physician-Superintendent from 1888 to 1911.[31] Lectures had been started at Bethlem by Alexander Morison in 1823 and the Hospital had held the first MPA examination in 1886, but little further encouragement was given.[32] The medical staff had offered clinical demonstrations and taught at other hospitals since the mid-nineteenth century (see Chapter 24), but the decision to hold lectures was motivated by an awareness that Bethlem needed to keep pace with developments elsewhere. The LCC's newly founded Maudsley Hospital had been running courses for the Diploma in Psychological Medicine (DPM) since September 1919.[33] Bethlem had initially viewed the Maudsley's foundation in 1907 with detachment, but by 1920 Bethlem's Physician-Superintendent, John Porter-Phillips, was concerned that the Maudsley represented a threat. As a past-member of the MPA's education committee, he explained to Lionel Faudel-Phillips, the domineering Treasurer, that 'something must be done in the near future in order that Bethlem may still retain a position in the front rank of teaching Institutions'. He even hinted that the University of London was anxious that Bethlem 'should maintain its position as the premier Hospital in the domain of psychiatry not only as regards to treatment but in teaching and research'.[34] The Medical Committee were concerned that lectures would interfere with treatment, but Porter-Phillips's enthusiasm proved contagious.[35]

Letters were sent to doctors at other mental hospitals by Porter-Phillips, who wanted them to teach at Bethlem. The response was patchy. When the lecturing staff were appointed in 1921 Bethlem's former and current medical officers predominated. In addition, several prominent psychiatrists and psychologists agreed to join. These included Alfred Tredgold, a controversial expert on mental deficiency; W. H. R. Rivers, the first psychologist for the Royal Flying Corps and director of the psychology laboratory at University College Hospital; and William Brown, a pioneer in experimental psychology.[36] In presenting his syllabus, Porter-Phillips paid close attention to the Maudsley. He shaped Bethlem's course accordingly, 'in order that [the hospital] may be recognised as a teaching centre in connection with the diploma for psychological medicine of the London University'.[37] Where the Maudsley charged fifteen guineas so too did Bethlem, although it was anticipated that the Hospital's 'more comprehensive syllabus' would allow it to attract more students.[38] Bethlem did not offer its own examinations, but the lectures matched the requirements of the University of London, Cambridge, Manchester, Durham, Leeds and the Conjoint Board.[39] Clinical instruction was made more formal and offered every morning, except Wednesdays, for an additional fee.[40]

The University of London was not approached for formal recognition of Bethlem as a school of the University until 1923 in order to allow time for the lectures to become established.[41] On investigation, the University suggested that more cohesion was needed before Bethlem could be considered. However, its inspectors were

> satisfied that the Hospital affords ample facilities for clinical instruction in all types of mental disorder, and probably there is no place in the United Kingdom which could be developed more readily into a leading School of Psychiatry.

The lecturing staff was seen as 'distinguished' and it was believed that Bethlem was 'actively prosecuting research', although little was published.[42] When the Governors were informed that the Maudsley had already been recognized by the University, they decided to ignore their previous concerns about the extent of the University's influence and meet its requirements.[43] A medical Advisory Committee was established to run the school and the University gave its official recognition in July 1924.[44] Links were now established with the West End Hospital for Nervous Diseases, Queen Square. The aim was to provide a comprehensive course that would embrace both psychiatry and neurology, a link that was part of a constant rhetoric that sought to stress psychiatry's connection with organic medicine.[45] The prospectus claimed that Bethlem was a centre for 'the teaching and practice of Psychological Medicine'.[46] Reality did not match expectations. When Desmond Curran joined as a house physician in October 1928, he found that he received little formal tuition and relied on the matron for advice.[47] Despite this, the medical school was initially successful. Between May and July 1925, Fifty-two students from Guy's, fifty-five from St Thomas's, 135 from St Bartholomew's and thirty from the Royal Free Hospital attended.[48] The large numbers should be no surprise: students from Guy's and St Thomas's were charged a special rate of 10s 6d per session, and those from medical schools where a Bethlem medical officer held a post could attend free at first.[49]

Problems started in 1927 when Bethlem's outpatient department was closed.[50] Lecturers saw the closure as 'suicidal' and feared that it would cause Bethlem to surrender its teaching and reputation.[51] However, when the University was approached it found that the decision had no impact on Bethlem's teaching status.[52] In retrospect, by closing the department the Governors had removed an important part of the medical school. It had placed '*most valuable material at the disposal of the teaching staff*' and enhanced the school's reputation, attracting distinguished lecturers, impressed with the pioneering service, and students.[53] Without the department the medical school could no longer claim to be providing the same facilities or extensive training as the Maudsley. As a result, Bethlem became less attractive, a position accelerated by the move. Tredgold wrote to Porter-Phillips in 1928 to express his anxiety. He pointed to a steady decline in attendance, where at the Maudsley twenty to twenty-four students were registered annually. Tredgold advised that 'as things are it seems to me hopeless to attempt to compete against the Maudsley'. John Worsfold, the long-serving secretary, had echoed similar sentiments in 1927.[54] Porter-Phillips was loath to accept their assessment, but even in 1927 he was aware 'that the future of Bethlem Hospital depends entirely on the status it maintains in the "academic and medical point of view"'.[55] By 1947 these views had achieved a new relevance. He was aware that where Bethlem had 'held a higher position and afforded greater attractions than Maudsley Hospital' the situation had been reversed.[56] The Maudsley's close links with the LCC provided privileged access to a network of regular vacancies in the LCC's asylums. By 1938 the Rockefeller Foundation could explain that the Maudsley offered 'advanced training to the personnel of the entire (mental) hospital system of the Council'.[57] Bethlem could not offer the same professional opportunities.

The Governors, however, were not daunted, though they did not provide a lecture theatre in the new Hospital because of the fall in applicants. Attempts were made to encourage affiliation with other mental hospitals, but by September 1931 the Medical Committee was informed that affiliation would only start once 'the reliability of the work at Bethlem Hospital becomes known'.[58] In the same year only two students attended. Because of the lecturers' reluctance to travel to Bethlem to teach such small numbers, it was decided that they could lecture 'at such centres as the lecturers may select'.[59] The postgraduate side of the medical school now largely ceased to function and the remaining teaching was conducted away from the Hospital. The move provided new research facilities in the Wakefield Unit, but no research funding or teaching facilities. It isolated the medical school at a time when it was already facing intense competition from the Maudsley. The Maudsley was closer to London, had a better reputation, and a dynamic school. Bethlem, no matter what the rhetoric, could offer none of this. Neither students nor staff seemed prepared to travel to Monks Orchard. To promote attendance, Porter-Phillips suggested that tea should be served after each lecture.[60] Even this was not enough. Porter-Phillips was only too aware that 'owing to our removal from Town it has not been found easy to organise our formerly successful course of instruction'.[61] To overcome this problem, discussions were held with the West End Hospital and St Bartholomew's, where Porter-Phillips was a lecturer, to provide a central London site.[62] The West End Hospital proved reluctant to cooperate, while discussions with St Bartholomew's were protracted and an agreement was not reached until 1936. The arrangement allowed all clinical demonstrations to be held at Bethlem with St Bartholomew's providing the lectures. The agreement did not bring the anticipated influx of students. In the 1937 autumn session only four suitable candidates applied.[63] The DPM course continued to be offered each year, but with few applicants it did not run again. War saw clinical demonstrations ending when London's medical schools were evacuated and travel restricted.[64] As a result, the sixteen lecturers were not re-elected in 1941.[65] So keen were the Governors to attract students after the war that when St Thomas's students were sent to Bethlem for ten weeks of clinical instruction they agreed to pay the travel expenses.[66]

The reorganization of postgraduate education in the University of London, in response to the 1944 Goodenough Report, provided an opportunity for the University to re-evaluate its teaching needs. The Report was the most important statement on medical education since 1918 and resulted in the formation of the British Postgraduate Medical Federation.[67] With concerns that there were already too many teaching hospitals in London, Bethlem was excluded. Bethlem had not benefited from the immediate post-war boom in student numbers or doctors returning from the war, and its medical school was by now moribund. Hamilton was pessimistic. He believed that the University would not include Bethlem as a school because it was not part of the Federation and did not prepare students for a degree.[68] His assessment proved correct. The Governors were not in a position to protest and did not consider it. In comparison the Maudsley had developed its medical school, even throughout the difficult wartime period when the hospital was evacuated to Mill Hill and the Belmont Hospital, Sutton. Aubrey Lewis, Edward Mapother's successor and the Maudsley's clinical director, recognized in 1942 that the hospital's future depended on its teaching role.[69] His views were prophetic. Lewis believed that the Maudsley should become the training ground for all doctors who wanted to work in the LCC's mental health service. Above all 'teaching and research' had to 'remain in the forefront of [the Maudsley's] activities' so that it could play an important role in shaping London's psychiatric services.[70] Under his guidance both these aspects were developed. By 1944 the Maudsley had started to provide psychiatric training for demobilized doctors, establishing further links with the LCC's asylums, Tavistock Clinic, Guy's, and the West End Hospital.[71] The Goodenough Committee felt that the Maudsley occupied 'a special place in psychiatric work'. It recommended that it should play a prominent role in the British Postgraduate Medical Federation, a view shared by the University Grants Committee.[72] Based on these views, the University decided to recognize the Maudsley's medical school as its postgraduate psychiatric teaching hospital in 1946. The school was renamed the Institute of Psychiatry in 1948.[73] It was recognized, however, that the Maudsley could not train all the psychiatrists needed and that facilities would have to be found elsewhere. In 1946 no decision had been made where these would be found.[74]

The University of London's decisions left the two rivals in very different positions. Bethlem had effectively isolated itself and its medical school with the move to Monks Orchard. The Maudsley had risen in status, overshadowing Bethlem. With the passing of the 1946 Act the situation for Bethlem was no longer one of prestige. Now it appeared one of survival. Stripped of its teaching status, Bethlem was in danger of being absorbed in the 'general health service of the country'.[75]

THE RICH AND THE VIRILE: THE MERGER OF BETHLEM AND THE MAUDSLEY

It was not until May 1947, while the final arrangements for the anniversary celebrations were being made, that Bethlem's Governors were finally presented with a scheme to save the Hospital. A new climate now existed in the Hospital. With the death of Charles Wakefield in 1940 and Faudel-Phillips in 1941 much of the administrative old guard had gone.[76] When Porter-Phillips finally resigned in October 1944 after thirty years, he was replaced by Hamilton, the senior Assistant Physician. He was younger and more dynamic. Under Wilkinson, Gerald Coke (the Treasurer since 1941), and Hamilton, Bethlem became more flexible and willing to compromise.

In March 1947 Coke approached Lewis to discuss how Bethlem might be improved. Lewis made several straightforward suggestions that were accepted by the House Committee.[77] Coke's meeting with Lewis marked an end to the Hospital's vocal antagonism to the Maudsley. Bethlem, it seemed, now felt it had much to learn from its rival. By March informal discussions had started between Coke, the Hospital's solicitor, Hamilton and Wilkinson over Bethlem's future. This small group quickly recognized that the Governors had few options if they wanted to preserve their independence. From these discussions the idea emerged that Bethlem could resist the changes embodied in the 1946 Act only by merging with a teaching hospital. The Maudsley was the obvious choice. No suggestion was made that a general teaching hospital should be approached because this presented the danger that Bethlem would become nothing more than a department. Coke wrote to Sir Arthur Rucker to learn the Ministry of Health's position and was informed that the Ministry would support any merger.[78] No consideration was given to the option that Bethlem could opt out of the new service and establish itself as a private, non-NHS mental hospital.[79] At one level, the proposal appeared a panic measure. Bethlem had always valued its traditions, viewing the Maudsley as a rival. When the Maudsley suggested in 1929 that they should cooperate over a child guidance clinic, Bethlem had rather priggishly rejected the offer.[80] Now the Maudsley offered the one thing Bethlem needed. Marked differences existed between the two hospitals' management and funding. Bethlem had a proud history of charitable independence; the Maudsley was dependent on the LCC.[81] However, there were similarities that made the partnership less unlikely. Bethlem was not the antithesis of the Maudsley. Both saw themselves as hospitals, not as asylums. They were committed to the early treatment of mental illness, favouring acute cases over the chronic, and each preferred voluntary patients. Each had something to gain.

At some point between March and May 1947, Lewis visited Bethlem at Coke's invitation. Lewis felt that the Hospital was entirely suitable for teaching, partly because it had the most 'up-to-date buildings of any mental hospital in the world', while its large endowments allowed freedom for research. He even intimated that the University would be in favour of such a move.[82] Between 1939 and 1945, Lewis had developed his ideas on the future of London's mental health service. He recognized the problems of the existing system and predicted that the Maudsley would have to develop links with other institutions.[83] However, when the Maudsley returned to Denmark Hill in 1945 problems were apparent. Many county and borough mental hospitals finished the war with their services run down, accommodation over-crowded, and suffering from serious staff shortages.[84] At the Maudsley these institutional problems were complicated by the wartime split between the two sites. Different practices had emerged at Belmont and Mill Hill that divided the staff between those interested in psychotherapy and those committed to physical treatment. Mapother's death in 1940 complicated the situation and left the Maudsley without guidance. Frustration and tension developed, especially as Lewis was trying to force the Maudsley to adopt a general teaching hospital structure.[85] Many of those who had been at Belmont became dissatisfied with Lewis's control and left to take up clinical posts in other teaching hospitals, seriously depleting the staff.[86] As if this was not enough, the medical superintendent's reports pointed to other 'major difficulties'. Accommodation at Denmark Hill was cramped and urgent work was needed on the nurses' accommodation and school. The psychological staff did not have an adequate laboratory and the number of students was limited by the lack of space. Patients even had to be sent to King's College Hospital for X-rays.[87] It was only in August 1947 that the Board of Control felt that the Maudsley was beginning to return to its pre-war position 'as a centre of activity in the fields of teaching, research, and treatment'.[88]

Lewis, aggressively sceptical and erudite, may have been flattered by Coke's approach, but he clearly realized the advantages.[89] Making little effort to become involved in the shaping of the new NHS, Lewis's interest focused solely on the Maudsley.[90] Concerned to promote teaching and research and 'to help his pupils in their careers, especially those doctors returning from the war', the merger offered Lewis a unique opportunity.[91] In Lewis's view, it allowed him to shape both institutions along the lines he wanted. At a time when the Maudsley was being criticized for its inadequate accommodation, Bethlem provided access to what the *Lancet* considered was 'the proper sort of surrounds for mentally sick people' and one that aided 'a higher recovery rate', something the Maudsley was committed to.[92] Bethlem offered a thoroughly modern and spacious hospital with an additional 250 beds and 240 acres ripe for development. Bethlem also promised something more fundamental, the accumulated wealth of seven centuries. By 1947 Bethlem's investments, excluding land, amounted to £276,233 with an annual income of over £36,000.[93] For William Sargant, a part-time consultant at the Maudsley and self-proclaimed apostle of physical treatment in Britain, such a dowry left the Maudsley 'goggle-eyed'.[94] Under the merger Bethlem would keep these endowments, and with exchequer funding to run the hospitals they would provide an additional reserve that Lewis realized could be spent on research. Lewis had been better at attracting funding than Mapother, but both were frustrated by the Maudsley's reliance on the LCC, which itself was hampered by the continuing problems of local government finance. Many at the Maudsley anticipated that the same problems would be encountered under the NHS. Access to Bethlem's endowed funds would remove any problem, allowing Lewis to develop both hospital and medical school.

In 1979 Sir Denis Hill looked back: 'The one, Royal Bethlem, was very old and very rich. The other, Maudsley, was very young and very poor.'[95] With the passing of the 1946 Act Bethlem needed the Maudsley's teaching status to survive on what it felt were its own terms; the Maudsley needed the accommodation and Bethlem's endowments. Those under Lewis's tutelage could not 'afford to go against his wishes', and he became a prime force in shaping the merger.[96] On both sides it was a marriage of convenience, though Bethlem's position appeared more urgent.

With Lewis keen to promote the merger and the Ministry of Health sympathetic, Coke presented the Governors with his suggestions in May 1947. At this point, neither the Maudsley nor the LCC had been officially approached. Coke reassured the Governors that his suggestions were only tentative and that no legal steps could be taken towards amalgamation until 5 July 1948, the NHS's appointed day. He did recommend the creation of a joint committee to plan the merger however. The Governors were effectively presented with little choice. They had hoped that Bethlem would 'occupy a position commensurate with its dignity' in the new service. The merger was presented as the only way this could be achieved. After discussing the Maudsley's reputation and the belief that Bethlem could dominate the administration, the Governors gave their unqualified support.[97] A letter was immediately sent to Lewis outlining Coke's suggestions. Lewis discussed the proposals with Mary Ormerod, the level-headed chair of the LCC's Mental Hospitals Committee and of the Maudsley Subcommittee, and Lord Latham, leader of the LCC. They saw the matter as 'one of reality, not of convenience', and gave their cautious support.[98] Lewis hoped 'very much that the suggested Joint Committee will soon be able to go ahead with the detailed plan for the amalgamation', but the Mental Hospitals Committee did not discuss the issue until June. Allen Daley, Medical Officer of Health for the LCC, reported that Bethlem was a 'distinguished [institution] . . . built to modern standards and is very well equipped'. He emphasized that the Maudsley would gain much-needed 'additional accommodation and so would increase the range and variety of clinical material and laboratory space'.[99] The committee therefore agreed to Lewis's proposal. It recognized that 'by its association with the Maudsley Hospital . . . [Bethlem] would increase the range and variety of clinical material available for instruction . . . [and] would gain from association with the premier English postgraduate school in psychiatry'. The General Purposes Committee was asked to appoint four members from the Mental Hospitals Committee and Maudsley Sub-committee of which Ormerod proved the key figure.[100] Lewis was not mentioned, but he had already assumed an active part in the discussions. The LCC gave the matter no further consideration, caught up as it was in the discussions over regionalization.[101]

Many were aware at Bethlem's seven-hundredth anniversary celebrations that the Hospital had started negotiations with the Maudsley. In recognition the Maudsley's medical staff were invited to attend the garden party. The doctors, used to cramped conditions at Denmark Hill, 'were amazed at the extent and beauty of the grounds'.[102] Queen Mary's attendance can be seen as an indication of her continued support for the Hospital and as part of the royal family's attempts to 'bolster morale' among charitable medical institutions after the passing of the NHS Act. Queen Mary shared a similar assessment of the Act as Bethlem's Governors, both viewing it as 'an act of vandalism comparable to the dissolution of the monasteries'.[103] The Act had produced an atmosphere of uncertainty, accounting for the low-keyed nature of the celebrations. Sir Bracewell Smith, Lord Mayor of London, referred to 'a new era' that promised to ensure Bethlem's 'preeminence in the mental world'. The aim was to 'develop from this amalgamation, on the one side a Hospital with a world-wide reputation for the teaching of postgraduate psychiatry and on the other a Hospital which is capable of great expansion as a teaching and research centre'. This would create 'an entity that will be capable of leading the world in psychiatric teaching' and have the teaching status Bethlem so vitally needed. The hope was that 'the old lady at 700' could go forward with 'the good wishes of all those who have at [their] heart the welfare of the Hospital' and not be swallowed anonymously by the NHS.[104]

Little public attention was paid to developments at the two hospitals – the *Nursing Mirror* was one of the few journals to announce the merger.[105] It became lost in the events surrounding the creation of the NHS. The changes at Bethlem and the Maudsley appeared unimportant, and with other hospitals merging at the same time it was not even a unique event.[106] No-one seemed to realize that the merger would have a crucial bearing on psychiatric training and research. Even within the two hospitals little attention was paid to the amalgamation outside the Joint Committee. It became the broker between Bethlem, the LCC and the Maudsley in the difficult task of merging 'two so very different hospitals, the one rich in history and tradition, well endowed, beautifully sited, the other thrusting, somewhat brash, poor and ugly'.[107] The Joint Committee first met on 11 July 1947 and from the start Bethlem was under-represented. To the LCC's four representatives, Lewis was added, nominally to represent the University of London. No representative was present from Bethlem's medical staff, and it was Lewis that dominated the medical planning. Coke, however, was pleased with the small size of the committee and guided proceedings as its chair.[108] Between July and December 1947 it met five times before the less active Joint Transitional Committee was appointed at the Ministry of Health's behest. This committee was designed to match the Ministry of Health's guidelines for the organization of a teaching hospital board of governors. Both Bethlem and the Maudsley elected three representatives; the remaining fourteen were appointed by the University of London, the South East Regional Hospital Board, in which the new institution would be located, and the Ministry of Health.[109] The committee was to ease the transition to the new Board of Governors, but it was the Joint Committee that hammered out the administrative details. Bethlem's management structure became the model and all committee meetings were initially held at Bridewell.[110] It was recognized that Bethlem had an accumulated administrative experience that would prove useful to the new institution, especially over estate management. Here Bethlem could dominate. It was decided that an Estates Management and Investment Committee, similar to the Hospital's Estate and Finance Subcommittee, would be appointed and of its twelve members six would be from Bethlem.[111] All Bethlem's administrative officers were elected to comparable posts in the new hospital and once Bevan and the Home Office had accepted that NHS hospitals could accept royal patronage, Queen Mary was nominated patron.[112]

Problems were encountered over the new name. Embarrassingly Queen Mary felt that the Hospital should be named after her. Sir Allen Daley came to the rescue, noting that while 'Royal' should certainly be in the title it was important to keep the hospitals' names.[113] The Governors suggested the 'Post-Graduate Hospital for Psychiatry incorporating the Bethlem Royal Hospital and the Maudsley Hospital', but it was recognized that this too cumbersome and it was shortened to 'The Royal Post-Graduate Hospital for Psychiatry'.[114] The Ministry of Health immediately objected. It argued that the name was too exclusive, given that 'other psychiatric teaching hospitals will, in due course, be established'.[115] The Ministry preferred the 'Bethlem–Maudsley Royal Hospital', arguing that many would welcome the retention of the two names, though it was worried that the association with Bethlem might deter some patients. The committee was dissatisfied and felt that further discussion was needed.[116] After due consideration, it was decided to simplify matters and call the new hospital the 'Bethlem Royal Hospital and the Maudsley Hospital'. Unofficially it became known as the Joint Hospital.[117]

Where Bethlem secured the administrative structure it wanted, Lewis's ideas on the new medical management prevailed. On Lewis's suggestion, Hamilton was packed off to America to study the mental hospital system there. With Bethlem's Physician-Superintendent absent, Lewis thereby gave himself more room for manoeuvre. He believed that staffing should match the needs of a teaching hospital, and therefore the Maudsley's needs, and not those of a mental hospital. High salaries would be used to attract the best staff. This, according to Lewis, had been Henry Maudsley's and Mapother's legacy. He proposed that, like the Maudsley, the post of Medical Superintendent should be abandoned in favour of a House Governor, arguing that the running of a mental hospital needed an administrator, not a clinician over-burdened with administrative duties. Daley disagreed. The two views represented the two poles in the late nineteenth- and twentieth-century debates on the desired administrative officer for a mental hospital. The medical and psychiatric profession generally asserted that medical influence was crucial in hospital management. Lewis went against this because he felt a doctor's time could be better spent treating patients and undertaking research than running a hospital. Many in the profession seeking control over their working environment disagreed, but in the Joint Hospital Lewis's views dominated, fitting with the Ministry of Health's aim 'to reduce to a minimum the time given by medical staff to administrative duties'.[118] The removal of the Physician-Superintendent ended Bethlem's hierarchical system of medical government, splitting the functions between the House Governor and a medical committee. Staff were to be given greater autonomy and responsibility, although they remained answerable to the Governors. Bethlem appointed Kenneth Johnson in June 1948, executive officer of the LCC's mental health service, to fill the post of House Governor and gave the position considerable authority.[119] The autocratic Johnson did not encourage an informal atmosphere and was always known as 'Mr Johnson'. His long association with the LCC and the Maudsley, however, did ensure that this was mostly in the Maudsley's favour. Further problems were encountered over the exact number of doctors needed. Lewis argued that the number should be determined by the amount of outpatient work, teaching and research. No mention was made of Bethlem's requirements. The Joint Committee realized that it would be best to consider staffing once the budgets from the Ministry of Health and University were known, but it provisionally recommended a staffing structure identical to the Maudsley's. This matched Lewis's proposals, and Bethlem's Governors seemed to accept the argument that the Maudsley was the more dynamic clinical hospital of the two.

Before the merger came into force, cooperation started at a medical level. Felix Post was seconded from the Maudsley in January 1948 and Hamilton started to attend the Maudsley's outpatient department.[120] Professor Nevin, professor of psychiatric medicine at the Maudsley, wanted to centre all biochemical research at Bethlem and start joint research work before the appointed day. Because of delays with the LCC, it was decided that Bethlem should spend £2,500 on new research equipment.[121] Lewis had larger projects in mind, but was less successful at spending Bethlem's money before July 1948. He approached Coke in November 1947 with a scheme to found a Child Guidance Clinic at Farnborough Hospital in Kent. The Maudsley had established links with similar LCC clinics, but now Lewis was asking Bethlem to fund a new venture outside London. He estimated that the clinic would cost £3,800 per annum to run, of which £2,200 would be provided from patient fees.[122] The Governors initially offered their support, but on further investigation found that Bethlem's charter prevented them from funding any clinic outside the Hospital.[123] Less pre-merger cooperation existed at an administrative level. In April 1948 Ormerod, as the chair designate of the Joint Hospital's House Committee, was allowed to attend meetings of Bethlem's House Committee so she could familiarize herself with the Hospital's work. Deeply committed to the Maudsley, she did not take an active role and this was not repeated elsewhere.[124] The Governors wanted to run Bethlem on their own terms for as long as possible. At the last meeting of the House Committee, five days before the merger, it was recorded that Bethlem had been run with 'efficiency and courtesy'.[125] The hope was that this would be continued in the Hospital's future.

ADJUSTING TO CHANGE: THE FIRST YEARS OF THE JOINT HOSPITAL

In a confidential report in 1949, the merger was seen as providing complementary, not duplicating, services.[126] According to the first House Governor, the two hospitals were 'gradually fused together, so that [by 1953] they were more like two wards of one hospital than separate entities'. This was symbolized in the new coat of arms (Plate 30.1). A certain poetic licence was adopted with the pickaxe of the Maudsley family, to which Henry Maudsley was not apparently related, and the dragon supporters of the City of London 'imposed' upon a revised version of Bethlem's arms. In the marriage of the two hospitals, Bethlem 'brought the fine buildings at Monks Orchard and the accumulated wealth of centuries, and [the] Maudsley the revivifying influence of a virile teaching hospital of international reputation'.[127] However, the new coat of arms might be seen as a metaphor for the Joint Hospital's early development. In the new health service the voluntary system was forced upon the former local authority hospitals. This did not happen at the Joint Hospital. Where Bethlem had provided the administrative model, this was quickly eroded. In 1951 meetings were transferred from the Bridewell's offices to the Guildhall and the secretarial work moved to the Maudsley.[128] With the transfer of the administration to Denmark Hill it became clear that it was no longer necessary to have a part-time secretary and a House Governor. It was admitted that this had promoted a smooth transition, but the Governors decided that Malcolm Hewitt, Bridewell and Bethlem's clerk since 1939, was spending too much time working for Bridewell. Hewitt was asked to retire, and

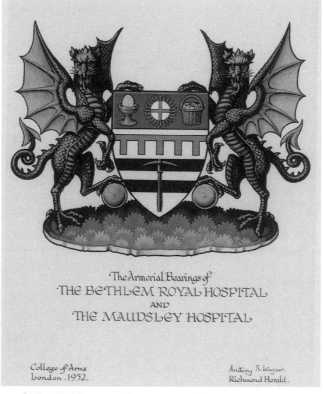

The Armorial Bearings of
THE BETHLEM ROYAL HOSPITAL
AND
THE MAUDSLEY HOSPITAL

College of Arms
London. 1952.

Anthony R. Wagner.
Richmond Herald.

Plate 30.1 Arms of The Bethlem Royal Hospital and The Maudsley Hospital, as granted by Letters Patent in 1951. Bethlem Royal Hospital Archives and Museum.

the post of House Governor and secretary were combined.[129] In terms of the medical administration, the Maudsley dominated. Its twenty-two doctors swamped Bethlem's small medical staff. At one point it was even suggested that those doctors who at worked at Monks Orchard should be excluded from the Medical Committee.[130] Changes were quickly made. Of Bethlem's old medical staff, only Hamilton remained; Duncan Whittaker, the senior Assistant Physician, had resigned in protest over what he felt was the lack of opportunity for him in the new Hospital.[131] No member of the Maudsley's staff lost their post.

Lewis's influence was considerable. At the second meeting of the Board of Governors he presented plans for the new medical organization. With the treatment of 'early and recoverable' cases occurring solely at the Maudsley, Bethlem would be used for other psychiatric services. This was a recognition of the practical problems of Bethlem's location and the absence of an outpatient department at Monks Orchard. Many of Bethlem's staff and former Governors did not see it like this. Further room for pathological and psychological work in the Wakefield Unit was to be provided by the removal of the out-dated 'ultra-violet, douche and other installations'. All neurosurgical work would be transferred to the new neurosurgical unit that the Maudsley was trying to establish with Guy's. Under his plans, Bethlem would become a home to psychotic children, senile patients, chronic schizophrenics, those needing long-term treatment, and those suffering from organic mental illness. This involved a complete change in the nature of Bethlem's patients.[132] Bethlem would become less like the hospital it had striven to be, and more like the asylums that it and the Maudsley had looked down on. For Lewis, reorganization would allow the full range of mental illness to be treated, though he envisaged that arrangements should remain flexible.[133] The Finance and General Purposes Committee accepted Lewis's views without argument. Staunch resistance over senile patients came from Miss Robinson, the Matron. Lewis had 'a tremendous stand-up fight with Matron . . . who was against the beautiful, recently private Bethlem being occupied by these nasty old people'.[134] Coke shared Robinson's concerns and felt that there was a

> need to bear in mind that owing to the more congenial surroundings at Monks
> Orchard the type of patient to be sent there should so far as possible be those
> who could appreciate and derive most benefit from their surroundings.

He was trying to defend Bethlem's traditional character, but in both cases Lewis won.[135] His idea of flexibility was unintentionally incorporated when it was decided to review the arrangements after a year, and it took several years before a permanent ward structure emerged.

The changes generated a considerable anxiety and resentment at Bethlem, with the Maudsley being viewed as arrogant and domineering. One of the main areas of bitterness was the large amount that was spent on the Maudsley. In the 1949/50 estimates of the £81,200 allocated for capital projects, only 10.4 per cent was to be spent on Bethlem.[136] The decision in 1949 that any improvement to the Institute of Psychiatry constituted 'an improvement to the Hospital buildings' allowed the Governors to recommend that the Hospital should pay for these improvements. It was a decision that ultimately led to the Joint Hospital providing £60,000 per annum from Bethlem's endowments to help fund the Institute's long-term building plan.[137] Bethlem's staff and former Governors recognized that the Maudsley was being improved out of Bethlem's endowments. Few were at first prepared to consider that Bethlem provided a physical environment superior to the Maudsley's. Spending on the Maudsley was vitally needed to raise standards, with wards even in the late 1960s still seen as a disgrace.

Bethlem found it hard to adjust to the new arrangement. The hope in 1947 that it would dominate the new institution quickly faded. The Maudsley proved to be another Bridewell. Bethlem was not at first considered an important part of the Joint Hospital's teaching or research.[138] Dissatisfaction was present at all levels. According to Felix Post 'there was an exodus of staff from Bethlem, which became short staffed', providing opportunities for Lewis's protégés.[139] Within five months of the merger, Coke resigned as chairman, citing 'increased pressure of business and call on his time in connection with the work for the South West Regional Board'. Although there is no direct evidence to suggest that he resigned because he was unhappy with the new arrangements, he did express a muted hostility to many decisions being made and was quickly removed from the House Committee on which he had planned to remain for a further year.[140] His resignation further weakened Bethlem's position. Ormerod became the new chair of the Board and the position of those connected to the LCC and the Maudsley was strengthened. By 1955 no members of Bethlem's former medical or governing body were on the Board, which was dominated by representatives from the LCC, Maudsley and the Institute of Psychiatry.

Lewis too quickly became frustrated.[141] In a confidential memorandum in 1949, the problems confronting the new Hospital were recognized and it was felt that the merger had been 'incompletely realised'. Lewis believed that the services provided did not require a joint hospital. He realized that the residue of 'pre-July staff at Bethlem fear change and are in a suspicious or reluctant mood'. Lewis did not attempt to understand these feelings or blame his own decisions in creating this tension, believing that friction would dissipate.[142] Others were equally dissatisfied. Sargant resigned in February 1949. At the time he explained his action as a matter of principle because the merger had produced decisions that divided the old staff from those joining or rejoining the Hospital.[143] He expected 'further differences', particularly over the allocation of beds and the degree of centralization.[144] He opposed Lewis's conception of the new Hospital, wanting the Maudsley to mirror the more porous model of the West End Hospital, but some of his grievances were real. An initial ruling that doctors should attend at least three times a week at 48-hour intervals was widely seen as impractical and was quickly reversed.[145] Problems existed throughout the Joint Hospital. Besides a reluctant and anxious Bethlem, it was difficult to determine which consultant was in charge of which patients, especially when they were transferred between the two sites. Beds were often 'avoidably empty', and Lewis believed that the Hospital 'would be in a most embarrassing position if there was any scrutiny of the use of our beds, with the result that we might be forced to submit to a degree of dictation from outside as to admissions'.[146]

CONCLUSION

The merger of Bethlem and the Maudsley had been designed as a 'marriage of tradition and progress' to solve a number of problems facing both hospitals.[147] What both institutions gained in trying to solve problems created new ones that took over a decade to overcome. Bethlem had swapped one partner for a new one, setting in motion changes that altered the nature and purpose of the Hospital. The result was a legacy of anxiety and resentment at Bethlem that lasted into the 1960s, particularly over the issue of finance. The solution in 1948 was not perfect, but at the time it appeared the only viable one. Over time both hospitals grew closer together and the initial teething problems were overcome. However, in joining with the Maudsley, Bethlem had become something different. Sargant, who became a critic of the merger after his resignation, felt that Bethlem, 'instead of remaining the most ancient and famous mental hospital in the world, with an historical personality of its own . . . became what was in fact an appendage of the Maudsley'.[148] His views, though biased, reflected reality. Bethlem had sacrificed the independence that it had been able to build up, and returned to a similar position to the one that had existed in the sixteenth century when the Hospital was linked with Bridewell.

NOTES

1 For London's experience during wartime see: Joanna Mack and Steve Humphries, *Making of Modern London: London at War* (London: Sidgwick & Jackson, 1985); J. Neville, *The Blitz: London Then and Now* (London: Hodder & Stoughton, 1990); and Philip Zeigler, *London at War* (London: Sinclair-Stevenson, 1995).

2 See C. Dunn, *The Emergency Medical Service* (London: HMSO, 1953).

3 House Committee, 20 September 1939; General Correspondence: Letter from Ablewhite, 10 September 1941.

4 Mack and Humphries, *op. cit.* 128–35.

5 Physician-Superintendent's Report, 9 August 1944.

6 *BMJ*, 2 (1947), 25.

7 *Beckenham & Penge Advertiser*, 3 July 1947, 1.

8 *Ibid.* 3 July 1947, 1; General Correspondence: Letter from Cooper to Hewitt, 16 June 1947.

9 For the development of the National Health Service see: Brian Abel Smith, *The Hospitals 1800–1948* (London: Heinemann, 1964); H. Eckstein, *The English Health Service: Its Origins, Structure and Achievements* (Cambridge, Mass.: Harvard University Press, 1958); D. Fox, *Health, Politics and Health Politics* (Princeton: Princeton University Press, 1986); F. Honigsbaum, *Health, Happiness and Security: The Creation of the National Health Service* (London: Routledge, 1989); J. E. Pater, *Making of the National Health Service* (London: King's Fund, 1981); Charles Webster, *Problems of Health Care: The National Health Service Before 1957* (London: HMSO, 1988). Charles Webster, 'Conflict and Consensus: Explaining the British Health Service', *Twentieth Century British History*, i (1990), 115–51 provides a historiographical discussion.

10 *Beckenham & Penge Advertiser*, 3 July 1947, 1

11 See José Harris, 'Some Aspects of Social Policy in Britain during the Second World War', in W. J. Mommsen (ed.), *Emergence of the Welfare State in Britain and Germany* (London: Croom Helm, 1981), 247–62.

12 Cited in J. Allsop, 'Health: From Seamless Service to Patchwork Quilt', in David Gladstone (ed.), *British Social Welfare: Past, Present and Future* (London: UCL Press, 1995), 98.

13 *Hansard*, H. of C., vol. 388, col. 1401, 15 April 1943.

14 *Lancet*, 1 (1945), 763–5.

15 Kathleen Jones, *A History of the Mental Health Service* (London: Routledge, 1972), 275–6.

16 Charles Webster (ed.), *Aneurin Bevan on the National Health Service* (Oxford: Wellcome Unit for the History of Medicine, 1991), 63.

17 See Daniel Fox, 'The National Health Service and the Second World War: The Elaboration of Consensus', in H. L. Smith (ed.), *War and Social Change: British Society in the Second World War* (Manchester: Manchester University Press, 1986), 32–57; Rodney Lowe, 'The Second World War Consensus and the Foundations of the Welfare State', *Twentieth Century British History*, i (1990), 152–82, or D. Kavanagh and P. Morris, *Consensus Politics from Atlee to Thatcher* (London: Basil Blackwell, 1989).

18 Cited in Frank Prochaska, *Philanthropy and the Hospitals of London: The King's Fund, 1897–1990* (Oxford: Clarendon Press, 1992), 159, 234.

19 House Committee, 27 February 1946.

20 *Ibid.* 10 April 1946.

21 *Nursing Mirror*, 28 June 1947, 224; *Hospital & Social Service Journal*, 23 July 1948, 54.

22 Jones, *op. cit.* 277.

23 Kathleen Jones, *Asylums and After* (London: Athlone Press, 1993), 144, 147–8.

24 *Public Assistance Journal*, 21 May 1948, 325.

25 Webster, 'Conflict and Consensus', 147.

26 Geoffrey Rivett, *Development of the London Hospital System* (London: OUP, 1986), 266.

27 Cited in Abel Smith, *op. cit.* 279.

28 *Public Assistance Journal*, 20 February 1948, 123.

29 Cited in Rivett, *op. cit.* 266, 267.

30 *Lancet*, 1 (1946), 839.

31 *Lancet*, 2 (1910), 831.

32 John Crammer, 'Training and Education in British Psychiatry', in Hugh Freeman and German Berrios (eds), *150 Years of British Psychiatry: The Aftermath* (London: Athlone Press, 1996), 220; Peter Nolan, 'Mental Health Nursing in Great Britain', in *ibid.* 178.

33 For the origins and foundation of the Maudsley, see Patricia Allderidge, 'The Foundation of the Maudsley Hospital', in German Berrios and Hugh Freeman (eds), *150 Years of British Psychiatry* (London: Gaskell, 1991), 79–88.

34 General Correspondence: Letter from Porter-Phillips to Faudel-Phillips, 26 October 1920.

35 Medical Committee, 6 April 1920.

36 Court of Governors, 25 April 1921.

37 Medical Committee, 22 October 1920.

38 *Ibid.* 6 July 1921.

39 'A Course of Lectures and Practical Instruction for the Diploma in Psychological Medicine granted by various Universities'.

40 *BMJ*, 2 (1922), 444.

41 General Committee, 13 March 1923.

42 1923 Report of Inspectors of Research, Teaching and Equipment.

43 Medical Committee, 2 January 1924.

44 Court of Governors, 28 April 1924.

45 General Committee, 12 December 1927.

46 Court of Governors, 23 February 1925.

47 *Bethlem & Maudsley Gazette*, Spring 1979, 8.

48 Medical Committee, 7 October 1925.

49 Court of Governors, 27 April 1925.

50 See Chapter 29, pp. 555–8.

51 Outpatient Department Papers: Letter from Danvers to Porter-Phillips, 22 July 1927.

52 *Ibid.* Letter from Faudel-Phillips to Worsfold, 30 July 1927.

53 Medical Subcommittee, 6 April 1927.

54 Outpatient Department Papers: Letter from Worsfold to Faudel-Phillips, 26 August 1927.

55 Medical Subcommittee, 29 September 1927.

56 *Ibid.* 4 April 1928.

57 Aubrey Lewis Papers, Box 5: Future of the Maudsley, Draft Memorandum, 6 August 1942.

58 Medical Committee, 16 September 1931.

59 *Ibid.* 7 January 1931.

60 *Ibid.* 30 March 1932.

61 *1935 Bethlem Annual Report*, 14.

62 Medical Committee, 30 November 1932.

63 *Ibid.* 25 March 1936.

64 *1940 Bethlem Annual Report*, 17.

65 Court of Governors, 9 April 1941.

66 General Correspondence: Memorandum, 18 April 1946.

67 See Negley Harte, *The University of London, 1836–1986* (London: Athlone Press, 1986), 242–3; Rivett, *op. cit.* 257–60, 282–4.

68 House Committee, 7 November 1945.

69 Lewis was born in 1900 in South Australia, qualifying in medicine in 1923 from the University of Adelaide. He served as a registrar at the University until 1926 when he was awarded a Rockefeller Fellowship to study psychiatry. With Rockefeller funding he visited Boston and the Phipps Clinic at Johns Hopkins, extending the Fellowship to carry on work at the National Hospital, Queen Square and in Berlin and Heidelberg in 1927. In 1928 Lewis joined the Maudsley, initially on a research grant, until he was made a member of staff, becoming clinical director in 1936. Since December 1932 he had been a recognized teacher of the University of London, though had taught since 1929. Between 1935 and 1945 he was a consultant psychiatrist at the British Postgraduate Medical School and taught psychiatric social workers at LSE from 1931. Lewis remained active during the war, developing his ideas on social psychiatry and the role of the mental health services. He was a civilian consultant in psychiatry to the RAF, a member of the Army Psychiatric Advisory Committee, on the Brain Injuries Committee of the MRC, the Scientific Advisory Committee of the Wartime Social Survey, and the Selection Committee for Nuffield Medical Fellowships: Aubrey Lewis Papers, Box 10: Copy of Application to the University of London Chair of Psychiatry, *c.* October 1945; Letter from Michael Shepherd, 3 April 1978; *The Times*, 22 January 1975, 14.

70 Aubrey Lewis Papers, Box 5: Future of the Maudsley.

71 *Ibid.* Box 12: Report of the Work of the Sub-Dean's Office, 1947.

72 *1949–50 Institute of Psychiatry Annual Report*, 2.

73 LCC Archive, Greater London Record Office (hereafter LCC Archive), LCC Mental Hospital Committee, LCC/MIN/606: 16 March 1948.

74 Aubrey Lewis Papers, Box 5: Letter from Daley, 25 July 1946.

75 General Committee, 13 May 1947.

76 Court of Governors, 28 January and 9 April 1941.

77 *Ibid.* 26 March 1947.

78 *Ibid.* 13 May 1947.

79 Nearly two hundred 'disclaimed hospitals' did elect to remain outside the NHS: See *The Times*, 1 April 1948, 2.

80 Medical Committee, 3 April 1929.

81 Allderidge, *op. cit.* 84.

82 General Committee, 13 May 1947.

83 Aubrey Lewis Papers, Box 5: Future of the Maudsley.

84 *1948 Board of Control Annual Report*, 3.

85 *British Journal of Psychiatry*, April 1975, 5–6.

86 LCC Archive, Maudsley Subcommittee Papers, LCC/MIN/1238.

87 Aubrey Lewis Papers, Box 10: Letter from Lewis to the director of the British Postgraduate Medical Federation, 11 November 1946.

88 *1947 Board of Control Annual Report*.

89 Foulkes Papers, Contemporary Medical Archives Centre (hereafter Foulkes Papers),

PP/SHF/B.11: Letter from Taylor to Foulkes, 24 October 1949; Aubrey Lewis Papers, Box 10: Letter from Michael Shepherd, 3 April 1978.

90 Ann Dally, *A Doctor's Story* (London: Macmillan, 1990), 43.

91 Foulkes Papers, PP/SHF/B.11: Letter from Taylor, 24 October 1949; Aubrey Lewis Papers, Box 10: Letter from Michael Shepherd, 3 April 1978.

92 *Lancet*, 2 (1947), 24.

93 Statement of Accounts and Balance Sheet, 1947.

94 William Sargant, *The Unquiet Mind* (London: Heinemann, 1967), 141.

95 Denis Hill, 'Origins of the Joint Hospital' (Unpublished Paper, 1979), 1.

96 Foulkes Papers, PP/SHF/B.11: Letter from Taylor, 24 October 1949; Aubrey Lewis Papers, Box 10: Letter from Michael Shepherd, 3 April 1978.

97 General Committee, 13 May 1947.

98 Aubrey Lewis Papers, Box 12: Letter from Lewis to Coke, 22 May 1947; *Bethlem & Maudsley Gazette*, March 1958, 4.

99 Aubrey Lewis Papers, Box 12: Letter from Lewis to Coke, 19 May 1947; LCC Archive, Mental Hospitals Committee, LCC/MIN/606: 17 June 1947.

100 Aubrey Lewis Papers, Box 12: Letter from Lewis to Coke, 19 May 1947; LCC Archive, Mental Hospitals Committee, LCC/MIN/606: 17 June 1947.

101 LCC Archive, Maudsley Subcommittee, LCC/MIN/1236.

102 Hill, *op. cit.*

103 Frank Prochaska, *Royal Bounty: The Making of a Welfare Monarchy* (New Haven, Conn. and London: Yale University Press, 1995), 234.

104 Anniversary Papers: Letter from Hewitt to the Lord Mayor, 24 June 1947.

105 *Nursing Mirror*, 5 July 1947, 242.

106 *Hospital*, 43 (1947), 528.

107 *Bethlem & Maudsley Gazette*, September 1962, 290.

108 Aubrey Lewis Papers, Box 12: Letter from Coke to Lewis, 23 June 1947.

109 Joint Transitional Committee, 26 February 1948.

110 Court of Governors, 24 June 1948.

111 Joint Committee, 11 July 1947.

112 See Prochaska, *Royal Bounty*, 236–7, for a discussion of the initial problems of royal patronage under the NHS.

113 Hill, *op. cit.* 3.

114 General Committee, 10 June 1947.

115 Aubrey Lewis Papers, Box 5: Letter from Ministry of Health to Coke, 19 April 1948.

116 Joint Transitional Committee, 22 April 1948.

117 *Ibid.* 24 May 1948.

118 Joint Committee, 14 August 1947; cited in Abel Smith, *op. cit.* 494.

119 Court of Governors, 28 February 1948.

120 Physician-Superintendent Weekly Reports, 14 January 1948.

121 House Committee, 12 August 1947.

122 *Ibid.* 5 November 1947.

123 General Committee, 9 December 1947.

124 *Ibid.* 13 April 1948.

125 House Committee, 30 June 1948.

126 Aubrey Lewis Papers, Box 5.

127 *Bethlem & Maudsley Gazette*, May 1953, 15.

128 Board of Governors, 21 May 1951.

129 Finance & General Purposes Committee, 21 May 1951.

130 Blacker Papers: Letter from Nevin to Blacker, 7 July 1948.

131 Joint Committee, 4 December 1947.

132 See Chapter 33, pp. 664–71.

133 Aubrey Lewis Papers: Circular Letter, 21 June 1948.

134 Greg Wilkinson (ed.), *Talking About Psychiatry* (London: Gaskell, 1993), 169.

135 Board of Governors, 26 July 1948.

136 1950 Estimate of Expenditure and Income.
137 Board of Governors, 11 July and 13 March 1949.
138 *1949 Board of Control Annual Report.*
139 Wilkinson, *op. cit.* 166.
140 Board of Governors, 1 November 1948 and 6 December 1948.
141 *British Journal of Psychiatry*, April 1975, 5–6.
142 Aubrey Lewis Papers, Box 5: Confidential Memorandum, *c.* 1949.
143 Sargant Papers, Contemporary Medical Archives Centre, PP/WWS/B.1/1: Letter from Hewitt, 16 March 1949.
144 *Ibid.*: Letter from Sargant to Hewitt, February 1949.
145 *Ibid.*: Letter from Sargant to Harris, 12 January 1949.
146 See Bed Allocation Working Party, 1971–91.
147 *Nursing Mirror*, 7 November 1958, 425.
148 Sargant, *The Unquiet Mind*, 141.

MANAGING MILLIONS
Administration and finance, 1901–82

——— •◆• ———

The creation of the National Health Service (NHS) and the merger with the Maudsley marked a turning point in Bethlem's history. However, continuities remained. Bethlem kept its endowments and management ethos, while the merger mirrored the previous connection with Bridewell (see Chapter 5). Where much has been written, not least by contemporaries, about how Bethlem was supposedly administered before 1815, no attention has been paid to the twentieth century. New research on the economic history of healthcare has started to address how institutional healthcare was managed and financed, but gaps remain. Apart from several institutional histories, twentieth-century mental hospitals have been neglected in favour of accounts of legislative change or therapeutic advance.[1] Research has ignored their administration and finance. In terms of Bethlem's management, the period between 1900 and the formation of the Special Health Authority (SHA) in 1982 was one of continuity and change, of internal development and external pressure, of prosperity and financial anxiety.

A VOLUNTARY ETHOS

Between 1900 and 1948 Bethlem was run along similar lines to other voluntary organizations. Administration was divided into three levels: the Governors, the Physician-Superintendent, and those in charge of the day-to-day routine. In the latter, the Steward managed the domestic side, a clerk of the works oversaw maintenance, a head gardener supervised the grounds, the Matron organized the nurses, and a clerk dealt with the paperwork and endowments. They were the most junior level of the Hospital's management, but excluded from the minutes, their authority is hard to assess. The role of the Physician-Superintendent is easier to determine. Andrew Scull asserts that the medical profession gained control of the asylum from the early nineteenth century. Medical Superintendents, as local government employees, were given considerable authority over what was seen as the mundane daily management, provided they presented annual reports and kept expenditure within reasonable bounds.[2] In no other field of institutional healthcare was the profession given such managerial control. However, a price was paid. Medical Superintendents had to become administrative Jacks-of-all-trades, reducing their involvement in the patients' management. The desired role of the Medical Superintendent came under increased debate after 1900, not least by the Board of Control, but it remained 'doubtful whether in any branch of the profession medical men are required to undertake duties so entirely alien to their proper calling'.[3]

Apart from the name, at Bethlem the Physician-Superintendent's post was no different from those in other mental hospitals. Each Physician-Superintendent's time was taken up by private practice, teaching, and committee meetings. None had any training in administration. Where doctors in general hospitals could consult manuals such as Stone's influential *Hospital Organisation and Management*, Medical Superintendents had little to guide them except their management committees and, when problems occurred, the Board of Control.[4] The post's administrative duties were extensive. At Bethlem, the Physician-Superintendent was expected to 'have authority over every official and servant . . . and shall be responsible for the general condition of the Hospital and the well-being of the Patients'. In addition 'he shall possess authority as to the classification, employment, amusement, instruction and general treatment of the patients'. Every part of the Hospital had to be visited at least once during the day and at 'uncertain hours' at night, more to keep an eye on the staff than on the patients. Regular reports were expected as was attendance at every weekly meeting of the House Committee and Medical Committee.[5] The Physician-Superintendent's impact on management was therefore extensive and his recommendations were invariably accepted, although often only after considerable discussion. Theophilus Hyslop and William Henry Stoddart were concerned to improve the Hospital's physical environment, but it was John Porter-Phillips who dominated the medical administration in the interwar period. Dedicated to the Hospital, he delayed his retirement and remained at Bethlem from 1914 to 1944. Active in the administration and taking a leading role in the planning of the Monks Orchard Hospital, he cautiously pressed for the adoption of new medical practices. Not all took kindly to his approach. In 1917 Wyatt Smith, temporary Assistant Physician, took it upon himself to investigate the food after complaints had been received about its repetitiveness and temperature. Wyatt Smith's investigation was symptomatic of his attitude to Bethlem's management. 'An undercurrent of disloyalty' was attributed to him and this was seen to have taken the 'form of verbal disparagement of and innuendo against the administrative actions' of Porter-Phillips. It was decided that Wyatt Smith should resign and Porter-Phillips was supported, but the Physician-Superintendents were rarely given a free hand.[6] Their authority was constrained by the Governors.

Control of the Hospital continued to rest with the Governors of Bridewell and Bethlem. However, although the two institutions were administered by the same body, the situation had been reversed. The President, Treasurer, surveyor, solicitor, and secretary continued to hold joint appointments, and the Governors carried on meeting in New Bridge Street, Blackfriars, but now it was Bethlem that commanded most of their attention. A charitable mental hospital with extensive estates needed a greater level of administrative involvement than either the King Edward's School or Bridewell, which existed mainly as a collection of offices in New Bridge Street and endowed estates. It is therefore possible to speak of Bethlem's administrative structure in the twentieth century.

County and borough mental hospitals were managed by individual committees of visitors who, after 1890, were drawn from county councillors responsible to local government and the ratepayers. In London, after the formation of the London County Council (LCC) in 1888, the administration was transferred to the Mental Hospitals Committee with each asylum managed by a subcommittee. The situation was different in the registered hospitals. Founded through voluntary effort they were run as separate charities but were bound by statutory provisions. All psychiatric institutions were under the nominal authority of the Board of Control. As the first charitable institution in England for the mentally ill, Bethlem provided a further variant, which had more in common with the capital's voluntary hospitals. With no subscribers and few benefactors no attempt had been made to mimic the nineteenth-century 'subscriber democracy' adopted at other charitable institutions.[7] Instead, Bridewell and Bethlem, along with Guy's and St Bartholomew's, were managed by self-perpetuating oligarchies. New Governors were elected by the existing Governors. To be nominated a candidate had to contribute at least fifty guineas, an amount similar to that requested by other London hospitals. This was not the only way to be elected; the President and Treasurer were able to appoint six Governors annually between them.[8] Governors continued to be drawn largely from the City of London's administration through the Court of Alderman and Common Council and remained predominately male until after 1948 when women started to play an active role. Bethlem's former senior medical officers were encouraged to continue their links with the Hospital and were made Governors. Many remained active in the management, a fact that assisted the Physician-Superintendents when pressing for change.

The notion that financial commitment was naturally linked to managerial responsibility was a powerful concept in voluntary institutions. The admission of paying patients shifted Bethlem away from its charitable origins, but the Governors continued to base their authority on an 'other-regarding' voluntary ethic.[9] Hospitals had been the 'flagships' of the Victorian benevolent system and until 1948 Bethlem continued to internalize their administrative ethos. The Governors followed voluntarism's sense of personal service, altruism, paternalism, and charity without rationalizing their actions or explaining their motives.[10] With Bethlem moved out of City politics and a governorship not carrying the former social cachet or financial advantage, the Hospital's Governors were motivated largely by a sense of duty or charity. No attempt was made to see patients through a 'deserving' ideology, partly because the charitable nexus had been broken by the admission of paying patients. Patients were sometimes referred to as 'guests' and the Governors felt responsible for their care, comfort and cure, if not their salvation and morality. Where Governors were expected to make donations they were first required to contribute their time, a situation more in line with the increased emphasis placed on personal and community services in twentieth-century philanthropy.[11] Not all took up their charge with equal enthusiasm. Committee meetings were often poorly attended unless an important decision was being made regarding the Hospital's future.[12] In the 1930s on average only three to four Governors out of nine attended the bi-weekly House Committee and during the two world wars attendance fell. Management therefore continued to be via a small clique, a situation Hayes Newington, psychiatrist and owner of Ticehurst, had praised in his late nineteenth-century vision of a utopian asylum and one common to voluntary organizations.[13] For A. J. P. Taylor such 'active people of England ... provided the ground swell of history', but this did not apply to those who managed Bethlem.[14] Where voluntarism was increasingly seen by some as an 'odious expression of social oligarchy', lacking the resources or coordination to deal with social problems, such concerns did not interest Bethlem's Governors.[15] They did not bring the debates about the role of the 'active citizen' or the 'active state' into the Hospital and appeared uninterested in national and metropolitan discussions over the structure of healthcare.[16] No attempt was made to cooperate with county and borough mental hospitals, but financial and administrative support was given to mental healthcare charities.[17] Bethlem was not part of Beveridge's 'moving frontier' of welfare.[18]

All voluntary hospitals organized their Governors into a court that sat periodically to discuss the institution's business. Bridewell and Bethlem were no exception. In theory the Court of Governors ran the hospital, elected the officers, and made the decisions. In practice, with every Governor entitled to attend and the committee meeting four times a year, managerial responsibility had been transferred to the smaller General Committee. From its creation in 1737 this had gradually taken over the management. With even the General Committee being too large and meeting too infrequently for effective administration, further streamlining had occurred to create a well-attended Estates Committee, which discussed every aspect of the Hospitals' property, and subcommittees to manage Bethlem and King Edward's School.[19] However, the Bethlem Subcommittee, renamed the House Committee in 1929, was the real managerial force ensuring that Bethlem's influence extended throughout the administration. Only over endowments did it not exercise direct control. What the Bethlem Subcommittee decided, the General Committee discussed and approved, and the Court of Governors eventually sanctioned.

Many hospital histories have justly been criticized as histories of prominent men, but at Bethlem between 1900 and 1948 it was the Hospital's five treasurers and four presidents who dominated. This was true of earlier periods of the Hospital's development. The President was seen as the 'chief ruler' responsible for the entire administration, with the Treasurer 'considered next in rank'. At Bridewell and Bethlem the President was more than a figurehead or the honorary post it had been in the past. In the twentieth century each post-holder took an active interest, but like other metropolitan hospitals, it was the Treasurer who ran the institution. The Treasurer had always had a considerable influence on Bethlem. Represented on every committee, his opinions were respected by the Governors and, given the small number involved in decision-making, he was the *de facto* executive authority.

For Bethlem's administration, the nineteenth century ended with James Alfred Copeland's retirement in 1920. He had been Treasurer, apart from a short interval between 1896 and 1900 when he resigned on health grounds, since 1865 ensuring considerable administrative continuity.[20] For the *City Press* and *Morning Post*, Copeland's departure marked the end of an era. Having served Bethlem for so long, he died a year after retiring.[21] Copeland had a reforming role in the nineteenth century, and with his retirement the opportunity was taken to revise the Treasurer's duties. Consequently official recognition was given to the fact that the Treasurer was the executive officer, and Copeland's successor, Lionel Faudel-Phillips (see Plate 31.1),

Plate 31.1 Sir Lionel Faudel-Phillips, Treasurer to Bethlem (1920–40), oil on canvas by Oswald Birley, 1931. Reproduced by permission of the Bethlem Royal Hospital Archives and Museum, with acknowledgements to the Bethlem and Maudsley NHS Trust.

benefited from the increased authority. He used this to his full advantage in guiding Bethlem until his death in 1941. In Copeland, the Hospital had found a conscientious, progressive and scientific-minded officer; under Faudel-Phillips the administration became more autocratic. Both, however, were committed to Bethlem and sought to serve it in every way possible, at times to the neglect of their respective family businesses. From an important City Jewish merchant family, Faudel-Phillips did not share his family's enthusiasm for the Jewish community, but did follow his father in playing an active part in local politics in the family home of Hertford.[22] Most of his energy went into Bethlem. Faudel-Phillips would frequently visit the wards, arriving through the kitchens where his pet aversion was dripping taps.[23] Politically Conservative by nature, Faudel-Phillips was inclined to be authoritarian. Not always easy to approach, it took over fifteen years before he and Porter-Phillips were on first-name terms. More financially minded than previous Treasurers, he was willing to make unpopular decisions to save money. Faudel-Phillips's main achievement was in persuading the Governors to rebuild Bethlem.[24] 'The conception of the new hospital', according to the Hospital's magazine, 'originated entirely in the mind of our Treasurer, and it was through his foresight and desire for progress that the new hospital at Monks Orchard was conceived and completed'.[25] What the writer neglected to mention was that Faudel-Phillips had also been prepared to force the resignation of any member of staff who criticized the new building. When Faudel-Phillips died in 1941, Monks Orchard was seen as a fitting memorial to all the hard work he had invested.

Family connections remained strong. As in the eighteenth century, particular families dominated. This was clearly seen in the selection of Treasurers. Copeland had been appointed by his father, Alderman William Taylor Copeland, Governor since 1829 and President between 1861 and 1868.[26] Rumours reported that William Copeland's last words to his son had been 'Alfred . . . don't forget the hospitals.' Copeland was eager to take on the mantle.[27] Similarly, Faudel-Phillips's family had 'worked nobly and unselfishly for three generations' for Bethlem, and his father, Sir George Faudel-Phillips, had been President from 1896 to 1912.[28] This was a traditional feature of hospital administration, where wealthy families and prominent City business interests dominated.[29]

By the start of the twentieth century, Bethlem's traditional links with the City of London had weakened. Only over the Hospital's move was the City's cooperation necessary to transfer the lease. As noted, Governors continued to be drawn from the Court of Aldermen and Common Council, but Bethlem had withdrawn from City politics. In the City's fight against the LCC's political control of London, politics had moved on and the power of the Crown had been redirected.[30] Charities no longer provided an important political arena. The City could exert its influence through other channels and was no longer so interested in using charities to advance its interests or dispense its patronage. Bethlem retained its Conservative bias, but by the late nineteenth century it existed as an independent charity. Informal links with the City of London, however, were maintained. Copeland was a senior liveryman of the Goldsmiths' Company and his father had been Lord Mayor. Lionel Faudel-Phillips was one of his Majesty's Lieutenants of the City of London, and like his grandfather and father, a Master of the Spectacle Makers.[31] These connections were used to attract donations from the City companies. Links with the City were more actively preserved through Bethlem's President, who on appointment had to be Lord Mayor, the City's highest office. The connection was mainly one-sided. Bethlem's presidents had distinguished careers in the City's administration before taking up their post at the

Hospital, where they generally remained until poor health or old age made them retire. In Sir George Faudel-Phillips, Bethlem found an active and civic-minded President; one who was 'clever and convincing as a speaker in serious mood, but undoubtedly, shone . . . when indulging in banter and genial cynicism'.[32] Sir George's role in the nineteenth century has been discussed earlier, but in the twentieth century he presided over a period of modernization. He was instrumental in pressing for new heating, lighting and drainage and encouraged a general improvement in the wards. Bethlem was the last civic duty from which he retired. Sir Charles Wakefield, his successor, believed that 'to his keen perception and penetration the hospitals [Bridewell and Bethlem] owe many of the steps which have brought them to their present position'.[33]

Wakefield, President between 1916 and 1941, was equally distinguished. Although deeply committed to the City, he was highly active in Bethlem's management.[34] Rigorously prompt and thorough, Wakefield was both stern and compassionate and as a man of business he worked well with Faudel-Phillips. Described by the *City Press* as 'one of the greatest benefactors of the Royal Hospitals', when Bethlem launched its building appeal in 1928 Wakefield headed the list with a donation of £25,000.[35] He had earlier made a series of donations to ensure that Bethlem could 'procure one of the best and most modern [X-ray] installations in London'.[36] Both donations reflected his extensive philanthropy and passion for technology, given his ownership of Wakefield & Co. the producers of Castrol oil. In recognition of his benevolence, Wakefield was awarded a CBE and made Honorary Freeman of the City in 1935, an honour previously only bestowed on royalty. Unlike his quiet wife, he disliked idleness. When Lord Mayor between 1915 and 1916 he played an energetic part in London's recruitment campaign and prowled the roof of Mansion House during air-raids, mindful of his responsibilities as a trustee of St Paul's. Wakefield was a keen promoter of the Empire and Anglo-American relations, taking part in various international deputations including the 1923 Sulgrave Delegation to the United States.[37] He and his wife were 'both believers in fresh air and simple living'. This perhaps explains his unqualified support for Bethlem's move to Monks Orchard and his interest in the sports club, to which he donated a pavilion in honour of George VI's coronation.[38]

Wakefield died in 1940 and Lionel Faudel-Phillips followed early in 1941. Little was said in the press about Faudel-Phillips, but Wakefield's death was seen as the 'passing of a man who in public and private life had dignified the title of citizenship'.[39] In both obituaries only fleeting reference was made to their work at Bethlem. However, their deaths marked an important change in the Hospital. Given the wartime circumstances it was decided to split the Treasurer's post between Edmund Stone, a dedicated Governor since 1902, and John Worsfold, the recently retired secretary, until a formal appointment could be made.[40] The decision was seen as a wartime expedient, but was a sensible move given their intimate knowledge of Bethlem's management. A similar division occurred in the Hospital's presidency. Immediately after Wakefield's death the Lord Mayor was approached, but not to fill the post of President. Instead this was offered to Queen Mary who accepted having opened the new Hospital in 1930. Royal support was felt to be beneficial to Bethlem given Queen Mary's sympathy for the Hospital and high profile.[41] The Governors made full use of the opportunity and each successive President has been a member of the royal family. Aware that a royal President could not take an active role in management, the Lord Mayor, Sir George Wilkinson, was made Vice-President.[42] With a return to peace, Stone and Worsfold resigned in November 1945 and Gerald Coke, a cousin of Faudel-Phillips, became Treasurer.[43] Coke had been a Governor since the 1930s and was a staunch defender of Bethlem's interests, but he was also a realist. Coke's appointment marked a new spirit in the Hospital, allowing Bethlem to adapt to the changes discussed in Chapter 29.

It is not easy to pass a verdict on Bethlem's management between 1900 and 1948. The administrative work of the Hospital expanded, mainly in response to legislative changes, but even with new typewriters and telephones there was no corresponding professionalization. All the administrative details, rent collection, and minute taking was undertaken by the secretary, who had to be present at every meeting. Not entitled to a voice in the management it is uncertain how much authority he exerted. Certainly Worsfold, secretary from 1911 to 1939, was respected. On his retirement he was made a Governor and then joint Treasurer in 1941. Where it is unlikely that the secretary could initiate policy, he could influence it. He was not the only administrative officer. By the 1930s Bethlem employed a secretary, steward, clerk of the works, head gardener, auditor, surveyor, and a solicitor.[44] Each had to present regular reports, but deprived of a management role it was the Governors, or more precisely the Treasurer, who validated their decisions and decided policy.

A protective voluntary ethos underpinned the entire management. Bethlem remained an insular institution before 1948. Administration was dominated by a small group headed by active Presidents and Treasurers. Management was cautious rather than dynamic, but it was responsive. When problems surfaced or the Board of Control pointed to deficiencies the Governors willingly responded, a relationship clearly seen in the planning of the new Hospital. Bethlem was better at reacting to the Board of Control's suggestion than many other psychiatric institutions. In a hospital that prided itself on being at the forefront of psychiatry any other course of action was impossible. Without real powers of enforcement and facing resistance from local authorities, the Board of Control stimulated change through advice, encouragement and criticism.[45] This was clearly seen in the relentless encouragement it gave to outpatient clinics from the 1920s onwards. At Bethlem pressure from the Board was aided by a concern for patient comfort. This lay behind many of the Governors' decisions. The Governors did listen to the advice of their medical staff, but they always made it clear that they were the ones who really ran Bethlem.

PROPERTY AND PROSPERITY: 1901–48

In the period before 1948 Bethlem was spared the financial problems that haunted London's voluntary hospitals. Where hospitals appeared to stumble from one financial crisis to the next, forcing state intervention in 1921, Bethlem's Governors could be confident about their financial position.[46] The Hospital did experience some of the same financial pressures facing other hospitals and between 1900 and 1948 expenditure increased as Bethlem developed and admissions rose (see Figure 31.1).

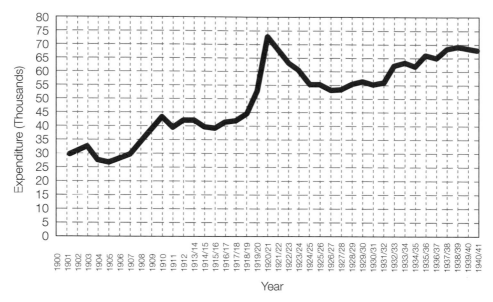

Figure 31.1 Expenditure, 1901–41

Table 31.1 Expenditure (per cent), 1910–44

		1910	1914/15	1920/1	1925/6	1930/1	1935/6	1940/1	1943/4
Maintenance	Provisions	22.4	19.5	19.5	20.6	7.0	13.1	15.6	11.3
	Medical	2.8	1.4	1.7	2.3	1.0	1.8	1.5	1.4
	Domestic	16.9	12.6	16.0	14.4	14.0	10.7	11.7	12.3
	Building	15.9	12.2	21.0	8.0	3.8	8.5	5.6	5.7
	Salaries	28.3	34.0	34.6	48.4	48.5	59.3	59.2	63.4
	Other	4.2	2.8	2.4	3.2	2.9	2.8	2.1	1.8
Administration		4.1	3.1	1.2	1.5	1.6	1.6	1.1	1.0
Extraordinary		5.4	14.4	3.6	1.6	21.2	2.2	3.2	3.1

Source: Statement of Accounts
Note: 'Extraordinary' expenditure was a term hospitals used to cover items of non-recurring expenditure. This included money spent on new medical equipment or repairs. The idea was that this would be separated from normal expenditure to prevent the view that those managing the hospital were extravagant. At Bethlem the large amounts spent on furnishing the new Hospital in 1930/1 were included under this heading.

Table 31.1 outlines the principal items of expenditure. Although the Governors provided patients with every comfort they were not extravagant and avoided debt. With most of the administration on a voluntary basis and no need to advertise for funds, management costs remained low.[47] Equally, a small amount was spent on medicine and surgical equipment. Treatments were limited until the 1930s and while sedation, psychological testing, hydrotherapy and electrotherapy played an important role these therapies were inexpensive to provide once the equipment had been bought. Patient care, however, required a large and expensive nursing establishment. While the amount spent on nursing rose, institutional costs fell. At most hospitals this proved an important item of expenditure as patients had to be fed and the building heated, lit and repaired. At Southwark the Governors actively strove to modernize and repair a building that was increasingly proving old-fashioned. The move to Monks Orchard cut maintenance costs and removed the need to make substantial structural alterations. In addition Park Farm, once compensation claims had been settled with the previous tenant, provided an important source of food.[48] The Farm was run as a commercial venture and offered limited employment to a minority of patients. The dairy herd supplied Bethlem with milk, and chickens ensured a regular supply of eggs until 1942 when it became more economical to buy in eggs.[49] Most mental hospitals had their own farms and vegetable gardens on which patients worked, but with the farm run commercially, Bethlem could take full advantage of what was produced.

Income was more than able to keep pace with expenditure (see Figure 31.2). In only four years did expenditure exceed income, with the largest deficits occurring in connection to the decision to build a new hospital. Bethlem proved a flexible and profitable institution, but this did not prevent anxiety. The move forced several financial strategies to meet spiralling costs and recoup the investments sold.[50] In 1932 part of the Hospital's property in Piccadilly had to be mortgaged to cover the overdraft and the possibility of a £125,000 loan was discussed.[51] Careful financial management ensured that the endowed income was not dramatically diminished,

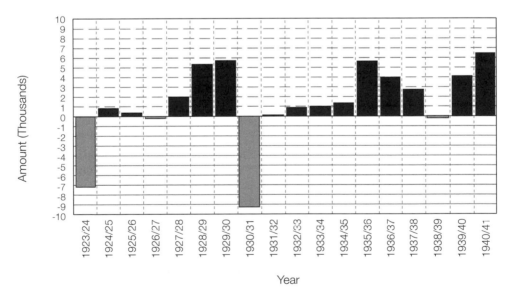

Figure 31.2 Excess of income over expenditure, 1923/4–1940/1 *Source:* Statement of Accounts

though a high level of debt remained. By the mid-1930s anxiety had lessened, but the Governors continued to make every effort to increase income and economies were regularly implemented. Not all were successful. In 1927 it was decided to burn Bothal Nuts in the furnaces instead of coke to save money. The scheme was quickly abandoned, for although Bothal Nuts were considerably cheaper they produced less heat.[52] After the move, the need for economy became more pressing. The Governors kept a careful account of every financial detail and prided themselves on their management. However, problems continued to occur. In 1928 discrepancies were found and Bertram & Mitcham, the Hospital's accountants, were blamed. After investigation it was revealed that Mitcham had recently spent over £1,200 on a house and a car. Faudel-Phillips was concerned that the auditors had not detected the 'falsification' sooner. Bertram was a friend of the Lord Mayor, who counselled against legal action. With Bethlem preparing to launch a building appeal Faudel-Phillips and Wakefield agreed with the Mayor to avoid any bad publicity.[53] This time Bethlem skirted public embarrassment and the Governors, already concerned about the lack of funds, became more conscientious in their control.

Bethlem's income came from three principal sources: estates, investments and paying patients, but other sources of funding existed as indicated in Table 31.2.

Table 31.2 Income (per cent), 1900–45

	1900–5	1906–10	1911–15	1916–20	1921–5	1926–30	1931–5	1936–40	1941–5
Balance	15.6	21.1	0.0	0.0	0.0	0.0	0.0	0.0	0.0
Rental	55.5	53.1	76.3	54.0	49.2	57.5	55.1	59.0	50.4
Dividends	10.6	2.3	3.4	15.1	26.3	19.1	8.1	3.2	4.6
Patients	12.5	11.9	17.5	12.9	22.8	21.5	34.4	35.4	42.7
Charity	0.7	0.6	1.4	1.1	1.7	1.1	0.5	0.5	0.6
Sales	2.2	8.4	1.3	16.9	0.0	0.8	1.9	1.9	0.0
Reclaimed tax	2.8	2.4	0.0	0.0	0.0	0.0	0.0	0.0	0.0
Other	0.1	0.2	0.1	0.0	0.0	0.0	0.0	0.0	1.7

Source: Statement of Accounts

However, where other sources of funding continued to be attracted, over time Bethlem's reliance on endowments and paying patients increased. Other London hospitals were in a position where financial circumstances forced them to develop new sources of funding. At Bethlem the reverse happened. There was no need to develop other resources because the Hospital was a small institution with substantial endowments, while payment from patients could be raised to meet financial needs.

Bethlem benefited in the twentieth century from the charity of the past. Seventeenth- and eighteenth-century benefactors through their gifts of land and money had made Bethlem into an endowed institution, but it was not the richest endowed hospital in London. By 1947 St Thomas's had endowments worth £1.3m and St Bartholomew's was even richer.[54] In comparison, Bethlem had £136,601 2s 10d in saving bonds, annuities and consolidated stock, a further £79,632 in mortgages and equipment, property at Monks Orchard worth £60,000, and extensive estates in Kent and London. Rental and building leases from these estates provided over 50 per cent of the income. Between 1900 and 1940 rental income rose from £23,552 13s to £40,278 3s 8d. It was unaffected by the economic slump from 1920 to 1921 and the 1930s depression, falling only during the Second World War when bombing damaged much of Bethlem's property in London.[55] Immediate 'first-aid' repairs were made to prevent further deterioration; full repairs were postponed until compensation was received under the 1941 War Damage Act. Not all settlements were made quickly.[56] It was the tenants' responsibility to inform the Governors of any damage and it was not uncommon for rent demands to be returned with a note explaining that the property had been bombed. All rent deemed irrecoverable was initially written off and after the war attempts were made to recover it.[57] In 1944 Malcolm Hewitt, the clerk, feared that Bethlem faced an 'unhopeful' financial position, estimating that estate income had fallen by £11,700. When the Hospital was bombed in 1944, the wartime loss of revenue was felt to be sufficient for the Governors seriously to consider closing Bethlem.[58] An emergency package was put together to prevent this from happening and rental income quickly began to recover after 1945.

Bethlem acted as landowner, estate developer, and landlord with the secretary responsible for collecting rents and the surveyor for managing estates. With Bethlem favouring non-residential property and farms, the Governors were spared the problems that Government rent controls brought in the interwar period.[59] Their prime concern was the income generated not the tenants, unlike other corporate landowners. Tenants were encouraged to make improvements, but though limited financial support was provided, no policy of modernization was adopted.[60] When leases were due to expire the property was inspected and if it was decided that too much needed to be spent on repairs it was sold. The Governors did monitor neighbouring developments to make sure they did not have a harmful effect. Whereas a skating rink and cinema were supported at Waltham Cross because they would raise the value of the Hospital's adjacent property, the Governors' attitude was less favourable towards the five houses built nearby because 'they might be detrimental to the estate'.[61] In 1937 they complained that their property in North London was being turned into flats and sublet, until it was discovered that the structural changes had improved properties and ensured that tenants remained longer.[62] Considerable attention, however, was paid to the Piccadilly estate, the most profitable land Bethlem held, where a more active management style existed.

Property outside London was gradually sold. Faith in agricultural land declined after the late nineteenth-century agricultural depression when England's gross annual land value fell by 23 per cent between 1879 and 1893.[63] By the 1940s Bethlem's only substantial agricultural estates were those tied up in the Kent farms, which were kept for the profitable mineral rights beneath them. The Lincolnshire Estate was sold in 1918 since the reinvestment would 'yield an income so greatly in excess of that now derived'.[64] Only the London estates were expanded. A 40 per cent fall in property values in the Edwardian period meant that real estate was cheap to buy.[65] Experience showed that given the capital's 'appetite for increase', incessant demand for property, and growing economy, property was a profitable investment.[66] Problems with finding suitable business premises to buy in the mid-1930s created some discussion over whether Bethlem should broaden its interests, but this was rejected.[67] Even those estates like Waltham Cross, originally on the outskirts of London, were sold to developers to take advantage of the capital's continued suburban sprawl and interwar housing boom.[68] The continued growth of Margate and Westgate as seaside resorts created new interests. John Glover-Kinde's song 'I do like to be beside the seaside' reflected the popularity of seaside resorts at the start of the twentieth century, encouraged by the growth of the railways.[69] Margate had won a reputation for vulgarity in the nineteenth century due to the number of working-class day trippers from London who went there by steampacket. Continued popularity ensured expansion. Unlike Waltham Cross, the demand for land in Margate, Westgate and later Ramsgate from Bethlem's Garlinge Estate required the Governors to become actively involved in planning.[70] Where painters found the tawdriness and holiday-camp atmosphere appealing, the Governors tried to protect the value of their property and ensure that suitable middle-class houses was built.[71] Like many twentieth-century aristocratic landlords, Bethlem wanted others to take the risks.[72] The Governors' powers were therefore limited in that they were dependent upon offers from potential builders. They had more influence over the local corporation. This was true of other landowners who were not easily thwarted by civic authorities trying to assume a larger role.[73] Margate Corporation had to apply to Bethlem whenever its developments cut across the Hospital's land. Development in neighbouring Westgate on the Westbrook Estate to raise money for the new Hospital, and then on Cliffs End Farm in the 1930s, produced more concern. Initially there was little demand and the Governors considered making advances to builders to encourage development.[74] When Cliffs End Farm was developed, a depressed economy, poor drainage, and the slowness of Ramsgate Corporation created further problems. On all their seaside estates, the Governors not only developed land for building leases by providing roads and sewers but also contributed funds to provide facilities like Margate's pavilion.[75] It made financial sense to spend money on services. Where unimproved land on the west edge of the Westbrook estate could be sold for £4,500, by spending £3,000 the Governors raised its estimated value to £10,500.[76] Bethlem's main interest was always with income.

Where property rose in value, investments had a mixed financial fortune. Linked to Britain's economic performance, investments fluctuated with the economy. Dividends rose to a high point in 1927 when £600,000 was invested, producing an income of £13,626 8s 5d.[77] The Governors were always concerned to find the best investment and bought and sold accordingly. Any money not used for maintenance or improvement was either placed in a sinking fund, deposited with the bankers, or used to buy additional investments or property. National economic problems in the 1930s saw the emphasis shift, and the amount raised from dividends fell to £3,222 7s 10d in 1945.[78] The 1929 Wall Street Crash did not have the same repercussions in Britain as it did in America or continental Europe, but a decline in international trade and a currency crisis depressed confidence and led the Governors to change their financial strategy.[79] The Governors took advantage of rising rents encouraged by the 1930s housing boom and the progressive abolition of rent controls and invested in freehold property. With such resources the Governors had no need to seek loans, organize special appeals, run up large debts, or delay development. All they had to do was sell investments to raise the necessary money. Few London hospitals were in such a fortunate position. However, under pressure from the Charity Commission this was not allowed to adversely affect revenue. When large portions of the endowments were sold a series of sinking funds were created and set annual payments made into them until the investment had been repaid.[80] Both internal and external forces were working to ensure that Bethlem's income did not decline.

Rents and dividends could not meet expenditure, especially as they proved relatively inelastic. The Governors therefore looked to their patients. Bethlem had always admitted paying-patients and with a financial crisis in voluntary hospitals more institutions came to rely on patient payments and contribution schemes.[81] The issue remained controversial, but in psychiatric institutions payment had been an acceptable principle since the growth of private madhouses in the eighteenth century.[82] The Charity Commission had formally agreed to the admission of paying patients to Bethlem in 1882. Where this was initially only to be to unoccupied beds, the number was extended to a maximum of eighty in 1921 provided they were admitted 'in a manner which shall not be inconsistent with the said general purpose of the hospital'.[83] The Commission did not consider patient charges a permanent feature, and the Governors had to reapply for permission every five years. In 1927 they suggested a permanent scheme under which half the patients could be admitted at five guineas.[84] The Charity Commission was cautious, but agreed, although formal approval was not granted until 1932.[85] While the Commission was prepared to accept the Governors' intentions, they were aware that this would be difficult to enforce and allowed them regularly to exceed the limit.[86] Problems were encountered in securing payment. After Captain Pike's refusal to pay the entire cost of his son's treatment in 1910, the Governors instructed their solicitor to insert a clause in the admission form whereby the liability 'to defray such reasonable expenses' was agreed to by the patient's friends or relatives.[87] The clause did nothing more than guarantee that Bethlem was involved in an increased number of legal actions to recover payment.[88] To prevent this problem in the short-lived outpatient department, an almoner from the Central Association for Mental Health was appointed in 1923 to investigate each patient to see if they were able to pay.[89] By the 1920s a greater acceptance of the principle of payment in medical care meant that the Governors had fewer difficulties in collecting fees, allowing them to become more lenient. Writing to a concerned member of the public in 1938, the Governors explained that

> patients' friends often make rather optimistic promises of contributions but the Committee is always willing to consider a re-adjustment when the friends begin to appreciate that mental illness is invariably a long one and makes greater financial calls than they had expected.[90]

The income derived from patients was an important and flexible source of finance. Between 1900 and 1945 patient payments rose by £17,478, representing 40 per cent of Bethlem's income by the end of the Second World War.[91] Most registered hospitals, with few other resources, were forced to raise fees to meet rising expenditure. Bethlem had more room for manoeuvre, but given the overriding interest to protect long-term income patient charges were used to raise the level of funding. This was seen in 1920 when the collapse of the post-war restocking boom prompted financial anxiety and saw the Governors pressing the Charity Commission for permission to admit more paying patients.[92] The same solution was adopted in 1944 when Bethlem was bombed. In an attempt to meet the cost of rebuilding, the Governors approached the relatives of all those patients paying two guineas per week and asked if they could pay more.[93] An application was also submitted to the Charity Commission to raise the maximum patient fee from five to seven guineas. The Commission agreed, but even when the repair work was completed it was decided not to return the payments to their previous level. Income rose as a result by 17.9 per cent.[94] Bethlem did not come to rely on payment from patients, but when problems were encountered it was to patients that the Governors turned to raise money.

In contrast with other charitable institutions, only a small portion of Bethlem's funds came from benevolent contributions. Where *Whitaker's Almanack* for 1934 could point to the continued flow of charity 'despite the shrinkage in values due to the general depression, and the very high taxation', Bethlem found no need to compete for charitable funds.[95] This was valuable as support for mental healthcare was not a popular object for philanthropy. The City livery companies continued to contribute, although at times the Governors had to write to remind them of Bethlem's good work.[96] The Goldsmiths' Company were consistent in their support, and while they donated 'some armour of Persian origin' in 1936 most of their contributions were designed to encourage scientific study.[97] Donations, however, came mainly from relatives and friends of patients and from patients themselves, grateful for the care Bethlem had provided. Eric Miller was particularly generous. He gave £1,000 in 1916 to fund the Miller Relief Fund to help discharged patients in recognition of care the Hospital had given to his father.[98] Others were more unusual in their benevolence: in 1908 one patient donated his false teeth; the friends of another in 1931 gave a bird bath.[99] The practice continued after the creation of the NHS, with the number of small contributions from patients and their relatives increasing. Avoiding publicity, Bethlem attracted few large donations or charitable bequests between 1900 and 1948. This reflected the structure of the metropolitan benevolent economy. Posthumous philanthropy had become unpopular and in the twentieth century an active form of giving was encouraged through personal participation, subscriptions and donations.[100] In comparison to the nineteenth century, the number of bequests fell. Between 1901 and 1955 Bethlem received twenty-nine separate legacies amounting to a total of £7,208 and shared eight bequests with Bridewell amounting to £205,568. No bequest was accepted if it came with the condition that a patient had to be treated. Apart from a few large legacies most gave small amounts – suggesting that many came from patients, their relatives or those connected to the Hospital like Wakefield, who left Bethlem £100,000 in 1941, the largest amount given in the twentieth century. Not all gave money: when the chaplain and historian Geoffrey O'Donoghue died, he left copies of his two books and their copyright.[101] The Governors, secure in the knowledge that they did not have to rely on charity, welcomed all these gifts and made no distinction between them.

Bethlem entered the NHS in 1948 a profitable institution, free from debt, and confident about its financial position. Other London hospitals found themselves in very different circumstances, reducing hostility to the NHS. The Hospital benefited from seven centuries of accumulated wealth, and property continued to be the most important source of funding. The move created problems. It pushed Bethlem further away from its charitable origins by increasing the reliance on paying-patients, but a shift had already occurred in the late nineteenth century. Financial decisions were not made rashly and often considerable deliberation was taken to decide the course of action. With a loose financial strategy the Governors worked consistently to raise the Hospital's income.

ADMINISTERING THE JOINT HOSPITAL: 1949–74

The NHS was the most popular service in the post-war welfare state. For many the two terms were synonymous. However, despite the NHS's public popularity doubts emerged in the 1950s about its practical ability to deliver healthcare. For the historian Rodney Lowe, the NHS represented an opportunity missed, not seized.[102] It did not 'dissipate old problems', merely placed them in a new context as old ideas and existing buildings survived.[103] Increasingly it became the centre of political, financial and administrative debates. Bethlem was at once part of these debates and on the margins. In 1948 more than half the hospital beds in England and Wales were in mental hospitals, but mental healthcare was assigned a low priority. In addition, Bethlem's new status as part of London's only postgraduate psychiatric teaching hospital gave it a privileged position and placed it among a group of hospitals that were treated separately from the rest of the service.[104] However, where Bethlem was inward-looking before 1948, after the NHS's appointed day it had to fit within a national structure and respond to external pressures.

Aneurin Bevan's National Health Service established a tripartite division. The country was divided into regions managed by Regional Hospital Boards (RHB) whose members were selected by the Minster of Health. These RHBs appointed management committees that ran individual hospitals. The Joint Hospital's teaching status ensured a different structure. Although part of the South East Metropolitan Regional Hospital Board (SEMRHB), the Joint Hospital was administered by a separate Board of Governors. It acted as the Hospital's RHB and management committee, dealing directly with the Ministry.[105] Like Bethlem's previous administration, the Board cherished its autonomy but could not avoid outside influence. The Ministry of Health selected its Governors, although it recognized Bethlem's long association with the City and continued to appoint aldermen. Neither could the Board sell any land nor spend more than £30,000 without the Ministry's approval.[106] Further influence was exerted by the University of London and SEMRHB, which had four representatives each. The Governors had to work with both bodies, and often closely with SEMRHB and its successor the South East Thames Regional Health Authority, in planning new units. New schemes were often hindered by problems with regional finance and approval. The relationship with Camberwell Health Authority over the planning of the district service was more frustrating.[107] Delays occurred and plans had to be scaled down in response to outside concerns. The Ministry of Health had a wider impact. Through a series of statutory instructions it helped shape the Joint Hospital where direct intervention in the management was seen as unnecessary. The Board of Control had encouraged therapeutic developments; the Ministry of

Health focused on financial concerns and the wider structure of the NHS. It remained 'confident that the [Joint Hospital's] Board will continue to give their unremitting attention to all measures designed to increase efficiency and secure economy'.[108] The Governors agreed, but friction over funding and staffing soon emerged with the Governors constantly pressing for more money and additional registrars. A confrontational stance was avoided because the Governors could use Bethlem's endowments to supplement Exchequer funds. Bethlem in merging with the Maudsley had sought independence, but where it was freed from the control of a RHB it still had to work within the NHS and answer to the Ministry of Health.

The administration of the new Board was based on the NHS (designation of teaching hospitals (No. 2)) Order, but it had parallels with Bethlem's pre-1948 management. With the Board of Governors meeting four times a year, management was delegated to a smaller Finance and General Purposes Committee, which met monthly. After twenty-eight years in the LCC, the Joint Hospital's first House Governor, Kenneth Johnson, was suspicious of management by committee. He believed in 'a committee of one, the one being myself', but the increased work needed to run two hospitals and meet the Ministry of Health's requirements ensured a large administrative structure.[109] To reduce the amount of work dealt with by the Committee a House Committee was established to manage the domestic administration while a Medical Committee, on which all the consultants were represented, supervised the medical administration. The Medical Committee also liaised with the Institute of Psychiatry and with Guy's over the management of the joint neurosurgical unit.[110] 'Mutual independence' was the aim and under Aubrey Lewis this was achieved by virtue of his role in founding the two institutions. This allowed him to dominate the medical administration and the style and management of the Institute. He encouraged a critical research atmosphere in both institutions. After his retirement, his management style was seen as unsuitable. Under Sir Denis Hill the Institute moved away from the Joint Hospital. It remained 'at arms length' in the 1970s due to problems over reciprocal payments and psychological services.[111] In the Joint Hospital, sub-committees were created *ad hoc*, increasing the size of the administration, slowing development, and making it more cumbersome. The situation was common to the NHS. The 1968 Farquharson–Lang Report felt that 'hospital authorities were concerning themselves over much with detail at the expense of broad policy. There was a proliferation of sub-committees, and meetings went on for hours discussing matters that ought to have been decided by officers'. It singled out house committees as particularly susceptible to discussing trivia.[112] The Joint Hospital was prone to the same problem. Hierarchies existed at all levels and the amount of bureaucracy and paperwork mounted, provoking frustration.

Management was supposed to be more democratic. In reality the situation was different. Represented on every committee, the chair of the Board of Governors exerted considerable influence much like Bethlem's President before 1948. Where the Board's chair remained an important position, it was under Mary Ormerod and her successor Lord Sandon that the post exerted its greatest influence. As a key figure in uniting the two hospitals, Ormerod was the obvious choice when Coke resigned in 1948. Elected to the LCC in 1946, having worked for the Ministry of Economic Welfare during the war, she had taken an immediate interest in mental healthcare, becoming the chair of the Mental Hospitals Committee and of the Maudsley Sub-committee.[113] Ormerod specialized in taking a direct approach, and with an 'inexhaustible reserve of energy' promoted patient care. Never stinting from a meeting or function, she was active outside the Joint Hospital as a member of the South West RHB and dedicated to her LCC constituency in Hackney.[114] On her retirement in 1965 Sandon was appointed. Eldest son of the Earl of Harroway, Sandon was an Etonian with a business background. Treasurer of the Institute of Psychiatry since 1954, he was keen to foster closer links between the two institutions and set out to promote a harmonious hospital. As managing director of Coutts' Bank since 1949, Sandon brought his financial experience to the Hospital and was more sympathetic to investments than property.[115] With his resignation in 1973 the chair of the Board of Governors seemed to take a less active role.

It was the House Governor, however, who effectively ran the Joint Hospital. Aubrey Lewis had insisted that the position of Physician-Superintendent be abolished in favour of a lay administrator to free the consultants from management. By removing the Physician-Superintendent a non-medical alternative was created. The 1954 Bradbeer Report on the NHS's internal administration saw the 'hospital administrator paramount in the lay administration of his own hospital'. In most hospitals the House Governor 'lost ground to functional specialists', but this was not true at Bethlem.[116] Lewis, in pressing for the post, did not anticipate that the House Governorship would become a position of considerable influence. Kenneth Johnson had been appointed by Bethlem's Governors before the merger and proved 'amusing, vigorous and intellectually active'.[117] As the first House Governor he had negotiated considerable influence. He could dismiss any member of staff and even over doctors he was answerable only to the chair of the Medical Committee. Johnson was inclined to be autocratic and promoted a very efficient hospital. He believed that plans should be opposed until those presenting the proposals convinced him that they were adamant, but he was not narrow-minded and was interested in the patients. Johnson did not always work well with the medical staff. Morale was low and junior doctors were antagonized by his attempt to implement a clocking-on system. Johnson retired in 1962 to be replaced by the more dynamic and Oxford-educated Leslie (or Nicki) Paine. He was appointed to improve cooperation between the two institutions and raise the Hospital's profile, given his literary background. Coming from the United Cambridge Hospitals, where he had been the deputy secretary, he had attended the only course run by the King's Fund Hospital Administrative Staff College. Under Paine a new attitude developed where administrators and clinicians were seen as equal. Morale improved. Where he was unable to promote the tripartite organization he wanted, he did bring Bethlem and the Maudsley closer together. The medical staff favoured Paine, although the nurses were not so satisfied with their level of influence. Eloquent and blessed with considerable skills as an administrator, he was keen to foster others' ideas and gave the impression that staff needs were as important as patient needs.[118]

By the 1960s the Joint Hospital was seen as a 'multifactorial pluralistic community' which was 'morbidly introspective'.[119] At the Maudsley intellectual life dominated, sometimes at the expense of the patients. This was not true of Bethlem where a sense of suburban calm and a less academic climate prevailed. Bethlem might have provided the original administrative drive behind the Joint Hospital, but it was initially an 'appendage of the Maudsley', as noted in Chapter 29, run by Johnson's academic but inept assistant.[120] With most consultants based at the Institute of Psychiatry and Denmark Hill, where all the teaching occurred, the Maudsley received most of the attention. In 1970 Paine admitted that since 1948 most of the money had been spent on the Maudsley.[121] A similar situation had existed when Bethlem was joined with Bridewell. Bethlem's semi-rural location and the problems of travelling to Monks Orchard did not help. The Governors were aware of the situation and had appointed Paine to redress the balance. This was not a reflection of the medical work undertaken at Monks Orchard, which had some of the most distinguished clinicians in the Hospital. In terms of general policy, however, continuities remained with Bethlem's pre-1948 administration. The new Board shared Bethlem's sense of paternalism. It used the endowments to provide 'some moderate conveniences or luxuries for the patients in the Hospital and some additional facilities for the staff'.[122] Efforts were made to improve and modernize the Joint Hospital and provide a high level of care, although the presence of the Maudsley increasingly shifted this towards clinical services.

PRESSURE OF NATIONAL REFORM: 1974–82

By 1974 Bevan's initial structure had changed considerably. The Ministry of Health wanted clear lines of communication, while doctors were becoming dissatisfied with a system that was filling hospitals with unsuitable long-stay patients.[123] After a long process of discussion, reforms were suggested where the idea of 'effective management' was central.[124] Bethlem 'acknowledged weaknesses in the present organisation', but like many in the health service the Governors opposed the nature of the reforms.[125] Their main concerns were independence and adequate funding, with the belief that it would be difficult to fit postgraduate teaching hospitals with their national and international role into any proposed regional structure.[126] However, the Governors were prepared to consider a possible federation of teaching hospitals, a suggestion put forward by the Ministry of Health in 1967 in an attempt to promote efficient planning.[127] It was a common view among teaching hospitals as they strove to maintain their independence. The Teaching Hospitals Association fought successfully for the postgraduate teaching hospitals to be excluded from the reorganization under an exemption order where it failed to maintain independence elsewhere. Reorganization went ahead without the postgraduate teaching hospitals, creating 'a Byzantine structure in which there were too many tiers of administration'.[128] Paine viewed the entire process as 'a bad example of a good idea' that had produced 'an intricately woven magic carpet that just won't fly'.[129]

The 1974 NHS Reorganisation Act did indirectly affect the Joint Hospital's management. Reorganization failed to remove the top-heavy administration, but it did embody a new management philosophy.[130] Since 1968 the Ministry of Health had been pressing for a simple committee structure, and discussions in the health service stimulated interest in how the Joint Hospital was administered. With six standing committees and numerous subcommittees responsibilities were duplicated. Some effort had been made to simplify the administration, but by 1971 Paine was beginning to feel that the management was too cumbersome. He undertook a study of the United Oxford Hospital where a '1980'-style management system had been established to bridge the gap between the ward and the board room. Paine was cautiously impressed and recommended an increased level of delegation.[131] It was not until 1973 that a Policy Subcommittee was established to draw up proposals for reform. These were circulated in 1975 and news quickly spread. The continued existence of the Board with direct access to the Department of Health and Social Security (DHSS), the Ministry of Health's successor, was seen as the best solution. Support was given to the idea of multidisciplinary management teams to promote consensus management.[132] The administration was simplified and the medical staff were given a greater role. A Strategic Planning Group was to plan major capital projects and the allocation of resources. To assist the Board, a Financial Policy Committee was created along with a Management Team of Officers (MTO) broadly modelled on the Area Management Teams of single district areas. The MTO took over some of the Hospital Committee's functions, with the rest passed to the House Governor. These two committees, along with the Medical Executive Committee discussed in Chapter 32, became the Hospitals' main governing bodies.[133] Initially the MTO met every two weeks to implement the reforms and plan a district psychiatric inpatient service, but gradually it became absorbed in the medical and domestic management. It seldom initiated measures, referring matters to individual committees and providing a multidisciplinary forum in which policy was discussed and recommendations made.

After the 1974 reorganization a limited revision followed in 1982 after the White Paper *Patients First*.[134] In line with the 1979 Royal Commission on the NHS, Area Health Authorities were removed in a reorganization that left the service unsettled. The Joint Hospital, critical of the NHS's administration, could not this time escape outside reform. With the exemption order due to expire in 1979, the future role of the postgraduate teaching hospitals came under increasing examination. In 1977 the DHSS revived the idea of an 'overlord postgraduate health authority' and suggested an alternative where postgraduate hospitals could be joined in a series of special health authorities.[135] Discussions with the postgraduate teaching hospitals were prolonged and it was not until 1980 that the London Advisory Group was established to visit each hospital. Influenced by the University of London, the Group recommended which postgraduate hospitals could be merged with general hospitals. It also suggested that the larger hospitals like the Joint Hospital should continue to be managed by Boards of Governors, reconstituted as SHAs. The Joint Hospital welcomed the suggestion mainly because it advocated continued independent management.[136] In response, the DHSS pressed for the creation of seven SHAs of which the Joint Hospital was one. Paine placed considerable hope in the move.[137]

Wixley, chair since 1980, was right in predicting a 'good degree of continuity' in the new Bethlem Royal Hospital and Maudsley Hospital Health Authority as the SHA was formally called.[138] The Joint Hospital was one of the last SHAs to have its chairman appointed. Although Wixley was replaced by Dr Ivan Clout, an unwelcome appointee of the Ministry of Health, twelve of the Board's nineteen members and the existing administrative officers were reappointed.[139] Despite the smaller size of the committee, representation was broadened. Of the nineteen members two had to be hospital consultants, one a general practitioner, another a consultant appointed from 'an appropriate specialty outside the hospital'. Nurses were represented by one member, with the Regional Health Authority, University of London, Institute of Psychiatry and health service trade union able to nominate members. The responsibilities of the MTO were broadened to cover housing and planning. Bethlem's past was not forgotten. It was left to the discretion of the Secretary of State to nominate one member from the Common Council of the City of London.[140] Continuity existed in the administration of the endowments. The possibility of creating a special trust was discussed in the belief that this would allow efficient management and avoid the party political influence that had increasingly come to concern the Governors. By a narrow majority it was decided that the SHA would manage the endowments.[141] A new committee was established that worked in a similar fashion to the Financial Policy Committee. Continuity was provided with Bethlem's pre-NHS management where it was the main Governing body that not only ran the Hospital but also managed its funds.

Gradually the view that Bethlem had its 'own particular and different contribution' to make to the Joint Hospital became accepted.[142] By the late 1960s Bethlem had become a home to leading departments in alcoholism, drug dependency, geriatrics and inpatient psychotherapy. They helped raise Bethlem's status in the Joint Hospital, while Paine had successfully encouraged more cooperation. In 1971 the Forward Planning Group saw Bethlem as the best location for specialist services. The Board realized that there was a 'need to consider future major developments at the joint hospital (ie including Bethlem) and not merely on the Maudsley Hospital site'.[143] More attention was paid to Bethlem and the need to develop services and improve conditions, especially for the staff. However, the development of the district commitment and District Services Centre at Denmark Hill ensured that the Maudsley retained its important position. Staff at Monks Orchard continued to complain into the 1980s that Bethlem was often neglected, not least in the *Bethlem & Maudsley Gazette*.

FINANCIAL ANXIETY AND THE NHS: 1948–82

The NHS brought other changes. Where the Maudsley benefited from the increased financial security Bethlem's endowments offered, Bethlem became more insecure. The Joint Hospital was reliant on Exchequer income and encountered external restraints on finance that had not previously affected Bethlem. Exchequer grants paradoxically instilled a sense of anxiety about the level of funding. Before 1948 it was income that was Bethlem's prime concern; with the NHS the emphasis shifted to expenditure.

Beveridge had assumed that the cost of healthcare was finite, but experiences quickly showed that he was wrong. The NHS proved more expensive than anticipated, prompting a perpetual crisis. One writer felt that administrators were in an 'Alice-in-Wonderland position: run as hard as they might they were always overtaken by costs'.[144] Bevan strenuously defended the NHS against cuts, but the need for restrictions quickly became apparent.[145] The 1956 Guillebaud Committee showed that expenditure had risen by 70 per cent since 1948, although it found no grounds for charges of extravagance. Many labelled the Report a 'bluebook full of whitewash' and those on the political Right began to argue that Britain could not afford the extensive service planned for.[146] Faced with a restrictive Treasury it was necessary to introduce charges to meet rising expenditure, encouraged by spiralling pharmaceutical costs and 'an appetite for hospitalisation'.[147] Further problems were encountered in the mid-1970s, with the oil crisis in 1973 accelerating the underlying rate of inflation and thus encouraging public expenditure cuts that hit the NHS. The Resource Allocation Working Party (RAWP) drew up a formula in 1976 that directed funding away from the well-endowed regions in London and the South East to poorly endowed regions.[148] This limited the regional funds available to the Joint Hospital and created problems for the creation of regional units at Bethlem. The history of the NHS might be seen as one of tension between health needs, financial resources, and the amount successive governments were willing to spend.

National constraints on funding affected the income available to the Joint Hospital, with the Ministry of Health and its successors making continuous attempts from the mid-1950s to reduce spending. Where Denis Hill could point to 'a great wave of enthusiasm in the mental hospitals', mental healthcare needed 'more money, more buildings, more steel and more staff' than was forthcoming.[149] The fear in 1947 that they would find it difficult to compete for resources increasingly became a reality within the 'Cinderella Service' of mental healthcare.[150] The Ministry of Health itself admitted that mental hospitals between 1948 and 1954 received 'a smaller portion than was reasonable'. Even with an expanded level of capital spending they received only 28.1 per cent of the NHS budget by 1955/6.[151] The problem continued to plague the mental healthcare sector. Consequently the politician David Owen admitted in 1976 that a 'low cost mentality' was needed, with a 'willingness to make and mend'.[152]

'In the interests of the future administration' of the Joint Hospital, the day-to-day financial administration was passed to a finance officer in 1949, but financial decisions rested with the Governors. Once problems with the duplication of accounts, dispersion of records, and defects in the allocation of expenditure had been overcome, the Governors attempted to control their resources.[153] Finance now took on two aspects: the management of Bethlem's endowments, and control of the income received from the Exchequer. It was the latter which provided the main source of funding and created the most problems. Estimates were submitted annually based on the previous five months' spending and after a process of negotiation funding was allocated. To meet rising expenditure, concessions and additional funding were sought – often with reasonable success. However, this was not enough to remove financial anxiety. From 1954 onwards the Governors started to complain that 'the overall allocation of Exchequer money to the Health Service was not sufficient to meet ... the demands by the various hospital authorities'.[154] They preferred to overspend and warned of potential reductions in services. Economies were necessary from the start with salaries reduced, recruitment restricted and various schemes set up to raise additional revenue from the staff. One of the more innovative economies was the use of outside firms from 1957 onwards to provide the catering at Bethlem. The decision to contract-out catering produced a considerable saving and marked the start of contractual agreements with private businesses twenty-two years before it became the DHSS's policy to encourage such moves.[155] However, economies were never enough to solve the financial pressures facing the Joint Hospital. In 1973 the auditor complained about the lack of financial control, but it was not resource management that lay at the heart of the problem.[156] The Joint Hospital's nature and demands from the consultants prompted 'creeping growth', raising expenditure while pressure was exerted centrally to reduce spending.[157]

The NHS had a huge impact on Bethlem's expenditure: in the first year spending was twenty times higher for the Joint Hospital than it had been for Bethlem in 1947.[158] The expansion of the Hospital, rising costs, and increased medical expenditure ensured that between 1950 and 1971 spending increased from £416,395 to £2,350,890. Unplanned financial requests created unwelcome strain on resources. Renovations to Bethlem's wards were scaled down, projects were delayed, and in 1980 it was decided to use the money set aside to reopen Tyson House West after renovations to finance a non-recurring revenue programme.[159] By the 1970s the Governors had become cautious about opening units without firm funding guarantees. To meet these difficulties legal concerns were put aside and endowments used to fund 'any deficiencies arising from the reduction of the Exchequer allocation'.[160] It had taken Paine considerable effort to convince the Governors that this was possible. This created a dilemma. To generate the funds needed property had to be sold, but the most saleable properties were those that brought the largest revenue at a time when inflation in the building industry, coupled with a decline in the markets, was creating concern. The Joint Hospital was presented with little choice. In 1975 the DHSS informed all mental hospitals that 'there will be effectively no room for initiating new developments unless the cost can be found from savings or from redeployment within existing services'.[161] Cuts followed and the Governors pressed for a better assessment of funding priorities. In 1980 the Finance Policy Committee recommended a 1 per cent saving. The MTO saw a blanket reduction as unfeasible and suggested a higher degree of involvement from clinical teams in making savings.[162] Overspending and economies became a regular feature of the Joint Hospital's finances.

Particular problems were encountered over capital projects. Most of the NHS's capital spending went on minor modernization projects and on general and district hospitals after the 1962 *Hospital Plan*, not on mental hospitals. The allocation of the 'mental million' for capital projects in mental hospitals from 1953 onwards did little to improve the situation.[163] The Governors at first felt that it was the Government's job to pay for new buildings. Paine overcame the Governors' caution and gradually convinced them that endowments could be used, with any money reclaimed invested. He felt that any other policy would be a betrayal of the patients. St Thomas's had paved the way. When it sought clarification on the 1948 Act it found that endowments could legitimately be used for hospital accommodation and medical and nursing services as long as it was remembered that 'hospital services are services to be rendered to the public at large, and not services to be rendered to the staff'.[164] While the Joint Hospital's Board did try to attract as much capital funding as possible, it worked with the knowledge that Bethlem's endowments could be used. By the 1980s, endowed income was sufficient to fund building without touching the capital. For example, where the DHSS allocated £400,000 for capital projects in 1980, an additional £1.1m was found from the endowments.[165] Major projects like the District Services Centre, the Community Centre at Monks Orchard, and the Institute of Psychiatry's new building were made possible through this mix of funding. However, where the Governors were prepared to take such action, they were not willing to over-commit the Hospital's endowments. They worked at improving the 'Endowment Fund income so as to provide possible funds for major building developments'.[166] With many Governors from City backgrounds, a cautious policy was adopted and Bethlem's previous policy of continual reassessment of investments continued to ensure the best rate of interest. In 1961 it was decided to divide investments between free and restricted assets. The sum of £100,000 was released for reinvestment to take advantage of Britain's high growth rate and low inflation. The decision created an immediate fall in income, but the move into shares spread the Hospital's investment portfolio and made it more responsive to market changes.[167] With the formation of the Financial Policy Committee in 1976 it was decided that the previous 'negative and passive policy' should be abandoned, with £250,000 made available for short-term investment.[168] Where the Governors continued to oversee the investment policy, they came to rely increasingly on the advice of their stockbrokers.

Property remained the key to the endowments. Management remained in the hands of consulting surveyors who were used to 'undertake the general supervision and management of the Board's town and country properties and farms'.[169] Some problems were encountered over ownership, resulting in the threat of legal action from Bridewell in 1955.[170] Income was set aside and investments sold to buy freehold and leasehold properties in central London, a move that went against the Chancellor of the Exchequer's advice in 1956. The Governors took advantage of post-war rebuilding. With few estates left to develop they concentrated their interests on offices and business premises, partly because by the mid-1950s there was 'a considerable falling off' of residential properties in London.[171] The government's 'Stop-Go' economic policy in the 1950s and 1960s, and rising living standards, made property a more attractive investment. Paine was also aware that with many 99-year leases due to be renegotiated in the 1970s, the Hospital could make substantial gains. To prevent the burden of unexpected expenditure, sinking funds were created to cover 'rebuilding . . . amortisation of leases and any other potential loses'.[172] Estates that produced a low return or needed extensive repairs were sold. The policy brought 'a considerable increase in the rents'.[173] By 1980 rental income had reached £360,000, while only £48,000 was raised from dividends.[174] The overriding interest was to maintain the Piccadilly estate, which generated a third of the endowed income, and to avoid selling property that would involve a major fall in revenue. This concern was ignored when funds were urgently needed. To fund building projects either short-term leaseholds or mortgages were sought, with sinking funds created to meet any potential loss.[175] Personal commitment may have declined in the management of the endowments, but the policy objectives had not changed since 1900.

Bethlem moved from a period of prosperity to one of anxiety. The financial concerns of the NHS and central government now had a direct bearing on the Hospital's development. It was not a situation that had been anticipated in 1948. The Governors consistently tried to improve the amount allocated by the Exchequer and worked to save money without cutting services. They were not always successful. However, Bethlem's endowments ensured that the Joint Hospital did not face the same degree of anxiety experienced at other institutions. They provided a reserve of funds that could be used to expand services and supplement Exchequer revenue. Increasingly the Joint Hospital found itself in a position where this was necessary. Without the endowments many developments in the Joint Hospital would have been severely underfunded or unable to happen. Even with them many projects had to be scaled down. These financial problems were to become worse in the 1980s.

CONCLUSION

Bethlem had moved from a profitable bastion of voluntarism to part of a prestigious NHS psychiatric teaching hospital facing national financial restrictions and cuts. Much had changed in the process, especially after the merger when Bethlem found itself in a subordinated position again. Bethlem weathered both internal and external administrative transformations and managed to retain its identity with some aspects of the Hospital's pre-1948 ethos remaining central to the administration of the Joint Hospital. The clearest continuities were seen in the management of the endowments, where the aim was always to protect the integrity of the Piccadilly estate and raise income. The formation of the SHA did not fundamentally alter the nature of the Joint Hospital, but considerable changes followed its creation which will be discussed in the concluding chapter. Bethlem had proved itself an adaptable institution, not least because its long history gave the Joint Hospital advantages that helped support and fund its continued expansion.

NOTES

1 See for example, Richard Hunter and Ida Macalpine, *Psychiatry for the Poor: 1851 Colney Hatch Asylum – Friern Hospital 1973* (London: Dawson, 1974); Elizabeth Malcolm, *Swift's Hospital: A History of St Patrick's Hospital Dublin* (Dublin: Gill & Macmillan, 1989), and John Crammer, *Asylum History* (London: Gaskell, 1990).

2 Andrew Scull, *The Most Solitary of Afflictions: Madness and Society in Britain 1700–1900* (New Haven and London: Yale University Press, 1993), 245–7.

3 *Lancet*, 4 (1904), 1795.

4 J. Stone, *Hospital Organisation and Management* (London: Faber & Gwyer, 1927).

5 1932 Rules & Orders, 42–4.

6 Bethlem Subcommittee, 19 September 1917.

7 See R. J. Morris, *Class, Sect and Party: The Making of the British Middle Class, Leeds 1820–50* (Manchester: Manchester University Press, 1990), 184.

8 1932 Rules & Orders, 2.

9 Geoffrey Finlayson, 'A Moving Frontier: Voluntarism and the State in British Social Welfare 1911–1949', *Twentieth Century British History*, i (1990), 183–206, p. 183.

10 Alan Kidd, 'Philanthropy and the "Social History Paradigm"', *Social History*, xxi (1996), 180–92, discusses the various historical and sociological interpretations of philanthropy.

11 Jane Lewis, 'The Boundary Between Voluntary and Statutory Social Services in the Late Nineteenth and Early Twentieth Centuries', *Historical Journal*, xxxix (1996), 155–77.

12 Large numbers of Governors attended the meeting in 1924 when it was decided to move

the Hospital. A similarly high attendance was recorded when Gerald Coke, the Treasurer, announced his plans to merge Bethlem with the Maudsley in 1947.

13 Charlotte MacKenzie, *Psychiatry for the Rich: A History of Ticehurst Private Asylum* (London: Routledge, 1992), 167.

14 A. J. P. Taylor, *English History 1914–1945* (Oxford: OUP, 1965), 175.

15 Cited in Finlayson, *op. cit.* 188.

16 See Geoffrey Rivett, *Development of the London Hospital System 1823–1982* (London: OUP, 1986), 194–9.

17 Bethlem was a firm supporter of the Mental After Care Association (MACA), founded in 1879 by Reverend Henry Hawkins, chaplain of Colney Hatch Asylum, to provide support, domiciliary care, and work for patients once they had been discharged (Records of the Association are held at the CMAC, Wellcome Institute, London). Charles Wakefield, as Bethlem's President, was also president of the MACA in the interwar period, believing that it was society's 'moral obligation' to protect patients from the shock of re-entering the community: *City Press*, 13 March 1920, 3. Bethlem regularly provided donations and a venue for the MACA's meetings. Other examples of Bethlem's charity included the financial support it gave in 1926 to the *Daily Mail*'s Wireless Fund, a scheme run to provide hospital wards with radios. Bethlem not only made a donation, but also benefited from the scheme: General Committee, 12 July 1926.

18 *Hansard*, H. of L., vol. 163 (1949), col. 163.

19 1932 Rules & Orders, 3–11.

20 *City Press*, 14 February 1920, 2.

21 Court of Governors, 8 March 1920.

22 *Jewish Chronicle*, 5 January 1923, 5; *Hertfordshire Chronicle*, 17 November 1928.

23 Vicki Hayward, 'Bethlem in the 1930s' (Unpublished article, 1982), 5.

24 See Chapter 29.

25 *Orchard Leaves*, Autumn 1936, 3.

26 *City Press*, 14 February 1920, 2.

27 *Ibid.*

28 *Orchard Leaves*, October 1934, 1.

29 Keir Waddington, 'Finance, Philanthropy and the Hospital: Metropolitan Hospitals 1850–1898' (unpublished Ph.D. Thesis, University of London, 1995), ch. 5.

30 See Frank Prochaska, *Royal Bounty: Making of a Welfare Monarchy* (New Haven, Conn. and London: Yale University Press, 1995).

31 *Orchard Leaves*, Autumn 1936, 3.

32 *City Press*, 30 December 1922, 5.

33 *Under the Dome*, 25 March 1923, 3.

34 *Dictionary of National Biography, 1941–1950* (Oxford: OUP, 1959), 914.

35 *City Press*, 7 December 1934, 13.

36 *1919 Bethlem Annual Report*, 18.

37 *City Press*, 26 July 1935, 9–11.

38 *Orchard Leaves*, Summer 1937, 1.

39 *The Times*, 25 January 1941, 5.

40 General Committee, 25 March 1941.

41 Court of Governors, 28 January 1941; Prochaska, *op. cit.* 220–5.

42 General Committee, 25 March 1941.

43 *Ibid.* 11 November 1945.

44 1932 Rules & Orders.

45 See, for example, Crammer, *op. cit.* 67. The Board of Control's predecessor, the Lunacy Commission, had fulfilled a similar role: D. Mellett, 'Bureaucracy and Mental Illness', *Medical History*, xxv (1981), 221–50.

46 For the development of hospital finance see Waddington, *op. cit.*, especially ch. 9 for the financial problems of the early twentieth century, while Rivett, *op. cit.* 184–91, provides a further analysis.

47 Where St Thomas's Hospital spent £4,402 3s 11d on administration in 1920, of which most

went of fund-raising, Bethlem spent £844 5s 7d: St Thomas's Hospital Archive, Greater London Record Officer (hereafter St Thomas's Archive), H1/St/A59/A24; Bethlem Hospital 1920/1 Statement of Accounts.

48 Monks Orchard Farm Papers: Letter from Elgar to Headington, 28 March 1927.

49 *Ibid.*: Letter from Ablewhite to Worsfold, 24 December 1934; 24 November 1938; Letter from Hewitt to Wilkinson, 8 July 1942.

50 See Chapter 29, pp. 553–5.

51 Court of Governors, 29 February 1932 and 11 July 1932.

52 Bethlem Subcommittee, 6 July 1927.

53 General Committee, 9 July 1928.

54 St Thomas's Archive, H1/ST/A59/A/24 and A59/A/51.

55 1900–1945 Statement of Accounts.

56 In 1960 the Governors were still trying to reach a provisional agreement with the War Damage Commission over the King's Arms, St George's Road: Finance and General Purposes Committee Presented Papers: 4 January 1960, Appendix F.

57 Estates Committee, 25 June 1941 and 4 September 1945.

58 House Committee, 23 August 1944.

59 Martin Daunton, 'Housing', in F. M. L. Thompson (ed.), *Cambridge Social History of Britain* 2 (Cambridge: CUP, 1990), vol. ii, 232–3.

60 See Mona Paton, 'Corporate East End Landlords: The Example of the London Hospital and the Mercers Company', *London Journal*, xviii (1983), 113–28.

61 Estates Committee, 25 May 1910 and 23 January 1901.

62 *Ibid.* 9 October 1937 and 9 June 1938.

63 RC on Agricultural Depression, *PP* 1897 xv, 22–3.

64 Estate Committee, 8 May 1918.

65 Daunton, *op. cit.* 226.

66 Cited in D. J. Olsen, *The Growth of Victorian London* (London: Batsford, 1976), 28; David Green, 'The Metropolitan Economy', in Keith Hoggart and David Green (eds), *London: A New Metropolitan Geography* (London: Edward Arnold, 1991), 8–33.

67 Estates Committee, 9 March 1934.

68 Alan Jackson, *Semi-Detached London* (London: Allen & Unwin, 1973); John Burnett, *A Social History of Housing* (London: Routledge, 1993), 252.

69 P. Waller, *Town, City and Nation: England 1850–1914* (Oxford: OUP, 1983), 131. For the development and popularity of seaside resorts see John Walton, *The English Seaside Resort* (Leicester: Leicester University Press, 1983).

70 The estate had been left to Bethlem in 1695 by John Edmanson, sailmaker of London. Originally the property consisted of about 120 acres, but by the 1930s the size had been slightly reduced by coastal erosion.

71 A similar policy was adopted by other landowners, see Bernard Nurse, 'Planning a London Suburban Estate: Dulwich 1882–1920', *London Journal*, xix (1994), 54–70. Over time many found they had to be flexible as they were 'tightly circumscribed by the commercial realities . . . and ineffective in turning back contrary tides': F. M. L. Thompson, *The Rise of Suburbia* (Leicester: Leicester University Press, 1982), 18. From the minutes, it would appear that Bethlem was not overly concerned once the houses had been built. Its building leases were a desired ideal rather than a rigid set of rules.

72 David Cannadine, *Lords and Landlords: The Aristocracy and the Towns, 1774–1967* (Leicester: Leicester University Press, 1980), 421–3.

73 Waller, *op. cit.* 138–9.

74 Estates Committee, 7 March 1924.

75 *Ibid.* 3–4 February 1913.

76 *Ibid.* 10 April 1931.

77 1900–1927 Statement of Accounts.

78 1928–1945 Statement of Accounts.

79 For the impact of the 1930s depression on British economy see D.H.Aldcroft, *The British Economy: The Years of Turmoil, 1920–1951* (Brighton: Wheatsheaf, 1986).

80 For example, when new heating and lighting was installed in 1911/12, with radiators throughout the Hospital costing £8,050, a heating sinking fund was established to which £400 was paid annually: Court of Governors, 27 February 1911.

81 Steve Cherry, 'Beyond National Health Insurance. The Voluntary Hospitals and Hospital Contributory Schemes: A Regional Study', *Social History of Medicine*, v (1992), 455–82.

82 See Brian Abel Smith, *The Hospitals* (London: Heinemann, 1964), 317; William Parry-Jones, *Trade in Lunacy: A Study of Private Madhouses in England in the Eighteenth and Nineteenth Centuries* (London: Routledge & Kegan Paul, 1971).

83 Bethlem Subcommittee, 2 March 1921.

84 Court of Governors, 27 June 1927.

85 *Ibid.* 29 February 1932.

86 Charity Commission Papers: Letter from Worsfold, 23 June 1927.

87 Bethlem Subcommittee, 4 May 1910.

88 It was not an uncommon experience: see Jonathan Andrews, 'Bedlam Revisited: A History of Bethlem Hospital *c.* 1600–*c.*1750.' (University of London, unpublished Ph.D. Thesis, 1991), 170–1.

89 Bethlem Subcommittee, 21 February 1923. Almoners had been introduced in the 1890s as part of an attempt to reduce what contemporaries believed was an abuse of the London outpatient departments by patients who could afford to pay: see Keir Waddington, 'Unsuitable Cases', *Medical History* (forthcoming, 1998).

90 General Correspondence: Letter to Jenks, 25 March 1938.

91 1900–1945 Statement of Accounts.

92 General Committee, 14 June 1920.

93 House Committee, 4 October 1944.

94 General Committee, 11 February 1945.

95 Cited in Finlayson, *op. cit.* 196.

96 General Correspondence: Letter from Worsfold to the Fishmongers' Company, 12 March 1936.

97 *Ibid.*: Letter from Porter-Phillips, 28 February 1936.

98 Miller Relief Fund Papers: Letter from Miller to Copeland, 15 November 1918.

99 Bethlem Subcommittee, 19 August 1908 and 18 February 1931.

100 See Donna Andrew, *Philanthropy and Police: London Charity in the Eighteenth Century* (Oxford: OUP, 1989).

101 Legacy Books, 1727–1925; 1925–55.

102 Rodney Lowe, *Welfare State in Britain Since 1945* (London: Macmillan, 1993).

103 T. Butler, *Mental Health, Social Policy and the Law* (Basingstoke: Macmillan, 1985), 119.

104 See Chapter 30 for Bethlem's merger with the Maudsley.

105 Brian Watkin, *National Health Service: The First Phase, 1948–1974 and After* (London: Allen & Unwin, 1978), 23–5.

106 Standing Orders, 5.

107 See Chapter 33.

108 Finance & General Purposes Committee, 7 March 1955.

109 Blacker Papers: Letter from Johnson to Blacker, 8 March 1949.

110 Standing Orders, 11–18.

111 Finance & General Purposes Committee Presented Papers: 1 February 1971.

112 Watkin, *op. cit.* 106.

113 *Bethlem & Maudsley Gazette*, March 1958, 4.

114 *Ibid.* June 1965, 55–6.

115 *Ibid.* March 1966, 32.

116 Watkin, *op. cit.*

117 *Bethlem & Maudsley Gazette*, September 1962, 29.

118 *Ibid.* Autumn 1985, 25.

119 *Ibid.* June 1963, 54.

120 *Ibid.* November 1965, 94.

121 Finance & General Purposes Committee Presented Papers: 2 November 1970, Appendix D.

122 Finance & General Purposes Committee, 23 January 1950.

123 See Lowe, *op. cit.* 301–4.

124 Cited in Roger Hadley and Stephen Hatch, *Social Welfare and the Failure of the State* (London 1981).

125 Board of Governors, 7 October 1968.

126 Finance & General Purposes Committee Presented Papers: 23 March 1970, Appendix G.

127 Board of Governors Presented Papers: 6 April 1970; 3 April 1967, Appendix H.

128 Lowe, *op. cit.* 186. Reorganization has been discussed extensively elsewhere: see Ruth Levitt, *Reorganised National Health Service* (London: Croom Helm, 1976); S. Brown, *Reorganising the National Health Service* (Oxford: OUP, 1979); while Vicente Navarro, *Class Struggle, the State and Medicine* (London: Martin Robertson & Co., 1978), 50–65, attributes change to forces outside the NHS.

129 *Lancet,* 2 (1976), 1130–1.

130 Kathleen Jones, *The Making of Social Policy In Britain* (London: Athlone, 1991), 177.

131 Board of Governors Presented Papers: 5 April 1971.

132 *Ibid.,* 7 April 1975.

133 Board of Governors, 6 October 1976.

134 Nicholas Timmins, *Five Giants: Biography of the Welfare State* (London: HarperCollins, 1995), 385.

135 Board of Governors Presented Papers: 3 April 1967, Appendix H; 16 May 1977.

136 Board of Governors, 6 April 1981.

137 Rivett, *op. cit.* 337–9.

138 Board of Governors, 1 March 1982.

139 SHA, 29 March 1982.

140 Finance & General Purposes Committee Presented Papers: 16 September 1987, Appendix A.

141 Board of Governors, 1 March 1982.

142 *Bethlem & Maudsley Gazette*, Winter 1969, 2.

143 Finance & General Purposes Committee Presented Papers: 20 September 1971, Appendix K; Board of Governors, 4 January 1971.

144 Pauline Gregg, *The Welfare State* (London: George Harrap, 1967), 189.

145 For the conflicts between 1948 and Bevan's retirement in 1951 see Michael Foot, *Aneurin Bevan*, vol. ii (London: Davies Poynter, 1973) or P. Williams, *Hugh Gaitskell* (London: 1979).

146 Jones, *op. cit.* 152; cited in Lowe, *op. cit.* 180.

147 For the financial problems facing the NHS in its first decade, see Charles Webster, *Problems of Health Care: The National Health Service Before 1957* (London: HMSO, 1988), 133–84; *Twentieth Century*, Autumn 1962, 171.

148 Julian Le Grand, David Winter and Francis Woolley, 'The National Health Service: Safe in Whose Hands?', in John Hills (ed.), *The State of Welfare: The Welfare State in Britain since 1974* (Oxford: Clarendon Press, 1990), 89.

149 Denis Hill, *Psychiatry in Medicine: Retrospect and Prospect* (Nuffield Provincial Hospitals Trust, 1969), 13; Webster, *op. cit.* 329.

150 Andrew Land, Rodney Lowe and Noel Whiteside, *Development of the Welfare State 1939–1951* (London: HMSO, 1992), 128; Jones, *op. cit.* 154.

151 Webster, *op. cit.* 338.

152 David Owen, *In Sickness and in Health* (London: Quartet Books, 1976), 143.

153 Finance & General Purposes Committee, 10 July 1950.

154 *Ibid.* 29 March 1954.

155 The decision had not been an ideological one but had been brought about after problems with attracting suitable catering staff to work at Bethlem. This saw an immediate decrease in the amount spent on food: Finance & General Purposes Committee Presented Papers: 5 November 1956, Appendix E.

156 *Ibid.*: 7 May 1973, Appendix I/1.

157 Financial Policy Committee, 20 September 1976.

158 1959 Estimate of Maintenance Expenditure and Income.

159 Board of Governors, 14 April 1980.
160 Finance & General Purposes Committee, 22 June 1970.
161 Finance & General Purposes Committee Presented Papers: 16 June 1975, Appendix G.
162 MTO, 30 September 1980.
163 Webster, *op. cit.* 338–9.
164 Finance & General Purposes Committee, 23 January 1950.
165 Financial Policy Committee, 24 March 1980.
166 Finance & General Purposes Committee Presented Papers: 2 May 1966, Appendix I.
167 *Ibid.* 9 January 1961.
168 Board of Governors Presented Papers: 26 April 1976, Appendix F.
169 Finance & General Purposes Committee, 12 January 1953.
170 *Ibid.* 4 July 1955.
171 Finance & General Purposes Committee Presented Papers: 27 September 1954, Appendix B/1.
172 *Ibid.* 6 March 1961, Appendix D.
173 *Ibid.* 2 September 1957, Appendix D/2.
174 Financial Policy Committee, 7 January 1980.
175 *Ibid.* 29 March 1971.

SERVING BETHLEM

Medical and nursing staff, 1901–82

——— •◆• ———

In the history of psychiatry those who have worked in mental hospitals have often been marginalized. For the psychiatric profession, it is the nineteenth century that has attracted most attention.[1] Andrew Scull has argued that Medical Superintendents dominated the asylum by 1900, allowing the institution to become the basis of their authority. The psychiatrist John Crammer has alternatively asserted that a psychiatric profession did not emerge until the twentieth century.[2] Certainly by the late nineteenth century, doctors controlled the asylum and had their own professional organization, the Medico-Psychological Association (MPA), and journal, the *Journal of Mental Science*. Psychiatrists, however, continued to lag behind the rest of the medical profession and many of the trappings of professionalization were acquired after 1900.[3] Few historians have turned their attention to these issues, and Medical Superintendents and leaders in the field dominate accounts. Little has been said about the twentieth century in general, the employment of women, or those who did most of the clinical work.[4] Even less attention has been paid to the role of the mental nurse.[5] It was first noted in 1960 that the history of mental nursing had been neglected and this was repeated in 1980 and 1996.[6] One historian who has addressed this question has suggested that a society that isolated the mentally ill also inevitably marginalized those who cared for them. He went on to argue that 'the men and women who nurse the mentally disturbed seldom achieve public attention except as a result of scandal or a case of alleged ill treatment'.[7] However, mental nurses were the backbone of the institution. Where they possessed little power to determine how the asylum was run, they did exercise considerable influence over the patients' lives. Here more attention has been paid at Bethlem with the publication of David Russell's *Scenes from Bedlam*.[8] He deals with nursing in the Hospital from 1247 to the twentieth century, providing much useful information in a neglected field.

Twentieth-century Bethlem did not become the focus of scandal or more positive professional interest, except over its outpatient department and new building. Until 1948 the Hospital provided a working environment for both the medical and nursing staff similar to that in other mental hospitals, but without the added pressure of overcrowding. It offered a meeting place for the MPA and other professional bodies, but failed to play a major role in the formation of either profession. After the creation of the National Health Service (NHS), as part of the Joint Hospital, Bethlem attracted little professional concern as it was on the Institute of Psychiatry and the Maudsley that interest focused. However, more than any other aspect of Bethlem's twentieth-century history, considerable changes occurred within the nursing and medical staff.

WORKING FOR BETHLEM

At the start of the twentieth century a career in psychiatry was not viewed as an attractive prospect. The work was 'monotonous, uninteresting and without adequate responsibility [which] leads to the stunting of ambition and a gradual loss of interest in scientific medicine'.[9] In many mental hospitals the Medical Superintendents did little of the clinical work, delegating the task to overworked junior staff. A similar situation existed at Bethlem. The Physician-Superintendents rarely visited the wards and relied heavily on the assistant physicians and house physicians. For junior staff, asylums presented an often depressing atmosphere where opportunities were limited and doctors hedged in by restrictive practices. At Bethlem, salaries remained low before 1948 in comparison to other institutions. It was not surprising therefore that the medical staff, already in a field 'divorced from ordinary medical education and practice', regularly complained of financial insecurity and pressed for higher wages.[10] Invariably, to keep doctors or attract suitable candidates, the Governors were forced to agree. They were more cautious, however, about allowing their staff too much professional freedom for fear that Bethlem's work might suffer. As a result, junior doctors were permitted only to make private consultations in London between 1903 and 1911 after protests had been received that this was forcing 'medical officers waiting on for pensions'.[11] Where doctors in general hospitals used their institutional connections to extend their private practices, restrictions were not unusual for London's mental hospitals.[12] When it became clear that some staff were using this to build up private careers before leaving the Hospital, the Governors clamped down and limited outside consultation to the Physician-Superintendent and Senior Assistant Physician.[13] This did not seriously affect junior doctors' careers. Few opportunities existed for private psychiatric consultations, with faith maintained in institutional treatment until the 1950s. According to the psychoanalyst Ernest Jones the only psychiatrists in private practice in the interwar period 'were those who had retired from the position of superintendent at Bethlehem'.[14]

For the junior staff, working at Bethlem did have some advantages. With 200 to 250 beds the Hospital was not overcrowded and the Governors had a paternalistic attitude. Junior doctors did have to abide by a rigid set of professional regulations, but restrictions on their personal lives were not oppressive and the accommodation and food were of a high standard. The senior and junior assistant physicians were expected to hold both medical and surgical qualifications and have some experience in the 'treatment of mental and nervous disorders'. These qualifications were frequently overlooked. Rule eighteen pointed to the level of the junior doctors' clinical duties. It stipulated that they had to keep the Physician-Superintendent informed of any change 'in the condition of the patients' and of matters 'affecting the welfare of the establishment'.[15] One was expected to be in charge of the male patients, the other the female patients. Complaints were raised in 1934 that the layout of the Monks Orchard Hospital increased the 'time and energy expended' and calls were made for an additional medical officer. The Governors were 'not persuaded that the Hospital was inadequately staffed', especially as the assistant physicians were helped by two house physicians, appointed for six months to extend their training.[16] When suitable candidates proved difficult to attract to Monks Orchard, a salaried junior and senior post were created in 1931 and the amount paid frequently raised to make the posts more attractive.[17] Under the direction of the Assistant Physician the house physicians were expected to examine and treat every patient and keep the case notes.[18] John Porter-Phillips, the Physician-Superintendent from 1911 to 1944, was not, however, convinced of their value. He worried about the standard of their work and competence. Although outspoken on the subject, he did little to alter the situation, and the house physicians continued to do most of the clinical work.[19] With no medical library and ineffectual guidance from the senior medical officers, many did the best they could during their six months at Bethlem.

Doctors made two ward rounds: one in the morning, the other in the evening. They were followed round by the charge nurse with a 'blotting pad, prescription book and inkwell', but this was ended when an inkwell was dropped ruining 'the doctor's spats'.[20] Work was not arduous. Denis Hill, a house physician before 1939, explained that 'one felt, and indeed one was, overworked if the morning round cut into leisurely sherry before lunch'.[21] Life at the other mental hospitals was very different. However, Bethlem was no backwater. Several doctors who went on to become leading psychiatrists held posts in the Hospital either as house physicians or as medical officers early in their careers. For example, Thomas Beaton, the open-minded Assistant Physician between 1920 and 1926, had worked at the Maudsley before coming to Bethlem. His work focused on neurosis after his wartime experiences at Chatham Hospital, and at Bethlem he developed his interest in academic psychiatry whilst teaching in the medical school. Unable to secure a teaching post in the University of London, he became Medical Superintendent in Portsmouth.[22] Here he established an integrated health service and aided the Board of Control in passing the 1930 Mental Treatment Act.[23] Denis Hill, who went on to play a leading role in the Joint Hospital and Institute of Psychiatry, Desmond Curran, and Felix Post, a key figure in the development of psychogeriatric treatment in Britain, had all been house physicians at Bethlem. In terms of clinical material and facilities, the Hospital had much to offer.

Bethlem shared the medical and psychiatric profession's views about the employment of female doctors. The medical profession was antagonistic to the inclusion of women, espousing medical theories that stressed their supposed inferiority. Psychiatrists, particularly the gloomy Henry Maudsley and Bethlem's George Savage, provided additional rationales that confirmed social prejudices and accepted gendered roles.[24] The MPA did not admit women until 1894, and then only after heated debate. In 1898 there were only eight women doctors working in English asylums and the London County Council (LCC) did not sanction the employment of female doctors until 1927.[25] Bethlem's Governors decided to employ a female doctor earlier than the LCC. Mary Barkas became the Hospital's first female house physician in 1919. Barkas had trained in New Zealand before coming to England to study medicine at St Mary's Hospital and the London School of Medicine for Women where Porter-Phillips was a lecturer. Porter-Phillips recommended her appointment and the Governors had agreed to overcome the shortage of 'suitable' male applicants during wartime.[26] Her work at Bethlem stimulated her interest in psychiatry. She went on to take her Diploma in Psychological Medicine (DPM) in 1923, becoming an assistant medical officer at the Maudsley where she specialized in psychotherapy.[27] Other than Barkas's brief spell as house physician, no further female applicant was considered until 1945 when Elizabeth Lobl was appointed assistant medical officer. Little is known about Lobl except that she had studied in Vienna. She left Bethlem in 1950 for the Tavistock Clinic in response to the absence of opportunities for any of the Hospital's medical staff in the Joint Hospital. At Bethlem, the Governors saw the employment of women doctors as a stop-gap until a man could be found.

The junior medical staff did not work alone. All prescriptions were drawn up and dispensed by a pharmacist who attended daily, after one house physician poisoned six patients in 1914. When it was found that doctors were using the pharmacy for their own ends, the dispenser was instructed to ensure that all drugs 'are ordered . . . for the patients in the Hospital'.[28] In 1912 a pathologist was appointed because of the complexity 'of the investigations of Mental Disease, and the little leisure which is at the disposal of existing Medical Staff'. Between 1913 and 1947 the position was held by Clement Lovell, who had been a house physician before his appointment. The outbreak of the Second World War ensured that he remained at Bethlem after his retirement. He worked alone despite growing demand and carried out all the bacteriological testing. Lovell's main interest, however, was in measuring the surface tension of blood, but his findings attracted little attention.[29] New forms of treatment encouraged the Governors to appoint additional staff. Through the work of William Brown, Wilde Reader in Mental Philosophy and director of the Hospital's psychological laboratory, Bethlem became an important centre for psychological research.[30] With the development of ultra-light treatment and hydrotherapy at Monks Orchard a physiotherapist was appointed in 1931.

One area where Bethlem was slow to develop was in inpatient services. Only at Aubrey Lewis's insistence, as Clinical Director of the Maudsley, during the final stages of the merger, was Muriel Norris from Sussex County Council appointed in 1947 as the Hospital's first psychiatric social worker. Much of the work had previously been undertaken by the nurses.[31] The use of psychiatric social workers was developed rapidly after 1948. A car was bought in 1950 to help them travel between the two sites and patients' homes and by 1957 the Joint Hospital had fourteen psychiatric social workers, most of whom were based at the Maudsley.[32] Often undervalued by doctors and facing problems in making their voice heard, they furnished an important service for patients. Social workers were available to advise every patient and were present to help with the family and personal problems caused by admission. They helped patients with their entitlement to state benefits and informed them how claims could be made. Responsibility for the social workers was transferred to Southwark Social Services under the 1974 NHS Reorganisation Act. Changes in the structure of social work in Southwark and financial difficulties prompted a crisis in the 1980s.[33] Concern had been raised in 1982 over the freezing of posts, and in 1988 Eric Byers, the Special Health Authority's (SHA) general manager, warned of a 50 per cent cut in social workers.[34] The Medical Committee, aware that this was an attempt to save money, passed a vote of no confidence. This did little.[35] Southwark Social Services only managed to antagonize and the Governors found themselves increasingly unable to rely on Southwark when it withdrew its social workers from the SHA to meet its commitments elsewhere. In an attempt to meet part of the problem, a Care Approach Programme was established in 1991 to help patients in the community.[36] The emphasis placed on the Patient's Charter by John Major's Conservative Government saw the Joint Hospital establishing other services. In 1990 a patient information service was set up to provide a friendly resource network for patients and their relatives. It aimed to give information on legislation, accommodation, medication, mental health groups, employment, education, leisure, and even supplied refreshments.[37]

When Lovell was hired in 1913, it was also decided to appoint several honorary consultants. The decision was made because it was felt to be cheaper than paying visiting doctors a consulting fee to provide surgical, dental, ophthalmic, anaesthetic and other services not covered by the medical staff.[38] They attended Bethlem regularly, or were called in when necessary, and the patient charged accordingly. After the move, once attempts to find suitable doctors in Croydon had failed, they had to be paid more before they were prepared to travel to Monks Orchard.[39] Following experience gained in 'asylum war hospitals', the Board of Control realized that consultants were vital to provide the necessary specialist services normally unavailable in a mental hospital.[40] General hospitals had adopted a similar practice in the nineteenth century. Bethlem was among the first mental hospitals to appoint honorary consultants and realized early 'that no Mental Hospital can possibly carry on successful investigation and treatment without the expert aid of trained specialists'.[41]

THE PHYSICIAN-SUPERINTENDENTS: 1901–48

Although it was the house physicians and assistant physicians who undertook most of the work, it was the four resident Physician-Superintendents between 1900 and 1948 who set Bethlem's medical character. Unlike the Medical Superintendents described by Montagu Lomax in his *Experiences of an Asylum Doctor*, they were not irresponsible, lazy or mean.[42] From the evidence available it would appear that all tried to promote the comfort of patients, if not of staff. Strict discipline was maintained, but support was given to nurses' professional organizations in an attempt to raise the standard of care. The title of Medical Superintendent was avoided, partly because it was associated with the county and borough asylums. Calling the post 'physician' associated the holder with that section of the medical profession which treated upper- and middle-class patients and viewed itself as a medical and social elite. This was felt to be more in line with Bethlem's character. Before 1948, when the post was dissolved in Lewis's new medical administration, the Physician-Superintendent played an influential role in the Hospital's development. Theophilus Hyslop and the urbane William Henry Stoddart had interests outside Bethlem and sought to build up their private practices. Porter-Phillips was wedded to the Hospital and spent his entire career at Bethlem. John Hamilton was more dynamic, interested in the new physical treatments and even after the merger continued to work at Monks Orchard, defending Bethlem's interests.

The Physician-Superintendent was expected to hold a DPM and be a fellow of the Royal College of Physicians. It was considered essential that he have five years' experience and be willing to live in the Hospital. Although not mentioned in the regulations, it was assumed that the officer would be male. No other office could be held, although the holder was permitted to undertake private practice and 'to give a yearly course of lectures on psychological medicine at not more than one of the recognised London Schools of Medicine'. The post, however, was not well paid and Physician-Superintendents needed these outside interests to increase their salary. In 1903 Bethlem's Physician-Superintendent was offered board and £950 per annum; at Manchester Hospital the salary was £2,500 including board, and the same amount was paid at Morningside Hospital, Edinburgh.[43] In response, the Governors raised the salary at regular intervals, but even by the 1940s the Physician-Superintendent was still paid below what Morningside offered in 1903. Neither was the salary in proportion to the considerable administrative duties the Physician-Superintendent was expected to undertake, as noted in Chapter 31. The regulations ensured that the Physician-Superintendent had little chance to intervene directly in the patients' treatment. After 1935 no mention was made of his having to classify all admissions nor was he expected to offer advice to patients on their discharge. He was, however, expected to discipline the staff, attend all post-mortems and supervise research.[44] Appointed internally from the senior assistant physicians and with most having trained under former Physician-Superintendents, Bethlem had a closed medical hierarchy. Connections between the Physician-Superintendents remained close. Hyslop and Stoddart had worked with Percy Smith and Maurice Craig; Porter-Phillips had held posts under his predecessors. All played a role in the MPA and sat on its committees. Bethlem may have avoided publicity, but its Physician-Superintendents, if not active in research, were active in the psychiatric profession and tempered their ideas with the realities of the Hospital and institutional inertia.

Hyslop bridged the nineteenth and twentieth centuries, holding the post of Physician-Superintendent from 1888 to 1911. He was closely associated with Bethlem, but under him little changed in the medical management. He continued the practices of his predecessors and the traditions established by William Charles Hood (see Chapter 26). A man of cool judgment and seductive rhetoric with 'untiring energy', Hyslop wanted to attract paying and voluntary patients, improving the conditions in the wards.

Hyslop had other interests. Keen to follow George Savage and Percy Smith before him, he was conscious that he needed to establish his own private practice before he could resign.[45] In 1903 he persuaded the Governors to reverse a 1888 ruling that prevented any doctor employed at Bethlem from undertaking private practice. For the remaining eight years before he resigned he conscientiously built up his private practice in London, much to the Governors' annoyance.[46] An accomplished athlete, musician, prolific writer, and painter who exhibited at the Royal Academy, he 'achieved outstanding merit in everything he touched'.[47] With so many concerns and a growing private practice that included Virginia Woolf, it is surprising that Hyslop found time to attend Bethlem. Like Savage before him, he was interested in degeneracy and eugenics. He believed that the English race was the highest point on the evolutionary scale, but worried that alcohol, trade unions, education, and female suffrage were damaging the race.[48] Post-impressionism, Cubism and Futurism were particular subjects of scorn. Unable to appreciate such art, Hyslop viewed it as insane and did not rest in publicizing his views to a wider audience.[49] He extended his concern to the mentally ill, where he adopted a sociological perspective that avoided clinical preoccupations or medical factors. For him patients were failed citizens who needed to be re-educated.[50] These ideas were not the exclusive preserve of the radical right, but were part of a more pervasive view shared by socialists and progressive liberals before the First World War.[51] After leaving Bethlem, he established a successful private practice, but started to suffer from anxiety after 1918 and a nervous tic haunted him until he died.

William Stoddart, who held the post from 1911 to 1914, was a more unlikely figure to become Physician-Superintendent. A pupil of Hyslop, he was a vast, portly figure, conducting his 'ward rounds in morning coat and top hat'. Apparently lazy, affable and always well dressed, he enjoyed good food, good wine and idle days on the river.[52] Despite his casual manner little escaped his lively eyes. The butt of many jokes, Stoddart's appearance did not reflect the important role he played in the development of psychotherapy in Britain. In his influential *The Mind and its Disorders* he introduced psychodynamic and Freudian ideas to his earlier Kraepelinian views and encouraged others to follow.[53] At Bethlem he encouraged staff to use psychotherapy, making it one of the first mental hospitals to implement a modified version of Freud's ideas. However, in other respects the therapeutic regime he encouraged differed little from that of his predecessors. He did press the Governors to insist that all nurses should sit the MPA's mental nursing examination, but other than this he encouraged few changes.

Porter-Phillips's appointment in 1914 marked a break with the past. Although he had trained under Hyslop and worked with Stoddart, he had a more modern approach and was passionately interested in the work undertaken at Bethlem. Porter-Phillips was a keen publicist for the Hospital and sought to have the slogan 'Bethlem means *curable*' adopted, sensitive as he was to the Hospital's reputation and popular image. He presided over a period of greater change, not only in psychiatry but also in the Hospital where he was responsible for many of the advances.

Born John Porter Phillips he altered his surname to Porter-Phillips late in life. Having attended University College Hospital and Guy's, he spent his entire working career at Bethlem, being first appointed as a house physician in 1907. He did not confine his attention solely to the Hospital. While Physician-Superintendent he had a small private practice and held lecturing posts at the London School of Medicine for Women and St Bartholomew's.[54] Responsible for the creation of Bethlem's medical school, he was keen to encourage research into the psychology and pathology of mental illness, while his enthusiasm for focal sepsis persuaded others to concentrate on a biological approach.[55] However, where he wanted to use the Hospital to improve the scientific basis of psychiatry, the research produced at Bethlem was disappointing. He finally retired in 1944 after thirty years, daunted by the prospect of rebuilding Monks Orchard after it had been hit by three German V-1 rockets in July and August. The Governors applauded his 'unanswering loyalty'.[56] Porter-Phillips was intensely loyal. He promoted Bethlem in all quarters and formed the 'Dog & Duck Club' (see Plate 32.1) in 1924 to encourage contact between former medical staff. However, he

Plate 32.1 Menu for the inaugural dinner of the Dog and Duck Club, 1924, a dining club for past and present Bethlem medical staff, showing John Porter-Phillips, Physician to Bethlem (1914–44). Reproduced by permission of the Bethlem Royal Hospital Archives and Museum.

was rarely unanswering.[57] Known as 'P.P.' he was a 'handsome man with a charming manner and a sympathetic attitude which made him popular with his patients'. Dignified with a 'calm distinguished bearing', he gave 'confidence to worried people', but could also prove stubborn and opinionated.[58] Staff whom he did not like saw him as a tyrant.[59] In fostering the creation of the outpatient department and the introduction of occupational therapy he was willing to bully the Governors into adopting his ideas. Of all his achievements he shared the Treasurer's pride in the Monks Orchard Hospital, having been intimately connected with its planning. Porter-Phillips's long period of office provoked frustration among the junior doctors concerned about their prospects of promotion. The assistant physicians felt that it placed them in a 'subordinate position'.[60] It was a common complaint in mental hospitals and in 1937 the Board of Control expressed concern that doctors remained in some posts too long, limiting the chances of promotion of able younger men.[61] A certain relief was felt when he retired. The Governors recognized his long service by adding him to their number and he continued to attend committee meetings until his death in 1946.

Hamilton joined the senior staff in 1934 from Holloway Sanatorium to replace the existing Assistant Physician after an argument over the amount of work doctors were expected to do.[62] He brought with him an enthusiasm for physical treatment and encouraged the introduction of cardiazol, electroconvulsive therapy and leucotomy. Seen as a generous man with a deep concern for people, he was always willing to offer help in a professional or personal capacity.[63] Truculent at times, Hamilton had a progressive attitude. He played a leading role in the decision to merge with the Maudsley, although he was sent to America at Lewis's suggestion when most of the planning was undertaken. He remained at Bethlem after 1948, and many felt he continued the Hospital's old style approach to patients until he retired. Nurses at Monks Orchard continued to treat him as the Physician-Superintendent, but Hamilton did not attempt to exploit this attitude. Throughout his career he remained interested in clinical psychiatry and did not contribute a large part to the research undertaken at the Institute of Psychiatry. In 1967 he was taken seriously ill while on holiday in Europe and was admitted to a Swiss hospital before being transferred to London. As a mark of respect for his long service he was made Emeritus Physician and a tree was planted in the grounds when he died in the same year.[64]

DOCTORS AND THE NHS

Hamilton's death marked a break with Bethlem's pre-1948 attitude, although the real change had come in 1948. Other mental hospitals took much of their pre-NHS character with them into the new service, but with the post of Physician-Superintendent replaced by a House Governor and Bethlem's medical staff swamped by the Maudsley's, change came earlier to the Hospital. The removal of the post ensured that a clinician no longer ran the Hospital and few doctors in the Joint Hospital were now permanently based at Monks Orchard. The NHS reduced the prestige, power and financial advantage of the medical staff, although it simultaneously provided an opportunity for them to advance their self-interests.[65] Within the new system, mental hospitals were frequently viewed as a 'Cinderella' service. Bethlem was in a different position, benefiting from its renewed teaching status. Those working at Monks Orchard gained financially, with salaries rising immediately. With the merger, the Hospital grew from an institution with three permanent doctors to become part of the Hospital with a professor of psychiatry, an assistant clinical director, five full-time and nine part-time consultants, six full-time and five part-time junior physicians, fifteen registrars and nine house physicians.[66] By 1949 this had increased to include twenty-two senior and twenty-two junior registrars.[67] As new units were developed, more consultants were created. The Joint Hospital's expansion was constrained, however, by the national 'chronic personnel shortage', with the Mental Health Standing Advisory Committee pointing to a 20 per cent shortage of hospital doctors by 1954. The number of registrars was limited and there was considerable wastage.[68] With a dearth of training facilities, the Joint Hospital did not suffer as severely as other hospitals. The Institute of Psychiatry effectively ensured a ready supply of psychiatrists at various stages of training to staff the hospitals. Restraints on the number of registrar posts, however, promoted friction with the Ministry of Health. Problems were found in attracting doctors to work at Monks Orchard, despite the presence of leading regional and national units. Communications between the two sites were poor and Bethlem was felt to be a long way from the Institute of Psychiatry. Many doctors at the Maudsley regarded being sent to Monks Orchard as being placed in the 'B' stream and an indication that Lewis was losing interest in a registrar. Lewis himself rarely visited Bethlem and an apocryphal story has it that on one occasion when he did his ulcer reacted badly, making him severely ill and discouraging him from returning. Denis Hill, Lewis's successor, was more interested in Monks Orchard. He pressed for the extension of academic facilities at Bethlem and in 1967 twelve beds from the professorial unit were transferred from the Maudsley to the Hospital.[69] There was hostility to the move, with some consultants worried about its effect on the Institute given their unwillingness to travel to Monks Orchard. Discussions proved protracted. One idea that emerged was the need for an academic centre at Bethlem. Planning proved fraught over how the centre should work and who should use it. Little progress was made, although a small library was provided.[70] The Governors presented their own solution, carrying out a programme of improvements to Bethlem's accommodation and social amenities from 1971 onwards while wards were renovated. It was believed that this was necessary before further clinical units could be established there. The aim was to stop the falling morale and sense of isolation at Bethlem, and the first measure introduced was the provision of a better bus service.[71]

Working practices immediately changed with the merger. Doctors were no longer expected to leave after lunch and were encouraged to fill their spare time with research or further study. Cooperation with the nurses was actively encouraged.[72] This, as the Hospital Advisory Service made clear in 1973, was not always the case and nurses complained about the lack of cooperation. Lewis's practice of admission and discharge conferences was introduced throughout the Hospital, along with a journal club. No attempt was made to remove the medical hierarchy. Junior doctors were constantly reminded that it was the consultants who had ultimate responsibility, but within reason they were encouraged to try new ideas. There was, however, a disease of 'note taking', which at times concealed a therapeutic nihilism that the lack of an overriding ethos encouraged. The environment was more relaxed at Bethlem than the Maudsley. Tea was an important part of night rounds and procedures were routinized, with doctors not always easy to find. A sense of community existed, encouraged by the presence of staff houses in Monks Orchard Road. Here doctors felt separated from the Joint Hospital but part of a wider community. They made full use of the farm and the grounds were seen as almost idyllic. Many recalled that Bethlem was a happier place to work than the Maudsley.

Some changes caused by the merger quickly provoked dissatisfaction. The introduction of a pay slip system in 1951 by the autocratic House Governor Kenneth Johnson to provide audit controls for the Ministry of Health, aroused opposition. At first it was suggested that doctors should clock in and out, but after a passionate attack by Henry Ray, a consultant, an alternative was suggested where every doctor had to make a monthly declaration of their hours. Registrars felt distrusted. Permanent staff were worried by the implication that some lacked a 'sense of duty and responsibility'. They disliked the fact that it encouraged an attitude of 'so many hours for so much pay'.[73] The entire issue became one of responsibility and professional integrity. Senior staff feared that the system would damage morale.[74] The Medical Committee discussed the issue in detail, but eventually admitted that the Governors had a right to be aware of the staffing situation. The doctors gave way, but continued to protest by refusing to fill in the form.[75] Matters reached a head in 1960 when a new neurosurgical house surgeon, after a long ward duty, reacted strongly when asked if he had carried out his duties. Feelings were already running high over the October reappointments. The junior staff demanded change. On investigation, the Governors found that the system had not worked well. Some registrars 'had omitted to return any pay slips over periods of several years, apparently without anyone noticing'.[76] It was decided after much discussion to stop the practice and relations between doctors and the Governors subsequently improved.

To manage the medical administration, a Medical Committee was created in 1948 which every consultant was entitled to attend. Junior doctors were excluded. Initially the Medical Committee had an advisory role, but with the consultants represented on every committee and Lewis playing a leading role in the shaping of the Joint Hospital and Institute of Psychiatry, medical influence was assured. Concern was expressed in 1949 that with the Committee meeting for over two hours and involving thirty consultants up to 'sixty doctor-hours' were being wasted. In response Charles Blacker, who was permanently concerned about the time spent on administration, called for more subcommittees to limit the business discussed by the Medical Committee.[77] His arguments were accepted, leading ironically to a proliferation of subcommittees, increasing the size of the administration. Johnson found this extension of medical representation alarming and believed that part of his job was to resist demands.[78] This changed under his successor Leslie (or Nicki) Paine who was popular with the doctors. He believed that their decisions should be backed if they were reasonable and money available. Paine's support coincided with pressure from the Ministry of Health from the late-1960s to extend the medical element in administration. Efforts to establish joint staff consultative committees on the lines recommended by the Whitley Council, however, were unsuccessful. Instead, informal meetings, with the heads of departments accompanied by one member of their staff, were established on an experimental basis at Bethlem in 1965.[79] The junior medical staff were not satisfied. From the mid-1960s they pressed for greater representation, aware that the Joint Hospital was dominated by Governors and consultants in a structure where registrars were canvassed only every four months. Communications did improve and in 1969 their pressure began to produce results. At the insistence of Denis Hill and J. C. McLean, the junior medical staff were given greater influence. They believed that junior doctors should have more say in how the Hospital was managed. Partly this was a reaction to the regime Lewis had established. Hill and McLean's suggestions meant that the Medical Committee had to be increased by four members, the Hospital Committee by one coopted member, with the junior staff able to nominate one member to the Board.[80] At a different level, cocktail parties were held four times a year from 1974 onwards to allow the Governors to meet the staff on a regular basis.[81] After these changes, and under Paine, it was felt that the Joint Hospital had a democratic management structure, at least for the medical staff.

In response to the 1967 Cogwheel reports, so named because of the design on the covers, the Ministry of Health encouraged the formation of medical executive committees. The idea was to strengthen the medical administration and promote a more rational use of beds, closer cooperation and better use of resources. It was anticipated that hospital administrators would delegate more decisions to their doctors. Progress was slow. Where the Joint Hospital established its Medical Executive Committee (MEC) in 1972, only half the hospitals in England and Wales had one by 1973.[82] At the Joint Hospital the aim of the Cogwheel reports had already been partly fulfilled through the existing Medical Committee. The reports did, however, provide an opportunity to reorganize the medical administration. Paine had first suggested the need for change, and the medical staff recognized in 1971 that an intolerable situation had arisen where expansion meant that meetings could be attended by up to seventy doctors. Under these conditions the medical administration had become 'slow, time consuming and inefficient'. At one point, professional administrators were suggested.[83] This was rejected in favour of a management structure where the Medical Committee would provide the broad representation, while a smaller MEC consisting of the House Governor, Chief Nursing Officer, and representatives from the junior staff, would form an executive body.[84] Honorary consultants were excluded, a matter that became the subject of recurring debate. Under these arrangements most of the decision-making passed to the MEC, although it was never an exclusive body. Doctors were welcome to attend if an issue was discussed that affected them. After three years the new structure was found to be 'a considerable improvement on the previous system'.[85] Administration was not simplified however. Further committees were appointed to deal with different aspects of the Joint Hospital's medical management. For example, the Bed Allocation Working Party was set up in 1971 to plan ward movements and the opening of new units. It decided who would have what beds where, aiming to raise the occupancy rate and limit the number of consultants on the wards. This was a response to the Hospital Advisory Service report. It found that doctors tended to dominate 'decisions regarding patient care', causing delays in treatment and a poor use of nurses.[86]

The situation changed in the 1980s. The creation of the SHA in 1982 saw a reduction in medical representation. Staff felt increasingly 'patronised and ignored' by a chairman who saw the patients as 'psychiatric layabouts'.[87] A rhetoric of cooperation came to replace the cooperation that had existed in reality, with many doctors blaming the management for NHS cuts. The morale built up under Paine dissipated and tension developed, mostly because of outside pressure and changes in the NHS.

NURSING THE MENTALLY ILL: 1901–82

Doctors, both before and after 1948, did not deal with the patients on a daily basis. They visited the wards and dealt with problems when they emerged, but they were not the backbone of the institution. According to Samuel Beckett's fictional account of 1930s Bethlem in *Murphy*, patients saw 'so much of the nurses and so little of the doctors, it was natural that they should regard the former as their persecutors and the latter as their saviour'.[88] Several patients agreed: one accusing the Governors and medical staff in 1924 of having 'nothing like full knowledge of what actually takes place in a patient's treatment'.[89] This was true of many mental hospitals before 1948. Nurses formed the largest group working in the mental healthcare sector.[90] Where general nursing was traditionally a largely female preserve, mental nursing was mixed with male staff valued for their strength to deal with difficult patients and protect other staff. They acted as gatekeepers between patients and doctors, a position that gave them considerable influence over the patients' lives. Doctors working in large mental hospitals frequently had to follow their advice. At Bethlem, nurses had a lower social status than the patients and, with the Governors concerned to promote patient comfort, they tried to ensure that nurses showed the 'utmost tenderness'. Beckett pointed to further characteristics. In his view they also had to show no initiative in a job where they were not paid to 'take an interest in the patients, but to fetch for them, carry for them and clean up after them'.[91] Nurses were held responsible for every escape, accident or suicide and were seen as an important part of Bethlem's moral fabric.[92] Discharge was immediate, no matter how many years of good service, when they were seen to fail in these duties.

One nurse remembers that nepotism remained an important part of the selection procedure in pre-NHS Bethlem. Nurses joined through the 'good offices of a Governor' and unlike other mental hospitals not 'because one played cricket, football or a musical instrument'.[93] Beckett satirized the situation when he mentioned the seven male relations of Thomas Clinch filling various posts.[94] Although an exaggeration, some nurses continued the Monros' tradition of having several family members working in the Hospital. The Cantle family proved particularly prominent: both Edward and Alfred Cantle worked at Bethlem, as did Edward's daughter and son. Family connections remained important at another level. When Miss Kough resigned as Matron in 1905 for a surprise wedding, the new appointee was already familiar with the Hospital as her brother had been a house physician and her family made regular visits to Bethlem.[95] This was not believed to have affected the quality of the nursing. In 1919 the Matron sternly informed the Governors that 'my staff has been chosen with the greatest care, and I feel sure you will find them efficient, capable, educated and well trained'.[96] At most hospitals the selection process depended on the 'supposed and expected ability of a matron to recognise on sight a potentially "good nurse"'.[97] Not all Bethlem's nurses matched these requirements. For example, when male nurse Essex was placed in charge of a ward he suffered a nervous breakdown, but was allowed to continue work because he was 'a zealous, conscientious and efficient worker in a junior position'.[98] Some qualities were valued more than others.

Generally nurses arrived with some experience, either of a mental or general hospital. Mental nursing, however, was rarely a first career choice. Informal training was provided on the wards by more experienced staff or newly qualified doctors in an effort to raise the standard of work. Stoddart was keen to encourage training. The MPA had met at Bethlem in 1885 to discuss certificated training for mental nurses, but it was not until 1913 that the Governors decided that all nurses should be prepared for the MPA examination.[99] Bethlem was slow to follow other mental hospitals. In 1899, 100 asylums were participating in the MPA's training scheme, but even when training was introduced at Bethlem the Governors remained reluctant to train male staff for fear that they would prove temporary.[100] Each nurse was lent a copy of the MPA's *Handbook for Nurses* and required to sit the preliminary examination in the first year before completing the three-year course. A focus on the actual work of the Hospital was provided only in the third year, although student nurses were used as cheap labour in the wards.[101] Additional training was given. Between 1913 and 1922 each probationary nurse was required to sit the St John's Ambulance Brigade's first aid certificate after six months to qualify for the permanent staff.[102] To encourage nurses to take these examinations and continue working in the Hospital, a bonus scheme was introduced in 1919. On passing the exam, each nurse was given a medal (see Plate 32.2), a two-shilling pay rise and a further two shillings after five years. This did not solve the problem, and a picture emerges of a high turnover of women beginning and leaving training.[103] As a result, the Governors decided to switch to the General Nursing Council's (GNC) examination in 1931. The GNC had been formed in 1920 and tried to cooperate with the MPA, insisting in 1923 on a common preliminary examination.[104] This eased the task of introducing the new examination. Bethlem had been recognized as an approved training hospital under the 1919 Nurses Registration Act and a sister tutor was appointed to help nurses study, given the Hospital's poor success rate. Although the Governors continued to recognize the MPA's qualification, they no longer promoted the course, believing that the GNC syllabus provided better training and higher status. In recognition, a five-guinea bonus was awarded to those who passed and agreed to work for a further two years.[105] Pressure from the nurses and continuing difficulties with finding suitable candidates persuaded the Governors to end the financial distinction between the two examinations in 1941.[106] A permanent shortage of nurses, however, ensured that it was not always possible to release them for training. The Governors believed that their first duty was always to the patients.

In 1900 Bethlem had a nursing staff of thirty male and thirty-five female nurses; this rose to forty-one and fifty-two respectively by 1933, dropping only during the Second World War.[107] Like all mental hospitals, Bethlem had a high turnover of staff, partly because of the lack of knowledge and motivation, poor conditions and low status. Between 1915 and 1940 Bethlem employed 593 nurses, with 75 per cent working for less than two years. After 1930 a higher percentage stayed for longer,

Plate 32.2 Medal awarded to Bethlem nurses on passing the examination of the Royal Medico-Psychological Association, presented to Winifred Gladys Caesar in 1931. Reproduced by permission of the Bethlem Royal Hospital Archives and Museum.

reflecting improved conditions at Monks Orchard and higher unemployment.[108] Junior or untrained staff were frequently left in charge of the wards, creating anxiety for the medical staff. The most promising nurses left to undertaken general training. Others left to get married or because they feared they would 'become mental' if they stayed.[109] During the First and Second World Wars resignations increased. Female nurses were uneasy about being in London; many male staff left to join the Royal Army Medical Corps while others resigned given the prospect of higher wartime wages elsewhere. Those who remained tended to do so for long periods. Sister Jackson was extraordinary even by the standards of those who stayed at Bethlem: on her retirement in 1909 she had worked at the Hospital for thirty-nine years without a day absent.[110] Nurses like Jackson were the exception. Where women would quickly pass through the institution, men tended to stay longer despite the low wages. They were attracted by the security of hospital employment and sports facilities. The

Matron was keen to dismiss nurses whom she considered unsuitable. A good nurse was expected to know his/her own mind, have self-control, a good knowledge of physical and mental hygiene, and a good '*character*'. Those who lacked these qualities or struck patients in frustration were immediately suspended while their case was investigated. The frequency of reported incidents against patients, however, was low. When an assault was reported, it was usually felt that the patient was 'delusional', with the Governors arguing that their staff were 'qualified and trained to perform their duties in a proper and efficient manner'.[111] Where nurses were blamed, it was felt that they were unsuitable for an occupation where they were expected to set an example for the patients.[112] No difference was made for gender. This allowed an individualistic assessment of the problem of wastage and removed the blame from the institution.

Staffing levels created a constant concern. All mental hospitals complained about a shortage of nurses and the situation became the 'most disturbing and intractable problem in the Mental Health Service'.[113] During the First World War many left to join the services. Nationally in 1915, 42 per cent of asylum staff had volunteered and at Bethlem the number of nurses was reduced by a third.[114] To keep those who remained, hours were shortened and leave extended. The situation improved in the interwar period, but the Treasurer could still anxiously report in 1924 that 'the problem of recruiting suitable women for our Nursing Staff is still unresolved'. It was believed that the situation was so acute on the female site that it was 'seriously limiting the work of the Hospital'.[115] This was a problem facing many hospitals. Mental hospitals did, however, benefit from the 1930s depression. With high levels of unemployment, work in a mental hospital became attractive for the security it offered. The difficulties of the First World War were repeated in the Second. In 1942 the shortage of staff ensured that Gresham Two had to be closed. To overcome the situation, forty part-time nurses were appointed in 1947. They worked 30 per cent fewer hours than the full-time staff and it was felt that 'their employment has made a very considerable difference to the biggest hospital problem of the present time'.[116] The situation did not change after 1948. In 1954 it was estimated that mental hospitals were understaffed by 20 per cent on the male and 35 per cent on the female side. Nationally there was a growth of untrained nurses, and recruitment campaigns began in earnest. A call was made for mental hospitals to be 'jolted out of their rut', a comment that was not appreciated at the Joint Hospital. Recruitment campaigns had little success in an occupation facing low wages and poor conditions.[117] At the Joint Hospital these national problems were superimposed on the local situation. Courses were held to attract general nurses and financial incentives were offered. Agency nurses were used to overcome difficulties, creating friction with the nursing unions and provoking strikes. Accommodation and facilities were seen as providing barriers to recruitment, but even after considerable effort and extensive publicity, problems remained. Shortages were compounded by 'shorter hours, [staff training] days, and other administrative duties', which combined added 'further pressure on ward staff'.[118] The constant expansion of the Joint Hospital complicated the situation. As late as 1986 Bethlem had an 18 per cent vacancy rate and, with an annual turnover of 53 per cent, many nurses called for improvements in in-service training, support, conditions and career prospects.[119] To encourage the retention of staff more effort was focused on job-sharing, part-time work and the provision of crèches. Given the national situation and the continued low status of mental nursing the SHA found it could do little to improve the situation.[120]

The shortage of staff before 1948 might be explained by pay and working conditions. Mental nursing was not an attractive occupation. In 1900, nurses at Bethlem were paid £22 for the first year, after which their salary rose by £1 a year until it reached a maximum of £30.[121] A uniform, board and lodging were provided and for married staff a grant was given in lieu of accommodation.[122] At Lancaster County Asylum the lowest paid nurses earned £28 in 1887.[123] Even when payments in kind are considered, mental nurses were poorly paid. For example, an agricultural worker in the 1870s would earn approximately £37 a year, although mental nurses earned more than domestic servants.[124] The situation did gradually improve and Bethlem raised its wages to keep in line with other institutions. A survey undertaken in 1937 by the Mental Hospital Association showed that the average minimum wage for a male nurse in London was £91.[125] Nurses at Bethlem earned £2 more per year than their counterparts in the LCC and compared favourably with those working in other registered hospitals.[126] It was felt 'necessary to offer financial inducements to retain the services of [those staff] who are in a position to secure higher rates of pay in the exercise of their profession elsewhere'.[127] This translated into regular pay reviews. By the eve of the Second World War, concern about the level of pay saw the Governors taking firm action. Salaries were raised throughout the Hospital. Nurses now earned between £104 and £143 a year, staff nurses £148, and sisters £158.[128] The Governors also felt that it was their patriotic duty to make up the service pay to that offered at Bethlem of any member of staff who enlisted.[129] Mental hospitals started making cost-of-living increases to keep staff, and to match the LCC's three shilling per week increase Bethlem was forced to raise its salaries in 1940.[130] The Governors were anxious to match their pay against that found in other mental hospitals to prevent a rise in resignations under difficult wartime conditions where shortages made petty pilfering common. After 1948 the Governors lost their discretion over pay when they entered the NHS.

When the Duke of Connaught visited Bethlem in 1924 he was impressed that 'everything is done to make the life of the nurses congenial'.[131] Nurses had different experiences and many contemporaries viewed mental nursing as 'worse and more degrading than the lowest menial service'.[132] Work was often routine and unrewarding. One nurse at Bethlem took to verse to express her feelings:

> Let us then grin and bear it.
> Grumbling only makes things worse.
> Let us hope in the next world
> Nobody will want a nurse.[133]

All appointments were initially for six months; hours were long and staff were encouraged to use surnames, and the chances of promotion were remote. Here Bethlem shared a common mental hospital culture despite the support Robert Armstrong Jones, a Governor, gave to shorter hours and less monotony in his *Text Book of Mental and Sick Nursing*.[134] In the 1920s nurses were expected to work a 66-hour week, which included six hours for meals. During the Second World War a shortage of staff saw this rise to ninety-six per week and night nurses were persuaded to forgo their 'occasional evenings off'.[135] The day started at six when a sister would walk around ringing a bell to wake the nurses for work at seven. Work finished at eight, with every nurse expected to be in bed by eleven, although at Monks Orchard nurses used to get round this by leaving windows open.[136] For the night staff work started at 7.50 p.m., and until they finished at seven in the morning they were expected to 'perform their duties with the least possible noise'.[137] In industry legislation in the 1870s had limited the working day for women to eight hours. The Governors were sympathetic to the National Asylum Workers' Union but did not attempt to heed its calls for shorter hours, and one of the main reasons nurses gave for resigning was that their hours were too long.[138]

Under the control of the charge nurses and Matron, who were the main authorities in the wards, nurses were expected to care for the patients and do most of the cleaning, preferably by ten each morning.[139] New nurses did most of the menial work. However, they were not expected to serve the institution alone. Their prime task was to provide for the patients' comfort and ensure that no harm came to them. Here Bethlem differed from other mental hospitals, partly because of the type of patient admitted.[140] The families of paying patients expected certain standards, while voluntary boarders could leave the Hospital after giving seventy-two hours' notice. To ensure that all rooms were visited half-hourly, a clocking-in system was introduced in 1930. Clocks were situated every three rooms and each time the nurse clocked in it was registered in the Matron's office.[141] To relieve the nurses of some of their domestic duties, four cleaners were appointed in 1913. Their duties extended to the nurses' accommodation, but not to dusting unless a small bribe was offered. This was seen as a means to allow nurses to spend more time with the patients.[142] Ward duties were split: male nurses tended the male patients; female nurses the women. Female staff were never allowed to walk or talk with their male counterparts and it was a common sight at Monks Orchard in the 1930s to see 'males one side of the road and the females the opposite side'.[143] The Board of Control supported women nursing male patients, but the Governors stubbornly resisted pressure.[144] The situation changed only in the 1960s under the far-sighted nursing superintendent, Eileen Skellern. On each side the administration was duplicated, with the Matron and a senior male nurse in charge. Both had to ensure that the rules were enforced and staff properly trained. They supervised meals, admissions, distribution of medicine and the patients' time in the Hospital.[145] Discipline remained strict, a feature praised in the MPA's *Handbook for Attendants for the Insane*. One nurse was dismissed in 1923 for keeping 'her room in a disgraceful condition in spite of scolding and warning'.[146] Staff were not fined, as in the LCC asylums, for being late, but dismissed. The same penalty resulted from losing one of the many keys. Attendance at Chapel was compulsory and nurses were expected to inform on each other over any breach of conduct.[147]

Conditions of service and low pay were partly relieved by the Governors' paternalism. This extended to all staff but mainly focused on the nurses. Where staff could be dismissed on any number of disciplinary grounds, the Governors did try to look after those who remained. By the 1940s Bethlem offered similar benefits to those secured under the 1937 National Health Insurance Acts and 1931 Workmen's Compensation Act. Sick leave was granted for a maximum of three months in any year. Cases were dealt with individually, although more stringent investigations were introduced in 1935.[148] An additional grant was given to those who had to resign due to illness. The Hospital's registered status excluded it from the 1909 Asylum Workers Superannuation Act, but in 1919 the Governors, inspired by discussions within the British Hospital Association, introduced individually assessed pensions. Those working in mental hospitals could retire with a pension at 55 and it was seen as the Governors' moral duty to provide similar cover.[149] They were praised for their generosity, although there was some suggestion that nurses were uneasy about relying on individual assessment.[150] The creation of the Federated Superannuation Scheme in 1928 by the Royal National Pension Fund for Nurses inspired the Governors to consider creating a similar arrangement among the registered hospitals. Opposition discouraged them. They abandoned the idea in favour of improving their own pension arrangements.[151] Borrowing from the Federated Scheme and the 1909 Asylum Officers Superannuation Act, and using the information collected from the registered hospitals, the secretary put forward new proposals. He praised the Governors for their previous generosity, but admitted that with pensions now seen as a 'right' a scheme where the Governors assessed each case was unsuitable. Under new proposals in 1930, the retirement age was set at 65, although staff would be considered for pensions if over 55 (50 for women) or if they had problems discharging their duty.[152] Pensions would not, however, be granted to those dismissed or who worked in the Hospital for less than ten years. The Governors hoped that this would 'give the staff concerned an assurance as to their future'.[153] Pensions, however, still rested on the Governors' discretion and complaints were occasionally received about the level of support.

With the creation of the NHS, Bethlem's pension scheme became redundant, but a sense of paternalism continued. Here Bethlem's endowments played an important part. The Governors were always keen to promote staff training. Endowment funds were used to allow medical and nursing staff to attend conferences or extend their training. This was seen as a direct benefit to the Hospital, but money was also spent for the benefit of the staff in a less calculating manner. This included cheap seaside holidays at Hastings in the 1950s, retirement gifts, financial assistance for staff buying their own home or car, and removal expenses. National financial restrictions increasingly limited this paternalism to permanent staff, with applicants having to prove that their application for support was 'essential in the interests of the conduct of the Board's business'.[154]

Efforts were made to improve the conditions nurses lived under when Bethlem moved to Monks Orchard. The Board of Control believed that 'modern nursing demands an educated nurse and no pension scheme or other contingent advantages will make up for conditions of living which would generally be described as improper'.[155] At Southwark nurses were accommodated in the wards, a position considered unsuitable. At Monks Orchard a separate nurses' home was built, which many saw as 'our idea of heaven', despite the lack of heating. All the nurses' meals were eaten there, with the sisters having a separate dining room and maids serving them.[156] The male nurses were accommodated in a series of staff flats and houses built on Monks Orchard Road where maids cleaned and brought tea. Eight additional rooms were provided throughout the Hospital so that some nurses could be kept close by in case of emergency.[157] In the nurses' home, however, no thought had been given to the level of noise. This created serious problems for the night nurses, despite the provision of slippers for the day staff, until 1931 when after a series of complaints doors were added to separate their quarters. This was seen as a cheap alternative to carpeting.[158] Advantage was taken of the damage caused by the three German V-1 rockets that hit Bethlem in 1944 to improve conditions. A private lounge was added, additional lighting and a record player bought so that nurses could hold small dances, and the furniture was improved.[159] Heating remained a problem and nurses tended to use electrical fires that constantly fused the lights.[160] By 1975 conditions had again deteriorated to resemble a 'seaside hotel in mid-December'.[161] Nurses, however, continued to prefer the nurses' home at Bethlem to the accommodation offered in Princess Marina House, which tended to segregated nurses into small groups. To improve facilities an extensive programme of modernization was carried out, but fewer nurses chose to be accommodated at the Hospital.[162]

After 1948, further efforts were made to provide additional staff accommodation near Bethlem. This greatly encouraged the sense of community at Monks Orchard. The Governors could never provide enough accommodation and 'requests [were] received every quarter' from newly appointed staff for housing. A proposal was made in 1957 that they should spend £40,000 to build further staff flats, but this was shelved in favour of buying additional houses.[163] Each purchase was seen as 'a wise investment' as well as providing additional accommodation.[164] By 1975 the Joint Hospital owned 111 'residential units' at or near Bethlem. Long-serving staff were encouraged to move out of the Hospital to reduce the sense of institutionalism. It was found that it was the nurses who were in greatest need of accommodation, with at least thirty extra rooms needed at Bethlem to aid recruitment. A private agreement was reached with the Colebrooke Housing Association to provide fifty houses for the Hospital's use in return for land on Monks Orchard Road.[165] Rents were kept deliberately low, despite pressure from the Department of Health and Social Security (DHSS) and the auditor.

The move to Monks Orchard had other effects, encouraging the growth of staff facilities. A sports club had first been suggested by Porter-Phillips in 1931, but it was not until 1932 that he canvassed the staff.[166] Mental hospitals in the interwar period became associated with first-rate sports facilities with inter-asylum football and cricket matches generating loyalty to the institution. They provided an outlet for the frustrations generated by working in an asylum.[167] At Bethlem, sixty-eight nurses wrote to the Governors in 1932 to express their willingness 'to join a club for games and recreation'. Porter-Phillips suggested that patient and staff facilities should be split, but his ideas were seen as too grand.[168] John Worsfold, the secretary, proposed a more modest start. Aware that with limited resources following rebuilding

> it has to be borne in mind that the grounds of the Hospital cannot be at once brought to the perfect pitch that many clubs and recreation grounds now attain, but a disposition to use and enjoy what is available will provide the incentive in all concerned for improvement . . .

At one point it was suggested that the sale of tobacco and chocolate might be used to fund the venture.[169] After initial discussion, the inaugural meeting of the Bethlem

Sports Club was held in July 1932.[170] Membership initially cost five shillings and by May 1933, 102 staff had joined.[171] Nurses were encouraged to play tennis and bowls and only hockey was seen as an entirely female sport. Uniforms had to be worn at all times.[172] Cricket became central to the club's activities and matches were regularly organized between the staff and patients and with other local clubs. By 1936 Bethlem had five tennis courts, and a pavilion was donated in 1937 by the health-conscious President, Charles Wakefield. Before the outbreak of war, teams were fielded in tennis, cricket, football and bowls with each being able to look forward to a full season of fixtures. By 1943 the nurses were becoming restless and complained that they found their 'conditions of life somewhat tedious'. The Matron suggested that a social club should be formed to supplement the sporting activities. Porter-Phillips was concerned about the 'gradual and perhaps insidious expansion of freedom' this might encourage, but the Governors supported the suggestion.[173] The two clubs were combined in 1950 after the merger with the Maudsley and a club for the whole Joint Hospital was created. To support the club, the Governors reluctantly gave £150 and hoped that it would become self-supporting.[174] From the start, staff were encouraged to use the facilities at Monks Orchard. In 1957 these were extended when a gymnasium was built, and further facilities including a swimming pool were added when the Community Centre was opened in 1964 by Princess Marina, patron of the Joint Hospital. Under Paine financial support was extended as a way of improving morale. Here Bethlem consistently outstripped the Maudsley which, in 1973, 'had among the worst hospital social and recreational facilities'.[175] With more facilities and a greater sense of community, Bethlem had a higher membership and dominated committees.[176] At first, with many of the Maudsley's staff living in London, it was felt that 'party activities are not really required' and sporting activities dominated. The annual sports day, started in 1953 to mark Elizabeth II's coronation, became the highlight of the year until it was replaced by a fete in 1958.[177] A change of emphasis in the 1960s saw the club becoming less athletic and more artistic, although the bowls section continued to flourish. However, there was a 'lack of spontaneous interest in the club' and attendance fell, an occurrence blamed on the lack of facilities at the Maudsley.[178] Attempts to reverse the decline produced only temporary improvement, but the club continued to function and do well in the London Mental Hospitals Sports Association.

NURSING AT THE JOINT HOSPITAL

The creation of the Joint Hospital saw several changes. At a numerical level the number of nurses rose from 300 in 1953 to 745 in 1984.[179] Despite the increase and a move away from a small and personal atmosphere, those visiting Bethlem continued to find it a 'great pleasure to work in these beautiful and peaceful surroundings'.[180] Some anxiety was encountered among the male nurses at Monks Orchard shortly after the merger; they feared that nursing sisters would take over the running of the wards and felt discriminated against, as the Governors insisted that no-one could manage a ward unless they had a dual qualification in general and mental nursing. Few male nurses had this qualification, but Johnson dismissed their concerns.[181] In other areas tension was reduced. Nurses were consulted in decisions to a greater degree than before. The night pegging clocks, which had been used to check on staff making their rounds, were removed. Discipline remained stringent however.[182] Most of the training was transferred to the Maudsley, although student nurses continued to be based at Bethlem for short periods. All nurses were expected to attend training days from 1964 onwards to keep them abreast of the latest developments.[183] In many areas the Joint Hospital led in the development of nurses' education and therapeutic duties. A quasi-independent training school was established that engineered its own postgraduate and joint-degree courses to match the changing demands placed on psychiatric nursing.[184] The GNC encouraged experimentation but was always cautious of the courses proposed by the Joint Hospital and often obstructionist, criticizing the Governors for not providing training in the care of long-stay cases.

In the wards, hours were gradually reduced, but nurses who had been at Bethlem before 1948 resented the Maudsley and complaints were frequent:

> These long long hours are still my lot,
> Any shorter shift have been quite forgot,
> Instead if being a National Health Flunky,
> I'd have been better to have been born a monkey.[185]

Nurses did not always feel appreciated in a doctor-dominated culture, despite Skellern's efforts to extend their role. They had little to do with the consultants, who were seen as a nuisance, but proved friendly to the junior doctors and added much to Bethlem's sense of community. Night nurses tended to become isolated and were blamed for problems that occurred during the day. The introduction of a shift system did improve matters. It ensured that nurses were no longer expected to work an 11-hour day. A. Oppenheim and B. Eeman, in their study of the nursing at the Joint Hospital in 1951/2, found that at Bethlem more than twice as much time was spent caring for the patients than at the Maudsley where more time was spent on domestic duties. The distribution of duties remained strictly hierarchical, with the situation aided at Bethlem by a higher level of domestic help. Nurses at Monks Orchard did spend less time in contact with the medical staff than their counterparts at the Maudsley. This reflected the Maudsley's proximity to the Institute of Psychiatry and the higher number of doctors working there.[186] A two-shift system operated at Bethlem with all grades of nurses starting at the same time. This was preferred to the Maudsley's three-shift system where nurses felt that 'one is forever rushing to get things ready for the next shift'.[187] Practices at both hospitals were standardized in 1958 when a three-shift system was also adopted at Monks Orchard.[188] By the 1980s the shift system and pressure from the Whitley Council ensured that working hours were reduced to an 8-hour day.

An important change was seen with the introduction of a non-uniform policy in the 1970s. Changes in ward management, with the introduction of an open-door policy and moves towards therapeutic communities, created new attitudes and a new type of nursing.[189] In 1971 the Nursing Committee recommended a 'no uniform' policy, except for nurses on night duty and in the Neurosurgical Unit, Emergency Clinic and Ward 7. This reflected attitudes in these wards. It was decided that the decision to wear a uniform rested with the individual.[190] Students felt patients got used to seeing staff without uniforms, believing that it was the nursing that was most important, and argued that the absence of a uniform promoted a more comfortable environment. The charge nurses agreed and felt that the 'ward atmosphere improved since not wearing uniforms'. Of the 273 nurses questioned, 60 per cent were against uniforms, though a number were worried about the expense of wearing their own clothes.[191] The Governors responded by providing £25 Marks and Spencer vouchers, although they warned that 'jeans and perhaps maxi-dresses will not be considered suitable'.[192] The adoption of the policy was seen as a daring decision and provoked considerable discussion. Many male Governors felt that 'the gentle female with her fair hand soothing the brow or taking the pulse could be far more effective in uniform'.[193] Hostility was expressed in some units but the decision was not reversed. Attention returned to the standards of dress in 1989. Freedom was allowed provided it was kept within what the SHA decided were reasonable bounds.[194]

A shortage of nurses, as noted above, created constant problems, which were increased by the imposition of manpower targets from 1983 onwards. The SHA resisted pressure from the DHSS, feeling that manpower targets impinged 'on the duty of the authority to manage the affairs of the Hospital'.[195] Resistance did not prove effective and appointments were frozen. These hit nursing levels hardest and fears increased about the possibility of 'a considerable reduction in the services provided in the joint hospital'.[196] By 1988 a series of cuts to meet external financial restrictions had reduced nursing to a 'dangerously low level'.[197] In response nurses had become more militant, expressing their grievances over conditions, where they were forced to work longer hours to cover staffing cuts, and pay. Morale remained low throughout the NHS. Industrial action by Confederation of Health Service Employees and the National Union of Public Employees over the Government's pay freeze and conditions in the mid-1970s and 1980s created difficulties for the Joint Hospital. Pay became a catalyst for action with nurses wanting more influence over admissions, especially with the number of violent cases increasing. Admissions were reduced, the attendance of day patients limited, and strain was felt in all units. With the nurses protesting largely against the use of agency nurses, several strikes were held that reduced the Hospital to a skeleton staff. Where the DHSS pressed for reductions from salaries for those staff undertaking industrial action and the GNC threatened legal proceedings for 'professional misconduct', the Board of Governors was sympathetic.[198] Junior doctors realized that the nurses had a legitimate grievance and argued for moderation. Cooperation was secured over emergency cases; an agreement was reached and agency nurses withdrawn. The Governors worked hard at maintaining good relations with the unions, although some resented their continuing involvement in management.[199]

To ease staffing problems and help the nurses in the wards, a voluntary help scheme was established in 1974 under Julia Birley, the wife of the Dean of the Institute of Psychiatry. Interest had been generated by the 1970 Aves Report, and the King Edward Hospital Fund for London had offered its support from 1972 onwards. The need for voluntary helpers in the Joint Hospital was only slowly recognized. When the post of volunteer help organizer was advertised in 1973, 200 hospitals already operated similar schemes. The aim was to fill the gaps left by staff shortages and encourage active community involvement. Volunteers were seen as complementary, not as substitutes. Nurses favoured the scheme, although some were worried about confidentiality, but unions remained uncertain.[200] Problems were encountered with recruiting suitable volunteers for the Maudsley, but these did not exist at Bethlem. By 1976 there were sixty-seven volunteers working in the Hospital, visiting lonely patients, organizing hobby groups and helping with the library.[201] Most came to Bethlem to learn about mental illness and frequently applied for nursing posts. Each year a cocktail party was organized by the Governors to thank the volunteers. The scheme owed much to Birley's enthusiasm and when she resigned as coordinator in 1981 she was replaced by two part-time coordinators, one of whom was based at Monks Orchard.[202]

Nurses did start to play a more active role in patient treatment.[203] The psycho-pharmacological revolution of the 1950s created some concern that the role of the nurse would be reduced, but developments in other areas created contrary pressures.[204] Encouraged by the ideas associated with the open-door policy, therapeutic community, and multidisciplinary teams, contact between nurses and patients at a therapeutic level increased. With the growth of community care, nurses began to move outside the Hospital and the Joint Hospital established a community psychiatric nursing programme. Nurses were rarely consulted about these changes. In the Joint Hospital dissatisfaction was expressed in the 1970s about the lack of training and the number of domestic duties nurses were still expected to perform.[205] Nurses distributed the medicines and persuaded the patients to take them. They made appointments with social workers and psychologists and ensured that patients kept them. Overall they kept 'the doctor behaving as a doctor, and the social worker as a social worker and so on', promoting continuity of care in an increasingly complex therapeutic setting.[206]

With their role expanding, a major problem nurses faced was the increased level of violence in the Joint Hospital. A change in drug use and a move away from sedation, which had kept many patients manageable before 1948, imposed a greater strain on the ward staff. New units were added to Bethlem, like the Drug Dependence Unit, Hilda Lewis House, Medium Secure Unit, and the Intensive Care Area in Fitzmary that demanded intensive nursing of difficult patients.[207] A feeling developed in the 1970s that the number of violent incidents was increasing and that 'insufficient regard is paid by some members of the medical staff to the difficulties and even dangers that can result in the wards'.[208] Investigations found that schizophrenics and those repeatedly admitted presented particular problems. In response, the Board of Governors adopted the National Association for Mental Health's guidelines. It recommended that patients should be restrained sparingly and a complaints procedure established to relieve grievances. The guidelines also advised that doctors should discuss management issues with nursing staff, with all violent patients kept under constant review.[209] The issue provoked considerable debate. Nurses felt that doctors should share the responsibility for managing violent patients and called for more communication.[210] The MEC presented a set of proposals where doctors would consult the nursing officer on duty over violent patients, monitor incidents, and promote discussions so that experiences could be learnt from.[211] In 1976 it was suggested that all incidents should be reported to the police, a practice that was increasingly used. By 1979 the MEC was aware these procedures were not always followed. The Governors recognized the adverse effects this was having on recruitment and stressed the need to create a safe environment.[212] Nurses suggested that it might become necessary to employ security guards and firmly believed that they should be closely involved in admissions so that violence might be prevented. To monitor the level of violence a 'Violent Incident Register' was established in 1976.[213] An emergency bleep system was introduced in 1979 and staff training in dealing with violence developed, with each site having its own 'crash' team to respond immediately to each incident.[214] Despite these measures, and growing cooperation between nursing and medical staff, the number of violent incidents continued to rise. By the 1980s, nurses were beginning to see violence as part of their work. Nurses were the subject of 65 per cent of assaults in 1988, 11 per cent of which required treatment. Those trained to deal with violence felt able to cope, but suggested that the measures set up to prevent violence were limited by a lack of resources and staff shortages.[215]

Just as the role, working conditions and problems facing nurses changed in the Joint Hospital, so too did their position in the Hospital's management. Whereas before 1948 the Physician-Superintendent had consulted the Matron, after the merger the Matron, renamed the Nursing Superintendent, was invited to attend committee meetings. This provided a degree of representation. It was the 1967 Salmon Report, however, which did much to reshape the structure of nursing. The Report had found that nationally nurses were inadequately represented at meetings and complained that nursing administration was frequently authoritarian. At the Joint Hospital, a Nursing Committee had been established in 1958 with representatives from the medical and nursing staff. It dealt with all matters relating to nursing from organization to recruitment. Under the Salmon Report, nursing administrators were divided into several grades to reflect their level of responsibility, with the Chief Nursing Officer primarily a management post. Once problems of finding suitable candidates for the most senior Salmon appointments had been overcome, the structure was set up at a national level. In the Joint Hospital it was believed that Salmon would promote the growth of therapeutic communities, extending the nurse's role and encouraging representation. The hope was that it would stimulate a greater definition of roles and remove some non-nursing duties.[216] Concern was expressed over the creation of a new middle-management grade and the Report's recommendations were cautiously implemented in 1972 at considerable expense.[217] In line with the Salmon Report the superintendent of nursing became the Chief Nursing Officer. Weekly meetings were introduced between the Chief Nursing Officer and senior nurses and the Nursing Committee was expanded to include three Governors. Nurses in charge of individual units were now expected to hold weekly meetings and these were encouraged at ward level, increasing in theory the level of nurse participation in management.[218] The Chief Nursing Officer was now invited to all meetings of the Medical Committee and not just those where nursing issues were raised. The Nursing Committee was, however, cautious when it came to extending representation to the student nurses who wanted to follow the lead of junior doctors.[219] According to Skellern, it created higher levels of stress. It made nurses become more dissatisfied with the conditions they worked under.[220] Changes in the Joint Hospital's administration altered these arrangements. Reorganization in 1976 made the Nursing Committee redundant. Responsibility was transferred to the Board of Governors and the Management

Team of Officers, on which the Chief Nursing Officer was represented. The Chief Nursing Officer or her deputy now became directly involved in the administration of the entire hospital.

The role of Bethlem's nurses had changed considerably during the twentieth century. They moved from ill-trained staff who were expected to care, comfort and control the patients, to highly trained staff who played an increasing role in the therapeutic regime. Nurses at Bethlem, however, experienced no golden age. Problems remained and a constant shortage of staff was experienced. Conditions, pay and hours did improve and discipline was relaxed, but grievances over these issues continued to surface. Nurses often felt undervalued and excluded. In management their voice, even after 1948, was not a major force in the administration. Over time nursing became more of an occupation than a vocation. Nurses spent less time in the Hospital and were not expected to be resident, while financial restraints reduced the Governors' paternalism. Bethlem's status, first as a semi-private registered hospital and then as part of a teaching hospital and SHA, created a situation that differed from many other mental hospitals. But though Bethlem was never an ideal hospital, it always offered conditions that were better than many others.

TO CARE FOR WHOM?

The creation of the SHA in 1982 changed the situation at Bethlem for both the medical and nursing staff. Physical changes were less significant than the changes in attitude and management structure, with many alterations being forced on the Joint Hospital by the NHS. For the patients there were no immediate changes. Where the medical staff defined the therapeutic regime and the nurses provided the backbone of the Hospital, the patients provided the reason for the institution's existence. Their presence often went unrecorded in the minutes, a situation heightened by the increased level of management in the NHS. Once more, marked differences and continuities can be seen, with the Joint Hospital marking the start of radical shifts in the type of patients admitted. Understanding the type of patient admitted to Bethlem in the twentieth century, and the treatments they were given, is a harder task than explaining the position of the medical staff and nurses; but who did Bethlem aim to provide care for? This question and the nature of treatment will be addressed in the following chapters.

NOTES

1 See M. Donnelly, *Managing the Mind* (London: Tavistock Press, 1983); J. Busfield, *Managing Madness* (London: Unwin, 1986); or the more challenging Andrew Scull, *The Most Solitary of Afflictions: Madness and Society in Britain, 1700–1900* (New Haven, Conn. and London: Yale University Press, 1993).
2 John Crammer, *Asylum History* (London: Gaskell, 1990).
3 See Eliot Freidson, *Professional Powers* (Chicago: University of Chicago Press, 1986) and *Profession of Medicine* (New York and London: Harper & Row, 1970).
4 For the continuing process of the professionalization of psychiatry in the twentieth

century see Trevor Turner, '"Not Worth Powder and Shot": The Public Profile of the Medico-Psychological Association', in German Berrios and Hugh Freeman (eds), *150 Years of British Psychiatry* (London: Gaskell, 1991), or John Howells, 'The Establishment of the Royal College of Psychiatrists', in *ibid.* 117–34.

5 The situation has been very different for general nursing and the Nightingale revolution: see Brian Abel Smith, *A History of the Nursing Profession* (London: Heinemann, 1960), who looks at the professionalization of nursing largely from a general nursing perspective.

6 See Alexander Walk, 'History of Mental Nursing', *JMS*, 107 (1961), 1–17; Mick Carpenter, 'Asylum Nursing Before 1914', in Celia Davies (ed.), *Rewriting Nursing History* (London: Croom Helm, 1980), 123–46; Peter Nolan, 'Mental Health Nursing in Great Britain', in Hugh Freeman and German Berrios (eds), *150 Years of British Psychiatry: The Aftermath* (London: Athlone, 1996), 171–92.

7 Carpenter, *op. cit.*, 123.

8 David Russell, *Scenes from Bedlam* (London: Baillière Tindall, 1996).

9 Cited in Andrew Scull, 'Focal Sepsis and Psychosis: The Career of Thomas Chivers Graves', in Hugh Freeman and German Berrios (eds), *150 Years of British Psychiatry: The Aftermath* (London: Athlone, 1996), 519.

10 *JMS*, 60 (1914), 667–9.

11 1902 Report on Consultations Etc in Hospitals for the Insane.

12 See M. J. Peterson, *The Medical Profession in Mid-Victorian London* (Berkeley: University of California Press, 1978); Anne Digby, *Making a Medical Living: Doctors and Patients in the English Market for Medicine, 1720–1911* (Cambridge: CUP, 1994).

13 General Committee, 13 March 1911. After the merger with the Maudsley, private practice was again restricted and limited to only those consultants working in the neurosurgical unit. The rationale was that this would allow doctors in other units to concentrate on teaching and research.

14 Ernest Jones, *Free Associations* (New York: Basic Books, 1959), 123.

15 1932 Rules & Orders, 45.

16 Mackenzie Papers: Minutes, 25 April 1934.

17 Court of Governors, 29 June 1931.

18 1935 House Physician Rules.

19 Physician-Superintendent's Report, 20 April 1920.

20 *Bethlem & Maudsley Gazette*, June 1959, 20.

21 *Ibid.* December 1966, 17.

22 *Charing Cross Hospital Gazette*, 62 (1964–5), 234.

23 Hugh Freeman, 'Portsmouth Mental Health Service', *The Medical Officer*, cvii (1962), 149–51.

24 See Elaine Showalter, *The Female Malady: Women, Madness, and English Culture, 1839–1980* (London: Virago, 1987), 101–44.

25 For a discussion of women's role in the psychiatric profession see Charlotte MacKenzie, 'Women and Psychiatric Professionalisation, 1780–1914', in London Feminist History Group, *Sexual Dynamics of History* (London: Pluto Press, 1985).

26 This was seen in other fields of medical practice. During the war women gained valuable experience in areas where they had been excluded, but as Leah Leneman in 'Medical Women at War, 1914–1918', *Medical History*, xxxviii (1994), 160–77, notes, 'none of this valuable experience advanced [female doctors'] career prospects' (p. 177) with a return to peacetime conditions and the demobilization of male doctors.

27 *BMJ*, 1 (1959), 1592.

28 Bethlem Subcommittee, 7 June 1922.

29 *BMJ*, 2 (1937), 656–9.

30 See Chapter 34, pp. 684–8.

31 Bethlem Subcommittee, 30 July 1947.

32 Finance & General Purposes Committee, 27 February 1950; Board of Governors, 4 February 1957.

33 Finance and General Purposes Committee, 18 March 1974.

34 Board of Governors, 1 March 1982; SHA, 11 January 1988.
35 Medical Committee Presented Papers: 19 December 1988, MCD 15/88.
36 *Ibid.* 18 November 1991, MCD 23/91.
37 Executive Group Presented Papers: 28 June 1990, Appendix B.
38 Court of Governors, 26 February 1912; General Committee, 11 November 1912.
39 Medical Committee, 16 April 1930.
40 *1924 Board of Control Annual Report*, 23.
41 *1928 Bethlem Annual Report*, 11.
42 Montagu Lomax, *Experiences of an Asylum Doctor* (London: Allen & Unwin, 1922).
43 1902 Report on Consultations etc. in Hospitals for the Insane.
44 1935 Physician-Superintendent's Rules.
45 General Correspondence: Letter from Hyslop, 21 March 1902.
46 General Committee, 9 January 1911.
47 *BMJ*, 1 (1933), 347.
48 See Stephen Trombley, *'All that Summer She was Mad: Virginia Woolf and Her Doctors* (London: Junction Books, 1981), 95–6, 209–40.
49 *Nineteenth Century*, 69 (1911), 270–81.
50 *BMJ*, 2 (1905), 941–2; T. Hyslop, *Mental Handicaps in Art* (London: Baillière, 1927).
51 Michael Freeden, 'Eugenics and Progressive Thought', *Historical Journal*, xxii (1979), 645–71.
52 Malcolm Pines, 'Development of the Psychodynamic Movement', in German Berrios and Hugh Freeman (eds), *150 Years of British Psychiatry* (London: Gaskell, 1991), 209.
53 William Stoddart, *The Mind and its Disorders* (London: Lewis, 1908).
54 *Munk's Roll*, vol. iv, 1826–1925, 582.
55 See *BMJ*, 2 (1912), 1705–6.
56 Court of Governors, 17 October 1944.
57 *Under the Dome*, Spring 1935, 3–4.
58 *Lancet*, 1 (1946), 365.
59 Mackenzie Papers: Letter from Porter-Phillips, 30 April 1934.
60 *Ibid.*: Staffing of Bethlem Hospital, 26 April 1934.
61 *1937 Board of Control Annual Report*, 4.
62 Mackenzie Papers: Letter from Worsfold to Mackenzie, 3 May 1934.
63 *BMJ*, 1 (1971), 676–6.
64 Board of Governors, 2 October 1967.
65 Charles Webster, *Problems of Health Care: Health Service Since the War* (London: HMSO, 1988), 332.
66 Joint Committee, 25 July 1947.
67 Board of Governors, 11 July 1949.
68 Webster, *op. cit.* 332–3.
69 General Purposes Subcommittee, 20 July 1967.
70 MEC Presented Papers: 5 July 1973, ECD 93/73.
71 Board of Governors Presented Papers: 5 July 1971, Appendix J/1.
72 *Notes for the Guidance of Medical Officers* (1951).
73 General Purposes Subcommittee, 13 April 1950.
74 *Ibid.* 5 June 1950.
75 Medical Committee, 5 June 1950.
76 *Bethlem & Maudsley Gazette*, March 1961, 52.
77 Medical Committee, 2 May 1949.
78 Blacker Papers: Letter from Johnson to Blacker, 8 March 1949.
79 Board of Governors, 6 December 1965.
80 *Ibid.* 6 October 1969.
81 *Ibid.* 1 July 1974.
82 Brian Watkin, *The National Health Service: The First Phase, 1948–1974 and After* (London: Allen & Unwin, 1978), 115.
83 Medical Committee, 7 October 1971.

84 General Purposes Subcommittee, 15 November 1971.
85 Medical Committee, 23 June 1975.
86 Finance & General Purposes Committee Presented Papers: 16 June 1973, Appendix E/1.
87 *Bethlem & Maudsley Gazette*, Summer 1986, 11.
88 Samuel Beckett, *Murphy* (London: Picador, 1973), 91–2.
89 General Correspondence: Letter to Worsfold, 23 December 1924.
90 See Peter Nolan, *A History of Mental Health Nursing* (London: Chapman & Hall, 1993).
91 Beckett, *op. cit.* 91–2.
92 1932 Rules & Orders, 2.
93 *Bethlem & Maudsley Gazette*, June 1959, 19.
94 Beckett, *op. cit.* 93.
95 *Under the Dome*, September 1905, 108.
96 General Correspondence: Letter to the Montagu Nursing Cooperation, 24 September 1919.
97 Christopher Maggs, 'Nurse Recruitment to Four Provincial Hospitals', in Celia Davies (ed.), *Rewriting Nursing History* (London: Croom Helm, 1980), 37.
98 General Correspondence: Letter from Porter-Phillips, 9 December 1927.
99 E. Santos and E. Stainbrook, 'A History of Psychiatric Nursing in the Nineteenth Century', *JMS*, iv (1949), 58.
100 Carpenter, *op. cit.* 32; *1913 Bethlem Annual Report*, 11–12.
101 For the growth of the MPA's examination and the development of mental nursing, see Walk, *op. cit.* 1–17.
102 Bethlem Subcommittee, 16 July 1913.
103 This was seen at other hospitals: see Maggs, *op. cit.* 32–3.
104 Court of Governors, November 1919.
105 *Ibid.* 29 June 1931.
106 *Ibid.* 24 November 1941.
107 *1901 Bethlem Annual Report*, 53; *1933 Bethlem Annual Report*, 17.
108 1915–1937 Nurses Registers.
109 1915–1921 Nurses Registers, 8.
110 *Under the Dome*, 30 September 1909, 127.
111 General Correspondence: Letter from Worsfold, 22 February 1926.
112 Carpenter, *op. cit.* 128.
113 *1945 Board of Control Annual Report*, 2.
114 Kathleen Jones, *Asylums and After* (London: Athlone Press, 1993), 124.
115 1923/4 Treasurer's Report.
116 *1947 Bethlem Annual Report*, 6.
117 Webster, *op. cit.* 334–7.
118 Nursing Committee Presented Papers: 30 April 1969, Appendix C.
119 Executive Group Presented Papers: 27 August 1987, Appendix I.
120 *Ibid.* 18 December 1986.
121 Bethlem Subcommittee, January 1901.
122 General Committee, 13 November 1922.
123 Carpenter, *op. cit.* 131.
124 *British Labour Statistics* (London: HMSO, 1971), 38.
125 Nurses' Pay Papers: Letter from the Mental Hospitals Association, 16 February 1938.
126 See Nesta Roberts, *Cheadle Royal Hospital* (Altrincham: John Sherratt & Sons, 1967), 120.
127 Bethlem Subcommittee, 2 June 1915.
128 *Ibid.* 23 March 1938.
129 It was a practice adopted by other hospitals: see C. Andrews, *The Dark Awakening* (London: Cox & Wyman, 1978), 217.
130 Nurses' Pay Papers: Letter from Hewitt, 28 November 1940.
131 *Daily Telegraph*, 6 August 1924.
132 Cited in Carpenter, *op. cit.* 134.
133 *Under the Dome*, 25 June 1919, 5.

134 Robert Armstrong Jones, *Text Book of Mental and Sick Nursing* (London: Scientific Press, 1907).
135 General Committee, 10 February 1943.
136 Vicki Hayward, 'Bethlem in the 1930s' (unpublished article, 1982), 1.
137 1932 Rules & Orders, 8.
138 For the growth of the union, see F. Adams, 'From Association to Union', *British Journal of Sociology*, xx (1969), 11–26.
139 General Correspondence: Memorandum from Hearder, 28 February 1932.
140 Nolan, 'Mental Health Nursing in Great Britain', 181.
141 Hayward, *op. cit.* 2
142 General Committee, 19 May 1913.
143 Hayward, *op. cit.* 6.
144 Walk, *op. cit.* 13.
145 1911 and 1935 Senior Male Nurse Rules; 1916 and 1935 Matron's Rules.
146 1921–1924 Nurses Registers, 34.
147 1932 Rules & Orders, 2.
148 Bethlem Subcommittee, 20 March 1935.
149 Pension Correspondence: Further Report of the Clerk on Pensions, April 1919.
150 Court of Governors, 28 April 1919.
151 Pension Correspondence: Letter from Worsfold, 1 November 1929.
152 *Ibid.*: Staff Retirement Scheme, August 1929.
153 *Ibid.*: Letter from Worsfold to Ablewhite, 20 March 1930; Letter from Faudel-Phillips, 3 March 1930.
154 Finance & General Purposes Committee, 3 May 1965.
155 *1929 Board of Control Annual Report*, 9.
156 Hayward, *op. cit.* 1.
157 Bethlem Subcommittee, 27 May 1931.
158 *Ibid.* 16 September 1931.
159 *Ibid.* 5 June 1946.
160 *Bethlem & Maudsley Gazette*, June 1954, 139.
161 House Committee Presented Papers: 26 February 1975, Appendix C.
162 Finance & General Purposes Committee Presented Papers: 14 December 1974, Appendix I.
163 Finance & General Purposes Committee, 4 July 1955 and 1 July 1957.
164 Board of Governors, 14 June 1976.
165 Finance & General Purposes Committee, 27 October 1975.
166 Sports Club Papers: Letter from Porter-Phillips, 17 July 1931; 15 January 1932.
167 Nolan, *A History of Mental Health Nursing*, 155.
168 Sports Club Papers: Letter from Porter-Phillips, 2 February 1932.
169 *Ibid.*: Letter from Worsfold to Ablewhite, 10 February 1932.
170 *Ibid.*: Letter from Worsfold to Faudel-Phillips, 1 March 1932.
171 *Ibid.*: Letter from Porter-Phillips, 6 March 1933.
172 *Orchard Leaves*, Winter 1935, 9.
173 General Correspondence: Letter from Porter-Phillips to Coke, 13 December 1943.
174 Hospital Committee, 29 November 1950.
175 *Bethlem & Maudsley Gazette*, Summer 1973, 24.
176 Annual General Meeting of the Sports and Social Club, 9 November 1953.
177 *Bethlem & Maudsley Gazette*, March 1954, 122; May 1953, 33.
178 Annual General Meeting of the Sports and Social Club, 20 October 1955.
179 *Bethlem & Maudsley Gazette*, August 1953, 19; MTO, 15 May 1984.
180 *Bethlem News-sheet*, 1973.
181 Board of Governors, 6 December 1948.
182 House Committee, 6 October 1948.
183 Nursing Committee Presented Papers: 21 January 1970, Appendix C/1. For the Joint Hospitals' leading training role, see Russell, *op. cit.* 170–4.
184 Board of Governors, 25 July 1955.

185 *Bethlem & Maudsley Gazette*, March 1957, 300.
186 A. Oppenheim and B. Eeman, *The Function and Training of Mental Nurses* (London: Chapman & Hall, 1955), 32, 49–50.
187 *Ibid.* 63.
188 Nursing Committee Presented Papers: 28 October 1958, Appendix A.
189 See Chapter 34, pp. 695–9.
190 Nursing Committee, 5 November 1973.
191 Finance & General Purposes Committee Presented Papers: 5 November 1973, Appendix B.
192 Nursing Committee, 25 July 1973.
193 Priscilla Norman, *In the Way of Understanding* (Godalming: Foxbury Press, 1982), 181.
194 Executive Group Presented Papers, 23 March 1989, Appendix E.
195 SHA, 12 September 1983.
196 MTO, 21 August 1984.
197 *Ibid.* 24 March 1988.
198 *Ibid.* 20 April 1982. For political activism at the Joint Hospital, see Russell, *op. cit.* 176–9.
199 Board of Governors, 7 October 1974.
200 House Committee Presented Papers: 12 September 1973, Appendix D/3.
201 Board of Governors Presented Papers: 6 September 1976, Appendix I.
202 MTO, 17 February 1981.
203 See Chapter 34, pp. 698–9.
204 Nolan, *A History of Mental Health Nursing*, 118.
205 Finance & General Purposes Committee Presented Papers: 16 June 1973, Appendix E/1.
206 *Bethlem & Maudsley Gazette*, Summer 1970, 29.
207 See Chapter 33.
208 MEC, 5 June 1975.
209 Nursing Committee Presented Papers: 22 January 1975, Appendix B/3.
210 Management of Violence Papers: Letter from Skellern, 4 May 1972.
211 *Care of Patients with Violent Behaviour* (1973).
212 Board of Governors, 16 January 1979.
213 MTO (Policy), 18 September 1984.
214 Working Party on Violence, 25 July 1984.
215 *Bethlem & Maudsley Gazette*, Spring 1988, 39–40.
216 Nursing Committee Presented Papers: 18 January 1967, Appendix A/1.
217 Board of Governors, 10 April 1972.
218 Nursing Committee, 25 October 1972.
219 *Ibid.* 26 January 1972.
220 Eileen Skellern Papers: 'Nurses: Second Class Citizens?' (Unpublished paper, *c.* 1970).

CHAPTER THIRTY-THREE

'IN A PRESUMABLY CURABLE CONDITION'

The character of admissions in the twentieth century

——— •◦• ———

Williams Charles Hood's mid-nineteenth-century reforms (see Chapter 26) had done much to alter the character of admissions to Bethlem. In the eighteenth century the Hospital had lost its status as England's only public asylum, and Hood increased the emphasis to the 'educated classes in a presumably curable condition'.[1] However, was the admission policy really as clear-cut as this? The formation of the Joint Hospital in 1948 changed the situation, although with statistics for Bethlem and the Maudsley combined it becomes harder to separate Bethlem's experiences. The purpose of this chapter is to attempt to determine how many patients were admitted, who they were, and what changes occurred.

ADMITTING THE MENTALLY ILL

Bethlem's admission procedure mirrored practices at other psychiatric institutions. Until 1948, patients were admitted on a daily basis by the house physicians, their decisions validated by the assistant physicians. Patients had their personal belongings recorded on admission by the Steward and afterwards their mental and physical condition was examined. They were then taken to the ward that best reflected their mental condition and the level of supervision needed. Bethlem's former medical officers and local practitioners were prominent in referring cases, but the extent of family influence is uncertain. It was the family who decided when institutional care was needed, with doctors sanctioning their decision. Those who referred patients to Bethlem did so because they were familiar with the institution. Medical authority, however, did not dominate. Their judgment was constrained by Bethlem's regulations, which remained unaltered until 1948. These stipulated that patients could not be admitted if they were 'unlikely to prove curable', showed signs of physical illness, or required permanent nursing. The emphasis was on early treatment of acute cases. Patients who had been discharged and were unable to prove continuous mental health for twelve months were excluded. All patients were to be discharged after twelve months.[2] In reality the doctors were given considerable leeway. Exceptions were made, especially over the definition of 'acute' and length of stay. 'Actively suicidal' patients were admitted, as were those suffering from General Paralysis of the

Insane (GPI), a condition that generally resulted in dementia and death. Occasionally, cases like Herbert A—, a civil servant described as 'hopeless' and 'impervious' to treatment, were admitted – but not regularly.[3] Some patients also remained for more than twelve months. The Governors were not prepared to submit to family pressure to keep patients for longer than this, unless no immediate alternative was found. Nor were they keen to discharge patients against medical advice even when they had been in the Hospital for over a year. In the 1930s, 30 per cent of patients spent between one and two years in Bethlem. According to Desmond Curran, a house physician in 1928, most of these were 'burnt-out schizophrenics'.[4] In the 1940s the number fell in response to new, more effective physical treatments with few patients staying for more than six months. Even when the regulations were ignored the Governors retained the final decision. Each Governor could recommend an applicant for admission, and frequently relatives of patients would write asking them to intercede, stressing the patient's exemplary character, deserving nature, or lack of funds. However, unable themselves to make a professional evaluation of a patient's psychiatric condition they relied on the judgment of their medical staff.

Bethlem's incurable establishment, funded from Edward Barkham's bequest of property in Lincolnshire in 1729, created further exceptions to the normal pattern. From 1866 patients deemed incurable were not admitted to the Hospital, although those found incurable after admission and where other arrangements could not be made, were maintained on the recommendation of the medical staff. It was often a fine distinction. In 1918 the position of the incurable department changed when Barkham's Lincolnshire property was sold.[5] The decision had been made because the Governors felt that the department had become increasingly anachronistic. It was argued that it was no longer necessary to admit incurables because they could be cared for in county and borough asylums, while the money spent on their maintenance denied treatment to other patients. John Worsfold, the secretary, had expressed this point clearly to John Porter-Phillips, the long-serving Physician-Superintendent, in 1922. He argued that 'any step with a view to the authorization of the retention of Incurable patients would appear to be a retrograde one'.[6] The sale of the Lincolnshire estate did not produce the immediate discharge of all incurables. It was decided that Bethlem would still provide limited care, but no incurable patient would be admitted without private funding. In 1920 the number maintained was further reduced to twenty and by 1923 this had fallen to sixteen.[7] The Governors remained sympathetic, aware of their historic obligation. Cases were individually assessed, but the number of incurables admitted started to fall. In 1930 only four male and three female incurables remained at Bethlem, the last being admitted in March 1917. None was considered bed-ridden and Porter-Phillips saw no problem in transferring them when the new buildings opened in 1930.[8] The Governors continued to feel a responsibility for their care, but after the move they were adamant that no more should be admitted. Under these conditions, the number gradually fell as patients died, or occasionally made miraculous recoveries. By 1948 Malcolm Hewitt, Worsfold's successor, could report that only three incurables remained, all of whom were in their seventies. With Bethlem planning to merge with the Maudsley, the Governors discussed the possibility of discharging these remaining patients. Although Hewitt advised that this was possible, no decision was reached.[9] A series of decisions ensured that the incurable establishment was run down, but it was the death of the few remaining incurables that finally ended Bethlem's care of such cases and not a conscious policy.

Registered hospitals provided care for only a small proportion of those admitted to psychiatric institutions. In terms of size they were unable to compete with the larger county and borough asylums, most of which had over five hundred beds. On average, registered hospitals admitted fewer than 3 per cent of the total number of patients. Bethlem was one of the largest. The Southwark hospital had 200 beds and in the 1930 building this was increased to 250. However, the Treasurer realized in 1934 that despite expansion, 230 patients 'represents almost as many cases as can be accepted'.[10] Bed capacity had an important bearing on admissions, with patients having to be turned away in 1902 because Bethlem was full.[11] Admissions fluctuated widely as illustrated in Figures 33.1 and 33.2. The number treated did, however, gradually increase: rising from 203 in 1900 to 338 in 1947. While institutional care may have been a last resort for many, Bethlem remained a relatively popular institution because of its hotel-like conditions, apparent success rate, and comparatively low charges. It was not a 'dumping ground for the sick whom nobody wanted' like many other contemporary institutions.[12] In 1911 William Stoddart, the newly appointed Physician-Superintendent, found that 'an enormous amount of the Medical Officer's time is occupied in listening to the pathetic tales of applicants'.[13] Nine years later his successor could point to the same problem: 'Bethlem proves by its numerical returns to be eminently successful and must be undoubtedly attractive to prospective patients.'[14]

Bethlem's experiences must be placed in a national context. Contemporaries

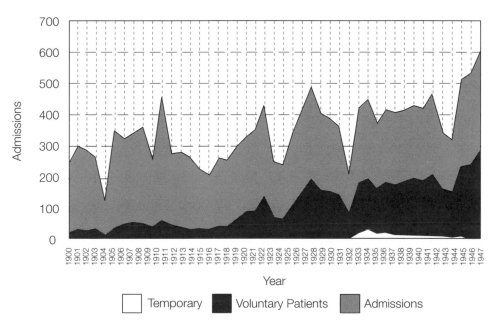

Figure 33.1 Admissions, 1900–47 *Source:* Annual Reports

pointed to a frightening increase in the incidence of mental illness, with the number of notified cases rising from 36,480 in 1859 to 140,466 in 1915.[15] During the interwar years the number continued to climb after a fall during the First World War, rising from 116,700 in 1919 to 150,300 by 1934.[16] The Board of Control struggled to alleviate anxiety, presenting a series of explanations that played down the significance of this rise. It stressed a fall in mortality and revived nineteenth-century claims that the increase reflected an accumulation of chronic cases. Andrew Scull's argument that the rapid institutional growth of the nineteenth century 'created the increased demand for its own service' does not really apply to the early twentieth century.[17] The changing nature of society made it less tolerant to its more awkward members, but such an explanation does not match Bethlem's experiences. At Bethlem, the rise reflected improvements in psychiatric practice, which made institutional care more acceptable and appear more effective. With the development of convulsion treatments in the late 1930s, doctors became more confident in their ability to treat mental illness. Discharge rates improved. This could not mitigate the stigma of treatment, but given Bethlem's preference for recoverable cases it did mean that more patients could be admitted.

Fluctuations in admissions can be explained in social and institutional terms. War had an important bearing. The First and Second World Wars saw a national fall in civilian admissions: between 1939 and 1945 the number of patients fell from 132,950 to 127,386.[18] Registered hospitals suffered from the creation of the Emergency Medical Service that served to divert psychiatric casualties and civilian cases to county and borough mental hospitals. In London, wartime evacuation further reduced the number of metropolitan patients, while restrictions on travel affected suburban Bethlem.[19] Admissions immediately recovered with the end of both wars, a fact Porter-Phillips attributed to the strain of adapting to peacetime conditions.[20] In the interwar period other factors were at work. The publication of Montagu Lomax's *Experiences of an Asylum Doctor* in 1921 damaged confidence in the asylum system. It provided a caesura in Bethlem's post-war increase in admissions. Faith was quickly restored by the medical profession's attack on Lomax and the appointment of a Royal Commission that found cause for concern but little substance to the accusations. Institutional events were superimposed on these national trends. The fall in admissions in 1904 was caused by the closure of the Hospital. After fires at Colney Hatch and in a Chicago theatre in 1903 the Governors felt that they had to 'make the safety of the inmates from fire absolutely assured'.[21] Between February and September no patients were admitted and those already in the Hospital were transferred to other institutions.[22] A similar fall between 1928 and 1930 was caused by Bethlem's move to Monks Orchard. Admissions were scaled down from 1928 until the Hospital was closed in May 1930. No patients were admitted until October. The new building removed the need to close wards for improvements until the 1960s, promoting a more stable pattern of admissions.

Figure 33.1 does not accurately show the number of new cases, but with a low readmission rate most were only admitted once to Bethlem. This contrasts sharply with institutions like the London County Council's (LCC) Colney Hatch where there was a 31 per cent readmission rate between 1895 and 1927.[23] Exceptions can be found: Emily B——, 'expressionless and mute', was first treated in 1905; by 1932 she had been admitted eleven times.[24] Such cases were unusual. The creation of the Joint Hospital changed this: in the triennial period 1949–51, 10.7 per cent of patients had been readmitted, but only 1 per cent more than three times.[25] By 1960 the readmission rate had risen to 22 per cent.[26] Patients suffering from anxiety or depression were twice as likely to return and Bethlem provided beds for most of these patients. With the introduction of the revolving door policy and moves to community care from the 1960s onwards, readmission for short periods of treatment or assessment became more common. This did not mean that admission to Bethlem was the patient's first experience of mental illness (see Table 33.1). In cases where patients had a history of

Table 33.1 Previous episodes, 1900–16

Year	Number of patients having previous episodes				
	1	2	3	4	5+
1900	32	11	6	4	—
1901	39	13	6	2	3
1902	158	44	18	2	6
1903	35	12	10	7	—
1904	21	3	8	6	3
1905	52	14	7	4	5
1906	49	14	5	1	4
1907	166	17	10	—	—
1908	52	10	11	—	—
1909	42	8	11	—	—
1910	51	11	12	—	—
1911	29	11	7	—	—
1912	36	9	11	—	—
1913	36	9	20	—	—
1914	26	10	9	—	—
1915	12	4	8	—	—
1916	29	6	6	—	—

Source: Annual Reports

mental illness, the time between the onset of the attack and admission was shorter, especially if they were violent, than in cases where no previous mental illness had been recorded. Given the stigma surrounding certification, certified patients were more likely to spend longer outside the Hospital before they were admitted.

A main characteristic of admissions, clearly shown in Figure 33.2, was the fall in certified patients and corresponding rise in voluntary admissions. The 1890 Lunacy Act set the parameters for admission, providing a legal system where a patient had to be certified insane.[27] Under the Act, asylums became 'a last resort for the insane rather than a means to their recovery'.[28] Registered hospitals differed. While they were

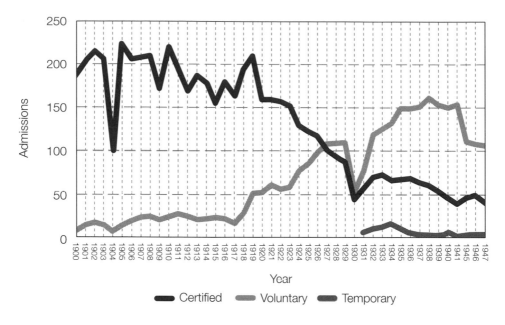

Figure 33.2 Average number of resident patients, 1900–47 *Source:* Annual Reports

not exempt from the workings of the Act they were allowed to admit patients free from certification. The 1890 Act recognized a practice that had been established in 1853 and extended to registered hospitals in 1879. At Bethlem the Governors quickly realized the importance of this category and prided themselves on being one of the 'pioneers' of uncertified cases.[29] The 1930 Mental Treatment Act extended the voluntary principle to all hospitals. For Clive Unsworth this was to 'shift the question from that of legal safeguards to that of early treatment'.[30] Many in the medical profession saw it as a relaxation of 'the numerous barriers preventing the intelligent treatment' of mental illness.[31] It did little to reduce the stigma of certification, but provided two new avenues of treatment: voluntary and temporary. Temporary patients were those unable to express a preference for treatment yet 'likely to benefit' from a period of admission that could last up to six months.[32] At Bethlem it was believed that they had an unfavourable prognosis and for the few admitted little treatment was given. Nationally the number of temporary patients remained 'disappointingly small'.[33] The voluntary category was a move 'in the direction of treating the mentally ill on comparable terms to the physically ill'.[34] Voluntary patients had to have the power of volition and apply for treatment in writing, while they could discharge themselves after giving seventy-two hours' notice. The distinction was not one of social status or degree of illness but of volition. The voluntary category increasingly became the favoured form of admission, widening the gap between more and less progressive institutions.[35]

Despite the *Lancet*'s disparaging comment that for 'the average man . . . a patient must be very insane indeed if he were of his own free will to seek admission', the 1930 Act stimulated the admission of voluntary patients.[36] The Board of Control offered encouragement, and by 1938 voluntary patients accounted for 35.2 per cent of admissions in England and Wales.[37] Many who would have avoided treatment until certification was necessary were now admitted under this category. Doctors in county and borough mental hospitals were initially cautious, but in registered hospitals the Act encouraged an existing admission category. Few psychiatric institutions could compete with Bethlem, which had more than 75 per cent of its admissions on a voluntary basis. Bethlem had favoured early treatment of acute cases since the late nineteenth century, and a trend had been established before 1930 with voluntary admissions tripling between 1923 and 1939. Not every patient was aware of their status or even location. Alexander A—, admitted in August 1924 believing he received messages from footballs, 'knew only by the address of a letter received here that he is in BRH'.[38] For the Board of Control this was a matter of real concern and it pressed for patients to be provided with more information.[39] At Bethlem it is uncertain what motives were behind this, but given the aim to treat cases quickly it did not arise from a desire to maintain paying patients for profit. It is more likely that patients were admitted as voluntary cases to avoid stigma where elsewhere they would have been be certified.

John Hamilton, the new Physician-Superintendent in 1941, wrote to the Board of Control in 1947 expressing concern that Bethlem's impending merger with the Maudsley would restrict voluntary patients.[40] He feared that association with a LCC asylum, even one like the Maudsley that had never admitted certified patients, would remove Bethlem's right to select its own cases. Hamilton's worries were unfounded. When plans for the Joint Hospital were being finalized, it was decided that, because of the stipulations in Henry Maudsley's will, only voluntary patients could be admitted. The first edition of *Notes for the Guidance of Medical Officers* explained in 1951 that the Joint Hospital admitted patients on the same basis as a general hospital. Staff were expected 'to assure patients that in entering the hospital they are not jeopardising their liberty and that they will never be forced to remain if they wish to leave'.[41] Doctors were warned that because the Hospital was not 'designated' a mental hospital it could not receive certified or temporary patients. The internal document advised that when it was necessary to certify a patient they first had to be discharged. Patients who presented no difficulty could be admitted with few procedures, although they were expected to sign a declaration of willingness. Potentially difficult patients had to be formally admitted to prevent later complications. Staff were advised to adopt a 'safe line', with decisions based on general prognosis and behaviour. Special arrangements for interesting cases, however, were made at the insistence of Aubrey Lewis, the Professor of Psychiatry and leading force in the Joint Hospital. Most of these were admitted to the neurosurgical unit.[42] The 1963 *Handbook for the Guidance of Doctors* added little to these guidelines. Taking account of the 1959 Mental Health Act, more organized procedures were established to deal with patients who required an observation or a 28-day emergency order, the two new forms of compulsory treatment that replaced certification. Doctors were now encouraged to work with a psychiatric social worker to find a suitable hospital for these patients.[43]

This practice continued until 1970 when the Joint Hospital started to admit patients under observation or emergency orders. The 1959 Act had led to discussion about the admission of certified patients, but it was changes in the administration of healthcare in south London that stimulated the need to revise the existing admissions policy. In response, a Joint District Psychiatric Services Working Party was established to plan new responsibilities with King's College Hospital. It discussed the closure of the observation unit at St Francis's Hospital, which had been under King's control and received emergency cases for the region. St Francis's had admitted patients under the two compulsory orders and it was decided that the Joint Hospital should take over responsibility. According to John Gunn, Professor of Forensic Psychiatry, difficulties in the Joint Hospital made this move more acceptable. The process where patients were transferred 'at a very inopportune moment' created frustration, requiring change to the 'pioneer Maudsley policies'.[44] Others realized that by preventing the admission of these patients the Joint Hospital was wasting interesting clinical material.[45] At the time the Medical Committee was cautious, but the Governors decided to ignore its concerns and admitted patients under observation and emergency orders, although those under Section 26 who required compulsory treatment for more than twenty-eight days were excluded.[46] After some initial confusion over who was responsible for signing section papers, a procedure developed where every admission was discussed by the consultant and senior nursing staff responsible. To prevent too great a strain on the nurses a limit of fifteen patients was set. By 1977 this was regularly exceeded.[47] A connection was maintained with Broadmoor Special Hospital and was later extended when its Professorial Unit became part of the Institute of Psychiatry. The Joint Hospital agreed to take some of Broadmoor's patients in return for corresponding admission rights.[48] Once the principle of legal detention was accepted the Joint Hospital adapted its procedures with each change in legislation. By 1987 between 100 and 110 patients were regularly 'detained under various sections' of the 1983 Mental Health Act and Bethlem reputedly had 'the highest number of detained patients in the country'.[49] The Special Health Authority (SHA), the successor to the Joint Hospital, felt that 'depriving a person of his liberty . . . [was] a serious matter and it's therefore important that we operate the Act as efficiently and as humanely as possible'. The result was an increase in paperwork and regular visits from the Mental Health Act Commissioners to monitor the Hospitals' work.[50]

CHARACTERIZING PATIENTS: 1901–48

Who were these patients? Throughout Bethlem's history famous patients had been admitted and the twentieth century was no exception. These have included, for example, the artist Louis Wain and the writer Antonia White. Wain was the son of a salesman for a textile firm whose depictions of humanized cats had become popular from the 1880s onwards. Always eccentric, Wain started to show signs of mental disorder in 1914. He became suspicious, abusive and violent, changes blamed on a fall from a train. In June 1924 he was certified and admitted to Springfield where the doctors considered him schizophrenic. Here he remained until the following year when, after a campaign led by admirers of his work, including H. G. Wells and the Labour leader Ramsey Macdonald, he was transferred to Bethlem. At Bethlem Wain proved quiet and cooperative, busying himself with his drawings. Cats remained

Plate 33.1 Louis Wain, *Edge of the Wood*, 1928, gouache on paper. Reproduced by permission of the Bethlem Royal Hospital Archives and Museum.

prominent, but he also developed an interest in painting brightly coloured landscapes. At Christmas the nurses asked him to make some contribution. In response, he decorated the ward mirror with gleeful cats facing each other across a Christmas pudding. The mirror was used annually. Wain remained in Bethlem until 1930 when he was transferred to Napsbury, dying in 1939.[51] The novelist Antonia White had a more traumatic time when she was admitted for ten months in 1922, as shown in her book *Beyond the Glass*. Her experiences helped shape her later writings and influenced her portrayal of mental hospitals. However, not every patient proved to be famous. How can they therefore be characterized?

According to Showalter, in the twentieth century 'we know that women are the majority of clients for private and public psychiatric hospitals'.[52] In 1915, of the 137,188 cases of notified mental illness in England and Wales, 53.8 per cent were female. The proportion had not substantially changed by 1946.[53] Bethlem reflected this national trend. Women outnumbered men, but the disparity fluctuated.[54] Whereas in 1907 58.5 per cent of admissions were female, in 1937 it was 69.4 per cent. Overall 58.2 per cent of patients in the 1920s and 61.5 per cent in the 1930s were female. This reinforced the fact that women outnumbered men in the general population by 8–9 per cent in this period. For historians like Showalter, such figures reflected women's vulnerability to mental illness, given the social expectations they faced.[55] These pressures were often greatest when the patient was married. Single patients did dominate, a fact Drs Blacker and Gore attributed to mental illness militating against marriage and the absence of familial support.[56] Between 1900 and 1916 only a third of the patients admitted to Bethlem were married, but this proportion was higher among women. Married women represented approximately two-thirds of all female admissions. In the triennial period 1967–9, while 38 per cent of male patients were married this was 51 per cent for female patients.[57] Numerous explanations can be found for this difference, but it might be suggested that a married woman suffering from mental illness was more of a burden and less tolerated and so more likely to be admitted.

Bethlem, unlike the Maudsley, rigidly excluded children and adolescents until 1948. Patients were rarely admitted if they were under 20, with only between 5 and 8 per cent aged between 16 and 20. Equally an effort was made to discourage those over 60 in the belief that cure was unlikely. While the medical staff were prepared to admit patients like Frederick W—, aged 74, with senile dementia in 1939, the number of these patients remained small.[58] The encouragement given to curable and paying patients discouraged both young and old alike and the median age remaining stable at 41 years between 1900 and 1947. The creation of an adolescent unit and a psychogeriatric unit at Monks Orchard in 1948 did not materially change the emphasis. Before 1948 most patients were aged between 25 and 54, with the greatest number in the 35–44 age range. Table 33.2 shows a similar pattern for the period 1949 to 1969.

Table 33.2 Age of patients (per cent), 1949–69

Year	16–24		25–34		35–44		45–54		55–64		65 +	
	M	F	M	F	M	F	M	F	M	F	M	F
1949–51	19.0	15.9	32.4	27.4	22.3	24.1	14.4	16.7	8.5	9.6	3.4	6.3
1952–54	15.9	14.1	31.9	28.1	23.0	23.3	15.2	16.2	8.8	9.9	5.2	6.4
1955–57	17.4	14.0	28.4	27.9	24.4	22.7	15.9	15.7	8.9	11.4	5.0	8.3
1958–60	17.4	16.1	23.5	24.3	22.1	21.8	17.2	16.6	12.4	11.6	7.4	9.7
1961–63	23	19	20	22	21	21	17	17	12	12	7	9
1964–66	24	25	22	21	21	20	16	15	11	10	6	9
1967–69	32	29	22	23	16	16	16	13	8	9	6	10

Source: Triennial Statistical Reports

It was not until the 1960s that there was a real shift. Despite a national trend that favoured a rise in patients over 65 (rising from 16.4 per cent in 1944 to 20.1 per cent in 1954), patients at the Joint Hospital became younger.[59] This was linked to the changing nature of the Joint Hospital, with the creation of specialized units that favoured younger patients and a change in policy in the psychogeriatrics unit (see pp. 666–7).

It is harder to determine patients' social backgrounds. In 1917 the Board of Control reported that registered hospitals had become institutions for patients 'who are able to make liberal payments and for such as being educated and refined but of limited means'.[60] This view has been confirmed by Anne Digby's work on the York Retreat. Others have seen a more rigid class division emerging in the early-Victorian period between county and borough asylums and private and registered hospitals.[61] However, can this generalization be applied to Bethlem? Hood's reforms had helped exclude the admission of pauper patients, and a decision to allow the medical staff to undertake private practice in 1903 promoted a 'better class of patients in London [to] come within range of the Hospital'.[62] Porter-Phillips saw Bethlem as a refuge for those who could not afford a private asylum.[63] Worsfold was more optimistic. He believed that 'the generality of patients ... are of the educated classes'.[64] However, the Governors remained concerned about the type of patient they admitted. With hindsight this proved unjustified. A study of the annual reports and a sample of the occupations listed in the case notes add a social dimension to admissions. David Glass warned in 1940 that 'a very large arbitrary element is involved in grouping occupations'. Assumptions have to be made so that a general impression of the social structure can be gained. Banks, in his work on the occupational structure of the nineteenth century, showed that the categories used in the 1911 Census are the most reliable guide (see Table 33.3).[65] Bethlem's records do not present the same problems

Table 33.3 1911 Census classification scheme

Class	Classification	Occupations (sample)
I	Professional occupations	Clergy, clerks, law, medicine, property owning, public service, teaching, etc.
II	Intermediate occupations	Butchers, bakers, drapers, grocers, haberdashers, ironmongers, publishers, pensioners, shopkeepers.
III	Skilled occupations	Bricklaying, carpenters, domestic (indoor), footwear, gunsmiths, hairdressers, printing, plasterers, plumbers, seamen, tailors, waiters, etc.
IV	Semi-skilled occupations	Agriculture, brewers, coopers, domestic (outdoor), fishermen, furriers, laundry, machinist, millers, postmen, sculptors, tanners, warehousemen, etc.
V	Unskilled occupations	Bargemen, cabmen, costermongers, labourers, mining, porters, sugar refiners, etc.

Source: Simon Szreter, *Fertility, Class and Gender in Britain, 1860–1940* (Cambridge: CUP, 1996) Appendix D

as census returns, but information about patients' occupations was rarely precise and often omitted. Occupations were invariably assigned on the opinion of the house physician, or in female cases either not recorded or based on their father's or spouse's occupation. Usually it is not clear to what extent the occupation listed corresponds to the patient's current or former occupation. What is produced is no more than an impression, but it is a revealing one (see Table 33.4). For the period 1901 to 1915 admissions and rhetoric matched. Whereas all mental hospitals admitted a mixed

Table 33.4 Social class (per cent), 1901–15

Class	Year		
	1901–5	*1906–10*	*1911–15*
I	65.4	55.8	60.9
II	15.1	25.9	13.3
III	10.4	5.8	5.9
IV	2.1	1.5	7.5
V	0.3	1.7	1.3
Unknown	6.7	9.3	11.1

Source: Annual Reports

clientele, classes I and II clearly dominated at Bethlem. By comparison, these classes represented only 29.1 per cent in the 1911 Census. A similar picture is produced by sampling admissions at quinquennial intervals where between 58 and 69.3 per cent of patients came from classes I and II. The numerical signification of these classes was reduced by the high incidence of unrecorded occupation. Where this might suggest private means, it more likely reflects the poor mental condition of some patients or laxity by the admitting officer. What does appear clear is that there was a preponderance of patients from the middle and upper ranks of society. Bethlem did not admit large numbers of patients of independent means as these were attracted to private institutions. However, it was successful in attracting professionals, ensuring that it remained a hospital for the educated and middle classes, at least until the creation of the National Health Service (NHS).

Certain forces were at work before 1948 to maintain this occupational structure. Applications from friends and relatives frequently stressed that Bethlem's reputation had been important in convincing them to apply. The stigma surrounding certification, felt most strongly in the upper and middle classes, and Bethlem's encouragement of voluntary patients made the Hospital an ideal 'last resort'. While no references were made to the Hospital's hotel-like conditions, this must have been a prominent consideration, with patients from classes I and II attracted by the high standards. The Governors projected an image that cast Bethlem as a leading psychiatric institution employing modern treatments (see Chapter 28). It paraded its high recovery rate and in asserting that it was an institution for the educated classes created a self-fulfilling prophecy.

Bethlem's increasing preference for paying patients guaranteed that patients would be from those classes who could afford to contribute to the cost of their care. All potential applicants were given a physical and financial examination on admission; those deemed able to pay were expected to contribute. Bethlem did retain a charitable dimension, but the number of free patients gradually fell: in 1900, 82.6 per cent of admissions were treated free of charge; by the end of the First World War this had fallen to 60.8 per cent. To meet the cost of the Monks Orchard Hospital, patient charges were increased and the medical staff encouraged to admit more paying

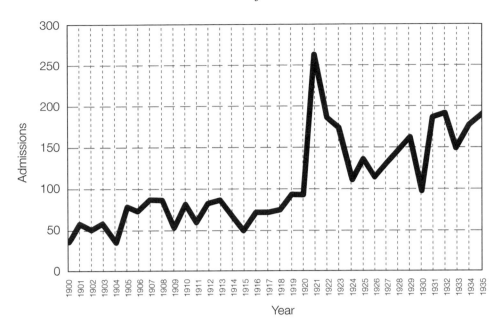

Figure 33.3 Admission of paying patients 1900–35 *Source:* Annual Reports

patients.[66] Between 1927 and 1931 the number of free patients therefore fell from 47.6 to 22 per cent, reaching 15.6 per cent by 1935. Bethlem's experiences were symptomatic of trends at other registered hospitals. The Governors rationalized their decision to admit more paying patients by claiming that their charges were comparatively low, extending a semblance of private care to middle-class patients who would otherwise have been admitted to county and borough mental hospitals. Charges rose from two guineas per week in 1900 to five after the move, reaching seven guineas in 1945. Fees were initially to cover the cost of maintenance. They were extended to include the cost of transfer to another institution and in 1938, in response to the high cost of the new convulsion therapies, an additional fee was introduced for any special treatment.[67] In comparison to other registered hospitals even Bethlem's highest fee was subsidized by the charity's funds. In the 1920s where Bethlem charged a maximum of three guineas per week, Bootham Park, York, expected four guineas; Riverhead House, Sevenoaks, eight. This was an incentive for those seeking a semblance of private care to send their friends or relatives to Bethlem. However, even Bethlem's charges would have been too high for many. Weekly wage rates did rise by a third, but average annual earnings were £80 in Edwardian England.[68] According to an analysis of income in 1938 some 88 per cent earned less than £5 per week, of whom 31 per cent had incomes less than £2 10s.[69] The average earnings for professionals in class I did rise from £349 to £741 between 1913/14 and 1936/7, but a skilled worker's wages only rose from £189 to £197.[70] Sickness and mental illness were unpredictable events; ones that many contemporaries realized placed a considerable financial strain on those affected. For those in classes III–V mental illness could not be budgeted for and Bethlem's charges would have been too high. Those in classes I and II were better placed to afford the Hospital's fees and more inclined to pay, given their hostility to county and borough mental hospitals.

Between 1900 and 1948 Bethlem's Governors could only be heartened by this pattern of admissions. In general, patients matched the regulation criteria, with the statistically ideal patient being a middle-aged woman from London's upper or middle ranks of society, suffering from a mild mental illness, who was prepared to attend the Hospital on a voluntary basis. However, this did not mean that the Governors were inflexible. At Bethlem there was always room for the chronic and those cases that did not match the standard admission pattern. Bethlem's most important contribution, however, was the encouragement it gave to voluntary admissions before many other institutions, including the Maudsley, had started to admit patients on a voluntary basis. As discussed below, the formation of the Joint Hospital emphasized some of these trends and established new ones, but in many ways the merger and the NHS ended Bethlem's exclusive nature.

A METROPOLITAN INSTITUTION?

In other respects, Bethlem continued to draw its character from London. The growth of county and borough asylums in the nineteenth century reduced the Hospital's national role. It was a situation the York Retreat had faced in the nineteenth century.[71] In 1905 74.3 per cent of Bethlem's patients came from London.[72] The Mental Welfare Association was sufficiently worried to complain in 1924 about the Hospital's apparent preference for metropolitan patients.[73] No attempt was made to modify the situation and the creation of the NHS did not bring fundamental change. While Edward Hare, editor of the *Triennial Statistical Reports*, argued that the Joint Hospital was 'like other teaching hospitals in that its patients are drawn from a population that cannot be defined in geographical' terms, the NHS and the merger concentrated admissions from the capital.[74] In the triennial period 1949–51, 86 per cent of patients came from London. Of these, 82 per cent were from south London with most of the non-metropolitan patients continuing to come from Kent, Middlesex and Surrey.[75]

In the 1960s pressure built up for the Joint Hospital to 'undertake a district responsibility for a defined local area'. Interest was produced by the growing emphasis on community services and the passing of the 1959 Mental Health Act, which allowed psychiatric patients to be treated in general hospitals in an effort to make mental healthcare an integral part of the NHS.[76] Projects had been started in Croydon and Lancashire and pressure was added by the Teaching Hospitals Association and the Ministry of Health, which believed that teaching hospitals should define their catchment areas.[77] Given Lewis's active encouragement of social psychiatry, a district commitment was seen by some as providing a fertile ground for research.[78] Discussions were started in 1964 when the Joint Hospital took part in the planning of an emergency service at St Francis's Hospital, but this was abandoned when it became apparent that the Regional Health Board (RHB) had planned for King's to take over responsibility for St Francis's.[79] Despite mounting pressure from Lewis's successor, Denis Hill, who did not really realize the full implications of his ideas, and despite suggestions for increased cooperation with King's, it was not until 1967 that responsibility for psychiatric inpatients in South Southwark was transferred from Camberwell Health Authority to the Joint Hospital. Camberwell had already been identified in 1958 as a possible area where the Hospital might start an experiment in providing domiciliary care and treatment.[80] The area was chosen because of changes in the health district managed by King's and because the Maudsley bordered the former borough of Camberwell. Staff had also conducted detailed research in the area. Opposition to the decision slowed development. A cabal within the medical staff saw the Joint Hospital as a national institution and wanted to protect its teaching nature, believing that a district commitment would 'gradually and surely reduce [it] to being a provider for local needs'.[81] These concerns were dismissed, but resistance took time to subside.

District services were slow to develop, hampered by changes in local government, administrative delays, and a resistance to change. At first only 126 beds were allocated.[82] A District Services Centre was then haltingly developed at the Maudsley to provide 'a psychiatric rehabilitation service', and cooperation with King's Health District and Camberwell Health Authority was extended.[83] Some discussion was held over the need to provide Bethlem with its own district commitment to Croydon, but this was abandoned in the face of opposition. Links were established with St Francis's, Cane Hill Hospital, and Southwark Health District where the Joint Hospital used Southwark's day centres and hostel accommodation.[84] The District Services Centre took over the role of St Francis's after its closure and the district commitment was extended in 1981. In 1983 the admission policy was altered so that patients from South Southwark became a 'priority group'.[85] The Camberwell Register of Patients, the first such research project, suggested new schemes and shaped the formation of Government policy, leading to further pressure to develop community services. When the Health Advisory Service visited Camberwell Health District in 1983 as part of its attempts to reduce the extent of institutionalization, it found 'a picture of an unsatisfactory, uneven and uncoordinated psychiatric service which is failing to meet the needs of mentally ill people in this community'. This was partly blamed on underfunding in the King's Health District and on the division of services between the SHA and district Health Authority. The Health Advisory Service recommended that the dichotomy of services should be ended. It wanted the SHA to provide a unified psychiatric service for the whole district in partnership with the London Boroughs of Lambeth and South Southwark.[86] Both the SHA and the Camberwell Health Authority expressed hostility to the Health Advisory Service's report, arguing that it was too narrow. The SHA, however, was more interested in the overall proposals and took the lead. After detailed negotiations smoothed the differences between the two organizations and reassured staff that research and teaching would not be 'adversely affected', the SHA took over responsibility for community services in South Southwark in 1988.[87] Despite initial concern over funding and hostility in the SHA, the district commitment was extended in 1991 to cover East Lambeth after the closure of Cane Hill and moves to transfer beds from the Dulwich North Hospital. In effect, the SHA was now commissioned by the Camberwell Health Authority under the 1990 NHS and Community Care Act to provide the mental health services for the district. This was the final fulfilment of the Health Advisory Service's recommendations. The hope was that the SHA would 'pursue innovative developments in service, research, comprehensive teaching and training', opening the way to 'community focused care'.[88] New services like the Alcohol Dependence Service had to be planned to overcome the low priority Southwark and Lambeth local authorities had assigned to mental health.[89] The SHA was now forced to look beyond the Hospital care it had provided to develop alternatives to inpatient admission.

The effect of the changes was to strengthen the metropolitan bias. It was felt that to be 'solely dependent on that service would be incompatible with the continuance and development of [the Joint Hospital's] major functions'.[90] However, most patients continued to come from south-east and south-west London, especially those areas near the Maudsley. By 1972 some of the medical staff were beginning to worry that the increasing number of Camberwell patients prevented admissions from other areas.[91] Others feared that 'this policy is leading us . . . to change completely the whole purpose of this hospital', a move that was felt would have 'disastrous consequences'.[92] Although these claims were dismissed, problems began to emerge. In 1975 only 9 per cent of Bethlem's patients came from outside Camberwell and, between 1981 and 1985, 73 per cent of all patients admitted came from the South East Thames region.[93] Bed occupancy fell where local general practitioners wrongly believed that the Joint Hospital had become solely reserved for Camberwell patients. To prevent this, doctors were reminded that it was important to admit non-Camberwell patients and 'green warnings' were introduced on wards to limit their admission when a threshold number was reached.[94] The move to provide institutional facilities for Camberwell produced a gradual silting-up of the wards with chronic patients, reflecting the experiences of nineteenth-century county and borough asylums. Added to this was the reluctance of referring districts to take patients back.[95] This made it difficult to discharge patients. Any assumption of a national or regional service, like the planning of a Mental Impairment Evaluation and Treatment Service at Bethlem in 1983 (see p. 669), was seen as a 'worthwhile new development' given the shrinking of the Hospital's catchment area.[96] The Joint Hospital had an international reputation and national and regional status, but this could not counter the high number of patients who continued to be drawn from Bethlem and the Maudsley's traditional catchment areas.

By 1989 serious consideration was being given to the position at Bethlem. Concern was expressed that Bethlem was becoming the 'poor relation in the partnership'. With services being transferred to the Maudsley many were beginning to feel that Monks Orchard was being 'run down'.[97] To avoid this problem, the Bethlem Site Estates Control Plan was produced to design a new role for Monks Orchard. It proposed that Bethlem should become the 'focus of the SHA's National and Regional services and that as few District Services be provided at Bethlem as possible'.[98] In doing so the emphasis shifted from London to the region and the nation, although in 1990 the 'vast majority' of patients continued to come from the South East Thames Region.[99]

ALL CHANGE: ADMISSIONS AND THE JOINT HOSPITAL, 1948–90s

As the number of patients admitted rose, reaching 834 a year to Bethlem by 1990/1, a change occurred in the type of patient treated.[100] After the NHS's appointed day,

Bethlem, even as part of a privileged postgraduate teaching hospital, could not maintain its exclusive character. The most noticeable change came with the adoption of a district responsibility where the Hospital became more concerned 'than hitherto with the care and management of patients with recurrent or chronic disorders'.[101] It was believed that in drawing patients from Camberwell after 1970 inpatient care was democratized, but a change had already started in 1948. Inpatients did have a higher social status than outpatients, but a comparison of Table 33.4 with Table 33.5 shows

Table 33.5 Social class of inpatients admitted to the Joint Hospital (per cent), 1949–69

Year	Class									
	I		II		III		IV		V	
	M	F	M	F	M	F	M	F	M	F
1949–51	9.5	6.4	18.5	15.6	49.2	63.9	11.0	10.6	11.8	3.5
1952–54	5.7	3.3	14.6	15.8	52.9	57.9	11.3	16.6	15.5	6.4
1955–57	6.7	3.6	15.1	16.3	52.6	57.7	10.2	14.7	15.4	7.7
1958–60	7.1	2.0	15.7	14.8	50.5	56.6	9.6	17.5	17.1	9.1
1961–63	5	—	14	—	52	—	13	—	16	—
1964–66	6	—	19	—	43	—	15	—	17	—
1967–69	7	—	17	—	43	—	16	—	17	—

Source: Triennial Statistical Reports

that the proportion of patients from the educated middle classes had fallen. A similar preference for patients from class III was shown in Bethlem's day hospital and adolescent unit.[102] Why had this happened? Hare blamed the fall in social status on the establishment of the Emergency Clinic at the Maudsley in 1958, which he believed attracted those poorer patients prone to mental illness.[103] The NHS had a more long-term impact. According to Charles Webster, official historian of the NHS, although the service 'achieved only limited equalisation of services, it provided the less well-off with a variety of forms of care to which previously they had only limited access'.[104] This had not been Bethlem's ambition. In reluctantly accepting the NHS, the Governors had to work within the framework of providing a free service open to all. The effect was to broaden the social class of admissions. Admissions were now more likely to reflect the social class background of London as a whole. After the assumption of a district responsibility in 1970 a further change occurred. Camberwell was seen as 'a relatively stable working-class area not characterised by great poverty, social isolation or social mobility' in 1974, but there was an awareness that the area was in decline.[105] Admissions came to reflect the social and ethnic structure of South Southwark and East Lambeth.

The nature of patients admitted equally changed. Immediately after the merger

Aubrey Lewis saw that it was necessary to redefine the type of cases treated at Bethlem. Lewis aimed to ensure that the Joint Hospital, as a national research institution, admitted the full range of mental illness to allow a comprhensive medical education. For him Bethlem offered the main area for development. Everything was to be subservient to teaching and research so that in 1962 one member of the staff could comment that 'although of course the joint hospital did provide treatment facilities its primary function was to provide for teaching needs'.[106] It was a legacy that persisted. Lewis felt that a diagnostic division of patients was unsuitable and favoured organization along the lines of 'social behaviour, sex, age, and the requirements of research'.[107] The main substance of Lewis's plans was accepted.[108]

Within a matter of months Bethlem became the home to patients who had previously been discouraged: the young, the old, the chronic and the psychotic. Monks Orchard increasingly came to treat patients who needed the more long-term programmes of care that the Maudsley could not provide, given the overcrowded conditions. Felix Post at first thought that he was supported 'because of my brilliant promise', but it soon became clear that Lewis 'really appointed me because he was thinking of having a department for old age psychiatry'.[109] At the time this was 'an almost revolutionary proposal; as neither of the now joint hospitals had . . . taken on the care of "chronic cases"'.[110] Post achieved international acclaim through the unit and was considered to have founded old-age psychiatry. Initially he had a few beds in a general ward, but by 1951 Gresham was converted to a psychogeriatric unit and it seemed like 'the whole place was more or less devoted to people over 60'.[111] The unit was 'fully operational' by 1952 and a decision was made to exclude those patients who merely needed nursing care and could be treated adequately elsewhere. Further alterations were made in 1976. The lowest age of admission was raised from 60 to 70 after Post informed the Medical Executive Committee that 'many specialised psychogeriatric problems did not occur in patients aged less than 70'. Patients between 60 and 70 were now cared for in the general psychiatric wards.[112] With 30 to 40 per cent of patients over 60 admitted to mental hospitals, the unit was seen as essential in providing training.[113] Bethlem's distance from London created problems, and services were later developed at St Francis's and Cane Hill in South East London, the latter for patients whose deterioration had become persistent.[114]

At the other extreme an adolescent unit was established. In 1948 the British Psychological Society discussed the problems of sending 'youngsters who require treatment to a mental hospital amongst adult patients'. Staff at the Joint Hospital took note and decided to establish a special unit following the lead set by St Ebba's Hospital.[115] The Governors were cautious. According to Priscilla Norman, a Governor between 1951 and 1975, they feared 'the damage these youngsters could do in the grounds, besides annoying the patients'.[116] Bethlem's Tyson ward was the obvious choice as no alterations were needed, and the Governors gave way. In 1949 a 'boys' ward of seventeen beds was established followed by an eighteen-bed 'girls' ward in 1950 for adolescents over the age of eleven.[117] These were the first adolescent inpatient wards to be established in England: between 1949 and 1963 admissions rose from 250 a year to 314. The Governors' initial concerns were justified and there were doubts in 1954 about whether the unit should continue to function. Adolescent patients, despite on average only spending four months in the Hospital, created problems. Every effort was made to control their behaviour, but staff tried to avoid them and the consultant in charge in the 1950s proved irritable and difficult to work with.[118] Adolescents regularly goaded the nurses, and in 1953 the high number of thefts at Bethlem was blamed on them.[119] When Tyson was renovated to provide a better environment many of these problems were reduced.

Other changes occurred. Bethlem, with its 240 acres, became the ideal location for many of these new departments given the cramped conditions at the Maudsley, even after the Institute of Psychiatry moved to its new buildings in 1967. Paying patients were excluded from Monks Orchard, despite Lewis's plans to turn Witley into a private patients' unit.[120] All neurosurgical cases were transferred to the Maudsley where a Neurosurgical Unit was established with Guy's Hospital. This became the jewel in the Hospital's crown, a source of income and prestige, even after the initial rationale for the unit had disappeared. Further changes followed as the Joint Hospital was unable to remain static and new departments were added. As early as 1974 Michael Rutter in the Medical Research Council's (MRC) Child Psychiatry Unit warned that Bethlem was 'becoming a collection of highly specialised units'. He feared that it was becoming known as 'the place which caters for all the difficult patients whom other places won't take'.[121] A brief outline of the major units established shows how Bethlem moved further away from its pre-NHS pattern of admissions, partly justifying Rutter's concerns.

Following the developments immediately after the merger, a day hospital was added in 1956 when the *Evening Standard*'s lease of Bethlem's sports ground expired, allowing the cricket pavilion to be used as a day hospital. In the same year the widely publicized Worthing Experiment was started where Graylingwell Hospital, Chichester established a day hospital at Worthing.[122] Mental health planners, faced with a shortage of funds, favoured such facilities and encouraged them, but between 1948 and 1958 only twenty day hospitals were established.[123] At the Joint Hospital it was felt that they maintained better contact between patients and their homes, improved morale by shortening treatment times, and allowed more patients to be treated. Others argued that day hospitals lowered costs, although there was some scepticism about this claim.[124] The new unit was named 'Dayholme'. With its own tennis courts and 'delightful situation, facing extensive parkland' it was more self-contained than the Maudsley's, founded two years earlier. The unit offered treatment with a particular emphasis on group psychotherapy and patient participation.[125] Patients arrived each weekday morning, having lunch and tea in the unit before returning home in the evening. Dayholme was dominated by the need to readjust patients to living at home and retained some of Bethlem's old character, with patients having a higher social status than those at the Maudsley. Kenneth Johnson, the first House Governor, felt that such units had a considerable future, especially as they conferred no official stigma, but the Medical Committee assigned Dayholme a low priority. Concern was raised about its viability in 1966 after several years of low referrals, restrictions on staffing, and the fact that therapeutic communities existed elsewhere in the Joint Hospital. It was felt that the ward should be run down and facilities extended at the Maudsley.[126] After much deliberation, Dayholme was closed, although some day facilities were provided in a day ward in Bethlem's recreation hall until 1971.[127] The decision proved unpopular. The *Beckenham & Penge Advertiser* saw the closure as 'a blow to the mental health facilities in the area', and the last link with the pre-1948 pattern of admissions was severed.[128]

Interest in the problems of addiction in the late 1960s, particularly after the publication of the 1965 Brian Report pointed to an increase in drug use, brought further change. Nine beds were already continuously used for addiction treatment in the Joint Hospital, while the Institute of Psychiatry was establishing a research department. It was felt that because 'drug addicts are not popular patients and cause difficulties in the general psychiatric ward' there was 'a reluctance to admit them for treatment; a tendency for ward problems to develop around them and to the drug addict being rejected by medical and nursing staff'. On these grounds, Denis Hill argued that a special unit was needed.[129] With the Maudsley facing a shortage of beds, Bethlem was suggested. Monks Orchard was not seen as ideal, given its distance from the Institute and concerns about the shortage of beds, but it was felt that because the Witley Wards were unsuitable for general cases and needed renovation they offered the best and cheapest solution. Bethlem became one of eleven hospitals taking part in a Government scheme to encourage inpatient care 'to fight the country's mounting drug addiction problem'. The aim 'was to contain the spread of addiction and to obviate recourse to illicit supplies'.[130] Difficulties over finance delayed development, but the Governors decided to go ahead provided the 'treatment of patients suffering from other conditions is safeguarded'.[131] Work progressed quickly. Philip Connell, consultant adviser to the Ministry of Health on drugs, was appointed consultant, marking a shift from his previous interest in child and adolescent psychiatry. The new unit was opened in Witley in 1968 as the Drug Dependency Clinical Research and Treatment Unit.[132] Witley was divided into two: ten beds in Witley Two were for oral or inhalation drug users; eleven in Witley Three for those who used injectable drugs. The Unit itself was unusual in that it looked at soft and hard drug usage whereas other units focused on heroin.[133] Hostility was not reduced and problems were encountered, with the patients proving 'demanding and manipulative' and often 'aggressive'. It did, however, appear in *Counter Culture*, a guide to how to live free in London. The unit was shown as the ideal place to acquire up to six months' free care in hotel-like conditions, winning fame in 'hippy folk-lore'.[134] Bed occupancy did remain high, but by 1977 the number of patients in Witley Two had fallen and the distinction between the two wards was abolished. By the 1980s, 80–90 patients were admitted each year and in 1985 the Drug Abuse Working Party reported that 'the pressure on the inpatient services has increased'. This was attributed to the 'increasing misuse of opioid drugs and the ready availability of heroin in the black market'.[135]

In 1971 a unit for children with learning disabilities was opened by Princess Alexandra on her first visit as Bethlem's patron. The new unit built on the work of Professors Tizard and O'Connor in the MRC Social Psychiatry Unit. They had looked at the frequency of mental disability in the community, linking with the South East Metropolitan Regional Hospital Board's interest in extending services for 'mentally disabled children'.[136] The need for such a unit had first been mentioned in 1961, given the changes initiated by the 1959 Mental Health Act. At the time a proposed unit was included in the Hospital's building plan, but not given a high priority.[137] It was not until 1967 that it was reluctantly decided to site the new unit at Bethlem. When finally opened, it was named Hilda Lewis House in memory of Lewis's wife, who had worked extensively with disturbed children.[138] Patients ranging from 4–18 years old stayed at Bethlem during the week, going home at weekends, with the unit working 'to teach them the basic needs of everyday life'. The long-term aim was 'to intervene earlier with children with behavioural and other specific handicaps . . . and so prevent long-term hospitalisation wherever possible'.[139] In all, the unit had twenty-four beds and two mother-and-baby rooms with a pioneering mother-and-baby unit later developed in Fitzmary. No attempt was made to offer long-term care.[140] Problems were encountered in the late 1980s. Hilda Lewis House had been planned as a community-based service, and with the growth of the district commitment it increasingly took more seriously disturbed patients, reducing its effectiveness. Opposition also existed to the behavioural approach it adopted, placing the unit at the centre of conflict between various psychiatric disciplines. The fabric of Hilda Lewis House was also proving expensive to maintain at a time when the SHA was facing financial restrictions, while with nursing shortages in other areas it was proving labour intensive.[141] On these grounds, and because the consultant in charge was retiring, it was decided to suspend inpatient services in 1991. The Medical Committee did not welcome the decision, especially when, through a misunderstanding, the out-reach services were also run down.[142]

In 1987 the work of Hilda Lewis House was supplemented by the opening of the Mental Impairment Evaluation and Treatment Service (MIETS) in Tyson West One. It was part of the South East Thames Regional Health Authority's (SETRHA) plans to fund two special needs units after patients at Darenth Park Hospital were moved into the community.[143] The Chief Nursing Officer was at first uncertain about establishing 'a further special unit' given recruitment problems, but with SETRHA promising part of a £1 million funding initiative these concerns were quickly dismissed. It was felt that in providing a unit as part of a regional initiative, the Joint Hospital would be taking a 'lead in the development of understanding in the most complicated and least understood areas of psychiatry'.[144] Admission was reserved for mentally impaired adults with specific behavioural and psychiatric problems. In practice this meant that most patients referred were aggressive or exhibited anti-social behaviour, creating a unit with the highest reported level of violence in the Hospital.[145] MIETS aimed to work with community services for the mentally disabled and provide advice on long-term treatment and placement needs. To prevent MIETS from silting up, the maximum period of stay was limited to eighteen months and SETRHA accepted final responsibility for all patients.[146]

Whereas the creation of these units modified the type of patient admitted, none attracted as much attention as the decision to establish a medium-secure unit. Discussions were started with the Department of Health and Social Security (DHSS) in 1974 over the possible location of a secure unit at Bethlem.[147] They marked the beginning of negotiations that 'would restore a traditional role to Bethlem which persisted right up to the opening of the Broadmoor Criminal Lunatics' Asylum'.[148] The Ministry of Health had tried to encourage the creation of secure units after the 1961 Emery Commission predicted that maximum security hospitals were in danger of becoming overcrowded. However, it was not until 1974, after scandals connected to several patients discharged from Broadmoor, that the interim Butler Report recommended 'that every region should have a secure hospital unit of up to 100 beds'. Similar proposals had been made before. Open-door policies created a need for secure units to remove the seriously disturbed from open wards and provide the directed care these patients needed.[149] The Joint Hospital under Gibbens, Peter Scott and John Gunn became a leading centre for the study of forensic psychiatry with interest first expressed in the idea of a secure unit in 1961. A working party under Denis Hill, himself a member of the Butler Committee, recommended a 73-bed secure male unit.[150] Initially the working party's suggestions were unacceptable, with many concerned about the size of the unit. This was a major rebuff for Hill. Modern forensic psychiatry had only really emerged in the 1950s and was greeted with hostility, especially as it dealt with patients for whom few wanted to accept responsibility.[151] Hill asked John Gunn, a member of the Special Hospital Research Unit at the Institute of Psychiatry, to head another working party. After lengthy consultation with the staff and important concessions that later led to problems, this put forward a revised version of Hill's suggestions. It recommended that a smaller, 36-bed mixed unit 'with high standards and a rapid turnover would be more valuable than a large stagnant institution'.[152] Gunn felt that 'the attraction of the scheme is that the service would be flexible and sensitive at each point through from the security hospitals to the community level to match the needs of patients'.[153] SETRHA used the interest at the Joint Hospital to advance its own plans. With the promises of funding from Barbara Castle, Secretary of State for Social Services, after the Butler Report, Regional Health Authorities now became interested.[154] Influenced by Gunn, SETRHA identified Bethlem as the place where a central unit for the region could be built as part of a £2 million 'interlocking rehabilitation scheme', linked to five smaller clinics in the region. The unit at Bethlem would provide the nucleus of the new service. Many felt that it was about time that institutions like the Joint Hospital undertook some dirty work to justify their privileged position.[155] It was not until September 1976 that a joint bid was presented to the DHSS. Although the scheme had broad implications for the type of patients that could be admitted, it was felt that 'hospitals and prisons have been housing such people for years'.[156] It overlooked that this had not been the case at Bethlem. Local residents were alarmed. One commented:

> it is rather frightening. We have inmates now from Bethlem knocking on our door. Only the other day a young woman came along who was obviously very disturbed. She said she had got over the fence and was too frightened to go back . . . I am not frightened of mentally disturbed people like this, but I admit I do feel nervous when I hear that mentally ill criminals are to be treated there.[157]

While staff recognized the need for the Joint Hospital to lead the field, they shared local concerns. According to the *Bethlem & Maudsley Gazette* there were 'the usual nightmare fantasies of being taken over by a deluge of vicious and dangerous patients'. The concern was a realistic one. Since 1970 the number of violent incidents had increased, with 'yellow warnings' introduced in 1976 to restrict the admission of disturbed patients to understaffed wards.[158] Staff were worried that a secure unit would only increase the problem.

To prevent the scheme from collapsing, a new working party was established to investigate concerns that 'the nature of the Bethlem Royal Hospital would be changed, and the young relatively defenceless patients at Bethlem would be put at risk'. The working party, driven by Gunn's enthusiasm, saw the need for a secure unit at Bethlem as vital, especially as regional plans were encountering difficulties. When hospitals were approached invariably someone would raise the case of Myra Hindley, the Moors murderer, and insist that their hospital was unsuitable for such cases. Bethlem was shown as taking a pioneering role. It expected that the new unit would be for referrals from court assessment, difficult detained patients, patients on probation, and patients returning to the community from Special Hospitals.[159] Psychopathic patients were to be excluded. It was expected that Bethlem would admit those patients who could not be treated in SETRHA's regional clinics or in ordinary units.[160] With promises of funding from the DHSS, extensive discussions within the Joint Hospital and visits to other secure units, it was decided to go ahead with the scheme, involving the Hospital in an extensive public relations campaign.[161] This did not reduce anxiety. Continuing negotiations with SETRHA over finance and the need for revenue savings slowed planning. As an interim measure Tyson West One, already empty through lack of funds, was converted into a secure unit and opened in 1980 by Jimmy Savile, himself sympathetic to mentally disturbed offenders, to reduce public hostility.[162] While a limited service was run from Tyson and secure units underway at Cane Hill, Oakwood and Bexley, lengthy negotiations continued with SETRHA. It was not until October 1980 that the Authority finally agreed to provide part of the funds.[163] This was only enough to support fifteen beds and it was decided to restrict admissions to those who were believed to be most likely to benefit. Unable to rely on funding from SETRHA given the financial restrictions facing the region, Ivan Clout, chair of the SHA, convinced the DHSS to supply funds direct to the SHA. With a mix of DHSS, SETRHA and endowed funds, a well-designed 30-bed unit, named after Denis Hill, was planned. After the usual delays it was opened in 1985.[164] Even after the unit had opened, SETRHA refused to reconsider its revenue allocation. It was only through the sale of eight beds to the North East Thames RHA, behind in its own plans to develop a secure service, that all thirty beds were opened.[165] Opposition had ensured that the unit did not become the focus of forensic psychiatry for the region as initially anticipated. Admission policy was set to regional needs and favoured clinical rather than diagnostic or legal needs. In theory patients were admitted only if they were not a danger to the public and the nursing staff felt they were manageable. Only a small proportion of female and adolescent patients were expected, with no admissions made on an emergency basis.[166] The Unit continued to be 'blighted by funding problems' and it proved difficult to finance all the beds.[167]

CONCLUSION

In 1986 the Bethlem Task Force, established to investigate changes at Monks Orchard, received reports about 'a change of emphasis at Bethlem'. Concern was raised that more patients 'in an acute phase of their illness are now admitted to Bethlem than previously'. This was placing a strain on the Intensive Care Area in Fitzmary, which was in urgent need of expansion.[168] Changes were made, but nothing was done to reverse the trend. The creation of a Drug Dependency Clinical Research and Treatment Unit, Hilda Lewis House, MIETS, and the Denis Hill Unit had done much to alter the type of patient admitted. The transition was gradual, but with each new department Bethlem moved further away from its pre-NHS pattern of admissions. An ideal statistical type now became harder to define. Bethlem had come far from the first admission of mentally ill patients in the fourteenth century, but the period of greatest change was from 1948 onwards. With Bethlem never a static institution, it should be no surprise that it adapted to the changing needs of psychiatry to provide a home to new type of patients.

NOTES

1 Bethlem Subcommittee, 9 October 1930.
2 1932 Rules & Orders.
3 1941 Case Notes: Male Case 5.
4 *Bethlem & Maudsley Gazette*, Autumn 1982, 6.
5 Court of Governors, 31 July 1918.
6 Incurable Establishment Papers: Letter from Worsfold to Porter-Phillips, 22 February 1922.
7 General Committee, 18 January 1920.
8 Incurable Establishment Papers: Letter from Porter-Phillips to Faudel-Phillips, 5 May 1930.
9 *Ibid.*: Letter from Hewitt to Coke, 12 February 1948.
10 1934/5 Treasurer's Report.
11 *1902 Bethlem Annual Report*, 37.
12 Richard Hunter and Ida Macalpine, *Psychiatry for the Poor: 1851 Colney Hatch Asylum – Friern Hospital 1973* (London: Dawson, 1974), 174.
13 *1911 Bethlem Annual Report*, 4.
14 *1920 Bethlem Annual Report*, 8.
15 *1914 Board of Control Annual Report*, 7.
16 *1945 Board of Control Annual Report*, 11.
17 See Andrew Scull, *The Most Solitary of Afflictions: Madness and Society in Britain, 1700–1900* (New Haven, Conn.: Yale University Press, 1993), 338–52, 363.
18 *1945 Board of Control Annual Report*, 11.
19 See T. Crosby, *Impact of Civilian Evacuation in the Second World War* (London: Croom Helm, 1986).
20 *1919 Bethlem Annual Report*, 8.
21 *City Press*, January 1904.
22 Court of Governors, 8 February 1904.
23 Hunter and Macalpine, *op. cit.* 53.
24 1939 Case Notes: Female Case 109.
25 *1949–51 Triennial Statistical Report*, 35.
26 *1958–60 Triennial Statistical Report*, 7–8.
27 Much has been written on mental health legislation. For a full discussion of the legal dimension of mental healthcare the most comprehensive study is Clive Unsworth, *The Politics of Mental Health Legislation* (Oxford: OUP, 1987). Kathleen Jones, *Asylums and After* (London: Athlone, 1993), especially 93–125, offers a more concise analysis, seeing mental health legislation as a balance between medicine and legalism. Phil Fennell, *Treatment Without Consent: Law, Psychiatry and the Treatment of Mentally Disordered People Since 1845* (London: Routledge, 1996), relates legislation to treatment, while Joan Busfield, *Managing Madness: Changing Ideas and Practice* (London: Hutchinson, 1986), links change to psychiatric developments outside the asylum and changes in the state's welfare provision.

28 T. Butler, *Mental Health, Social Policy and the Law* (Basingstoke: Macmillan, 1985), 68.

29 General Correspondence: Letter from Faudel-Phillips to Henriques, 17 May 1929.

30 Unsworth, *op. cit.* 126

31 *Lancet*, 2 (1922), 492.

32 Cited in Jones, *op. cit.* 136.

33 *1932 Board of Control Annual Report*, 2.

34 Busfield, *op. cit.* 340.

35 Butler, *op. cit.* 97.

36 *Lancet*, 2 (1924), 709.

37 Jones, *op. cit.* 136.

38 1925 Case Notes: Case 2.

39 *1921 Board of Control Annual Report*, 51.

40 Board of Control Correspondence: Letter to the Board of Control, 11 June 1947.

41 *Bethlem & Maudsley Gazette*, November 1965, 74.

42 *Notes for the Guidance of Medical Officers* (1951).

43 *Handbook for the Guidance of Doctors* (1963).

44 Special Assessment and Supervision Service Correspondence: Letter from John Gunn, 12 July 1985.

45 Medical Committee, 18 December 1967.

46 Board of Governors, 1 January 1968.

47 MTO, 18 January 1977.

48 Hospital Committee, 3 December 1975.

49 MEC Presented Papers: 2 April 1987, ECD 23/87.

50 *Mental Health Act Guidelines*, 1.

51 See R. Dale, *Louis Wain: The Man Who Drew Cats* (London: Michael O'Mara Books Limited, 1991), 88–100.

52 Elaine Showalter, *The Female Malady: Women, Madness and English Culture 1830–1980* (London: Virago, 1987), 3.

53 *1915 Board of Control Annual Report*, 1; *1946 Bethlem Annual Report*, 5–6.

54 Anne Digby, *Madness, Morality and Medicine: A Study of the York Retreat 1796–1914* (Cambridge: CUP, 1985), 174–5, has seen a similar situation at the York Retreat in the nineteenth century.

55 B. R. Mitchell and P. Deane, *Abstract of British Historical Statistics* (Cambridge: CUP, 1971), 6; Showalter, *op. cit.*

56 *1949–51 Triennial Statistical Report*, 17.

57 *1967–69 Triennial Statistical Report*, 13.

58 1945 Case Notes: Male Case 47.

59 Charles Webster, *Problems of Health Care: The National Health Service Before 1957* (London: HMSO, 1988), 339.

60 *1917 Board of Control Annual Report*, 48.

61 Digby, *op. cit.* 183–5; L. Smith, '"Levelled to the Same Common Standard?" Social Class in the Lunatic Asylum, 1780–1860', in Owen Ashton, Robert Fyson and Stephen Roberts (eds), *Duty of Discontent: Essays for Dorothy Thompson* (London: Mansell, 1996), 142–66.

62 General Correspondence: Letter from Hyslop, 21 March 1902.

63 *1914 Bethlem Annual Report*, 8.

64 General Correspondence: Letter from Worsfold, 6 June 1921.

65 Cited in J. Banks, 'The Social Structure of the Nineteenth Century as seen through Census', in R. Lawton (ed.), *Census and Social Structure* (London: Cass, 1978), 196, 190–5.

66 Bethlem Subcommittee, 3 September 1930.

67 Court of Governors, 2 May 1938.

68 R. Price and G. Bain, 'Labour Force', in A.Halsey (ed.), *British Social Trends since 1900* (London: Macmillan, 1988); Paul Thompson, *The Edwardians: The Remaking of British Society* (London: Routledge, 1992), 5.

69 John Stevenson, *British Social History 1914–1945* (London: Penguin, 1984), 119.

70 Guy Routh, *Occupation and Pay in Great Britain 1906–1979* (Cambridge: CUP, 1980), 64, 88.

71 Digby, *op. cit.* 178.
72 *1905 Bethlem Annual Report*, 74.
73 General Correspondence: Letter from the Mental Welfare Association, 18 February 1924.
74 *1958–60 Triennial Statistical Report*, 1.
75 *1949–51 Triennial Statistical Report*, 101–3.
76 Different interpretations have been placed on the reasons behind community care and these are discussed in Chapter 34, pp. 701–2.
77 Geoffrey Rivett, *Development of the London Hospital System* (London: OUP, 1986), 301–4.
78 *Bethlem & Maudsley Gazette*, Summer 1968, 6.
79 Board of Governors, 1 June 1964 and 7 December 1965.
80 General Purposes Subcommittee, 3 December 1959.
81 Medical Committee Presented Papers: 24 July 1972, MCD 64/72.
82 Medical Committee, 23 October 1967.
83 See District Services Centre Working Party, 1970–1988.
84 SHA and King's Joint Policy Committee, 1979–1983; *1970–75 Triennial Statistical Report*, 19.
85 MEC, 7 July 1983.
86 1984 Health Advisory Service Report.
87 MEC Presented Papers: 5 June 1986, ECD 63/86.
88 Local People in Mind Development Group, 7 April 1989.
89 Planning Steering Group, 27 March 1986.
90 MEC Presented Papers: 6 April 1972, ECD 7/72.
91 Board of Governors, 10 April 1972.
92 Medical Committee Presented Papers: 24 July 1972, MCD 64/72.
93 *1970–75 Triennial Statistical Reports*, 35; Medical Committee Presented Papers: 9 February 1987, MCD 6/87.
94 MTO, 14 February and 15 August 1978.
95 Board of Governors, 14 September 1987.
96 MTO (Policy), 18 October 1983.
97 Bethlem Estates Control Plan, 20 October 1989.
98 *Ibid.* 5 September 1991.
99 SHA, 10 September 1991.
100 *1991 Joint Report*, 38.
101 *1967–69 Triennial Statistical Report*, 1.
102 *1955–57 Triennial Statistical Report*, 72; *1961–63 Triennial Statistical Report*, 42–43.
103 *1961–63 Triennial Statistical Report*, 9.
104 Webster, *op. cit.* 397.
105 J. King and A. Hailey, *Evaluating a Community Psychiatric Service* (London: OUP, 1972).
106 Hospital Committee, 14 March 1962.
107 Aubrey Lewis Papers, Box 5: Circular Letter, 21 June 1948.
108 Board of Governors, 26 July 1948.
109 Greg Wilkinson (ed.), *Talking About Psychiatry* (London: Gaskell, 1993), 163, 169.
110 *Bethlem & Maudsley Gazette*, March 1955, 270.
111 Wilkinson, *op. cit.* 163, 169.
112 MEC, 3 March 1976.
113 *Bethlem & Maudsley Gazette*, March 1955, 271.
114 *1970–75 Triennial Statistical Reports*, 23.
115 *Bethlem & Maudsley Gazette*, May 1953, 9.
116 Priscilla Norman, *In the Way of Understanding* (Godalming: Foxbury Press, 1982), 179.
117 *1961–63 Triennial Statistical Report*, 42.
118 Medical Committee, 3 May 1954.
119 House Committee, 11 November 1953.
120 Board of Governors, 6 September 1948. At first the exclusion affected the whole hospital, but when the Neurosurgical Unit at the Maudsley was opened a certain number of pay beds were included. In the 1970s when Barbara Castle was pressing for the phasing out of pay

beds, the Governors supported the medical staff and pressed hard for the Neurosurgical Unit not to be affected.

121 Working Party on Forensic Unit at Bethlem, 8 November 1974.
122 Almont Lindsey, *Socialised Medicine in England and Wales* (London: OUP, 1962), 310.
123 Webster, *op. cit.* 340.
124 General Purposes Subcommittee, 22 January 1953.
125 *Beckenham Journal*, 8 August 1958,
126 Hospital Committee, 12 January 1966.
127 Board of Governors Presented Papers: 6 February 1966, Appendix E.
128 *Beckenham & Penge Advertiser*, 9 December 1971.
129 Board of Governors Presented Papers: 3 April 1967, Appendix E/4.
130 *Beckenham & Penge Advertiser*, 1 February 1968, 2.
131 Board of Governors, 2 January 1967.
132 *Ibid.* 2 October 1967.
133 *Beckenham & Penge Advertiser*, 6 June 1968, 3.
134 *Sunday Telegraph*, 29 March 1970, 4.
135 Drug Abuse Working Party, 11 March 1985.
136 *Bethlem & Maudsley Gazette*, Spring 1972, 31–2.
137 Medical Committee, 24 April 1961.
138 Board of Governors, 6 April 1970.
139 *Nursing Mirror*, 14 November 1974, 52.
140 *Beckenham Journal*, 4 June 1971, 4.
141 MTO Presented Papers: 16 April 1985, MTD 31/85
142 Medical Committee, 29 January 1991.
143 Mental Handicap Development Working Party, 14 January 1983.
144 Medical Committee Presented Papers: 19 December 1983, MCD 23/83.
145 MEC, 7 December 1989.
146 *Joint Hospital Messenger*, September 1988.
147 Board of Governors, 7 July 1975.
148 Working Party on Forensic Unit, 27 December 1973.
149 Board of Governors Presented Papers: 6 September 1976, Appendix J.
150 Working Party in Forensic Unit, 4 October 1974.
151 Henry Rollin, 'Forensic Psychiatry in England', in Hugh Freeman and German Berrios (eds), *150 Years of British Psychiatry: The Aftermath* (London: Athlone, 1996), 261–5.
152 Working Party in Forensic Unit, 3 January 1975.
153 *Nursing Mirror*, 16 September 1976, 34.
154 *Bethlem & Maudsley Gazette*, Summer 1985, 4.
155 *Ibid.* Summer 1980, 11.
156 Board of Governors Presented Papers: 6 September 1976, Appendix J.
157 *Beckenham Journal & Kentish Times*, 23 September 1976, 1.
158 MTO, 18 January 1977.
159 *Bethlem & Maudsley Gazette*, Summer 1985, 4, 6.
160 Medium Secure Unit CNO File: Draft Operational Policy, 24 October 1977.
161 Board of Governors, 14 January 1980.
162 *Inter Nos*, Winter 1980, 6.
163 Board of Governors, 8 September 1980.
164 See Central Clinic Project Team, 1981–1982; Central Clinic Commissioning Team, 1982–1985.
165 SHA, 9 July 1984.
166 *Bethlem & Maudsley Gazette*, Summer 1985, 9.
167 Executive Committee Presented Papers: 21 December 1988, Appendix B.
168 Bethlem Task Force, 19 November 1986.

CHAPTER THIRTY-FOUR

TEMPERING MADNESS
Patients and the treatment of mental illness in twentieth-century Bethlem

——— .◆. ———

Many have argued that the everyday voices of the mentally ill have been silenced by institutional psychiatry. For Michel Foucault and the anti-psychiatry movement this became the hidden purpose at the heart of the mental hospital.[1] The nature of the institution and the illness has often deprived psychiatric patients of a voice. References to Bethlem's day-to-day management do not appear because there was no need to explain to those intimately connected to the Hospital how it worked. It is a problem common to many institutions. From this it might appear impossible to reconstruct how patients were treated. However, evidence can be gleaned from the rules, case notes, and personal memories to provide a glimpse of Bethlem's changing therapeutic regime.

CARE, SEDATION AND RESTRAINT

At the turn of the twentieth century, psychiatrists were far from optimistic about their ability to cure. It was only in 1913 that the *Lancet* could feel sufficiently confident to explain that 'psychiatry is beginning to awake from its lethargy'. On the other hand, the Medico-Psychological Association (MPA) continued to see psychiatry 'in a decidedly inferior position to practically every other branch of medicine'.[2] Britain was not the most fertile ground for psychological medicine in 1900 and many of the developments were to take place in continental Europe. Most references to psychiatry lacked the sanguine attitude that the growth of a biochemical and scientific approach had brought to other fields of medicine.[3] In 1901 the Lunacy Commission reported:

> with a slow but steady increase of the average lunacy population year by year ... the conviction is slowly being strengthened that with all our boasted scientific and medical progress ... the cure of insanity as a whole has fallen behind expectations.[4]

Others worried that there was an attitude that 'no special skill or experience is needed in the treatment of mental disorder'.[5] In a paper, 'The Present State of Mental Science', one doctor lamented that 'though medical science has made great advances during the nineteenth century, our knowledge of the *mental* functions of the brain is comparatively still obscure'.[6] Much was to change. In medicine the interwar period was one of consolidation; in psychiatry it was one of development. New therapies were devised that finally appeared to offer a cure.

In Edwardian Bethlem, few would have predicted these developments. The Hospital was no backwater, although treatment had remained unaltered since the 1880s. When a reporter for the *London Argus* visited the Hospital in 1904 he left with the view that nothing 'is left undone which will tend to purge the brain of its brooding melancholy'.[7] The Board of Control asserted that Bethlem carried out 'work of varied interest and of great benefit to the community'.[8] A paradox existed. The Hospital for Nervous Diseases, the short-lived outpatient department, and an early emphasis on voluntary admissions were pioneering. Bethlem also led in the early application of psychoanalytical and psychological methods. However, the Hospital was not always at the forefront of psychiatry as the Governors liked to claim. An early interest in psychotherapy and psychology did not prevent recreation and sedation remaining the 'master methods'. Here Bethlem was not alone. Other mental hospitals relied on comparable therapeutic regimes and the Board of Control constantly complained that 'more might be done to effect recovery'.[9] At Bethlem, an enthusiasm for modern equipment did not mean that new treatments were quickly adopted, at least until the 1930s. Some discoveries like the alleged benefits of prolonged sleep were ignored.[10] By the mid-1930s the situation had changed. The previous interest in bacteriological infection, sedation, recreation and psychological testing declined. Attention now turned to physical treatments and occupational therapy, partly in response to patient pressure. Psychiatrists greeted these developments with often unreasoning enthusiasm, but at Bethlem they were introduced reluctantly. The interest displayed in measuring mental ability and John Porter-Phillips's long tenure as Physician-Superintendent (1914–44) provided a critical environment for the reception of these new methods. In addition, a small medical staff and the admission of middle-class and paying patients discouraged experimentation. This limited the treatments that could be used. However, once the new convulsion therapies had been popularized, pressure increased from patients for their adoption, overcoming the Governors' reluctance and Porter-Phillips's scepticism.

Care and sedation provided the main underlying tenets of Bethlem's therapeutic regime until the 1930s. A regimen, unaltered since the late nineteenth century, was used to cure or at least prevent patients from brooding on their condition. Here similarities existed between Bethlem's institutional culture and that found in other psychiatric institutions.[11] Admission itself had become a form of treatment in the nineteenth century with the growth of the asylum system. Although psychiatry was rarely praised, the asylum was a source of professional pride, and psychiatry remained institutionally rooted until the reaction against mental hospitals in the 1950s.[12] For a mental hospital in the early twentieth century it was hard to escape accepted practices of patient management where the ethos of moral treatment had been reduced to administrative routine. Bethlem's rules provided a carefully regulated environment. Each part of the patient's day was planned and every day was the same. Patients were woken between six and seven with a cup of tea when the nurses would 'unlock the bed-room doors of all patients . . . fit to be at large' before breakfast at eight. After breakfast they were either set to work cleaning, underwent special treatment and occupational therapy, or were expected to amuse themselves. Lunch was at one, and in the afternoon the morning routine was repeated until the patients were returned to the ward at four. After tea they were encouraged to read or 'take up other amusements' until nine when they were put to bed, their clothes removed from the rooms, and the doors locked. Patients were expected to conform to these rules and were prevented from exercising 'any authority' over each other.[13]

Like all mental hospitals, the sexes were segregated and difficult patients were grouped together, creating problems for the nurses. Bethlem retained a flexible ward arrangement and patients were moved around inside the institution according to their mental condition. Improvement saw transfer to a ward where more freedom was allowed. Convalescent cases were sent to a separate ward. The aim was to return the patient to a normal life. A limited system of parole was in operation, but most patients were not allowed to leave the ward unaccompanied. Observation was not perfect. Escapes and suicides occurred weekly, and after a patient drowned in one of the Monks Orchard lakes these were filled in.[14] To reduce the risk of suicide, windows could be opened only a few inches, stairwells were fenced, fireguards were locked, and even the bath taps had keys.[15] The jangle of keys was heard constantly. Everywhere patients went they were treated like children by benign but authoritarian nurses.[16] The medical staff adopted a behavioural assessment of recovery, popularized in the nineteenth century, and spoke in terms of patients having to 'obey' the nurses.[17] They viewed mental illness as a failure of will that a moral–pastoral environment could reinvigorate. Patients had to be seen to accept the rules and moderate their behaviour accordingly if they wanted to be discharged. Their gradual improvement was marked by references to participation in ward life or the fact that they had taken up sport or reading. Considerable emphasis was placed on personal hygiene. One nurse remembered: 'we had to train everyone and take them to the toilet'; those who remained 'dirty in their habits' were likely to be discharged uncured.[18] Discipline was seen as an important part of the therapeutic regime.

Despite similarities with other psychiatric institutions, Bethlem managed to modify the mental hospital environment. Voluntary and paying patients and their relatives expected high standards. Patients were not therefore housed in large wards or viewed as convenient labour. Single rooms were provided and attempts were made to make them comfortable. One nurse recalls that the wards were 'cosy' and 'beautifully furnished', filled with flowers from the greenhouses. All the bedrooms at Monks Orchard were 'equipped with a Lloyd Loom chair, water jug, and washbasin and lockers'.[19] In 1934 the Board of Control enthusiastically noted 'the thoroughly sympathetic attitude of the nursing staff and of the consideration shown to the personal wishes of the patients'.[20] When other mental hospitals were being attacked after the publication of Lomax's *Experiences of an Asylum Doctor*, Bethlem was praised. The Governors' habit of making unannounced visits helped ensure that everything was kept in good order. Such was Bethlem's atmosphere that many mistook it for a private or general hospital. Patient experiences did not always match these views. The author Antonia White gave a fictional account of her treatment at Bethlem, where she had spent ten months in 1922, in *Beyond the Glass*. She wrote of being confined in a locked cell with 'whitewashed and dirty' walls where she was forcibly fed, heavily drugged, and strait-jacketed. Nurses were shown as roughly handling patients in an environment that was oppressively Victorian.[21] Letters from patients complaining about how they were stripped, pummelled, and forcibly given 'unknown medicines' help support White's account.[22] Some even threatened suicide 'if not removed', a strategy that proved counterproductive and led to further confinement in a padded room.[23] This was more like the Bedlam of old, but actual reports of harsh treatment were uncommon. Medical and nursing staff reflecting on their time at Bethlem in the 1930s talked about a caring institution. Some patients described 'a clinging confidence that betokens real affection' between the nurses and patients.[24] Patients were allowed to dress how they pleased. Those suffering from paranoia were reassured. Doors were left open if the patient became frightened. Patients appeared to be talking about different institutions, but both experiences were possible.

Before 1948, every patient admitted to Bethlem was sedated no matter what their mental illness or behaviour. Like Rhys Williams before him, George Savage had experimented with various drugs at Bethlem and their enthusiasm for sedation continued. Several standard preparations were used. These included sulphonal, a powerful tranquillizer developed in the 1880s and used until the 1950s, and foul-tasting paraldehyde, 'the safest, cheapest and most convenient of all forms of chemical restraint'.[25] Hyoscine was prescribed in the 1930s to deal with 'head-banging, rubbing, and pulling out of hair, relentless picking away of the skin causing sepsis'.[26] Ovaltine was also used to help patients sleep, and in extreme cases chloroform was administered. In line with developments in other hospitals and the growth of the pharmaceutical industry, the staff increasingly favoured the use of barbiturates like the hypnotic veronal and the milder medinal, allowing patients to sleep deeply and wake refreshed. No distinction was made between voluntary and certified patients. All these drugs were efficient at calming excitement and promoting sleep. They were not, however, seen as offering anything other than a temporary relief of symptoms. Depressed patients were prescribed stimulants. This mainly took the form of brandy and whisky until benzedrine, a drug that produced a sense of euphoria and was used experimentally in the treatment of schizophrenia, started to be prescribed in the 1930s. Along with rest, exercise and diet these drugs formed a common armamentarium for Edwardian psychiatry. Mistakes were occasionally made in prescription. In 1914 six patients died after one house physician accidentally administered undiluted amylene hydrate. Miss Gair was immediately appointed as a dispenser to prevent a recurrence, though it was her shorthand and typing skills that were favoured over her pharmaceutical knowledge. She worked as the dispenser for a year until she was replaced by a qualified pharmacist from the Royal South London Dispensary. Gair remained as Porter-Phillips's secretary and more careful attention was paid to prescribing.[27] Blood tests were used to prevent over-medication, though many patients stayed on these drugs for months. Several did complain that the combination made them drunk and one noted that it was 'the hottest cocktail she had ever had'.[28] The staff ignored these complaints and relied on sedation to calm patients, making them easier to manage and more amenable to psychological methods. This did not mean that Bethlem was a peaceful environment, and many were disturbed 'by the wailing and noise at night'.[29]

Other forms of treatment were used, but until the 1920s these were mainly prescribed for depression. A modified form of Weir Mitchell's rest cure was in use, where patients were nursed in bed and bound by a regime of rest, seclusion and a nourishing diet. There is no evidence to support the view that it was limited to female patients or those suffering from neurasthenia.[30] Savage and Sir Maurice Craig had recommended the treatment to Virginia Woolf and used the same methods at Bethlem from the 1890s onwards. As Woolf explains in *Mrs Dalloway*, the treatment was almost like a living death.[31] Geoffrey O'Donoghue, the chaplain, felt there was a more serious concern. In 1916 he complained that the rest cure was preventing patients from attending chapel.[32] By the 1920s neurologists began to question the effectiveness of the cure. At Bethlem this translated into less interest in keeping patients in bed and attention shifted to mechanically stimulating patients.

When sedation or rest did not work, electrotherapy and massage were suggested. Electrotherapy had been pioneered by Wilhelm Erb in Germany and became widely popular. It was believed that electricity restored depleted nerves, and although the treatment was unpleasant, it was not painful.[33] Electrotherapy was first used at Bethlem in 1919 and three nurses were sent to Guy's Hospital for training.[34] Between 1919 and 1927 electrotherapy and massages were given to 117 patients in the out-patient department.[35] In the main Hospital the two therapies were seldom combined and the medical staff were criticized for not making wider use of them.[36] Alastair MacGregor, a doctor at Bethlem in the 1930s, explained that electrotherapy was useful in treating mental fatigue, though he was aware that tact was needed as some patients were frightened by the apparatus.[37] Hope was also placed in ultraviolet light. Mental hospitals had started using ultraviolet light in 1923 and the Board of Control encouraged its use as thoroughly modern.[38] Silverston and Thomas at Lancaster Mental Hospital believed it was a 'general tonic treatment of the insane', but at Bethlem the doctors were not at first enthusiastic and equipment was installed only in 1932 when it was mainly used with convalescent patients.[39] Doses remained small, often no more than a minute, especially as patients objected to any skin irritation.[40] More money was spent on providing hydrotherapy treatment after the Board of Control noted the absence of such facilities at Southwark, although there is evidence that hot and cold baths were used as a form of treatment in the late nineteenth century.[41] Hydrotherapy had established itself as the main competitor to electro-therapy in the early twentieth century, developing into a medical speciality dealing with the therapeutic effects of baths, douches, wet packs, and steam.[42] At Monks Orchard a shower bath was used in Fitzmary One where 'a hessian hammock was in situ in the bath with jets of controlled warm water entering the bath from both sides'.[43] This was the most popular form of hydrotherapy and similar practices were used at the Maudsley in the 1930s.[44] Treatment was given to restless patients for anything up to an hour. In addition, Porter-Phillips advocated the use of lactic acid bacillus from soured milk. He argued that it reduced the amount of toxins absorbed in the intestine, promoted an increase in weight, and shortened 'the duration of illness'.[45] The staff were not enthusiastic. None of these treatments proved effective and were given only to a few patients. In 1948 Aubrey Lewis, Professor of Psychiatry at the Maudsley, pronounced all these treatments old-fashioned when he outlined his ideas for the medical administration of the Joint Hospital. He felt that 'modern methods . . . do not require the continued use of the ultra-violet, douche and other installations' and insisted that they be removed to make more room for the patho-logical laboratory.[46] Facilities, however, remained on the wards until the 1960s and some older nurses keenly demonstrated their use to junior staff.

After the controversies at Bethlem in the 1880s, enthusiasm for restraint and seclusion was not dulled. Savage's successors did not express his unrepentant faith in restraint, but they did see certain forms as permissible. The resurgence of restraint from the 1890s onwards did not end debate. In the 1920s the whole 'question of seclusion' still 'bristle[d] with difficulties'.[47] Attempts were made by Bethlem's Gov-ernors to reduce both methods of control. Neither was referred to in the 1935 rules, but practice differed. Patients in an excited condition who could not be sedated, or showed 'excessive violence', were removed to a padded or 'quiet' room. Suicidal patients were placed on a 'tab' and visited every fifteen minutes. Continuous con-finement was avoided and if patients proved too difficult to manage they were discharged. When Bethlem moved in 1930 it was initially felt that 'other methods of control' could be used, but it was quickly found that this was not possible. Between 1928 and 1965, ninety-two patients were restrained, 40 per cent of these between 1928 and 1937. Most were restrained 'to prevent self injury or harm' or for 'surgical reasons'. Restraint was limited to 'soft-padded gloves', with 'strong clothing' used when patients refused to remain dressed. After 1950 the methods changed. Violent patients were now locked in their rooms for periods of up to six hours, or placed in a 'quiet room'. Lewis considered these 'quiet rooms' an embarrassment. He thought that 'as long as they are available, they will be used' and pressed for their removal. The medical staff supported Lewis, but the nurses were anxious about the management of 'acutely disturbed patients'. The Medical Committee disagreed and proposed that, despite fears of increased sedation, the 'quiet rooms' should be closed for a trial period of six months.[48] After the trial a report saw the continued need for 'quiet rooms', but by 1954 seclusion had declined and the 'quiet rooms' had fallen into disuse, given moves to relax the Hospital's regime and provide open wards and therapeutic communities (see pp. 695–9). Between 1955 and 1962 only eight patients were placed under some form of restraint.[49] The seclusion policy came under review in 1985. Staff were reminded that it 'was a serious matter to interfere with any patient's freedom'. Seclusion now took several forms: detention to prevent patients from leaving the Hospital, seclusion in a locked room, segregation in an unlocked room, and restrictions to limit the patient's freedom.[50] The procedure remained controversial and the decision of what to do with seriously disturbed or violent patients continued to prove difficult.

The physical treatments and forms of management outlined above were part of the standard forms of therapy available to psychiatrists. Bethlem did not contribute to their development, merely incorporating them into its therapeutic regime. Here the Hospital was not controversial and used these treatments to a lesser extent than other mental hospitals. Procedures were modified after the merger with the Maudsley and the psychopharmacological revolution, but they provided continuity with Bethlem's pre-National Health Service (NHS) regime.

A PREOCCUPATION WITH TEETH

Other forms of treatment did prove controversial. In the climate of therapeutic self-doubt at the start of the twentieth century, American psychiatrist Henry Cotton attempted to bring 'asylum medicine' into the mainstream. The result, according to Andrew Scull, was a gothic tale of modern medicine.[51] Cotton built on Adolph Meyer's psychobiological approach, convinced of the value of physical treatments. He developed his ideas on 'focal sepsis', drawing on the discovery that General Paralysis of the Insane (GPI) was caused by syphilis to embrace a bacteriological view where mental illness was caused by infections travelling to the brain. Cotton earnestly believed that the mentally ill were physically sick. Critical of psychotherapy, he felt that many lesions had gone unnoticed because they were not acute disorders and could be detected only by radiological and bacteriological examination. He advocated radical surgery to remove the infection and so the madness. At Trenton State Hospital, Cotton was at first preoccupied with patients' teeth, but his interest quickly extended to the entire body, often with fatal results. In England, given the continuing disdain with which psychiatrists viewed psychotherapy and the success of bacteriology, similar ideas had been expressed. Despite dubious statistics, Cotton's theory was praised, but opposition in America quickly mounted. Meyer presented a critical report and Cotton responded with a nervous breakdown.[52] Where the focal sepsis theory proved contentious in America, psychiatrists in England were enthusiastic. This encouraged Cotton. In 1927 a joint meeting of the MPA and British Medical Association (BMA) gave a powerful endorsement and called for operating theatres in all mental hospitals. Not all institutions were convinced: at the Maudsley focal sepsis was rejected in favour of a psychoanalytical and hereditary approach. Enthusiasm started to wane in the 1930s. Despite extensive research at St Andrew's Hospital, Northampton Hospital, and Birmingham Mental Hospital under Thomas Chivers Graves, psychiatrists were beginning to have doubts. Interest was slow to subside, especially outside London with the doctors at Birmingham remaining stubborn adherents. With the introduction of convulsion therapies focal sepsis no longer seemed relevant, given the new sense of therapeutic optimism, so that by 1941 'medicine in general had rather abandoned focal sepsis'.[53]

Bethlem did not embrace every aspect of Cotton's work, but led by Porter-Phillips the medical staff accorded focal sepsis a significant part in treatment.[54] In 1920 he explained that at Bethlem more attention was now being paid to the 'physical side of mental illness'. He felt that 'it is absolutely essential that in the first instance a searching physical examination should be made in order to discover the [physical] causal factors and eliminate them if possible'.[55] Enemas were given to '[sluice] the intestines' and efforts were made to simulate the immune system to fight the infection through injections of 'TAB', a typhoid vaccine often inducing nausea and fever.[56] The main emphasis, however, was on patients' teeth. To further treatment, William Bulleid, former assistant dental bacteriologist at Guy's Hospital, was appointed dental surgeon in 1922.[57] From Bulleid's appointment the work of the dental department 'increased considerably . . . owing to the fact [that] in quite a number of cases one has realised that certain diseases of the teeth and consequent oral sepsis play an important part in the aetiology of mental disorder'.[58] In 1926 Porter-Phillips confidently explained that

> such a very large number of patients are admitted with marked dental disease that treatment must often be resorted to at once. This is most essential as one has to consider the possible role this focal sepsis plays in the causation of mental disorder.[59]

Bulleid was seen as offering valuable assistance to the medical staff. By 1925 all patients had their teeth examined. The medical staff could point to their own successes that appeared to justify the theory. Not all patients appreciated the doctors' enthusiasm: dental work was extremely painful and frequently led to further infection.

Interest in focal sepsis persisted at Bethlem longer than at many other institutions. However, from the mid-1930s less emphasis was being placed on the theory. Porter-Phillips's enthusiasm declined as he became more interested in psychological examinations and occupational therapy. The focal sepsis rationale for dental work did not entirely disappear. He was still prepared to look to physical factors and recommended in 1936 that 'particular attention should be paid to the complete examination of the blood, urine and excreta'.[60] In 1941 Bulleid, now distracted from his work by his patriotic obligations to the wartime Emergency Medical Service, was still able to recommend that 'teeth should be removed'.[61] Of the ninety-eight female patients discharged in 1943, 45 per cent received some form of dental treatment, although by the 1940s the link between poor teeth and mental illness was less clear in the case notes. Attention had gradually shifted from focal sepsis dentistry to dental conservation and sight tests in an attempt to help maintain patients' general health. Where Bethlem's interest in patients' teeth did not contribute to their cure, it at least ensured that when patients were discharged those teeth they had left had received expert attention.

THE START OF PRACTICAL TREATMENT?

While Bethlem was concentrating on focal sepsis, other institutions had started to adopt malarial treatment for patients suffering from General Paralysis of the Insane (GPI). A long-term consequence of syphilis, GPI was not the 'paradigm-disease' that some have believed, but it produced a vivid picture of madness and a marked decline that resulted in death.[62] Nearly every patient admitted to Bethlem by the 1920s was given a Wassermann test to determine if they had contracted syphilis, and those exhibiting signs of the illness had their genitals examined. If GPI was diagnosed, no effective treatment was available, although experiments were made with intercranial injections of salvarsanized serum, a treatment for syphilis. In 1917 Julius Wagner-Jauregg in Vienna discovered that it was possible to treat GPI with a malaria-induced fever to eradicate the syphilitic spirochaete in the blood.[63] Malarial therapy was first used in England at the Whittingham Mental Hospital in 1922 and Wagner-Jauregg's method was quickly adopted, shaking the 'nihilistic outlook of clinical psychiatry'.[64] Within three years malarial therapy had been adopted at forty-three mental hospitals, although attempts to apply the treatment to schizophrenics met with little success. Public health concerns were voiced when it was found that English mosquitoes could become infected, but the high mortality was invariably overlooked in the belief that patients would die anyhow. Bethlem had first investigated alternatives to malarial therapy in 1923. NAB injections, a treatment for syphilis, were given to patients with GPI and interest switched to malarial therapy only in 1925 when no improvement was seen.[65] At first patients were sent to the West End Hospital for Nervous Diseases, Queen Square, for 'an injection of malarial blood' to remove the danger of having infected mosquitoes in the wards, before malarial infected blood was used to inoculate patients. Early experiences were not encouraging. It was felt that the treatment only offered 'a slight hope of complete cure'.[66] However, there was little opportunity to use malarial therapy. Chronic cases were discouraged at Bethlem and few GPI patients were admitted. The treatment was virtually monopolized by county and borough mental hospitals, especially in London where the London County Council's (LCC) Horton Hospital had its own malarial ward. By 1944 the therapy had been replaced by penicillin. Malaria therapy was continued at the Maudsley, but at Bethlem there was no need to persist with a treatment that had proved marginal in its therapeutic regime.

Despite the faith in focal sepsis, Bethlem did not cut itself off from other developments. Where the medical staff ignored some of the more unusual treatments like feeding brains to stuporous schizophrenics, interest was shown in psychology and psychotherapy.[67] Freud's ideas gained a certain notoriety before 1914, if not clinical enthusiasm.[68] Bethlem's Physician-Superintendent William Henry Stoddart, as noted in Chapter 32, played an important role in encouraging the acceptance of psychotherapy. Apart from his own interest, he encouraged the pathologist to hypnotize patients. Building on the work of Charcot and Janet in France on the treatment of hysterical patients, it was believed that through hypnosis traumatic memories could be uncovered. Freud had himself first employed hypnosis until he found that patients could be persuaded to talk in full consciousness, during which he urged them not to choose or censor their speech (free association). Psychotherapy was widely greeted with hostility in the medico-psychological community and was seen as 'incompatible with the traditional professional conception of the doctor's moral/pastoral responsibilities'.[69] The public were more receptive and were weaned on a diluted form of Freudianism that was more optimistic and less sexually oriented.[70] Stoddart made Bethlem one of the first mental hospitals in England to use Freud's approach.

The First World War greatly encouraged a growing awareness of psychological techniques and an eclectic psychotherapy wary of Freudian excess. Some have argued that these developments effectively transformed post-war psychiatry and created a new attitude that led to the more liberal 1930 Mental Treatment Act. Interest was not sufficient to encourage the development of office psychiatry and few institutional services were created.[71] Extensive psychotherapy was developed at the Cassel Hospital, Richmond and the Tavistock Clinic (Bloomsbury), while the Maudsley under Edward Mapother established a psychotherapy unit and was keen to encourage 'unprejudiced trials of every form of treatment'.[72] Bethlem was not as open-minded, but did not dismiss Freud's talking-cure. Psychotherapy continued to have influential opponents including Sir Robert Armstrong Jones, one of Bethlem's Governors and Lord Chancellor Visitor in Lunacy.[73] He attacked Stoddart in 1926 and, coincidentally, none of Bethlem's doctors flaunted their psychodynamic ideas. Psychotherapy,

684

however, continued to be used on the wards and there was no reluctance to discuss sex. Doctors joining Bethlem after the war started using suggestion to convince patients that their condition was not hopeless. In the medical school William Brown, a pioneer in experimental psychology and Wilde Reader in Mental Philosophy at Oxford, and William Rivers, who treated Siegfried Sassoon for shell-shock, held lecturing posts. Encouraged by their experiences with shell-shocked soldiers and the importance of dream analysis, they were both proponents of a modified Freudian approach.[74] Their work at Bethlem was limited to teaching and psychometric testing, as noted below, but they helped create a sympathetic environment. Psychotherapy was employed with depressed patients, but taking into account the often advanced nature of the illness before admission many staff became frustrated when improvement was not seen, given the 'attention lavished'.[75] This matched the more pessimistic assessments outside the Hospital. Although it was felt that some success was encountered, no special arrangements were made until 1936 when Bernard Armitage, house physician and medical adviser to the Antwerp Olympic games, was appointed as a psychotherapeutic officer. The appointment was made because it was felt that psychotherapy had become common in mental hospitals and not because of an underlying faith in the treatment.[76]

Like psychotherapy, interest in psychology was stimulated by wartime experiences.[77] The two approaches are difficult to separate, but at Bethlem a clear distinction was made. Psychiatrists had shown some interest in psychology since the nineteenth century and in the interwar period Spearman's work on mental measurement impressed leading psychiatrists, including Mapother. He felt that psychologists should work alongside clinicians, using their methods of mental testing to aid diagnosis. This was the approach adopted at Bethlem. Outside the mental hospital these ideas were popularized by Cyril Burt, Professor of Psychology at the University of London from 1932. His theories of intelligence demonstrated to a wider audience the relevance of psychology to social problems.[78] Edgar Miller, Professor of Clinical Psychology at the University of Leicester, has argued that clinical psychology did not really have a firm place in mental healthcare until the creation of the NHS. He suggests that Blackburn and Vernon at the Maudsley were the first psychologists to be employed in a mental hospital before 1939.[79] He has ignored developments at Bethlem where a consultant psychologist was appointed in 1923. Experiences with shell-shock had shown the value of psychological methods, and Porter-Phillips was keen to include psychology in the medical school's syllabus. Brown and Rivers were added to the lecturing staff and contributed an important part to its distinguished character.[80] At first they had little to do with the Hospital, but under pressure from Brown, Porter-Phillips started to realize the wider application of their methods. He began pushing in 1922 for the appointment of a psychological consultant, aware that psychological investigations could be useful in the early stages of mental illness, asserting that 'it is a matter of considerable importance that this branch of psychological medicine should not be in any way neglected'. The Governors agreed and appointed Brown because he held 'well balanced views of this difficult subject'.[81] Porter-Phillips and Brown next pressed for a psychological laboratory. The Governors were reluctant, especially as the Treasurer had recently announced the need to build a new hospital (see Chapter 29). They believed that a laboratory would benefit only the medical school, but Porter-Phillips convinced them that services would be available to the medical staff. Brown was duly made director of the psychological laboratory in 1932.[82] Progress was slow. Cooperation did not always exist between the director of the department and the rest of the medical staff. No attempt was made to adopt anything other than a psychometric approach and on admission each patient underwent word-association and intelligence tests. Regular complaints were made that American tests were too easy for Bethlem's patients. Tests were subsequently modified and new ones devised. Meetings were held at the Hospital by the British Psychological Society to discuss these findings, and several joint projects were started with University College Hospital.

With the introduction of convulsion treatments psychometric tests were used with less frequency. Interest was revived after the creation of the Joint Hospital in 1948. The Institute of Psychiatry, able to attract leading psychologists, was one of three institutions to run a postgraduate course in clinical psychology in the 1950s. After the dismissal of the director of the psychological department in 1948, no psychologists held a post at Bethlem and services were provided by the Institute.[83] All patients were given vocabulary tests on admission. Other cognitive and personality tests were now considered a special treatment and required consultation with the Institute. Rising demand made psychology students at the Institute feel like 'a pair of hands'. Senior staff worried that they were devoting a 'disproportionate amount of their available time on case-work'. To solve the problem, the Medical Committee urged in 1970 that more attention should be given to the selection of cases.[84] Psychological services were split into two: type one would be available for all patients; type two for those who required extensive treatment.[85] The distribution of psychological services and the question of payment to the Institute remained fraught.

Psychotherapy underwent a similar expansion, building on the experiences of the Maudsley's unit. Lewis was slightly sceptical, but Denis Hill saw psychotherapy as an important part of psychiatry that all doctors should use. Sigmund Foulkes, the renowned group therapist, taught methods where the psychiatrist would be part of a group but not its leader, while Wilhelm Hoffer, Heinz Wolff and Murray Jackson tried to encourage psychoanalytical ideas.[86] At Bethlem intensive group psychotherapy was provided from 1960 in Tyson West Two under Robert Hobson, who had been pressing for a psychotherapy unit since the previous year.[87] When plans were made to close the day ward in 1971, Hobson suggested the creation of a day-unit and special hostel. The Medical Committee, concerned to minimize the effects of the closure, suggested a psychotherapeutic community for ten patients.[88] Bethlem's old recreation hall was used and renamed the Charles Hood Unit, a name Hobson felt appropriate given the 'emphasis he placed upon social and moral treatment'. The aim was to create a therapeutic community to reduce dependence. Where at first it was seen as an experiment, the unit quickly proved its worth.[89] When Hobson left in 1974 to take up a post in Manchester, the unit went through a period of uncertainty, closing in 1978. Psychotherapy services were transferred to a small ward in Tyson West and then to the Maudsley in 1987, but by the late 1970s psychodrama, Gestalt therapy, group therapy and transactional analysis were in regular use throughout Bethlem. Psychodrama was based an Aristotelian views of catharsis and aimed to use a series of situations to resolve tensions, while through Gestalt therapy patients were taught to personify the warring parts of their mind and invent a dialogue in which they could come to agreement.[90] In these therapeutic games patients were encouraged to shed their inhibitions and express their feelings in active or symbolic ways. Such therapies had a bad reputation as an outlet for middle-class boredom, but staff argued that they provided an important means to stimulate learning and personal development.[91] As experience accumulated it became evident that these methods were not suited to every patient. Some did not see nurses' interventions as helpful and became frustrated with ward groups, whose purpose was not always clear. With 220 separate weekly groups by 1984, staff felt there was too much emphasis on group therapy and many of the methods were disliked by patients.[92]

Behavioural psychotherapy provided an important area of development. British psychologists were among the first to exploit the ideas put forward in 1958 by Joseph Wolpe in *Psychotherapy by Reciprocal Inhibition*, which brought behavioural therapy to the fore. The Institute of Psychiatry and the Maudsley became leading centres for these ideas through the work of Jones, Meyer and Eysenck, who founded the journals, *Behaviour Research* and *Therapy*, in 1963. Formally started in the Joint Hospital in 1964, behavioural therapy based its claim on the principle of conditioning and learning. Experience quickly showed that it was the treatment of choice for phobias and obsessive-compulsive disorders and had much to offer patients with sexual problems. There was no wish, however, 'to claim these behavioural techniques offer a "cure-all" for psychiatric disorders'.[93] Eysenck, no stranger to controversy, commented that 'few people who were not present . . . can have any conception of the condemnation, the opposition, or the downright hostility these new methods aroused'. The introduction of behavioural therapy marked a shift from the earlier diagnosis and intelligence testing approach. Eysenck explained that it filled the void left by the overthrow of Freudian methods and promised remarkable cures.[94] In the Joint Hospital the acceptance of behavioural therapy owed much to the work of Jack Rachman and Isaac Marks, who from Tyson West Two ran the behavioural programme.

At Bethlem treatment mainly focused on the nurse-therapist scheme established by Marks. The shortage of trained therapists meant that many neurotic patients went without adequate treatment and placed a burden on the NHS. Opposition was encountered from the nursing superintendent, Governors and some of the medical staff who were uncertain whether it was appropriate that nurses should be trained in psychotherapy and treat sexual problems. Marks compromised and stressed that none of the treatments involved the nurses becoming sexual objects.[95] Once the principle of nurse-therapists was accepted, Marks extended the training scheme between 1970 and 1975 to cover sexual problems by proving its success and arguing that it cut down the chance of readmission for sexual problems not treated at the Hospital. Permanent support was secured from the Department of Health and Social Security in 1975, allowing the Hospital to become the leading centre for the training of nurse therapists. Patients with phobias were exposed to their fears and taught to confront them. Group work was used for obsessive-compulsive disorders, while patients with 'sexual dysfunction or deviation' were encouraged to communicate before being gradually exposed to sexual situations.[96] Some attempt was made to provide shame aversion therapy for exhibitionists in 1979, but the Ethical Committee felt that the treatment was unsuitable, while at the Maudsley the use of shock aversion therapy for alcoholism aroused strong criticism.[97] From the 1980s a self-help model was adopted.

Treatment was not limited to Marks's behavioural unit. Nurse-therapists worked in several units. In Hilda Lewis House, children were given a reinforcer (usually chocolate) to strengthen the lessons learnt during treatment, and punished with short periods of seclusion.[98]

Bethlem's enthusiasm for psychological methods did not prevent an interest in other forms of treatment from developing before 1948. Entertainment and recreation remained central to Bethlem's therapeutic regime, once George Tuthill had introduced them as a form of treatment in the nineteenth century (see Chapter 24). Both were important parts of moral restraint and asylum orthodoxy and provided the basis for the development of formal occupational therapy in the 1930s. Hunter and Macalpine believed that they did 'much to repair the public image of asylums as places where patients were unwillingly detained, if not maltreated'.[99] At Bethlem, the Governors continued to ensure that patients were 'fully and agreeably occupied'. Entertainments and recreation served an important social and curative function to help resocialize patients and keep them amused.[100] One nurse remembers that 'we tried to keep everyone occupied . . . they played cards, table tennis, did knitting, [and] sewing'.[101] The Governors believed that by providing pianos and a library, they were stimulating the patients and 'bringing fresh activity into institutional life.'[102] The installation of radios in the wards in 1926 was greeted with widespread enthusiasm. One patient wrote: 'ours was a splendid instrument, giving speech and song in a manner as limpid and crystal clear as a stream . . . and every listener was still'.[103] In addition, an active programme was provided throughout the year. Entertainments proved 'extremely popular and provided material for conversation for days after the event', with trips to Epsom in the summer and concerts and plays on Friday evenings in the winter.[104] O'Donoghue offered lantern-slide lectures, which proved particularly popular, as did the Fancy Dress Ball which quickly became the highlight of the Hospital's year. For the dramatic performances professional companies were avoided in favour of amateur dramatic companies. Bethlem proved a critical audience and one poor performance was enough for a society not to be invited back. Every effort was made to avoid anything that had a serious character and the emphasis was on entertainment and distraction. Staff were expected to attend and contribute where necessary. Even more attention was paid to outdoor recreation (Plate 34.1). Sport played a prominent part in mental hospital life, particularly football and cricket. Facilities were gradually developed for both staff and patients and a sports club was formed in 1933. At first the Governors aimed to involve patients, especially through the daily cricket matches, but increasingly the club supported purely staff activities.[105]

The regular programme of entertainments and sport did not keep every patient occupied. Frustration developed and in the 1920s Porter-Phillips began to suggest that more structured occupation was needed. The idea that patients should work was not new. Pinel, Tuke and Conolly had all seen the value of occupation in moral therapy, but in most nineteenth-century asylums this had been translated into work to increase the efficiency of the institution rather than aid recovery. Bethlem had used similar methods until the 1880s when work was scaled down, given the class of patients admitted. Formal training and an ideology of occupational therapy took longer to develop. In 1919 David Henderson, medical superintendent at Gartnavel Royal Mental Hospital, Glasgow, introduced the first formal occupational therapy

Plate 34.1 Patients playing bowls, *c.* 1910. Reproduced by permission of the Bethlem Royal Hospital Archives and Museum.

classes and presented an influential paper to the MPA in 1924.[106] The Board of Control added its support, finding it 'distressing to go round the wards and find scores of patients left to deteriorate in wearisome idleness'.[107] From 1923 onwards, the Board pressed mental hospitals to found departments, and when a training school was established at Bristol in 1930 facilities existed for training staff. At Bethlem, basket-making had been started in 1907 to relieve depression and patients were employed in the wards, but not to the degree found in other mental hospitals.[108] Work did not agree with the Hospital's bourgeois character. Plans for a 'therapeutic workshop' had been shelved in 1927 in the interests of economy, a situation the architects considered a serious omission given that occupational therapy was 'considered by most modern practitioners as [an] essential curative agency'.[109] Increasingly complaints from paying patients spurred Bethlem into action. In 1932 five patients wrote to the Governors to explain that their

> recovery is very greatly retarded by having nothing to do beyond billiards and draughts. We sit about from morning till night, with meals and medicines as the only variety. Is it not possible to give us some light manual occupation to take our thoughts off ourselves and which might be of some practical use?[110]

Porter-Phillips used this to persuade the Governors to appoint the energetic Nora Pollard as an occupational therapist. Early therapy concentrated on diversions and recreational activities and Bethlem was no exception. Part of the laundry block was converted and training in seventeen different crafts was provided, with gardening included when weather permitted. Work continued to be highly gendered and attendance was highest on the female side. Despite the emphasis placed on acute cases and the shift in attention to early intervention through convulsion therapies, occupational therapy remained an important part of the therapeutic routine. Classes were a success: by 1939, 317 patients attended the department and 'so interested do most of them become that extra work has to be supplied to take back to the wards'.[111] Renamed the Arts and Crafts Department in 1935, a training programme was started two years later where students would receive nine months' training and board in lieu of pay. Cooperation with the Occupational Therapy and Training Centre at Merton Rise from 1944 onwards increased the number of students.[112] Occupational therapy was extended and the boundaries with physical exercise were blurred when the department started to organize physical fitness classes and folk dancing.[113] Work was regularly entered in the Surrey Handicrafts Exhibition and several prizes were won.[114] The Board of Control was pleased with the progress made and was encouraged that even the 'seriously mentally disturbed and lost [were] induced to take an active part in simple musical exercises and games'. It was sure that 'this is a development of real importance'.[115]

After the merger occupational therapy was extended. The Medical Research Council Social Psychiatry Unit at the Institute of Psychiatry, and Aubrey Lewis's interest, stimulated occupational therapy. Lewis felt that 'within the hospital it provides the patient with satisfaction and brings him into close and cooperative contact with other people in relationships that are familiar to him'.[116] Professors Tizard and O'Connor in the Institute emphasized the value of training for the mentally retarded and persuaded local businesses to provide simple subcontract work.[117] Ironically an Industrial Rehabilitation Unit was not established at the Maudsley until the 1960s. No effort was made to provide a similar service at Bethlem, although the Joint Hospital continued to work with local firms and charities to provide industrial therapy outside the Hospital.[118] Most of the work at Bethlem took place in the occupational therapy department or in the wards. Each patient was assessed and programmes were tailored to individual needs. Some limited work on the farm was offered. Although the House Governor argued that it met the need for outdoor employment, the Governors resisted pressure from the Ministry of Health to sell land because it was 'essential to ensure reasonable seclusion and sites for development of future buildings'.[119] A patients' sports day was held annually until 1970 when it was stopped because of lack of interest. Inter-ward sports competitions flourished in the 1970s, but had all but died out by 1986. Whereas nurses suggested the need for more outings, many were aware that there was little for patients to do at the weekends, a problem that continued into the 1990s.[120] No attempt was made to offer the same detailed programme of entertainments that had existed before 1948. Therapy now aimed at getting patients back to work. For those geriatric patients who spent a long period at Bethlem an 'Over 60 Club' was formed that, by promoting outings, mirrored Bethlem's previous efforts.[121] Financial support was also given to an ex-patients' club, which organized social activities, lectures and film shows in the Maudsley's outpatient department.

The new Community Centre at Monks Orchard increased the work undertaken by the department. Initially planned in 1957, it was the first new building development at

Bethlem since 1930. The aim was 'to provide a place where patients can get together in pleasant and interesting surroundings, and so speed their recovery'. In view of this 'great attention was paid to the decoration and design and furnishing' in order to avoid the antiseptic atmosphere of a hospital.[122] With new facilities, the occupational therapy department could now offer classes in typing and shorthand, cooking and housecraft, dressmaking, art, music, printing and duplicating. The old building continued to be used for carpentry, metalwork, pottery, and car maintenance.[123] The development of art and music therapy in the 1970s, originally as a focus for group therapy, saw the emphasis shift from work therapy and skills training.

Despite the growth of provision, concern was voiced in 1968 that its value was not properly understood by doctors.[124] Attendance was low. When the head occupational therapist retired in 1975 a working party was established to put forward a 'radical reappraisal'. It found that the Joint Hospital did not have a good reputation for occupational therapy and that staff had low expectations. Facilities at Bethlem were seen as inadequate, and the working party pointed to a lack of organization. At the Maudsley the situation was worse.[125] It was decided in 1977 to reorganize the department and more emphasis was placed on rehabilitation and home management. An Intake Assessment Area was provided, along with a work area to prepare patients for work, and a Home Management Unit to stimulate home management skills.[126] Relaxation classes were added in the mid-1980s.[127] Each area had its own specialist therapist, with nine additional therapists appointed to Bethlem's wards. Greater cooperation with other staff was encouraged.[128]

SHOCKING PATIENTS BACK TO HEALTH

Where Bethlem was developing psychotherapy, psychometric testing and occupational therapy, malarial treatment had given 'renewed credence to treatments of mental disorder which relied on administering a severe blow to the patient's physical being'.[129] Sedation made patients more amenable to psychological methods, but in the 1930s physical treatments came to the fore. Attention now turned increasingly to schizophrenia, although it was found during the early 1940s that the new therapies were more effective in the affective disorders. The use of cardiazol (later triazol) was first reported in 1934, insulin coma in 1935 and electroconvulsive therapy (ECT) in 1938. The background to these treatments has been extensively discussed elsewhere.[130] Apart from insulin, all produced a series of controlled fits in an attempt to recreate an epileptic fit in the belief that there was a negative correlation between schizophrenia and epilepsy, a reaction against over-complex psychodynamic ideas.[131] The theory proved erroneous, but when they were reported these treatments were quickly adopted, almost uncritically.

Convulsion by injections of cardiazol was introduced in 1934 by the Hungarian Ladislas Meduna. The Board of Control invited experimentation in 1937, brushing aside concerns that the treatment involved physical risk.[132] This was to become a common approach as psychiatrists appeared desperate for effective treatments. The Board was keen to have cardiazol adopted because it offered the prospect of treating schizophrenia, the main contributor to overcrowding in mental hospitals. The medical staff at Bethlem, led by the Senior Assistant Physician, eagerly took up the invitation, replacing cardiazol in 1939 with triazol, a drug that produced a similar fit with fewer unpleasant effects. Initially limited to female schizophrenics, it gradually became a universal therapy. Neither treatment was tried immediately on admission. Normal therapies were used first for one to two months before cardiazol or triazol was given. The treatment was frightening, producing anxiety and the feeling of impending death before the fit and could induce uncontrolled seizures. Understandably some were terrified and refused further injections. Porter-Phillips was, however, sceptical about the recovery rate and uncertain about the therapeutic rationale or prospect of stable recovery. John Hamilton, the Senior Assistant Physician, was more optimistic. He felt that with a 61 per cent recovery rate it was 'possible to treat a greater number of patients within a prescribed time with the same number of beds'. For him this was sufficient justification.[133] Given the apparent effectiveness of cardiazol and triazol, even if only short term, the medical staff put their doubts aside and widely adopted the treatment.

Where the medical staff were slow to embrace some treatments, Bethlem was one of the first institutions to start using insulin coma therapy. Insulin had been isolated in 1922 and apart from its use with diabetics it had been used to quieten psychiatric patients and build up their weight. The Austrian Manfred Sakel, working with the vague theory that a loss of sugar would act as a tonic to the brain, developed a procedure in 1935 where insulin was used to sink patients into unconsciousness from which they would be roused.[134] The risks created initial concern, but these were put aside when it became clear that the treatment worked. The Board of Control announced the use of insulin in 1936, but the treatment had been introduced in Edinburgh and Bethlem in 1935, four years before the LCC approved its use in its hospitals.[135] Insulin therapy required considerable nursing and skill to avoid a prolonged coma. Hamilton was anxious about the after-effects and advised that all hospitals should follow Bethlem's lead and use continuous observation.[136] The numbers treated at Bethlem were therefore small (see Table 34.1). Patients were collected from the wards at seven and transferred to insulin beds in the Wakefield Unit where they would be treated, going back to the wards after lunch. War made it difficult to obtain insulin and glucose and, where other hospitals found new methods to induce the coma, the Governors at Bethlem decided to discontinue the treatment. It was

Table 34.1 Number of patients given insulin therapy, 1945–8

Year	Male	Female	Number treated	
			Recovered	*Relieved*
1945	5	8	7	2
1946	15	24	18	8
1947	19	26	30	10
1948	24	24	16	14

Source: Insulin Treatment Summary

restarted in 1946 when the procedure was already beginning to be attacked. The Medical Committee of the Joint Hospital expressed dissatisfaction with Bethlem's arrangements in 1949, and a special insulin unit like the one at the Maudsley was established in Tyson West Two.[137] The ward was run by an authoritarian nurse who prided herself on keeping the unit clean and patients regimented. After the treatment, patients would sit around doing little, but attempts to introduce group therapy met staunch resistance. When research showed that the same effects could be produced by barbiturate narcosis, and more effective treatment could be secured by neuroleptic drugs, the use of insulin coma declined and the unit was closed in 1960.[138]

While Bethlem was extending its use of triazol, a less distressing form of convulsion therapy using an electric shock to the brain was developed in Italy by Ugo Cerletti, Professor of Psychiatry in Rome, and his assistant Lucio Bini. The procedure, which owed more to Bini than Cerletti, became known as ECT and spread rapidly. Initially no attempt was made to assess the therapeutic value of the method and it was felt to have the same effect as cardiazol.[139] Everywhere the electroshock machine was introduced it occasioned great enthusiasm, even after examinations revealed that in some patients it produced crushed vertebrae. ECT revolutionized the treatment of depression and mania, but in some patients it left a lifelong horror of treatment.[140] With Porter-Phillips unsure about the benefits of triazol, Bethlem started using ECT in 1940 whereas the LCC initially proved reluctant.[141] Triazol had become unobtainable with the outbreak of war and Porter-Phillips was optimistic about ECT, aware that it had far 'less unpleasant features' despite complaints of headaches and vomiting.[142] ECT was also cheaper and easier to administer and came to dominate treatment. Prolonged treatment was avoided and ECT was given in short bursts until an improvement was seen. The medical staff were not guided by any particular diagnosis and it was not given to every patient, although women were twice as likely to undergo a course of ECT. Consent was sought from friends and relatives, but this did not stop them complaining when injuries occurred. Many expressed gratitude that it had 'shortened [the] attack so much' and others even appeared to enjoy it.[143] The machine

> was the size of a small cinema organ, its top a rather bewildering array of dials and switches. Although the machine was fearsome to us nurses and doctors to begin with, the fears of patients about convulsion treatment became unusual and outright refusal rare.[144]

ECT provided Bethlem with an effective therapy that reduced treatment times and allowed a reduction in the amount of sedatives prescribed. At the same time it meant that the Governors and medical staff were less inclined to admit difficult patients if others could be quickly discharged. Of the 146 patients discharged in 1941, only eighteen were reported to have been difficult and of these only five had to be restrained.

Unlike the other forms of convulsion therapy, ECT survived the war and the merger. It remained the anchor of treatment until drugs started to offer better means of therapy. More attention was turned to its administration. Given the attacks the antipsychiatry movement made on ECT, concerns were raised in 1969 that the treatment was not undertaken in 'accordance with current recommendations for good practice' at the Joint Hospital. To solve the problem a working party was appointed. It found that ECT was administered under the general supervision of a consultant with a senior registrar and registrar present. The working party was concerned that the registrars were not sufficiently qualified to give the anaesthetic and recommended the appointment of an anaesthetist.[145] Difficulties were encountered. The junior staff did not see the importance of the treatment and often failed to attend sessions. It was admitted that ECT, even if it went well, which was rare, proved nerve-racking. The Medical Executive Committee therefore recommended that it could only be administered to one patient at a time in a separate room.[146] A special hut was provided, with sound proofing added in 1976 to limit the noise transmitted to the waiting room which had been distressing patients.[147] ECT was eventually centralized at Bethlem in the Wakefield Unit and treatment underwent a resurgence in the 1980s. ECT is still used in the Joint Hospital for schizophrenia when antipsychotic drugs fail. The main modern use, however, is for depression when medication proves ineffective, and as an emergency treatment.

Before 1954, ECT was the Hospital's most effective form of treatment, but when it failed or patients reacted adversely, Bethlem's medical staff considered using leucotomy (or lobotomy) after 1944.[148] The operation, where the frontal lobes of the brain were damaged by surgery, became a historical embarrassment by the 1960s, but it 'was not a medical abberation, spawned in ignorance', rather a part of the mainstream of medicine that built on increasing research into the chemistry of the brain and cerebral localization.[149] Dogged by controversy from the start, the technique was first developed in Portugal in 1935 by the Nobel prize winner, Moniz. Hospitals initially proved cautious about the spectacular results reported with disturbed patients. However, the need for a treatment that worked with the most intractable cases convinced many of the efficacy of a procedure that promised to resocialize a subgroup of patients otherwise doomed to institutionalism. Concerns about mortality and the risk of permanent damage to the patient's personality were overlooked because it was felt that it could not make the patient any worse. Here was a repeat of the early attitude to malarial therapy. As the Harvard neurologist Stanley Cobb noted in 1949, 'seldom in the history of medicine has a laboratory observation been so quickly adopted and dramatically translated into a therapeutic procedure', a transition eased by the influential support leucotomy received.[150] By 1947, ninety-seven mental hospitals had adopted the treatment and more radical forms were developed. Treatment was not motivated by diagnosis, but by the failure of other methods and behavioural problems.[151] By 1940s standards the operation was seen as good clinical medicine, encouraging the development of a more scientific methodology.[152]

The Board of Control's visitors to Bethlem in 1942 commented that whereas the use of ECT was relatively new 'it is intended shortly to introduce leucotomy for certain cases'.[153] Porter-Phillips remained sceptical about the treatment.[154] The Governors were cautious and agreed only in 1946 to allow the operation after their insurance company had arranged cover.[155] Formal approval did not match practice: the first leucotomy was performed at the Hospital in 1944. Mita R— was obsessional and suicidal, even with ECT, and after two years at Bethlem a leucotomy was insisted on. The improvement was 'most dramatic', allowing Mita to be discharged after six weeks.[156] Four more operations took place in 1945. Treatment was limited to those suffering from schizophrenia and paraphrenia, a subtype of schizophrenia identified by Kraepelin in 1913 that was characterized by a higher degree of violation.[157] The treatment put considerable pressure on the nurses as patients were reduced to a childlike state and required intensive behavioural and psychological retraining. Pressure did not come from Bethlem's medical staff, but from patients and their relatives. Leucotomies, however, were reserved for difficult cases, especially those who were abusive. Consent was sought before the operation and a special fee of thirty shillings was charged for the consultant surgeon to attend. A similar practice was used at other hospitals where the medical staff lacked the surgical skill to perform the operation. The creation of the joint neurosurgical unit with Guy's Hospital after the merger stopped all neurosurgical operations at Bethlem. Operations were transferred to the Maudsley, which became an important centre for psychosurgery. Enthusiasm eventually declined with the development of neuroleptic drugs, and by 1967 the treatment had been largely abandoned and new surgical procedures developed.

Porter-Phillips remained cautious about these new treatments, preferring a psychobiological and psychological approach. Hamilton on the other hand, as the Senior Assistant Physician and then Physician-Superintendent, was mainly responsible for their introduction and became a keen advocate of psychosurgery. Both ECT and leucotomy became 'orthodox and popular' and such treatments did change the psychiatrist's image to that of a healer.[158] 'One may question whether shock treatments do any good to the patients,' wrote Louis Casamajor, a New York psychiatrist, in 1943, 'but there can be no doubt that they have done an enormous amount of good to psychiatry.'[159] Successes heartened Bethlem's medical staff and allowed them to be more optimistic about recovery. By 1947 46.4 per cent of the certified patients were given ECT, 8.9 per cent insulin therapy, and 19.6 per cent a leucotomy.[160] These new forms of treatment shifted the balance in active therapy from the male to the female patients. They also had a wider impact, allowing Bethlem to catch up with the other London mental hospitals in terms of treatment.

OPEN DOORS AND THERAPEUTIC COMMUNITIES

Enthusiasm for physical treatments continued after 1948. According to John Crammer, barbiturates were in wide use in the Joint Hospital in the 1950s and ECT was the main anchor for treatment.[161] Even Lewis's support for social psychiatry did not dull enthusiasm. Although a battle was fought over the value of such physical treatments, the Joint Hospital was more successful at combining different approaches than the Maudsley had been immediately after the Second World War.[162] Here a larger hospital with two sites became an advantage. Friction existed, but the Joint Hospital remained a broad church. A medical and biomedical approach, however, remained important. Such an approach was encouraged by the psychopharmacological revolution of the 1950s that, as will be noted, allowed psychiatry to move beyond the institution. Other methods were adopted that altered how patients were managed and treated. The development of an open-door policy, mixed wards, therapeutic communities and multidisciplinary teams did not occur separately. These movements were interlinked and built on the new sense of optimism after the war. They were not the sum of post-war psychiatry. The development of new drugs and means of investigation led to what Robin Murray has termed the 'decade of the brain', where mental illness has been increasingly treated as a genetically influenced disorder of brain chemistry. This marked a further shift from the post-war emphasis on social psychiatry. Only by detailing the extensive research undertaken at the Joint Hospital and the Institute of Psychiatry would it be possible to give an accurate picture of these developments. This is clearly beyond the scope of this volume. Instead, to avoid complicated lists of drug names and their effects, the aim is to look at the broader changes in patient management and treatment that surrounded these developments.

With the formation of the NHS, Denis Hill felt a new spirit had come to infuse mental healthcare. The NHS brought at least an extra hour in bed for the patients, and changes in psychiatry ensured a relaxation of Bethlem's routine. Others shared Hill's assessment, believing that it 'tended to reduce the barriers between the mental hospitals and society'.[163] Staff in the Joint Hospital felt that 'mental hospitals every-where are undergoing at the present time a stimulating and exhilarating experience – a rethinking of the patient's needs and a replanning of the ways in which these may best be satisfied'.[164] The authoritarian nature of the nursing at Bethlem, however, took longer to change. The NHS saw an improvement in the physical conditions found in the county and borough mental hospitals, but at Bethlem much of the hotel-like character remained.[165] Monks Orchard provided a calm and pleasant environ-ment, free of the congestion and anxieties of the Maudsley. When the wards were seen as 'gloomy and somewhat old fashioned' in 1966 a programme of renovation was started to bring Bethlem in line with the recently modernized Maudsley.[166] Only the Intensive Care Area in Fitzmary remained a 'bleak and depressing place', partly because of the nature of the patients admitted.[167] Governors visiting the wards continued to be impressed with the level of sympathy extended to the patients. When the Mental Health Act Commissioners visited Bethlem in 1990 they were 'much impressed by the atmosphere of efficiency and dedication'.[168] The Joint Hospital was able to maintain high standards of care by drawing on Bethlem's endowments.

For Hill the new spirit was symbolized by the open-door policy.[169] Unlocked doors were not new. In some mental hospitals wards had been unlocked in the 1920s, but Thomas Rees's publicity at Warlingham Park encouraged others to follow.[170] At the time there was little theorizing and the decision seemed motivated mainly by a grow-ing awareness of asylum conditions. Rees held that the mentally ill were not a race apart and emphasized that the opening of doors marked a return to a more caring attitude where patients were seen as people. He even suggested that this was a return to moral therapy.[171] The opening of doors appeared to be an end in itself and many hailed an immediate improvement in staff–patient relationships. By the 1950s, the open-door policy was 'sweeping the hospitals of the Western world'. The movement came to be associated with doctors like David Clark at Fulbourn and a reluctant nursing staff who were often opposed to the decision. This was not the case at Bethlem. Fears on the part of the nurses were genuine, and the decision to open wards required courage as they had previously been held responsible for any escape. Most doctors were reluctant to proceed with a full open-door policy and many institutions established a flexible regime. Some locked wards were retained and few hospitals remained entirely open, with fences maintained and a more vigorous treatment of absconders.[172]

The issue of open wards at Bethlem was first raised in 1949. It was felt 'a little anachronistic' in a hospital that admitted only voluntary patients that wards should be locked. Voluntary patients were free to discharge themselves and many resented the semi-custodial atmosphere. Warren recommended that more consideration should be given to the open-ward principle to solve this problem, although he recognized that the shortage of nurses might present difficulties. He felt that any change should be introduced gradually and proposed that Fitzmary Two should be opened. This suggestion was adopted.[173] Patients from this ward were allowed access to the grounds from nine to four and to the ward garden until dusk. They were prohibited from visiting other wards and permission from a doctor was needed to leave the grounds.[174] Gresham Two followed in May 1950, and each time a ward was opened it was done only after lengthy consultation.[175] Unfortunately the records say little about how this process was achieved or the difficulties that were encountered, although the number of thefts did, coincidentally, rise.

At the same time as doors were being opened, wards were being mixed after an experiment in Tyson West One in 1951.[176] This was not extended to the adolescent unit until 1979 after earlier public embarrassment when two teenage patients eloped to Tunbridge Wells.[177] Strict controls were maintained in the Drug Dependence Unit and Medium Secure Unit. Here patients were separated from the rest of the Hospital, the former mixing only during occupational therapy.[178] Whereas an open-door policy and mixed wards existed throughout Bethlem by the 1960s, the nurses' home was still double-locked.[179] However, it was not until 1966 that wards remained unlocked until ten. When Priscilla Norman, a Governor between 1951 and 1975, visited Bethlem she felt that the practice appeared 'to be working well and was acceptable to nearly all staff'. She went on to comment that few problems had been encountered and those that had were nothing compared to the hazards posed by 'foxes and badgers'.[180] A 'custodial approach', however, was still seen. It was felt that nurses showed a 'traditionalism and resistance to change' and 'protective and security measures' were in force. Patients were expected to sign a ward book on leaving the ward, and ward passes that allowed a maximum of 48 hours' leave were in operation until 1974.[181] The decision to open wards stimulated a large programme of occupational therapy to keep patients in the Hospital, while it increased the burden on the staff who were now expected to know their patients better.[182] By 1978 the medical staff had returned to the view that locked wards were necessary, given the type of patient being sent to Bethlem. The Management Team of Officers were not entirely convinced that this was the solution to the problems posed by disturbed patients.[183] The increased admission of disturbed patients and the rise in the number of violent incidents overrode these concerns. Many of the new units at Bethlem, like Hilda Lewis House and the Mental Impairment Evaluation and Treatment Service, could not run on an entirely open-door policy. For these patients some restrictions were found necessary. The creation of an interim medium-secure unit in Tyson West One in 1980 produced a unit where locked doors were implicit.[184] Gradually doors were locked once more throughout the Hospital.

Open wards were part of an environmental response to mental illness to reduce tension and the sense of institutionalism. Therapeutic communities were a similar reaction, and the two were often linked. The idea of a therapeutic community had grown out of wartime experiences and the dynamics perceived in group psychotherapy. The term was first used by Tom Main who, with his colleagues in Northfield Military Hospital, advocated 'a therapeutic setting with a spontaneous and emotionally structured ... organisation to which all staff and patients engaged'.[185] The aim was for equality, where all patients and staff would participate in the running of the community. Main took his ideas to Cassel Hospital, while the charismatic Maxwell Jones ran the Social Rehabilitation Unit funded by the Ministry of Labour at Belmont Hospital. Jones became the leading proponent of the therapeutic community.[186] Through ward groups and regular meetings therapeutic communities tried to give patients more freedom and mitigate the resentment of being sent to a mental hospital. To achieve this nurses were assigned a greater therapeutic role. Progress was slow as patients adapted and staff became used to ward meetings and criticism by patients.[187] Open-door policies aimed to provide an alternative to detention; the therapeutic community assumed that detention was a prelude to care.

It is hard to gain a clear picture of developments in the Joint Hospital. Ward practices were rarely mentioned in the minutes. What is clear is that at Bethlem not every aspect of the therapeutic community was adopted. Instead, a general approach and not a therapeutic community proper was adopted and applied in the treatment of alcoholism, drug addiction and for adolescent disorders, where it was seen as particularly useful.[188] Several staff had worked with Maxwell Jones at Mill Hill and Dartford. Lewis was a firm supporter of social psychiatry and Foulkes had applied his group therapy to the work at Northfield. They were keen to encourage the development of therapeutic communities. Bethlem's day hospital incorporated some of these ideas and in 1960 Robert Hobson established the first therapeutic community at Monks Orchard in the newly redecorated Tyson West Two.[189] The idea was gradually adopted by other units, like the Drug Dependence Unit, partly due to Eileen Skellern's encouragement. She was appointed Matron in 1963, having had considerable experience of therapeutic communities. Skellern had worked with Maxwell Jones at Belmont, where she had been in charge of the Social Rehabilitation Unit, and at the Social Therapy Unit at Cassel.[190] She believed that a routine should not be forced on patients and recommended that nurses should establish a relationship with a small group of patients and treat them with warmth and respect, encouraging them to express themselves.[191] Skellern brought her ideas into the Joint Hospital and worked easily with those interested in psychotherapy, fostering an enhanced role for psychiatric nurses. She helped stimulate training in this field. More attention was turned to the patients' day and further facilities were provided. Enthusiasm began to wane in the late 1960s because the movement had not produced the 'comprehensive revolution in the social organisation of custodial institutions which many idealists sought'.[192] The approach that therapeutic communities encouraged, however, lived on in a modified form and became incorporated into the psychiatric regime of the Joint Hospital.

One area where the therapeutic community persisted was the emphasis it placed on the role of the nurse in treatment. In the Joint Hospital and elsewhere this led to the growth of multidisciplinary teams. When Hilda Lewis House was opened in 1971, each child had its own interdisciplinary team of a nurse, doctor, occupational therapist, teacher and social worker.[193] Multidisciplinary teams became standard. Several nurses did complain that the rhetoric of constant cooperation in patient care did not often exist in practice. They felt that 'doctors often appear cynical or casual and do not seem to be interested', while the half-hourly ward meeting was insufficient to cover anything up to thirty patients.[194] Similar views were echoed by the Hospital Advisory Service in 1973. Its report pointed to a degree of 'doctor domination' that limited the effectiveness of multidisciplinary teams. Only one consultant was seen to invite nurses to ward conferences. Junior doctors commented that more encouragement should be given to the ward staff to relate to their patients 'in such a way as to reduce the need for both physical and pharmacological constraints and restrictive rituals'. The report did, however, identify that more positive teamwork existed at Bethlem.[195] The solution was to encourage additional ward groups and a greater degree of nurse participation. After the report, inter-disciplinary staff meetings and patient/staff meetings were established on all wards on a weekly basis.[196] Multidisciplinary teams, despite periodic opposition from the junior medical staff who were concerned about their own role, became the vogue. Cuts in Southwark Social Services in the late 1980s, however, left 'major gaps', arousing hostility in the Joint Hospital.

PSYCHOPHARMACOLOGICAL REVOLUTION AND COMMUNITY CARE

All three of these approaches owed something to the new emphasis placed on pharmacological solutions and controls for mental illness. On the tenth anniversary of the NHS one member of the House of Commons commented that 'tranquillisers . . . have given infinitely more freedom to these patients', and pointed to a dramatic change.[197] Psychiatrists continued to be optimistic in the 1960s that drugs would be developed to combat every form of mental illness, an optimism that was failing by the 1990s. The profession had been seeking a pharmaceutical panacea since the mid-nineteenth century, and drug therapies were not new. In the 1930s psychiatrists like Erich Guttman and Walter Maclay at the Maudsley had experimented with the use of mescaline and LSD. Tests with LSD after 1945, however, were overshadowed by the development of a new group of drugs that took the psychiatric profession by storm.

Michael Shepherd believed that the introduction of chlorpromazine to Britain in 1953 transformed psychiatry.[198] Even William Sargant, the self-proclaimed apostle of physical treatment, admitted that this phenothiazine derivative, which appeared to reduce the symptoms of psychoses without impairing consciousness, was 'a wonder drug'.[199] Trials showed that chlorpromazine produced rapid sedation in schizophrenic and manic cases with patients developing an indifference both to their surroundings and symptoms, reducing tension, anxiety and the need for intensive nursing. It appeared to offer a cure in some cases of schizophrenia, a general reduction of symptoms in all cases, and the ability to discharge nearly all schizophrenics. Treatment times were shortened and institutionalization seemed less necessary. By the end of 1954 chlorpromazine was hailed as a revolutionary breakthrough, launching an 'era of psychopharmacology'.[200] Only the diehards continued to go against the 'fashionable pharmacotherapy'.[201] Pharmaceutical companies rushed to produce a whole range of drugs with similar effects to cash in on chlorpromazine's success. According to Fennell:

> never again would 'advances in psychiatry' come from therapeutic entrepreneurs . . . Innovation would henceforth be pioneered in the laboratories of drug companies. Psychiatric hospitals became extensions of those laboratories where the effects of the drugs on humans could be monitored. Psychiatrists became the customers and researchers of the pharmaceutical companies and this fortified psychiatry's already pronounced dependence on drugs.[202]

The first of the tricyclics, so called because of their chemical composition, and the neuroleptics drugs were developed in 1957, narrowly missing being discarded as useless.[203] Both transformed the treatment of depression, filling the vacuum left by the growing disillusionment with the empirical methods of physical treatment. Further tricyclic, neuroleptic and psychoactive drugs were developed (mostly outside the recognized neuroscientific and psychiatric centres like Oxford, Cambridge, the Maudsley and the Institute of Psychiatry) in the gold rush of discovery of the 1970s.[204] Prozac (fluoxetine) is only among the most recent and the most hyped by the media to be developed. For some Prozac, used in the treatment of depression, presents new dangers and has been perceived as the beginning of a new 'cosmetic psychopharmacology' first seen with the introduction of diazepam (Valium) in 1963.[205] With this new psychopharmacology, many felt that psychiatry had emerged from the dark ages with the promise that hazardous and irreversible treatments could be eliminated. Like the convulsion therapies of the 1930s, side-effects were frequently ignored because the benefits appeared too great. By 1977 psychoactive drugs accounted for 25 per cent of NHS prescriptions.[206] Freedom to prescribe was curtailed in 1985 by the publication of the Government's limited list of brand-name drugs considered ineffective or over-priced. The BMA was incensed, but many hospitals (including the Joint Hospital) had already used their own lists in an attempt to save money.[207]

The arrival of chlorpromazine saw a marked change in the Joint Hospital. Where only 15 per cent of patients were given some form of drug therapy in 1952, the introduction of chlorpromazine saw this rise to 40 per cent in 1957; by 1969 38 per cent of patients were given antidepressants, 37 per cent phenothiazine. Doctors remained cautious. They were advised against automatically prescribing new expensive drugs, but by the 1970s the full range of drugs was used and the number of discharges had subsequently swollen. The balance shifted from physical treatments and more attention was given to follow-up clinics, day wards, and domiciliary visits.[208] Changes had occurred by the 1970s and monitoring increased. An attempt was made to prevent the hoarding of sedatives by not informing patients about the nature or dose of the drugs prescribed.[209] Addictive barbiturates had been replaced and where chlorpromazine continued to be prescribed attention turned to tricyclic drugs. There was a firm belief that prescriptions should not be extended for more than two months, when the case should be re-evaluated.[210] The senior nursing officer reported in 1974 that 'extensive drug use had released many patients from the bondage of their suffering and has allowed a large number of patients who 20 years ago would have been condemned to a life in hospital to take part in society'. He went on to explain that 'drugs ease the burden on the staff. The freedom that mentally ill patients now enjoy would be impossible without the use of drugs'.[211] It is undeniable that the tricyclics, neuroleptics and antipsychotics did have a major impact on the Joint Hospital. Every unit used medication in some form, either to reduce the symptoms or to make patients more amenable to psychological or psychotherapeutic methods. The Joint Hospital was not a zealot for these new methods. An active research programme was maintained to monitor the short- and long-term effects of drugs, and an enlightened nursing regime, especially in the treatment of eating disorders, was preferred. Where this suggests links with Bethlem's pre-NHS experiences, the biggest difference is that psychiatrists felt more optimistic about their ability to treat mental illness and not just relieve its symptoms. Disillusionment now turned to Government policy and areas outside the mental hospital.

Psychotropic drugs gave psychiatry a recognizable medical form of treatment. They were popular with psychiatrists on these grounds and because they required little knowledge of the patient's background. They were also popular with patients. Some have attributed the growth of community care to this psychopharmacological revolution, a view shared by the 1990 White Paper *Caring for People*.[212] However, the reasons for the shift in emphasis to favour non-institutional care are not so straightforward. Deinstitutionalization started before the psychopharmacological revolution, although new drugs made treatment outside the Hospital easier. Where therapeutic changes contributed, other forces were at work. Faced with a crisis of funding and accommodation in mental healthcare it should be no surprise that 'many mental health planners became enthusiastic about forms of therapy permitting more rapid turn-over of patients'.[213] A local shortage of nurses encouraged these trends. In psychiatry more attention was turned to social psychiatry with the creation of day hospitals and outpatient clinics, which seemed to promise a more caring and family-oriented approach.[214] The 1959 Mental Health Act helped legitimize these services through the support it gave to informal admissions, promoting the view that patients need not be detained to undergo treatment. Encouragement was also given by the 1962 *Hospital Plan*, which called for a 45 per cent reduction in mental hospital beds and suggested that community care for the physically and mentally disabled and the elderly should replace expensive institutional care.[215] In 1976 a further consultative document explained that community care was a 'low cost solution', a statement that did not always prove true in reality.[216] Where new drug therapies and economics played a part, so too did changes in social attitudes. Attacks on asylums were nothing new in the 1950s, but after Russell Barton's popularization of 'institutional neurosis' they multiplied.[217]

Led by Ronald Laing, a psychiatrist at Gartnavel, and the South African David Cooper, the British anti-psychiatry movement went on to characterize care in a psychiatric hospital as bad, while films like *Family Life* (1971) and *One Flew over the Cuckoo's Nest* (1975) mobilized public feeling against mental hospitals. Psychiatrists and outside critics no longer viewed the mental hospital as the ideal or desirable location for treatment. The psychopharmacological revolution enabled patients to be treated outside mental hospitals, the NHS's financial problems created a need to find cheaper means of care, and ideological concerns showed mental hospitals as undesirable and even damaging.

Development, however, was slow. Financial restrictions limited the idealistic vision of community care. Although the resident mental hospital population fell by approximately 33,000 between 1961 and 1970 it had not been halved by 1975 as predicted.[218] Plans were often made to empty hospitals while little thought was paid to the services that should replace them, adding to professional and public disillusionment. These views were confirmed by the Audit Commission's 1986 report. It saw that many vulnerable people, highlighted by the ever-growing problem of homelessness, were being left 'without care and at serious personal risk'.[219] When a survey was conducted at the Joint Hospital in 1990, most of the consultants felt that the growth of community care was one of the most destructive influences of the previous fifty years.[220] The slow and troubled development of community care did not see a withering away of psychiatry but forced it to develop in new areas. For the historian Kathleen Jones, the NHS 'has been shedding any responsibility for mental illness which cannot be dealt with by a few days in hospital to adjust medication'.[221] The death of Ben Silcock in the Lion's enclosure of London Zoo in 1993 only seemed to highlight the problems.

Bethlem's experiences as part of the Joint Hospital were different. The antipsychiatry movement had little impact on the Joint Hospital, while it was slow to adopt national policy. Although aware of the need to develop community services in the mid-1960s, it was only from 1988 that the Special Health Authority's (SHA) district commitment was extended to include community services.[222] Paradoxically, because of its teaching status and links with the Institute of Psychiatry, the SHA could extend its services and take over those offered in other mental hospitals rather than having its beds closed and buildings sold. Encouraged by the 1975 White Paper, *Better Services for the Mentally Ill*, services were extended although problems with funding and a lack of knowledge of what needed to be done slowed development.[223] Over thirty years before the 1990 White Paper, *Caring for People*, which called for a 'mixed economy of care', the Governors had started working with other state and voluntary organizations to provide a district service.[224] In 1960 Mary Ormerod, the chair of the Board of Governors, commented that 'it was difficult to see how more could be done for the community', but projects continued to be developed, reflecting the support Bethlem had given to voluntary organizations before the NHS.[225] Most of these projects, like the Community Psychiatric Nurse Service, Daily Living Programme for schizophrenics, the first of its kind in Europe, or the Adolescent Outreach Service, were organized through the Maudsley's District Service Centre. One project that did develop out of Bethlem's experiences was the creation of summer play schemes for mentally disturbed children in 1982 by Lotte Mason, a social worker in Hilda Lewis House. This evolved into the Community Development Project for the Mentally Handicapped. The Project organized summer play schemes for up to sixty children, along with after-school play centres, four weekend clubs, holiday schemes, mothers' groups, and baby-sitting and child-minding services. The results were encouraging. It was felt that children who had been on the scheme were easier to manage, and 'without exception all families who used the project spoke warmly and enthusiastically of it'.[226]

Community care and the problems and anxieties it has produced have become central to late twentieth-century psychiatry, and the Joint Hospital has adapted accordingly by organizing and extending its services in the community. Negotiations were frequently fraught, but in many ways the Joint Hospital was praised for providing a model, if troubled service.

SUCCESS?

How successful were these treatments in returning Bethlem's patients to health? Whether a patient recovered or not was a subjective judgment. The terminology used by the Board of Control did not allow precise measurement. Doctors at Bethlem complained about the category 'not improved', which did not allow room for marginal improvement.[227] The Hospital preferred to use the more pessimistic term 'uncured'. Given this fact, the Hospital's average recovery rate of 50 per cent between 1900 and 1948 must be treated with caution. Differences existed between voluntary, certified and temporary patients, as shown in Figure 34.1. Voluntary patients always did better than those admitted under certification. This often reflected the more advanced nature of the mental disorder in certified patients before admission was sought. Surprisingly, the introduction of new treatments in the 1930s made no appreciable difference to the recovery rate, despite the optimism they generated, although patients given ECT did noticeably better than those given the other forms of convulsion therapies. However, with these therapies treatment times declined and patients were less likely to be readmitted. The recovery rate was generally more favourable in registered hospitals, but the average at Bethlem was still high. For example, at the

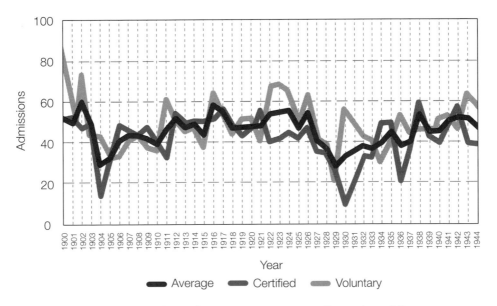

Figure 34.1 Comparison of recovery rates, 1900–44 *Source:* Annual Reports

Cheadle Royal the recovery rate was 37 per cent between 1908 and 1927, and other registered hospitals showed similar figures.[228] In county and borough mental hospitals the recovery ranged between 25 and 35 per cent in the interwar period, and at the Maudsley this was closer to 28 per cent. The Board of Control sought to justify this by claiming that the low figures were a consequence of the rigorous standards set.[229] Bethlem's high recovery rate was linked not to the treatment adopted but to the type of patients admitted, where acute rather than chronic cases were favoured. The merger and the psychopharmacological revolution did not at first appreciably raise the recovery rate. Between 1949 and 1969, on average, 50 per cent of patients left the Joint Hospital recovered, 32 per cent improved.[230] Figures are not available for the period after 1969. These figures conceal different outcomes according to gender or illness. Women were more likely to recover than men. Patients with depression had the highest chance of recovery (74 per cent) along with those with various psychoses (70 per cent), while only 37 per cent of schizophrenics made a full recovery. New drugs have meant, however, that more patients were discharged only to return on a revolving-door policy.

By the creation of the NHS trust in 1994, Bethlem had seen many changes to its therapeutic regime that matched the broad development of psychiatry in the twentieth century. The Joint Hospital's broad church gave full scope to treatment, but it is interesting to note that even before 1948 Bethlem's recovery rate made it one of the most therapeutically successful mental hospitals in England. Where this was not always owed to the therapies used it had much to do with the careful nursing regime in operation and the type of patients treated.

NOTES

1 For the anti-psychiatry movement see Digby Tantam, 'The Anti-Psychiatry Movement', in German Berrios and Hugh Freeman (eds), *150 Years of British Psychiatry* (London: Gaskell, 1991), 333–47.

2 *Lancet*, 2 (1913), 1333; *JMS*, 60 (1914), 675.

3 A. Youngson, *Scientific Revolution in Victorian Medicine* (London: Croom Helm, 1979), is just one of many historians who have pointed to the growth of scientific medicine, though Christopher Lawrence in 'Incommunicable Knowledge: Science, Technology and the Clinical Art in Britain 1850–1914', *Journal of Contemporary History*, xx (1985), 503–20, has argued that bedside practice did not match scientific rhetoric.

4 *Lancet*, 2 (1901), 380.

5 *Lancet*, 1 (1903), 133–4; *JMS*, 46 (1900), 781.

6 *JMS*, 47 (1901), 293

7 *London Argus*, 15 October 1904, 28; 1929/30 Treasurer's Report.

8 *Daily Telegraph*, 6 August 1924, 12.

9 *1935 Board of Control Annual Report*, 3.

10 See G. Windholtz and L. Witterspoon, 'Sleep as a Cure for Schizophrenia', *History of Psychiatry*, iv (1993), 83–93.

11 Kathleen Jones, 'Culture of the Mental Hospital', in German Berrios and Hugh Freeman (eds), *150 Years of British Psychiatry* (London: Gaskell, 1991), 22–3.

12 Clive Unsworth, *Politics of Mental Health Legislation* (Oxford: Clarendon Press, 1987), 60.

13 1932 Rules & Orders, 11.

14 Bethlem Subcommittee, 30 March 1932.

15 *BMJ*, 2 (1979), 429.
16 1932 Rules & Orders, 4–5.
17 P. Phippard, 'Demented, but Clean and Useful' (Unpublished MA Dissertation, University of York, 1992).
18 Vicki Hayward, 'Bethlem in the 1930s' (Unpublished article, 1982), 6.
19 *Ibid.* 2, 7.
20 Board of Control Correspondence: Letter from Porter-Phillips, 3 October 1931.
21 Antonia White, *Beyond the Glass* (London: Virago, 1954), 211–12.
22 General Correspondence: Letter to Wakefield, 6 February 1927.
23 1910 Case Notes: Male Case 27.
24 *London Argus*, 15 October 1904, 48; *Pearson's Weekly*, 30 May 1912, 1159.
25 W. L. Jones, *Ministering to Minds Diseased* (London: Heinemann, 1983), 42–3, cited in Phil Fennell, *Treatment without Consent: Law, Psychiatry and the Treatment of Mentally Disordered People Since 1845* (London: Routledge, 1996), 121.
26 *BMJ*, 2 (1979), 429.
27 Medical Subcommittee, 7 December 1915.
28 1933 Case Notes: Case 116.
29 1939 Case Notes: Female Case 85.
30 See Simon Wessely, 'Neurasthenia and Fatigue Syndromes', in German Berrios and Roy Porter (eds), *History of Clinical Psychiatry* (London: Athlone, 1995), 536–8.
31 Virginia Woolf, *Mrs Dalloway* (London: Hogarth Press, 1990), 83–7.
32 *Under the Dome*, 25 March 1916, 11.
33 Elliot Valenstein, *Great and Desperate Cures: The Rise and Decline of Psychosurgery and Other Radical Treatments for Mental Illness* (New York: Basic Books, 1986), 24.
34 General Committee, 14 April 1919.
35 1919–1927 Massage and Electrical Treatment Book.
36 Medical Subcommittee, 21 April 1920.
37 *British Journal of Physical Medicine*, 10 February 1934.
38 *1925 Board of Control Annual Report*, 13.
39 *1928 Board of Control Annual Report*, 31.
40 *British Journal of Physical Medicine*, 10 February 1934.
41 *1924 Bethlem Annual Report*, 24.
42 Valenstein, *op. cit.* 27.
43 Hayward, *op. cit.* 4.
44 *Bethlem & Maudsley Gazette*, Spring 1975, 9.
45 *JMS*, 56 (1910), 422–30.
46 Aubrey Lewis Papers, Box 5: Circular from Lewis, 21 June 1948.
47 Fennell, *op. cit.* 48–65; *Daily Telegraph*, 12 September 1921, 12.
48 Medical Committee, 19 November 1951.
49 1928–1962 Register of Mechanical Restraint and Seclusion.
50 Medical Committee Presented Papers: 11 March 1985, MCD 6/85.
51 Andrew Scull, 'Desperate Remedies: A Gothic Tale of Madness and Modern Medicine', *Psychological Medicine* 17 (1987), 561–77; Valenstein, *op. cit.* 37–43.
52 Scull, *op. cit.* 561–7.
53 *JMS*, 87 (1941), 526.
54 Porter-Phillips had been interested in the bacteriological dimension of mental illness for some time, having submitted a thesis in 1910 on the 'Bacterial Origins of General Paralysis'. In 1936 he continued to support these views though he had modified his stance to embrace a much broader physical aetiology of mental illness: *Practitioner*, July–December 1936, 36–48.
55 *1920 Bethlem Annual Report*, 10, 47–8.
56 House Committee, 28 May 1930; similar practices were being undertaken by Graves in Birmingham: Andrew Scull, 'Focal Sepsis and Psychosis: The Career of Thomas Chivers Graves', in Hugh Freeman and German Berrios (eds), *150 Years of British Psychiatry: The Aftermath* (London: Athlone, 1996), 527–8.

57 *1922 Annual Report*, 11; while at Bethlem Bulleid wrote two textbooks, *Practical Dental Histology and Bacteriology* (London: John Bale Sons & Danielsson, 1924) and *Textbook of Bacteriology for Dental Students* (London: William Heinemann, 1926), which highlighted his interest in infection and bacteriology but made no mention of focal sepsis in mental illness.

58 *Souvenir of Bethlem Hospital* (c. 1924), 9–10.

59 *1926 Bethlem Annual Report*, 13.

60 *Practitioner*, July–December 1936, 48.

61 1941 Case Notes: Male Case 1.

62 German Berrios, 'Dementia', in German Berrios and Roy Porter (eds), *History of Clinical Psychiatry* (London: Athlone, 1995), 39.

63 See Juliet Hurn, 'History of General Paralysis of the Insane, 1850–1950' (unpublished Ph.D. Thesis, University of London, 1997).

64 Hans Hoff, 'Invention of Insulin Shock Treatment', in Max Rinkel (ed.), *Biological Treatment of Mental Illness* (New York: Page, 1966), 47.

65 1925 Case Notes: Case 113.

66 1927 Case Notes: Case 17, 77.

67 *1932 Board of Control Annual Report*, 100.

68 The literature on Freud is vast. It includes the hagiography of Ernest Jones, *The Life and Works of Siegmund Freud*, vols 1–3 (London: Huber, 1953–7); or accounts by P. Gay, *Freud: A Life for Our Time* (London: Dent, 1981); P. Grosskurth, *Secret Ring* (London: Jonathan Cape, 1991) and A. Storr, *Freud* (Oxford: OUP, 1992), to name but a few.

69 Malcolm Pines, 'Development of the Psychodynamic Movement', in German Berrios and Hugh Freeman (eds), *150 Years of British Psychiatry* (London: Gaskell, 1991), 208.

70 Dean Rapp, 'The Early Discovery of Freud by the British General Educated Public', *Social History of Medicine*, iii (1990), 217–43.

71 See Harold Mersky, 'Shellshock', in German Berrios and Hugh Freeman (eds), *150 Years of British Psychiatry* (London: Gaskell, 1991), 261–4, while M. Stone, 'Shellshock and the Psychologists', in W. F. Bynum, Roy Porter and Michael Shepherd (eds), *Anatomy of Madness* (London: Tavistock, 1985), vol. ii, 242–71, argues differently.

72 See H. Dicks, *50 Years of the Tavistock Clinic* (London: Routledge, 1970); 1923 Maudsley Hospital Superintendent Report.

73 Pines, *op. cit.* 218–19.

74 Rapp, *op. cit.* 235.

75 1921 Case Notes: Case 8.

76 *1913 Bethlem Annual Report*, 17; Medical Subcommittee, 12 February 1936.

77 For the development of clinical psychology, see J. Reisman, *A History of Clinical Psychology* (New York: Hemisphere, 1991), who adopts a largely American perspective.

78 Roy Porter, 'Two Cheers for Psychiatry!', in Hugh Freeman and German Berrios (eds), *150 Years of British Psychiatry: The Aftermath* (London: Athlone, 1996), 387.

79 Edgar Miller, 'Twentieth Century British Clinical Psychology and Psychiatry', in Hugh Freeman and German Berrios (eds), *150 Years of British Psychiatry: The Aftermath* (London: Athlone, 1996), 157–61.

80 Rapp, *op. cit.* 235.

81 General Correspondence: Letter from Porter-Phillips, 24 October 1922.

82 Medical Subcommittee, 26 January and 6 July 1927.

83 Miller, *op. cit.* 162.

84 Medical Committee, 28 September 1970.

85 MEC, 6 April 1972.

86 Pines, *op. cit.* 226.

87 Bethlem Subcommittee, 9 November 1959.

88 Board of Governors, 4 October 1971.

89 MEC Presented Papers: 4 January 1973, ECD 205/72.

90 Jones, *Ministering to Minds Diseased*, 76.

91 *Bethlem & Maudsley Gazette*, Summer 1979, 20.

92 MEC Presented Papers: 7 December 1989, ECD 107/89. See Stuart Sutherland, *Breakdown* (London: Weidenfield & Nicolson, 1976), who describes his frustration with ward groups.

93 *1970–1975 Triennial Statistical Reports*, 135.

94 *Bethlem & Maudsley Gazette*, Winter 1983, 4–5.

95 Board of Governors Presented Papers: 3 July 1972, Appendix G/1.

96 *1970–1975 Triennial Statistical Reports*, 51–4.

97 MEC Presented Papers: 5 July 1979, ECD 73/79; *Guardian*, 10 January 1970, 1.

98 *Nursing Mirror*, 14 November 1974, 50–1.

99 Richard Hunter and Ida Macalpine, *Psychiatry for the Poor: 1851 Colney Hatch Asylum – Friern Hospital 1973* (London: Dawson, 1974), 45.

100 *Daily Telegraph*, 6 August 1924, 12.

101 Hayward, *op. cit.* 7.

102 *1932 Rules & Orders*, 40; *1947 Board of Control Annual Report*, 4.

103 *Under the Dome*, 25 March 1927, 28.

104 Physician-Superintendent's Report, 14 December 1935.

105 See Chapter 32, pp. 637–8.

106 Douglas Bennett, 'Work and Occupation for the Mentally Ill', in Hugh Freeman and German Berrios (eds), *150 Years of British Psychiatry: The Aftermath* (London: Athlone, 1996), 194.

107 *1931 Board of Control Annual Report*, 9.

108 *Under the Dome*, 30 September 1907, 108.

109 General Correspondence: Letter from Cheston to Faudel-Phillips, 3 May 1929.

110 *Ibid.*: Letter to Robertson, 1932.

111 *1939 Bethlem Annual Report*, 13; *1932 Bethlem Annual Report*, 11–12.

112 General Correspondence: Letter from Hewitt to Porter-Phillips, 22 March 1944.

113 *1937 Bethlem Annual Report*, 9.

114 *Orchard Leaves*, Winter 1935, 7.

115 Visitors' Book, 18 February 1937.

116 Aubrey Lewis, 'Resettlement of Chronic Schizophrenics', in *Congress Report of the Second International Congress for Psychiatry* (Zurich: Orell Fussli, 1957), 223–8.

117 Bennett, *op. cit.* 198.

118 For example, in 1973 the Governors gave the newly formed Camberwell Rehabilitation Association £28,000 to buy a property for a sheltered workshop to complement the Hospital's own Industrial Rehabilitation Unit: Board of Governors, 1 October 1973 and 6 January 1975.

119 House Committee, 9 June 1954.

120 *Ibid.* 11 March 1970.

121 *Bethlem & Maudsley Gazette*, September 1954, 182.

122 *Beckenham & Penge Advertiser*, 16 July 1964, 1.

123 *Bethlem & Maudsley Gazette*, June 1964, 64–5.

124 *Ibid.* Winter 1968, 20–2.

125 Occupational Therapy Working Party, 21 June 1976.

126 *Ibid.* 25 November 1977.

127 *Bethlem & Maudsley Gazette*, Summer 1985, 13.

128 Occupational Therapy Working Party, 25 November 1977.

129 Fennell, *op. cit.* 129.

130 Valenstein, *op. cit.* 46–61, Fennell, *op. cit.* 48–169, and Jones, *Ministering to Minds Diseased*, discuss the development of these treatments; see below for individual therapies.

131 M. Gelder, 'Adolph Meyer and his Influence on British Psychiatry', in German Berrios and Hugh Freeman (eds), *150 Years of British Psychiatry* (London: Gaskell, 1991), 419–35.

132 *1937 Board of Control Annual Report*, 3.

133 *1939 Bethlem Annual Report*, 9–10.

134 See F. Jones, 'Insulin Treatment in Psychiatry', *History of Psychiatry*, iii (1992), 221–35.

135 LCC Archive, Greater London Record Office, LCC Mental Hospitals Committee:

Maudsley Orders, Council Resolutions, 16 May 1939; William Sargant, *The Unquiet Mind* (London: Heinemann, 1967), 78.

136 *Lancet*, 2 (1937), 1074–5.

137 Medical Committee, 17 January 1949.

138 *Lancet*, 1 (1957), 607; *Bethlem & Maudsley Gazette*, March 1960, 14.

139 German Berrios, 'Early Electroconvulsive Therapy in Britain, France and Germany', in Hugh Freeman and German Berrios (eds), *150 Years of British Psychiatry: The Aftermath* (London: Athlone, 1996), 10.

140 Jones, *Ministering to Minds Diseased*, 25–6.

141 Sargant, *op. cit.* 81–2.

142 *1940 Bethlem Annual Report*, 7.

143 1941 Cases Notes: Female Case 30; Male Case 35.

144 *BMJ*, 2 (1979), 430.

145 Board of Governors Presented Papers: 6 January 1969, Appendix F.

146 MEC Presented Papers: 4 December 1975, ECD 155/75.

147 MTO, 12 October 1976.

148 See German Berrios, 'Psychosurgery in Britain and Elsewhere', in Hugh Freeman and German Berrios (eds), *150 Years of British Psychiatry: The Aftermath* (London: Athlone, 1996), 180–96; Valenstein*, op. cit.* provides an extensive discussion, while David Shutts, *Lobotomy: Resort of the Knife* (New York: Nostrand Reinhold, 1982), offers a similar account and more particularly a study of Walter Freeman, an obsessive advocate of psychosurgery.

149 Valenstein, *op. cit.* 4.

150 Cited in Jack Pressman, 'Sufficient Promise: John Fulton and the Origins of Psychosurgery', *Bulletin of the History of Medicine*, lxviii (1988), 4, 20.

151 D. Crossley, 'The Introduction of Leucotomy', *History of Psychiatry*, iv (1993), 554–5.

152 Jack Pressman, 'Uncertain Promise: Psychosurgery and the Development of Scientific Psychiatry in America' (unpublished Ph.D. Thesis, university of Pennsylvania, 1986).

153 Visitors' Book, 20 January 1942.

154 House Committee, 6 May 1942.

155 General Committee, 12 November 1946.

156 Board of Control Correspondence: Circular 958, March 1945.

157 Physician-Superintendent's Report, 12 September 1945; P. Hoff, 'Kraepelin', in German Berrios and Roy Porter (eds), *History of Clinical Psychiatry* (London: Athlone, 1995), 272.

158 Crossley, *op. cit.* 553.

159 *JNMD*, 98 (1943), 407.

160 1947 Case Notes.

161 *Bethlem & Maudsley Gazette*, Autumn 1984, 5.

162 *Ibid.* Winter 1983, 33.

163 Almont Lindsey, *Socialised Medicine in England and Wales* (London: OUP, 1962), 307.

164 *Croydon Advertiser*, 7 November 1958, 6.

165 Brian Watkin, *National Health Service: The First Phase, 1948–1974 and After* (London: Allen & Unwin, 1978), 75–83.

166 House Committee Presented Papers: 9 March 1966, Appendix B.

167 SHA, 9 July 1990.

168 MEC Presented Papers: 6 September 1990, ECD 83/90.

169 Denis Hill, *Psychiatry in Medicine* (London: Nuffield Provincial Hospitals Trust, 1969), 13.

170 C. Andrews, *The Dark Awakening* (London: Cox & Wyman, 1978), 227. Warlingham Park was not the first open hospital. Dingleton Hospital, Melrose, led the way and was completely opened by 1949 following a three-year transitionary period. It was followed by Mapperley Hospital, Nottingham, in 1951 with Warlingham Park only open by 1954, although two wards for persistent absconders remained closed: *Lancet*, 2 (1962), 188–90; *Lancet*, 2 (1954), 953–4.

171 *JMS*, 103 (1957), 303–13.

172 Liam Clarke, 'Open Doors in British Mental Hospitals', *History of Psychiatry*, iv (1993), 527–51.

173 Medical Committee, 5 September 1949.
174 General Purposes Subcommittee, 1 November 1949.
175 Bethlem Subcommittee, 1 September 1950.
176 General Purposes Subcommittee, 1 February 1951. The Maudsley was slow to follow the lead taken at Bethlem. Only in 1968 was the first ward mixed at the Maudsley and they were still considered experimental in 1970: General Purposes Subcommittee, 2 April 1970.
177 *Empire News & Sunday Chronicle*, 4 September 1960.
178 Executive Group, 26 February 1987.
179 *Bethlem & Maudsley Gazette*, December 1960, 22.
180 House Committee Presented Papers: 12 October 1966, Appendix E/2.
181 Board of Governors Presented Papers: 2 July 1973, Appendix H/1.
182 *Bethlem & Maudsley Gazette*, Autumn 1984, 7.
183 MTO, 7 November 1978.
184 See Chapter 33, pp. 669–71.
185 Cited in Jones, *Ministering to Minds Diseased*, 74.
186 D. Millard, 'Maxwell Jones and the Therapeutic Community', in Hugh Freeman and German Berrios (eds), *150 Years of British Psychiatry: The Aftermath* (London: Athlone, 1996), 582–3.
187 For the development of a therapeutic community at the Cheadle Royal see N. Roberts, *Cheadle Royal Hospital* (Altrincham: John Sherratt & Sons, 1967), 151–4.
188 *British Journal of Psychiatry*, cxi (1965), 947–54.
189 *Bethlem & Maudsley Gazette*, March 1961, 97.
190 *Ibid.* June 1963, 38–9.
191 See *Nursing Times*, 22 February 1957, 209–11.
192 Millard, *op. cit.* 596.
193 *Nursing Mirror*, 14 November 1974, 50.
194 *Bethlem & Maudsley Gazette*, June 1957, 10–11.
195 Finance & General Purposes Committee Presented Papers: 16 June 1973, Appendix E/1.
196 Board of Governors Presented Papers: 1 April 1974, Appendix E/2.
197 *Hansard*, H. of C., vol. 592 (1958), col. 1479.
198 Michael Shepherd, 'Neurolepsis and the Psychopharmacological Revolution', *History of Psychiatry*, v (1994), 89.
199 Sargant, *op. cit.* 149.
200 *JMS*, 105 (1959), 1020–31.
201 Shepherd, *op. cit.* 93, 94.
202 Fennell, *op. cit.* 158–9.
203 Jones, *Ministering to Minds Diseased*, 46–7.
204 David Healy, 'History of British Psychopharmacology', in Hugh Freeman and German Berrios (eds), *150 Years of British Psychiatry: The Aftermath* (London: Athlone, 1996), 61–88.
205 Peter Kramer, *Listening to Prozac* (New York: Penguin, 1993), xvi.
206 N. Rose, 'Psychiatry', in P. Miller and N. Rose (eds), *The Power of Psychiatry* (Cambridge: Polity Press, 1986), 69.
207 Nicholas Timmins, *Five Giants: Biography of the Welfare State* (London: HarperCollins, 1995), 412–13.
208 *Bethlem & Maudsley Gazette*, Autumn 1984, 7.
209 *Handbook for the Guidance of Doctors*, 20.
210 *Bethlem & Maudsley Gazette*, Spring 1972, 20.
211 *Orpington Times & Kentish Times*, 5 September 1974, 3.
212 See Rose, *op. cit.* 54–6.
213 Charles Webster, *Problems of Health Care: The National Health Service Before 1957* (London: HMSO, 1988), 340.
214 Developments in Britain were paralleled by international developments, although work in America had a cold reception in Britain and programmes in Italy in the 1970s showed that the replacement of mental hospitals with diagnosis and cure units was difficult to replicate outside Trieste: Kathleen Jones, *Asylum and After* (London: Athlone, 1993), 216–21.

215 Watkin, *op. cit.* 62–3.
216 Douglas Bennett, 'Drive Towards the Community', in German Berrios and Hugh Freeman (eds), *150 Years of British Psychiatry* (London: Gaskell, 1991), 321; Andrew Scull, *Decarceration: Community Treatment and the Deviant: A Radical View* (New Jersey: Prentice-Hall, 1974).
217 Russell Barton, *Institutional Neurosis* (Bristol: Wright, 1959).
218 Jones, *Asylum and After*, 187.
219 Timmins, *op. cit.* 417.
220 *Bethlem & Maudsley Gazette*, Spring 1990, 9.
221 Jones, *Asylum and After*, 250–1.
222 See Chapter 33, pp. 662–4.
223 Audrey Leathard, *Health Care Provision* (London: Chapman & Hall, 1990), 48.
224 MEC Presented Papers: 4 January 1990, ECD 7/90. For example, in 1971 the Governors agreed to give £1,000 to the Windsor Walk Housing Association, an organization established under the guidance of James Birley at the Maudsley, to help refurbish a hostel for clinically handicapped psychiatric patients: Board of Governors Presented Papers: 5 April 1971, Appendix B/2.
225 *Nursing Times*, 28 October 1960, 1344–5; see Chapter 31.
226 *Bethlem & Maudsley Gazette*, Summer 1982, 16–18.
227 Board of Control Correspondence: Letter from Porter-Phillips, 20 October 1938.
228 Roberts, *op. cit.* 132.
229 *1928 Board of Control Annual Report*, 2.
230 *1949–1969 Triennial Statistical Reports*.

FROM SHA TO NHS TRUST,
1982–94

——— •❖• ———

OUTSIDE PRESSURE

Outside Bethlem, which was part of the Special Health Authority (SHA), the 1982 National Health Service (NHS) reorganization was an admission that earlier reforms had not been effective. Where it brought immediate changes the ambition of efficient management became a constant concern, sponsoring further developments not restructuring. Reorganization was followed by a drive to bring the perceived efficiency of the business world into healthcare. Sir Roy Griffiths, a governmental adviser from the Sainsbury's food chain, was appointed to look into the NHS's management structure. In the SHA, doctors felt that such business ideas were ill-suited to clinical services and worried that patients would not be put first. Griffiths concluded that 'if Florence Nightingale were carrying her lamp through the corridors of the NHS today, she would almost certainly be searching for the people in charge'.[1] He recommended the need for a clear management structure where clinicians would be more closely involved through a unit administration. The Report also suggested the need for general managers to ensure that decisions were made.[2] Griffiths's ideas were not new and had been anticipated by Leslie Paine, the Joint Hospital's second House Governor, and by the King Edward's Hospital Fund in 1967. The SHA was cautious, believing it had already carried out most of the Report's suggestions. The Management Team of Officers (MTO) feared that the 'appointment of general managers may introduce into the organisation and administration of Health Services an element of autocracy that we would see as unacceptable'.[3] However, the SHA did support the idea of extending doctors' management role.

At first the DHSS consulted hospitals, but this was abruptly halted in June 1984. Health authorities were instructed to prepare guidelines for new general managers by the end of September. It was felt that this could be best achieved in the SHA by merging the role of the general manager with that of the chairman of the MTO. In reality this meant that the popular House Governor, Paine, would become the general manager and play a major role in defining the function of the new post.[4] It was believed that this would minimize further disruption. The DHSS considered Paine ineligible because he had only three years before his retirement, forcing him to retire early. In his place Eric Byers, a member of the British Institute of Management and the district administrator for Tunbridge Wells Health Authority, was appointed.

From a business background, he was committed to cost-effectiveness and public accountability, aware that the SHA was not in a position to waste money. Byers aimed to reorganize the SHA on a more businesslike basis. He believed his role was to break down traditional hierarchy structures, aware that this would sometimes place him in a difficult position, especially when unpopular decisions had to be made.[5] Byers did not have a favourable position to work from, with many resenting the changes being forced on the SHA. Some even argued that the changes aimed to remove control from doctors to reduce expenditure.[6] On the other hand, the adoption of management budgeting in 1984 and the growth of the Resource Management Initiative did bring clinicians into management. The SHA took a leading role in setting up such a scheme and by 1988 had six resource directors. At Bethlem the Drug Dependence Unit, Mental Impairment Evaluation and Treatment Service, and Denis Hill Unit each had a resource director. Despite criticism from the Confederation of Health Service Employees, staff at the SHA were optimistic about resource management and wanted greater levels of local control.[7]

Further change followed in 1986. Byers sought to create a single administration for Bethlem and the Maudsley. A Head of Clinical Services, answerable to the General Manager, was appointed. The relationship between the new post and the chair of the Medical Committee was unclear and it was initially decided to combine the post for a year on an experimental basis.[8] A Clinical Advisory Group followed in 1990 to assist the General Manager and Head of Clinical Services through a non-executive multi-disciplinary body that aimed to give a balance of clinical and academic backgrounds. Doctors remained uncertain about the new structure. Byers informed them that if they wanted to influence management 'they would have to get involved'.[9] The Medical Executive Committee (MEC) saw the problem of 'divided responsibility' and worried that some clinicians were 'spending too much time on management responsibilities'. Others believed that it gave more responsibility but little actual power, concerns that re-emerged throughout the 1990s with doctors worried about their authority.[10] Nurses felt more aggrieved. The Griffiths Report reversed some of the managerial implications of the Salmon structure and reduced nurses' influence.[11] This merged with concerns over poor pay and status, long hours and lack of support, promoting strike action.[12] A functional split occurred with separate managers for different kinds of service, while a new management rhetoric of performance indicators and quality assurance was ushered in. Everything had to be quantifiable and accountable. Doctors disliked the transformation and blamed the SHA.

By 1988 it was felt that the SHA was going through a 'bad phase'. Criticism had mounted since 1986, with some clinicians seeing the changes initiated by the Griffiths Report as 'not working' with planning slow and 'long drawn out'.[13] They disliked the work that management budgeting produced, pointing to the arbitrary nature of charging and the erosion of the Medical Committee's influence.[14] In turn, it was felt that the academic staff at the Maudsley were more concerned with 'building up their own . . . empires' and there was an awareness that stronger links were needed with the Institute of Psychiatry.[15] There was a clear need for the latter as decisions made in one institution were having resource implications for the other. Cooperation was promoted through the creation of a Joint Committee and the appointment of Trevor Owen (who like Byers had a business background) as chair of the SHA and the

Institute. He felt he could bring his business experience to two institutions 'stuffed full of people who have expertise in medicine'. Owen, however, did not intend to intervene directly, having faith in Byers's ability.[16]

Problems in the SHA were matched by problems in the NHS. Health standards were improving, but this was not always apparent as a sense of crisis evolved. Health-care professionals were becoming vocal in their criticism. Public dissatisfaction, par-ticularly over waiting lists, was increasing, and the media was highlighting the NHS's shortcomings. Suspicion mounted that Margaret Thatcher's Conservative Govern-ment wanted to privatize health care, leading to a sharp increase in interest in Britain by American health companies.[17] The Government responded in 1989 with the lavish launch of *Working for Patients*. There was nothing in the White Paper about the Special Health Authorities or mental health directly, but the document aroused concern at Bethlem. Many felt that it proposed placing financial considerations at the heart of clinical decisions. Others warned that it ran the risk of breaking down familiar health services.[18] Produced in the middle of a funding crisis, *Working for Patients* contained no recommendations for increased resources or an expansion of private funding. How-ever, where it promised that the NHS would 'continue to be available to all', the White Paper called for the creation of an internal market, a solution proposed in 1984 by American academic, Professor Enthoven.[19] The 1990 NHS and Community Care Act was the result. Doctors moved to defend the NHS where they had previously attacked it, but with the British Medical Association marginalized they could do little. The Act contained the provision for hospitals to opt out of the NHS and to develop services on contract.[20] Large hospitals were encouraged to become independent trusts and compete for patients and resources. In response the SHA underwent a process of administrative change. A new slimmed SHA was created with the Hospital run as two units: a National Service Unit and a Community Unit. A further sub-division occurred to created financial autonomous resource management units. Clinical involvement in management was encouraged through the formation of nine clinical directorates. Emphasis shifted to 'quality assurance'.[21] Management was modelled on the private sector with the creation of a new Board of twelve executive and twelve non-executive members. The inclusion of Lambeth into the Hospital's district responsibility further extended management. The new Board's mission statement aimed to make the SHA into the 'flagship for psychiatry'.[22]

The NHS's continued popularity prevented privatization.[23] However, under the 1990 Act central control was replaced by an internal market. At the district level a division occurred between purchasing agencies and providers with contracts for care negotiated annually. Consequently, anxiety was institutionalized with health providers like the SHA dependent on annual contracts. This was to be the 'hidden hand' of the market, with the management working to maximize patient care while minimizing the cost of delivery in order to survive.[24] The emphasis was on district commitments, where the ideal was that money would follow the patient. The changes appeared the most radical since the 1946 Act. In the SHA, competition was seen as inappropriate to healthcare with fears that it would create instability. Byers was not as pessimistic, feeling that contract funding might provide some incentive to develop new services and projects. He envisaged the SHA offering 'high quality specialist services' and compared the Hospital to the 'Marks and Spencer' end of the market.[25] To achieve this, Byers was aware that considerable cooperation was needed from the staff. Others criticized the absence of accountability. Many found flaws in the new system. A poll in the *Daily Telegraph* showed that a large portion of the public did not believe the NHS was safe in the Conservatives' hands.[26] Expectations were slow to adapt to the new environment. Without clear guidelines health authorities underwent a process of 'learning by doing'.[27] Problems were blamed on the new system from the start and the Government went on the defensive when accusations of 'creeping privatisation' were made.[28]

The idea that hospitals should become independent trusts gathered momentum. Part of the inspiration came from the old ideas of voluntarism where hospitals were run independently by their Governors.[29] The voluntary ethos had been seen as ill-suited to the needs of mass healthcare in post-war Britain, but in the late 1980s the idea was reinterpreted. Trusts allowed Government to distance itself from local difficulties through local managers. Pressure was exerted on hospitals and authorities to form trusts, although the two trust flagships, Guy's Hospital and the Bradford Hospitals, were experiencing problems.[30] The SHA was reluctant to follow Guy's lead and shared the Royal College of Psychiatrists' concern about self-government. When the idea of opting out was first announced in 1989, the SHA's official response was 'that the time for expressing an interest was [not] right due to the uncertainty of funding arrangements'.[31] Outside pressure, however, forced the Hospital to follow suit in 1994. Rumours circulated that the Department of Health and Social Security had warned that an SHA could be appointed that did want a trust.[32] In response Owen resigned, breaking the formal link with the Institute of Psychiatry, although cooperation continued. Doctors were anxious about what appeared to be uncharted waters and feared that the Hospital's academic bias would limit its ability to compete. The Nursing Advisory Committee compared the proposals to a 'dark tunnel'. It worried about the impact on nursing and the increased costs involved, fearing a 'discontinuity of care'.[33] The Trust had a mixed reception with most of the medical staff unsympathetic. The SHA's decision must be set against national experiences, with 90 per cent of NHS services of all hospitals and community services becoming self-managing through 440 Trusts.[34] Problems were encountered, especially in London where the high cost of care created a shortfall in contracts, generating financial problems that threatened the survival of some institutions.

AN EVERLASTING FUNDING CRISIS?

Despite economic recovery in the 1980s, welfare became subject to the 'ideological blizzard' of Thatcherite policies.[35] Public expenditure on welfare as part of the Gross Domestic Product fell, although the trend had been started under James Callaghan's Labour Government.[36] Under the Conservatives, real expenditure on the NHS rose from £17.7bn in 1980/1 to £20.6bn seven years later.[37] This is not, however, a good measure of the financial pressures experienced by the NHS. Where Britain's system was the most cost-effective in Europe, expenditure was rising with demand, while capital funding remained low. Under these conditions, funding remained static at a time when the proportion of income spent on different sectors was changing, leading to feelings of resource starvation in the hospital sector as beds began to close, especially in London.[38]

With NHS funding restricted, the SHA faced further problems. Regional allocation for South East Thames Regional Health Authority in the Resources Allocation Working Party (RAWP) formula fell from 10 per cent of the revenue available in 1979/80 to 3 per cent in 1987/8. RAWP became an effective way of equalizing misery. This had an impact on the regional services the SHA was committed to, limiting funding and reducing cover. In addition, where the Labour Government had identified mental healthcare as a priority in its 1976 White Paper, the Conservatives reaffirmed this priority but restricted funding. In mental healthcare spending was increasingly diverted from institutional services to programmes that encouraged community care.[39] For the SHA, the period from 1982 onwards presented mounting financial problems common to NHS hospitals. Many felt that the Hospital was being underfunded, a position that forced the SHA 'to avoid developments with recurring revenue consequences, which was not in accord with the hospital's role as an innovator'.[40] Anxiety existed at all levels, with staff reacting with 'bewilderment and fury' to cuts.[41] The DHSS recognized the problem in 1986, but it suggested no solution other than unpopular cost improvement schemes. After attempts to scale down non-clinical services, the MEC was instructed to recommend cuts to clinical services that would be 'least damaging to patient care'.[42] The medical staff opposed cuts, forcing Byers into an unpopular position. Units with a low bed occupancy rate were temporarily closed, particularly at weekends and Christmas, and staff formed an Action Group to protest. The Group did not always share the management's stance, while the SHA adopted a non-confrontational approach that sought ways round cuts to minimize their effects.[43] Efforts were made to freeze spending, although further pressure was added by the financial problems facing the Institute of Psychiatry, with falling university funding forcing the SHA to provide an increased level of support from its endowments.[44] Pressure was placed on hospitals to privatize services to reduce spending. Here the Joint Hospital was ahead of other institutions and had started to contract-out services in the 1950s.[45] Income generation projects were discussed, while resource monitoring was introduced to ensure that what funds were available were spent wisely.[46] The bullish Ivan Clout, as chair of the SHA, was placed in a position where he constantly had to reassure staff that services would be protected. Clout's promises could not always be kept. Cuts proved inevitable, leaving the Contingency Working Party in an unenviable position of having to decide where savings could be made. Most of these affected the more expensive services at the Maudsley.[47] The MTO was aware that by funding one development others would lose, creating competition for resources. With funding now moving into the internal market and based on weighted population and contracts any reduction in activity would be reflected in a budget reduction. The Use of Resources Working Party, which replaced the Contingency Working Party in 1989, was aware of the need for diplomacy given the 'delicate nature of the matter'. It did, however, point to a 'common feeling that there was an individual responsibility to save money in minor ways'.[48] To reduce expenditure, locum cover was cut. When staff went sick or on holiday it was not therefore always possible to provide locums, which 'inevitably reduced the level of clinical services'.[49] At the same time, more money was spent on staff training and development. Staffing shortages became common to all units at Bethlem, increasing concerns about the level of violence.

Anxiety mounted with the stock market crash of 1987. Byers, like Paine, was keen to use endowments and property was sold to substitute the reduction in Exchequer funding.[50] The original restrictions on endowments had by now been forgotten, and in an institution unwilling to remain static endowed income was poured into development plans and new units. To raise money, the SHA invested heavily during the boom of the early 1980s, selling property to take advantage of rising share prices.[51] Control over Bethlem's endowments had largely passed from those running the Hospital to the SHA's stockbrokers who advised the Investments Subcommittee and Property Subcommittee on what action to take. An aggressive policy was adopted despite the Investment Committee's innate sense of caution, but the 1987 crash wiped out the capital gains made over the previous five years.[52] A mix of investments and property ensured that the effects of the crash had been reduced, and a more cautious policy was adopted. Pressure on resources made the Governors aware that they had to use their contacts in the City to promote goodwill to increase the flow of charitable donations.[53] More support had been given to the role of charity in the NHS since 1980, with charitable funding no longer providing the extras. The SHA continued to manage Bethlem's endowments with care, but where more attention was given to charity the endowed funds available obviated the need to launch a public appeal like other hospitals.[54]

The 1988 Health and Medicines Act gave health authorities more powers to raise income from the sale of their services. This created an early form of Enthoven's internal market, while London's teaching hospitals had already started charging other districts for treating their patients. The internal market in creating a purchaser–provider split aimed to remove the traditional restrictions of annual budgets.[55] The stress given to care in the community further aimed to transfer part of the financial burden of care from the NHS to local authorities. At the same time, the Government was committed to a policy of 'making the best use of available resources'.[56] Authorities were expected to make efficiency savings to the equivalent of a 0.5 per cent cash increase. It became the only way that improvements and additional resources could be found. This was clearly seen in the SHA, with a concerted effort made to encourage efficiency savings. In an attempt to control spending, it was decided in 1990 that all patients from 1 April 1991 should be linked to a specific contract as the SHA approached the new internal market.[57] Gradually it was admitted that with the financial situation unlikely to improve services had to be reduced. To decide where cuts would occur usage, clinical relevance, teaching, research, recruitment and potential were assessed. However, it found that no unit was dispensable and even low-ranking units were seen as important for the SHA's 'corporate purpose'.[58] Continued cuts had a demoralizing effect. Financial concerns came to dominate decisions far more than before. By 1992, the Medical Committee 'felt disempowered and disaffected and feared that the practice of second-rate psychiatry was now taking place'.[59] Under these circumstance, the Hospital struggled to provide the best possible care and services with the resources available.

AND BEYOND THE TRUST?

With the SHA approaching trust status, Byers did admit that

> we are in a greater period of uncertainty now then ever before. We are engaged
> in a process that identified winners, losers and the priorities which we will need
> to acknowledge in order to survive. It's changing the beast quickly [that] worries
> me – and I fear it could be a long dog-fight![60]

As for the internal market, it was seen as both a threat and an opportunity. The threat
came from the SHA's location in a costly inner London area, pointing to the need to
develop cost-effective and cost-attractive services that purchasers of healthcare
wanted to buy in an environment where all institutions were facing mounting anxiety.
Four years after the adoption of trust status uncertainties still prevailed as the
Hospital sought to adapt and adjust its services.

NOTES

1　Cited in Nicholas Timmins, *The Five Giants: A Biography of the Welfare State* (London: Harper-Collins, 1995), 409.
2　SHA Presented Papers: 14 November 1983, Appendix E.
3　*Ibid.* 9 January 1984, Appendix H.
4　*Ibid.* 10 September 1984, Appendix A.
5　*Bethlem & Maudsley Gazette*, Winter 1985, 44, 33.
6　See R. Flynn, *Structures of Control in Health Management* (London: Routledge, 1992), and B. Davey and J. Popay (eds), *Dilemmas in Health Care* (Birmingham: Open University Press, 1993).
7　MEC Presented Papers: 7 July 1988, ECD 63/88; 5 October 1989, ECD 88/89.
8　Medical Committee, 17 March 1986 and 9 February 1987.
9　MEC Presented Papers: 8 January 1987, ECD 2/87.
10　MEC, 2 June 1988.
11　See Chapter 32, pp. 628–30.
12　R. Rowden, 'The Griffiths Report: What Might it Mean to Nursing?', *Journal of Clinical Nursing*, iii (1986), 272–3.
13　Medical Committee, 16 January 1986.
14　*Ibid.* 31 October 1988.
15　Ann Dally, *A Doctor's Story* (London: Macmillan, 1990), 264.
16　*Bethlem & Maudsley Gazette*, Summer 1989, 32.
17　In 1985 Charter Medical Ltd, an American company involved in the private provision of hospital services, particularly in the psychiatric field, approached the SHA. It wanted to establish links with the SHA and the Institute of Psychiatry and proposed that land at Monks Orchard could be used to provide a private hospital and staff training centre (SHA, 14 January 1985). In a climate where the DHSS wanted surplus hospital land sold, the SHA was under pressure to consider such proposals, while in the Maudsley's development plan the sale of land was seen as an important source of funding. The MEC had its reservations and wanted other options to be explored before Charter's bid was taken further (SHA, 13 January 1986). A number believed that the only way to fund the Maudsley's redevelopment would be to agree to Charter's proposals, especially as the original lease stipulated that Monks Orchard could be used only for the care of the mentally ill. Junior staff protested and the issue aroused hostility in the Hospital and in the medical press, provoking far-reaching discussions. Charter, however, was more interested in its negotiations with the Institute and

in November 1985 decided to cease negotiations with the SHA to prevent the 'crossing lines of two very separate matters' (SHA Presented Papers: 11 November 1985).

18 MEC Presented Papers: 4 May 1989, ECD 51/89.

19 Julian Le Grand, David Winter and Francis Woolley, 'The National Health Service: Safe in Whose Hands?', in John Hills (ed.), *The State of Welfare: The Welfare State in Britain since 1974* (Oxford: Clarendon Press, 1990), 93; Alain Enthoven, *Refections on the Management of the National Health Service* (London: Nuffield Provincial Hospital Trust, Occasional Paper 5, 1985).

20 Kathleen Jones, *The Making of Social Policy in Britain* (London: Athlone, 1991), 195.

21 *1990 Joint Annual Report*, 33–4.

22 *1991 Joint Annual Report*, 5, 19.

23 Michael Hill, *The Welfare State in Britain* (London: Edward Elgar, 1993), 137.

24 Judith Allsop, 'Health: From Seamless Service to Patchwork Quilt', in David Gladstone (ed.), *British Social Welfare* (London: UCL Press, 1995), 98, 113.

25 *Bethlem & Maudsley Gazette*, Autumn 1993, 21.

26 Aubrey Leathard, *Health Care Provision* (London: Chapman & Hall, 1990), 156–77.

27 Chris Ham, Frank Honigsbaum and David Thompson, 'Priority Setting for Health Gain', in A. Oakley and A. Williams (eds), *Politics of the Welfare State* (London: UCL Press, 1994), 99.

28 Timmins, *op. cit.* 482.

29 See Chapter 31.

30 John Mohan, *A National Health Service? Restructuring of Health Care in Britain Since 1979* (London: Macmillan, 1995), 210.

31 Medical Committee, 19 June 1989.

32 *Ibid.* 15 February 1993.

33 SHA Presented Papers: 8 May 1989, Appendix K.

34 Allsop, *op. cit.* 113.

35 Charles Webster, 'Conservatives and Consensus: The Politics of the National Health Service, 1951–1964', in A. Oakley and A. Williams (eds), *Politics of the Welfare State* (London: UCL Press, 1994), 54–74, argues that this did not mark a considerable change as for the Conservatives 'the NHS was among the least regarded of the social services: it was the first candidate offered for sacrifice in the search for economies in public expenditure'.

36 Hill, *op. cit.* 124.

37 Le Grand *et al.*, *op. cit.* 95.

38 Leathard, *op. cit.* 141.

39 Le Grand *et al.*, *op. cit.* 112–13, 117.

40 SHA, 10 March 1986.

41 *Bethlem & Maudsley Gazette*, Summer 1986, 10.

42 SHA, 8 September 1986.

43 MTO, 23 October 1986.

44 Finance & Policy Committee, 20 October 1982 and 23 July 1986.

45 See Chapter 31.

46 Finance & Policy Committee, 25 January 1989.

47 1986 Contingency Working Party Report.

48 Use of Resources Working Party, 19 May 1988 and 29 June 1989.

49 SHA, 8 July 1985.

50 Finance & Policy Committee, 19 May 1987.

51 Property Subcommittee, 29 October 1986.

52 SHA, 9 November 1987.

53 Property Subcommittee, 16 September 1987.

54 Mohan, *op. cit.* 177.

55 *Ibid.* 6.

56 Cited in Le Grand *et al.*, *op. cit.* 110.

57 Working Party on the Reduction of Clinical Services, 11 April 1990.

58 Priorities in Clinical Services Working Party, 15 November 1990.

59 Medical Committee, 21 September 1992.

60 *Bethlem & Maudsley Gazette*, Autumn 1993, 22.

CHAPTER THIRTY-SIX

CONCLUSION

——— ·◆· ———

As has just been shown, twentieth-century Bethlem proved able to find ways and means to resist all manner of pressures applied to it to abandon its independence and its own ways, and thus succeeded in avoiding disappearing into the common soup of the nation's psychiatric services. The Governors strove mightily to give Bethlem a rebirth at Monks Orchard; and their dexterous diplomacy ensured that the threats to its autonomy posed by the coming of the National Health Service were overcome by marriage with the Maudsley. Partly as a consequence of that, the risk of extinction by closure – the fate of so many other recent institutions – was averted.[1] Yet the great irony has been that, in this process of saving the institution, the very name was lost, and almost by inadvertence: as of 1991 the institution has been officially known simply as 'The Maudsley'. Does Bethlem still really exist, one might ask, if it no longer has its name? In some respects, the institution might have been well advised to shed its name a couple of centuries ago when 'Bedlam' really was synonymous with corruption, cruelty and craziness; it is odd that the name has been dropped in an age in which it has ceased to be offensive.

Matters of names and realities, institutions and images, of course raise the eternal question Heraclitus posed – one that applies particularly acutely to the historian of institutions: the problem of continuity and change, the question of identity. One cannot step into the same river twice, observed that ancient Greek philosopher. Should we, in other words, be talking about Bethlem as if it had some fundamental essence or at least a continuing unfolding? In one sense the answer must be 'yes', since, like a single living human being, its activities have been unbroken. Whatever else has happened, since 1247 Bethlem has never been shut, pulled down, bolted and barred, abolished and refounded. In another sense, the answer must be 'no', since, unlike a growing human who is programmed in a certain way by the laws of genetics, biochemistry and physiology, the actual course of Bethlem's development was utterly unpredictable and the outcome of contingency. Its entire history is a saga of might-have-beens: it might never have taken in lunatics in the first place; it might have been finally closed by the Henrician Reformation. Today, undergoing what Eric Byers has called a 'greater period of uncertainty than ever before', who can say what its future might be? Certainly not its historians.

Like the endlessly patched quilt or the endlessly darned sock, it has certainly always

719

been altering its appearance. It began as a pan-European religious foundation. Its fortunes became a pawn in multinational politics, and then part of the identity of the City of London and its Corporation. On the way, it chanced to become a refuge for lunatics – and thereby, as Bedlam, to represent lunacy to the nation. In the nineteenth century Bethlem participated in the medicalization of insanity, it ceased to be Bedlam and became bourgeois, cast off its paupers, moved out of London and, well over 700 years old, in a bid for immortality or at least rejuvenation, finally sealed the knot with the macho Maudsley. Not least in this saga of assumed identities, our age of deinstitutionalization has not seen Bethlem closed down. In other words, Bethlem has continually changed places and changed faces. Yet it has also been permeated by mythologies of permanence: the Bedlam image that dogged it, the nepotistic traditionalism that led to the four Monros, or the Revd Bowen's suggestion that it had a pedigree going back to pre-Conquest times.

What is it that makes institutions perpetuate themselves, assume a life of their own? And how does that affect those associated with them in the shorter term? An institution like Bethlem has both inertia and momentum. Those connected with it and society at large affect its direction. It is the perfect embodiment of Karl Marx's great truth: men make their own history but not under circumstances of their own making.

NOTES

1 Peter Barham, *Closing the Asylum: The Mental Patient in Modern Society* (London: Penguin Books, 1992).

PART V

APPENDICES

APPENDIX 1

MASTERS, WARDENS OR KEEPERS OF BETHLEM, 1247–1633

Appointed by	Name	Date	Source(s)
Bishop of Bethlem	??	1247–c.1290	
Bishop of Bethlem	Thomas de Doncastre	fl. 1292?–3	CPR 1290–2/473, CCR 1288–96/316
,,	William de Banham	fl. 1330	CLB E/251
,,	Philip Dene	fl. 1339	CPMR 1323–64/110–1
,,	John Matheu de Nortone[1]	fl. 1342–46	CPR 1340–3/482, CLB F/154, 155
Sir John Darcy?	John de Wilton[2]	fl. 1348	CPR 1348–50/181
Bishop of Bethlem	Robert Mannyel	fl. 1364	CPR 1361–4/477
Sir John Beauchamp?	William [. . .]	fl. 1367	CPR 1367–70/68–9
Sir James Audley?	William Tytte	fl. 1380	CPR 1377–81/431, C270/22, 4
City of London	John Gardyner, chaplain	1381	CLB H/165
The King	Robert Lincoln[3]	1388/9	CPR 1385–9/526
,,	Rober Dale, chaplain	1423	CPR 1422–9/135
,,	Edward Atherton[4]	1437	CPR 1436–41/17
,,	John Arundel[5]	1457	CPR 1452–61/338
,,	Thomas Henry DD	1459	CPR 1452–61/484
,,	John Brown[6]	1459	CPR 1452–61/485
,,	John Smeethe clerk	1470	CPR 1467–77/233
,,	John Brown	fl. 1477	Ghall 9171/6, 28v
,,	John Davyson[7]	pre-1479	CPR 1476–85/166
,,	Walter Bate ⎫ William Hobbs[8] ⎬	1479	CPR 1476–85/166
,,	Thomas Maudesley[9]	1485	CPR 1485–94/7
,,	Thomas Deinman[10]	1494	CPR 1485–94/471
,,	Matthew Baker[11]	1504	CPR 1494–1509/349
,,	John Cavalari[12]	1512/3	CSP H8, iii/10, ibid. i/16
,,	George Bulleyn[13]	1529	CSP Henry 8, iv, 2598
,,	Peter Mewtys[14]	fl. 1537–46	CA Rep. 10/5, Mun. Bk., 47v

cont.

Appointed by	Name	Date	Source(s)
City of London	Edward Alleyn, innholder[15]	fl. 1555	*CA Rep.* 12/2/483v, Mun. Bk./30v/60–1
,,	Richard Minnes, draper[16]	1561	*CA Rep.* 14/524
,,	Edward Rest, grocer[17]	pre-1571	*CA Rep.* 17/162v
,,	John Mell	1571	*CA Rep.* 17/162v
,,	Rowland Sleforth, clothworker	1579	*CA Rep.* 20/23
,,	John Parrott, draper	1598	*CA Rep.* 24/311
,,	Richard Lansdale, draper	1605	*CA Rep.* 27/14
,,	John Grimkin, painter	1614	*CA Rep.* 31/2/347v
,,	Thomas Jenner, fishmonger	1614	*CA Rep.* 31/2/424
,,	Helkiah Crooke MD	1619–33	BCGM 6/110

Notes:

1 [Matheu] de Norton: possibly to be identified with John de Norton, Chancellor of Salisbury, 1361: *Calendar of Entries in the Papal Registers . . .: Petitions*, 379.

2 Wilton: possibly to be identified with John de Wilton, Chancellor of Salisbury in 1352: *Calendar of Entries in the Papal Registers . . .: Petitions*, 235.

3 Lincoln: 'King's clerk'.

4 Atherton: 'Clerk of the [King's] Closet'.

5 Arundel: 'King's Chaplain'; also Physician to Henry VI, Bishop of Chichester, 1458.

6 Brown: probably one of the Chamberlains of the Exchequer, 1447; appointed one of the Receivers of the lands of various rebels, including the Earl of Warwick (the Kingmaker), in 1460, but cooperated with the government of the usurper, Edward IV, apparently becoming sufficiently identified with the Yorkist regime to be replaced during the restoration of Henry VI in 1470 and then to recover his office again, presumably when Edward IV seized back the throne in 1471: *Calendar of Patent Rolls 1446–52*, 60, 166–7; *Calendar of Patent Rolls 1452–61*, 572.

7 Davyson: Keeper of the Hanaper, 1467–73; by 1476, Dean of Salisbury: *Calendar of Patent Rolls 1467–77*, 47, 563.

8 Hobbs: Surgeon to Henry VI in the 1450s, when the King lost his reason (see Chapter 7).

9 Maudesley: 'King's Clerk'.

10 Deinman: 'Doctor of good arts and in medicines, for services to the King's mother.'

11 Baker: 'Esquire for the Body.' He was a parishioner of St Saviour's Southwark when he died in 1513, and his will makes no mention of Bethlem (although he left money for his executors to distribute in alms as they saw fit): *PRO PROB* 11/17/18.

12 For a discussion of Cavalari and his connections, see Chapter 5.

13 Bulleyn: 'Esquire of the Body'; Queen Anne Boleyn's brother, Viscount Rochford (see Chapter 5).

14 Mewtys: 'Gentleman of the Privy Chamber.' His 1526 will, in which he is described as 'of Westham, Essex', makes no mention of Bethlem, but his executors were given goods to sell and distribute in alms as he saw fit: *PRO PROB* 11/414/23.

15 Alleyn: 'innholder', *BRHLA* Muniment Book, fols. 61–2. Father of the actor of the same name (see Chapter 10). His will of 1570 describes him as a parishioner of St Botolph's Bishopsgate. He left no bequests or legacies in alms; his witnesses all subscribed their marks rather than signatures.

16 Minnes: Mayor's Porter.

17 Died June/July 1571: no mention of Bethlem in his will: *Gball* 9171/16/67v–8.

APPENDIX 2

BETHLEM AND BRIDEWELL PRESIDENTS 1606–1793

Name	Dates	Reason
Sir Thomas Bennett	1606 – b. 1613	Unknown
Sir Thomas Middleton	1613 – b. 15 Sept. 1631	Deceased
Sir Rowland Heylin	15 Sept. 1631 – c. 9 March 1632	Deceased
Sir George Whitmore	12 March 1632 – 15 Sept. 1642	Resigned as sick
Sir John Wollaston	15 Sept. 1642 – c. 17 Oct. 1649	Resigned, having been elected President of Christ's
Sir Christopher Packe	9 Nov. 1649 – b. 1660	Unknown
Sir Richard Browne (Bt.)	b. 1660 – b. 22 Oct. 1669	Deceased
Sir William Turner	22 Oct. 1669 – 14 Nov. 1688	Resigned, having also resigned as an alderman
Sir James Smyth	14 Nov. 1688 – 4 July 1689	Replaced, having declined election unless City approve
Sir Henry Tulse	4 July 1689 – 9 July 1689	Resigned 'in regard of other publike businesse'
Sir Robert Jeffery/Geoffrey	9 July 1689 – 28 Aug. 1690	Resigned in favour of Turner's re-election
Sir William Turner	28 Aug. 1690 – b. 17 March 1693	Deceased
Sir Robert Jeffery/Geoffrey	17 March 1693 – b. 15 March 1704	Deceased
Sir Samuel Dashwood	15 March 1704 – b. 26 Aug. 1705	Deceased
Sir Thomas Rawlinson	22 Sept. 1705 – b. 26 Nov. 1708	Deceased
Sir William Withers	15 Dec. 1708 – b. 21 Feb. 1721	Deceased
Sir Samuel Garrard (Bt.)	10 March 1721 – b. 7 May 1725	Deceased
Rt Hon Humphrey Parsons, Esq.	5 Aug. 1725 – b. 23 Jan. 1747	Deceased
Rt Hon William Benn, Esq.	28 Jan. 1747 – b. 11 Sept. 1755	Deceased
Sir Richard Glynn (Bt.)	25 Sept. 1755 – b. 3 Feb. 1773	Deceased
Walter Rawlinson, Esq.	11 Feb. 1773 – b. 1777	Unknown
Brackley Kennett, Esq.	1777 – b. 24 May 1782	Deceased
Brass Crosby, Esq.	7 June 1782 – b. 1793	Deceased

Key: b. = by; *c.* = *circa*

APPENDIX 3

BETHLEM AND BRIDEWELL APOTHECARIES, 1634–1816

Ralph Yardley	1634 – b. 16 Jan. 1656	Deceased
James James	16 Jan. 1656 – b. 15 March 1678	Deceased
Jeremy Lester	15 March 1678 – b. 11 Dec. 1685	Deceased
John Pelling	a. 11 Dec. 1685 – b. 5 April 1689	Deceased
William Dickenson	19 April 1689 – b. 20 March 1696	Deceased
John Adams	27 March 1696 – b. 18 Feb. 1715	Deceased
Widow Adams (temp.)	25 Feb. 1715 – 25 March 1715	Replaced
William Elderton	25 March 1715 – b. 22 May 1751	Replaced
John Winder (resident)	22 May 1751 – b. 25 June 1772	Resigned
John Gozna (resident)	9 July 1772 – b. 11 July 1795	Deceased
Thomas Gozna (temp.)	b. 11 July 1795 – 30 July 1795	Replaced
John Haslam (resident)	30 July 1795 – 15 May 1816	Not re-elected
	19 June 1816	Replaced

Key: b. = by; a. = after

APPENDIX 4

BETHLEM AND BRIDEWELL PHYSICIANS, 1619–1816

Helkiah Crooke		13 April 1619 – 24 May 1633	Dismissed
Othewell Meverall		c. 1634 – 13 July 1648	Deceased
Thomas Nurse		21 July 1648 – 9 June 1667	Deceased
Thomas Allen		26 June 1667 – b. 19 Dec. 1684	Deceased
Edward Tyson		19 Dec. 1684 – 1 Aug. 1708	Deceased
Richard Hale		10 Sept. 1708 – 26 Sept. 1728	Deceased
James Monro	(sole)	9 Oct. 1728 – 21 June 1751	
	(joint)	21 June 1751 – 3/4 Nov. 1752	Deceased
John Monro	(joint)	21 June 1751 – 3/4 Nov. 1752	
	(sole)	5 Nov. 1752 – 19 July 1787	
	(joint)	19 July 1287 – 27 Dec. 1791	Deceased
Thomas Monro	(joint)	19 July 1787 – 27 Dec. 1791	
	(sole)	27 Dec. 1791 – June 1816	Resigned

Key: b. = by; *c.* = circa; joint = serving jointly as physician; sole = serving alone

APPENDIX 5

BETHLEM AND BRIDEWELL SURGEONS, 1629–1815

John Quince	23 Dec 1629 –	
William Wright	– b. 6 July 1632	Deceased
	(3 Dec. 1630	Ord. Dismissed)
Edward Sey	1633	
Samuel Sambrooke	6 July 1632 – b. 21 Jan. 1643	Deceased
John Meredith	21 Jan. 1643 – March 1656	Deceased
Edmund Higgs	2 April 1656 – 10 June 1669	Retired (age)
Jeremy Higgs	10 June 1669 – b. 7 April 1693	Deceased
Christopher Talman	7 April 1693 – b. 19 March 1708	Deceased
Richard Blackstone	16 April 1708 – b. 17 Dec. 1714	Deceased
John Wheeler	17 Dec. 1714 – b. 4 Dec. 1741	Deceased
Charles Wheeler	11 Dec. 1741 – b. 28 Oct. 1761	Deceased
Henry Wentworth	4 Nov. 1761 – b. 2 March 1769	Deceased
Richard Crowther	9 March 1769 – b. 22 Jan. 1789	Deceased
Bryan Crowther	5 Feb. 1789 – 1815	Deceased

Key: b. = by

APPENDIX 6

BETHLEM MEDICAL OFFICERS, 1783–1900

Physicians
John Monro, 1751–91 (joint: 1751–2; 1787–91)
Thomas Monro, 1787–1816 (joint: 1787–91)
Edward Thomas Monro, 1816–55 (joint)
George Leman Tuthill, 1816–35 (joint)
Alexander Morrison, 1835–53 (joint) (post replaced by Resident Physician)

Apothecaries
John Gozna, 1772–95
John Haslam, 1795–1816
George Wallet, 1816–19
Edward Wright, 1819–30
John Thomas, 1830–45
William Wood, 1845–52
William Helps,* 1852–62
W. Rhys Williams,* 1862–6 (post replaced by Assistant Medical Officer)

Resident Physician-Superintendents
William Charles Hood, 1852–62 (Treasurer: 1868–70 (died))
William Helps,* 1862–5
W. Rhys Williams,* 1865–78
George Henry Savage,* 1878–88
Robert Percy Smith,* 1888–98
Theophilus B. Hyslop,* 1898–1910

Assistant Medical Officers
Henry Law Kempthorne, 1866–70
Henry Rayner, 1870–?
George Henry Savage,* 1872–8
W.E. Ramsden Wood, 1878–85

Robert Percy Smith,* 1885–8
Theophilus B. Hyslop,* 1888–98
Maurice Craig,* 1898–1907

Surgeons
Bryan Crowther, 1789–1815 (died in office)
William Lawrence, 1816–67

Note: * denotes held other post in Hospital.

APPENDIX 7

TWENTIETH-CENTURY BETHLEM OFFICERS

President
Sir George Faudel-Phillips, 1897–1912
Sir Thomas Boor Crosby, 1912–16
Sir Charles Wakefield, 1916–40
Queen Mary, 1944–53
Princess Marina, 1955–68
Princess Alexandra, 1968–

Vice-President
Sir George Wilkinson, 1945–8

Treasurer
Sir James Alfred Copeland, 1865–96, 1900–20
Sir Lionel Faudel-Phillips, 1920–41
Edmund Stone, 1941–5
John Worsfold, 1941–5
Gerald Coke, 1945–8 (post abolished in 1948)

Clerk
Henry (?) Brewer, 1866–1911
John Worsfold, 1911–39
Malcolm Hewitt, 1939–51

House Governor
Kenneth Johnson, 1948–62
Leslie Paine, 1962–85 (post abolished in 1985)

General Manager
Eric Byers, 1985-

Physician-Superintendent
Theophilus Bulkeley Hyslop, 1888–1911
William Stoddart, 1911–14
John Porter-Phillips, 1914–44
John Hamilton, 1944–8 (post abolished in 1948)

Senior Assistant Physician
Maurice Craig, 1899–1907
William Stoddart, 1907–11
John Porter-Phillips, 1911–14
Ralph Brown, 1914–16
Leslie Hilgrove MacCarthy, 1919–20
Thomas Beaton, 1920–6
Murdo Mackenzie, 1926–34
John Hamilton, 1934–44
Duncan Whittaker, 1944–8

Junior Assistant Physician
William Stoddart, 1899–1907
John Porter-Phillips, 1907–11
Ralph Brown, 1911–14
Leslie Hilgrove MacCarthy, 1914
Henry Travers Jones, 1914–15
Frederick Wilfred Sass, 1915–16
John Noel Sergeant, 1915–16
George Herman Monrad-Krohin, 1916–17
Frank Wyatt-Smith, 1916–17
Desmond MacManus, 1918–19
Geoffery Cobb, 1919–21
Macpherson Lawrie, 1921–3
Murdo Mackenzie, 1923–6
Francis Eliot Fox, 1926
David Robertson, 1926–35
Duncan Whittaker, 1936–44
Peter Fry, 1945
Elizabeth Lobl, 1945–8

NAME INDEX

—— •◆• ——

Note: page numbers in italics refer to illustrations

SUBJECT INDEX

———— •◆• ————

Note: page numbers in italics refer to illustrations or tables